The Wiley Blackwell Anthology of African American Literature

Volume 1

1746–1920

About the website

www.wiley.com/go/jarrett

The Wiley Blackwell Anthology of African American Literature companion website features a wealth of resources created by the authors to help you use this book in university courses, whether you are an instructor or a student.

For Instructors and Students

- **Q & A with Gene Andrew Jarrett,** Editor of *The Wiley Blackwell Anthology of African American Literature*
- **Guide to Literary Categories** provides an alternative thematic table of contents
- **Useful Websites for Students** featuring links to a host of companion multimedia materials
- **Key Issues and Themes** for each author and period, including questions for reflection
- **Glossary**
- **Timeline**

For Instructors

- **Useful Websites for Instructors** featuring links to a host of multimedia materials useful for sparking classroom discussion
- **Key Issues and Themes with Teaching Suggestions** designed to help instructors build their syllabi and plan their class lectures
- **Sample Syllabi**

The Wiley Blackwell Anthology of African American Literature

Volume 1

1746–1920

EDITED BY GENE ANDREW JARRETT

WILEY Blackwell

This edition first published 2014

Registered Office
John Wiley & Sons, Ltd, The Atrium, Southern Gate, Chichester, West Sussex, PO19 8SQ, UK

Editorial Offices
350 Main Street, Malden, MA 02148–5020, USA
9600 Garsington Road, Oxford, OX4 2DQ, UK
The Atrium, Southern Gate, Chichester, West Sussex, PO19 8SQ, UK

For details of our global editorial offices, for customer services, and for information about how to apply for permission to reuse the copyright material in this book please see our website at www.wiley.com / wiley-blackwell.

Library of Congress Cataloging-in-Publication Data

The Wiley Blackwell Anthology of African American Literature: Volume 1, 1746–1920 / edited by Gene Andrew Jarrett.
pages cm. – (Blackwell anthologies)
Includes index. ISBN 978-0-470-65800-0 (hardback) – ISBN 978-0-470-65799-7 (paper)
1. American literature–African American authors. I. Jarrett, Gene Andrew, 1975– editor of compilation.
PS153.N5W486 2014
810.9′896073–dc23

2013033149

A catalogue record for this book is available from the British Library.

Cover image: Volume 1: Lois Mailou Jones, *Babelle*, Paris 1937, oil on canvas, 21 3/4 × 18 1/2 inches. Courtsey of Lois Mailou Jones Pierre-Noel Trust, Gift from the Trust to Mint Museum of Art, Charlotte, North Carolina USA.
Cover design by Richard Boxall Design Associates

Set in 10/12.5pt Dante by SPi Publisher Services, Pondicherry, India
Printed in Singapore by Ho Printing Singapore Pte Ltd

1 2014

Table of Contents (by Chronology)

Part 2 The Literatures of Slavery and Freedom: *c*.1830–1865 137

Part 3 The Literatures of Reconstruction, Racial Uplift, and the New Negro: *c.*1865–1920 491

Editorial Advisory Board

Preface

The Wiley Blackwell Anthology of African American Literature is a comprehensive collection of poems, short stories, novellas, novels, plays, autobiographies, and essays authored by New World Africans and African Americans from the eighteenth century until the present. Published in two volumes, it is the first such anthology to be fundamentally conceived for both classroom and online education in the twenty-first century. Of equal importance, the anthology marks a special way of distinguishing the canon from the tradition of African American literature; a more diverse way of representing the lives and literatures of the African diaspora in the United States; and an advanced, if ironic, way of recognizing the ambivalent expressions of race not just in these first decades of the new millennium, but in generations long ago.

Admittedly, this two volume anthology is presenting a canon. It argues that most of the texts of African American literature selected here have been – or should be – adopted, analyzed, written about, and taught within introductory and specialized courses. Yet this canon, like all useful canons, is provisional. It has incorporated the legendary authors who, after a period of obscurity, now deserve special recognition; and it has included the recent, emerging authors who have so upended traditional paradigms that they likewise warrant attention. Long-lasting literary anthologies earn the trust of teachers, students, and scholars by balancing the editorial projects of celebrating the best and welcoming the avant-garde of *belles lettres*. Aiming to join this hallowed group, *The Wiley Blackwell Anthology of African American Literature* seeks to represent a canon that retains its scholarly and pedagogical worth over time, with each subsequent edition.

In subtle but significant ways, the arrangement of literary works in this anthology does differ from what one is likely to discover in fellow anthologies. Evident in the chronological table of contents, the publication dates of literary works – as opposed to the dates on which the authors were born – determine the sequence in which the authors are introduced. (In only a few cases where multiple works by a single author are included, the initial publication date of the first work determines their collective placement in the anthology.) The rationale for this arrangement is straightforward. A handful of authors may share the same decade of birth and belong to the same generation, for example, but these facts do not guarantee that their major writings and publications will cluster in the same moment of literary history. Only six months in 1825 separate the births of Harriet E. Wilson and Frances Ellen Watkins Harper, but over three decades separate Wilson's publication of *Our Nig* in 1859 and Harper's *Iola Leroy* in 1892. Periodizing literary works according to authorial birthdates also bodes poorly for those who had written multiple literary works across multiple historical periods. Although W.E.B. Du Bois had lived from 1868 to 1963, he published *Africa in Battle against Colonialism, Racialism, Imperialism* in 1960, creating a potential discrepancy between the literary periodizations of his birthdate and one of the final works of his career. (The selection of Du Bois's writings for this anthology does not face as extreme a scenario, but he is, in fact, the only author included in both volumes to mitigate the problem of periodization posed by literary longevity.)

The birthdate periodization of literature also threatens to mischaracterize authors who released their best literature not exactly when their generational contemporaries were most productive and publicized. This scenario bespeaks the legacy of Toni Morrison. Although her first three novels, *The Bluest Eye* (1970), *Sula* (1974), and *Song of Solomon* (1977), appeared in the second half of the Black Arts Movement of the 1960s and 1970s, she does not represent this movement as much as her 1931 birthdate would suggest. (By contrast, the other authors born in Morrison's decade of birth, such as LeRoi Jones/Amiri Baraka, Adrienne Kennedy, Larry Neal, and Sonia Sanchez, peaked in celebrity during this movement, with which they openly affiliated.) This anthology's renewed focus on the actual historical sequence and patterns of African American literature helps to redress the commonplace inconsistencies of canonical periodization.

After extensive instructional, scholarly, commercial, and collaborative research, reliable metrics have been developed to ensure that the texts readers encounter in the following pages are those that either are actually being adopted in the classroom in great numbers or have come to embody legitimate reasons why they should be. Copyright expenses and restrictions and practical word count limits posed the greatest challenges to fulfilling this anthology's mission of reprinting all the texts most ideal for teaching and learning. The data on course adoptions, commercial sales, scholarly citations, and historical acclaim (or lack thereof) helped to calibrate this anthology's selection of African American literature. The result is a list of authors whose statures are in proper proportion to each other and whose lives and literatures remain especially meaningful today. Regularly monitoring and adjusting these data over time will help keep as negligible as possible the divide between how teachers and students are examining African American literature in the classroom and how experts are doing so in the scholarly field.

Even if this anthology succeeds in harmonizing scholarship and pedagogy, the gamut of specialties intrinsic to each mode of inquiry must be addressed. Scholars and teachers – and, by extension, students – are more specialized now than ever before. Specialties may include, first, a century or a movement in African American literature's history, such as the "long" nineteenth or twentieth centuries, the New Negro Renaissance, modernism, postmodernism, or the contemporary period; second, a literary form or genre, as specific as poetry, drama, performance, or science fiction; and, third, a methodology such as diaspora, transnationalism, psychoanalysis, performance, print culture, or literary history. The stratification inherent to African American literary studies translates into the comparable stratifications of English and of African American/Africana curricula. The students who try to understand the diversity of courses emerging from these circumstances are also more predisposed than ever before to technologically advanced, multimedia, and online education.

The scholarly and pedagogic ecosystem of *The Wiley Blackwell Anthology of African American Literature* has been carefully constructed and deeply integrated to meet the contemporary and evolving demands of educational specialization and technology. Along with the typical preface, volume introductions, period introductions, headnotes, textual annotations, glossary, and timeline, this anthology features after every author's headnote a copious scholarly bibliography of articles, book chapters, books, and edited collections published recently (usually within the past two decades) and capturing the latest approaches to the author, the text, or the circumstances of literary production. This anthology features information pointing students and instructors to the website (www.wiley.com/go/jarrett). Maintained by Wiley Blackwell, the website will in turn refer to this anthology, yet it is also specially designed to enhance the experiences of readers with this anthology. In addition, it will provide new material such as syllabi, classroom discussion questions and paper topics, reorganizations of the table of contents, audio and video links, links to Wiley Blackwell's own online library, and links to other relevant websites. The ecosystem includes the print and electronic versions of this anthology alongside Wiley Blackwell's *A Companion to African American Literature*, a comprehensive overview of the scholarly field from the eighteenth century to the present. Comprising close to 30 article-length essays and embracing the full range of African American literature, the collection explores this literature's forms, themes, genres, contexts, and major authors, while presenting the latest critical approaches. This ecosystem of scholarship and pedagogy are suited to take full advantage of the multiple ways in which African American literature is being consumed and circulated today.

Rare for a comprehensive anthology of African American literature, the structural division of *The Wiley Blackwell Anthology of African American Literature* into two volumes advances the study of African American literature. (Previously, Howard University Press published *The New Cavalcade: African American Writing from 1760 to the Present*, edited by Arthur P. Davis, J. Saunders Redding, and Joyce Ann Joyce, in two volumes in 1991, but since then it has been out of print.) We are now in an age when introductory or survey courses on this literature, similar to those on broader American literature, are taught over multiple semesters, not just one. We are also in an age when specialized courses tend to revolve around historical periods far shorter than the sestercentennial life of African American literature. The two-volume format of the print and electronic editions of this anthology ideally accounts for these changing circumstances.

Pedagogy and scholarship dictate today, just as they did during the academic maturation of American literature anthologies in the 1970s and 1980s, that a comprehensive anthology of African American literature must be portable enough to cater to the specialized needs of teachers and students who may wish to mix and match each volume within a course. The two-volume format also enhances this anthology's self-sufficiency. Few, if any, competing anthologies reprint more long works than this one. Many of the selected works in Volume 1 alone – including those of John Marrant, Frederick Douglass, William Wells Brown, Harriet E. Wilson, Harriet Jacobs, Pauline E. Hopkins, Charles W. Chesnutt, W.E.B. Du Bois, and James Weldon Johnson – would have been excerpted for an anthology, but here they are reprinted in their entireties. Although facing at times exorbitant copyright expenses and gross restrictions, even Volume 2 exhibits a remarkable share of fully reprinted long works, such as those by Jean Toomer, Nella Larsen, Amiri Baraka, Adrienne Kennedy, August Wilson, and Rita Dove.

Logically and evenly split at the outset of the New Negro Renaissance, the two volumes of *The Wiley Blackwell Anthology of African American Literature* mark an important step toward a refined organization of literary texts according to more appropriate periods of African American literary history, dividing them into seven sections that accurately depict intellectual, cultural, and political movements. Specifically, Volume 1 reprints African American literature from its beginnings to 1920; its three sections span the early national period, the antebellum and Civil War periods, and the New Negro period. Proceeding from 1920 to the present, Volume 2 includes four sections: the New Negro Renaissance; modernism and civil rights; nationalism and the Black Aesthetic; and the contemporary period. Showcasing the literature of 70 authors spread across both volumes, this may not be the largest anthology in terms of the number of pages. Nor may it be the most comprehensive in terms of the number of authors and texts. Nonetheless, it encourages sustained, close reading to take advantage of its inclusion of not only more reprints of entire long works but also longer selections of major works than any other anthology of its kind. At the same time, this anthology concedes – as all anthologies do – that as much as it can function on its own to anchor introductory or specialized courses to assigned readings in African American literature, it still can serve to complement an instructor's independent adoption of separate books, whose large size, copyright costs, and page restrictions prohibit their inclusion in any anthology.

Concerned as it is with reprinting African American literature, this anthology of course affirms the political attitude of previous anthologies, even as it tries to pave a new road ahead. In recognizing African American literature as a crucial part of American literature, this anthology recalls the academic growth of early anthologies from, on the one hand, advocating for the inclusion of the "major writers of America" in English Department curricula toward, on the other, tailoring the canon to accommodate the historical and contemporary realities of "race," among other categories of diversity. Over the years these comprehensive anthologies of American literature accumulated more and more African American writers who wrote literary texts that, with presumable racial authenticity, depict the underrepresented experiences of African Americans.

The 1990s marked a turning point. In this decade, a consensus of scholars and instructors argued rightly that this incremental accumulation of African American writers and experiences in the American canon practically did not – and theoretically could not – account for the centuries-long lives and literatures of New World Africans and African Americans. Comprehensive anthologies emerged to fill the void – both to declare a tradition of African American literature and, because they were indeed anthologies, to represent a canon of this literature at the same time. *The Wiley Blackwell Anthology of African American Literature* likewise asserts the centrality of race to the American canon; reaffirms the salience of New World African and African American experiences in United States (and world) literary history; and celebrates the comprehensive array of literary examples attesting to these qualities.

Yet this anthology resists the particular conflation of "tradition-building" and "canon formation" found in fellow comprehensive anthologies of African American literature. This conflation anoints texts with canonical significance only insofar as they attest to the traditional heritage and genealogy of "blackness," such as the spirituals, gospel, work songs, folklore, the blues, proverbs, sermons, prayers, orations, jazz, black urban vernacular, and rap lyrics that people of African descent created, circulated, and consumed. It goes without saying that all comprehensive anthologies of African American literature should refer to the cultural traditions of the black vernacular. This one does as well. One cannot fully comprehend the selected writings of Frederick Douglass and W.E.B. Du Bois without appreciating work songs and the spirituals; those of Phillis Wheatley, Jupiter Hammon, and Harriet Jacobs without proverbs, sermons, and prayers; those of Charles W. Chesnutt, Paul Laurence Dunbar, Zora Neale Hurston, and Alice Walker without folklore; those of James Weldon Johnson, Langston Hughes, Sterling A. Brown, and Michael S. Harper without jazz and the blues; and those of Gwendolyn Brooks, Amiri Baraka, Lucille Clifton, and Gloria Naylor without codes of black urban vernacular. In this anthology, more connections and overlaps of this sort are made across African American literary history.

The fact remains, however, that contemporary specialists have now begun on their own to compile and republish examples of the black vernacular, providing readers with a selection more copious, a background more thorough, than what is possible in even the most comprehensive anthologies of African American literature.[1] As these independent collections rightly continue to make the case that texts of black vernacular culture deserve more scholarly and classroom attention, *The Wiley Blackwell Anthology of African American Literature* seeks to play a role more complementary than substitutive. Belletristic texts are selected here mainly for their pedagogic, scholarly, and intellectual value in literary studies, which, in countless cases, includes the black vernacular. But this approach is not preoccupied with justifying the canonical inclusion of any and all notable texts for the sake of reestablishing an authentic tradition of African American literature in the name of the black vernacular. African American literature is more complex and diverse than that. Indeed, the selected fiction and essays of Frank J. Webb, Jean Toomer, George S. Schuyler, Samuel Delany, Toni Morrison, and Charles S. Johnson unsettle traditional conceptions of race that presume the unvariegated quintessence of African American literature, experiences, communities, and politics.

The Wiley Blackwell Anthology of African American Literature thus marks a new, long-awaited turn in the tone, structure, and purpose of canon formation. No longer must a comprehensive anthology sound an existential urgency to disprove condemnations of the tradition or canonicity of African American literature. No longer must it bear the burden of representing all versions of the written and spoken word communicated by "the race." And no longer should it presume the hunger of contemporary readers for authentic racial self-reflection. Rather, this kind of anthology should delight in an ironic corpus of literature that, at one moment, asserts the shared diasporic experience and history of African Americans yet, at another, wonders whether this assertion rings hollow as often as it rings true. In the new millennium, the ambivalent life, literature, and literary historiography of race demand this canonical turn.

Notes

[1] Specialized books republishing examples of the black vernacular include *The Anthology of Rap* (Yale University Press, 2010), edited by Adam Bradley and Andrew Du Bois; *African American Folktales: Stories from Black Traditions in the New World* (Pantheon, 1985), edited by Roger D. Abrahams; *Talkin' to Myself: Blues Lyrics, 1921–1942* (Routledge, 2005), edited by Michael Taft; *The Oxford Book of Spirituals* (Oxford University Press, 2002), edited by Moses Hogan; and *Preaching with Sacred Fire: An Anthology of African American Sermons, 1750 to the Present* (W. W. Norton & Company, 2010), edited by Martha Simmons and Frank A. Thomas.

Introduction

Volume 1 of *The Wiley Blackwell Anthology of African American Literature* reprints African American literature from its beginnings in the middle of the eighteenth century, just before the Revolutionary War, to the early twentieth century, around the end of World War I. Featuring 22 different writers, the volume divides into three chronological sections – the early national period, the antebellum and Civil War periods, and the New Negro period – that best periodize the historical circumstances under which New World Africans and African Americans in the United States and across the world wrote creative or intellectual literature. The broad issues described in this volume include the crises of slavery and freedom in American society; the tension between individual rights and government; the subjugation of African Americans; and the intellectual, literary, and political strategies by which African Americans articulated these issues for various readers.

The first section of Volume 1, "The Literatures of Africa, Middle Passage, and Slavery," reprints writings from Lucy Terry's 1746 poem about an Indian attack in Massachusetts to David Walker's 1829 polemic to his fellow African Americans. In this section, we realize the degree to which slavery drove the growth and prosperity of early America. Slaves were a crucial presence in the nation's labor force and economic expansion. But little consensus existed over the fundamental issues of liberty and slavery, independence and rule, and the interpretation of republicanism and the individual liberties that it signified. The issues were contested along regional, class, and racial lines. By the dawn of the nineteenth century, the enslavement of peoples of African descent and the violent displacement of Native Americans had become constitutive practices in a country once divided over the republican ideas of Revolution. The early national literature published during this time reflected the contested nature of freedom and slavery at the heart of the country's founding, and thus was preoccupied with defining the structural framework of republican citizenship and government. The historical circumstances and the prevailing literary interrogations of freedom and liberty, individual rights and central government helped lay the political foundations for New World African and early African American literatures.

The next section, "The Literatures of Slavery and Freedom," features texts published from Omar ibn Said's 1831 autobiographical story of being a slave in North Carolina to Harriet Jacobs's 1861 episodic narrative about a "slave girl." During these three decades, slavery grew so much that, by the Civil War's outset, African Americans had become one of the largest enslaved populations in world history. The cotton industry relied on the subjugation and exploitation of enslaved African Americans.

Southern politicians spearheaded legislation that increased the area in which slavery could exist in the country, even as the "peculiar institution" grew controversial in North America and declined in the rest of the Atlantic world. The paradoxical quality of the nation's antebellum era lies in its creation of permanent liberal institutions – ranging from the public school to civil rights praxis – alongside the enduring contradictions of racial inequality, nativism, and sectionalism. The economic, political, and social circumstances under which slavery thrived shaped writers of the American Renaissance, who took stock of the changes in the young nation yet sought to construct a quintessentially American self independent of the British colonial past. For certain African American writers, however, slavery and freedom were not merely the literary tropes of sentimentalism that also attained commercial prominence. The realities of enslavement and racial subjugation informed their experiences of America and, in turn, instilled their desire to write autobiographical narratives and novels about slavery, for example, that challenge both southern slavery and its institutional perpetuation of white supremacist ideology.

The final section of Volume 1, "The Literatures of Reconstruction, Racial Uplift, and the New Negro," covers writings beginning with Frank J. Webb's two 1870 *New Era* Gothic and love stories and ending with James Weldon Johnson's 1912 anonymous novel purporting to be the autobiography of a "colored man" passing as white. The close of over two centuries of slavery on the North American continent and the ensuing emancipation of four million African Americans promised a radical rethinking of citizenship through Radical Reconstruction in the South. African American men held public office in the same states where they had previously been property. New representative governments, composed of freed people and their white allies, drafted state constitutions that created the first public education system in the South, abolished imprisonment for debt, and expanded suffrage to all men. Yet white resistance and violence countered the optimism of Reconstruction in the former Confederacy, and escalated sharply after federal troops withdrew from the South a little over a decade after the Civil War. The southern reinstatement of the laws disfranchising, segregating, and subjugating African Americans thereupon commenced. African Americans were committed to literary realism as they registered their sense of the racial violence, disfranchisement, and segregation that had spread in the aftermath of Reconstruction, as well as of an American literary culture that sought to restrict their images to derogatory stereotypes. By the arrival of World War I, debates raged among African American writers and intellectuals over the best means of racial uplift in light of these political and cultural conditions.

Every section of Volume 1 contains a pedagogical and scholarly apparatus. Each has an introduction with three main goals: to paint in broad strokes the social, cultural, intellectual, political, economic, and international circumstances of the United States at a particular moment in history; to outline briefly the relationship of these circumstances to the nature of American literature being written and published at that time; and, finally, to indicate the potential implications of these broader literary and historical forces on the formal and thematic principles of African American literature. Next, a biographical and critical headnote introduces each selected author, describing the full trajectory of the author's thinking and writing to put the selected text in proper perspective. After the headnote is a bibliography that advises teachers and students on the most relevant journal articles, book chapters, books, and edited collections of scholarly essays they should consider for "further reading." This scholarly bibliography has been honed down to recognize only scholarship published recently (such as within the past two decades) and specializing on the author or the selected text. The bibliography also almost always views as a complementary resource the recent essays published in Wiley Blackwell's *A Companion to African American Literature*. Volume 1 is not the most comprehensive selection of African American literature published from the beginnings to 1920 – but it does not intend to be. Rather, the authors and texts, which, with few exceptions, are laid out in chronological order and selected with citation and commercial research in mind, together capture the complexity and range of African American literary history up to the modern era.

Principles of Selection and Editorial Procedures

The Wiley Blackwell Anthology of African American Literature is carefully designed to incorporate as many reprints of entire works, and as many longer selections of major works, as possible. Between the genesis and publication of the anthology, multiple stages of peer-review assessed its mission, structure, contents, and viability. Professors at colleges and universities were consulted to comment on and help revise the anthology and its corresponding website, while the Editorial Advisory Board contributed deeper critical engagement with the anthology's principles of selection. The outcome of this collaboration is an anthology that, despite the breadth and depth afforded by its two-volume format, focuses not on being the most comprehensive collection of African American literature in terms of the number of authors and texts. Rather, it concentrates on encouraging instructors to cultivate the sustained, close reading of any combination of the 70 authors, but with recognition that students, teachers, and scholars are now more specialized than ever before in analyzing movements, genres, or methodologies. The anthology can function alone in introductory or specialized courses, and it can complement an instructor's independent adoption of separate books.

The principles of selection have sought to balance the availability of African American literature with its affordability. On the one hand, the anthology provides a representative yet diverse range of belletristic texts for literary study. The responses of external evaluators and of the Editorial Advisory Board, coupled with reliable metrics mined from extensive scholarly and commercial data, helped to refine the anthology's table of contents. The texts readers encounter in the following pages thus are actually being adopted in the classroom in great numbers. New archival discoveries and the discernible cultural turn in higher education toward realizing the ambivalent life, literature, and literary historiography of race also necessitate this anthology's implicit argument that certain other exemplary texts should likewise be adopted.

On the other hand, this anthology seeks to ensure that the purchase of one volume or both volumes of the anthology remains within the financial means of students. Editorial decisions to feature entire novels, plays, and collections of poems by individual authors inevitably faced the challenges of accounting for their large size in terms of word count; paying their copyright costs if in the private domain; and, in the latter case, accommodating copyright owners or their agents who understandably wish to winnow down the anthology's selection so that it does not detract from the separate, independent sales of these entire texts. Even on a smaller textual scale, such as the short stories and individual poems of renowned authors, these structural limitations played a role in the editorial decision to include or exclude them. All comprehensive anthologies, past and present, have had to endure circumstances in which the pedagogic and intellectual arguments to include entire texts ran up against the practical and budgetary arguments to excerpt or exclude them. The current edition and format of *The Wiley Blackwell Anthology of African American Literature* represent the successful negotiation of these conditions. The comprehensive list of esteemed authors and texts is herein more available, affordable, and portable than ever before, for both classroom and online use.

Compiling and editing the selected literature followed a series of guidelines and procedures. The reprintings of primary texts largely hew to original editions. For the benefit of readers, the texts have been lightly edited to correct errors of spelling, punctuation, syntax, and capitalization born in the original editions. Where no semantic meaning is involved in the change, typographic elements have been made consistent across the volumes and arabic numbering has been used in preference to roman. Annotative footnotes (which are enumerated by the editor) occasionally include these corrections or translate incomprehensibly archaic language into contemporary form. More often, they define obscure words; explain complex or meaningful phrases; and trace the historical significance of individuals, groups, places, and events. When known, the year of first publication, which generally dictates the chronological order of the contents, follows each selection on the right-hand side, sometimes adjoined to the year of a subsequent, revised edition. If relevant, the year of composition is also provided on the left-hand side.

Acknowledgments

The Wiley Blackwell Anthology of African American Literature was the most difficult editorial project I have ever taken up in my career. In the past I have compiled and reprinted the writings of canonical and obscure African American authors; edited and published the essays of contemporary scholars; and along the way dealt with the literary estates or agencies of authors whose works still exist in the private domain and require copyright permission for republication. Preparing this two-volume anthology demanded that I recall these experiences and endure them again. Doing so was equivalent to putting together multiple kinds of collections in one, and addressing a large group of collaborators and constituencies with varying interests and needs in this enterprise. Unenviable to some, this was no small task.

Yet multiple things helped bring everyone together, in the spirit of consensus and contribution. There was either a deep-seated admiration for the literatures of New World Africans and African Americans from centuries ago to the present; an ineluctable sense of belonging to, and support of, this historic community of writers; or an abiding commitment to examining and circulating this literary corpus on behalf of higher education both in the United States and around the world. Or, the sentiment included all the above. This shared focus inspired me as I tried to shepherd this project from inception to conclusion, as did the opportunity to work closely with great literary artists and critics, academic instructors, scholars, editors, and students.

Located in both England and the United States, an outstanding group of editors and staff at Wiley Blackwell advocated for this enormous and complex book, and I wish to thank them here. Emma Bennett, Executive Editor/Publisher of Literature, was receptive to my idea, first proposed in 2009, of a new comprehensive anthology of African American literature released in multivolume format. She was patient and considerate as we hammered out contractual details about the parameters and resources of the project. Our regular conversations since then were crucial to the anthology's current shape and focus. Ben Thatcher, Project Editor, skillfully managed the project's unwieldy materials. With an eye always to buoying my soul, he eloquently negotiated with copyright holders and literary estates and agencies so that I did not have to enter the fray. Deirdre Ilkson, Senior Development Editor, and Bridget Jennings, Senior Editorial Assistant, helped to usher the project to completion, especially in the final stages. Possessing a keen eye, Giles Flitney patiently copy-edited these very long volumes, and worked with me to resolve issues both big and small. Finally, Felicity Marsh managed the project with a steady hand that kept me at ease at all times.

My literary agent, Wendy Strothman, of the Strothman Agency, LLC, meticulously worked on my behalf during the very important and time-consuming negotiation with Wiley Blackwell over the contractual details of the project.

The anthology would not be where or what it is today without the members of the Editorial Advisory Board. They generously gave their time and insight, their advice and encouragement, cooperating with me and the countless staff, either at the publisher or at my home institution, Boston University, working on my behalf. By name I thank them again here, even though they are already spotlighted on another page in the front matter: Daphne A. Brooks, Joanna Brooks, Margo Natalie Crawford, Madhu Dubey, Michele Elam, Philip Gould, George B. Hutchinson, Marlon B. Ross, Cherene M. Sherrard-Johnson, James Edward Smethurst, Werner Sollors, John Stauffer, Jeffrey Allen Tucker, and Ivy G. Wilson. Over the course of preparing this anthology I also consulted several other professors, most notably, Brent Hayes Edwards, Harryette Mullen, Lawrence P. Jackson, William Maxwell and Margaret B. Wilkerson.

The essays in Wiley Blackwell's *A Companion to African American Literature* (2010) figure prominently in the scholarly rationale or apparatus for the anthology. I thank their authors here (some also appearing above): Vincent Carretta, James Sidbury, Frances Smith Foster, Kim D. Green, Michael J. Drexler, Ed White, Joanna Brooks, Tyler Mabry, Philip Gould, Maurice S. Lee, Robert S. Levine, Ivy G. Wilson, Marlon B. Ross, Andreá N. Williams, Shirley Moody-Turner, Michelle Ann Stephens, Cherene M. Sherrard-Johnson, Mark Christian Thompson, Michelle Yvonne Gordon, Keith D. Leonard, James Edward Smethurst, Glenda Carpio, Madhu Dubey, Robin V. Smiles, Jeffrey Allen Tucker, Theresa Delgadillo, Guy Mark Foster, and Arlene R. Keizer. Finally, the many professors and instructors who responded to questionnaires and solicitations about the anthology were invaluable.

Completing this project would have been impossible without my former and current research assistants at Boston University. John Barnard diligently worked on the project at a very early organizational stage. Kerri Greenidge possesses exhaustive knowledge of African American cultural, political, and intellectual history, and her tireless application of this knowledge to the project was a godsend. Iain Bernhoft demonstrated remarkable acumen, discipline, and leadership as he handled the anthology's literary and scholarly materials and served as interlocutor between me and Wiley Blackwell. Joyce Kim generously and energetically came onto the project very late in the process to help rescue the preparation of key parts of the anthology. Anne Austin, as Department Administrator, helped to keep me organized and attentive as I necessarily attended to my other duties as Professor and Chair of the Department of English. And I thank my colleagues and administrators at Boston University for their longstanding support.

This anthology builds on the previous accomplishments of teachers, writers, scholars, and anthologists of African American literature. I express gratitude to the selected writers and their literary estates and agencies willing to work with us to include their writings. I also extend thanks to the editors of fellow anthologies who provided advice as I consulted them on the viability of this project: Henry Louis Gates, Jr, William L. Andrews, Robert S. Levine, Ivy Schweitzer, and Richard Yarborough.

My longtime wife and best friend, Renée, has long believed in me; she was the first to support this project; and she encouraged me as I tried to finish it. I thank her; our lovely children, Nyla, Noah, and Nadia; and the rest of our family who supported me all the while, from beginning to end.

A book of this complexity and magnitude will inevitably have factual and conceptual errors. Even though everyone above contributed to this anthology in some way, I accept ultimate responsibility and apologize for any such errors that happen to wind their way into print.

Table of Contents (by Genre)

Poetry

Autobiography

Essay

Drama

Fiction

Novel or Novella

Part One

The Literatures of Africa, Middle Passage, and Slavery

*c.*1746–1830

Introduction

When the French and Indian War ended with the Treaty of Paris in 1763, Great Britain gained control over eastern North America from Nova Scotia to Georgia. In these colonies over 1.5 million people resided, a diverse mixture of Europeans, Africans, and Native Americans. By 1830, early America, now spreading westward across the Allegheny Mountains from the 13 original colonies on the Atlantic coast, contained 12 million inhabitants.

Early America's growth and prosperity were inextricable from slavery. Since the first British colonists arrived at Jamestown, Virginia, in 1607, colonial America evolved from what one historian has called a "society with slaves" – one in which slaves were one form of labor among many, and slavery was not confined to people of African descent – into a prosperous slave society that produced £2.8 million per annum for the British crown on the eve of the American Revolution. Slavery permeated all aspects of colonial America, from Puritan Massachusetts, where slavery was first legalized in 1641, to New York City, home to the largest enslaved population outside of the South. A little over a century later, in 1750, 20% of those living in the North American colonies were enslaved, the majority of them (61%) living in Virginia and Maryland, where their muscle provided the hard labor in the Chesapeake's rapidly expanding tobacco economy.

In eighteenth-century America, little consensus existed over fundamental issues of liberty and slavery, independence and rule. Only seven of the 13 colonies attended the 1754 Albany Congress, where Benjamin Franklin promoted a plan for a unified colonial government. All seven colonies rejected the plan, and Franklin lamented that "the colonial assemblies … were narrowly provincial in outlook, mutually jealous, and suspicious of any central taxing authority." Later, southern delegates to the Continental Congress objected to Thomas Jefferson's initial draft of the Declaration of Independence over a reference to slavery being forced on the colonies by the British Crown. Even after the Treaty of Paris ended the Revolutionary War in 1783, and the American Constitution was drafted in 1787, interpretation of republicanism and the individual liberties that it signified were hotly contested along regional, class, and racial lines. The federal Constitution itself partly responded to arguments over the protection of slavery and the Congressional

The Wiley Blackwell Anthology of African American Literature: Volume 1, 1746–1920, First Edition.
Edited by Gene Andrew Jarrett.

representation of slaveholding states. The document that resulted – based on the premise of "provid[ing] for the common defense, promot[ing] the general welfare, and secur[ing] the blessings of liberty" – provided for three-fifths of all slaves to be counted in each state's Congressional representation, extended the slave trade for 20 years, and allowed the federal government to aid in the recapture of fugitives slaves, all without mentioning the word "slavery." By the time America emerged from the War of 1812 and entered a market revolution fueled by southern plantations, northern manufacturing, and westward expansion, the enslavement of peoples of African descent and the violent removal of Native Americans had become constitutive practices in a country once divided over the ideas of republican Revolution.

American literature published between 1750 and 1830 reflected the contested nature of freedom and slavery at the heart of the country's founding. This literature evolved in two primary phases that sentimental literature and culture would connect by way of antislavery discourse: the moral and political proselytizing of Enlightenment doctrine, and the romanticism of the early republic that flourished following the acquisition of Louisiana Territory in 1803 and American victory over Britain in the War of 1812. The first originated in the theological exhortations of the Great Awakening, which swept through New England and beyond with George Whitefield's 1739 tour of the Atlantic seaboard. Jonathan Edwards's *Sinners in the Hand of an Angry God* (1741) articulated God's grace as a sentiment that could be felt through personal conversion, partly anticipating the sentimental literature of the mid-nineteenth century. Yet after Edwards's 1750 removal from his Northampton, Massachusetts, church, colonial printing presses increasingly published moral essays that used the language of individualism, liberty, and equality to argue against British oppression. While texts like Samson Occom's *Sermon at the Execution of Moses Paul* (1772) preached morality and the evils of liquor, radical political tracts became increasingly popular. The tracts were also easily accessible, released in the 50 newspapers and 40 magazines produced on American soil. The colonial press provided a rare unifying institution for colonial subjects, most living within 50 miles of the Atlantic coast, where port cities published pamphlets and sermons from correspondents across the Atlantic world.

The most famous example of Enlightenment proselytizing was Thomas Paine's *Common Sense*, published in January 1776. When it appeared in the newspaper *The American Crisis*, Paine's appeal to "love of mankind" spread to cities and towns across the colonies and was read before George Washington's troops that December. With the conclusion of the War of Independence and the creation of a central government, American letters became preoccupied with defining the structural framework of a republican government, most notably through political essays, known as the Federalist Papers, published in 1787 and 1788 under the pseudonym "Publius" by John Jay, Alexander Hamilton, and James Madison. The nationalism born of the Revolutionary War inclined toward literature that exalted civic virtues and readers' devotion to liberty, good government, and republican principles. Joel Barlow's *Columbiad* (1807) celebrated the birth of the young nation, while Richard Emmons's *The Fredoniad; or, Independence Preserved* (1827) likewise ascribed to the War of 1812 classical epic status.

In the first decades of the nineteenth century, though, most Americans were more familiar with Greco-Roman history and British romantic writers than with American authors like Benjamin Franklin or Charles Brockden Brown. Problems of accessibility plagued American literature – most American works were scarce or incompletely printed, while British texts were printed in coastal cities within weeks of their London publications. Particularly after trade was restored following the War of 1812, European literature was readily available to American readers, and newspapers in Boston, Philadelphia, New York, and Charleston had correspondents in European cities and post offices with cheap mailing rates for printed materials. After the Erie Canal was completed in 1825, the ease of trade between eastern seaboard and expanding west ensured American exposure to William Wordsworth and Samuel Taylor Coleridge, Lord George Gordon Byron and Percy Bysshe Shelley.

National copyright law was in place by 1790, but not until 1891 did writers secure the legal right to international sales of their published works. Thus, throughout most of the nineteenth century, American printers could publish inexpensive versions of British texts, such as those of the beloved Sir Walter Scott, without having to pay royalties. Scott helped to make fiction respectable in America (rather than a frivolous and immoral temptation); his historical *Waverley* novels, published between 1814 and 1832, elevated the dignity of the novelistic form and helped pave the way for popular American writers like James Fenimore Cooper, Washington Irving, Lydia Maria Child, and Catharine Maria Sedgwick. Works like Cooper's *The Pioneers* (1823) and Child's *Hobomok* (1824) helped to popularize fiction focused on American history. Perhaps the most celebrated American writer of the time was Washington Irving, whose *Sketch Book of Geoffrey Crayon, Gent.* (1819–1820), which included "Rip Van Winkle" and "The Legend of Sleepy Hollow," won wide acclaim. Although he spent many years in England and Spain, Irving's works displayed a nationalism highlighted by their setting in rural American villages rather than an idealized European past.

The historical circumstances and the prevailing literary interrogations of freedom and liberty, individual rights and central government helped lay the political foundations for New World African and early African American literatures. The fact that early American slavery was a byproduct of the larger Atlantic world meant that the first published literature by people of African descent reflected the revivalism and personal deliverance of the Great Awakening, not so much the militant demands for racial equality espoused by Maria Stewart, among others, in the 1830s. James Ukawsaw Gronniosaw's 1772 autobiography, the first such text published by an African in Britain, uses the language of personal salvation and individual enlightenment to trace his journey from West African royalty to Dutch captivity and Christian education in colonial New York. As the first slave narrative, it established the spiritual awakening as a major theme of New World African literature of the late eighteenth and early nineteenth centuries. Early African American literature also homed in on the inherent contradictions of American republicanism. Since people of African descent across the Americas were widely deemed unworthy of "the natural rights of man," many of the spiritual journeys detailed in certain early texts served rhetorically to assert the humanity of Africans and, of equal importance, their qualification for admission to the early national polity. Harrowing tales of transatlantic journeys and intercultural discovery characterize Briton Hammon's *Narrative of the Uncommon Sufferings and Surprizing Deliverance of Briton Hammon, a Negro Man* (1760) and Olaudah Equiano's *Interesting Narrative of the Life of Olaudah Equiano, or Gustavus Vassa, The African, Written by Himself* (1789), while John Marrant's story of ministering to colonial slaves after experiencing conversion by George Whitefield combines themes of individual redemption with subversive challenges to racial inferiority.

Phillis Wheatley, a young woman kidnapped from her West African homeland and sold in Boston while still a child, further inaugurated a canon with her 1773 book *Poems on Various Subjects*. Although Lucy Terry, a fellow New England slave, wrote the ballad "Bars Fight" in 1746, and Jupiter Hammon's "An Evening Thought" appeared as a broadside in 1761, Wheatley was the first African American to publish a book and receive international acclaim for her talent. While these late eighteenth-century authors did not deal explicitly with "race" as we now know it, their employment of the popular tropes of personal deliverance and spiritual awakening argued powerfully against those who denied people of African descent access to Revolutionary discourse. These authors proved highly adept at using early print culture and republican rhetoric to assert their rights, even as the likes of George Washington banned non-white soldiers from his colonial Army in early 1775, and Thomas Jefferson justified American slavery and white supremacy in *Notes on the State of Virginia*, published exactly a decade later.

Early African American pamphlets also typified political activism, penned, as they were, by male and female leaders of free black northern communities increasingly encountering racism and racial discrimination. In 1794, for instance, over 10 years before he founded the first African American Protestant denomination in the United States, Richard Allen published his *Narrative of the Proceedings of the Black People During the Late Awful Calamity in Philadelphia* to counter white accusations that the city's African or African American residents profited from the 1793 Yellow Fever Epidemic by plundering the homes of sick whites who fled to the countryside. By the time John Brown Russwurm and Samuel Cornish founded *Freedom's Journal* in New York City in 1827, free African Americans used the claims to freedom and equality espoused in their literature to "plead [their] own cause" through a thriving independent press. David Walker's incendiary *Appeal to the Coloured Citizens of the World* (1829) was perhaps the most notable fruit of these publishing efforts. Although *Freedom's Journal* ended in 1829, it laid the foundations for a northern press that nurtured African American cultural and political identity independent of white denigration and southern slavery. Even as popular works like James Fenimore Cooper's *Leatherstocking Tales* established distinctly American tropes for a rapidly developing national literature, then, an inherently political African American literature emerged to challenge this nationalism.

The cultural and ideological complexity of New World African and African American authors, along with the formal and thematic diversity of their writings, demonstrate the limitations of the contemporary term "African American literature" for describing the earliest stage of the tradition. The term is fraught with contradiction, failing to realize that English-speaking authors of African descent, such as Briton Hammon, John Marrant, Olaudah Equiano, and Phillis Wheatley, were perhaps more transatlantic or international than exclusively New World or national in their identity. In addition to the movement enforced by the intercontinental slave trade, the voluntary travels of the authors across and around the Atlantic shaped their conceptions of "Africa" and "America." Against the backdrop of the rise of plantation slavery in the British American colonies between the mid-seventeenth century and the late eighteenth century, coupled with the provisional self-definition of Africans and their descendants during this period, the social effacement of slavery made African identity interchangeable with more New World terms as "Negro" and "black." However, Africa still remained a distinct trope for authors of African descent, including Equiano and Wheatley. The trope suggested an imaginative reorientation to the traumas of the past, the struggles of the present, and the promises of the future, even as the material experiences of Africa itself continued to dissipate as a personal or collective reference point at the dawn of the nineteenth century.

Lucy Terry (*c*.1730–1821)

A longtime New England resident of African descent, Lucy Terry achieved literary fame only after her death, when her poem "Bars Fight" was published in Josiah Gilbert Holland's *History of Western Massachusetts* in 1855. Prior to its publication, the poem had been preserved orally by Deerfield, Massachusetts, residents in their memory of the 1746 Abenaki Indian attack. Born in Africa but sold into slavery as an infant, Terry was purchased in Bristol, Rhode Island, by Ensign Ebenezer Wells of Deerfield, whose church she joined in 1744. Twelve years later, she married a free black man named Abijah Prince, a veteran of the French and Indian War who purchased her freedom. Granted his own freedom because of his military service, Prince owned three parcels of land in northern Massachusetts and Vermont. In 1760, the Princes settled in Guilford, Vermont, where their six children were born; a son, Cesar Prince, fought in the Revolutionary War. In addition to properties in Northfield and Guilford (the latter left to Prince by his former employer, Deacon Samuel Field), Abijah Prince owned 100 acres in Sunderland, Vermont, a town he helped found.

Over the next 50 years, Lucy Terry gained a reputation as a skilled orator. She was also a vigilant protector of her family's interests in the predominantly white region. In 1785, after a group of white neighbors attacked the Princes' property in Guilford, Lucy Terry and her husband appealed to Vermont's governor for help; he ruled that the town's selectmen must protect the Princes from attack. Her three-hour argument before the State Supreme Court on behalf of a disputed land claim earned Terry praise from the leading white attorneys of the state during the 1790s. She died in 1821, more than three decades before her poem was published. "Bars Fight" is the first poem written by a woman of African descent in what would become the United States.

Further reading

Adams, Catherine and Elizabeth H. Pleck. *Love of Freedom: Black Women in Colonial and Revolutionary New England*. New York: Oxford University Press, 2010. Ch. 2.

Brown, Lois. "Memorial Narratives of African Women in Antebellum New England." *Legacy* 20.1&2 (2003): 38–61.

Cima, Gay Gibson. *Early American Women Critics: Performance, Religion, Race*. New York: Cambridge University Press, 2006. Ch. 2.

De Lancey, Frenzella E. "Teaching Four African American Female Poets in Context: Lucy Terry, Phillis Wheatley, Frances E.W. Harper, and Sonia Sanchez." *Teaching African American Women's Writing*. Ed. Gina Wisker. Basingstoke, England: Palgrave Macmillan, 2010. 75–86.

Gerzina, Gretchen Holbrook. *Mr. and Mrs. Prince: How an Extraordinary Eighteenth-Century Family Moved Out of Slavery and Into Legend*. New York: Amistad/HarperCollins, 2008.

Harris, Sharon M. *Executing Race: Early American Women's Narratives of Race, Society, and the Law*. Columbus: Ohio State University Press, 2005. Ch. 6.

Langley, April C.E. *The Black Aesthetic Unbound: Theorizing the Dilemma of Eighteenth-Century African American Literature*. Columbus: Ohio State University Press, 2008. Ch. 4.

The Wiley Blackwell Anthology of African American Literature: Volume 1, 1746–1920, First Edition.
Edited by Gene Andrew Jarrett.

Bars[1] Fight

August, 'twas the twenty-fifth,
Seventeen hundred forty-six,
The Indians did in ambush lay,
Some very valiant[2] men to slay,

The names of whom I'll not leave out:
Samuel Allen like a hero fout,[3]
And though he was so brave and bold,
His face no more shall we behold.

Eleazor Hawks was killed outright,
Before he had time to fight –
Before he did the Indians see,
Was shot and killed immediately.

Oliver Armsden he was slain,
Which caused his friends much grief and pain.
Simeon Arsden they found dead
Not many rods[4] distant from his head.

Adonijah Gillet, we do hear,
Did lose his life which was so dear.
John Sadler fled across the water,
And thus escaped the dreadful slaughter.

Eunice Allen see the Indians coming,
And hopes to save herself by running;
And had not her petticoats stopped her,
The awful creatures had not catched her,

Nor tommy hawked her on the head,
And left her on the ground for dead.
Young Samuel Allen, Oh, lack-a-day!
Was taken and carried to Canada.

1746 1855

Notes

[1] *Bars* meadows.

[2] *Original reads*: valient [ed.].

[3] *fout* fought.

[4] *rod* unit of measurement.

Briton Hammon (dates unknown)

An Atlantic Creole, Briton Hammon embodies the transnational lives of people of African descent in the pre-Revolutionary Americas. His journeys took him from Boston to Florida, Cuba, Jamaica, and England. While New Englanders Lucy Terry and Phillis Wheatley had personal and familial ties to the region's intellectual elite, Hammon's relationship to the region, and the New World African community within it, is less certain. Even more than Wheatley and Terry (not to mention fellow traveler Olaudah Equiano), Briton Hammon's history is difficult to trace. All that scholars know about Hammon comes from his *Narrative of the Uncommon Sufferings and Surprizing Deliverance of Briton Hammon, a Negro Man*. Whether he was born a slave or free, in America or Africa, and how old he was when he wrote his famous text – all remain unclear. What is known is that his 1760 work was perhaps the first published autobiographical work by an African American, appearing 13 years before Phillis Wheatley's *Poems on Various Subjects* was published in London.

According to his *Narrative*, Hammon left Massachusetts for Jamaica with the permission of his master, a merchant named General Winslow. Hammon was the sole survivor when his ship was first wrecked on a reef then raided by Caribbean native pirates off the Florida coast on Christmas Day in 1747. He escaped captivity by fleeing to a Spanish schooner, only to be imprisoned four years in Cuba for refusing to serve in the Spanish navy. After being released from prison, he worked briefly in Cuba before escaping his Spanish captors by signing on to a London-bound naval ship. In London he was reunited with his master, General Winslow, after almost 13 years apart. Winslow helped Hammon publish his narrative when the men returned together to Boston. Just as Hammon's experiences qualify him as an Atlantic Creole, outside of readymade national categories, so too does his *Narrative* invite a number of classifications, incorporating elements of Indian captivity narrative, spiritual autobiography, and travel narrative.

Further reading

Carretta, Vincent. "Back to the Future: Eighteenth-Century Transatlantic Black Authors." *A Companion to African American Literature*. Ed. Gene Andrew Jarrett. Malden, MA: Wiley-Blackwell, 2010. 11–24.

Desrochers, Robert Jr. "'Surprizing Deliverance'? Slavery and Freedom, Language, and Identity in the Narrative of Briton Hammon, 'A Negro Man'." *Genius in Bondage: Literature of the Early Black Atlantic*. Eds. Vincent Carretta and Philip Gould. Lexington: University Press of Kentucky, 2001. 153–174.

Foster, Frances Smith and Kim D. Green. "Ports of Call, Pulpits of Consultation: Rethinking the Origins of African American Literature." *A Companion to African American Literature*. Ed. Gene Andrew Jarrett. Malden, MA: Wiley-Blackwell, 2010. 45–58.

Sekore, John. "Briton Hammon, the Indian Captivity Narrative, and the African American Slave Narrative." *When Brer Rabbit Meets Coyote: African–Native American Literature*. Ed. Jonathan Brennan. Urbana: University of Illinois Press, 2003. 141–157.

Vollaro, Daniel. "Sixty Indians and Twenty Canoes: Briton Hammon's Unreliable Witness to History." *Native South* 2 (2009): 133–147.

Weyler, Karen A. "Race, Redemption, and Captivity in *A Narrative of the Lord's Wonderful Dealings with John Marrant, a Black and Narrative of the Uncommon Sufferings and Surprizing Deliverance of Briton Hammon a Negro Man.*" *Genius in Bondage: Literature of the Early Black Atlantic*. Eds. Vincent Carretta and Philip Gould. Lexington: University Press of Kentucky, 2001. 39–53.

The Wiley Blackwell Anthology of African American Literature: Volume 1, 1746–1920, First Edition.
Edited by Gene Andrew Jarrett.

Narrative of the Uncommon Sufferings and Surprizing Deliverance of Briton Hammon, a Negro Man

NARRATIVE of the UNCOMMON SUFFERINGS AND Surprizing DELIVERANCE OF BRITON HAMMON, *A Negro Man – Servant to GENERAL WINSLOW,*[1] *of* Marshfield, *in NEW-ENGLAND; Who returned to* Boston, *after having been absent almost Thirteen Years. CONTAINING An Account of the many Hardships he underwent from the Time he left his Master's House, in the Year 1747, to the Time of his Return to* Boston. *How he was Castaway in the Capes of* Florida *– the horrid Cruelty and inhuman Barbarity of the* Indians *in murdering the whole Ship's Crew – the Manner of his being carry'd by them into Captivity. Also, An Account of his being Confined Four Years and Seven Months in a close Dungeon – And the remarkable Manner in which he met with his* good old Master in London; *who returned to* New-England, *a Passenger, in the same Ship. BOSTON,* Printed and Sold by [John] GREEN & [Joseph] RUSSELL,[2] in Queen-Street, 1760.

TO THE READER,
AS my Capacities and Condition of Life are very low, it cannot be expected that I should make those Remarks on the Sufferings I have met with, or the kind Providence of a good GOD for my Preservation, as one in a higher Station; but shall leave that to the Reader as he goes along, and so I shall only relate Matters of Fact as they occur to my Mind –

On Monday, 25th Day of *December*, 1747, with the leave of my Master,[3] I went from *Marshfield*, with an Intention to go a Voyage to Sea, and the next Day, the 26th, got to *Plymouth*, where I immediately ship'd myself on board of a Sloop,[4] Capt. *John Howland*, Master,[5] bound to *Jamaica* and the *Bay*[6] – We sailed from *Plymouth* in a short Time, and after a pleasant Passage of about 30 Days, arrived at *Jamaica;* we were[7] detain'd at *Jamaica* only 5 Days, from whence we sailed for the *Bay*, where we arrived safe in 10 Days. We loaded our Vessel with Logwood,[8] and sailed from the *Bay* the 25th Day of May following, and the 15th Day of *June*, we were cast away on *Cape Florida*,[9] about 5 Leagues[10] from the Shore; being now destitute of every Help, we knew not what to do or what Course to take in this our sad Condition – The Captain was advised, intreated, and beg'd on, by every Person on board, to heave over but only 20 Ton of the *Wood*, and we should get

Notes

1 *GENERAL WINSLOW* Major-General John Winslow (1703–1774) of colonial Massachusetts.

2 *GREEN & RUSSELL* John Green and Joseph Russell published several local Boston newspapers together, such as the *Boston Evening Post* and the *Boston Post-Boy*.

3 *Master* While one could argue that Hammon was actually a freeman and is using "master" in terms of having servants, not slaves, it seems more likely that Hammon was actually enslaved.

4 *Sloop* a small, single-mast vessel.

5 *John Howland, Master* Howland is the captain of the ship, not Hammon's master.

6 *the Bay* of Honduras or the Bay of Campeachy; both are located in the Gulf of Mexico.

7 *Original reads*: we was detain'd [ed.].

8 *Logwood* Native to the Gulf of Mexico, logwood is a natural source of dye.

9 *Cape Florida* At this time, Florida was a Spanish colony.

10 *5 Leagues* about 17 miles.

11 *the Mate and Nine Hands* A mate holds a higher position than a hand.

12 *tarry* remain.

clear, which if he had done, might have sav'd his Vessel and Cargo, and not only so, but his own Life, as well as the Lives of the Mate and Nine Hands,[11] as I shall presently relate.

After being upon this Reef two Days, the Captain order'd the Boat to be hoisted out, and then ask'd who were willing to tarry[12] on board? The whole Crew was for going on Shore at this Time, but as the Boat would not carry 12 persons at once, and to prevent any Uneasiness, the Captain, a Passenger, and one Hand tarry'd on board, while the Mate, with Seven Hands besides myself, were order'd to go on Shore in the Boat, which as soon as we had reached, one half were to be Landed, and the other four to return to the Sloop, to fetch the Captain and the others on Shore. The Captain order'd us to take with us our Arms, Ammunition, Provisions and Necessaries for Cooking, as also a Sail to make a Tent of, to shelter us from the Weather; after having left the Sloop we stood towards the Shore, and being within Two Leagues of the same, we espy'd a Number of Canoes, which we at first took to be Rocks, but soon found our Mistake, for we perceiv'd they moved towards us; we presently saw an English Colour[13] hoisted in one of the Canoes, at the Sight of which we were not a little rejoiced, but on our advancing yet nearer, we found them, to our very great Surprize, to be *Indians* of which there were Sixty; being now so near them we could not possibly make our Escape; they soon came up with and boarded us, took away all our Arms, Ammunition, and Provision. The whole Number of Canoes (being about Twenty) then made for the Sloop, except Two which they left to guard us, who order'd us to follow on with them; the Eighteen which made for the Sloop, went so much faster than we that they got on board above Three Hours before we came along side, and had kill'd Captain *Howland*, the Passenger and the other hand; we came to the Larboard side of the Sloop, and they order'd us round to the Starboard,[14] and as we were passing round the Bow, we saw the whole Number of *Indians*, advancing forward and loading their Guns, upon which the Mate said, *"my Lads we are all dead Men"* and before we had got round, they discharged their Small Arms upon us, and kill'd Three of our hands, viz.[15] *Reuben Young* of *Cape-Cod*, Mate; *Joseph Little* and *Lemuel Doty* of *Plymouth*, upon which I immediately jump'd overboard, choosing[16] rather to be drowned, than to be kill'd by those barbarous and inhuman Savages. In three or four Minutes after, I heard another Volley[17] which dispatched the other five, viz. *John Nowland*, and *Nathaniel Rich*, both belonging to *Plymouth*, and *Elkanah Collymore*, and *James Webb*, Strangers, and *Moses Newmock*, Molatto.[18] As soon as they had kill'd the whole of the People, one of the Canoes paddled after me, and soon came up with me, hauled[19] me into the Canoe, and beat me most terribly with a Cutlass,[20] after that they tied[21] me down, then this Canoe stood for the Sloop again and as soon as she came along side, the *Indians* on board the Sloop betook themselves to their Canoes, then set the Vessel on Fire, making a prodigious shouting and hallowing like so many Devils. As soon as the Vessel was burnt down to the Water's edge, the *Indians* stood for the Shore, together with our Boat, on board of which they put 5 hands. After we came to the Shore, they led me to their Huts,[22] where I expected nothing but immediate Death, and as they spoke broken English, were often telling me, while coming from the Sloop to the Shore, that they intended to roast me alive.

Notes

[13] *English Colour* a flag indicating English loyalty.

[14] *Larboard ... Starboard* the left-hand and right-hand sides of the ship.

[15] *viz* namely (abbreviation of the Latin word *videlicet*).

[16] *Original reads*: chusing [ed.].

[17] *Volley* discharge of gunfire.

[18] *Molatto* mulatto: one who is of black and white descent.

[19] *Original reads*: hawled [ed.].

[20] *Cutlass* a short, curved sword.

[21] *Original reads*: ty'd [ed.].

[22] *Original reads*: Hutts [ed.].

[23] *Original reads*: they were better to me then my Fears [ed.].

But the Providence of God order'd it other ways, for He appeared for my Help, *in this Mount of Difficulty*, and they were better to me than[23] my Fears, and soon unbound me, but set a Guard over me every Night. They kept me with them about five Weeks, during which Time they us'd me pretty well, and gave me boil'd Corn, which was what they often eat themselves. The Way I made my Escape from these Villains was this; A Spanish Schooner[24] arriving there from *St. Augustine*,[25] the Master of which, whose Name was *Romond*, asked the *Indians* to let me go on board his Vessel, which they granted, and the Captain, knowing me very well, weigh'd Anchor and carry'd me off to the *Havanna*,[26] and after being there four Days the *Indians* came after me, and insisted on having *me* again, as I was their Prisoner – They made Application to the Governor,[27] and demanded me again from him; in answer to which the Governor told them, that as they had put the whole Crew to Death, they should not have me again, and so paid them Ten Dollars for me, adding, that he would not have them kill any Person hereafter, but take as many of them as they could, of those that should be cast away, and bring them to him for which he would pay them Ten Dollars a-head. At the *Havanna* I lived with the Governor in the Castle about a Twelve-month, where I was walking thro' the Street, I met with a Press-Gang[28] who immediately prest me, and put me into Gaol,[29] and with a Number of others I was confin'd till next Morning, when we were all brought out, and ask'd who would go on board the King's Ships, four of which having been lately built, were bound to *Old-Spain*, and on my refusing to serve on board, they put me in a close Dungeon, where I was confin'd *Four Years and seven months*; during which time I often made application to the Governor, by Persons who came to see the Prisoners, but they never acquainted him with it, nor did he know all this Time what became of me, which was the means of my being confin'd there so long. But kind Providence so order'd it, that after I had been in this Place so long as the Time mention'd above the Captain of a Merchantman,[30] belonging to *Boston*, having sprung a Leak was obliged to put into the *Havanna* to rest, and while he was at Dinner at Mrs. *Betty Howard's*, she told the Captain of my deplorable Condition, and said she would be glad, if he could by some means or other relieve me; The Captain told Mrs. *Howard* he would use his best Endeavours for my Relief and Enlargement.

Accordingly, after Dinner, [the Captain] came to the Prison, and ask'd the Keeper if he might see me; upon his Request I was brought out of the Dungeon, and after the Captain had Interrogated me, told me, he would intercede with the Governor for my Relief out of that miserable Place, which he did, and the next Day the Governor sent an order to release me; I lived with the Governor about a Year after I was delivered from the Dungeon, in which Time I endeavour'd three Times to make my Escape, the last of which proved effectual; the first Time I got on board of Captain *Marsh*, an *English* Twenty Gun Ship, with a Number of others, and lay on board conceal'd that Night; and the next Day the Ship being under sail, I thought myself safe, and so made my Appearance upon Deck, but as soon as we were discovered the Captain ordered the Boat out, and sent us all on Shore – I intreated the Captain to let me, in particular, tarry on board, begging, and crying to him, to commiserate my unhappy Condition, and

Notes

[24] *Schooner* a two-masted ship.

[25] *St. Augustine* port city in northeastern Florida occupied by the Spanish.

[26] *Havanna* Havana, the capital of Cuba.

[27] *the Governor* Francisco Antonio Cajigal de la Vega was the governor of Cuba from 1747–1760.

[28] *Press-Gang* a group commissioned by the government to impress ("prest") or draft men into the naval forces.

[29] *Gaol* jail. *Original reads*: Goal [ed.].

[30] *Merchantman* a cargo ship.

added, that I had been confin'd almost five Years in a close Dungeon, but the Captain would not hearken to any Intreaties, for fear of having the Governor's Displeasure, and so I was obliged to go on Shore.

After being on Shore another Twelvemonth, I endeavour'd to make my Escape the second Time, by trying to get on board of a Sloop bound to *Jamaica*, and as I was going from the City to the Sloop, was unhappily taken by the Guard, and ordered back to the Castle, and there confined. However, in a short Time I was set at Liberty, and order'd with a Number of others to carry the Bishop[31] from the Castle, thro' the Country, to confirm the old People, baptize Children, &c. for which he receives large Sums of Money. I was employ'd in this Service about Seven Months, during which Time I lived very well, and then returned to the Castle again, where I had my Liberty to walk about the City, and do Work for myself – The *Beaver*, an *English* Man of War[32] then lay in the Harbour, and having been informed by some of the Ship's Crew that she was to sail in a few Days, I had nothing now to do, but to seek an Opportunity how I should make my Escape.

Accordingly one Sunday Night the Lieutenant of the Ship with a Number of the Barge Crew were in a Tavern, and Mrs. *Howard* who had before been a Friend to me, interceded with the Lieutenant to carry me on board: the Lieutenant said he would with all his Heart, and immediately I went on board in the Barge. The next Day the *Spaniards* came along side the *Beaver*, and demanded me again, with a Number of others who had made their Escape from them, and got on board the Ship, but just before I did; but the Captain, who was a true *Englishman*, refus'd them, and said he could not answer it, to deliver up any *Englishman* under *English* Colours. In a few Days we set Sail for *Jamaica*, where we arrived safe, after a short and pleasant Passage.

After being at *Jamaica* a short Time we sail'd for *London*, as convoy to a Fleet of Merchantmen, who all arrived safe in the *Downs*,[33] I was turned over to another Ship, the *Arcenceil*,[34] and there remained about a Month. From this Ship I went on board the *Sandwich* of 90 Guns; on board the *Sandwich*, I tarry'd 6 Weeks, and then was order'd on board the *Hercules*, Capt. *John Porter*, a 74 Gun Ship, we sail'd on a Cruize, and met with a *French* 84 Gun Ship, and had a very smart Engagement,[35] in which about 70 of our Hands were Kill'd and Wounded, the Captain lost his Leg in the Engagement, and I was Wounded in the Head by a small Shot. We should have taken this Ship, if they had not cut away the most of our Rigging; however, in about three Hours after, a 64 Gun Ship, came up with and took her – I was discharged from the *Hercules* the 12th Day of *May* 1759 (having been on board of that Ship 3 Months) on account of my being disabled in the Arm, and render'd incapable of Service, after being honourably paid the Wages due to me. I was put into the *Greenwich* Hospital where I stay'd and soon recovered. I then ship'd myself a Cook on board Captain *Martyn*, an arm'd Ship in the King's Service. I was on board this Ship almost Two Months, and after being paid my Wages, was discharg'd in the Month of *October*. After my discharge from Captain *Martyn*, I was taken sick in *London* of a Fever, and was confin'd about 6 Weeks, where I expended all my Money, and left in very poor Circumstances; and unhappy for me I knew nothing

Notes

31 *carry the Bishop* Eight people literally carried the Bishop, Pedro Augustín Morell de Santa Cruz, in a red velvet chair.

32 *Man of War* a powerful warship.

33 *the Downs* in the North Sea, near the English Channel.

34 *the Arcenceil* a French 50-gun ship captured by the English in 1756.

35 *a very smart Engagement* a battle.

36 *Guinea* Africa.

37 *a publick House* a tavern.

of my *good Master's* being in *London* at this my very difficult Time. After I got well of my sickness, I ship'd myself on board of a large Ship bound to *Guinea*[36], and being in a publick House[37] one Evening, I overheard a Number of Persons talking about Rigging a Vessel bound to *New-England*, I ask'd them to what Part of *New-England* this Vessel was bound? They told me, to *Boston;* and having ask'd them who was Commander? they told me, Capt. *Watt*; in a few Minutes after this the Mate of the Ship came in, and I ask'd him if Captain Watt did not want a Cook, who told me he did, and that the Captain would be in, in a few Minutes; and in about half an Hour the Captain came in, and then I ship'd myself at once, after begging off from the Ship bound to *Guinea;* I work'd on board Captain *Watt's* Ship almost Three Months, before she sail'd, and one Day being at Work in the Hold, I overheard some Persons on board mention the Name of *Winslow*, at the Name of which I was very inquisitive, and having ask'd what *Winslow* they were talking about? They told me it was *General Winslow;* and that he was one of the Passengers, I ask'd them what *General Winslow*? For I never knew *my good Master*, by that Title before; but after enquiring more particularly I found it must be *Master*, and in a few Days' Time the Truth was joyfully verify'd by a happy Sight of his Person, which so overcome me, that I could not speak to him for some Time – *My good Master* was exceeding glad to see me, telling me that I was like one arose from the Dead; for he thought I had been Dead a great many Years, having heard nothing of me for almost Thirteen Years.

I think I have not deviated from Truth, in any particular of this my Narrative, and tho' I have omitted a great many Things, yet what is wrote may suffice to convince the Reader, that I have been most grievously afflicted, and yet thro' the Divine Goodness, as miraculously preserved, and delivered out of many Dangers; of which I desire to retain a *grateful Remembrance*, as long as I live in the World.

And now, That in the Providence of that GOD, who delivered his Servant David out of the Paw of the Lion and out of the Paw of the Bear,[38] *I am freed from a* long *and* dreadful Captivity, among worse Savages than they; *And am return'd to my* own Native Land, to Shew how Great Things the Lord hath done for Me; *I would call upon all Men, and Say*, O Magnify[39] the Lord with Me, and let us Exalt his Name together! – O that Men would Praise the Lord for His Goodness, and for his Wonderful Works to the Children of Men!

1760

Notes

[38] *the Paw of the Lion and out of the Paw of the Bear* 1 Samuel 17:37; "The Lord that delivered me out of the paw of the lion, and out of the paw of the bear, he will deliver me out of the hand of this Philistine [Goliath]."

[39] *Original reads*: Magnifie [ed.].

Phillis Wheatley (*c.*1753–1784)

Kidnapped from her native West Africa as a small child and sold into slavery, Phillis Wheatley built the reputation of being the most famous woman of African descent in the Revolutionary-era Atlantic World. This stature is doubly remarkable given that Wheatley died in the poverty and obscurity that characterized the lives of most of her fellow colonial New Englanders of color. While her prodigious talent gained her access to a world most New World Africans could scarcely imagine, her poetry could never fully quell the Enlightenment rhetoric of the inherent inferiority of Africans. In his 1785 *Notes on the State of Virginia*, Thomas Jefferson used Wheatley's verses not as an example of American literature, but as evidence of the degraded condition of a race whose humanity was deemed questionable. "Religion indeed has produced a Phyllis Whately [*sic*] but it could not produce a poet," he wrote, while misspelling her name. "The compositions published under her name are below the dignity of criticism." Yet, from the moment her *Poems on Various Subjects, Religious and Moral* appeared in 1773, Wheatley has had a seminal place in the canon of African American literature, even as statesmen like Jefferson denied the possibility of such a canon's existence.

Phillis Wheatley was born around 1753 in West Africa. The year of her birth is approximate: when she arrived in Boston, in 1761, her missing front baby teeth led her white captors to surmise that she was between seven and eight years old. From the few descriptions of her homeland provided in her poetry, scholars have concluded that she was probably from Gambia, a member of the Fulani tribe, her family perhaps part of the Muslim elite. In Boston she was purchased by the wealthy merchant John Wheatley, who named her for the slave ship that had carried her to Massachusetts (*The Phillis*). John Wheatley purchased her to serve his wife, but it was soon clear that the child possessed a keen intellect that confounded the racial assumptions on which slavery was predicated. Phillis's quick grasp of English (she learned the language in a matter of months) prompted the Wheatleys to recognize her talents. In deference to her precociousness and delicate health, they delegated most of her duties to other slaves in the household and encouraged her to study the Bible, Latin, Greek, and classical literature under the tutelage of their daughter Mary.

In a form of patronage that would become a pattern in the careers of African American writers well into the twentieth century, Phillis Wheatley was educated in the libraries of some of the leading white Congregationalist intellectuals in colonial America. Attending Boston's Old South Church with the Wheatleys, Phillis had access to the church's extensive library, bequeathed to the congregation by Thomas Prince, the previous minister. Prince's 1,500-volume collection was one of the largest in colonial America, and provided Wheatley with access to many of the classical authors referenced in her writing. Other mentors and tutors to Wheatley included Joseph Sewell, pastor at Old South Church and son of the famous diarist, Samuel Sewall; Samuel Cooper, minister at Boston's Brattle Street meetinghouse; and Mather Byles, the Wheatleys' neighbor and Cotton Mather's nephew, whose library was second only to that of the Old South Church in its scope. Immersed in such an environment of classical education and constant intellectual engagement, Phillis excelled as a student of Greek and Latin, doing scriptural exegesis just a few short years after arriving from Africa. At the age of 12 she sent a letter to

The Wiley Blackwell Anthology of African American Literature: Volume 1, 1746–1920, First Edition.
Edited by Gene Andrew Jarrett.

Mohegan minister Samson Occom, and also around the same time formed a lasting bond with Rhode Island slave Obour Tanner. In 1767, Wheatley published her first poem in the *Newport Mercury*, "On Messrs. Hussey and Coffin," a meditation on their safe delivery from a hurricane.

Over the next five years, Wheatley's reputation as a poet spread throughout New and Old England with her 1768 poem, "To the King's Most Excellent Majesty," which praised George III's repeal of the Stamp Act, and a 1770 elegy for the Rev. George Whitefield, one of the founders of Methodism. Yet neither these successes nor an ode to the fallen heroes of the Boston Massacre (including the mixed-race Crispus Attucks) could inoculate Wheatley against prejudicial suspicions that she was not the author of her poems. In a legend that has been called "the primal scene of African American letters," a court of Boston's most respected political and literary leaders – including John Hancock and Massachusetts Governor Thomas Hutchinson – called upon Wheatley in 1772 to give an oral defense of her literary authenticity. Recent scholarship has questioned the historical veracity of such a scene, suggesting instead that the noteworthy signatures attesting to her authorship that appear in the preface of her *Poems on Various Subjects, Religious and Moral* were instead collected by an enterprising Wheatley at a town meeting. Although conflicting, both stories attest to Wheatley's pluck and tenacity in defending her poetry against racist assumptions.

Poems on Various Subjects, Religious and Moral was first released in London, where the Countess of Huntingdon assisted Wheatley in finding a publisher. In 1773, while in London with the Wheatleys' son, Nathaniel, she was feted by British royalty, including Brook Watson, the future Lord Mayor of London, and by Benjamin Franklin. Her success also eventually inspired John Wheatley to grant Wheatley her freedom. When the book appeared in the colonies in 1774, Wheatley became the fifth American woman, and only the second American woman poet (after Anne Bradstreet), to have work appear in print for a public audience. In October of the following year, she wrote a poem honoring General George Washington, which she mailed to the commander-in-chief. Washington responded by inviting Wheatley to visit him at his headquarters in Cambridge, Massachusetts, and she did so in early 1776.

Lamentably, Wheatley's fame could neither speed her subsequent efforts to publish nor protect her from poverty. In 1778, her former master John Wheatley died. The limited financial support that he provided dried up. Shortly thereafter she married the Bostonian John Peters, an African American man of many professions but little success, and the couple entered a period of economic and personal hardship that contrasted with Wheatley's previous life of relative privilege. Her efforts in drumming up subscribers for a second volume of poems came to naught. She gave birth to three children who died in infancy. After John Peters was imprisoned for debt, Wheatley's poverty deepened. She died in 1784, shortly after delivering her third child.

Further reading

Balkun, Mary McAleer. "Phillis Wheatley's Construction of Otherness and the Rhetoric of Performed Ideology." *African American Review* 36.1 (2002): 121–135.

Brooks, Joanna. "Our Phillis, Ourselves." *American Literature* 82.1 (2010): 1–28.

Carretta, Vincent. *Phillis Wheatley: Biography of a Genius in Bondage*. Athens: University of Georgia Press, 2011.

Erkkila, Betsy. "Phillis Wheatley and the Black American Revolution." *Feminist Interventions in Early American Studies*. Ed. Mary C. Carruth. Tuscaloosa: University of Alabama Press, 2006. 161–182.

Gates, Henry Louis, Jr. *The Trials of Phillis Wheatley*. New York: Basic Books, 2003.

Harris, Will. "Phillis Wheatley, Diaspora Subjectivity, and the African American Canon." *MELUS: The Journal of the Society for the Study of the Multi-Ethnic Literature of the United States* 33.3 (2008): 29–43.

Shields, John C. *Phillis Wheatley's Poetics of Liberation*. Knoxville: University of Tennessee Press, 2008.

Shields, John C. *Phillis Wheatley and the Romantics*. Knoxville: University of Tennessee Press, 2010.

Shields, John C. and Eric D. Lamore, eds. *New Essays on Phillis Wheatley*. Knoxville: University of Tennessee Press, 2011.

Sidbury, James. "Africa in Early African American Literature." *A Companion to African American Literature*. Ed. Gene Andrew Jarrett. Malden, MA: Wiley-Blackwell, 2010. 25–44.

Slauter, Eric. "Neoclassical Culture in a Society with Slaves: Race and Rights in the Age of Wheatley." *Early American Studies: An Interdisciplinary Journal* 2.1 (2004): 81–122.

Thorn, Jennifer. "Phillis Wheatley's Ghosts: The Racial Melancholy of New England Protestants." *Eighteenth Century: Theory and Interpretation* 50.1 (2009): 73–99.

Waldstreicher, David. "The Wheatleyan Moment." *Early American Studies: An Interdisciplinary Journal* 9.3 (2011): 522–551.

To Maecenas[1]

From *Poems on Various Subjects, Religious and Moral*

MAECENAS, you, beneath the myrtle[2] shade,
Read o'er what poets sung, and shepherds play'd.
What felt those poets but you feel the same?
Does not your soul possess the sacred flame?
Their noble strains your equal genius shares
In softer language, and diviner airs.

While ***Homer*** paints lo! circumfus'd in air,
Celestial Gods in mortal forms appear;
Swift as they move hear each recess rebound,
Heav'n quakes, earth trembles, and the shores resound.
Great Sire of verse, before my mortal eyes,
The lightnings blaze across the vaulted skies,
And, as the thunder shakes the heav'nly plains,
A deep-felt horror thrills through all my veins.
When gentler strains demand thy graceful song,
The length'ning line moves languishing along.
When great *Patroclus* courts *Achilles'* aid,[3]
The grateful tribute of my tears is paid;
Prone on the shore he feels the pangs of love,
And stern *Pelides*[4] tend'rest passions move.

Great *Maro's*[5] strain in heav'nly numbers flows,
The *Nine*[6] inspire, and all the bosom glows.
O could I rival thine and *Virgil's* page,
Or claim the *Muses* with the *Mantuan* Sage;[7]
Soon the same beauties should my mind adorn,
And the same ardors in my soul should burn:

Notes

To Maecenas

[1] *Maecenas* a Roman aristocrat (74–78 BC) and patron of the poets Horace and Virgil.

[2] *myrtle* an evergreen shrub, sacred to the goddess of love, Venus.

[3] *Patroclus/Achilles* the Greek hero of Homer's *Iliad*; Patroclus was his beloved companion.

[4] *Pelides* Achilles (son of Peleus).

[5] *Maro* the family name of Virgil.

[6] *The Nine* the nine Muses, goddesses who inspire art.

[7] *Mantuan Sage* i.e., Virgil, who was born in Mantua.

Then should my song in bolder notes arise,
And all my numbers pleasingly surprize;
But here I sit, and mourn a grov'ling mind
That fain would mount, and ride upon the wind.

Not you, my friend, these plaintive strains become,
Not you, whose bosom is the *Muses* home;
When they from tow'ring *Helicon*[8] retire,
They fan in you the bright immortal fire,
But I less happy, cannot raise the song,
The fault'ring music dies upon my tongue.

The happier *Terence*[9] all the choir inspir'd,
His soul replenish'd, and his bosom fir'd;
But say, ye *Muses*, why this partial grace,
To one alone of *Afric's* sable race;
From age to age transmitting thus his name
With the first glory in the rolls of fame?

Thy virtues, great *Maecenas!* shall be sung
In praise of him, from whom those virtues sprung:
While blooming wreaths around thy temples spread,
I'll snatch a laurel from thine honour'd head,
While you indulgent smile upon the deed.

As long as *Thames*[10] in streams majestic flows,
Or *Naiads*[11] in their oozy beds repose,
While *Phoebus*[12] reigns above the starry train,
While bright *Aurora*[13] purples o'er the main,
So long, great Sir, the muse thy praise shall sing,
So long thy praise shall make *Parnassus*[14] ring:
Then grant, *Maecenas*, thy paternal rays,
Hear me propitious, and defend my lays.

To the University of Cambridge,[1] in New-England

From *Poems on Various Subjects, Religious and Moral*

WHILE an intrinsic ardor prompts to write,
The muses promise to assist my pen;
'Twas not long since I left my native shore

Notes

[8] *Helicon* a mountain in Greece where the Muses reputedly live.
[9] *Terence* a Roman comic playwright (*c.*190–159 BC).
[10] *Thames* the river of London.
[11] *Naiads* nymphs of Greek folklore, said to inhabit rivers and streams.
[12] *Phoebus* Apollo, a Greek god associated with the sun.
[13] *Aurora* the Roman goddess of dawn.
[14] *Parnassus* a sacred Greek mountain associated with Apollo and the Muses.

To the University of Cambridge, in New-England
[1] *Cambridge* i.e., Harvard College.

The land of errors, and *Egyptian* gloom:
Father of mercy, 'twas thy gracious hand
Brought me in safety from those dark abodes.

Students, to you 'tis giv'n to scan the heights
Above, to traverse the ethereal space,
And mark the systems of revolving worlds.
Still more, ye sons of science ye receive
The blissful news by messengers from heav'n,
How *Jesus'* blood for your redemption flows.
See him with hands out-stretcht upon the cross;
Immense compassion in his bosom glows;
He hears revilers, nor resents their scorn:
What matchless mercy in the Son of God!
When the whole human race by sin had fall'n,
He deign'd to die that they might rise again,
And share with him in the sublimest skies,
Life without death, and glory without end.

Improve your privileges while they stay,
Ye pupils, and each hour redeem, that bears
Or good or bad report of you to heav'n.
Let sin, that baneful evil to the soul,
By you be shunn'd, nor once remit your guard;
Suppress the deadly serpent in its egg.
Ye blooming plants of human race divine,
An *Ethiop*[2] tells you 'tis your greatest foe;
Its transient sweetness turns to endless pain,
And in immense perdition sinks the soul.

On Being Brought from Africa to America

From *Poems on Various Subjects, Religious and Moral*

'TWAS mercy brought me from my *Pagan* land,
Taught my benighted soul to understand
That there's a God, that there's a *Saviour* too:
Once I redemption neither sought nor knew.
Some view our sable race with scornful eye,
"Their colour is a diabolic die."
Remember, *Christians, Negros,* black as *Cain,*[1]
May be refin'd, and join th' angelic train.

Notes

[2] *Ethiop* of Ethiopia; a black African.

ON BEING BROUGHT FROM AFRICA TO AMERICA

[1] *Cain* son of Adam and Eve, "marked" by God after murdering his brother, Abel.

On the Death of the Rev. Dr. Sewell.[1] 1769

From *Poems on Various Subjects, Religious and Moral*

ERE yet the morn its lovely blushes spread,
See *Sewell* number'd with the happy dead.
Hail, holy man, arriv'd th' immortal shore,
Though we shall hear thy warning voice no more.
Come, let us all behold with wishful eyes
The saint ascending to his native skies;
From hence the prophet wing'd his rapt'rous way
To the blest mansions in eternal day.
Then begging for the Spirit of our God,
And panting eager for the same abode,
Come, let us all with the same vigour rise,
And take a prospect of the blissful skies;
While on our minds *Christ's* image is imprest,
And the dear Saviour glows in ev'ry breast.
Thrice happy saint! to find thy heav'n at last,
What compensation for the evils past!

Great God, incomprehensible, unknown
By sense, we bow at thine exalted throne.
O, while we beg thine excellence to feel,
Thy sacred Spirit to our hearts reveal,
And give us of that mercy to partake,
Which thou hast promis'd for the *Saviour's* sake!

"*Sewell* is dead." Swift-pinion'd[2] *Fame* thus cry'd.
"Is *Sewell* dead," my trembling tongue reply'd,
O what a blessing in his flight deny'd!
How oft for us the holy prophet pray'd!
How oft to us the Word of Life convey'd!
By duty urg'd my mournful verse to close,
I for his tomb this epitaph compose.

"Lo, here a Man, redeem'd by *Jesus'* blood,
A sinner once, but now a saint with God;
Behold ye rich, ye poor, ye fools, ye wise,
Nor let his monument your heart surprize;
'Twill tell you what this holy man has done,
Which gives him brighter lustre than the sun.
Listen, ye happy, from your seats above.
I speak sincerely, while I speak and love,
He sought the paths of piety and truth,

Notes

On the Death of the Rev. Dr. Sewell. 1769

[1] *Dr. Sewell* the minister of Old South Church in Boston, where the Wheatley family worshipped.

[2] *pinion* the flight feathers of a bird's wing.

By these made happy from his early youth!
In blooming years that grace divine he felt,
Which rescues sinners from the chains of guilt.
Mourn him, ye indigent, whom he has fed,
And henceforth seek, like him, for living bread;
Ev'n *Christ*, the bread descending from above,
And ask an int'rest in his saving love.
Mourn him, ye youth, to whom he oft has told
God's gracious wonders from the times of old.
I, too have cause this mighty loss to mourn,
For he my monitor will not return.
O when shall we to his blest state arrive?
When the same graces in our bosoms thrive."

On the Death of the Rev. Mr. George Whitefield.[1] 1770

From *Poems on Various Subjects, Religious and Moral*

HAIL, happy saint, on thine immortal throne,
Possest of glory, life, and bliss unknown;
We hear no more the music of thy tongue,
Thy wonted auditories cease to throng.
Thy sermons in unequall'd accents flow'd,
And ev'ry bosom with devotion glow'd;
Thou didst in strains of eloquence refin'd
Inflame the heart, and captivate the mind.
Unhappy we the setting sun deplore,
So glorious once, but ah! it shines no more.

Behold the prophet in his tow'ring flight!
He leaves the earth for heav'n's unmeasur'd height,
And worlds unknown receive him from our sight.
There *Whitefield* wings with rapid course his way,
And sails to *Zion* through vast seas of day.
Thy pray'rs, great saint, and thine incessant cries
Have pierc'd the bosom of thy native skies.
Thou moon hast seen, and all the stars of light,
How he has wrestled with his God by night.
He pray'd that grace in ev'ry heart might dwell,
He long'd to see *America* excel;
He charg'd its youth that ev'ry grace divine
Should with full lustre in their conduct shine;
That Saviour, which his soul did first receive,

Notes

ON THE DEATH OF THE REV. MR. GEORGE WHITEFIELD. 1770

[1] Rev. George Whitefield English Methodist minister (1714–1770), a famed evangelist called the "Voice of the Great Awakening" in America.

The greatest gift that ev'n a God can give,
He freely offer'd to the num'rous throng,
That on his lips with list'ning pleasure hung.

"Take him, ye wretched, for your only good,
Take him ye starving sinners, for your food;
Ye thirsty, come to this life-giving stream,
Ye preachers, take him for your joyful theme;
Take him my dear *Americans*, he said,
Be your complaints on his kind bosom laid:
Take him, ye *Africans*, he longs for you,
Impartial Saviour is his title due:
Wash'd in the fountain of redeeming blood,
You shall be sons, and kings, and priests to God."

Great *Countess*,[2] we *Americans* revere
Thy name, and mingle in thy grief sincere;
New England deeply feels, the *Orphans* mourn,
Their more than father will no more return.

But, though arrested by the hand of death,
Whitefield no more exerts his lab'ring breath,
Yet let us view him in th' eternal skies,
Let ev'ry heart to this bright vision rise;
While the tomb safe retains its sacred trust,
Till life divine re-animates his dust.

On the Death of a Young Lady of Five Years of Age

From *Poems on Various Subjects, Religious and Moral*

FROM dark abodes to fair ethereal[1] light
Th' enraptur'd innocent has wing'd her flight;
On the kind bosom of eternal love
She finds unknown beatitude above.
This know, ye parents, nor her loss deplore,
She feels the iron hand of pain no more;
The dispensations of unerring grace,
Should turn your sorrows into grateful praise;
Let then no tears for her henceforward flow,
No more distress'd in our dark vale below.

Her morning sun, which rose divinely bright,
Was quickly mantled with the gloom of night;
But hear in heav'n's blest bow'rs[2] your *Nancy* fair,

Notes

[2] *Great Countess* the Countess of Huntingdon, Selina Shirley Hastings (1707–1791), a religious revivalist and supporter of Whitefield.

On the Death of a Young Lady of Five Years of Age

[1] *Original reads*: etherial [ed.].

[2] *bow'rs* idyllic shady places or bedrooms.

And learn to imitate her language there.
"Thou, Lord, whom I behold with glory crown'd,
By what sweet name, and in what tuneful sound
Wilt thou be prais'd? Seraphic[3] pow'rs are faint
Infinite love and majesty to paint.
To thee let all their grateful voices raise,
And saints and angels join their songs of praise."

Perfect in bliss she from her heav'nly home
Looks down, and smiling beckons you to come;
Why then, fond parents, why these fruitless groans?
Restrain your tears, and cease your plaintive moans.
Freed from a world of sin, and snares, and pain,
Why would you wish your daughter back again?
No – bow resign'd. Let hope your grief control,
And check the rising tumult of the soul.
Calm in the prosperous, and adverse day,
Adore the God who gives and takes away;
Eye him in all, his holy name revere,
Upright your actions, and your hearts sincere,
Till having sail'd through life's tempestuous sea,
And from its rocks, and boist'rous billows free,
Yourselves, safe landed on the blissful shore,
Shall join your happy babe to part no more.

On Recollection

From *Poems on Various Subjects, Religious and Moral*

MNEME[1] begin. Inspire, ye sacred nine,[2]
Your vent'rous *Afric* in her great design.
Mneme, immortal pow'r, I trace thy spring:
Assist my strains, while I thy glories sing:
The acts of long departed years, by thee
Recover'd, in due order rang'd we see:
Thy pow'r the long-forgotten calls from night,
That sweetly plays before the *fancy's* sight.

Mneme in our nocturnal visions pours
The ample treasure of her secret stores;
Swift from above she wings her silent flight
Through *Phoebe's*[3] realms, fair regent of the night;

Notes

[3] *Seraphic* angelic.

On Recollection

[1] *Mneme* the muse of memory.

[2] *sacred nine* the nine Muses, goddesses who inspire art.

[3] *Phoebe* a Greek goddess associated with the moon.

And, in her pomp of images display'd,
To the high-raptur'd poet gives her aid,
Through the unbounded regions of the mind,
Diffusing light celestial and refin'd.
The heav'nly *phantom* paints the actions done
By ev'ry tribe beneath the rolling sun.

Mneme, enthron'd within the human breast,
Has vice condemn'd, and ev'ry virtue blest.
How sweet the sound when we her plaudit hear?
Sweeter than music to the ravish'd ear,
Sweeter than *Maro's*[4] entertaining strains
Resounding through the groves, and hills, and plains.
But how is *Mneme* dreaded by the race,
Who scorn her warnings and despise her grace?
By her unveil'd each horrid crime appears,
Her awful hand a cup of wormwood[5] bears.
Days, years mispent, O what a hell of woe!
Hers the worst tortures that our souls can know.

Now eighteen years their destin'd course have run,
In fast succession round the central sun.
How did the follies of that period pass
Unnotic'd, but behold them writ in brass!
In Recollection see them fresh return,
And sure 'tis mine to be asham'd, and mourn.

O *Virtue*, smiling in immortal green,
Do thou exert thy pow'r, and change the scene;
Be thine employ to guide my future days,
And mine to pay the tribute of my praise.

Of *Recollection* such the pow'r enthron'd
In ev'ry breast, and thus her pow'r is own'd.
The wretch, who dar'd the vengeance of the skies,
At last awakes in horror and surprize,
By her alarm'd, he sees impending fate,
He howls in anguish, and repents too late.
But O! what peace, what joys are hers t'impart
To ev'ry holy, ev'ry upright heart!
Thrice blest the man, who, in her sacred shrine,
Feels himself shelter'd from the wrath divine!

Notes

[4] *Maro* i.e., Virgil, the epic Roman poet.

[5] *wormwood* a shrub with a bitter, herbal taste (associated with grief).

On Imagination

From *Poems on Various Subjects, Religious and Moral*

THY various works, imperial queen, we see,
How bright their forms! how deck'd with pomp by thee!
Thy wond'rous acts in beauteous order stand,
And all attest how potent is thine hand.

From *Helicon's*[1] refulgent heights attend,
Ye sacred choir, and my attempts befriend:
To tell her glories with a faithful tongue,
Ye blooming graces, triumph in my song.

Now here, now there, the roving *Fancy* flies,
Till some lov'd object strikes her wand'ring eyes,
Whose silken fetters all the senses bind,
And soft captivity involves the mind.

Imagination! who can sing thy force?
Or who describe the swiftness of thy course?
Soaring through air to find the bright abode,
Th' empyreal[2] palace of the thund'ring God,
We on thy pinions can surpass the wind,
And leave the rolling universe behind:
From star to star the mental optics rove,
Measure the skies, and range the realms above.
There in one view we grasp the mighty whole,
Or with new worlds amaze th' unbounded soul.

Though W*inter* frowns to *Fancy's* raptur'd eyes
The fields may flourish, and gay scenes arise;
The frozen deeps may break their iron bands,
And bid their waters murmur o'er the sands.
Fair *Flora*[3] may resume her fragrant reign,
And with her flow'ry riches deck the plain;
Sylvanus[4] may diffuse his honours round,
And all the forest may with leaves be crown'd:
Show'rs may descend, and dews their gems disclose,
And nectar sparkle on the blooming rose.

Such is thy pow'r, nor are thine orders vain,
O thou the leader of the mental train:
In full perfection all thy works are wrought,

Notes

ON IMAGINATION

[1] *Helicon* a mountain in Greece where the Muses (the "sacred choir") reputedly live.

[2] *empyreal* heavenly.

[3] *Flora* Roman goddess of flowering plants.

[4] *Sylvanus* a Roman god of woods and fields.

And thine the sceptre o'er the realms of thought.
Before thy throne the subject-passions bow,
Of subject-passions sov'reign ruler Thou,
At thy command joy rushes on the heart,
And through the glowing veins the spirits dart.

Fancy might now her silken pinions try
To rise from earth, and sweep th' expanse on high;
From *Tithon's* bed now might *Aurora*[5] rise,
Her cheeks all glowing with celestial dies,[6]
While a pure stream of light o'er flows the skies.
The monarch of the day I might behold,
And all the mountains tipt with radiant gold,
But I reluctant leave the pleasing views,
Which *Fancy* dresses to delight the *Muse*;
Winter austere forbids me to aspire,
And northern tempests damp the rising fire;
They chill the tides of *Fancy's* flowing sea,
Cease then, my song, cease the unequal lay.[7]

To the Right Honourable William,[1] Earl of Dartmouth, His Majesty's Principal Secretary of State for North-America, &c.

From *Poems on Various Subjects, Religious and Moral*

HAIL, happy day, when, smiling like the morn,
Fair *Freedom* rose *New-England* to adorn:
The northern clime beneath her genial ray,
Dartmouth, congratulates thy blissful sway:
Elate with hope her race no longer mourns,
Each soul expands, each grateful bosom burns,
While in thine hand with pleasure we behold
The silken reins, and *Freedom's* charms unfold.
Long lost to realms beneath the northern skies
She shines supreme, while hated *faction* dies:
Soon as appear'd the *Goddess* long desir'd,
Sick at the view, she lanquish'd and expir'd;
Thus from the splendors of the morning light
The owl in sadness seeks the caves of night.

Notes

[5] *Aurora* the Roman goddess of the dawn; Tithonus was her Trojan lover.

[6] *dies* colors.

[7] *lay* ballad.

To the Right Honourable William, Earl of Dartmouth, His Majesty's Principal Secretary of State for North-America, &c

[1] William Legge (1731–1801), 2nd Earl of Dartmouth.

No more, *America*, in mournful strain
Of wrongs, and grievance unredress'd complain,
No longer shalt thou dread the iron chain,
Which wanton *Tyranny* with lawless hand
Had made, and with it meant t'enslave the land.

Should you, my lord, while you peruse my song,
Wonder from whence my love of *Freedom* sprung,
Whence flow these wishes for the common good,
By feeling hearts alone best understood,
I, young in life, by seeming cruel fate
Was snatch'd from *Afric's* fancy'd happy seat:
What pangs excruciating must molest,
What sorrows labour in my parent's breast?
Steel'd was that soul and by no misery mov'd
That from a father seiz'd his babe belov'd:
Such, such my case. And can I then but pray
Others may never feel tyrannic sway?

For favours past, great Sir, our thanks are due,
And thee we ask thy favours to renew,
Since in thy pow'r, as in thy will before,
To sooth the griefs, which thou did'st once deplore.
May heav'nly grace the sacred sanction give
To all thy works, and thou for ever live
Not only on the wings of fleeting *Fame*,
Though praise immortal crowns the patriot's name.
But to conduct to heav'ns refulgent fane,
May fiery coursers[2] sweep th' ethereal plain,
And bear thee upwards to that blest abode,
Where, like the prophet,[3] thou shalt find thy God.

To S.M.,[1] a Young *African* Painter, on Seeing His Works

From *Poems on Various Subjects, Religious and Moral*

TO show the lab'ring bosom's deep intent,
And thought in living characters to paint,
When first thy pencil did those beauties give,
And breathing figures learnt from thee to live,
How did those prospects give my soul delight,
A new creation rushing on my sight?
Still, wond'rous youth! each noble path pursue,
On deathless glories fix thine ardent view:
Still may the painter's and the poet's fire

Notes

[2] *coursers* horses.

[3] *prophet* Elijah, carried up to heaven in a fiery chariot (2 Kings 2.11).

To S.M., a Young *African* Painter, on Seeing His Works

[1] *S.M.* Scipio Moorhead, a Bostonian slave whose only surviving work is a portrait of Wheatley.

To aid thy pencil, and thy verse conspire!
And may the charms of each seraphic[2] theme
Conduct thy footsteps to immortal fame!
High to the blissful wonders of the skies
Elate thy soul, and raise thy wishful eyes.
Thrice happy, when exalted to survey
That splendid city, crown'd with endless day,
Whose twice six gates on radiant hinges ring:
Celestial *Salem*[3] blooms in endless spring.

Calm and serene thy moments glide along,
And may the muse inspire each future song!
Still, with the sweets of contemplation bless'd,
May peace with balmy wings your soul invest!
But when these shades of time are chas'd away,
And darkness ends in everlasting day,
On what seraphic pinions shall we move,
And view the landscapes in the realms above?
There shall thy tongue in heav'nly murmurs flow,
And there my muse with heav'nly transport glow:
No more to tell of *Damon's*[4] tender sighs,
Or rising radiance of *Aurora's*[5] eyes,
For nobler themes demand a nobler strain,
And purer language on th' ethereal plain.
Cease, gentle muse! the solemn gloom of night
Now seals the fair creation from my sight.

A Farewell[1] to America to Mrs. S.W.[2]

From *Poems on Various Subjects, Religious and Moral*

ADIEU, *New-England's* smiling meads, 1
Adieu, the flow'ry plain:
I leave thine op'ning charms, O spring,
And tempt the roaring main.[3]

In vain for me the flow'rets rise, 2
And boast their gaudy pride,
While here beneath the northern skies
I mourn for *health* deny'd.

Notes

[2] *seraphic* angelic.
[3] *Salem* Heavenly Jerusalem, the divine city.
[4] *Damon* a mythological figure of true friendship, who pledged his life for his friend Pythias.
[5] *Aurora* the Roman goddess of the dawn.

A Farewell to America to Mrs. S.W.
[1] *Original reads*: Farewel [ed.].
[2] *S.W.* Susannah Wheatley, the poet's mistress.
[3] *main* the open ocean.

Celestial maid of rosy hue, 3
O let me feel thy reign!
I languish till thy face I view,
Thy vanish'd joys regain.

Susannah mourns, nor can I bear 4
To see the crystal show'r,
Or mark the tender falling tear
At sad departure's hour;

Nor unregarding can I see 5
Her soul with grief opprest:
But let no sighs, no groans for me,
Steal from her pensive breast.

In vain the feather'd warblers sing, 6
In vain the garden blooms,
And on the bosom of the spring
Breathes out her sweet perfumes,

While for *Britannia's* distant shore 7
We sweep the liquid plain,
And with astonish'd eyes explore
The wide-extended main.

Lo! *Health* appears! celestial dame! 8
Complacent and serene,
With *Hebe's*[4] mantle o'er her Frame,
With soul-delighting mein.[5]

To mark the vale where *London* lies 9
With misty vapours crown'd,
Which cloud *Aurora's*[6] thousand dyes,
And veil her charms around,

Why, *Phoebus*,[7] moves thy car so slow? 10
So slow thy rising ray?
Give us the famous town to view
Thou glorious king of day!

For thee, *Britannia*, I resign 11
New-England's smiling fields;
To view again her charms divine,
What joy the prospect yields!

Notes

[4] *Hebe* Greek goddess of youth.
[5] *mein* countenance, expression.
[6] *Aurora* the Roman goddess of dawn.
[7] *Phoebus* Apollo, god of the sun.

But thou! Temptation hence away, 12
With all thy fatal train
Nor once seduce my soul away,
By thine enchanting strain.

Thrice happy they, whose heav'nly shield 13
Secures their souls from harms,
And fell *Temptation* on the field
Of all its pow'r disarms!

1773

Jupiter Hammon (1711–c.1806)

By the time Jupiter Hammon (unrelated to Briton Hammon) wrote "An Address to Miss Phillis Wheatly [*sic*], Ethiopian Poetess, in Boston, Who Came from Africa at Eight Years of Age, and Soon Became Acquainted with the Gospel of Jesus Christ" on August 4, 1778, recognizing, by way of biblical references, the "Ethiopian Poetess" of Boston for her literary gift and her dedication to God, he was a respected writer and orator, whose 1760 poem "An Evening Thought: Salvation by Christ, with Penitential Cries" made him the first published poet of African descent in American history. Like Wheatley, Jupiter Hammon witnessed first-hand the promises and disappointments of American independence as a slave on Long Island, and as a leader in New York's African Society. In his 1787 "Address to the Negroes in the State of New York," Hammon preached conservative patience, a call reprinted by one of the nation's first antislavery groups, the Pennsylvania Society for Promoting the Abolition of Slavery. At a time when New York had yet to draft its gradual emancipation policy for the state's slaves, Hammon counseled obedience to God, and posited that poverty and hardship would surely follow if they were suddenly freed and left to their own limited devices.

A slave on Lloyd's Neck in Queens, Long Island, Hammon received a fine education, with access to Henry Lloyd's library. As an adult, he worked alongside his master, Henry Lloyd, and was often sent to New York City to negotiate lucrative agricultural trade deals on Lloyd's behalf. The Christian faith that Hammon proclaimed in "An Evening Thought" informed all his writing; in addition to his biblically inflected verse, he published several evangelical sermons. When Henry Lloyd died, Hammon continued to serve under his master's son, Joseph Lloyd, a patriot who fled with Jupiter to Connecticut after the British invaded New York City. At war's end, Jupiter returned to the Lloyd manor on Long Island, where he continued to write poetry until his death sometime around 1806.

Further reading

Bell, Bernard W. *Bearing Witness to African American Literature: Validating and Valorizing Its Authority, Authenticity, and Agency*. Detroit: Wayne State University Press, 2012. Ch. 2.

Bernier, Celeste-Marie. "'Iron Arguments': Spectacle, Rhetoric and the Slave Body in New England and British Antislavery Oratory." *European Journal of American Culture* 26.1 (2007): 57–78.

Brooks, Joanna and Tyler Mabry. "Religion in Early African American Literature." *A Companion to African American Literature*. Ed. Gene Andrew Jarrett. Malden, MA: Wiley-Blackwell, 2010. 75–89.

Guruswamy, Rosemary Fithian. "'Thou Hast the Holy Word': Jupiter Hammon's Regards to Phillis Wheatley." *Genius in Bondage: Literature of the Early Black Atlantic*. Eds. Vincent Carretta and Philip Gould. Lexington: University Press of Kentucky, 2001. 190–198.

Langley, April C.E. *The Black Aesthetic Unbound: Theorizing the Dilemma of Eighteenth-Century African American Literature*. Columbus: The Ohio State University Press, 2008. Ch. 4.

May, Cedrick. *Evangelism and Resistance in the Black Atlantic, 1760–1835*. Athens: University of Georgia Press, 2008. Ch. 1.

Nydam, Arlen. "Numerological Tradition in the Works of Jupiter Hammon." *African American Review* 40.2 (2006): 207–220.

The Wiley Blackwell Anthology of African American Literature: Volume 1, 1746–1920, First Edition.
Edited by Gene Andrew Jarrett.

An Address to Miss Phillis Wheatly, Ethiopian Poetess, in Boston, Who Came from Africa at Eight Years of Age, and Soon Became Acquainted with the Gospel of Jesus Christ

Miss WHEATLY; pray give leave to express as follows:

O Come you pious youth! adore 1
The wisdom of thy God,
In bringing thee from distant shore,
To learn his holy word,
Eccles. 7.

Thou mightst been left behind, 2
Amidst a dark abode;
God's tender mercy still combin'd,
Thou hast the holy word.
Psal. 135:2, 3.

Fair wisdom's ways are paths of peace, 3
And they that walk therein,
Shall reap the joys that never cease,
And Christ shall be their king.
Psal. 1:1, 2; Prov. 3:7.

God's tender mercy brought thee here, 4
Tost[1] o'er the raging main;
In Christian faith thou hast a share,
Worth all the gold of Spain.
Psal. 103:1, 3, 4.

While thousands tossed by the sea, 5
And others settled down,
God's tender mercy set thee free
From dangers still unknown.
Death.

That thou a pattern still might be, 6
To youth of Boston town,
The blessed Jesus set thee free,
From every sinful wound.
2 Cor. 5:10.

The blessed Jesus, who came down, 7
Unveil'd[2] his sacred face,
To cleanse the soul of every wound,
And give repenting grace.
Rom. 5:21.

Notes

[1] *Tost* tossed.

[2] *Original reads*: Unvail'd [ed.].

That we poor sinners may obtain 8
The pardon of our sin;
Dear blessed Jesus now constrain,
And bring us flocking in.
Psal. 34:6, 7, 8.

Come you, Phillis, now aspire, 9
And seek the living God,
So step by step thou mayst go higher,
Till perfect in the word.
Matth. 7:7, 8.

While thousands mov'd to distant shore, 10
And others left behind,
The blessed Jesus still adore,
Implant this in thy mind.
Psal. 89:1.

Thou hast left the heathen shore, 11
Thro' mercy of the Lord,
Among the heathen live no more,
Come magnify thy God.
Psal. 34:1, 2, 3.

I pray the living God may be, 12
The shepherd of thy soul;
His tender mercies still are free,
His mysteries to unfold.
Psal. 80:1, 2, 3.

Thou, Phillis, when thou hunger hast, 13
Or pantest for thy God;
Jesus Christ is thy relief,
Thou hast the holy word.
Psal. 13:1, 2, 3.

The bounteous mercies of the Lord, 14
Are hid beyond the sky,
And holy souls that love his word,
Shall taste them when they die.
Psal. 16:10, 11.

These bounteous mercies are from God, 15
The merits of his Son;
The humble soul that loves his word,
He chooses for his own.
Psal. 34:15.

Come, dear Phillis, be advis'd, 16
To drink Samaria's flood:[3]
There nothing is that shall suffice,
But Christ's redeeming blood.
John 4:13, 14.

While thousands muse with earthly toys, 17
And range about the street,
Dear Phillis, seek for heaven's joys,
Where we do hope to meet.
Matth. 6:33.

When God shall send his summons down, 18
And number saints together,
Blest angels chant, (triumphant sound)
Come live with me for ever.
Psal. 116:15.

The humble soul shall fly to God, 19
And leave the things of time,
Start forth as 'twere at the first word,
To taste things more divine.
Matth. 5:3, 8.

Behold! the soul shall waft away, 20
Whene'er we come to die,
And leave its cottage made of clay,
In twinkling of an eye.
1 Cor. 15:51, 52, 53.

Now glory be to the Most High, 21
United praises given,
By all on earth, incessantly,
And all the host of heav'n.
Psal. 150:6.

Composed by JUPITER HAMMON, a Negro Man belonging to Mr. Joseph Lloyd, of Queen's Village on Long-Island, now in Hartford.

The above lines are published by the Author, and a number of his friends, who desire to join with him in their best regards to Miss Wheatly.

1778

Notes

[3] *Samaria's flood* At a well in Samaria, Jesus contrasts water drawn from a well with the metaphorical water of salvation that he offers.

John Marrant (1755–1791)

Perhaps the signal event in John Marrant's life was chancing to hear a sermon delivered by George Whitefield, an evangelist and one of the founders of Methodism (later eulogized by Phillis Wheatley). Born free in New York City, Marrant suffered his father's death and had to move to the South, where he interacted with the gentry of Georgia and of Charleston, South Carolina. In 1768, Marrant heard Whitefield preach and experienced a profound conversion. He struck out into the wilderness alone, seeking spiritual inspiration and trusting that God would provide for him. Nevertheless, he was captured by Cherokees and sentenced to death. Marrant claims in his autobiography that he was reprieved after the miraculous conversion of his would-be executioner. For two years he lived with the Cherokees, Creeks, Catawbas, and Housaws before he returned to Charleston and conducted missionary work with local slaves. Unrecognized by his family, who still resided in the region, Marrant worked as a free carpenter, contracting his work on local plantations and ministering to slaves over the objections of white slave owners. During the Revolutionary War, the Royal Navy conscripted him to serve six years. He subsequently trained as a Methodist minister with the Countess of Huntingdon's Connexion, an evangelical sect that had separated from the Church of England in 1783. In 1785, he was ordained in Bath, England, and that year, dated July 18, the story that he had told of his conversion and captivity appeared in print, titled *A Narrative of the Lord's Wonderful Dealings with John Marrant, a Black*.

Published in London with the help of Methodist Reverend William Aldridge, *Narrative* achieved remarkable popularity and went through 17 editions, although Marrant saw little profit from these largely unauthorized reprintings. The year 1785 also marks when Marrant ministered to a congregation in Nova Scotia comprising black loyalist refugees from New York, Charleston, and Savannah who had fled after the Revolutionary War. The destitute congregation in Birchtown could not support Marrant long, however; of necessity he moved to Boston in 1787. He became chaplain of the Prince Hall Grand Lodge in 1788, and returned to Nova Scotia to marry Elizabeth Herries. In 1790 he journeyed once again to England, where he published his *Journal*, an account of his missionary work over the previous four years.

In 1791, Marrant died in Islington, a suburb of London. Around this time the Sierra Leone Company had begun to relocate Nova Scotia's black loyalists to the West African coast. Marrant had been highly influential in propagating a vision of an exodus to an African Zion, which his successors and congregation attempted to carry out. Even after his death, his missionary work lived on in the ill-fated British settlement. Indeed, in 1800, black Huntingdonians led an unsuccessful rebellion against the Sierra Leone Company for its attempts to exploit the migrants' labor.

Further reading

Brooks, Joanna. *American Lazarus: Religion and the Rise of African American and Native American Literatures*. New York: Oxford University Press, 2003.

Dillon, Elizabeth Maddock. "John Marrant Blows the French Horn: Print, Performance, and the Making of Publics in Early African American Literature." *Early African American Print Culture*. Eds. Lara Langer Cohen and Jordan Alexander Stein. Philadelphia: University of Pennsylvania Press, 2012. 318–339.

The Wiley Blackwell Anthology of African American Literature: Volume 1, 1746–1920, First Edition.
Edited by Gene Andrew Jarrett.

Eileen Razzari. *Piety and Dissent: Race, Gender, Biblical Rhetoric in Early American Autobiography.* erst: University of Massachusetts Press, 2008. Ch. 3.

May, Cedrick. *Evangelism and Resistance in the Black Atlantic, 1760–1835.* Athens: University of Georgia Press, 2008. Ch. 3.

Miles, Tiya. "'His Kingdom for a Kiss': Indians and Intimacy in the Narrative of John Marrant." *Haunted by Empire: Geographies of Intimacy in North American History.* Ed. Ann Laura Stoler. Durham: Duke University Press, 2006. 163–188.

Montgomery, Benilde. "Recapturing John Marrant." *When Brer Rabbit Meets Coyote: African–Native American Literature.* Ed. Jonathan Brennan. Urbana: University of Illinois Press, 2003. 158–167.

Saillant, John. "'Wipe away All Tears from Their Eyes': John Marrant's Theology in the Black Atlantic, 1785–1808." *Journal of Millennial Studies* 1.2 (1999).

A Narrative of the Lord's Wonderful Dealings with John Marrant, a Black

I JOHN MARRANT, born June 15th, 1755, in New-York, in North-America, with these gracious dealings of the Lord with me to be published, in hopes they may be useful to others, to encourage the fearful, to confirm the wavering, and to refresh the hearts of true believers. My father died when I was little more than four years of age, and before I was five my mother removed from New-York to St. Augustine,[1] about seven hundred miles[2] from that city. Here I was sent to school, and taught to read and spell; after we had resided here about eighteen months, it was found necessary to remove to Georgia, where we remained; and I was kept to school until I had attained my eleventh year. The Lord spoke to me in my early days, by these removes, if I could have understood him, and said, "Here we have no continuing city."[3] We left Georgia, and went to Charles-Town, where it was intended I should be put apprentice to some trade. Some time after I had been in Charles-Town, as I was walking one day, I passed by a school, and heard music and dancing, which took my fancy very much, and I felt a strong inclination to learn the music. I went home, and informed my sister, that I had rather learn to play upon music than go to a trade. She told me she could do nothing in it, until she had acquainted my mother with my desire. Accordingly she wrote a letter concerning it to my mother, which, when she read, the contents were disapproved of by her, and she came to Charles-Town to prevent it. She persuaded me much against it, but her persuasions were fruitless. Disobedience either to God or man, being one of the fruits of sin,[4] grew out from me in early buds. Finding I was set upon it, and resolved to learn nothing else, she agreed to it, and went with me to speak to the man, and to settle upon the best terms with him she could. He insisted upon twenty pounds down, which was paid, and I was engaged to stay with him eighteen months, and my mother to find me everything[5] during that term. The first day I went to him he put the violin into my hand, which pleased me much, and, applying close, I learned very fast, not only to play, but to dance also; so that in six months I was able to play for the whole school. In the evenings after the scholars were dismissed, I used to resort to the bottom of our garden, where it was customary for some musicians to assemble to blow the French-horn. Here my improvement was so rapid, that in a twelve-month's time I became master both of the violin and of the French-horn, and was much respected

Notes

[1] *St. Augustine* port city in northeastern Florida.

[2] *about seven hundred miles* actually closer to one thousand miles.

[3] *"here we have no continuing city"* Hebrews 13:14.

[4] *fruits of sin* Galatians 5:19–21.

[5] *Original reads*: every thing [ed.].

by the Gentlemen and Ladies whose children attended the school, as also by my master: This opened to me a large door of vanity and vice, for I was invited to all the balls and assemblies that were held in the town, and met with the general applause of the inhabitants. I was a stranger to want, being supplied with as much money as I had any occasion for; which my sister observing said, "You have now no need of a trade." I was now in my thirteenth year, devoted to pleasure and drinking in iniquity like water; a slave to every vice suited to my nature and to my years. The time I had engaged to serve my master being expired, he persuaded me to stay with him, and offered me anything,[6] or any money, not to leave him. His intreaties proving ineffectual, I quitted his service, and visited my mother in the country; with her I staid two months, living without God or hope in the world, fishing and hunting on the Sabbath-day.[7] Unstable as water I returned to town, and wished to go to some trade. My sister's husband being informed of my inclination provided me with a master, on condition that I should serve him one year and a half on trial, and afterwards be bound, if he approved of me. Accordingly I went, but every evening I was sent for to play music,[8] somewhere or another; and I often continued out very late, sometimes all night, so as to render me incapable of attending my master's business the next day; yet in this manner I served him a year and four months, and was much approved of by him. He wrote a letter to my mother to come and have me bound, and whilst my mother was weighing the matter in her own mind, the gracious purposes of God, respecting a perishing sinner, were now to be disclosed. One evening I was sent for in a very particular manner to go and play for some Gentlemen, which I agreed to do, and was on my way to fulfil my promise; and passing by a large meeting house I saw many lights in it, and crowds[9] of people going in. I enquired what it meant, and was answered by my companion, that a crazy man was hallooing[10] there; this raised my curiosity to go in, that I might hear what he was hallooing about. He persuaded me not to go in, but in vain. He then said, "If you will do one thing I will go in with you." I asked him what that was?. He replied, "Blow the French-horn among them." I liked the proposal well enough, but expressed my fears of being beaten for disturbing them; but upon his promising to stand by and defend me, I agreed. So we went, and with much difficulty got within the doors. I was pushing the people to make room, to get the horn off my shoulder to blow it, just as Mr. Whitefield[11] was naming his text, and looking round, and, as I thought, directly upon me, and pointing with his finger, he uttered these words, "PREPARE TO MEET THY GOD, O ISRAEL."[12] The Lord accompanied the word with such power, that I was struck to the ground, and lay both speechless and senseless near half an hour. When I came a little to,[13] I found two men attending me, and a woman throwing water in my face, and holding a smelling-bottle to my nose; and when something more recovered, every word I heard from the minister was like a parcel of swords thrust into me, and what added to my distress, I thought I saw the devil on every side of me. I was constrained in the bitterness of my spirit to halloo out in the midst of the congregation, which disturbing them, they took me away; but finding I could neither walk nor stand,[14] they carried me as far as the vestry,[15] and there

Notes

6 *Original reads*: any thing [ed.].

7 *Original reads*: sabbath-day [ed.].

8 *Original reads*: play on music [ed.].

9 *Original reads*: crouds [ed.].

10 *hallooing* shouting.

11 *Mr. Whitefield* Methodist preacher John Whitefield (1714–1770), one of the founders of the Great Awakening religious movement.

12 *"Prepare to meet thy God, O Israel"* Amos 4:12.

13 *Original reads*: When I was come a little too [ed.].

14 *Original reads*: neither walk or stand [ed.].

15 *vestry* room attached to the chapel in which records and clergy robes are kept.

I remained till the service was over. When the people were dismissed Mr. Whitefield came into the vestry, and being told of my condition he came immediately, and the first word he said to me was, "JESUS CHRIST HAS GOT THEE AT LAST." He asked where I lived, intending to come and see me the next day; but recollecting he was to leave the town the next morning, he said he could not come himself, but would send another minister; he desired them to get me home, and then taking his leave of me, I saw him no more. When I reached my sister's house, being carried by two men, she was very uneasy to see me in so distressed a condition. She got me to bed, and sent for a doctor, who came immediately, and after looking at me, he went home, and sent me a bottle of mixture, and desired her to give me a spoonful every two hours; but I could not take anything[16] the doctor sent, nor indeed keep in bed; this distressed my sister very much, and she cried out, "The lad will surely die." She sent for two other doctors, but no medicine they prescribed could I take. No, no; it may be asked, a wounded spirit who can cure? as well as who can bear? In this distress of soul I continued for three days without any food, only a little water now and then. On the fourth day, the minister* Mr. Whitefield had desired to visit me, came to see me, and being directed upstairs, when he entered the room, I thought he made my distress much worse. He wanted to take hold of my hand, but I durst not give it to him. He insisted upon taking hold of it, and I then got away from him on the other side of the bed; but being very weak I fell down, and before I could recover he came to me and took me by the hand, and lifted me up, and after a few words desired to go to prayer. So he fell upon his knees, and pulled me down also; after he had spent some time in prayer he rose up, and asked me now how I did; I answered, much worse; he then said, "Come, we will have the old thing over again," and so we kneeled down a second time, and after he had prayed earnestly we got up, and he said again, "How do you do now?"[17] I replied worse and worse, and asked him if he intended to kill me? "No, no, said he, you are worth a thousand dead men, let us try the old thing over again," and so falling upon our knees, he continued in prayer a considerable time, and near the close of his prayer, the Lord was pleased to set my soul at perfect liberty, and being filled with joy I began to praise the Lord immediately; my sorrows were turned into peace, and joy, and love. The minister said, "How is it now?" I answered, all is well, all happy. He then took his leave of me; but called every day for several days afterwards, and the last time he said, "Hold fast that thou hast already obtained,'till Jesus Christ come."[18] I now read the Scriptures very much. My master sent often to know how I did, and at last came himself, and finding me well, asked me if I would not come to work again? I answered no. He asked me the reason, but receiving no answer he went away. I continued with my sister about three weeks, during which time she often asked me to play upon the violin for her, which I refused; then she said I was crazy and mad, and so reported it among the neighbours, which opened the mouths of all around against me. I then resolved to go to my mother, which was eighty-four miles from Charles-Town. I was two days on my journey home, and enjoyed much communion with God on the road, and had occasion to mark the gracious interpositions of his kind providence as I passed along. The third day I arrived at my mother's house, and was well received. At supper they sat down to eat without asking the Lord's blessing, which caused me to burst out into tears. My mother asked me what was the matter? I answered, I wept because they sat down to

Notes

* Mr. HALL, a Baptist Minister at Charles-Town.

[16] *Original reads*: any thing [ed.].

[17] *Original reads*: "How to you do now;" [ed.].

[18] *"Hold fast that …"* Revelations 2:25.

supper without asking the Lord's blessing. She bid me, with much surprise, to ask a blessing. I remained with her fourteen days without interruption; the Lord pitied me, being a young soldier. Soon, however, Satan began to stir up my two sisters and brother, who were then at home with my mother; they called me every name but that which was good. The more they persecuted me, the stronger I grew in grace. At length my mother turned against me also, and the neighbours joined her, and there was not a friend to assist me, or that I could speak to; this made me earnest with God. In these circumstances, being the youngest but one of our family, and young in Christian experience, I was tempted so far as to threaten my life; but reading my Bible one day, and finding that if I did destroy myself I could not come where God was, I betook myself to the fields, and some days staid put from morning to night to avoid the persecutors. I staid one time two days without any food, but seemed to have clearer views into the spiritual things of God. Not long after this I was sharply tried, and reasoned the matter within myself, whether I should turn to my old courses of sin and vice, or serve and cleave to the Lord; after prayer to God, I was fully persuaded in my mind, that if I turned to my old ways I should perish eternally. Upon this I went home, and finding them all as hardened, or worse than before, and everybody saying I was crazy; but a little sister I had, about nine years of age, used to cry when she saw them persecute me, and continuing so about five weeks and three days, I thought it was better for me to die than to live among such people. I rose one morning very early, to get a little quietness and retirement, I went into the woods, and staid till eight o'clock in the morning; upon my return I found them all at breakfast; I passed by them, and went up-stairs without any interruption; I went upon my knees to the Lord, and returned him thanks; then I took up a small pocket Bible and one of Dr. Watts's[19] hymn books, and passing by them went out without one word spoken by any of us. After spending some time in the fields I was persuaded to go from home altogether. Accordingly I went over the fence, about half a mile from our house, which divided the inhabited and cultivated parts of the country from the wilderness. I continued travelling in the desert[20] all day without the least inclination of re-turning back. About evening I began to be surrounded with wolves; I took refuge from them on a tree, and remained there all night. About eight o'clock next morning I descended from the tree, and returned God thanks for the mercies of the night. I went on all this day without any thing to eat or drink. The third day, taking my Bible out of my pocket, I read and walked for some time, and then being wearied and almost spent I sat down, and after resting awhile I rose to go forward; but had not gone above a hundred yards when something tripped me up, and I fell down; I prayed to the Lord upon the ground that he would command the wild beasts to devour me, that I might be with him in glory. I made this request to God the third and part of the fourth day. The fourth day in the morning, descending from my usual lodging, a tree, and having nothing all this time to eat, and but a little water to drink, I was so feeble that I tumbled half way down the tree, not being able to support myself, and lay upon my back on the ground an hour and a half, praying and crying; after which, getting a little strength, and trying to stand upright to walk, I found myself not able; then I went upon my hands and knees, and so crawled till I reached a tree that was tumbled down, in order to get across it, and there I prayed with my body leaning upon it above an hour, that the Lord would take me to himself. Such nearness to God I then enjoyed, that I willingly resigned myself into his hands. After some time I thought I was strengthened, so I got across the tree without my feet

Notes

[19] *Dr. Watts* Isaac Watts, prolific English hymnist (1674–1748).

[20] *Original reads*: desart [ed.].

or hands touching the ground; but struggling I fell over on the other side, and then thought the Lord will now answer my prayer, and take me home: But the time was not come. After lying[21] there a little, I rose, and looking about, saw at some distance bunches of grass, called deer-grass; I felt a strong desire to get at it; though I rose, yet it was only on my hands and knees, being so feeble, and in this manner I reached the grass. I was three-quarters of an hour going in this form twenty yards. When I reached it I was unable to pull it up, so I bit it off like a horse, and prayed the Lord to bless it to me, and I thought it the best meal I ever had in my life, and I think so still, it was so sweet. I returned my God hearty thanks for it, and then lay down about an hour. Feeling myself very thirty, I prayed the Lord to provide me with some water: Finding I was something strengthened I got up, and stood on my feet, and staggered from one tree to another, if they were near each other, otherwise the journey was too long for me. I continued moving so for some time, and at length passing between two trees, I happened to fall upon some bushes, among which were a few large hollow leaves, which had caught and contained the dews of the night, and lying low among the bushes, were not exhaled by the solar rays; this water in the leaves fell upon me as I tumbled down and was lost, I was now tempted to think the Lord had given me water from Heaven, and I had wasted it. I then prayed the Lord to forgive me. What poor unbelieving creatures we are! though we are assured the Lord will supply all our needs. I was presently directed to a puddle of water very muddy, which some wild pigs had just left; I kneeled down, and asked the Lord to bless it to me, so I drank both mud and water mixed together, and being satisfied I returned the Lord thanks, and went on my way rejoicing. This day was much chequered with wants and supplies, with dangers and deliverances. I continued travelling on for nine days, feeding upon grass, and not knowing whither I was going; but the Lord Jesus Christ was very present, and that comforted me through all. The next morning, having quitted my customary lodging, and returned thanks to the Lord for my preservation through the night, reading and travelling on, I passed between two bears, about twenty yards distance from each other. Both sat and looked at me, but I felt no fear; and after I had passed them, they both went the same way from me without growling, or the least apparent uneasiness. I went and returned God thanks for my escape, who had tamed the wild beasts of the forest, and made them friendly to me: I rose from my knees and walked on; singing hymns of praise to God, about five o'clock in the afternoon, and about 55 miles from home, right through the wilderness. As I was going on, and musing upon the goodness of the Lord, an Indian hunter, who stood at some distance, saw me; he hid himself behind a tree; but as I passed along he bolted out, and put his hands on my breast, which surprised me a few moments. He then asked me where I was going? I answered I did not know, but where the Lord was pleased to guide me. Having heard me praising God before I came up to him, he enquired who I was talking to? I told him I was talking to my Lord Jesus; he seemed surprised, and asked me where he was? for he did not see him there. I told him he could not be seen with bodily eyes. After a little more talk, he insisted upon taking me home; but I refused, and added, that I would die rather than return home. He then asked me if I knew how far I was from home? I answered, I did not know; you are 55 miles and a half, says he, from home. He farther asked me how I did to live? I said I was supported by the Lord. He asked me how I slept? I answered, the Lord provided me with a bed every night; he further enquired what preserved me from being devoured by the wild beasts? I replied, the Lord Jesus Christ

Notes

[21] *Original reads*: laying [ed.].

kept me from them. He stood astonished, and said, you say the Lord Jesus Christ do this, and do that, and do everything[22] for you, he must be a very fine man, where is he? I replied, he is here present. To this he made me no answer, only said, I know you, and your mother and sister and upon a little further conversation I found he did know them, having been used in winter to sell skins in our town. This alarmed me, and I wept for fear he would take me home by force; but when he saw me so affected, he said he would not take me home if I would go with him. I objected against that, for fear he would rob me of my comfort and communion with God: But at last, being much pressed, I consented to go. Our employment for ten weeks and three days was killing deer, and taking off their skins by day, which we afterwards hung on the trees to dry till they were sent for; the means of defence and security against our nocturnal enemies, always took up the evenings: We collected a number of large bushes, and placed them nearly in a circular form, which uniting at the extremity, afforded us both a verdant covering, and a sufficient shelter from the night dews. What moss we could gather was strewed upon the ground, and this composed our bed. A fire was kindled in the front of our temporary lodging room, and fed with fresh fuel all night, as we slept and watched by turns; and this was our defence from the dreadful animals, whole shining eyes and tremendous roar we often saw and heard during the night.

By constant conversation with the hunter, I acquired a fuller knowledge of the Indian tongue: This, together with the sweet communion I enjoyed with God, I have considered as a preparation for the great trial I was soon after to pass through.

The hunting season being now at an end, we left the woods, and directed our course towards a large Indian town, belonging to the Cherokee nation; and having reached it, I said to the hunter, they will not suffer me to enter in. He replied, as I was with him, nobody would interrupt me.

There was an Indian fortification all round the town, and a guard placed at each entrance. The hunter passed one of these without molestation, but I was stopped by the guard and examined. They asked me where I came from, and what was my business there? My companion of the woods attempted to speak for me, but was not permitted; he was taken away, and I saw him no more. I was now surrounded by about 50 men, and carried to one of their chiefs to be examined by him. When I came before him, he asked me what was my business there? I told him I came there with a hunter, whom I met with in the woods. He replied, "Did I not know that whoever came there without giving a better account of themselves than I did, was to be put to death?" I said I did not know it. Observing that I answered him so readily in his own language, he asked me where I learnt it? To this I returned no answer, but burst out into a flood of tears, and calling upon my Lord Jesus. At this he stood astonished, and expressed a concern for me, and said I was young. He asked me who my Lord Jesus was? – To this I gave him no answer, but continued praying and weeping. Addressing himself to the officer who stood by him, he said he was sorry; but it was the law, and it must not be broken. I was then ordered to be taken away, and put into a place of confinement. They led me from their court into a low dark place, and thrust me into it, very dreary and dismal; they made fast the door, and set a watch. The judge sent for the executioner, and gave him his warrant for my execution in the afternoon of the next day. The executioner came, and gave me notice of it, which made me very happy, as the near prospect of death made me hope for a speedy deliverance from the body: And truly this dungeon

Notes

[22] *Original reads*: every thing [ed.].

became my chapel, for the Lord Jesus did not leave me in this great trouble, but was very present, so that I continued blessing him, and singing his praises all night without ceasing: The watch hearing the noise, informed the executioner that somebody had been in the dungeon with me all night; upon which he came in to see and to examine, with a great torch lighted in his hand, who it was I had with me; but finding nobody, he turned round, and asked me who it was? I told him it was the Lord Jesus Christ; but he made no answer; turned away, went out, and locked the door. At the hour appointed for my execution I was taken out and led to the destined spot, amidst a vast number of people. I praised the Lord all the way we went, and when we arrived at the place I understood the kind of death I was to suffer, yet, blessed be God, none of those things moved me. The executioner showed me a basket of turpentine wood, stuck full of small pieces, like skewers; he told me I was to be stripped naked, and laid down in the basket, and these sharp pegs were to be stuck into me, and then set on fire, and when they had burnt to my body* I was to be turned on the other side, and served in the same manner, and then to be taken by four men and thrown into the flame, which was to finish the execution. I burst into tears, and asked what I had done to deserve so cruel a death! To this he gave me no answer. I cried out, Lord, if it be thy will that it should be so, thy will be done:[23] I then asked the executioner to let me go to prayer; he asked me to whom? I answered, to the Lord my God; he seemed surprized, and asked me where he was? I told him he was present; upon which he gave me leave. I desired them all to do as I did, so I fell down upon my knees, and mentioned to the Lord his delivering of the three children in the fiery furnace, and of Daniel in the lion's den,[24] and had close communion with God. I prayed in English a considerable time, and about the middle of my prayer, the Lord impressed a strong desire upon my mind turn into their language, and pray in their tongue. I did so, and with remarkable liberty, which wonderfully affected the people. One circumstance was very singular, and strikingly displays the power and grace of God. I believe the executioner was savingly converted to God. He rose from his knees, and embraced me round the middle, and was unable to speak for about five minutes; the first words he expressed, when he had utterance, were, "No man shall hurt thee till thou hast been to the king."

I was taken away immediately, and as we passed along, and I was reflecting upon the deliverance which the Lord had wrought out for me, and hearing the praises which the executioner was singing to the Lord, I must own I was utterly at a loss to find words to praise him. I broke out in these words, what can't the Lord Jesus do! and what power is like unto his! I will thank thee for what is passed, and trust thee for what is to come. I will sing thy praise with my feeble tongue whilst life and breath shall last, and when I fail to sound thy praises here, I hope to sing them round thy throne above: And thus, with unspeakable joy, I sung two verses of Dr. Watts's hymns:

"My God, the spring of all my joys,[25]
The life of my delights;
The glory of my brightest days,
And comfort of my nights.

Notes

* These pegs were to be kindled at the opposite end from the body.

[23] *thy will be done* similar to Jesus's prayer to God to follow through with his crucifixion (Luke 22:42).

[24] *the three children in the fiery furnace, and of Daniel in the lion's den* see the book of Daniel, in which God miraculously intervenes in saving Shadrach, Meshach and Abednego (Daniel 3) and Daniel from the lions (Daniel 6).

[25] *"My God, the spring ... rising sun."* from the hymn "My God, the Spring of All My Joys" (1707) by Isaac Watts.

In darkest shades, if thou appear,
My dawning is begun;
Thou art my soul's bright morning star,
And thou my rising sun."

Passing by the judge's door, he stopped us, and asked the executioner why he brought me back? The man fell upon his knees and begged he would permit me to be carried before the king, which being granted, I went on, guarded by two hundred soldiers with bows and arrows. After many windings I entered the king's outward chamber, and after waiting some time he came to the door, and his first question was, how came I there? I answered, I came with a hunter whom I met with in the woods, and who persuaded me to come there. He then asked me how old I was? I told him not fifteen. He asked me how I was supported before I met with this man? I answered, by the Lord Jesus Christ, which seemed to confound him. He turned round, and asked me if he lived where I came from? I answered, yes; and here also. He looked about the room, and said he did not see him; but I told him I felt him. The executioner fell upon his knees, and intreated the king, and told him what he had felt of the same Lord. At this instant the king's eldest daughter came into the chamber, a person about 19 years of age, and stood at my right-hand. I had a Bible in my hand, which she took out of it, and having opened it, she kissed it, and seemed much delighted with it. When she had put it into my hand again, the king asked me what it was? and I told him, the name of my God was recorded there; and, after several questions, he bid me read it; which I did, particularly the 53d chapter of Isaiah, in the most solemn manner I was able; and also the 26th chapter of Matthew's Gospel;[26] and when I pronounced the name of Jesus, the particular effect it had upon me was observed by the king. When I had finished reading, he asked me why I read those names,* with so much reverence? I told him, because the Being to whom those names belonged made heaven and earth, and I and he; this he denied. I then pointed to the sun, and asked him who made the sun, and moon, and stars, and preserved them in their regular order? He said there was a man in their town that did it. I laboured as much as I could to convince him to the contrary. His daughter took the book out of my hand a second time; she opened it, and kissed it again; her father bid her give it to me, which she did; but said, with much sorrow, the book would not speak to her. The executioner then fell upon his knees, and begged the king to let me go to prayer, which being granted, we all went upon our knees, and now the Lord displayed his glorious power. In the midst of the prayer some of them cried out, particularly the king's daughter, and the man who ordered me to be executed, and several others seemed under deep conviction of sin: This made the king very angry; he called me a witch, and commanded me to be thrust into the prison, and to be executed the next morning. This was enough to make me think, as old Jacob once did, "All these things are against me";[27] for I was dragged away, and thrust into the dungeon with much indignation; but God, who never forsakes his people, was with me. Though I was weak in body, yet was I strong in the spirit: The Lord works, and who shall let it? The executioner went to the king, and assured him, that if he put me to death, his daughter would never be well. They used the skill of all their doctors that afternoon and night; but physical prescriptions were useless. In the morning the executioner

Notes

* Or what those parts were which seemed to affect me so much, not knowing what I read, as he did not understand the English language.

[26] Isaiah 53 and Matthew 26 both concern themselves with the persecution of Jesus.

[27] *"All these things are against me"* Genesis 42:36.

came to me, and, without opening the prison door, called to me, and hearing me answer, said, "Fear not, thy God who delivered thee yesterday, will deliver thee to-day." This comforted me very much, especially to find he could trust the Lord. Soon after I was fetched out; I thought it was to be executed; but they led me away to the king's chamber with much bodily weakness, having been without food two days. When I came into the king's presence, he said to me, with much anger, if I did not make his daughter and that man well, I should be laid down and chopped into pieces before him. I was not afraid, but the Lord tried my faith sharply. The king's daughter and the other person were brought out into the outer chamber, and we went to prayer; but the heavens were locked up to my petitions. I besought the Lord again, but received no answer: I cried again, and he was intreated. He said, "Be it to thee as thou wilt":[28] the Lord appeared most lovely and[29] glorious; the king himself was awakened, and the others set at liberty. A great change took place among the people; the king's house became God's house; the soldiers were ordered away, and the poor condemned prisoner had perfect liberty, and was treated like a prince. Now the Lord made all my enemies to become my great friends. I remained nine weeks in the king's palace, praising God day and night: I was never out but three days all the time. I had assumed the habit of the country, and was dressed much like the king, and nothing was too good for me. The king would take *off* his golden ornaments, his chain and bracelets, like a child, if I objected to them, and lay them aside. Here I learnt to speak their tongue in the highest stile.

I began now to feel an inclination growing upon me to go farther on, but none to return home. The king being acquainted with this, expressed his fears of my being used ill by the next Indian nation, and, to prevent it, sent 50 men, and a recommendation to the king, with me. The next nation was called the Creek Indians, at 60 miles distance. Here I was received with kindness, owing to the king's influence, from whom I had parted; here I staid five weeks. I next visited the Catawar Indians, at about 55 miles distance from the others: Lastly, I went among the Housaw Indians, 80 miles distant from the last mentioned; here I staid seven weeks. These nations were then at peace with each other, and I passed among them without danger, being recommended from one to the other. When they recollect that the white people drove them from the American shores, the three first nations have often united, and murdered all the white people in the back settlements which they could lay hold of, man, woman, and child. I had not much reason to believe any of these three nations were savingly wrought upon, and therefore I returned to the Cherokee nation, which took me up eight weeks. I continued with my old friends seven weeks and two days.

I now and then found, that my affections to my family and country were not dead; they were sometimes very sensibly[30] felt, and at last strengthened into an invincible desire of returning home. The king was much against it; but feeling the same strong bias towards my country, after we had asked Divine direction, the king consented, and accompanied me 60 miles with 140 men. I went to prayer three times before we could part, and then he sent 40 men with me a hundred miles farther; I went to prayer, and then took my leave of them, and passed on my way. I had 70 miles now to go to the back settlements of the white people. I was surrounded very soon with wolves again, which made my old lodging both necessary and welcome. However it was not long, for in two days I reached the settlements, and on the third I found a house: It was about

Notes

[28] *"Be it to thee as thou wilt"* Jesus speaks these words to a woman whom he heals because of her great faith (Matthew 15:28).

[29] *Original reads*: an [ed.].

[30] *sensibly* deeply.

dinner-time, and as I came up to the door the family saw me, were frightened, and ran away. I sat down to dinner alone, and ate[31] very heartily, and, after returning God thanks, I went to see what had become of the family. I found means to lay hold of a girl that stood peeping at me from behind a barn. She fainted away, and it was upwards of an hour before she recovered; it was nine o'clock before I could get them all to venture in, they were so terrified.

My dress was purely in the Indian stile; the skins of wild beasts composed my garments, my head was set out in the savage manner, with a long pendant down my back, a sash round my middle without breeches, and a tomahawk[32] by my side. In about two days they became sociable. Having visited three or four other families, at the distance of 16 or 20 miles, I got them altogether to prayer on the Sabbath days, to the number of 17 persons. I said with them six weeks, and they expressed much sorrow when I left them. I was now one hundred and twelve miles from home. On the road I sometimes met with a house, then I was hospitably entertained; and when I met with none, a tree lent me the use of its friendly shelter and protection from the prowling beasts of the woods during the night. The God of mercy and grace supported me thus for eight days, and on the ninth I reached my uncle's house.

The following particulars, relating to the manner in which I was made known to my family, are less interesting; and yet, perhaps, some readers would not forgive their omission: I shall, however, be as brief as I can. I asked my uncle for a lodging, which he refused. I enquired how far the town was off; three quarters of a mile, said he. Do you know Mrs. Marrant and family, and how the children do? was my next question. He said he did, they were all well, but one was lately lost; at this I turned my head and wept. He did not know me, and upon refusing again to lodge me, I departed. When I reached the town it was dark, and passing by a house where one of my old schoolfellows lived, I knocked at the door; he came out, and asked me what I wanted? I desired a lodging, which was granted: I went in, but was not known. I asked him if he knew Mrs. Marrant, and how the family were? He said, he had just left them, they were all well; but a young lad, with whom he went to school, who, after he had quitted school, went to Charles-Town to learn some trade; but came home crazy, and rambled in the woods, and was torn in pieces by the wild beasts. How do you know, said I, that he was killed by wild beasts? I, and his brother, and uncle, and others, said he, went three days into the woods in search of him, and found his carcase torn, and brought it home, and buried it, and they are now in mourning for him. This affected me very much, and I wept; observing it, he said, what is the matter? I made no answer. At supper they sat down without craving a blessing, for which I reproved them; this so affected the man, that I believe it ended in a sound conversion. Here is a wild man, says he, come out of the woods to be a witness for God, and to reprove our ingratitude and stupefaction! After supper I went to prayer, and then to bed. Rising a little before day-light, and praising the Lord, as my custom was, the family were surprised, and got up: I staid with them till nine o'clock, and then went to my mother's house in the next street. The singularity of my dress drew every body's eyes upon me, yet none knew me. I knocked at my mother's door; my sister opened it, and was startled at my appearance. Having expressed a desire to see Mrs. Marrant, I was answered, she was not very well and that my business with her could be done by the person at the door, who also attempted to shut me out, which I prevented. My mother being called, I went in, and sat down, a mob of people being round the door. My mother asked, "what is your business"; only

Notes

[31] *Original reads*: eat [ed.].

[32] *Original reads*: tomohawk [ed.].

to see you, said I. She was much obliged to me, but did not know me. I asked, how are your children? how are your two sons? She replied, her daughters were in good health, of her two sons one was well, and with her, but the other – unable to contain, she burst into a flood of tears, and retired. I was overcome, and wept much; but nobody knew me. This was an affecting scene! Presently my brother came in: He enquired, who I was, and what I was? My sister did not know; but being uneasy at my presence, they contrived to get me out of the house, which, being over-heard by me, I resolved not to stir. My youngest sister, eleven years of age, came in from school, and knew me the moment she saw me: She goes into the kitchen, and tells the woman her brother was come, but her news finding no credit there she returns, passes through the room where I sat, made a running curtsey, and says to my eldest sister in the next room, it is my brother! She was then called a foolish girl, and threatened; the child cried, and insisted upon it. She went crying up-stairs to my mother, and told her; but neither would my mother believe her. At last they said to her, if it be your brother, go and kiss him, and ask him how he does? She ran and clasped me round the neck, and, looking me in the face, said, "Are not you my brother John?" I answered yes, and wept. I was then made known to all the family, to my friends, and acquaintances, who received me, and were glad, and rejoiced:* Thus the dead was brought to life again; thus the lost was found.[33] I shall now close the Narrative, with only remarking a few incidents in my life, until my connection with my Right Honourable patroness, the Countess of HUNTINGDON.[34]

I remained with my relations till the commencement of the American troubles.[35] I used to go and hear the word of God, if any Gospel ministers came into the country, though at a considerable distance, and thereby got acquainted with a few poor people, who feared God in Will's Town, and Borough-Town, Dorchester Town, and other places thereabouts; and in those places we used to meet and associate together for Christian conversation, and, at their request, I frequently went to prayer with them, and at times enjoyed much of the Lord's presence among them; and yet, reader, my soul was got into a declining state. Don't forget our Lord's exhortation, "What I say unto you, I say unto all, WATCH."[36]

About this time I was an eye-witness of the remarkable conversion of a child seven and a half years old, named Mary Scott, which I shall here mention, in hopes the Lord may make it useful and profitable to my young readers. Her parents lived in the house adjoining to my sister's. One day, as I was returning from my work, and passing by the school where she was instructed, I saw the children coming out, and stop'd and looked among them for her, to take her home in my hand; but not seeing her among those that were coming out, I supposed she was gone before, and went on towards home; when passing by the church-yard, which was in my way, I saw her very busy walking from one tomb to another, and went to her, and asked her what she was doing there? She told me, that in the lesson she had set her at school that morning, in the Twentieth of the Revelations, she read, "I saw the dead, small and great, stand before God," &c. and she had been measuring the graves with a tape she then held in her hand, to see if there were any so small as herself among them, and that she had found six that were shorter. I then said, and what of that? She answered, "I shall die, Sir." I told her I knew she would, but hoped she would live till she was grown a woman; but she continued

Notes

* I had been absent from them about 23 months.

[33] *thus the lost was found* conjugation of words spoken by the prodigal son's father after his return (Luke 15:24).

[34] *Countess of HUNTINGDON* Selina, Countess of Huntingdon (1707–1791), founded a society of evangelical churches in 1783.

[35] *American troubles* the American Revolution.

[36] *"What I say unto you … WATCH"* Mark 13:37.

to express her desire to depart, and be with Christ, rather than to live till she was grown up. I then took her by the hand and brought her home with me. After this, she was observed to be always very solid and thoughtful, and that passage appeared always to be fresh upon her mind. I used frequently to be with her when in town and at her request we often read and prayed together, and she appeared much affected. She never afterwards was seen out at play with other children; but spent her leisure time in reading God's word and prayer. In about four months after this she was taken ill, and kept her room about three weeks; when first taken, she told me she should never come down stairs alive. I frequently visited her during her illness, and made light of what she said about her dying so soon; but in the last week *of* her illness she said to me, in a very solemn manner, "Sir, I shall die before Saturday-night." The physicians attended her, but she took very few (if any) medicines, and appeared quite calm and resigned to God's will. On Friday morning, which was the day she died, I visited her, and told her that I hoped she would not die so soon as she said; but she told me that she should certainly die before six o'clock that evening. About five o'clock I visited her again. She was then sitting in a chair, and reading in her Bible, to all appearance pretty well recovered. After setting with her about a quarter of an hour, she got up, and desired me to go down, and send her mother up with a clean shift[37] for her, which I did; and after a little time, when I went up again, I found her lying on the bed, with her eyes fixed up to Heaven; when, turning herself and seeing me, she said, "Mr. Marrant, don't you see that pretty town, and those fine people, how they shine like gold?[38] – O how I long to be with my Lord and his redeemed Children in Glory!" and then turning to her parents and two sisters (who were all present, having by her desire been called to her) she shook hands with them, and bade them farewell; desiring them not to lament for her when she was dead, for she was going to that fine place, where God would wipe away all tears[39] from her eyes, and she should sing Hallelujahs to God and the Lamb for ever and ever, and where she hoped afterwards to meet them; and then turning again to me, she said, "Farewell, and God bless you," and then fell asleep in the arms of Jesus. This afterwards proved the conversion of her mother.

In those troublesome times, I was pressed on board the Scorpion sloop of war, as their musician, as they were told I could play on music.[40] I continued in his majesty's service six years and eleven months; and with shame confess, that a lamentable stupor crept over all my spiritual vivacity, life and vigour; I got cold and dead. My gracious God, my dear Father in his dear Son, roused me every now and then by dangers and deliverances. I was at the siege of Charles-Town,[41] and passed through many dangers. When the town was taken, my old royal benefactor and convert, the king of the Cherokee Indians, riding into the town with general Clinton,[42] saw me, and knew me: He alighted off his horse,* and came to me; said he was glad to see me; that his daughter was very happy, and sometimes longed to get out of the body.

Some time after this I was cruising about in the American seas, and cannot help mentioning a singular deliverance I had from the most imminent danger, and the use

Notes

* Though it is unusual for Indians to have a horse, yet the king accompanied the general on the present successful occasion riding on horse-back. If the king wished to serve me, there was no opportunity; the town being taken on Friday afternoon, Saturday an express arrived from the commander in chief at New York, for a large detachment, or the town would fall into the hands of the Americans, which hurried us away on Sunday morning.

[37] *shift* dress.

[38] *"pretty town … gold"* Revelation 21:18–21 describes Heaven as golden.

[39] *God would wipe away all tears* Revelation 21:4.

[40] *Original reads*: play on music [ed.].

[41] *siege of Charles-Town* The siege of Charleston was a major battle in the American Revolution fought in May 1780.

[42] *general Clinton* British general Henry Clinton (1730–1795).

the Lord made of it to me. We were overtaken by a violent storm; I was washed overboard, and thrown on again; dashed into the sea a second time, and tossed upon deck again. I now fastened a rope round my middle, as a security against being thrown into the sea again; but, alas! forgot to fasten it to any part of the ship; being carried away the third time by the fury of the waves, when in the sea, I found the rope both useless and an incumbrance. I was in the sea the third time about eight minutes, and the sharks came round me in great numbers; one of an enormous size, that could easily have taken me into his mouth at once, passed and rubbed against my side. I then cried more earnestly to the Lord than I had done for some time; and he who heard Jonah's prayer,[43] did not shut out mine, for I was thrown aboard again; these were the means the Lord used to revive me, and I began now to set out afresh.

I was in the engagement with the Dutch off the Dogger Bank,[44] on board the Princess-Amelia, of 84 guns.* We had a great number killed and wounded; the deck was running with blood; six men were killed, and three wounded, stationed at the same gun with me; my head and face were covered with the blood and brains of the slain: I was wounded, but did not fall, till a quarter of an hour before the engagement ended, and was happy during the whole of it. After being in the hospital three months and 16 days, I was sent to the West-Indies on board a ship of war, and, after cruising in those seas, we returned home as a convoy. Being taken ill of my old wounds, I was put into the hospital at Plymouth, and had not been there long, when the physician gave it as his opinion, that I should not be capable of serving the king again; I was therefore discharged, and came to London, where I lived with a respectable and pious merchant three years,† who was unwilling to part with me. During this time I saw my call to the ministry fuller and clearer; had a feeling concern for the salvation of my countrymen; I carried them constantly in the arms of prayer and faith to the throne of grace, and had continual sorrow in my heart for my brethren, for my kinsmen, according to the flesh. I wrote a letter to my brother, who returned me an answer, in which he prayed some ministers would come and preach to them, and desired me to shew it to the minister whom I attended. I used to exercise my gifts on a Monday evening in prayer and exhortation, and was approved of, and ordained at Bath. Her Ladyship[45] having seen the letter from my brother in Nova-Scotia, thought Providence called me there: To which place I am now bound, and expect to sail in a few days.

I have now only to entreat the earnest prayers of all my kind Christian friends, that I may be carried safe there; kept humble, made faithful, and successful; that strangers may hear of and run to Christ; that Indian tribes may stretch out their hands to God; that the black nations may be made white in the blood of the Lamb; that vast multitudes of hard tongues, and of a strange speech, may learn the language of Canaan, and sing the song of Moses, and of the Lamb; and, anticipating the glorious prospect, may we all with fervent hearts, and willing tongues, sing hallelujah; the kingdoms of the world are become the kingdoms of our God, and of his Christ. Amen and Amen.

1785

Notes

* This action was on the 5th of August, 1781.

† About three years; it might have been a few weeks over or under.

[43] *Jonah's prayer* The prophet Jonah was swallowed and then spit out by a whale (see the Book of Jonah).

[44] *Dogger Bank* the Battle of Dogger Bank between the Dutch and the English.

[45] *Her Ladyship* the Countess of Huntingdon.

Olaudah Equiano (1745–1797)

Immanuel Kant wrote in his 1784 essay "What Is Enlightenment?" that the term "enlightenment," broadly speaking, meant the freedom to use one's own intelligence, beyond religious, political, and social orthodoxies of the day. He may as well have been talking about Olaudah Equiano. Even more than American polymath Benjamin Franklin, Equiano used his own intelligence to craft an identity and challenge prevailing assumptions about what a person of African descent meant in a world that excluded this kind of person from the realm of human reason. Fusing travel narrative with autobiography and social protest, Equiano's 1789 *Interesting Narrative of the Life of Olaudah Equiano, or Gustavus Vassa, the African, Written by Himself* influenced African American literature well into the nineteenth century. This influence was undiminished by the fact that his *Narrative* was first published in England, that Equiano himself spent more time on the high seas and in the transatlantic British empire than in colonial North America, and that questions remained – and still remain – concerning the facts of his biography.

In his *Interesting Narrative,* Equiano writes that he was born in an Igbo village (in present-day Nigeria), and that at the age of 11 he and his younger sister were kidnapped and forced into slavery in a neighboring village. The two children eventually landed in the hands of European slave traders who transported them to Barbados. From there, Equiano was shipped to Virginia, and he never saw his sister or his family again. While Equiano writes movingly of his idyllic village youth and of the harrowing brutalities of the Middle Passage, scholars have cast some doubt on the veracity of these accounts, pointing to baptismal records and naval muster rolls linking Equiano's birth to South Carolina. If true, this revision of Equiano's history serves to emphasize the rhetorical savvy that underwrites his self-presentation: he made powerful use of his story in promoting the egalitarian principles that most Enlightened men denied to people of African descent. Equiano's story of his kidnapping, his constant abuse at the hands of white slave traders, and the horrors of the Middle Passage all constituted the most famous account of the slave trade, written by a person of African descent, in British history.

In Virginia, a Royal Navy Lieutenant named Michael Pascal purchased Equiano and named him Gustavus Vassa. Like his namesake, a sixteenth-century Swedish nobleman who rose to become king of his country, Equiano/Vassa would become a great leader within London's Afro-British community after purchasing his freedom in 1766. In his time as Pascal's personal servant, Equiano was present at various battles of the French and Indian War. Pascal eventually sent Equiano to a sister's home in England, where he attended school for the first time and converted to Christianity. Equiano was baptized in Westminster's St Margaret's Church.

Equiano's education and his faith did not immunize him against betrayal, however. Pascal promised Equiano both a share of prize money from the Crown and freedom in reward for his wartime assistance, then delivered neither. Instead, Pascal sold Equiano to one Captain James Doran, who transported him to the island of Montserrat prior to selling him again, in 1762, to a Philadelphia merchant and Quaker named Robert King. While working for King, the

The Wiley Blackwell Anthology of African American Literature: Volume 1, 1746–1920, First Edition.
Edited by Gene Andrew Jarrett.

enterprising Equiano was permitted to earn his own money, and was promised that he could buy his freedom for 40 pounds, which he did by 1766. Although King moved to make Equiano a business partner, the young man declined the offer and returned to Britain, where the recent Somerset Case made it harder for free men of color to be re-enslaved. Equiano had narrowly escaped re-enslavement in Georgia. Like many former slaves, Equiano found his status less problematic in Europe than it was in the Americas.

In spite of having bought his own freedom, Equiano encountered many whites who sought to label him as slave because he was of African descent. Even after traveling through the Americas, Turkey, and the Mediterranean, he was almost kidnapped while waiting for his ship to depart from England. And after sailing with the Phipps Expedition in search of the Northwest Passage in 1773, he was re-enslaved for a time while managing a plantation on the Mosquito Shore of present-day Honduras. When denied promised wages while working in Jamaica, Equiano elected to resettle in Britain in 1777. There, he immersed himself in the abolitionist movement alongside white British civil servant and scholar Granville Sharp.

The British abolition movement in the late eighteenth century was principally concerned with ending the slave trade, although men like Sharp used this crusade to argue against inequality in many forms. Equiano joined a group of London Africans that included Ottobah Cugoano, a former slave whose group, the Sons of Africa, wrote protests against the slave trade for local newspapers. Cugoano published his own treatise, *Thoughts and Sentiments on the Evil of Slavery and Commerce of the Human Species*, in 1787, but Equiano above all transformed his own experience of slavery and the slave trade into a rallying cry for British antislavery efforts with his *Interesting Narrative* in 1789. With Cugoano, Equiano was part of a politically active group of Britons that also included poet William Blake and Radical reformer Thomas Hardy. Just as John Marrant had benefitted from the support of the Countess of Huntingdon, Equiano earned white abolitionist patronage as he toured the United Kingdom on behalf of the abolition movement. By 1788, his connections to British royalty led to his involvement with what would become the Sierra Leone Company, Granville Sharp's government-supported project that sought resettlement of the poor on the western coast of Africa. Equiano was eventually dismissed from the project, but not before his *Interesting Narrative* became a best-seller; it went through numerous editions before it appeared in the United States in 1791, and was also translated into Dutch, German, and Russian in the early 1790s.

Equiano's later years were less eventful than his early life of high seas travel and exploration, but he continued to fight against inequality. Aside from abolition, he worked for the London Corresponding Society with his longtime friend, Thomas Hardy. The organization sought extension of the franchise to working men, and incurred the wrath of British officials in a conservative reaction to the violence of the French Revolution. Equiano married Englishwoman Susannah Cullen in Cambridgeshire in 1792 and had two daughters, one of whom, Joanna, inherited the estate after his death in 1797.

Further reading

Boulukos, George. *The Grateful Slave: The Emergence of Race in Eighteenth-Century British and American Culture*. New York: Cambridge University Press, 2008. Ch. 5.

Bugg, John. "The Other Interesting Narrative: Olaudah Equiano's Public Book Tour." *PMLA: Publications of the Modern Language Association of America* 121.5 (2006): 1424–1442.

Carretta, Vincent. *Equiano, the African: Biography of a Self-Made Man*. Athens: University of Georgia Press, 2005.

Carretta, Vincent. "Back to the Future: Eighteenth-Century Transatlantic Black Authors." *A Companion to African American Literature*. Ed. Gene Andrew Jarrett. Malden, MA: Wiley-Blackwell, 2010. 11–24.

Davidson, Cathy. "Olaudah Equiano, Written by Himself." *Novel: A Forum on Fiction* 40.1–2 (2006–2007): 18–51.

Elmer, Jonathan. *On Lingering and Being Last: Race and Sovereignty in the New World*. Bronx: Fordham University Press, 2008. Ch. 2.

Field, Emily Donaldson. "'Excepting Himself': Olaudah Equiano, Native Americans, and the Civilizing Mission." *MELUS: The Journal of the Society for the Study of the Multi-Ethnic Literature of the United States* 34.4 (2009): 15–38.

Finseth, Ian Frederick. Shades of Green: Visions of Nature in the Literature of American Slavery. Athens: University of Georgia Press, 2009. Ch. 2.

Gould, Philip. *Barbaric Traffic: Commerce and Antislavery in the Eighteenth-Century Atlantic World*. Cambridge: Harvard University Press, 2003. Ch. 3.

Lovejoy, Paul E. "Olaudah Equiano o Vassa: What's in a Name?" *Atla Literary, Cultural, and Historical Persp* (2012): 165–184.

M'Baye, Babacar. *The Trickster Comes West: Pan-Africa Influence in Early Black Diasporan Narratives*. Jackson: University Press of Mississippi, 2009. Ch. 3.

Molesworth, Jesse M. "Equiano's 'Loud Voice': Witnessing the Performance of *The Interesting Narrative*." *Texas Studies in Literature and Language* 48.2 (2006): 123–144.

Pudaloff, Ross J. "No Change Without Purchase: Olaudah Equiano and the Economies of Self and Market." *Early American Literature* 40.3 (2005): 499–527.

Wilay, Michael. "Consuming Africa: Geography and Identity in Olaudah Equiano's *Interesting Narrative*." *Studies in Romanticism* 44.2 (2005): 165–179.

Extracts from Interesting Narrative of the Life of Olaudah Equiano, or Gustavus Vassa, the African, Written by Himself

Chapter 1

The Author's account of his country, and their manners and customs – Administration of justice – Embrenché – Marriage ceremony, and public entertainments[1] *– Mode of living – Dress – Manufactures – Buildings – Commerce – Agriculture – War and Religion – Superstition of the natives – Funeral ceremonies of the priests or magicians – Curious mode of discovering poison – Some hints concerning the origin of the Author's countrymen, with the opinions of different writers on that subject.*

I BELIEVE it is difficult for those who publish their own memoirs to escape the imputation of vanity; nor is this the only disadvantage under which they labour; it is also their misfortune, that whatever is uncommon is rarely, if ever, believed; and what is obvious we are apt to turn from with disgust, and to charge the writer with impertinence. People generally think those memoirs only worthy to be read or remembered which abound in great or striking events; those, in short, which in a high degree excite either admiration or pity: all others they consign to contempt and oblivion. It is, therefore, I confess, not a little hazardous, in a private and obscure individual, and a stranger too, thus to solicit the indulgent attention of the public; especially when I own I offer here the history of neither a saint, a hero, nor a tyrant. I believe there are a few events in my life which have not happened to many; it is true the incidents of it are numerous; and, did I consider myself an European, I might say my sufferings were great; but, when I compare my lot with that of most of my countrymen, I regard myself as a *particular favourite of Heaven*, and acknowledge the mercies of Providence in every occurrence of my life. If, then, the following narrative does not appear sufficiently interesting to engage general attention, let my motive be some excuse for its publication.

Notes

[1] *Original reads*: entertaiments [ed.].

I am not so foolishly vain as to expect from it either immortality or literary reputation. If it affords any satisfaction to my numerous friends, at whose request it has been written, or in the smallest degree promotes the interest of humanity, the ends for which it was undertaken will be fully attained, and every wish of my heart gratified. Let it therefore be remembered that, in wishing to avoid censure, I do not aspire to praise.

That part of Africa, known by the name of Guinea, to which the trade for slaves is carried on, extends along the coast above 3,400 miles, from Senegal to Angola, and includes a variety of kingdoms. Of these the most considerable is the kingdom of Benin,[2] both as to extent and wealth, the richness and cultivation of the soil, the power of its king, and the number and warlike disposition of the inhabitants. It is situated nearly under the line[3] and extends along the coast about 170 miles, but runs back into the interior part of Africa to a distance hitherto I believe unexplored by any traveller; and seems only terminated at length by the empire of Abyssinia,[4] near 1,500 miles from its beginning. This kingdom is divided into many provinces or districts: in one of the most remote and fertile of which, called Eboe,[5] I was born, in the year 1745, in a charming fruitful vale, named Essaka. The distance of this province from the capital of Benin and the sea coast must be very considerable; for I had never heard of white men or Europeans, nor of the sea; and our subjection to the king of Benin was little more than nominal; for every transaction of the government, as far as my slender observation extended, was conducted by the chiefs or elders of the place. The manners and government of a people who have little commerce with other countries are generally very simple; and the history of what passes in one family or village may serve as a specimen of the whole nation. My father was one of those elders or chiefs I have spoken of, and was styled Embrenché;[6] a term, as I remember, importing the highest distinction, and signifying in our language a mark of grandeur. This mark is conferred on the person entitled to it, by cutting the skin across at the top of the forehead, and drawing it down to the eye-brows; and, while it is in this situation, applying a warm hand, and rubbing it until it shrinks up into a thick *weal*[7] across the lower part of the forehead. Most of the judges and senators were thus marked; my father had long borne it: I had seen it conferred on one of my brothers, and I was also *destined* to receive it by my parents. Those Embrenché, or chief men, decided disputes and punished crimes; for which purpose they always assembled together. The proceedings were generally short; and in most cases the law of retaliation prevailed. I remember a man was brought before my father, and the other judges, for kidnapping a boy; and, although he was the son of a chief or senator, he was condemned to make recompense by a man or woman slave. Adultery, however, was sometimes punished with slavery or death; a punishment which I believe is inflicted on it throughout most of the nations of Africa: so sacred among them is the honour of the marriage bed, and so jealous are they of the fidelity of their wives. Of this I recollect an instance. A woman was convicted before the judges of adultery, and delivered over, as the custom was, to her husband to be punished. Accordingly he determined to put her to death: but it being found, just before her execution, that she had an infant at her breast; and no woman being prevailed on to perform the part of a nurse, she was spared on account of the child. The men, however, do not preserve the same constancy to their wives, which they expect from them; for they indulge in a plurality, though seldom in more than two. Their mode of marriage is thus: both

Notes

[2] *Benin* a country in West Africa.

[3] *under the line* below the equator.

[4] *Abyssinia* the ancient name of Ethiopia.

[5] *Eboe* Ibo/Igbo.

[6] *Embrenché* a mark distinguishing tribal leaders.

[7] *weal* a welt.

parties are usually betrothed when young by their parents (though I have known the males to betroth themselves). On this occasion a feast is prepared, and the bride and bridegroom stand up in the midst of all their friends, who are assembled for the purpose, while he declares she is thenceforth to be looked upon as his wife, and that no other person is to pay any addresses to her. This is also immediately proclaimed in the vicinity, on which the bride retires from the assembly. Some time after, she is brought home to her husband, and then another feast is made, to which the relations of both parties are invited: her parents then deliver her to the bridegroom, accompanied with a number of blessings, and at the same time they tie round her waist a cotton string of the thickness of a goose-quill, which none but married women are permitted to wear: she is now considered as completely his wife; and at this time the dowry is given to the new married pair, which generally consists of portions of land, slaves, and cattle, household goods, and implements of husbandry. These are offered by the friends of both parties; besides which the parents of the bridegroom present gifts to those of the bride, whose property she is looked upon before marriage; but after it she is esteemed the sole property of her husband. The ceremony being now ended, the festival begins, which is celebrated with bonfires, and loud acclamations of joy, accompanied with music and dancing.

We are almost a nation of dancers, musicians, and poets. Thus every great event, such as a triumphant return from battle, or other cause of public rejoicing, is celebrated in public dances, which are accompanied with songs and music suited to the occasion. The assembly is separated into four divisions, which dance either apart or in succession, and each with a character peculiar to itself. The first division contains the married men, who in their dances frequently exhibit feats of arms, and the representation of a battle. To these succeed the married women, who dance in the second division. The young men occupy the third; and the maidens the fourth. Each represents some interesting scene of real life, such as a great achievement, domestic employment, a pathetic story, or some rural sport; and as the subject is generally founded on some recent event, it is therefore ever new. This gives our dances a spirit and variety which I have scarcely seen elsewhere. We have many musical instruments, particularly drums of different kinds, a piece of music which resembles a guitar, and another much like a stickado.[8] These last are chiefly used by betrothed virgins, who play on them on all grand festivals.

As our manners are simple, our luxuries are few. The dress of both sexes is nearly the same. It generally consists of a long piece of calico, or muslin, wrapped loosely round the body, somewhat in the form of a Highland plaid. This is usually dyed blue, which is our favourite colour. It is extracted from a berry, and is brighter and richer than any I have seen in Europe. Besides this, our women of distinction wear golden ornaments, which they dispose with some profusion on their arms and legs. When our women are not employed with the men in tillage, their usual occupation is spinning and weaving cotton, which they afterwards dye, and make into garments. They also manufacture earthen vessels, of which we have many kinds. Among the rest tobacco pipes, made after the same fashion, and used in the same manner, as those in Turkey.

Our manner of living is entirely plain; for as yet the natives are unacquainted with those refinements in cookery which debauch the taste: bullocks, goats, and poultry supply the greatest part of their food. These constitute likewise the principal wealth of the country, and the chief articles of its commerce. The flesh is usually stewed in a pan.

Notes

8 *stickado* a musical instrument similar to a xylophone.

To make it savory, we sometimes use also pepper, and other spices, and we have salt made of wood ashes. Our vegetables are mostly plantains, eadas,[9] yams, beans, and Indian corn. The head of the family usually eats alone; his wives and slaves have also their separate tables. Before we taste food, we always wash our hands: indeed our cleanliness on all occasions is extreme; but on this it is an indispensable ceremony. After washing, libation is made, by pouring out a small portion of the drink on the floor, and tossing a small quantity of the food in a certain place, for the spirits of departed relations, which the natives suppose to preside over their conduct, and guard them from evil. They are totally unacquainted with strong or spiritous liquours; and their principal beverage is palm wine. This is got from a tree of that name, by tapping it at the top, and fastening a large gourd to it; and sometimes one tree will yield three or four gallons in a night. When just drawn it is of a most delicious sweetness; but in a few days it acquires a tartish and more spirituous flavour: though I never saw anyone[10] intoxicated by it. The same tree also produces nuts and oil. Our principal luxury is in perfumes; one sort of these is an odoriferous wood of delicious fragrance: the other a kind of earth; a small portion of which thrown into the fire diffuses a most powerful odour. We beat this wood into powder, and mix it with palm-oil; with which both men and women perfume themselves.

In our buildings we study convenience rather than ornament. Each master of a family has a large square piece of ground, surrounded with a moat or fence, or enclosed with a wall made of red earth tempered, which, when dry, is as hard as brick. Within this are his houses to accommodate his family and slaves; which, if numerous, frequently present the appearance of a village. In the middle stands the principal building, appropriated to the sole use of the master, and consisting of two apartments; in one of which he sits in the day with his family, the other is left apart for the reception of his friends. He has besides these a distinct apartment in which he sleeps, together with his male children. On each side are the apartments of his wives, who have also their separate day and night houses. The habitations of the slaves and their families are distributed throughout the rest of the enclosure. These houses never exceed one story in height; they are always built of wood, or stakes driven into the ground, crossed with wattles,[11] and neatly plastered within, and without. The roof is thatched with reeds. Our day houses are left open at the sides; but those in which we sleep are always covered, and plastered in the inside, with a composition mixed with cow-dung, to keep off the different insects which annoy us during the night. The walls and floors also of these are generally covered with mats. Our beds consist of a platform, raised three or four feet from the ground, on which are laid skins, and different parts of a spongy[12] tree called plantain.[13] Our covering is calico or muslin, the same as our dress. The usual seats are a few logs of wood; but we have benches, which are generally perfumed, to accommodate strangers; these compose the greater part of our household furniture. Houses so constructed and furnished require but little skill to erect them. Every man is a sufficient architect for the purpose. The whole neighbourhood afford their unanimous assistance in building them, and, in return, receive and expect no other recompense than a feast.

As we live in a country where nature is prodigal of her favours, our wants are few and easily supplied; of course we have few manufactures. They consist for the most

Notes

[9] *eadas* an edible tuberous plant (also called a coco-yam).

[10] *Original reads*: any one [ed.].

[11] *wattles* a weave of sticks and twigs.

[12] *Original reads*: spungy [ed.].

[13] *Original reads*: plaintain [ed.].

part of calicoes, earthen ware, ornaments, and instruments of war and husbandry. But these make no part of our commerce, the principal articles of which, as I have observed, are provisions. In such a state money is of little use; however we have some small pieces of coin, if I may call them such. They are made something like an anchor; but I do not remember either their value or denomination. We have also markets, at which I have been frequently with my mother. These are sometimes visited by stout, mahogany-coloured men from the south west of us: we call them *Oye-Eboe*, which term signifies red men living at a distance. They generally bring us firearms, gunpowder, hats, beads, and dried fish. The last we esteemed a great rarity, as our waters were only brooks and springs. These articles they barter with us for odoriferous woods and earth, and our salt of wood-ashes. They always carry slaves through our land; but the strictest account is exacted of their manner of procuring them before they are suffered to pass. Sometimes indeed we sold slaves to them, but they were only prisoners of war, or such among us as had been convicted of kidnapping, or adultery, and some other crimes which we esteemed heinous. This practice of kidnapping induces me to think, that, notwithstanding all our strictness, their principal business among us was to trepan[14] our people. I remember too they carried great sacks along with them, which, not long after, I had an opportunity of fatally seeing applied to that infamous purpose.

Our land is uncommonly rich and fruitful, and produces all kinds of vegetables in great abundance. We have plenty of Indian corn, and vast quantities of cotton and tobacco. Our pine apples grow without culture; they are about the size of the largest sugarloaf, and finely flavoured. We have also spices of different kinds, particularly pepper; and a variety of delicious fruits which I have never seen in Europe; together with gums of various kinds, and honey in abundance. All our industry is exerted to improve those blessings of nature. Agriculture is our chief employment; and everyone,[15] even the children and women, are engaged in it. Thus we are all habituated to labour from our earliest years. Everyone[16] contributes something to the common stock; and as we are unacquainted with idleness, we have no beggars. The benefits of such a mode of living are obvious. The West-India planters prefer the slaves of Benin or Eboe to those of any other part of Guinea, for their hardiness, intelligence, integrity, and zeal. Those benefits are felt by us in the general healthiness of the people, and in their vigour and activity; I might have added too in their comeliness. Deformity is indeed unknown amongst us, I mean that of shape. Numbers of the natives of Eboe now in London might be brought in support of this assertion; for, in regard to complexion, ideas of beauty are wholly relative. I remember while in Africa to have seen three negro children, who were tawny, and another quite white, who were universally regarded by myself and the natives in general, as far as related to their complexions, as deformed. Our women too were, in my eyes at least, uncommonly graceful, alert, and modest to a degree of bashfulness; nor do I remember to have ever heard of an instance of incontinence amongst them before marriage. They are also remarkably cheerful. Indeed cheerfulness and affability are two of the leading characteristics of our nation.

Our tillage is exercised in a large plain or common, some hours walk from our dwellings, and all the neighbours resort thither in a body. They use no beasts of husbandry; and their only instruments are hoes, axes, shovels, and beaks, or pointed iron to dig with. Sometimes we are visited by locusts, which come in large clouds, so as to

Notes

[14] *trepan* ensnare or trick.

[15] *Original reads*: every one [ed.].

[16] *Original reads*: every one [ed.].

darken the air, and destroy our harvest. This however happens rarely, but when it does, a famine is produced by it. I remember an instance or two wherein this happened. This common is ofttimes[17] the theatre of war; and therefore when our people go out to till their land, they not only go in a body, but generally take their arms with them, for fear of a surprise; and when they apprehend an invasion they guard the avenues to their dwellings, by driving sticks into the ground, which are so sharp at one end as to pierce the foot, and are generally dipt in poison. From what I can recollect of these battles, they appear to have been irruptions of one little state or district on the other, to obtain prisoners or booty. Perhaps they were incited to this by those traders who brought the European goods I mentioned amongst us. Such mode of obtaining slaves in Africa is common; and I believe more are procured this way, and by kidnapping, than any other. When a trader wants slaves, he applies to a chief for them, and tempts him with his wares. It is not extraordinary, if on this occasion he yields to the temptation with as little firmness, and accepts the price of his fellow creature's liberty with as little reluctance, as the enlightened merchant. Accordingly, he falls on his neighbours, and a desperate battle ensues. If he prevails, and takes prisoners, he gratifies his avarice by selling them; but, if his party be vanquished, and he falls into the hands of the enemy, he is put to death: for, as he has been known to foment their quarrels, it is thought dangerous to let him survive, and no ransom can save him, though all other prisoners may be redeemed. We have firearms, bows and arrows, broad two-edged swords and javelins; we have shields also, which cover a man from head to foot. All are taught the use of the weapons. Even our women are warriors, and march boldly out to fight along with the men. Our whole district is a kind of militia: on a certain signal given, such as the firing of a gun at night, they all rise in arms and rush upon their enemy. It is perhaps something remarkable, that when our people march to the field, a red flag or banner is borne before them. I was once a witness to a battle in our common. We had been all at work in it one day as usual when our people were suddenly attacked. I climbed a tree at some distance, from which I beheld the fight. There were many women as well as men on both sides; among others my mother was there and armed with a broad sword. After fighting for a considerable time with great fury, and many had been killed, our people obtained the victory, and took their enemy's Chief prisoner. He was carried off in great triumph, and, though he offered a large ransom for his life, he was put to death. A virgin of note among our enemies had been slain in the battle, and her arm was exposed in our market-place, where our trophies were always exhibited. The spoils were divided according to the merit of the warriors. Those prisoners which were not sold or redeemed we kept as slaves: but how different was their condition from that of the slaves in the West-Indies! With us they do no more work than other members of the community, even their master. Their food, clothing,[18] and lodging were nearly the same as theirs, except that they were not permitted to eat with those who were free born and there was scarce any other difference between them, than a superior degree of importance which the head of a family possesses in our state, and that authority which, as such, he exercises over every part of his household. Some of these slaves have even slaves under them, as their own property, and for their own use.

As to religion, the natives believe that there is one Creator of all things, and that he lives in the sun, and is girded round with a belt, that he may never eat or drink; but, according to some, he smokes a pipe, which is our own favourite luxury. They believe

Notes

[17] *Original reads*: oftimes [ed.].

[18] *Original reads*: cloathing [ed.].

he governs events, especially our deaths or captivity; but, as for the doctrine of eternity, I do not remember to have ever heard of it: some however believe in the transmigration of souls in a certain degree. Those spirits, which are not transmigrated, such as our dear friends or relations, they believe always attend them, and guard them from the bad spirits of their foes. For this reason, they always, before eating, as I have observed, put some small portion of the meat, and pour some of their drink, on the ground for them; and they often make oblations[19] of the blood of beasts or fowls at their graves. I was very fond of my mother, and almost constantly with her. When she went to make these oblations at her mother's tomb, which was a kind of small solitary thatched house, I sometimes attended her. There she made her libations, and spent most of the night in cries and lamentations. I have been often extremely terrified on these occasions. The loneliness of the place, the darkness of the night, and the ceremony of libation, naturally awful and gloomy, were heightened by my mother's lamentations; and these, concurring with the doleful cries of birds, by which these places were frequented, gave an inexpressible terror to the scene.

We compute the year from the day on which the sun crosses the line, and, on its setting that evening, there is a general shout throughout the land; at least I can speak from my own knowledge throughout our vicinity. The people at the same time make a great noise with rattles, not unlike the basket rattles used by children here, though much larger, and hold up their hands to heaven for a blessing. It is then the greatest offerings are made; and those children whom our wise men foretell will be fortunate are then presented to different people. I remember many used to come to see me, and I was carried about to others for that purpose. They have many offerings, particularly at full moons; generally two at harvest, before the fruits are taken out of the ground: and, when any young animals are killed, sometimes they offer up part of them as a sacrifice. These offerings, when made by one of the heads of a family, serve for the whole. I remember we often had them at my father's and my uncle's, and their families have been present. Some of our offerings are eaten with bitter herbs. We had a saying among us to anyone[20] of a cross temper, "That if they were to be eaten, they should be eaten with bitter herbs."

We practised circumcision like the Jews, and made offerings and feasts on that occasion in the same manner as they did. Like them also, our children were named from some event, some circumstance, or fancied foreboding at the time of their birth. I was named *Olaudah*, which, in our language, signifies vicissitude, or fortunate also; one favoured, and having a loud voice and well spoken. I remember we never polluted the name of the object of our adoration; on the contrary, it was always mentioned with the greatest reverence; and we were totally unacquainted with swearing, and all those terms of abuse and reproach which find the way so readily and copiously into the languages of more civilized people. The only expressions of that kind I remember were "May you rot, or may you swell, or may a beast take you."

I have before remarked, that the natives of this part of Africa are extremely cleanly. This necessary habit of decency was with us a part of religion, and therefore we had many purifications and washings; indeed almost as many, and used on the same occasions, if my recollection does not fail me, as the Jews. Those that touched the dead at any time were obliged to wash and purify themselves before they could enter a dwelling-house. Every woman too, at certain times, was forbidden to come into a

Notes

[19] *oblations* offerings.

[20] *Original reads*: any one [ed.].

dwelling-house, or touch any person, or anything[21] we ate. I was so fond of my mother I could not keep from her, or avoid touching her at some of those periods, in consequence of which I was obliged to be kept out with her, in a little house made for that purpose, till offering was made, and then we were purified.

Though we had no places of public worship, we had priests and magicians, or wise men. I do not remember whether they had different offices, or whether they were united in the same persons but they were held in great reverence by the people. They calculated our time, and foretold events, as their name imported, for we called them Ah-affoe-way-cah, which signifies calculators, or yearly men, our year being called Ah-affoe. They wore their beards; and, when they died, they were succeeded by their sons. Most of their implements and things of value were interred along with them. Pipes and tobacco were also put into the grave with the corpse, which was always perfumed and ornamented; and animals were offered in sacrifice to them. None accompanied their funerals but those of the same profession or tribe. These buried them after sunset, and always returned from the grave by a different way from that which they went.

These magicians were also our doctors or physicians. They practised bleeding by cupping,[22] and were very successful in healing wounds and expelling poisons. They had likewise some extraordinary method of discovering jealousy, theft, and poisoning; the success of which no doubt they derived from their unbounded influence over the credulity and superstition of the people. I do not remember what those methods were, except that as to poisoning. I recollect an instance or two, which I hope it will not be deemed impertinent here to insert, as it may serve as a kind of specimen of the rest, and is still used by the negroes in the West Indies. A young woman had been poisoned, but it was not known by whom; the doctors ordered the corpse to be taken up by some persons, and carried to the grave. As soon as the bearers had raised it on their shoulders, they seemed seized with some sudden impulse, and ran to and fro', unable to stop themselves. At last, after having passed through a number of thorns and prickly bushes unhurt, the corpse fell from them close to a house, and defaced it in the fall: and the owner being taken up, he immediately confessed the poisoning.

The natives are extremely cautious about poison. When they buy any eatable the seller kisses it all round before the buyer, to shew him it is not poisoned; and the same is done when any meat or drink is presented, particularly to a stranger. We have serpents of different kinds, some of which are esteemed ominous when they appear in our houses, and these we never molest. I remember two of those ominous snakes, each of which was as thick as the calf of a man's leg, and in colour resembling a dolphin in the water, crept at different times into my mother's night-house, where I always lay with her, and coiled themselves into folds, and each time they crowed like a cock. I was desired by some of our wise men to touch these, that I might be interested in the good omens, which I did, for they were quite harmless, and would tamely suffer themselves to be handled; and then they were put into a large open earthen pan, and set on one side of the highway. Some of our snakes, however, were poisonous: one of them crossed the road one day when I was standing on it, and passed between my feet, without offering to touch me, to the great surprise of many who saw it; and these incidents were accounted by the wise men, and likewise by my mother and the rest of the people, as remarkable omens in my favour.

Notes

[21] *Original reads*: any thing [ed.].

[22] *cupping* drawing blood by means of a heated glass cup.

Such is the imperfect sketch my memory has furnished me with of the manners and customs of a people among whom I first drew my breath. And here I cannot forbear suggesting what has long struck me very forcibly, namely, the strong analogy which even by this sketch, imperfect as it is, appears to prevail in the manners and customs of my countrymen, and those of the Jews, before they reached the Land of Promise, and particularly the patriarchs,[23] while they were yet in that pastoral state which is described in Genesis – an analogy, which alone would induce me to think that the one people had sprung from the other. Indeed this is the opinion of Dr. Gill,[24] who, in his commentary on Genesis, very ably deduces the pedigree of the Africans from Afer and Afra, the descendants of Abraham by Keturah his wife and concubine (for both these titles are applied to her). It is also conformable to the sentiments of Dr. John Clarke,[25] formerly Dean of Sarum, in his Truth of the Christian Religion: both these authors concur in ascribing to us this original. The reasonings of these gentlemen are still further confirmed by the Scripture Chronology of the Rev. Arthur Bedford; and if any further corroboration were required, this resemblance in so many respects is a strong evidence in support of the opinion. Like the Israelites in their primitive state, our government was conducted by our chiefs, our judges, our wise men, and elders; and the head of a family with us enjoyed a similar authority over his household with that which is ascribed to Abraham and the other patriarchs. The law of retaliation obtained almost universally with us as with them: and even their religion appeared to have shed upon us a ray of its glory, though broken and spent in its passage, or eclipsed by the cloud with which time, tradition, and ignorance might have enveloped it: for we had our circumcision (a rule I believe peculiar to that people): we had also our sacrifices and burnt-offerings, our washings and purifications, on the same occasions as they had.

As to the difference of colour between the Eboan Africans and the modern Jews, I shall not presume to account for it. It is a subject which has engaged the pens of men of both genius and learning, and is far above my strength. The most able and Reverend Mr. T. Clarkson, however, in his much-admired Essay on the Slavery and Commerce of the Human Species,[26] has ascertained the cause, in a manner that at once solves every objection on that account, and, on my mind at least, has produced the fullest conviction. I shall therefore refer to that performance for the theory, contenting myself with extracting a fact as related by Dr. Mitchel. "The Spaniards, who have inhabited America, under the torrid zone, for any time, are become as dark coloured as our native Indians of Virginia, *of which I myself have been a witness*. There is also another instance of a Portuguese settlement at Mitomba, a river in Sierra Leona,[27] where the inhabitants are bred from a mixture of the first Portuguese discoverers with the natives, and are now become, in their complexion, and in the woolly quality of their hair, *perfect negroes*, retaining however a smattering of the Portuguese language."[28]

These instances, and a great many more which might be adduced, while they shew how the complexions of the same persons vary in different climates, it is hoped may

Notes

[23] *patriarchs* in the Bible, Abraham, Isaac, Jacob and his sons; to them God promises Canaan, or the "Land of Promise" (cf. Genesis 15:18 and 17:8).

[24] *Dr. Gill* John Gill (1697–1771), English pastor and theologian, author of *An Exposition of the Old Testament* (1763–1766).

[25] Dr. John Clarke (1682–1757), Dean of Salisbury, England. *The Truth of the Christian Religion* (1711) was a text by Hugo Grotius that Clarke translated.

[26] *Reverend Mr. T. Clarkson ... much admired Essay... Human Species* Thomas Clarkson (1760–1846), English abolitionist. His "Essay on the Slavery and Commerce of the Human Species" was published in 1786.

[27] *Sierra Leona* a Portuguese slave port on the West African coast.

[28] *"The Spaniards ... language."* From the closing lines of John Mitchel's essay, "Causes of the Different Colours of Persons in Different Climates," printed in *The Philosophical Transactions (From the Year 1743, to the Year 1750) Abridged, and Disposed under General Heads* (London: Lockyer Davis and Charles Reymers, 1756).

tend also to remove the prejudice that some conceive against the natives of Africa on account of their colour. Surely the minds of the Spaniards did not change with their complexions! Are there not causes enough to which the apparent inferiority of an African may be ascribed, without limiting the goodness of God, and supposing he forbore to stamp understanding on certainly his own image, because "carved in ebony?" Might it not naturally be ascribed to their situation? When they come among Europeans, they are ignorant of their language, religion, manners, and customs. Are any pains taken to teach them these? Are they treated as men? Does not slavery itself depress the mind, and extinguish all its fire, and every noble sentiment? But, above all, what advantages do not a refined people possess over those who are rude and uncultivated? Let the polished and haughty European recollect that *his* ancestors were once, like the Africans, uncivilized, and even barbarous. Did Nature make *them* inferior to their sons? and should *they too* have been made slaves? Every rational mind answers, No. Let such reflections as these melt the pride of their superiority into sympathy for the wants and miseries of their sable[29] brethren, and compel them to acknowledge, that understanding is not confined to feature or colour. If, when they look round the world, they feel exultation, let it be tempered with benevolence to others, and gratitude to God, "who hath made of one blood all nations of men for to dwell on all the face of the earth;[30] and whose wisdom is not our wisdom, neither are our ways his ways."

Chapter 2

The Author's birth and parentage – His being kidnapped with his sister – Their separation – Surprise at meeting again – Are finally separated – Account of the different places and incidents the Author met with till his arrival on the coast – The effect the sight of a slave-ship had on him – He sails for the West-Indies – Horrors of a slave-ship – Arrives at Barbadoes, where the cargo is sold and dispersed.

I HOPE the reader will not think I have trespassed on his patience in introducing myself to him with some account of the manners and customs of my country. They had been implanted in me with great care, and made an impression on my mind, which time could not erase, and which all the adversity and variety of fortune I have since experienced served only to rivet and record: for, whether the love of one's country be real or imaginary, or a lesson of reason, or an instinct of nature, I still look back with pleasure on the first scenes of my life, though that pleasure has been for the most part mingled with sorrow.

I have already acquainted the reader with the time and place of my birth. My father, besides many slaves, had a numerous family, of which seven lived to grow up, including myself and a sister, who was the only daughter. As I was the youngest of the sons, I became, of course, the greatest favourite with my mother, and was always with her; and she used to take particular pains to form my mind. I was trained up from my earliest years in the arts of agriculture and war: my daily exercise was shooting and throwing javelins; and my mother adorned me with emblems, after the manner of our greatest warriors. In this way I grew up till I was turned the age of eleven, when an end

Notes

[29] *sable* black.

[30] *"who hath made one blood of all nations ... the earth"* Acts 17:26.

was put to my happiness in the following manner: Generally, when the grown people in the neighbourhood were gone far in the fields to labour, the children assembled together in some of the neighbours' premises to play; and commonly some of us used to get up a tree to look out for any assailant, or kidnapper, that might come upon us; for they sometimes took those opportunities of our parents' absence, to attack and carry off as many as they could seize. One day, as I was watching at the top of a tree in our yard, I saw one of those people come into the yard of our next neighbour but one, to kidnap, there being many stout young people in it. Immediately, on this, I gave the alarm of the rogue, and he was surrounded by the stoutest of them, who entangled him with cords, so that he could not escape till some of the grown people came and secured him. But, alas! ere long it was my fate to be thus attacked, and to be carried off, when none of the grown people were nigh. One day, when all our people were gone out to their works as usual, and only I and my dear sister were left to mind the house, two men and a woman got over our walls, and in a moment seized us both; and, without giving us time to cry out, or make resistance, they stopped our mouths, tied our hands, and ran off with us into the nearest wood: and continued to carry us as far as they could, till night came on, when we reached a small house, where the robbers halted for refreshment, and spent the night. We were then unbound, but were unable to take any food; and, being quite overpowered by fatigue and grief, our only relief was some sleep, which allayed our misfortune for a short time. The next morning we left the house, and continued travelling all the day. For a long time we had kept the woods, but at last we came into a road which I believed I knew. I had now some hopes of being delivered; for we had advanced but a little way before I discovered some people at a distance, on which I began to cry out for their assistance; but my cries had no other effect than to make them tie me faster, and stop my mouth, and then they put me into a large sack. They also stopped my sister's mouth, and tied her hands; and in this manner we proceeded till we were out of the sight of these people. When we went to rest the following night they offered us some victuals;[31] but we refused them; and the only comfort we had was in being in one another's arms all that night, and bathing each other with our tears. But, alas! we were soon deprived of even the smallest comfort of weeping together. The next day proved a day of greater sorrow than I had yet experienced; for my sister and I were then separated, while we lay clasped in each other's arms. It was in vain that we besought them not to part us: she was torn from me, and immediately carried away, while I was left in a state of distraction not to be described. I cried and grieved continually; and for several days I did not eat anything[32] but what they forced into my mouth. At length, after many days travelling, during which I had often changed masters, I got into the hands of a chieftain, in a very pleasant country. This man had two wives and some children, and they all used me extremely well, and did all they could to comfort me; particularly the first wife, who was something like my mother. Although I was a great many days journey from my father's house, yet these people spoke exactly the same language with us. This first master of mine, as I may call him, was a smith, and my principal employment was working his bellows, which were the same kind as I had seen in my vicinity. They were in some respects not unlike the stoves here in gentlemen's kitchens; and were covered over with leather; and in the middle of that leather a stick was fixed, and a person stood up, and worked it, in the same manner as is done to pump water out of a cask with a hand-pump. I believe it was gold he worked, for it was of a lovely bright yellow

Notes

[31] *victuals* food.

[32] *Original reads*: any thing [ed.].

colour, and was worn by the women on their wrists and ankles.[33] I was there I suppose about a month, and they at last used to trust me some little distance from the house. This liberty I used in embracing every opportunity to inquire the way to my own home: and I also sometimes, for the same purpose, went with the maidens, in the cool of the evenings, to bring pitchers of water from the springs for the use of the house. I had also remarked where the sun rose in the morning, and set in the evening, as I had travelled along; and I had observed that my father's house was towards the rising of the sun. I therefore determined to seize the first opportunity of making my escape, and to shape my course for that quarter; for I was quite oppressed and weighed down by grief after my mother and friends; and my love of liberty, ever great, was strengthened by the mortifying circumstance of not daring to eat with the free-born children, although I was mostly their companion. While I was projecting my escape one day, an unlucky event happened, which quite disconcerted my plan, and put an end to my hopes. I used to be sometimes employed in assisting an elderly woman slave to cook and take care of the poultry; and one morning, while I was feeding some chickens, I happened to toss a small pebble at one of them, which hit it on the middle, and directly killed it. The old slave, having soon after missed the chicken, inquired after it; and on my relating the accident (for I told her the truth, because my mother would never suffer me to tell a lie) she flew into a violent passion, threatened that I should suffer for it; and, my master being out, she immediately went and told her mistress what I had done. This alarmed me very much, and I expected an instant correction, which to me was uncommonly dreadful; for I had seldom been beaten at home. I therefore resolved to fly; and accordingly I ran into a thicket that was hard by, and hid myself in the bushes. Soon afterwards my mistress and the slave returned, and, not seeing me, they searched all the house, but, not finding me, and I not making answer when they called to me, they thought I had run away, and the whole neighbourhood was raised in the pursuit of me. In that part of the country (as well as ours) the houses and villages were skirted with woods, or shrubberies, and the bushes were so thick, that a man could readily conceal himself in them, so as to elude the strictest search. The neighbours continued the whole day looking for me, and several times many of them came within a few yards of the place where I lay hid. I expected every moment, when I heard a rustling among the trees, to be found out, and punished by my master; but they never discovered me, though they were often so near that I even heard their conjectures as they were looking about for me; and I now learned from them, that any attempt to return home would be hopeless. Most of them supposed I had fled towards home; but the distance was so great, and the way so intricate, that they thought I could never reach it, and that I should be lost in the woods. When I heard this I was seized with a violent panic, and abandoned myself to despair. Night too began to approach, and aggravated all my fears. I had before entertained hopes of getting home, and I had determined when it should be dark to make the attempt; but I was now convinced it was fruitless, and I began to consider that, if possibly I could escape all other animals, I could not those of the human kind; and that, not knowing the way, I must perish in the woods. Thus was I like the hunted deer:

Ev'ry leaf and ev'ry whisp'ring breath
Convey'd a foe, and ev'ry foe a death.[34]

Notes

[33] *Original reads*: ancles [ed.].

[34] *Ev'ry leaf … a death* an approximation of lines from *Cooper's Hill* (1642), by English poet John Denham (1615–1669).

I heard frequent rustlings among the leaves; and, being pretty sure they were snakes, I expected every instant to be stung by them. This increased my anguish, and the horror of my situation became now quite insupportable. I at length quitted the thicket, very faint and hungry, for I had not eaten or drank anything[35] all the day, and crept to my masters kitchen, from whence I set out at first, and which was an open shed, and laid myself down in the ashes, with an anxious wish for death to relieve me from all my pains. I was scarcely awake in the morning when the old woman slave, who was the first up, came to light the fire, and saw me in the fire-place. She was very much surprised to see me, and could scarcely believe her own eyes. She now promised to intercede for me, and went for her master, who soon after came, and, having slightly reprimanded me, ordered me to be taken care of, and not ill-treated.

Soon after this my master's only daughter and child by his first wife sickened and died, which affected him so much that for some time he was almost frantic, and really would have killed himself had he not been watched and prevented. However, in a small time afterwards he recovered, and I was again sold. I was now carried to the left of the sun's rising, through many dreary wastes and dismal woods, amidst the hideous roarings of wild beasts. The people I was sold to used to carry me very often, when I was tired, either on their shoulders or on their backs. I saw many convenient well-built sheds along the roads, at proper distances, to accommodate the merchants and travellers, who lay in those buildings along with their wives, who often accompany them; and they always go well armed.

From the time I left my own nation I always found somebody that understood me till I came to the sea coast. The languages of different nations did not totally differ, nor were they so copious as those of the Europeans, particularly the English. They were therefore easily learned; and, while I was journeying thus through Africa, I acquired two or three different tongues. In this manner I had been travelling for a considerable time, when one evening, to my great surprise, whom should I see brought to the house where I was but my dear sister. As soon as she saw me she gave a loud shriek, and ran into my arms. I was quite overpowered; neither of us could speak, but, for a considerable time, clung to each other in mutual embraces, unable to do anything[36] but weep. Our meeting affected all who saw us; and indeed I must acknowledge, in honour of those sable destroyers of human rights, that I never met with any ill treatment, or saw any offered to their slaves, except tying them, when necessary, to keep them from running away. When these people knew we were brother and sister they indulged us to be together; and the man, to whom I supposed we belonged, lay with us, he in the middle, while she and I held one another by the hands across his breast all night; and thus for a while we forgot our misfortunes in the joy of being together: but even this small comfort was soon to have an end; for scarcely had the fatal morning appeared, when she was again torn from me for ever! I was now more miserable, if possible, than before. The small relief which her presence gave me from pain was gone, and the wretchedness of my situation was redoubled by my anxiety after her fate, and my apprehensions lest her sufferings should be greater than mine, when I could not be with her to alleviate them. Yes, thou dear partner of all my childish sports! thou sharer of my joys and sorrows! happy should I have ever esteemed myself to encounter every misery for you, and to procure your freedom by the sacrifice of my own. Though you were early forced from my arms, your image has been always

Notes

[35] *Original reads*: any thing [ed.].

[36] *Original reads*: any thing [ed.].

riveted[37] in my heart, from which neither *time nor fortune* have been able to remove it: so that, while the thoughts of your sufferings have damped my prosperity, they have mingled with adversity, and increased its bitterness. To that heaven which protects the weak from the strong, I commit the care of your innocence and virtues, if they have not already received their full reward; and if your youth and delicacy have not long since fallen victims to the violence of the African trader, the pestilential stench of a Guinea ship, the seasoning in the European colonies, or the lash and lust of a brutal and unrelenting overseer.

I did not long remain after my sister. I was again sold, and carried through a number of places, till, after travelling a considerable time, I came to a town called Tinmah, in the most beautiful country I had yet seen in Africa. It was extremely rich, and there were many rivulets which flowed through it; and supplied a large pond in the center of the town, where the people washed. Here I first saw and tasted cocoa nuts, which I thought superior to any nuts I had ever tasted before; and the trees, which were loaded, were also interspersed amongst the houses, which had commodious shades adjoining, and were in the same manner as ours, the insides being neatly plastered and white-washed. Here I also saw and tasted for the first time sugar-cane. Their money consisted of little white shells, the size of the finger nail: they are known in this country by the name of *core*, I was sold here for one hundred and seventy-two of them by a merchant who lived and brought me there. I had been about two or three days at his house, when a wealthy widow, a neighbour of his, came there one evening, and brought with her an only son, a young gentleman about my own age and size. Here they saw me; and, having taken a fancy to me, I was bought of the merchant, and went home with them. Her house and premises were situated close to one of those rivulets I have mentioned, and were the finest I ever saw in Africa: they were very extensive, and she had a number of slaves to attend her. The next day I was washed and perfumed, and when meal-time came, I was led into the presence of my mistress, and ate and drank before her with her son. This filled me with astonishment: and I could scarce help expressing my surprise that the young gentleman should suffer[38] me, who was bound, to eat with him who was free; and not only so, but that he would not at any time either eat or drink till I had taken first, because I was the eldest, which was agreeable to our custom. Indeed everything[39] here, and all their treatment of me, made me forget that I was a slave. The language of these people resembled ours so nearly, that we understood each other perfectly. They had also the very same customs as we. There were likewise slaves daily to attend us, while my young master and I, with other boys, sported with our darts and bows and arrows, as I had been used to do at home. In this resemblance to my former happy state I passed about two months, and I now began to think I was to be adopted into the family, and was beginning to be reconciled to my situation, and to forget by degrees my misfortunes, when all at once the delusion vanished; for, without the least previous knowledge, one morning early, while my dear master and companion was still asleep, I was awakened out of my reverie to fresh sorrow, and hurried away even among the uncircumcised.

Thus, at the very moment I dreamed of the greatest happiness, I found myself most miserable: and it seemed as if fortune wished to give me this taste of joy only to render the reverse more poignant. The change I now experienced was as painful as it was sudden and unexpected. It was a change indeed from a state of bliss to a scene which is

Notes

[37] *Original reads*: rivetted [ed.].

[38] *suffer* allow.

[39] *Original reads*: every thing [ed.].

inexpressible by me, as it discovered to me an element I had never before beheld, and till then had no idea of, and wherein such instances of hardship and cruelty continually occurred as I can never reflect on but with horror.

All the nations and people I had hitherto passed through resembled our own in their manners, customs and language: but I came at length to a country, the inhabitants of which differed from us in all those particulars. I was very much struck with this difference, especially when I came among a people who did not circumcise, and eat without washing their hands. They cooked also in iron pots, and had European cutlasses[40] and cross bows, which were unknown to us, and fought with their fists among themselves. Their women were not so modest as ours, for they eat, and drank, and slept with their men. But, above all, I was amazed to see no sacrifices or offerings among them. In some of those places the people ornamented themselves with scars, and likewise filed their teeth very sharp. They wanted sometimes to ornament me in the same manner, but I would not suffer them; hoping that I might sometime[41] be among a people who did not thus disfigure themselves, as I thought they did. At last, I came to the banks of a large river, which was covered with canoes, in which the people appeared to live with their household utensils and provisions of all kinds. I was beyond measure astonished at this, as I had never before seen any water larger than a pond or a rivulet; and my surprise was mingled with no small fear when I was put into one of these canoes, and we began to paddle and move along the river. We continued going on thus till night; and when we came to land, and made fires on the banks, each family by themselves, some dragged their canoes on shore, others staid and cooked in theirs, and laid in them all night. Those on the land had mats, of which they made tents, some in the shape of little houses: In these we slept; and after the morning meal we embarked again, and proceeded as before. I was often very much astonished to see some of the women, as well as the men, jump into the water, dive to the bottom, come up again, and swim about. Thus I continued to travel, sometimes by land, sometimes by water, through different countries, and various nations, till, at the end of six or seven months after I had been kidnapped, I arrived at the sea coast. It would be tedious and uninteresting to relate all the incidents which befell[42] me during this journey, and which I have not yet forgotten; of the various hands I passed through, and the manners and customs of all the different people among whom I lived: I shall therefore only observe, that, in all the places where I was, the soil was exceedingly rich; the pomkins,[43] eadas, plantains, yams, &c. &c. were in great abundance, and of incredible size. There were also vast quantities of different gums, though not used for any purpose; and everywhere[44] a great deal of tobacco. The cotton even grew quite wild; and there was plenty of red wood. I saw no mechanics whatever in all the way, except such as I have mentioned. The chief employment in all these countries was agriculture, and both the males and females, as with us, were brought up to it, and trained in the arts of war.

The first object which saluted my eyes when I arrived on the coast was the sea, and a slave-ship, which was then riding at anchor, and waiting for its cargo. These filled me with astonishment, which was soon converted into terror, which I am yet at a loss to describe, nor the then feelings of my mind. When I was carried on board I was immediately handled, and tossed up, to see if I were sound, by some of the crew; and I was now persuaded that I had gotten into a world of bad spirits, and that they were going

Notes

[40] *cutlasses* short curved swords.

[41] *Original reads*: some time [ed.].

[42] *Original reads*: befel [ed.].

[43] *pomkins* pumpkins.

[44] *Original reads*: every where [ed.].

to kill me. Their complexions too differing so much from ours, their long hair, and the language they spoke, which was very different from any I had ever heard, united to confirm me in this belief. Indeed, such were the horrors of my views and fears at the moment, that, if ten thousand worlds had been my own, I would have freely parted with them all to have exchanged my condition with that of the meanest slave in my own country. When I looked round the ship too, and saw a large furnace of copper boiling, and a multitude of black people of every description chained together, every one of their countenances expressing dejection and sorrow, I no longer doubted of my fate, and, quite overpowered with horror and anguish, I fell motionless on the deck and fainted. When I recovered a little, I found some black people about me, who I believed were some of those who brought me on board, and had been receiving their pay; they talked to me in order to cheer me, but all in vain. I asked them if we were not to be eaten by those white men with horrible looks, red faces, and long hair? They told me I was not; and one of the crew brought me a small portion of spirituous liquor in a wine glass; but, being afraid of him, I would not take it out of his hand. One of the blacks therefore took it from him and gave it to me, and I took a little down my palate, which, instead of reviving me, as they thought it would, threw me into the greatest consternation at the strange feeling it produced, having never tasted any such liquor before. Soon after this, the blacks who brought me on board went off, and left me abandoned to despair. I now saw myself deprived of all chance of returning to my native country, or even the least glimpse of hope of gaining the shore, which I now considered as friendly: and I even wished for my former slavery in preference to my present situation, which was filled with horrors of every kind, still heightened by my ignorance of what I was to undergo. I was not long suffered to indulge my grief; I was soon put down under the decks, and there I received such a salutation in my nostrils as I had never experienced in my life; so that with the loathsomeness of the stench, and crying together, I became so sick and low that I was not able to eat, nor had I the least desire to taste anything.[45] I now wished for the last friend, Death, to relieve me; but soon, to my grief, two of the white men offered me eatables; and, on my refusing to eat, one of them held me fast by the hands, and laid me across, I think, the windlass,[46] and tied my feet, while the other flogged me severely. I had never experienced anything[47] of this kind before; and although, not being used to the water, I naturally feared that element the first time I saw it; yet, nevertheless, could I have got over the nettings, I would have jumped over the side, but I could not; and, besides, the crew used to watch us very closely who were not chained down to the decks, lest we should leap into the water; and I have seen some of these poor African prisoners most severely cut for attempting to do so, and hourly whipped for not eating. This indeed was often the case with myself. In a little time after, amongst the poor chained men, I found some of my own nation, which in a small degree gave ease to my mind. I inquired of these what was to be done with us? they gave me to understand we were to be carried to these white people's country to work for them. I then was a little revived, and thought, if it were no worse than working, my situation was not so desperate: but still I feared I should be put to death, the white people looked and acted, as I thought, in so savage a manner; for I had never seen among any people such instances of brutal cruelty; and this not only shewn towards us blacks, but also to some of the whites themselves. One white man in particular I saw, when we were permitted to be on deck, flogged

Notes

45 *Original reads*: any thing [ed.].

46 *windlass* a winch.

47 *Original reads*: any thing [ed.].

so unmercifully with a large rope near the foremast, that he died in consequence of it; and they tossed him over the side as they would have done a brute. This made me fear these people the more; and I expected nothing less than to be treated in the same manner. I could not help expressing my fears and apprehensions to some of my countrymen: I asked them if these people had no country, but lived in this hollow place the ship? they told me they did not, but came from a distant one. "Then," said I, "how comes it in all our country we never heard of them?" They told me, because they lived so very far off. I then asked where were their women? had they any like themselves! I was told they had: "And why," said I, "do we not see them?" they answered, because they were left behind. I asked how the vessel could go? they told me they could not tell; but that there were cloths put upon the masts by the help of the ropes I saw, and then the vessel went on; and the white men had some spell or magic they put in the water when they liked in order to stop the vessel. I was exceedingly amazed at this account, and really thought they were spirits. I therefore wished much to be from amongst them, for I expected they would sacrifice me: but my wishes were vain; for we were so quartered that it was impossible for any of us to make our escape. While we staid on the coast I was mostly on deck; and one day, to my great astonishment, I saw one of these vessels coming in with the sails up. As soon as the whites saw it, they gave a great shout, at which we were amazed; and the more so as the vessel appeared larger by approaching nearer. At last she came to an anchor in my sight, and when the anchor was let go, I and my countrymen who saw it were lost in astonishment to observe the vessel stop; and were now convinced it was done by magic. Soon after this the other ship got her boats out, and they came on board of us, and the people of both ships seemed very glad to see each other. Several of the strangers also shook hands with us black people, and made motions with their hands, signifying, I suppose, we were to go to their country; but we did not understand them. At last, when the ship we were in had got in all her cargo, they made ready with many fearful noises, and we were all put under deck, so that we could not see how they managed the vessel. But this disappointment was the least of my sorrow. The stench of the hold while we were on the coast was so intolerably loathsome, that it was dangerous to remain there for any time, and some of us had been permitted to stay on the deck for the fresh air; but now that the whole ship's cargo were confined together, it became absolutely pestilential. The closeness of the place, and the heat of the climate, added to the number in the ship, which was so crowded that each had scarcely room to turn himself, almost suffocated us. This produced copious perspirations, so that the air soon became unfit for respiration, from a variety of loathsome smells, and brought on a sickness among the slaves, of which many died, thus falling victims to the improvident avarice, as I may call it, of their purchasers. This wretched situation was again aggravated by the galling of the chains, now become insupportable; and the filth of the necessary tubs,[48] into which the children often fell, and were almost suffocated. The shrieks of the women, and the groans of the dying, rendered the whole a scene of horror almost inconceivable.[49] Happily perhaps for myself I was soon reduced so low here that it was thought necessary to keep me almost always on deck; and from my extreme youth I was not put in fetters. In this situation I expected every hour to share the fate of my companions, some of whom were almost daily brought upon deck at the point of death, which I began to hope would soon put an end to my miseries. Often did I think many of the inhabitants of the deep much more happy than myself; I envied them the freedom they enjoyed, and as often

Notes

[48] *necessary tubs* latrines.

[49] *Original reads*: inconceiveable [ed.].

wished I could change my condition for theirs. Every circumstance I met with served only to render my state more painful, and heighten my apprehensions, and my opinion of the cruelty of the whites. One day they had taken a number of fishes; and when they had killed and satisfied themselves with as many as they thought fit, to our astonishment who were on the deck, rather than give any of them to us to eat, as we expected, they tossed the remaining fish into the sea again, although we begged and prayed for some as well as we could, but in vain; and some of my countrymen, being pressed by hunger, took an opportunity, when they thought no one saw them, of trying to get a little privately; but they were discovered, and the attempt procured them some very severe floggings.

One day, when we had a smooth sea, and moderate wind, two of my wearied countrymen, who were chained together (I was near them at the time), preferring death to such a life of misery, somehow made through the nettings, and jumped into the sea: immediately another quite dejected fellow, who, on account of his illness, was suffered to be out of irons, also followed their example; and I believe many more would very soon have done the same, if they had not been prevented by the ship's crew, who were instantly alarmed. Those of us that were the most active were, in a moment, put down under the deck; and there was such a noise and confusion amongst the people of the ship as I never heard before, to stop her, and get the boat out to go after the slaves. However, two of the wretches were drowned, but they got the other, and afterwards flogged him unmercifully, for thus attempting to prefer death to slavery. In this manner we continued to undergo more hardships than I can now relate; hardships which are inseparable from this accursed trade. Many a time we were near suffocation, from the want of fresh air, which we were often without for whole days together. This, and the stench of the necessary tubs, carried off many. During our passage I first saw flying fishes, which surprised me very much: they used frequently to fly across the ship, and many of them fell on the deck. I also now first saw the use of the quadrant.[50] I had often with astonishment seen the mariners make observations with it, and I could not think what it meant. They at last took notice of my surprise; and one of them, willing to increase it, as well as to gratify my curiosity, made me one day look through it. The clouds appeared to me to be land, which disappeared as they passed along. This heightened my wonder: and I was now more persuaded than ever that I was in another world, and that everything[51] about me was magic. At last we came in sight of the island of Barbadoes, at which the whites on board gave a great shout, and made many signs of joy to us. We did not know what to think of this; but as the vessel drew nearer we plainly saw the harbour, and other ships of different kinds and sizes: and we soon anchored amongst them off Bridge Town.[52] Many merchants and planters now came on board, though it was in the evening. They put us in separate parcels, and examined us attentively. They also made us jump, and pointed to the land, signifying we were to go there. We thought by this we should be eaten by these ugly men, as they appeared to us; and, when soon after we were all put down under the deck again, there was much dread and trembling among us, and nothing but bitter cries to be heard all the night from these apprehensions, insomuch that at last the white people got some old slaves from the land to pacify us. They told us we were not to be eaten, but to work, and were soon to go on land, where we should see many of our country people. This report eased us much; and sure enough, soon after we were landed, there came to us

Notes

[50] *quadrant* an instrument that measures a star's altitude to determine one's position at sea.

[51] *Original reads*: every thing [ed.].

[52] *Bridge Town* Bridgetown, the capital of Barbados, an island in the Caribbean.

Africans of all languages. We were conducted immediately to the merchant's yard, where we were all pent up together like so many sheep in a fold, without regard to sex or age. As every object was new to me, everything[53] I saw filled me with surprise. What struck me first was, that the houses were built with bricks, in stories, and in every other respect different from those I have seen in Africa:[54] but I was still more astonished on seeing people on horseback. I did not know what this could mean; and indeed I thought these people were full of nothing but magical arts. While I was in this astonishment, one of my fellow prisoners spoke to a countryman of his about the horses, who said they were the same kind they had in their country. I understood them, though they were from a distant part of Africa, and I thought it odd I had not seen any horses there; but afterwards, when I came to converse with different Africans, I found they had many horses amongst them, and much larger than those I then saw. We were not many days in the merchant's custody before we were sold after their usual manner, which is this: On a signal given (as the beat of a drum), the buyers rush at once into the yard where the slaves are confined, and make choice of that parcel they like best. The noise and clamour with which this is attended, and the eagerness visible in the countenances of the buyers, serve not a little to increase the apprehensions of the terrified Africans, who may well be supposed to consider them as the ministers of that destruction to which they think themselves devoted. In this manner, without scruple, are relations and friends separated, most of them never to see each other again. I remember in the vessel in which I was brought over, in the men's apartment, there were several brothers, who, in the sale, were sold in different lots; and it was very moving on this occasion to see and hear their cries at parting. O, ye nominal Christians! might not an African ask you, learned you this from your God? who says unto you, Do unto all men as you would men should do unto you?[55] Is it not enough that we are torn from our country and friends to toil for your luxury and lust of gain? Must every tender feeling be likewise sacrificed to your avarice? Are the dearest friends and relations, now rendered more dear by their separation from their kindred, still to be parted from each other, and thus prevented from cheering the gloom of slavery with the small comfort of being together and mingling their sufferings and sorrows? Why are parents to lose their children, brothers their sisters, or husbands their wives? Surely this is a new refinement in cruelty, which, while it has no advantage to atone for it, thus aggravates distress, and adds fresh horrors even to the wretchedness of slavery.

Chapter 3

The Author is carried to Virginia – His[56] distress – Surprise at seeing a picture and a watch – Is bought by Captain Pascal, and sets out for England – His terror during the voyage – Arrives in England – His wonder at a fall of snow – Is sent to Guernsey, and in some time goes on board a ship of war with his master – Some account of the expedition against Louisbourg, under the command of Admiral Boscawen, in 1758.

I NOW totally lost the small remains of comfort I had enjoyed in conversing with my countrymen; the women too, who used to wash and take care of me, were all gone different ways, and I never saw one of them afterwards.

Notes

[53] *Original reads*: every thing [ed.].

[54] *Original reads*: from in those I have seen in Africa [ed.].

[55] *Do unto all men … you?* a paraphrase of Matthew 7:12, commonly called the "golden rule."

[56] *Original reads*: his [ed.].

I stayed in this island for a few days; I believe it could not be above a fortnight; when I and some few more slaves, that were not saleable among the rest, from very much fretting, were shipped off in a sloop for North America. On the passage we were better treated than when we were coming from Africa, and we had plenty of rice and fat pork. We were landed up a river a good way from the sea, about Virginia county, where we saw few or none of our native Africans, and not one soul who could talk to me. I was a few weeks weeding grass, and gathering stones in a plantation; and at last all my companions were distributed different ways, and only myself was left. I was now exceedingly miserable, and thought myself worse off than any of the rest of my companions; for they could talk to each other, but I had no person to speak to that I could understand. In this state I was constantly grieving and pining, and wishing for death, rather than anything[57] else. While I was in this plantation, the gentleman, to whom I supposed the estate belonged, being unwell, I was one day sent for to his dwelling house to fan him: when I came into the room where he was, I was very much affrighted at some things I saw, and the more so as I had seen a black woman slave as I came through the house, who was cooking the dinner, and the poor creature was cruelly loaded with various kinds of iron machines; she had one particularly on her head, which locked her mouth so fast that she could scarcely speak; and could not eat nor drink. I was much astonished and shocked at this contrivance, which I afterwards learned was called the iron muzzle. Soon after I had a fan put into my hand, to fan the gentleman while he slept; and so I did indeed with great fear. While he was fast asleep I indulged myself a great deal in looking about the room, which to me appeared very fine and curious. The first object that engaged my attention was a watch which hung on the chimney, and was going. I was quite surprised at the noise it made, and was afraid it would tell the gentleman anything[58] I might do amiss: and when I immediately after observed a picture hanging in the room, which appeared constantly to look at me, I was still more affrighted, having never seen such things as these before. At one time I thought it was something relative to magic; and not seeing it move, I thought it might be some way the whites had to keep their great men when they died, and offer them libations as we used to do our friendly spirits. In this state of anxiety I remained till my master awoke, when I was dismissed out of the room, to my no small satisfaction and relief, for I thought that these people were all made of wonders. In this place I was called Jacob; but on board the African snow[59] I was called Michael. I had been some time in this miserable, forlorn, and much dejected state, without having anyone[60] to talk to, which made my life a burden, when the kind and unknown hand of the Creator (who in very deed leads the blind in a way they know not) now began to appear, to my comfort; for one day the captain of a merchant ship, called the Industrious Bee, came on some business to my master's house. This gentleman, whose name was Michael Henry Pascal, was a lieutenant in the royal navy, but now commanded this trading ship, which was somewhere in the confines of the county many miles off. While he was at my master's house it happened that he saw me, and liked me so well that he made a purchase of me. I think I have often heard him say he gave thirty or forty pounds sterling for me; but I do not now remember which. However, he meant me for a present to some of his friends in England; and I was sent accordingly from the house of my then master (one Mr. Campbell) to the place where the ship lay; I was conducted on horseback by an elderly black man (a mode of travelling which appeared

Notes

[57] *Original reads*: any thing [ed.].

[58] *Original reads*: any thing [ed.].

[59] *snow* a ship with two masts.

[60] *Original reads*: any one [ed.].

very odd to me). When I arrived I was carried on board a fine large ship, loaded with tobacco, &c. and just ready to sail for England. I now thought my condition much mended; I had sails to lie on, and plenty of good victuals to eat; and everybody[61] on board used me very kindly, quite contrary to what I had seen of any white people before; I therefore began to think that they were not all of the same disposition. A few days after I was on board we sailed for England. I was still at a loss to conjecture my destiny. By this time, however, I could smatter a little imperfect English; and I wanted to know as well as I could where we were going. Some of the people of the ship used to tell me they were going to carry me back to my own country, and this made me very happy. I was quite rejoiced at the idea of going back; and thought if I should get home what wonders I should have to tell. But I was reserved for another fate, and was soon undeceived when we came within sight of the English coast. While I was on board this ship, my captain and master named me *Gustavus Vasa*.[62] I at that time began to understand him a little, and refused to be called so, and told him as well as I could that I would be called Jacob; but he said I should not, and still called me Gustavus; and when I refused to answer to my new name, which at first I did, it gained me many a cuff; so at length I submitted, and by which I have been known ever since. The ship had a very long passage; and on that account we had very short allowance of provisions. Towards the last we had only one pound and a half of bread per week, and about the same quantity of meat, and one quart of water a day. We spoke with only one vessel the whole time we were at sea, and but once we caught a few fishes. In our extremities the captain and people told me in jest they would kill and eat me, but I thought them in earnest, and was depressed beyond measure, expecting every moment to be my last. While I was in this situation one evening they caught, with a good deal of trouble, a large shark, and got it on board. This gladdened my poor heart exceedingly, as I thought it would serve the people, to eat instead of their eating me; but very soon, to my astonishment, they cut off a small part of the tail, and tossed the rest over the side. This renewed my consternation; and I did not know what to think of these white people; I very much feared they would kill and eat me. There was on board the ship a young lad who had never been at sea before, about four or five years older than myself: his name was Richard Baker. He was a native of America, had received an excellent education, and was of a most amiable temper. Soon after I went on board he shewed me a great deal of partiality and attention, and in return I grew extremely fond of him. We at length became inseparable; and for the space of two years, he was of very great use to me, and was my constant companion and instructor. Although this dear youth had many slaves of his own, yet he and I have gone through many sufferings together on shipboard; and we have many nights lain in each other's bosoms when we were in great distress. Thus such a friendship was cemented between us as we cherished till his death, which, to my very great sorrow, happened in the year 1759, when he was up the Archipelago,[63] on board his majesty's ship the Preston: an event which I have never ceased to regret, as I lost at once a kind interpreter, an agreeable companion, and a faithful friend; who, at the age of fifteen, discovered a mind superior to prejudice; and who was not ashamed to notice, to associate with, and to be the friend and instructor of one who was ignorant, a stranger, of a different complexion, and a slave! My master

Notes

[61] *Original reads*: every body [ed.].

[62] Gustavus Vasa (1496–1560), a Swedish nobleman who fought to win independence from Danish rule, and was subsequently King Gustavus I (1523–1560).

[63] *Archipelago* the Greek islands.

had lodged in his mother's house in America: he respected him very much, and made him always eat with him in the cabin. He used often to tell him jocularly that he would kill and eat me. Sometimes he would say to me – the black people were not good to eat, and would ask me if we did not eat people in my country. I said, No: then he said he would kill Dick (as he always called him) first, and afterwards me. Though this hearing relieved my mind a little as to myself, I was alarmed for Dick, and whenever he was called I used to be very much afraid he was to be killed; and I would peep and watch to see if they were going to kill him: nor was I free from this consternation till we made the land. One night we lost a man overboard; and the cries and noise were so great and confused, in stopping the ship, that I, who did not know what was the matter, began, as usual, to be very much afraid, and to think they were going to make an offering with me, and perform some magic; which I still believed they dealt in. As the waves were very high, I thought the Ruler of the seas was angry, and I expected to be offered up to appease him. This filled my mind with agony, and I could not any more that night close my eyes again to rest. However, when day-light appeared, I was a little eased in my mind; but still every time I was called I used to think it was to be killed. Some time after this we saw some very large fish, which I afterwards found were called grampusses.[64] They looked to me extremely terrible, and made their appearance just at dusk, and were so near as to blow the water on the ship's deck. I believed them to be the rulers of the sea; and, as the white people did not make any offerings at any time, I thought they were angry with them; and, at last, what confirmed my belief was, the wind just then died away, and a calm ensued, and in consequence of it the ship stopped going. I supposed that the fish had performed this, and I hid myself in the fore-part of the ship, through fear of being offered up to appease them, every minute peeping and quaking; but my good friend Dick came shortly towards me, and I took an opportunity to ask him, as well as I could, what these fish were? Not being able to talk much English, I could but just make him understand my question; and not at all, when I asked him if any offerings were to be made to them? However, he told me these fish would swallow anybody;[65] which sufficiently alarmed me. Here he was called away by the captain, who was leaning over the quarter-deck railing and looking at the fish; and most of the people were busied in getting a barrel of pitch[66] to light, for them to play with. The captain now called me to him, having learned some of my apprehensions from Dick; and having diverted himself and others for some time with my fears, which appeared ludicrous enough in my crying and trembling, he dismissed me. The barrel of pitch was now lighted and put over the side into the water: by this time it was just dark, and the fish went after it; and, to my great joy, I saw them no more.

However, all my alarms began to subside when we got sight of land; and at last the ship arrived at Falmouth,[67] after a passage of thirteen weeks. Every heart on board seemed gladdened on our reaching the shore, and none more than mine. The captain immediately went on shore, and sent on board some fresh provisions, which we wanted very much: we made good use of them, and our famine was soon turned into feasting, almost without ending. It was about the beginning of the spring 1757 when I arrived in England, and I was near twelve years of age at that time. I was very much struck with the buildings and the pavement of the streets in Falmouth; and, indeed, any object I saw filled me with new surprise. One morning, when I got upon deck, I saw it covered all over with the snow that fell over-night: as I had never seen

Notes

[64] *grampusses* small whales.

[65] *Original reads*: any body [ed.].

[66] *pitch* tar.

[67] *Falmouth* English port city.

anything[68] of the kind before, I thought it was salt; so I immediately ran down to the mate, and desired him, as well as I could, to come and see how somebody in the night had thrown salt all over the deck. He, knowing what it was, desired me to bring some of it down to him: accordingly I took up a handful of it, which I found very cold indeed; and when I brought it to him he desired me to taste it. I did so, and I was surprised beyond measure. I then asked him what it was? he told me it was snow: but I could not in any wise understand him. He asked me if we had no such thing in my country? and I told him, No. I then asked him the use of it, and who made it; he told me a great man in the heavens, called God: but here again I was to all intents and purposes at a loss to understand him; and the more so, when a little after I saw the air filled with it, in a heavy shower, which fell down on the same day. After this I went to church; and having never been at such a place before, I was again amazed at seeing and hearing the service. I asked all I could about it; and they gave me to understand it was worshipping God, who made us and all things. I was still at a great loss, and soon got into an endless field of inquiries, as well as I was able to speak and ask about things. However, my little friend Dick used to be my best interpreter; for I could make free with him, and he always instructed me with pleasure: and from what I could understand by him of this God, and in seeing these white people did not sell one another, as we did, I was much pleased; and in this I thought they were much happier than we Africans. I was astonished at the wisdom of the white people in all things I saw; but was amazed at their not sacrificing, or making any offerings, and eating with unwashed hands, and touching the dead. I likewise could not help remarking the particular slenderness of their women, which I did not at first like; and I thought they were not so modest and shamefaced as the African women.

I had often seen my master and Dick employed in reading; and I had a great curiosity to talk to the books, as I thought they did; and so to learn how all things had a beginning: for that purpose I have often taken up a book, and have talked to it, and then put my ears to it, when alone, in hopes it would answer me; and I have been very much concerned when I found it remained silent.

My master lodged at the house of a gentleman in Falmouth, who had a fine little daughter about six or seven years of age, and she grew prodigiously fond of me; insomuch that we used to eat together, and had servants to wait on us. I was so much caressed by this family that it often reminded me of the treatment I had received from my little noble African master. After I had been here a few days, I was sent on board of the ship; but the child cried so much after me that nothing could pacify her till I was sent for again. It is ludicrous enough, that I began to fear I should be betrothed to this young lady; and when my master asked me if I would stay there with her behind him, as he was going away with the ship, which had taken in the tobacco again? I cried immediately, and said I would not leave him. At last, by stealth, one night I was sent on board the ship again; and in a little time we sailed for Guernsey,[69] where she was in part owned by a merchant, one Nicholas Doberry. As I was now amongst a people who had not their faces scarred, like some of the African nations where I had been, I was very glad I did not let them ornament me in that manner when I was with them. When we arrived at Guernsey, my master placed me to board and lodge with one of his mates, who had a wife and family there; and some months afterwards he went to England, and left me in the care of this mate, together with my friend Dick. This mate had a little daughter aged about five or six years, with whom I used to be much delighted.

Notes

[68] *Original reads*: any thing [ed.].

[69] *Guernsey* an island in the English Channel.

I had often observed, that when her mother washed her face it looked very rosy; but when she washed mine it did not look so; I therefore tried oftentimes myself if I could not by washing make my face of the same colour as my little play-mate (Mary), but it was all in vain; and I now began to be mortified at the difference in our complexions. This woman behaved to me with great kindness and attention; and taught me everything[70] in the same manner as she did her own child, and indeed in every respect treated me as such. I remained here till the summer of the year 1757, when my master, being appointed first lieutenant of his Majesty's ship the Roebuck, sent for Dick and me, and his old mate: on this we all left Guernsey, and set out for England in a sloop bound for London. As we were coming up towards the Nore, where the Roebuck lay, a man of war's boat came along side to press[71] our people; on which each man ran to hide himself. I was very much frightened at this, though I did not know what it meant, or what to think or do. However, I went and hid myself also under a hencoop. Immediately the press-gang came on board with their swords drawn, and searched all about, pulled the people out by force, and put them into the boat. At last I was found out also; the man that found me held me up by the heels while they all made their sport of me, I roaring and crying out all the time most lustily; but at last the mate, who was my conductor, seeing this, came to my assistance, and did all he could to pacify me; but all to very little purpose, till I had seen the boat go off. Soon afterwards we came to the Nore, where the Roebuck lay; and, to our great joy, my master came on board to us, and brought us to the ship. I was amazed indeed to see the quantity of men and the guns. However my surprise began to diminish, as my knowledge increased; and I ceased to feel those apprehensions and alarms which had taken such strong possession of me when I first came among the Europeans, and for some time after. I began now to pass to an opposite extreme; I was so far from being afraid of anything[72] new which I saw, that, after I had been some time in this ship, I even began to long for an engagement. My griefs too, which in young minds are not perpetual, were now wearing away; and I soon enjoyed myself pretty well, and felt tolerably easy in my present situation. There were[73] a number of boys on board, which still made it more agreeable; for we were always together, and a great part of our time was spent in play. I remained in this ship a considerable time, during which we made several cruises, and visited a variety of places: among others we were twice in Holland, and brought over several persons of distinction from it, whose names I do not now remember. On the passage, one day, for the diversion of those gentlemen, all the boys were called on the quarter-deck, and were paired proportionably, and then made to fight; after which the gentleman gave the combatants from five to nine shillings each. This was the first time I ever fought with a white boy; and I never knew what it was to have a bloody nose before. This made me fight most desperately; I suppose considerably more than an hour; and at last, both of us being weary, we were parted. I had a great deal of this kind of sport afterwards, in which the captain and the ship's company used very much to encourage me. Sometime afterwards the ship went to Leith, in Scotland, from thence to the Orkneys,[74] where I was surprised in seeing scarcely any night; and from thence we sailed with a great fleet, full of soldiers, for England. All this time we had never come to an engagement, though we were frequently cruising off the coast of France; during which we chased many vessels, and took in all seventeen prizes.[75] I had been learning

Notes

[70] *Original reads*: every thing [ed.].

[71] *press* force into military service.

[72] *Original reads*: any thing [ed.].

[73] *Original reads*: was [ed.].

[74] *Orkneys* islands north of Scotland.

[75] *prizes* captured enemy warships or cargo.

many of the manoeuvres of the ship during our cruise; and I was several times made to fire the guns.

One evening, off Havre de Grace, just as it was growing dark, we were standing off shore, and met with a fine large French-built frigate. We got all things immediately ready for fighting; and I now expected I should be gratified in seeing an engagement, which I had so long wished for in vain. But the very moment the word of command was given to fire, we heard those on board the other ship cry "Haul down the jib"; and in that instant she hoisted English colours. There was instantly with us an amazing cry of – "Avast!" or "stop firing!" and I think one or two guns had been let off, but happily they did no mischief. We had hailed them several times; but they not hearing, we received no answer, which was the cause of our firing. The boat was then sent on board of her, and she proved to be the Ambuscade man of war, to my no small disappointment. We returned to Portsmouth, without having been in any action, just at the trial of Admiral Byng[76] (whom I saw several times during it); and my master, having left the ship, and gone to London for promotion, Dick and I were put on board the Savage sloop of war, and we went in her to assist in bringing off the St. George man of war, that had run ashore somewhere on the coast. After staying a few weeks on board the Savage, Dick and I were sent on shore at Deal, where we remained some short time, till my master sent for us to London, the place I had long desired exceedingly to see. We therefore both with great pleasure got into a waggon, and came to London, where we were received by a Mr. Guerin, a relation of my master. This gentleman had two sisters, very amiable ladies, who took much notice and great care of me. Though I had desired so much to see London, when I arrived in it I was unfortunately unable to gratify my curiosity; for I had at this time the chilblains[77] to such a degree that I could not stand for several months, and I was obliged to be sent to St. George's Hospital. There I grew so ill, that the doctors wanted to cut my left leg off at different times, apprehending a mortification;[78] but I always said I would rather die than suffer it; and happily (I thank God) I recovered without the operation. After being there several weeks, and just as I had recovered, the small-pox broke out on me, so that I was again confined; and I thought myself now particularly unfortunate. However, I soon recovered again: and by this time my master having been promoted to be first lieutenant of the Preston man of war of fifty guns, then new at Deptford, Dick and I were sent on board her, and soon we went to Holland to bring over the late Duke of Cumberland to England. While I was in this ship an incident happened, which though trifling, I beg leave to relate, as I could not help taking particular notice of it, and considering it then as a judgment of God. One morning a young man was looking up to the fore-top, and in a wicked tone, common on shipboard, d——d his eyes about something. Just at the moment some small particles of dirt fell into his left eye, and by the evening it was very much inflamed. The next day it grew worse; and within six or seven days he lost it. From this ship my master was appointed a lieutenant on board the Royal George. When he was going he wished me to stay on board the Preston, to learn the French horn; but the ship being ordered for Turkey, I could not think of leaving my master, to whom I was very warmly attached; and I told him, if he left me behind it would break my heart. This prevailed on him to take me with him; but he left Dick on

Notes

[76] *Portsmouth ... Admiral Byng* an English seaport; John Byng (1704–1757), an English naval officer court martialed and executed for suffering defeat at French hands in the Seven Years' War.

[77] *chilblains* inflammation of the extremities caused by cold weather.

[78] *mortification* gangrene.

board the Preston, whom I embraced at parting for the last time. The Royal George was the largest ship I had ever seen; so that when I came on board of her I was surprised at the number of people, men, women, and children, of every denomination; and the largeness of the guns, many of them also of brass, which I had never seen before. Here were also shops or stalls of every kind of goods, and people crying their different commodities about the ship as in a town. To me it appeared a little world, into which I was again cast without a friend, for I had no longer my dear companion Dick. We did not stay long here. My master was not many weeks on board before he got an appointment to be sixth lieutenant of the Namur, which was then at Spithead, fitting up for Vice-Admiral Boscawen, who was going with a large fleet on an expedition against Louisbourgh.[79] The crew of the Royal George were turned over to her, and the flag of that gallant Admiral was hoisted on board, the blue at the maintop gallant-mast head. There was a very great fleet of men of war of every description assembled together for this expedition, and I was in hopes soon to have an opportunity of being gratified with a sea-fight. All things being now in readiness, this mighty fleet (for there was also Admiral Cornish's fleet in company, destined for the East Indies) at last weighed anchor, and sailed. The two fleets continued in company for several days, and then parted; Admiral Cornish, in the Lenox, having first saluted our Admiral in the Namur, which he returned. We then steered for America; but, by contrary winds, we were driven to Teneriffe,[80] where I was struck with its noted peak. Its prodigious height, and its form, resembling a sugar loaf, filled me with wonder. We remained in sight of this island some days, and then proceeded for America, which we soon made, and got into a very commodious harbour called St. George, in Halifax,[81] where we had fish in great plenty, and all other fresh provisions. We were here joined by different men of war and transport ships with soldiers; after which, our fleet being increased to a prodigious number of ships of all kinds, we sailed for Cape Breton in Nova Scotia. We had the good and gallant General Wolfe[82] on board our ship, whose affability made him highly esteemed and beloved by all the men. He often honoured me, as well as other boys, with marks of his notice; and saved me once a flogging for fighting with a young gentleman. We arrived at Cape Breton in the summer of 1758: and here the soldiers were to be landed, in order to make an attack upon Louisbourgh. My master had some part in superintending the landing; and here I was in a small measure gratified in seeing an encounter between our men and the enemy. The French were posted on the shore to receive us, and disputed our landing for a long time: but at last they were driven from their trenches, and a complete landing was effected. Our troops pursued them as far as the town of Louisbourgh. In this action many were killed on both sides. One thing remarkable I saw this day; A lieutenant of the Princess Amelia, who, as well as my master, superintended the landing, was giving the word of command, and while his mouth was open a musket ball went through it, and passed out at his cheek. I had that day in my hand the scalp of an Indian king, who was killed in the engagement: the scalp had been taken off by an Highlander.[83] I saw this king's ornaments too, which were very curious, and made of feathers.

Our land forces laid siege to the town of Louisbourgh, while the French men of war were blocked up in the harbour by the fleet, the batteries[84] at the same time playing

Notes

[79] *Louisbourgh* a French fortress on the St. Lawrence River in Quebec.

[80] *Teneriffe* Tenerife, in the Canary Islands.

[81] Halifax, Nova Scotia.

[82] *General Wolfe* James Wolfe (1727–1759), a celebrated British army officer.

[83] *Highlander* a Scotsman.

[84] *batteries* groupings of guns.

upon them from the land. This they did with such effect, that one day I saw some of the ships set on fire by the shells from the batteries, and I believe two or three of them were quite burnt. At another time, about fifty boats belonging to the English men of war, commanded by Captain George Balfour of the Aetna fireship, and Mr. Laforey, another junior captain, attacked and boarded the only two remaining French men of war in the harbour. They also set fire to a seventy-gun ship, but they brought off a sixty-four, called the Bienfaisant. During my stay here I had often an opportunity of being near Captain Balfour, who was pleased to notice me, and liked me so much that he often asked my master to let him have me, but he would not part with me; and no consideration would have induced me to leave him. At last Louisbourgh was taken, and the English men of war came into the harbour before it, to my very great joy; for I had now more liberty of indulging myself, and I went often on shore. When the ships were in the harbour, we had the most beautiful procession on the water I ever saw. All the admirals and captains of the men of war, full dressed, and in their barges, well ornamented with pendants, came alongside of the Namur. The Vice-admiral then went on shore in his barge, followed by the other officers in order of seniority, to take possession, as I suppose, of the town and fort. Some time after this the French governor and his lady, and other persons of note, came on board our ship to dine. On this occasion our ships were dressed with colours of all kinds, from the topgallant-mast head to the deck; and this, with the firing of guns, formed a most grand and magnificent spectacle.

As soon as everything[85] here was settled, Admiral Boscawen sailed with part of the fleet for England, leaving some ships behind with Rear Admirals Sir Charles Hardy and Durell. It was now winter; and one evening, during our passage home, about dusk, when we were in the channel, or near soundings, and were beginning to look for land, we descried seven sail of large men of war, which stood off shore. Several people on board of our ship said, as the two fleets were (in forty minutes from the first sight) within hail of each other, that they were English men of war; and some of our people even began to name some of the ships. By this time both fleets began to mingle, and our admiral ordered his flag to be hoisted. At that instant, the other fleet, which were French, hoisted their ensigns, and gave us a broadside as they passed by. Nothing could create greater surprise and confusion among us than this. The wind was high, the sea rough, and we had our lower and middle deck guns housed in, so that not a single gun on board was ready to be fired at any of the French ships. However, the Royal William and the Somerset, being our sternmost ships, became a little prepared, and each gave the French ships a broadside as they passed by. I afterwards heard this was a French squadron, commanded by Mons. Conflans; and certainly had the Frenchman known our condition, and had a mind to fight us, they might have done us great mischief. But we were not long before we were prepared for an engagement. Immediately many things were tossed overboard; the ships were made ready for fighting as soon as possible; and about ten at night we had bent a new main sail, the old one being split. Being how in readiness for fighting, we wore ship, and stood after the French fleet, who were one or two ships in number more than we. However, we gave them chase, and continued pursuing them all night; and at day-light we saw six of them, all large ships of the line, and an English East-Indiaman, a prize they had taken. We chased them all day till between three and four o'clock in the evening, when we came up with, and passed within a musquet shot of one seventy-four gun ship and the Indiaman also, who now

Notes

[85] *Original reads*: every thing [ed.].

hoisted her colours, but immediately hauled them down again. On this we made a signal for the other ships to take possession of her; and, supposing the man of war would likewise strike, we cheered, but she did not; though if we had fired into her, from being so near, we must have taken her. To my utter surprise the Somerset, who was the next ship a-stern of the Namur, made way likewise; and, thinking they were sure of this French ship, they cheered in the same manner, but still continued to follow us. The French Commodore was about a gun-shot a-head of all, running from us with all speed; and about four o'clock he carried his fore-top-mast overboard. This caused another loud cheer with us; and a little after the top-mast came close by us; but, to our great surprise, instead of coming up with her, we found she went as fast as ever, if not faster. The sea grew now much smoother; and the wind lulling, the seventy-four gun ship we had passed came again by us in the very same direction, and so near, that we heard her people talk as she went by; yet not a shot was fired on either side; and about five or six o'clock, just as it grew dark, she joined her Commodore. We chased all night; but the next day they were out of sight, so that we saw no more of them; and we only had the old Indiaman (called Carnarvon I think) for our trouble. After this, we stood in for the channel, and soon made the land; and, about the close of the year 1758–9, we got safe to St. Helen's. Here the Namur ran a-ground; and also another large ship a-stern of us; but, by starting our water, and tossing many things overboard to lighten her, we got the ships off without any damage. We stayed for a short time at Spithead, and then went into Portsmouth harbour to refit; from whence the Admiral went to London; and my master and I soon followed, with a press-gang, as we wanted some hands to complete our complement.

Chapter 4

The Author is baptized – Narrowly escapes drowning – Goes on an expedition to the Mediterranean – Incidents he met with there – Is witness to an engagement between some English and French ships – A particular account of the celebrated engagement between Admiral Boscawen and Mons. Le Clue, off Cape Logas, in August 1759 – Dreadful explosion of a French ship – The Author sails for England – His master appointed to the command of a fire-ship – Meets[86] *a negro boy, from whom he experiences much benevolence – Prepares for an expedition against Belle-Isle – A remarkable story of a disaster which befell*[87] *his ship – Arrives at Belle-Isle – Operations of the landing and siege – The Author's danger and distress, with his manner of extricating himself – Surrender of Belle-Isle – Transactions afterwards on the coast of France – Remarkable instance of kidnapping – The Author returns to England – Hears a talk of peace, and expects his freedom – His ship sails for Deptford to be paid off and when he arrives there he is suddenly seized by his master, and carried forcibly on board a West India ship, and sold.*

IT was now between three and four years since I first came to England, a great part of which I had spent at sea; so that I became inured to that service, and began to consider myself as happily situated; for my master treated me always extremely well; and my attachment and gratitude to him were very great. From the various scenes I had beheld on ship-board, I soon grew a stranger to terror of every kind, and was, in that respect at least, almost an Englishman. I have often reflected with surprise that I never felt half the alarm at any of the numerous dangers I have been in, that I was filled with at the

Notes

[86] *Original reads*: meets [ed.].

[87] *Original reads*: befel [ed.].

first sight of the Europeans, and at every act of theirs, even the most trifling, when I first came among them, and for some time afterwards. That fear, however, which was the effect of my ignorance, wore away as I began to know them. I could now speak English tolerably well, and I perfectly understood everything[88] that was said. I now not only felt myself quite easy with these new countrymen, but relished their society and manners. I no longer looked upon them as spirits, but as men superior to us; and therefore I had the stronger desire to resemble them; to imbibe their spirit, and imitate their manners; I therefore embraced every occasion of improvement; and every new thing that I observed I treasured up in my memory. I had long wished to be able to read and write; and for this purpose I took every opportunity to gain instruction, but had made as yet very little progress. However, when I went to London with my master, I had soon an opportunity of improving myself, which I gladly embraced. Shortly after my arrival, he sent me to wait upon the Miss Guerins, who had treated me with much kindness when I was there before; and they sent me to school.

While I was attending these ladies, their servants told me I could not go to heaven, unless I was baptized. This made me very uneasy; for I had now some faint idea of a future state: accordingly I communicated my anxiety to the eldest Miss Guerin, with whom I was become a favourite, and pressed her to have me baptized; when, to my great joy, she told me I should. She had formerly asked my master to let me be baptized, but he had refused; however, she now insisted on it; and he, being under some obligation to her brother, complied with her request; so I was baptized at St. Margaret's church, Westminster, in February 1759, by my present name. The clergyman, at the same time, gave me a book, called a guide to the Indians, written by the Bishop of Sodor and Man.[89] On this occasion, Miss Guerin and her brother did me the honour to stand as godfather and godmother, and afterwards gave me a treat. I used to attend these ladies about the town, in which service I was extremely happy; as I had thus very many opportunities of seeing London, which I desired of all things. I was sometimes, however, with my master at his rendezvous-house, which was at the foot of Westminster bridge. Here I used to enjoy myself in playing about the bridge stairs, and often in the watermen's wherries[90] with other boys. On one of these occasions there was another boy with me in a wherry, and we went out into the current of the river; while there, two more stout boys came to us in another wherry, and, abusing us for taking the boat, desired me to get into the other wherry-boat. Accordingly I went to get out of the wherry I was in; but just as I had got one of my feet into the other boat, the boys shoved it off, so that I fell into the Thames and, not being able to swim, I should unavoidably have been drowned, but for the assistance of some watermen, who providentially came to my relief.

The Namur being again got ready for sea, my master, with his gang, was ordered on board; and, to my no small grief, I was obliged to leave my school-master, whom I liked very much, and always attended while I stayed in London, to repair on board with my master. Nor did I leave my kind patronesses, the Miss Guerins, without uneasiness and regret. They often used to teach me to read, and took great pains to instruct me in the principles of religion, and the knowledge of God. I therefore parted from those amiable ladies with reluctance; after receiving from them many friendly cautions how to conduct myself, and some valuable presents.

Notes

88 *Original reads*: every thing [ed.].

89 *guide to the Indians ... Bishop of Sodor and Man* Bishop Thomas Wilson (1697–1755) wrote *An Essay toward an Instruction for the Indians* (1740). Sodor and Man (the Hebrides and the Isle of Mann) are islands off the Scottish coast.

90 *wherries* rowboats.

When I came to Spithead, I found we were destined for the Mediterranean, with a large fleet, which was now ready to put to sea. We only waited for the arrival of the admiral, who soon came on board; and about the beginning of the spring 1759, having weighed anchor and got under way, sailed for the Mediterranean; and in eleven days from the Land's End,[91] we got to Gibraltar. While we were here I used to be often on shore, and got various fruits in great plenty, and very cheap.

I had frequently told several people, in my excursions on shore, the story of my being kidnapped with my sister, and of our being separated, as I have related before; and I had as often expressed my anxiety for her fate, and my sorrow at having never met her again. One day, when I was on shore, and mentioning these circumstances to some persons, one of them told me he knew where my sister was, and if I would accompany him, he would bring me to her. Improbable as this story was, I believed it immediately, and agreed to go with him, while my heart leaped for joy; and, indeed, he conducted me to a black young woman, who was so like my sister that, at first sight, I really thought it was she; but I was quickly undeceived; and, on talking to her, I found her to be of another nation.

While we lay here the Preston came in from the Levant.[92] As soon as she arrived, my master told me I should now see my old companion Dick, who was gone in her when she sailed for Turkey. I was much rejoiced at this information, and expected every minute to embrace him; and when the captain came on board of our ship, which he did immediately after, I ran to enquire about my friend; but, with inexpressible sorrow, I learned from the boat's crew that the dear youth was dead! and that they had brought his chest, and all his other things to my master: these he afterwards gave to me, and I regarded them as a memorial of my friend, whom I loved and grieved for as a brother.

While we were at Gibraltar I saw a soldier hanging by the heels at one of the moles.[93] I thought this a strange sight, as I had seen a man hanged in London by his neck. At another time I saw the master of a frigate towed to shore on a grating, by several of the men of war's boats, and discharged the fleet, which I understood was a mark of disgrace for cowardice. On board the same ship a sailor was also hung up at the main-yard-arm.

After lying at Gibraltar for some time, we sailed up the Mediterranean, a considerable way above the gulf of Lyons:[94] where we were one night overtaken by a terrible gale of wind, much greater than any I had ever yet experienced. The sea ran so high that, though all the guns were well housed, there was great reason to fear their getting loose, the ship rolled so much; and if they had, it must have proved our destruction. After we had cruised here for a short time, we came to Barcelona, a Spanish sea-port, remarkable for its silk manufactories. Here the ships were all to be watered; and my master, who spoke different languages, and used often to interpret for the admiral, superintended the watering of ours. For that purpose he and the officers of the other ships, who were on the same service, had tents pitched in the bay; and the Spanish soldiers were stationed along the shore, I suppose to see that no depredations were committed by our men.

I used constantly to attend my master, and I was charmed with this place. All the time of our stay it was like a fair with the natives, who brought us fruits of all kinds, and sold them to us much cheaper than I had got them in England. They used also to bring wine down to us in hog and sheep skins, which diverted me very much. The

Notes

[91] *Land's End* the westernmost outcrop of England.

[92] *the Levant* Syria or the Eastern Mediterranean.

[93] *moles* piers.

[94] *gulf of Lyons* by southern France.

Spanish officers here treated our officers with great politeness and attention; and some of them, in particular, used to come often to my master's tent to visit him; where they did sometimes divert themselves by mounting me on the horses or mules, so that I could not fall, and setting them off at full gallop; my imperfect skill in horsemanship all the while affording them no small entertainment. After the ships were watered, we returned to our old station of cruizing off Toulon, for the purpose of intercepting a fleet of French men of war that lay there. One Sunday, in our cruize, we came off a place where there were two small French frigates lying in shore; and our admiral, thinking to take or destroy them, sent two ships in after them – the Culloden and the Conqueror. They soon came up to the Frenchmen, and I saw a smart fight here, both by sea and land: for the frigates were covered by batteries, and they played upon our ships most furiously, which they as furiously returned, and for a long time a constant firing was kept up, on all sides, at an amazing rate. At last one frigate sunk; but the people escaped, though not without much difficulty: and a little after some of the people left the other frigate also, which was a mere wreck. However, our ships did not venture to bring her away, they were so much annoyed from the batteries, which raked them both in going and coming; their topmasts were shot away, and they were otherwise so much shattered, that the admiral was obliged to send in many boats to tow them back to the fleet. I afterwards sailed with a man who fought in one of the French batteries during the engagement, and he told me our ships had done considerable mischief that day on shore, and in the batteries.

After this we sailed for Gibraltar, and arrived there about August 1759. Here we remained with all our sails unbent, while the fleet was watering and doing other necessary things. While we were in this situation, one day the admiral, with most of the principal officers, and many people of all stations, being on shore, about seven o'clock in the evening we were alarmed by signals from the frigates stationed for that purpose; and in an instant there was a general cry that the French fleet was out, and just passing through the straights. The admiral immediately came on board with some other officers; and it is impossible to describe the noise, hurry, and confusion, throughout the whole fleet, in bending their sails, and slipping their cables; many people and ship's boats were left on shore in the bustle. We had two captains on board of our ship, who came away in the hurry and left their ships to follow. We shewed lights from the gunwales to the main-top-mast-head; and all our lieutenants were employed amongst the fleet to tell the ships not to wait for their captains, but to put the sails to the yards, slip their cables and follow us; and in this confusion of making ready for fighting, we set out for sea in the dark after the French fleet. Here I could have exclaimed with Ajax,

> Oh Jove! O father! if it be thy will
> That we must perish, we thy will obey,
> But let us perish by the light of day.[95]

They had got the start of us so far that we were not able to come up with them during the night; but at day-light we saw seven sail of ships of the line some miles a-head. We immediately chased them till about four o'clock in the evening, when our ships came up with them; and though we were about fifteen large ships, our gallant admiral only

Notes

[95] *"Oh Jove! O Father … light of day"* from a translation of the *Iliad* by English poet Alexander Pope (1680–1744). Ajax is a mighty warrior in Homer's poem.

fought them with his own division, which consisted of seven; so that we were just ship for ship. We passed by the whole of the enemy's fleet in order to come at their commander, Mons. La Clue, who was in the Ocean, an eighty-four gun ship: as we passed they all fired on us; and at one time three of them fired together, continuing to do so for some time. Notwithstanding which our admiral would not suffer a gun to be fired at any of them, to my astonishment; but made us lie on our bellies on the deck till we came quite close to the Ocean, who was a-head of them all; when we had orders to pour the whole three tiers into her at once.

The engagement now commenced with great fury on both sides: the Ocean immediately returned our fire, and we continued engaged with each other for some time; during which I was frequently stunned with the thundering of the great guns, whose dreadful contents hurried many of my companions into awful eternity. At last the French line was entirely broken, and we obtained the victory, which was immediately proclaimed with loud huzzas and acclamations. We took three prizes, La Modeste, of sixty-four guns, and Le Temeraire and Centaur, of seventy-four guns each. The rest of the French ships took to flight with all the sail they could crowd. Our ship being very much damaged, and quite disabled from pursuing the enemy, the admiral immediately quitted her, and went in the broken, and only boat we had left, on board the Newark, with which, and some other ships, he went after the French. The Ocean, and another large French ship, called the Redoutable, endeavouring to escape, ran ashore at Cape Logas, on the coast of Portugal; and the French admiral and some of the crew got ashore; but we, finding it impossible to get the ships off, set fire to them both. About midnight I saw the Ocean blow up, with a most dreadful explosion. I never beheld a more awful scene. About the space of a minute, the midnight seemed turned into day by the blaze, which was attended with a noise louder and more terrible than thunder, that seemed to rend every element around us.

My station during the engagement was on the middle deck, where I was quartered with another boy, to bring powder to the aftermost gun; and here I was a witness of the dreadful fate of many of my companions, who, in the twinkling of an eye, were dashed in pieces, and launched into eternity. Happily I escaped unhurt, though the shot and splinters flew thick about me during the whole fight. Towards the latter part of it my master was wounded, and I saw him carried down to the surgeon; but, though I was much alarmed for him, and wished to assist him, I dared not leave my post. At this station my gun-mate (a partner in bringing powder for the same gun) and I ran a very great risk for more than half an hour of blowing up the ship. For, when we had taken the cartridges out of the boxes, the bottoms of many of them proving rotten, the powder ran all about the deck, near the match-tub: we scarcely had water enough at the last to throw on it. We were also, from our employment, very much exposed to the enemy's shots; for we had to go through nearly the whole length of the ship to bring the powder. I expected therefore every minute to be my last; especially when I saw our men fall so thick about me; but, wishing to guard as much against the dangers as possible, at first I thought it would be safest not to go for the powder till the Frenchmen had fired their broadside; and then, while they were charging, I could go and come with my powder: but immediately afterwards I thought this caution was fruitless; and, cheering myself with the reflection that there was a time allotted for me to die as well as to be born, I instantly cast off all fear or thought whatever of death, and went through the whole of my duty with alacrity; pleasing myself with the hope, if I survived the battle, of relating it and the dangers I had escaped to the Miss Guerins, and others, when I should return to London.

Our ship suffered very much in this engagement; for, besides the number of our killed and wounded, she was almost torn to pieces, and our rigging so much shattered, that our mizen-mast, main-yard, &c. hung over the side of the ship; so that we were obliged to get many carpenters and others, from some of the ships of the fleet, to assist in setting us in some tolerable order; and, notwithstanding which, it took us some time before we were completely refitted; after which we left Admiral Broderick to command, and we, with the prizes, steered for England. On the passage, and as soon as my master was something recovered of his wounds, the Admiral appointed him captain of the Aetna fire-ship, on which he and I left the Namur, and went on board of her at sea. I liked this small ship very much. I now became the captain's steward, in which situation I was very happy, for I was extremely well treated by all on board, and I had leisure to improve myself in reading and writing. The latter I had learned a little before I left the Namur, as there was a school on board. When we arrived at Spithead, the Aetna went into Portsmouth harbour to refit, which being done, we returned to Spithead, and joined a large fleet that was thought to be intended against the Havannah. But about that time the king died; whether that prevented the expedition I know not; but it caused our ship to be stationed at Cowes, in the Isle of Wight,[96] till the beginning of the year sixty-one. Here I spent my time very pleasantly; I was much on shore all about this delightful island, and found the inhabitants very civil.

While I was here, I met with a trifling incident which surprised me agreeably. I was one day in a field belonging to a gentleman who had a black boy about my own size; this boy having observed me from his master's house, was transported at the sight of one of his own countrymen, and ran to meet me with the utmost haste. I not knowing what he was about, turned a little out of his way at first, but to no purpose; he soon came close to me, and caught hold of me in his arms as if I had been his brother, though we had never seen each other before. After we had talked together for some time, he took me to his master's house, where I was treated very kindly. This benevolent boy and I were very happy in frequently seeing each other, till about the month of March 1761, when our ship had orders to fit out again for another expedition. When we got ready, we joined a very large fleet at Spithead, commanded by Commodore Keppel, destined against Belle-Isle;[97] and having a number of transport ships in company, with troops on board, to make a descent on the place, we sailed once more in quest of fame. I longed to engage in new adventures, and to see fresh wonders.

I had a mind on which everything[98] uncommon made its full impression, and every event which I considered as marvellous. Every extraordinary escape, or signal deliverance, either of myself or others, I looked upon to be effected by the interposition of Providence. We had not been above ten days at sea before an incident of this kind happened; which, whatever credit it may obtain from the reader, made no small impression upon my mind.

We had on board a gunner, whose name was John Mondle, a man of very indifferent morals. This man's cabin was between the decks, exactly over where I lay, a-breast of the quarter-deck ladder. One night, the 5th of April, being terrified with a dream, he awoke in so great a fright that he could not rest in his bed any longer, nor even remain in his cabin; and he went upon deck about four o'clock in the morning extremely agitated. He immediately told those upon the deck of the agonies of his mind, and the dream which occasioned it; in which he said he had seen many things very awful, and had been warned by St. Peter to repent, who told him his time was short. This he said had greatly alarmed him, and he was determined to alter his life. People generally

Notes

[96] *Isle of Wight* in the English Channel.

[97] *Belle-Isle* off the French coast.

[98] *Original reads*: every thing [ed.].

mock the fears of others when they are themselves in safety; and some of his shipmates who heard him only laughed at him. However, he made a vow that he never would drink strong liquors again; and he immediately got a light, and gave away his sea-stores of liquor. After which, his agitation still continuing, he began to read the scriptures, hoping to find some relief; and soon afterwards he laid himself down again on his bed, and endeavoured to compose himself to sleep, but to no purpose; his mind still continuing in a state of agony. By this time it was exactly half after seven in the morning; I was then under the half deck at the great cabin door; and all at once I heard the people in the waist cry out most fearfully – "The Lord have mercy upon us! We are all lost! The Lord have mercy upon us!" – Mr. Mondle hearing the cries, immediately ran out of his cabin; and we were instantly struck by the Lynne, a forty-gun ship, Captain Clerk, which nearly ran us down. This ship had just put about, and was by the wind, but had not got full head-way, or we must all have perished; for the wind was brisk. However, before Mr. Mondle had got four steps from his cabin door, she struck our ship, with her cutwater, right in the middle of his bed and cabin, and ran it up to the combings of the quarter deck hatchway, and above three feet below water, and in a minute there was not a bit of wood to be seen where Mr. Mondle's cabin stood; and he was so near being killed, that some of the splinters tore his face. As Mr. Mondle must inevitably have perished from this accident, had he not been alarmed in the very extraordinary way I have related, I could not help regarding this as an awful interposition of Providence for his preservation. The two ships for some time swinged alongside of each other; for ours being a fire-ship, our grappling-irons[99] caught the Lynne every way, and the yards and rigging went at an astonishing rate. Our ship was in such a shocking condition that we all thought she would instantly go down, and everyone[100] ran for their lives, and got as well as they could on board the Lynne; but our lieutenant being the aggressor, he never quitted the ship. However, when we found she did not sink, immediately, the captain came on board again and encouraged our people to return and try to save her. Many of them came back, but some would not venture. Some of the ships in the fleet, seeing our situation, immediately sent their boats to our assistance; but it took us the whole day to save the ship with all their help. And by using every possible means, particularly frapping her together with many hawsers,[101] and putting a great quantity of tallow below water where she was damaged, she was kept together; but it was well we did not meet with any gales of wind, or we must have gone to pieces; for we were in such a crazy condition that we had ships to attend us till we arrived at Belle-Isle, the place of our destination; and then we had all things taken out of the ship, and she was properly repaired. This escape of Mr. Mondle, which he, as well as myself, always considered as a singular act of Providence, I believe had a great influence on his life and conduct ever afterwards.

Now that I am on this subject, I beg leave to relate another instance or two which strongly raised my belief of the particular interposition of Heaven, and which might not otherwise have found a place here, from their insignificance. I belonged for a few days, in the year 1758, to the Jason, of fifty-four guns, at Plymouth; and one night, when I was on board, a woman, with a child at her breast, fell from the upper deck down into the hold, near the keel. Everyone[102] thought that the mother and child must be both dashed to pieces; but, to our great surprise, neither of them was hurt. I myself

Notes

[99] *grappling irons* clawed instrument used in naval warfare for holding and boarding enemy ships.

[100] *Original reads*: every one [ed.].

[101] *frapping her together with many hawsers* binding with large ropes.

[102] *Original reads*: every one [ed.].

one day fell headlong from the upper deck of the Aetna down the after-hold, when the ballast was out; and all who saw me fall called out I was killed; but I received not the least injury. And in the same ship a man fell from the mast-head on the deck without being hurt. In these, and in many more instances, I thought I could very plainly trace the hand of God, without whose permission a sparrow cannot fall. I began to raise my fear from man to him alone, and to call daily on his holy name with fear and reverence: and I trust he heard my supplications, and graciously condescended to answer me according to his holy word, and to implant the seeds of piety in me, even one of the meanest[103] of his creatures.

When we had refitted our ship, and all things were in readiness for attacking the place, the troops on board the transports were ordered to disembark; and my master, as a junior captain, had a share in the command of the landing. This was on the 12th of April. The French were drawn up on the shore, and had made every disposition to oppose the landing of our men, only a small part of them this day being able to effect it; most of them, after fighting with great bravery, were cut off, and General Crawford, with a number of others, were taken prisoners. In this day's engagement we had also our lieutenant killed.

On the 21st of April we renewed our efforts to land the men, while all the men of war were stationed along the shore to cover it, and fired at the French batteries and breastworks,[104] from early in the morning till about four o'clock in the evening, when our soldiers effected a safe landing. They immediately attacked the French; and, after a sharp encounter, forced them from the batteries. Before the enemy retreated, they blew up several of them, lest they should fall into our hands. Our men then proceeded to besiege the citadel, and my master was ordered on shore to superintend the landing of all the materials necessary for carrying on the siege; in this service I mostly attended him. While I was there I went about to different parts of the island; and one day, particularly, my curiosity almost cost me my life. I wanted very much to see the mode of charging the mortars, and letting off the shells, and for that purpose I went to an English battery that was but a very few yards from the walls of the citadel. There indeed I had an opportunity of completely gratifying myself in seeing the whole operation, and that not without running a very great risk, both from the English shells that burst while I was there, but likewise from those of the French. One of the largest of their shells bursted within nine or ten yards of me: there was a single rock close by, about the size of a butt;[105] and I got instant shelter under it in time to avoid the fury of the shell. Where it burst the earth was torn in such a manner that two or three butts might easily have gone into the hole it made, and it threw great quantities of stones and dirt to a considerable distance. Three shot were also fired at me, and another boy who was along with me, one of them in particular seemed

> Wing'd with red lightning and impetuous rage;[106]

for, with a most dreadful sound, it hissed close by me, and struck a rock at a little distance, which it shattered to pieces. When I saw what perilous circumstances I was in, I attempted to return the nearest way I could find, and thereby I got between the English and the French centinels. An English serjeant, who commanded the outposts,

Notes

[103] *meanest* lowliest.

[104] *breastworks* temporary fortification.

[105] *butt* a large cask.

[106] *Wing'd with red lightning … rage* from John Milton's (1608–1674) epic poem, *Paradise Lost* (1.175).

seeing me, and surprised how I came there (which was by stealth along the sea-shore), reprimanded me very severely for it, and instantly took the centinel off his post into custody, for his negligence in suffering me to pass the lines. While I was in this situation I observed at a little distance a French horse belonging to some islanders, which I thought I would now mount, for the greater expedition of getting off. Accordingly, I took some cord which I had about me, and making a kind of bridle of it, I put it round the horse's head, and the tame beast very quietly suffered me to tie him thus and mount him. As soon as I was on the horse's back I began to kick and beat him, and try every means to make him go quick, but all to very little purpose: I could not drive him out of a slow pace. While I was creeping along, still within reach of the enemy's shot, I met with a servant well mounted on an English horse. I immediately stopped; and, crying, told him my case; and begged of him to help me, and this he effectually did: for, having a fine large whip, he began to lash my horse with it so severely, that he set off full speed with me towards the sea, while I was quite unable to hold or manage him. In this manner I went along till I came to a craggy precipice. I now could not stop my horse; and my mind was filled with apprehensions of my deplorable fate, should he go down the precipice, which he appeared fully disposed to do: I therefore thought I had better throw myself off him at once, which I did immediately with a great deal of dexterity, and fortunately escaped unhurt. As soon as I found myself at liberty, I made the best of my way for the ship, determined I would not be so fool-hardy again in a hurry.

We continued to besiege the citadel till June, when it surrendered. During the siege I have counted above sixty shells and carcases in the air at once. When this place was taken I went through the citadel, and in the bomb-proofs under it, which were cut in the solid rock; and I thought it a surprising place, both for strength and building: notwithstanding which our shots and shells had made amazing devastation, and ruinous heaps all around it.

After the taking of this island, our ships, with some others commanded by Commodore Stanhope, in the Swiftsure, went to Basse-road, where we blocked up a French fleet. Our ships were there from June till February following; and in that time I saw a great many scenes of war, and stratagems on both sides, to destroy each other's fleet. Sometimes we would attack the French with some ships of the line; at other times with boats; and frequently we made prizes. Once or twice the French attacked us, by throwing shells with their bomb-vessels; and one day, as a French vessel was throwing shells at our ships, she broke from her springs behind the Isle of Rhe: the tide being complicated, she came within a gun-shot of the Nassau; but the Nassau could not bring a gun to bear upon her, and thereby the Frenchman got off. We were twice attacked by their fire-floats,[107] which they chained together, and then let them float down with the tide; but each time we sent boats with grapplings, and towed them safe out of the fleet.

We had different commanders while we were at this place, Commodores Stanhope, Dennis, Lord Howe, &c. From thence, before the Spanish war began, our ship and the Wasp sloop, were sent to St. Sebastian, in Spain, by Commodore Stanhope; and Commodore Dennis afterwards sent our ship as a cartel to Bayonne in France; after which we went in February 1762, to Belle-Isle, and there stayed till the summer, then we left it, and returned to Portsmouth.

Notes

[107] *fire-floats* barges loaded with explosives with which to sink enemy ships.

After our ship was fitted out again for service, in September she went to Guernsey, where I was very glad to see my old hostess, who was now a widow, and my former little charming companion her daughter. I spent some time here very happily with them, till October, when we had orders to repair to Portsmouth. We parted from each other with a great deal of affection, and I promised to return soon, and see them again, not knowing what all-powerful fate had determined for me. Our ship having arrived at Portsmouth, we went into the harbour, and remained there till the end of November, when we heard great talk about peace; and, to our very great joy, in the beginning of December we had orders to go up to London with our ship, to be paid off. We received this news with loud huzzas, and every other demonstration of gladness; and nothing but mirth was to be seen through every part of the ship. I too was not without my share of the general joy on this occasion. I thought now of nothing but being freed, and working for myself, and thereby getting money to enable me to get a good education; for I always had a great desire to be able at least to read and write; and while I was on shipboard I had endeavoured to improve myself in both. While I was in the Aetna particularly, the captain's clerk taught me to write, and gave me a smattering of arithmetic as far as the rule of three.[108] There was also one Daniel Queen, about forty years of age, a man very well educated, who messed[109] with me on board this ship, and he likewise dressed and attended the captain. Fortunately this man soon became very much attached to me, and took very great pains to instruct me in many things. He taught me to shave and dress hair a little, and also to read in the Bible, explaining many passages to me, which I did not comprehend. I was wonderfully surprised to see the laws and rules of my country written almost exactly here; a circumstance which I believe tended to impress our manners and customs more deeply on my memory. I used to tell him of this resemblance; and many a time we had sat up the whole night together at this employment. In short he was like a father to me; and some even used to call me after his name; they also styled me the black Christian. Indeed I almost loved him with the affection of a son. Many things I have denied myself that he might have them; and when I used to play at marbles, or any other game, and won a few halfpence, or got any little money, which I did sometimes, for shaving anyone,[110] I used to buy him a little sugar or tobacco, as far as my stock of money would go. He used to say, that he and I never should part; and that when our ship was paid off, as I was as free as himself or any other man on board, he would instruct me in his business, by which I might gain a good livelihood. This gave me new life and spirits, and my heart burned within me, while I thought the time long till I obtained my freedom: for though my master had not promised it to me, yet besides the assurances I had received that he had no right to detain me, he always treated me with the greatest kindness, and reposed in me an unbounded confidence; he even paid attention to my morals; and would never suffer me to deceive him, or tell lies, of which he used to tell me the consequences; and that if I did so, God would not love me; so that from all this tenderness, I had never once supposed, in all my dreams of freedom, that he would think of detaining me any longer than I wished.

In pursuance of our orders we sailed from Portsmouth for the Thames, and arrived at Deptford the 10th of December; where we cast anchor just as it was high water. The ship was up about half an hour, when my master ordered the barge to be manned; and all in an instant, without having before given me the least reason to

Notes

[108] *rule of three* in mathematics, finding the fourth term when three are given.

[109] *messed* ate.

[110] *Original reads*: any one [ed.].

suspect anything[111] of the matter, he forced me into the barge, saying, I was going to leave him, but he would take care I should not. I was so struck with the unexpectedness of this proceeding, that for some time I could not make a reply, only I made an offer to go for my books and chest of clothes, but he swore I should not move out of his sight; and if I did he would cut my throat, at the same time taking his hanger.[112] I began, however, to collect myself: and, plucking up courage, I told him I was free, and he could not by law serve me so. But this only enraged him the more; and he continued to swear, and said he would soon let me know whether he would or not, and at that instant sprung himself into the barge from the ship, to the astonishment and sorrow of all on board. The tide, rather unluckily for me, had just turned downward, so that we quickly fell down the river along with it, till we came among some outward-bound West-Indiamen; for he was resolved to put me on board the first vessel he could get to receive me. The boat's crew, who pulled against their will, became quite faint at different times, and would have gone ashore; but he would not let them. Some of them strove then to cheer me, and told me he could not sell me, and that they would stand by me, which revived me a little, and encouraged my hopes; for as they pulled along he asked some vessels to receive me, and they would not. But, just as we had got a little below Gravesend, we came alongside of a ship which was going away the next tide for the West Indies; her name was the Charming Sally, Capt. James Doran; and my master went on board and agreed with him for me; and in a little time I was sent for into the cabin. When I came there, Captain Doran asked me if I knew him. I answered that I did not; "Then," said he, "you are now my slave." I told him my master could not sell me to him, nor to anyone[113] else. "Why," said he, "did not your master buy you?" I confessed he did. But I have served him, said I, many years, and he has taken all my wages and prize-money, for I only got one sixpence during the war; besides this I have been baptized; and by the laws of the land no man has a right to sell me: and I added, that I had heard a lawyer, and others at different times, tell my master so. They both then said that those people who told me so were not my friends: but I replied – It was very extraordinary that other people did not know the law as well as they. Upon this Captain Doran said I talked too much English; and if I did not behave myself well, and be quiet, he had a method on board to make me. I was too well convinced of his power over me to doubt what he said: and my former sufferings in the slave-ship presenting themselves to my mind, the recollection of them made me shudder. However, before I retired, I told them that as I could not get any right among men here, I hoped I should hereafter in Heaven; and I immediately left the cabin, filled with resentment and sorrow. The only coat I had with me my master took away with him, and said, "If your prize-money had been 10,000£ I had a right to it all, and would have taken it." I had about nine guineas, which during my long sea-faring life, I had scraped together from trifling perquisites[114] and little ventures; and I hid it that instant, lest my master should take that from me likewise, still hoping that by some means or other I should make my escape to the shore, and indeed some of my old shipmates told me not to despair, for they would get me back again; and that, as soon as they could get their pay, they would immediately come to Portsmouth to me, where this ship was going: but, alas! all my hopes were baffled, and the hour of my deliverance was yet far off. My master, having soon concluded his bargain with the captain, came out of the cabin, and

Notes

111 *Original reads*: any thing [ed.].

112 *hanger* short sword.

113 *Original reads*: any one [ed.].

114 *perquisites* tips.

he and his people got into the boat, and put off: I followed them with aching eyes as long as I could, and when they were out of sight I threw myself on the deck, with a heart ready to burst with sorrow and anguish.

Chapter 5

The Authors reflections on his situation – Is deceived by a promise of being delivered – His despair at sailing for the West Indies – Arrives at Montserrat, where he is sold to Mr. King – Various interesting instances of oppression, cruelty, and extortion, which the Author saw practised upon the slaves in the West-Indies during his captivity, from the year 1763 to 1766 – Address to the planters.

THUS, at the moment I expected all my toils to end, was I plunged, as I supposed, in a new slavery: in comparison of which all my service hitherto had been perfect freedom; and whose horrors, always present to my mind, now rushed on it with tenfold aggravation. I wept very bitterly for some time: and began to think that I must have done something to displease the Lord, that he thus punished me so severely. This filled me with painful reflections on my past conduct; I recollected that on the morning of our arrival at Deptford I had rashly sworn that as soon as we reached London I would spend the day in rambling and sport. My conscience smote me for this unguarded expression: I felt that the Lord was able to disappoint me in all things, and immediately considered my present situation as a judgment of Heaven on account of my presumption in swearing: I therefore, with contrition of heart, acknowledged my transgression to God, and poured out my soul before him with unfeigned repentance, and with earnest supplications I besought him not to abandon me in my distress, nor cast me from his mercy for ever. In a little time my grief, spent with its own violence, began to subside; and after the first confusion of my thoughts was over, I reflected with more calmness on my present condition: I considered that trials and disappointments are sometimes for our good, and I thought God might perhaps have permitted this in order to teach me wisdom and resignation; for he had hitherto shadowed me with the wings of his mercy, and by his invisible but powerful hand brought me the way I knew not. These reflections gave me a little comfort, and I rose at last from the deck with dejection and sorrow in my countenance, yet mixed with some faint hope that the Lord would appear for my deliverance.

Soon afterwards, as my new master was going ashore, he called me to him, and told me to behave myself well, and do the business of the ship the same as any of the rest of the boys, and that I should fare the better for it; but I made him no answer. I was then asked if I could swim, and I said, No. However I was made to go under the deck, and was well watched. The next tide the ship got under way, and soon after arrived at the Mother Bank, Portsmouth; where she waited a few days for some of the West India convoy. While I was here I tried every means I could devise among the people of the ship to get me a boat from the shore, as there was none suffered to come along side of the ship; and their own, whenever it was used, was hoisted in again immediately. A sailor on board took a guinea from me on pretence of getting me a boat; and promised me, time after time, that it was hourly to come off. When he had the watch upon deck I watched also; and looked long enough, but all in vain; I could never see either the boat or my guinea again. And what I thought was still the worst of all, the fellow gave information, as I afterwards found, all the while to the mates of my intention to go off, if I could in any way do it; but, rogue-like, he never told them he had got a guinea from me to procure my escape. However, after we had sailed, and his trick was made known to the ship's crew, I had some satisfaction in seeing him detested and despised by them all for his behaviour to me. I was still in hopes that my old shipmates would not forget their promise to come for me to Portsmouth; and they did at last, but not till the day before we sailed, some of them did come there, and sent me off some oranges, and other tokens of their regard. They also sent me word they would come off to me themselves the next day or the day after; and a lady also, who lived in Gosport, wrote to me that she would come and take me out of the ship at the same time. This lady had been once very intimate with my former master; I used to sell and take care of a great deal of property for her in different ships; and in return she always shewed great friendship for me; and used to tell my master that she would take me away to live with her: but unfortunately for me, a disagreement soon afterwards took place between them; and she was succeeded in my master's good graces by another lady, who appeared sole mistress of the Aetna, and mostly lodged on board. I was not so great a favourite with this lady as with the former; she had conceived a pique against me on some occasion when she was on board, and she did not fail to instigate my master to treat me in the manner he did.

However the next morning, the 30th of December, the wind being brisk and easterly, the Aeolus frigate, which was to escort the convoy, made a signal for sailing. All the ships then got up their anchors; and, before any of my friends had an opportunity to come off to my relief, to my inexpressible anguish, our ship had got under way. What tumultuous emotions agitated my soul when the convoy got under sail, and I, a prisoner on board, now without hope! I kept my swimming eyes upon the land, in a state of unutterable grief; not knowing what to do, and despairing how to help myself. While my mind was in this situation, the fleet sailed on, and in one day's time I lost sight of the wished-for land. In the first expressions of my grief I reproached my fate, and wished I had never been born. I was ready to curse the tide that bore us, the gale that wafted my prison, and even the ship that conducted us; and I called on death to relieve me from the horrors I felt and dreaded, that I might be in that place

Where slaves are free, and men oppress no more,
Fool that I was, inur'd so long to pain,
To trust to hope, or dream of joy again.

Now dragg'd once more beyond the western main,
To groan beneath some dastard planter's chain;
Where my poor countrymen in bondage wait
The long enfranchisement of a ling'ring fate:
Hard ling'ring fate! while, ere the dawn of day,
Rous'd by the lash, they go their cheerless way;
And as their souls with shame and anguish burn,
Salute with groans unwelcome morn's return,
And, chiding ev'ry hour the slow-pac'd sun,
Pursue their toils till all his race is run.
No eye to mark their suff'rings with a tear;
No friend to comfort, and no hope to cheer:
Then, like the dull unpity'd brutes, repair
To stalls as wretched, and as coarse a fare;
Thank heaven one day of mis'ry was o'er,
Then sink to sleep, and wish to wake no more.[115]

Notes

[115] *Where slaves are free ... and wish to wake no more.* From *The Dying Negro, A Poetical Epistle, Supposed to Be Written by a Black (Who Lately Shot Himself on Board a Vessel in the River Thames;) to His Intended Wife* (1773), a hugely popular poem by Thomas Day (1748–1789) and John Bicknell.

The turbulence of my emotions, however, naturally gave way to calmer thoughts, and I soon perceived what fate had decreed no mortal on earth could prevent. The convoy sailed on without any accident, with a pleasant gale and smooth sea, for six weeks, till February, when one morning the Aeolus ran down a brig, one of the convoy, and she instantly went down and was ingulfed in the dark recesses of the ocean. The convoy was immediately thrown into great confusion till it was day-light; and the Aeolus was illuminated with lights to prevent any farther mischief. On the 13th of February 1763, from the mast-head, we descried our destined island Montserrat;[116] and soon after I beheld those

> Regions of sorrow, doleful shades, where peace
> And rest can rarely dwell. Hope never comes
> That comes to all, but torture without end
> Still urges.[117]

At the sight of this land of bondage, a fresh horror ran through all my frame, and chilled me to the heart. My former slavery now rose in dreadful review to my mind, and displayed nothing but misery, stripes, and chains; and, in the first paroxysm of my grief, I called upon God's thunder, and his avenging power, to direct the stroke of death to me, rather than permit me to become a slave, and to be sold from lord to lord.

In this state of my mind our ship came to an anchor, and soon after discharged her cargo. I now knew what it was to work hard; I was made to help to unload and load the ship. And, to comfort me in my distress in that time, two of the sailors robbed me of all my money, and ran away from the ship. I had been so long used to an European climate that at first I felt the scorching West-India sun very painful, while the dashing surf would toss the boat and the people in it frequently above high-water mark. Sometimes our limbs were broken with this, or even attended with instant death, and I was day by day mangled and torn.

About the middle of May, when the ship was got ready to sail for England, I all the time believing that Fate's blackest clouds were gathering over my head, and expecting their bursting would mix me with the dead, captain Doran sent for me ashore one morning, and I was told by the messenger that my fate was then determined. With trembling steps and fluttering heart I came to the captain, and found with him one Mr. Robert King, a Quaker[118] and the first merchant in the place. The captain then told me my former master had sent me there to be sold; but that he had desired him to get me the best master he could, as he told him I was a very deserving boy, which Captain Doran said he found to be true, and if he were to stay in the West Indies he would be glad to keep me himself; but he could not venture to take me to London, for he was very sure that when I came there I would leave him. I at that instant burst out a crying, and begged much of him to take me to England with him, but all to no purpose. He told me he had got me the very best master in the whole island, with whom I should be as happy as if I were in England, and for that reason he chose to let him have me, though he could sell me to his own brother-in-law for a great deal more money than what he got from this gentleman. Mr. King, my new master, then made a reply, and said the reason he had bought me was on account of my good character; and, as he had not the least doubt of my good behaviour, I should be very well off with him. He

Notes

[116] *Montserrat* an island in the West Indies.

[117] *Regions of sorrow … Still Urges* Milton, *Paradise Lost* 1.65–68.

[118] *Original reads*: quaker [ed.].

also told me he did not live in the West Indies, but at Philadelphia, where he was going soon; and, as I understood something of the rules of arithmetic, when we got there he would put me to school, and fit me for a clerk. This conversation relieved my mind a little, and I left those gentlemen considerably more at ease in myself than when I came to them; and I was very thankful to Captain Doran, and even to my old master, for the character they had given me; a character which I afterwards found of infinite service to me. I went on board again, and took my leave of all my shipmates; and the next day the ship sailed. When she weighed anchor I went to the waterside and looked at her with a very wishful and aching heart, and followed her with my eyes until she was totally out of sight. I was so bowed down with grief that I could not hold up my head for many months; and if my new master had not been kind to me, I believe I should have died under it at last. And indeed I soon found that he fully deserved the good character which Captain Doran had given me of him; for he possessed a most amiable disposition and temper, and was very charitable and humane. If any of his slaves behaved amiss, he did not beat or use them ill, but parted with them. This made them afraid of disobliging him; and as he treated his slaves better than any other man on the island, so he was better and more faithfully served by them in return. By this kind treatment I did at last endeavour to compose myself; and with fortitude, though moneyless, determined to face whatever fate had decreed for me. Mr. King soon asked me what I could do; and at the same time said he did not mean to treat me as a common slave. I told him I knew something of seamanship, and could shave and dress hair pretty well; and I could refine wines, which I had learned on shipboard, where I had often done it; and that I could write, and understood arithmetic tolerably well as far as the Rule of Three. He then asked me if I knew anything[119] of gauging;[120] and, on my answering that I did not, he said one of his clerks should teach me to gauge.

Mr. King dealt in all manner of merchandize, and kept from one to six clerks. He loaded many vessels in a year; particularly to Philadelphia, where he was born, and was connected with a great mercantile[121] house in that city. He had besides many vessels and droggers[122] of different sizes, which used to go about the island and other places to collect rum, sugar, and other goods. I understood pulling and managing those boats very well; and this hard work, which was the first that he set me to, in the sugar seasons, used to be my constant employment. I have rowed the boat, and slaved at the oars, from one hour to sixteen in the twenty-four; during which I had fifteen pence sterling per day to live on, though sometimes only ten pence. However, this was considerably more than was allowed to other slaves that used to work often with me, and belonged to other gentlemen on the island: these poor souls had never more than nine-pence a day, and seldom more than six-pence, from their masters or owners, though they earned them three or four pisterines[123] a day: for it is a common practice in the West Indies, for men to purchase slaves, though they have not plantations themselves, in order to let them out to planters and merchants, at so much a-piece by the day, and they give what allowance they choose out of this produce of their daily work to their slaves for subsistence; this allowance is often very scanty. My master often gave the owners of those slaves two and a half of these pieces per day, and found the poor fellows in victuals himself, because he thought their owners did not feed them well enough according to the work they did. The slaves used to like this very well, and as

Notes

119 *Original reads*: any thing [ed.].

120 *gauging* measuring.

121 *Original reads*: merchantile [ed.].

122 *droggers* slow boats.

123 *pisterines* coins, each with the value of a shilling.

they knew my master to be a man of feeling, they were always glad to work for him in preference to any other gentleman; some of whom, after they had been paid for these poor people's labours, would not give them their allowance out of it. Many times have I seen these unfortunate wretches beaten for asking for their pay; and often severely flogged by their owners if they did not bring them their daily or weekly money exactly to the time; though the poor creatures were obliged to wait on the gentlemen they had worked for, sometimes more than half the day, before they could get their pay; and this generally on Sundays, when they wanted the time for themselves. In particular, I knew a countryman of mine, who once did not bring the weekly money directly that it was earned; and though he brought it the same day to his master, yet he was staked to the ground for his pretended negligence, and was just going to receive a hundred lashes, but for a gentleman who begged him off fifty. This poor man was very industrious, and by his frugality had saved so much money, by working on shipboard, that he had got a white man to buy him a boat, unknown to his master. Some time after he had this little estate, the governor wanted a boat to bring his sugar from different parts of the island; and, knowing this to be a negro-man's boat, he seized upon it for himself, and would not pay the owner a farthing. The man on this went to his master, and complained to him of this act of the governor; but the only satisfaction he received was to be damned very heartily by his master, who asked him how dared any of his negroes to have a boat. If the justly-merited ruin of the governor's fortune could be any gratification to the poor man he had thus robbed, he was not without consolation. Extortion and rapine are poor providers; and some time after this, the governor died in the King's Bench,[124] in England, as I was told, in great poverty. The last war favoured this poor negro-man, and he found some means to escape from his Christian master; he came to England, where I saw him afterwards several times. Such treatment as this often drives these miserable wretches to despair, and they run away from their masters at the hazard of their lives. Many of them in this place, unable to get their pay when they have earned it, and fearing to be flogged as usual, if they return home without it, run away where they can for shelter, and a reward is often offered to bring them in dead or alive. My master used sometimes in these cases to agree with their owners, and to settle with them himself; and thereby he saved many of them a flogging.

Once, for a few days, I was let out to fit a vessel, and I had no victuals allowed me by either party; at last I told my master of this treatment, and he took me away from him. In many of the estates, on the different islands where I used to be sent for rum or sugar, they would not deliver it to me, or to any other negro; he was therefore obliged to send a white man along with me to those places; and then he used to pay him from six to ten pisterines a day. From being thus employed, during the time I served Mr. King, in going about the different estates on the island, I had all the opportunity I could wish for, to see the dreadful usage of the poor men; usage that reconciled me to my situation, and made me bless God for the hands into which I had fallen.

I had the good fortune to please my master in every department in which he employed me; and there was scarcely any part of his business, or household affairs, in which I was not occasionally engaged. I often supplied the place of a clerk, in receiving and delivering cargoes to the ships, in tending stores, and delivering goods; and, besides this, I used to shave and dress my master when convenient, and take care of his horse; and when it was necessary, which was very often, I worked likewise on board of different vessels of his. By these means I became very useful to my master, and saved him,

Notes

[124] *the King's Bench* a debtors prison in London.

as he used to acknowledge, above a hundred pounds a year. Nor did he scruple to say I was of more advantage to him than any of his clerks; though their usual wages in the West Indies are from sixty to a hundred pounds current a year.

I have sometimes heard it asserted, that a negro cannot earn his master the first cost; but nothing can be further from the truth. I suppose nine tenths of the mechanics throughout the West Indies are negro slaves; and I well know the coopers[125] among them earn two dollars a day; the carpenters the same, and oftentimes more; also the masons, smiths, and fishermen, &c. and I have known many slaves whose masters would not take a thousand pounds current for them. But surely this assertion refutes itself; for, if it be true, why do the planters and merchants pay such a price for slaves? And, above all, why do those, who make this assertion, exclaim the most loudly against the abolition of the slave trade? So much are we blinded, and to such inconsistent arguments are they driven by mistaken interest! I grant, indeed, that slaves are sometimes, by half-feeding, half-clothing,[126] overworking, and stripes, reduced so low, that they are turned out as unfit for service, and left to perish in the woods, or expire on a dunghill.

My master was several times offered by different gentlemen one hundred guineas for me; but he always told them he would not sell me, to my great joy: and I used to double my diligence and care for fear of getting into the hands of those men who did not allow a valuable slave the common support of life. Many of them used to find fault with my master for feeding his slaves so well as he did; although I often went hungry, and an Englishman might think my fare very indifferent; but he used to tell them he always would do it, because the slaves thereby looked better and did more work.

While I was thus employed by my master, I was often a witness to cruelties of every kind, which were exercised on my unhappy fellow slaves. I used frequently to have different cargoes of new negroes in my care for sale; and it was almost a constant practice with our clerks, and other whites, to commit violent depredations on the chastity of the female slaves; and these I was, though with reluctance, obliged to submit to at all times, being unable to help them. When we have had some of these slaves on board my master's vessels to carry them to other islands, or to America, I have known our mates to commit these acts most shamefully, to the disgrace, not of Christians only, but of men. I have even known them gratify their brutal passion with females not ten years old; and these abominations some of them practised to such scandalous excess, that one of our captains discharged the mate and others on that account. And yet in Montserrat I have seen a negro-man staked to the ground, and cut most shockingly, and then his ears cut off bit by bit, because he had been connected with a white woman who was a common prostitute: as if it were no crime in the whites to rob an innocent African girl of her virtue; but most heinous in a black man only to gratify a passion of nature, where the temptation was offered by one of a different colour, though the most abandoned woman of her species.

One Mr. Drummond told me that he had sold 41,000 negroes, and that he once cut off a negro-man's leg for running away. I asked him, if the man had died in the operation? How he, as a Christian, could answer for the horrid act before God? And he told me, answering was a thing of another world; but what he thought and did were policy. I told him that the Christian doctrine taught us to do unto others as we would that others should do unto us. He then said that his scheme had the desired effect – it cured that man and some others of running away.

Notes

[125] *coopers* barrel makers.

[126] *Original reads*: half-cloathing [ed.].

Another negro man was half hanged, and then burnt, for attempting to poison a cruel overseer. Thus by repeated cruelties are the wretched first urged to despair, and then murdered, because they still retain so much of human nature about them as to wish to put an end to their misery, and retaliate on their tyrants! These overseers are indeed for the most part persons of the worst character of any denomination of men in the West Indies. Unfortunately, many humane gentlemen, by not residing on their estates, are obliged to leave the management of them in the hands of these human butchers, who cut and mangle the slaves in a shocking manner on the most trifling occasions, and altogether treat them in every respect like brutes. They pay no regard to the situation of pregnant women, nor the least attention to the lodging of the field-negroes. Their huts, which ought to be well covered, and the place dry where they take their little repose, are often open sheds, built in damp places; so that, when the poor creatures return tired from the toils of the field, they contract many disorders, from being exposed to the damp air in this uncomfortable state, while they are heated, and their pores are open. This neglect certainly conspires with many others to cause a decrease in the births as well as in the lives of the grown negroes. I can quote many instances of gentlemen who reside on their estates in the West Indies, and then the scene is quite changed; the negroes are treated with lenity[127] and proper care, by which their lives are prolonged, and their masters are profited. To the honour of humanity, I knew several gentlemen who managed their estates in this manner; and they found that benevolence was their true interest. And, among many I could mention in several of the islands, I knew one in Montserrat whose slaves looked remarkably well, and never needed any fresh supplies of negroes; and there are many other estates, especially in Barbadoes, which, from such judicious treatment, need no fresh stock of negroes at any time. I have the honour of knowing a most worthy and humane gentleman, who is a native of Barbadoes, and has estates there. This gentleman has written a treatise on the usage of his own slaves. He allows them two hours for refreshment at midday;[128] and many other indulgencies and comforts, particularly in their lying;[129] and, besides this, he raises more provisions on his estate than they can destroy; so that by these attentions he saves the lives of his negroes, and keeps them healthy, and as happy as the condition of slavery can admit. I myself, as shall appear in the sequel, managed an estate, where, by those attentions, the negroes were uncommonly cheerful and healthy, and did more work by half than by the common mode of treatment they usually do. "For want, therefore, of such care and attention to the poor negroes, and otherwise oppressed as they are, it is no wonder that the decrease should require 20,000 new negroes annually to fill up the vacant places of the dead.

"Even in Barbadoes, notwithstanding those humane exceptions which I have mentioned, and others I am acquainted with, which justly make it quoted as a place where slaves meet with the best treatment, and need fewest recruits of any in the West Indies, yet this island requires 1,000 negroes annually to keep up the original stock, which is only 80,000. So that the whole term of a negro's life may be said to be there but sixteen years! and yet the climate here is in every respect the same as that from which they are taken, except in being more wholesome." Do the British colonies decrease in this manner? And yet what a prodigious difference is there between an English and West India climate.

Notes

[127] *lenity* leniency.

[128] *Original reads*: mid day [ed.].

[129] *lying* post-partum recovery.

While I was in Montserrat, I knew a negro man, named Emanuel Sankey, who endeavoured to escape from his miserable bondage, by concealing himself on board of a London ship: but fate did not favour the poor oppressed man; for being discovered when the vessel was under sail, he was delivered up again to his master. This *Christian master* immediately pinned the wretch down to the ground at each wrist and ankle, and then took some sticks of sealing-wax, and lighted them, and dropped it all over his back. There was another master who was noted for cruelty, and I believe he had not a slave but what had been cut, and had pieces fairly taken out of the flesh: and after they had been punished thus, he used to make them get into a long wooden box or case he had for that purpose, in which he shut them up during pleasure.[130] It was just about the height and breadth of a man; and the poor wretches had no room when in the case to move.

It was very common in several of the islands, particularly in St. Kitt's, for the slaves to be branded with the initial letters of their master's name, and a load of heavy iron hooks hung about their necks. Indeed, on the most trifling occasions they were loaded with chains, and often other instruments of torture were added. The iron muzzle, thumb-screws, &c. are so well known, as not to need a description, and were sometimes applied for the slightest faults. I have seen a negro beaten till some of his bones were broken, for only letting a pot boil over. It is not uncommon, after a flogging, to make slaves go on their knees, and thank their owners, and pray, or rather say, God bless them. I have often asked many of the men slaves (who used to go several miles to their wives, and late in the night, after having been wearied with a hard day's labour) why they went so far for wives, and why they did not take them of their own master's negro women, and particularly those who lived together as household slaves? Their answers have ever been – "Because when the master or mistress choose to punish the women, they make the husbands flog their own wives, and that they could not bear to do." Is it surprising that usage like this should drive the poor creatures to despair, and make them seek a refuge in death from those evils which render their lives intolerable – while,

> With shudd'ring horror pale, and eyes aghast,
> They view their lamentable lot, and find
> No rest![131]

This they frequently do. A negro man on board a vessel of my master's, while I belonged to her, having been put in irons for some trifling misdemeanor, and kept in that state for some days, being weary of life, took an opportunity of jumping overboard into the sea; however, he was picked up without being drowned. Another, whose life was also a burden to him, resolved to starve himself to death, and refused to eat any victuals: this procured him a severe flogging; and he also, on the first occasion which offered, jumped overboard at Charles Town, but was saved.

Nor is there any greater regard shewn to the little property than there is to the persons and lives of the negroes. I have already related an instance or two of particular oppression out of many which I have witnessed; but the following is frequent in all the islands. The wretched field slaves, after toiling all the day for an unfeeling owner, who gives them but little victuals, steal sometimes a few moments from rest or refreshment to gather some small portion of grass, according as their time will admit. This they

Notes

[130] *during pleasure* for as long as he wished.

[131] *With shudd'ring horror pale … no rest!* Milton, *Paradise Lost* 2.616–618.

commonly tie up in a parcel; either a bit's worth (sixpence) or half a bit's worth; and bring it to town, or to the market, to sell. Nothing is more common than for the white people on this occasion to take the grass from them without paying for it; and not only so, but too often also to my knowledge, our clerks, and many others, at the same time, have committed acts of violence on the poor, wretched, and helpless females, whom I have seen for hours stand crying to no purpose, and get no redress or pay of any kind. Is not this one common and crying sin, enough to bring down God's judgment on the islands? He tells us, the oppressor and the oppressed are both in his hands; and if these are not the poor, the broken-hearted, the blind, the captive, the bruised, which our Saviour speaks of,[132] who are they? One of these depredators once, in St. Eustatia,[133] came on board of our vessel, and bought some fowls and pigs of me; and a whole day after his departure with the things, he returned again and wanted his money back: I refused to give it, and, not seeing my captain on board, he began the common pranks with me; and swore he would even break open my chest and take my money. I therefore expected, as my captain was absent, that he would be as good as his word; and he was just proceeding to strike me, when fortunately a British seaman on board, whose heart had not been debauched by a West India climate, interposed and prevented him. But had the cruel man struck me, I certainly should have defended myself at the hazard of my life; for what is life to a man thus oppressed? He went away, however, swearing; and threatened that whenever he caught me on shore he would shoot me, and pay for me afterwards.

The small account in which the life of a negro is held in the West Indies is so universally known, that it might seem impertinent to quote the following extract, if some people had not been hardy enough of late to assert that negroes are on the same footing in that respect as Europeans. By the 329th Act, page 125, of the Assembly of Barbadoes, it is enacted, "That if any negro, or other slave, under punishment by his master, or his order, for running away, or any other crime or misdemeanor towards his said master, unfortunately shall suffer in life or member, no person whatsoever shall be liable to a fine; but if any man shall out of *wantonness, or only of bloody-mindedness, or cruel intention, wilfully kill a negro, or other slave, of his own, he shall pay into the public treasury fifteen pounds sterling*." And it is the same in most, if not all, of the West India islands. Is not this one of the many acts of the islands which call loudly for redress? And do not the assembly which enacted it, deserve the appellation of savages and brutes rather than of Christians and men? It is an act at once unmerciful, unjust, and unwise; which for cruelty would disgrace an assembly of those who are called barbarians; and for its injustice and *insanity* would shock the morality and common sense of a Samaide or a Hottentot.[134]

Shocking as this and many other acts of the bloody West India code at first view appear, how is the iniquity of it heightened when we consider to whom it may be extended. Mr. James Tobin,[135] a zealous labourer in the vineyard of slavery, gives an account of a French planter, of his acquaintance, in the island of Martinico,[136] who shewed him many Mulattoes working in the fields like beasts of burden; and he told

Notes

[132] *which our Saviour speaks of* Luke 4:8.

[133] *St. Eustatia* an island in the West Indies.

[134] *Samaide or a Hotentot* natives of Mongolia and South Africa, respectively.

[135] *James Tobin* West Indies planter who wrote *Cursory Remarks upon the Reverend Mr. Ramsay's Essay on the Treatment and Conversion of African Slaves in the Sugar Colonies* (1785), attacking the abolitionist James Ramsay (1733–1789).

[136] *Martinico* Martinique.

Mr. Tobin, these were all the produce of his own loins! And I myself have known similar instances. Pray, reader, are these sons and daughters of the French planter less his children by being begotten on black women! And what must be the virtue of those legislators, and the feelings of those fathers, who estimate the lives of their sons, however begotten, at no more than fifteen pounds, though they should be murdered, as the act says, *out of wantonness and bloody-mindedness*? But is not the slave trade entirely at war with the heart of man? And surely that which is begun, by breaking down the barriers of virtue, involves in its continuance destruction to every principle, and buries all sentiments in ruin!

I have often seen slaves, particularly those who were meagre, in different islands, put into scales and weighed, and then sold from three-pence to six-pence, or nine-pence a pound. My master, however, whose humanity was shocked at this mode, used to sell such by the lump. And at or after a sale, even those negroes born in the islands, it is not uncommon to see taken from their wives, wives taken from their husbands, and children from their parents, and sent off to other islands, and wherever else their merciless lords choose; and probably never more during life see each other! Oftentimes my heart has bled at these partings; when the friends of the departed have been at the water-side, and with sighs and tears have kept their eyes fixed on the vessel till it went out of sight.

A poor Creole negro I knew well, who, after having often been thus transported from island to island, at last resided in Montserrat. This man used to tell me many melancholy tales of himself. Generally, after he had done working for his master, he used to employ his few leisure moments to go fishing. When he had caught any fish, his master would frequently take them from him without paying him; and at other times some other white people would serve him in the same manner. One day he said to me, very movingly, "Sometimes when a white man take away my fish, I go to my master, and he get me my right; and when my master, by strength, take away my fishes, what me must do? I can't go to any body to be righted"; then, said the poor man, looking up above, "I must look up to God Mighty in the top for right." This artless tale moved me much, and I could not help feeling the just cause Moses had in redressing his brother against the Egyptian.[137] I exhorted the man to look up still to the God on the top, since there was no redress below. Though I little thought then that I myself should more than once experience such imposition, and need the same exhortation hereafter, in my own transactions in the islands; and that even this poor man and I should sometime[138] after suffer together in the same manner, as shall be related hereafter.

Nor was such usage as this confined to particular places or individuals: for, in all the different islands in which I have been (and I have visited no less than fifteen) the treatment of the slaves was nearly the same; so nearly indeed, that the history of an island, or even a plantation, with a few such exceptions as I have mentioned, might serve for a history of the whole. Such a tendency has the slave-trade to debauch men's minds, and harden them to every feeling of humanity! For I will not suppose that the dealers in slaves are born worse than other men – No! it is the fatality of this mistaken avarice, that it corrupts the milk of human kindness, and turns it into gall.[139] And, had the pursuits of those men been different, they might have been as generous, as tender-hearted, and just, as they are unfeeling, rapacious, and cruel. Surely this traffic cannot be good, which

Notes

[137] *the just cause Moses had in redressing his brother against the Egyptian* In Exodus 2:11–12, Moses kills an Egyptian that he sees beating a Hebrew slave.

[138] *Original reads*: some time [ed.].

[139] *the milk of human kindness, and turns it into gall* Shakespeare, *Macbeth* 1.5.18–49.

spreads like a pestilence, and taints what it touches! Which violates that first natural right of mankind, equality and independency, and gives one man a dominion over his fellows which God could never intend! For it raises the owner to a state as far above man as it depresses the slave below it; and, with all the presumption of human pride, sets a distinction between them, immeasurable in extent, and endless in duration! Yet how mistaken is the avarice even of the planters. Are slaves more useful by being thus humbled to the condition of brutes, than they would be if suffered to enjoy the privileges of men? The freedom which diffuses health and prosperity throughout Britain answers you – No. When you make men slaves, you deprive them of half their virtue, you set them, in your own conduct, an example of fraud, rapine, and cruelty, and compel them to live with you in a state of war; and yet you complain that they are not honest or faithful! You stupify them with stripes, and think it necessary to keep them in a state of ignorance; and yet you assert that they are incapable of learning; that their minds are such a barren soil or moor, that culture would be lost on them; and that they came from a climate, where nature (though prodigal of her bounties in a degree unknown to yourselves) has left man alone scant and unfinished, and incapable of enjoying the treasures she has poured out for him! An assertion at once impious and absurd. Why do you use those instruments of torture? Are they fit to be applied by one rational being to another? And are ye not struck with shame and mortification, to see the partakers of your nature reduced so low? But, above all, are there no dangers attending this mode of treatment? Are you not hourly in dread of an insurrection? Nor would it be surprising; for when

… No peace is given
To us enslav'd, but custody severe;
And stripes and arbitrary punishment
Inflicted – What peace can we return?
But to our power, hostility and hate;
Untam'd reluctance, and revenge, tho' slow,
Yet ever plotting how the conqueror least
May reap his conquest, and may least rejoice
In doing what we most in suff'ring feel.[140]

But, by changing your conduct, and treating your slaves as men, every cause of fear would be banished. They would be faithful, honest, intelligent and vigorous; and peace, prosperity, and happiness would attend you.

Chapter 10

The Author leaves Dr. Irving, and engages on board a Turkey ship – Account of a black man's being kidnapped on board, and sent to the West Indies, and the Author's fruitless endeavours to procure his freedom – Some account of the manner of the Author's conversion to the Faith of Jesus Christ.

OUR voyage to the North Pole being ended, I returned to London with Dr. Irving, with whom I continued for some time, during which I began seriously to reflect on the dangers I had escaped, particularly those of my last voyage, which made a lasting

Notes

[140] *No peace is given … we most in suffering feel* Milton, *Paradise Lost* 2.232–240.

impression on my mind, and, by the grace of God, proved afterwards a mercy to me: it caused me to reflect deeply on my eternal state, and to seek the Lord with full purpose of heart ere it be too late. I rejoiced greatly; and heartily thanked the Lord for directing me to London, where I was determined to work out my own salvation, and, in so doing, procure a title to heaven; being the result of a mind blinded by ignorance and sin.

In process of time I left my master, Doctor Irving, the purifier of waters. I lodged in Coventry-court, Haymarket, where I was continually oppressed and much concerned about the salvation of my soul, and was determined (in my own strength) to be a first-rate Christian. I used every means for this purpose; and, not being able to find any person amongst those with whom I was then acquainted that acquiesced with me in point of religion, or, in scripture language, that would shew me any good, I was much dejected, and knew not where to seek relief; however, I first frequented the neighbouring churches, St. James's and others, two or three times a day, for many weeks: still I came away dissatisfied: something was wanting that I could not obtain, and I really found more heart-felt relief in reading my bible at home than in attending the church; and, being resolved to be saved, I pursued other methods. First I went among the people called Quakers, whose meeting at times was held in silence, and I remained as much in the dark as ever. I then searched into the Roman Catholic principles, but was not in the least edified. I, at length, had recourse to the Jews, which availed me nothing, as the fear of eternity daily harassed my mind and I knew not where to seek shelter from the wrath to come. However, this was my conclusion, at all events, to read the Four Evangelists,[141] and whatever sect or party I found adhering thereto, such I would join. Thus I went on heavily without any guide to direct me the way that leadeth to eternal life. I asked different people questions about the manner of going to heaven, and was told different ways. Here I was much staggered, and could not find any at that time more righteous than myself, or indeed so much inclined to devotion. I thought we should not all be saved (this is agreeable to the holy scriptures), nor would all be damned. I found none among the circle of my acquaintance that kept holy the Ten Commandments. So righteous was I in my own eyes, that I was convinced I excelled many of them in that point, by keeping eight out of ten; and finding those, who in general termed themselves Christians, not so honest or so good in their morals as the Turks. I really thought the Turks were in a safer way of salvation than my neighbours; so that between hopes and fears I went on, and the chief comforts I enjoyed were in the musical French-horn, which I then practised, and also dressing of hair. Such was my situation some months, experiencing the dishonesty of many people here. I determined at last to set out for Turkey, and there to end my days. It was now early in the spring 1774. I sought for a master, and found a Captain John Hughes, commander of a ship called Anglicania, fitting out in the river Thames, and bound to Smyrna in Turkey. I shipped myself with him as a steward; at the same time I recommended to him a very clever black man, John Annis, as a cook. This man was on board the ship near two months doing his duty; he had formerly lived many years with Mr. William Kirkpatrick, a gentleman of the island of St. Kitts,[142] from whom he parted by consent, though he afterwards tried many schemes to inveigle the poor man. He had applied to many captains, who traded to St. Kitt's, to trepan him; and when all their attempts and schemes of kidnapping proved abortive, Mr. Kirkpatrick came to our ship at Union-stairs,

Notes

[141] *the Four Evangelists* Matthew, Mark, Luke, and John, the writers of the four gospels in the New Testament.

[142] *St. Kitt's* a West Indies island.

on Easter Monday, April the 4th, with two wherry-boats and six men, having learned that the man was on board; and tied, and forcibly took him away from the ship, in the presence of the crew and the chief mate, who had detained him after he had information to come away. I believe this was a combined piece of business; but, be that as it may, it certainly reflected great disgrace on the mate, and captain also, who, although they had desired the oppressed man to stay on board, yet notwithstanding this vile act on the man who had served him, he did not in the least assist to recover him, or pay me a farthing of his wages, which was about five pounds. I proved the only friend he had, who attempted to regain him his liberty, if possible, having known the want of liberty myself. I sent, as soon as I could, to Gravesend, and got knowledge of the ship in which he was; but unluckily she had sailed the first tide after he was put on board. My intention was then immediately to apprehend Mr. Kirkpatrick, who was about setting off for Scotland; and having obtained a *habeas corpus*[143] for him, and got a tipstaff[144] to go with me to St. Paul's Church yard, where he lived; he, suspecting something of this kind, set a watch to look out. My being known to them obliged me to use the following deception: I whitened my face, that they might not know me, and this had the desired effect. He did not go out of his house that night, and next morning I contrived a well-plotted stratagem, notwithstanding he had a gentleman in his house to personate him. My direction to the tipstaff had the desired effect; he got admittance into the house, and conducted him to a judge, according to the writ. When he came there, his plea was, that he had not the body in custody, on which he was admitted to bail. I proceeded immediately to that well-known philanthropist, Granville Sharp, Esq.[145] who received me with the utmost kindness, and gave me every instruction that was needful on the occasion. I left him in full hopes that I should gain the unhappy man his liberty, with the warmest sense of gratitude towards Mr. Sharp for his kindness. But, alas! my attorney proved unfaithful; he took my money, lost me many months employ, and did not the least good in the cause; and when the poor man arrived at St. Kitts, he was, according to custom, staked to the ground with four pins through a cord, two on his wrists, and two on his ankles,[146] was cut and flogged most unmercifully, and afterwards loaded cruelly with irons about his neck. I had two very moving letters from him while he was in this situation; and I made attempts to go after him at a great hazard, but was sadly disappointed: I also was told of it by some very respectable families, now in London, who saw him in St. Kitt's, in the same state, in which he remained till kind death released him out of the hands of his tyrants. During this disagreeable business, I was under strong convictions of sin, and thought that my state was worse than any man's; my mind was unaccountably disturbed; I often wished for death, though, at the same time, convinced I was altogether unprepared for that awful summons: suffering much by villains in the late cause, and being much concerned about the state of my soul, these things (but particularly the latter) brought me very low; so that I became a burden to myself, and viewed all things around me as emptiness and vanity, which could give no satisfaction to a troubled conscience. I was again determined to go to Turkey, and resolved, at that time, never more to return to England. I engaged as steward on board a Turkeyman (the Wester Hall, Capt. Lina), but was prevented by means of my late captain, Mr. Hughes, and others. All this appeared to be against me, and the only comfort I then experienced was in reading the Holy Scriptures, where I saw that

Notes

143 *Habeas corpus* a legal writ requiring a person under imprisonment to be brought before a judge (to determine the legality of his captivity).

144 *tipstaff* a constable.

145 Granville Sharp (1735–1813), English abolitionist.

146 *Original reads*: ancles [ed.].

"there is no new thing under the sun," Ecclesiastes i. 9.[147] and what was appointed for me I must submit to. Thus I continued to travel in much heaviness, and frequently murmured against the Almighty, particularly in his providential dealings; and, awful to think! I began to blaspheme, and wished often to be anything[148] but a human being. In these severe conflicts the Lord answered me by awful "visions of the night, when deep sleep falleth upon men, in slumberings upon the bed," Job xxxiii. 15. He was pleased, in much mercy, to give me to see, and in some measure understand, the great and awful scene of the Judgment-day, that "no unclean person, no unholy thing, can enter into the kingdom of God," Ephesians v. 5.[149] I would then, if it had been possible, have changed my nature with the meanest worm on the earth, and was ready to say to the mountains and rocks, "fall on me," Revelation vi. 16.[150] But[151] all in vain. I then, in the greatest agony, requested the divine Creator, that he would grant me a small space of time to repent of my follies and vile iniquities, which I felt were grievous. The Lord, in his manifold mercies, was pleased to grant my request, and being yet in a state of time, the sense of God's mercies was so great on my mind when I awoke, that my strength entirely failed me for many minutes, and I was exceedingly weak. This was the first spiritual mercy I ever was sensible of, and being on praying ground, as soon as I recovered a little strength, and got out of bed and dressed myself I invoked heaven from my inmost soul, and fervently begged that God would never again permit me to blaspheme his most holy name. The Lord, who is long-suffering, and full of compassion to such poor rebels as we are, condescended to hear and answer. I felt that I was altogether unholy, and saw clearly what a bad use I had made of the faculties I was endowed with: they were given me to glorify God with; I thought, therefore, I had better want them here, and enter into life eternal, than abuse them and be cast into hell fire. I prayed to be directed, if there were any holier persons than those with whom I was acquainted, that the Lord would point them out to me. I appealed to the searcher of hearts, whether I did not wish to love him more, and serve him better. Notwithstanding all this, the reader may easily discern, if a believer, that I was still in nature's darkness. At length I hated the house in which I lodged, because God's most holy name was blasphemed in it; then I saw the word of God verified, viz. "Before they call, I will answer; and while they are yet speaking, I will hear."[152]

I had a great desire to read the Bible the whole day at home; but not having a convenient place for retirement, I left the house in the day, rather than stay amongst the wicked ones; and that day, as I was walking, it pleased God to direct me to a house where there was an old sea-faring man, who experienced much of the love of God shed abroad in his heart. He began to discourse with me; and, as I desired to love the Lord, his conversation rejoiced me greatly; and indeed I had never heard before the love of Christ to believers set forth in such a manner, and in so clear a point of view. Here I had more questions to put to the man than his time would permit him to answer: and in that memorable hour there came in a Dissenting Minister;[153] he joined our discourse, and asked me some few questions; among others, where I heard the gospel preached? I knew not what he meant by hearing the gospel; I told him I had read the gospel: and he asked me where I went to church, or whether I went at all, or not? To which I replied, "I attended St. James's, St. Martins, and St. Ann's, Soho." – "So," said he,

Notes

[147] *Original reads*: Eccles.[iastes] i. 9. [ed.].

[148] *Original reads*: any thing [ed.].

[149] *Original reads*: Ephe[sians]. v. 5. [ed.].

[150] *Original reads*: Rev[elation]. vi. 16. [ed.].

[151] *Original reads*: but [ed.].

[152] *"Before they call ... I will hear"* Isaiah 65:24.

[153] *Dissenting Minister* Methodist.

"you are a churchman?" I answered, I was. He then invited me to a love feast[154] at his chapel that evening. I accepted the offer, and thanked him; and soon after he went away. I had some further discourse with the old Christian, added to some profitable reading, which made me exceedingly happy. When I left him he reminded me of coming to the feast; I assured him I would be there. Thus we parted, and I weighed over the heavenly conversation that had passed between these two men, which cheered my then heavy and drooping spirit more than anything[155] I had met with for many months. However, I thought the time long in going to my supposed banquet. I also wished much for the company of these friendly men; their company pleased me much; and I thought the gentleman very kind in asking me, a stranger, to a feast; but how singular did it appear to me, to have it in a chapel! When the wished for hour came I went, and happily the old man was there, who kindly seated me, as he belonged to the place. I was much astonished to see the place filled with people, and no signs of eating and drinking. There were many ministers in the company. At last they began by giving out hymns, and between the singing, the ministers engaged in prayer: in short, I knew not what to make of this sight, having never seen anything[156] of the kind in my life before now. Some of the guests began to speak their experience, agreeable to what I read in the Scriptures: much was said by every speaker of the providence of God, and his unspeakable mercies to each of them. This I knew in a great measure, and could most heartily join them. But when they spoke of a future state, they seemed to be altogether certain of their calling and election of God; and that no one could ever separate them from the love of Christ, or pluck them out of his hands. This filled me with utter consternation, intermingled with admiration. I was so amazed as not to know what to think of the company; my heart was attracted, and my affections were enlarged: I wished to be as happy as them, and was persuaded in my mind that they were different from the world "that lieth in wickedness," 1 John v. 19. Their language and singing, &c. did well harmônize; I was entirely overcome, and wished to live and die thus. Lastly, some persons produced some neat baskets full of buns, which they distributed about; and each person communicated with his neighbour, and sipped water out of different mugs, which they handed about to all who were present. This kind of Christian fellowship I had never seen, nor ever thought of seeing on earth; it fully reminded me of what I had read in the Holy Scriptures of the primitive Christians, who loved each other and broke bread, in partaking of it, even from house to house. This entertainment (which lasted about four hours) ended in singing and prayer. It was the first soul-feast I ever was present at. These last twenty-four hours produced me things, spiritual and temporal, sleeping and waking, judgment and mercy, that I could not but admire the goodness of God, in directing the blind, blasphemous sinner in the path that he knew not of, even among the just; and instead of judgment he has shewed mercy, and will hear and answer the prayers and supplications of every returning prodigal;

O! to grace how great a debtor
Daily I'm constrain'd to be.[157]

After this I was resolved to win heaven, if possible; and if I perished, I thought it should be at the feet of Jesus, in praying to him for salvation. After having been an eye-witness

Notes

[154] *love feast* Evangelical service commemorating Christ's Last Supper.

[155] *Original reads*: any thing [ed.].

[156] *Original reads*: any thing [ed.].

[157] *O! to grace how great a debtor … to be* "Come, Thou Fountain of Every Blessing," a hymn by Robert Robinson (1735–1790).

to some of the happiness which attended those who feared God, I knew not how, with any propriety, to return to my lodgings, where the name of God was continually profaned, at which I felt the greatest horror; I paused in my mind for some time, not knowing what to do; whether to hire a bed elsewhere, or go home again. At last, fearing an evil report might arise, I went home, with a farewell to card-playing and vain-jesting, &c. I saw that time was very short, eternity long, and very near; and I viewed those persons alone blessed, who were found ready at midnight-call, or when the Judge of all, both quick and dead, cometh.

The next day I took courage, and went to Holborn, to see my new and worthy acquaintance, the old man, Mr. C——; he, with his wife, a gracious woman, were at work at silk-weaving; they seemed mutually happy, and both quite glad to see me, and I more to see them. I sat down, and we conversed much about soul matters, &c. Their discourse was amazingly delightful, edifying, and pleasant. I knew not at last how to leave this agreeable pair, till time summoned me away. As I was departing, they lent me a little book, entitled "The Conversion of an Indian."[158] It was in questions and answers. The poor man came over the sea to London, to enquire after the Christian's God, who (through rich mercy) he found, and had not his journey in vain. The above book was of great use to me, and at that time was a means of strengthening my faith; however, in parting, they both invited me to call on them when I pleased. This delighted me, and I took care to make all the improvement from it I could: and so far I thanked God for such company and desires. I prayed that the many evils I felt within might be done away, and that I might be weaned from my former carnal acquaintances. This was quickly heard and answered, and I was soon connected with those whom the Scripture calls the excellent of the earth. I heard the gospel preached, and the thoughts of my heart and actions were laid open by the preachers, and the way of salvation by Christ alone was evidently set forth. Thus I went on happily for near two months; and I once heard, during this period, a reverend gentleman, Mr. Green, speak of a man who had departed this life in full assurance of his going to glory. I was much astonished at the assertion, and did very deliberately inquire how he could get at this knowledge. I was answered fully, agreeably to what I read in the oracles of truth; and was told also, that if I did not experience the new birth, and the pardon of my sins, thro' the blood of Christ, before I died, I could not enter the kingdom of heaven. I knew not what to think of this report, as I thought I kept eight commandments out of ten; then my worthy interpreter told me I did not do it, nor could I; and he added, that no man ever did or could keep the commandments, without offending in one point. I thought this sounded very strange, and puzzled me much for many weeks; for I thought it a hard saying. I then asked my friend Mr. L——d, who was clerk in a chapel, why the commandments of God were given, if we could not be saved by them? To which he replied, "The law is a school-master to bring us to Christ," who alone could, and did keep the commandments, and fulfilled all their requirements for his elect people, even those to whom he had given a living faith, and the sins of those chosen vessels *were already* atoned for and forgiven them whilst living; and if I did not experience the same before my exit, the Lord would say at that great day to me, "Go, ye cursed," &c. &c. for God would appear faithful in his judgments to the wicked, as he would be faithful in shewing mercy to those who were ordained to it before the world was; therefore Christ Jesus seemed to be all in all to that man's soul. I was much wounded at this discourse,

Notes

158 *"The Conversion of an Indian"* Lawrence Harlow, *The Conversion of the Indian, in a Letter to a Friend* (1774).

and brought into such a dilemma as I never expected. I asked him, if he was to die that moment, whether he was sure to enter the kingdom of God; and added, "Do you *know* that your sins are forgiven you?" he answered in the affirmative. Then confusion, anger, and discontent seized me, and I staggered much at this sort of doctrine; it brought me to a stand, not knowing which to believe, whether salvation by works, or by faith only in Christ. I requested him to tell me how I might know when my sins were forgiven me. He assured me he could not, and that none but God alone could do this. I told him it was very mysterious; but he said it was really matter of fact, and quoted many portions of Scripture immediately to the point, to which I could make no reply. He then desired me to pray to God to shew me these things. I answered that I prayed to God every day. He said, "I perceive you are a churchman." I answered, I was. He then entreated me to beg of God, to shew me what I was, and the true state of my soul. I thought the prayer very short and odd; so we parted for that time. I weighed all these things over, and could not help thinking how it was possible for a man to know his sins were forgiven him in this life. I wished that God would reveal this selfsame thing to me. In a short time after this, I went to Westminster chapel; the late Rev. Dr. Peckwell preached from Lamentations. iii 39.[159] It was a wonderful sermon; he clearly shewed that a living man had no cause to complain for the punishments of his sins; he evidently justified the Lord in all his dealings with the sons of men; he also shewed the justice of God in the eternal punishment of the wicked and impenitent. The discourse seemed to me like a two-edged sword cutting all ways; it afforded me much joy, intermingled with many fears about my soul; and when it was ended, he gave it out that he intended, the ensuing week, to examine all those who meant to attend the Lord's table. Now I thought much of my good works, and, at the same time, was doubtful of my being a proper object to receive the sacrament: I was full of meditation till the day of examining. However, I went to the chapel, and, though much distressed, I addressed the reverend gentleman, thinking, if I was not right, he would endeavour to convince me of it. When I conversed with him, the first thing he asked me was, What I knew of Christ? I told him I believed in him, and had been baptized in his name. "Then," said he, "when were you brought to the knowledge of God; and how were you convinced of sin?" I knew not what he meant by these questions; I told him I kept eight commandments out of ten; but that I sometimes swore on board of ship, and sometimes when on shore, and broke the Sabbath.[160] He then asked me if I could read; I answered, "Yes." – "Then," said he, "do you read in the Bible, he that offends in one point is guilty of all?"[161] I said, "Yes." Then he assured me, that one sin unatoned[162] for was as sufficient to damn a soul, as one leak was to sink a ship. Here I was struck with awe; for the minister exhorted me much, and reminded me of the shortness of time, and the length of eternity, and that no unregenerate soul, or anything[163] unclean, could enter the kingdom of Heaven.

He did not admit me as a communicant; but recommended me to read the scriptures, and hear the word preached; not to neglect fervent prayer to God, who has promised to hear the supplications of those who seek him in godly sincerity; so I took my leave of him, with many thanks, and resolved to follow his advice, so far as the Lord would condescend to enable me. During this time I was out of employ, nor was

Notes

159 Lamentations 3.39, "Wherefore doth a living man complain, a man for the punishment of his sins?" *Original reads*: Lam[entations]. iii 39 [ed.].

160 *Original reads*: sabbath [ed.].

161 *he that offends in one point is guilty of all?* James 2:10.

162 *Original reads*: unattoned [ed.].

163 *Original reads*: any thing [ed.].

likely to get a situation suitable for me, which obliged me to go once more to sea. I engaged as steward of a ship called the Hope, Captain Richard Strange, bound from London to Cadiz in Spain. In a short time after I was on board, I heard the name of God much blasphemed, and I feared greatly lest I should catch the horrible infection. I thought if I sinned again, after having life and death set evidently before me, I should certainly go to hell. My mind was uncommonly chagrined, and I murmured much at God's providential dealings with me, and was discontented with the commandments, that I could not be saved by what I had done; I hated all things, and wished I had never been born; confusion seized me, and I wished to be annihilated. One day I was standing on the very edge of the stern of the ship, thinking to drown myself; but this scripture was instantaneously impressed on my mind, "That no murderer hath eternal life abiding in him," I John iii. 15. Then I paused, and thought myself the unhappiest man living. Again, I was convinced that the Lord was better to me than I deserved, and I was better off in the world than many. After this I began to fear death; I fretted, mourned, and prayed, till I became a burden to others, but more so to myself. At length I concluded to beg my bread on shore, rather than go again to sea amongst a people who feared not God, and I entreated the captain three different times to discharge me; he would not, but each time gave me greater encouragement to continue with him, and all on board shewed me very great civility: notwithstanding all this, I was unwilling to embark again. At last some of my religious friends advised me, by saying it was my lawful calling, consequently it was my duty to obey, and that God was not confined to place, &c. particularly Mr. G. Smith, the governor of Tothill-fields, Bridewell,[164] who pitied my case, and read the eleventh chapter of the Hebrews to me, with exhortations. He prayed for me, and I believe that he prevailed on my behalf, as my burden was then greatly removed, and I found a heartfelt resignation to the will of God. The good man gave me a pocket Bible, and Alleine's Alarm to the Unconverted.[165] We parted, and the next day I went on board again. We sailed for Spain, and I found favour with the captain. It was the fourth of the month of September when we sailed from London, and we had a delightful voyage to Cadiz, where we arrived the twenty-third of the same month. The place is strong, commands a fine prospect, and is very rich. The Spanish galleons[166] frequent that port, and some arrived whilst we were there. I had many opportunities of reading the Scriptures. I wrestled hard with God in fervent prayers, who had declared in his word that he would hear the groanings and deep sighs of the poor in spirit. I found this verified to my utter astonishment and comfort in the following manner: On the morning of the 6th of October (I pray you to attend) all that day, I thought I should see or hear something supernatural. I had a secret impulse on my mind of something that was to take place, which drove me continually for that time to a throne of grace. It pleased God to enable me to wrestle with him, as Jacob did:[167] I prayed that if sudden death were to happen, and I perished, it might be at Christ's feet.

In the evening of the same day, as I was reading and meditating on the fourth chapter of the Acts, twelfth verse,[168] under the solemn apprehensions of eternity, and

Notes

[164] *Mr. G. Smith ... Tothill-fields, Bridewell* George Smith (d. 1784); Tothill fields, Bridewell was a London prison.

[165] *Alleine's Alarm to the Unconverted* Joseph Alleine's evangelization treatise, *An Alarme to Unconverted Sinners* (1674).

[166] *galleons* large warships.

[167] *wrestle with him, as Jacob did* Genesis 32:24–30.

[168] Acts 4:12, "Neither is there salvation in any other: for there is none other name under heaven given among men, whereby we must be saved."

reflecting on my past actions, I began to think I had lived a moral life, and that I had a proper ground to believe I had an interest in the divine favour; but still meditating on the subject, not knowing whether salvation was to be had partly for our own good deeds, or solely as the sovereign gift of God: in this deep consternation the Lord was pleased to break in upon my soul with his bright beams of heavenly light, and in an instant, as it were, removing the veil, and letting light into a dark place, Isaiah. xxv. 7.[169] I saw clearly, with the eye of faith, the crucified Saviour bleeding on the cross on Mount Calvary: the Scriptures became an unsealed book, I saw myself a condemned criminal under the law, which came with its full force to my conscience, and when "the commandment came sin revived, and I died."[170] I saw the Lord Jesus Christ in his humiliation, loaded and bearing my reproach, sin, and shame. I then clearly perceived, that by the deed of the law no flesh living could be justified. I was then convinced, that by the first Adam sin came, and by the second Adam (the Lord Jesus Christ) all that are saved must be made alive. It was given me at that time to know what it was to be born again, John iii. 5. I saw the eighth chapter to the Romans, and the doctrines of God's decrees verified, agreeable to his eternal, everlasting and unchangeable purposes. The word of God was sweet to my taste, yea sweeter than honey and the honey comb. Christ was revealed to my soul as the chiefest among ten thousand. These heavenly moments were really as life to the dead, and what John calls an earnest of the Spirit. This was indeed unspeakable, and, I firmly believe, undeniable by many. Now every leading providential circumstance that happened to me, from the day I was taken from my parents to that hour, was then, in my view, as if it had but just then occurred. I was sensible of the invisible hand of God, which guided and protected me, when in truth I knew it not: still the Lord pursued me although I slighted and disregarded it; this mercy melted me down. When I considered my poor wretched state, I wept, seeing what a great debtor I was to sovereign free grace. Now the Ethiopian was willing to be saved by Jesus Christ, the sinner's only surety, and also to rely on none other person or thing for salvation. Self was obnoxious, and good works he had none; for it is God that worketh in us both to will and to do. Oh! the amazing things of that hour can never be told – it was joy in the Holy Ghost! I felt an astonishing change; the burden of sin, the gaping jaws of hell, and the fears of death, that weighed me down before, now lost their horror; indeed I thought death would now be the best earthly friend I ever had. Such were my grief and joy, as, I believe, are seldom experienced. I was bathed in tears, and said, What am I, that God should thus look on me, the vilest of sinners? I felt a deep concern for my mother and friends, which occasioned me to pray with fresh ardour; and, in the abyss of thought, I viewed the unconverted people of the world in a very awful state, being without God and without hope.

It pleased God to pour out on me the spirit of prayer and the grace of supplication, so that in loud acclamations I was enabled to praise and glorify his most holy name. When I got out of the cabin, and told some of the people what the Lord had done for me, alas! who could understand me or believe my report! None but to whom the arm of the Lord was revealed. I became a barbarian to them in talking of the love of Christ: his name was to me as ointment poured forth; indeed it was sweet to my soul, but to them a rock of offence. I thought my case singular, and

Notes

[169] *Original reads*: Isa[iah]. xxv. 7. [ed.].

[170] *"the commandment came sin revived, and I died."* Romans 7:9.

every hour a day until I came to London, for I much longed to be with some to whom I could tell of the wonders of God's love towards me, and join in prayer to him whom my soul loved and thirsted after. I had uncommon commotions within, such as few can tell aught about. Now the Bible was my only companion and comfort; I prized it much, with many thanks to God that I could read it for myself, and was not left to be tossed about or led by man's devices and notions. The worth of a soul cannot be told. May the Lord give the reader an understanding in this. Whenever I looked in the Bible I saw things new, and many texts were immediately applied to me with great comfort; for I knew that to me was the word of salvation sent. Sure I was that the Spirit which indited the word opened my heart to receive the truth of it as it is in Jesus – that the same Spirit enabled me to act with faith upon the promises which were precious to me, and enabled me to believe to the salvation of my soul. By free grace I was persuaded that I had a part and lot in the first resurrection, and was enlightened with the "light of the living," Job xxxiii. 30. I wished for a man of God, with whom I might converse; my soul was like the chariots of Aminadab,[171] Canticles vi. 12. These, among others, were the precious promises that were so powerfully applied to me: "All things whatsoever ye shall ask in prayer, believing, ye shall receive," Matthew. xxi. 22.[172] "Peace I leave with you, my peace I give unto you," John xiv. 27. I saw the blessed Redeemer to be the fountain of life, and the well of salvation. I experienced him to be all in all; he had brought me by a way that I knew not, and he had made crooked paths straight. Then in his name I set up his Ebenezer,[173] [5]saying, Hitherto He hath helped me: and could say to the sinners about me, Behold what a Saviour I have! Thus I was, by the teaching of that all glorious Deity, the great One in Three, and Three in One, confirmed in the truths of the Bible; those oracles of everlasting truth, on which every soul living must stand or fall eternally, agreeably to Acts iv. 12. "Neither is there salvation in any other, for there is no other name under heaven given among men whereby we must be saved, but only Jesus Christ." May God give the reader a right understanding in these facts! "To him that believeth, all things are possible, but to them that are unbelieving, nothing is pure," Titus i. 15.

During this period we remained at Cadiz until our ship got laden. We sailed about the 4th of November; and, having a good passage, we arrived in London the month following, to my comfort, with heart-felt gratitude to God, for his rich and unspeakable mercies.

On my return, I had but one text which puzzled me, or that the devil endeavoured to buffet me with, viz. Romans. xi. 6.[174] and as I had heard of the Rev. Mr. Romaine,[175] and his great knowledge in the Scriptures, I wished much to hear him preach. One day I went to Blackfriars church, and, to my great satisfaction and surprise, he preached from that very text. He very clearly shewed the difference between human works and free election, which is according to God's sovereign will and pleasure. These glad tidings set me entirely at liberty, and I went out of the church rejoicing, seeing my spots were those of God's children. I went to Westminster chapel, and saw some of my old friends, who were glad when they perceived the wonderful

Notes

[171] *Aminadab* a biblical figure named in genealogies.

[172] *Original reads*: Matt[hew]. xxi. 22. [ed.].

[173] *set up his Ebenezer* literally "stone of help." In 1 Samuel 7:12, the prophet Samuel raises a large stone to commemorate God's help in defeating the Philistines.

[174] Romans 6:6, "And if by grace, then it is no longer of works; otherwise grace is no longer grace. But if it is of works, it is no longer grace; otherwise work is no longer work." *Original reads*: Rom[ans]. xi. 6.

[175] *Mr. Romaine* William Romaine (1714–1795), English theologian.

change that the Lord had wrought in me, particularly Mr. G. Smith, my worthy acquaintance, who was a man of a choice spirit, and had great zeal for the Lord's service. I enjoyed his correspondence till he died in the year 1784. I was again examined in that same chapel, and was received into church-fellowship amongst them: I rejoiced in spirit, making melody in my heart to the God of all my mercies. Now my whole wish was to be dissolved, and to be with Christ – but, alas! I must wait my appointed time.

Chapter 12

Different transactions of the author's life till the present time – His application to the late Bishop of London to be appointed a missionary to Africa – Some account of his share in the conduct of the late expedition to Sierra Leona – Petition to the Queen – Conclusion.

Such were the various scenes which I was a witness to, and the fortune I experienced until the year 1777. Since that period my life has been more uniform, and the incidents of it fewer, than in any other equal number of years preceding; I therefore hasten to the conclusion of a narrative, which I fear the reader may[176] think already sufficiently tedious.

I had suffered so many impositions in my commercial transactions in different parts of the world, that I became heartily disgusted with the seafaring life, and I was determined not to return to it, at least for some time. I therefore once more engaged in service shortly after my return, and continued for the most part in this situation until 1784.

Soon after my arrival in London, I saw a remarkable circumstance relative to African complexion, which I thought so extraordinary, that I beg leave just to mention it: A white negro woman, that I had formerly seen in London and other parts, had married a white man, by whom she had three boys, and they were every one mulattoes, and yet they had fine light hair. In 1779 I served Governor Macnamara, who had been a considerable time on the coast of Africa. In the time of my service, I used to ask frequently other servants to join me in family prayers; but this only excited their mockery. However, the Governor, understanding that I was of a religious turn, wished to know of what religion I was; I told him I was a protestant of the church of England, agreeable to the thirty-nine articles[177] of that church, and that whomsoever I found to preach according to that doctrine, those I would hear. A few days after this, we had some more discourse on the same subject: the Governor spoke to me on it again, and said that he would, if I chose, as he thought I might be of service in converting my countrymen to the Gospel faith, get me sent out as a missionary to Africa. I at first refused going, and told him how I had been served on a like occasion by some white people the last voyage I went to Jamaica, when I attempted (if it were the will of God) to be the means of converting the Indian prince; and I said I supposed they would serve me worse than Alexander the coppersmith[178] did St. Paul, if I should attempt to go amongst them in Africa. He told me not to fear, for he would apply to the Bishop of London to get me ordained. On these terms I consented to the Governor's proposal to go to

Notes

[176] *Original reads*: my [ed.].

[177] *thirty-nine articles* the doctrinal statements of the Church of England, first issued in 1563.

[178] *Alexander the coppersmith* Cf. 1 Timothy 1:18–20 and 2 Timothy 4:14.

Africa, in hope of doing good if possible amongst my countrymen; so, in order to have me sent out properly, we immediately wrote the following letters to the late Bishop of London:

To the Right Reverend Father in God, ROBERT, *Lord Bishop of London*:

The MEMORIAL of GUSTAVUS VASSA SHEWETH,

That your memorialist is a native of Africa, and has a knowledge of the manners and customs of the inhabitants of that country.

That your memorialist has resided in different parts of Europe for twenty-two years last past, and embraced the Christian faith in the year 1759.

That your memorialist is desirous of returning to Africa as a missionary, if encouraged by your Lordship, in hopes of being able to prevail upon his countrymen to become Christians; and your memorialist is the more induced to undertake the same, from the success that has attended the like undertakings when encouraged by the Portuguese through their different settlements on the coast of Africa, and also by the Dutch; both governments encouraging the blacks, who, by their education are qualified to undertake the same, and are found more proper than European clergymen, unacquainted with the language and customs of the country.

Your memorialist's only motive for soliciting the office of a missionary is that he may be a means, under God, of reforming his countrymen and persuading them to embrace the Christian religion. Therefore your memorialist humbly prays your Lordship's encouragement and support in the undertaking.

Gustavus Vassa.

At Mr. Guthrie's, taylor,
No. 17, Hedge-lane.

MY LORD,

I have resided near seven years on the coast of Africa, for most part of the time as commanding officer. From the knowledge I have of the country and its[179] inhabitants, I am inclined to think that the within plan will be attended with great success, if countenanced by your Lordship. I beg leave further to represent to your Lordship, that the like attempts, when encouraged by other governments, have met with uncommon success; and at this very time I know a very respectable character a black priest at Cape Coast Castle. I know the within named Gustavus Vassa, and believe him a moral good man.

I have the honour to be,
My Lord,
Your Lordship's
Humble and obedient servant,
Matt. MacNamara.

Grove, 11th March 1779.

This letter was also accompanied by the following from Doctor Wallace, who had resided in Africa for many years, and whose sentiments on the subject of an African mission were the same with Governor Macnamara's.[180]

Notes

[179] *Original reads*: it's [ed.].

[180] *Original reads*: Governor: Macnamara's. [ed.].

March 13, 1779.

My Lord,

I have resided near five years on Senegambia[181] on the coast of Africa, and have had the honour of filling very considerable employments in that province. I do approve of the within plan, and think the undertaking very laudable and proper, and that it deserves your Lordship's protection and encouragement, in which case it must be attended with the intended success.

I am,
My Lord,
Your Lordship's
Humble and obedient servant,
Thomas Wallace.

With these letters, I waited on the Bishop by the Governor's desire, and presented them to his Lordship. He received me with much condescension and politeness; but, from some certain scruples of delicacy, declined to ordain me.

My sole motive for thus dwelling on this transaction, or inserting these papers, is the opinion which gentlemen of sense and education, who are acquainted with Africa, entertain of the probability of converting the inhabitants of it to the faith of Jesus Christ, if the attempt were countenanced by the legislature.

Shortly after this I left the Governor, and served a nobleman in the Devonshire militia, with whom I was encamped at Coxheath for some time; but the operations there were too minute and uninteresting to make a detail of.

In the year 1783, I visited eight counties in Wales, from motives of curiosity. While I was in that part of the country I was led to go down into a coal-pit in Shropshire, but my curiosity nearly cost me my life; for while I was in the pit the coals fell in, and buried one poor man, who was not far from me: upon this I got out as fast as I could, thinking the surface of the earth the safest part of it.

In the spring 1784 I thought of visiting old ocean again. In consequence of this I embarked as steward on board a fine new ship called the London, commanded by Martin Hopkin, and sailed for New-York. I admired this city very much; it is large and well-built, and abounds with provisions of all kinds. While we lay here a circumstance happened which I thought extremely singular: One day a malefactor was to be executed on a gallows; but with a condition that if any woman, having nothing on but her shift, married the man under the gallows, his life was to be saved. This extraordinary privilege was claimed; a woman presented herself; and the marriage ceremony was performed. Our ship having got laden we returned to London in January 1785. When she was ready again for another voyage, the captain being an agreeable man, I sailed with him from hence in the spring, March 1785, for Philadelphia. On the fifth of April we took our departure from the Land's-end, with a pleasant gale; and about nine o'clock that night the moon shone bright, the sea was smooth, while our ship was going free by the wind, at the rate of about four or five miles an hour. At this time another ship was going nearly as fast as we on the opposite point, meeting us right in the teeth, yet none on board observed either ship until we struck each other forcibly head and head, to the astonishment and consternation of both crews. She did us much damage, but I believe we did her more; for when we passed by each other, which we

Notes

181 *Senegambia* a region covering parts of present-day Senegal, Gambia, and Mali.

did very quickly, they called to us to bring to, and hoist out our boat, but we had enough to do to mind ourselves; and in about eight minutes we saw no more of her. We refitted as well as we could the next day and proceeded on our voyage, and in May arrived at Philadelphia. I was very glad to see this favourite old town once more; and my pleasure was much increased in seeing the worthy Quakers[182] freeing and easing the burthens of many of my oppressed African brethren. It rejoiced my heart when one of these friendly people took me to see a free-school they had erected for every denomination of black people, whose minds are cultivated here and forwarded to virtue; and thus they are made useful members of the community. Does not the success of this practice say loudly to the planters in the language of scripture – "Go ye and do likewise?"[183]

In October 1785 I was accompanied by some of the Africans, and presented this address of thanks to the gentlemen called Friends or Quakers, in Gracechurch-Court Lombard-Street:

GENTLEMEN,

By reading your book, entitled a Caution to Great Britain and her Colonies,[184] concerning the Calamitous State of the enslaved Negroes: We the poor, oppressed, needy, and much-degraded negroes, desire to approach you with this address of thanks, with our inmost love and warmest acknowledgment; and with the deepest sense of your benevolence, unwearied labour, and kind interposition, towards breaking the yoke of slavery, and to administer a little comfort and ease to thousands and tens of thousands of very grievously afflicted, and too heavy burthened negroes.

Gentlemen, could you, by perseverance, at last be enabled, under God, to lighten in any degree the heavy burthen of the afflicted, no doubt it would, in some measure, be the possible means, under God, of saving the souls of many of the oppressors; and, if so, sure we are that the God, whose eyes are ever upon all his creatures, and always rewards every true act of virtue, and regards the prayers of the oppressed, will give to you and yours those blessings which it is not in our power to express or conceive, but which we, as a part of those captived, oppressed, and afflicted people, most earnestly wish and pray for.

These gentlemen received us very kindly, with a promise to exert themselves on behalf of the oppressed Africans, and we parted.

While in town I chanced once to be invited to a Quaker's[185] wedding. The simple and yet expressive mode used at their solemnizations is worthy of note. The following is the true form of it:

After the company have met they have seasonable exhortations by several of the members; the bride and bridegroom stand up, and, taking each other by the hand in a solemn manner, the man audibly declares to this purpose:

"Friends, in the fear of the Lord, and in the presence of this assembly, whom I desire to be my witnesses, I take this my friend, M.N. to be my wife; promising, through

Notes

182 *Original reads*: quakers [ed.].

183 *"Go ye and do likewise?"* Luke 10:37.

184 *a Caution to Great Britain and her Colonies* Anthony Benezet (1713–1784), *A Caution and Warning to Great Britain and Her Colonies* (1766).

185 *Original reads*: quaker's [ed.].

divine assistance, to be unto her a loving and faithful husband till death separate us:" and the woman makes the like declaration. Then the two first sign their names to the record, and as many more witnesses as have a mind. I had the honour to subscribe mine to a register in Gracechurch-Court, Lombard-Street.

We returned to London in August; and our ship not going immediately to sea, I shipped as a steward in an American ship called the Harmony, Captain John Willet, and left London in March 1786, bound to Philadelphia. Eleven days after sailing we carried our foremast away. We had a nine weeks passage, which caused our trip not to succeed well, the market for our goods proving bad; and, to make it worse, my commander began to play me the like tricks as others too often practise on free negroes in the West Indies. But I thank God I found many friends here, who in some measure prevented him. On my return to London in August I was very agreeably surprised to find that the benevolence of government had adopted the plan of some philanthropic individuals to send the Africans from hence to their native quarter; and that some vessels were then engaged to carry them to Sierra Leone; an act which redounded to the honour of all concerned in its promotion, and filled me with prayers and much rejoicing. There was then in the city a select committee of gentlemen for the black poor, to some of whom I had the honour of being known; and, as soon as they heard of my arrival they sent for me to the committee. When I came there they informed me of the intention of government; and as they seemed to think me qualified to superintend part of the undertaking, they asked me to go with the black poor to Africa. I pointed out to them many objections to my going; and particularly I expressed some difficulties on the account of the slave dealers, as I would certainly oppose their traffic in the human species by every means in my power. However these objections were over-ruled by the gentlemen of the committee, who prevailed on me to go, and recommended me to the honourable Commissioners[186] of his Majesty's Navy as a proper person to act as commissary for government in the intended expedition; and they accordingly appointed me in November 1786 to that office, and gave me sufficient power to act for the government in the capacity of commissary, having received my warrant and the following order.

By the principal Officers and Commissioners of his Majesty's Navy.

WHEREAS you were directed, by our warrant of the 4th of last month, to receive into your charge from Mr. Irving the surplus provisions remaining of what was provided for the voyage, as well as the provisions for the support of the black poor, after the landing at Sierra Leone, with the clothing,[187] tools, and all other articles provided at government's expense; and as the provisions were laid in at the rate of two months for the voyage, and for four months after the landing, but the number embarked being so much less than was expected, whereby there may be a considerable surplus of provisions, clothing, &c. These are, in addition to former orders, to direct and require you to appropriate or dispose of such surplus to the best advantage you can for the benefit of government, keeping and rendering to us a faithful account of what you do herein. And for your guidance in preventing any white persons going, who are not intended to have the indulgence of being carried thither, we send by herewith a list of those recommended by the Committee for the black poor as proper persons to be permitted to embark, and acquaint you that you are not to suffer any others to go

Notes

[186] *Original reads*: Comssimioners [ed.].

[187] *Original reads*: cloathing [ed.].

who do not produce a certificate from the committee for the black poor, of their having their permission for it. For which this shall be your warrant. Dated at the Navy Office, January 16, 1787.

J. Hinslow
Geo. Marsh,
W. Palmer.

To Mr. Gustavus Vassa, Commissary of Provisions and Stores for the Black Poor going to Sierra Leone.

I proceeded immediately to the execution of my duty on board the vessels destined for the voyage, where I continued till the March following.

During my continuance in the employment of government, I was struck with the flagrant abuses committed by the agent, and endeavored to remedy them, but without effect. One instance, among many which I could produce, may serve as a specimen. Government had ordered to be provided all necessaries (slops,[188] as they are called, included) for 750 persons; however, not being able to muster more than 426, I was ordered to send the superfluous slops, &c. to the king's stores at Portsmouth; but, when I demanded them for that purpose from the agent, it appeared they had never been bought, though paid for by government. But that was not all, government were not the only objects of peculation;[189] these poor people suffered infinitely more; their accommodations were most wretched; many of them wanted beds, and many more clothing[190] and other necessaries. For the truth of this, and much more, I do not seek credit from my own assertion. I appeal to the testimony of Capt. Thompson, of the Nautilus, who convoyed us, to whom I applied in February 1787 for a remedy, when I had remonstrated to the agent in vain, and even brought him to be a witness of the injustice and oppression I complained of. I appeal also to a letter written by these wretched people, so early as the beginning of the preceding January, and published in the Morning Herald of the 4th of that month, signed by twenty of their chiefs.

I could not silently suffer government to be thus cheated, and my countrymen plundered and oppressed, and even left destitute of the necessaries for almost their existence. I therefore informed the Commissioners of the Navy of the agent's proceeding; but my dismission was soon after procured, by means of a gentleman in the city, whom the agent, conscious of his peculation, had deceived by letter, and whom, moreover, empowered the same agent to receive on board, at the government expense, a number of persons as passengers, contrary to the orders I received. By this I suffered a considerable loss in my property: however, the commissioners was satisfied with my conduct, and wrote to Capt. Thompson, expressing their approbation of it.

Thus provided, they proceeded on their voyage; and at last, worn out by treatment, perhaps not the most mild, and wasted by sickness, brought on by want of medicine, cloths,[191] bedding, &c. they reached Sierra Leone just at the commencement of the rains. At that season of the year it is impossible to cultivate the lands; their provisions therefore were exhausted before they could derive any benefit from agriculture; and it is not surprising that many, especially the lascars,[192] whose constitutions are very tender, and who had been cooped up in the ships from October to June, and accommodated in the manner I have mentioned, should be so wasted by their confinement as not long to survive it.

Notes

[188] *slops* sailor's clothes and bedding.

[189] *peculation* embezzlement.

[190] *Original reads*: cloathing [ed.].

[191] *Original reads*: cloaths [ed.].

[192] *lascars* soldiers.

Thus ended my part of the long-talked-of expedition to Sierra Leone; an expedition which, however unfortunate in the event, was humane and politic in its design, nor was its failure owing to government: everything was done on their part; but there was evidently sufficient mismanagement attending the conduct and execution of it to defeat its success.

I should not have been so ample in my account of this transaction, had not the share I bore in it been made the subject of partial animadversion, and even my dismission from my employment thought worthy of being made by some a matter of public triumph. The motives which might influence any person to descend to a petty contest with an obscure African, and to seek gratification by his depression, perhaps it is not proper here to inquire into or relate, even if its detection were necessary to my vindication; but I thank Heaven it is not. I wish to stand by my own integrity, and not to shelter myself under the impropriety of another; and I trust the behavior of the Commissioners of the Navy to me entitle me to make this assertion; for after I had been dismissed, March 24, I drew up a memorial thus:

To *the Right Honourable the Lords Commissioners of his Majesty's Treasury*:
The Memorial and Petition of GUSTAVUS VASSA a black Man, late Commissary to the black Poor going to Africa.
HUMBLY SHEWETH,

That your Lordships' memorialist was, by the Honourable the Commissioners of his Majesty's Navy, on the 4th of December last, appointed to the above employment by warrant from that board;

That he accordingly proceeded to the execution of his duty on board of the Vernon, being of the ships appointed to proceed to Africa with the above poor;

That your memorialist, to his great grief and astonishment, received a letter of dismission from the Honourable Commissioners of the Navy, by your Lordships' orders;

That, conscious of having acted with the most perfect fidelity and the greatest assiduity in discharging the trust reposed in him, he is altogether at a loss to conceive the reasons of your Lordships' having altered the favourable opinion you were pleased to conceive of him, sensible that your Lordships would not proceed to so severe a measure without some apparent good cause; he therefore has every reason to believe that his conduct has been grossly misrepresented to your Lordships; and he is the more confirmed in his opinion, because, by opposing measures of others concerned in the same expedition, which tended to defeat your Lordships' humane intentions, and to put the government to a very considerable additional expense, he created a number of enemies, whose misrepresentations, he has too much reason to believe, laid the foundation of his dismission. Unsupported by friends, and unaided by the advantages of a liberal education, he can only hope for redress from the justice of his cause, in addition to the mortification of having been removed from his employment, and the advantage which he reasonably might have expected to have derived there from. He has had the misfortune to have sunk a considerable part of his little property in fitting himself out, and in other expenses arising out of his situation, an account of which he here annexes. Your memorialist will not trouble your Lordships with a vindication of any part of his conduct, because he knows not of what crimes he is accused; he, however, earnestly entreats that you will be pleased to direct an inquiry into his behaviour during the time he acted in the public service; and, if it be found that his dismission arose from false representations, he is confident that in your Lordships' justice he shall find redress.

Your petitioner therefore humbly prays that your Lordships will take his case into consideration, and that you will be pleased to order payment of the above referred-to account, amounting to 32£ 4 s. and also the wages intended, which is most humbly submitted.

London, May 12, 1787.

The above petition was delivered into the hands of their Lordships, who were kind enough, in the space of some few months afterwards, without hearing, to order me 50£ sterling – that is, 18£ wages for the time (upwards of four months) I acted a faithful part in their service. Certainly the sum is more than a free negro would have had in the western colonies!!!

March the 21st, 1788, I had the honour of presenting the Queen with a petition on behalf of my African brethren, which was received most graciously by her Majesty:

To the QUEEN's most Excellent Majesty.

MADAM,

Your Majesty's well known benevolence and humanity emboldens me to approach your royal presence, trusting that the obscurity of my situation will not prevent your Majesty from attending to the sufferings for which I plead.

Yet I do not solicit your royal pity for my own distress; my sufferings, although numerous, are in a measure forgotten. I supplicate your Majesty's compassion for millions of my African countrymen, who groan under the lash of tyranny in the West Indies.

The oppression and cruelty exercised to the unhappy negroes there, have at length reached the British legislature, and they are now deliberating on its redress; even several persons of property in slaves in the West Indies, have petitioned parliament against its continuance, sensible that it is as impolitic as it is unjust – and what is inhuman must ever be unwise.

Your Majesty's reign has been hitherto distinguished by private acts of benevolence and bounty; surely the more extended the misery is, the greater claim it has to your Majesty's compassion, and the greater must be your Majesty's pleasure in administering to its relief.

I presume, therefore, gracious Queen, to implore your interposition with your royal consort, in favour of the wretched Africans; that, by your Majesty's benevolent influence, a period may now be put to their misery; and that they may be raised from the condition of brutes, to which they are at present degraded, to the rights and situation of freemen, and admitted to partake of the blessings of your Majesty's happy government; so shall your Majesty enjoy the heart-felt pleasure of procuring happiness to millions, and be rewarded in the grateful prayers of themselves, and of their posterity.

And may the all-bountiful Creator shower on your Majesty, and the Royal Family, every blessing that this world can afford, and every fulness of joy which divine revelation has promised us in the next.

I am your Majesty's most dutiful and devoted servant to command,

Gustavus Vassa,
The Oppressed Ethiopian.[193]

No.53, Baldwin's Gardens.

Notes

[193] *Original reads*: Ethiopean [ed.].

The negro consolidated act,[194] made by the assembly of Jamaica last year, and the new act of amendment now in agitation there, contain a proof of the existence of those charges that have been made against the planters relative to the treatment of their slaves.

I hope to have the satisfaction of seeing the renovation of liberty and justice resting on the British government, to vindicate the honour of our common nature. These are concerns which do not perhaps belong to any particular office: but, to speak more seriously to every man of sentiment, actions like these are the just and sure foundation of future fame; a reversion, though remote, is coveted by some noble minds as a substantial good. It is upon these grounds that I hope and expect the attention of gentlemen in power. These are designs consonant to the elevation of their rank, and the dignity of their stations: they are ends suitable to the nature of a free and generous government, and, connected with views of empire and dominion, suited to the benevolence and solid merit of the legislature. It is a pursuit of substantial greatness. May the time come – at least the speculation to me is pleasing – when the sable people shall gratefully commemorate the auspicious era of extensive freedom. Then shall those persons particularly be named with praise and honour, who generously proposed and stood forth in the cause of humanity, liberty, and good policy; and brought to the ear of the legislature designs worthy of royal patronage and adoption. May Heaven make the British senators the dispersers of light, liberty, and science, to the uttermost parts of the earth: then will be glory to God on the highest, on earth peace, and good-will to men: Glory, honour, peace, &c. to every soul of man that worketh good, to the Britons first, (because to them the Gospel is preached) and also to the nations. "Those that honour their Maker have mercy on the poor."[195] "It is righteousness exalteth a nation: but sin is a reproach to any people; destruction shall be to the workers of iniquity, and the wicked shall fall by their own wickedness."[196] May the blessings of the Lord be upon the heads of all those who commiserated the cases of the oppressed negroes, and the fear of God prolong their days; and may their expectations be filled with gladness! "The liberal devise liberal things, and by liberal things shall stand." Isaiah xxxii. 8. They can say with pious Job, "Did not I weep for him that was in trouble? was not my soul grieved for the poor?" Job xxx. 25.

As the inhuman traffic of slavery is to be taken into the consideration of the British legislature, I doubt not, if a system of commerce was established in Africa, the demand for manufactures would most rapidly augment, as the native inhabitants will insensibly adopt the British fashions, manners, customs, &c. In proportion to the civilization, so will be the consumption of British manufactures.

The wear and tear of a continent, nearly twice as large as Europe, and rich in vegetable and mineral productions, is much easier conceived than calculated.

A case in point. It cost the Aborigines of Britain little or nothing in clothing, &c. The difference between their forefathers and the present generation, in point of consumption, is literally infinite. The supposition is most obvious. It will be equally immense in Africa—The same cause, viz. civilization, will ever have the same effect.

It is trading upon safe grounds. A commercial intercourse with Africa opens an inexhaustible source of wealth to the manufacturing interests of Great Britain, and to all which the slave trade is an objection.

If I am not misinformed, the manufacturing interest is equal, if not superior, to the landed interest, as to the value, for reasons which will soon appear. The abolition of

Notes

194 *negro consolidated act* The Jamaica Consolidated Slave Act of 1788 mandated that slave owners grant their slaves land and the time to maintain it; specified humane standards of food and rest for slaves; and outlawed various forms of cruelty once inflicted by masters.

195 *"Those that honour … poor"* Proverbs 14:31.

196 *"It is righteousness … wickedness"* Proverbs 14:34.

slavery, so diabolical, will give a most rapid extension of manufactures, which is totally and diametrically opposite to what some interested people assert.

The manufacturers of this country must and will, in the nature and reason of things, have a full and constant employ by supplying the African markets.

Population, the bowels and surface of Africa, abound in valuable and useful returns; the hidden treasures of centuries will be brought to light and into circulation. Industry, enterprize, and mining, will have their full scope, proportionably as they civilize. In a word, it lays open an endless field of commerce to the British manufactures and merchant adventurer. The manufacturing interest and the general interests are synonymous. The abolition of slavery would be in reality an universal good.

Tortures, murder, and every other imaginable barbarity and iniquity, are practised upon the poor slaves with impunity. I hope the slave trade will be abolished. I pray it may be an event at hand. The great body of manufacturers, uniting in the cause, will considerably facilitate and expedite it; and, as I have already stated, it is most substantially their interest and advantage, and as such the nation's at large, (except those persons concerned in the manufacturing neck-yokes, collars, chains, hand-cuffs, leg-bolts, drags, thumbscrews, iron muzzles, and coffins; cats,[197] scourges, and other instruments of torture used in the slave trade). In a short time one sentiment alone will prevail, from motives of interest as well as justice and humanity. Europe contains one hundred and twenty millions of inhabitants. Query – How many millions doth Africa contain? Supposing the Africans, collectively and individually, to expend 5£ a head in raiment and furniture yearly when civilized, &c. an immensity beyond the reach of imagination!

This I conceive to be a theory founded upon facts, and therefore an infallible one. If the blacks were permitted to remain in their own country, they would double themselves every fifteen years. In proportion to such increase will be the demand for manufactures. Cotton and indigo grow spontaneously in most parts of Africa; a consideration this of no small consequence to the manufacturing towns of Great Britain.[198] It opens a most immense, glorious, and happy prospect – the clothing, &c. of a continent ten thousand miles in circumference, and immensely rich in productions of every denomination in return for manufactures.

I have only therefore to request the reader's indulgence and conclude. I am far from the vanity of thinking there is any merit in this narrative: I hope censure will be suspended, when it is considered that it was written by one who was as unwilling as unable to adorn the plainness of truth by the colouring of imagination. My life and fortune have been extremely chequered, and my adventures various. Even those I have related are considerably abridged. If any incident in this little work should appear uninteresting and trifling to most readers, I can only say, as my excuse for mentioning it, that almost every event of my life made an impression on my mind and influenced my conduct. I early accustomed myself to look for the hand of God in the minutest occurrence, and to learn from it a lesson of morality and religion; and in this light every circumstance I have related was to me of importance. After all, what makes any event important, unless by its observation we become better and wiser, and learn "to do justly, to love mercy, and to walk humbly before God?"[199] To those who are possessed of this spirit, there is scarcely any book or incident so trifling that does not afford some profit, while to others the experience of ages seems of no use; and even to pour out to them the treasures of wisdom is throwing the jewels of instruction away.

1789, 1791

Notes

[197] *cat* cat-o'-nine-tails, a type of whip.

[198] *Original reads*: Baitain [ed.].

[199] *"to do justly … before God?"* Micah 6:8.

David Walker (c.1785–1830)

Prior to publishing his 1829 *Appeal in Four Articles; Together with a Preamble, to the Coloured Citizens of the World, but in Particular and Very Expressly, to Those of the United States of America,* David Walker witnessed two of the most significant events in the antebellum American antislavery movement. The first was the failed revolt of Denmark Vesey in 1822, and the second, four years later, was the founding of the first all-black abolitionist organization in America, the Massachusetts General Colored Association. While Vesey's preempted insurrection in Charleston, South Carolina, would have been the largest slave revolt in American history, the Massachusetts General Colored Association would have been the preeminent militant reform organization in antebellum America had not the New England Anti-Slavery Society overshadowed it. These two movements epitomize opposing currents in African American abolitionist discourse: violent, slave-led insurrection based in the South, and organized, institution-based agitation for racial equality led by free blacks in the North. Each finds expression in David Walker's *Appeal.*

The child of a free mother and slave father in Wilmington, North Carolina, Walker grew up free but constantly constrained by and reminded of the degradations of slavery. He became familiar with organized resistance through the small free African American community in Charleston, which centered on the African Methodist Episcopal Church, organized by Vesey in 1817. Walker left South Carolina after Vesey's conspiracy was betrayed and Vesey and others were tried and hanged. After traveling widely, he settled in Boston around 1825, married, and set up a secondhand clothing business. In the politically active, small African American community that resided on the north slope of Beacon Hill, Walker quickly became a prominent figure, delivering antislavery speeches and serving as a general agent for *Freedom's Journal.* Operated by Samuel Cornish and John Browne Russwurm, *Freedom's Journal* became the first black newspaper produced in the United States when it was published in New York City in 1827. Walker was a member of Boston's African Methodist Episcopal Zion Church, not to mention a founding member of the Massachusetts General Colored Association.

Walker's political activism found fullest expression in his *Appeal.* Titled in an ironic echo of the American Constitution, Walker's *Appeal* both took to task the Founding Fathers (particularly Thomas Jefferson in his 1785 book *Notes on the State of Virginia*) and anticipated the fiery invective and black nationalism of the antebellum era. The *Appeal* set off a firestorm of controversy, particularly among slaveholders in the South. The year after its release, Walker died under suspicious circumstances (indeed, while a reward was out in Georgia for his death). He died without seeing the full impact his radical politics had on the abolition movement, and just a year before Nat Turner's uprising. He also died without seeing his son, Edward G. Walker, who was born three months after his death. In 1866, Edward went on to become the first African American elected to the Massachusetts state legislature.

Further reading

Ammons, Elizabeth. *Brave New Words: How Literature Will Save the Planet.* Iowa City: University of Iowa Press, 2010. Ch. 2.

Apap, Chris. "'Let No Man of Us Budge One Step': David Walker and the Rhetoric of African American

The Wiley Blackwell Anthology of African American Literature: Volume 1, 1746–1920, First Edition.
Edited by Gene Andrew Jarrett.

Emplacement." *Early American Literature* 46.2 (2011): 319–350.

Burrow, Rufus, Jr. *God and Human Responsibility: David Walker and Ethical Prophecy*. Macon: Mercer University Press, 2003.

Dinius, Marcy J. "'Look!! Look!!! at This!!!!': The Racial Typography of David Walker's *Appeal*." *PMLA: Publications of the Modern Language Association of America* 126.1 (2011): 55–72.

Engels, Jeremy. "Friend or Foe?: Naming the Enemy." *Rhetoric & Public Affairs* 12.1 (2009): 37–64.

Finseth, Ian. "David Walker, Nature's Nation, and Early African-American Separatism." *Mississippi Quarterly: The Journal of Southern Cultures* 54.3 (2001): 337–362.

Hinks, Peter P. *To Awaken My Afflicted Brethren: David Walker and the Problem of Antebellum Slave Resistance*. University Park: Pennsylvania State University Press, 1997.

Jarrett, Gene Andrew. *Representing the Race: A New Political History of African American Literature*. New York: New York University Press, 2011. Ch. 1.

Levine, Robert S. *Dislocating Race and Nation: Episodes in Nineteenth-Century American Literary Nationalism*. Chapel Hill: University of North Carolina Press, 2008. Ch. 2.

Levine, Robert S. "African American Literary Nationalism." *A Companion to African American Literature*. Ed. Gene Andrew Jarrett. Malden, MA: Wiley-Blackwell, 2010. 119–132.

Extracts from Appeal in Four Articles; Together with a Preamble, to the Coloured Citizens of the World, but in Particular and Very Expressly, to Those of the United States of America

Article 1

Our Wretchedness in Consequence of Slavery

My beloved brethren: The Indians of North and of South America – the Greeks – the Irish, subjected under the king of Great Britain – the Jews, that ancient people of the Lord – the inhabitants of the islands of the sea – in fine, all the inhabitants of the earth (except, however, the sons of Africa) are called *men*, and of course are, and ought to be free. But we, (coloured people) and our children are *brutes!!* and of course are, and *ought to be* SLAVES to the American people and their children forever!! to dig their mines and work their farms; and thus go on enriching them, from one generation to another with our *blood* and our *tears!!!!*

I promised in a preceding page to demonstrate to the satisfaction of the most incredulous, that we (coloured people of these United States of America) are the *most wretched, degraded* and *abject* set of beings that *ever lived* since the world began, and that the white Americans having reduced us to the wretched state of *slavery*, treat us in that condition *more cruel* (they being an enlightened and Christian people) than any heathen nation did any people whom it had reduced to our condition. These affirmations are so well confirmed in the minds of all unprejudiced men, who have taken the trouble to read histories, that they need no elucidation from me. But to put them beyond all doubt, I refer you in the first place to the children of Jacob, or of Israel in Egypt, under Pharaoh and his people. Some of my brethren do not know who Pharaoh and the Egyptians were – I know it to be a fact, that some of them take the Egyptians to have been a gang of *devils*, not knowing any better, and that they (Egyptians) having got possession of the Lord's people, treated them *nearly* as cruel as *Christian Americans* do us, at the present day. For the information of such, I would only mention that the Egyptians, were Africans or coloured people, such as we are – some of them yellow and others dark – a mixture of Ethiopians and the natives of Egypt – about the same as you see the coloured people of the United States at the present day – I say, I call your attention then, to the children of Jacob, while I point out particularly to you his son Joseph, among the rest, in Egypt.

"And Pharaoh, said unto Joseph, … thou shalt be over my house, and according unto thy word shall all my people be ruled: only in the throne will I be greater than thou.*

"And Pharaoh said unto Joseph, see, I have set thee over all the land of Egypt."†

"And Pharaoh said unto Joseph, I am Pharaoh, and without thee shall no man lift up his hand or foot in all the land of Egypt."‡

Now I appeal to heaven and to earth, and particularly to the American people themselves, who cease not to declare that our condition is not *hard*, and that we are comparatively satisfied to rest in wretchedness and misery, under them and their children. Not, indeed, to show me a coloured President, a Governor, a Legislator, a Senator, a Mayor, or an Attorney at the Bar. But to show me a man of colour, who holds the low office of Constable, or one who sits in a Juror Box, even on a case of one of his wretched brethren, throughout this great Republic!! – But let us pass Joseph the son of Israel a little farther in review, as he existed with that heathen nation.

"And Pharaoh called Joseph's name Zaphnathpaaneah; and he gave him to wife Asenath the daughter of Potipherah priest of On. And Joseph went out over all the land of Egypt."ʃ

Compare the above, with the American institutions. Do they not institute laws to prohibit us from marrying the whites? I would wish, candidly, however, before the Lord, to be understood, that I would not give a *pinch of snuff* to be married to any white person I ever saw in all the days of my life. And I do say it, that the black man, or man of colour, who will leave his own colour (provided he can get one, who is good for anything[ʳ]) and marry a white woman, to be a double slave to her, just because she is *white*, ought to be treated by her as he surely will be, viz: as a NIGGER!!!! It is not, indeed, what I care about inter-marriages with the whites, which induced me to pass this subject in review; for the Lord knows, that there is a day coming when they will be glad enough to get into the company of the blacks, notwithstanding, we are, in this generation, levelled by them, almost on a level with the brute creation: and some of us they treat even worse than they do the brutes that perish. I only made this extract to show how much lower we are held, and how much more cruel we are treated by the Americans, than were the children of Jacob, by the Egyptians – We will notice the sufferings of Israel some further, under *heathen Pharaoh*, compared with ours under the *enlightened Christians of America*.

"And Pharaoh spoke unto Joseph, saying, thy father and thy brethren are come unto thee:

"The land of Egypt is before thee: in the best of the land make thy father and brethren to dwell; in the land of Goshen let them dwell: and if thou knowest any men of activity among them, then make them rulers over my cattle."ǁ

I ask those people who treat us so *well*, Oh! I ask them, where is the most barren spot of land which they have given unto us? Israel had the most fertile land in all Egypt. Need I mention the very notorious fact, that I have known a poor man of colour, who laboured night and day, to acquire a little money, and having acquired it, he vested it in a small piece of land, and got him a house erected thereon, and having paid for the whole, he moved his family into it, where he was suffered to remain but nine months, when he was cheated out of his property by a white man, and driven out of door! And is not this the case generally? Can a man of colour buy a piece of land and keep it

Notes

* Genesis 41:39–40.

† Genesis 41:41.

‡ Genesis 41:44.

ʃ Genesis 41:45.

ǁ Genesis 47:5–6.

ʳ *Original reads*: any thing [ed.].

peaceably? Will not some white man try to get it from him, even if it is in a *mud hole?* I need not comment any further[2] on a subject, which all, both black and white, will readily admit. But I must, really, observe that in this very city, when a man of colour dies, if he owned any real estate it most generally falls into the hands of some white person. The wife and children of the deceased may weep and lament if they please, but the estate will be kept snug enough by its white possessor.

But to prove farther that the condition of the Israelites was better under the Egyptians than ours is under the whites. I call upon the professing Christians, I call upon the philanthropist, I call upon the very tyrant himself, to show me a page of history, either sacred or profane, on which a verse can be found, which maintains that the Egyptians heaped the *insupportable insult* upon the children of Israel, by telling them that they were not of the *human family*. Can the whites deny this charge? Have they not, after having reduced us to the deplorable condition of slaves under their feet, held us up as descending originally from the tribes of *Monkeys* or *Orang-Outangs*? O! my God! I appeal to every man of feeling – is not this insupportable? Is it not heaping the most gross insult upon our miseries, because they have got us under their feet and we cannot help ourselves? Oh! pity us we pray thee, Lord Jesus, Master. Has Mr. Jefferson declared to the world, that we are inferior to the whites both in the endowments of our bodies and our minds?[3] It is indeed surprising, that a man of such great learning, combined with such excellent natural parts, should speak so of a set of men in chains. I do not know what to compare it to, unless, like putting one wild deer in an iron cage, where it will be secured, and hold another by the side of the same, then let it go, and expect the one in the cage to run as fast as the one at liberty. So far, my brethren, were the Egyptians from heaping these insults upon their slaves, that Pharaoh's daughter took Moses, a son of Israel for her own, as will appear by the following.

"And Pharaoh's daughter said unto her [Moses' mother], take this child away, and nurse it for me, and I will pay thee thy wages. And the woman took the child [Moses] and nursed it.

"And the child grew, and she brought him unto Pharaoh's daughter and he became her son. And she called his name Moses: and she said because I drew him out of the water."*

In all probability, Moses would have become Prince Regent to the throne, and no doubt, in process of time but he would have been seated on the throne of Egypt. But he had rather suffer shame, with the people of God, than to enjoy pleasures with that wicked people for a season. O! that the coloured people were long since of Moses' excellent disposition, instead of courting favour with and telling news and lies to our *natural enemies*, against each other – aiding them to keep their hellish chains of slavery upon us. Would we not long before this time, have been respectable men, instead of such wretched victims of oppression as we are? Would they be able to drag our mothers, our fathers, our wives, our children and ourselves, around the world in chains and handcuffs as they do, to dig up gold and silver for them and theirs? This question, my brethren, I leave for you to digest; and may God Almighty force it home to your hearts. Remember that unless you are united, keeping your tongues within your teeth, you will be afraid to trust your secrets to each other, and thus perpetuate our miseries under the *Christians!!!!*

Notes

* Exodus 2:9–10.

[2] *Original reads*: farther [ed.].

[3] *"Has Mr. Jefferson ... our bodies and our minds?"* Walker is responding to Thomas Jefferson's *Notes on the State of Virginia* (1785), in which he judges those of African descent to be physically and mentally inferior to whites.

☞ Addition – Remember, also to lay humble at the feet of our Lord and Master Jesus Christ, with prayers and fastings. Let our enemies go on with their butcheries, and at once fill up their cup. Never make an attempt to gain our freedom or *natural right*, from under our cruel oppressors and murderers, until you see your way clear† – when that hour arrives and you move, be not afraid or dismayed; for be you assured that Jesus Christ the King of heaven and of earth who is the God of justice and of armies will surely go before you. And those enemies who have for hundreds of years stolen our *rights*, and kept us ignorant of Him and His divine worship, He[4] will remove. Millions of whom, are this day, so ignorant and avaricious, that they cannot conceive how God can have an attribute of justice, and show mercy to us because it pleased Him to make us black – which colour, Mr. Jefferson calls unfortunate!!!!!! As though we are not as thankful to our God, for having made us as it pleased himself, as they, (the whites,) are for having made them white. They think because they hold us in their infernal chains of slavery, that we wish to be white, or of their color – but they are dreadfully deceived – we wish to be just as it pleased our Creator to have made us, and no avaricious and unmerciful wretches, have any business to make slaves of, or hold us in slavery. How would they like for us to make slaves of, and hold them in cruel slavery, and murder them as they do us? – But are[5] Mr. Jefferson's assertions true? viz. "that it is unfortunate for us that our Creator has been pleased to make us *black*." We will not take his say so, for the fact. The world will have an opportunity to see whether it is unfortunate for us, that our Creator *has made us* darker than the *whites*.

Fear not the number and education of our *enemies*, against whom we shall have to contend for our lawful right; guaranteed to us by our Maker; for why should we be afraid, when God is, and will continue (if we continue humble) to be, on our side?

The man who would not fight under our Lord and Master Jesus Christ, in the glorious and heavenly cause of freedom and of God – to be delivered from the most wretched, abject and servile slavery, that ever a people was afflicted with since the foundation of the world, to the present day – ought to be kept with all of his children or family, in slavery, or in chains, to be butchered by his *cruel enemies*.☜

I saw a paragraph, a few years since, in a South Carolina paper, which, speaking of the barbarity of the Turks, it said: "The Turks are the most barbarous people in the world – they treat the Greeks more like *brutes* than human beings." And in the same paper was an advertisement, which said: "Eight well-built Virginia and Maryland *Negro fellows* and four *wenches* will positively be *sold* this day, *to the highest bidder!*" And what astonished me still more was to see in this same *humane* paper!! the cuts of three men, with clubs and budgets[6] on their backs, and an advertisement offering a considerable sum of money for their apprehension and delivery. I declare, it is really so amusing to hear the Southerners and Westerners of this country talk about *barbarity*, that it is positively enough to make a man *smile*.

Notes

† It is not to be understood here, that I mean for us to wait until God shall take us by the hair of our heads and drag us out of abject wretchedness and slavery, nor do I mean to convey the idea for us to wait until our enemies shall make preparations, and call us to seize those preparations, take it away from them, and put everything before us to death, in order to gain our freedom which God has given us. For you must remember that we are men as well as they. God has been pleased to give us two eyes, two hands, two feet, and some sense in our heads as well as they. They have no more right to hold us in slavery than we have to hold them; we have just as much right, in the sight of God, to hold them and their children in slavery and wretchedness, as they have to hold us, and no more.

4 *Original reads*: he [ed.].

5 *Original reads*: is [ed.].

6 *budgets* leather pouches or bags.

The sufferings of the Helots among the Spartans were somewhat severe, it is true, but to say that theirs were as severe as ours among the Americans I do most strenuously deny – for instance, can any man show me an article on a page of ancient history which specifies that the Spartans chained and handcuffed the Helots, and dragged them from their wives and children, children from their parents, mothers from their suckling babes, wives from their husbands, driving them from one end of the country to the other? Notice the Spartans were heathens, who lived long before our Divine Master made his appearance in the flesh. Can Christian Americans deny these barbarous cruelties? Have you not, Americans, having subjected us under you, added to these miseries, by insulting us in telling us to our face, because we are helpless, that we are not of the human family? I ask you, O! Americans, I ask you, in the name of the Lord, can you deny these charges? Some perhaps may deny, by saying that they never thought or said that we were not men. But do not actions speak louder than words? Have they not made provisions for the Greeks, and Irish? Nations who have never done the least thing for them, while *we*, who have enriched their country with our blood and tears – have dug up gold and silver for them and their children, from generation to generation, and are in more miseries than any other people under heaven, are not seen but by comparatively a handful of the American people? There are, indeed, more ways to kill a dog, besides choking it to death with butter. Further – The Spartans or Lacedaemonians, had some frivolous pretext for enslaving the Helots, for they (Helots), while being free inhabitants of Sparta, stirred up an intestine commotion, and were, by the Spartans subdued, and made prisoners of war. Consequently, they and their children were condemned to perpetual slavery.

I have been for years troubling the pages of historians, to find out what our fathers have done to the *white Christians of America*, to merit such condign punishment as they have inflicted on them, and do continue to inflict on us their children. But I must aver that my researches have hitherto been to no effect. I have, therefore, come to the immoveable conclusion that they (Americans) have and do continue to punish us for nothing else, but for enriching them and their country. For I cannot conceive of anything else. Nor will I ever believe otherwise, until the Lord shall convince me.

The world knows that slavery as it existed among the Romans (which was the primary cause of their destruction) was, comparatively speaking, no more than a *cypher*, when compared with ours under the Americans. Indeed I should not have noticed the Roman slaves, had not the very learned and penetrating Mr. Jefferson said, "when a master was murdered, all his slaves in the same house, or within hearing, were condemned to death." – Here let me ask Mr. Jefferson (but he is gone to answer at the bar of God, for the deeds done in his body while living), I therefore ask the whole American people, had I not rather die, or be put to death, than to be a slave to any tyrant, who takes not only my own, but my wife and children's lives by the inches? Yea, would I meet death with avidity far! far!! in preference to such *servile submission* to the murderous hands of tyrants. Mr. Jefferson's very severe remarks on us have been so extensively argued upon by men whose attainments in literature I shall never be able to reach, that I would not have meddled with it, were it not to solicit each of my brethren, who has the spirit of a man, to buy a copy of Mr. Jefferson's "Notes on Virginia," and put it in the hand of his son. For let no one of us suppose that the refutations which have been written by our white friends are enough – they are *whites* – *we are blacks*. We, and the world wish to see the charges of Mr. Jefferson refuted by the blacks *themselves*, according to their chance; for we must remember that what the whites have written respecting this subject is other men's labours, and did not emanate from the blacks. I know well, that there are some talents and learning among the coloured people of this country, which we have not a chance to develop,[7] in consequence of oppression; but our oppression ought not to hinder us from acquiring all we can. For we will have a chance to develop[8] them by and by. God will not suffer us, always to be oppressed. Our sufferings will come to an *end*, in spite of all the Americans this side of *eternity*. Then we will want all the learning and talents among ourselves, and perhaps more, to govern ourselves. "Every dog must have its day," the American's is coming to an end.

But let us review Mr. Jefferson's remarks respecting us some further. Comparing our miserable fathers, with the learned philosophers of Greece, he says: "Yet notwithstanding these and other discouraging circumstances among the Romans, their slaves were often their rarest artists. They excelled too, in science, insomuch as to be usually employed as tutors to their master's children; Epictetus, Terence and Phaedrus,[9] were slaves – but they were of the race of whites. It is not their *condition* then, but *nature*, which has produced the distinction." See this, my brethren!! Do you believe that this assertion is swallowed by millions of the whites? Do you know that Mr. Jefferson was one of as great characters as ever lived among the whites? See his writings for the world, and public labours for the United States of America. Do you believe that the assertions of such a man will pass away into oblivion unobserved by this people and the world?

If you do you are much mistaken – See how the American people treat us – have we souls in our bodies? Are we men who have any spirits at all? I know that there are many *swell- bellied* fellows among us, whose greatest object is to fill their stomachs. Such I do not mean – I am after those who know and feel, that we are MEN, as well as other people; to them, I say, that unless we try to refute Mr. Jefferson's arguments respecting us, we will only establish them.

But the slaves among the Romans. Everybody[10] who has read history knows that as soon as a slave among the Romans obtained his freedom, he could rise to the greatest eminence in the State, and there was no law instituted to hinder a slave from buying his freedom. Have not the Americans instituted laws to hinder us from obtaining our freedom? Do any deny this charge? Read the laws of Virginia, North Carolina, &c. Further: have not the Americans instituted laws to prohibit a man of colour from obtaining and holding any office whatever, under the government of the United States of America? Now, Mr. Jefferson tells us, that our condition is not so hard, as the slaves were under the Romans!!!!!!

It is time for me to bring this article to a close. But before I close it, I must observe to my brethren that at the close of the first Revolution in this country with Great Britain, there were but thirteen States in the Union, now there are twenty-four, most of which are slave-holding States, and the whites are dragging us around in chains and in handcuffs, to their new States and Territories to work their mines and farms, to enrich them and their children – and millions of them believing firmly that we being a little darker than they, were made by our Creator to be an inheritance to them and their children for ever – the same as a parcel of *brutes*.

Are we MEN!! – I ask you, O my brethren! are we MEN? Did our Creator make us to be slaves to dust and ashes like ourselves? Are they not dying worms as well as we?

Notes

[7] *Original reads*: develope [ed.].

[8] *Original reads*: develope [ed.].

[9] *Epictetus, Terence, and Phaedrus* respectively: a Greek Stoic philosopher (AD 55–135), a Roman dramatist (195–159 BC), and Roman fabulist (15 BC–AD 50).

[10] *Original reads*: Every body [ed.].

Have they not to make their appearance before the tribunal of Heaven, to answer for the deeds done in the body, as well as we? Have we any other Master but Jesus Christ alone? Is he not their Master as well as ours? What right then, have we to obey and call any other Master, but Himself? How we could be so *submissive* to a gang of men, whom we cannot tell whether they are *as good* as ourselves or not, I never could conceive. However, this is shut up with the Lord, and we cannot precisely tell – but I declare, we judge men by their works.

The whites have always been an unjust, jealous, unmerciful, avaricious and bloodthirsty set of beings, always seeking after power and authority. We view them all over the confederacy of Greece, where they were first known to be anything[11] (in consequence of education) we see them there, cutting each other's throats – trying to subject each other to wretchedness and misery – to effect which they used all kinds of deceitful, unfair, and unmerciful means. We view them next in Rome, where the spirit of tyranny and deceit raged still higher. We view them in Gaul,[12] Spain, and in Britain. In fine, we view them all over Europe, together with what were scattered about in Asia and Africa, as heathens, and we see them acting more like devils than accountable men. But some may ask, did not the blacks of Africa, and the mulattoes of Asia, go on in the same way as did the whites of Europe. I answer, no – they never were half so avaricious, deceitful and unmerciful as the whites, according to their knowledge.

But we will leave the whites or Europeans as heathens, and take a view of them as Christians, in which capacity we see them as cruel, if not more so than ever. In fact, take them as a body, they are ten times more cruel, avaricious and unmerciful than ever they were; for while they were heathens, they were bad enough it is true, but it is positively a fact that they were not quite so audacious as to go and take vessel loads of men, women and children, and in cold blood, and through devilishness, throw them into the sea, and murder them in all kind of ways. While they were heathens, they were too ignorant for such barbarity. But being Christians, enlightened[13] and sensible, they are completely prepared for such hellish cruelties. Now suppose God were to give them more sense, what would they do? If it were possible, would they not *dethrone* Jehovah and seat themselves upon His[14] throne? I therefore, in the name and fear of the Lord God of Heaven and of earth, divested of prejudice either on the side of my colour or that of the whites, advance my suspicion of them, whether they are *as good by nature* as we are or not. Their actions, since they were known as a people, have been the reverse, I do indeed suspect them, but this, as I before observed, is shut up with the Lord, we cannot exactly tell, it will be proved in succeeding generations. The whites have had the essence of the gospel as it was preached by my master and his apostles – the Ethiopians have not, who are to have it in its meridian splendor – the Lord will give it to them to their satisfaction. I hope and pray my God, that they will make good use of it, that it may be well with them.*

Notes

* It is my solemn belief, that if ever the world becomes Christianized (which must certainly take place before long), it will be through the means, under God of the *Blacks*, who are now held in wretchedness, and degradation, by the white *Christians* of the world, who before they learn to do justice to us before our Maker – and be reconciled to us, and reconcile us to them, and by that means have clear consciences before God and man – send out Missionaries to convert the Heathens, many of whom after they cease to worship gods, which neither see nor hear, become ten times more the children of Hell, then ever they were. Why, what is the reason? Why, the reason is obvious, they must learn to do justice at home, before they go into distant lands, to display their charity, Christianity, and benevolence; when they learn to do justice, God will accept their offering (no man may think that I am against Missionaries for I am not, my object is to see justice done at home, before we go to convert the Heathens.)

11 *Original reads*: any thing [ed.].

12 *Gaul* France.

13 *Original reads*: enlighted [ed.].

14 *Original reads*: his [ed.].

Article 2

Our Wretchedness in Consequence of Ignorance

Ignorance, my brethren, is a mist, low down into the very dark and almost impenetrable abyss in which our fathers for many centuries have been plunged. The Christians, and enlightened of Europe, and some of Asia, seeing the ignorance and consequent degradation of our fathers, instead of trying to enlighten them by teaching them that religion and light with which God had blessed them, they have plunged them into wretchedness ten thousand times more intolerable than if they had left them entirely to the Lord, and to add to their miseries, deep down into which they have plunged them tell them, that they are an *inferior* and *distinct race* of beings, which they will be glad enough to recall and swallow by and by. Fortune and misfortune, two inseparable companions, lay rolled up in the wheel of events, which have from the creation of the world, and will continue to take place among men until God shall dash worlds together.

When we take a retrospective view of the arts and sciences – the wise legislators – the Pyramids, and other magnificent buildings – the turning of the channel of the river Nile, by the sons of Africa or of Ham,[15] among whom learning originated, and was carried thence into Greece, where it was improved upon and refined. Thence among the Romans, and all over the then enlightened parts of the world, and it has been enlightening the dark and benighted minds of men from then, down to this day. I say, when I view retrospectively, the renown of that once mighty people, the children of our great progenitor I am indeed cheered. Yea further, when I view that mighty son of Africa, Hannibal,[16] one of the greatest generals of antiquity, who defeated and cut off so many thousands of the white Romans or murderers, and who carried his victorious arms to the very gate of Rome, and I give it as my candid opinion, that had Carthage been well united and had given him good support, he would have carried that cruel and barbarous city by storm. But they were dis-united, as the coloured people are now, in the United States of America, the reason our natural enemies are enabled to keep their feet on our throats.

Beloved brethren – here let me tell you, and believe it, that the Lord our God, as true as He[17] sits on His[18] throne in heaven, and as true as our Saviour died to redeem the world, will give you a Hannibal, and when the Lord shall have raised him up, and given him to you for your possession, O my suffering brethren! remember the divisions and consequent sufferings of *Carthage* and of *Hayti*.[19] Read the history particularly of Hayti, and see how they were butchered by the whites, and do you take warning. The person whom God shall give you, give him your support and let him go his length, and behold in him the salvation of your God. God will, indeed, deliver you through him from your deplorable and wretched condition under the Christians of America. I charge you this day before my God to lay no obstacle in his way, but let him go.

The whites want slaves, and want us for their slaves, but some of them will curse the day they ever saw us. As true as the sun ever shone in its meridian splendor, my colour will root some of them out of the very face of the earth. They shall have enough of making slaves of, and butchering, and murdering us in the manner which they have.

Notes

[15] *sons of … Ham* In the Bible, Ham is a son of Noah, and legendary forefather of the people of Africa and the Middle East.

[16] Hannibal (247–182 BC), the legendary general and military strategist of ancient Carthage, who in the Second Punic War invaded Italy and almost conquered Rome.

[17] *Original reads*: he [ed.].

[18] *Original reads*: his [ed.].

[19] *Hayti* The Haitian Revolution (1791–1804) was the only slave revolt that resulted in the founding of a state; however, in the years following the revolution, Haiti was rife with division and infighting.

No doubt some may say that I write with a bad spirit, and that I being a black, wish these things to occur. Whether I write with a bad or a good spirit, I say if these things do not occur in their proper time, it is because the world in which we live does not exist, and we are deceived with regard to its existence – It is immaterial however to me, who believe, or who refuse – though I should like to see the whites repent peradventure God may have mercy on them. Some, however, have gone so far that their cup must be filled.

But what need have I to refer to antiquity, when Hayti, the glory of the blacks and terror of tyrants, is enough to convince the most avaricious and stupid of wretches – which is at this time, and I am sorry to say it, plagued with that scourge of nations, the Catholic religion; but I hope and pray God that she may yet rid herself of it, and adopt in its stead the Protestant faith; also, I hope that she may keep peace within her borders and be united, keeping a strict look out for tyrants, for if they get the least chance to injure her, they will avail themselves of it, as true as the Lord lives in heaven. But one thing which gives me joy is, that they are men who would be cut off to a man, before they would yield to the combined forces of the whole world – in fact, if the whole world was combined against them, it could not do anything[20] with them, unless the Lord delivers them up.

Ignorance and treachery one against the other – a grovelling servile and abject submission to the lash of tyrants, we see plainly, my brethren, are not the natural elements of the blacks, as the Americans try to make us believe; but these are misfortunes which God has suffered our fathers to be enveloped in for many ages, no doubt in consequence of their disobedience to their Maker, and which do, indeed, reign at this time among us, almost to the destruction of all other principles: for I must truly say, that ignorance, the mother of treachery and deceit, gnaws into our very vitals. Ignorance, as it now exists among us, produces a state of things, Oh my Lord! too horrible to present to the world. Any man who is curious to see the full force of ignorance developed among the coloured people of the United States of America has only to go into the southern and western states of this confederacy, where, if he is not a tyrant, but has the feelings of a human being, who can feel for a fellow creature, he may see enough to make his very heart bleed! He may see there, a son take his mother, who bore almost the pains of death to give him birth, and by the command of a tyrant, strip her as naked as she came into the world, and apply the cow-hide to her, until she falls a victim to death in the road! He may see a husband take his dear wife, not unfrequently in a pregnant state, and perhaps far advanced, and beat her for an unmerciful wretch, until his infant falls a lifeless lump at her feet! Can the Americans escape God Almighty? If they do, can He[21] be to us a God of Justice? God is just, and I know it – for He[22] has convinced me to my satisfaction – I cannot doubt Him.[23] My observer may see fathers beating their sons, mothers their daughters, and children their parents, all to pacify the passions of unrelenting tyrants. He may also, see them telling news and lies, making mischief one upon another. These are some of the productions of ignorance, which he will see practised among my dear brethren, who are held in unjust slavery and wretchedness, by avaricious and unmerciful tyrants, to whom, and their hellish deeds, I would suffer my life to be taken before I would submit. And when my curious observer comes to take notice of those who are said to be free (which assertion I deny), and who are

Notes

[20] *Original reads*: any thing [ed.].

[21] *Original reads*: he [ed.].

[22] *Original reads*: he [ed.].

[23] *Original reads*: him [ed.].

making some frivolous pretentions to common sense, he will see that branch of ignorance among the slaves assuming a more cunning and deceitful course of procedure. He may see some of my brethren in league with tyrants, selling their own brethren into *hell upon earth*, not dissimilar to the exhibitions in Africa, but in a more secret, servile and abject manner. Oh Heaven! I am full!!! I can hardly move my pen!!!! and as I expect some will try to put me to death, to strike terror into others, and to obliterate from their minds the notion of freedom, so as to keep my brethren the more secure in wretchedness, where they will be permitted to stay but a short time (whether tyrants believe it or not) – I shall give the world a development of facts, which are already witnessed in the courts of heaven. My observer may see some of those ignorant and treacherous creatures (coloured people) sneaking about in the large cities, endeavouring to find out all strange coloured people, where they work and where they reside, asking them questions, and trying to ascertain whether they are runaways or not, telling them, at the same time, that they always have been, are, and always will be, friends to their brethren; and, perhaps, that they themselves are absconders, and a thousand such treacherous lies to get the better information of the more ignorant!!! There have been and are at this day in Boston, New-York, Philadelphia, and Baltimore, coloured men, who are in league with tyrants, and who receive a great portion of their daily bread, of the moneys which they acquire from the blood and tears of their more miserable brethren, whom they scandalously delivered into the hands of our *natural enemies!!!!!!*

To show the force of degraded ignorance and deceit among us some farther, I will give here an extract from a paragraph, which may be found in the Columbian Centinel[24] of this city, for September 9, 1829, on the first page of which, the curious may find an article, headed

"AFFRAY AND MURDER." *"Portsmouth, (Ohio) Aug. 22, 1829.*

"A most shocking outrage was committed in Kentucky, about eight miles from this place, on 14th inst. A negro driver, by the name of Gordon, who had purchased in Maryland about sixty negroes, was taking them, assisted by an associate named Allen, and the wagoner who conveyed the baggage, to the Mississippi. The men were handcuffed and chained together, in the usual manner for driving those poor wretches, while the women and children were suffered to proceed without incumbrance. It appears that, by means of a file the negroes, unobserved, had succeeded in separating the iron which bound their hands, in such a way as to be able to throw them off at any moment. About 8 o'clock in the morning, while proceeding on the state road leading from Greenup to Vanceburg, two of them dropped their shackles and commenced a fight, when the wagoner (Petit) rushed in with his whip to compel them to desist. At this moment, every negro was found to be perfectly at liberty; and one of them seizing a club, gave Petit a violent blow on the head, and laid him dead at his feet; and Allen, who came to his assistance, met a similar fate, from the contents of a pistol fired by another of the gang. Gordon was then attacked, seized and held by one of the negroes, whilst another fired twice at him with a pistol, the ball of which each time grazed his head, but not proving effectual, he was beaten with clubs, and left for dead. They then commenced pillaging the wagon, and with an axe split open the trunk of Gordon, and rifled it of the money, about $2,400. Sixteen of the negroes then took to the woods; Gordon,

Notes

[24] *Columbian Centinel* a Boston newspaper (1790–1840).

in the meantime,[25] not being materially injured, was enabled, by the assistance of one of the women, to mount his horse and flee; pursued, however, by one of the gang on another horse, with a drawn pistol; fortunately he escaped with his life barely, arriving at a plantation, as the negro came in sight; who then turned about and retreated.

"The neighbourhood was immediately rallied, and a hot pursuit given – which, we understand, has resulted in the capture of the whole gang and the recovery of the greatest part of the money. Seven of the negro men and one woman, it is said were engaged in the murders, and will be brought to trial at the next court in Greenupsburg."

Here my brethren, I want you to notice particularly in the above article, the *ignorant* and *deceitful actions* of this coloured woman. I beg you to view it candidly, as for ETERNITY!!!! Here a *notorious wretch*, with two other confederates had SIXTY of them in a gang, driving them like *brutes* – the men all in chains and hand-cuffs, and by the help of God they got their chains and hand-cuffs thrown off, and caught two of the wretches and put them to death, and beat the other until they thought he was dead, and left him for dead; however, he deceived them, and rising from the ground, this *servile woman* helped him upon his horse, and he made his escape. Brethren, what do you think of this? Was it the natural *fine feelings* of this woman, to save such a wretch alive? I know that the blacks, take them half enlightened and ignorant, are more humane and merciful than the most enlightened and refined European that can be found in all the earth. Let no one say that I assert this because I am prejudiced on the side of my colour, and against the whites or Europeans. For what I write, I do it candidly, for my God and the good of both parties: Natural observations have taught me these things; there is a solemn awe in the hearts of the blacks, as it respects *murdering* men:* whereas the whites, (though they are great cowards) where they have the advantage, or think that there are any prospects of getting it, they murder all before them, in order to subject men to wretchedness and degradation under them. This is the natural result of pride and avarice. But I declare, the actions of this black woman are really insupportable. For my own part, I cannot think it was anything[26] but servile deceit, combined with the most gross ignorance: for we must remember that *humanity*, *kindness* and the *fear of the Lord*, does not consist in protecting *devils*. Here is a set of wretches, who had SIXTY of them in a gang, driving them around the country like *brutes*, to dig up gold and silver for them (which they will get enough of yet). Should the lives of such creatures be spared? Are God and Mammon in league? What has the Lord to do with a gang of desperate wretches, who go *sneaking about the country like robbers* – light upon his people wherever they can get a chance, binding them with chains and hand-cuffs, beat and murder them as they would *rattlesnakes*? Are they not the Lord's enemies? Ought they not to be destroyed? Any person who will save such wretches from destruction is fighting against the Lord, and will receive his just recompense. The black men acted like *blockheads*. Why did they not make sure of the wretch? He would have made sure of them, if he could. It is just the way with black men – eight white men can frighten fifty of them; whereas, if you can only get courage into the blacks, I do declare it, that one good black man can put to death six white men; and I give it as a fact, let twelve black men get well armed for battle, and they will kill and put to flight fifty whites. The reason is, the blacks, once you get them started, they glory in death. The whites have had us under them for more than three centuries, murdering, and treating us like brutes; and, as Mr. Jefferson wisely said, they have never *found us out* – they do not know,

Notes

* Which is the reason the whites take advantage of us.

[25] *Original reads*: mean time [ed.].

[26] *Original reads*: any thing [ed.].

indeed, that there is an unconquerable disposition in the breasts of the blacks, which, when it is fully awakened and put in motion, will be subdued, only with the destruction of the animal existence. Get the blacks started, and if you do not have a gang of tigers and lions to deal with, I am a deceiver of the blacks and of the whites. How sixty of them could let that wretch escape unkilled, I cannot conceive – they will have to suffer as much for the two whom, they secured, as if they had put one hundred to death: if you commence, make sure work – do not trifle, for they will not trifle with you – they want us for their slaves, and think nothing of murdering us in order to subject us to that wretched condition – therefore, if there is an *attempt* made by us, kill or be killed. Now, I ask you, had you not rather be killed than to be a slave to a tyrant, who takes the life of your mother, wife, and dear little children? Look upon your mother, wife and children, and answer God Almighty; and believe this, that it is no more harm for you to kill a man who is trying to kill you, than it is for you to take a drink of water when thirsty; in fact, the man who will stand still and let another murder him, is worse than an infidel, and, if he has common sense, ought not to be pitied. The actions of this deceitful and ignorant coloured woman, in saving the life of a desperate wretch, whose avaricious and cruel object was to drive her, and her companions in miseries through the country like cattle, to make his fortune on their carcasses, are but too much like that of thousands of our brethren in these states: if anything[27] is whispered by one which has any allusion to the melioration of their dreadful condition, they run and tell tyrants, that they may be enabled to keep them the longer in wretchedness and miseries. Oh! coloured people of these United States, I ask you, in the name of that God who made us, have we, in consequence of oppression, nearly lost the spirit of man, and, in no very trifling degree, adopted that of brutes? Do you answer, no? I ask you, then, what set of men can you point me to, in all the world, who are so abjectly employed by their oppressors as we are by our *natural enemies*? How can, Oh! how can those enemies but say that we and our children are not of the HUMAN FAMILY, but were made by our Creator to be an inheritance to them and theirs for ever? How can the slaveholders but say that they can bribe the best coloured person in the country, to sell his brethren for a trifling sum of money, and take that atrocity to confirm them in their avaricious opinion, that we were made to be slaves to them and their children? How could Mr. Jefferson but say, "I advance it therefore as a suspicion only, that the blacks, whether originally a distinct race, or made distinct by time and circumstances, are *inferior* to the whites in the endowments both of body and mind?" – "It," says he, "is not against experience to suppose, that different species of the same genius, or varieties of the same species, may possess different qualifications." [Here, my brethren, listen to him.]

☞"Will not a lover of natural history, then, one who views the gradations in all the races of *animals* with the eye of philosophy, excuse an effort to keep those in the department of MAN as *distinct* as nature has formed them?" – I hope you will try to find out the meaning of this verse – its widest sense and all its bearings: whether you do or not, remember the whites do. This very verse, brethren, having emanated from Mr. Jefferson, a much greater philosopher the world never afforded, has in truth injured us more, and has been as great a barrier to our emancipation as anything[28] that has ever been advanced against us. I hope you will not let it pass unnoticed. He goes on further, and says: "This *unfortunate* difference of colour, and *perhaps* of *faculty*, is a powerful obstacle to

Notes

[27] *Original reads*: any thing [ed.].

[28] *Original reads*: any thing [ed.].

the emancipation of these people. Many of their advocates, while they wish to vindicate the liberty of human nature are anxious also to preserve its *dignity* and *beauty*. Some of these, embarrassed by the question, 'What further is to be done with them?' join themselves in opposition with those who are actuated by sordid avarice only." Now I ask you candidly, my suffering brethren in time, who are candidates for the eternal worlds, how could Mr. Jefferson but have given the world these remarks respecting us, when we are so submissive to them, and so much servile deceit prevail among ourselves – when we so *meanly* submit to their murderous lashes, to which neither the Indians nor any other people under Heaven would submit? No, they would die to a man, before they would suffer such things from men who are no better than themselves, and *perhaps not so good*. Yes, how can our friends but be embarrassed, as Mr. Jefferson says, by the question, "What further is to be done with these people?" For while they are working for our emancipation, we are, by our treachery, wickedness and deceit, working against ourselves and our children – helping ours, and the enemies of God, to keep us and our dear little children in their infernal chains of slavery!!! Indeed, our friends cannot but relapse and join themselves "with those who are actuated by *sordid avarice* only!!!!" For my own part, I am glad Mr. Jefferson has advanced his positions for your sake; for you will either have to contradict or confirm him by your own actions, and not by what our friends have said or done for us; for those things are other men's labours, and do not satisfy the Americans, who are waiting for us to prove to them ourselves, that we are MEN, before they will be willing to admit the fact; for I pledge you my sacred word of honour that Mr. Jefferson's remarks respecting us, have sunk deep into the hearts of millions of the whites, and never will be removed this side of eternity. For how can they, when we are confirming him every day, by our *groveling submissions* and *treachery?* I aver, that when I look over these United States of America, and the world, and see the ignorant deceptions and consequent wretchedness of my brethren, I am brought off-times[29] solemnly to a stand, and in the midst of my reflections I exclaim to my God, "Lord didst thou make us to be slaves to our brethren, the whites?" But when I reflect that God is just, and that millions of my wretched brethren would meet death with glory – yea, more, would plunge into the very mouths of cannons and be torn into particles as minute as the atoms which compose the elements of the earth, in preference to a mean submission to the lash of tyrants, I am with streaming eyes compelled to shrink back into nothingness before my Maker, and exclaim again, thy will be done, O Lord God Almighty.

Men of colour, who are also of sense, for you particularly is my APPEAL designed. Our more ignorant brethren are not able to penetrate its value. I call upon you therefore to cast your eyes upon the wretchedness of your brethren, and to do your utmost to enlighten them – *go to work and enlighten your brethren!* – Let the Lord see you doing what you can to rescue them and yourselves from degradation. Do any of you say that you and your family are free and happy, and what have you to do with the wretched slaves and other people? So can I say, for I enjoy as much freedom as any of you, if I am not quite as well off as the best of you. Look into our freedom and happiness, and see of what kind they are composed!! They are of the very lowest kind – they are the very *dregs!* – they are the most servile and abject kind, that ever a people was in possession of! If any of you wish to know how FREE you are, let one of you start and go through the southern and western States of this country, and unless you travel as a slave to a white man (a servant is a *slave* to the man whom he serves) or have your free papers (which if you

Notes

[29] *Original reads*: oftimes [ed.].

are not careful they will get from you), if they do not take you up and put you in jail, and if you cannot give good evidence of your freedom, sell you into eternal slavery, I am not a living man: or any man of colour, immaterial who he is, or where he came from, if he is not *the fourth from the negro race!!* (as we are called) the white Christians of America will serve him the same, they will sink him into wretchedness and degradation for ever while he lives. And yet some of you have the hardihood to say that you are free and happy! May God have mercy on your freedom and happiness!! I met a coloured man in the street a short time since, with a string of boots on his shoulders; we fell into conversation, and in course of which, I said to him, what a miserable set of people we are! He asked, why? Said I, we are so subjected under the whites, that we cannot obtain the comforts of life, but by cleaning their boots and shoes, old clothes, waiting on them, shaving them &c. Said he, (with the boots on his shoulders) "I am completely happy!!! I never want to live any better or happier than when I can get a plenty of boots and shoes to clean!!!" Oh! how can those who are actuated by avarice only, but think, that our Creator made us to be an inheritance to them for ever, when they see that our greatest glory is centered in such mean and low objects? Understand me, brethren, I do not mean to speak against the occupations by which we acquire enough and sometimes scarcely that, to render ourselves and families comfortable through life. I am subjected to the same inconvenience, as you all. My objections are, to our *glorying* and being *happy* in such low employments; for if we are men, we ought to be thankful to the Lord for the past, and for the future. Be looking forward with thankful hearts to higher attainments than *wielding the razor* and *cleaning boots and shoes*. The man whose aspirations are not *above*, and even *below* these, is, indeed, ignorant and wretched enough. I advanced it therefore to you, not as a *problematical*, but as an unshaken and for ever immovable *fact*, that your full glory and happiness, as well as all other coloured people under Heaven, shall never be fully consummated, but with the *entire emancipation of your enslaved brethren all over the world*. You may therefore, go to work and do what you can to rescue, or join in with tyrants to oppress them and yourselves, until the Lord shall come upon you all like a thief in the night. For I believe it is the will of the Lord that our greatest happiness shall consist in working for the salvation of our whole body. When this is accomplished a burst of glory will shine upon you, which will indeed astonish you and the world. Do any of you say this never will be done? I assure you that God will accomplish it – if nothing else will answer, he will hurl tyrants and devils into *atoms* and make way for his people. But O my brethren! I say unto you again, you must go to work and prepare the way of the Lord.

There is a great work for you to do, as trifling as some of you may think of it. You have to prove to the Americans and the world, that we are MEN, and not *brutes*, as we have been represented, and by millions treated. Remember, to let the aim of your labours among your brethren, and particularly the youths, be the dissemination of education and religion.* It is lamentable, that many of our children go to school, from four until they are eight or ten, and sometimes fifteen years of age, and leave school knowing but a little more about the grammar of their language than a horse does about handling a musket – and not a few of them are really so ignorant, that they are unable to answer a person correctly, general questions in geography, and to hear them

Notes

* Never mind what the ignorant ones among us may say, many of whom when you speak to them for their good, and try to enlighten their minds, laugh at you, and perhaps tell you plump to your face, that they want no instruction from you or any other Niger, and all such aggravating language. Now if you are a man of understanding and sound sense, I conjure you in the name of the Lord, and of all that is good, to impute their actions to ignorance, and wink at their follies, and do your very best to get around them some way or other, for remember they are your brethren; and I declare to you that it is for your interests to teach and enlighten them.

read, would only be to disgust a man who has a taste for reading; which, to do well, as trifling as it may appear to some (to the ignorant in particular), is a great part of learning. Some few of them may make out to scribble tolerably well, over a half sheet of paper, which I believe has hitherto been a powerful obstacle in our way, to keep us from acquiring knowledge. An ignorant father, who knows no more than what nature has taught him, together with what little he acquires by the senses of hearing and seeing, finding his son able to write a neat hand, sets it down for granted that he has as good learning as anybody;[30] the young, ignorant gump, hearing his father or mother, who perhaps may be ten times more ignorant, in point of literature, than himself, extolling his learning, struts about, in the full assurance, that his attainments in literature are sufficient to take him through the world, when, in fact, he has scarcely any learning at all!!!!

I promiscuously fell in conversation once, with an elderly coloured man on the topics of education, and of the great prevalency of ignorance among us: Said he, "I know that our people are very ignorant but my son has a good education: I spent a great deal of money on his education: he can write as well as any white man, and I assure you that no one can fool him," &c. Said I, what else can your son do, besides writing a good hand? Can he post a set of books in a mercantile manner? Can he write a neat piece of composition in prose or in verse? To these interrogations he answered in the negative. Said I, did your son learn, while he was at school, the width and depth of English Grammar? To which he also replied in the negative, telling me his son did not learn those things. Your son, said I, then, has hardly any learning at all – he is almost as ignorant, and more so, than many of those who never went to school one day in all their lives. My friend got a little put out, and so walking off, said that his son could write as well as any white man. Most of the coloured people, when they speak of the education of one among us who can write a neat hand, and who perhaps knows nothing but to scribble and puff pretty fair on a small scrap of paper, immaterial whether his words are grammatical, or spelt correctly, or not; if it only looks beautiful, they say he has as good an education as any white man – he can write as well as any white man, &c. The poor, ignorant creature, hearing this, he is ashamed, forever after to let any person see him humbling himself to another for knowledge but going about trying to deceive those who are more ignorant than himself, he at last falls an ignorant victim to death in wretchedness. I pray that the Lord may undeceive my ignorant brethren, and permit them to throw away pretensions, and seek after the substance of learning. I would crawl on my hands and knees through mud and mire, to the feet of a learned man, where I would sit and humbly supplicate him to instil into me, that which neither devils nor tyrants could remove, only with my life – for coloured people to acquire learning in this country, makes tyrants quake and tremble on their sandy foundation. Why, what is the matter? Why, they know that their infernal deeds of cruelty will be made known to the world. Do you suppose one man of good sense and learning would submit himself, his father, mother, wife and children, to be slaves to a wretched man like himself, who, instead of compensating him for his labours, chains, hand-cuffs and beats him and family almost to death, leaving life enough in them, however, to work for, and call him master? No! no! he would cut his devilish throat from ear to ear and well do slave-holders know it. The bare name of educating the coloured people, scares our cruel oppressors almost to death. But if they do not have enough to be frightened for yet, it will be, because they can always keep us ignorant, and because God approbates their cruelties, with which they have been for centuries murdering us. The whites shall have enough of the blacks, yet as true as God sits on his throne in Heaven.

Notes

[30] *Original reads*: any body [ed.].

Some of our brethren are so very full of learning, that you cannot mention anything[31] to them which they do not know better than yourself!! – nothing is strange to them!! – they knew everything[32] years ago! – if anything[33] should be mentioned in company where they are, immaterial how important it is respecting us or the world, if they had not divulged it; they make light of it, and affect to have known it long before it was mentioned and try to make all in the room, or wherever you may be, believe that your conversation is nothing!! – not worth hearing! All this is the result of ignorance and ill-breeding; for a man of good-breeding, sense and penetration, if he had heard a subject told twenty times over, and should happen to be in company where one should commence telling it again, he would wait with patience on its narrator, and see if he would tell it as it was told in his presence before – paying the most strict attention to what is said, to see if any more light will be thrown on the subject: for all men are not gifted alike in telling, or even hearing the most simple narration. These ignorant, vicious, and wretched men contribute almost as much injury to our body as tyrants themselves, by doing so much for the promotion of ignorance amongst us; for they, making such pretensions to knowledge, such of our youth as are seeking after knowledge, and can get access to them, take them as criterions to go by, who will lead them into a channel, where, unless the Lord blesses them with the privilege of seeing their folly, they will be irretrievably lost forever, while in time!!!

I must close this article by relating the very heart-rending fact, that I have examined school-boys and young men of colour in different parts of the country, in the most simple parts of Murray's English Grammar,[34] and not more than one in thirty was able to give a correct answer to my interrogations. If anyone[35] contradicts me, let him step out of his door into the streets of Boston, New-York, Philadelphia, or Baltimore (no use to mention any other, for the Christians are too charitable further south or west!) – I say, let him who disputes me, step out of his door into the streets of either of those four cities, and promiscuously collect one hundred school-boys, or young men of colour, *who have been to school*, and who are considered by the coloured people to have received an excellent education, because, perhaps, some of them can write a good hand, but who, notwithstanding their neat writing, may be almost as ignorant, in comparison, as a horse – And, I say it, he will hardly find (in this enlightened day, and in the midst of this *charitable* people) five in one hundred, who are able to correct the false grammar of their language – The cause of this almost universal ignorance among us, I appeal to our schoolmasters to declare. Here is a fact, which I this very minute take from the mouth of a young coloured man, who has been to school in this state (Massachusetts) nearly nine years, and who knows grammar this day, *nearly* as well as he did the day he first entered the school-house under a white master. This young man says: "My master would never allow me to study grammar." I asked him, why? "The school committee," said he "forbid the coloured children learning grammar – they would not allow any but the white children to study grammar." It is a notorious fact, that the major part of the white Americans have, ever since we have been among them, tried to keep us ignorant, and make us believe that God made us and our children to be slaves to them and theirs. *Oh! my God, have mercy on Christian Americans!!!*

1829

Notes

31 *Original reads*: any thing [ed.].

32 *Original reads*: every thing [ed.].

33 *Original reads*: any thing [ed.].

34 *Murray's English Grammar* Lindley Murray's (1745–1826) *English Grammar* was one of the most widely used grammar textbooks of the nineteenth century in the United States and Britain.

35 *Original reads*: any one [ed.].

Part Two

The Literatures of Slavery and Freedom

*c.*1830–1865

Introduction

When Andrew Jackson ushered in the "age of the common man" with his election to the presidency in 1828, America had grown remarkably since it declared independence from England in 1776. Still, the country was overwhelmingly Protestant and western European, and coalescing along the Atlantic coast. But by 1860 the nation was undergoing a seismic shift. America had been economically, politically, and culturally transformed by the annexation of Texas, the War with Mexico, the Gold Rush and westward expansion, and by the arrival on its shores of German, Irish Catholic, and Chinese immigrants. Abraham Lincoln's election to the presidency in 1860 spurred the secession of southern states, a collective movement that threatened to tear the nation asunder.

In the meantime, the population of people of African descent rose from two million to four million, or almost 13% of the national population. Native Americans were far from the "vanished Indian" that James Fenimore Cooper romanticized in his 1826 novel *The Last of the Mohicans*, but generations of disease inherited from Europe, warfare, and forced displacement reduced their numbers to less than 500,000 by 1860, the Civil War's eve. Hence African Americans were the largest non-white population in North America. As the market revolution connected increasingly far-flung American territories through such new technology as the first railroads, built in 1826, and Samuel Morse's telegraph, appearing in 1844, the agricultural and small manufacturing economy of the early republic grew into a sprawling network of industrial production in no small part due to slavery and the cotton industry in the South.

Contrary to Thomas Jefferson's belief that slavery would eventually end with the spread of white yeoman farmers and African deportation, the exact opposite happened. Slavery grew and, by 1860, African Americans had become one of the largest enslaved populations in world history. In 1820, the amount of cotton produced in the South amounted to 600,000 bales. Three decades later, that number reached four million. Relying on the subjugation and exploitation of enslaved African Americans, cotton simultaneously supported the textile industry in New England, a profitable interstate slave trade, and a manufacturing boom from Pittsburgh, Pennsylvania, to Cincinnati, Ohio. With significant representation in Congress (thanks, in part, to the

The Wiley Blackwell Anthology of African American Literature: Volume 1, 1746–1920, First Edition.
Edited by Gene Andrew Jarrett.

notorious "three-fifths compromise" that granted each man an extra three votes in the House of Representatives and the presidential Electoral College for every five slaves he owned), southern politicians spearheaded legislation that increased the area in which slavery could exist.

Even as politicians facilitated slavery's expansion, the "peculiar institution" grew controversial in North America and declined in the rest of the Atlantic world. The Missouri Compromise in 1820 prevented slavery from spreading above the 36°30' parallel in the Louisiana Territory. But the lucrative slave economies in such southern states as Mississippi, Alabama, Louisiana, and Arkansas grew, and the Mexican–American War prompted expansion to the Pacific coast. Invigorating debates over the national spread of slavery, these circumstances led to the birth of the Free Soil Party, dedicated to halting the spread of slavery, and precipitated the demise of the Whig Party by 1854. Abolitionists, speaking in radical rhetoric, tried to convince slaveholding Americans of the immorality and misery of slavery. Many of these reformers were part of a Second Great Awakening, exemplified in the evangelism of Charles Grandison Finney rather than the revivalism of Jonathan Edwards, that regarded slavery as a major sin of the new age. By 1859, when the radical John Brown attacked Harper's Ferry, Virginia, these reformers had created the first college to admit African Americans and women (Oberlin, founded in 1835, in Ohio), and launched the first national women's rights movement at Seneca Falls in 1848. The paradoxical quality of the nation's antebellum era, then, lies in its creation of permanent liberal institutions – the public school, evangelical Christianity, civil rights movements – alongside the enduring contradictions of racial inequality, nativism, and sectionalism.

Though few white writers outside of the northern antislavery press explicitly wrote against slavery, the authors of the American Renaissance were nonetheless shaped by the economic, political, and social circumstances under which slavery thrived. The cotton kingdom promoted the expansion of the textile industry in New England, and the ensuing demand for labor led rural New Englanders to move from family farms to urban factories during the 1830 s and 1840 s. The economic changes wrought by industrialization created a cultural landscape ripe for both the dark romanticism of Herman Melville and Nathaniel Hawthorne and the transcendentalism of Ralph Waldo Emerson and Henry David Thoreau. As these American writers took stock of the changes in the young nation, they sought to construct a quintessentially American self that was independent of the British colonial past. In *Nature* (1836), Ralph Waldo Emerson famously calls upon readers to "build their own world," one based on "a poetry and philosophy of insight and not of tradition."

In addition to transcendentalism, the radical abolitionist movement influenced American writers. When William Lloyd Garrison published the first issue of Boston's *The Liberator* in 1831, he channeled the militancy of fellow activist David Walker to spread abolitionism across the North. Calling for the immediate and total abolition of slavery, along with a reassessment of America's supposed commitment to liberty and equality, *The Liberator* was the longest running antislavery publication in the country, inspiring dozens of newspapers that employed many of the leading authors of the era. Poet John Greenleaf Whittier edited Washington's *The National Era*, which serialized Harriet Beecher Stowe's 1852 novel *Uncle Tom's Cabin*. Like James Russell Lowell and Henry Wadsworth Longfellow, Whittier was an early convert to Garrisonian abolitionism. Whittier's 1833 manifesto "Justice and Expediency" called for slavery's end and "an immediate surrender of baneful prejudice to Christian love." A founder of the antislavery Liberty Party in 1839, he wrote poems that enraged slavery's supporters. (Four years earlier, an angry mob savagely beat him.) In 1857, he helped to found, with other reformers including Lowell, Stowe, and Emerson himself, *The Atlantic Monthly*.

The periodical provided space for Whittier's bestselling and commercially acclaimed long narrative poem "Snow-Bound" (1866).

Whittier's commercial success and the creation of literary magazines like *The Atlantic* (whereas *Harper's* was first published in New York in 1850) were part of another development in antebellum American literature – the rise of the bestselling and nationally serialized American author. Although Susanna Rowson's *Charlotte Temple* (1794) sold 1.5 million copies throughout the nineteenth century (thus predating *Uncle Tom's Cabin* as first bestseller in the United States), the British-born Rowson's story of seduction was published first in London in 1792. The story was also part of the sentimental tradition that flourished alongside romanticism – often with much great commercial success – in the antebellum era. Novels like Susan Warner's *The Wide, Wide World* (1850) and Fanny Fern's syndicated columns reached audiences and sales figures far in excess of what Nathaniel Hawthorne or Herman Melville enjoyed (a fact which sheds light on Hawthorne's famed diatribe about America being "wholly given over to a damned mob of scribbling women").

Galvanized into existence by the passage of the Fugitive Slave Law in 1850, Stowe's *Uncle Tom's Cabin* was the apotheosis of not only the sentimental tradition and abolitionist literature but also nationwide commercial success. *Uncle Tom's Cabin* sold 350,000 copies in its first year, and its influence on the slavery debate is encapsulated in 1862, when Abraham Lincoln greets Stowe and, almost in apocryphal fashion, calls her "the little lady who started this big war." Stowe's novel also provoked a new, if antithetical, genre – the "anti-Tom" novel – in which southern writers, such as Mary Henderson Eastman, countered Stowe with the proslavery *Aunt Phillis' Cabin* (1852). In the century and a half since Stowe's novel appeared, other contemporaneous works have supplanted it in the American canon, such as Melville's *Moby-Dick* (1851). Though scorned by his contemporaries, Melville has since been embraced by modernists and postmodernists. Still, Stowe's iconic work and sentimental politics defined popular American literature on the eve of the Civil War.

For certain African American writers, slavery and freedom were not merely sentimental literary tropes. The realities of enslavement and racial subjugation informed their experiences of America. By extension, their literature sought to challenge both southern slavery and its institutional perpetuation of white supremacist ideology. The most popular and persuasive literary form was the antebellum slave narrative. Unlike their early nineteenth century forebears who described personal journeys of deliverance through spiritual autobiographies, slave narratives depicted on behalf of the abolitionist cause African American journeys from slavery to freedom. From 1825 to 1865, over 80 slave narratives were published, most in antislavery newspapers or in pamphlets sold on the antislavery speakers' circuit. Some helped popularize sentimental novels by white authors. Solomon Northup's *Twelve Years a Slave* (1853), for instance, is believed to be the true story of Stowe's Uncle Tom.

White abolitionists also often introduced, edited, and vouched for slave narratives. Narratives written by men and women who became eloquent and influential abolitionist leaders in their own right have most endured the test of time. Three of the most important words of Frederick Douglass's *Narrative of the Life of Frederick Douglass, an American Slave. Written by Himself.* (1845) were those that completed the title. "Written by Himself" signifies his ascent from slavery to freedom, but also his quest for intellectual education, self-mastery, and rhetorical expression. Endorsed by Wendell Phillips and William Lloyd Garrison, Douglass gained international fame as an orator, newspaper editor, and activist for abolitionism and women's rights. Similarly, William Wells Brown's 1849 *Narrative* helped to launch the former slave into a lucrative public speaking career in which he could publish works outside of the slave narrative genre, such as his novel *Clotel; or, The President's Daughter* (1853) and the 1858 play *The Escape; or, a Leap for Freedom*. Harriet Jacob's *Incidents in the Life of a Slave Girl. Written by Herself.* (1861) was serialized in Horace Greeley's *New-York Tribune* and supported by Lydia Maria Child.

The popularity of reform and sentimental literature in the antebellum North meant that even African American texts written outside of the slave narrative genre owed their success to antislavery publications and institutions of protest within the northern free African American community. By 1860, over 450,000 African Americans, or 11% of the total African American population, were free. But systemic racial discrimination meant that most free people lived in tightly knit communities in coastal cities like Boston, New York, and Philadelphia – places that were also centers of the publishing industry. Although the first novel by a person of African descent was *The Mulatto* (1837), by New Orleans native Victor Séjour and published in France, this proved anomalous. Unlike Séjour, most African American writers lived in the urban North and had deep connections to both the free black communities in which they lived and the antislavery networks that surrounded these communities.

Thus a novel like William Wells Brown's *Clotel* went through multiple editions, including serialization in the *Weekly Anglo-African*, an African American magazine based in New York City. Likewise, writers like Maria Stewart, Jarena Lee, and Nancy Prince published political speeches, religious sermons, and travel narratives after first establishing themselves within their own communities. Stewart's *Religion and the Pure Principles of Morality* (1831) appeared after she gained local renown in Boston's black community. An upshot of the antebellum developments in publishing, literary circulation, and speaking was that the decade immediately preceding the Civil War witnessed an early renaissance in African American literature. In the powerful testimony of Douglass, the adoption and repurposing of popular sentimental tropes by Brown and Jacobs, the fiction of Harriet Wilson, or the political and theoretical writing of Martin Delany, African American literature formed a constitutive and vital element of American literature as a whole. All of antebellum African American literature may be seen as a form of nation-making, a way for the enslaved and the free to interrogate the racial politics of the democratic "self-reliance" espoused by leading American authors of the age.

Framed by the rise of American antislavery societies and the period of the Civil War, antebellum antislavery literature by Brown, Jacobs, and Douglass also demonstrate an economic sophistication in which their critiques of slave capitalism anticipated the anxieties of white, bourgeois, and Protestant readers who were experiencing the modernization of the North. The renaissance of African American literature in the 1850s, distinguished by the novels of Brown, Frank J. Webb, Harriet Wilson, and Martin Delany, indicated an evolution across multiple genres, ranging from the slave narrative and the novel to drama and poetry, buoyed, in part, by the special coalescence of ideological, economic, and political forces as slavery became increasingly untenable and as the country began to brace for the Civil War.

In the mid-nineteenth century, nationalism was one of the great ideological forces that African American writers had claimed as their own and had concomitantly expressed in literature. Sown in the early part of the nineteenth century, the seeds of African American literary nationalism blossomed into the antebellum era, inviting present-day study not because of the clarity of its compelling argument for a black nation within the US nation. Rather, nationalism – which intrigued Walker and Delany, most notably – demands new explanations of its sometimes conflicting, sometimes compatible, set of biological, cultural, political, and spiritual doctrines. That diverse set of ideologies complicates the one-to-one relationship between racial nationalism, on the one hand, and African American literature, on the other.

Omar ibn Said (1770–1864)

Of the 12 million Africans transported to the Americas through the transatlantic slave trade between the sixteenth and nineteenth centuries, about one-fifth were Muslims. Omar ibn Said was one of them, and his 1831 *Autobiography of Omar ibn Said, Slave in North Carolina* is the earliest preserved Muslim manuscript written in America. Although scholars have long believed that Said converted to Christianity in 1820, and in the *Autobiography* he writes of replacing his Mohammedan prayers with those about "Our Father," the precise character of his faith is ambiguous. Evidence suggests that Said maintained some degree of spiritual autonomy by continuing to write in Arabic. In addition to his *Autobiography* and Koranic translations, he wrote a dedication to Allah in the front of his Bible, and Surat An-Nasr, a prayer calling for the conversion of unbelievers to Islam, on the back of a card dated 1857. (The fact that the English caption on the card identifies the Arabic inscription as "the Lord's Prayer," and evidence of Said's Christian piety, also hints at a subversive element in his religiosity.)

Omar ibn Said was born in Futa Toro, a region along the present-day middle Senegal River in West Africa. He was Fullah, a Bedouin people in Yemen, and his family was highly respected for its Muslim faith. Said had extensive knowledge of Christianity and Judaism as a result of his travels through Timbuktu and Cairo, which he visited during his pilgrimage to Mecca. In 1807, he was captured, enslaved, and taken to America where a cruel master in Charleston, South Carolina, briefly owned him. Said soon fled, taking refuge in a church in Fayetteville, South Carolina, but there he was recaptured and thrown in jail as a runaway slave. Since he was unable to communicate in English, he wrote in Arabic on his jail cell wall with charcoal, petitioning for his freedom. His pleas were neither understood nor answered.

Eventually, Said was sold to General Owen of Fayetteville, North Carolina. With the Owen family, Said was called various names, including Uncle Moreau and Prince Omeroh. By his own accounts they respected his erudition and treated him very kindly, both obtaining for him an Arabic translation of the Bible and allowing him ample time to write and study. In 1831 he wrote his narrative, and transcribed pieces from the Koran from memory. He died in 1864, at the age of 94, without ever seeing his original homeland again.

Further reading

Alryyes, Ala. "Introduction: 'Arabic Work,' Islam, and American Literature." *A Muslim American Slave: The Life of Omar ibn Said*. Ed. Ala Alryyes. Madison: University of Wisconsin Press, 2011. 3–46.

Austin, Allan D. "Contemporary Contexts for Omar's *Life* and Life." A Muslim American Slave: The Life of Omar ibn Said. Ed. Ala Alryyes. Madison: University of Wisconsin Press, 2011. 133–151.

Diouf, Sylviane A. "'God Does not Allow Kings to Enslave Their People': Islamic Reformists and the Transatlantic Slave Trade." A Muslim American Slave: The Life of Omar ibn Said. Ed. Ala Alryyes. Madison: University of Wisconsin Press, 2011. 162–181.

Huntwick, John. "'I Wish to Be Seen in Our Land Called Afrika': Umar b. Sayyid's Appeal to Be Released from Slavery." Journal of Arabic and Islamic Studies 5 (2003–2004): 63–77.

Marfo, Florence. "African Muslims in African American Literature." Callaloo 32.4 (2009): 1213–1222.

Osman, Ghada. "Representing the West in the Arabic Language: The Slave Narrative of Omar ibn Said." Journal of Islamic Studies 15.3 (2004): 331–343.

The Wiley Blackwell Anthology of African American Literature: Volume 1, 1746–1920, First Edition.
Edited by Gene Andrew Jarrett.

Autobiography of Omar ibn Said, Slave in North Carolina

In the name of God, the merciful, the gracious. God grant his blessing upon our Prophet Mohammed. Blessed be He in whose hands is the kingdom and who is Almighty; who created death and life that he might test You; for he is exalted; he is the forgiver (of sins), who created seven heavens one above the other. Do you discern anything trifling in creation? Bring back your thoughts. Do you see anything worthless? Recall your vision in earnest. Turn your eye inward for it is diseased. God has adorned the heavens and the world with lamps, and has made us missiles for the devils, and given us for them a grievous punishment, and to those who have disbelieved their Lord, the punishment of hell and pains of body. Whoever associates with them shall hear a boiling caldron, and what is cast therein may fitly represent those who suffer under the anger of God. Ask them if a prophet has not been sent unto them. They say, "Yes; a prophet has come to us, but we have lied to him." We said, "God has not sent us down anything, and you are in grievous error." They say, "If we had listened and been wise we should not now have been suffering the punishment of the Omniscient." So they confess they have sinned in destroying the followers of the Omniscient. Those who fear their Lord and profess his name, they receive pardon and great honor. Guard your words, (ye wicked), make it known that God is all-wise in all his manifestations. Do you not know from the creation that God is full of skill? that He has made for you the way of error, and you have walked therein, and have chosen to live upon what your god Nasûr has furnished you? Believe on Him who dwells in heaven, who has fitted the earth to be your support and it shall give you food. Believe on Him who dwells in Heaven, who has sent you a prophet, and you shall understand what a teacher (He has sent you). Those that were before them deceived them (in regard to their prophet). And how came they to reject him? Did they not see in the heavens above them, how the fowls of the air receive with pleasure that which is sent them? God looks after all. Believe ye: it is He who supplies your wants, that you may take his gifts and enjoy them, and take great pleasure in them. And now will you go on in error, or walk in the path of righteousness. Say to them, "He who regards you with care, and who has made for you the heavens and the earth and gives you prosperity, Him you think little of. This is He that planted you in the earth, and to whom you are soon to be gathered." But they say, "If you are men of truth, tell us when shall this promise be fulfilled?" Say to them, "Does not God know? and am not I an evident Prophet?" When those who disbelieve shall see the things draw near before their faces, it shall then be told them, "These are the things about which you made inquiry." Have you seen that God has destroyed me or those with me? or rather that He has shewn us mercy? And who will defend the unbeliever from a miserable punishment? Say, "Knowledge is from God." Say, "Have you not seen that your water has become impure? Who will bring you fresh water from the fountain?"

From Omar to Sheikh Hunter

O Sheikh Hunter,[1] I cannot write my life because I have forgotten much of my own language, as well as of the Arabic. Do not be hard upon me, my brother. To God let many thanks be paid for his great mercy and goodness.

Notes

[1] *O Sheikh Hunter* It is unclear who this person is. A "sheikh" is an Arabic honorific for an elder or scholar.

In the name of God, the Gracious, the Merciful. Thanks be to God, supreme in goodness and kindness and grace, and who is worthy of all honor, who created all things for his service, even man's power of action and of speech.

You asked me to write my life. I am not able to do this because I have much forgotten my own, as well as the Arabic language. Neither can I write very grammatically or according to the true idiom. And so, my brother, I beg you, in God's name, not to blame me, for I am a man of weak eyes, and of a weak body.

My name is Omar ibn Seid. My birthplace was Fut Tûr,[2] between the two rivers. I sought knowledge under the instruction of a Sheikh called Mohammed Seid, my own brother, and Sheikh Soleiman Kembeh, and Sheikh Gabriel Abdal. I continued my studies twenty-five years, and then returned to my home where I remained six years. Then there came to our place a large army, who killed many men, and took me, and brought me to the great sea, and sold me into the hands of the Christians, who bound me and sent me on board a great ship and we sailed upon the great sea a month and a half, when we came to a place called Charleston in the Christian language. There they sold me to a small, weak, and wicked man called Johnson, a complete infidel, who had no fear of God at all. Now I am a small man, and unable to do hard work so I fled from the hand of Johnson and after a month came to a place called Fayd-il.[3] There I saw some great houses (churches). On the new moon I went into a church to pray. A lad saw me and rode off to the place of his father and informed him that he had seen a black man in the church. A man named Handah[4] and another man with him on horseback, came attended by a troop of dogs. They took me and made me go with them twelve miles to a place called Fayd-il, where they put me into a great house from which I could not go out. I continued in the great house (which, in the Christian language, they called *jail)* sixteen days and nights. One Friday the jailor came and opened the door of the house and I saw a great many men, all Christians, some of whom called out to me, "What is your name? Is it Omar or Seid?" I did not understand their Christian language. A man called Bob Mumford took me and led me out of the jail, and I was very well pleased to go with them to their place. I stayed at Mumford's four days and nights, and then a man named Jim Owen, son-in-law of Mumford, having married his daughter Betsey, asked me if I was willing to go to a place called Bladen. I said, Yes, I was willing. I went with them and have remained in the place of Jim Owen until now.

Before[5] I came into the hand of Gen. Owen a man by the name of Mitchell came to buy me. He asked me if I were willing to go to Charleston City. I said "*No, no, no, no, no, no, no,* I not willing to go to Charleston. I stay in the hand of Jim Owen."

O ye people of North Carolina, O ye people of S. Carolina, O ye people of America all of you; have you among you any two such men as Jim Owen and John Owen? These men are good men. What food they eat they give to me to eat. As they clothe themselves they clothe me. They permit me to read the gospel of God, our Lord, and Saviour, and King; who regulates all our circumstances, our health and wealth, and who bestows his mercies willingly, not by constraint. According to power I open my heart, as to a great light, to receive the true way, the way of the Lord Jesus the Messiah.

Before I came to the Christian country, my religion was the religion of "Mohammed, the Apostle of God – may God have mercy upon him and give him peace." I walked to the mosque[6] before day-break, washed my face and head and hands and feet. I prayed

Notes

[2] *Fut Tûr* or Futa Toro, located along the Senegal River and encompassing both northern Senegal and southern Mauritania.

[3] *Fayd-il* Fayetteville, North Carolina.

[4] *Handah* possibly Hunter.

[5] *Before* given the context, "After" would appear to be correct here.

[6] *mosque* Islamic place of worship.

at noon, prayed in the afternoon, prayed at sunset, prayed in the evening. I gave alms every year, gold, silver, seeds, cattle, sheep, goats, rice, wheat, and barley. I gave tithes of all the above-named things. I went every year to the holy war against the infidels. I went on pilgrimage to Mecca,[7] as all did who were able. My father had six sons and five daughters, and my mother had three sons and one daughter. When I left my country I was thirty-seven years old; I have been in the country of the Christians twenty-four years. Written AD 1831.

O ye people of North Carolina, O ye people of South Carolina, O all ye people of America – The first son of Jim Owen is called Thomas, and his sister is called Masa-jein.[8] This is an excellent family.

Tom Owen and Nell Owen have two sons and a daughter. The first son is called Jim and the second John. The daughter is named Melissa.

Seid Jim Owen and his wife Betsey have two sons and five daughters. Their names are Tom, and John, and Mercy, Miriam, Sophia, Margaret and Eliza. This family is a very nice family. The wife of John Owen is called Lucy and an excellent wife she is. She had five children. Three of them died and two are still living.

O ye Americans, ye people of North Carolina – have you, have you, have you, have you, have you among you a family like this family, having so much love to God as they?

Formerly I, Omar, loved to read the book of the Koran the famous. General Jim Owen and his wife used to read the gospel, and they read it to me very much – the gospel of God, our Lord, our Creator, our King, He that orders all our circumstances, health and wealth, willingly, not constrainedly, according to his power. Open thou my heart to the gospel, to the way of uprightness. Thanks to the Lord of all worlds, thanks in abundance. He is plenteous in mercy and abundant in goodness.

For the law was given by Moses but grace and truth were by the Jesus, the Messiah.

When I was a Mohammedan I prayed thus: "Thanks be to God, Lord of all worlds, the merciful, the gracious, Lord of the day of Judgment, thee we serve, on thee we call for help. Direct us in the right way, the way of those on whom thou hast had mercy, with whom thou hast not been angry and who walk not in error. Amen." But now I pray "Our Father," etc., in the words of our Lord Jesus the Messiah.

I reside in this our country by reason of great necessity. Wicked men took me by violence and sold me to the Christians. We sailed a month and a half on the great sea to the place called Charleston in the Christian land. I fell into the hands of a small, weak and wicked man, who feared not God at all nor did he read (the gospel) at all nor pray.

I was afraid to remain with a man so depraved and who committed so many crimes and I ran away. After a month our Lord God brought me forward to the hand of a good man, who fears God, and loves to do good, and whose name is Jim Owen and whose brother is called Col. John Owen. These are two excellent men. I am residing in Bladen County.

I continue in the hand of Jim Owen who never beats me, nor scolds me. I neither go hungry nor naked, and I have no hard work to do. I am not able to do hard work for I am a small man and feeble. During the last twenty years I have known no want in the hand of Jim Owen.

1831

Notes

[7] *Mecca* the birthplace of Mohammed, located in today's Saudi Arabia.

[8] *Masa-jein* possibly Martha Jane.

Frederick Douglass (1818–1895)

In "Frederick Douglass," a poem included in his 1895 book *Majors and Minors*, Paul Laurence Dunbar eulogizes the man as "no soft-tongued apologist; / He spoke straight-forward, fearlessly uncowed; / The sunlight of his truth dispelled the mist / And set in bold relief each dark-hued cloud." After spending the first 20 years of his life as the property of other men, Douglass broke new ground for African Americans, not just literarily but also politically. He was the only African American to attend the 1848 Seneca Falls Convention that launched the first wave of American feminism. In 1872, he was the first African American man placed on a vice-presidential ticket (alongside the first female presidential nominee, Victoria Woodhull). And in 1888, he was the first African American to receive a vote for President of the United States on a major party's roll call. To be sure, racial and political controversies dogged him later in life (his second marriage to Helen Pitts, a white woman, in 1884, for instance, led many to accuse him of racial infidelity). Yet Douglass's uncompromising push for human equality nonetheless distinguished his career as an abolitionist, author, and statesman.

He was born Frederick August Washington Bailey in Talbot County, Maryland. After his mother died when he was seven, he was sent to the Wye House Plantation, under overseer Aaron Anthony. When Anthony died, he was given as a present to Lucretia Auld, who sent him to Baltimore to serve her brother-in-law, Hugh Auld. With the Aulds, Douglass learned the power of literacy when his new mistress, Sophia Auld, began to teach him how to read the alphabet. When her husband found out, he put a stop to the lessons for fear that it would "spoil" his property. Still, Douglass secretly continued his studies by enlisting white neighborhood school children, and by paying attention to the handwriting of white men for whom he worked. A quarrel between Hugh and Thomas Auld (the legal owner) precipitated Douglass's return to his boyhood plantation, where Thomas decided to farm him out to a notorious slave breaker, Edward Covey, to curb his rebellious spirit. In a momentous scene, Covey's cruel treatment of Douglass led to a fight between the two men, in which the 16-year-old slave emerged victorious. Douglass was later sent to William Freeland's plantation, where he gained his first experience as a community leader by teaching fellow slaves in a weekly Sunday school. Again, plantation owners broke up this attempt at slave self-education, and, once again, Douglass's defiance continued. While with Freeland, he made his first attempt at escape. Success would finally come three years later in 1838 in Baltimore.

Douglass refuses to reveal the details of his flight to freedom in his 1845 *Narrative of the Life of Frederick Douglass, an American Slave. Written by Himself*. He feared that they would risk the enterprise and safety of fellow African Americans and their white allies to the devices of slaveholding authorities. Later, Douglass revealed that he escaped with the help of his future first wife, Anna Murray (a free black woman in Baltimore), and a network of African American sailors. Taking a train out of Baltimore on September 3, 1838, he arrived the next day in New York City, where he sent for Murray and gained assistance from local African American abolitionist David Ruggles. Douglass and Murray were married on September 15, 1838, a union that lasted over 40 years and

The Wiley Blackwell Anthology of African American Literature: Volume 1, 1746–1920, First Edition.
Edited by Gene Andrew Jarrett.

produced five children. The couple soon settled in New Bedford, Massachusetts, where they joined the local African American church and abolitionist community.

In New Bedford, Douglass took an active role in the movement that would define his public career. By 1841, as a subscriber to William Lloyd Garrison's *The Liberator*, Douglass delivered his first antislavery speech before the Massachusetts Anti-Slavery Society's annual convention at Nantucket's African Meeting House. His natural ability as an orator led him to participate in the American Anti-Slavery Society's Hundred Conventions project, a six-month tour through abolitionist circles in the East and Midwest. On this trip Douglass encountered violent attacks by anti-abolitionist crowds. In Pendleton, Indiana, a mob chased and beat him, and it probably would have killed him if not for the help of a local Quaker family.

Motivated by insinuations that a man of his gifts could never have grown up a slave, Douglass penned his *Narrative* in 1845, when it also instantly became a best-seller around the world. Worried that the accompanying publicity would make him vulnerable to recapture, white abolitionist friends encouraged Douglass to go on a lecture tour of Great Britain shortly after the release of this narrative. During his two-year tour of England, Scotland, and Ireland – on which he met Irish nationalist Daniel O'Connell, and British abolitionist Thomas Clarkson – Douglass was finally legally freed after British supporters raised money to purchase him from Thomas Auld. By 1847, he was back in Rochester, New York, where he launched the publication of his newspaper, *The North Star*, which he would continue to write for and publish until 1863. It was here that he published his novella, *The Heroic Slave*, in 1853.

During the 1850s, as America lurched towards the Civil War, Douglass broke with his former ally and mentor, William Lloyd Garrison, who also wrote the preface to the 1845 *Narrative*. They had quarreled over Douglass's newspaper ventures, and by 1851, when Douglass merged *The North Star* with Gerrit Smith's *Liberty Party Paper* to create *Frederick Douglass' Paper*, the ideological differences and the increasingly adversarial personal relationship between Douglass and Garrison proved too great to mend. This split gave Douglass cause to reassess his goals and philosophy of reform. Out of this reflection came an expanded version of his autobiography, *My Bondage and My Freedom*, in 1855. Throughout the decade Douglass's radicalism increased, even having ties to John Brown. Although he did not approve of John Brown's 1859 raid on Harper's Ferry, Douglass fled briefly to Canada to avoid investigation by white authorities. By the time Abraham Lincoln's Emancipation Proclamation authorized the enlistment of African Americans into the Union Army in 1863, Douglass was back in Massachusetts, where he actively recruited young African American men for the Fifty-Fourth Infantry. His son and namesake, Frederick Douglass, Jr, enlisted in the Fifty-Fourth, and gained renown in his own right for participating in the infantry's famed attack on Fort Wagner, South Carolina.

After the war, Douglass supported the Republican program for suffrage and civil rights, and was awarded with an appointment as president of the Freedman's Savings Bank. He also served as consul to Haiti and chargé d'affaires for the Dominican Republic, but left after two years over disagreements with the Ulysses S. Grant presidential administration over US policy in that country. In 1870, his last newspaper, the *New National Era*, appeared in Washington, DC, where he moved after a fire destroyed his Rochester home in 1872. Although his governmental appointments and lecture circuit prominence ensured comfortable final decades of his life, the last 20 years in particular, as documented in the last and most comprehensive edition of his autobiography, *The Life and Times of Frederick Douglass* (1881, 1892), witnessed his transition to highly respected relic of a quickly fading past. Douglass's opposition to African American migration from the South during the 1879 Exoduster movement, the failure of the Freedman's Bank, and his marriage to a white woman left him vulnerable to criticism by a younger generation of African Americans frustrated by his perceived conservatism and the failed promise of Southern Reconstruction. He died in 1895 just hours after speaking at a National Council of Women meeting in Washington, DC.

Further reading

Bromell, Nick. "A 'Voice from the Enslaved': The Origins of Frederick Douglass's Political Philosophy of Democracy." *American Literary History* 23.4 (2011): 697–723.

Buccola, Nicholas. *The Political Thought of Frederick Douglass: In Pursuit of American Liberty*. New York: New York University Press, 2012.

Chaney, Michael A. "Heartfelt Thanks to *Punch* for the Picture: Frederick Douglass and the Transnational Jokework of Slave Caricature." *American Literature* 82.1 (2010): 57–90.

Dinius, Marcy. *The Camera and the Press: American Visual and Print Culture in the Age of the Daguerreotype*. Philadelphia: University of Pennsylvania Press, 2012. Ch. 6.

Gooding-Williams, Robert. *In the Shadow of Du Bois: Afro-Modern Political Thought in America*. Cambridge: Harvard University Press, 2009.

Lee, Maurice S., ed. *The Cambridge Companion to Frederick Douglass*. New York: Cambridge University Press, 2009.

Lee, Maurice S. "The 1850s: The First Renaissance of Black Letters." A Companion to African American Literature. Ed. Gene Andrew Jarrett. Malden, MA: Wiley-Blackwell, 2010. 103–118.

Levine, Robert S. and Samuel Otter, eds. *Frederick Douglass and Herman Melville: Essays in Relation*. Chapel Hill: University of North Carolina Press, 2008.

Meyers, Peter C. *Frederick Douglass: Race and the Rebirth of American Liberalism*. Lawrence: University Press of Kansas, 2008.

Newman, Lance. "Free Soil and the Abolitionist Forests of Frederick Douglass's 'The Heroic Slave'." *American Literature* 81.1 (2009): 127–152.

Oakes, John. *The Radical and the Republican: Frederick Douglass, Abraham Lincoln, and the Triumph of Antislavery Politics*. New York: Norton, 2007.

Polyné, Millery. *From Douglass to Duvalier: U.S. African Americans, Haiti, and Pan Americanism, 1870–1964*. Gainesville: University Press of Florida, 2010. Ch. 1.

Ramsey, William M. "Frederick Douglass, Southerner." *The Southern Literary Journal* 40.1 (2007): 19–38.

Stauffer, John. *Giants: The Parallel Lives of Frederick Douglass and Abraham Lincoln*. New York: Twelve, 2008.

Wilson, Ivy G. "On Native Ground: Transnationalism, Frederick Douglass, and 'The Heroic Slave'." *PMLA: Publications of the Modern Language Association of America* 121.2 (2006): 453–468.

Narrative of the Life of Frederick Douglass, an American Slave. Written by Himself.

Preface[1]

IN the month of August, 1841, I attended an anti-slavery convention in Nantucket, at which it was my happiness to become acquainted with FREDERICK DOUGLASS, the writer of the following Narrative. He was a stranger to nearly every member of that body; but, having recently made his escape from the southern prison-house of bondage, and feeling his curiosity excited to ascertain the principles and measures of the abolitionists – of whom, he had heard a somewhat vague description while he was a slave – he was induced to give his attendance, on the occasion alluded to, though at that time a resident in New Bedford.

Notes

NARRATIVE OF THE LIFE OF FREDERICK DOUGLASS, AN AMERICAN SLAVE. WRITTEN BY HIMSELF.

[1] Preface by William Lloyd Garrison (1805–1879), American abolitionist and journalist.

Fortunate, most fortunate occurrence! – fortunate for the millions of his manacled brethren, yet panting for deliverance from their awful thraldom! – fortunate for the cause of negro emancipation, and of universal liberty! – fortunate for the land of his birth, which he has already done so much to save and bless! – fortunate for a large circle of friends and acquaintances, whose sympathy and affection he has strongly secured by the many sufferings he has endured, by his virtuous traits of character, by his ever-abiding remembrance of those who are in bonds, as being bound with them! – fortunate for the multitudes, in various parts of our republic, whose minds he has enlightened on the subject of slavery, and who have been melted to tears by his pathos, or roused to virtuous indignation by his stirring eloquence against the enslavers of men! – fortunate for himself, as it at once brought him into the field of public usefulness, "gave the world assurance of a MAN,"[2] quickened the slumbering energies of his soul, and consecrated him to the great work of breaking the rod of the oppressor, and letting the oppressed go free!

I shall never forget his first speech at the convention – the extraordinary emotion it excited in my own mind – the powerful impression it created upon a crowded auditory, completely taken by surprise – the applause which followed from the beginning to the end of his felicitous remarks. I think I never hated slavery so intensely as at that moment; certainly, my perception of the enormous outrage which is inflicted by it, on the godlike nature of its victims, was rendered far more clear than ever. There stood one, in physical proportion and stature commanding and exact – in intellect richly endowed – in natural eloquence a prodigy – in soul manifestly "created but a little lower than the angels"[3] – yet a slave, ay, a fugitive slave – trembling for his safety, hardly daring to believe that on the American soil, a single white person could be found who would befriend him at all hazards, for the love of God and humanity! Capable of high attainments as an intellectual and moral being – needing nothing but a comparatively small amount of cultivation to make him an ornament to society and a blessing to his race – by the law of the land, by the voice of the people, by the terms of the slave code, he was only a piece of property, a beast of burden, a chattel personal, nevertheless!

A beloved friend from New Bedford prevailed on Mr. DOUGLASS to address the convention. He came forward to the platform with a hesitancy and embarrassment, necessarily the attendants of a sensitive mind in such a novel position. After apologizing for his ignorance, and reminding the audience that slavery was a poor school for the human intellect and heart, he proceeded to narrate some of the facts in his own history as a slave, and in the course of his speech gave utterance to many noble thoughts and thrilling reflections. As soon as he had taken his seat, filled with hope and admiration, I rose, and declared that PATRICK HENRY,[4] of revolutionary fame, never made a speech more eloquent in the cause of liberty, than the one we had just listened to from the lips of that hunted fugitive. So I believed at that time – such is my belief now. I reminded the audience of the peril which surrounded this self-emancipated young man at the North – even in Massachusetts, on the soil of the Pilgrim Fathers, among the descendants of revolutionary sires; and I appealed to them, whether they would ever allow him to be carried back into slavery – law or no law, constitution or no constitution. The response was unanimous and in thunder-tones – "NO!" "Will you succor and protect him as a brother-man – a resident of the old Bay State?"[5] "YES!" shouted

Notes

[2] *"assurance of a* MAN" Shakespeare, *Hamlet* 3.4.62.

[3] *"created but a little lower than the angels"* Psalm 8:5.

[4] Patrick Henry (1736–1799), American orator and revolutionary-era politician best known for his declaration, "Give me liberty, or give me death!"

[5] *Bay State* Massachusetts.

the whole mass, with an energy so startling, that the ruthless tyrants south of Mason and Dixon's line might almost have heard the mighty burst of feeling, and recognized it as the pledge of an invincible determination, on the part of those who gave it, never to betray him that wanders, but to hide the outcast, and firmly to abide the consequences.

It was at once deeply impressed upon my mind, that, if Mr. Douglass could be persuaded to consecrate his time and talents to the promotion of the anti-slavery enterprise, a powerful impetus would be given to it, and a stunning blow at the same time inflicted on northern prejudice against a colored complexion. I therefore endeavored to instil hope and courage into his mind, in order that he might dare to engage in a vocation so anomalous and responsible for a person in his situation; and I was seconded in this effort by warm-hearted friends, especially by the late General Agent of the Massachusetts Anti-Slavery Society, Mr. John A. Collins, whose judgment in this instance entirely coincided with my own. At first, he could give no encouragement; with unfeigned diffidence, he expressed his conviction that he was not adequate to the performance of so great a task; the path marked out was wholly an untrodden one; he was sincerely apprehensive that he should do more harm than good. After much deliberation, however, he consented to make a trial; and ever since that period, he has acted as a lecturing agent, under the auspices either of the American or the Massachusetts Anti-Slavery Society. In labors he has been most abundant; and his success in combating prejudice, in gaining proselytes, in agitating the public mind, has far surpassed the most sanguine expectations that were raised at the commencement of his brilliant career. He has borne himself with gentleness and meekness, yet with true manliness of character. As a public speaker, he excels in pathos, wit, comparison, imitation, strength of reasoning, and fluency of language. There is in him that union of head and heart, which is indispensable to an enlightenment of the heads and a winning of the hearts of others. May his strength continue to be equal to his day! May he continue to "grow in grace, and in the knowledge of God," that he may be increasingly serviceable in the cause of bleeding humanity, whether at home or abroad!

It is certainly a very remarkable fact, that one of the most efficient advocates of the slave population, now before the public, is a fugitive slave, in the person of Frederick Douglass; and that the free colored population of the United States are as ably represented by one of their own number, in the person of Charles Lenox Remond,[6] whose eloquent appeals have extorted the highest applause of multitudes on both sides of the Atlantic. Let the calumniators of the colored race despise themselves for their baseness and illiberality of spirit, and henceforth cease to talk of the natural inferiority of those who require nothing but time and opportunity to attain to the highest point of human excellence.

It may, perhaps, be fairly questioned, whether any other portion of the population of the earth could have endured the privations, sufferings and horrors of slavery, without having become more degraded in the scale of humanity than the slaves of African descent. Nothing has been left undone to cripple their intellects, darken their minds, debase their moral nature, obliterate all traces of their relationship to mankind; and yet how wonderfully they have sustained the mighty load of a most frightful bondage, under which they have been groaning for centuries! To illustrate the effect of slavery on the white man – to show that he has no powers of endurance, in such a condition, superior to those of his black brother – Daniel O'Connell,[7] the distinguished advocate of

Notes

[6] Charles Lenox Remond (1810–1873), a free-born African American lecturer and abolitionist.

[7] Daniel O'Connell (1775–1847), Irish political leader known as "the Liberator," who fought for Catholic emancipation and Irish independence.

universal emancipation, and the mightiest champion of prostrate but not conquered Ireland, relates the following anecdote in a speech delivered by him in the Conciliation Hall, Dublin, before the Loyal National Repeal Association, March 31, 1845. "No matter," said Mr. O'Connell, "under what specious term it may disguise itself, slavery is still hideous. *It has a natural, an inevitable tendency to brutalize every noble faculty of man*. An American sailor, who was cast away on the shore of Africa, where he was kept in slavery for three years, was, at the expiration of that period, found to be imbruted and stultified – he had lost all reasoning power; and having forgotten his native language, could only utter some savage gibberish between Arabic and English, which nobody could understand, and which even he himself found difficulty in pronouncing. So much for the humanizing influence of THE DOMESTIC INSTITUTION!" Admitting this to have been an extraordinary case of mental deterioration, it proves at least that the white slave can sink as low in the scale of humanity as the black one.

Mr. DOUGLASS has very properly chosen to write his own Narrative, in his own style, and according to the best of his ability, rather than to employ someone[8] else. It is, therefore, entirely his own production; and, considering how long and dark was the career he had to run as a slave – how few have been his opportunities to improve his mind since he broke his iron fetters – it is, in my judgment, highly creditable to his head and heart. He who can peruse it without a tearful eye, a heaving breast, an afflicted spirit – without being filled with an unutterable abhorrence of slavery and all its abettors, and animated with a determination to seek the immediate overthrow of that execrable system – without trembling for the fate of this country in the hands of a righteous God, who is ever on the side of the oppressed, and whose arm is not shortened that it cannot save – must have a flinty heart, and be qualified to act the part of a trafficker "in slaves and the souls of men." I am confident that it is essentially true in all its statements; that nothing has been set down in malice, nothing exaggerated, nothing drawn from the imagination; that it comes short of the reality, rather than overstates a single fact in regard to SLAVERY AS IT IS. The experience of FREDERICK DOUGLASS, as a slave, was not a peculiar one; his lot was not especially a hard one; his case may be regarded as a very fair specimen of the treatment of slaves in Maryland, in which State it is conceded that they are better fed and less cruelly treated than in Georgia, Alabama, or Louisiana. Many have suffered incomparably more, while very few on the plantations have suffered less, than himself. Yet how deplorable was his situation! what terrible chastisements were inflicted upon his person! what still more shocking outrages were perpetrated upon his mind! with all his noble powers and sublime aspirations, how like a brute was he treated, even by those professing to have the same mind in them that was in Christ Jesus! to what dreadful liabilities was he continually subjected! how destitute of friendly counsel and aid, even in his greatest extremities! how heavy was the midnight of woe which shrouded in blackness the last ray of hope, and filled the future with terror and gloom! what longings after freedom took possession of his breast, and how his misery augmented, in proportion as he grew reflective and intelligent – thus demonstrating that a happy slave is an extinct man! how he thought, reasoned, felt, under the lash of the driver, with the chains upon his limbs! what perils he encountered in his endeavors to escape from his horrible doom! and how signal have been his deliverance and preservation in the midst of a nation of pitiless enemies!

This Narrative contains many affecting incidents, many passages of great eloquence and power; but I think the most thrilling one of them all is the description DOUGLASS

Notes

[8] *Original reads*: some one [ed.].

gives of his feelings, as he stood soliloquizing respecting his fate, and the chances of his one day being a freeman, on the banks of the Chesapeake Bay – viewing the receding vessels as they flew with their white wings before the breeze, and apostrophizing them as animated by the living spirit of freedom. Who can read that passage, and be insensible to its pathos and sublimity? Compressed into it is a whole Alexandrian library[9] of thought, feeling, and sentiment – all that can, all that need be urged, in the form of expostulation, entreaty, rebuke, against that crime of crimes – making man the property of his fellow-man! O, how accursed is that system, which entombs the godlike mind of man, defaces the divine image, reduces those who by creation were crowned with glory and honor to a level with four-footed beasts, and exalts the dealer in human flesh above all that is called God! Why should its existence be prolonged one hour? Is it not evil, only evil, and that continually? What does its presence imply but the absence of all fear of God, all regard for man, on the part of the people of the United States? Heaven speed its eternal overthrow!

So profoundly ignorant of the nature of slavery are many persons, that they are stubbornly incredulous whenever they read or listen to any recital of the cruelties which are daily inflicted on its victims. They do not deny that the slaves are held as property; but that terrible fact seems to convey to their minds no idea of injustice, exposure to outrage, or savage barbarity. Tell them of cruel scourgings, of mutilations and brandings, of scenes of pollution and blood, of the banishment of all light and knowledge, and they affect to be greatly indignant at such enormous exaggerations, such wholesale misstatements, such abominable libels on the character of the southern planters! As if all these direful outrages were not the natural results of slavery! As if it were less cruel to reduce a human being to the condition of a thing, than to give him a severe flagellation, or to deprive him of necessary food and clothing! As if whips, chains, thumb-screws, paddles, bloodhounds, overseers, drivers, patrols, were not all indispensable to keep the slaves down, and to give protection to their ruthless oppressors! As if, when the marriage institution is abolished, concubinage, adultery, and incest, must not necessarily abound; when all the rights of humanity are annihilated, any barrier remains to protect the victim from the fury of the spoiler; when absolute power is assumed over life and liberty, it will not be wielded with destructive sway! Skeptics of this character abound in society. In some few instances, their incredulity arises from a want of reflection; but, generally, it indicates a hatred of the light, a desire to shield slavery from the assaults of its foes, a contempt of the colored race, whether bond or free. Such will try to discredit the shocking tales of slaveholding cruelty which are recorded in this truthful Narrative; but they will labor in vain. Mr. DOUGLASS has frankly disclosed the place of his birth, the names of those who claimed ownership in his body and soul, and the names also of those who committed the crimes which he has alleged against them. His statements, therefore, may easily be disproved, if they are untrue.

In the course of his Narrative, he relates two instances of murderous cruelty – in one of which a planter deliberately shot a slave belonging to a neighboring plantation, who had unintentionally gotten within his lordly domain in quest of fish; and in the other, an overseer blew out the brains of a slave who had fled to a stream of water to escape a bloody scourging. Mr. DOUGLASS states that in neither of these instances was anything[10] done by way of legal arrest or judicial investigation. The Baltimore

Notes

[9] *Alexandrian library* The library at Alexandria, Egypt, was the preeminent center and storehouse for learning in the ancient world.

[10] *Original reads*: any thing [ed.].

American, of March 17, 1845, relates a similar case of atrocity, perpetrated with similar impunity – as follows: "*Shooting a Slave*. We learn, upon the authority of a letter from Charles county, Maryland, received by a gentleman of this city, that a young man, named Matthews, a nephew of General Matthews, and whose father, it is believed, holds an office at Washington, killed one of the slaves upon his father's farm by shooting him. The letter states that young Matthews had been left in charge of the farm; that he gave an order to the servant, which was disobeyed, when he proceeded to the house, *obtained a gun, and, returning, shot the servant*. He immediately, the letter continues, fled to his father's residence, where he still remains unmolested." Let it never be forgotten, that no slaveholder or overseer can be convicted of any outrage perpetrated on the person of a slave, however diabolical it may be, on the testimony of colored witnesses, whether bond or free. By the slave code, they are adjudged to be as incompetent to testify against a white man, as though they were indeed a part of the brute creation. Hence, there is no legal protection in fact, whatever there may be in form, for the slave population; and any amount of cruelty may be inflicted on them with impunity. Is it possible for the human mind to conceive of a more horrible state of society?

The effect of a religious profession on the conduct of southern masters is vividly described in the following Narrative, and shown to be anything[11] but salutary. In the nature of the case, it must be in the highest degree pernicious. The testimony of Mr. Douglass, on this point, is sustained by a cloud of witnesses, whose veracity is unimpeachable. "A slaveholder's profession of Christianity is a palpable imposture. He is a felon of the highest grade. He is a man-stealer. It is of no importance what you put in the other scale."

Reader! are you with the man-stealers in sympathy and purpose, or on the side of their down-trodden victims? If with the former, then are you the foe of God and man. If with the latter, what are you prepared to do and dare in their behalf? Be faithful, be vigilant, be untiring in your efforts to break every yoke, and let the oppressed go free. Come what may – cost what it may – inscribe on the banner which you unfurl to the breeze, as your religious and political motto – "No Compromise with Slavery! No Union with Slaveholders!"

WM. Lloyd Garrison.

Boston, *May* 1, 1845.

LETTER FROM WENDELL PHILLIPS, ESQ.[12]

Boston, *April* 22, 1845.

My Dear Friend:

You remember the old fable of "The Man and the Lion," where the lion complained that he should not be so misrepresented "when the lions wrote history."

I am glad the time has come when the "lions write history." We have been left long enough to gather the character of slavery from the involuntary evidence of the masters. One might, indeed, rest sufficiently satisfied with what, it is evident, must be, in general, the results of such a relation, without seeking farther to find whether they have followed in every instance. Indeed, those who stare at the half-peck of corn a

Notes

[11] *Original reads*: any thing [ed.].

[12] Wendell Phillips (1811–1884), American abolitionist and orator.

week, and love to count the lashes on the slave's back, are seldom the "stuff" out of which reformers and abolitionists are to be made. I remember that, in 1838, many were waiting for the results of the West India experiment,[13] before they could come into our ranks. Those "results" have come long ago; but, alas! few of that number have come with them, as converts. A man must be disposed to judge of emancipation by other tests than whether it has increased the produce of sugar – and to hate slavery for other reasons than because it starves men and whips women – before he is ready to lay the first stone of his anti-slavery life.

I was glad to learn, in your story, how early the most neglected of God s children waken to a sense of their rights, and of the injustice done them. Experience is a keen teacher; and long before you had mastered your A B C, or knew where the white sails of the Chesapeake were bound, you began, I see, to gauge the wretchedness of the slave, not by his hunger and want, not by his lashes and toil, but by the cruel and blighting death which gathers over his soul.

In connection with this, there is one circumstance which makes your recollections peculiarly valuable, and renders your early insight the more remarkable. You come from that part of the country where we are told slavery appears with its fairest features. Let us hear, then, what it is at its best estate – gaze on its bright side, if it has one; and then imagination may task her powers to add dark lines to the picture, as she travels southward to that (for the colored man) Valley of the Shadow of Death, where the Mississippi sweeps along.

Again, we have known you long, and can put the most entire confidence in your truth, candor, and sincerity. Everyone[14] who has heard you speak has felt, and, I am confident, everyone[15] who reads your book will feel, persuaded that you give them a fair specimen of the whole truth. No one-sided portrait – no wholesale complaints – but strict justice done, whenever individual kindliness has neutralized, for a moment, the deadly system with which it was strangely allied. You have been with us, too, some years, and can fairly compare the twilight of rights, which your race enjoy at the North, with that "noon of night" under which they labor south of Mason and Dixon's line. Tell us whether, after all, the half-free colored man of Massachusetts is worse off than the pampered slave of the rice swamps!

In reading your life, no one can say that we have unfairly picked out some rare specimens of cruelty. We know that the bitter drops, which even you have drained from the cup, are no incidental aggravations, no individual ills, but such as must mingle always and necessarily in the lot of every slave. They are the essential ingredients, not the occasional results, of the system.

After all, I shall read your book with trembling for you. Some years ago, when you were beginning to tell me your real name and birthplace, you may remember I stopped you, and preferred to remain ignorant of all. With the exception of a vague description, so I continued, till the other day, when you read me your memoirs. I hardly knew, at the time, whether to thank you or not for the sight of them, when I reflected that it was still dangerous, in Massachusetts, for honest men to tell their names! They say the fathers, in 1776, signed the Declaration of Independence with the halter about their necks. You, too, publish your declaration of freedom with danger compassing you around. In all the broad lands which the Constitution of the United States overshadows,

Notes

[13] *West India experiment* the abolition of slavery in the British Empire.

[14] *Original reads*: Every one [ed.].

[15] *Original reads*: every one [ed.].

there is no single spot – however narrow or desolate – where a fugitive slave can plant himself and say, "I am safe." The whole armory of Northern Law has no shield for you. I am free to say that, in your place, I should throw the MS. into the fire.

You, perhaps, may tell your story in safety, endeared as you are to so many warm hearts by rare gifts, and a still rarer devotion of them to the service of others. But it will be owing only to your labors, and the fearless efforts of those who, trampling the laws and Constitution of the country under their feet, are determined that they will "hide the outcast," and that their hearths shall be, spite of the law, an asylum for the oppressed, if, sometime[16] or other, the humblest may stand in our streets, and bear witness in safety against the cruelties of which he has been the victim.

Yet it is sad to think, that these very throbbing hearts which welcome your story, and form your best safeguard in telling it, are all beating contrary to the "statute in such case made and provided." Go on, my dear friend, till you, and those who, like you, have been saved, so as by fire, from the dark prison-house, shall stereotype these free, illegal pulses into statutes; and New England, cutting loose from a bloodstained Union, shall glory in being the house of refuge for the oppressed; till we no longer merely "*hide* the outcast," or make a merit of standing idly by while he is hunted in our midst; but, consecrating anew the soil of the Pilgrims as an asylum for the oppressed, proclaim our *welcome* to the slave so loudly, that the tones shall reach every hut in the Carolinas, and make the broken-hearted bondman leap up at the thought of old Massachusetts.

God speed the day!
Till then, and ever,
Yours truly,
Wendell Phillips

FREDERICK DOUGLASS.

Narrative of the Life of Frederick Douglass

Chapter 1

I was born in Tuckahoe, near Hillsborough, and about twelve miles from Easton, in Talbot county, Maryland. I have no accurate knowledge of my age, never having seen any authentic record containing it. By far the larger part of the slaves know as little of their ages as horses know of theirs, and it is the wish of most masters within my knowledge to keep their slaves thus ignorant. I do not remember to have ever met a slave who could tell of his birthday. They seldom come nearer to it than planting-time, harvest-time, cherry-time, springtime, or fall-time. A want of information concerning my own was a source of unhappiness to me even during childhood. The white children could tell their ages. I could not tell why I ought to be deprived of the same privilege. I was not allowed to make any inquiries of my master concerning it. He deemed all such inquiries on the part of a slave improper and impertinent, and evidence of a restless spirit. The nearest estimate I can give makes me now between twenty-seven and twenty-eight years of age. I come to this, from hearing my master say, sometime[17] during 1835, I was about seventeen years old.

Notes

[16] *Original reads*: some time [ed.].

[17] *Original reads*: some time [ed.].

My mother was named Harriet Bailey. She was the daughter of Isaac and Betsey Bailey, both colored, and quite dark. My mother was of a darker complexion than either my grandmother or grandfather.

My father was a white man. He was admitted to be such by all I ever heard speak of my parentage. The opinion was also whispered that my master was my father; but of the correctness of this opinion, I know nothing; the means of knowing was withheld from me. My mother and I were separated when I was but an infant – before I knew her as my mother. It is a common custom, in the part of Maryland from which I ran away, to part children from their mothers at a very early age. Frequently, before the child has reached its twelfth month, its mother is taken from it, and hired out on some farm a considerable distance off, and the child is placed under the care of an old woman, too old for field labor. For what this separation is done, I do not know, unless it be to hinder the development of the child's affection toward its mother, and to blunt and destroy the natural affection of the mother for the child. This is the inevitable result.

I never saw my mother, to know her as such, more than four or five times in my life; and each of these times was very short in duration, and at night. She was hired by a Mr. Stewart, who lived about twelve miles from my home. She made her journeys to see me in the night, travelling the whole distance on foot, after the performance of her day's work. She was a field hand, and a whipping is the penalty of not being in the field at sunrise, unless a slave has special permission from his or her master to the contrary – a permission which they seldom get, and one that gives to him that gives it the proud name of being a kind master. I do not recollect of ever seeing my mother by the light of day. She was with me in the night. She would lie down with me, and get me to sleep, but long before I waked she was gone. Very little communication ever took place between us. Death soon ended what little we could have while she lived, and with it her hardships and suffering. She died when I was about seven years old, on one of my master's farms, near Lee's Mill. I was not allowed to be present during her illness, at her death, or burial. She was gone long before I knew anything[18] about it. Never having enjoyed, to any considerable extent, her soothing presence, her tender and watchful care, I received the tidings of her death with much the same emotions I should have probably felt at the death of a stranger.

Called thus suddenly away, she left me without the slightest intimation of who my father was. The whisper that my master was my father, may or may not be true; and, true or false, it is of but little consequence to my purpose whilst the fact remains, in all its glaring odiousness, that slaveholders have ordained, and by law established, that the children of slave women shall in all cases follow the condition of their mothers; and this is done too obviously to administer to their own lusts, and make a gratification of their wicked desires profitable as well as pleasurable; for by this cunning arrangement, the slaveholder, in cases not a few, sustains to his slaves the double relation of master and father.

I know of such cases; and it is worthy of remark that such slaves invariably suffer greater hardships, and have more to contend with, than others. They are, in the first place, a constant offence to their mistress. She is ever disposed to find fault with them; they can seldom do anything[19] to please her; she is never better pleased than when she sees them under the lash, especially when she suspects her husband of showing to his mulatto children favors which he withholds from his black slaves. The master is frequently compelled to sell this class of his slaves, out of deference to the feelings of his white wife; and, cruel as the deed may strike anyone[20] to be, for a man to sell his own

Notes

[18] *Original reads*: any thing [ed.].

[19] *Original reads*: any thing [ed.].

[20] *Original reads*: any one [ed.].

children to human flesh-mongers, it is often the dictate of humanity for him to do so; for, unless he does this, he must not only whip them himself, but must stand by and see one white son tie up his brother, of but few shades darker complexion than himself, and ply the gory lash to his naked back; and if he lisp one word of disapproval, it is set down to his parental partiality, and only makes a bad matter worse, both for himself and the slave whom he would protect and defend.

Every year brings with it multitudes of this class of slaves. It was doubtless in consequence of a knowledge of this fact, that one great statesman of the south predicted the downfall of slavery by the inevitable laws of population. Whether this prophecy is ever fulfilled or not, it is nevertheless plain that a very different-looking class of people are springing up at the south, and are now held in slavery, from those originally brought to this country from Africa; and if their increase will do no other good, it will do away the force of the argument, that God cursed Ham,[21] and therefore American slavery is right. If the lineal descendants of Ham are alone to be scripturally enslaved, it is certain that slavery at the south must soon become unscriptural; for thousands are ushered into the world, annually, who, like myself, owe their existence to white fathers, and those fathers most frequently their own masters.

I have had two masters. My first master's name was Anthony. I do not remember his first name. He was generally called Captain Anthony – a title which, I presume, he acquired by sailing a craft on the Chesapeake Bay. He was not considered a rich slaveholder. He owned two or three farms, and about thirty slaves. His farms and slaves were under the care of an overseer. The overseer's name was Plummer. Mr. Plummer was a miserable drunkard, a profane swearer, and a savage monster. He always went armed with a cowskin[22] and a heavy cudgel. I have known him to cut and slash the women's heads so horribly, that even master would be enraged at his cruelty, and would threaten to whip him if he did not mind himself. Master, however, was not a humane slaveholder. It required extraordinary barbarity on the part of an overseer to affect him. He was a cruel man, hardened by a long life of slaveholding. He would at times seem to take great pleasure in whipping a slave. I have often been awakened at the dawn of day by the most heart-rending shrieks of an own aunt of mine, whom he used to tie up to a joist, and whip upon her naked back till she was literally covered with blood. No words, no tears, no prayers, from his gory victim, seemed to move his iron heart from its bloody purpose. The louder she screamed, the harder he whipped; and where the blood ran fastest, there he whipped longest. He would whip her to make her scream, and whip her to make her hush; and not until overcome by fatigue, would he cease to swing the blood-clotted cowskin. I remember the first time I ever witnessed this horrible exhibition. I was quite a child, but I well remember it. I never shall forget it whilst I remember anything.[23] It was the first of a long series of such outrages, of which I was doomed to be a witness and a participant. It struck me with awful force. It was the blood-stained gate, the entrance to the hell of slavery, through which I was about to pass. It was a most terrible spectacle. I wish I could commit to paper the feelings with which I beheld it.

This occurrence took place very soon after I went to live with my old master, and under the following circumstances. Aunt Hester went out one night – where or for

Notes

[21] *cursed Ham* (Genesis 9:20–27) Noah curses his son Ham and his descendants to be slaves; this passage was put to dubious purpose to justify the enslavement of dark-skinned peoples in the modern era.

[22] *cowskin* whip.

[23] *Original reads*: any thing [ed.].

what I do not know – and happened to be absent when my master desired her presence. He had ordered her not to go out evenings, and warned her that she must never let him catch her in company with a young man, who was paying attention to her, belonging to Colonel Lloyd. The young man's name was Ned Roberts, generally called Lloyd's Ned. Why master was so careful of her, may be safely left to conjecture. She was a woman of noble form, and of graceful proportions, having very few equals, and fewer superiors, in personal appearance among the colored or white women of our neighborhood.

Aunt Hester had not only disobeyed his orders in going out, but had been found in company with Lloyd's Ned; which circumstance, I found, from what he said while whipping her, was the chief offence. Had he been a man of pure morals himself, he might have been thought interested in protecting the innocence of my aunt; but those who knew him will not suspect him of any such virtue. Before he commenced whipping Aunt Hester, he took her into the kitchen, and stripped her from neck to waist, leaving her neck, shoulders, and back entirely naked. He then told her to cross her hands, calling her at the same time a d——d b——h. After crossing her hands, he tied them with a strong rope, and led her to a stool under a large hook in the joist, put in for the purpose. He made her get upon the stool, and tied her hands to the hook. She now stood fair for his infernal purpose. Her arms were stretched up at their full length, so that she stood upon the ends of her toes. He then said to her, "Now, you d——d b——h, I'll learn you how to disobey my orders!" and after rolling up his sleeves, he commenced to lay on the heavy cowskin, and soon the warm, red blood (amid heart-rending shrieks from her, and horrid oaths from him) came dripping to the floor. I was so terrified and horror-stricken at the sight, that I hid myself in a closet, and dared not venture out till long after the bloody transaction was over. I expected it would be my turn next. It was all new to me. I had never seen anything[24] like it before. I had always lived with my grandmother on the outskirts of the plantation, where she was put to raise the children of the younger women. I had therefore been, until now, out of the way of the bloody scenes that often occurred on the plantation.

Chapter 2

My master's family consisted of two sons, Andrew and Richard; one daughter, Lucretia, and her husband, Captain Thomas Auld. They lived in one house, upon the home plantation of Colonel Edward Lloyd. My master was Colonel Lloyd's clerk and superintendent. He was what might be called the overseer of the overseers. I spent two years of childhood on this plantation in my old master's family. It was here that I witnessed the bloody transaction recorded in the first chapter; and as I received my first impressions of slavery on this plantation, I will give some description of it, and of slavery as it there existed. The plantation is about twelve miles north of Easton, in Talbot country, and is situated on the border of Miles River. The principal products raised upon it were tobacco, corn, and wheat. These were raised in great abundance; so that, with the products of this and the other farms belonging to him, he was able to keep in almost constant employment a large sloop, in carrying them to market at Baltimore. This sloop was named Sally Lloyd, in honor of one of the colonel's daughters. My master's son-in-law, Captain Auld, was master of the vessel; she was otherwise

Notes

[24] *Original reads*: any thing [ed.].

manned by the colonel's own slaves. Their names were Peter, Isaac, Rich, and Jake. These were esteemed very highly by the other slaves, and looked upon as the privileged ones of the plantation; for it was no small affair, in the eyes of the slaves, to be allowed to see Baltimore.

Colonel Lloyd kept from three to four hundred slaves on his home plantation, and owned a large number more on the neighboring farms belonging to him. The names of the farms nearest to the home plantation were Wye Town and New Design. Wye Town was under the overseership of a man named Noah Willis. New Design was under the overseership of a Mr. Townsend. The overseers of these, and all the rest of the farms, numbering over twenty, received advice and direction from the managers of the home plantation. This was the great business place. It was the seat of government for the whole twenty farms. All disputes among the overseers were settled here. If a slave was convicted of any high misdemeanor, became unmanageable, or evinced a determination to run away, he was brought immediately here, severely whipped, put on board the sloop, carried to Baltimore, and sold to Austin Woolfolk, or some other slave-trader, as a warning to the slaves remaining.

Here, too, the slaves of all the other farms received their monthly allowance of food, and their yearly clothing. The men and women slaves received, as their monthly allowance of food, eight pounds of pork, or its equivalent in fish, and one bushel of corn meal. Their yearly clothing consisted of two coarse linen shirts, one pair of linen trousers, like the shirts, one jacket, one pair of trousers for winter, made of coarse negro cloth, one pair of stockings, and one pair of shoes, the whole of which could not have cost more than seven dollars. The allowance of the slave children was given to their mothers, or the old women having the care of them. The children unable to work in the field had neither shoes, stockings, jackets, nor trousers given to them; their clothing consisted of two coarse linen shirts per year. When these failed them, they went naked until the next allowance-day. Children from seven to ten years old, of both sexes, almost naked, might be seen at all seasons of the year.

There were no beds given the slaves, unless one coarse blanket be considered such, and none but the men and women had these. This, however, is not considered a very great privation. They find less difficulty from the want of beds, than from the want of time to sleep; for when their day's work in the field is done, the most of them having their washing, mending, and cooking to do, and having few or none of the ordinary facilities for doing either of these, very many of their sleeping hours are consumed in preparing for the field the coming day; and when this is done, old and young, male and female, married and single, drop down side by side, on one common bed – the cold, damp floor – each covering himself or herself with their miserable blankets; and here they sleep till they are summoned to the field by the driver's horn. At the sound of this, all must rise, and be off to the field. There must be no halting; everyone[25] must be at his or her post; and woe betides them who hear not this morning summons to the field; for if they are not awakened by the sense of hearing, they are by the sense of feeling: no age nor sex finds any favor. Mr. Severe, the overseer, used to stand by the door of the quarter, armed with a large hickory stick and heavy cowskin, ready to whip anyone[26] who was so unfortunate as not to hear, or, from any other cause, was prevented from being ready to start for the field at the sound of the horn.

Mr. Severe was rightly named: he was a cruel man. I have seen him whip a woman, causing the blood to run half an hour at the time; and this, too, in the midst of her

Notes

[25] *Original reads*: every one [ed.].

[26] *Original reads*: any one [ed.].

crying children, pleading for their mother's release. He seemed to take pleasure in manifesting his fiendish barbarity. Added to his cruelty, he was a profane swearer. It was enough to chill the blood and stiffen the hair of an ordinary man to hear him talk. Scarce a sentence escaped him but that was commenced or concluded by some horrid oath. The field was the place to witness his cruelty and profanity. His presence made it both the field of blood and of blasphemy. From the rising till the going down of the sun, he was cursing, raving, cutting, and slashing among the slaves of the field, in the most frightful manner. His career was short. He died very soon after I went to Colonel Lloyd's; and he died as he lived, uttering, with his dying groans, bitter curses and horrid oaths. His death was regarded by the slaves as the result of a merciful providence.

Mr. Severe's place was filled by a Mr. Hopkins. He was a very different man. He was less cruel, less profane, and made less noise, than Mr. Severe. His course was characterized by no extraordinary demonstrations of cruelty. He whipped, but seemed to take no pleasure in it. He was called by the slaves a good overseer.

The home plantation of Colonel Lloyd wore the appearance of a country village. All the mechanical operations for all the farms were performed here. The shoemaking and mending, the blacksmithing, cartwrighting, coopering, weaving, and grain-grinding, were all performed by the slaves on the home plantation. The whole place wore a business-like aspect very unlike the neighboring farms. The number of houses, too, conspired to give it advantage over the neighboring farms. It was called by the slaves the *Great House Farm*. Few privileges were esteemed higher, by the slaves of the out-farms, than that of being selected to do errands at the Great House Farm. It was associated in their minds with greatness. A representative could not be prouder of his election to a seat in the American Congress, than a slave on one of the out-farms would be of his election to do errands at the Great House Farm. They regarded it as evidence of great confidence reposed in them by their overseers; and it was on this account, as well as a constant desire to be out of the field from under the driver's lash, that they esteemed it a high privilege, one worth careful living for. He was called the smartest and most trusty fellow, who had this honor conferred upon him the most frequently. The competitors for this office sought as diligently to please their overseers, as the office-seekers in the political parties seek to please and deceive the people. The same traits of character might be seen in Colonel Lloyd's slaves, as are seen in the slaves of the political parties.

The slaves selected to go to the Great House Farm, for the monthly allowance for themselves and their fellow-slaves, were peculiarly enthusiastic. While on their way, they would make the dense old woods, for miles around, reverberate with their wild songs, revealing at once the highest joy and the deepest sadness. They would compose and sing as they went along, consulting neither time nor tune. The thought that came up, came out – if not in the word, in the sound; and as frequently in the one as in the other. They would sometimes sing the most pathetic sentiment in the most rapturous tone, and the most rapturous sentiment in the most pathetic tone. Into all of their songs they would manage to weave something of the Great House Farm. Especially would they do this, when leaving home. They would then sing most exultingly the following words:–

> "I am going away to the Great House Farm!
> O, yea! O, yea! O!"

This they would sing, as a chorus, to words which to many would seem unmeaning jargon, but which, nevertheless, were full of meaning to themselves. I have sometimes thought that the mere hearing of those songs would do more to impress some minds with the horrible character of slavery, than the reading of whole volumes of philosophy on the subject could do.

I did not, when a slave, understand the deep meaning of those rude and apparently incoherent songs. I was myself within the circle; so that I neither saw nor heard as those without might see and hear. They told a tale of woe which was then altogether beyond my feeble comprehension; they were tones loud, long, and deep; they breathed the prayer and complaint of souls boiling over with the bitterest anguish. Every tone was a testimony against slavery, and a prayer to God for deliverance from chains. The hearing of those wild notes always depressed my spirit, and filled me with ineffable sadness. I have frequently found myself in tears while hearing them. The mere recurrence to those songs, even now, afflicts me; and while I am writing these lines, an expression of feeling has already found its way down my cheek. To those songs I trace my first glimmering conception of the dehumanizing character of slavery. I can never get rid of that conception. Those songs still follow me, to deepen my hatred of slavery, and quicken my sympathies for my brethren in bonds. If anyone[27] wishes to be impressed with the soul-killing effects of slavery, let him go to Colonel Lloyd's plantation, and, on allowance-day, place himself in the deep pine woods, and there let him, in silence, analyze the sounds that shall pass through the chambers of his soul – and if he is not thus impressed, it will only be because "there is no flesh in his obdurate heart."[28]

I have often been utterly astonished, since I came to the north, to find persons who could speak of the singing, among slaves, as evidence of their contentment and happiness. It is impossible to conceive of a greater mistake. Slaves sing most when they are most unhappy. The songs of the slave represent the sorrows of his heart; and he is relieved by them, only as an aching heart is relieved by its tears. At least, such is my experience. I have often sung to drown my sorrow, but seldom to express my happiness. Crying for joy, and singing for joy, were alike uncommon to me while in the jaws of slavery. The singing of a man cast away upon a desolate island might be as appropriately considered as evidence of contentment and happiness, as the singing of a slave; the songs of the one and of the other are prompted by the same emotion.

Chapter 3

Colonel Lloyd kept a large and finely cultivated garden, which afforded almost constant employment for four men besides the chief gardener (Mr. M'Durmond). This garden was probably the greatest attraction of the place. During the summer months, people came from far and near – from Baltimore, Easton, and Annapolis – to see it. It abounded in fruits of almost every description, from the hardy apple of the north to the delicate orange of the south. This garden was not the least source of trouble on the plantation. Its excellent fruit was quite a temptation to the hungry swarms of boys, as well as the older slaves, belonging to the colonel, few of whom had the virtue or the vice to resist it. Scarcely a day passed, during the summer, but that some slave had to take the lash for stealing fruit. The colonel had to resort to all kinds of stratagems to keep his slaves out of the garden. The last and most successful one was that of tarring his fence all around; after which, if a slave was caught with any tar upon his person, it

Notes

[27] *Original reads*: any one [ed.].

[28] *"There is no flesh in his obdurate heart"* The lines come from "The Time-Piece" (2.8), a section of English poet William Cowper's (1731–1800) long poem, *The Task* (1785).

was deemed sufficient proof that he had either been into the garden, or had tried to get in. In either case, he was severely whipped by the chief gardener. This plan worked well; the slaves became as fearful of tar as of the lash. They seemed to realize the impossibility of touching *tar* without being defiled.

The colonel also kept a splendid riding equipage. His stable and carriage-house presented the appearance of some of our large city livery establishments. His horses were of the finest form and noblest blood. His carriage-house contained three splendid coaches, three or four gigs, besides dearborns and barouches[29] of the most fashionable style.

This establishment was under the care of two slaves – old Barney and young Barney – father and son. To attend to this establishment was their sole work. But it was by no means an easy employment; for in nothing was Colonel Lloyd more particular than in the management of his horses. The slightest inattention to these was unpardonable, and was visited upon those, under whose care they were placed, with the severest punishment; no excuse could shield them, if the colonel only suspected any want of attention to his horses – a supposition which he frequently indulged, and one which, of course, made the office of old and young Barney a very trying one. They never knew when they were safe from punishment. They were frequently whipped when least deserving, and escaped whipping when most deserving it. Everything[30] depended upon the looks of the horses, and the state of Colonel Lloyd's own mind when his horses were brought to him for use. If a horse did not move fast enough, or hold his head high enough, it was owing to some fault of his keepers. It was painful to stand near the stable-door, and hear the various complaints against the keepers when a horse was taken out for use. "This horse has not had proper attention. He has not been sufficiently rubbed and curried, or he has not been properly fed; his food was too wet or too dry; he got it too soon or too late; he was too hot or too cold; he had too much hay, and not enough of grain; or he had too much grain, and not enough of hay; instead of old Barney's attending to the horse, he had very improperly left it to his son." To all these complaints, no matter how unjust, the slave must answer never a word. Colonel Lloyd could not brook any contradiction from a slave. When he spoke, a slave must stand, listen, and tremble; and such was literally the case. I have seen Colonel Lloyd make old Barney, a man between fifty and sixty years of age, uncover his bald head, kneel down upon the cold, damp ground, and receive upon his naked and toil-worn shoulders more than thirty lashes at the time. Colonel Lloyd had three sons – Edward, Murray, and Daniel – and three sons-in-law, Mr. Winder, Mr. Nicholson, and Mr. Lowndes. All of these lived at the Great House Farm, and enjoyed the luxury of whipping the servants when they pleased, from old Barney down to William Wilkes, the coach-driver. I have seen Winder make one of the house-servants stand off from him a suitable distance to be touched with the end of his whip, and at every stroke raise great ridges upon his back.

To describe the wealth of Colonel Lloyd would be almost equal to describing the riches of Job. He kept from ten to fifteen house-servants. He was said to own a thousand slaves, and I think this estimate quite within the truth. Colonel Lloyd owned so many that he did not know them when he saw them; nor did all the slaves of the out-farms know him. It is reported of him, that, while riding along the road one day, he met a colored man, and addressed him in the usual manner of speaking to colored people on the public highways of the south: "Well, boy, whom do you belong to?" "To Colonel Lloyd," replied the slave. "Well, does the colonel treat you well?"

Notes

[29] *coaches … barouches* various types of carriages.

[30] *Original reads*: Every thing [ed.].

"No, sir," was the ready reply. "What, does he work you too hard?" "Yes, sir." "Well, don't he give you enough to eat?" "Yes, sir, he gives me enough, such as it is."

The colonel, after ascertaining where the slave belonged, rode on; the man also went on about his business, not dreaming that he had been conversing with his master. He thought, said, and heard nothing more of the matter, until two or three weeks afterwards. The poor man was then informed by his overseer that, for having found fault with his master, he was now to be sold to a Georgia trader. He was immediately chained and handcuffed; and thus, without a moment's warning, he was snatched away, and forever sundered, from his family and friends, by a hand more unrelenting than death. This is the penalty of telling the truth, of telling the simple truth, in answer to a series of plain questions.

It is partly in consequence of such facts, that slaves, when inquired of as to their condition and the character of their masters, almost universally say they are contented, and that their masters are kind. The slaveholders have been known to send in spies among their slaves, to ascertain their views and feelings in regard to their condition. The frequency of this has had the effect to establish among the slaves the maxim, that a still tongue makes a wise head. They suppress the truth rather than take the consequences of telling it, and in so doing prove themselves a part of the human family. If they have anything[31] to say of their masters, it is generally in their masters' favor, especially when speaking to an untried man. I have been frequently asked, when a slave, if I had a kind master, and do not remember ever to have given a negative answer; nor did I, in pursuing this course, consider myself as uttering what was absolutely false; for I always measured the kindness of my master by the standard of kindness set up among slaveholders around us. Moreover, slaves are like other people, and imbibe prejudices quite common to others. They think their own better than that of others. Many, under the influence of this prejudice, think their own masters are better than the masters of other slaves; and this, too, in some cases, when the very reverse is true. Indeed, it is not uncommon for slaves even to fall out and quarrel among themselves about the relative goodness of their masters, each contending for the superior goodness of his own over that of the others. At the very same time, they mutually execrate their masters when viewed separately. It was so on our plantation. When Colonel Lloyd's slaves met the slaves of Jacob Jepson, they seldom parted without a quarrel about their masters; Colonel Lloyd's slaves contending that he was the richest, and Mr. Jepson's slaves that he was the smartest, and most of a man. Colonel Lloyd's slaves would boast his ability to buy and sell Jacob Jepson. Mr. Jepson's slaves would boast his ability to whip Colonel Lloyd. These quarrels would almost always end in a fight between the parties, and those that whipped were supposed to have gained the point at issue. They seemed to think that the greatness of their masters was transferable to themselves. It was considered as being bad enough to be a slave; but to be a poor man's slave was deemed a disgrace indeed!

Chapter 4

Mr. Hopkins remained but a short time in the office of overseer. Why his career was so short, I do not know, but suppose he lacked the necessary severity to suit Colonel Lloyd. Mr. Hopkins was succeeded by Mr. Austin Gore, a man possessing, in an eminent degree, all those traits of character indispensable to what is called a first-rate overseer.

Notes

[31] *Original reads*: any thing [ed.].

Mr. Gore had served Colonel Lloyd, in the capacity of overseer, upon one of the out-farms, and had shown himself worthy of the high station of overseer upon the home or Great House Farm.

Mr. Gore was proud, ambitious, and persevering. He was artful, cruel, and obdurate. He was just the man for such a place, and it was just the place for such a man. It afforded scope for the full exercise of all his powers, and he seemed to be perfectly at home in it. He was one of those who could torture the slightest look, word, or gesture, on the part of the slave, into impudence, and would treat it accordingly. There must be no answering back to him; no explanation was allowed a slave, showing himself to have been wrongfully accused. Mr. Gore acted fully up to the maxim laid down by slaveholders – "It is better that a dozen slaves suffer under the lash, than that the overseer should be convicted, in the presence of the slaves, of having been at fault." No matter how innocent a slave might be – it availed him nothing, when accused by Mr. Gore of any misdemeanor. To be accused was to be convicted, and to be convicted was to be punished; the one always following the other with immutable certainty. To escape punishment was to escape accusation; and few slaves had the fortune to do either, under the overseership of Mr. Gore. He was just proud enough to demand the most debasing homage of the slave, and quite servile enough to crouch, himself, at the feet of the master. He was ambitious enough to be contented with nothing short of the highest rank of overseers, and persevering enough to reach the height of his ambition. He was cruel enough to inflict the severest punishment, artful enough to descend to the lowest trickery, and obdurate enough to be insensible to the voice of a reproving conscience. He was, of all the overseers, the most dreaded by the slaves. His presence was painful; his eye flashed confusion; and seldom was his sharp, shrill voice heard, without producing horror and trembling in their ranks.

Mr. Gore was a grave man, and, though a young man, he indulged in no jokes, said no funny words, seldom smiled. His words were in perfect keeping with his looks, and his looks were in perfect keeping with his words. Overseers will sometimes indulge in a witty word, even with the slaves; not so with Mr. Gore. He spoke but to command, and commanded but to be obeyed; he dealt sparingly with his words, and bountifully with his whip, never using the former where the latter would answer as well. When he whipped, he seemed to do so from a sense of duty, and feared no consequences. He did nothing reluctantly, no matter how disagreeable; always at his post, never inconsistent. He never promised but to fulfil. He was, in a word, a man of the most inflexible firmness and stone-like coolness.

His savage barbarity was equalled only by the consummate coolness with which he committed the grossest and most savage deeds upon the slaves under his charge. Mr. Gore once undertook to whip one of Colonel Lloyd's slaves, by the name of Demby. He had given Demby but few stripes, when, to get rid of the scourging, he ran and plunged himself into a creek, and stood there at the depth of his shoulders, refusing to come out. Mr. Gore told him that he would give him three calls, and that, if he did not come out at the third call, he would shoot him. The first call was given. Demby made no response, but stood his ground. The second and third calls were given with the same result. Mr. Gore then, without consultation or deliberation with any one, not even giving Demby an additional call, raised his musket to his face, taking deadly aim at his standing victim, and in an instant poor Demby was no more. His mangled body sank out of sight, and blood and brains marked the water where he had stood.

A thrill of horror flashed through every soul upon the plantation, excepting Mr. Gore. He alone seemed cool and collected. He was asked by Colonel Lloyd and my old master, why he resorted to this extraordinary expedient. His reply was, (as well as I can remember,) that Demby had become unmanageable. He was setting a dangerous example to the other slaves – one which, if suffered to pass without some such demonstration on his part, would finally lead to the total subversion of all rule and order upon the plantation. He argued that if one slave refused to be corrected, and escaped with his life, the other slaves would soon copy the example; the result of which would be, the freedom of the slaves, and the enslavement of the whites. Mr. Gore's defence was satisfactory. He was continued in his station as overseer upon the home plantation. His fame as an overseer went abroad. His horrid crime was not even submitted to judicial investigation. It was committed in the presence of slaves, and they of course could neither institute a suit, nor testify against him; and thus the guilty perpetrator of one of the bloodiest and most foul murders goes unwhipped of justice, and uncensured by the community in which he lives. Mr. Gore lived in St. Michael's, Talbot county, Maryland, when I left there; and if he is still alive, he very probably lives there now; and if so, he is now, as he was then, as highly esteemed and as much respected as though his guilty soul had not been stained with his brother's blood.

I speak advisedly when I say this – that killing a slave, or any colored person, in Talbot country, Maryland, is not treated as a crime, either by the courts or the community. Mr. Thomas Lanman, of St. Michael's, killed two slaves, one of whom he killed with a hatchet, by knocking his brains out. He used to boast of the commission of the awful and bloody deed. I have heard him do so laughingly, saying, among other things, that he was the only benefactor of his country in the company, and that when others would do as much as he had done, we should be relieved of "the d——d niggers."

The wife of Mr. Giles Hick, living but a short distance from where I used to live, murdered my wife's cousin, a young girl between fifteen and sixteen years of age, mangling her person in the most horrible manner, breaking her nose and breastbone with a stick, so that the poor girl expired in a few hours afterward. She was immediately buried, but had not been in her untimely grave but a few hours before she was taken up and examined by the coroner, who decided that she had come to her death by severe beating. The offence for which this girl was thus murdered was this – She had been set that night to mind Mrs. Hick's baby, and during the night she fell asleep, and the baby cried. She, having lost her rest for several nights previous, did not hear the crying. They were both in the room with Mrs. Hicks. Mrs. Hicks, finding the girl slow to move, jumped from her bed, seized an oak stick of wood by the fireplace, and with it broke the girl's nose and breastbone, and thus ended her life. I will not say that this most horrid murder produced no sensation in the community. It did produce sensation, but not enough to bring the murderess to punishment. There was a warrant issued for her arrest, but it was never served. Thus she escaped not only punishment, but even the pain of being arraigned before a court for her horrid crime.

Whilst I am detailing bloody deeds which took place during my stay on Colonel Lloyd's plantation, I will briefly narrate another, which occurred about the same time as the murder of Demby by Mr. Gore.

Colonel Lloyd's slaves were in the habit of spending a part of their nights and Sundays in fishing for oysters, and in this way made up the deficiency of their scanty allowance. An old man belonging to Colonel Lloyd, while thus engaged, happened to get beyond the limits of Colonel Lloyd's, and on the premises of Mr. Beal Bondly. At this trespass, Mr. Bondly took offence, and with his musket came down to the shore, and blew its deadly contents into the poor old man.

Mr. Bondly came over to see Colonel Lloyd the next day, whether to pay him for his property, or to justify himself in what he had done, I know not. At any rate, this whole fiendish transaction was soon hushed up. There was very little said about it at all, and nothing done. It was a common saying, even among little white boys, that it was worth a half-cent to kill a "nigger," and a half-cent to bury one.

Chapter 5

As to my own treatment while I lived on Colonel Lloyd's plantation, it was very similar to that of the other slave children. I was not old enough to work in the field, and there being little else than field work to do, I had a great deal of leisure time. The most I had to do was to drive up the cows at evening, keep the fowls out of the garden, keep the front yard clean, and run errands[32] for my old master's daughter, Mrs. Lucretia Auld. The most of my leisure time I spent in helping Master Daniel Lloyd in finding his birds, after he had shot them. My connection with Master Daniel was of some advantage to me. He became quite attached to me, and was a sort of protector of me. He would not allow the older boys to impose upon me, and would divide his cakes with me.

I was seldom whipped by my old master, and suffered little from anything[33] else than hunger and cold. I suffered much from hunger, but much more from cold. In hottest summer and coldest winter, I was kept almost naked – no shoes, no stockings, no jacket, no trousers, nothing on but a coarse tow linen shirt, reaching only to my knees. I had no bed. I must have perished with cold, but that, the coldest nights, I used to steal a bag which was used for carrying corn to the mill. I would crawl into this bag, and there sleep on the cold, damp, clay floor, with my head in and feet out. My feet have been so cracked with the frost, that the pen with which I am writing might be laid in the gashes.

We were not regularly allowanced. Our food was coarse corn meal boiled. This was called *mush*. It was put into a large wooden tray or trough, and set down upon the ground. The children were then called, like so many pigs, and like so many pigs they would come and devour the mush; some with oyster-shells, others with pieces of shingle, some with naked hands, and none with spoons. He that ate fastest got most; he that was strongest secured the best place; and few left the trough satisfied.

I was probably between seven and eight years old when I left Colonel Lloyd's plantation. I left it with joy. I shall never forget the ecstasy with which I received the intelligence that my old master (Anthony) had determined to let me go to Baltimore, to live with Mr. Hugh Auld, brother to my old master's son-in-law, Captain Thomas Auld. I received this information about three days before my departure. They were three of the happiest days I ever enjoyed. I spent the most part of all these three days in the creek, washing off the plantation scurf, and preparing myself for my departure.

The pride of appearance which this would indicate was not my own. I spent the time in washing, not so much because I wished to, but because Mrs. Lucretia had told me I must get all the dead skin off my feet and knees before I could go to Baltimore; for the people in Baltimore were very cleanly, and would laugh at me if I looked dirty. Besides, she was going to give me a pair of trousers, which I should not put on unless I got all the dirt off me. The thought of owning a pair of trousers was great indeed! It was almost a sufficient motive, not only to make me take off what would be called by pig-drovers the mange, but the skin itself. I went at it in good earnest, working for the first time with the hope of reward.

The ties that ordinarily bind children to their homes were all suspended in my case. I found no severe trial in my departure. My home was charmless; it was not home to me; on parting from it, I could not feel that I was leaving anything[34] which I could have enjoyed by staying. My mother was dead; my grandmother lived far off, so that

Notes

[32] *Original reads*: run of errands [ed.].

[33] *Original reads*: any thing [ed.].

[34] *Original reads*: any thing [ed.].

I seldom saw her. I had two sisters and one brother that lived in the same house with me; but the early separation of us from our mother had well-nigh blotted the fact of our relationship from our memories. I looked for home elsewhere, and was confident of finding none which I should relish less than the one which I was leaving. If, however, I found in my new home hardship, hunger, whipping, and nakedness, I had the consolation that I should not have escaped any one of them by staying. Having already had more than a taste of them in the house of my old master, and having endured them there, I very naturally inferred my ability to endure them elsewhere, and especially at Baltimore; for I had something of the feeling about Baltimore that is expressed in the proverb, that "being hanged in England is preferable to dying a natural death in Ireland." I had the strongest desire to see Baltimore. Cousin Tom, though not fluent in speech, had inspired me with that desire by his eloquent description of the place. I could never point out anything[35] at the Great House, no matter how beautiful or powerful, but that he had seen something at Baltimore far exceeding, both in beauty and strength, the object which I pointed out to him. Even the Great House itself, with all its pictures, was far inferior to many buildings in Baltimore. So strong was my desire, that I thought a gratification of it would fully compensate for whatever loss of comforts I should sustain by the exchange. I left without a regret, and with the highest hopes of future happiness.

We sailed out of Miles River for Baltimore on a Saturday morning. I remember only the day of the week, for at that time I had no knowledge of the days of the month, nor the months of the year. On setting sail, I walked aft, and gave to Colonel Lloyd's plantation what I hoped would be the last look. I then placed myself in the bows of the sloop, and there spent the remainder of the day in looking ahead, interesting myself in what was in the distance rather than in things nearby[36] or behind.

In the afternoon of that day, we reached Annapolis, the capital of the State. We stopped but a few moments, so that I had no time to go on shore. It was the first large town that I had ever seen, and though it would look small compared with some of our New England factory villages, I thought it a wonderful place for its size – more imposing even than the Great House Farm!

We arrived at Baltimore early on Sunday morning, landing at Smith's Wharf, not far from Bowley's Wharf. We had on board the sloop a large flock of sheep; and after aiding in driving them to the slaughter-house of Mr. Curtis on Louden Slater's Hill, I was conducted by Rich, one of the hands belonging on board of the sloop, to my new home in Alliciana Street, near Mr. Gardner's ship-yard, on Fells Point.

Mr. and Mrs. Auld were both at home, and met me at the door with their little son Thomas, the care of whom I had been given.[37] And here I saw what I had never seen before; it was a white face beaming with the most kindly emotions; it was the face of my new mistress, Sophia Auld. I wish I could describe the rapture that flashed through my soul as I beheld it. It was a new and strange sight to me, brightening up my pathway with the light of happiness. Little Thomas was told, there was his Freddy – and I was told to take care of little Thomas; and thus I entered upon the duties of my new home with the most cheering prospect ahead.

I look upon my departure from Colonel Lloyd's plantation as one of the most interesting events of my life. It is possible, and even quite probable, that but for the mere circumstance of being removed from that plantation to Baltimore, I should have

Notes

[35] *Original reads*: any thing [ed.].

[36] *Original reads*: near by [ed.].

[37] *Original reads*: to take care of whom I had been given. [ed.].

to-day, instead of being here seated by my own table, in the enjoyment of freedom and the happiness of home, writing this Narrative, been confined in the galling chains of slavery. Going to live at Baltimore laid the foundation, and opened the gateway, to all my subsequent prosperity. I have ever regarded it as the first plain manifestation of that kind providence which has ever since attended me, and marked my life with so many favors. I regarded the selection of myself as being somewhat remarkable. There were a number of slave children that might have been sent from the plantation to Baltimore. There were those younger, those older, and those of the same age. I was chosen from among them all, and was the first, last, and only choice.

I may be deemed superstitious, and even egotistical, in regarding this event as a special interposition of divine Providence in my favor. But I should be false to the earliest sentiments of my soul, if I suppressed the opinion. I prefer to be true to myself, even at the hazard of incurring the ridicule of others, rather than to be false, and incur my own abhorrence. From my earliest recollection, I date the entertainment of a deep conviction that slavery would not always be able to hold me within its foul embrace; and in the darkest hours of my career in slavery, this living word of faith and spirit of hope departed not from me, but remained like ministering angels to cheer me through the gloom. This good spirit was from God, and to him I offer thanksgiving and praise.

Chapter 6

My new mistress proved to be all she appeared when I first met her at the door – a woman of the kindest heart and finest feelings. She had never had a slave under her control previously to myself, and prior to her marriage she had been dependent upon her own industry for a living. She was by trade a weaver; and by constant application to her business, she had been in a good degree preserved from the blighting and dehumanizing effects of slavery. I was utterly astonished at her goodness. I scarcely knew how to behave towards her. She was entirely unlike any other white woman I had ever seen. I could not approach her as I was accustomed to approach other white ladies. My early instruction was all out of place. The crouching servility, usually so acceptable a quality in a slave, did not answer when manifested toward her. Her favor was not gained by it; she seemed to be disturbed by it. She did not deem it impudent or unmannerly for a slave to look her in the face. The meanest slave was put fully at ease in her presence, and none left without feeling better for having seen her. Her face was made of heavenly smiles, and her voice of tranquil music.

But, alas! this kind heart had but a short time to remain such. The fatal poison of irresponsible power was already in her hands, and soon commenced its infernal work. That cheerful eye, under the influence of slavery, soon became red with rage; that voice, made all of sweet accord, changed to one of harsh and horrid discord; and that angelic face gave place to that of a demon.

Very soon after I went to live with Mr. and Mrs. Auld, she very kindly commenced to teach me the A, B, C. After I had learned this, she assisted me in learning to spell words of three or four letters. Just at this point of my progress, Mr. Auld found out what was going on, and at once forbade Mrs. Auld to instruct me further, telling her, among other things, that it was unlawful, as well as unsafe, to teach a slave to read. To use his own words, further, he said, "If you give a nigger an inch, he will take an ell. A nigger should know nothing but to obey his master – to do as he is told to do. Learning would *spoil* the best nigger in the world. Now," said he, "if you teach that nigger (speaking of myself) how to read, there would be no keeping him. It would forever unfit him to be a slave. He would at once become unmanageable, and of no value to his master. As to himself, it could do him no good, but a great deal of harm. It would make him discontented and unhappy." These words sank deep into my heart, stirred up sentiments within that lay slumbering, and called into existence an entirely new train of thought. It was a new and special revelation, explaining dark and mysterious things, with which my youthful understanding had struggled, but struggled in vain. I now understood what had been to me a most perplexing difficulty – to wit, the white man's power to enslave the black man. It was a grand achievement, and I prized it highly. From that moment, I understood the pathway from slavery to freedom. It was just what I wanted, and I got it at a time when I the least expected it. Whilst I was saddened by the thought of losing the aid of my kind mistress, I was gladdened by the invaluable instruction which, by the merest accident, I had gained from my master. Though conscious of the difficulty of learning without a teacher, I set out with high hope, and a fixed purpose, at whatever cost of trouble, to learn how to read. The very decided manner with which he spoke, and strove to impress his wife with the evil consequences of giving me instruction, served to convince me that he was deeply sensible of the truths he was uttering. It gave me the best assurance that I might rely with the utmost confidence on the results which, he said, would flow from teaching me to read. What he most dreaded, that I most desired. What he most loved, that I most hated. That which to him was a great evil, to be carefully shunned, was to me a great good, to be diligently sought; and the argument which he so warmly urged, against my learning to read, only served to inspire me with a desire and determination to learn. In learning to read, I owe almost as much to the bitter opposition of my master, as to the kindly aid of my mistress. I acknowledge the benefit of both.

I had resided but a short time in Baltimore before I observed a marked difference, in the treatment of slaves, from that which I had witnessed in the country. A city slave is almost a freeman, compared with a slave on the plantation. He is much better fed and clothed, and enjoys privileges altogether unknown to the slave on the plantation. There is a vestige of decency, a sense of shame, that does much to curb and check those outbreaks of atrocious cruelty so commonly enacted upon the plantation. He is a desperate slaveholder, who will shock the humanity of his non-slaveholding neighbors with the cries of his lacerated slave. Few are willing to incur the odium attaching to the reputation of being a cruel master; and above all things, they would not be known as not giving a slave enough to eat. Every city slaveholder is anxious to have it known of him, that he feeds his slaves well; and it is due to them to say, that most of them do give their slaves enough to eat. There are, however, some painful exceptions to this rule. Directly opposite to us, on Philpot Street, lived Mr. Thomas Hamilton. He owned two slaves. Their names were Henrietta and Mary. Henrietta was about twenty-two years of age, Mary was about fourteen; and of all the mangled and emaciated creatures I ever looked upon, these two were the most so. His heart must be harder than stone, that could look upon these unmoved. The head, neck, and shoulders of Mary were literally cut to pieces. I have frequently felt her head, and found it nearly covered with festering sores, caused by the lash of her cruel mistress. I do not know that her master ever whipped her, but I have been an eye-witness to the cruelty of Mrs. Hamilton. I used to be in Mr. Hamilton's house nearly every day. Mrs. Hamilton used to sit in a large chair in the middle of the room, with a heavy cowskin always by her side, and scarce an hour passed during the day but was marked by the blood of one of these slaves. The girls seldom passed her without her saying, "Move faster, you *black gip!*" at the same time giving them a blow with the cowskin over the head or shoulders, often drawing the blood. She would then say, "take that, you *black gip*" – continuing, "If you don't move faster, I'll move you!" Added to the cruel lashings to which these slaves were subjected, they were kept nearly half-starved. They seldom knew what it was to eat a full meal. I have seen Mary contending with the pigs for the offal thrown into the street. So much was Mary kicked and cut to pieces, that she was oftener called "*pecked*" than by her name.

Chapter 7

I LIVED in Master Hugh's family about seven years. During this time I succeeded in learning to read and write. In accomplishing this, I was compelled to resort to various stratagems. I had no regular teacher. My mistress, who had kindly commenced to instruct me, had, in compliance with the advice and direction of her husband, not only ceased to instruct, but had set her face against my being instructed by anyone[38] else. It is due, however, to my mistress to say of her, that she did not adopt this course of treatment immediately. She at first lacked the depravity indispensable to shutting me up in mental darkness. It was at least necessary for her to have some training in the exercise of irresponsible power, to make her equal to the task of treating me as though I were a brute.

My mistress was, as I have said, a kind and tender-hearted woman; and in the simplicity of her soul she commenced, when I first went to live with her, to treat me as she supposed one human being ought to treat another. In entering upon the duties of a slaveholder, she did not seem to perceive that I sustained to her the relation of a mere chattel, and that for her to treat me as a human being was not only wrong, but dangerously so. Slavery proved as injurious to her as it did to me. When I went there, she was a pious, warm, and tenderhearted woman. There was no sorrow or suffering for which she had not a tear. She had bread for the hungry, clothes for the naked, and comfort for every mourner that came within her reach. Slavery soon proved its ability to divest her of these heavenly qualities. Under its influence, the tender heart became stone, and the lamblike disposition gave way to one of tiger-like fierceness. The first step in her downward course was in her ceasing to instruct me. She now commenced to practise her husband's precepts. She finally became even more violent in her opposition than her husband himself. She was not satisfied with simply doing as well as he had commanded; she seemed anxious to do better. Nothing seemed to make her more angry than to see me with a newspaper. She seemed to think that here lay the danger. I have had her rush at me with a face made all up of fury, and snatch from me a newspaper, in a manner that fully revealed her apprehension. She was an apt woman; and a little experience soon demonstrated, to her satisfaction, that education and slavery were incompatible with each other.

From this time I was most narrowly watched. If I was in a separate room any considerable length of time, I was sure to be suspected of having a book, and was at once called to give an account of myself. All this, however, was too late. The first step had been taken. Mistress, in teaching me the alphabet, had given me the *inch*, and no precaution could prevent me from taking the *ell*.

The plan which I adopted, and the one by which I was most successful, was that of making friends of all the little white boys whom I met in the street. As many of these as I could, I converted into teachers. With their kindly aid, obtained at different times and in different places, I finally succeeded in learning to read. When I was sent on errands,[39] I always took my book with me, and by going one part of my errand quickly,

Notes

[38] *Original reads*: any one [ed.].

[39] *Original reads*: sent of errands [ed.].

I found time to get a lesson before my return. I used also to carry bread with me, enough of which was always in the house, and to which I was always welcome; for I was much better off in this regard than many of the poor white children in our neighborhood. This bread I used to bestow upon the hungry little urchins, who, in return, would give me that more valuable bread of knowledge. I am strongly tempted to give the names of two or three of those little boys, as a testimonial of the gratitude and affection I bear them; but prudence forbids; not that it would injure me, but it might embarrass them; for it is almost an unpardonable offence to teach slaves to read in this Christian country. It is enough to say of the dear little fellows, that they lived on Philpot Street, very near Durgin and Bailey's ship-yard. I used to talk this matter of slavery over with them. I would sometimes say to them, I wished I could be as free as they would be when they got to be men. "You will be free as soon as you are twenty-one, *but I am a slave for life!* Have not I as good a right to be free as you have?" These words used to trouble them; they would express for me the liveliest sympathy, and console me with the hope that something would occur by which I might be free.

I was now about twelve years old, and the thought of being *a slave for life* began to bear heavily upon my heart. Just about this time, I got hold of a book entitled "The Columbian Orator."[40] Every opportunity I got, I used to read this book. Among much of other interesting matter, I found in it a dialogue between a master and his slave. The slave was represented as having run away from his master three times. The dialogue represented the conversation which took place between them, when the slave was retaken the third time. In this dialogue, the whole argument in behalf of slavery was brought forward by the master, all of which was disposed of by the slave. The slave was made to say some very smart as well as impressive things in reply to his master – things which had the desired though unexpected effect; for the conversation resulted in the voluntary emancipation of the slave on the part of the master.

In the same book, I met with one of Sheridan's[41] mighty speeches on and in behalf of Catholic emancipation. These were choice documents to me. I read them over and over again with unabated interest. They gave tongue to interesting thoughts of my own soul, which had frequently flashed through my mind, and died away for want of utterance. The moral which I gained from the dialogue was the power of truth over the conscience of even a slaveholder. What I got from Sheridan was a bold denunciation of slavery, and a powerful vindication of human rights. The reading of these documents enabled me to utter my thoughts, and to meet the arguments brought forward to sustain slavery; but while they relieved me of one difficulty, they brought on another even more painful than the one of which I was relieved. The more I read, the more I was led to abhor and detest my enslavers. I could regard them in no other light than a band of successful robbers, who had left their homes, and gone to Africa, and stolen us from our homes, and in a strange land reduced us to slavery. I loathed them as being the meanest as well as the most wicked of men. As I read and contemplated the subject, behold! that very discontentment which Master Hugh had predicted would follow my learning to read had already come, to torment and sting my soul to unutterable anguish. As I writhed under it, I would at times feel that learning to read had been a curse rather than a blessing. It had given me a view of my wretched condition, without the remedy. It opened my eyes to the horrible pit, but to no ladder upon which to

Notes

[40] *The Columbian Orator* (1797) was a popular collection of writings, poems, and dialogues used as a pedagogical tool for the instruction of writing and rhetoric.

[41] *Sheridan* Richard Brinsley Sheridan (1751–1816), Irish playwright and politician.

get out. In moments of agony, I envied my fellow-slaves for their stupidity. I have often wished myself a beast. I preferred the condition of the meanest reptile to my own. Anything,[42] no matter what, to get rid of thinking! It was this everlasting thinking of my condition that tormented me. There was no getting rid of it. It was pressed upon me by every object within sight or hearing, animate or inanimate. The silver trump of freedom had roused my soul to eternal wakefulness. Freedom now appeared, to disappear no more forever. It was heard in every sound, and seen in everything.[43] It was ever present to torment me with a sense of my wretched condition. I saw nothing without seeing it, I heard nothing without hearing it, and felt nothing without feeling it. It looked from every star, it smiled in every calm, breathed in every wind, and moved in every storm.

I often found myself regretting my own existence, and wishing myself dead; and but for the hope of being free, I have no doubt but that I should have killed myself, or done something for which I should have been killed. While in this state of mind, I was eager to hear anyone[44] speak of slavery. I was a ready listener. Every little while, I could hear something about the abolitionists. It was some time before I found what the word meant. It was always used in such connections as to make it an interesting word to me. If a slave ran away and succeeded in getting clear, or if a slave killed his master, set fire to a barn, or did anything[45] very wrong in the mind of a slaveholder, it was spoken of as the fruit of *abolition*. Hearing the word in this connection very often, I set about learning what it meant. The dictionary afforded me little or no help. I found it was "the act of abolishing"; but then I did not know what was to be abolished. Here I was perplexed. I did not dare to ask anyone[46] about its meaning, for I was satisfied that it was something they wanted me to know very little about. After a patient waiting, I got one of our city papers, containing an account of the number of petitions from the north, praying for the abolition of slavery in the District of Columbia, and of the slave trade between the States. From this time I understood the words *abolition* and *abolitionist*, and always drew near when that word was spoken, expecting to hear something of importance to myself and fellow-slaves. The light broke in upon me by degrees. I went one day down on the wharf of Mr. Waters; and seeing two Irishmen unloading a scow of stone, I went, unasked, and helped them. When we had finished, one of them came to me and asked me if I were a slave. I told him I was. He asked, "Are ye a slave for life?" I told him that I was. The good Irishman seemed to be deeply affected by the statement. He said to the other that it was a pity so fine a little fellow as myself should be a slave for life. He said it was a shame to hold me. They both advised me to run away to the north; that I should find friends there, and that I should be free. I pretended not to be interested in what they said, and treated them as if I did not understand them; for I feared they might be treacherous. White men have been known to encourage slaves to escape, and then, to get the reward, catch them and return them to their masters. I was afraid that these seemingly good men might use me so; but I nevertheless remembered their advice, and from that time I resolved to run away. I looked forward to a time at which it would be safe for me to escape. I was too young to think of doing so immediately; besides, I wished to learn how to write, as I might have occasion to write my own pass. I consoled myself with the hope that I should one day find a good chance. Meanwhile, I would learn to write.

Notes

[42] *Original reads*: every thing [ed.].

[43] *Original reads*: any thing [ed.].

[44] *Original reads*: any one [ed.].

[45] *Original reads*: any thing [ed.].

[46] *Original reads*: any one [ed.].

The idea as to how I might learn to write was suggested to me by being in Durgin and Bailey's ship-yard, and frequently seeing the ship carpenters, after hewing, and getting a piece of timber ready for use, write on the timber the name of that part of the ship for which it was intended. When a piece of timber was intended for the larboard side, it would be marked thus – "L." When a piece was for the starboard side, it would be marked thus – "S." A piece for the larboard side forward, would be marked thus – "L. F." When a piece was for starboard side forward, it would be marked thus – "S. F." For larboard aft, it would be marked thus – "L. A." For starboard aft, it would be marked thus – "S. A." I soon learned the names of these letters, and for what they were intended when placed upon a piece of timber in the ship-yard. I immediately commenced copying them, and in a short time was able to make the four letters named. After that, when I met with any boy who I knew could write, I would tell him I could write as well as he. The next word would be, "I don't believe you. Let me see you try it." I would then make the letters which I had been so fortunate as to learn, and ask him to beat that. In this way I got a good many lessons in writing, which it is quite possible I should never have gotten in any other way. During this time, my copy-book was the board fence, brick wall, and pavement; my pen and ink was a lump of chalk. With these, I learned mainly how to write. I then commenced and continued copying the Italics in Webster's Spelling Book,[47] until I could make them all without looking on the book. By this time, my little Master Thomas had gone to school, and learned how to write, and had written over a number of copybooks. These had been brought home, and shown to some of our near neighbors, and then laid aside. My mistress used to go to class meeting at the Wilk Street meeting-house every Monday afternoon, and leave me to take care of the house. When left thus, I used to spend the time in writing in the spaces left in Master Thomas's copy-book, copying what he had written. I continued to do this until I could write a hand very similar to that of Master Thomas. Thus, after a long, tedious effort for years, I finally succeeded in learning how to write.

Chapter 8

In a very short time after I went to live at Baltimore, my old master's youngest son Richard died; and in about three years and six months after his death, my old master, Captain Anthony, died, leaving only his son, Andrew, and daughter, Lucretia, to share his estate. He died while on a visit to see his daughter at Hillsborough. Cut off thus unexpectedly, he left no will as to the disposal of his property. It was therefore necessary to have a valuation of the property, that it might be equally divided between Mrs. Lucretia and Master Andrew. I was immediately sent for, to be valued with the other property. Here again my feelings rose up in detestation of slavery. I had now a new conception of my degraded condition. Prior to this, I had become, if not insensible to my lot, at least party so. I left Baltimore with a young heart overborne with sadness, and a soul full of apprehension. I took passage with Captain Rowe, in the schooner Wild Cat, and, after a sail of about twenty-four hours, I found myself near the place of my birth. I had now been absent from it almost, if not quite, five years. I, however, remembered the place very well. I was only about five years old when I left it, to go and live with my old master on Colonel Lloyd's plantation; so that I was now between ten and eleven years old.

Notes

[47] *Webster's Spelling Book* Noah Webster (1758–1843) was an American lexicographer instrumental in systematizing language and scholarship in the United States; his *Spelling* book first appeared in 1783.

We were all ranked together at the valuation. Men and women, old and young, married and single, were ranked with horses, sheep, and swine. There were horses and men, cattle and women, pigs and children, all holding the same rank in the scale of being, and were all subjected to the same narrow examination. Silvery-headed age and sprightly youth, maids and matrons, had to undergo the same indelicate inspection. At this moment, I saw more clearly than ever the brutalizing effects of slavery upon both slave and slaveholder.

After the valuation, then came the division. I have no language to express the high excitement and deep anxiety which were felt among us poor slaves during this time. Our fate for life was now to be decided. We had no more voice in that decision than the brutes among whom we were ranked. A single word from the white men was enough – against all our wishes, prayers, and entreaties – to sunder forever the dearest friends, dearest kindred, and strongest ties known to human beings. In addition to the pain of separation, there was the horrid dread of falling into the hands of Master Andrew. He was known to us all as being a most cruel wretch – a common drunkard, who had, by his reckless mismanagement and profligate dissipation, already wasted a large portion of his father's property. We all felt that we might as well be sold at once to the Georgia traders, as to pass into his hands; for we knew that that would be our inevitable condition – a condition held by us all in the utmost horror and dread.

I suffered more anxiety than most of my fellow-slaves. I had known what it was to be kindly treated; they had known nothing of the kind. They had seen little or nothing of the world. They were in very deed men and women of sorrow, and acquainted with grief. Their backs had been made familiar with the bloody lash, so that they had become callous; mine was yet tender; for while at Baltimore I got few whippings, and few slaves could boast of a kinder master and mistress than myself; and the thought of passing out of their hands into those of Master Andrew – a man who, but a few days before, to give me a sample of his bloody disposition, took my little brother by the throat, threw him on the ground, and with the heel of his boot stamped upon his head till the blood gushed from his nose and ears – was well calculated to make me anxious as to my fate. After he had committed this savage outrage upon my brother, he turned to me, and said that was the way he meant to serve me one of these days – meaning, I suppose, when I came into his possession.

Thanks to a kind Providence, I fell to the portion of Mrs. Lucretia, and was sent immediately back to Baltimore, to live again in the family of Master Hugh. Their joy at my return equaled their sorrow at my departure. It was a glad day to me. I had escaped a worse than lion's jaws. I was absent from Baltimore, for the purpose of valuation and division, just about one month, and it seemed to have been six.

Very soon after my return to Baltimore, my mistress, Lucretia, died, leaving her husband and one child, Amanda; and in a very short time after her death, Master Andrew died. Now all the property of my old master, slaves included, was in the hands of strangers – strangers who had had nothing to do with accumulating it. Not a slave was left free. All remained slaves, from the youngest to the oldest. If any one thing in my experience, more than another, served to deepen my conviction of the infernal character of slavery, and to fill me with unutterable loathing of slaveholders, it was their base ingratitude to my poor old grandmother. She had served my old master faithfully from youth to old age. She had been the source of all his wealth; she had peopled his plantation with slaves; she had become a great grandmother in his service. She had rocked him in infancy, attended him in childhood, served him through life, and at his death wiped from his icy brow the cold death-sweat, and closed his eyes forever. She was nevertheless left a slave – a slave for life – a slave in the hands of strangers; and in their hands she saw her children, her grandchildren, and her great-grandchildren, divided, like so many sheep, without being gratified with the small privilege of a single word, as to their or her own destiny. And, to cap the climax of their base ingratitude and fiendish barbarity, my grandmother, who was now very old, having outlived my old master and all his children, having seen the beginning and end of all of them, and her present owners finding she was of but little value, her frame already racked with the pains of old age, and complete helplessness fast stealing over her once active limbs, they took her to the woods, built her a little hut, put up a little mud-chimney, and then made her welcome to the privilege of supporting herself there in perfect loneliness; thus virtually turning her out to die! If my poor old grandmother now lives, she lives to suffer in utter loneliness; she lives to remember and mourn over the loss of children, the loss of grandchildren, and the loss of great-grandchildren. They are, in the language of the slave's poet, Whittier,[48] –

"Gone, gone, sold and gone
To the rice swamp dank and lone,
Where the slave-whip ceaseless swings,
Where the noisome insect stings,
Where the fever-demon strews
Poison with the falling dews,
Where the sickly sunbeams glare
Through the hot and misty air –
Gone, gone, sold and gone
To the rice swamp dank and lone,
From Virginia hills and waters –
Woe is me, my stolen daughters!"

The hearth is desolate. The children, the unconscious children, who once sang and danced in her presence, are gone. She gropes her way, in the darkness of age, for a drink of water. Instead of the voices of her children, she hears by day the moans of the dove, and by night the screams of the hideous owl. All is gloom. The grave is at the door. And now, when weighed down by the pains and aches of old age, when the head inclines to the feet, when the beginning and ending of human existence meet, and helpless infancy and painful old age combine together – at this time, this most needful time, the time for the exercise of that tenderness and affection which children only can exercise towards a declining parent – my poor old grandmother, the devoted mother of twelve children, is left all alone, in yonder little hut, before a few dim embers. She stands – she sits – she staggers – she falls – she groans – she dies – and there are none of her children or grandchildren present, to wipe from her wrinkled brow the cold sweat of death, or to place beneath the sod her fallen remains. Will not a righteous God visit for these things?

In about two years after the death of Mrs. Lucretia, Master Thomas married his second wife. Her name was Rowena Hamilton. She was the eldest daughter of Mr. William Hamilton. Master now lived in St. Michael's. Not long after his marriage, a misunderstanding took place between himself and Master Hugh; and as a means of punishing his brother, he took me from him to live with himself at St. Michael's. Here I underwent another most painful separation. It, however, was not so severe as the one

Notes

[48] *Whittier* John Greenleaf Whittier (1807–1892), American poet and abolitionist; the poem quoted is "The Farewell of a Virginia Slave Mother to Her Daughters Sold into Southern Bondage" (1838).

I dreaded at the division of property; for, during this interval, a great change had taken place in Master Hugh and his once kind and affectionate wife. The influence of brandy upon him, and of slavery upon her, had effected a disastrous change in the characters of both; so that, as far as they were concerned, I thought I had little to lose by the change. But it was not to them that I was attached. It was to those little Baltimore boys that I felt the strongest attachment. I had received many good lessons from them, and was still receiving them, and the thought of leaving them was painful indeed. I was leaving, too, without the hope of ever being allowed to return. Master Thomas had said he would never let me return again. The barrier betwixt himself and brother he considered impassable.

I then had to regret that I did not at least make the attempt to carry out my resolution to run away; for the chances of success are tenfold greater from the city than from the country.

I sailed from Baltimore for St. Michael's in the sloop Amanda, Captain Edward Dodson. On my passage, I paid particular attention to the direction which the steamboats took to go to Philadelphia. I found, instead of going down, on reaching North Point they went up the bay, in a north-easterly direction. I deemed this knowledge of the utmost importance. My determination to run away was again revived. I resolved to wait only so long as the offering of a favorable opportunity. When that came, I was determined to be off.

Chapter 9

I HAVE now reached a period of my life when I can give dates. I left Baltimore, and went to live with Master Thomas Auld, at St. Michael's, in March, 1832. It was now more than seven years since I lived with him in the family of my old master, on Colonel Lloyd's plantation. We of course were now almost entire strangers to each other. He was to me a new master, and I to him a new slave. I was ignorant of his temper and disposition; he was equally so of mine. A very short time, however, brought us into full acquaintance with each other. I was made acquainted with his wife not less than with himself. They were well matched, being equally mean and cruel. I was now, for the first time during a space of more than seven years, made to feel the painful gnawings of hunger – something which I had not experienced since I left Colonel Lloyd's plantation.[49] It went hard enough with me then, when I could look back to no period at which I had enjoyed a sufficiency. It was tenfold harder after living in Master Hugh's family, where I had always had enough to eat, and of that which was good. I have said Master Thomas was a mean man. He was so. Not to give a slave enough to eat, is regarded as the most aggravated development of meanness even among slaveholders. The rule is, no matter how coarse the food, only let there be enough of it. This is the theory; and in the part of Maryland from which I came, it is the general practice – though there are many exceptions. Master Thomas gave us enough of neither coarse nor fine food. There were four slaves of us in the kitchen – my sister Eliza, my aunt Priscilla, Henny, and myself; and we were allowed less than a half of a bushel of corn-meal per week, and very little else, either in the shape of meat or vegetables. It was not enough for us to subsist upon. We were therefore reduced to the wretched necessity

Notes

[49] *Original reads*: a something which I had not experienced before since I left Colonel Lloyd's plantation [ed.].

of living at the expense of our neighbors. This we did by begging and stealing, whichever came handy in the time of need, the one being considered as legitimate as the other. A great many times have we poor creatures been nearly perishing with hunger, when food in abundance lay mouldering in the safe and smoke-house,[50] and our pious mistress was aware of the fact; and yet that mistress and her husband would kneel every morning, and pray that God would bless them in basket and store!

Bad as all slaveholders are, we seldom meet one destitute of every element of character commanding respect. My master was one of this rare sort. I do not know of one single noble act ever performed by him. The leading trait in his character was meanness; and if there were any other element in his nature, it was made subject to this. He was mean; and, like most other mean men, he lacked the ability to conceal his meanness. Captain Auld was not born a slaveholder. He had been a poor man, master only of a Bay craft. He came into possession of all his slaves by marriage; and of all men, adopted slaveholders are the worst. He was cruel, but cowardly. He commanded without firmness. In the enforcement of his rules, he was at times rigid, and at times lax. At times, he spoke to his slaves with the firmness of Napoleon and the fury of a demon; at other times, he might well be mistaken for an inquirer who had lost his way. He did nothing of himself. He might have passed for a lion, but for his ears. In all things noble which he attempted, his own meanness shone most conspicuous. His airs, words, and actions, were the airs, words, and actions of born slaveholders, and, being assumed, were awkward enough. He was not even a good imitator. He possessed all the disposition to deceive, but wanted the power. Having no resources within himself, he was compelled to be the copyist of many, and being such, he was forever the victim of inconsistency; and of consequence he was an object of contempt, and was held as such even by his slaves. The luxury of having slaves of his own to wait upon him was something new and unprepared for. He was a slaveholder without the ability to hold slaves. He found himself incapable of managing his slaves either by force, fear, or fraud. We seldom called him "master"; we generally called him "Captain Auld," and were hardly disposed to title him at all. I doubt not that our conduct had much to do with making him appear awkward, and of consequence fretful. Our want of reverence for him must have perplexed him greatly. He wished to have us call him master, but lacked the firmness necessary to command us to do so. His wife used to insist upon our calling him so, but to no purpose. In August, 1832, my master attended a Methodist camp-meeting[51] held in the Bay-side, Talbot county, and there experienced religion. I indulged a faint hope that his conversion would lead him to emancipate his slaves, and that, if he did not do this, it would, at any rate, make him more kind and humane. I was disappointed in both these respects. It neither made him to be humane to his slaves, nor to emancipate them. If it had any effect on his character, it made him more cruel and hateful in all his ways; for I believe him to have been a much worse man after his conversion than before. Prior to his conversion, he relied upon his own depravity to shield and sustain him in his savage barbarity; but after his conversion, he found religious sanction and support for his slaveholding cruelty. He made the greatest pretensions to piety. His house was the house of prayer. He prayed morning, noon, and night. He very soon distinguished himself among his brethren, and was soon made a

Notes

[50] *safe and smoke-house* for storing and curing meats, respectively.

[51] *Methodist camp-meeting* Camp meetings were temporary camps to which people would travel to hear itinerant preachers; they were a feature of frontier life and of the Second Great Awakening.

class-leader and exhorter. His activity in revivals was great, and he proved himself an instrument in the hands of the church in converting many souls. His house was the preachers' home. They used to take great pleasure in coming there to put up; for while he starved us, he stuffed them. We have had three or four preachers there at a time. The names of those who used to come most frequently while I lived there, were Mr. Storks, Mr. Ewery, Mr. Humphry, and Mr. Hickey. I have also seen Mr. George Cookman at our house. We slaves loved Mr. Cookman. We believed him to be a good man. We thought him instrumental in getting Mr. Samuel Harrison, a very rich slaveholder, to emancipate his slaves; and by some means got the impression that he was laboring to effect the emancipation of all the slaves. When he was at our house, we were sure to be called in to prayers. When the others were there, we were sometimes called in and sometimes not. Mr. Cookman took more notice of us than either of the other ministers. He could not come among us without betraying his sympathy for us, and, stupid as we were, we had the sagacity to see it.

While I lived with my master in St. Michael's, there was a white young man, a Mr. Wilson, who proposed to keep a Sabbath school for the instruction of such slaves as might be disposed to learn to read the New Testament. We met but three times, when Mr. West and Mr. Fairbanks, both class-leaders, with many others, came upon us with sticks and other missiles, drove us off, and forbade us to meet again. Thus ended our little Sabbath school in the pious town of St. Michael's.

I have said my master found religious sanction for his cruelty. As an example, I will state one of many facts going to prove the charge. I have seen him tie up a lame young woman, and whip her with a heavy cowskin upon her naked shoulders, causing the warm red blood to drip; and, in justification of the bloody deed, he would quote this passage of Scripture – "He that knoweth his master's will, and doeth it not, shall be beaten with many stripes."[52]

Master would keep this lacerated young woman tied up in this horrid situation four or five hours at a time. I have known him to tie her up early in the morning, and whip her before breakfast; leave her, go to his store, return at dinner, and whip her again, cutting her in the places already made raw with his cruel lash. The secret of master's cruelty toward "Henny" is found in the fact of her being almost helpless. When quite a child, she fell into the fire, and burned herself horribly. Her hands were so burnt that she never got the use of them. She could do very little but bear heavy burdens. She was to master a bill of expense; and as he was a mean man, she was a constant offence to him. He seemed desirous of getting the poor girl out of existence. He gave her away once to his sister; but, being a poor gift, she was not disposed to keep her. Finally, my benevolent master, to use his own words, "set her adrift to take care of herself." Here was a recently-converted man, holding on upon the mother, and at the same time turning out her helpless child, to starve and die! Master Thomas was one of the many pious slaveholders who hold slaves for the very charitable purpose of taking care of them.

My master and I[53] had quite a number of differences. He found me unsuitable to his purpose. My city life, he said, had had a very pernicious effect upon me. It had almost ruined me for every good purpose, and fitted me for everything[54] which was bad. One of my greatest faults was that of letting his horse run away, and go down to his father-in-law's farm, which was about five miles from St. Michael's. I would then have to go after it. My reason for this kind of carelessness, or carefulness, was that I could always

Notes

[52] *"He that knoweth ... stripes"* Luke 12:47.

[53] *Original reads*: myself [ed.].

[54] *Original reads*: every thing [ed.].

get something to eat when I went there. Master William Hamilton, my master's father-in-law, always gave his slaves enough to eat. I never left there hungry, no matter how great the need of my speedy return. Master Thomas at length said he would stand it no longer. I had lived with him nine months, during which time he had given me a number of severe whippings, all to no good purpose. He resolved to put me out, as he said, to be broken; and, for this purpose, he let me for one year to a man named Edward Covey. Mr. Covey was a poor man, a farm-renter. He rented the place upon which he lived, as also the hands with which he tilled it. Mr. Covey had acquired a very high reputation for breaking young slaves, and this reputation was of immense value to him. It enabled him to get his farm tilled with much less expense to himself than he could have had it done without such a reputation. Some slaveholders thought it not much loss to allow Mr. Covey to have their slaves one year, for the sake of the training to which they were subjected, without any other compensation. He could hire young help with great ease, in consequence of this reputation. Added to the natural good qualities of Mr. Covey, he was a professor of religion – a pious soul – a member and a class-leader in the Methodist church. All of this added weight to his reputation as a "nigger-breaker." I was aware of all the facts, having been made acquainted with them by a young man who had lived there. I nevertheless made the change gladly; for I was sure of getting enough to eat, which is not the smallest consideration to a hungry man.

Chapter 10

I LEFT Master Thomas's house, and went to live with Mr. Covey, on the 1st of January, 1833. I was now, for the first time in my life, a field hand. In my new employment, I found myself even more awkward than a country boy appeared to be in a large city. I had been at my new home but one week before Mr. Covey gave me a very severe whipping, cutting my back, causing the blood to run, and raising ridges on my flesh as large as my little finger. The details of this affair are as follows: Mr. Covey sent me, very early in the morning of one of our coldest days in the month of January, to the woods, to get a load of wood. He gave me a team of unbroken oxen. He told me which was the in-hand ox, and which the off-hand one.[55] He then tied the end of a large rope around the horns of the in-hand ox, and gave me the other end of it, and told me, if the oxen started to run, that I must hold on upon the rope. I had never driven oxen before, and of course I was very awkward. I, however, succeeded in getting to the edge of the woods with little difficulty; but I had got a very few rods into the woods, when the oxen took fright, and started full tilt, carrying the cart against trees, and over stumps, in the most frightful manner. I expected every moment that my brains would be dashed out against the trees. After running thus for a considerable distance, they finally upset the cart, dashing it with great force against a tree, and threw themselves into a dense thicket. How I escaped death, I do not know. There I was, entirely alone, in a thick wood, in a place new to me. My cart was upset and shattered, my oxen were entangled among the young trees, and there was none to help me. After a long spell of effort, I succeeded in getting my cart righted, my oxen disentangled, and again yoked to the cart. I now proceeded with my team to the place where I had, the day before,

Notes

[55] *in-hand ox and the off-hand one* the oxen on the left and the right side of the yoke.

been chopping wood, and loaded my cart pretty heavily, thinking in this way to tame my oxen. I then proceeded on my way home. I had now consumed one half of the day. I got out of the woods safely, and now felt out of danger. I stopped my oxen to open the woods gate; and just as I did so, before I could get hold of my ox-rope, the oxen again started, rushed through the gate, catching it between the wheel and the body of the cart, tearing it to pieces, and coming within a few inches of crushing me against the gate-post. Thus twice, in one short day, I escaped death by the merest chance. On my return, I told Mr. Covey what had happened, and how it happened. He ordered me to return to the woods again immediately. I did so, and he followed on after me. Just as I got into the woods, he came up and told me to stop my cart, and that he would teach me how to trifle away my time, and break gates. He then went to a large gum-tree, and with his axe cut three large switches, and, after trimming them up neatly with his pocket-knife, he ordered me to take off my clothes. I made him no answer, but stood with my clothes on. He repeated his order. I still made him no answer, nor did I move to strip myself. Upon this he rushed at me with the fierceness of a tiger, tore off my clothes, and lashed me till he had worn out his switches, cutting me so savagely as to leave the marks visible for a long time after. This whipping was the first of a number just like it, and for similar offences.

I lived with Mr. Covey one year. During the first six months, of that year, scarce a week passed without his whipping me. I was seldom free from a sore back. My awkwardness was almost always his excuse for whipping me. We were worked fully up to the point of endurance. Long before day we were up, our horses fed, and by the first approach of day we were off to the field with our hoes and ploughing teams. Mr. Covey gave us enough to eat, but scarce time to eat it. We were often less than five minutes taking our meals. We were often in the field from the first approach of day till its last lingering ray had left us; and at saving-fodder time,[56] midnight often caught us in the field binding blades.[57]

Covey would be out with us. The way he used to stand it, was this. He would spend the most of his afternoons in bed. He would then come out fresh in the evening, ready to urge us on with his words, example, and frequently with the whip. Mr. Covey was one of the few slaveholders who could and did work with his hands. He was a hard-working man. He knew by himself just what a man or a boy could do. There was no deceiving him. His work went on in his absence almost as well as in his presence; and he had the faculty of making us feel that he was ever present with us. This he did by surprising us. He seldom approached the spot where we were at work openly, if he could do it secretly. He always aimed at taking us by surprise. Such was his cunning, that we used to call him, among ourselves, "the snake." When we were at work in the cornfield, he would sometimes crawl on his hands and knees to avoid detection, and all at once he would rise nearly in our midst, and scream out, "Ha, ha! Come, come! Dash on, dash on!" This being his mode of attack, it was never safe to stop a single minute. His comings were like a thief in the night. He appeared to us as being ever at hand. He was under every tree, behind every stump, in every bush, and at every window, on the plantation. He would sometimes mount his horse, as if bound to St. Michael's, a distance of seven miles, and in half an hour afterwards you would see him coiled up in the corner of the wood-fence, watching every motion of the slaves. He would, for this purpose, leave his horse tied up in the woods. Again, he would sometimes walk up to us, and give us orders as though he was upon the point of starting on

Notes

[56] *saving-fodder time* harvest season.

[57] *binding blades* tying up bundles of grain.

a long journey, turn his back upon us, and make as though he was going to the house to get ready; and, before he would get half way thither, he would turn short and crawl into a fence-corner, or behind some tree, and there watch us till the going down of the sun.

Mr. Covey's *forte* consisted in his power to deceive. His life was devoted to planning and perpetrating the grossest deceptions. Everything[58] he possessed in the shape of learning or religion, he made conform to his disposition to deceive. He seemed to think himself equal to deceiving the Almighty. He would make a short prayer in the morning, and a long prayer at night; and, strange as it may seem, few men would at times appear more devotional than he. The exercises of his family devotions were always commenced with singing; and, as he was a very poor singer himself, the duty of raising the hymn generally came upon me. He would read his hymn, and nod at me to commence. I would at times do so; at others, I would not. My non-compliance would almost always produce much confusion. To show himself independent of me, he would start and stagger through with his hymn in the most discordant manner. In this state of mind, he prayed with more than ordinary spirit. Poor man! such was his disposition, and success at deceiving, I do verily believe that he sometimes deceived himself into the solemn belief, that he was a sincere worshipper of the most high God; and this, too, at a time when he may be said to have been guilty of compelling his woman slave to commit the sin of adultery. The facts in the case are these: Mr. Covey was a poor man; he was just commencing in life; he was only able to buy one slave; and, shocking as is the fact, he bought her, as he said, for *a breeder*. This woman was named Caroline. Mr. Covey bought her from Mr. Thomas Lowe, about six miles from St. Michael's. She was a large, able-bodied woman, about twenty years old. She had already given birth to one child, which proved her to be just what he wanted. After buying her, he hired a married man of Mr. Samuel Harrison, to live with him one year; and him he used to fasten up with her every night! The result was, that, at the end of the year, the miserable woman gave birth to twins. At this result Mr. Covey seemed to be highly pleased, both with the man and the wretched woman. Such was his joy, and that of his wife, that nothing they could do for Caroline during her confinement was too good, or too hard, to be done. The children were regarded as being quite an addition to his wealth.

If at any one time of my life more than another, I was made to drink the bitterest dregs of slavery, that time was during the first six months of my stay with Mr. Covey. We were worked in all weathers. It was never too hot or too cold; it could never rain, blow, hail, or snow, too hard for us to work in the field. Work, work, work, was scarcely more the order of the day than of the night. The longest days were too short for him, and the shortest nights too long for him. I was somewhat unmanageable when I first went there, but a few months of this discipline tamed me. Mr. Covey succeeded in breaking me. I was broken in body, soul, and spirit. My natural elasticity was crushed, my intellect languished, the disposition to read departed, the cheerful spark that lingered about my eye died; the dark night of slavery closed in upon me; and behold a man transformed into a brute!

Sunday was my only leisure time. I spent this in a sort of beast-like stupor, between sleep and wake, under some large tree. At times I would rise up, a flash of energetic freedom would dart through my soul, accompanied with a faint beam of hope, that flickered for a moment, and then vanished. I sank down again, mourning over my

Notes

[58] *Original reads*: every thing [ed.].

wretched condition. I was sometimes prompted to take my life, and that of Covey, but was prevented by a combination of hope and fear. My sufferings on this plantation seem now like a dream rather than a stern reality.

Our house stood within a few rods of the Chesapeake Bay, whose broad bosom was ever white with sails from every quarter of the habitable globe. Those beautiful vessels, robed in purest white, so delightful to the eye of freemen, were to me so many shrouded ghosts, to terrify and torment me with thoughts of my wretched condition. I have often, in the deep stillness of a summer's Sabbath, stood all alone upon the lofty banks of that noble bay, and traced, with saddened heart and tearful eye, the countless number of sails moving off to the mighty ocean. The sight of these always affected me powerfully. My thoughts would compel utterance; and there, with no audience but the Almighty, I would pour out my soul's complaint, in my rude way, with an apostrophe to the moving multitude of ships:–

"You are loosed from your moorings, and are free; I am fast in my chains, and am a slave! You move merrily before the gentle gale, and I sadly before the bloody whip! You are freedom's swift-winged angels, that fly round the world; I am confined in bands of iron! O that I were free! O, that I were on one of your gallant decks, and under your protecting wing! Alas! betwixt me and you, the turbid waters roll. Go on, go on. O that I could also go! Could I but swim! If I could fly! O, why was I born a man, of whom to make a brute! The glad ship is gone; she hides in the dim distance. I am left in the hottest hell of unending slavery. O God, save me! God, deliver me! Let me be free! Is there any God? Why am I a slave? I will run away. I will not stand it. Get caught, or get clear, I'll try it. I had as well die with ague as the fever. I have only one life to lose. I had as well be killed running as die standing. Only think of it; one hundred miles straight north, and I am free! Try it? Yes! God helping me, I will. It cannot be that I shall live and die a slave. I will take to the water. This very bay shall yet bear me into freedom. The steamboats steered in a north-east course from North Point. I will do the same; and when I get to the head of the bay, I will turn my canoe adrift, and walk straight through Delaware into Pennsylvania. When I get there, I shall not be required to have a pass; I can travel without being disturbed. Let but the first opportunity offer, and, come what will, I am off. Meanwhile, I will try to bear up under the yoke. I am not the only slave in the world. Why should I fret? I can bear as much as any of them. Besides, I am but a boy, and all boys are bound to someone.[59] It may be that my misery in slavery will only increase my happiness when I get free. There is a better day coming."

Thus I used to think, and thus I used to speak to myself; goaded almost to madness at one moment, and at the next reconciling myself to my wretched lot.

I have already intimated that my condition was much worse, during the first six months of my stay at Mr. Covey's, than in the last six. The circumstances leading to the change in Mr. Covey's course toward me form an epoch in my humble history. You have seen how a man was made a slave; you shall see how a slave was made a man. On one of the hottest days of the month of August, 1833, Bill Smith, William Hughes, a slave named Eli, and myself, were engaged in fanning wheat.[60] Hughes was clearing the fanned wheat from before the fan, Eli was turning, Smith was feeding, and I was carrying wheat to the fan. The work was simple, requiring strength rather than intellect; yet, to one entirely unused to such work, it came very hard. About three o'clock of that day, I broke down; my strength failed me; I was seized with a violent aching of the head, attended with extreme dizziness; I trembled in every limb. Finding what was

Notes

[59] *Original reads*: some one [ed.].

[60] *fanning wheat* separating wheat from chaff.

coming, I nerved myself up, feeling it would never do to stop work. I stood as long as I could stagger to the hopper with grain. When I could stand no longer, I fell, and felt as if held down by an immense weight. The fan of course stopped; everyone[61] had his own work to do; and no one could do the work of the other, and have his own go on at the same time.

Mr. Covey was at the house, about one hundred yards from the treading-yard where we were fanning. On hearing the fan stop, he left immediately, and came to the spot where we were. He hastily inquired what the matter was. Bill answered that I was sick, and there was no one to bring wheat to the fan. I had by this time crawled away under the side of the post and rail-fence by which the yard was enclosed, hoping to find relief by getting out of the sun. He then asked where I was. He was told by one of the hands. He came to the spot, and, after looking at me awhile, asked me what was the matter. I told him as well as I could, for I scarce had strength to speak. He then gave me a savage kick in the side, and told me to get up. I tried to do so, but fell back in the attempt. He gave me another kick, and again told me to rise. I again tried, and succeeded in gaining my feet; but, stooping to get the tub with which I was feeding the fan, I again staggered and fell. While down in this situation, Mr. Covey took up the hickory slat with which Hughes had been striking off the half-bushel measure, and with it gave me a heavy blow upon the head, making a large wound, and the blood ran freely; and with this again told me to get up. I made no effort to comply, having now made up my mind to let him do his worst. In a short time after receiving this blow, my head grew better. Mr. Covey had now left me to my fate. At this moment I resolved, for the first time, to go to my master, enter a complaint, and ask his protection. In order to do this,[62] I must that afternoon walk seven miles; and this, under the circumstances, was truly a severe undertaking. I was exceedingly feeble; made so as much by the kicks and blows which I received, as by the severe fit of sickness to which I had been subjected. I, however, watched my chance, while Covey was looking in an opposite direction, and started for St. Michael's. I succeeded in getting a considerable distance on my way to the woods, when Covey discovered me, and called after me to come back, threatening what he would do if I did not come. I disregarded both his calls and his threats, and made my way to the woods as fast as my feeble state would allow; and thinking I might be overhauled by him if I kept the road, I walked through the woods, keeping far enough from the road to avoid detection, and near enough to prevent losing my way. I had not gone far before my little strength again failed me. I could go no farther. I fell down, and lay for a considerable time. The blood was yet oozing from the wound on my head. For a time I thought I should bleed to death; and think now that I should have done so, but that the blood so matted my hair as to stop the wound. After lying there about three quarters of an hour, I nerved myself up again, and started on my way, through bogs and briers, barefooted and bareheaded, tearing my feet sometimes at nearly every step; and after a journey of about seven miles, occupying some five hours to perform it, I arrived at master's store. I then presented an appearance enough to affect any but a heart of iron. From the crown of my head to my feet, I was covered with blood. My hair was all clotted with dust and blood; my shirt was stiff with blood. My legs and feet were torn in sundry places with briers and thorns, and were also covered with blood. I suppose I looked like a man who had escaped a den of wild beasts, and barely escaped them. In this state I appeared before my master, humbly entreating him to interpose his authority for my protection. I told him all the circumstances as well as I could, and

Notes

[61] *Original reads*: every one [ed.].

[62] *Original reads*: In order to this [ed.].

it seemed, as I spoke, at times to affect him. He would then walk the floor, and seek to justify Covey by saying he expected I deserved it. He asked me what I wanted. I told him, to let me get a new home; that as sure as I lived with Mr. Covey again, I should live with but to die with him; that Covey would surely kill me; he was in a fair way for it. Master Thomas ridiculed the idea that there was any danger of Mr. Covey's killing me, and said that he knew Mr. Covey; that he was a good man, and that he could not think of taking me from him; that, should he do so, he would lose the whole year's wages; that I belonged to Mr. Covey for one year, and that I must go back to him, come what might; and that I must not trouble him with any more stories, or that he would himself *get hold of me*. After threatening me thus, he gave me a very large dose of salts, telling me that I might remain in St. Michael's that night, (it being quite late,) but that I must be off back to Mr. Covey's early in the morning; and that if I did not, he would *get hold of me*, which meant that he would whip me. I remained all night, and, according to his orders, I started off to Covey's in the morning, (Saturday morning,) wearied in body and broken in spirit. I got no supper that night, or breakfast that morning. I reached Covey's about nine o'clock; and just as I was getting over the fence that divided Mrs. Kemp's fields from ours, out ran Covey with his cowskin, to give me another whipping. Before he could reach me, I succeeded in getting to the cornfield; and as the corn was very high, it afforded me the means of hiding. He seemed very angry, and searched for me a long time. My behavior was altogether unaccountable. He finally gave up the chase, thinking, I suppose, that I must come home for something to eat; he would give himself no further trouble in looking for me. I spent that day mostly in the woods, having the alternative before me – to go home and be whipped to death, or stay in the woods and be starved to death. That night, I fell in with Sandy Jenkins, a slave with whom I was somewhat acquainted. Sandy had a free wife, who lived about four miles from Mr. Covey's; and it being Saturday, he was on his way to see her. I told him my circumstances, and he very kindly invited me to go home with him. I went home with him, and talked this whole matter over, and got his advice as to what course it was best for me to pursue. I found Sandy an old adviser. He told me, with great solemnity, I must go back to Covey; but that before I went, I must go with him into another part of the woods, where there was a certain *root*, which, if I would take some of it with me, carrying it *always on my right side*, would render it impossible for Mr. Covey, or any other white man, to whip me. He said he had carried it for years; and since he had done so, he had never received a blow, and never expected to while he carried it. I at first rejected the idea, that the simple carrying of a root in my pocket would have any such effect as he had said, and was not disposed to take it; but Sandy impressed the necessity with much earnestness, telling me it could do no harm, if it did no good. To please him, I at length took the root, and, according to his direction, carried it upon my right side. This was Sunday morning. I immediately started for home; and upon entering the yard gate, out came Mr. Covey on his way to a meeting.[63] He spoke to me very kindly, bade me drive the pigs from a lot nearby,[64] and passed on towards the church. Now, this singular conduct of Mr. Covey really made me begin to think that there was something in the *root* which Sandy had given me; and had it been on any other day than Sunday, I could have attributed the conduct to no other cause than the influence of that root; and as it was, I was half inclined to think the *root* to be something more than I at first had taken it to be. All went well till Monday morning. On this morning, the virtue of the *root* was fully tested. Long before daylight, I was

Notes

[63] *Original reads*: on his way to meeting [ed.].

[64] *Original reads*: near by [ed.].

called to go and rub, curry, and feed, the horses. I obeyed, and was glad to obey. But whilst thus engaged, whilst in the act of throwing down some blades from the loft, Mr. Covey entered the stable with a long rope; and just as I was half out of the loft, he caught hold of my legs, and was about tying me. As soon as I found what he was up to, I gave a sudden spring, and as I did so, he holding to my legs, I was brought sprawling on the stable floor. Mr. Covey seemed now to think he had me, and could do what he pleased; but at this moment – from whence came the spirit I don't know – I resolved to fight; and, suiting my action to the resolution, I seized Covey hard by the throat; and as I did so, I rose. He held on to me, and I to him. My resistance was so entirely unexpected, that Covey seemed taken all aback. He trembled like a leaf. This gave me assurance, and I held him uneasy, causing the blood to run where I touched him with the ends of my fingers. Mr. Covey soon called out to Hughes for help. Hughes came, and, while Covey held me, attempted to tie my right hand. While he was in the act of doing so, I watched my chance, and gave him a heavy kick close under the ribs. This kick fairly sickened Hughes, so that he left me in the hands of Mr. Covey. This kick had the effect of not only weakening Hughes, but Covey also. When he saw Hughes bending over with pain, his courage quailed. He asked me if I meant to persist in my resistance. I told him I did, come what might; that he had used me like a brute for six months, and that I was determined to be used so no longer. With that, he strove to drag me to a stick that was lying just out of the stable door. He meant to knock me down. But just as he was leaning over to get the stick, I seized him with both hands by his collar, and brought him by a sudden snatch to the ground. By this time, Bill came. Covey called upon him for assistance. Bill wanted to know what he could do. Covey said, "Take hold of him, take hold of him!" Bill said his master hired him out to work, and not to help to whip me; so he left Covey and me[65] to fight our own battle out. We were at it for nearly two hours. Covey at length let me go, puffing and blowing at a great rate, saying that if I had not resisted, he would not have whipped me half so much. The truth was, that he had not whipped me at all. I considered him as getting entirely the worst end of the bargain; for he had drawn no blood from me, but I had from him. The whole six months afterwards, that I spent with Mr. Covey, he never laid the weight of his finger upon me in anger. He would occasionally say, he didn't want to get hold of me again. "No," thought I, "you need not; for you will come off worse than you did before."

This battle with Mr. Covey was the turning-point in my career as a slave. It rekindled the few expiring embers of freedom, and revived within me a sense of my own manhood. It recalled the departed self-confidence, and inspired me again with a determination to be free. The gratification afforded by the triumph was a full compensation for whatever else might follow, even death itself. He only can understand the deep satisfaction which I experienced, who has himself repelled by force the bloody arm of slavery. I felt as I never felt before. It was a glorious resurrection, from the tomb of slavery, to the heaven of freedom. My long-crushed spirit rose, cowardice departed, bold defiance took its place; and I now resolved that, however long I might remain a slave in form, the day had passed forever when I could be a slave in fact. I did not hesitate to let it be known of me, that the white man who expected to succeed in whipping, must also succeed in killing me.

From this time I was never again what might be called fairly whipped, though I remained a slave four years afterwards. I had several fights, but was never whipped.

Notes

[65] *Original reads*: myself [ed.].

It was for a long time a matter of surprise to me why Mr. Covey did not immediately have me taken by the constable to the whipping-post, and there regularly whipped for the crime of raising my hand against a white man in defence of myself. And the only explanation I can now think of does not entirely satisfy me; but such as it is, I will give it. Mr. Covey enjoyed the most unbounded reputation for being a first-rate overseer and negro-breaker. It was of considerable importance to him. That reputation was at stake; and had he sent me – a boy about sixteen years old – to the public whipping-post, his reputation would have been lost; so, to save his reputation, he suffered me to go unpunished.

My term of actual service to Mr. Edward Covey ended on Christmas day, 1833. The days between Christmas and New Year's Day[66] are allowed as holidays; and, accordingly, we were not required to perform any labor, more than to feed and take care of the stock. This time we regarded as our own, by the grace of our masters; and we therefore used or abused it nearly as we pleased. Those of us who had families at a distance, were generally allowed to spend the whole six days in their society. This time, however, was spent in various ways. The staid, sober, thinking and industrious ones of our number would employ themselves in making corn-brooms, mats, horse-collars, and baskets; and another class of us would spend the time in hunting opossums, hares, and coons. But by far the larger part engaged in such sports and merriments as playing ball, wrestling, running foot-races, fiddling, dancing, and drinking whisky; and this latter mode of spending the time was by far the most agreeable to the feelings of our masters. A slave who would work during the holidays was considered by our masters as scarcely deserving them. He was regarded as one who rejected the favor of his master. It was deemed a disgrace not to get drunk at Christmas; and he was regarded as lazy indeed, who had not provided himself with the necessary means, during the year, to get whisky enough to last him through Christmas.

From what I know of the effect of these holidays upon the slave, I believe them to be among the most effective means in the hands of the slaveholder in keeping down the spirit of insurrection. Were the slaveholders at once to abandon this practice, I have not the slightest doubt it would lead to an immediate insurrection among the slaves. These holidays serve as conductors, or safety-valves, to carry off the rebellious spirit of enslaved humanity. But for these, the slave would be forced up to the wildest desperation; and woe betide the slaveholder, the day he ventures to remove or hinder the operation of those conductors! I warn him that, in such an event, a spirit will go forth in their midst, more to be dreaded than the most appalling earthquake.

The holidays are part and parcel of the gross fraud, wrong, and inhumanity of slavery. They are professedly a custom established by the benevolence of the slaveholders; but I undertake to say, it is the result of selfishness, and one of the grossest frauds committed upon the down-trodden slave. They do not give the slaves this time because they would not like to have their work during its continuance, but because they know it would be unsafe to deprive them of it. This will be seen by the fact, that the slaveholders like to have their slaves spend those days just in such a manner as to make them as glad of their ending as of their beginning. Their object seems to be, to disgust their slaves with freedom, by plunging them into the lowest depths of dissipation. For instance, the slaveholders not only like to see the slave drink of his own accord, but will adopt various plans to make him drunk. One plan is, to make bets on their slaves, as to who can drink the most whisky without getting drunk; and in this way they succeed in

Notes

[66] *Original reads*: New Year's day [ed.].

getting whole multitudes to drink to excess. Thus, when the slave asks for virtuous freedom, the cunning slaveholder, knowing his ignorance, cheats him with a dose of vicious dissipation, artfully labelled with the name of liberty. The most of us used to drink it down, and the result was just what might be supposed: many of us were led to think that there was little to choose between liberty and slavery. We felt, and very properly too, that we had almost as well be slaves to man as to rum. So, when the holidays ended, we staggered up from the filth of our wallowing, took a long breath, and marched to the field – feeling, upon the whole, rather glad to go, from what our master had deceived us into a belief was freedom, back to the arms of slavery.

I have said that this mode of treatment is a part of the whole system of fraud and inhumanity of slavery. It is so. The mode here adopted to disgust the slave with freedom, by allowing him to see only the abuse of it, is carried out in other things. For instance, a slave loves molasses; he steals some. His master, in many cases, goes off to town, and buys a large quantity; he returns, takes his whip, and commands the slave to eat the molasses, until the poor fellow is made sick at the very mention of it. The same mode is sometimes adopted to make the slaves refrain from asking for more food than their regular allowance. A slave runs through his allowance, and applies for more. His master is enraged at him; but, not willing to send him off without food, gives him more than is necessary, and compels him to eat it within a given time. Then, if he complains that he cannot eat it, he is said to be satisfied neither full nor fasting, and is whipped for being hard to please! I have an abundance of such illustrations of the same principle, drawn from my own observation, but think the cases I have cited sufficient. The practice is a very common one.

On the first of January, 1834, I left Mr. Covey, and went to live with Mr. William Freeland, who lived about three miles from St. Michael's. I soon found Mr. Freeland a very different man from Mr. Covey. Though not rich, he was what would be called an educated southern gentleman. Mr. Covey, as I have shown, was a well-trained negro-breaker and slave-driver. The former (slaveholder though he was) seemed to possess some regard for honor, some reverence for justice, and some respect for humanity. The latter seemed totally insensible to all such sentiments. Mr. Freeland had many of the faults peculiar to slaveholders, such as being very passionate and fretful; but I must do him the justice to say, that he was exceedingly free from those degrading vices to which Mr. Covey was constantly addicted. The one was open and frank, and we always knew where to find him. The other was a most artful deceiver, and could be understood only by such as were skilful enough to detect his cunningly-devised frauds. Another advantage I gained in my new master was, he made no pretensions to, or profession of, religion; and this, in my opinion, was truly a great advantage. I assert most unhesitatingly, that the religion of the south is a mere covering for the most horrid crimes – a justifier of the most appalling barbarity – a sanctifier of the most hateful frauds – and a dark shelter under which the darkest, foulest, grossest, and most infernal deeds of slaveholders find the strongest protection. Were I to be again reduced to the chains of slavery, next to that enslavement, I should regard being the slave of a religious master the greatest calamity that could befall me. For of all slaveholders with whom I have ever met, religious slaveholders are the worst. I have ever found them the meanest and basest, the most cruel and cowardly, of all others. It was my unhappy lot not only to belong to a religious slaveholder, but to live in a community of such religionists. Very near Mr. Freeland lived the Rev. Daniel Weeden, and in the same neighborhood lived the Rev. Rigby Hopkins. These were members and ministers in the Reformed Methodist Church. Mr. Weeden owned, among others, a woman slave, whose name I have forgotten. This woman's back, for weeks, was kept literally raw, made so by the lash of this merciless, *religious* wretch. He used to hire hands. His maxim was, Behave well or behave ill, it is the duty of a master occasionally to whip a slave, to remind him of his master's authority. Such was his theory, and such his practice.

Mr. Hopkins was even worse than Mr. Weeden. His chief boast was his ability to manage slaves. The peculiar feature of his government was that of whipping slaves in advance of deserving it. He always managed to have one or more of his slaves to whip every Monday morning. He did this to alarm their fears, and strike terror into those who escaped. His plan was to whip for the smallest offences, to prevent the commission of large ones. Mr. Hopkins could always find some excuse for whipping a slave. It would astonish one, unaccustomed to a slaveholding life, to see with what wonderful ease a slaveholder can find things, of which to make occasion to whip a slave. A mere look, word, or motion – a mistake, accident, or want of power – are all matters for which a slave may be whipped at any time. Does a slave look dissatisfied? It is said, he has the devil in him, and it must be whipped out. Does he speak loudly when spoken to by his master? Then he is getting high-minded, and should be taken down a button-hole lower. Does he forget to pull off his hat at the approach of a white person? Then he is wanting in reverence, and should be whipped for it. Does he ever venture to vindicate his conduct, when censured for it? Then he is guilty of impudence – one of the greatest crimes of which a slave can be guilty. Does he ever venture to suggest a different mode of doing things from that pointed out by his master? He is indeed presumptuous, and getting above himself; and nothing less than a flogging will do for him. Does he, while ploughing, break a plough – or, while hoeing, break a hoe? It is owing to his carelessness, and for it a slave must always be whipped. Mr. Hopkins could always find something of this sort to justify the use of the lash, and he seldom failed to embrace such opportunities. There was not a man in the whole county, with whom the slaves who had the getting their own home, would not prefer to live, rather than with this Rev. Mr. Hopkins. And yet there was not a man anywhere[67] round, who made higher professions of religion, or was more active in revivals – more attentive to the class, love-feast, prayer and preaching meetings, or more devotional in his family – that prayed earlier, later, louder, and longer – than this same reverend slave-driver, Rigby Hopkins.

But to return to Mr. Freeland, and to my experience while in his employment. He, like Mr. Covey, gave us enough to eat; but, unlike Mr. Covey, he also gave us sufficient time to take our meals. He worked us hard, but always between sunrise and sunset. He required a good deal of work to be done, but gave us good tools with which to work. His farm was large, but he employed hands enough to work it, and with ease, compared with many of his neighbors. My treatment, while in his employment, was heavenly, compared with what I experienced at the hands of Mr. Edward Covey.

Mr. Freeland was himself the owner of but two slaves. Their names were Henry Harris and John Harris. The rest of his hands he hired. These consisted of myself, Sandy Jenkins,* and Handy Caldwell. Henry and John were quite intelligent, and in a very little while after I went there, I succeeded in creating in them a strong desire to learn how to read. This desire soon sprang up in the others also. They very soon mustered up some old spelling-books, and nothing would do but that I must keep a Sabbath school. I agreed to do so, and accordingly devoted my Sundays to teaching these my

Notes

* This is the same man who gave me the roots to prevent my being whipped by Mr. Covey. He was "a clever soul." We used frequently to talk about the fight with Covey, and as often as we did so, he would claim my success as the result of the roots which he gave me. This superstition is very common among the more ignorant slaves. A slave seldom dies but that his death is attributed to trickery.

[67] *Original reads*: any where [ed.].

loved fellow-slaves how to read. Neither of them knew his letters when I went there. Some of the slaves of the neighboring farms found what was going on, and also availed themselves of this little opportunity to learn to read. It was understood, among all who came, that there must be as little display about it as possible. It was necessary to keep our religious masters at St. Michael's unacquainted with the fact, that, instead of spending the Sabbath in wrestling, boxing, and drinking whisky, we were trying to learn how to read the will of God; for they had much rather see us engaged in those degrading sports, than to see us behaving like intellectual, moral, and accountable beings. My blood boils as I think of the bloody manner in which Messrs. Wright Fairbanks and Garrison West, both class-leaders, in connection with many others, rushed in upon us with sticks and stones, and broke up our virtuous little Sabbath school, at St. Michael's – all calling themselves Christians! humble followers of the Lord Jesus Christ! But I am again digressing.

I held my Sabbath school at the house of a free colored man, whose name I deem it imprudent to mention; for, should it be known, it might embarrass him greatly, though the crime of holding the school was committed ten years ago. I had at one time over forty scholars, and those of the right sort, ardently desiring to learn. They were of all ages, though mostly men and women. I look back to those Sundays with an amount of pleasure not to be expressed. They were great days to my soul. The work of instructing my dear fellow-slaves was the sweetest engagement with which I was ever blessed. We loved each other, and to leave them at the close of the Sabbath was a severe cross indeed. When I think that these precious souls are to-day shut up in the prison-house of slavery, my feelings overcome me, and I am almost ready to ask, "Does a righteous God govern the universe? and for what does he hold the thunders in his right hand, if not to smite the oppressor, and deliver the spoiled out of the hand of the spoiler?" These dear souls came not to Sabbath school because it was popular to do so, nor did I teach them because it was reputable to be thus engaged. Every moment they spent in that school, they were liable to be taken up, and given thirty-nine lashes. They came because they wished to learn. Their minds had been starved by their cruel masters. They had been shut up in mental darkness. I taught them, because it was the delight of my soul to be doing something that looked like bettering the condition of my race. I kept up my school nearly the whole year I lived with Mr. Freeland; and, besides[68] my Sabbath school, I devoted three evenings in the week, during the winter, to teaching the slaves at home. And I have the happiness to know, that several of those who came to Sabbath school learned how to read; and that one, at least, is now free through my agency.

The year passed off smoothly. It seemed only about half as long as the year which preceded it. I went through it without receiving a single blow. I will give Mr. Freeland the credit of being the best master I ever had, *till I became my own master*. For the ease with which I passed the year, I was, however, somewhat indebted to the society of my fellow-slaves. They were noble souls; they not only possessed loving hearts, but brave ones. We were linked and interlinked with each other. I loved them with a love stronger than anything[69] I have experienced since. It is sometimes said that we slaves do not love and confide in each other. In answer to this assertion, I can say, I never loved any or confided in any people more than my fellow-slaves, and especially those with whom I lived at Mr. Freeland's. I believe we would have died for each other. We never undertook to do anything,[70] of any importance, without a mutual consultation. We never

Notes

[68] *Original reads*: beside [ed.].

[69] *Original reads*: any thing [ed.].

[70] *Original reads*: any thing [ed.].

moved separately. We were one; and as much so by our tempers and dispositions, as by the mutual hardships to which we were necessarily subjected by our condition as slaves.

At the close of the year 1834, Mr. Freeland again hired me of my master, for the year 1835. But, by this time, I began to want to live *upon free land* as well as *with Freeland*; and I was no longer content, therefore, to live with him or any other slaveholder. I began, with the commencement of the year, to prepare myself for a final struggle, which should decide my fate one way or the other. My tendency was upward. I was fast approaching manhood, and year after year had passed, and I was still a slave. These thoughts roused me – I must do something. I therefore resolved that 1835 should not pass without witnessing an attempt, on my part, to secure my liberty. But I was not willing to cherish this determination alone. My fellow-slaves were dear to me. I was anxious to have them participate with me in this, my life-giving determination. I therefore, though with great prudence, commenced early to ascertain their views and feelings in regard to their condition, and to imbue their minds with thoughts of freedom. I bent myself to devising ways and means for our escape, and meanwhile strove, on all fitting occasions, to impress them with the gross fraud and inhumanity of slavery. I went first to Henry, next to John, then to the others. I found, in them all, warm hearts and noble spirits. They were ready to hear, and ready to act when a feasible plan should be proposed. This was what I wanted. I talked to them of our want of manhood, if we submitted to our enslavement without at least one noble effort to be free. We met often, and consulted frequently, and told our hopes and fears, recounted the difficulties, real and imagined, which we should be called on to meet. At times we were almost disposed to give up, and try to content ourselves with our wretched lot; at others, we were firm and unbending in our determination to go. Whenever we suggested any plan, there was shrinking – the odds were fearful. Our path was beset with the greatest obstacles; and if we succeeded in gaining the end of it, our right to be free was yet questionable – we were yet liable to be returned to bondage. We could see no spot, this side of the ocean, where we could be free. We knew nothing about Canada. Our knowledge of the north did not extend farther than New York; and to go there, and be forever harassed with the frightful liability of being returned to slavery – with the certainty of being treated tenfold worse than before – the thought was truly a horrible one, and one which it was not easy to overcome. The case sometimes stood thus: At every gate through which we were to pass, we saw a watchman – at every ferry a guard – on every bridge a sentinel – and in every wood a patrol. We were hemmed in upon every side. Here were the difficulties, real or imagined – the good to be sought, and the evil to be shunned. On the one hand, there stood slavery, a stern reality, glaring frightfully upon us – its robes already crimsoned with the blood of millions, and even now feasting itself greedily upon our own flesh. On the other hand, away back in the dim distance, under the flickering light of the north star, behind some craggy hill or snow-covered mountain, stood a doubtful freedom – half frozen – beckoning us to come and share its hospitality. This in itself was sometimes enough to stagger us; but when we permitted ourselves to survey the road, we were frequently appalled. Upon either side we saw grim death, assuming the most horrid shapes. Now it was starvation, causing us to eat our own flesh; now we were contending with the waves, and were drowned; now we were overtaken, and torn to pieces by the fangs of the terrible bloodhound. We were stung by scorpions, chased by wild beasts, bitten by snakes, and finally, after having nearly reached the desired spot – after swimming rivers, encountering wild beasts, sleeping in the woods, suffering hunger and nakedness – we were overtaken by our pursuers, and, in our resistance, we were shot dead upon the spot! I say, this picture sometimes appalled us, and made us

"rather bear those ills we had,
Than fly to others, that we knew not of."[71]

In coming to a fixed determination to run away, we did more than Patrick Henry, when he resolved upon liberty or death. With us it was a doubtful liberty at most, and almost certain death if we failed. For my part, I should prefer death to hopeless bondage.

Sandy, one of our number, gave up the notion, but still encouraged us. Our company then consisted of Henry Harris, John Harris, Henry Bailey, Charles Roberts, and myself. Henry Bailey was my uncle, and belonged to my master. Charles married my aunt: he belonged to my master's father-in-law, Mr. William Hamilton.

The plan we finally concluded upon was, to get a large canoe belonging to Mr. Hamilton, and upon the Saturday night previous to Easter holidays, paddle directly up the Chesapeake Bay. On our arrival at the head of the bay, a distance of seventy or eighty miles from where we lived, it was our purpose to turn our canoe adrift, and follow the guidance of the north star till we got beyond the limits of Maryland. Our reason for taking the water route was, that we were less liable to be suspected as runaways; we hoped to be regarded as fishermen; whereas, if we should take the land route, we should be subjected to interruptions of almost every kind. Anyone[72] having a white face, and being so disposed, could stop us, and subject us to examination.

The week before our intended start, I wrote several protections, one for each of us. As well as I can remember, they were in the following words, to wit:–

"This is to certify that I, the undersigned, have given the bearer, my servant, full liberty to go to Baltimore, and spend the Easter holidays. Written with mine own hand, &c., 1835.

William Hamilton,
Near St. Michael's, in Talbot county, Maryland."

We were not going to Baltimore; but, in going up the bay, we went toward Baltimore, and these protections were only intended to protect us while on the bay.

As the time drew near for our departure, our anxiety became more and more intense. It was truly a matter of life and death with us. The strength of our determination was about to be fully tested. At this time, I was very active in explaining every difficulty, removing every doubt, dispelling every fear, and inspiring all with the firmness indispensable to success in our undertaking; assuring them that half was gained the instant we made the move; we had talked long enough; we were now ready to move; if not now, we never should be; and if we did not intend to move now, we had as well fold our arms, sit down, and acknowledge ourselves fit only to be slaves. This, none of us were prepared to acknowledge. Every man stood firm; and at our last meeting, we pledged ourselves afresh, in the most solemn manner, that, at the time appointed, we would certainly start in pursuit of freedom. This was in the middle of the week, at the end of which we were to be off. We went, as usual, to our several fields of labor, but with bosoms highly agitated with thoughts of our truly hazardous undertaking. We tried to conceal our feelings as much as possible; and I think we succeeded very well.

Notes

[71] *"bear the ills … know not"* Shakespeare, *Hamlet* 3.1.81–82. [72] *Original reads*: any one [ed.].

After a painful waiting, the Saturday morning, whose night was to witness our departure, came. I hailed it with joy, bring what of sadness it might. Friday night was a sleepless one for me. I probably felt more anxious than the rest, because I was, by common consent, at the head of the whole affair. The responsibility of success or failure lay heavily upon me. The glory of the one, and the confusion of the other, were alike mine. The first two hours of that morning were such as I never experienced before, and hope never to again. Early in the morning, we went, as usual, to the field. We were spreading manure; and all at once, while thus engaged, I was overwhelmed with an indescribable feeling, in the fulness of which I turned to Sandy, who was nearby,[73] and said, "We are betrayed!" "Well," said he, "that thought has this moment struck me." We said no more. I was never more certain of anything.[74]

The horn was blown as usual, and we went up from the field to the house for breakfast. I went for the form, more than for want of anything[75] to eat that morning. Just as I got to the house, in looking out at the lane gate, I saw four white men, with two colored men. The white men were on horseback, and the colored ones were walking behind, as if tied. I watched them a few moments till they got up to our lane gate. Here they halted, and tied the colored men to the gatepost. I was not yet certain as to what the matter was. In a few moments, in rode Mr. Hamilton, with a speed betokening great excitement. He came to the door, and inquired if Master William was in. He was told he was at the barn. Mr. Hamilton, without dismounting, rode up to the barn with extraordinary speed. In a few moments, he and Mr. Freeland returned to the house. By this time, the three constables rode up, and in great haste dismounted, tied their horses, and met Master William and Mr. Hamilton returning from the barn; and after talking awhile, they all walked up to the kitchen door. There was no one in the kitchen but myself and John. Henry and Sandy were up at the barn. Mr. Freeland put his head in at the door, and called me by name, saying, there were some gentlemen at the door who wished to see me. I stepped to the door, and inquired what they wanted. They at once seized me, and, without giving me any satisfaction, tied me – lashing my hands closely together. I insisted upon knowing what the matter was. They at length said, that they had learned I had been in a "scrape," and that I was to be examined before my master; and if their information proved false, I should not be hurt.

In a few moments, they succeeded in tying John. They then turned to Henry, who had by this time returned, and commanded him to cross his hands. "I won't!" said Henry, in a firm tone, indicating his readiness to meet the consequences of his refusal. "Won't you?" said Tom Graham, the constable. "No, I won't!" said Henry, in a still stronger tone. With this, two of the constables pulled out their shining pistols, and swore, by their Creator, that they would make him cross his hands or kill him. Each cocked his pistol, and, with fingers on the trigger, walked up to Henry, saying, at the same time, if he did not cross his hands, they would blow his damned heart out. "Shoot me, shoot me!" said Henry; "you can't kill me but once. Shoot, shoot – and be damned! *I won't be tied!*" This he said in a tone of loud defiance; and at the same time, with a motion as quick as lightning, he with one single stroke dashed the pistols from the hand of each constable. As he did this, all hands fell upon him, and, after beating him some time, they finally overpowered him, and got him tied.

During the scuffle, I managed, I know not how, to get my pass out, and, without being discovered, put it into the fire. We were all now tied; and just as we were to leave

Notes

[73] *Original reads*: near by [ed.].

[74] *Original reads*: any thing [ed.].

[75] *Original reads*: any thing [ed.].

for Easton jail, Betsy Freeland, mother of William Freeland, came to the door with her hands full of biscuits, and divided them between Henry and John. She then delivered herself of a speech, to the following effect:– addressing herself to me, she said, "*You devil! You yellow devil!* it was you that put it into the heads of Henry and John to run away. But for you, you long-legged mulatto devil! Henry nor John would never have thought of such a thing." I made no reply, and was immediately hurried off towards St. Michael's. Just a moment previous to the scuffle with Henry, Mr. Hamilton suggested the propriety of making a search for the protections which he had understood Frederick had written for himself and the rest. But, just at the moment he was about carrying his proposal into effect, his aid was needed in helping to tie Henry; and the excitement attending the scuffle caused them either to forget, or to deem it unsafe, under the circumstances, to search. So we were not yet convicted of the intention to run away.

When we got about half way to St. Michael's, while the constables having us in charge were looking ahead, Henry inquired of me what he should do with his pass. I told him to eat it with his biscuit, and own nothing; and we passed the word around, "*Own nothing;*" and "*Own nothing!*" said we all. Our confidence in each other was unshaken. We were resolved to succeed or fail together, after the calamity had befallen us as much as before. We were now prepared for anything.[76] We were to be dragged that morning fifteen miles behind horses, and then to be placed in the Easton jail. When we reached St. Michael's, we underwent a sort of examination. We all denied that we ever intended to run away. We did this more to bring out the evidence against us, than from any hope of getting clear of being sold; for, as I have said, we were ready for that. The fact was, we cared but little where we went, so we went together. Our greatest concern was about separation. We dreaded that more than anything[77] this side of death. We found the evidence against us to be the testimony of one person; our master would not tell who it was; but we came to a unanimous decision among ourselves as to who their informant was. We were sent off to the jail at Easton. When we got there, we were delivered up to the sheriff, Mr. Joseph Graham, and by him placed in jail. Henry, John, and myself, were placed in one room together – Charles, and Henry Bailey, in another. Their object in separating us was to hinder concert.

We had been in jail scarcely twenty minutes, when a swarm of slave traders, and agents for slave traders, flocked into jail to look at us, and to ascertain if we were for sale. Such a set of beings I never saw before! I felt myself surrounded by so many fiends from perdition. A band of pirates never looked more like their father, the devil. They laughed and grinned over us, saying, "Ah, my boys! we have got you, haven't we?" And after taunting us in various ways, they one by one went into an examination of us, with intent to ascertain our value. They would impudently ask us if we would not like to have them for our masters. We would make them no answer, and leave them to find out as best they could. Then they would curse and swear at us, telling us that they could take the devil out of us in a very little while, if we were only in their hands.

While in jail, we found ourselves in much more comfortable quarters than we expected when we went there. We did not get much to eat, nor that which was very good; but we had a good clean room, from the windows of which we could see what was going on in the street, which was very much better than though we had been placed in one of the dark, damp cells. Upon the whole, we got along very well, so far

Notes

[76] *Original reads*: any thing [ed.].

[77] *Original reads*: any thing [ed.].

as the jail and its keeper were concerned. Immediately after the holidays were over, contrary to all our expectations, Mr. Hamilton and Mr. Freeland came up to Easton, and took Charles, the two Henrys, and John, out of jail, and carried them home, leaving me alone. I regarded this separation as a final one. It caused me more pain than anything[78] else in the whole transaction. I was ready for anything[79] rather than separation. I supposed that they had consulted together, and had decided that, as I was the whole cause of the intention of the others to run away, it was hard to make the innocent suffer with the guilty; and that they had, therefore, concluded to take the others home, and sell me, as a warning to the others that remained. It is due to the noble Henry to say, he seemed almost as reluctant at leaving the prison as at leaving home to come to the prison. But we knew we should, in all probability, be separated, if we were sold; and since he was in their hands, he concluded to go peaceably home.

I was now left to my fate. I was all alone, and within the walls of a stone prison. But a few days before, and I was full of hope. I expected to have been safe in a land of freedom; but now I was covered with gloom, sunk down to the utmost despair. I thought the possibility of freedom was gone. I was kept in this way about one week, at the end of which, Captain Auld, my master, to my surprise and utter astonishment, came up, and took me out, with the intention of sending me, with a gentleman of his acquaintance, into Alabama. But, from some cause or other, he did not send me to Alabama, but concluded to send me back to Baltimore, to live again with his brother Hugh, and to learn a trade.

Thus, after an absence of three years and one month, I was once more permitted to return to my old home at Baltimore. My master sent me away, because there existed against me a very great prejudice in the community, and he feared I might be killed.

In a few weeks after I went to Baltimore, Master Hugh hired me to Mr. William Gardner, an extensive ship-builder, on Fell's Point. I was put there to learn how to calk. It, however, proved a very unfavorable place for the accomplishment of this object. Mr. Gardner was engaged that spring in building two large man-of-war brigs, professedly for the Mexican government. The vessels were to be launched in the July of that year, and in failure thereof, Mr. Gardner was to lose a considerable sum; so that when I entered, all was hurry. There was no time to learn anything.[80] Every man had to do that which he knew how to do. In entering the ship-yard, my orders from Mr. Gardner were, to do whatever the carpenters commanded me to do. This was placing me at the beck and call of about seventy-five men. I was to regard all these as masters. Their word was to be my law. My situation was a most trying one. At times I needed a dozen pair of hands. I was called a dozen ways in the space of a single minute. Three or four voices would strike my ear at the same moment. It was – "Fred., come help me to cant this timber here." – "Fred., come carry this timber yonder." – "Fred., bring that roller here." – "Fred., go get a fresh can of water." – "Fred., come help saw off the end of this timber." – "Fred., go quick, and get the crowbar." – "Fred., hold on the end of this fall." – "Fred., go to the blacksmith's shop, and get a new punch." – "Hurra, Fred.! run and bring me a cold chisel." – "I say, Fred., bear a hand, and get up a fire as quick as lightning under that steam-box." – "Halloo, nigger! come, turn this grindstone." – "Come, come! move, move! and *bowse*[81] this timber forward." – "I say, darky, blast your eyes, why don't you heat up some pitch?" – "Halloo! halloo! halloo!" (Three voices at the same time.) "Come here! – Go there! – Hold on where you are! Damn you, if you move, I'll knock your brains out!"

Notes

[78] *Original reads*: any thing [ed.].

[79] *Original reads*: any thing [ed.].

[80] *Original reads*: any thing [ed.].

[81] *bowse* haul.

This was my school for eight months; and I might have remained there longer, but for a most horrid fight I had with four of the white apprentices, in which my left eye was nearly knocked out, and I was horribly mangled in other respects. The facts in the case were these: Until a very little while after I went there, white and black ship-carpenters worked side by side, and no one seemed to see any impropriety in it. All hands seemed to be very well satisfied. Many of the black carpenters were freemen. Things seemed to be going on very well. All at once, the white carpenters knocked off, and said they would not work with free colored workmen. Their reason for this, as alleged, was, that if free colored carpenters were encouraged, they would soon take the trade into their own hands, and poor white men would be thrown out of employment. They therefore felt called upon at once to put a stop to it. And, taking advantage of Mr. Gardner's necessities, they broke off, swearing they would work no longer, unless he would discharge his black carpenters. Now, though this did not extend to me in form, it did reach me in fact. My fellow-apprentices very soon began to feel it degrading to them to work with me. They began to put on airs, and talk about the "niggers" taking the country, saying we all ought to be killed; and, being encouraged by the journeymen, they commenced making my condition as hard as they could, by hectoring me around, and sometimes striking me. I, of course, kept the vow I made after the fight with Mr. Covey, and struck back again, regardless of consequences; and while I kept them from combining, I succeeded very well; for I could whip the whole of them, taking them separately. They, however, at length combined, and came upon me, armed with sticks, stones, and heavy handspikes. One came in front with a half brick. There was one at each side of me, and one behind me. While I was attending to those in front, and on either side, the one behind ran up with the handspike, and struck me a heavy blow upon the head. It stunned me. I fell, and with this they all ran upon me, and fell to beating me with their fists. I let them lay on for a while, gathering strength. In an instant, I gave a sudden surge, and rose to my hands and knees. Just as I did that, one of their number gave me, with his heavy boot, a powerful kick in the left eye. My eyeball seemed to have burst. When they saw my eye closed, and badly swollen, they left me. With this I seized the handspike, and for a time pursued them. But here the carpenters interfered, and I thought I might as well give it up. It was impossible to stand my hand against so many. All this took place in sight of not less than fifty white ship-carpenters, and not one interposed a friendly word; but some cried, "Kill the damned nigger! Kill him! kill him! He struck a white person." I found my only chance for life was in flight. I succeeded in getting away without an additional blow, and barely so; for to strike a white man is death by Lynch law[82] – and that was the law in Mr. Gardner's ship-yard; nor is there much of any other out of Mr. Gardner's ship-yard.

I went directly home, and told the story of my wrongs to Master Hugh; and I am happy to say of him, irreligious as he was, his conduct was heavenly, compared with that of his brother Thomas under similar circumstances. He listened attentively to my narration of the circumstances leading to the savage outrage, and gave many proofs of his strong indignation at it. The heart of my once overkind mistress was again melted into pity. My puffed-out eye and blood-covered face moved her to tears. She took a chair by me, washed the blood from my face, and, with a mother's tenderness, bound up my head, covering the wounded eye with a lean piece of fresh beef. It was almost compensation for my suffering to witness, once more, a manifestation of kindness

Notes

[82] *Lynch law* to be subject to lynching prior to any due process.

from this, my once affectionate old mistress. Master Hugh was very much enraged. He gave expression to his feelings by pouring out curses upon the heads of those who did the deed. As soon as I got a little the better of my bruises, he took me with him to Esquire Watson's, on Bond Street, to see what could be done about the matter. Mr. Watson inquired who saw the assault committed. Master Hugh told him it was done in Mr. Gardner's ship-yard, at mid-day, where there were a large company of men at work. "As to that," he said, "the deed was done, and there was no question as to who did it." His answer was, he could do nothing in the case, unless some white man would come forward and testify. He could issue no warrant on my word. If I had been killed in the presence of a thousand colored people, their testimony combined would have been insufficient to have arrested one of the murderers. Master Hugh, for once, was compelled to say this state of things was too bad. Of course, it was impossible to get any white man to volunteer his testimony in my behalf, and against the white young men. Even those who may have sympathized with me were not prepared to do this. It required a degree of courage unknown to them to do so; for just at that time, the slightest manifestation of humanity toward a colored person was denounced as abolitionism, and that name subjected its bearer to frightful liabilities. The watchwords of the bloody-minded in that region, and in those days, were, "Damn the abolitionists!" and "Damn the niggers!" There was nothing done, and probably nothing would have been done if I had been killed. Such was, and such remains, the state of things in the Christian city of Baltimore.

Master Hugh, finding he could get no redress, refused to let me go back again to Mr. Gardner. He kept me himself, and his wife dressed my wound till I was again restored to health. He then took me into the ship-yard of which he was foreman, in the employment of Mr. Walter Price. There I was immediately set to calking, and very soon learned the art of using my mallet and irons. In the course of one year from the time I left Mr. Gardner's, I was able to command the highest wages given to the most experienced calkers. I was now of some importance to my master. I was bringing him from six to seven dollars per week. I sometimes brought him nine dollars per week: my wages were a dollar and a half a day. After learning how to calk, I sought my own employment, made my own contracts, and collected the money which I earned. My pathway became much more smooth than before; my condition was now much more comfortable. When I could get no calking to do, I did nothing. During these leisure times, those old notions about freedom would steal over me again. When in Mr. Gardner's employment, I was kept in such a perpetual whirl of excitement, I could think of nothing, scarcely, but my life; and in thinking of my life, I almost forgot my liberty. I have observed this in my experience of slavery – that whenever my condition was improved, instead of its increasing my contentment, it only increased my desire to be free, and set me to thinking of plans to gain my freedom. I have found that, to make a contented slave, it is necessary to make a thoughtless one. It is necessary to darken his moral and mental vision, and, as far as possible, to annihilate the power of reason. He must be able to detect no inconsistencies in slavery; he must be made to feel that slavery is right; and he can be brought to that only when he ceases to be a man.

I was now getting, as I have said, one dollar and fifty cents per day. I contracted for it; I earned it; it was paid to me; it was rightfully my own; yet, upon each returning Saturday night, I was compelled to deliver every cent of that money to Master Hugh. And why? Not because he earned it – not because he had any hand in earning it – not because I owed it to him – nor because he possessed the slightest shadow of a right to it; but solely because he had the power to compel me to give it up. The right of the grim-visaged pirate upon the high seas is exactly the same.

Chapter 11

I NOW come to that part of my life during which I planned, and finally succeeded in making, my escape from slavery. But before narrating any of the peculiar circumstances, I deem it proper to make known my intention not to state all the facts connected with the transaction. My reasons for pursuing this course may be understood from the following: First, were I to give a minute statement of all the facts, it is not only possible, but quite probable, that others would thereby be involved in the most embarrassing difficulties. Secondly, such a statement would most undoubtedly induce greater vigilance on the part of slaveholders than has existed heretofore among them; which would, of course, be the means of guarding a door whereby some dear brother bondman might escape his galling chains. I deeply regret the necessity that impels me to suppress anything[83] of importance connected with my experience in slavery. It would afford me great pleasure indeed, as well as materially add to the interest of my narrative, were I at liberty to gratify a curiosity, which I know exists in the minds of many, by an accurate statement of all the facts pertaining to my most fortunate escape. But I must deprive myself of this pleasure, and the curious of the gratification which such a statement would afford. I would allow myself to suffer under the greatest imputations which evil-minded men might suggest, rather than exculpate myself, and thereby run the hazard of closing the slightest avenue by which a brother slave might clear himself of the chains and fetters of slavery.

I have never approved of the very public manner in which some of our western friends have conducted what they call the *underground railroad*, but which, I think, by their open declarations, has been made most emphatically the *upperground railroad*. I honor those good men and women for their noble daring, and applaud them for willingly subjecting themselves to bloody persecution, by openly avowing their participation in the escape of slaves. I, however, can see very little good resulting from such a course, either to themselves or the slaves escaping; while, upon the other hand, I see and feel assured that those open declarations are a positive evil to the slaves remaining, who are seeking to escape. They do nothing towards enlightening the slave, whilst they do much towards enlightening the master. They stimulate him to greater watchfulness, and enhance his power to capture his slave. We owe something to the slaves south of the line as well as to those north of it; and in aiding the latter on their way to freedom, we should be careful to do nothing which would be likely to hinder the former from escaping from slavery. I would keep the merciless slaveholder profoundly ignorant of the means of flight adopted by the slave. I would leave him to imagine himself surrounded by myriads of invisible tormentors, ever ready to snatch from his infernal grasp his trembling prey. Let him be left to feel his way in the dark; let darkness commensurate with his crime hover over him; and let him feel that at every step he takes, in pursuit of the flying bondman, he is running the frightful risk of having his hot brains dashed out by an invisible agency. Let us render the tyrant no aid; let us not hold the light by which he can trace the footprints of our flying brother. But enough of this. I will now proceed to the statement of those facts, connected with my escape, for which I am alone responsible, and for which no one can be made to suffer but myself.

In the early part of the year 1838, I became quite restless. I could see no reason why I should, at the end of each week, pour the reward of my toil into the purse of my

Notes

[83] *Original reads*: any thing [ed.].

master. When I carried to him my weekly wages, he would, after counting the money, look me in the face with a robber-like fierceness, and ask, "Is this all?" He was satisfied with nothing less than the last cent. He would, however, when I made him six dollars, sometimes give me six cents, to encourage me. It had the opposite effect. I regarded it as a sort of admission of my right to the whole. The fact that he gave me any part of my wages was proof, to my mind, that he believed me entitled to the whole of them. I always felt worse for having received any thing; for I feared that the giving me a few cents would ease his conscience, and make him feel himself to be a pretty honorable sort of robber. My discontent grew upon me. I was ever on the look-out for means of escape; and, finding no direct means, I determined to try to hire my time, with a view of getting money with which to make my escape. In the spring of 1838, when Master Thomas came to Baltimore to purchase his spring goods, I got an opportunity, and applied to him to allow me to hire my time. He unhesitatingly refused my request, and told me this was another stratagem by which to escape. He told me I could go nowhere but that he could get me; and that, in the event of my running away, he should spare no pains in his efforts to catch me. He exhorted me to content myself, and be obedient. He told me, if I would be happy, I must lay out no plans for the future. He said, if I behaved myself properly, he would take care of me. Indeed, he advised me to complete thoughtlessness of the future, and taught me to depend solely upon him for happiness. He seemed to see fully the pressing necessity of setting aside my intellectual nature, in order to contentment in slavery. But in spite of him, and even in spite of myself, I continued to think, and to think about the injustice of my enslavement, and the means of escape.

About two months after this, I applied to Master Hugh for the privilege of hiring my time. He was not acquainted with the fact that I had applied to Master Thomas, and had been refused. He too, at first, seemed disposed to refuse; but, after some reflection, he granted me the privilege, and proposed the following terms: I was to be allowed all my time, make all contracts with those for whom I worked, and find my own employment; and, in return for this liberty, I was to pay him three dollars at the end of each week; find myself in calking tools, and in board and clothing. My board was two dollars and a half per week. This, with the wear and tear of clothing and calking tools, made my regular expenses about six dollars per week. This amount I was compelled to make up, or relinquish the privilege of hiring my time. Rain or shine, work or no work, at the end of each week the money must be forthcoming, or I must give up my privilege. This arrangement, it will be perceived, was decidedly in my master's favor. It relieved him of all need of looking after me. His money was sure. He received all the benefits of slaveholding without its evils; while I endured all the evils of a slave, and suffered all the care and anxiety of a freeman. I found it a hard bargain. But, hard as it was, I thought it better than the old mode of getting along. It was a step towards freedom to be allowed to bear the responsibilities of a freeman, and I was determined to hold on upon it. I bent myself to the work of making money. I was ready to work at night as well as day, and by the most untiring perseverance and industry, I made enough to meet my expenses, and lay up a little money every week. I went on thus from May till August. Master Hugh then refused to allow me to hire my time longer. The ground for his refusal was a failure on my part, one Saturday night, to pay him for my week's time. This failure was occasioned by my attending a camp meeting about ten miles from Baltimore. During the week, I had entered into an engagement with a number of young friends to start from Baltimore to the camp ground early Saturday evening; and being detained by my employer, I was unable to get down to Master Hugh's without disappointing the company. I knew that Master Hugh was in no special need of the money that night. I therefore decided to go to camp meeting, and upon my return pay him the three dollars. I staid at the camp meeting one day longer than I intended when I left. But as soon as I returned, I called upon him to pay him what he considered his due. I found him very angry; he could scarce restrain his wrath. He said he had a great mind to give me a severe whipping. He wished to know how I dared go out of the city without asking his permission. I told him I hired my time, and while I paid him the price which he asked for it, I did not know that I was bound to ask him when and where I should go. This reply troubled him; and, after reflecting a few moments, he turned to me, and said I should hire my time no longer; that the next thing he should know of, I would be running away. Upon the same plea, he told me to bring my tools and clothing home forthwith. I did so; but instead of seeking work, as I had been accustomed to do previously to hiring my time, I spent the whole week without the performance of a single stroke of work. I did this in retaliation. Saturday night, he called upon me as usual for my week's wages. I told him I had no wages; I had done no work that week. Here we were upon the point of coming to blows. He raved, and swore his determination to get hold of me. I did not allow myself a single word; but was resolved, if he laid the weight of his hand upon me, it should be blow for blow. He did not strike me, but told me that he would find me in constant employment in future. I thought the matter over during the next day, Sunday, and finally resolved upon the third day of September, as the day upon which I would make a second attempt to secure my freedom. I now had three weeks during which to prepare for my journey. Early on Monday morning, before Master Hugh had time to make any engagement for me, I went out and got employment of Mr. Butler, at his ship-yard near the drawbridge, upon what is called the City Block, thus making it unnecessary for him to seek employment for me. At the end of the week, I brought him between eight and nine dollars. He seemed very well pleased, and asked me why I did not do the same the week before. He little knew what my plans were. My object in working steadily was to remove any suspicion he might entertain of my intent to run away; and in this I succeeded admirably. I suppose he thought I was never better satisfied with my condition than at the very time during which I was planning my escape. The second week passed, and again I carried him my full wages; and so well pleased was he, that he gave me twenty-five cents, (quite a large sum for a slaveholder to give a slave,) and bade me to make a good use of it. I told him I would.

Things went on without very smoothly indeed, but within there was trouble. It is impossible for me to describe my feelings as the time of my contemplated start drew near. I had a number of warm-hearted friends in Baltimore – friends that I loved almost as I did my life – and the thought of being separated from them forever was painful beyond expression. It is my opinion that thousands would escape from slavery, who now remain, but for the strong cords of affection that bind them to their friends. The thought of leaving my friends was decidedly the most painful thought with which I had to contend. The love of them was my tender point, and shook my decision more than all things else. Besides the pain of separation, the dread and apprehension of a failure exceeded what I had experienced at my first attempt. The appalling defeat I then sustained returned to torment me. I felt assured that, if I failed in this attempt, my case would be a hopeless one – it would seal my fate as a slave forever. I could not hope to get off with anything[84] less than the severest punishment, and being placed beyond the means of escape. It required no very vivid imagination to depict the most frightful scenes through which I should have to pass, in case I failed. The wretchedness of

Notes

[84] *Original reads*: any thing [ed.].

slavery, and the blessedness of freedom, were perpetually before me. It was life and death with me. But I remained firm, and, according to my resolution, on the third day of September, 1838, I left my chains, and succeeded in reaching New York without the slightest interruption of any kind. How I did so – what means I adopted – what direction I travelled, and by what mode of conveyance – I must leave unexplained, for the reasons before mentioned.

I have been frequently asked how I felt when I found myself in a free State. I have never been able to answer the question with any satisfaction to myself. It was a moment of the highest excitement I ever experienced. I suppose I felt as one may imagine the unarmed mariner to feel when he is rescued by a friendly man-of-war from the pursuit of a pirate. In writing to a dear friend, immediately after my arrival at New York, I said I felt like one who had escaped a den of hungry lions. This state of mind, however, very soon subsided; and I was again seized with a feeling of great insecurity and loneliness. I was yet liable to be taken back, and subjected to all the tortures of slavery. This in itself was enough to damp the ardor of my enthusiasm. But the loneliness overcame me. There I was in the midst of thousands, and yet a perfect stranger; without home and without friends, in the midst of thousands of my own brethren – children of a common Father, and yet I dared not to unfold to any one of them my sad condition. I was afraid to speak to anyone[85] for fear of speaking to the wrong one, and thereby falling into the hands of money-loving kidnappers, whose business it was to lie in wait for the panting fugitive, as the ferocious beasts of the forest lie in wait for their prey. The motto which I adopted when I started from slavery was this – "Trust no man!" I saw in every white man an enemy, and in almost every colored man cause for distrust. It was a most painful situation; and, to understand it, one must needs experience it, or imagine himself in similar circumstances. Let him be a fugitive slave in a strange land – a land given up to be the hunting-ground for slaveholders – whose inhabitants are legalized kidnappers – where he is every moment subjected to the terrible liability of being seized upon by his fellow-men, as the hideous crocodile seizes upon his prey! – I say, let him place himself in my situation – without home or friends – without money or credit – wanting shelter, and no one to give it – wanting bread, and no money to buy it – and at the same time let him feel that he is pursued by merciless men-hunters, and in total darkness as to what to do, where to go, or where to stay – perfectly helpless both as to the means of defence and means of escape – in the midst of plenty, yet suffering the terrible gnawings of hunger – in the midst of houses, yet having no home – among fellow-men, yet feeling as if in the midst of wild beasts, whose greediness to swallow up the trembling and half-famished fugitive is only equalled by that with which the monsters of the deep swallow up the helpless fish upon which they subsist – I say, let him be placed in this most trying situation – the situation in which I was placed – then, and not till then, will he fully appreciate the hardships of, and know how to sympathize with, the toil-worn and whip-scarred fugitive slave.

Thank Heaven, I remained but a short time in this distressed situation. I was relieved from it by the humane hand of Mr. David Ruggles,[86] whose vigilance, kindness, and perseverance, I shall never forget. I am glad of an opportunity to express, as far as words can, the love and gratitude I bear him. Mr. Ruggles is now afflicted with blindness, and is himself in need of the same kind offices which he was once so forward in the performance of toward others. I had been in New York but a few days, when

Notes

[85] *Original reads*: any one [ed.].

[86] Mr. David Ruggles (1810–1849), African American printer and antislavery activist.

Mr. Ruggles sought me out, and very kindly took me to his boarding-house at the corner of Church and Lespenard Streets. Mr. Ruggles was then very deeply engaged in the memorable *Darg* case,[87] as well as attending to a number of other fugitive slaves, devising ways and means for their successful escape; and, though watched and hemmed in on almost every side, he seemed to be more than a match for his enemies.

Very soon after I went to Mr. Ruggles, he wished to know of me where I wanted to go; as he deemed it unsafe for me to remain in New York. I told him I was a calker, and should like to go where I could get work. I thought of going to Canada; but he decided against it, and in favor of my going to New Bedford, thinking I should be able to get work there at my trade. At this time, Anna,[*] my intended wife, came on; for I wrote to her immediately after my arrival at New York, (notwithstanding my homeless, houseless, and helpless condition,) informing her of my successful flight, and wishing her to come on forthwith. In a few days after her arrival, Mr. Ruggles called in the Rev. J.W.C. Pennington,[88] who, in the presence of Mr. Ruggles, Mrs. Michaels, and two or three others, performed the marriage ceremony, and gave us a certificate, of which the following is an exact copy:–

"THIS may certify, that I joined together in holy matrimony Frederick Johnson[†] and Anna Murray, as man and wife, in the presence of Mr. David Ruggles and Mrs. Michaels.

JAMES W.C. PENNINGTON.

New York, Sept. 15, 1838."

Upon receiving this certificate, and a five-dollar bill from Mr. Ruggles, I shouldered one part of our baggage, and Anna took up the other, and we set out forthwith to take passage on board of the steamboat John W. Richmond for Newport, on our way to New Bedford. Mr. Ruggles gave me a letter to a Mr. Shaw in Newport, and told me, in case my money did not serve me to New Bedford, to stop in Newport and obtain further assistance; but upon our arrival at Newport, we were so anxious to get to a place of safety, that, notwithstanding we lacked the necessary money to pay our fare, we decided to take seats in the stage, and promise to pay when we got to New Bedford. We were encouraged to do this by two excellent gentlemen, residents of New Bedford, whose names I afterward ascertained to be Joseph Ricketson and William C. Taber. They seemed at once to understand our circumstances, and gave us such assurance of their friendliness as put us fully at ease in their presence. It was good indeed to meet with such friends, at such a time. Upon reaching New Bedford, we were directed to the house of Mr. Nathan Johnson, by whom we were kindly received, and hospitably provided for. Both Mr. and Mrs. Johnson took a deep and lively interest in our welfare. They proved themselves quite worthy of the name of abolitionists. When the stage-driver found us unable to pay our fare, he held on upon our baggage as security for the debt. I had but to mention the fact to Mr. Johnson, and he forthwith advanced the money.

We now began to feel a degree of safety, and to prepare ourselves for the duties and responsibilities of a life of freedom. On the morning after our arrival at New Bedford, while at the breakfast-table, the question arose as to what name I should be called by. The name given me by my mother was, "Frederick Augustus Washington Bailey."

Notes

* She was free.

† I had changed my name from Frederick *Bailey* to that of *Johnson*.

87 *the memorable Darg case* In 1838, Ruggles was beaten and arrested for abetting the escape of Thomas Hughes, a slave of John P. Darg, a Virginia slaveholder.

88 James W.C. Pennington (1807–1870) an African American lecturer and Congregationalist minister who, like Douglass, escaped from slavery in Maryland as a young man.

I, however, had dispensed with the two middle names long before I left Maryland, so that I was generally known by the name of "Frederick Bailey." I started from Baltimore bearing the name of "Stanley." When I got to New York, I again changed my name to "Frederick Johnson," and thought that would be the last change. But when I got to New Bedford, I found it necessary again to change my name. The reason of this necessity was, that there were so many Johnsons in New Bedford, it was already quite difficult to distinguish between them. I gave Mr. Johnson the privilege of choosing me a name, but told him he must not take from me the name of "Frederick." I must hold on to that, to preserve a sense of my identity. Mr. Johnson had just been reading the "Lady of the Lake,"[89] and at once suggested that my name be "Douglass." From that time until now I have been called "Frederick Douglass"; and as I am more widely known by that name than by either of the others, I shall continue to use it as my own.

I was quite disappointed at the general appearance of things in New Bedford. The impression which I had received respecting the character and condition of the people of the north, I found to be singularly erroneous. I had very strangely supposed, while in slavery, that few of the comforts, and scarcely any of the luxuries, of life were enjoyed at the north, compared with what were enjoyed by the slaveholders of the south. I probably came to this conclusion from the fact that northern people owned no slaves. I supposed that they were about upon a level with the non-slaveholding population of the south. I knew *they* were exceedingly poor, and I had been accustomed to regard their poverty as the necessary consequence of their being non-slaveholders. I had somehow imbibed the opinion that, in the absence of slaves, there could be no wealth, and very little refinement. And upon coming to the north, I expected to meet with a rough, hard-handed, and uncultivated population, living in the most Spartan-like simplicity, knowing nothing of the ease, luxury, pomp, and grandeur of southern slaveholders. Such being my conjectures, any one acquainted with the appearance of New Bedford may very readily infer how palpably I must have seen my mistake.

In the afternoon of the day when I reached New Bedford, I visited the wharves, to take a view of the shipping. Here I found myself surrounded with the strongest proofs of wealth. Lying at the wharves, and riding in the stream, I saw many ships of the finest model, in the best order, and of the largest size. Upon the right and left, I was walled in by granite warehouses of the widest dimensions, stowed to their utmost capacity with the necessaries and comforts of life. Added to this, almost everybody[90] seemed to be at work, but noiselessly so, compared with what I had been accustomed to in Baltimore. There were no loud songs heard from those engaged in loading and unloading ships. I heard no deep oaths or horrid curses on the laborer. I saw no whipping of men; but all seemed to go smoothly on. Every man appeared to understand his work, and went at it with a sober, yet cheerful earnestness, which betokened the deep interest which he felt in what he was doing, as well as a sense of his own dignity as a man. To me this looked exceedingly strange. From the wharves I strolled around and over the town, gazing with wonder and admiration at the splendid churches, beautiful dwellings, and finely-cultivated gardens; evincing an amount of wealth, comfort, taste, and refinement, such as I had never seen in any part of slaveholding Maryland.

Everything[91] looked clean, new, and beautiful. I saw few or no dilapidated houses, with poverty-stricken inmates; no half-naked children and barefooted women, such as

Notes

[89] *"Lady of the Lake"* an 1810 poem by Scottish novelist and poet Sir Walter Scott (1771–1832); in it, Sir James Douglas is a Scottish nobleman and outlaw.

[90] *Original reads*: every body [ed.].

[91] *Original reads*: every thing [ed.].

I had been accustomed to see in Hillsborough, Easton, St. Michael's, and Baltimore. The people looked more able, stronger, healthier, and happier, than those of Maryland. I was for once made glad by a view of extreme wealth, without being saddened by seeing extreme poverty. But the most astonishing as well as the most interesting thing to me was the condition of the colored people, a great many of whom, like me,[92] had escaped thither as a refuge from the hunters of men. I found many, who had not been seven years out of their chains, living in finer houses, and evidently enjoying more of the comforts of life, than the average of slaveholders in Maryland. I will venture to assert that my friend Mr. Nathan Johnson (of whom I can say with a grateful heart, "I was hungry, and he gave me meat; I was thirsty, and he gave me drink; I was a stranger, and he took me in"[93]) lived in a neater house; dined at a better table; took, paid for, and read, more newspapers; better understood the moral, religious, and political character of the nation – than nine tenths of the slaveholders in Talbot county, Maryland. Yet Mr. Johnson was a working man. His hands were hardened by toil, and not his alone, but those also of Mrs. Johnson. I found the colored people much more spirited than I had supposed they would be. I found among them a determination to protect each other from the blood-thirsty kidnapper, at all hazards. Soon after my arrival, I was told of a circumstance which illustrated their spirit. A colored man and a fugitive slave were on unfriendly terms. The former was heard to threaten the latter with informing his master of his whereabouts. Straightway a meeting was called among the colored people, under the stereotyped notice, "Business of importance!" The betrayer was invited to attend. The people came at the appointed hour, and organized the meeting by appointing a very religious old gentleman as president, who, I believe, made a prayer, after which he addressed the meeting as follows: *"Friends, we have got him here, and I would recommend that you young men just take him outside the door, and kill him!"* With this, a number of them bolted at him; but they were intercepted by some more timid than themselves, and the betrayer escaped their vengeance, and has not been seen in New Bedford since. I believe there have been no more such threats, and should there be hereafter, I doubt not that death would be the consequence.

I found employment, the third day after my arrival, in stowing a sloop with a load of oil. It was new, dirty, and hard work for me; but I went at it with a glad heart and a willing hand. I was now my own master. It was a happy moment, the rapture of which can be understood only by those who have been slaves. It was the first work, the reward of which was to be entirely my own. There was no Master Hugh standing ready, the moment I earned the money, to rob me of it. I worked that day with a pleasure I had never before experienced. I was at work for myself and newly-married wife. It was to me the starting-point of a new existence. When I got through with that job, I went in pursuit of a job of calking; but such was the strength of prejudice against color, among the white calkers, that they refused to work with me, and of course I could get no employment.* Finding my trade of no immediate benefit, I threw off my calking habiliments, and prepared myself to do any kind of work I could get to do. Mr. Johnson kindly let me have his wood-horse and saw, and I very soon found myself a plenty of work. There was no work too hard – none too dirty. I was ready to saw wood, shovel coal, carry the hod, sweep the chimney, or roll oil casks – all of which I did for nearly three years in New Bedford, before I became known to the anti-slavery world.

Notes

* I am told that colored persons can now get employment at calking in New Bedford – a result of anti-slavery effort.

[92] *Original reads*: any thing [ed.].

[93] *"I was hungry … and he took me in"* Matthew 25:35.

In about four months after I went to New Bedford, there came a young man to me, and inquired if I did not wish to take the "Liberator."[94] I told him I did; but, just having made my escape from slavery, I remarked that I was unable to pay for it then. I, however, finally became a subscriber to it. The paper came, and I read it from week to week with such feelings as it would be quite idle for me to attempt to describe. The paper became my meat and my drink. My soul was set all on fire. Its sympathy for my brethren in bonds – its scathing denunciations of slaveholders – its faithful exposures of slavery – and its powerful attacks upon the upholders of the institution – sent a thrill of joy through my soul, such as I had never felt before!

I had not long been a reader of the "Liberator," before I got a pretty correct idea of the principles, measures and spirit of the anti-slavery reform. I took right hold of the cause. I could do but little; but what I could, I did with a joyful heart, and never felt happier than when in an anti-slavery meeting. I seldom had much to say at the meetings, because what I wanted to say was said so much better by others. But, while attending an anti-slavery convention at Nantucket, on the 11th of August, 1841, I felt strongly moved to speak, and was at the same time much urged to do so by Mr. William C. Coffin, a gentleman who had heard me speak in the colored people's meeting at New Bedford. It was a severe cross, and I took it up reluctantly. The truth was, I felt myself a slave, and the idea of speaking to white people weighed me down. I spoke but a few moments, when I felt a degree of freedom, and said what I desired with considerable ease. From that time until now, I have been engaged in pleading the cause of my brethren – with what success, and with what devotion, I leave those acquainted with my labors to decide.

Appendix

I FIND, since reading over the foregoing Narrative, that I have, in several instances, spoken in such a tone and manner, respecting religion, as may possibly lead those unacquainted with my religious views to suppose me an opponent of all religion. To remove the liability of such misapprehension, I deem it proper to append the following brief explanation. What I have said respecting and against religion, I mean strictly to apply to the *slaveholding religion* of this land, and with no possible reference to Christianity proper; for, between the Christianity of this land, and the Christianity of Christ, I recognize the widest possible difference – so wide, that to receive the one as good, pure, and holy, is of necessity to reject the other as bad, corrupt, and wicked. To be the friend of the one, is of necessity to be the enemy of the other. I love the pure, peaceable, and impartial Christianity of Christ: I therefore hate the corrupt, slaveholding, women-whipping, cradle-plundering, partial and hypocritical Christianity of this land. Indeed, I can see no reason, but the most deceitful one, for calling the religion of this land Christianity. I look upon it as the climax of all misnomers, the boldest of all frauds, and the grossest of all libels. Never was there a clearer case of "stealing the livery of the court of heaven to serve the devil in."[95] I am filled with unutterable loathing when I contemplate the religious pomp and show, together with the horrible inconsistencies, which everywhere[96] surround me. We have men-stealers for ministers, women-whippers for missionaries, and cradle-plunderers for church members. The man who wields the blood-clotted cowskin during the week fills the pulpit on Sunday,

Notes

[94] *the "Liberator"* abolitionist newspaper edited by William Lloyd Garrison.

[95] *"stealing the livery … devil in."* from *The Course of Time* (1827) by Robert Pollok (1798–1827).

[96] *Original reads*: every where [ed.].

and claims to be a minister of the meek and lowly Jesus. The man who robs me of my earnings at the end of each week meets me as a class-leader on Sunday morning, to show me the way of life, and the path of salvation. He who sells my sister, for purposes of prostitution, stands forth as the pious advocate of purity. He who proclaims it a religious duty to read the Bible denies me the right of learning to read the name of the God who made me. He who is the religious advocate of marriage robs whole millions of its sacred influence, and leaves them to the ravages of wholesale pollution. The warm defender of the sacredness of the family relation is the same that scatters whole families – sundering husbands and wives, parents and children, sisters and brothers – leaving the hut vacant, and the hearth desolate. We see the thief preaching against theft, and the adulterer against adultery. We have men sold to build churches, women sold to support the gospel, and babes sold to purchase Bibles for the *poor heathen! all for the glory of God and the good of souls!* The slave auctioneer's bell and the church-going bell chime in with each other, and the bitter cries of the heart-broken slave are drowned in the religious shouts of his pious master. Revivals of religion and revivals in the slave-trade go hand in hand together. The slave prison and the church stand near each other. The clanking of fetters and the rattling of chains in the prison, and the pious psalm and solemn prayer in the church, may be heard at the same time. The dealers in the bodies and souls of men erect their stand in the presence of the pulpit, and they mutually help each other. The dealer gives his blood-stained gold to support the pulpit, and the pulpit, in return, covers his infernal business with the garb of Christianity. Here we have religion and robbery the allies of each other – devils dressed in angels' robes, and hell presenting the semblance of paradise.

"Just God! and these are they,[97]
 Who minister at thine altar, God of right!
Men who their hands, with prayer and blessing, lay
 On Israel's ark of light.[98]
"What! preach, and kidnap men?
 Give thanks, and rob thy own afflicted poor?
Talk of thy glorious liberty, and then
 Bolt hard the captive's door?

"What! servants of thy own
 Merciful Son, who came to seek and save
The homeless and the outcast, fettering down
 The tasked and plundered slave!

"Pilate and Herod friends![99]
 Chief priests and rulers, as of old, combine!
Just God and holy! is that church which lends
 Strength to the spoiler thine?"

The Christianity of America is a Christianity, of whose votaries it may be as truly said, as it was of the ancient scribes and Pharisees, "They bind heavy burdens, and

Notes

[97] John Greenleaf Whittier's antislavery poem "Clerical Oppressors" (1836).

[98] *Israel's ark of light* the Ark of the Covenant, containing the tablets of the law.

[99] *Pilate and Herod* the two authority figures who sanction the crucifixion of Christ, Pontius Pilate as Roman prefect of Judea, Herod Antipas as tetrarch of Galilee.

grievous to be borne, and lay them on men's shoulders, but they themselves will not move them with one of their fingers. All their works they do for to be seen of men. They love the uppermost rooms at feasts, and the chief seats in the synagogues, … and to be called of men, Rabbi, Rabbi. But woe unto you, scribes and Pharisees, hypocrites! for ye shut up the kingdom of heaven against men; for ye neither go in yourselves, neither suffer ye them that are entering to go in. Ye devour widows' houses, and for a pretence make long prayers; therefore ye shall receive the greater damnation. Ye compass sea and land to make one proselyte, and when he is made, ye make him twofold more the child of hell than yourselves. Woe unto you, scribes and Pharisees, hypocrites! for ye pay tithe of mint, and anise, and cumin, and have omitted the weightier matters of the law, judgment, mercy, and faith; these ought ye to have done, and not to leave the other undone. Ye blind guides! which strain at a gnat, and swallow a camel. Woe unto you, scribes and Pharisees, hypocrites! for ye make clean the outside of the cup and of the platter; but within, they are full of extortion and excess. Woe unto you, scribes and Pharisees, hypocrites! for ye are like unto whited sepulchres, which indeed appear beautiful outward, but are within full of dead men's bones, and of all uncleanness. Even so ye also outwardly appear righteous unto men, but within ye are full of hypocrisy and iniquity."[100]

Dark and terrible as is this picture, I hold it to be strictly true of the overwhelming mass of professed Christians in America. They strain at a gnat, and swallow a camel. Could anything[101] be more true of our churches? They would be shocked at the proposition of fellowshipping a *sheep*-stealer; and at the same time they hug to their communion a *man*-stealer, and brand me with being an infidel, if I find fault with them for it. They attend with Pharisaical strictness to the outward forms of religion, and at the same time neglect the weightier matters of the law, judgment, mercy, and faith. They are always ready to sacrifice, but seldom to show mercy. They are they who are represented as professing to love God whom they have not seen, whilst they hate their brother whom they have seen. They love the heathen on the other side of the globe. They can pray for him, pay money to have the Bible put into his hand, and missionaries to instruct him; while they despise and totally neglect the heathen at their own doors.

Such is, very briefly, my view of the religion of this land; and to avoid any misunderstanding, growing out of the use of general terms, I mean, by the religion of this land, that which is revealed in the words, deeds, and actions, of those bodies, north and south, calling themselves Christian churches, and yet in union with slaveholders. It is against religion, as presented by these bodies, that I have felt it my duty to testify.

I conclude these remarks by copying the following portrait of the religion of the south, (which is, by communion and fellowship, the religion of the north,) which I soberly affirm is "true to the life," and without caricature or the slightest exaggeration. It is said to have been drawn, several years before the present anti-slavery agitation began, by a northern Methodist preacher, who, while residing at the south, had an opportunity to see slaveholding morals, manners, and piety, with his own eyes. "Shall I not visit for these things? saith the Lord. Shall not my soul be avenged on such a nation as this?"[102]

Notes

[100] *"They bind heavy burdens … full of hypocrisy and iniquity"* Matthew 23:4–28. In this passage, Jesus denounces the hypocrisy of the Pharisees, a party in Judaism that emphasized strict forms of religious observance.

[101] *Original reads*: any thing [ed.].

[102] *"Shall I not visit … such a nation as this?"* Jeremiah 5:9.

"A PARODY[103]

"Come, saints and sinners, hear me tell
How pious priests whip Jack and Nell,
And women buy and children sell,
And preach all sinners down to hell,
 And sing of heavenly union.

"They'll bleat and baa, dona like goats,
Gorge down black sheep, and strain at motes,
Array their backs in fine black coats,
Then seize their negroes by their throats,
 And choke, for heavenly union.

"They'll church you if you sip a dram,
And damn you if you steal a lamb;
Yet rob old Tony, Doll, and Sam,
Of human rights, and bread and ham;
 Kidnapper's heavenly union.

"They'll loudly talk of Christ's reward,
And bind his image with a cord,
And scold, and swing the lash abhorred,
And sell their brother in the Lord
 To handcuffed heavenly union.

"They'll read and sing a sacred song,
And make a prayer both loud and long,
And teach the right and do the wrong,
Hailing the brother, sister throng,
 With words of heavenly union.

"We wonder how such saints can sing,
Or praise the Lord upon the wing,
Who roar, and scold, and whip, and sting,
And to their slaves and mammon cling,
 In guilty conscience union.

"They'll raise tobacco, corn, and rye,
And drive, and thieve, and cheat, and lie,
And lay up treasures in the sky,
By making switch and cowskin fly,
 In hope of heavenly union.

"They'll crack old Tony on the skull,
And preach and roar like Bashan bull,[104]

Notes

[103] Parody of "Heavenly Union," a popular Southern hymn.

[104] *Bashan bull* Psalm 22:12, "strong bulls of Bashan have encircled me."

Or braying ass, of mischief full,
Then seize old Jacob by the wool,
  And pull for heavenly union.

"A roaring, ranting, sleek man-thief,
Who lived on mutton, veal, and beef,
Yet never would afford relief
To needy, sable sons of grief,
  Was big with heavenly union.

"'Love not the world,' the preacher said,
And winked his eye, and shook his head;
He seized on Tom, and Dick, and Ned,
Cut short their meat, and clothes, and bread,
  Yet still loved heavenly union.

"Another preacher whining spoke
Of One whose heart for sinners broke:
He tied old Nanny to an oak,
And drew the blood at every stroke,
  And prayed for heavenly union.

"Two others oped their iron jaws,
And waved their children-stealing paws;
There sat their children in gewgaws;
By stinting negroes' backs and maws,
  They kept up heavenly union.

"All good from Jack another takes,
And entertains their flirts and rakes,
Who dress as sleek as glossy snakes,
And cram their mouths with sweetened cakes;
  And this goes down for union."

Sincerely and earnestly hoping that this little book may do something toward throwing light on the American slave system, and hastening the glad day of deliverance to the millions of my brethren in bonds – faithfully relying upon the power of truth, love, and justice, for success in my humble efforts – and solemnly pledging myself anew to the sacred cause – I subscribe myself,

Frederick Douglass.

1845

What to the Slave Is the Fourth of July?: An Address Delivered in Rochester, New York, on 5 July 1852

Mr. President, Friends and Fellow Citizens: He who could address this audience without a quailing sensation, has stronger nerves than I have. I do not remember ever to have appeared as a speaker before any assembly more shrinkingly, nor with greater distrust of my ability, than I do this day. A feeling has crept over me, quite unfavorable to the exercise of my limited powers of speech. The task before me is one which requires much previous thought and study for its proper performance. I know that apologies of this sort are generally considered flat and unmeaning. I trust, however, that mine will not be so considered. Should I seem at ease, my appearance would much misrepresent me. The little experience I have had in addressing public meetings, in country school houses, avails me nothing on the present occasion.

The papers and placards say, that I am to deliver a 4th of July oration.[1] This certainly sounds large, and out of the common way, for me. It is true that I have often had the privilege to speak in this beautiful Hall, and to address many who now honor me with their presence. But neither their familiar faces, nor the perfect gage I think I have of Corinthian Hall, seems to free me from embarrassment.

The fact is, ladies and gentlemen, the distance between this platform and the slave plantation, from which I escaped, is considerable – and the difficulties to be overcome in getting from the latter to the former, are by no means slight. That I am here to-day is, to me, a matter of astonishment as well as of gratitude. You will not, therefore, be surprised, if in what I have to say, I evince no elaborate preparation, nor grace my speech with any high sounding exordium. With little experience and with less learning, I have been able to throw my thoughts hastily and imperfectly together; and trusting to your patient and generous indulgence, I will proceed to lay them before you.

This, for the purpose of this celebration, is the 4th of July. It is the birthday of your National Independence, and of your political freedom. This, to you, is what the Passover was to the emancipated people of God. It carries your minds back to the day, and to the act of your great deliverance; and to the signs, and to the wonders, associated with that act, and that day. This celebration also marks the beginning of another year of your national life; and reminds you that the Republic of America is now 76 years old. I am glad, fellow-citizens, that your nation is so young. Seventy-six years, though a good old age for a man, is but a mere speck in the life of a nation. Three score years and ten is the allotted time for individual men; but nations number their years by thousands. According to this fact, you are, even now, only in the beginning of your national career, still lingering in the period of childhood. I repeat, I am glad this is so. There is hope in the thought, and hope is much needed, under the dark clouds which lower above the horizon. The eye of the reformer is met with angry flashes, portending disastrous times; but his heart may well beat lighter at the thought that America is young, and that she is still in the impressible stage of her existence. May he not hope that high lessons of wisdom, of justice and of truth, will yet give direction to her destiny? Were the nation older, the patriot's heart might be sadder, and the reformer's brow heavier. Its future might be shrouded in gloom, and the hope of its prophets go out in sorrow. There is consolation in the thought that America is young. Great streams are not easily turned from channels, worn deep in the course of ages. They may sometimes rise in

Notes

"What to the Slave Is the Fourth of July?"

[1] *Original reads*: 4th July oration [ed.].

quiet and stately majesty, and inundate the land, refreshing and fertilizing the earth with their mysterious properties. They may also rise in wrath and fury, and bear away, on their angry waves, the accumulated wealth of years of toil and hardship. They, however, gradually flow back to the same old channel, and flow on as serenely as ever. But, while the river may not be turned aside, it may dry up, and leave nothing behind but the withered branch, and the unsightly rock, to howl in the abyss-sweeping wind, the sad tale of departed glory. As with rivers so with nations.

Fellow-citizens, I shall not presume to dwell at length on the associations that cluster about this day. The simple story of it is that, 76 years ago, the people of this country were British subjects. The style and title of your "sovereign people" (in which you now glory) was not then born. You were under the British Crown. Your fathers esteemed the English Government as the home government; and England as the fatherland. This home government, you know, although a considerable distance from your home, did, in the exercise of its parental prerogatives, impose upon its colonial children, such restraints, burdens and limitations, as, in its mature judgement, it deemed wise, right and proper.

But, your fathers, who had not adopted the fashionable idea of this day, of the infallibility of government, and the absolute character of its acts, presumed to differ from the home government in respect to the wisdom and the justice of some of those burdens and restraints. They went so far in their excitement as to pronounce the measures of government unjust, unreasonable, and oppressive, and altogether such as ought not to be quietly submitted to. I scarcely need say, fellow-citizens, that my opinion of those measures fully accords with that of your fathers. Such a declaration of agreement on my part would not be worth much to anybody. It would, certainly, prove nothing, as to what part I might have taken, had I lived during the great controversy of 1776. To say *now* that America was right, and England wrong, is exceedingly easy. Everybody can say it; the dastard, not less than the noble brave, can flippantly discant on the tyranny of England towards the American Colonies. It is fashionable to do so; but there was a time when to pronounce against England, and in favor of the cause of the colonies, tried men's souls. They who did so were accounted in their day, plotters of mischief, agitators and rebels, dangerous men. To side with the right, against the wrong, with the weak against the strong, and with the oppressed against the oppressor! *here* lies the merit, and the one which, of all others, seems unfashionable in our day. The cause of liberty may be stabbed by the men who glory in the deeds of your fathers. But, to proceed.

Feeling themselves harshly and unjustly treated by the home government, your fathers, like men of honesty, and men of spirit, earnestly sought redress. They petitioned and remonstrated; they did so in a decorous, respectful, and loyal manner. Their conduct was wholly unexceptionable. This, however, did not answer the purpose. They saw themselves treated with sovereign indifference, coldness and scorn. Yet they persevered. They were not the men to look back.

As the sheet anchor takes a firmer hold, when the ship is tossed by the storm, so did the cause of your fathers grow stronger, as it breasted the chilling blasts of kingly displeasure. The greatest and best of British statesmen admitted its justice, and the loftiest eloquence of the British Senate came to its support. But, with that blindness which seems to be the unvarying characteristic of tyrants, since Pharoah and his hosts were drowned in the Red Sea, the British Government persisted in the exactions complained of.

The madness of this course, we believe, is admitted now, even by England; but we fear the lesson is wholly lost on our present rulers.

Oppression makes a wise man mad. Your fathers were wise men, and if they did not go mad, they became restive under this treatment. They felt themselves the victims of grievous wrongs, wholly incurable in their colonial capacity. With brave men there is always a remedy for oppression. Just here, the idea of a total separation of the colonies from the crown was born! It was a startling idea, much more so, than we, at this distance of time, regard it. The timid and the prudent (as has been intimated) of that day, were, of course, shocked and alarmed by it.

Such people lived then, had lived before, and will, probably, ever have a place on this planet; and their course, in respect to any great change, (no matter how great the good to be attained, or the wrong to be redressed by it), may be calculated with as much precision as can be the course of the stars. They hate all changes, but silver, gold and copper change! Of this sort of change they are always strongly in favor.

These people were called Tories[2] in the days of your fathers; and the appellation, probably, conveyed the same idea that is meant by a more modern, though a somewhat less euphonious term, which we often find in our papers, applied to some of our old politicians.

Their opposition to the then dangerous thought was earnest and powerful; but, amid all their terror and affrighted vociferations against it, the alarming and revolutionary idea moved on, and the country with it.

On the 2d of July, 1776, the old Continental Congress, to the dismay of the lovers of ease, and the worshippers of property, clothed that dreadful idea with all the authority of national sanction. They did so in the form of a resolution; and as we seldom hit upon resolutions, drawn up in our day, whose transparency is at all equal to this, it may refresh your minds and help my story if I read it.

> "Resolved, That these united colonies *are*, and of right, ought to be free and Independent States; that they are absolved from all allegiance to the British Crown; and that all political connection between them and the State of Great Britain *is*, and ought to be, dissolved."

Citizens, your fathers made good that resolution. They succeeded; and today you reap the fruits of their success. The freedom gained is yours; and you, therefore, may properly celebrate this anniversary. The 4th of July is the first great fact in your nation's history – the very ring-bolt in the chain of your yet undeveloped destiny.

Pride and patriotism, not less than gratitude, prompt you to celebrate and to hold it in perpetual remembrance. I have said that the Declaration of Independence is the RING-BOLT to the chain of your nation's destiny; so, indeed, I regard it. The principles contained in that instrument are saving principles. Stand by those principles, be true to them on all occasions, in all places, against all foes, and at whatever cost.

From the round top of your ship of state, dark and threatening clouds may be seen. Heavy billows, like mountains in the distance, disclose to the leeward huge forms of flinty rocks! That *bolt* drawn, that *chain* broken, and all is lost. *Cling to this day – cling to it*, and to its principles, with the grasp of a storm-tossed mariner to a spar at midnight.

The coming into being of a nation, in any circumstances, is an interesting event. But, besides general considerations, there were peculiar circumstances which make the advent of this republic an event of special attractiveness.

The whole scene, as I look back to it, was simple, dignified and sublime. The population of the country, at the time, stood at the insignificant number of three millions.

Notes

[2] *Original reads*: tories [ed.].

The country was poor in the munitions of war. The population was weak and scattered, and the country a wilderness unsubdued. There were then no means of concert and combination, such as exist now. Neither steam nor lightning had then been reduced to order and discipline. From the Potomac to the Delaware was a journey of many days. Under these, and innumerable other disadvantages, your fathers declared for liberty and independence and triumphed.

Fellow Citizens, I am not wanting in respect for the fathers of this republic. The signers of the Declaration of Independence were brave men. They were great men too – great enough to give fame to a great age. It does not often happen to a nation to raise, at one time, such a number of truly great men. The point from which I am compelled to view them is not, certainly, the most favorable; and yet I cannot contemplate their great deeds with less than admiration. They were statesmen, patriots and heroes, and for the good they did, and the principles they contended for, I will unite with you to honor their memory.

They loved their country better than their own private interests; and, though this is not the highest form of human excellence, all will concede that it is a rare virtue, and that when it is exhibited, it ought to command respect. He who will, intelligently, lay down his life for his country, is a man whom it is not in human nature to despise. Your fathers staked their lives, their fortunes, and their sacred honor, on the cause of their country. In their admiration of liberty, they lost sight of all other interests.

They were peace men; but they preferred revolution to peaceful submission to bondage. They were quiet men; but they did not shrink from agitating against oppression. They showed forbearance; but that they knew its limits. They believed in order; but not in the order of tyranny. With them, nothing was "*settled*" that was not right. With them, justice, liberty and humanity were "*final*"; not slavery and oppression. You may well cherish the memory of such men. They were great in their day and generation. Their solid manhood stands out the more as we contrast it with these degenerate times.

How circumspect, exact and proportionate were all their movements! How unlike the politicians of an hour! Their statesmanship looked beyond the passing moment, and stretched away in strength into the distant future. They seized upon eternal principles, and set a glorious example in their defence. Mark them!

Fully appreciating the hardship to be encountered, firmly believing in the right of their cause, honorably inviting the scrutiny of an on-looking world, reverently appealing to heaven to attest their sincerity, soundly comprehending the solemn responsibility they were about to assume, wisely measuring the terrible odds against them, your fathers, the fathers of this republic, did, most deliberately, under the inspiration of a glorious patriotism, and with a sublime faith in the great principles of justice and freedom, lay deep the corner-stone of the national superstructure, which has risen and still rises in grandeur around you.

Of this fundamental work, this day is the anniversary. Our eyes are met with demonstrations of joyous enthusiasm. Banners and pennants wave exultingly on the breeze. The din of business, too, is hushed. Even Mammon[3] seems to have quitted his grasp on this day. The ear-piercing fife and the stirring drum unite their accents with the ascending peal of a thousand church bells. Prayers are made, hymns are sung, and sermons are preached in honor of this day; while the quick martial tramp of a great and multitudinous nation, echoed back by all the hills,

Notes

[3] *Mammon* greed for money, personified as a false god.

valleys and mountains of a vast continent, bespeak the occasion one of thrilling and universal interest – a nation's jubilee.

Friends and citizens, I need not enter further into the causes which led to this anniversary. Many of you understand them better than I do. You could instruct me in regard to them. That is a branch of knowledge in which you feel, perhaps, a much deeper interest than your speaker. The causes which led to the separation of the colonies from the British crown have never lacked for a tongue. They have all been taught in your common schools, narrated at your firesides, unfolded from your pulpits, and thundered from your legislative halls, and are as familiar to you as household words. They form the staple of your national poetry and eloquence.

I remember, also, that, as a people, Americans are remarkably familiar with all facts which make in their own favor. This is esteemed by some as a national trait – perhaps a national weakness. It is a fact, that whatever makes for the wealth or for the reputation of Americans, and can be had *cheap*! will be found by Americans. I shall not be charged with slandering Americans, if I say I think the American side of any question may be safely left in American hands.

I leave, therefore, the great deeds of your fathers to other gentlemen whose claim to have been regularly descended will be less likely to be disputed than mine!

The Present

My business, if I have any here to-day, is with the present. The accepted time with God and his cause is the ever-living now.

> "Trust no future, however pleasant,
> Let the dead past bury its dead;
> Act, act in the living present,
> Heart within, and God overhead."[4]

We have to do with the past only as we can make it useful to the present and to the future. To all inspiring motives, to noble deeds which can be gained from the past, we are welcome. But now is the time, the important time. Your fathers have lived, died, and have done their work, and have done much of it well. You live and must die, and you must do your work. You have no right to enjoy a child's share in the labor of your fathers, unless your children are to be blest by your labors. You have no right to wear out and waste the hard-earned fame of your fathers to cover your indolence. Sydney Smith[5] tells us that men seldom eulogize the wisdom and virtues of their fathers, but to excuse some folly or wickedness of their own. This truth is not a doubtful one. There are illustrations of it near and remote, ancient and modern. It was fashionable, hundreds of years ago, for the children of Jacob to boast, we have "Abraham to our father,"[6] when they had long lost Abraham's faith and spirit. That people contented themselves under the shadow of Abraham's great name, while they repudiated the deeds which made his name great. Need I remind you that a similar thing is being done all over this country to-day? Need I tell you that the Jews are not the only people who

Notes

4 *"Trust … overhead"* an excerpt of Henry Wadworth Longfellow's poem "A Psalm of Life."

5 Sydney Smith (1771–1845), an English satirist and Anglican cleric.

6 *"Abraham … father"* Abraham was Hebrew patriarch from whom all Jews trace their descent.

built the tombs of the prophets, and garnished the sepulchres of the righteous? Washington could not die till he had broken the chains of his slaves. Yet his monument is built up by the price of human blood, and the traders in the bodies and souls of men, shout – "We have Washington to *our father.*" Alas! that it should be so; yet so it is.

> "The evil that men do, lives after them,
> The good is oft' interred with their bones."[7]

Fellow-citizens, pardon me, allow me to ask, why am I called upon to speak here to-day? What have I, or those I represent, to do with your national independence? Are the great principles of political freedom and of natural justice, embodied in that Declaration of Independence, extended to us? And[8] am I, therefore, called upon to bring our humble offering to the national altar, and to confess the benefits and express devout gratitude for the blessings resulting from your independence to us?

Would to God, both for your sakes and ours, that an affirmative answer could be truthfully returned to these questions! Then would my task be light, and my burden easy and delightful. For *who* is there so cold, that a nation's sympathy could not warm him? Who so obdurate and dead to the claims of gratitude, that would not thankfully acknowledge such priceless benefits? Who so stolid and selfish, that would not give his voice to swell the hallelujahs of a nation's jubilee, when the chains of servitude had been torn from his limbs? I am not that man. In a case like that, the dumb might eloquently speak, and the "lame man leap as an hart."[9]

But, such is not the state of the case. I say it with a sad sense of the disparity between us. I am not included within the pale of this glorious anniversary! Your high independence only reveals the immeasurable distance between us. The blessings in which you, this day, rejoice, are not enjoyed in common. The rich inheritance of justice, liberty, prosperity and independence, bequeathed by your fathers, is shared by you, not by me. The sunlight that brought life and healing to you, has brought stripes and death to me. This Fourth [of] July is *yours*, not *mine*. *You* may rejoice, *I* must mourn. To drag a man in fetters into the grand illuminated temple of liberty, and call upon him to join you in joyous anthems, were inhuman mockery and sacrilegious irony. Do you mean, citizens, to mock me, by asking me to speak today? If so, there is a parallel to your conduct. And let me warn you that it is dangerous to copy the example of a nation whose crimes, towering up to heaven, were thrown down by the breath of the Almighty, burying that nation in irrecoverable ruin! I can to-day take up the plaintive lament of a peeled and woe-smitten people!

"By the rivers of Babylon, there we sat down. Yea! we wept when we remembered Zion. We hanged our harps upon the willows in the midst thereof. For there, they that carried us away captive, required of us a song; and they who wasted us required of us mirth, saying, Sing us one of the songs of Zion. How can we sing the Lord's song in a strange land? If I forget thee, O Jerusalem, let my right hand forget her cunning. If I do not remember thee, let my tongue cleave to the roof of my mouth."[10]

Fellow-citizens; above your national, tumultuous joy, I hear the mournful wail of millions! whose chains, heavy and grievous yesterday, are, to-day, rendered more intolerable by the jubilee shouts that reach them. If I do forget, if I do not faithfully remember those bleeding children of sorrow this day, "may my right hand forget her cunning,

Notes

[7] *"The evil ... their bones"* Shakespeare, *Julius Caesar* 3.2.76.

[8] *Original reads*: and [ed.].

[9] *"lame ... hart"* Isaiah 35:6.

[10] *"By the rivers ... mouth"* Psalm 137:1–6.

and may my tongue cleave to the roof of my mouth!" To forget them, to pass lightly over their wrongs, and to chime in with the popular theme, would be treason most scandalous and shocking, and would make me a reproach before God and the world. My subject, then fellow-citizens, is AMERICAN SLAVERY. I shall see, this day, and its popular characteristics, from the slave's point of view. Standing, there, identified with the American bondman, making his wrongs mine, I do not hesitate to declare, with all my soul, that the character and conduct of this nation never looked blacker to me than on this 4th of July! Whether we turn to the declarations of the past, or to the professions of the present, the conduct of the nation seems equally hideous and revolting. America is false to the past, false to the present, and solemnly binds herself to be false to the future. Standing with God and the crushed and bleeding slave on this occasion, I will, in the name of humanity which is outraged, in the name of liberty which is fettered, in the name of the constitution and the Bible, which are disregarded and trampled upon, dare to call in question and to denounce, with all the emphasis I can command, everything that serves to perpetuate slavery – the great sin and shame of America! "I will not equivocate; I will not excuse"; I will use the severest language I can command; and yet not one word shall escape me that any man, whose judgement is not blinded by prejudice, or who is not at heart a slaveholder, shall not confess to be right and just.

But I fancy I hear someone[II] of my audience say, it is just in this circumstance that you and your brother abolitionists fail to make a favorable impression on the public mind. Would you argue more, and denounce less, would you persuade more, and rebuke less, your cause would be much more likely to succeed. But, I submit, where all is plain there is nothing to be argued. What point in the anti-slavery creed would you have me argue? On what branch of the subject do the people of this country need light? Must I undertake to prove that the slave is a man? That point is conceded already. Nobody doubts it. The slaveholders themselves acknowledge it in the enactment of laws for their government. They acknowledge it when they punish disobedience on the part of the slave. There are seventy-two crimes in the State of Virginia, which, if committed by a black man, (no matter how ignorant he be), subject him to the punishment of death; while only two of the same crimes will subject a white man to the like punishment. What is this but the acknowledgement that the slave is a moral, intellectual and responsible being? The manhood of the slave is conceded. It is admitted in the fact that Southern statute books are covered with enactments forbidding, under severe fines and penalties, the teaching of the slave to read or to write. When you can point to any such laws, in reference to the beasts of the field, then I may consent to argue the manhood of the slave. When the dogs in your streets, when the fowls of the air, when the cattle on your hills, when the fish of the sea, and the reptiles that crawl, shall be unable to distinguish the slave from a brute, *then* will I argue with you that the slave is a man!

For the present, it is enough to affirm the equal manhood of the negro race. Is it not astonishing that, while we are ploughing, planting and reaping, using all kinds of mechanical tools, erecting houses, constructing bridges, building ships, working in metals of brass, iron, copper, silver and gold; that, while we are reading, writing and cyphering, acting as clerks, merchants and secretaries, having among us lawyers, doctors, ministers, poets, authors, editors, orators and teachers; that, while we are engaged in all manner of enterprises common to other men, digging gold in

Notes

[II] *Original reads*: some one [ed.].

California, capturing the whale in the Pacific, feeding sheep and cattle on the hill-side, living, moving, acting, thinking, planning, living in families as husbands, wives and children, and, above all, confessing and worshipping the Christian's God, and looking hopefully for life and immortality beyond the grave, we are called upon to prove that we are men!

Would you have me argue that man is entitled to liberty? that he is the rightful owner of his own body? You have already declared it. Must I argue the wrongfulness of slavery? Is that a question for Republicans? Is it to be settled by the rules of logic and argumentation, as a matter beset with great difficulty, involving a doubtful application of the principle of justice, hard to be understood? How should I look to-day, in the presence of Americans, dividing, and subdividing a discourse, to show that men have a natural right to freedom? speaking of it relatively, and positively, negatively, and affirmatively. To do so, would be to make myself ridiculous, and to offer an insult to your understanding. There is not a man beneath the canopy of heaven, that does not know that slavery is wrong *for him*.

What, am I to argue that it is wrong to make men brutes, to rob them of their liberty, to work them without wages, to keep them ignorant of their relations to their fellow men, to beat them with sticks, to flay their flesh with the lash, to load their limbs with irons, to hunt them with dogs, to sell them at auction, to sunder their families, to knock out their teeth, to burn their flesh, to starve them into obedience and submission to their masters? Must I argue that a system thus marked with blood, and stained with pollution, is *wrong*? No! I will not. I have better employments for my time and strength, than such arguments would imply.

What, then, remains to be argued? Is it that slavery is not divine; that God did not establish it; that our doctors of divinity are mistaken? There is blasphemy in the thought. That which is inhuman, cannot be divine! *Who* can reason on such a proposition? They that can, may; I cannot. The time for such argument is past.

At a time like this, scorching irony, not convincing argument, is needed. O! had I the ability, and could I reach the nation's ear, I would, to-day, pour out a fiery stream of biting ridicule, blasting reproach, withering sarcasm, and stern rebuke. For it is not light that is needed, but fire; it is not the gentle shower, but thunder. We need the storm, the whirlwind, and the earthquake. The feeling of the nation must be quickened; the conscience of the nation must be roused; the propriety of the nation must be startled; the hypocrisy of the nation must be exposed; and its crimes against God and man must be proclaimed and denounced.

What, to the American slave, is your 4th of July? I answer: a day that reveals to him, more than all other days in the year, the gross injustice and cruelty to which he is the constant victim. To him, your celebration is a sham; your boasted liberty, an unholy license; your national greatness, swelling vanity; your sounds of rejoicing are empty and heartless; your denunciations of tyrants, brass fronted impudence; your shouts of liberty and equality, hollow mockery; your prayers and hymns, your sermons and thanksgivings, with all your religious parade, and solemnity, are, to him, mere bombast, fraud, deception, impiety, and hypocrisy – a thin veil to cover up crimes which would disgrace a nation of savages. There is not a nation on the earth guilty of practices, more shocking and bloody, than are the people of these United States, at this very hour.

Go where you may, search where you will, roam through all the monarchies and despotisms of the old world, travel through South America, search out every abuse, and when you have found the last, lay your facts by the side of the everyday practices of this nation, and you will say with me, that, for revolting barbarity and shameless hypocrisy, America reigns without a rival.

The Internal Slave Trade

Americans! your republican politics, not less than your republican religion, are flagrantly inconsistent. You boast of your love of liberty, your superior civilization, and your pure Christianity, while the whole political power of the nation (as embodied in the two great political parties), is solemnly pledged to support and perpetuate the enslavement of three millions of your countrymen. You hurl your anathemas at the crowned headed tyrants of Russia and Austria, and pride yourselves on your Democratic institutions, while you yourselves consent to be the mere *tools* and *bodyguards* of the tyrants of Virginia and Carolina. You invite to your shores fugitives of oppression from abroad, honor them with banquets, greet them with ovations, cheer them, toast them, salute them, protect them, and pour out your money to them like water; but the fugitives from your own land you advertise, hunt, arrest, shoot and kill. You glory in your refinement and your universal education; yet you maintain a system as barbarous and dreadful as ever stained the character of a nation – a system begun in avarice, supported in pride, and perpetuated in cruelty. You shed tears over fallen Hungary, and make the sad story of her wrongs the theme of your poets, statesmen and orators, till your gallant sons are ready to fly to arms to vindicate her cause against her oppressors; but, in regard to the ten thousand wrongs of the American slave, you would enforce the strictest silence, and would hail him as an enemy of the nation who dares to make those wrongs the subject of public discourse! You are all on fire at the mention of liberty for France or for Ireland; but are as cold as an iceberg at the thought of liberty for the enslaved of America. You discourse eloquently on the dignity of labor; yet, you sustain a system which, in its very essence, casts a stigma upon labor. You can bare your bosom to the storm of British artillery to throw off a threepenny tax on tea; and yet wring the last hard-earned farthing from the grasp of the black laborers of your country. You profess to believe "that, of one blood, God made all nations of men to dwell on the face of all the earth," and hath commanded all men, everywhere to love one another; yet you notoriously hate, (and glory in your hatred), all men whose skins are not colored like your own. You declare, before the world, and are understood by the world to declare, that you *"hold these truths to be self-evident, that all men are created equal; and are endowed by their Creator with certain inalienable rights; and that, among these are, life, liberty, and the pursuit of happiness"*; and yet, you hold securely, in a bondage which, according to your own Thomas Jefferson, *"is worse than ages of that which your fathers rose in rebellion to oppose," a seventh part* of the inhabitants of your country.

Fellow-citizens! I will not enlarge further on your national inconsistencies. The existence of slavery in this country brands your republicanism as a sham, your humanity as a base pretence, and your Christianity as a lie. It destroys your moral power abroad; it corrupts your politicians at home. It saps the foundation of religion; it makes your name a hissing, and a by-word to a mocking earth. It is the antagonistic force in your government, the only thing that seriously disturbs and endangers your *Union*. It fetters your progress; it is the enemy of improvement, the deadly foe of education; it fosters pride; it breeds insolence; it promotes vice; it shelters crime; it is a curse to the earth that supports it; and yet, you cling to it, as if it were the sheet anchor of all your hopes. Oh! be warned! be warned! a horrible reptile is coiled up in your nation's bosom; the venomous creature is nursing at the tender breast of your youthful republic; *for the love of God, tear away*, and fling from you the hideous monster, and *let the weight of twenty millions crush and destroy it forever*!

The Constitution

Allow me to say, in conclusion, notwithstanding the dark picture I have this day presented of the state of the nation, I do not despair of this country. There are forces in operation, which must inevitably work the downfall of slavery. *"The arm of the Lord is not shortened,"* and the doom of slavery is certain. I, therefore, leave off where I began, with *hope*. While drawing encouragement from the Declaration of Independence, the great principles it contains, and the genius of American Institutions, my spirit is also cheered by the obvious tendencies of the age. Nations do not now stand in the same relation to each other that they did ages ago. No nation can now shut itself up from the surrounding world, and trot round in the same old path of its fathers without interference. The time *was* when such could be done. Long established customs of hurtful character could formerly fence themselves in, and do their evil work with social impunity. Knowledge was then confined and enjoyed by the privileged few, and the multitude walked on in mental darkness. But a change has now come over the affairs of mankind. Walled cities and empires have become unfashionable. The arm of commerce has borne away the gates of the strong city. Intelligence is penetrating the darkest corners of the globe. It makes its pathway over and under the sea, as well as on the earth. Wind, steam, and lightning are its chartered agents. Oceans no longer divide, but link nations together. From Boston to London is now a holiday excursion. Space is comparatively annihilated. Thoughts expressed on one side of the Atlantic are distinctly heard on the other.

The far off and almost fabulous Pacific rolls in grandeur at our feet. The Celestial Empire, the mystery of ages, is being solved. The fiat of the Almighty, *"Let there be Light,"* has not yet spent its force. No abuse, no outrage whether in taste, sport or avarice, can now hide itself from the all-pervading light. The iron shoe, and crippled foot of China must be seen, in contrast with nature. *Africa must rise and put on her yet unwoven garment. "Ethiopia shall stretch out her hand unto God."* In the fervent aspirations of William Lloyd Garrison, I say, and let every heart join in saying it:

God speed the year of jubilee
  The wide world o'er!
When from their galling chains set free,
Th' oppress'd shall vilely bend the knee,
And wear the yoke of tyranny
  Like brutes no more.
That year will come, and freedom's reign,
To man his plundered rights again
  Restore.

God speed the day when human blood
  Shall cease to flow!
In every clime be understood,
The claims of human brotherhood,
And each return for evil, good,
  Not blow for blow;
That day will come all feuds to end,
And change into a faithful friend
  Each foe.

God speed the hour, the glorious hour,
  When none on earth
Shall exercise a lordly power,
Nor in a tyrant's presence cower;
But all to manhood's stature tower,
  By equal birth!
THAT HOUR WILL COME, to each, to all,
And from his prison-house, the thrall
  Go forth.

Until that year, day, hour, arrive,
With head, and heart, and hand I'll strive,
To break the rod, and rend the gyve,
The spoiler of his prey deprive –
  So witness Heaven!
And never from my chosen post,
Whate'er the peril or the cost,
  Be driven.

1852

William Wells Brown (1814–1884)

When William Wells Brown published *Clotel; or, The President's Daughter* in London in 1853, the novel marked a banner achievement in a literary career that already included a bestselling 1847 slave narrative and a pioneering 1852 work of African American travel writing. By his death in 1884, Brown had written eight books and two plays, making him one of the most prolific African American authors of the antebellum era. Like Frederick Douglass and other African American writers of his generation, Brown used his experiences as a slave and fugitive, Underground Railroad conductor, and abolitionist orator to create the hallmark forms and themes of mid-century African American literature.

William was born a slave in Lexington, Kentucky, his mother a slave and his father a white relative of her owner, but he moved to St Louis, Missouri, as a young child. His owner, John Young, was a physician. Through his work as a house servant in Young's practice, William developed a life-long interest in medicine. William worked in local taverns, on farms, and, in a position foreshadowing his abolitionist future, as a hand-boy in the printing office of abolitionist editor Elijah Lovejoy. He was eventually purchased by Enoch Price, a St Louis commission merchant and steamboat owner. Price took the slave with him on travels up and down the Ohio River. After one failed attempt to flee (with his mother), William escaped slavery for good on New Year's Day in 1834 while his boat was docked in Cincinnati, Ohio. In Central Ohio, he was befriended by Wells Brown, a white Quaker whose name he took as he embarked on a life of freedom.

Now called William Wells Brown, the young man lived in Cleveland and married a free woman, Elizabeth Schooner (or Spooner), before moving to Buffalo, New York, the city in which he would establish himself as a lecturer and conductor on the Underground Railroad. The marriage was not a happy one, however. By 1847 the couple separated. The two daughters remained with Brown as he traveled abroad; one of the children, Josephine, became Brown's first biographer. Between 1836 and 1845, while living in Buffalo and the nearby town of Farmington, Brown worked on Lake Erie steamboats, using them to transport fugitive slaves to Canada. Over a seven-month period in 1842, he smuggled about 70 fugitive slaves across the border. He actively lectured for the local temperance community, and also became a lecturing agent for the Western New York Anti-Slavery Society. By the time he took custody of his two daughters and moved to Boston in 1847, he had four years of experience as a respected orator on the regional circuit of antislavery speakers. As a member of the Massachusetts Anti-Slavery Society, Brown eventually traveled to Paris with the American Peace Society's delegation to the International Peace Congress.

Between 1849 and 1854, Brown toured Europe, speaking on behalf of America's abolition movement. Over this five-year period, Brown traveled thousands of miles and gave hundreds of antislavery lectures from Paris to London. In London, actually, his crowning achievement, *Clotel*, was published in 1853. As it did for other authors of African descent, the English publishing market proved more receptive than the American counterpart. *Clotel* sold well in England, building on the success of his best-selling 1847 *Narrative of William Wells Brown, an*

The Wiley Blackwell Anthology of African American Literature: Volume 1, 1746–1920, First Edition.
Edited by Gene Andrew Jarrett.

American Slave. Written by Himself. The novel *Clotel* went through three editions in 14 years, including a serialized version, *Miralda; or, the Beautiful Quadroon,* that was published in the *Anglo-African* newspaper. But Brown's success in Europe could not shield him from the threat of re-enslavement in the United States. After the passage of the 1850 Fugitive Slave Law, he hesitated to return home for fear of re-enslavement. Luckily for Brown, British abolitionist friends raised enough money to purchase him from his owner (as they had for Frederick Douglass previously). He returned to America in late 1854.

The last two decades of Brown's life were as literarily prolific as the first 20 years of his freedom. In addition to working as a recruiter for the Union Army during the Civil War, he published the first play by an African American, *The Escape; or, a Leap for Freedom* in 1858. His last four non-fiction works described African American triumph in the Civil War, and assessed the prospects of racial equality during Reconstruction. These later works cast African American history as an integral part of the United States: *The Negro in the American Rebellion* (1867), *The Rising Son; or, The Antecedents and Advancement of the Colored Race* (1874), and *My Southern Home: or, The South and Its People* (1880), the last of which resulted from Brown's tour of the former Confederacy in 1879 and 1880.

Brown's second marriage, to Massachusetts native Annie Elizabeth Gray, in 1860, led him to spend his final years in Cambridge and Chelsea, Massachusetts, where he practiced medicine and lectured on temperance. When he died in 1884, public services held in the abolitionist North Russell Street African Methodist Episcopal Zion Church in Boston accommodated over a thousand mourners.

Further reading

Baraw, Charles. "William Wells Brown, *Three Years in Europe*, and Fugitive Tourism." *African American Review* 44.3 (2011): 453–470.

Carpio, Glenda. *Laughing Fit to Kill: Black Humor in the Fiction of Slavery*. New York: Oxford University Press, 2008. Ch. 1.

Chaney, Michael A. *Fugitive Vision: Slave Image and Black Identity in Antebellum Narrative*. Bloomington: Indiana University Press, 2007. Ch. 3.

Ernest, John. "William Wells Brown Maps the South in *My Southern Home: Or, the South and Its People*." *Southern Quarterly: A Journal of the Arts in the South* 45.3 (2008): 88–107.

Frye, Katie. "The Case against Whiteness in William Wells Brown's *Clotel*." *Mississippi Quarterly: The Journal of Southern Cultures*, 62.3–4 (2009): 527–540.

Hooper, M. Clay. "'It Is Good to Be Shifty': William Wells Brown's Trickster Critique of Black Autobiography." *Modern Language Studies* 38.2 (2009): 28–45.

James, Jennifer. "'Civil' War Wounds: William Wells Brown, Violence, and the Domestic Narrative." *African American Review* 39.1–2 (2005): 39–54.

Lee, Maurice S. "The 1850s: The First Renaissance of Black Letters." *A Companion to African American Literature*. Ed. Gene Andrew Jarrett. Malden, MA: Wiley-Blackwell, 2010. 103–118.

Lucasi, Stephen. "William Wells Brown's *Narrative* & Traveling Subjectivity." *African American Review* 41.3 (2007): 521–539.

Schell, Jennifer. "'This Life Is a Stage': Performing the South in William Wells Brown's *Clotel or, the President's Daughter*." *Southern Quarterly: A Journal of the Arts in the South* 45.3 (2008): 48–69.

Schoolman, Martha. "Violent Places: *Three Years in Europe* and the Question of William Wells Brown's Cosmopolitanism." ESQ: *A Journal of the American Renaissance* 58.1 (2012): iv–35.

Stewart, Carole Lynn. "A Transnational Temperance Discourse? William Wells Brown, Creole Civilization, and Temperate Manners." *Journal of Transnational American Studies* 3.1 (2011): 1–25.

Wilson, Ivy G. *Specters of Democracy: Blackness and the Aesthetics of Politics in the Antebellum U.S.* New York: Oxford University Press, 2011. Ch. 2.

Narrative of William Wells Brown, an American Slave. Written by Himself.[1]

Note to the Fourth American Edition

Three editions of this work, consisting in all of eight thousand copies, were sold in less than eighteen months from the time the first edition was published. No antislavery work has met with a more rapid sale in the United States than this narrative. The present edition is published to meet the demand now existing for the work.

The Publisher

Note to the Present Edition

THE present Narrative was first published in Boston (U.S.) in July, 1847, and eight thousand copies were sold in less than eighteen months from the time of its publication. This rapid sale may be attributed to the circumstance, that for three years preceding its publication, I had been employed as a lecturing agent by the American Anti-Slavery[2] Society; and I was thus very generally known throughout the free states[3] of the Great Republic, as one who had spent the first twenty years of his life as a slave, in her southern house of bondage.

In visiting Great Britain I had two objects in view. Firstly, I have been chosen as a delegate by "the American Peace Committee for a Congress of Nations," to attend the Peace Convention to be held in Paris during the last week of the present month (August, 1849). Many of the most distinguished American Abolitionists considered it a triumphant evidence of the progress of their principles, that one of the oppressed coloured race – one who is even now, by the constitution of the United States, a slave – should have been selected for this honourable office; and were therefore very desirous that I should attend. Secondly, I wished to follow up the work of my friends and fellow-labourers, Charles Lenox Remond[4] and Frederick Douglass,[5] and to lay before the people of Great Britain and Ireland the wrongs that are still committed upon the slaves and the free coloured people of America. The rapid increase of communication between the two sides of the Atlantic has brought them so close together, that the personal intercourse between the British people and American slaveowners is now very great; and the slaveholder, crafty and politic, as deliberate tyrants generally are, rarely leaves the shores of Europe without attempting at least to assuage the prevalent hostility against his beloved "peculiar institution." The influence of the Southern States of America is mainly directed to the maintenance and propagation of the system of slavery in their own and in other countries. In the pursuit of this object, every consideration of religion, liberty, national strength, and social order is made to give way, and hitherto they have been very successful. The actual number of the slaveholders is small, but their union is complete, so that they form a dominant oligarchy in the United States. It is my desire, in common with every abolitionist, to diminish their influence, and this can only be effected by the promulgation of truth, and the cultivation of a correct public sentiment at home and abroad. Slavery cannot be let alone. It is aggressive, and must either be succumbed to, or put down.

Notes

NARRATIVE OF WILLIAM WELLS BROWN, AN AMERICAN SLAVE. WRITTEN BY HIMSELF.

[1] Fourth American edition, published in 1850.

[2] *Original reads*: Anti-slavery [ed.].

[3] *Original reads*: Free States [ed.].

[4] Charles Lenox Remond (1810–1873), abolitionist during the Civil War.

[5] *Original reads*: Douglas [ed.].

It has been suggested that my narrative is somewhat deficient in dates. From my total want of education previous to my escape from slavery, I am unable to give them with much accuracy. The ignorance of the American slaves is, with rare exceptions, intense; and the slaveholders generally do their utmost to perpetuate this mental darkness. The perpetuation of slavery depends upon it. Whatever may be said of the physical condition of the slaves, it is undeniable that if they were not kept in a state of intellectual, religious, and moral degradation, they could be retained as slaves no longer.

In conclusion, I ask the attention of the reader to the Resolutions of the coloured citizens of Boston, and to the other documents in reference to myself, which will be found at the end of the book. Of the latter, two are from the pen of WILLIAM LLOYD GARRISON, that faithful and indefatigable friend of the oppressed, whose position, as the Pioneer of the anti-slavery movement, has secured to him – more than to any other American abolitionist – the gratitude of the coloured race and a world-wide reputation.

William Wells Brown

Newcastle-upon-Tyne,
January 1st, 1850

Letter from Edmund Quincy, Esq

Dedham, July 1, 1847

To WILLIAM W. BROWN
MY DEAR FRIEND: I heartily thank you for the privilege of reading the manuscript of your Narrative. I have read it with deep interest and strong emotion. I am much mistaken if it be not greatly successful and eminently useful. It presents a different phase of the infernal slave-system from that portrayed in the admirable story of Mr. Douglass, and gives us a glimpse of its hideous cruelties in other portions of its domain.

Your opportunities of observing the workings of this accursed system have been singularly great. Your experiences in the Field, in the House, and especially on the River in the service of the slave-trader, Walker, have been such as few individuals have had – no one, certainly, who has been competent to describe them. What I have admired, and marvelled at, in your Narrative, is the simplicity and calmness with which you describe scenes and actions which might well "move the very stones to rise and mutiny" against the National Institution which makes them possible.

You will perceive that I have made very sparing use of your flattering permission to alter what you had written. To correct a few errors, which appeared to be merely clerical ones, committed in the hurry of composition under unfavorable circumstances, and to suggest a few curtailments, is all that I have ventured to do. I should be a bold man, as well as a vain one, if I should attempt to improve your descriptions of what you have seen and suffered. Some of the scenes are not unworthy of De Foe[6] himself.

I trust and believe that your Narrative will have a wide circulation. I am sure it deserves it. At least, a man must be differently constituted from me, who can rise from the perusal of your Narrative without feeling that he understands slavery better, and hates it worse, than he ever did before.

I am, very faithfully and respectfully,
Your friend,
Edmund Quincy

Notes

[6] Daniel Defoe (1660–1731), English author of 1719 novel *Robinson Crusoe*.

Preface

WHEN I first published this Narrative, the public had no evidence whatever that I had been a slave, except my own story. As soon as the work came from the press, I sent several copies to slaveholders residing at the South, with whom I was acquainted; and among others, one to Mr. Enoch Price, the man who claims my body and soul as his property, and from whom I had run away. A few weeks after the Narrative was sent, Edmund Quincy, Esq. received the following letter from Mr. Price. It tells its own story, and forever settles the question of my having been a slave. Here is the letter:

St. Louis, Jan. 10th, 1848

SIR: I received a pamphlet, or a Narrative, so called on the title-page, of the Life of William W. Brown, a fugitive slave, purporting to have been written by himself; and in his book I see a letter from you to said William W. Brown. This said Brown is named Sanford; he is a slave belonging to me, and ran away from me the first day of January, 1834. Now I see many things in his book that are not true, and a part of it as near true as a man could recollect after so long a time I purchased him of Mr. S. Willi, the last of September, 1833. I paid six hundred and fifty dollars for him. If I had wanted to speculate on him, I could have sold him for three times as much as I paid for him. I was offered two thousand dollars for him, in New Orleans, at one time, and fifteen hundred dollars for him, at another time, in Louisville, Kentucky. But I would not sell him. I was told that he was going to run away, the day before he ran away, but I did not believe the man, for I had so much confidence in Sanford. I want you to see him, and see if what I say is not the truth. I do not want him as a slave, but I think that his friends, who sustain him and give him the right hand of fellowship, or he himself, could afford to pay my agent in Boston three hundred and twenty-five dollars, and I will give him free papers, so that he may go wherever he wishes to. Then he can visit St. Louis, or any other place he may wish.

This amount is just half that I paid for him. Now, if this offer suits Mr. Brown, and the Anti-Slavery Society of Boston, or Massachusetts, let me know, and I will give you the name of my agent in Boston, and forward the papers, to be given to William W. Brown as soon as the money is paid.

Yours respectfully,
E. Price

TO EDMUND QUINCY, Esq.

Mr. Price says that he sees many things in my book which are not true, and a part of it as near true as a man could recollect after so long a time. As I was with Mr. Price only three months, and have devoted only six pages to him and his family, he can know but little about my narrative, except that part which speaks of him. But I am willing to avail myself of his testimony, for he says that a part of it is true.

But I cannot accept of Mr. Price's offer to become a purchaser of my body and soul. God made me as free as he did Enoch Price, and Mr. Price shall never receive a dollar from me or my friends with my consent.

W. W. Brown

Boston, October, 1848

Chapter 1

I WAS born in Lexington, Ky. The man who stole me as soon as I was born, recorded the births of all the infants which he claimed to be born his property, in a book which he kept for that purpose. My mother's name was Elizabeth. She had seven children, viz.:[7] Solomon, Leander, Benjamin, Joseph, Millford, Elizabeth, and myself. No two of us were children of the same father. My father's name, as I learned from my mother, was George Higgins. He was a white man, a relative of my master, and connected with some of the first families in Kentucky.

My master owned about forty slaves, twenty-five of whom were field hands. He removed from Kentucky to Missouri when I was quite young, and settled thirty or forty miles above St. Charles, on the Missouri, where, in addition to his practice as a physician, he carried on milling, merchandizing and farming. He had a large farm, the principal productions of which were tobacco and hemp. The slave cabins were situated on the back part of the farm, with the house of the overseer, whose name was Grove Cook, in their midst. He had the entire charge of the farm, and having no family, was allowed a woman to keep house for him, whose business it was to deal out the provisions for the hands.

A woman was also kept at the quarters to do the cooking for the field hands, who were summoned to their unrequited toil every morning at four o'clock, by the ringing of a bell, hung on a post near the house of the overseer. They were allowed half an hour to eat their breakfast, and get to the field. At half past four a horn was blown by the overseer, which was the signal to commence work; and everyone[8] that was not on the spot at the time, had to receive ten lashes from the negro-whip, with which the overseer always went armed. The handle was about three feet long, with the butt-end filled with lead, and the lash, six or seven feet in length, made of cow-hide, with platted wire on the end of it. This whip was put in requisition very frequently and freely, and a small offence on the part of a slave furnished an occasion for its use. During the time that Mr. Cook was overseer, I was a house servant – a situation preferable to that of a field hand, as I was better fed, better clothed, and not obliged to rise at the ringing of the bell, but about half an hour after. I have often laid and heard the crack of the whip, and the screams of the slave. My mother was a field hand, and one morning was ten or fifteen minutes behind the others in getting into the field. As soon as she reached the spot where they were at work, the overseer commenced whipping her. She cried, "Oh! pray – Oh! pray – Oh! pray" – these are generally the words of slaves, when imploring mercy at the hands of their oppressors. I heard her voice, and knew it, and jumped out of my bunk, and went to the door. Though the field was some distance from the house, I could hear every crack of the whip, and every groan and cry of my poor mother. I remained at the door, not daring to venture any further. The cold chills ran over me, and I wept aloud. After giving her ten lashes, the sound of the whip ceased, and I returned to my bed, and found no consolation but in my tears. Experience has taught me that nothing can be more heart-rending than for one to see a dear and beloved mother or sister tortured, and to hear their cries, and not be able to render them assistance. But such is the position which an American slave occupies.

My master, being a politician, soon found those who were ready to put him into office, for the favors he could render them; and a few years after his arrival in Missouri he was elected to a seat in the legislature. In his absence from home everything was left

Notes

[7] *viz* namely (abbreviation for *videlicet*).

[8] *Original reads*: every one [ed.].

in charge of Mr. Cook, the overseer, and he soon became more tyrannical and cruel. Among the slaves on the plantation was one by the name of Randall. He was a man about six feet high, and well-proportioned, and known as a man of great strength and power. He was considered the most valuable and able-bodied slave on the plantation; but no matter how good or useful a slave may be, he seldom escapes the lash. But it was not so with Randall. He had been on the plantation since my earliest recollection, and I had never known of his being flogged. No thanks were due to the master or overseer for this. I have often heard him declare that no white man should ever whip him – that he would die first.

Cook, from the time that he came upon the plantation, had frequently declared that he could and would flog any nigger that was put into the field to work under him. My master had repeatedly told him not to attempt to whip Randall, but he was determined to try it. As soon as he was left sole dictator, he thought the time had come to put his threats into execution. He soon began to find fault with Randall, and threatened to whip him if he did not do better. One day he gave him a very hard task – more than he could possibly do; and at night, the task not being performed, he told Randall that he should remember him the next morning. On the following morning, after the hands had taken breakfast, Cook called out to Randall, and told him that he intended to whip him, and ordered him to cross his hands and be tied. Randall asked why he wished to whip him. He answered, because he had not finished his task the day before. Randall said that the task was too great, or he should have done it. Cook said it made no difference – he should whip him. Randall stood silent for a moment, and then said, "Mr. Cook, I have always tried to please you since you have been on the plantation, and I find you are determined not to be satisfied with my work, let me do as well as I may. No man has laid hands on me, to whip me, for the last ten years, and I have long since come to the conclusion not to be whipped by any man living." Cook, finding by Randall's determined look and gestures, that he would resist, called three of the hands from their work, and commanded them to seize Randall, and tie him. The hands stood still – they knew Randall – and they also knew him to be a powerful man, and were afraid to grapple with him. As soon as Cook had ordered the men to seize him, Randall turned to them, and said – "Boys, you all know me; you know that I can handle any three of you, and the man that lays hands on me shall die. This white man can't whip me himself, and therefore he has called you to help him." The overseer was unable to prevail upon them to seize and secure Randall, and finally ordered them all to go to their work together.

Nothing was said to Randall by the overseer for more than a week. One morning, however, while the hands were at work in the field, he came into it, accompanied by three friends of his, Thompson, Woodbridge and Jones. They came up to where Randall was at work, and Cook ordered him to leave his work, and go with them to the barn. He refused to go; whereupon he was attacked by the overseer and his companions, when he turned upon them, and laid them, one after another, prostrate on the ground. Woodbridge drew out his pistol, and fired at him, and brought him to the ground by a pistol ball. The others rushed upon him with their clubs, and beat him over the head and face, until they succeeded in tying him. He was then taken to the barn, and tied to a beam. Cook gave him over one hundred lashes with a heavy cow-hide, had him washed with salt and water, and left him tied during the day. The next day he was untied, and taken to a blacksmith's shop, and had a ball and chain attached to his leg. He was compelled to labor in the field, and perform the same amount of work that the other hands did. When his master returned home, he was much pleased to find that Randall had been subdued in his absence.

Chapter 2

Soon afterwards, my master removed to the city of St. Louis, and purchased a farm four miles from there, which he placed under the charge of an overseer by the name of Friend Haskell. He was a regular Yankee from New England. The Yankees are noted for making the most cruel overseers.

My mother was hired out in the city, and I was also hired out there to Major Freeland, who kept a public house. He was formerly from Virginia, and was a horse-racer, cock-fighter, gambler, and withal an inveterate drunkard. There were ten or twelve servants in the house, and when he was present, it was cut and slash – knock down and drag out. In his fits of anger, he would take up a chair, and throw it at a servant; and in his more rational moments, when he wished to chastise one, he would tie them up in the smoke-house, and whip them; after which, he would cause a fire to be made of tobacco stems, and smoke them. This he called "*Virginia play*."

I complained to my master of the treatment which I received from Major Freeland; but it made no difference. He cared nothing about it, so long as he received the money for my labor. After living with Major Freeland five or six months, I ran away, and went into the woods back of the city; and when night came on, I made my way to my master's farm, but was afraid to be seen, knowing that if Mr. Haskell, the overseer, should discover me, I should be again carried back to Major Freeland; so I kept in the woods. One day, while in the woods, I heard the barking and howling of dogs, and in a short time they came so near that I knew them to be the bloodhounds of Major Benjamin O'Fallon. He kept five or six, to hunt runaway slaves with.

As soon as I was convinced that it was them, I knew there was no chance of escape. I took refuge in the top of a tree, and the hounds were soon at its base, and there remained until the hunters came up in a half or three quarters of an hour afterwards. There were two men with the dogs, who, as soon as they came up, ordered me to descend. I came down, was tied, and taken to St. Louis jail. Major Freeland soon made his appearance, and took me out, and ordered me to follow him, which I did. After we returned home, I was tied up in the smoke-house, and was very severely whipped. After the major had flogged me to his satisfaction, he sent out his son Robert, a young man eighteen or twenty years of age, to see that I was well smoked. He made a fire of tobacco stems, which soon set me to coughing and sneezing. This, Robert told me, was the way his father used to do to his slaves in Virginia. After giving me what they conceived to be a decent smoking, I was untied and again set to work.

Robert Freeland was a "chip off the old block."[9] Though quite young, it was not unfrequently that he came home in a state of intoxication. He is now, I believe, a popular commander of a steamboat on the Mississippi river. Major Freeland soon after failed in business, and I was put on board the steamboat Missouri, which plied between St. Louis and Galena. The commander of the boat was William B. Culver. I remained on her during the sailing season, which was the most pleasant time for me that I had ever experienced. At the close of navigation I was hired to Mr. John Colburn, keeper of the Missouri Hotel. He was from one of the free states; but a more inveterate hater of the negro I do not believe ever walked God's green earth. This hotel was at that time one of the largest in the city, and there were employed in it twenty or thirty servants, mostly slaves.

Mr. Colburn was very abusive, not only to the servants, but to his wife also, who was an excellent woman, and one from whom I never knew a servant to receive a

Notes

[9] *Original reads*: "chip of the old block." [ed.].

harsh word; but never did I know a kind one to a servant from her husband. Among the slaves employed in the hotel was one by the name of Aaron, who belonged to Mr. John F. Darby, a lawyer. Aaron was the knife-cleaner. One day, one of the knives was put on the table, not as clean as it might have been. Mr. Colburn, for this offence, tied Aaron up in the wood-house, and gave him over fifty lashes on the bare back with a cow-hide, after which, he made me wash him down with rum. This seemed to put him into more agony than the whipping. After being untied he went home to his master, and complained of the treatment which he had received. Mr. Darby would give no heed to anything he had to say, but sent him directly back. Colburn, learning that he had been to his master with complaints, tied him up again, and gave him a more severe whipping than before. The poor fellow's back was literally cut to pieces; so much so, that he was not able to work for ten or twelve days.

There was, also, among the servants, a girl whose master resided in the country. Her name was Patsey. Mr. Colburn tied her up one evening, and whipped her until several of the boarders came out and begged him to desist. The reason for whipping her was this. She was engaged to be married to a man belonging to Major William Christy, who resided four or five miles north of the city. Mr. Colburn had forbid her to see John Christy. The reason of this was said to be the regard which he himself had for Patsey. She went to a meeting[10] that evening, and John returned home with her. Mr. Colburn had intended to flog John, if he came within the inclosure; but John knew too well the temper of his rival, and kept at a safe distance – so he took vengeance on the poor girl. If all the slave-drivers had been called together, I do not think a more cruel man than John Colburn – and he too a northern man – could have been found among them.

While living at the Missouri hotel, a circumstance occurred which caused me great unhappiness. My master sold my mother, and all her children, except myself. They were sold to different persons in the city of St. Louis.

Chapter 3

I was soon after taken from Mr. Colburn's, and hired to Elijah P. Lovejoy,[11] who was at that time publisher and editor of the "St. Louis Times." My work, while with him, was mainly in the printing office, waiting on the hands, working the press, &c. Mr. Lovejoy was a very good man, and decidedly the best master that I had ever had. I am chiefly indebted to him, and to my employment in the printing office, for what little learning I obtained while in slavery.

Though slavery is thought, by some, to be mild in Missouri, when compared with the cotton, sugar and rice growing states, yet no part of our slave-holding country is more noted for the barbarity of its inhabitants than St. Louis. It was here that Col. Harney, a United States officer, whipped a slave woman to death. It was here that Francis McIntosh, a free colored man from Pittsburg, was taken from the steamboat Flora and burned at the stake. During a residence of eight years in this city, numerous cases of extreme cruelty came under my own observation – to record them all would occupy more space than could possibly be allowed in this little volume. I shall, therefore, give but a few more in addition to what I have already related.

Notes

[10] *Original reads*: went to meeting [ed.].

[11] Elijah Lovejoy (1802–1837), abolitionist murdered by a pro-slavery mob.

Capt. J.B. Brant, who resided near my master, had a slave named John. He was his body servant, carriage driver, &c. On one occasion, while driving his master through the city – the streets being very muddy, and the horses going at a rapid rate – some mud spattered upon a gentleman by the name of Robert More. More was determined to be revenged. Some three or four months after this occurrence, he purchased John, for the express purpose, as he said, "to tame the d——d nigger." After the purchase he took him to a blacksmith's shop, and had a ball and chain fastened to his leg, and then put him to driving a yoke of oxen, and kept him at hard labor, until the iron around his leg was so worn into the flesh, that it was thought mortification[12] would ensue. In addition to this, John told me that his master whipped him regularly three times a week for the first two months – and all this to *"tame him."* A more noble-looking man than he was not to be found in all St. Louis, before he fell into the hands of More; and a more degraded and spirit-crushed looking being was never seen on a southern plantation, after he had been subjected to this *"taming"* process for three months. The last time that I saw him, he had nearly lost the entire use of his limbs.

While living with Mr. Lovejoy, I was often sent on errands to the office of the "Missouri Republican," published by Mr. Edward Charless. Once, while returning to the office with type,[13] I was attacked by several large boys, sons of slave-holders, who pelted me with snow-balls. Having the heavy form of type in my hands, I could not make my escape by running; so I laid down the type and gave them battle. They gathered around pelting me with stones and sticks, until they overpowered me, and would have captured me, if I had not resorted to my heels. Upon my retreat they took possession of the type; and what to do to regain it I could not devise. Knowing Mr. Lovejoy to be a very humane man, I went to the office and laid the case before him. He told me to remain in the office. He took one of the apprentices with him and went after the type, and soon returned with it; but on his return informed me that Samuel McKinney had told him he would whip me, because I had hurt his boy. Soon after, McKinney was seen making his way to the office by one of the printers, who informed me of the fact, and I made my escape through the back door.

McKinney, not being able to find me on his arrival, left the office in a great rage, swearing that he would whip me to death. A few days after, as I was walking along Main street, he seized me by the collar, and struck me over the head five or six times with a large cane, which caused the blood to gush from my nose and ears in such a manner that my clothes were completely saturated with blood. After beating me to his satisfaction he let me go, and I returned to the office so weak from the loss of blood that Mr. Lovejoy sent me home to my master. It was five weeks before I was able to walk again. During this time it was necessary to have someone[14] to supply my place at the office, and I lost the situation.

After my recovery, I was hired to Capt. Otis Reynolds, as a waiter on board the steamboat Enterprise, owned by Messrs. John and Edward Walsh, commission merchants at St. Louis. This boat was then running on the upper Mississippi. My employment on board was to wait on gentlemen, and the captain being a good man, the situation was a pleasant one to me – but in passing from place to place, and seeing new faces every day, and knowing that they could go where they pleased, I soon became unhappy, and several times thought of leaving the boat at some landing-place, and trying to make my escape to Canada, which I had heard much about as a place where the slave might live, be free, and be protected.

Notes

[12] *mortification* gangrene.

[13] *type* small blocks with characters used in printing.

[14] *Original reads*: some one [ed.].

But whenever such thoughts would come into my mind, my resolution would soon be shaken by the remembrance that my dear mother was a slave in St. Louis, and I could not bear the idea of leaving her in that condition. She had often taken me upon her knee, and told me how she had carried me upon her back to the field when I was an infant – how often she had been whipped for leaving her work to nurse me – and how happy I would appear when she would take me into her arms. When these thoughts came over me, I would resolve never to leave the land of slavery without my mother. I thought that to leave her in slavery, after she had undergone and suffered so much for me, would be proving recreant[15] to the duty which I owed to her. Besides this, I had three brothers and a sister there – two of my brothers having died.

My mother, my brothers Joseph and Millford, and my sister Elizabeth, belonged to Mr. Isaac Mansfield, formerly from one of the free states, (Massachusetts, I believe.) He was a tinner by trade, and carried on a large manufacturing establishment. Of all my relatives, mother was first and sister next. One evening, while visiting them, I made some allusion to a proposed journey to Canada, and sister took her seat by my side, and taking my hand in hers, said, with tears in her eyes –

"Brother, you are not going to leave mother and your dear sister here without a friend, are you?"

I looked into her face, as the tears coursed swiftly down her cheeks, and bursting into tears myself, said –

"No, I will never desert you and mother!"

She clasped my hand in hers, and said –

"Brother, you have often declared that you would not end your days in slavery. I see no possible way in which you can escape with us; and now, brother, you are on a steamboat where there is some chance for you to escape to a land of liberty. I beseech you not to let us hinder you. If we cannot get our liberty, we do not wish to be the means of keeping you from a land of freedom."

I could restrain my feelings no longer, and an outburst of my own feelings caused her to cease speaking upon that subject. In opposition to their wishes, I pledged myself not to leave them in the hand of the oppressor. I took leave of them, and returned to the boat, and lay down in my bunk; but "sleep departed from mine eyes, and slumber from mine eyelids."[16]

A few weeks after, on our downward passage, the boat took on board, at Hannibal, a drove of slaves, bound for the New Orleans market. They numbered from fifty to sixty, consisting of men and women from eighteen to forty years of age. A drove of slaves on a southern steamboat, bound for the cotton or sugar regions, is an occurrence so common, that no one, not even the passengers, appears[17] to notice it, though they clank their chains at every step. There was, however, one in this gang that attracted the attention of the passengers and crew. It was a beautiful girl, apparently about twenty years of age, perfectly white, with straight light hair and blue eyes. But it was not the whiteness of her skin that created such a sensation among those who gazed upon her – it was her almost unparalleled beauty. She had been on the boat but a short time, before the attention of all the passengers, including the ladies, had been called to her, and the common topic of conversation was about the beautiful slave-girl. She was not in chains. The man who claimed this article of human merchandise was a Mr. Walker – a well-known slave-trader, residing in St. Louis. There was a general anxiety

Notes

[15] *recreant* disloyal.

[16] *"sleep departed … eyelids"* Genesis 31:40.

[17] *Original reads*: appear [ed.].

among the passengers and crew to learn the history of the girl. Her master kept close by her side, and it would have been considered impudent for any of the passengers to have spoken to her, and the crew were not allowed to have any conversation with them. When we reached St. Louis, the slaves were removed to a boat bound for New Orleans, and the history of the beautiful slave-girl remained a mystery.

I remained on the boat during the season, and it was not an unfrequent occurrence to have on board gangs of slaves on their way to the cotton, sugar and rice plantations of the south.

Toward the latter part of the summer Captain Reynolds left the boat, and I was sent home. I was then placed on the farm, under Mr. Haskell, the overseer. As I had been some time out of the field, and not accustomed to work in the burning sun, it was very hard; but I was compelled to keep up with the best of the hands.

I found a great difference between the work in a steamboat cabin and that in a corn-field.

My master, who was then living in the city, soon after removed to the farm, when I was taken out of the field to work in the house as a waiter. Though his wife was very peevish, and hard to please, I much preferred to be under her control than the overseer's. They brought with them Mr. Sloane, a Presbyterian minister; Miss Martha Tulley, a niece of theirs from Kentucky; and their nephew William. The latter had been in the family a number of years, but the others were all newcomers.

Mr. Sloane was a young minister, who had been at the South but a short time, and it seemed as if his whole aim was to please the slaveholders, especially my master and mistress. He was intending to make a visit during the winter, and he not only tried to please them, but I think he succeeded admirably. When they wanted singing, he sang;[18] when they wanted praying, he prayed; when they wanted a story told, he told a story. Instead of his teaching my master theology, my master taught theology to him. While I was with Captain Reynolds my master "got religion," and new laws were made on the plantation. Formerly we had the privilege of hunting, fishing, making splint brooms, baskets, &c., on Sunday; but this was all stopped. Every Sunday we were all compelled to attend a meeting.[19] Master was so religious that he induced some others to join him in hiring a preacher to preach to the slaves.

Chapter 4

My master had family worship, night and morning. At night the slaves were called in to attend; but in the mornings they had to be at their work, and master did all the praying. My master and mistress were great lovers of mint julep, and every morning a pitcher-full was made, of which they all partook freely, not excepting little master William. After drinking freely all round they would have family worship, and then breakfast. I cannot say but I loved the julep as well as any of them, and during prayer was always careful to seat myself close to the table where it stood, so as to help myself when they were all busily engaged in their devotions. By the time prayer was over, I was about as happy as any of them. A sad accident happened one morning. In helping myself, and at the same time keeping an eye on my old mistress, I accidentally let the pitcher fall upon the floor, breaking it in pieces, and spilling the contents. This was a bad affair for me; for as soon as prayer was over, I was taken and severely chastised.

Notes

18 *Original reads*: sung [ed.].

19 *Original reads*: to attend meeting [ed.].

My master's family consisted of himself, his wife, and their nephew, William Moore. He was taken into the family when only a few weeks of age. His name being that of my own, mine was changed for the purpose of giving precedence to his, though I was his senior by ten or twelve years. The plantation being four miles from the city, I had to drive the family to church. I always dreaded the approach of the Sabbath; for, during service, I was obliged to stand by the horses in the hot, broiling sun, or in the rain, just as it happened.

One Sabbath, as we were driving past the house of D.D. Page, a gentleman who owned a large baking establishment, as I was sitting upon the box of the carriage, which was very much elevated, I saw Mr. Page pursuing a slave around the yard with a long whip, cutting him at every jump. The man soon escaped from the yard, and was followed by Mr. Page. They came running past us, and the slave, perceiving that he would be overtaken, stopped suddenly, and Page stumbled over him, and falling on the stone pavement, fractured one of his legs, which crippled him for life. The same gentleman, but a short time previous, tied up a woman of his, by the name of Delphia, and whipped her nearly to death; yet he was a deacon in the Baptist church, in good and regular standing. Poor Delphia! I was well acquainted with her and called to see her while upon her sick bed; and I shall never forget her appearance. She was a member of the same church with her master.

Soon after this, I was hired out to Mr. Walker, the same man whom I have mentioned as having carried a gang of slaves down the river on the steamboat Enterprise. Seeing me in the capacity of a steward on the boat, and thinking that I would make a good hand to take care of slaves, he determined to have me for that purpose; and finding that my master would not sell me, he hired me for the term of one year.

When I learned the fact of my having been hired to a negro speculator, or a "soul driver," as they are generally called among slaves, no one can tell my emotions. Mr. Walker had offered a high price for me, as I afterwards learned, but I suppose my master was restrained from selling me by the fact that I was a near relative of his. On entering the service of Mr. Walker, I found that my opportunity of getting to a land of liberty was gone, at least for the time being. He had a gang of slaves in readiness to start for New Orleans, and in a few days we were on our journey. I am at a loss for language to express my feelings on that occasion. Although my master had told me that he had not sold me, and Mr. Walker had told me that he had not purchased me, I did not believe them; and not until I had been to New Orleans, and was on my return, did I believe that I was not sold.

There was on the boat a large room on the lower deck, in which the slaves were kept, men and women, promiscuously[20] – all chained two and two, and a strict watch kept that they did not get loose; for cases have occurred in which slaves have got off their chains, and made their escape at landing-places, while the boats were taking in wood – and with all our care, we lost one woman who had been taken from her husband and children, and having no desire to live without them, in the agony of her soul jumped overboard, and drowned herself. She was not chained.

It was almost impossible to keep that part of the boat clean.

On landing at Natchez, the slaves were all carried to the slave-pen, and there kept one week, during which time several of them were sold. Mr. Walker fed his slaves well. We took on board at St. Louis several hundred pounds of bacon (smoked meat) and corn-meal, and his slaves were better fed than slaves generally were in Natchez, so far as my observation extended.

Notes

[20] *promiscuously* indiscriminately.

At the end of a week, we left for New Orleans, the place of our final destination, which we reached in two days. Here the slaves were placed in a negro-pen, where those who wished to purchase could call and examine them. The negro-pen is a small yard, surrounded by buildings, from fifteen to twenty feet wide, with the exception of a large gate with iron bars. The slaves are kept in the buildings during the night, and turned out into the yard during the day. After the best of the stock was sold at private sale at the pen, the balance were taken to the Exchange Coffee-House Auction Rooms, kept by Isaac L. McCoy, and sold at public auction. After the sale of this lot of slaves, we left New Orleans for St. Louis.

Chapter 5

On our arrival at St. Louis I went to Dr. Young, and told him that I did not wish to live with Mr. Walker any longer. I was heart-sick at seeing my fellow-creatures bought and sold. But the Dr. had hired me for the year, and stay I must. Mr. Walker again commenced purchasing another gang of slaves. He bought a man of Colonel John O'Fallon, who resided in the suburbs of the city. This man had a wife and three children. As soon as the purchase was made, he was put in jail for safe keeping, until we should be ready to start for New Orleans. His wife visited him while there, several times, and several times when she went for that purpose was refused admittance.

In the course of eight or nine weeks Mr. Walker had his cargo of human flesh made up. There was in this lot a number of old men and women, some of them with gray locks. We left St. Louis in the steamboat Carlton, Captain Swan, bound for New Orleans. On our way down, and before we reached Rodney, the place where we made our first stop, I had to prepare the old slaves for market. I was ordered to have the old men's whiskers shaved off, and the grey hairs plucked out where they were not too numerous, in which case he had a preparation of blacking to color it, and with a blacking brush we would put it on. This was new business to me, and was performed in a room where the passengers could not see us. These slaves were also taught how old they were by Mr. Walker, and after going through the blacking process they looked ten or fifteen years younger; and I am sure that some of those who purchased slaves of Mr. Walker were dreadfully cheated, especially in the ages of the slaves which they bought.

We landed at Rodney, and the slaves were driven to the pen in the back part of the village. Several were sold at this place, during our stay of four or five days, when we proceeded to Natchez. There we landed at night, and the gang were put in the warehouse until morning, when they were driven to the pen. As soon as the slaves are put in these pens, swarms of planters may be seen in and about them. They knew when Walker was expected, as he always had the time advertised beforehand when he would be in Rodney, Natchez, and New Orleans. These were the principal places where he offered his slaves for sale.

When at Natchez the second time, I saw a slave very cruelly whipped. He belonged to a Mr. Broadwell, a merchant who kept a store on the wharf. The slave's name was Lewis. I had known him several years, as he was formerly from St. Louis. We were expecting a steamboat down the river, in which we were to take passage for New Orleans. Mr. Walker sent me to the landing to watch for the boat, ordering me to inform him on its arrival. While there I went into the store to see Lewis. I saw a slave in the store, and asked him where Lewis was. Said he, "They have got Lewis hanging between the heavens and the earth." I asked him what he meant by that. He told me to go into the warehouse and see. I went in, and found Lewis there. He was tied up to a beam, with his toes just touching the floor. As there was no one in the warehouse but himself, I inquired the reason of his being in that situation. He said Mr. Broadwell had sold his wife to a planter six miles from the city, and that he had been to visit her – that he went in the night, expecting to return before daylight, and went without his master's permission. The patrol had taken him up before he reached his wife. He was put in jail, and his master had to pay for his catching and keeping, and that was what he was tied up for.

Just as he finished his story, Mr. Broadwell came in, and inquired what I was doing there. I knew not what to say, and while I was thinking what reply to make he struck me over the head with the cowhide, the end of which struck me over my right eye, sinking deep into the flesh, leaving a scar which I carry to this day. Before I visited Lewis he had received fifty lashes. Mr. Broadwell gave him fifty lashes more after I came out, as I was afterwards informed by Lewis himself.

The next day we proceeded to New Orleans, and put the gang in the same negro-pen which we occupied before. In a short time the planters came flocking to the pen to purchase slaves. Before the slaves were exhibited for sale, they were dressed and driven out into the yard. Some were set to dancing, some to jumping, some to singing, and some to playing cards. This was done to make them appear cheerful and happy. My business was to see that they were placed in those situations before the arrival of the purchasers, and I have often set them to dancing when their cheeks were wet with tears. As slaves were in good demand at that time, they were all soon disposed of, and we again set out for St. Louis.

On our arrival, Mr. Walker purchased a farm five or six miles from the city. He had no family, but made a housekeeper of one of his female slaves. Poor Cynthia! I knew her well. She was a quadroon,[21] and one of the most beautiful women I ever saw. She was a native of St. Louis, and bore an irreproachable character for virtue and propriety of conduct. Mr. Walker bought her for the New Orleans market, and took her down with him on one of the trips that I made with him. Never shall I forget the circumstances of that voyage! On the first night that we were on board the steamboat, he directed me to put her into a state-room he had provided for her, apart from the other slaves. I had seen too much of the workings of slavery not to know what this meant. I accordingly watched him into the state-room, and listened to hear what passed between them. I heard him make his base offers, and her reject them. He told her that if she would accept his vile proposals, he would take her back with him to St. Louis, and establish her as his housekeeper on his farm. But if she persisted in rejecting them, he would sell her as a field hand on the worst plantation on the river. Neither threats nor bribes prevailed, however, and he retired, disappointed of his prey.

The next morning poor Cynthia told me what had passed, and bewailed her sad fate with floods of tears. I comforted and encouraged her all I could; but I foresaw but too well what the result must be. Without entering into any further particulars, suffice it to say that Walker performed his part of the contract at that time. He took her back to St. Louis, established her as his mistress and housekeeper at his farm, and before I left, he had two children by her. But, mark the end! Since I have been at the North, I have been credibly informed that Walker has been married, and, as a previous measure, sold poor Cynthia and her four children (she having had two more since I came away) into hopeless bondage!

He soon commenced purchasing to make up the third gang. We took the steamboat,[22] and went to Jefferson City, a town on the Missouri river. Here we landed, and

Notes

[21] *quadroon* one who is one-quarter black.

[22] *Original reads*: took steamboat [ed.].

took the stage[23] for the interior of the state. He bought a number of slaves as he passed the different farms and villages. After getting twenty-two or twenty-three men and women, we arrived at St. Charles, a village on the banks of the Missouri. Here he purchased a woman who had a child in her arms, appearing to be four or five weeks old.

We had been travelling by land for some days, and were in hopes to have found a boat at this place for St. Louis, but were disappointed. As no boat was expected for some days, we started for St. Louis by land. Mr. Walker had purchased two horses. He rode one, and I the other. The slaves were chained together, and we took up our line of march, Mr. Walker taking the lead, and I bringing up the rear. Though the distance was not more than twenty miles, we did not reach it the first day. The road was worse than any that I have ever travelled.

Soon after we left St. Charles the young child grew very cross, and kept up a noise during the greater part of the day. Mr. Walker complained of its crying several times, and told the mother to stop the child's d——d[24] noise, or he would. The woman tried to keep the child from crying, but could not. We put up at night with an acquaintance of Mr. Walker, and in the morning, just as we were about to start, the child again commenced crying. Walker stepped up to her, and told her to give the child to him. The mother tremblingly obeyed. He took the child by one arm, as you would a cat by the leg, walked into the house, and said to the lady,

"Madam, I will make you a present of this little nigger; it keeps such a noise that I can't bear it."

"Thank you, sir," said the lady.

The mother, as soon as she saw that her child was to be left, ran up to Mr. Walker, and falling upon her knees, begged him to let her have her child; she clung around his legs, and cried, "Oh, my child! my child! master, do let me have my child! oh, do, do, do! I will stop its crying if you will only let me have it again." When I saw this woman crying for her child so piteously, a shudder – a feeling akin to horror – shot through my frame. I have often since in imagination heard her crying for her child –

None but those who have been in a slave state, and who have seen the American slave-trader engaged in his nefarious traffic, can estimate the sufferings their victims undergo. If there is one feature of American slavery more abominable than another, it is that which sanctions the buying and selling of human beings. The African slave-trade was abolished by the American Congress some twenty years since; and now, by the laws of the country, if an American is found engaged in the African slave-trade, he is considered a pirate; and if found guilty of such, the penalty would be death.

Although the African slave-trader has been branded as a pirate, men are engaged in the traffic in slaves in this country, who occupy high positions in society, and hold offices of honor in the councils of the nation; and not a few have made their fortunes by this business.

After the woman's child had been given away, Mr. Walker commanded her to return into the ranks with the other slaves. Women who had children were not chained, but those that had none were. As soon as her child was disposed of she was chained in the gang.

The following song I have often heard the slaves sing, when about to be carried to the far south. It is said to have been composed by a slave.

Notes

[23] *Original reads*: took stage [ed.].

[24] *d——d* damned.

"See these poor souls from Africa
Transported to America;
We are stolen, and sold to Georgia –
Will you go along with me?
We are stolen, and sold to Georgia –
Come sound the jubilee!

See wives and husbands sold apart,
Their children's screams will break my heart –
There's a better day a coming –
Will you go along with me?
There's a better day a coming,
Go sound the jubilee!

O, gracious Lord ! when shall it be,
That we poor souls shall all be free?
Lord, break them slavery powers –
Will you go along with me?
Lord, break them slavery powers,
Go sound the jubilee!

Dear Lord, dear Lord, when slavery'll cease,
Then we poor souls will have our peace –
There's a better day a coming –
Will you go along with me?
There's a better day a coming,
Go sound the jubilee!"

We finally arrived at Mr. Walker's farm. He had a house built during our absence to put slaves in. It was a kind of domestic jail. The slaves were put in the jail at night, and worked on the farm during the day. They were kept here until the gang was completed, when we again started for New Orleans, on board the steamboat North America, Capt. Alexander Scott. We had a large number of slaves in this gang. One, by the name of Joe, Mr. Walker was training up to take my place, as my time was nearly out, and glad was I. We made our first stop at Vicksburg, where we remained one week and sold several slaves.

Mr. Walker, though not a good master, had not flogged a slave since I had been with him, though he had threatened me. The slaves were kept in the pen, and he always put up at the best hotel, and kept his wines in his room, for the accommodation of those who called to negotiate with him for the purchase of slaves. One day, while we were at Vicksburg, several gentlemen came to see him for that purpose, and as usual the wine was called for. I took the tray and started around with it, and having accidentally filled some of the glasses too full, the gentlemen spilled the wine on their clothes as they went to drink. Mr. Walker apologized to them for my carelessness, but looked at me as though he would see me again on this subject.

After the gentlemen had left the room, he asked me what I meant by my carelessness, and said that he would attend to me. The next morning he gave me a note to carry to the jailer, and a dollar in money to give to him. I suspected that all was not right, so I went down near the landing, where I met with a sailor, and, walking up to him, asked him if he would be so kind as to read the note for me. He read it over, and then looked at me. I asked him to tell me what was in it. Said he,

"They are going to give you hell."

"Why?" said I.

He said, "This is a note to have you whipped, and says that you have a dollar to pay for it."

He handed me back the note, and off I started. I knew not what to do, but was determined not to be whipped. I went up to the jail – took a look at it, and walked off again. As Mr. Walker was acquainted with the jailer, I feared that I should be found out if I did not go, and be treated in consequence of it still worse.

While I was meditating on the subject, I saw a colored man about my size walk up, and the thought struck me in a moment to send him with my note. I walked up to him, and asked him who he belonged to. He said he was a free man, and had been in the city but a short time. I told him I had a note to go into the jail, and get a trunk to carry to one of the steamboats; but was so busily engaged that I could not do it, although I had a dollar to pay for it. He asked me if I would not give him the job. I handed him the note and the dollar, and off he started for the jail.

I watched to see that he went in, and as soon as I saw the door close behind him, I walked around the corner, and took my station, intending to see how my friend looked when he came out. I had been there but a short time, when a colored man came around the corner, and said to another colored man with whom he was acquainted –

"They are giving a nigger scissors[25] in the jail."

"What for?" said the other. The man continued,

"A nigger came into the jail, and asked for the jailer. The jailer came out, and he handed him a note, and said he wanted to get a trunk. The jailer told him to go with him, and he would give him the trunk. So he took him into the room, and told the nigger to give up the dollar. He said a man had given him the dollar to pay for getting the trunk. But that lie would not answer. So they made him strip himself, and then they tied him down, and are now whipping him."

I stood by all the while listening to their talk, and soon found out that the person alluded to was my customer. I went into the street opposite the jail, and concealed myself in such a manner that I could not be seen by anyone[26] coming out. I had been there but a short time, when the young man made his appearance, and looked around for me. I, unobserved, came forth from my hiding-place, behind a pile of brick, and he pretty soon saw me, and came up to me complaining bitterly, saying that I had played a trick upon him. I denied any knowledge of what the note contained, and asked him what they had done to him. He told me in substance what I heard the man tell who had come out of the jail.

"Yes," said he, "they whipped me and took my dollar, and gave me this note."

He showed me the note which the jailer had given him, telling him to give it to his master. I told him I would give him fifty cents for it – that being all the money I had. He gave it to me and took his money. He had received twenty lashes on his bare back, with the negro-whip.

I took the note and started for the hotel where I had left Mr. Walker. Upon reaching the hotel, I handed it to a stranger whom I had not seen before, and requested him to read it to me. As near as I can recollect, it was as follows:

"Dear Sir: By your direction, I have given your boy twenty lashes. He is a very saucy boy, and tried to make me believe that he did not belong to you, and I put it on to him well for lying to me.

I remain

Your obedient servant."

Notes

[25] *scissors* a lashing.

[26] *Original reads*: any one [ed.].

It is true that in most of the slave-holding cities, when a gentleman wishes his servants whipped, he can send him to the jail and have it done. Before I went in where Mr. Walker was, I wet my cheeks a little, as though I had been crying. He looked at me, and inquired what was the matter. I told him that I had never had such a whipping in my life, and handed him the note. He looked at it and laughed – "And so you told him that you did not belong to me?" "Yes, sir," said I. "I did not know that there was any harm in that." He told me I must behave myself, if I did not want to be whipped again.

This incident shows how it is that slavery makes its victims lying and mean; for which vices it afterwards reproaches them, and uses them as arguments to prove that they deserve no better fate. Had I entertained the same views of right and wrong which I now do, I am sure I should never have practised the deception upon that poor fellow which I did. I know of no act committed by me while in slavery which I have regretted more than that; and I heartily desire that it may be at some time or other in my power to make him amends for his vicarious sufferings in my behalf.

Chapter 6

In a few days we reached New Orleans, and arriving there in the night, remained on board until morning. While at New Orleans this time, I saw a slave killed; an account of which has been published by Theodore D. Weld,[27] in his book entitled "Slavery as it is." The circumstances were as follows. In the evening, between seven and eight o'clock, a slave came running down the levee,[28] followed by several men and boys. The whites were crying out, "Stop that nigger! stop that nigger!" while the poor panting slave, in almost breathless accents, was repeating, "I did not steal the meat – I did not steal the meat." The poor man at last took refuge in the river. The whites who were in pursuit of him ran[29] on board of one of the boats to see if they could discover him. They finally espied him under the bow of the steamboat Trenton. They got a pike-pole, and tried to drive him from his hiding place. When they would strike at him he would dive under the water. The water was so cold, that it soon became evident that he must come out or be drowned.

While they were trying to drive him from under the bow of the boat or drown him, he would in broken and imploring accents say, "I did not steal the meat; I did not steal the meat. My master lives up the river. I want to see my master. I did not steal the meat. Do let me go home to master." After punching him, and striking him over the head for some time, he at last sunk in the water, to rise no more alive.

On the end of the pike-pole with which they were striking him was a hook, which caught in his clothing, and they hauled him up on the bow of the boat. Some said he was dead; others said he was *"playing possum"*; while others kicked him to make him get up; but it was of no use – he was dead.

As soon as they became satisfied of this, they commenced leaving, one after another. One of the hands on the boat informed the captain that they had killed the man, and that the dead body was lying on the deck. The captain came on deck, and said to those who were remaining, "You have killed this nigger; now take him off of my boat." The captain's name was Hart. The dead body was dragged on shore

Notes

[27] Theodore D. Weld (1803–1896), American abolitionist.

[28] *levee* dike.

[29] *Original reads*: run [ed.].

and left there. I went on board of the boat where our gang of slaves were, and during the whole night my mind was occupied with what I had seen. Early in the morning I went on shore to see if the dead body remained there. I found it in the same position that it was left the night before. I watched to see what they would do with it. It was left there until between eight and nine o'clock, when a cart, which takes up the trash out of the streets, came along, and the body was thrown in, and in a few minutes more was covered over with dirt which they were removing from the streets. During the whole time, I did not see more than six or seven persons around it, who, from their manner, evidently regarded it as no uncommon occurrence.

During our stay in the city I met with a young white man with whom I was well acquainted in St. Louis. He had been sold into slavery, under the following circumstances. His father was a drunkard, and very poor, with a family of five or six children. The father died, and left the mother to take care of and provide for the children as best she might. The eldest was a boy, named Burrill, about thirteen years of age, who did chores in a store kept by Mr. Riley, to assist his mother in procuring a living for the family. After working with him two years, Mr. Riley took him to New Orleans to wait on him while in that city on a visit, and when he returned to St. Louis, he told the mother of the boy that he had died with the yellow fever. Nothing more was heard from him, no one supposing him to be alive. I was much astonished when Burrill told me his story. Though I sympathized with him I could not assist him. We were both slaves. He was poor, uneducated, and without friends; and, if living, is, I presume, still held as a slave.

After selling out this cargo of human flesh, we returned to St. Louis, and my time was up with Mr. Walker. I had served him one year, and it was the longest year I ever lived.

Chapter 7

I WAS sent home, and was glad enough to leave the service of one who was tearing the husband from the wife, the child from the mother, and the sister from the brother – but a trial more severe and heart-rending than any which I had yet met with awaited me. My dear sister had been sold to a man who was going to Natchez, and was lying in jail, awaiting the hour of his departure. She had expressed her determination to die, rather than go to the far south, and she was put in jail for safe-keeping. I went to the jail the same day that I arrived, but as the jailer was not in I could not see her.

I went home to my master, in the country, and the first day after my return he came where I was at work, and spoke to me very politely. I knew from his appearance that something was the matter. After talking to me about my several journeys to New Orleans with Mr. Walker, he told me that he was hard pressed for money, and as he had sold my mother and all her children except me, he thought it would be better to sell me than any other one, and that as I had been used to living in the city, he thought it probable that I would prefer it to a country life. I raised up my head, and looked him full in the face. When my eyes caught his he immediately looked to the ground. After a short pause, I said,

"Master, mother has often told me that you are a near relative of mine, and I have often heard you admit the fact; and after you have hired me out, and received, as I once heard you say, nine hundred dollars for my services – after receiving this large sum, will you sell me to be carried to New Orleans or some other place?"

"No," said he, "I do not intend to sell you to a negro-trader. If I had wished to have done that, I might have sold you to Mr. Walker for a large sum, but I would not sell you to a negro-trader. You may go to the city, and find you a good master."

"But," said I, "I cannot find a good master in the whole city of St. Louis."

"Why?" said he.

"Because there are no good masters in the state."

"Do you not call me a good master?"

"If you were you would not sell me."

"Now I will give you one week to find a master in, and surely you can do it in that time."

The price set by my evangelical master upon my soul and body was the trifling sum of five hundred dollars. I tried to enter into some arrangement by which I might purchase my freedom; but he would enter into no such arrangement.

I set out for the city with the understanding that I was to return in a week with someone[30] to become my new master. Soon after reaching the city, I went to the jail, to learn if I could once more see my sister; but could not gain admission. I then went to mother, and learned from her that the owner of my sister intended to start for Natchez in a few days.

I went to the jail again the next day, and Mr. Simonds, the keeper, allowed me to see my sister for the last time. I cannot give a just description of the scene at that parting interview. Never, never can be erased from my heart the occurrences of that day! When I entered the room where she was, she was seated in one corner, alone. There were four other women in the same room, belonging to the same man. He had purchased them, he said, for his own use. She was seated with her face towards the door where I entered, yet she did not look up until I walked up to her. As soon as she observed me she sprung up, threw her arms around my neck, leaned her head upon my breast, and, without uttering a word, burst into tears. As soon as she recovered herself sufficiently to speak, she advised me to take mother, and try to get out of slavery. She said there was no hope for herself – that she must live and die a slave. After giving her some advice, and taking from my finger a ring and placing it upon hers, I bade her farewell forever, and returned to my mother, and then and there made up my mind to leave for Canada as soon as possible.

I had been in the city nearly two days, and as I was to be absent only a week, I thought best to get on my journey as soon as possible. In conversing with mother, I found her unwilling to make the attempt to reach a land of liberty, but she counselled me to get my liberty if I could. She said, as all her children were in slavery, she did not wish to leave them. I could not bear the idea of leaving her among those pirates, when there was a prospect of being able to get away from them. After much persuasion I succeeded in inducing her to make the attempt to get away.

The time fixed for our departure was the next night. I had with me a little money that I had received, from time to time, from gentlemen for whom I had done errands. I took my scanty means and purchased some dried beef, crackers and cheese, which I carried to mother, who had provided herself with a bag to carry it in. I occasionally thought of my old master, and of my mission to the city to find a new one. I waited with the most intense anxiety for the appointed time to leave the land of slavery, in search of a land of liberty.

The time at length arrived, and we left the city just as the clock struck nine. We proceeded to the upper part of the city, where I had been two or three times during the day, and selected a skiff[31] to carry us across the river. The boat was not

Notes

[30] *Original reads*: some one [ed.].

[31] *skiff* small boat.

mine, nor did I know to whom it did belong; neither did I care. The boat was fastened with a small pole, which, with the aid of a rail, I soon loosened from its moorings. After hunting round and finding a board to use as an oar, I turned to the city, and bidding it a long farewell, pushed off my boat. The current running very swift, we had not reached the middle of the stream before we were directly opposite the city.

We were soon upon the Illinois shore, and, leaping from the boat, turned it adrift, and the last I saw of it, it was going down the river at good speed. We took the main road to Alton, and passed through just at daylight, when we made for the woods, where we remained during the day. Our reason for going into the woods was that we expected that Mr. Mansfield (the man who owned my mother) would start in pursuit of her as soon as he discovered that she was missing. He also knew that I had been in the city looking for a new master, and we thought probably he would go out to my master's to see if he could find my mother, and in so doing, Dr. Young might be led to suspect that I had gone to Canada to find a purchaser.

We remained in the woods during the day, and as soon as darkness overshadowed the earth, we started again on our gloomy way, having no guide but the NORTH STAR. We continued to travel by night, and secrete ourselves in the woods by day; and every night, before emerging from our hiding-place, we would anxiously look for our friend and leader – the NORTH STAR. And in the language of Pierpont[32] we might have exclaimed,

"Star of the North! while blazing day
Pours round me its full tide of light,
And hides thy pale but faithful ray,
I, too, lie hid, and long for night.
For night – I dare not walk at noon,
Nor dare I trust the faithless moon,
Nor faithless man, whose burning lust
For gold hath riveted my chain;
No other leader can I trust
But thee, of even the starry train;
For, all the host around thee burning,
Like faithless man, keep turning, turning.

In the dark top of southern pines
I nestled, when the driver's horn
Called to the field, in lengthening lines,
My fellows, at the break of morn.
And there I lay, till thy sweet face
Looked in upon my 'hiding place,'
Star of the North!
Thy light, that no poor slave deceiveth,
Shall set me free."

Notes

[32] *Pierpont* from "The Fugitive Slave's Apostrophe to the North Star" (1840) by John Pierpont (1785–1866).

Chapter 8

As we travelled towards a land of liberty, my heart would at times leap for joy. At other times, being, as I was, almost constantly on my feet, I felt as though I could travel no further. But when I thought of slavery, with its democratic whips – its republican chains – its evangelical blood-hounds, and its religious slave-holders – when I thought of all this paraphernalia of American democracy and religion behind me, and the prospect of liberty before me, I was encouraged to press forward, my heart was strengthened, and I forgot that I was tired or hungry.

On the eighth day of our journey, we had a very heavy rain, and in a few hours after it commenced we had not a dry thread upon our bodies. This made our journey still more unpleasant. On the tenth day, we found ourselves entirely destitute of provisions, and how to obtain any we could not tell. We finally resolved to stop at some farmhouse, and try to get something to eat. We had no sooner determined to do this than we went to a house and asked them for some food. We were treated with great kindness, and they not only gave us something to eat, but gave us provisions to carry with us. They advised us to travel by day and lie by at night. Finding ourselves about one hundred and fifty miles from St. Louis, we concluded that it would be safe to travel by daylight, and did not leave the house until the next morning. We travelled on that day through a thickly settled country, and through one small village. Though we were fleeing from a land of oppression, our hearts were still there. My dear sister and two beloved brothers were behind us, and the idea of giving them up, and leaving them forever, made us feel sad. But with all this depression of heart, the thought that I should one day be free, and call my body my own, buoyed me up, and made my heart leap for joy. I had just been telling my mother how I should try to get employment as soon as we reached Canada, and how I intended to purchase us a little farm, and how I would earn money enough to buy sister and brothers, and how happy we would be in our own FREE HOME – when three men came up on horseback, and ordered us to stop.

I turned to the one who appeared to be the principal man, and asked him what he wanted. He said he had a warrant to take us up. The three immediately dismounted, and one took from his pocket a handbill, advertising us as runaways, and offering a reward of two hundred dollars for our apprehension and delivery in the city of St. Louis. The advertisement had been put out by Isaac Mansfield and John Young.

While they were reading the advertisement, mother looked me in the face, and burst into tears. A cold chill ran over me, and such a sensation I never experienced before, and I hope never to again. They took out a rope and tied me, and we were taken back about six miles, to the house of the individual who appeared to be the leader. We reached there about seven o'clock in the evening, had supper, and were separated for the night. Two men remained in the room during the night. Before the family retired to rest, they were all called together to attend prayers. The man who but a few hours before had bound my hands together with a strong cord, read a chapter from the Bible, and then offered up prayer, just as though God had sanctioned the act he had just committed upon a poor, panting, fugitive slave.

The next morning a blacksmith came in, and put a pair of handcuffs on me, and we started on our journey back to the land of whips, chains and Bibles. Mother was not tied, but was closely watched at night. We were carried back in a wagon, and after four days' travel, we came in sight of St. Louis. I cannot describe my feelings upon approaching the city.

As we were crossing on the ferry,[33] Mr. Wiggins, the owner of the ferry, came up to me, and inquired what I had been doing that I was in chains. He had not heard that I had run away. In a few minutes we were on the Missouri side, and were taken directly to the jail. On the way thither, I saw several of my friends, who gave me a nod of recognition as I passed them. After reaching the jail, we were locked up in different apartments.

Chapter 9

I HAD been in jail but a short time when I heard that my master was sick, and nothing brought more joy to my heart than that intelligence. I prayed fervently for him – not for his recovery, but for his death. I knew he would be exasperated at having to pay for my apprehension, and knowing his cruelty, I feared him. While in jail, I learned that my sister Elizabeth, who was in prison when we left the city, had been carried off four days before our arrival.

I had been in jail but a few hours when three negro-traders, learning that I was secured thus for running away, came to my prison-house and looked at me, expecting that I would be offered for sale. Mr. Mansfield, the man who owned mother, came into the jail as soon as Mr. Jones, the man who arrested us, informed him that he had brought her back. He told her that he would not whip her, but would sell her to a negro-trader, or take her to New Orleans himself. After being in jail about one week, master sent a man to take me out of jail, and send me home. I was taken out and carried home, and the old man was well enough to sit up. He had me brought into the room where he was, and as I entered, he asked me where I had been? I told him I had acted according to his orders. He had told me to look for a master, and I had been to look for one. He answered that he did not tell me to go to Canada to look for a master. I told him that as I had served him faithfully, and had been the means of putting a number of hundreds of dollars into his pocket, I thought I had a right to my liberty. He said he had promised my father that I should not be sold to supply the New Orleans market, or he would sell me to a negro-trader.

I was ordered to go into the field to work, and was closely watched by the overseer during the day, and locked up at night. The overseer gave me a severe whipping on the second day that I was in the field. I had been at home but a short time, when master was able to ride to the city; and on his return he informed me that he had sold me to Samuel Willi, a merchant tailor. I knew Mr. Willi. I had lived with him three or four months some years before, when he hired me of my master.

Mr. Willi was not considered by his servants as a very bad man, nor was he the best of masters. I went to my new home, and found my new mistress very glad to see me. Mr. Willi owned two servants before he purchased me – Robert and Charlotte. Robert was an excellent white-washer, and hired his time from his master, paying him one dollar per day, besides taking care of himself. He was known in the city by the name of Bob Music. Charlotte was an old woman, who attended to the cooking, washing, &c. Mr. Willi was not a wealthy man, and did not feel able to keep many servants around his house; so he soon decided to hire me out, and as I had been accustomed to service in steamboats, he gave me the privilege of finding such employment.

Notes

[33] *Original reads*: crossing the ferry [ed.].

I soon secured a situation on board the steamer Otto, Capt. J.B. Hill, which sailed from St. Louis to Independence, Missouri. My former master, Dr. Young, did not let Mr. Willi know that I had run away, or he would not have permitted me to go on board a steamboat. The boat was not quite ready to commence running, and therefore I had to remain with Mr. Willi. But during this time, I had to undergo a trial for which I was entirely unprepared. My mother, who had been in jail since her return until the present time, was now about being carried to New Orleans, to die on a cotton, sugar, or rice plantation!

I had been several times to the jail, but could obtain no interview with her. I ascertained, however, the time the boat in which she was to embark would sail, and as I had not seen mother since her being thrown into prison, I felt anxious for the hour of sailing to come. At last, the day arrived when I was to see her for the first time after our painful separation, and, for aught that I knew, for the last time in this world!

At about ten o'clock in the morning I went on board of the boat, and found her there in company with fifty or sixty other slaves. She was chained to another woman. On seeing me, she immediately dropped her head upon her heaving bosom. She moved not, neither did she weep. Her emotions were too deep for tears. I approached, threw my arms around her neck, kissed her, and fell upon my knees, begging her forgiveness, for I thought myself to blame for her sad condition; for if I had not persuaded her to accompany me, she would not then have been in chains.

She finally raised her head, looked me in the face, (and such a look none but an angel can give!) and said, *"My dear son, you are not to blame for my being here. You have done nothing more nor less than your duty. Do not, I pray you, weep for me. I cannot last long upon a cotton plantation. I feel that my heavenly Master will soon call me home, and then I shall be out of the hands of the slave-holders!"*

I could bear no more – my heart struggled to free itself from the human form. In a moment she saw Mr. Mansfield coming toward that part of the boat, and she whispered into my ear, *"My child, we must soon part to meet no more this side of the grave. You have ever said that you would not die a slave; that you would be a freeman. Now try to get your liberty! You will soon have no one to look after but yourself!"* and just as she whispered the last sentence into my ear, Mansfield came up to me, and with an oath, said, "Leave here this instant; you have been the means of my losing one hundred dollars to get this wench back" – at the same time kicking me with a heavy pair of boots. As I left her, she gave one shriek, saying, "God be with you!" It was the last time that I saw her, and the last word I heard her utter.

I walked on shore. The bell was tolling. The boat was about to start. I stood with a heavy heart, waiting to see her leave the wharf. As I thought of my mother, I could but feel that I had lost

"—— the glory of my life,
My blessing and my pride!
I half forgot the name of slave,
When she was by my side."[34]

The love of liberty that had been burning in my bosom had well-nigh gone out. I felt as though I was ready to die. The boat moved gently from the wharf, and while she glided down the river, I realized that my mother was indeed

Notes

[34] "*—— the glory … by my side*" from George W. Clark's "The Bereaved Father," published in *The Liberty Minstrel.*

"Gone – gone – sold and gone,
To the rice swamp, dank and lone!"[35]

After the boat was out of sight I returned home; but my thoughts were so absorbed in what I had witnessed, that I knew not what I was about half of the time. Night came, but it brought no sleep to my eyes.

In a few days, the boat upon which I was to work being ready, I went on board to commence. This employment suited me better than living in the city, and I remained until the close of navigation; though it proved anything but pleasant. The captain was a drunken, profligate,[36] hard-hearted creature, not knowing how to treat himself, or any other person.

The boat, on its second trip, brought down Mr. Walker, the man of whom I have spoken in a previous chapter, as hiring my time. He had between one and two hundred slaves, chained and manacled. Among them was a man that formerly belonged to my old master's brother, Aaron Young. His name was Solomon. He was a preacher, and belonged to the same church with his master. I was glad to see the old man. He wept like a child when he told me how he had been sold from his wife and children.

The boat carried down, while I remained on board, four or five gangs of slaves. Missouri, though a comparatively new state, is very much engaged in raising slaves to supply the southern market. In a former chapter, I have mentioned that I was once in the employ of a slave-trader, or driver, as he is called at the south. For fear that some may think that I have misrepresented a slave-driver, I will here give an extract from a paper published in a slave-holding state, Tennessee, called the "Millennial Trumpeter."

> "Droves of negroes, chained together in dozens and scores, and hand-cuffed, have been driven through our country in numbers far surpassing any previous year, and these vile slave-drivers and dealers are swarming like buzzards around a carrion. Through this county, you cannot pass a few miles in the great roads without having every feeling of humanity insulted and lacerated by this spectacle, nor can you go into any county or any neighborhood, scarcely, without seeing or hearing of some of these despicable creatures, called negro-drivers.
>
> "Who is a negro-driver? One whose eyes dwell with delight on lacerated bodies of helpless men, women and children; whose soul feels diabolical raptures at the chains, and hand-cuffs, and cart-whips, for inflicting tortures on weeping mothers torn from helpless babes, and on husbands and wives torn asunder forever!"

Dark and revolting as is the picture here drawn, it is from the pen of one living in the midst of slavery. But though these men may cant about negro-drivers, and tell what despicable creatures they are, who is it, I ask, that supplies them with the human beings that they are tearing asunder? I answer, as far as I have any knowledge of the state where I came from, that those who raise slaves for the market are to be found among all classes, from Thomas H. Benton[37] down to the lowest political demagogue who may be able to purchase a woman for the purpose of raising stock, and from the doctor of divinity down to the most humble lay member in the church.

Notes

[35] *"Gone ... dank and lone!"* from "The Farewell" by abolitionist and poet John Greenleaf Whittier (1807–1892); also set to music by Clark in *The Liberty Minstrel* (published by Clark as "Gone, Sold and Gone").

[36] *profligate* wasteful.

[37] Thomas H. Benton (1782–1858), Missouri senator.

It was not uncommon in St. Louis to pass by an auction-stand, and behold a woman upon the auction-block, and hear the seller crying out, *"How much is offered for this woman? She is a good cook, good washer, a good obedient servant. She has got religion!"* Why should this man tell the purchasers that she has religion? I answer, because in Missouri, and as far as I have any knowledge of slavery in the other states, the religious teaching consists in teaching the slave that he must never strike a white man; that God made him for a slave; and that, when whipped, he must not find fault – for the Bible says, "He that knoweth his master's will and doeth it not, shall be beaten with many stripes!" And slaveholders find such religion very profitable to them.

After leaving the steamer Otto, I resided at home, in Mr. Willi's family, and again began to lay my plans for making my escape from slavery. The anxiety to be a freeman would not let me rest day or night. I would think of the northern cities that I had heard so much about – of Canada, where so many of my acquaintances had found a refuge. I would dream at night that I was in Canada, a freeman, and on waking in the morning, weep to find myself so sadly mistaken.

"I would think of Victoria's domain,
And in a moment I seemed to be there!
But the fear of being taken again,
Soon hurried me back to despair."

Mr. Willi treated me better than Dr. Young ever had; but instead of making me contented and happy, it only rendered me the more miserable, for it enabled me better to appreciate liberty. Mr. Willi was a man who loved money as most men do, and without looking for an opportunity to sell me, he found one in the offer of Captain Enoch Price, a steamboat owner and commission merchant, living in the city of St. Louis. Captain Price tendered seven hundred dollars, which was two hundred more than Mr. Willi had paid. He therefore thought best to accept the offer. I was wanted for a carriage driver, and Mrs. Price was very much pleased with the captain's bargain. His family consisted of himself, wife, one child, and three servants, besides myself – one man and two women.

Mrs. Price was very proud of her servants, always keeping them well dressed, and as soon as I had been purchased, she resolved to have a new carriage. And soon one was procured, and all preparations were made for a turn-out in grand style, I being the driver.

One of the female servants was a girl some eighteen or twenty years of age, named Maria. Mrs. Price was very soon determined to have us united, if she could so arrange matters. She would often urge upon me the necessity of having a wife, saying that it would be so pleasant for me to take one in the same family! But getting married, while in slavery, was the last of my thoughts; and had I been ever so inclined, I should not have married Maria, as my love had already gone in another quarter. Mrs. Price soon found out that her efforts at this match-making between Maria and me[38] would not prove successful. She also discovered (or thought she had) that I was rather partial to a girl named Eliza, who was owned by Dr. Mills. This induced her at once to endeavor the purchase of Eliza, so great was her desire to get me a wife!

Before making the attempt, however, she deemed it best to talk to me a little upon the subject of love, courtship, and marriage. Accordingly, one afternoon she called me

Notes

[38] *Original reads*: myself [ed.].

into her room – telling me to take a chair and sit down. I did so, thinking it rather strange, for servants are not very often asked thus to sit down in the same room with the master or mistress. She said that she had found out that I did not care enough about Maria to marry her. I told her that was true. She then asked me if there was not a girl in the city that I loved. Well, now, this was coming into too close quarters with me! People, generally, don't like to tell their love stories to everybody that may think fit to ask about them, and it was so with me. But, after blushing a while and recovering myself, I told her that I did not want a wife. She then asked me if I did not think something of Eliza. I told her that I did. She then said that if I wished to marry Eliza, she would purchase her if she could.

I gave but little encouragement to this proposition, as I was determined to make another trial to get my liberty, and I knew that if I should have a wife, I should not be willing to leave her behind; and if I should attempt to bring her with me, the chances would be difficult for success. However, Eliza was purchased, and brought into the family.

Chapter 10

But the more I thought of the trap laid by Mrs. Price to make me satisfied with my new home, by getting me a wife, the more I determined never to marry any woman on earth until I should get my liberty. But this secret I was compelled to keep to myself, which placed me in a very critical position. I must keep upon good terms with Mrs. Price and Eliza. I therefore promised Mrs. Price that I would marry Eliza; but said that I was not then ready. And I had to keep upon good terms with Eliza for fear that Mrs. Price would find out that I did not intend to get married.

I have here spoken of marriage, and it is very common among slaves themselves to talk of it. And it is common for slaves to be married; or at least to have the marriage ceremony performed. But there is no such thing as slaves being lawfully married. There has never yet a case occurred where a slave has been tried for bigamy. The man may have as many women as he wishes, and the women as many men; and the law takes no cognizance of such acts among slaves. And in fact some masters, when they have sold the husband from the wife, compel her to take another.

There lived opposite Captain Price's, Doctor Farrar, well known in St. Louis. He sold a man named Ben to one of the traders. He also owned Ben's wife, and in a few days he compelled Sally (that was her name) to marry Peter, another man belonging to him. I asked Sally why she married Peter so soon after Ben was sold. She said because master made her do it.

Mr. John Calvert, who resided near our place, had a woman named Lavinia. She was quite young, and a man to whom she was about to be married was sold, and carried into the country near St. Charles, about twenty miles from St. Louis. Mr. Calvert wanted her to get a husband; but she had resolved not to marry any other man, and she refused. Mr. Calvert whipped her in such a manner that it was thought she would die. Some of the citizens had him arrested, but it was soon hushed up. And that was the last of it. The woman did not die, but it would have been the same if she had.

Captain Price purchased me in the month of October, and I remained with him until December, when the family made a voyage to New Orleans, in a boat owned by himself, and named the "Chester." I served on board as one of the stewards. On arriving at New Orleans, about the middle of the month, the boat took in freight for Cincinnati; and it was decided that the family should go up the river in her, and what was of more interest to me, I was to accompany them.

The long looked for opportunity to make my escape from slavery was near at hand.

Captain Price had some fears as to the propriety of taking me near a free state, or a place where it was likely I could run away, with a prospect of liberty. He asked me if I had ever been in a free state. "Oh yes," said I, "I have been in Ohio; my master carried me into that state once, but I never liked a free state."

It was soon decided that it would be safe to take me with them, and what made it more safe, Eliza was on the boat with us, and Mrs. Price, to try me, asked if I thought as much as ever of Eliza. I told her that Eliza was very dear to me indeed, and that nothing but death should part us. It was the same as if we were married. This had the desired effect. The boat left New Orleans, and proceeded up the river.

I had at different times obtained little sums of money, which I had reserved for a "rainy day." I procured some cotton cloth, and made me a bag to carry provisions in. The trials of the past were all lost in hopes for the future. The love of liberty, that had been burning in my bosom for years, and had been well-nigh extinguished, was now resuscitated. At night, when all around was peaceful, I would walk the decks, meditating upon my happy prospects.

I should have stated that, before leaving St. Louis, I went to an old man named Frank, a slave, owned by a Mr. Sarpee. This old man was very distinguished (not only among the slave population, but also the whites) as a fortune-teller. He was about seventy years of age, something over six feet high, and very slender. Indeed, he was so small around his body that it looked as though it was not strong enough to hold up his head.

Uncle Frank was a very great favorite with the young ladies, who would go to him in great numbers to get their fortunes told. And it was generally believed that he could really penetrate into the mysteries of futurity. Whether true or not, he had the *name*, and that is about half of what one needs in this gullible age. I found Uncle Frank seated in the chimney corner, about ten o'clock at night. As soon as I entered, the old man left his seat. I watched his movement as well as I could by the dim light of the fire. He soon lit a lamp, and coming up, looked me full in the face, saying, "Well, my son, you have come to get uncle to tell your fortune, have you?" "Yes," said I. But how the old man should know what I came for, I could not tell. However, I paid the fee of twenty-five cents, and he commenced by looking into a gourd, filled with water. Whether the old man was a prophet, or the son of a prophet, I cannot say; but there is one thing certain, many of his predictions were verified.

I am no believer in soothsaying; yet I am sometimes at a loss to know how Uncle Frank could tell so accurately what would occur in the future. Among the many things he told was one which was enough to pay me for all the trouble of hunting him up. It was that I *should be free!* He further said that in trying to get my liberty I would meet with many severe trials. I thought to myself any fool could tell me that!

The first place in which we landed in a free state was Cairo, a small village at the mouth of the Ohio River.[39] We remained here but a few hours, when we proceeded to Louisville. After unloading some of the cargo, the boat started on her upward trip. The next day was the first of January. I had looked forward to New Year's Day[40] as the commencement of a new era in the history of my life. I had decided upon leaving the peculiar institution that day.

During the last night that I served in slavery I did not close my eyes a single moment. When not thinking of the future, my mind dwelt on the past. The love of a dear mother, a dear sister, and three dear brothers, yet living, caused me to shed many tears.

Notes

[39] *Original reads*: Ohio river [ed.].

[40] *Original reads*: New Year's day [ed.].

If I could only have been assured of their being dead, I should have felt satisfied; but I imagined I saw my dear mother in the cotton-field, followed by a merciless task-master, and no one to speak a consoling word to her! I beheld my dear sister in the hands of a slave-driver, and compelled to submit to his cruelty! None but one placed in such a situation can for a moment imagine the intense agony to which these reflections subjected me.

Chapter 11

AT last the time for action arrived. The boat landed at a point which appeared to me the place of all others to start from. I found that it would be impossible to carry anything with me but what was upon my person. I had some provisions, and a single suit of clothes, about half worn. When the boat was discharging her cargo, and the passengers engaged carrying their baggage on and off shore, I improved the opportunity to convey myself with my little effects on land. Taking up a trunk, I went up the wharf, and was soon out of the crowd. I made directly for the woods, where I remained until night, knowing well that I could not travel, even in the state of Ohio, during the day, without danger of being arrested.

I had long since made up my mind that I would not trust myself in the hands of any man, white or colored. The slave is brought up to look upon every white man as an enemy to him and his race; and twenty-one years in slavery had taught me that there were traitors, even among colored people. After dark, I emerged from the woods into a narrow path, which led me into the main travelled road. But I knew not which way to go. I did not know north from south, east from west. I looked in vain for the North Star; a heavy cloud hid it from my view. I walked up and down the road until near midnight, when the clouds disappeared, and I welcomed the sight of my friend – truly the slave's friend – the North Star!

As soon as I saw it, I knew my course, and before daylight I travelled twenty or twenty-five miles. It being in the winter, I suffered intensely from the cold; being without an overcoat and my other clothes rather thin for the season. I was provided with a tinder-box, so that I could make up a fire when necessary. And but for this, I should certainly have frozen to death; for I was determined not to go to any house for shelter. I knew of a man belonging to Gen. Ashly, of St. Louis, who had run away near Cincinnati, on the way to Washington, but had been caught and carried back into slavery; and I felt that a similar fate awaited me, should I be seen by anyone.[41] I travelled at night, and lay by during the day.

On the fourth day my provisions gave out, and then what to do I could not tell. Have something to eat I must; but how to get it was the question! On the first night after my food was gone, I went to a barn on the road-side and there found some ears of corn. I took ten or twelve of them, and kept on my journey. During the next day, while in the woods, I roasted my corn and feasted upon it, thanking God that I was so well provided for.

My escape to a land of freedom now appeared certain, and the prospects of the future occupied a great part of my thoughts. What should be my occupation, was a subject of much anxiety to me; and the next thing what should be my name? I have before stated that my old master, Dr. Young, had no children of his own, but had with

Notes

[41] *Original reads*: any one [ed.].

him a nephew, the son of his brother, Benjamin Young. When this boy was brought to Dr. Young, his name being William, the same as mine, my mother was ordered to change mine to something else. This, at the time, I thought to be one of the most cruel acts that could be committed upon my rights; and I received several very severe whippings for telling people that my name was William, after orders were given to change it. Though young, I was old enough to place a high appreciation upon my name. It was decided, however, to call me "Sandford," and this name I was known by, not only upon my master's plantation, but up to the time that I made my escape. I was sold under the name of Sandford.

But as soon as the subject came to my mind, I resolved on adopting my old name of William, and let Sandford go by the board, for I always hated it. Not because there was anything peculiar in the name; but because it had been forced upon me. It is sometimes common, at the south, for slaves to take the name of their masters. Some have a legitimate right to do so. But I always detested the idea of being called by the name of either of my masters. And as for my father, I would rather have adopted the name of "Friday,"[42] and been known as the servant of some Robinson Crusoe, than to have taken his name. So I was not only hunting for my liberty, but also hunting for a name; though I regarded the latter as of little consequence, if I could but gain the former. Travelling along the road, I would sometimes speak to myself, sounding my name over, by way of getting used to it, before I should arrive among civilized human beings. On the fifth or six day, it rained very fast, and froze about as fast as it fell, so that my clothes were one glare of ice. I travelled on at night until I became so chilled and benumbed – the wind blowing into my face – that I found it impossible to go any further, and accordingly took shelter in a barn, where I was obliged to walk about to keep from freezing.

I have ever looked upon that night as the most eventful part of my escape from slavery. Nothing but the providence of God, and that old barn, saved me from freezing to death. I received a very severe cold, which settled upon my lungs, and from time to time my feet had been frostbitten, so that it was with difficulty I could walk. In this situation I travelled two days, when I found that I must seek shelter somewhere, or die.

The thought of death was nothing frightful to me, compared with that of being caught, and again carried back into slavery. Nothing but the prospect of enjoying liberty could have induced me to undergo such trials, for

"Behind I left the whips and chains,
Before me were sweet Freedom's plains!"

This, and this alone, cheered me onward. But I at last resolved to seek protection from the inclemency of the weather, and therefore I secured myself behind some logs and brush, intending to wait there until someone[43] should pass by; for I thought it probable that I might see some colored person, or, if not, someone[44] who was not a slaveholder; for I had an idea that I should know a slaveholder as far as I could see him.

The first person that passed was a man in a buggy-wagon. He looked too genteel for me to hail him. Very soon another passed by on horseback. I attempted to speak to him, but fear made my voice fail me. As he passed, I left my hiding-place, and was approaching the road, when I observed an old man walking towards me, leading

Notes

[42] *"Friday"* the servant of Robinson Crusoe in Daniel Defoe's novel (1719).

[43] *Original reads*: some one [ed.].

[44] *Original reads*: some one [ed.].

a white horse. He had on a broad-brimmed hat and a very long coat, and was evidently walking for exercise. As soon as I saw him, and observed his dress, I thought to myself, "You are the man that I have been looking for!" Nor was I mistaken. He was the very man!

On approaching me, he asked me if I were not a slave.[45] I looked at him some time, and then asked him if he knew of anyone[46] who would help me, as I was sick. He answered that he would; but again asked, if I was not a slave. I told him I was. He then said that I was in a very pro-slavery neighborhood, and if I would wait until he went home, he would get a covered wagon for me. I promised to remain. He mounted his horse, and was soon out of sight.

After he was gone, I meditated whether to wait or not; being apprehensive that he had gone for someone[47] to arrest me. But I finally concluded to remain until he should return; removing some few rods to watch his movements. After a suspense of an hour and a half or more, he returned with a two-horse covered wagon, such as are usually seen under the shed of a Quaker meeting-house on Sundays and Thursdays; for the old man proved to be a Quaker of the George Fox[48] stamp.

He took me to his house, but it was some time before I could be induced to enter it; not until the old lady came out, did I venture into the house. I thought I saw something in the old lady's cap that told me I was not only safe, but welcome, in her house. I was not, however, prepared to receive their hospitalities. The only fault I found with them was their being too kind. I had never had a white man to treat me as an equal, and the idea of a white lady waiting on me at the table was still worse! Though the table was loaded with the good things of this life, I could not eat. I thought if I could only be allowed the privilege of eating in the kitchen I should be more than satisfied!

Finding that I could not eat, the old lady, who was a "Thompsonian,"[49] made me a cup of "composition," or "number six"; but it was so strong and hot, that I called it "*number seven!*" However, I soon found myself at home in this family. On different occasions, when telling these facts, I have been asked how I felt upon finding myself regarded as a man by a white family; especially just having run away from one. I cannot say that I have ever answered the question yet.

The fact that I was in all probability a freeman, sounded in my ears like a charm. I am satisfied that none but a slave could place such an appreciation upon liberty as I did at that time. I wanted to see mother and sister, that I might tell them "I was free!" I wanted to see my fellow-slaves in St. Louis, and let them know that the chains were no longer upon my limbs. I wanted to see Captain Price, and let him learn from my own lips that I was no more a chattel, but a man! I was anxious, too, thus to inform Mrs. Price that she must get another coachman. And I wanted to see Eliza more than I did either Mr. or Mrs. Price!

The fact that I was a freeman – could walk, talk, eat and sleep, as a man, and no one to stand over me with the blood-clotted cow-hide – all this made me feel that I was not myself.

The kind friend that had taken me in was named Wells Brown. He was a devoted friend of the slave; but was very old, and not in the enjoyment of good health. After being by the fire awhile, I found that my feet had been very much frozen. I was seized

Notes

[45] *Original reads*: if I was not a slave [ed.].

[46] *Original reads*: any one [ed.].

[47] *Original reads*: some one [ed.].

[48] George Fox (1624–1691), one of the founders of the Quaker religion.

[49] "*Thompsonian*" alternative, herbalist medicine named after its founder Samuel Thomson (1769–1843).

with a fever, which threatened to confine me to my bed. But my Thompsonian friends soon raised me, treating me as kindly as if I had been one of their own children. I remained with them twelve or fifteen days, during which time they made me some clothing, and the old gentleman purchased me a pair of boots.

I found that I was about fifty or sixty miles from Dayton, in the State of Ohio, and between one and two hundred miles from Cleaveland,[50] on Lake Erie, a place I was desirous of reaching on my way to Canada. This I know will sound strangely to the ears of people in foreign lands, but it is nevertheless true. An American citizen was fleeing from a democratic, republican, Christian government, to receive protection under the monarchy of Great Britain. While the people of the United States boast of their freedom, they at the same time keep three millions of their own citizens in chains; and while I am seated here in sight of Bunker Hill Monument, writing this narrative, I am a slave, and no law, not even in Massachusetts, can protect me from the hands of the slaveholder!

Before leaving this good Quaker friend, he inquired what my name was besides William. I told him that I had no other name. "Well," said he, "thee must have another name. Since thee has got out of slavery, thee has become a man, and men always have two names."

I told him that he was the first man to extend the hand of friendship to me, and I would give him the privilege of naming me.

"If I name thee," said he, "I shall call thee Wells Brown, after myself."

"But," said I, "I am not willing to lose my name of William. As it was taken from me once against my will, I am not willing to part with it again upon any terms.

"Then," said he, "I will call thee William Wells Brown."

"So be it," said I; and I have been known by that name ever since I left the house of my first white friend, Wells Brown.

After giving me some little change, I again started for Canada. In four days I reached a public house, and went in to warm myself. I there learned that some fugitive slaves had just passed through the place. The men in the bar-room were talking about it, and I thought that it must have been me[51] they referred to, and I was therefore afraid to start, fearing they would seize me; but I finally mustered courage enough, and took my leave. As soon as I was out of sight, I went into the woods, and remained there until night, when I again regained the road, and travelled on until next day.

Not having had any food for nearly two days, I was faint with hunger, and was in a dilemma what to do, as the little cash supplied me by my adopted father, and which had contributed to my comfort, was now all gone. I however concluded to go to a farm-house, and ask for something to eat. On approaching the door of the first one presenting itself, I knocked, and was soon met by a man who asked me what I wanted. I told him that I would like something to eat. He asked me where I was from, and where I was going. I replied that I had come some way, and was going to Cleaveland.

After hesitating a moment or two, he told me that he could give me nothing to eat, adding, "that if I would work, I could get something to eat."

I felt bad, being thus refused something to sustain nature, but did not dare tell him that I was a slave.

Just as I was leaving the door, with a heavy heart, a woman, who proved to be the wife of this gentleman, came to the door, and asked her husband what I wanted. He did not seem inclined to inform her. She therefore asked me herself. I told her that

Notes

[50] *Cleaveland* Cleveland.

[51] *Original reads*: myself [ed.].

I had asked for something to eat. After a few other questions, she told me to come in, and that she would give me something to eat.

I walked up to the door, but the husband remained in the passage, as if unwilling to let me enter.

She asked him two or three times to get out of the way, and let me in. But as he did not move, she pushed him on one side, bidding me walk in! I was never before so glad to see a woman push a man aside! Ever since that act, I have been in favor of "woman's rights!"

After giving me as much food as I could eat, she presented me with ten cents, all the money then at her disposal, accompanied with a note to a friend, a few miles further on the road. Thanking this angel of mercy from an overflowing heart, I pushed on my way, and in three days arrived at Cleaveland, Ohio.

Being an entire stranger in this place, it was difficult for me to find where to stop. I had no money, and the lake being frozen, I saw that I must remain until the opening of the navigation, or go to Canada by way of Buffalo. But believing myself to be somewhat out of danger, I secured an engagement at the Mansion House, as a table waiter, in payment for my board. The proprietor, however, whose name was E.M. Segur, in a short time, hired me for twelve dollars a month; on which terms I remained until spring, when I found good employment on board a lake steamboat.

I purchased some books, and at leisure moments perused them with considerable advantage to myself. While at Cleaveland, I saw, for the first time, an anti-slavery newspaper. It was the "*Genius of Universal Emancipation*," published by Benjamin Lundy;[52] and though I had no home, I subscribed for the paper. It was my great desire, being out of slavery myself, to do what I could for the emancipation of my brethren yet in chains, and while on Lake Erie, I found many opportunities of "helping their cause along."

It is well known that a great number of fugitives make their escape to Canada, by way of Cleaveland; and while on the lakes, I always made arrangement to carry them on the boat to Buffalo or Detroit, and thus effect their escape to the "promised land." The friends of the slave, knowing that I would transport them without charge, never failed to have a delegation when the boat arrived at Cleaveland. I have sometimes had four or five on board at one time.

In the year 1842 I conveyed, from the first of May to the first of December, sixty-nine fugitives over Lake Erie to Canada. In 1843, I visited Malden, in Upper Canada, and counted seventeen in that small village, whom I had assisted in reaching Canada. Soon after coming north I subscribed for the Liberator, edited by that champion of freedom, William Lloyd Garrison.[53] I had heard nothing of the anti-slavery movement while in slavery, and as soon as I found that my enslaved countrymen had friends who were laboring for their liberation, I felt anxious to join them, and give what aid I could to the cause.

I early embraced the temperance[54] cause, and found that a temperance reformation was needed among my colored brethren. In company with a few friends, I commenced a temperance reformation among the colored people in the city of Buffalo, and labored three years, in which time a society was built up, numbering over five hundred out of a population of less than seven hundred.

Notes

[52] Benjamin Lundy (1789–1839), Quaker abolitionist and newspaper editor.

[53] William Lloyd Garrison (1805–1879), prominent abolitionist and founder of the American Anti-Slavery Society.

[54] *temperance* opposition to alcohol.

In the autumn, 1843, impressed with the importance of spreading anti-slavery truth, as a means to bring about the abolition of slavery, I commenced lecturing as an agent of the western New York Anti-Slavery Society, and have ever since devoted my time to the cause of my enslaved countrymen.

Chapter 12

During the autumn of 1836, a slaveholder by the name of Bacon Tate, from the State of Tennessee, came to the north in search of fugitives from slavery. On his arrival at Buffalo he heard of two of the most valuable of the slaves that he was in pursuit of. They were residing in St. Catharine's, in Upper Canada, some twenty-five miles from Buffalo. After hearing that they were in Canada, one would have supposed that Tate would have given up all hope of getting them. But not so. Bacon Tate was a man who had long been engaged in the slave-trade, and previous to that had been employed as a negro-driver. In these two situations he had gained the name of being the most complete "negro-breaker" in that part of Tennessee where he resided. He was as unfeeling and as devoid of principle as a man could possibly be. This made him the person, above all others, to be selected to be put on the track of the fugitive slave. He had not only been commissioned to catch Stanford and his wife, the two valuable slaves already alluded to, but he had the names of some twenty others.

Many slaves had made their escape from the vicinity of Nashville, and the slaveholders were anxious to have some caught, that they might make an example of them. And Tate, anxious to sustain his high reputation as a negro-catcher, left no stone unturned to carry out his nefarious objects.

Stanford and his little family were as happily situated as fugitives can be who make their escape to Canada in the cold season of the year. Tate, on his arrival at Buffalo, took lodgings at the Eagle Tavern, the best house at that time in the city. And here he began to lay his plans to catch and carry back into slavery those men and women who had undergone so much to get their freedom. He soon became acquainted with a profligate colored woman, who was a servant in the hotel, and who was as unprincipled as himself. This woman was sent to St. Catharine's, to spy out the situation of Stanford's family. Under the pretence of wishing to get board in the family, and at the same time offering to pay a week's board in advance, she was taken in. After remaining with them three or four days, the spy returned to Buffalo, and informed Tate how they were situated. By the liberal use of money, Tate soon found those who were willing to do his bidding. A carriage was hired, and four men employed to go with it to St. Catharine's, and to secure their victims during the night.

The carriage, with the kidnappers, crossed the Niagara River[55] at Black Rock, on Saturday evening, about seven o'clock, and went on its way towards St. Catharine's; no one suspecting in the least that they were after fugitive slaves. About twelve o'clock that night they attacked Stanford's dwelling by breaking in the door. They found the family asleep, and of course met with no obstacle whatever in tying, gagging, and forcing them into the carriage.

The family had one child about six weeks old. That was kept at its mother's breast, to keep it quiet. The carriage re-crossed the river, at the same place, the next morning at sunrise, and proceeded to Buffalo, where it remained a short time, and after changing

Notes

[55] *Original reads*: Niagara river [ed.].

horses and leaving some of its company, it proceeded on its journey. The carriage being closely covered, no one had made the least discovery as to its contents. But some time during the morning, a man, who was neighbor to Stanford, and who resided but a short distance from him, came on an errand; and finding the house deserted, and seeing the most of the family's clothes lying on the floor, and seeing here and there stains of blood, soon gave the alarm, and the neighbors started in every direction, to see if they could find the kidnappers. One man got on the track of the carriage, and followed it to the ferry at Black Rock, where he heard that it had crossed some three hours before. He went on to Buffalo, and gave the alarm to the colored people of that place. The colored people of Buffalo are noted for their promptness in giving aid to the fugitive slave. The alarm was given just as the bells were ringing for church. I was in company with five or six others, when I heard that a brother slave with his family had been seized and dragged from his home during the night previous. We started on a run for the livery-stable, where we found as many more of our own color trying to hire horses to go in search of the fugitives. There were two roads which the kidnappers could take, and we were at some loss to know which to take ourselves. But we soon determined to be on the right track, and so divided our company – one half taking the road to Erie, the other taking the road leading to Hamburgh.[56] I was among those who took the latter.

We travelled on at a rapid rate, until we came within half a mile of Hamburgh Corners, when we met a man on the side of the road on foot, who made signs to us to stop. We halted for a moment, when he informed us that the carriage that we were in pursuit of was at the public house, and that he was then in search of some of his neighbors, to assemble and to demand of the kidnappers the authority by which they were taking these people into slavery.

We proceeded to the tavern, where we found the carriage standing in front of the door, with a pair of fresh horses ready to proceed on their journey. The kidnappers, seeing us coming, took their victims into a room, and locked the door and fastened down the windows. We all dismounted, fastened our horses, and entered the house. We found four or five persons in the bar-room, who seemed to rejoice as we entered.

One of our company demanded the opening of the door, while others went out and surrounded the house. The kidnappers stationed one of their number at the door, and another at the window. They refused to let us enter the room, and the tavern-keeper, who was more favorable to us than we had anticipated, said to us, "Boys, get into the room in any way that you can; the house is mine, and I give you the liberty to break in through the door or window." This was all that we wanted, and we were soon making preparations to enter the room at all hazards. Those within had warned us that if we should attempt to enter, they would "shoot the first one." One of our company, who had obtained a crow-bar, went to the window, and succeeded in getting it under the sash, and soon we had the window up, and the kidnappers, together with their victims, in full view.

One of the kidnappers, while we were raising the window, kept crying at the top of his voice, "I'll shoot, I'll shoot!" but no one seemed to mind him. As soon as they saw that we were determined to rescue the slaves at all hazards, they gave up, one of their number telling us that we might "come in."

The door was thrown open, and we entered, and there found Stanford seated in one corner of the room, with his hands tied behind him, and his clothing, what little he had

Notes

56 *Hamburgh* Hamburg.

on, much stained with blood. Near him was his wife, with her child, but a few weeks old, in her arms. Neither of them had anything on except their night-clothes. They had both been gagged, to keep them from alarming the people, and had been much beaten and bruised when first attacked by the kidnappers. Their countenances lighted up the moment we entered the room.

The most of those who made up our company were persons who had made their escape from slavery, and who knew its horrors from personal experience, and who had left near and dear relatives behind them. And we knew how to "feel for those in bonds as bound with them."

The woman who had betrayed them, and who was in the house at the time they were taken, had been persuaded by Tate to go on with him to Tennessee. She had accompanied them from Canada, and we found her in the same room with Stanford and his wife. As soon as she found that we were about to enter the room, she ran under the bed. We knew nothing of her being in the room until Stanford pointed to the bed and said, "Under there is our betrayer." She was soon hauled out, and it was as much as some of us could do to keep the others from lynching her upon the spot. The curses came thick and fast from a majority of the company. But nothing attracted my attention at the time more than the look of Mrs. Stanford at the betrayer, as she sat before her. She did not say a word to her, but her countenance told the feelings of her inmost soul, and we could but think, that had she spoken to her, she would have said, "May the world deny thee a shelter! earth a home! the dust a grave! the sun his light! and Heaven her God!"

The betrayer begged us to let her go. I was somewhat disposed to comply with her request, but I found many to oppose me; in fact, I was entirely alone. My main reason for wishing to let her escape was that I was afraid that her life would be in danger. I knew that, if she was taken back to Buffalo or Canada, she would fall into the hands of an excited people, the most of whom had themselves been slaves. And they, being comparatively ignorant of the laws, would be likely to take the law into their own hands.

However, the woman was not allowed to escape, but was put into the coach, together with Stanford and his wife; and after an hour and a half's drive, we found ourselves in the city of Buffalo. The excitement which the alarm had created in the morning had broken up the meetings of the colored people for that day; and on our arrival in the city we were met by some forty or fifty colored persons. The kidnappers had not been inactive; for, on our arrival in the city, we learned that the man who had charge of the carriage and fugitives when we caught up with them, returned to the city immediately after giving the slaves up to us, and had informed Tate, who had remained behind, of what had occurred. Tate immediately employed the sheriff and his posse to re-take the slaves. So, on our arrival in Buffalo, we found that the main battle had yet to be fought. Stanford and his wife and child were soon provided with clothing and some refreshment, while we were preparing ourselves with clubs, pistols, knives, and other weapons of defence. News soon came[57] to us that the sheriff, with his under officers, together with some sixty or seventy men who were at work on the canal, were on the road between Buffalo and Black Rock, and that they intended to re-take the slaves when we should attempt to take them to the ferry to convey them to Canada. This news was anything but pleasant to us, but we prepared for the worst.

Notes

[57] *Original reads*: come [ed.].

We returned to the city about two o'clock in the afternoon, and about four we started for Black Rock ferry, which is about three miles below Buffalo. We had in our company some fifty or more able-bodied, resolute men, who were determined to stand by the slaves, and who had resolved, before they left the city, that if the sheriff and his men took the slaves, they should first pass over their dead bodies.

We started, and when about a mile below the city, the sheriff and his men came upon us, and surrounded us. The slaves were in a carriage, and the horses were soon stopped, and we found it advisable to take them out of the carriage, and we did so. The sheriff came forward, and read something purporting to be a "Riot Act," and at the same time called upon all good citizens to aid him in keeping the "peace." This was a trick of his, to get possession of the slaves. His men rushed upon us with their clubs and stones, and a general fight ensued. Our company had surrounded the slaves, and had succeeded in keeping the sheriff and his men off. We fought, and at the same time kept pushing on towards the ferry.

In the midst of the fight, a little white man made his appearance among us, and proved to be a valuable friend. His name was Pepper; and he proved himself a *pepper* to the sheriff and his posse that day. He was a lawyer; and as the officers would arrest any of our company, he would step up and ask the officer if he had a "warrant to take that man"; and as none of them had warrants, and could not answer affirmatively, he would say to the colored man, "He has no right to take you; knock him down." The command was no sooner given than the man would fall. If the one who had been arrested was not able to knock him down, some who were close by, and who were armed with a club or other weapon, would come to his assistance.

After it became generally known in our company that the "little man" was a lawyer, he had a tremendous influence with them. You could hear them cry out occasionally, "That's right, knock him down; the little man told you to do it, and he is a lawyer; he knows all about the law; that's right – hit him again! he is a white man, and he has done our color enough."

Such is but a poor representation of what was said by those who were engaged in the fight. After a hard-fought battle, of nearly two hours, we arrived at the ferry, the slaves still in our possession. On arriving at the ferry, we found that some of the sheriff's gang had taken possession of the ferry-boat. Here another battle was to be fought, before the slaves could reach Canada. The boat was fastened at each end by a chain, and in the scuffle for the ascendency, one party took charge of one end of the boat, while the other took the other end. The blacks were commanding the ferryman to carry them over, while the whites were commanding him not to. While each party was contending for power, the slaves were pushed on board, and the boat shoved from the wharf. Many of the blacks jumped on board of the boat, while the whites jumped on shore. And the swift current of the Niagara soon carried them off, amid the shouts of the blacks, and the oaths and imprecations of the whites. We on shore swung our hats and gave three cheers, just as a reinforcement came to the whites. Seeing the odds entirely against us in numbers, and having gained the great victory, we gave up without resistance, and suffered ourselves to be arrested by the sheriff's posse. However, we all remained on the shore until the ferry-boat had landed on the Canada side. As the boat landed, Stanford leaped on shore, and rolled over in the sand, and even rubbed it into his hair.

I did not accompany the boat over, but those who did informed us that Mrs. Stanford, as she stepped on the shore, with her child in her arms, exclaimed, "I thank God that I am again in Canada!" We returned to the city, and some forty of our company were lodged in jail, to await their trial the next morning.

And now I will return to the betrayer. On our return to Buffalo, she was given over to a committee of women, who put her in a room, and put a guard over her. Tate, who had been very active from the time that he heard that we had recaptured the carriage with the slaves, was still in the city. He was not with the slaves when we caught up with them at Hamburgh, nor was he to be found in the fight. He sent his hirelings, while he remained at the hotel drinking champagne. As soon as he found the slaves were out of his reach, he then made an offer of fifty dollars to any person who would find the betrayer. He pretended that he wished to save her from the indignation of the colored people. But the fact is, he had promised her that if she would accompany him to the south, that he would put her in a situation where she would be a lady. Poor woman! She was foolish enough to believe him; and now that the people had lost all sympathy for her, on account of her traitorous act, he still thought that, by pretending to be her friend, he could induce her to go to the south, that he might sell her. But those who had her in charge were determined that she should be punished for being engaged in this villanous transaction.

Several meetings were held to determine what should be done with her. Some were in favor of hanging her, others for burning her, but a majority were for taking her to the Niagara river, tying a fifty-six pound weight to her, and throwing her in. There seemed to be no way in which she could be reached by the civil law. She was kept in confinement three days, being removed to different places each night.

So conflicting were the views of those who had her in charge that they could not decide upon what should be done with her. However, there seemed to be such a vast majority in favor of throwing her into the Niagara River[58] that some of us, who were opposed to taking life, succeeded in having her given over to another committee, who, after reprimanding her, let her go.

Tate, in the meantime,[59] hearing that the colored people had resolved to take vengeance on him, thought it best to leave the city. On Monday, at ten o'clock, we were all carried before Justice Grosvenor; and of the forty who had been committed the evening before, twenty-five were held to bail to answer to a higher court. When the trials came on, we were fined more or less, from five to fifty dollars each.

During the fight no one was killed, though there were many broken noses and black eyes; one young man, who was attached to a theatrical corps, was so badly injured in the conflict that he died some three months after.

Thus ended one of the most fearful fights for human freedom that I ever witnessed. The reader will observe that this conflict took place on the Sabbath, and that those who were foremost in getting it up were officers of justice. The plea of the sheriff and his posse was that we were breaking the Sabbath by assembling in such large numbers to protect a brother slave and his wife and child from being dragged back into slavery which is far worse than death itself.

From *The Liberty Bell* of 1848

The American Slave-trade

By William Wells Brown

Of the many features which American slavery presents, the most cruel is that of the slave-trade. A traffic in the bodies and souls of native-born Americans is carried on in the slave-holding states to an extent little dreamed of by the great mass of the people in the non-slave-holding states. The precise number of slaves carried from the slave-raising

Notes

[58] *Original reads*: Niagara river [ed.].

[59] *Original reads*: mean time [ed.].

to the slave-consuming states we have no means of knowing. But it must be very great, as forty thousand were sold and carried out of the State of Virginia in one single year!

This heart-rending and cruel traffic is not confined to any particular class of persons. No person forfeits his or her character or standing in society by being engaged in raising and selling slaves to supply the cotton, sugar, and rice plantations of the south. Few persons who have visited the slave states have not, on their return, told of the gangs of slaves they had seen on their way to the southern market. This trade presents some of the most revolting and atrocious scenes which can be imagined. Slave-prisons, slave-auctions, handcuffs, whips, chains, bloodhounds, and other instruments of cruelty, are part of the furniture which belongs to the American slave-trade. It is enough to make humanity bleed at every pore, to see these implements of torture.

Known to God only is the amount of human agony and suffering which sends its cry from these slave-prisons, unheard or unheeded by man, up to His ear; mothers weeping for their children – breaking the night-silence with the shrieks of their breaking hearts. We wish no human being to experience emotions of needless pain, but we do wish that every man, woman, and child in New England could visit a southern slave-prison and auction-stand.

I shall never forget a scene which took place in the city of St. Louis, while I was in slavery. A man and his wife, both slaves, were brought from the country to the city, for sale. They were taken to the rooms of Austin & Savage, auctioneers. Several slave-speculators, who are always to be found at auctions where slaves are to be sold, were present. The man was first put up, and sold to the highest bidder. The wife was next ordered to ascend the platform. I was present. She slowly obeyed the order. The auctioneer commenced, and soon several hundred dollars were bid. My eyes were intensely fixed on the face of the woman, whose cheeks were wet with tears. But a conversation between the slave and his new master attracted my attention. I drew near them to listen. The slave was begging his new master to purchase his wife. Said he, "Master, if you will only buy Fanny, I know you will get the worth of your money. She is a good cook, a good washer, and her last mistress liked her very much. If you will only buy her how happy I shall be." The new master replied that he did not want her but if she sold cheap he would purchase her. I watched the countenance of the man while the different persons were bidding on his wife. When his new master bid on his wife you could see the smile upon his countenance, and the tears stop; but as soon as another would bid, you could see the countenance change and the tears start afresh. From this change of countenance one could see the workings of the inmost soul. But this suspense did not last long; the wife was struck off to the highest bidder, who proved not to be the owner of her husband. As soon as they became aware that they were to be separated, they both burst into tears; and as she descended from the auction-stand, the husband, walking up to her and taking her by the hand, said, "Well, Fanny, we are to part forever, on earth; you have been a good wife to me. I did all that I could to get my new master to buy you; but he did not want you, and all I have to say is, I hope you will try to meet me in heaven. I shall try to meet you there." The wife made no reply, but her sobs and cries told, too well, her own feelings. I saw the countenances of a number of whites who were present, and whose eyes were dim with tears at hearing the man bid his wife farewell.

Such are but common occurrences in the slave states. At these auction-stands, bones, muscles, sinews, blood and nerves, of human beings, are sold with as much indifference as a farmer in the north sells a horse or sheep. And this great American nation is, at the present time, engaged in the slave-trade. I have before me now the Washington "Union," the organ of the government, in which I find an advertisement of several slaves to be sold for the benefit of the government. They will, in all human probability, find homes among the rice-swamps of Georgia, or the cane-brakes of Mississippi.

With every disposition on the part of those who are engaged in it to veil the truth, certain facts have, from time to time, transpired, sufficient to show, if not the full amount of the evil, at least that it is one of prodigious magnitude. And what is more to be wondered at, is the fact that the greatest slave-market is to be found at the capital of the country! The American slave-trader marches by the capitol with his "coffle-gang," – the stars and stripes waving over their heads, and the constitution of the United States in his pocket!

The Alexandria Gazette, speaking of the slave-trade at the capital, says, "Here you may behold fathers and brothers leaving behind them the dearest objects of affection, and moving slowly along in the mute agony of despair; there, the young mother, sobbing over the infant whose innocent smile seems but to increase her misery. From some you will hear the burst of bitter lamentation, while from others, the loud hysteric laugh breaks forth, denoting still deeper agony. Such is but a faint picture of the American slave-trade."

Boston, Massachusetts.

Flight of the Bondman

Dedicated to William W. Brown,

And sung by the Hutchinsons.

by Elias Smith.

From the crack of the rifle and baying of hound,
  Takes the poor panting bondman his flight;
His couch through the day is the cold damp ground,
  But northward he runs through the night.

O, God speed the flight of the desolate slave,
  Let his heart never yield to despair;
There is room 'mong our hills for the true and the brave,
  Let his lungs breathe our free northern air!

O sweet to the storm-driven sailor the light,
  Streaming far o'er the dark swelling wave:
But sweeter by far 'mong the lights of the night,
  Is the star of the north to the slave.

Cold and bleak are our mountains and chilling our winds,
  But warm as the soft southern gales
Be the hands and the hearts which the hunted one finds,
  'Mong our hills and our own winter vales.

Then list to the 'plaint of the heart-broken thrall,
  Ye blood-hounds, go back to your lair;
May a free northern soil soon give freedom to *all*,
  Who shall breathe in its pure mountain air.

Freedom's Star

Respectfully Dedicated to William Wells Brown, as a testimony of regard for his uncompromising advocacy of the cause of his enslaved brothers and sisters, by D. B. Harris.

As I strayed from my cot at the close of the day,
I turned my fond gaze to the sky;
I beheld all the stars as so sweetly they lay,
And but one fixed my heart or my eye.

Shine on, northern star, thou 'rt beautiful and bright
To the slave on his journey afar;
For he speeds from his foes in the darkness of night,
Guided on by thy light, freedom's star.

On thee he depends when he threads the dark woods,
Ere the bloodhounds have hunted him back;
Thou leadest him on over mountains and floods,
With thy beams shining full on his track.

Unwelcome to him is the bright orb of day,
As it glides o'er the earth and the sea;
He seeks then to hide like a wild beast of prey,
But with hope, rests his heart upon thee.

May never a cloud overshadow thy face,
While the slave flies before his pursuer;
Gleam steadily on to the end of his race,
Till his body and soul are secure.

Lament of the Fugitive Slave

"My child, we must soon part, to meet no more this side of the grave. You have ever said that you would not die a slave; that you would be a free man. Now try to get your liberty!" W. W. Brown's Narrative.

I've wandered out beneath the moonlit heaven,
Lost mother! loved and dear,
To every beam a magic power seems given
To bring thy spirit near;
For though the breeze of freedom fans my brow,
My soul still turns to thee! oh, where art thou?

Where art thou, mother? I am weary thinking;
A heritage of pain and woe
Was thine – beneath it art thou slowly sinking,
Or hast thou perished long ago?
And doth thy spirit 'mid the quivering leaves above me,
Hover, dear mother, to guard and love me?

I murmur at my lot; in the white man's dwelling
  The mother there is found;
Or he may tell where spring-buds first are swelling
  Above her lowly mound;
But thou, – lost mother, every trace of thee
In the vast sepulchre of Slavery!

Long years have fled, since sad, faint-hearted,
  I stood on Freedom's shore,
And knew, dear mother, from thee I was parted,
  To meet thee never more;
And deemed the tyrant's chain with thee were better
Than stranger hearts and limbs without a fetter.

Yet blessings on thy Roman-mother spirit;
  Could I forget it, then,
The parting scene, and struggle not to inherit
  A freeman's birth-right once again?
O noble words! O holy love, which gave
Thee strength to utter them, a poor, heart-broken slave.

Be near me, mother, be thy spirit near me,
  Wherever thou may'st be;
In hours like this bend near that I may hear thee,
  And know that thou art free;
Summoned at length from bondage, toil and pain,
To God's free world, a world without a chain!

1847, 1850

The Escape; or, a Leap for Freedom: A Drama in Five Acts

Author's preface

This play is solely written for my own amusement, and not with the remotest thought that it would ever be seen by the public eye. I read it privately however, to a circle of my friends, and through them was invited to read it before a Literary Society. Since then, the Drama has been given in various parts of the country. By the earnest solicitation of some in whose judgment I have the greatest confidence, I now present it in printed form to the public. As I never aspired to be a dramatist, I ask no favor for it, and have little or no solicitude for its fate. If it is not readable, no word of mine can make it so: if it is, to ask favor for it would be needless.

The main features in the Drama are true. Glen and Melinda are actual characters, and still reside in Canada. Many of the incidents were drawn from my own experience of eighteen years at the South. The marriage ceremony, as performed in the second act, is still adhered to in many of the Southern States, especially in the farming districts.

The ignorance of the slave, as seen in the case of "Big Sally," is common wherever chattel slavery exists. The difficulties created in the domestic circle by the presence of beautiful slave women, as found in Dr. Gaines's family, is well understood by all who have ever visited the valley of the Mississippi.

The play, no doubt, abounds in defects, but as I was born in slavery and never had a day's schooling in my life, I owe the public no apology for my errors.

W.W.B.

Characters represented

Dr. Gaines, *proprietor of the farm at Muddy Creek.*
Rev. John Pinchen, *a clergyman.*
Dick Walker, *a slave speculator.*
Mr. Wildmarsh, *neighbor to Dr. Gaines.*
Major Moore, *a friend of Dr. Gaines.*
Mr. White, *a citizen of Massachusetts.*
Bill Jennings, *a slave speculator.*
Jacob Scragg, *overseer to Dr. Gaines.*
Mrs. Gaines, *wife of Dr. Gaines.*
Mr. and Mrs. Neal, and Daughter, *Quakers, in Ohio.*
Thomas, *Mr. Neal's hired man.*
Glen, *slave of Mr. Hamilton, brother-in-law of Dr. Gaines.*
Cato, Sam, Sampey, Melinda, Dolly, Susan, and Big Sally, *slaves of Dr. Gaines.*
Pete, Ned, and Bill,
Officers, Loungers, Barkeeper, *&c.*

Act I

Scene 1 – A sitting-room.

[Mrs. Gaines, *looking at some drawings* – Sampey, *a white slave,*[1] *stands behind the lady's chair.*

Enter Dr. Gaines, R.]

Dr. Gaines: Well, my dear, my practice is steadily increasing. I forgot to tell you that neighbor Wyman engaged me yesterday as his family physician; and I hope that the fever and ague, which is now taking hold of the people, will give me more patients. I see by the New Orleans papers that the yellow fever is raging there to a fearful extent. Men of my profession are reaping a harvest in that section of this year. I would that we could have a touch of the yellow fever here, for I think I could invent a medicine that would cure it. But the yellow fever is a luxury that we medical men in this climate can't expect to enjoy; yet we may hope for the cholera.

Mrs. Gaines: Yes, I would be glad to see it more sickly here, so that your business might prosper. But we are always unfortunate. Everybody[2] here seems to be in good health,

Notes

The Escape; or, a Leap for Freedom: A Drama in Five Acts

[1] *a white slave* Sampey has so much white blood within him that he appears to be white, but is nonetheless enslaved.

[2] *Original reads*: every body [ed.].

and I'm afraid that they'll keep so. However, we must hope for the best. We must trust in the Lord. Providence may possibly send some disease amongst us for our benefit.

[*Enter* Cato, R.]

Cato: Mr. Campbell is at de door, massa.
Dr. G: Ask him in, Cato.

[*Enter* Mr. Campbell, R.]

Dr. G: Good morning, Mr. Campbell. Be seated.
Mr. Campbell: Good morning, doctor. The same to you, Mrs. Gaines. Fine morning, this.
Mrs. G: Yes, sir; beautiful day.
Mr. C: Well, doctor, I've come to engage you for my family physician. I am tired of Dr. Jones. I've lost another very valuable nigger under his treatment; and, as my old mother used to say, "change of pastures makes fat calves."
Dr. G: I shall be most happy to become your doctor. Of course, you want me to attend to your niggers, as well as to your family?
Mr. C: Certainly, sir. I have twenty-three servants. What will you charge me by the year?
Dr. G: Of course, you'll do as my other patients do, send your servants to me when they are sick, if able to walk?
Mr. C: Oh, yes; I always do that.
Dr. G: Then I suppose I'll have to lump it, and say $500 per annum.
Mr. C: Well, then, we'll consider that matter settled; and as two of the boys are sick, I'll send them over. So I'll bid you good day, doctor. I would be glad if you came over some time, and bring Mrs. Gaines with you.
Dr. G: Yes, I will; and shall be glad if you pay us a visit, and bring with you Mrs. Campbell. Come over and spend the day.
Mr. C: I will. Good morning, doctor.

[*Exit* Mr. Campbell, R.]

Dr. G: There, my dear, what do you think of that? Five hundred dollars more added to our income. That's patronage worth having! And I am glad to get all the negroes I can to doctor, for Cato is becoming very useful to me in the shop. He can bleed, pull teeth, and do almost anything[3] that the blacks require. He can put up medicine as well as anyone.[4] A valuable boy, Cato!
Mrs. G: But why did you ask Mr. Campbell to visit you, and to bring his wife? I am sure I could never consent to associate with her, for I understand that she was the daughter of a tanner. You must remember, my dear, that I was born with a silver spoon in my mouth. The blood of the Wyleys runs in my veins. I am surprised that you should ask him to visit you at all; you should have known better.
Dr. G: Oh, I did not mean for him to visit me. I only invited him for the sake of compliments, and I think he so understood it; for I should be far from wishing you to associate with Mrs. Campbell. I don't forget, my dear, the family you were raised in, nor do I overlook my own family. My father, you know, fought by the side of Washington, and I hope someday[5] to have a handle[6] to my own name. I am certain Providence intended me for something higher than a medical man. Ah! by-the-by, I had forgotten that I have a couple of patients to visit this morning, I must go at once.

Notes

[3] *Original reads*: any thing [ed.].
[4] *Original reads*: any one [ed.].
[5] *Original reads*: some day [ed.].
[6] *handle* a title.

[*Exit* Dr. Gaines, R.]

[*Enter* Hannah, L.]

Mrs. G: Go, Hannah, and tell Dolly to kill a couple of fat pullets,[7] and to put the biscuit to rise. I expect brother Pinchen here this afternoon, and I want everything in order. Hannah, Hannah, tell Melinda to come here.

[*Exit* Hannah, L.]

We mistresses do have a hard time in this world; I don't see why the Lord should have imposed such heavy duties on us poor mortals. Well, it can't last always. I long to leave this wicked world, and go home to glory.

[*Enter* Melinda.]

I am to have company this afternoon, Melinda. I expect brother Pinchen here, and I want everything[8] in order. Go and get one of my new caps, with the lace border, and get out my scalloped-bottomed dimity[9] petticoat, and when you go out, tell Hannah to clean the white-handled knives, and see that not a speck is on them; for I want everything[10] as it should be while brother Pinchen is here.

[*Exit* Mrs. Gaines, L., Hannah, R.]

Scene 2 – Doctor's shop – Cato making pills.

[*Enter* Dr. Gaines, L.]

Dr. G: Well, Cato, have you made the batch of ointment that I ordered?

Cato: Yes, massa; I dun made de intment, an' now I is making the bread pills. De tater pills is up on the top shelf.

Dr. G: I am going out to see some patients. If any gentlemen call, tell them that I shall be in this afternoon. If any servants come, you attend to them. I expect two of Mr. Campbell's boys over. You see to them. Feel their pulse, look at their tongues, bleed them, and give each a dose of calomel.[11] Tell them to drink no cold water, and to take nothing but water gruel.

Cato: Yes, massa; I'll tend to 'em.

[*Exit* Dr. Gaines, L.]

Cato: I allers knowed I was a doctor, an' now de ole boss has put me at it, I muss change my coat. Ef any niggers comes in, I wants to look suspectable.[12] Dis jacket don't suit a doctor, I'll change it. [*Exit* Cato – *immediately returning in a long coat.*] Ah! now I looks like a doctor. Now I can bleed, pull teef, or cut off a leg. Oh! well, well, ef I aint put de pill stuff an' de intment stuff togedder. By golly, dat ole cuss will be mad when he finds it out, won't he? Nebber mind, I'll make it up in pills, and when de flour is on dem, he won't know what's in 'em; an' I'll make some new intment. Ah! yonder comes Campbell's Pete an' Ned; dems de ones massa sed was comin'. I'll see ef I looks right. [*Goes to the looking-glass and views himself.*] I em some punkins, ain't I? [*Knock at the door.*] Come in.

Notes

[7] *pullets* chickens.

[8] *Original reads*: every thing [ed.].

[9] *dimity* thin cotton fabric.

[10] *Original reads*: every thing [ed.].

[11] *calomel* white powder that acts as a diuretic.

[12] *suspectable* respectable.

[*Enter* Pete *and* Ned, R.]

Pete: Whar is de doctor?

Cato: Here I is; don't you see me?

Pete: But whar is de ole boss?

Cato: Dat's none you business. I dun tole you dat I is de doctor, an dat's enuff.

Ned: Oh! do tell us whar de doctor is. I is almos dead. Oh me! Oh dear me! I is so sick. [*Horrible faces.*]

Pete: Yes, do tell us; we don't want to stan here foolin'.

Cato: I tells you again dat I is de doctor. I larn de trade under massa.

Ned: Oh! well, den, give me somethin' to stop dis pain. Oh dear me! I shall die. [*He tries to vomit, but can't – ugly faces.*]

Cato: Let me feel your pulse. Now put out your tongue. You is berry sick. Ef you don't mine, you'll die. Come out in de shed, an' I'll bleed you. [*Exit all – re-enter.*]

Cato: Dar, now take dese pills, two in de mornin' and two at night, and ef you don't feel better, double de dose. Now, Mr. Pete, what's de matter wid you?

Pete: I is got de cole chills, an' has a fever in de night.

Cato: Come out, an' I'll bleed you.

[*Exit all – re-enter.*]

Now take dese pills, two in de mornin' and two at night, an' ef dey don't help you, double de dose. Ah! I like to forget to feel your pulse and look at your tongue. Put out your tongue. [*Feels his pulse.*] Yes, I tells by de feel ob your pulse dat I is gib you de right pills.

[*Enter* Mr. Parker's[13] Bill, L.]

Cato: What you come in dat door widout knockin' for?

Bill: My toof ache so, I didn't tink to knock. Oh, my toof! my toof! Whar is de doctor?

Cato: Here I is; don't you see me?

Bill: What! you de doctor, you brack[14] cuss! You looks like a doctor! Oh, my toof! my toof! Whar is de doctor?

Cato: I tells you I is de doctor. Ef you don't believe me, ax dese men. I can pull your toof in a minnit.

Bill: Well, den, pull it out. Oh, my toof! how it aches! Oh, my toof! [Cato *gets the rusty turnkeys.*]

Cato: Now lay down on your back.

Bill: What for?

Cato: Dat's de way massa does.

Bill: Oh, my toof! Well, den, come on. [*Lies down,* Cato *goes astraddle of* Bill*'s breast, puts the turnkeys on the wrong tooth, and pulls – Bill kicks, and cries out*] – Oh, do stop! Oh! oh! oh! [Cato *pulls the wrong tooth* – Bill *jumps up.*]

Cato: Dar, now, I tole you I could pull your toof for you.

Bill: Oh, dear me! Oh, it aches yet! Oh me! Oh, Lor-e-massy! You dun pull de wrong toof. Drat your skin! ef I don't pay you for this, you brack cuss! [*They fight, and turn over table, chairs, and bench –* Pete *and* Ned *look on.*]

[*Enter* Dr. Gaines, R.]

Dr. G: Why, dear me, what's the matter? What's this all about? I'll teach you a lesson, that I will. [*The* Doctor *goes at them with his cane.*]

Notes

13 *Original reads*: Parker's [ed.].

14 *brack* black.

CATO: Oh massa! he's to blame, sir. He's to blame. He struck me fuss.

BILL: No, sir; he's to blame; he pull de wrong toof. Oh, my toof! oh, my toof!

DR. G: Let me see your tooth. Open your mouth. As I live, you've taken out the wrong tooth. I am amazed. I'll whip you for this; I'll whip you well. You're a pretty doctor. Now lie down, Bill, and let him take out the right tooth; and if he makes a mistake this time, I'll cowhide him well. Lie down, Bill. [BILL *lies down, and* CATO *pulls the tooth.*] There now, why didn't you do that in the first place?

CATO: He wouldn't hole still, sir.

BILL: He lies, sir. I did hole still.

DR. G: Now go home, boys; go home.

[*Exit* PETE, NED *and* BILL,[15] L.]

DR. G: You've made a pretty muss of it, in my absence. Look at the table! Never mind, Cato; I'll whip you well for this conduct of yours today. Go to work now, and clear up the office.

[*Exit* DR. GAINES, R.]

CATO: Confound dat nigger! I wish he was in Ginny. He bite my finger and scratch my face. But didn't I give it to him? Well, den, I reckon I did. [*He goes to the mirror, and discovers that his coat is torn – weeps.*] Oh, dear me! Oh, my coat – my coat is tore! Dat nigger has tore my coat. [*He gets angry, and rushes about the room frantic.*] Cuss dat nigger! Ef I could lay my hands on him, I'd tare him all to pieces – dat I would. An' de ole boss hit me wid his cane after dat nigger tore my coat. By golly, I wants to fight somebody. Ef ole massa should come in now, I'd fight him. [*Rolls up sleeves.*] Let 'em come now, ef dey dare – ole massa, or any body else; I'm ready for 'em.

[*Enter* DR. GAINES, R.]

DR. G: What's all this noise here?

CATO: Nuffin', sir; only juss I is puttin' things to rights, as you tole me. I didn't hear any noise except de rats.

DR. G: Make haste, and come in; I want you to go to town.

[*Exit* DR. GAINES, R.]

CATO: By golly, de ole boss like to cotch me dat time, didn't he? But wasn't I mad? When I was mad, nobody can do nuffin' wid me. But here's my coat, tore to pieces. Cuss dat nigger! [*Weeps.*] Oh, my coat! oh, my coat! I rudder he had broke my head den to tore my coat. Drat dat nigger! Ef he ever comes here agin, I'll pull out every toof he's got in his head – dat I will.

[*Exit*, R.]

Scene 3 – A room in the quarters.

[*Enter* GLEN, L.]

GLEN: How slowly the time passes away. I've been waiting here two hours, and Melinda has not yet come. What keeps her, I cannot tell. I waited long and late for her last night, and when she approached, I sprang to my feet, caught her in my arms, pressed

Notes

[15] *Original reads*: Bill [ed.].

her to my heart, and kissed away the tears from her moistened cheeks. She placed her trembling hand in mine, and said, "Glen, I am yours; I will never be the wife of another." I clasped her to my bosom, and called God to witness that I would ever regard her as my wife. Old Uncle Joseph joined us in holy wedlock by moonlight; that was the only marriage ceremony. I look upon the vow as ever binding on me, for I am sure that a just God will sanction our union in heaven. Still, this man, who claims Melinda as his property, is unwilling for me to marry the woman of my choice, because he wants her himself. But he shall not have her. What will he say when he finds out that we are married, I cannot tell; but I am determined to protect my wife or die. Ah! here comes Melinda.

[*Enter* MELINDA, R.]

I am glad to see you, Melinda. I've been waiting long, and feared you would not come. Ah! in tears again?

MELINDA: Glen, you are always thinking I am in tears. But what did master say to-day?

GLEN: He again forbade our union.

MELINDA: Indeed! Can he be so cruel?

GLEN: Yes, he can be just so cruel.

MELINDA: Alas! alas! how unfeeling and heartless! But did you appeal to his generosity?

GLEN: Yes, I did; I used all the persuasive powers that I was master of but to no purpose; he was inflexible. He even offered me a new suit of clothes, if I would give you up; and when I told him that I could not, he said he would flog me to death if I ever spoke to you again.

MELINDA: And what did you say to him?

GLEN: I answered, that, while I loved life better than death, even life itself could not tempt me to consent to a separation that would make life an unchanging curse. Oh, I would kill myself, Melinda, if I thought that, for the sake of life, I could consent to your degradation. No, Melinda, I can die, but shall never live to see you the mistress of another man. But, my dear girl, I have a secret to tell you, and no one must know it but you. I will go out and see that no person is within hearing. I will be back soon.

[*Exit* GLEN, L.]

MELINDA: It is often said that the darkest hour of the night precedes the dawn. It is ever thus with the vicissitudes of human suffering. After the soul has reached the lowest depths of despair, and can no deeper plunge amid its rolling, foetid[16] shades, than the reactionary force of man's nature begin to operate, resolution takes the place of despondency, energy succeeds instead of apathy, and an upward tendency is felt and exhibited. Men then hope against power, and smile in defiance of despair. I shall never forget when first I saw Glen. It is now more than a year since he came here with his master, Mr. Hamilton. It was a glorious moonlight night in autumn. The wide and fruitful face of nature was silent and buried in repose. The tall trees on the borders of Muddy Creek waved their leafy branches in the breeze, which was wafted from afar, refreshing over hill and vale, over the rippling water, and the waving corn and wheat fields. The starry sky was studded over with a few light, flitting clouds, while the moon, as if rejoicing to witness the meeting of two hearts

Notes

[16] *foetid* fetid, or stinking.

that should be cemented by the purest love, sailed triumphantly along among the shifting vapors.

Oh, how happy I have been in my acquaintance with Glen! That he loves me, I do well believe it; that I love him, it is most true. Oh, how I would that those who think the slave incapable of the finer feelings could only see our hearts, and learn our thoughts – thoughts that we dare not utter in the presence of our masters! But I fear that Glen will be separated from me, for there is nothing too base and mean for masters to do, for the purpose of getting me entirely in his power. But, thanks to Heaven, he does not own Glen, and therefore cannot sell him. Yet he might purchase him from his brother-in-law, so as to send him out of the way. But here comes my husband.

[*Enter* Glen, L.]

Glen: I've been as far as the overseer's house, and all is quiet. Now, Melinda, as you are my wife, I will confide to you a secret. I've long been thinking of making my escape to Canada, and taking you with me. It is true that I don't belong to your master, but he might buy me from Hamilton, and then sell me out of the neighborhood.

Melinda: But we could never succeed in the attempt to escape.

Glen: We will make the trial, and show that we at least deserve success. There is a slave trader expected here next week, and Dr. Gaines would sell you at once if he knew that we were married. We must get ready and start, and if we can pass the Ohio river, we'll be safe on the road to Canada.

[*Exit*, R.]

Scene 4 – Dining-room.

[Rev. Mr. Pinchen *giving* Mrs. Gaines *an account of his experience as a minister* – Hannah *clearing away the breakfast table* – Sampey *standing behind* Mrs. Gaines' *chair*.]

Mrs. Gaines: Now, do give me more of your experience, brother Pinchen. It always does my soul good to hear religious experience. It draws me nearer and nearer to the Lord's side. I do love to hear good news from God's people.

Mr. Pinchen: Well, sister Gaines, I've had great opportunities in my time to study the heart of man. I've attended a great many camp-meetings, revival meetings, protracted meetings,[17] and death-bed scenes, and I am satisfied, sister Gaines, that the heart of man is full of sin, and desperately wicked. This is a wicked world, sister Gaines, a wicked world.

Mrs. G: Were you ever in Arkansas, brother Pinchen? I've been told that the people out there are very ungodly.

Mr. P: Oh yes, sister Gaines. I once spent a year at Little Rock, and preached in all the towns round about there; and I found some hard cases out there, I can tell you. I was once spending a week in a district where there were a great many horse thieves, and one night, somebody stole my pony. Well, I knowed it was no use to make a fuss, so I told brother Tarbox to say nothing about it, and I'd get my horse by preaching God's everlasting gospel; for I had faith in the truth, and knowed that my savior would not let me lose my pony. So the next Sunday I preached on horse-stealing,

Notes

[17] *protracted meetings* lengthy religious meetings that can last several days.

and told the brethren to come up in the evenin' with their hearts filled with the grace of God. So that night the house was crammed brim full of anxious souls, panting for the bread of life. Brother Bingham opened with prayer, and brother Tarbox followed, and I saw right off that we were gwine to have a blessed time. After I got 'em all pretty warmed up, I jumped on to one of the seats, stretched out my hands, and said, "I know who stole my pony; I've found out; and you are in here tryin' to make people believe that you've got religion; but you ain't got it. And if you don't take my horse back to brother Tarbox's pasture this very night, I'll tell your name right out in meetin' tomorrow night. Take my pony back, you vile and wretched sinner, and come up here and give your heart to God." So the next mornin', I went out to brother Tarbox's pasture, and sure enough, there was my bobtail pony. Yes, sister Gaines, there he was, safe and sound. Ha, ha, ha.

Mrs. G: Oh, how interesting, and how fortunate for you to get your pony! And what power there is in the gospel! God's children are very lucky. Oh, it is so sweet to sit here and listen to such good news from God's people! You Hannah, what are you doing standing there listening for, and neglecting your work? Never mind, my lady, I'll whip you well when I'm done here. Go at your work this moment, you lazy huzzy! Never mind, I'll whip you well. [*Aside*] Come, do go on, brother Pinchen, with your godly conversation. It is so sweet! It draws me nearer and nearer to the Lord's side.

Mr. P: Well, sister Gaines, I've had some mighty queer dreams in my time, that I have. You see, one night I dreamed that I was dead and in heaven, and such a place I never saw before. As soon as I entered the gates of the celestial empire I saw many old and familiar faces that I had seen before. The first person that I saw was good old Elder Pike, the preacher that first called my attention to religion. The next person I saw was Deacon Billings, my first wife's father, and then I saw a host of godly faces. Why, sister Gaines, you knowed Elder Goosbee, didn't you?

Mrs. G: Why, yes; did you see him there? He married me to my first husband.

Mr. P: Oh, yes, sister Gaines, I saw the old Elder, and he looked for all the world as if he had just come out of a revival meetin'.

Mrs. G: Did you see my first husband there, brother Pinchen?

Mr. P: No, sister Gaines, I didn't see brother Pepper there; but I've no doubt but that brother Pepper was there.

Mrs. G: Well, I don't know; I have my doubts. He was not the happiest man in the world. He was always borrowing trouble about something or another. Still, I saw some happy moments with Mr. Pepper. I was happy when I made his acquaintance, happy during our courtship, happy a while after our marriage, and happy when he died. [*Weeps.*]

Hannah: Massa Pinchen, did you see my ole man Ben up dar in hebben?

Mr. P: No, Hannah; I didn't go amongst the niggers.

Mrs. G: No, of course Pinchen didn't go amongst the blacks. What are you asking questions for? Never mind, my lady, I'll whip you well when I'm done here. I'll skin you from head to foot. [*Aside.*] Do go on with your heavenly conversation, brother Pinchen; it does my very soul good. This is indeed a precious moment for me. I do love to hear of God and Him crucified.

Mr. P: Well, sister Gaines, I promised sister Daniels that I'd come over and see her this morning, and have a little season of prayer with her, and I suppose I must go. I'll tell you more of my religious experience when I return.

Mrs. G: If you must go, then I'll have to let you; but before you do, I wish to get your advice upon a little matter that concerns Hannah. Last week, Hannah stole a goose, killed it, cooked it, and she and her man Sam had a fine time eating the goose; and her master and I would never have known a word about it, if it had not been for Cato, a faithful servant, who told his master. And then, you see, Hannah had to be severely whipped before she'd confess that she stole the goose. Next Sabbath is sacrament day, and I want to know if you think Hannah is fit to go to the Lord's supper after stealing the goose.

MR. P: Well, sister Gaines, that depends on circumstances. If Hannah has confessed that she stole the goose, and has been sufficiently whipped, and has begged her master's pardon, and thinks she'll never do the like again, why then I suppose she can go to the Lord's supper; for

"While the lamp holds out to burn,
The vilest sinner may return."

But she must be sure that she has repented, and won't steal any more.

MRS. G: Now, Hannah, do you hear that? For my own part, I don't think she's fit to go to the Lord's supper, for she had no occasion to steal the goose. We give our niggers plenty of good wholesome food. They have a full run to the meal tub, meat once a fortnight, and all the sour milk about the place, and I'm sure there's enough for anyone.[18] I do think that our niggers are the most ungrateful creatures in the world, that I do. They aggravate my life out of me.

HANNAH: I know, missis, dat I steal de goose, and massa whip me for it, and I confess it, and I is sorry for it. But, missis, I is gwine to de Lord's supper, next Sunday, kase I ain't agwine to turn my back on my bressed Lord an' Massa for no old tough goose, dat I ain't. [*Weeps.*]

MR. P: Well, sister Gaines, I suppose I must go over and see sister Daniels; she'll be waiting for me.

[*Exit* MR. PINCHEN, M.D.]

MRS. G: Now, Hannah, brother Pinchen is gone, do you get the cowhide and follow me to the cellar, and I'll whip you well for aggravating me as you have to-day. It seems as if I can never sit down to take a little comfort with the Lord, without you crossing me. The devil always puts it into your head to disturb me, just when I'm trying to serve the Lord. I've no doubt but that I'll miss going to heaven on your account. But I'll whip you well before I leave this world, that I will. Get the cowhide and follow me to the cellar.

[*Exit* MRS. GAINES *and* HANNAH, R.]

Act 2

Scene 1 – Parlor.

[DR. GAINES *at a table, letters and papers before him.*
Enter SAMPEY, L.]

SAMPEY: Dar's a gemman at de doe, massa, dat wants to see you, seer.
DR. GAINES: Ask him to walk in, Sampey.

Notes

[18] *Original reads*: any one [ed.].

[*Exit* SAMPEY, L.]

[*Enter* WALKER.][19]

WALKER: Why, how do you do Dr. Gaines? I em glad to see you, I'll swear.

DR. G: How do you do, Mr. Walker? I did not expect to see you up here so soon. What has hurried you?

WALK: Well, you see, doctor, I comes when I em not expected. The price of niggers is up, and I em gwine to take advantage of the times. Now, doctor, ef you've got any niggers that you wants to sell, I em your man. I am paying the highest price of any-body[20] in the market. I pay cash down, and no grumblin'.

DR. G: I don't know that I want to sell any of my people now. Still, I've got to make up a little money next month, to pay in bank; and another thing, the doctors say we are likely to have a touch of cholera this summer, and if that's the case, I suppose I had better turn as many of my slaves into cash as I can.

WALK: Yes, doctor, that is very true. The cholera is death on slaves, and a thousand dollars in your pocket is a great deal better than a nigger in the field, with cholera at his heels. Why, who is that coming up the lane? It's Mr. Wildmarsh, as I live! Jest the very man I wants to see.

[*Enter* MR. WILDMARSH.]

Why, how do you do squire? I was jest thinkin' about you.

WILDMARSH: How are you Mr. Walker? and how are you, doctor? I am glad to see you both looking so well. You seem in remarkably good health, doctor?

DR. G: Yes, Squire, I was never in the enjoyment of better health. I hope you left all well at Licking?

WILD: Yes, I thank you. And now, Mr. Walker, how goes times with you?

WALK: Well, you see, Squire, I em in good spirits. The price of niggers is up in the market, and I'm looking out for bargains; and I was just intendin' to come over to Lickin' to see you, to see if you had any niggers to sell. But it seems as ef the Lord knowed that I wanted to see you, and directed your steps over here. Now, Squire, ef you've got any niggers you wants to sell, I em your man. I am payin' the highest cash price of anybody[21] in the market. Now's your time, Squire.

WILD: No, I don't think I want to sell any of my slaves now. I sold a very valuable gal to Mr. Haskins last week. I tell you, she was a smart one. I got eighteen hundred dollars for her.

WALK: Why, Squire, how you do talk! Eighteen hundred dollars for one gal? She must have been a screamer to bring that price. What sort of a lookin' critter was she? I should like to have bought her.

WILD: She was a little of the smartest gal I've ever raised; that she was.

WALK: Then she was of your own raising, was she?

WILD: Oh, yes; she was raised on my place, and if I could have kept her three or four years longer, and taken her to the market myself, I am sure I could have sold her for three thousand dollars. But you see, Mr. Walker, my wife got a little jealous, and you know jealousy sets the women's heads a teetering, and so I had to sell the gal. She's got straight hair, blue eyes, prominent features, and is almost white. Haskins will make a spec, and no mistake.

Notes

[19] *Walker* also the name of the slave trader Brown worked for in his *Narrative*.

[20] *Original reads*: any body [ed.].

[21] *Original reads*: any body [ed.].

WALK: Why, Squire, was she that pretty little gal that I saw on your knee the day that your wife was gone, when I was at your place three years ago?

WILD: Yes, the same.

WALK: Well, now, Squire, I thought that was your daughter; she looked mightily like you. She was your daughter, wasn't she? You need not be ashamed to own it to me, for I am mum upon such matters.

WILD: You know, Mr. Walker, that people will talk, and when they talk, they say a great deal; and people did talk, and many said the gal was my daughter; and you know we can't help people's talking. But here comes the Rev. Mr. Pinchen; I didn't know that he was in the neighborhood.

WALK: It is Mr. Pinchen, as I live; jest the very man I wants to see.

[*Enter* MR. PINCHEN, R.]

Why, how do you do, Mr. Pinchen? What in the name of Jehu[22] brings you down here to Muddy Creek? Any camp-meetins, revival meetins, deathbed scenes, or anything[23] else in your line going on down there? How is religion prosperin' now, Mr. Pinchen? I always like to hear about religion.

MR. PIN: Well, Mr. Walker, the Lord's work is in good condition everywhere[24] now. I tell you, Mr. Walker, I've been in the gospel ministry these thirteen years, and I am satisfied that the heart of man is full of sin and desperately wicked. This is a wicked world, Mr. Walker, a wicked world, and we ought all of us to have religion. Religion is a good thing to live by, and we all want it when we die. Yes, sir, when the great trumpet blows, we ought to be ready. And a man in your business of buying and selling slaves needs religion more than anybody[25] else, for it makes you treat your people as you should. Now, there is Mr. Haskins – he is a slave-trader, like yourself. Well, I converted him. Before he got religion, he was one of the worst men to his niggers I ever saw; his heart was as hard as stone. But religion has made his heart as soft as a piece of cotton. Before I converted him, he would sell husbands from their wives, and seem to take delight in it; but now he won't sell a man from his wife, if he can get anyone[26] to buy both of them together. I tell you, sir, religion has done wonderful work for him.

WALK: I know, Mr. Pinchen, that I ought to have religion, and I feel that I am a great sinner; and whenever I get with pious people like you and the doctor, and Mr. Wildmarsh, it always makes me feel that I am a desperate sinner. I feel it the more, because I've got a religious turn of mind. I know that I would be happier with religion, and the first spare time I get, I am going to try to get it. I'll go to a protracted meeting, and I won't stop till I get religion. Yes, I'll scuffle with the Lord till I gets forgiven. But it always makes me feel bad to talk about religion, so I'll change the subject. Now, doctor, what about them thar niggers you thought you could sell me?

DR. GAINES: I'll see my wife, Mr. Walker, and if she is willing to part with Hannah, I'll sell you Sam and his wife, Hannah. Ah! here comes my wife; I'll mention it.

[*Enter* MRS. GAINES, L.]

Ah! my dear, I'm glad you've come. I was just telling Mr. Walker, that if you were willing to part with Hannah, I'd sell him Sam and Hannah.

Notes

[22] *Jehu* Israelite King (see 2 Kings 9).

[23] *Original reads*: any thing [ed.].

[24] *Original reads*: every where [ed.].

[25] *Original reads*: any body [ed.].

[26] *Original reads*: any one [ed.].

Mrs. G: Now, Dr. Gaines, I am astonished and surprised that you should think of such a thing. You know what trouble I've had in training up Hannah for a house servant, and now that I've got her so that she knows my ways, you want to sell her. Haven't[27] you niggers enough on the plantation to sell, without selling the servants from under my very nose?

Dr. G: Oh, yes, my dear; but I can spare Sam, and don't like to separate him from his wife; and I thought if you could let Hannah go, I'd sell them both. I don't like to separate husbands from their wives.

Mrs. G: Now, gentlemen, that's just the way with my husband. He thinks more about the welfare and comfort of his slaves, than he does of himself or his family. I am sure you need not feel so bad at the thought of separating Sam from Hannah. They've only been married eight months. And their attachment can't be very strong in that short time. Indeed, I shall be glad if you do sell Sam, for then I'll make Hannah *jump the broomstick*[28] with Cato, and I'll have them both here under my eye. I never will again let one of my house servants marry a field hand – never! For when night comes on, the servants are off to the quarters, and I have to holler and holler enough to split my throat before I can make them hear. And another thing: I want you to sell Melinda. I don't intend to keep that mulatto wench about the house any longer.

Dr. Gaines: My dear, I'll sell any servant from the place to suit you, except Melinda. I can't think of selling her – I can't think of it.

Mrs. G: I tell you that Melinda shall leave this house, or I'll go. There, now you have it. I've had my life tormented out of me by the presence of that yellow wench, and I'll stand it no longer. I know you love her more than you do me, and I'll – I'll – I'll write – write to my father. [*Weeps.*]

[*Exit* Mrs. Gaines, L.]

Walk: Why, doctor, your wife's a screamer, ain't she? Ha, ha, ha. Why, doctor, she's got a tongue of her own, ain't she? Why, doctor, it was only last week that I thought of getting a wife myself; but your wife has skeered the idea out my head. Now, doctor, if you wants to sell the gal, I'll buy her. Husband and wife should be on good terms, and your wife won't feel well till the gal is gone. Now, I'll pay you all she's worth, if you wants to sell.

Dr. G: No, Mr. Walker; the girl my wife spoke of is not for sale. My wife does not mean what she says, she's only a little jealous. I'll get brother Pinchen to talk to her, and get her mind upon religious matters and then she'll forget it. She's only a little jealous.

Walk: I tell you what, doctor, ef you call that a little jealous, I'd like to know what's a heap. I tell you, it will take something more than religion to set your wife right. You had better sell me the gal; I'll pay you cash down, and no grumblin'.

Dr. G: The girl is not for sale, Mr. Walker; but if you want two good, able-bodied servants, I'll sell you Sam and Big Sally. Sam is trustworthy, and Sally is worth more than her weight in gold for rough usage.

Walk: Well, doctor, I'll go out and take a look at 'em, for I never buys slaves without examining them well, because they are sometimes injured by over-work or underfeedin'. I don't say that is the case with yours, for I don't believe it is; but as I sell on honor, I must buy on honor.

Dr. G: Walk out, sir, and you can examine them to your heart's content. Walk right out, sir.

Notes

[27] *Original reads*: Hav n't [ed.].

[28] *jump the broomstick* an unofficial marriage ritual for slaves.

Scene 2 – View in front of the great house.

[*Examination of* SAM *and* BIG SALLY – DR. GAINES, WILDMARSH, MR. PINCHEN *and* WALKER *present.*]

WALK: Well, my boy, what's your name?

SAM: Sam, sir, is my name.

WALK: How old are you, Sam?

SAM: Ef I live to see next corn plantin' time, I'll be 27, or 30, or 35, or 40 – I don't know which, sir.

WALK: Ha, ha, ha. Well, doctor, this is a rather green boy. Well, mer feller, are you sound?

SAM: Yes, sir, I spec I is.

WALK: Open your mouth and let me see your teeth. I allers judge a nigger's age by his teeth, same as I does a hoss. Ah! pretty good set of grinders. Have you got a good appetite?

SAM: Yes, sir.

WALK: Can you eat your allowance?

SAM: Yes, sir, when I can get it.

WALK: Get out on the floor and dance; I want to see if you are supple.

SAM: I don't like to dance; I is got religion.

WALK: Oh, ho! you've got religion, have you? That's so much the better. I likes to deal in the gospel. I think he'll suit me. Now, mer gal, what's your name?

SALLY: I is Big Sally, sir.

WALK: How old are you, Sally?

SALLY: I don't know, sir; but I heard once dat I was born at pertater diggin' time.

WALK: Ha, ha, ha. Don't know how old you are! Do you know who made you?

SALLY: I hev heard who it is in de Bible dat made me, but I dun forget de gentman's name.

WALK: Ha, ha, ha. Well, doctor, this is the greenest lot of niggers I've seen for some time. Well, what do you ask for them?

DR. GAINES: You may have Sam for $1000, and Sally for $900. They are worth all I ask for them. You know I never banter, Mr. Walker. There they are; you can take them at that price, or let them alone, just as you please.

WALK: Well, doctor, I reckon I'll take 'em; but it's all they are worth. I'll put handcuffs on 'em and then I'll pay you. I likes to go according to Scripter. Scripter says ef eating meat will offend your brother, you must quit it; and I says, ef leavin' your slaves without the handcuffs will make 'em run away, you mus put the handcuffs on 'em. Now, Sam, don't you and Sally cry. I am of a tender heart, an it allers makes me feel bad to see people cryin'. Don't cry, and the first place I get to, I'll buy each of you a great big *ginger cake* – that I will. Now, Mr. Pinchen, I wish you were going down the river. I'd like to have your company, for I allers likes the company of preachers.

MR. PINCHEN: Well, Mr. Walker, I would be much pleased to go down the river with you, but it's too early for me. I expect to go to Natchez in four or five weeks, to attend a camp-meetin', and if you were going down then, I'd like it. What kind of niggers sells best in the Orleans market, Mr. Walker?

WALK: Why, field hands. Did you think of goin' in the trade?

MR. P: Oh, no; only it's a long ways down to Natchez, and I thought I'd just buy five or six niggers, and take 'em down and sell 'em to pay for my travellin' expenses. I only want to clear my way.

Scene 3 – Sitting-room – table and rocking-chair.

[*Enter* Mrs. Gaines, R., *followed by* Sampey]

Mrs. Gaines: I do wish your master would come; I want supper. Run to the gate, Sampey, and see if he is coming.

[*Exit* Sampey, L.]

That man is enough to break my heart. The patience of an angel could not stand it.

[*Enter* Sampey, L.]

Samp: Yes, missis, master is coming.

[*Enter* Dr. Gaines, L.]

[*The* Doctor *walks about with his hands under his coat, seeming very much elated.*]

Mrs. Gaines: Why, doctor, what is the matter?

Dr. Gaines: My dear, don't call me *doctor*.

Mrs. G: What should I call you?

Dr. G: Call me Colonel, my dear – Colonel. I have been elected Colonel of Militia, and I want you to call me by my right name. I always felt that Providence had designed me for something great, and He has just begun to shower His Blessings upon me.

Mrs. G: Dear me, I could never get to calling you Colonel; I've called you Doctor for the last twenty years.

Dr. G: Now, Sarah, if you will call me Colonel, other people will, and I want you to set the example. Come, my darling, call me Colonel, and I'll give you anything[29] you wish for.

Mrs. G: Well, as I want a new gold watch and bracelets, I'll commence now. Come, Colonel, we'll go to supper. Ah! now for my new shawl. [*Aside.*] Mrs. Lemme was here to-day, Colonel, and she had on, Colonel, one of the prettiest shawls, Colonel, I think, Colonel, that I ever saw, Colonel, in my life, Colonel. An there is only one, Colonel, in Mr. Watson's store, Colonel; and that, Colonel, will do, Colonel, for a Colonel's wife.

Dr. G: Ah! my dear, you never looked so much the lady since I've known you. Go, my darling, get the watch, bracelets, and shawl, and tell them to charge them to Colonel Gaines; and when you say "Colonel," always emphasize the word.

Mrs. G: Come, Colonel, let's go to supper.

Dr. G: My dear, you're a jewel – you are!

[*Exit*, R.]

[*Enter* Cato, L.]

Cato: Why, whar is massa and missis? I tought dey was here. Ah! by golly, yonder comes a mulatter gal: Yes, it's Mrs. Jones's Tapioca. I'll set up to dat gal, dat I will.

[*Enter* Tapioca, R.]

Good ebenin', Miss Tappy. How is your folks?

Tapioca: Pretty well, I tank you.

Cato: Miss Tappy, dis wanderin' heart of mine is yours. Come, take a seat! Please to squze my manners; love discommodes me. Take a seat. Now, Miss Tappy, I loves you; an ef you will jess marry me, I'll make you a happy husbands, dat I will. Come, take me as I is.

Notes

[29] *Original reads*: any thing [ed.].

TAP: But what will Big Jim say?

CATO: Big Jim! Why, let dat nigger go to Ginny. I want to know, now, if you is tinkin' about dat common nigger? Why, Miss Tappy, I is surstonished dat you should tink 'bout frowin' yousef away wid a common, ugly lookin' cuss like Big Jim, when you can get a fine lookin', suspectable man like me. Come, Miss Tappy, choose dis day who you have. Afore I go any furder, give me one kiss. Come, give me one kiss. Come, let me kiss you.

TAP: No you shan't – dare now! You shan't kiss me widout you is stronger den I is and I know you is dat. [*He kisses her.*]

[*Enter* DR. GAINES, R, *and hides.*]

CATO: Did you know, Miss Tappy, dat I is de head doctor 'bout dis house? I beats de ole boss all to pieces.

TAP: I hev heard dat you bleeds and pulls teef.

CATO: Yes, Miss Tappy; massa could not get along widout me, for massa was made a doctor by books; but I is a natral doctor. I was born a doctor, jess as Lorenzo Dow was born a preacher. So you see I can't be nuffin' but a doctor, while massa is a bunglin' ole cuss at de bissness.

DR. GAINES: [*in a low voice.*] Never mind; I'll teach you a lesson, that I will.

CATO: You see, Miss Tappy, I was gwine to say – Ah! but afore I forget, jess give me anudder kiss, jess to keep company wid de one dat you gave me jess now – dat's all. [*Kisses her.*] Now, Miss Tappy, duse you know de fuss time dat I seed you?

TAP: No, Mr. Cato, I don't.

CATO: Well, it was at de camp-meetin'. Oh, Miss Tappy, dat pretty red calliker[30] dress you had on dat time did de work for me. It made my heart flutter –

DR. G: [*low voice.*] Yes, and I'll make your black hide flutter.

CATO: Didn't I hear some noise? By golly, dar is teves[31] in dis house, and I'll drive 'em out. [*Takes a chair and runs at the* DOCTOR, *and knocks him down. The* DOCTOR *chases* CATO *around the table.*] Oh, massa, I didn't know 'twas you!

DR. G: You scoundrel! I'll whip you well. Stop! I tell you.

[*Curtain falls.*]

Act 3

Scene 1 – Sitting-room.

[MRS. GAINES, *seated in an arm chair, reading a letter.*

Enter HANNAH, L.]

MRS. GAINES: You need not tell me, Hannah, that you don't want another husband, I know better. Your master has sold Sam, and he's gone down the river, and you'll never see him again. So, go and put on your calico dress, and meet me in the kitchen. I intend for you to *jump the broomstick* with Cato. You need not tell me that you don't want another man. I know that there's no woman living that can be happy and satisfied without a husband.

HANNAH: Oh, missis, I don't want to jump de broomstick wid Cato. I don't love Cato; I can't love him.

Notes

[30] *calliker* calico.

[31] *teves* thieves.

Mrs. G: Shut up, this moment! What do you know about love? I didn't love your master when I married him, and people don't marry for love now. So go and put on your calico dress, and meet me in the kitchen.

[*Exit* Hannah, L.]

I am glad that the Colonel has sold Sam; now I'll make Hannah marry Cato, and I have them both here under my eye. And I am also glad that the Colonel has parted with Melinda. Still, I'm afraid that he is trying to deceive me. He took the hussy away yesterday, and says he sold her to a trader; but I don't believe it. At any rate, if she's in the neighborhood, I'll find her, that I will. No man ever fools me.

[*Exit* Mrs. Gaines, L.]

Scene 2 – The kitchen – slaves at work.

[*Enter* Hannah, R.]

Hannah: Oh, Cato, do go and tell missis dat you don't want to jump de broomstick with me – dat's a good man! Do, Cato; kase I nebber can love you. It was only last week dat massa sold my Sammy, and I don't want any udder man. Do go tell missis dat you don't want me.

Cato: No, Hannah, I ain't a gwine to tell missis no such thing, kase I does want you, and I ain't a-gwine to tell a lie for you ner nobody else. Dar, now you's got it! I don't see why you need to make so much fuss. I is better lookin' den Sam; an' I is a house servant, an' Sam was only a fiel' hand; so you ought to feel proud of a change. So go and do as missis tells you.

[*Exit* Hannah, L.]

Hannah needn't try to get me to tell a lie; I ain't a-gwine to do it, kase I dose want her, an' I is bin wantin' her dis long time, an' soon as massa sold Sam, I knowed I would get her. By golly, I is gwine to be a married man. Won't I be happy! Now, ef I could only jess run away from ole massa, an' get to Canada wid Hannah, den I'd show 'em who I was. Ah! dat reminds me of my song 'bout ole massa and Canada, an' I'll sing it fer yer. Dis is my moriginal hyme. It comed into my head one night when I was fass asleep under an apple tree, looking up at de moon. Now for my song:

[Air – "*Dandy Jim.*"]

Come all ye bondmen far and near,
Let's put a song in massa's ear,
It is a song for our poor race,
Who're whipped and trampled with disgrace.

Chorus.

My old massa tells me, Oh,
This is a land of freedom, Oh;
Let's take a look about and see if it's so,
Just as massa tells me, Oh.

He tells us of that glorious one,
I think his name was Washington,
How he did fight for liberty,
To save a threepence tax on tea. [*Chorus.*]

But now we look about and see
That we poor blacks are not so free;
We're whipped and thrashed about like fools,
And have no chance at common schools. [*Chorus.*]

They take our wives, insult and mock,
And sell our children on the block,
They choke us if we say a word,
And say that "niggers" shan't be heard. [*Chorus.*]

Our preachers, too, with whip and cord,
Command obedience in the Lord:
They say they learn it from the big book,
But for ourselves, we dare not look. [*Chorus.*]

There is a country far away,
I think they call it Canada,
And if we reach Victoria's shore,
They say that we are slaves no more.
  Now hasten, all bondmen, let us go,
  And leave this *Christian* country, Oh;
  Haste to the land of the British Queen,
  Where whips for negroes are not seen.
Now, if we go, we must take the night,
And never let them come in sight;
The bloodhounds will be on our track,
And woe[32] to us if they fetch us back.
  Now hasten all bondmen, let us go,
  And leave this *Christian* country, Oh;
  God help us to Victoria's shore,
  Where we are free and slaves no more!

[*Enter* MRS. GAINES, L.]

MRS. GAINES: Ah! Cato, you're ready, are you? Where is Hannah?

CATO: Yes, missis; I is bin waitin' dis long time. Hannah has been here tryin' to swade[32] me to tell you dat I don't want her; but I telled her dat you sed I must jump de broomstick wid her, an' I is gwine to mind you.

MRS. G: That's right, Cato; servants should always mind their masters and mistresses, without asking a question.

CATO: Yes, missis, I allers dose what you and massa tells me, an' axes nobody.

[*Enter* HANNAH, R.]

MRS. GAINES: Ah! Hannah; come we are waiting for you. Nothing can be done till you come.

HANNAH: Oh, missis, I don't[34] want to jump de broomstick wid Cato; I can't love him.

Notes

[32] *Original reads*: wo [ed.].

[33] *swade* persuade.

[34] *Original reads*: do n't [ed.].

Mrs. G: Shut up, this moment. Dolly, get the broom. Susan, you take hold of the other end. There, now hold it a little lower – there, a little higher. There, now, that'll do. Now Hannah, take hold of Cato's hand. Let Cato take hold of your hand.

Hannah: Oh, missis, do spare me. I don't[35] want to jump de broom stick wid Cato.

Mrs. G: Get the cowhide, and follow me to the cellar, and I'll whip you well. I'll let you know how to disobey my orders. Get the cowhide, and follow me to the cellar.

[*Exit* Mrs. Gaines *and* Hannah, R.]

Dolly: Oh, Cato, do go an' tell missis dat you don't want Hannah. Don't you here how she's whippin' her in de cellar. Do go an' tell missis dat you don't want Hannah, and den she'll stop whippin' her.

Cato: No, Dolly, I ain't a-gwine to do no such thing, kase ef I tell missis dat I don't want Hannah, den missis will whip me; an' I ain't a-gwine to be whipped fer you, ner Hannah, ner nobody else. No, I'll jump de broomstick wid every woman on de place, ef missis wants me to, before I'll be whipped.

Dolly: Cato, ef I was in Hannah's place, I'd see you in de bottomless pit before I'd live wid you, you great big wall-eyed,[36] empty-headed, knock-kneed fool. You're as mean as your devilish old missis.

Cato: Ef you don't[37] quit dat busin' me, Dolly, I'll tell missis as soon as she comes in, an' she'll whip you, you know she will.[*Enter* Mrs. Gaines *and* Hannah, R. Mrs. G. *fans herself with her handkerchief, and appears fatigued.*]

Mrs. G: You ought to be ashamed of yourself, Hannah, to make me fatigue myself in this way, to make you do your duty. It's very naughty in you, Hannah. Now, Dolly, you and Susan get the broom, and get out in the middle of the room. There, hold it a little lower – a little higher; there that'll do. Now, remember that this is a solemn occasion; you are going to jump into matrimony. Now, Cato, take hold of Hannah's hand. There, now, why couldn't[38] you let Cato take hold of your hand before? Now get ready, and when I count to three, do you jump. Eyes on the *broomstick!* All ready. One, two, three, and over you go. There, now you're husband and wife, and if you don't[39] live happily together, it's your own fault; for I am sure there's nothing to hinder it. Now, Hannah, come up to the house, and I'll give you some whiskey, and you can make some apple toddy, and you and Cato can have a fine time.[*Exit* Mrs. Gaines *and* Hannah, L.]

Dolly: I tell you what, Susan, when I get married, I is gwine to have a preacher to marry me. I aint' a-gwine to jump de broomstick. Dat will do for fiel' hands, but house servants ought to be 'bove dat.

Susan: Well, chile, you can't speck any ting else from ole missis. She come down from Carlina, from 'mong de poor white trash. She don't know any better. You can't speck nothin' more dan a jump from a frog. Missis says she is one of de akastocacy;[40] but she ain't no more of an akastocacy dan I is. Missis says she was born with a silver spoon in her mouf; ef she was, I wish it had a-choked her, dat's what I wish. Missis wanted to make Linda jump de broomstick wid Glen, but massa ain't a-gwine to let Linda jump de broomstick wid anyone. He's gwine to keep Linda fer heself.

Dolly: You know massa took Linda 'way las' night, an' tell missis dat he has sold her and sent her down the river; but I don't[41] believe he has sold her at all. He went ober towards

Notes

35 *Original reads*: do n't [ed.].
36 *wall-eyed* lazy-eyed.
37 *Original reads*: do n't [ed.].
38 *Original reads*: could n't [ed.].
39 *Original reads*: do n't [ed.].
40 *akastocacy* aristocracy.
41 *Original reads*: don't [ed.].

poplar farm, an' I tink Linda is ober dar right now. Ef she is dar, missis'll find it out, fer she tell'd massa las' night, dat ef Linda was in de neighborhood, she'd find her.

[*Exit* DOLLY *and* SUSAN.]

Scene 3 – Sitting room – chairs and table.

[*Enter* HANNAH, R.]

HANNAH: I don't keer what missis says; I don't like Cato, an' I won't live wid him. I always love my Sammy, an' I loves him now. [*Knock at the door – goes to the door.*]

[*Enter* MAJ. MOORE, M.D.]

Walk in, sir; take a seat. I'll call missis, sir; massa is gone away.

[*Exit* HANNAH, R.]

MAJ. MOORE: So I am here at last, and the Colonel is not at home. I hope his wife is a good-looking woman. I rather like fine-looking women, especially when their husbands are from home. Well, I've studied human nature to some purpose. If you wish to get the good will of a man, don't[42] praise his wife, and if you wish to gain the favor of a woman, praise her children, and swear that they are the picture of their father, whether they are or not. Ah! here comes the lady.

[*Enter* MRS. GAINES, R.]

MRS. G: Good morning, sir!

MAJ. M: Good morning, madam! I am Maj. Moore, of Jefferson. The Colonel and I had seats near each other in the last Legislature.

MRS. G: Be seated, sir. I think I've heard the Colonel speak of you. He's away now; but I expect him every moment. You're a stranger here, I presume?

MAJ. M: Yes, madam, I am. I rather like the Colonel's situation here.

MRS. G: It is thought to be a fine location.

[*Enter* SAMPEY, R.]

Hand me my fan, will you, Sampey? [SAMPEY *gets the fan and passes near the* MAJOR, *who mistakes the boy for the* COLONEL'*s son. He reaches out his hand.*]

MAJ. M: How do you do, bub? Madam, I should have known that this was the Colonel's son, if I had met him in California; for he looks so much like his papa.

MRS. G: [*To the boy.*] Get out of here this minute. Go[43] to the kitchen.

[*Exit* SAMPEY, R.]

That is one of the niggers, sir.

MAJ. M: I beg your pardon, madam; I beg your pardon.

MRS. G: No offence, sir; mistakes will be made. Ah! here comes the colonel.

[*Enter* DR. GAINES, M.D.]

DR. GAINES: Bless my soul, how are you, Major? I'm exceedingly pleased to see you. Be seated, be seated, Major.

MRS. G: Please excuse me, gentlemen; I must go and look after dinner, for I've no doubt that the Major will have an appetite for dinner, by the time it is ready.

Notes

[42] *Original reads*: do n't [ed.].

[43] *Original reads*: Got [ed.].

[*Exit* Mrs. Gaines, R.]

Maj. M: Colonel, I'm afraid I've played the devil here to-day.

Dr. G: Why, what have you done?

Maj. M: You see, Colonel, I always make it a point, wherever I go, to praise the children, if there are any, and so to-day, seeing one of your little children come in, and taking him to be your son, I spoke to your wife of the marked resemblance between you and the boy. I'm afraid I've insulted madam.

Dr. G: Oh! don't[44] let it trouble you. Ha, ha, ha. If you did call him my son, you didn't[45] miss much. Ha, ha, ha. Come, we'll take a walk, and talk over matters about old times.

[*Exit*, L.]

Scene 4 – Forest scenery.

[*Enter* Glen, L.]

Glen: Oh, how I want to see Melinda! My heart pants and my soul is moved whenever I hear her voice. Human tongue cannot tell how my heart yearns toward her. God! Thou who gavest me life, and implanted in my bosom the love of liberty, and gave me a heart to love, Oh, pity the poor outraged slave! Thou, who canst rend the veil of centuries, speak, Oh, speak, and put a stop to this persecution! What is death, compared to slavery? Oh, heavy curse, to have thoughts, reason, taste, judgment; conscience and passions like another man, and not have equal liberty to use them! Why was I born with a wish to be free, and still be a slave? Why should I call another man master? And my poor Melinda, she is taken away from me, and I dare not ask the tyrant where she is. It is childish to stand here weeping. Why should my eyes be filled with tears, when my brain is on fire? I will find my wife – I will; and woe[46] to him who shall try to keep me from her!

Scene 5 – Room in a small cottage on the poplar farm.

[*Ten miles from Muddy Creek, and owned by* Dr. Gaines.]

[*Enter* Melinda, R.]

Melinda: Here I am, watched, and kept a prisoner in this place. Oh, I would that I could escape, and once more get with Glen. Poor Glen! He does not know where I am. Master took the opportunity, when Glen was in the city with his master, to bring me here to this lonely place, and fearing that mistress would know where I was, he brought me here at night. Oh, how I wish I could rush into the arms of sleep! – that sweet sleep, which visits all alike, descending, like the dews of heaven upon the bond as well as the free. It would drive from my troubled brain the agonies of this terrible night.

[*Enter* Dr. Gaines, L.]

Dr. Gaines: Good evening, Melinda! Are you not glad to see me?

Melinda: Sir, how can I be glad to see the one who has made life a burden, and turned my sweetest moments into bitterness?

Notes

[44] *Original reads*: do n't [ed.].

[45] *Original reads*: did n't [ed.].

[46] *Original reads*: wo [ed.].

DR. G: Come, Melinda, no more reproaches! You know that I love you, and I have told you, and I tell you again, that if you will give up all idea of having Glen for a husband, I will set you free, let you live in this cottage, and be your own mistress, and I'll dress you like a lady. Come, now, be reasonable.

MELINDA: Sir, I am your slave; you can do as you please with the avails of my labor, but you shall never tempt me to swerve from the path of virtue.

DR. G: Now, Melinda, that black scoundrel Glen has been putting these notions into your head. I'll let you know that you are my property and I'll do as I please with you. I'll teach you that there is no limit to my power.

MELINDA: Sir, let me warn you that if you compass my ruin, a woman's bitterest curse will be laid upon your head, with all the crushing, withering weight that my soul can impart to it; a curse that shall cling to you throughout the remainder of your wretched life; a curse that shall haunt you like a spectre in your dreams by night, and attend upon you by day; a curse, too, that shall embody itself in the ghastly form of a woman whose chastity you will have outraged. Command me to bury myself in yonder stream, and I will obey you. Bid me to do anything else, but I beseech you not to commit a double crime – outrage a woman, and make her false to her husband.

DR. G: You got a husband! Who is your husband, and when were you married?

MELINDA: Glen is my husband, and I've been married four weeks. Old Uncle Joseph married us one night by moonlight. I see you are angry; I pray you not to injure my husband.

DR. G: Melinda, you shall never see Glen again. I have bought him from Hamilton, and I will return to Muddy Creek, and roast him at the stake. A black villain, to get into my way in that manner! Here I've come ten miles tonight to see you, and this is the way you receive me!

MELINDA: Oh, master, I beg you not to injure my husband! Kill me, but spare him! Do! do! he is my husband!

DR. G: You shall never see that black imp again, so good night, my lady! When I come again, you'll give me a more cordial reception. Good night!

[*Exit* DR. GAINES, L.]

MELINDA: I shall go distracted. I cannot remain here and know that Glen is being tortured on my account. I must escape from this place – I must – I must.

[*Enter* CATO, R.]

CATO: No, you ain't a-gwine to 'scape, nudder. Massa tells me to keep dese eyes on you, an' I is gwine to do it.

MELINDA: Oh, Cato, do let me get away! I beg you, do!

CATO: No; I tells you massa telled me to keep you safe; an' ef I let you go, massa will whip me.

[*Exit* CATO, L.]

[*Enter* MRS. GAINES, R.]

MRS. GAINES: Ah, you trollop! here you are! Your master had told me that he had sold you and sent you down the river, but I knew better; I knew it was a lie. And when he left home this evening, he said he was going to the city on business, and I knew that was a lie too, and determined to follow him, and see what he was up to. I rode all the way over here to-night. My side-saddle was lent out, and I had to ride ten miles bare-back, and I can scarcely walk; and your master has just left here. Now deny that, if you dare.

MELINDA: Madam, I will deny nothing which is true. Your husband has just gone from here, but God knows I am innocent of anything[47] wrong with him.

MRS. G: It's a lie! I know better. If you are innocent, what are you doing here, cooped up in this cottage by yourself? Tell me that!

MELINDA: God knows that I was brought here against my will, and I will beg that you will take me away.

MRS. G: Yes, Melinda, I will see that you are taken away, but it shall be after a fashion that you won't like. I know that your master loves you, and I intend to put a stop to it. Here, drink the contents of this vial – drink it!

MELINDA: Oh, you will not take my life – you will not!

MRS. G: Drink the poison this moment!

MELINDA: I cannot drink it.

MRS. G: I tell you to drink this poison at once. Drink it, or I will thrust this knife to your heart! The poison at once. Drink it, or I will thrust this knife to your heart! The poison or the dagger, this instant! [*She draws a dagger;* MELINDA *retreats, to the back of the room, and seizes a broom.*]

MELINDA: I will not drink this poison! [*They fight;* MELINDA *sweeps off* MRS. GAINES – *cap, combs and curls.*]

[*Curtain falls.*]

Act 4

Scene 1 – Interior of a dungeon – GLEN in chains.

GLEN: When I think of my unmerited sufferings, it almost drives me mad. I struck the doctor, and for that, I must remain here loaded with chains. But why did he strike me? He takes my wife from me, sends her off, and then comes back and beats me over the head with his cane. I did right to strike him back. I would have killed him. Oh! there is a volcano pent up in the hearts of the slaves of these Southern States that will burst forth ere long. When that day comes, woe[48] to those whom its unpitying fury may devour! I would be willing to die, if I could smite down with these chains every man who attempts to enslave his fellow-man.

[*Enter* SAMPEY, R.]

SAMPEY: Glen, I jess bin hear the massa call de oberseer, and I spec somebody is gwine to be whipped. Anudder thing: I know where massa took Linda to. He took her to de poplar farm, an' he went away las' night, an' missis she follow after massa, an' she ain't come back yet. I tell you, Glen, de debil will be to pay on dis place, but don't tell any body dat I tole you.

[*Exit* SAMPEY, R.]

Scene 2 – Parlor.

[DR. GAINES, *alone.*]

DR. GAINES: Yes, I will have the black rascal well whipped, and then I'll sell him. It was most fortunate for me that Hamilton was willing to sell him to me.

Notes

[47] *Original reads*: any thing [ed.].

[48] *Original reads*: wo [ed.].

[*Enter* Mr. Scragg, L.]

I have sent for you, Mr. Scragg. I want you to take Glen out of the dungeon, take him into the tobacco house, fasten him down upon the stretcher, and give him five hundred lashes upon his bare back; and when you have whipped him, feel his pulse, and report to me how it stands, an if he can bear any more, I'll have you give him an additional hundred or two as the case may be.

Scragg: I tell you, doctor, that suits me to a charm. I've long wanted to whip that nigger. When your brother-in-law came here to board, and brought that boy with him, I felt bad to see a nigger dressed up in such fine clothes, and I wanted to whip him right off. I tell you, doctor, I had rather whip that nigger than go to heaven, any day – that I had!

Dr. G: Go, Mr. Scragg, and do your duty. Don't spare the whip!

Scragg: I will, sir; I'll do it in order.

[*Exit* Scragg, L.]

Dr. G: Everything[49] works well now, and when I get Glen out of the way, I'll pay Melinda another visit, and she'll give me a different reception. But I wonder where my wife is? She left word that she was going to see her brother, but I am afraid that she has got on my track. That woman is the pest of my life. If there's any place in heaven for her, I'd be glad if the Lord would take her home, for I've had her too long already. But what noise is that? What can it be? What is the matter?

[*Enter* Scragg, L., *with face bloody*.]

Scragg: Oh, dear me! oh, my head! That nigger broke away from me, and struck me over the head with a stick. Oh, dear me! Oh!

Dr. G: Where is he, Mr. Scragg?

Scragg: Oh! sir, he jumped out of the window; he's gone. Oh! my head; he's cracked my skull. Oh, dear me, I'm kilt! Oh! oh! oh!

[*Enter* Slaves, R.]

Dr. G: Go, Dolly, and wash Mr. Scragg's head with some whiskey, and bind it up. Go at once. And Bob, you run over to Mr. Hall, and tell him to come with his hounds; we must go after the rascal.

[*Exit all except the* Doctor, R.]

This will never do. When I catch the scoundrel, I'll make an example of him; I'll whip him to death. Ah! here comes my wife. I wonder what she comes for now? I must put on a sober face, for she looks angry.

[*Enter* Mrs. Gaines, L.]

Ah! my dear, I am glad you've come, I've been so lonesome without you. Oh! Sarah, I don't[50] know what I should do if the Lord should take you home to heaven. I don't[51] think that I should be able to live without you.

Mrs. G: Dr. Gaines, you ought to be ashamed to sit there and talk in that way. You know very well that if the Lord should call me home to glory tonight, you'd jump for joy. But you need not think that I am going to leave this world before

Notes

[49] *Original reads*: every thing [ed.].

[50] *Original reads*: do n't [ed.].

[51] *Original reads*: do n't [ed.].

you. No; with the help of the Lord, I'll stay here to foil you in your meanness. I've been on your track, and a dirty track it is, too. You ought to be ashamed of yourself. See what promises you made me before we were married; and this is the way you keep your word. When I married you, everybody[52] said that it was a pity that a woman of my sweet temper should be linked to such a man as you. [*She weeps and wrings her hands.*]

DR. G: Come, my dear, don't[53] make a fool of yourself. Come, let's go to supper, an' a strong cup of tea will help your head.

MRS. G: Tea help my head! tea won't help my head! You're a brute of a man; I always knew I was a fool marrying you. There was Mr. Comstock, he wanted me, he loved me, and he said I was an angel, so he did; and he loved me, and he was rich; and mother always said that he loved me more than you, for when he used to kiss me, he always squeezed my hand. You never did such a thing in your life. [*She weeps and wrings her hands.*]

DR. G: Come, my dear, don't[54] act so foolish.

MRS. G: Yes; everything[55] I do is foolish. You're a brute of a man; I won't live with you any longer. I'll leave you – that I will. I'll go and see a lawyer, and get a divorce from you – so I will.

DR. G: Well, Sarah, if you want a divorce, you had better engage Mr. Barker. He's the best lawyer in town; and if you want some money to facilitate the business, I'll draw a check for you.

MRS. G: So you want me to get a divorce, do you? Well, I won't have a divorce; no, I'll never leave you, as long as the Lord spares me.

[*Exit* MRS. GAINES, R.]

Scene 3 – Forest at night – large tree.

[*Enter* MELINDA, L.]

MELINDA: This is indeed a dark night to be out and alone on this road. But I must find my husband, I must. Poor Glen! if he only knew that I was here, and could get to me, he would. What a curse slavery is! It separates husbands from their wives, and tears mothers from their helpless offspring, and blights all our hopes for this world. I must try to reach Muddy Creek before daylight, and seek out my husband. What's that I hear? – footsteps? I'll get behind this tree.

GLEN: It is so dark, I'm afraid I've missed the road. Still, this must be the right way to the poplar farm. I will soon be with her; and if I once get her in my arms, it will be a strong man that shall take her from me. Aye, a dozen strong men shall not be able to wrest her from my arms. [MELINDA *rushes from behind the tree.*]

MELINDA: Oh, Glen! It is my husband – it is!

GLEN: Melinda! Melinda! it is, it is. Oh God! I thank Thee for this manifestation of Thy kindness. Come, come, Melinda, we must go at once to Canada. I escaped from the overseer, whom Dr. Gaines sent to flog me. Yes, I struck him over the head with his own club, and I made the wine flow freely; yes, I pounded his old skillet well for him, and then jumped out of the window. It was a leap for freedom. Yes, Melinda, it was a leap for freedom. I've said "master" for the last time. I am free; I'm bound for

Notes

[52] *Original reads*: every body [ed.].

[53] *Original reads*: do n't [ed.].

[54] *Original reads*: do n't [ed.].

[55] *Original reads*: every thing [ed.].

Canada. Come, let's be off, at once, for the negro dogs will be put out upon our track. Let us once get beyond the Ohio River,[56] and all will be right.

[*Exit* R.]

Act 5

Scene 1 – Bar-room in the American hotel – travelers lounging in chairs, and at the bar.

[*Enter* Bill Jennings, R.]

Barkeeper: Why, Jennings, how do you do?

Jennings: Say Mr. Jennings, if you please.

Barkeeper: Well, Mr. Jennings, if that suits you better. How are times? We've been expecting you, for some days.

Jennings: Well, before I talk about the times, I want my horses put up, and want you to tell me where my niggers are to stay to-night. Sheds, stables, barns, and everything[57] else here, seems pretty full, if I am a judge.

Barkeeper: Oh! I'll see to your plunder.

1st Lounger: I say, Barkeeper, make me a brandy cocktail, strong. Why, how do[58] you do, Mr. Jennings?

Jennings: Pretty well, Mr. Peters. Cold evening, this.

1st Loun: Yes, this is cold. I heard you speak of your niggers. Have you got a pretty large gang?

Jennings: No, only thirty-three. But they are the best that the country can afford. I shall clear a few dimes, this trip. I hear that the price is up.

[*Enter* Mr. White, R.]

White: Can I be accommodated here to-night, landlord?

Barkeeper: Yes, sir; we've bed for man and beast. Go, Dick, and take the gentleman's coat and hat. [*To the* Waiter.] You're a stranger in these parts I rec'on.

White: Yes, I am a stranger here.

2d Loun: Where mout you come from, ef it's a far question?

White: I am from Massachusetts.

3rd Loun: I say, cuss Massachusetts!

White: I say, landlord, if this is the language that I am to hear, I would like to go into a private room.

Barkeeper: We ain't got no private room empty.

1st Loun: Maybe you're mad 'bout what I said 'bout your State. Ef you is, I've only to say that this is a free country, and people talks what they please; an' ef you don't[59] like it, you can better yourself.

White: Sir, if this is a free country, why do you have slaves here? I saw a gang at the door, as I came in.

2d Loun: He didn't[60] mean that this was a free country for niggers. He meant that it's free for white people. And another thing, ef you get to taking 'bout freedom for niggers, you'll catch what you won't like, mister. It's right for niggers to be slaves.

Notes

[56] *Original reads*: Ohio river [ed.].

[57] *Original reads*: every thing [ed.].

[58] *Original reads*: o [ed.].

[59] *Original reads*: do n't [ed.].

[60] *Original reads*: did n't [ed.].

WHITE: But I saw some white slaves.

1ST LOUN: Well, they're white niggers.

WHITE: Well, sir, I am from a free state,[61] and I thank God for it; for the worst act that a man can commit upon his fellow-man, is to make him a slave. Conceive of a mind, a living soul, with the germs of faculties which infinity cannot exhaust, as it first beams upon you in its glad morning of existence, quivering with life and joy, exulting in the glorious sense of its developing energies, beautiful, and brave, and generous, and joyous, and free – the clear spirit bathed in the auroral lights of its unconscious immortality – and then follow it in its dark and dreary passage through slavery, until oppression stifles and kills, one by one, every inspiration and aspiration of its being, until it becomes a dead soul entombed in a living frame!

3D LOUN: Stop that; stop that, I say. That's treason to the country; that's downright rebellion.

BARKEEPER: Yes, it is. And another thing – this is not a meeting-house.

1ST LOUN: Yes, if you talk such stuff as that, you'll get a chunk of cold lead in you, that you will.

[*Enter* DR. GAINES *and* SCRAGG, followed *by* CATO, R.]

DR. G: Gentlemen, I am in pursuit of two valuable slaves, and I will pay five hundred dollars for their arrest.

[*Exit* MR. WHITE, L.]

1ST LOUN: I'll bet a picayune[62] that your niggers have been stolen by that cussed feller from Massachusetts. Don't you see he's gone?

DR. G: Where is the man? If I can lay my hands on him, he'll never steal another nigger. Where is the scoundrel?

1ST LOUN: Let's go after the feller. I'll go with you. Come, foller me.

[*Exit all*, L., *except* CATO *and the* WAITER.]

CATO: Why don't you bring in massa's saddle-bags? What de debil you standin' dar for? You common country niggers don't know nuffin', no how. Go an' get massa's saddle-bags,[63] and bring 'em in.

[*Exit* SERVANT, R]

By golly! ebry body's gone, an' de bar-keeper too. I'll tend de bar myself now; an' de fuss gemman I waits on will be dis gemman of color. [*Goes behind the counter and drinks.*] Ah, dis is de stuff for me; it makes my head swim; it makes me happy right off. I'll take a little more.

[*Enter* BARKEEPER, L]

BARKEEPER: What are you doing behind that bar, you black cuss?

CATO: I is lookin' for massa's saddle-bags, sir. Is dey here?

BARKEEPER: But what were you drinking there?

CATO: Me drinkin'! Why, massa, you muss be mistaken. I ain't drink nuffin'.

BARKEEPER: You infernal whelp, to stand there and lie in that way!

CATO: Oh, yes, seer, I did tase dat coffee in dat bottle; dat's all I did.

Notes

[61] *Original reads*: free State [ed.].

[62] *picayune* Spanish five-cent coin.

[63] *Original reads*: nsaddle-bags [ed.].

[*Enter* Mr. White, L., *excited.*]

Mr. White: I say, sir, is there no place of concealment in your house? They are after me, and my life is in danger. Say sir, can't you hide me away?

Barkeeper: Well, you ought to hold your tongue when you come into our State.

Mr. White: But, sir, the Constitution gives me the right to speak my sentiments, at all times and in all places.

Barkeeper: We don't care for Constitution nor nothin' else. We made the Constitution, and we'll break it. But you had better hide away; they are coming, and they'll lynch you, that they will. Come with me; I'll hide you in the cellar. Foller me.

[*Exit* Barkeeper *and* White, L.]

[*Enter the* Mob, R.]

Dr. Gaines: If I can once lay my hands on that scoundrel, I'll blow a hole through his head.

Jennings: Yes, I say so too; for no one knows whose niggers are safe now-a-days. I must look after my niggers. Who is that I see in the distance? I believe it's that cussed Massachusetts feller. Come, let's go after him.

[*Exit the* Mob, R.]

Scene 2 – Forest at night.

[*Enter* Glen *and* Melinda, R.]

Melinda: I am so tired and hungry, that I cannot go further. It is so cloudy that we cannot see the North Star, and therefore cannot tell whether we're going to Canada, or further South. Let's sit down here.

Glen: I know we cannot see the North Star, Melinda, and I fear we've lost our way. But, see! the clouds are passing away, and it'll soon be clear. See! yonder is a star; yonder is another and another. Ah! yonder is the North Star, and we are safe!

"Star of the North! though night winds drift
  The fleecy drapery of the sky
Between thy lamp and me, I lift,
  Yea, lift with hope my sleepless eye,
To the blue heights wherein[64] thou dwellest,
And of a land of freedom tellest.

"Star of the North! while blazing day
  Pours round me its full tide of light,
And hides thy pale but faithful ray,
  I, too, lie hid, and long for night:
For night: I dare not walk at noon,
Nor dare I trust the faithless moon –

Notes

[64] *Original reads*: wherin [ed.].

"Nor faithless man, whose burning lust
For gold hath riveted my chain –
Nor other leader can I trust
But thee, of even the starry train;
For all the host around thee burning,
Like faithless man, keep turning, turning.

"I may not follow where thee go –
Star of the North! I look to thee
While on I press; for well I know,
Thy light and truth shall set me free –
Thy light, that no poor slave deceiveth;
Thy truth, that all my soul believeth.

"Thy beam is on the glassy breast
Of the still spring, upon whose brink
I lay me weary limbs to rest,
And bow my parching lips to drink.
Guide of the friendless negro's way,
I bless thee for this quiet ray!

"In the dark top of the southern pines
I nestled, when the Driver's horn
Called to the field, in lengthening lines,
My fellows, at the break of morn.
And there I lay till thy sweet face
Looked in upon "my hiding place."

"The tangled cane-break, where I crept
For shelter from the heat of noon,
And where, while others toiled, I slept,
Till wakening by the rising moon,
As its stalks felt the night wind free,
Gave me to catch a glimpse of thee.

"Star of the North! in bright array
The constellations round thee sweep,
Each holding on its nightly way,
Rising, or sinking in the deep,
And, as it hangs in mid heaven flaming,
The homage of some nation claiming.

"*This* nation to the eagle cowers;
Fit ensign! she's a bird of spoil –
Like worships like! for each devours
The earnings of another's toil.
I've felt her talons and her beak,
And now the gentler Lion seek.

"The Lion, at the Monarch's feet
Crouches, an' lays his mighty paw
Into her lap! – an emblem meet
Of England's Queen, and English law:
Queen, that hath made her islands free!
Law, that holds out its shield to me!

Star of the North! upon that shield
Thou shinest – Oh, for ever shine!
The negro, from the cotton field
Shall, then, beneath its orb recline,
And feed the Lion, couched before it,
Nor heed the Eagle, screaming o'er it!"

With the thoughts of servitude behind us, and the North Star before us, we will go forward with cheerful hearts. Come, Melinda, let's go on.

[*Exit*, L.]

Scene 3 – A street.

[*Enter* Mr. White, R.]

Mr. White: I am glad to be once more in a free State. If I am caught once again south of Mason and Dixon's line, I'll give them leave to lynch me. I came near losing my life. This is the way our[65] constitutional rights are trampled upon. But what care these men about Constitutions, or anything[66] else that does not suit them? But I must hasten on.

[*Exit*, L.]

[*Enter* Cato, *in disguise*, R.]

Cato: I wonder ef dis is me? By golly, I is free as a frog. But maybe I is mistaken; maybe dis ain't me. Cato, is that you? Yes, seer. Well, now it is me, an' I em a free man. But, stop! I muss change my name, kase ole massa might foller me, and somebody might tell him dat dey seed Cato; so I'll change my name, and den he won't know me ef he sees me. Now, what shall I call myself? I'm now in a suspectable part of de country, an' I muss have a suspectable name. Ah! I'll call myself Alexander Washington Napoleon Pompey Cæsar. Dar, now, dat's a good long, suspectable name, and everybody[67] will suspect me. Let me see; I wonder ef I can't make up a song on my escape? I'll try.

[Air – "*Dearest Mae.*"]

Now, freemen, listen to my song, a story I'll relate,
It happened in de valley of de ole Kentucky State:
Dey marched me out into de fiel', at every break of day,
And work me dar till late sunset, widout a cent of pay.

Notes

[65] *Original reads*: out [ed.].
[66] *Original reads*: any thing [ed.].
[67] *Original reads*: every body [ed.].

Chorus. Dey work me all de day,
Widout a bit of pay,
And thought, because dey fed me well,
I would not run away.

Massa gave me his ole coat, an' thought I'd happy be,
But I had my eye on de North Star, an' thought of liberty;
Ole massa lock de door, an' den he went to sleep,
I dress myself in his bess clothes, an' jump into de street.

Chorus. Dey work me all de day,
Widout a bit of pay,
So I took my flight, in the middle of de night,
When de sun was gone away.

Sed I, dis chile's a freeman now, he'll be a slave no more;
I travell'd faster all dat night, dan I ever did before.
I came up to a farmer's house, jest at de break of day,
And saw a white man standin' dar, sed he, "You are a runaway."

Chorus. Dey work me all day, &c.

I tole him I had left de whip, an' bayin' of de hound,
To a place where man is man, ef sich dar can be found;
Dat I had heard, in Canada, dat all mankind is free,
An' dat I was going dar in search of liberty.

Chorus. Dey work me all day, &c.

I've not committed any crime, why should I run away?
Oh! shame upon your laws, dat drive me off to Canada.
You loudly boast of liberty, an' say your State is free,
But ef I tarry in your midst, will you protect me?

Chorus. Dey work me all de day, &c.

[*Exit*, L.]

Scene 4 – Dining-room – table spread. Mrs. Neal *and* Charlotte.

Mrs. Neal: Thee may put the tea to draw, Charlotte. Thy father will be in soon, and we must have breakfast.

[*Enter* Mr. Neal, L.]

I think, Simeon, it is time that those people were called. Thee knows that they may be pursued, and we ought not to detain them long here.

Mr. Neal: Yes, Ruth, thou art right. Go, Charlotte, and knock on their chamber door, and tell them that breakfast is ready.

[*Exit* Charlotte, R.]

Mrs. N: Poor creatures! I hope they'll reach Canada in safety. They seem to be worthy persons.

[*Enter* CHARLOTTE, R.]

CHARLOTTE: I've called them, mother, and they'll be soon down. I'll put the breakfast on the table.

[*Enter* NEIGHBOR JONES, L.]

MR. N: Good morning, James. Thee has heard, I presume, that we have two very interesting persons in the house?

JONES: Yes, I heard that you had two fugitives by the Underground road, last night; and I've come over to fight for them, if any persons come to take them back.

[*Enter* THOMAS, R.]

MR. N: Go, Thomas, and harness up the horses and put them to the covered wagon, and be ready to take these people on, as soon as they get their breakfast. Go, Thomas, and hurry thyself.

[*Exit* THOMAS, R.]

And so thee wants to fight, this morning, James?

JONES: Yes; as you belongs to a society that don't believe in fighting, and I does believe in that sort of thing, I thought I'd come by and relieve you of that work, if there is any to be done.

[*Enter* GLEN *and* MELINDA, R.]

MR. N: Good morning, friends. I hope thee rested well, last night.

MRS. N: Yes, I hope thee had a good night's rest.

GLEN: I thank you, madam, we did.

MR. N: I'll introduce thee to our neighbor, James Jones. He's a staunch friend of thy people.

JONES: I am glad to see you. I've come over to render assistance, if any is needed.

MRS. N: Come, friends, take seats at the table. Thee'll take seats there. [*To* GLEN *and* MELINDA.] [*All take seats at the table.*] Does thee take sugar and milk in thy tea?

MELINDA: I thank you, we do.

JONES: I'll look at your *Tribune*, Uncle Simeon, while you're eating.

MR. N: Thee'll find it on the table.

MRS. N: I presume thee's anxious to get to thy journey's end?

GLEN: Yes, madam, we are. I am told that we are not safe in any of the free states.[68]

MR. N: I am sorry to tell them that that is too true. Thee will not be safe until thee gets on British soil. I wonder what keeps Thomas; he should have been here with the team.

[*Enter* THOMAS, L.]

THOMAS: All's ready; and I've written the prettiest song that was ever sung. I call it "The Underground Railroad."

MR. N: Thomas, thee can eat thy breakfast far better than thee can write a song, as thee calls it. Thee must hurry thyself, when I send thee for the horses, Thomas. Here lately, thee takes thy time.

THOMAS: Well, you see I've been writing poetry; that's the reason I've been so long. If you wish it, I'll sing it to you.

JONES: Do let us hear the song.

MRS. NEAL: Yes, if Thomas has written a ditty, do let us hear it.

Notes

[68] *Original reads*: free States [ed.].

Mr. Neal: Well, Thomas, if thee has a ditty, thee may recite it to us.

Thomas: Well, I'll give it to you. Remember that I call it "The Underground Railroad."

[Air – "*Waiting for the Wagon.*"]

Oh, where is the invention
Of this growing age,
Claiming the attention
Of statesman, priest, or sage,
In the many railways
Through the nation found,
Equal to the Yankees'
Railway under-ground?

Chorus. No one hears the whistle,
Or rolling of the cars,
While negroes ride to freedom
Beyond the stripes and stars.

On the Southern borders
Are the Railway stations,
Negroes get free orders
While on the plantations;
For all, of ev'ry color,
First-class cars are found,
While they ride to freedom
By Railway under-ground.

Chorus. No one hears the whistle, &c.

Masters in the morning
Furiously rage,
Cursing the inventions
Of this knowing age;
Order out the bloodhounds,
Swear they'll bring them back,
Dogs return exhausted,
Cannot find the track.

Chorus. No one hears the whistle, &c.

Travel is increasing,
Build a double track,
Cars and engines wanted,
They'll come, we have[69] no lack.
Clear the track of loafers,

Notes

[69] *Original reads*: hve [ed.].

See that crowded car!
Thousands passing yearly,
Stock is more than par.

Chorus. No one hears the whistle, &c.

JONES: Well done! That's a good song. I'd like to have a copy of them verses. [*Knock at the door.* CHARLOTTE *goes to the door, and returns.*]

[*Enter* CATO, L., *still in disguise.*]

MR. NEAL: Who is this we have? Another of the outcasts, I presume?

CATO: Yes, seer; I is gwine to Canada, an' I met a man, an' he tole me dat you would give me some wittals an' help me on de way. By golly! ef dar ain't Glen an' Melinda. Dey don't[70] know me in dese fine clothes. [*Goes up to them.*] Ah, chillen! I is one wid you. I golly, I is here too! [*They shake hands.*]

GLEN: Why, it is Cato, as I live!

MELINDA: Oh, Cato, I am so glad to see you! But how did you get here?

CATO: Ah, chile, I came wid ole massa to hunt you; an' you see I get tired huntin' you, an' I am now huntin' for Canada. I left de ole boss in de bed at de hotel; an' you see I thought, afore I left massa, I'd jess change clothes with him; so you see, I is fixed up – ha, ha, ha. Ah, chillen! I is gwine wid you.

MRS. NEAL: Come, sit thee down, and have some breakfast.

CATO: Thank you, madam, I'll do dat. [*Sits down and eats.*]

MR. NEAL: This is pleasant for thee to meet one of thy friends.

GLEN: Yes, sir, it is; I would be glad if we could meet more of them. I have a mother and sister still in slavery, and I would give worlds, if I possessed them, if by doing so I could release them from their bondage.

THOMAS: We are all ready, sir, an the wagon is waiting.

MRS. NEAL: Yes, thee had better start.

CATO: Ef any body tries to take me back to ole massa, I'll pull ebry toof out of dar heads, dat I will! As soon as I get to Canada, I'll set up a doctor shop, an won't I be poplar? Den I rec'on I will. I'll pull teef fer all de people in Canada. Oh, how I wish I had Hannah wid me! It makes me feel bad when I tink I ain't a-gwine to see my wife no more. But, come, chillen, let's be makin' tracks. Dey say we is most to de British side.

MR. NEAL: Yes, a few miles further, and you'll be safe beyond the reach of the Fugitive-Slave Law.

CATO: Ah, dat's de talk fer dis chile.

[*Exit,* M.D.]

Scene 5 – The Niagara River – a ferry.

[FERRYMAN, *fastening his small boat.*]

FERRYMAN*:* [*advancing, takes out his watch.*] I swan, if it ain't one o'clock. I thought it was dinner time. Now there's no one here, I'll go to dinner, and if anybody[71] comes, they can wait until I return. I'll go at once.

Notes

[70] *Original reads*: do n't [ed.].

[71] *Original reads*: any body [ed.].

[*Exit*, L.]

[*Enter* Mr. White, R., *with an umbrella.*]

Mr. White: I wonder where that ferryman is? I want to cross to Canada. It seems a little showery, or else the mist from the Falls is growing thicker. [*Takes out his sketch-book and pencils – sketches.*]

[*Enter* Cane pedlar, R.]

Pedlar: Want a good cane to-day, sir? Here's one from Goat island – very good, sir – straight and neat – only one dollar. I've a wife and nine small children – youngest is nursing, and the oldest only three years old. Here's a cane from Table Rock, sir. Please buy one! I've had no breakfast to-day: My wife's got the rheumatics, and the children's got the measles. Come, sir, do buy a cane! I've a lame shoulder, and can't work.

Mr. White: Will you stop your confounded talk, and let me alone? Don't you see that I am sketching? You've spoiled a beautiful scene for me, with your nonsense.

[*Enter* 2d Pedlar, R.]

2d Pedlar: Want any bead bags, or money purses? These are real Ingen[72] bags, made by the Black Hawk Ingens. Here's a pretty bag, sir, only 75 cents. Here's a money purse, 50 cents. Please, sir, buy something! My wife's got the fever and ague, and the house is full of children, and they're all sick. Come, sir, do help a worthy man!

Mr. White: Will you hold your tongue? You've spoiled some of the finest pictures in the world. Don't you see that I'm sketching?

[*Exit* Pedlars, R., *grumbling.*]

I am glad those fellows have gone; now I'll go a little further up the shore, and see if I can find another boat. I want to get over.

[*Exit*, L.]

[*Enter* Dr. Gaines, Scragg, *and an* Officer.]

Officer: I don't[73] think that your slaves have crossed yet, and my officers will watch the shore below here, while we stroll up the river. If once I get my hands on them, all the Abolitionists in the State shall not take them from me.

Dr. G: I hope they have not gone over, for I would not lose them for two hundred dollars, especially the gal.

[*Enter* 1st Pedlar.]

Pedlar: Wish to get a good cane, sir? This stick was cut on the very spot where Sam Patch jumped over the falls. Only fifty cents. I have a sick wife and thirteen children. Please buy a cane; I ain't had no dinner.

Officer: Get out of the way! Gentlemen, we'll go up the shore.

[*Exit*, L.]

[*Enter* Cato, R.]

Cato: I is loss fum de cumpny, but dis is de ferry, and I spec dey'll soon come. But didn't[74] we have a good time las' night in Buffalo? Dem dar Buffalo gals make my

Notes

[72] *Ingen* Indian.

[73] *Original reads*: do n't [ed.].

[74] *Original reads*: did n't [ed.].

heart flutter, dat dey did. But, tanks be to de Lord, I is got religion. I git it las' night in de meetin'. Before I got religion, I was a great sinner; I got drunk, an' took de name of de Lord in vain. But now I is a conwerted man; I is bound for hebben; I toats de witness in my bosom; I feel dat my name is wrote[75] in the book of life. But dem niggers in de Vince Street Church las' night shout an' make sich a fuss, dey gave me de headache. But, tank de lord, I is got religion, an' now I'll be a preacher, and den dey'll call me Rev. Alexander Washington Napoleon Pompey Cæsar. Now I'll preach and pull teef, bofe at de same time. Oh, how I wish I had Hannah wid me! Cuss ole massa, fer ef it warn't for him, I could have my wife wid me. Ef I hadn't[76] religion, I'd say "Damn ole massa!" but as I is a religious man, an' belongs to de church, I won't say no such thing. But who is dat I see comin'? Oh, it's a whole heap of people. Good Lord! what is de matter?

[*Enter* Glen *and* Melinda, L., *followed by* Officers.]

Glen: Let them come; I am ready for them. He that lays hands on me or my wife shall feel the weight of this club.

Melinda: Oh, Glen, let's die right here, rather than again go into slavery.

Officer: I am the United States Marshal. I have a warrant from the Commissioner to take you, and bring you before him. I command assistance.

[*Enter* Dr. Gaines, Scragg, *and* Officer, R.]

Dr. Gaines: Here they are. Down with the villain! Down with him! But don't[77] hurt the gal!

[*Enter* Mr. White, R.]

Mr. White: Why, bless me! These are the slaveholding fellows. I'll fight for freedom! [*Takes hold of his umbrella with both hands – The fight commences,*[78] *in which* Glen, Cato, Dr. Gaines, Scragg, White, *and the* Officers, *take part –* Ferryman *enters, and runs to his boat –* Dr. Gaines, Scragg, *and the* Officers *are knocked down,* Glen, Melinda *and* Cato *jump into the boat, and as it leaves the shore and floats away,* Glen *and* Cato *wave their hats, and shout loudly for freedom – Curtain falls.*]

The end

1858

Notes

[75] *Original reads*: rote [ed.].

[76] *Original reads*: had n't [ed.].

[77] *Original reads*: do n't [ed.].

[78] *Original reads*: commence [ed.].

Martin Robison Delany (1812–1885)

Of the various Back-to-Africa schemes developed in the decades before the American Civil War, Martin R. Delany's Niger River Valley experiment was the only one that earned a hearing before Britain's Royal Geographical Society. Although the Abbeokuta settlement for former African American slaves in present-day Nigeria never materialized, and indeed many of his visionary ambitions came to naught, Delany's ringing assertion of African American self-determination and nationhood inspired generations of black nationalists.

Martin Robison Delany was born free in present-day West Virginia. After neighbors threatened to imprison Delany's mother for hiring a Yankee peddler to teach her children how to read, the family fled to Chambersburg, Pennsylvania. As a young man in Pittsburgh, he attended night school at the local African Methodist Episcopal Church, and studied medicine with a doctor while working as an officer in the Pittsburgh Anti-Slavery Society. In addition to his medical practice, Delany began publishing a weekly newspaper, *The Mystery*, in 1843. His bold writing on race brought him to the attention of Frederick Douglass, who hired him as co-editor of *The North Star* in 1847. The partnership lasted two years, before Delany's increasingly apocalyptic tone and various quarrels drove them apart. In 1850, Delany was admitted to Harvard's medical school, but student protests and university pressure forced him to withdraw shortly thereafter. Enraged, Delany returned to Pittsburgh, where he came to reevaluate his commitment to racial integration. He decided to throw himself into the emigration movement. In 1854, two years after publishing *The Condition, Elevation, Emigration, and Destiny of the Colored People of the United States,* he spoke before the Emigration Convention in Cleveland. His actions speaking as loudly as his words, he moved his family to Chatham, Ontario, and then toured Central America and Hawaii on behalf of fellow black emigrationists.

The notion of African Americans as a "nation within a nation" was central to Delany's thought. *Blake; or The Huts of America* (serialized in the *Anglo-African Magazine* in 1859) clearly articulates this vision. The novel depicts a transnational coalition of blacks in Cuba working toward hemispheric revolution and self-determining nationhood. Although he continued to support emigration, the Civil War led him to cast his lot with the Union. In 1863, as his son headed south with the all-black Massachusetts Fifty-Fourth Regiment, Delany traveled throughout New England and the Midwest recruiting African Americans for the Union Army. Delany also held various government positions in Reconstruction-era South Carolina. He supported Charleston's Democratic gubernatorial candidate – Wade Hampton, a former Confederate officer and slaveholder – in 1876, thereby earning the wrath of angry freed people who accused him of political betrayal. Ultimately disgusted with Reconstruction's failures and clinging to hope in black emigration, he lost an 1884 lawsuit following the seizure of his Liberian Exodus Joint Stock Exchange Company as it carried emigrants to West Africa. He was living in Wilberforce, Ohio, pursuing Federal appointment in DC and seeking to finance his family's emigration to Liberia, when he died in 1885.

The Wiley Blackwell Anthology of African American Literature: Volume 1, 1746–1920, First Edition.
Edited by Gene Andrew Jarrett.

Further reading

Adeleke, Tunde. *Without Regard to Race: The Other Martin Robison Delany*. Jackson: University of Mississippi Press, 2003.

Biggio, Rebecca Skidmore. "The Specter of Conspiracy in Martin Delany's *Blake*." *African American Review* 42. 3/4 (2008): 439–454.

Chiles, Katy. "Within and without Raced Nations: Intratextuality, Martin Delany, and *Blake; or the Huts of America*." *American Literature* 80.2 (2008): 323–352.

Clymer, Jeffory A. "Martin Delany's *Blake* and the Transnational Politics of Property." *American Literary History* 15.4 (2003): 709–731.

Cole, Jean Lee. "Theresa and Blake: Mobility and Resistance in Antebellum African American Serialized Fiction." *Callaloo* 34.1 (2011): 158–175.

Doolen, Andy. "'Be Cautious of the Word "Rebel"': Race, Revolution, and Transnational History in Martin Delany's *Blake; or, The Huts of America*." *American Literature* 81.1 (2009): 153–179.

Nwankwo, Ifeoma Kiddoe. *Black Cosmopolitanism: Racial Consciousness and Transnational Identity in the Nineteenth-century Americas*. Philadelphia: University of Pennsylvania Press, 2005. Ch. 2.

Nwankwo, Ifeoma Kiddoe. "The Promises and Perils of US African American Hemispherism: Latin America in Martin Delany's *Blake* and Gayl Jones's *Mosquito*." *American Literary History* 18.3 (2006): 579–600.

Powell, Timothy. "Postcolonial Theory in an American Context: A Reading of Martin Delany's *Blake*." *The Pre-occupation of Postcolonial Studies*. Eds. Fawzia Afzal-Khan and Kalpana Seshadri-Crooks. Durham: Duke University Press, 2000. 347–365.

Reid, Mandy A. "Utopia Is in the Blood: The Bodily Utopias of Martin R. Delany and Pauline Hopkins." *Utopian Studies* 22.1 (2011): 91–103.

Shelby, Tommie. "Two Conceptions of Black Nationalism: Martin Delany on the Meaning of Black Political Solidarity." *Political Theory* 31.5 (2003): 664–692.

Tomek, Beverly. *Colonization and Its Discontents: Emancipation, Emigration, and Antislavery in Antebellum Pennsylvania*. New York: New York University Press, 2010. Ch. 7.

Extracts from The Condition, Elevation, Emigration, and Destiny of the Colored People of the United States

Chapter 1

Condition of Many Classes in Europe Considered

That there have been in all ages and in all countries, in every quarter of the habitable globe, especially among those nations laying the greatest claim to civilization and enlightenment, classes of people who have been deprived of equal privileges, political, religious and social, cannot be denied, and that this deprivation on the part of the ruling classes is cruel and unjust, is also equally true. Such classes have even been looked upon as inferior to their oppressors, and have ever been mainly the domestics and menials of society, doing the low offices and drudgery of those among whom they lived, moving about and existing by mere sufferance, having no rights nor privileges but those conceded by the common consent of their political superiors. These are historical facts that cannot be controverted, and therefore proclaim in tones more eloquently than thunder, the listful attention of every oppressed man, woman, and child under the government of the people of the United States of America.

In past ages there were many such classes, as the Israelites in Egypt, the Gladiators in Rome, and similar classes in Greece; and in the present age, the Gypsies[1] in Italy and Greece, the Cossacks[2] in Russia and Turkey, the Slavs[3] and Croats in the Germanic States, and the Welsh and Irish among the British, to say nothing of various other classes among other nations.

Notes

[1] *Original reads*: Gipsies [ed.].

[2] *Original reads*: Cossacs [ed.].

[3] *Original reads*: Sclaves [ed.].

That there has[4] in all ages, in almost every nation, existed a nation within a nation – a people who, although forming a part and parcel of the population, yet were from force of circumstances known by the peculiar position they occupied, forming in fact, by the deprivation of political equality with others, no part, or[5] if any, but a restricted part of the body politic of such nations – is also true.

Such then are the Poles in Russia, the Hungarians in Austria, the Scots,[6] Irish, and Welsh in the United Kingdom, and such also are the Jews, scattered throughout not only the length and breadth of Europe, but almost the habitable globe, maintaining their national characteristics, and looking forward in high hopes of seeing the day when they may return to their former national position of self-government and independence, let that be in whatever part of the habitable world it may. This is the lot of these various classes of people in Europe, and it is not our intention here to discuss the justice or injustice of the causes that have contributed to their degradation, but simply to set forth the undeniable facts, which are as glaring as the rays of a noonday's sun, thereby to impress them indelibly on the mind of every reader of this pamphlet.

It is not enough that these people are deprived of equal privileges by their rulers, but, the more effectually to succeed, the equality of these classes must be denied and their inferiority by nature as distinct races actually asserted. This policy is necessary to appease the opposition that might be interposed in their behalf. Wherever there is arbitrary rule, there must by necessity, on the part of the dominant classes, be superiority assumed.[7] To assume superiority is to deny the equality of others, and to deny their equality is to premise their incapacity for self-government. Let this once be conceded and there will be little or no sympathy for the oppressed, the oppressor being left to prescribe whatever terms, at the discretion of their government, to suit his own purpose.[8]

Such then is the condition of various classes in Europe; yes, nations, for centuries within nations, even without the hope of redemption among those who oppress them. And however unfavorable their condition, there is none more so than that of the colored people of the United States.

Chapter 2

Comparative Condition of the Colored People of the United States

The United States, untrue to her trust and unfaithful to her professed principles of republican equality, has also pursued a policy of political degradation to a large portion of her native born countrymen, and that class is the Colored People. Denied an equality not only of political but of natural rights, in common with the rest of our fellow citizens, there is no species of degradation to which we are not subject.

To be reduced to abject slavery is not enough,[9] the very thought of which should awaken every sensibility of our common nature; but those of their descendants who are freemen even in the non-slaveholding States, occupy the very same position politically, religiously, civilly and socially (with but few exceptions) as the bondman occupies in the slave States.

Notes

[4] *Original reads*: have [ed.].

[5] *Original reads*: and [ed.].

[6] *Original reads*: Scotch [ed.].

[7] *Original reads*: Wherever there is arbitrary rule, there must be necessity, on the part of the dominant classes, superiority be assumed [ed.].

[8] *Original reads*: at discretion for their government, suits his own purpose [ed.].

[9] *Original reads*: Reduced to abject slavery is not enough [ed.].

In those States, the bondman is disfranchised, and for the most part so are we. He is denied all civil, religious, and social privileges, except such as he gets by mere sufferance, and so are we. They have no part nor lot in the government of the country, neither have we. They are ruled and governed without representation, existing as mere nonentities among the citizens, and excrescences[10] on the body politic – a mere dreg in community, and so are we. Where then is our political superiority to the enslaved? There is none; neither are we superior[11] in any other relation to society, except that we are de facto masters of ourselves and joint rulers of our own domestic household, while the bondman's self is claimed by another, and his relation to his family denied him. What the unfortunate classes are in Europe, such are we in the United States, which is folly to deny, insanity not to understand, blindness not to see, and it is surely now full time[12] that our eyes were opened to these startling truths, which for ages have stared us full in the face.

It is time that we had become politicians, we mean, to understand the political economy and domestic policy of nations; that we had become as well as moral theorists, also the practical demonstrators of equal rights and self-government. Unless[13] we do, it is idle to talk about rights, it is mere chattering for the sake of being seen and heard – like the slave, saying something because his so-called "master" said it, and saying just what he told him to say. Have we not now sufficient intelligence among us to understand our true position, to realise our actual condition, and determine for ourselves what is best to be done? If we have not now, we never shall have, and should at once cease prating about our equality, capacity, and all that.

Twenty years ago, when the writer was a youth, his young and yet uncultivated mind was aroused, and his tender heart made to leap with anxiety in anticipation of the promises then held out by the prime movers in the cause of our elevation.

In 1830, the most intelligent and leading spirits among the colored men in the United States, such as James Forten, Robert Douglass, I. Bowers, A.D. Shadd, John Peck, Joseph Cassey, and John B. Vashon of Pennsylvania; John T. Hilton, Nathaniel and Thomas Paul, and James G. Barbodoes of Massachusetts; Henry Sipkins, Thomas Hamilton, Thomas L. Jennings, Thomas Downing, Samuel E. Cornish,[14] and others of New York; R. Cooley and others of Maryland, and representatives from other States which cannot now be recollected, the data not being at hand, assembled in the city of Philadelphia, in the capacity of a National Convention, to "devise ways and means for the bettering of our condition." These Conventions determined to assemble annually, much talent, ability, and energy of character being displayed; when, in 1831, at a sitting of the Convention in September, from their previous pamphlet reports, much interest having been created throughout the country, they were favored by the presence of a number of whites, some of whom were able and distinguished men, such

Notes

[10] *excrescences* a disfiguring outgrowth.

[11] *Original reads*: none, neither are we superior [ed.].

[12] *Original reads*: and surely now full time [ed.].

[13] *Original reads*: Except [ed.].

[14] James Forten (1766–1842), abolitionist and affluent businessman; Robert Douglass (1776–1849), a founder of Philadelphia's first African Presbyterian Church; Thomas I. Bowers (1826–1885), opera singer; Abraham Doras Shadd (1801–1882), founding member of the American Anti-Slavery Society and politician; John Peck (b. 1801), abolitionist; Joseph Cassey (1789–1848), a businessman and education activist; John B. Vashon (1790–1853), barber and abolitionist; John T. Hilton (1801–1864), a Boston activist and black Masonic leader; Nathaniel Paul (1793–1839) and Thomas Paul (1773–1831) were clergymen and abolitionists; James G. Barbadoes (c.1796–1841), a barber and abolitionist; Henry Sipkins (1788–1838), founded a number of African American societies and associations in New York; Thomas Hamilton (1823–1865), edited the *Anglo-African Magazine*; Thomas L. Jennings (1791–1859), dry cleaning inventor and abolitionist; George Thomas Downing (1819–1903), civil rights activist; Samuel E. Cornish (1795–1858), a founder of the American Anti-Slavery Society and editor of *Freedom's Journal*.

as Rev. R.R. Gurley, Arthur Tappan, Elliot Cresson, John Rankin, Simeon Jocelyn and others, among them William Lloyd Garrison,[15] then quite a young man, all of whom were staunch and ardent Colonizationists,[16] young Garrison at that time, doing his mightiest in his favorite work.

Among other great projects of interest brought before the convention at a previous sitting, was that of the expediency of a general emigration, as far as it was practicable, of the colored people to the British Provinces of North America. Another was that of raising sufficient means for the establishment and erection of a College for the proper education of the colored youth. These gentlemen, long accustomed to observation and reflection on the condition of their people, saw at once that there must necessarily be means used adequate to the end to be attained – that end being an unqualified equality with the ruling class of their fellow citizens. He saw that, as a class, the colored people of the country were ignorant, degraded, and oppressed, by far the greater portion of them being abject slaves in the South, the very condition of whom was almost enough, under the circumstances, to blast the remotest hope of success, and those who were freemen, whether in the South or North, occupied a subservient, servile, and menial position, considering it a favor to get into the service of the whites, and do their degrading offices. That the difference between the whites and themselves consisted in the superior advantages of the one over the other in point of attainments. That if a knowledge of the arts and sciences, the mechanical occupations, the industrial occupations, as farming, commerce, and all the various business enterprises, and learned professions were necessary for the superior position occupied by their rulers, it was also necessary for them. And very reasonably too, the first suggestion which occurred to them was the advantages of a location, then the necessity of a qualification. They reasoned with themselves that all distinctive differences made among men on account of their origin are[17] wicked, unrighteous, and cruel, and never shall receive countenance in any shape from us. Therefore, the first act of the measure[18] entered into by them was to protest, solemnly protest, against every unjust measure and policy in the country having for its object the proscription of the colored people, whether state, national, municipal, social, civil, or religious.

But being far-sighted, reflecting, discerning men, they took a political view of the subject, and determined for the good of their people to be governed in their policy according to the facts as they presented themselves. In taking a glance at Europe, they discovered there, however unjustly, as we have shown in another part of this pamphlet, that there are and have been numerous classes proscribed and oppressed, and it was not for them to cut short their wise deliberations, and arrest their proceedings in contention, as to the cause, whether on account of language, the color of eyes, hair, skin, or their origin of country – because all this is contrary to reason, a contradiction to common sense, at war with nature herself, and at variance with facts as they stare us every day in the face, among all nations, in every country – this being made the pretext as a matter of *policy* alone – a fact worthy of observation, that wherever the objects of oppression are the most easily distinguished by any peculiar or general characteristics,

Notes

[15] Rev. R.R. Gurley (1797–1872), head of the American Colonization Society; Arthur Tappan (1786–185), abolitionist and philanthropist; Elliot Cresson (1796–1854), philanthropist and merchant; John Rankin (1793–1886), minister, writer, and Underground Railroad conductor; Simeon Jocelyn (1799–1879), abolitionist and minister; William Lloyd Garrison (1805–1879), abolitionist, journalist, and reformer.

[16] *Colonizationists* advocates of the idea that emancipated slaves should colonize Africa rather than remain in the United States.

[17] *Original reads*: is [ed.].

[18] *Original reads*: therefore, the first acts of the measure [ed.].

these people are the more easily oppressed, because the war of oppression is the more easily waged against them. This is the case with the modern Jews and many other people who have strongly-marked, peculiar, or distinguishing characteristics. This arises in this wise. The policy of all those who proscribe any people induces them to select as the objects of proscription those who differ[19] as much as possible, in some particulars, from themselves. This is to ensure the greater success, because it engenders the greater prejudice, or in other words, elicits less interest on the part of the oppressing class, in their favor. This fact is well understood in national conflicts, as the soldier or civilian who is distinguished by his dress, mustache, or any other peculiar appendage would certainly prove himself a madman if he did not take the precaution to change his dress, remove his mustache, and conceal as much as possible his peculiar characteristics, to give him access among the repelling party.

This is mere policy, nature having nothing to do with it. Still, it is a fact, a great truth well worthy of remark, and as such I adduce[20] it for the benefit of those of our readers unaccustomed to an enquiry into the policy of nations.

In view of these truths, our fathers and leaders in our elevation discovered that as a policy we the colored people were selected as the subordinate class in this country, not on account of any actual or supposed inferiority on their part, but simply because, in view of all the circumstances of the case, they were the very best class that could be selected. They would have as readily had any other class as subordinates in the country as the colored people, but the condition of society *at the time* would not admit of it. In the struggle for American Independence there were among those who performed the most distinguished parts the most common-place peasantry of the Provinces. English, Danish, Irish, Scotch, and others, were among those whose names blazoned forth as heroes in the American Revolution. But a single reflection will convince us, that no course of policy could have induced the proscription of the parentage and relatives of such men as Benjamin Franklin[21] the printer, Roger Sherman[22] the cobbler, the tinkers, and others of the signers of the Declaration of Independence. But as they were determined to have a subservient class, it will readily be conceived that, according to the state of society at the time, the better policy on their part was to select some class, who, from their political position – however much they may have contributed their aid, as we certainly did, in the general struggle for liberty by force of arms – had[23] the least claims upon them, or who had the *least chance*, or was the *least potent* in urging their claims. This class of course was the colored people and Indians.

The Indians, who in the early settlement of the continent, before an African captive had ever been introduced thereon, were reduced to the most abject slavery, toiling day and night in the mines, under the relentless hands of heartless Spanish taskmasters, but being a race of people raised to the sports of fishing, the chase, and of war, were wholly unaccustomed to labor, and therefore sank[24] under the insupportable weight, two millions and a half having fallen victims to the cruelty of oppression and toil suddenly placed upon their shoulders. And it was only this that prevented their further[25] enslavement as a class, after the provinces were absolved from the British Crown. It is true that their general enslavement took place on the islands and in the mining districts of South America, where indeed, the Europeans continued to enslave them until a

Notes

[19] *Original reads*: differed [ed.].

[20] *Original reads*: and as such as adduce [ed.].

[21] Benjamin Franklin (1706–1790), American statesman, author, and inventor.

[22] Roger Sherman (1721–1793), American lawyer and politician.

[23] *Original reads*: who had [ed.].

[24] *Original reads*: sunk [ed.].

[25] *Original reads*: farther [ed.].

comparatively recent period; still, the design, the feeling, and inclination from policy, was the same to do so here, in this section of the continent.

Nor was it until their influence became too great, by the political position occupied by their brethren in the new republic, that the German and Irish peasantry ceased to be sold as slaves for a term of years fixed by law for the repayment of their passage-money, the descendants of these classes of people for a long time being held as inferiors in the estimation of the ruling class; and it was not until they assumed the rights and privileges guaranteed to them by the established policy of the country, among the leading spirits of whom were their relatives, that the policy towards them was discovered to be a bad one, and accordingly changed. Nor was it, as is frequently very erroneously asserted, by colored as well as white persons, that it was on account of hatred of the African,[26] or in other words, on account of hatred of his color,[27] that the African was selected as the subject of oppression in this country. This is sheer nonsense, being based on policy and nothing else, as shown in another place. The Indians, who being the most foreign to the sympathies of the Europeans on this continent, were selected in the first place, who, being unable to withstand the hardships, gave way before them.

But the African race had long been known to Europeans, in all ages of the world's history, as a long-lived, hardy race, subject to toil and labor of various kinds, subsisting mainly by traffic, trade, and industry, and consequently, being as foreign to the sympathies of the invaders of the continent as the Indians, they were selected, captured, brought here as a laboring class, and as a matter of policy held as such. Nor was the absurd idea of natural inferiority of the African ever dreamed of, until recently adduced by the slave-holders and their abettors in justification of the policy. This, with contemptuous indignation, we fling back into their face, as a scorpion to a vulture. And so did our patriots and leaders in the cause of regeneration know better, and never for a moment yielded to the base doctrine. But they had discovered the great fact, that a cruel policy was pursued towards our people, and that they possessed distinctive characteristics which made them the objects of proscription. These characteristics being strongly marked in the colored people, as in the Indians, by color, character of hair and so on, made them the more easily distinguished from other Americans, and the policies more effectually urged against us. For this reason they introduced the subject of emigration to Canada, and a proper institution for the education of the youth.

At this important juncture of their proceedings, the aforenamed[28] white gentlemen were introduced to the notice of the Convention, and after gaining permission to speak, expressed their gratification and surprise at the qualification and talent manifested by different members of the Convention, all expressing their determination to give the cause of the colored people more serious reflection. Mr. Garrison, the youngest of them all, and none the less honest on account of his youthfulness, being but 26 years of age at the time (1831), expressed his determination to change his course of policy at once, and espouse the cause of the elevation of the colored people here in their own country. We are not at present well advised upon this point, it now having escaped our memory, but we are under the impression that Mr. Jocelyn also at once changed his policy.

During the winter of 1832, Mr. Garrison issued his "Thoughts on African Colonization," and near about the same time, or shortly after, issued the first number

Notes

[26] *Original reads*: hatred to the African [ed.].

[27] *Original reads*: hatred to his color [ed.].

[28] *Original reads*: afore named [ed.].

of the "Liberator,"[29] in both of which his full convictions of the enormity of American slavery, and the wickedness of their policy towards the colored people, were fully expressed. At the sitting of the Convention in this year, a number, perhaps all, of these gentlemen were present, and those who had denounced the Colonization scheme and espoused the cause of the elevation of the colored people in this country, or the Anti-Slavery cause, as it was now termed, expressed themselves openly and without reserve.

Sensible of the high-handed injustice done to the colored people in the United States, and the mischief likely to emanate from the unchristian proceedings of the deceptious Colonization scheme, like all honest-hearted penitents, with the ardor only known to new converts, they entreated the Convention, whatever they did, not to entertain for a moment, the idea of recommending emigration to their people, nor the establishment of separate institutions of learning. They earnestly contended, and doubtless honestly meaning what they said, that they (the whites) had been our oppressors and injurers, they had obstructed our progress to the high positions of civilization, and now, it was their bounden duty to make full amends for the injuries thus inflicted on an unoffending people. They exhorted the Convention to cease; as they had laid on the burden, they would also take it off; as they had obstructed our pathway, they would remove the hindrance. In a word, as they had oppressed and trampled down the colored people, they would now elevate them. These suggestions and promises, good enough to be sure, after they were made, were accepted by the Convention – though some gentlemen were still in favor of the first project as the best policy, Mr. A.D. Shadd of West Chester, Pa., as we learn from himself, being one among that number – and ran[30] through the country like wildfire, no one thinking, and if he thought, daring to speak above his breath of going anywhere[31] out of certain prescribed limits, or of sending a child to school, if it should but have the name of "colored" attached to it, without the risk of being termed a "traitor" to the cause of his people, or an enemy to the Anti-Slavery cause.

At this important point in the history of our efforts, the colored men stopped suddenly, and with their hands thrust deep in their breeches-pockets, and their mouths gaping open, stood gazing with astonishment, wonder, and surprise at the stupendous moral colossal statues of our Anti-Slavery friends and brethren, who in the heat and zeal of honest hearts, from a desire to make atonement for the many wrongs inflicted, promised a great deal more than they have ever been able half to fulfill, in thrice the period in which they expected it. And in this, we have no fault to find with our Anti-Slavery friends, and here wish it to be understood that we are not laying anything[32] to their charge as blame, neither do we desire for a moment to reflect on them, because we heartily believe that all that they did at the time, they did with the purest and best of motives, and further believe that they now are, as they then were, the truest friends we have among the whites in this country. And we hope,[33] and desire, and request, that our people should always look upon *true* anti-slavery people, Abolitionists we mean, as their friends, until they have just cause for acting otherwise. It is true that the Anti-Slavery, like all good causes, has produced some recreants, but the cause itself is no more to be blamed for that, than Christianity is for the malconduct of any professing hypocrite, nor the society of Friends for the conduct of a broad-brimmed hat and shad-belly coated[34] horse thief,[35] because he spoke *thee* and *thou* before stealing the horse.

Notes

[29] *"The Liberator"* Garrison's antislavery newspaper, published in Boston from 1831–1865.

[30] *Original reads*: being one among that number – ran [ed.].

[31] *Original reads*: any where [ed.].

[32] *Original reads*: any thing [ed.].

[33] *Original reads*: And hope [ed.].

[34] *shad-belly coated* dressed in a style of coat worn by Quakers (the society of Friends).

[35] *Original reads*: horse thief [ed.].

But what is our condition even amidst our Anti-Slavery friends? And here, as our sole intention is to contribute to the elevation of our people, we must be permitted to express our opinion freely, without being thought uncharitable.

In the first place, we should look at the objects for which the Anti-Slavery cause was commenced, and the promises or inducements it held out at the commencement. It should be borne in mind that Anti-Slavery took its rise among *colored men* just at the time they were introducing their greatest projects for their own elevation, and that our Anti-Slavery brethren were converts of the colored men, in behalf of their elevation. Of course, it would be expected that being baptized into the new doctrines, their faith would induce them to embrace the principles therein contained with the strictest possible adherence.

The cause of dissatisfaction with our former condition was that we were proscribed, debarred, and shut out from every respectable position, occupying the places of inferiors and menials.

It was expected that Anti-Slavery, according to its professions, would extend to colored persons, as far as in the power of its adherents, those advantages nowhere else to be obtained among white men. That colored boys would get situations in their shops and stores, and every other advantage tending to elevate them as far as possible would be extended to them. At least, it was expected, that in Anti-Slavery establishments colored men would have the preference. Because there was no other ostensible object in view, in the commencement of the Anti-Slavery enterprise, than the *elevation* of the *colored man*, by facilitating his efforts in attaining equality[36] with the white man. It was urged, and it was true, that the colored people were susceptible of all that the whites were, and all that was required was to give them a fair opportunity, and they would prove their capacity. That it was unjust, wicked, and cruel, the result of an unnatural prejudice, that debarred them from places of respectability, and that public opinion could and should be corrected upon this subject. That it was only necessary to make a sacrifice of feeling, and an innovation on the customs of society, to establish a different order of things – that, as Anti-Slavery men, they were willing to make these sacrifices and determined to take the colored man by the hand, making common cause with him in affliction, and bear a part of the odium heaped upon him. That his cause was the cause of God – that "In as much as ye did it not unto the least of these my little ones, ye did it not unto me,"[37] and that as Anti-Slavery men, they would "do right if the heavens fell."[38] Thus was the cause espoused, and thus did we expect much. But in all this we were doomed to disappointment, sad, sad disappointment. Instead of realising what we had hoped for, we find ourselves occupying the very same position in relation to our Anti-Slavery friends, as we do in relation to the pro-slavery part of the community – a mere secondary, underling position, in all our relations to them, and anything[39] more than this is not a matter of course affair – it comes not by established anti-slavery custom or right, but like that which emanates from the pro-slavery portion of the community by mere sufferance.

It is true, that the "Liberator" office, in Boston, has got Elijah Smith, a colored youth, at the cases – the "Standard,"[40] in New York, a young colored man, and the "Freeman," in Philadelphia,[41] William Still,[42] another, in the publication office, as "packing clerk"; yet these are but three out of the hosts that fill these offices in their various

Notes

[36] *Original reads*: attaining to equality [ed.].

[37] *"In as much … not unto me"* Matthew 25:45.

[38] *"do right if the heavens fell"* a translation of a Latin legal phrase, *Fiat justitia ruat caelum*, suggesting that justice must be pursued regardless of consequences.

[39] *Original reads*: any thing [ed.].

[40] *"Standard"* the *National Anti-Slavery Standard* (1840–1870).

[41] *"Freeman," in Philadelphia* the *Pennsylvania Freeman* (1838–1854), edited by John Greenleaf Whittier.

[42] William Still (1821–1902), often called "the father of the Underground Railroad," writer and historian.

departments, all occupying places that could have been, and as we once thought, would have been, easily enough occupied by colored men. Indeed, we can have no other idea about anti-slavery in this country than that the legitimate persons to fill any and every position about an anti-slavery establishment are colored persons. Nor will it do to argue in extenuation that white men are as justly entitled to them as colored men; because white men do not from *necessity* become anti-slavery men in order to get situations; they, being white men, may occupy any position they are capable of filling – in a word, their chances are endless, every avenue in the country being opened to them. They do not therefore become abolitionists for the sake of employment – at least, it is not the song that anti-slavery sang,[43] in the first love of the new faith, proclaimed by its disciples.

And if it be urged that colored men are incapable as yet to fill these positions, all that we have to say is that the cause has fallen far short; almost equivalent to a failure of a tithe of what it promised to do in half the period of its existence, to this time, if it have not as yet, now a period of twenty years, raised up colored men enough to fill the offices within its patronage. We think it is not unkind to say, if it had been half as faithful to itself as it should have been – its professed principles, we mean – it could have reared and tutored from childhood colored men enough by this time for its own especial purpose. These we know could have been easily obtained, because colored people in general are favorable to the anti-slavery cause, and wherever there is an adverse manifestation, it arises from sheer ignorance; and we have now but comparatively few such among us. There is one thing certain, that no colored person, except such as would reject education altogether, would be averse[44] to putting their child with an anti-slavery person for educational advantages. This then could have been done. But it has not been done, and let the cause of it be whatever it may, and let whoever may be to blame, we are willing to let all that pass, and extend to our anti-slavery brethren the right-hand of fellowship, bidding them God-speed in the propagation of good and wholesome sentiments – for whether they are practically carried out or not, the profession are in themselves all right and good. Like Christianity, the principles are holy and of divine origin. And we believe, if ever a man started right, with pure and holy motives, Mr. Garrison did; and that, had he the power of making the cause what it should be, it would all be right, and there never would have been any cause for the remarks we have made, though in kindness, and with the purest of motives. We are, nevertheless, still occupying a miserable position in the community, wherever we live; and what we most desire is to draw the attention of our people to this fact, and point out what, in our opinion, we conceive to be a proper remedy.

Chapter 3

American Colonization

When we speak of colonization, we wish distinctly to be understood as speaking of the "American Colonization Society" – or that which is under its influence – commenced in Richmond, Virginia, in 1817, under the influence of Mr. Henry Clay of Ky., Judge Bushrod Washington of Va.,[45] and other Southern slaveholders, having for their express object, as their speeches and doings all justify us in asserting in good faith, the removal

Notes

[43] *Original reads*: sung [ed.].

[44] *Original reads*: adverse [ed.].

[45] Henry Clay (1777–1852) was a politician who served as congressman, senator, and Secretary of State; Judge Bushrod Washington (1762–1829) was a Supreme Court associate justice (and George Washington's nephew).

of the free colored people from the land of their birth, for the security of the slaves, as property to the slave propagandists.

This scheme had no sooner been propagated than the old and leading colored men of Philadelphia, Pa., with Richard Allen, James Forten, and others at their head, true to their trust and the cause of their brethren, summoned the colored people together, and then and there, in language and with voices pointed and loud, protested against the scheme as an outrage, having no other object in view than the benefit of the slave-holding interests of the country, and that as freemen, they would never prove recreant to the cause of their brethren in bondage by leaving them without hope of redemption from their chains. This determination of the colored patriots of Philadelphia was published in full, authentically, and circulated throughout the length and breadth of the country by the papers of the day. The colored people everywhere[46] received the news, and at once endorsed with heart and soul the doings of the Anti-Colonization Meeting of colored freemen. From that time forth, the colored people generally have had no sympathy with the colonization scheme, nor confidence in its leaders, looking upon them all as arrant hypocrites seeking every opportunity to deceive them. In a word, the monster was crippled in its infancy, and has never as yet recovered from the stroke. It is true that, like its ancient sire, which[47] was "more subtle than all the beasts of the field,"[48] it has inherited a large portion of his most prominent characteristic – an idiosyncrasy of the animal[49] – that enables him to entwine himself into the greater part of the Church and other institutions of the country, and, having once entered there, leave[50] his venom, which puts such a spell on the conductors of those institutions, that is only on condition that a colored person consents to go to the neighborhood of his kindred brother monster the boa, that he may find admission in the one or the other. We look upon the American Colonization Society as one of the most arrant enemies of the colored man, ever seeking to discomfit him, and envying him of every privilege that he may enjoy. We believe it to be anti-Christian in its character, and misanthropic in its pretended sympathies. Because if this were not the case, men could not be found professing morality and Christianity – as to our astonishment we have found them – who unhesitatingly say, "I know it is right" – that is, in itself – "to do" so and so, "and I am willing and ready to do it, but only on condition that you go to Africa." Indeed, a highly talented clergyman informed us in November last (three months ago), in the city of Philadelphia, that he was present when the Rev. Doctor J.P. Durbin, late President of Dickinson College,[51] called on Rev. Mr. P. or B. to consult him about going to Liberia to take charge of the literary department of a University[52] in contemplation, when the following conversation ensued: Mr. P. – "Doctor, I have as much and more than I can do here in educating the youth of our own country and preparing them for usefulness here at home." Dr. D. – "Yes, but do as you may, you can never be elevated here." Mr. P. – "Doctor, do you not believe that the religion of our blessed Redeemer Jesus Christ has morality, humanity, philanthropy, and justice enough in it to elevate us and enable us to obtain our rights in this our own country?" Dr. D. – "No, indeed, sir, I do not, and if you depend upon that, your hopes are vain!" Mr. P. – Turning to Doctor Durbin, looking him solemnly, though affectionately, in the face, remarked – "Well, Doctor Durbin, we both profess to be ministers of Christ; but dearly as I love the cause

Notes

[46] *Original reads*: every where [ed.].

[47] *Original reads*: that [ed.].

[48] *"more subtle than all the beasts of the field,"* Genesis 3:1.

[49] *Original reads*: an idiosyncrasy with the animal [ed.].

[50] *Original reads*: which having once entered there, leaves [ed.].

[51] John Price Durbin (1800–1876), a Methodist clergyman.

[52] *Original reads*: an University [ed.].

of my Redeemer, if for a moment I could entertain the opinion you do about Christianity, I would not serve him another hour!" We do not know, as we were not advised, that the Rev. Doctor added, in fine, "Well, you may quit now, for all your serving him will not avail against the power of the god (hydra) of Colonization." Will anyone[53] doubt for a single moment the justice of our strictures on colonization, after reading the conversation between the Rev. Dr. Durbin and the colored clergyman? Surely not. We can therefore make no account of it, but that of setting it down as being the worst enemy of the colored people.

Recently, there has been a strained effort in the city of New York on the part of the Rev. J.B. Pinney and others of the leading white Colonizationists,[54] to get up a movement among some poor pitiable colored men – we say pitiable, for certainly the colored persons who are at this period capable of loaning themselves to the enemies of their race, against the best interest of all that we hold sacred to that race, are pitiable in the lowest extreme, far beneath the dignity of an enemy, and therefore, we pass them by with the simple remark that this is the hobby that colonization is riding all over the country, as the "tremendous" access of colored people to their cause within the last twelve months. We should make another remark here perhaps, in justification of governor Pinney's New York allies – that is, report says that in the short space of some three or five months, one of his confidants benefited himself to the "reckoning" of from eleven to fifteen hundred dollars, or "such a matter," while others were benefited in sums "pretty considerable" but of a less "reckoning." Well, we do not know, after all, that they may not have quite as good a right to pocket part of the spoils of this "grab game" as anybody[55] else. However, they are of little consequence, as the ever watchful eye of those excellent gentlemen and faithful guardians of their people's rights – the *Committee of Thirteen*, consisting of Messrs. John J. Zuille,[56] *Chairman*, T. Joiner White, Philip A. Bell,[57] *Secretaries*, Robert Hamilton,[58] George T. Downing, Jeremiah Powers, John T. Raymond,[59] Wm. Burnett, James McCune Smith,[60] Ezekiel Dias, Junius C. Morel,[61] Thomas Downing, and Wm. J. Wilson,[62] – have properly chastised this pet-slave of Mr. Pinney, and made it "know its place" by keeping within the bounds of its master's enclosure.

In expressing our honest conviction of the designedly injurious character of the Colonization Society, we should do violence to our own sense of individual justice if we did not express the belief that there are some honest-hearted men, who not having seen things in the proper light, favor that scheme, simply as a means of elevating the colored people. Such persons, so soon as they become convinced of their error, immediately change their policy, and advocate the elevation of the colored people, anywhere and everywhere, in common with other men. Of such were the early abolitionists as before stated; and the great and good Dr. F.J. Lemoyne,[63] Gerrit Smith,[64] and Rev. Charles Avery,[65] and a host of others, who were Colonizationists before espousing the cause of our elevation here at home, and nothing but an honorable sense of justice

Notes

[53] *Original reads*: any one [ed.].

[54] *Original reads*: colonizationists [ed.].

[55] *Original reads*: any body [ed.].

[56] John J. Zuille (1814–1894), New York-based printer.

[57] Philip A. Bell (1808–1889), abolitionist and journalist.

[58] Robert Hamilton, journalist who wrote for, edited, and published *The Weekly Anglo-African*.

[59] John T. Raymond, a minister at Boston's African Meeting House.

[60] James McCune Smith (1813–1865), prominent physician and abolitionist.

[61] Junius C. Morel, Philadelphia abolitionist.

[62] Wm. J. Wilson, abolitionist writer.

[63] Francis Julius LeMoyne (1798–1879), a Pennsylvania philanthropist, physician, and underground railroad conductor.

[64] Gerrit Smith (1797–1874), a politician and radical abolitionist.

[65] Rev. Charles Avery (1784–1858), Pittsburgh businessman, abolitionist, and Methodist minister.

induces us to make these exceptions, as there are many good persons within our knowledge, whom we believe to be well-wishers of the colored people, who may favor colonization.* But the animal itself is the same "hydra-headed monster," let whomsoever may fancy to pet it. A serpent is a serpent, and none the less a viper because nestled in the bosom of an honest-hearted man. This the colored people must bear in mind, and keep clear of the hideous thing, lest its venom may be tested[66] upon them. But why deem any argument necessary to show the unrighteousness of colonization? Its very origin, as before shown – the source from whence it sprung being the offspring of slavery – is in itself sufficient to blast it in the estimation of every colored person in the United States who has sufficient intelligence to comprehend it.

We dismiss this part of the subject, and proceed to consider the mode and means of our elevation in the United States.

Chapter 4

Our Elevation in the United States

That very little comparatively as yet has been done to attain a respectable position as a class in this country will not be denied, and that the successful accomplishment of this end is also possible must also be admitted; but in what manner, and by what means, has long been, and is even now, by the best thinking minds among the colored people themselves, a matter of difference of opinion.

We believe in the universal equality of man, and believe in that declaration of God's word, in which it is there positively said that "God has made of one blood all the nations that dwell on the face of the earth."[69] Now, of "the nations that dwell on the face of the earth" – that is, all the people – there are one thousand millions of souls, and of this vast number of human beings, two-thirds are colored, from black, tending in complexion to the olive or that of the Chinese, with all the intermediate and admixtures of black and white, with the various "crosses," as they are physiologically but erroneously termed, to white. We are thus explicit in stating these points, because we are determined to be understood by all. We have then, two colored to one white person throughout the earth, and yet, singular as it may appear, according to the present geographical and political history of the world, the white race predominates over the colored; or in other words, wherever there is one white person, that one rules and governs two colored persons. This is a living undeniable truth, to which we call the especial attention of the colored reader in particular. Now there is a cause for this, as there is no effect without a cause, a comprehensible remediable cause. We all

Notes

* Benjamin Coates, Esq.,[1] a merchant of Philadelphia, we believe to be an honest-hearted man and real friend of the colored people, and a true, though as yet, rather undecided philanthropist. Mr. Coates, to our knowledge, has supported three or four papers published by colored men, for the elevation of colored people in the United States, and given, as he continues to do, considerable sums to their support. We have recently learned from him[67] that, though he still advocates Colonization simply as a means of elevating the colored race of the United States, he has[68] *left* the Colonization Society, and prefers seeing colored people located on this continent, to going to Liberia, or elsewhere off of it – though his zeal for the enlightenment of Africa is unabated, as every good man's should be; and we are satisfied that Mr. Coates is neither well understood, nor rightly appreciated by the friends of our cause. One thing we do know, that he left the Colonization Society because he could not conscientiously subscribe to its measures.

66 *Original reads*: test [ed.].

67 *Original reads*: himself [ed.].

68 *Original reads*: that he has [ed.].

69 *"God has made … of the earth"* Acts 17:26.

believe in the justice of God, that he is impartial, "looking upon his children with an eye of care,"[70] dealing out to them all the measure of his goodness; yet, how can we reconcile ourselves to the difference that exists between the colored and the white races, as they truthfully present themselves before our eyes? To solve this problem is to know the remedy; and to know it is but necessary in order successfully to apply it. And we shall but take the colored people of the United States as a fair sample of the colored races everywhere of the present age, as the arguments that apply to the one will apply to the other, whether Christians, Mahomedans, or pagans.

The colored races are highly susceptible of religion; it is a constituent principle of their nature, and an excellent trait in their character. But unfortunately for them, they carry it too far. Their hope is largely developed, and consequently, they usually stand still – hope in God, and really expect Him to do that for them which it is necessary they should do themselves. This is their great mistake, and arises from a misconception of the character and ways of Deity. We must know God, that is, understand His nature and purposes, in order to serve Him; and to serve Him well is but to know him rightly. To depend for assistance upon God is a *duty* and right; but to know when, how, and in what manner to obtain it is the key to this great Bulwark of Strength and Depository of Aid.

God himself is perfect; perfect in all his works and ways. He has means for every end; and every means used must be adequate to the end to be gained. God's means are laws – fixed laws of nature, a part of His own being, and as immutable, as unchangeable as Himself. Nothing can be accomplished but through the medium of, and conformable to, these laws.

They are *three* – and like God himself, represented in the three persons in the God-head – the *Spiritual*, *Moral* and *Physical* Laws.

That which is Spiritual can only be accomplished through the medium of the Spiritual law; that which is Moral, through the medium of the Moral law; and that which is Physical, through the medium of the Physical law. Other[71] than this, it is useless to expect anything.[72] If a person wants[73] a spiritual blessing, he must apply through the medium of the spiritual law – *pray* for it in order to obtain it. If they desire to do a moral good, they must apply through the medium of the moral law – exercise their sense and feeling of *right* and *justice* in order to effect it. If they want[74] to attain a physical end, they can only do so through the medium of the physical law – go to *work* with muscles, hands, limbs, might, and strength, and this, and nothing else, will attain it.

The argument that man must pray for what he receives is a mistake, and one that is doing the colored people especially, incalculable injury. That man must pray in order to get to Heaven, every Christian will admit – but a great truth we have yet got to learn, that he can live on earth whether he is religious or not, so that he conforms to the great law of God, regulating the things of earth; the great physical laws. It is only necessary, in order to convince our people of their error and palpable mistake in this matter, to call their attention to the fact that there are no people more religious in this country[75] than the colored people, and none so poor and miserable as they. That prosperity and wealth smiles upon the efforts of wicked white men, whom we know to utter the name of God with curses instead of praises. That among the slaves there are thousands of them religious, continually raising their voices, sending up their prayers

Notes

[70] *"looking upon his children with an eye of care"* Psalm 33.

[71] *Original reads*: Otherwise [ed.].

[72] *Original reads*: any thing [ed.].

[73] *Original reads*: Does a person want [ed.].

[74] *Original reads*: Do they want [ed.].

[75] *Original reads*: Country [ed.].

to God, invoking His aid in their behalf, asking for a speedy deliverance; but they are still in chains, although they have thrice suffered out their three score years and ten. That "God sendeth rain upon the just and unjust" should be sufficient to convince us that our success in life does not depend upon our religious character, but that the physical laws governing all earthly and temporary affairs benefit equally the just and the unjust. Any other doctrine than this is downright delusion, unworthy of a free people, and only intended for slaves. That all men and women should be moral, upright, good, and religious – we mean *Christians* – we would not utter a word against, and could only wish that it were so; but, what we here desire to do is to correct the long-standing error among a large body of the colored people in this country, that the cause of our oppression and degradation is the displeasure of God towards us, because of our unfaithfulness to Him. This is not true; because if God is just – and he is – there could be no justice in prospering white men with his fostering care, for more than two thousand years, in all their wickedness, while dealing out to the colored people the measure of his displeasure for not half the wickedness as that of the whites. Here then is our mistake, and let it forever henceforth be corrected. We are no longer slaves, believing any interpretation that our oppressors may give the word of God for the purpose of deluding us to the more easy subjugation; but freemen, comprising some of the first minds of intelligence and rudimental qualifications in the country. What then is the remedy for our degradation and oppression? This appears now to be the only remaining question – the means of successful elevation in this our own native land? This depends entirely upon the application of the means of Elevation.

Chapter 5

Means of Elevation

Moral theories have long been resorted to by us as a means of effecting the redemption of our brethren in bonds and the elevation of the free colored people in this country. Experience has taught us that speculations are not enough; that the *practical* application of principles adduced, the thing carried out, is the only true and proper course to pursue.

We have speculated and moralised much about equality – claiming to be as good as our neighbors, and everybody[76] else – all of which, may do very well in ethics, but not in politics. We live in society among men, conducted by men, governed by rules and regulations. However arbitrary, there are certain policies that regulate all well-organized institutions and corporate bodies. We do not intend here to speak of the legal political relations of society, for those are treated on elsewhere. The business and social, or voluntary and mutual, policies are those that now claim our attention. Society regulates itself – being governed by mind, which like water, finds its own level. "Like seeks like," is a principle in the laws of matter, as well as of mind. There is such a thing as inferiority of things, and positions; at least society has made them so; and while we continue to live among men, we must agree to all *just* measures – all those, we mean, that do not necessarily infringe on the rights of others. By the regulations of society, there is no equality of attainments. By this, we do not wish to be understood as advocating the actual equal attainments of every individual; but we mean to say,

Notes

[76] *Original reads*: every body [ed.].

that if these attainments be necessary for the elevation of the white man, they are necessary for the elevation of the colored man. That some colored men and women, in a like proportion to the whites, should be qualified in all the attainments possessed by them. It is one of the regulations of society the world over, and we shall have to conform to it or be discarded as unworthy of the associations of our fellows.

Cast our eyes about us and reflect for a moment and what do we behold! everything[77] that presents to view gives evidence of the skill of the white man. Should we purchase a pound of groceries, a yard of linen, a vessel of crockery-ware, a piece of furniture, the very provisions that we eat – all, all are the products of the white man, purchased by us from the white man; consequently, our earnings and means are all given to the white man.

Pass along the avenues of any city or town in which you live – behold the trading shops – the manufacturies[78] – see the operations of the various machinery – see the stagecoaches coming in, bringing the mails of intelligence – look at the railroads interlining every section, bearing upon them their mighty trains, flying with the velocity of the swallow, ushering in the hundreds of industrious, enterprising travellers. Cast again your eyes widespread over the ocean – see the vessels in every direction with their white sheets spread to the winds of heaven, freighted with the commerce, merchandise, and wealth of many nations. Look as you pass along through the cities, at the great and massive buildings – the beautiful and extensive structures of architecture – behold the ten thousand cupolas, with their spires all reared up towards heaven, intersecting the territory of the clouds – all standing as mighty living monuments to the industry,[79] enterprise, and intelligence of the white man. And yet, with all these living truths rebuking us with scorn, we strut about, place our hands akimbo, straighten up ourselves to our greatest height, and talk loudly about being "as good as anybody."[80] How do we compare with them? Our fathers are their coachmen, our brothers their cookmen, and ourselves their waiting-men. Our mothers their nurse-women, our sisters their scrub-women, our daughters their maid-women, and our wives their washer-women. Until colored men attain to a position above permitting their mothers, sisters, wives, and daughters to do the drudgery and menial offices of other men's wives and daughters, it is useless, it is nonsense, it is pitiable mockery to talk about equality and elevation in society. The world is looking upon us with feelings of commiseration, sorrow, and contempt. We scarcely deserve sympathy if we peremptorily refuse advice bearing upon our elevation.

We will suppose a case for argument: In this city reside two colored families, of three sons and three daughters each. At the head of each family there is an old father and mother. The opportunities of these families may or may not be the same for educational advantages – be that as it may, the children of the one go to school and become qualified for the duties of life. One daughter becomes school-teacher, another a mantua-maker,[81] and a third a fancy shop-keeper; while one son becomes a farmer, another a merchant, and a third a mechanic. All enter into business with fine prospects, marry respectably, and settle down in domestic comfort – while the six sons and daughters of the other family grow up without educational and business qualifications, and the highest aim they have is to apply to the sons and daughters of the first named family to hire for domestics! Would there be an equality here between the children of these

Notes

[77] *Original reads*: every thing [ed.].

[78] *manufacturies* manufacturers.

[79] *Original reads*: living monuments, of the industry [ed.].

[80] *Original reads*: any body [ed.].

[81] *mantua-maker* a mantua is a loose gown.

two families? Certainly not. This, then, is precisely the position of the colored people generally in the United States, compared with the whites. What is necessary to be done, in order to attain an equality, is to change the condition, and the person is at once changed. If, as before stated, a knowledge of all the various business enterprises, trades, professions, and sciences is necessary for the elevation of the white, a knowledge of them also is necessary for the elevation of the colored man; and he cannot be elevated without them.

White men are producers – we are consumers. They build houses, and we rent them. They raise produce, and we consume it. They manufacture clothes and wares, and we garnish ourselves with them. They build coaches, vessels, cars, hotels, saloons, and other vehicles and places of accommodation, and we deliberately wait until they have got them in readiness, then walk in and contend with as much assurance for a "right," as though the whole thing was bought by, paid for, and belonged to us. By their literary attainments they are the contributors to, authors, and teachers of literature, science, religion, law, medicine, and all other useful attainments that the world now makes use of. We have no reference to ancient times – we speak of modern things.

These are the means by which God intended man to succeed: and this discloses the secret of the white man's success, with all of his wickedness, over the head of the colored man, with all of his religion. We have been pointed and plain on this part of the subject, because we desire our readers to see persons and things in their true position. Until we are determined to change the condition of things, and raise ourselves above the position in which we are now prostrated, we must hang our heads in sorrow and hide our faces in shame. It is enough to know that these things are so; the causes we care little about. Those we have been examining, complaining about, and moralising over all our life time. This we are weary of. What we desire to learn now is how to effect a *remedy*; this we have endeavored to point out. Our elevation must be the result of *self-efforts*, and work of our *own hands*. No other human power can accomplish it. If we but determine it shall be so, it will be so. Let each one make the case his own, and endeavor to rival his neighbor in honorable competition.

These are the proper and only means of elevating ourselves and attaining equality in this country or any other, and it is useless, utterly futile, to think about going anywhere[82] unless[83] we are determined to use these as the necessary means of developing our manhood. The means are at hand, within our reach. Are we willing to try them? Are we willing to raise ourselves superior to the condition of slaves, or continue the meanest underlings, subject to the beck and call of every creature bearing a pale complexion? If we are, we had as well remained in the South as to have come to the North in search of more freedom. What was the object of our parents in leaving the south if it were not for the purpose of attaining equality in common with others of their fellow citizens, by giving their children access to all the advantages enjoyed by others? Surely this was their object. They heard of liberty and equality here, and they hastened on to enjoy it, and no people are more astonished and disappointed than they, who, for the first time, behold the position we occupy here in the free north[84] – what is called, and what they expect to find, the free States. They at once tell us, that they have as much liberty in the south as we have in the north – that there as free people, they are protected in their rights – that we have nothing more – that in other respects they have the same opportunity, indeed the preferred opportunity, of being their maids, servants,

Notes

[82] *Original reads*: any where [ed.].
[83] *Original reads*: except [ed.].
[84] *Original reads*: who for the first time, on beholding the position we occupy here in the free north [ed.].

cooks, waiters, and menials in general, there, as we have here – that had they known for a moment, before leaving, that such was to be the only position they occupied here, they would have remained where they were, and never left. Indeed, such is the disappointment in many cases that they immediately return back again, completely insulted at the idea of having us here at the north assume ourselves to be their superiors. Indeed, if our superior advantages of the free States do not induce and stimulate us to the higher attainments in life, what in the name of degraded humanity will do it? Nothing, surely nothing. If, in fine, the advantages of free schools in Massachusetts, New York, Pennsylvania, Ohio, Michigan, and wherever else we may have them, do not give us advantages and pursuits superior to our slave brethren, then are the unjust assertions of Messrs. Henry Clay, John C. Calhoun,[85] Theodore Frelinghuysen,[86] late Governor Poindexter of Mississippi,[87] George McDuffy,[88] Governor Hammond of South Carolina,[89] Extra Billy (present Governor) Smith, of Virginia,[90] and the host of our oppressors, slave-holders and others, true, that we are insusceptible and incapable of elevation to the more respectable, honorable, and higher attainments among white men. But this we do not believe – neither do you, although our whole life and course of policy in this country are such that it would seem to prove otherwise. The degradation of the slave parent has been entailed upon the child, induced by the subtle policy of the oppressor, in regular succession handed down from father to son – a system of regular submission and servitude, menialism and dependence, until it has become almost a physiological function of our system, an actual condition of our nature. Let this no longer be so, but let us determine to equal the whites among whom we live, not by declarations and unexpressed self-opinion, for we have always had enough of that, but by actual proof in acting, doing, and carrying out practically the measures of equality. Here is our nativity, and here have we the natural right to abide and be elevated through the measures of our own efforts.

Chapter 6

The United States Our Country

Our common country is the United States. Here were we born, here raised and educated; here are the scenes of childhood; the pleasant associations of our school-going days; the loved enjoyments of our domestic and fireside relations, and the sacred graves of our departed fathers and mothers, and from here will we not be driven by any policy that may be schemed against us.

We are Americans, having a birthright citizenship – natural claims upon the country – claims common to all others of our fellow citizens – natural rights, which may, by virtue of unjust laws, be obstructed, but never can be annulled. Upon these do we place ourselves, as immovably fixed as the decrees of the living God. But according to the economy that regulates the policy of nations, upon which rests the basis of justifiable claims to all freeman's rights, it may be necessary to take another view of, and enquire into the political claims of, colored men.

Notes

85 John C. Calhoun (1782–1850), South Carolina senator and Vice President under John Quincy Adams and Andrew Jackson (1825–1832).

86 Theodore Frelinghuysen (1787–1862), American politician who ran for Vice President on Henry Clay's Whig ticket in 1844.

87 George Poindexter (1779–1853).

88 George McDuffie (1790–1851), Governor of South Carolina.

89 James Henry Hammond (1807–1864).

90 William Smith (1797–1887), also a Major General in the Confederate States Army during the Civil War.

Chapter 17

Emigration of the Colored People of the United States

That there have been people in all ages, under certain circumstances, that may be benefited by emigration, will be admitted; and that there are circumstances under which emigration is absolutely necessary to their political elevation cannot be disputed.

This we see in the Exodus of the Jews from Egypt to the land of Judea; in the expedition of Dido and her followers from Tyro to Mauritania;[91] and not to dwell upon hundreds of modern European examples – also in the ever memorable emigration of the Puritans, in 1620, from Great Britain, the land of their birth, to the wilderness of the New World, at which may be fixed the beginning of emigration to this continent as a permanent residence.

This may be acknowledged; but to advocate the emigration of the colored people of the United States from their native homes is a new feature in our history, and at first view, may be considered objectionable, as pernicious to our interests. This objection is at once removed when reflecting on our condition as incontrovertibly shown in a foregoing part of this work. And we shall proceed at once to give the advantages to be derived from emigration, to us as a people, in preference to any other policy that we may adopt. This granted, the question will then be, Where shall we go? This we conceive to be all-important – of paramount consideration – and shall endeavor to show the most advantageous locality; and premise the recommendation with the strictest advice against any countenance whatever to the emigration scheme of the so called Republic of Liberia.

Chapter 23

A Glance at Ourselves – Conclusion

With broken hopes – sad devastation;
A race resigned *to* DEGRADATION!

We have said much to our young men and women about their vocation and calling; we have dwelt much upon the menial position of our people in this country. Upon this point we cannot say too much, because there is a seeming satisfaction and seeking after such positions manifested on their part, unknown to any other people. There appears to be a want of a sense of propriety or *self-respect* altogether inexplicable; because young men and women among us, many of whom have good trades and homes, adequate to their support, voluntarily leave them and seek positions, such as servants, waiting-maids, coachmen, nurses, cooks in gentlemen's kitchen, or such like occupations, when they can gain a livelihood at something more respectable or elevating in character. And the worse part of the whole matter is that they have become so accustomed to it, it has become so "fashionable," that it seems to have become second nature, and they really become offended when it is spoken against.

Among the German, Irish, and other European peasantry who come to this country, it matters not what they were employed at before and after they come; just so soon

Notes

[91] *Dido and her followers from Tyro to Mauritania* In Greco-Roman ancient history, Dido is the founder and first Queen of Carthage, having left her birthplace of Tyre (in Lebanon).

as they can better their condition by keeping shops, cultivating the soil, the young men and women going to night-schools, qualifying themselves for usefulness, and learning trades – they do so. Their first and last care, object, and aim is to better their condition by raising themselves above the condition that necessity places them in. We do not say too much when we say, as an evidence of the deep degradation of our race in the United States, that there are those among us, the wives and daughters, some of the *first ladies* (and who dare say they are not the "first," because they belong to the "first class" and associate where anybody[92] among us can?), whose husbands are industrious, able, and willing to support them, who voluntarily leave home and become chamber-maids and stewardesses upon vessels and steamboats, in all probability to enable them to obtain some more fine or costly article of dress or furniture.

We have nothing to say against those whom *necessity* compels to do these things, those who can do no better; we have only to do with those who can, and will not, or do not, do better. The whites are always in the advance, and we either standing still or retrograding; as that which does not go forward must either stand in one place or go back. The father in all probability is a farmer, mechanic, or man of some independent business; and the wife, sons, and daughters are chamber-maids, on vessels, nurses and waiting-maids, or coachmen and cooks in families. This is retrogradation. The wife, sons, and daughters should be elevated above this condition as a necessary consequence.

If we did not love our race superior to others, we would not concern ourselves[93] about their degradation; for the greatest desire of our heart is to see them stand on a level with the most elevated of mankind. No people are ever elevated above the condition of their *females*; hence, the condition of the *mother* determines the condition of the child. To know the position of a people it is only necessary to know the *condition* of their *females*; and despite themselves, they cannot rise above their level. Then what is our condition? Our *best ladies* being washerwomen, chamber-maids, children's traveling nurses, and common house servants, and menials, we are all a degraded, miserable people, inferior to any other people as a whole, on the face of the globe.

These great truths, however unpleasant, must be brought before the minds of our people in their[94] true and proper light, as we have been too delicate about them, and too long concealed them for fear of giving offence. It would have been infinitely better for our race if these facts had been presented before us half a century ago – we would have been now proportionably benefitted by it.

As an evidence of the degradation to which we have been reduced, we dare premise that this chapter will give offence to many, very many: and why? Because they may say, "He dared to say that the occupation of a *servant* is a degradation." It is not necessarily degrading; it would not be to one or a few people of a kind; but a *whole race of servants* are a degradation to that people.

Efforts made by men of qualifications for the toiling and degraded millions among the whites neither gives offence to that class, nor is it taken unkindly by them; but received with manifestations of gratitude, to know that they are thought to be, equally worthy of, and entitled to stand on a level with the elevated classes; and they have only got to be informed of the way to raise themselves, to make the effort and do so as far as they can. But how different with us. Speak of our position in society and it at once gives insult. Though we are servants, among ourselves we claim to be *ladies* and *gentlemen*, equal in standing, and as the popular expression goes, "Just as

Notes

[92] *Original reads*: any body [ed.].
[93] *Original reads*: ourself [ed.].
[94] *Original reads*: its [ed.].
[95] *Original reads*: any body [ed.].

good as anybody"[95] – and so believing, we make no efforts to rise[96] above the common level of menials; because the *best* being in that capacity, all are content with the position. We cannot at the same time be domestic and lady; servant and gentleman. We must be the one or the other. Sad, sad indeed, is the thought that hangs drooping in our mind when contemplating the picture drawn before us. Young men and women, "we write these things unto you, because ye are strong,"[97] because the writer, a few years ago, gave unpardonable offence to many of the young people of Philadelphia and other places, because he dared tell them that he thought too much of them to be content with seeing them the servants of other people. Surely, she that could be the mistress would not be the maid; neither would he that could be the master be content with being the servant; then why be offended when we point out to you the way that leads from the menial to the mistress or the master. All this we seem to reject with fixed determination, repelling with anger every effort on the part of our intelligent men and women to elevate us, with true Israelitish degradation, in reply to any suggestion or proposition that may be offered, "Who made thee a ruler and judge?"[98]

The writer is no "Public Man," in the sense in which this is understood among our people, but simply a humble[99] individual endeavoring to seek a livelihood by a profession obtained entirely by his own efforts, without relatives and friends able to assist him; except such friends as he gained by the merit of his course and conduct, which he here gratefully acknowledges; and whatever he has accomplished, other young men may, by making corresponding efforts, also accomplish.

We have advised an emigration to Central and South America, and even to Mexico and the West Indies, to those who prefer either of the last named places, all of which are free countries, Brazil being the only real slave-holding State in South America – there being nominal slavery in Dutch Guiana,[100] Peru, Buenos Ayres,[101] Paraguay, and Uruguay,[102] in all of which places colored people have equality in social, civil, political, and religious privileges; Brazil making it punishable with death to import slaves into the empire.

Our oppressors, when urging us to go to Africa, tell us that we are better adapted to the climate than they – that the physical condition of the constitution of colored people better endures the heat of warm climates than that of the whites; this we are willing to *admit*, without argument, without adducing the physiological reason why, that colored people can and do stand warm climates better than whites; and find an answer fully to the point in the fact, that they also stand *all other* climates, cold, temperate, and modified, that white people can stand; therefore, according to our oppressors' own showing, we are a *superior race*, being endowed with properties fitting us for *all parts* of the earth, while they are only adapted to *certain* parts. Of course, this proves our right and duty to live wherever we may *choose*; while the white race may only live where they *can*. We are content with the fact, and have ever claimed it. Upon this rock they and we shall ever agree.

Of the West India Islands,[103] Santa Cruz, belonging to Denmark;[104] Puerto Rico;[105] and Cuba with its little adjuncts, belonging to Spain, are the only slaveholding islands[106] among them – three-fifths of the whole population of Cuba being colored people,

Notes

[96] *Original reads*: raise [ed.].

[97] *"we write these things unto you, because ye are strong"* 1 John 2:14.

[98] *"Who made thee a ruler and judge?"* Acts 7:27.

[99] *Original reads*: an humble [ed.].

[100] *Dutch Guiana* modern-day Suriname.

[101] *Buenos Ayres* Buenos Aires, in Argentina.

[102] *Original reads*: Uraguay [ed.].

[103] *West India Islands* the West Indies.

[104] *Santa Cruz, belonging to Denmark* modern-day Saint Croix, US Virgin Islands.

[105] *Original reads*: Porto Rico [ed.].

[106] *Original reads*: Islands [ed.].

who cannot and will not much longer endure the burden and the yoke. They only want intelligent leaders of their own color, when they are ready at any moment to charge to the conflict – to liberty or death. The remembrance of the noble mulatto, PLACIDO,[107] the gentleman, scholar, poet, and intended Chief Engineer of the Army of Liberty and Freedom in Cuba; and the equally noble black, CHARLES BELAIR,[108] who was to have been Commander-in-Chief, who were shamefully put to death in 1844, by that living monster, Captain General O'Donnell,[109] is still fresh and indelible to the mind of every bondman of Cuba.

In our own country, the United States, there are *three million five hundred thousand slaves*; and we, the nominally free colored people, are *six hundred thousand* in number; estimating one-sixth to be men, we have *one hundred thousand* able-bodied freemen, which will make a powerful auxiliary in any country to which we may become adopted – an ally not to be despised by any power on earth. We love our country, dearly love her, but she doesn't[110] love us – she despises us, and bids us be gone,[111] driving us from her embraces; but we shall not go where she desires us; but when we do go, whatever love we have for her, we shall love the country none the less that receives us as her adopted children.

For the want of business habits and training, our energies have become paralyzed; our young men never think of business, any more than if they were so many bondmen, without the right to pursue any calling they may think most advisable. With our people in this country, dress and good appearances have been made the only test of gentleman and ladyship, and that vocation which offers the best opportunity to dress and appear well has generally been preferred, however menial and degrading, by our young people, without even, in the majority of cases, an effort to do better; indeed, in many instances, refusing situations equally lucrative and superior in position; but which would not allow as much display of dress and personal appearance. This, if we ever expect to rise, must be discarded from among us, and a high and respectable position assumed.

One of our great temporal curses is our consummate poverty. We are the poorest people, as a class, in the world of civilized mankind – abjectly, miserably poor, no one scarcely being able to assist the other. To this, of course, there are noble exceptions; but that which is common to, and the very process by which white men exist and succeed in life, is unknown to colored men in general. In any and every considerable community may be found someone[112] of our white fellow-citizens who is worth more than all the colored people in that community put together. We consequently have little or no efficiency. We must have means to be practically efficient in all the undertakings of life; and to obtain them, it is necessary that we should be engaged in lucrative pursuits, trades, and general business transactions. In order to be thus engaged, it is necessary that we should occupy positions that afford the facilities for such pursuits. To compete now with the mighty odds of wealth, social and religious preferences, and political influences of this country, at this advanced stage of its national existence, we never may expect. A new country, and new beginning, is the only true, rational, politic remedy for our disadvantageous position; and that country we have already pointed out, with triple golden advantages, all things considered, to that of any country to which it has been the province of man to embark.

Notes

[107] "Plácido" was the nom de plume of Cuban poet Gabriel de la Concepción Valdés (1809–1844).

[108] Charles Belair (1778–1802), one of Toussaint L'Ouverture's generals in the Haitian revolution. *Original reads*: Blair [ed.].

[109] Leopoldo O'Donnell (1809–1867), governor of Cuba (1843–1848).

[110] *Original reads*: don't [ed.].

[111] *Original reads*: begone [ed.].

[112] *Original reads*: some one [ed.].

Every other than we have, at various periods of necessity, been a migratory people; and all when oppressed, shown a greater abhorrence of oppression, if not a greater love of liberty, than we. We cling to our oppressors as the objects of our love. It is true that our enslaved brethren are here, and we have been led to believe that it is necessary for us to remain on that account. Is it true that all should remain in degradation, because a part are degraded? We believe no such thing. We believe it to be the duty of the Free to elevate themselves in the most speedy and effective manner possible; as the redemption of the bondman depends entirely upon the elevation of the freeman; therefore, to elevate the free colored people of America anywhere upon this continent forebodes the speedy redemption of the slaves. We shall hope to hear no more of so fallacious a doctrine – the necessity of the free remaining in degradation for the sake of the oppressed. Let us apply first the lever to ourselves; and the force that elevates us to the position of manhood's considerations and honors will cleft the manacle of every slave in the land.

When such great worth and talents – for want of a better sphere – of men like Rev. Jonathan Robinson, Robert Douglass,[113] Frederick A. Hinton,[114] and a hundred others that might be named, were permitted to expire in a barber-shop; and such living men as may be found in Boston, New York, Philadelphia, Baltimore, Richmond, Washington City, Charleston, (S.C.) New Orleans, Cincinnati, Louisville, St. Louis, Pittsburg, Buffalo, Rochester, Albany, Utica, Cleveland, Detroit, Milwaukie, Chicago, Columbus, Zanesville, Wheeling, and a hundred other places, confining themselves to barber-shops[115] and waiter-ships in hotels;[116] certainly the necessity of such a course as we have pointed out must be cordially acknowledged; appreciated by every brother and sister of oppression; and not rejected as heretofore, as though they preferred inferiority to equality. These minds must become "unfettered," and have "space to rise." This cannot be in their present positions. A continuance in any position becomes what is termed "Second Nature"; it begets an *adaptation*, and *reconciliation* of *mind* to such condition. It changes the whole physiological condition of the system, and adapts man and woman to a higher or lower sphere in the pursuits of life. The offspring of slaves and peasantry have the general characteristics of their parents, and nothing but a different course of training and education will change the character.

The slave may become a lover of his master, and learn to forgive him for continual deeds of maltreatment and abuse; just as the Spaniel would couch and fondle at the feet that kick him; because he has been taught to reverence them, and consequently, becomes adapted in body and mind to his condition. Even the shrubbery-loving Canary, and lofty-soaring Eagle, may be tamed to the cage, and learn to love it from habit of confinement. It has been so with us in our position among our oppressors; we have been so prone to such positions that we have learned to love them. When reflecting upon this all-important, and to us, all-absorbing subject, we feel in the agony and anxiety of the moment, as though we could cry out in the language of a Prophet of old: "Oh that my head were waters, and mine eyes a fountain of tears, that I might weep day and night for the" degradation "of my people! Oh that I had in the wilderness a lodging place of way-faring men; that I might leave my people, and go from them!"[117]

Notes

[113] Robert Douglass (1809–1887), an African American artist.

[114] Frederick A. Hinton (1804–1849), headed the American Moral Reform Society.

[115] *Original reads*: Barber-shops [ed.].

[116] *Original reads*: Hotels [ed.].

[117] *"Oh that my head were waters … go from them!"* Jeremiah 9:1–2.

The Irishman and German in the United States are very different persons to what they were when in Ireland and Germany, the countries of their nativity. There their spirits were depressed and downcast; but the instant they set their foot upon unrestricted soil, free to act and untrammeled to move, their physical condition undergoes a change, which in time becomes physiological, which is transmitted to the offspring, who, when born under such circumstances, is a decidedly different being to what it would have been had it been born under different circumstances.

A child born under oppression has all the elements of servility in its constitution; who, when born under favorable circumstances, has, to the contrary, all the elements of freedom and independence of feeling. Our children, then, may not be expected to maintain that position and manly bearing, born under the unfavorable circumstances with which we are surrounded in this country, that we so much desire. To use the language of the talented Mr. Whipper,[118] "they cannot be raised in this country, without being stoop shouldered." Heaven's pathway stands unobstructed, which will lead us into a Paradise of bliss. Let us go on and possess the land,[119] and the God of Israel will be our God.

The lessons of every school book, the pages of every history, and the columns of every newspaper, are so replete with stimuli to nerve us on to manly aspirations, that our young people will now refuse[120] to enter upon this great theatre of Polynesian adventure, and take their position on the stage of Central and South America, where a brilliant engagement, of certain and most triumphant success, in the drama of human equality awaits them; then, with the blood of *slaves*, they will write upon the lintel[121] of every door in sterling Capitals, to be gazed and hissed at by every passerby –

Doomed by the Creator
To servility and degradation;
The SERVANT of the *white man*,
And despised of every nation!

1852

Notes

[118] William Whipper (1804–1876), African American businessman and abolitionist.

[119] *Let us go on and possess the land* Deuteronomy 8:1.

[120] *Original reads*: and columns of every newspaper, are so replete with stimuli to nerve us on to manly aspirations, that those of our young people, who will now refuse [ed.].

[121] *Original reads*: with the blood of *slaves*, write upon the lintel [ed.].

Harriet E. Adams Wilson (1825–1900)

When Harriet Wilson died in Quincy, Massachusetts, in 1900, few of her contemporaries knew that the elderly woman had written one of the first African American novels in 1859. Rather, "Dr. Hattie E. Wilson, the trance medium" was known as a spiritualist and traveling lecturer who performed at camp meetings, in theaters, and in private homes across New England. A delegate to the American Association of Spiritualists in 1870 who shared the stage with feminist Victoria Woodhull, Wilson was also a housekeeper in one of Boston's South End boarding houses. Her early life as an author, however, most ushered her into the canon of African American literature, despite the fact that her novel, *Our Nig; or, Sketches from the Life of a Free Black* (1859), received scant attention until the scholar Henry Louis Gates, Jr unearthed her African American identity in the early 1980s.

Harriet Wilson was born in Milford, New Hampshire, the daughter of an African American cooper named Joshua Green, and an Irish washerwoman named Margaret Ann (or Adams) Smith. When her father died, the young Harriet fell into a state of poverty and disadvantage that would haunt her throughout her life. Margaret Smith abandoned her daughter at the home of a well-to-do Milford farmer, Nehemiah Hayward, Jr. Wilson became the Haywards' indentured servant, and the abuse heaped upon Frado by the Bellmont family in *Our Nig* mirrors Wilson's own treatment at the hands of her adoptive family. Like the tragic mulattoes of William Wells Brown's 1853 *Clotel*, Wilson's mixed-race background did little to shelter her from the abuse and animosity of the predominantly white surroundings.

At the end of her indenture, Harriet earned a living as a servant and seamstress, in various households around southern New Hampshire and Massachusetts. In 1851, she married Thomas Wilson, a Milford speaker on the antislavery circuit who later confided to Harriet that he had never been enslaved. Thomas Wilson's biographical fraud was a sign of things to come, and the marriage was marked by instability and tension. While pregnant with the couple's first and only child, Wilson found herself alone when her husband suddenly disappeared. Thrust once again into grinding poverty, she entered the Hillsborough County, New Hampshire, Poor Farm where she gave birth to her only son, George Mason Wilson, in 1852. Thomas Wilson briefly returned to his family, rescuing them from the Poor Farm and going to sea to earn money, but his sudden death forced Harriet to send young George back to the Poor Farm while she moved to Boston to earn a living. In Boston, she wrote *Our Nig*, a story of the racism and discrimination faced by free African Americans in the antebellum North. Unfortunately, whatever money Wilson received from her only novel came too late to save her seven-year-old son, who died at the Poor Farm in early 1860. Wilson herself spent three more years under the care of the Overseers of the Poor in Milford before she moved to Cambridge, Massachusetts, in 1867. There she reinvented herself as "the colored medium," becoming a fixture in the local Spiritualist movement and marrying for the second time. Her new husband, John Gallatin Robinson, was a Canadian apothecary 18 years younger than she was. The couple lived in Boston for a time before separating in the late 1870s.

Our Nig has a seminal place in the African American literary canon. With an August 18, 1859, copyright, it is the first novel published by an

The Wiley Blackwell Anthology of African American Literature: Volume 1, 1746–1920, First Edition.
Edited by Gene Andrew Jarrett.

African American in the United States (whereas William Wells Brown's *Clotel* and Frank J. Webb's 1857 *The Garies and Their Friends* were first published in England). It is notable for its portrayal of northern racism and economic exploitation of free African Americans, but also being a testament to the courage and faith of African American women in persevering through such hardships.

Further reading

Boggis, JerriAnne, Eve Allegra Raimon, and Barbara A. White, eds. *Harriet Wilson's New England: Race, Writing, and Region*. Durham: University of New Hampshire Press, 2007.

Borgstrom, Michael. *Minority Reports: Identity and Social Knowledge in Nineteenth-Century American Literature*. New York: Palgrave Macmillan, 2010. Ch. 1.

Dowling, David. *Capital Letters: Authorship in the Antebellum Literary Market*. Iowa City: University of Iowa Press, 2009. Ch. 1.

Ellis, R.J. *Harriet Wilson's Our Nig: A Cultural Biography of a 'Two-Story' African American Novel*. Amsterdam: Rodopi, 2003.

Ellis, R.J. and Henry Louis Gates, Jr. "'Grievances at the treatment she received': Harriet E. Wilson's Spiritualist Career in Boston, 1868–1900." *American Literary History* 24.2 (2012): 234–264.

Gomaa, Sally. "Writing to 'Virtuous' and 'Gentle' Readers: The Problem of Pain in Harriet Jacobs's *Incidents* and Harriet Wilson's *Sketches*." *African American Review* 43.2–3 (2009): 371–381.

Kilcup, Karen L. "Frado Taught A Naughty Ram: Animal and Human Natures in *Our Nig*." ELH 79.2 (2012): 341–368.

Lee, Maurice S. "The 1850s: The First Renaissance of Black Letters." *A Companion to African American Literature*. Ed. Gene Andrew Jarrett. Malden, MA: Wiley-Blackwell, 2010. 103–118.

Raimon, Eve Allegra. *The 'Tragic Mulatta' Revisited: Race and Nationalism in Nineteenth-Century Antislavery Fiction*. New Brunswick: Rutgers University Press, 2004. Ch. 4.

Santamarina, Xiomara. *Belabored Professions: Narratives of African American Working Womanhood*. Chapel Hill: University of North Carolina Press, 2005. Ch. 2.

Tompkins, Kyla Wazana. "'Everything 'Cept Eat Us': The Antebellum Black Body Portrayed as Edible Body." *Callaloo* 30.1 (2007): 201–224.

Our Nig; or, Sketches from the Life of a Free Black

Preface

In offering to the public the following pages, the writer confesses her inability to minister to the refined and cultivated, the pleasure supplied by abler pens. It is not for such these crude narrations appear. Deserted by kindred, disabled by failing health, I am forced to some experiment which shall aid me in maintaining myself and child without extinguishing this feeble life. I would not from these motives even palliate slavery at the South, by disclosures of its appurtenances[1] North. My mistress was wholly imbued with *southern* principles. I do not pretend to divulge every transaction in my own life, which the unprejudiced would declare unfavorable in comparison with treatment of legal bondmen; I have purposely omitted what would most provoke shame in our good anti-slavery friends at home.

My humble position and frank confession of errors will, I hope, shield me from severe criticism. Indeed, defects are so apparent it requires no skilful hand to expose them.

I sincerely appeal to my colored brethren universally for patronage, hoping they will not condemn this attempt of their sister to be erudite, but rally around me a faithful band of supporters and defenders.

H.E.W.

Notes

[1] *appurtenances* accessories.

Chapter 1

Mag Smith, My Mother

Oh, Grief beyond all other griefs, when fate
First leaves the young heart lone and desolate
In the wide world, without that only tie
For which it loved to live or feared to die;
Lorn as the hung-up lute, that ne'er hath spoken
Since the sad day its master-chord was broken![2]
Moore.

Lonely Mag Smith! See her as she walks with downcast eyes and heavy heart. It was not always thus. She *had* a loving, trusting heart. Early deprived of parental guardianship, far removed from relatives, she was left to guide her tiny boat over life's surges alone and inexperienced. As she merged into womanhood, unprotected, uncherished, uncared for, there fell on her ear the music of love, awakening an intensity of emotion long dormant. It whispered of an elevation before unaspired to; of ease and plenty her simple heart had never dreamed of as hers. She knew the voice of her charmer, so ravishing, sounded far above her. It seemed like an angel's, alluring her upward and onward. She thought she could ascend to him and become an equal. She surrendered to him a priceless gem, which he proudly garnered as a trophy, with those of other victims, and left her to her fate. The world seemed full of hateful deceivers and crushing arrogance. Conscious that the great bond of union to her former companions was severed, that the disdain of others would be insupportable, she determined to leave the few friends she possessed, and seek an asylum among strangers. Her offspring came unwelcomed, and before its nativity numbered weeks, it passed from earth, ascending to a purer and better life.

"God be thanked," ejaculated Mag, as she saw its breathing cease; "no one can taunt *her* with my ruin."

Blessed release! may we all respond. How many pure, innocent children not only inherit a wicked heart of their own, claiming life-long scrutiny and restraint, but are heirs also of parental disgrace and calumny, from which only long years of patient endurance in paths of rectitude can disencumber them.

Mag's new home was soon contaminated by the publicity of her fall; she had a feeling of degradation oppressing her; but she resolved to be circumspect, and try to regain in a measure what she had lost. Then some foul tongue would jest of her shame, and averted looks and cold greetings disheartened her. She saw she could not bury in forgetfulness her misdeed, so she resolved to leave her home and seek another in the place she at first fled from.

Alas, how fearful are we to be first in extending a helping hand to those who stagger in the mires of infamy; to speak the first words of hope and warning to those emerging into the sunlight of morality! Who can tell what numbers, advancing just far enough to hear a cold welcome and join in the reserved converse of professed reformers, disappointed, disheartened, have chosen to dwell in unclean places, rather than encounter these "holier-than-thou" of the great brotherhood of man!

Notes

[2] *"Oh, Grief beyond all other griefs … was broken!"* from the epic poem "Lalla Rookh" (1817) by Thomas Moore (1779–1852).

Such was Mag's experience; and disdaining to ask favor or friendship from a sneering world, she resolved to shut herself up in a hovel she had often passed in better days, and which she knew to be untenanted. She vowed to ask no favors of familiar faces; to die neglected and forgotten before she would be dependent on any. Removed from the village, she was seldom seen except as upon your introduction, gentle reader, with downcast visage, returning her work to her employer, and thus providing herself with the means of subsistence. In two years many hands craved the same avocation; foreigners who cheapened toil and clamored for a livelihood, competed with her, and she could not thus sustain herself. She was now above no drudgery. Occasionally old acquaintances called to be favored with help of some kind, which she was glad to bestow for the sake of the money it would bring her; but the association with them was such a painful reminder of by-gones, she returned to her hut morose and revengeful, refusing all offers of a better home than she possessed. Thus she lived for years, hugging her wrongs, but making no effort to escape. She had never known plenty, scarcely competency; but the present was beyond comparison with those innocent years when the coronet of virtue was hers.

Every year her melancholy increased, her means diminished. At last no one seemed to notice her, save a kind-hearted African, who often called to inquire after her health and to see if she needed any fuel, he having the responsibility of furnishing that article, and she in return mending or making garments.

"How much you earn dis week, Mag?" asked he one Saturday evening.

"Little enough, Jim. Two or three days without any dinner. I washed for the Reeds, and did a small job for Mrs. Bellmont; that's all. I shall starve soon, unless I can get more to do. Folks seem as afraid to come here as if they expected to get some awful disease. I don't[3] believe there is a person in the world but would be glad to have me dead and out of the way."

"No, no, Mag! don't[4] talk so. You shan't starve so long as I have barrels to hoop.[5] Peter Greene boards me cheap. I'll help you, if nobody else will."

A tear stood in Mag's faded eye. "I'm glad," she said, with a softer tone than before, "if there is *one* who isn't[6] glad to see me suffer. I b'lieve all Singleton wants to see me punished, and feel as if they could tell when I've been punished long enough. It's a long day ahead they'll set it, I reckon."

After the usual supply of fuel was prepared, Jim returned home. Full of pity for Mag, he set about devising measures for her relief. "By golly!" said he to himself one day – for he had become so absorbed in Mag's interest that he had fallen into a habit of musing aloud – "By golly! I wish she'd[7] *marry* me."

"Who?" shouted Pete Greene, suddenly starting from an unobserved corner of the rude shop.

"Where you come from, you sly nigger!" exclaimed Jim.

"Come, tell me, who is't?" said Pete; "Mag Smith, you want to marry?"

"Git out, Pete! and when you come in dis shop again, let a nigger know it. Don't[8] steal in like a thief."

Notes

[3] *Original reads*: do n't [ed.].

[4] *Original reads*: do n't [ed.].

[5] *barrels to hoop* The wooden slats of a barrel were bound together by metal hoops.

[6] *Original reads*: is n't [ed.].

[7] *Original reads*: she 'd [ed.].

[8] *Original reads*: Do n't [ed.].

Pity and love know little severance. One attends the other. Jim acknowledged the presence of the former, and his efforts in Mag's behalf told also of a finer principle.

This sudden expedient which he had unintentionally disclosed, roused his thinking and inventive powers to study upon the best method of introducing the subject to Mag.

He belted his barrels, with many a scheme revolving in his mind, none of which quite satisfied him, or seemed, on the whole, expedient. He thought of the pleasing contrast between her fair face and his own dark skin; the smooth, straight hair, which he had once, in expression of pity, kindly stroked on her now wrinkled but once fair brow. There was a tempest gathering in his heart, and at last, to ease his pent-up passion, he exclaimed aloud, "By golly!" Recollecting his former exposure, he glanced around to see if Pete was in hearing again. Satisfied on this point, he continued: "She'd be as much of a prize to me as she'd[9] fall short of coming up to the mark with white folks. I don't[10] care for past things. I've done things 'fore now I's 'shamed of. She's good enough for me, anyhow."[11]

One more glance about the premises to be sure Pete was away.

The next Saturday night brought Jim to the hovel again. The cold was fast coming to tarry its apportioned time. Mag was nearly despairing of meeting its rigor.

"How's the wood, Mag?" asked Jim.

"All gone; and no more to cut, anyhow,"[12] was the reply.

"Too bad!" Jim said. His truthful reply would have been, I'm glad. "Anything to eat in the house?" continued he.

"No," replied Mag.

"Too bad!" again, orally, with the same *inward* gratulation[13] as before.

"Well, Mag," said Jim, after a short pause, "you's down low enough. I don't[14] see but I've got to take care of ye. 'Sposin' we marry!"

Mag raised her eyes, full of amazement, and uttered a sonorous "What?"

Jim felt abashed for a moment. He knew well what were her objections.

"You's had trial of white folks, anyhow.[15] They run off and left ye, and now none of 'em come near ye to see if you's dead or alive. I's black outside, I know, but I's got a white heart inside. Which you rather have, a black heart in a white skin, or a white heart in a black one?"

"Oh, dear!" sighed Mag; "Nobody on earth cares for *me* – "

"I do," interrupted Jim.

"I can do but two things," said she, "beg my living, or get it from you."

"Take me, Mag. I can give you a better home than this, and not let you suffer so."

He prevailed; they married. You can philosophize, gentle reader, upon the impropriety of such unions, and preach dozens of sermons on the evils of amalgamation.[16] Want is a more powerful philosopher and preacher. Poor Mag. She has sundered another bond which held her to her fellows. She has descended another step down the ladder of infamy.

Notes

9 *Original reads*: she 'd [ed.].
10 *Original reads*: do n't [ed.].
11 *Original reads*: any how [ed.].
12 *Original reads*: any how [ed.].
13 *gratulation* a feeling of pleasure, joy, or gratification.
14 *Original reads*: do n't [ed.].
15 *Original reads*: any how [ed.].
16 amalgamation the uniting of two separate entities (inter-marriage).

Chapter 2

My Father's Death

Misery! we have known each other,
Like a sister and a brother,
Living in the same lone home
Many years – we must live some
Hours or ages yet to come.[17]
Shelley.

Jim, proud of his treasure – a white wife – tried hard to fulfil his promises; and furnished her with a more comfortable dwelling, diet, and apparel. It was comparatively a comfortable winter she passed after her marriage. When Jim could work, all went on well. Industrious, and fond of Mag, he was determined she should not regret her union to him. Time levied[18] an additional charge upon him, in the form of two pretty mulattos, whose infantile pranks amply repaid the additional toil. A few years, and a severe cough and pain in his side compelled him to be an idler for weeks together, and Mag had thus a reminder of by-gones. She cared for him only as a means to subserve her own comfort; yet she nursed him faithfully and true to marriage vows till death released her. He became the victim of consumption. He loved Mag to the last. So long as life continued, he stifled his sensibility to pain, and toiled for her sustenance long after he was able to do so.

A few expressive wishes for her welfare; a hope of better days for her; an anxiety lest they should not all go to the "good place"; brief advice about their children; a hope expressed that Mag would not be neglected as she used to be; the manifestation of Christian patience; these were *all* the legacy of miserable Mag. A feeling of cold desolation came over her, as she turned from the grave of one who had been truly faithful to her.

She was now expelled from companionship with white people; this last step – her union with a black – was the climax of repulsion.

Seth Shipley, a partner in Jim's business, wished her to remain in her present home; but she declined, and returned to her hovel again, with obstacles threefold more insurmountable[19] than before. Seth accompanied her, giving her a weekly allowance which furnished most of the food necessary for the four inmates. After a time, work failed; their means were reduced.

How Mag toiled and suffered, yielding to fits of desperation, bursts of anger, and uttering curses too fearful to repeat. When both were supplied with work, they prospered; if idle, they were hungry together. In this way their interests became united; they planned for the future together. Mag had lived an outcast for years. She had ceased to feel the gushings of penitence; she had crushed the sharp agonies of an awakened conscience. She had no longings for a purer heart, a better life. Far easier to descend lower. She entered the darkness of perpetual infamy. She asked not the rite of civilization or Christianity. Her will made her the wife of Seth. Soon followed scenes familiar and trying.

Notes

[17] *"Misery! We have known … to come"* from the poem "Invocation to Misery" (1839) by Percy Shelley, (1792–1822).

[18] *levied* imposed or collected.

[19] *Original reads*: iusurmountable [ed.].

"It's no use," said Seth one day; "we must give the children away, and try to get work in some other place."

"Who'll take the black devils?" snarled Mag.

"They're none of mine," said Seth; "what you growling about?"

"Nobody will want anything[20] of mine, or yours either," she replied.

"We'll make 'em, p'r'aps,"[21] he said. "There's Frado's six years old, and pretty, if she is yours, and white folks'll say so. She'd[22] be a prize somewhere," he continued, tipping his chair back against the wall, and placing his feet upon the rounds, as if he had much more to say when in the right position.

Frado, as they called one of Mag's children, was a beautiful mulatto, with long, curly black hair, and handsome, roguish eyes, sparkling with an exuberance of spirit almost beyond restraint.

Hearing her name mentioned, she looked up from her play, to see what Seth had to say of her.

"Wouldn't[23] the Bellmonts take her?" asked Seth.

"Bellmonts?" shouted Mag. "His wife is a right she-devil! and if – "

"Hadn't[24] they better be all together?" interrupted Seth, reminding her of a like epithet used in reference to her little ones.

Without seeming to notice him, she continued, "She can't keep a girl in the house over a week; and Mr. Bellmont wants to hire a boy to work for him, but he can't find one that will live in the house with her; she's so ugly, they can't."

"Well, we've got to make a move soon," answered Seth; "if you go with me, we shall go right off. Had you rather spare the other one?" asked Seth, after a short pause.

"One's as bad as t'other,"[25] replied Mag. "Frado is such a wild, frolicky thing, and means to do jest as she's[26] a mind to; she won't[27] go if she don't[28] want to. I don't[29] want to tell her she is to be given away."

"I will," said Seth. "Come here, Frado?"

The child seemed to have some dim foreshadowing of evil, and declined.

"Come here," he continued; "I want to tell you something."

She came reluctantly. He took her hand and said: "We're going to move, by-'m-bye; will you go?"

"No!" screamed she; and giving a sudden jerk which destroyed Seth's equilibrium, left him sprawling on the floor, while she escaped through the open door.

"She's a hard one," said Seth, brushing his patched coat sleeve. "I'd risk her at Bellmont's."

They discussed the expediency of a speedy departure. Seth would first seek employment, and then return for Mag. They would take with them what they could carry, and leave the rest with Pete Greene, and come for them when they were wanted. They were long in arranging affairs satisfactorily, and were not a little startled at the close of their conference to find Frado missing. They thought approaching night would bring her. Twilight passed into darkness, and she did not come. They thought she had understood their plans, and had, perhaps, permanently withdrawn. They could not rest

Notes

[20] *Original reads*: any thing [ed.].

[21] *p'r'aps* perhaps.

[22] *Original reads*: She 'd [ed.].

[23] *Original reads*: Would n't [ed.].

[24] *Original reads*: Had n't [ed.].

[25] *Original reads*: t' other [ed.].

[26] *Original reads*: she 's [ed.].

[27] *Original reads*: wo n't [ed.].

[28] *Original reads*: do n't [ed.].

[29] *Original reads*: do n't [ed.].

without making some effort to ascertain her retreat. Seth went in pursuit, and returned without her. They rallied others when they discovered that another little colored girl was missing, a favorite playmate of Frado's. All effort proved unavailing. Mag felt sure her fears were realized, and that she might never see her again. Before her anxieties became realities, both were safely returned, and from them and their attendant they learned that they went to walk, and not minding the direction soon found themselves lost. They had climbed fences and walls, passed through thickets and marshes, and when night approached selected a thick cluster of shrubbery as a covert[30] for the night. They were discovered by the person who now restored them, chatting of their prospects, Frado attempting to banish the childish fears of her companion. As they were some miles from home, they were kindly cared for until morning. Mag was relieved to know her child was not driven to desperation by their intentions to relieve themselves of her, and she was inclined to think severe restraint would be healthful.

The removal was all arranged; the few days necessary for such migrations passed quickly, and one bright summer morning they bade farewell to their Singleton hovel, and with budgets[31] and bundles commenced their weary march. As they neared the village, they heard the merry shouts of children gathered around the schoolroom, awaiting the coming of their teacher.

"Halloo!" screamed one, "Black, white, and yeller!" "Black, white, and yeller," echoed a dozen voices.

It did not grate so harshly on poor Mag as once it would. She did not even turn her head to look at them. She had passed into an insensibility no childish taunt could penetrate, else she would have reproached herself as she passed familiar scenes, for extending the separation once so easily annihilated by steadfast integrity. Two miles beyond lived the Bellmonts, in a large, old fashioned, two-story white house, environed[32] by fruitful acres, and embellished by shrubbery and shade trees. Years ago a youthful couple consecrated it as home; and after many little feet had worn paths to favorite fruit trees, and over its green hills, and mingled at last with brother man in the race which belongs neither to the swift or strong, the sire became grey-haired and decrepit,[33] and went to his last repose. His aged consort[34] soon followed him. The old homestead thus passed into the hands of a son, to whose wife Mag had applied the epithet "she-devil," as may be remembered. John, the son, had not in his family arrangements departed from the example of the father. The pastimes of his boyhood were ever freshly revived by witnessing the games of his own sons as they rallied about the same goal his youthful feet had often won; as well as by the amusements of his daughters in their imitations of maternal duties.

At the time we introduce them, however, John is wearing the badge of age. Most of his children were from home; some seeking employment; some were already settled in homes of their own. A maiden sister shared with him the estate on which he resided, and occupied a portion of the house.

Within sight of the house, Seth seated himself with his bundles and the child he had been leading, while Mag walked onward to the house leading Frado. A knock at the door brought Mrs. Bellmont, and Mag asked if she would be willing to let that child stop there while she went to the Reed's house to wash, and when she came back she

Notes

[30] *covert* shelter.

[31] *budgets* leather pouches or bags.

[32] *environed* surrounded.

[33] *Original reads*: decrepid [ed.].

[34] *consort* spouse.

would call and get her. It seemed a novel request, but she consented. Why the impetuous child entered the house, we cannot tell; the door closed, and Mag hastily departed. Frado waited for the close of day, which was to bring back her mother. Alas! it never came. It was the last time she ever saw or heard of her mother.

Chapter 3

A New Home for Me

Oh! did we but know of the shadows so nigh,
The world would indeed be a prison of gloom;
All light would be quenched in youth's eloquent eye,
And the prayer-lisping infant would ask for the tomb.
For if Hope be a star that may lead us astray,
And "deceiveth the heart," as the aged ones preach;
Yet 'twas Mercy that gave it, to beacon our way,
Though its halo illumes where it never can reach.[35]

Eliza Cook.

As the day closed and Mag did not appear, surmises were expressed by the family that she never intended to return. Mr. Bellmont was a kind, humane man, who would not grudge hospitality to the poorest wanderer, nor fail to sympathize with any sufferer, however humble. The child's desertion by her mother appealed to his sympathy,[36] and he felt inclined to succor[37] her. To do this in opposition to Mrs. Bellmont's wishes would be like encountering a whirlwind charged with fire, daggers and spikes. She was not as susceptible of fine emotions as her spouse. Mag's opinion of her was not without foundation. She was self-willed, haughty, undisciplined, arbitrary and severe. In common parlance, she was a *scold*, a thorough one. Mr. B. remained silent during the consultation which follows, engaged in by mother, Mary and John, or Jack, as he was familiarly called.

"Send her to the County House," said Mary, in reply to the query what should be done with her, in a tone which indicated self-importance in the speaker. She was indeed the idol of her mother, and more nearly resembled her in disposition and manners than the others.

Jane, an invalid daughter, the eldest of those at home, was reclining on a sofa apparently uninterested.

"Keep her," said Jack. "She's real handsome and bright, and not very black, either."

"Yes," rejoined Mary; "that's just like you, Jack. She'll[38] be of no use at all these three years, right under foot all the time."

"Poh! Miss Mary; if she should stay, it wouldn't[39] be two days before you would be telling the girls about *our* nig, *our* nig!" retorted Jack.

"I don't[40] want a nigger 'round *me*, do you, mother?" asked Mary.

"I don't[41] mind the nigger in the child. I should like a dozen better than one," replied her mother. "If I could make her do my work in a few years, I would keep her. I have

Notes

[35] *"Oh! Did we but know … can reach"* from the poem "The Future" by Eliza Cook (1818–1889).

[36] *Original reads*: symathy [ed.].

[37] *succor* help.

[38] *Original reads*: She 'll [ed.].

[39] *Original reads*: would n't [ed.].

[40] *Original reads*: do n't [ed.].

[41] *Original reads*: do n't [ed.].

so much trouble with girls I hire, I am almost persuaded if I have one to train up in my way from a child, I shall be able to keep them awhile. I am tired of changing every few months."

"Where could she sleep?" asked Mary. "I don't[42] want her near me."

"In the L chamber," answered the mother.

"How'll she get there?" asked Jack. "She'll be afraid to go through that dark passage, and she can't climb the ladder safely."

"She'll have to go there; it's good enough for a nigger," was the reply.

Jack was sent on horseback to ascertain if Mag was at her home. He returned with the testimony of Pete Greene that they were fairly departed, and that the child was intentionally thrust upon their family.

The imposition was not at all relished by Mrs. B., or the pert, haughty Mary, who had just glided into her teens.

"Show the child to bed, Jack," said his mother. "You seem most pleased with the little nigger, so you may introduce her to her room."

He went to the kitchen, and, taking Frado gently by the hand, told her he would put her in bed now; perhaps her mother would come the next night after her.

It was not yet quite dark, so they ascended the stairs without any light, passing through nicely furnished rooms, which were a source of great amazement to the child. He opened the door which connected with her room by a dark, unfinished passage-way. "Don't bump your head," said Jack, and stepped before to open the door leading into her apartment – an unfinished chamber over the kitchen, the roof slanting nearly to the floor, so that the bed could stand only in the middle of the room. A small half window furnished light and air. Jack returned to the sitting room with the remark that the child would soon outgrow those quarters.

"When she *does*, she'll outgrow the house," remarked the mother.

"What can she do to help you?" asked Mary. "She came just in the right time, didn't[43] she? Just the very day after Bridget left," continued she.

"I'll see what she can do in the morning," was the answer.

While this conversation was passing below, Frado lay, revolving in her little mind whether she would remain or not until her mother's return. She was of wilful, determined nature, a stranger to fear, and would not hesitate to wander away should she decide to. She remembered the conversation of her mother with Seth, the words "given away" which she heard used in reference to herself; and though she did not know their full import, she thought she should, by remaining, be in some relation to white people she was never favored with before. So she resolved to tarry, with the hope that mother would come and get her some time. The hot sun had penetrated her room, and it was long before a cooling breeze reduced the temperature so that she could sleep.

Frado was called early in the morning by her new mistress. Her first work was to feed the hens. She was shown how it was *always* to be done, and in no other way; any departure from this rule to be punished by a whipping. She was then accompanied by Jack to drive the cows to pasture, so she might learn the way. Upon her return she was allowed to eat her breakfast, consisting of a bowl of skimmed milk, with brown bread crusts, which she was told to eat, standing, by the kitchen table, and must not be over ten minutes about it. Meanwhile the family were taking their morning meal in the

Notes

[42] *Original reads*: do n't [ed.].

[43] *Original reads*: did n't [ed.].

dining-room. This over, she was placed on a cricket[44] to wash the common dishes; she was to be in waiting always to bring wood and chips, to run hither and thither from room to room.

A large amount of dish-washing for small hands followed dinner. Then the same after tea and going after the cows finished her first day's work. It was a new discipline to the child. She found some attractions about the place, and she retired to rest at night more willing to remain. The same routine followed day after day, with slight variation; adding a little more work, and spicing the toil with "words that burn," and frequent blows on her head. These were great annoyances to Frado, and had she known where her mother was, she would have gone at once to her. She was often greatly wearied, and silently wept over her sad fate. At first she wept aloud, which Mrs. Bellmont noticed by applying a raw-hide,[45] always at hand in the kitchen. It was a symptom of discontent and complaining which must be "nipped in the bud," she said.

Thus passed a year. No intelligence of Mag. It was now certain Frado was to become a permanent member of the family. Her labors were multiplied; she was quite indispensable, although but seven years old. She had never learned to read, never heard of a school until her residence in the family.

Mrs. Bellmont was in doubt about the utility of attempting to educate people of color, who were incapable of elevation. This subject occasioned a lengthy discussion in the family. Mr. Bellmont, Jane and Jack arguing for Frado's education; Mary and her mother objecting. At last Mr. Bellmont declared decisively that she *should* go to school. He was a man who seldom decided controversies at home. The word once spoken admitted of no appeal; so, notwithstanding Mary's objection that she would have to attend the same school she did, the word became law.

It was to be a new scene to Frado, and Jack had many queries and conjectures to answer. He was himself too far advanced to attend the summer school, which Frado regretted, having had too many opportunities of witnessing Miss Mary's temper to feel safe in her company alone.

The opening day of school came. Frado sauntered on far in the rear of Mary, who was ashamed to be seen "walking with a nigger." As soon as she appeared, with scanty clothing and bared feet, the children assembled, noisily publishing[46] her approach: "See that nigger," shouted one. "Look! look!" cried another. "I won't play with her," said one little girl. "Nor I neither," replied another.

Mary evidently relished these sharp attacks, and saw a fair prospect of lowering Nig where, according to her views, she belonged. Poor Frado, chagrined and grieved, felt that her anticipations of pleasure at such a place were far from being realized. She was just deciding to return home, and never come there again, when the teacher appeared, and observing the downcast looks of the child, took her by the hand, and led her into the school-room. All followed, and, after the bustle of securing seats was over, Miss Marsh inquired if the children knew "any cause for the sorrow of that little girl?" pointing to Frado. It was soon all told. She then reminded them of their duties to the poor and friendless; their cowardice in attacking a young innocent child; referred them to one who looks not on outward appearances, but on the heart. "She looks like a good girl; I think *I* shall love her, so lay aside all prejudice, and vie with each other in shewing kindness and good-will to one who seems different from you," were the

Notes

[44] *cricket* footstool.

[45] *raw-hide* whip.

[46] *Original reads*: published [ed.].

closing remarks of the kind lady. Those kind words! The most agreeable sound which ever meets the ear of sorrowing, grieving childhood.

Example rendered her words efficacious. Day by day there was a manifest change of deportment towards "Nig." Her speeches often drew merriment from the children; no one could do more to enliven their favorite pastimes than Frado. Mary could not endure to see her thus noticed, yet knew not how to prevent it. She could not influence her schoolmates as she wished. She had not gained their affections by winning ways and yielding points of controversy. On the contrary, she was self-willed, domineering; every day reported "mad" by some of her companions. She availed herself of the only alternative, abuse and taunts, as they returned from school. This was not satisfactory; she wanted to use physical force "to subdue her," to "keep her down."

There was, on their way home, a field intersected by a stream over which a single plank was placed for a crossing. It occurred to Mary that it would be a punishment to Nig to compel her to cross over; so she dragged her to the edge, and told her authoritatively to go over. Nig hesitated, resisted. Mary placed herself behind the child, and, in the struggle to force her over, lost her footing and plunged into the stream. Some of the larger scholars being in sight, ran, and thus prevented Mary from drowning and Frado from falling. Nig scampered home fast as possible, and Mary went to the nearest house, dripping, to procure a change of garments. She came loitering home, half crying, exclaiming, "Nig pushed me into the stream!" She then related the particulars. Nig was called from the kitchen. Mary stood with anger flashing in her eyes. Mr. Bellmont sat quietly reading his paper. He had witnessed too many of Miss Mary's outbreaks to be startled. Mrs. Bellmont interrogated Nig.

"I didn't[47] do it! I didn't[48] do it!" answered Nig, passionately, and then related the occurrence truthfully.

The discrepancy greatly enraged Mrs. Bellmont. With loud accusations and angry gestures she approached the child. Turning to her husband, she asked,

"Will you sit still, there, and hear that black nigger call Mary a liar?"

"How do we know but she has told the truth? I shall not punish her," he replied, and left the house, as he usually did when a tempest threatened to envelop him. No sooner was he out of sight than Mrs. B. and Mary commenced beating her inhumanly; then, propping her mouth open with a piece of wood, shut her up in a dark room, without any supper. For employment, while the tempest raged within, Mr. Bellmont went for the cows, a task belonging to Frado, and thus unintentionally prolonged her pain. At dark Jack came in, and seeing Mary, accosted her with, "So you thought you'd vent your spite on Nig, did you? Why can't you let her alone? It was good enough for you to get a ducking, only you did not stay in half long enough."

"Stop!" said his mother. "You shall never talk so before me. You would have that little nigger trample on Mary, would you? She came home with a lie; it made Mary's story false."

"What was Mary's story?" asked Jack.

It was related.

"Now," said Jack, sallying[49] into a chair, "the school-children happened to see it all, and they tell the same story Nig does. Which is most likely to be true, what a dozen agree they saw, or the contrary?"

Notes

[47] *Original reads*: did n't [ed.].

[48] *Original reads*: did n't [ed.].

[49] *sallying* rushing.

"It is very strange you will believe what others say against your sister," retorted his mother, with flashing eye. "I think it is time your father subdued you."

"Father is a sensible man," argued Jack. "He would not wrong a dog. Where *is* Frado?" he continued.

"Mother gave her a good whipping and shut her up," replied Mary.

Just then Mr. Bellmont entered, and asked if Frado was "shut up yet."

The knowledge of her innocence, the perfidy[50] of his sister, worked fearfully on Jack. He bounded from his chair, searched every room till he found the child; her mouth wedged apart, her face swollen, and full of pain.

How Jack pitied her! He relieved her jaws, brought her some supper, took her to her room, comforted her as well as he knew how, sat by her till she fell asleep, and then left for the sitting room. As he passed his mother, he remarked, "If that was the way Frado was to be treated, he hoped she would never wake again!" He then imparted her situation to his father, who seemed untouched, till a glance at Jack exposed a tearful eye. Jack went early to her next morning. She awoke sad, but refreshed. After breakfast Jack took her with him to the field, and kept her through the day. But it could not be so generally. She must return to school, to her household duties. He resolved to do what he could to protect her from Mary and his mother. He bought her a dog, which became a great favorite with both. The invalid, Jane, would gladly befriend her; but she had not the strength to brave the iron will of her mother. Kind words and affectionate glances were the only expressions of sympathy she could safely indulge in. The men employed on the farm were always glad to hear her prattle; she was a great favorite with them. Mrs. Bellmont allowed them the privilege of talking with her in the kitchen. She did not fear but she should have ample opportunity of subduing her when they were away. Three months of schooling, summer and winter, she enjoyed for three years. Her winter over-dress was a cast-off overcoat, once worn by Jack, and a sun-bonnet. It was a source of great merriment to the scholars, but Nig's retorts were so mirthful, and their satisfaction so evident in attributing the selection to "Old Granny Bellmont," that it was not painful to Nig or pleasurable to Mary. Her jollity was not to be quenched by whipping or scolding. In Mrs. Bellmont's presence she was under restraint; but in the kitchen, and among her schoolmates, the pent up fires burst forth. She was ever at some sly prank when unseen by her teacher, in school hours; not unfrequently some outburst of merriment, of which she was the originator,[51] was charged upon some innocent mate, and punishment inflicted which she merited. They enjoyed her antics so fully that any of them would suffer wrongfully to keep open the avenues of mirth. She would venture far beyond propriety, thus shielded and countenanced.

The teacher's desk was supplied with drawers, in which were stored his books and other *et ceteras* of the profession. The children observed Nig very busy there one morning before school, as they flitted in occasionally from their play outside. The master came; called the children to order; opened a drawer to take the book the occasion required; when out poured a volume of smoke. "Fire! fire!" screamed he, at the top of his voice. By this time he had become sufficiently acquainted with the peculiar odor, to know he was imposed upon. The scholars shouted with laughter to see the terror of the dupe, who, feeling abashed at the needless fright, made no very strict investigation, and Nig once more escaped punishment. She had provided herself with cigars,

Notes

[50] *perfidy* treachery.

[51] *Original reads*: original [ed.].

and puffing, puffing away at the crack of the drawer, had filled it with smoke, and then closed it tightly to deceive the teacher, and amuse the scholars.

The interim of terms was filled up with a variety of duties new and peculiar. At home, no matter how powerful the heat when sent to rake hay or guard the grazing herd, she was never permitted to shield her skin from the sun. She was not many shades darker than Mary now; what a calamity it would be ever to hear the contrast spoken of. Mrs. Bellmont was determined the sun should have full power to darken the shade which nature had first bestowed upon her as best befitting.

Chapter 4

A Friend for Nig

"Hours of my youth! when nurtured in my breast,
To love a stranger, friendship made me blest: –
Friendship, the dear peculiar bond of youth,
When every artless bosom throbs with truth;
Untaught by worldly wisdom how to feign,
And check each impulse with prudential reign;
When all we feel our honest souls disclose –
In love to friends, in open hate to foes;
No varnished tales the lips of youth repeat,
No dear-bought knowledge purchased by deceit."[52]
Byron.

With what differing emotions have the denizens of earth awaited the approach of to-day. Some sufferer has counted the vibrations of the pendulum impatient for its dawn, who, now that it has arrived, is anxious for its close. The votary of pleasure, conscious of yesterday's void, wishes for power to arrest time's haste till a few more hours of mirth shall be enjoyed. The unfortunate are yet gazing in vain for golden-edged clouds they fancied would appear in their horizon. The good man feels that he has accomplished too little for the Master, and sighs that another day must so soon close. Innocent childhood, weary of its stay, longs for another morrow; busy manhood cries, hold! hold! and pursues it to another's dawn. All are dissatisfied. All crave some good not yet possessed, which time is expected to bring with all its morrows.

Was it strange that, to a disconsolate child, three years should seem a long, long time? During school time she had rest from Mrs. Bellmont's tyranny. She was now nine years old; time, her mistress said, such privileges should cease.

She could now read and spell, and knew the elementary steps in grammar, arithmetic, and writing. Her education completed, as *she* said, Mrs. Bellmont felt that her time and person belonged solely to her. She was under her in every sense of the word. What an opportunity to indulge her vixen nature! No matter what occurred to ruffle her, or from what source provocation came, real or fancied, a few blows on Nig seemed to relieve her of a portion of ill-will.

These were days when Fido was the entire confidant of Frado. She told him her griefs as though he were human; and he sat so still, and listened so attentively, she

Notes

[52] *"Hours of my youth! … purchased by deceit"* from "Childish Recollections" (1852) by Lord Byron (1788–1824).

really believed he knew her sorrows. All the leisure moments she could gain were used in teaching him some feat of dog-agility, so that Jack pronounced him very knowing, and was truly gratified to know he had furnished her with a gift answering his intentions.

Fido was the constant attendant of Frado, when sent from the house on errands, going and returning with the cows, out in the fields, to the village. If ever she forgot her hardships it was in his company.

Spring was now retiring. James, one of the absent sons, was expected home on a visit. He had never seen the last acquisition of the family.[53] Jack had written faithfully of all the merits of his colored *protegé*, and hinted plainly that mother did not always treat her just right. Many were the preparations to make the visit pleasant, and as the day approached when he was to arrive, great exertions were made to cook the favorite viands, to prepare the choicest table-fare.

The morning of the arrival day was a busy one. Frado knew not who would be of so much importance; her feet were speeding hither and thither so unsparingly. Mrs. Bellmont seemed a trifle fatigued, and her shoes which had, early in the morning, a methodic squeak, altered to an irregular, peevish snap.

"Get some little wood to make the fire burn," said Mrs. Bellmont, in a sharp tone. Frado obeyed, bringing the smallest she could find.

Mrs. Bellmont approached her, and, giving her a box on her ear, reiterated the command.

The first the child brought was the smallest to be found; of course, the second must be a trifle larger. She well knew it was, as she threw it into a box on the hearth. To Mrs. Bellmont it was a greater affront, as well as larger wood, so she "taught her" with the raw-hide, and sent her the third time for "little wood."

Nig, weeping, knew not what to do. She had carried the smallest; none left would suit her mistress; of course further punishment awaited her; so she gathered up whatever came first, and threw it down on the hearth. As she expected, Mrs. Bellmont, enraged, approached her, and kicked her so forcibly as to throw her upon the floor. Before she could rise, another foiled the attempt, and then followed kick after kick in quick succession and power, till she reached the door. Mr. Bellmont and Aunt[54] Abby, hearing the noise, rushed in, just in time to see the last of the performance. Nig jumped up, and rushed from the house, out of sight.

Aunt Abby returned to her apartment, followed by John, who was muttering to himself.

"What were you saying?" asked Aunt Abby.

"I said I hoped the child never would come into the house again."

"What would become of her? You cannot mean *that*," continued his sister.

"I do mean it. The child does as much work as a woman ought to; and just see how she is kicked about!"

"Why do you have it so, John?" asked his sister.

"How am I to help it? Women rule the earth, and all in it."

"I think I should rule my own house, John" –

"And live in hell meantime," added Mr. Bellmont.

John now sauntered out to the barn to await the quieting of the storm.

Notes

[53] *Original reads*: to the family [ed.].

[54] *Original reads*: Anut [ed.].

Aunt Abby had a glimpse of Nig as she passed out of the yard; but to arrest her, or shew her that *she* would shelter her, in Mrs. Bellmont's presence, would only bring reserved wrath on her defenceless head. Her sister-in-law had great prejudices against her. One cause of the alienation was that she did not give her right in the homestead to John, and leave it forever; another was that she was a professor[55] of religion (so was Mrs. Bellmont); but Nab, as she called her, did not live according to her profession; another, that she *would* sometimes give Nig cake and pie, which she was never allowed to have at home. Mary had often noticed and spoken of her inconsistencies.

The dinner hour passed. Frado had not appeared. Mrs. B. made no inquiry or search. Aunt Abby looked long, and found her concealed in an outbuilding.[56] "Come into the house with me," implored Aunt Abby.

"I ain't going in any more," sobbed the child.

"What will you do?" asked Aunt Abby.

"I've got to stay out here and die. I ha'n't[57] got no mother, no home. I wish I was dead."

"Poor thing," muttered Aunt Abby; and slyly[58] providing her with some dinner, left her to her grief.

Jane went to confer with her Aunt about the affair; and learned from her the retreat. She would gladly have concealed her in her own chamber, and ministered to her wants; but she was dependent on Mary and her mother for care, and any displeasure caused by attention to Nig was seriously felt.

Toward night the coach brought James. A time of general greeting, inquiries for absent members of the family, a visit to Aunt Abby's room, undoing[59] a few delicacies for Jane, brought them to the tea hour.

"Where's Frado?" asked Mr. Bellmont, observing she was not in her usual place, behind her mistress' chair.

"I don't know, and I don't care. If she makes her appearance again, I'll take the skin from her body," replied his wife.

James, a fine looking young man, with a pleasant countenance, placid, and yet decidedly serious, yet not stern, looked up confounded. He was no stranger to his mother's nature; but years of absence had erased the occurrences once so familiar, and he asked, "Is this that pretty little Nig, Jack writes to me about, that you are so severe upon, mother?"

"I'll not leave much of her beauty to be seen, if she comes in sight; and now, John," said Mrs. B., turning to her husband, "you need not think you are going to learn her to treat me in this way; just see how saucy she was this morning. She shall learn her place."

Mr. Bellmont raised his calm, determined eye full upon her, and said, in a decisive manner: "You shall not strike, or scald, or skin her, as you call it, if she comes back again. Remember!" and he brought his hand down upon the table. "I have searched an hour for her now, and she is not to be found on the premises. Do *you* know where she is? Is she *your* prisoner?"

"No! I have just told you I did not know where she was. Nab has her hid somewhere, I suppose. Oh, dear! I did not think it would come to this; that my own husband would

Notes

[55] *professor* in this case, a believer.

[56] *outbuilding* shed.

[57] *Original reads*: ha' n't [ed.].

[58] *slyly* secretly.

[59] *undoing* revealing.

treat me so." Then came fast flowing tears, which no one but Mary seemed to notice. Jane crept into Aunt Abby's room; Mr. Bellmont and James went out of doors, and Mary remained to condole with her parent.

"Do you know where Frado is?" asked Jane of her aunt.

"No," she replied. "I have hunted everywhere. She has left her first hiding-place. I cannot think what has become of her. There comes Jack and Fido; perhaps he knows"; and she walked to a window near where James and his father were conversing together.

The two brothers exchanged a hearty greeting, and then Mr. Bellmont told Jack to eat his supper; afterward he wished to send him away. He immediately went in. Accustomed to all the phases of indoor storms, from a whine to thunder and lightning, he saw at a glance marks of disturbance. He had been absent through the day, with the hired men.

"What's the fuss?" asked he, rushing into Aunt Abby's.

"Eat your supper," said Jane; "go home, Jack."

Back again through the dining-room, and out to his father.

"What's the fuss?" again inquired he of his father.

"Eat your supper, Jack, and see if you can find Frado. She's not been seen since morning, and then she was kicked out of the house."

"I shan't eat my supper till I find her," said Jack, indignantly. "Come, James, and see the little creature mother treats so."

They started, calling, searching, coaxing, all their way along. No Frado. They returned to the house to consult. James and Jack declared they would not sleep till she was found.

Mrs. Bellmont attempted to dissuade them from the search. "It was a shame a little *nigger* should make so much trouble."

Just then Fido came running up, and Jack exclaimed, "Fido knows where she is, I'll bet."

"So I believe," said his father; "but we shall not be wiser unless we can outwit him. He will not do what his mistress forbids him."

"I know how to fix him," said Jack. Taking a plate from the table, which was still waiting, he called, "Fido! Fido! Frado wants some supper. Come!" Jack started, the dog followed, and soon capered on before, far, far into the fields, over walls and through fences, into a piece of swampy land. Jack followed close, and soon appeared to James, who was quite in the rear, coaxing and forcing Frado along with him.

A frail child, driven from shelter by the cruelty of his mother, was an object of interest to James. They persuaded her to go home with them, warmed her by the kitchen fire, gave her a good supper, and took her with them into the sitting-room.

"Take that nigger out of my sight," was Mrs. Bellmont's command, before they could be seated.

James led her into Aunt Abby's, where he knew they were welcome. They chatted awhile until Frado seemed cheerful; then James led her to her room, and waited until she retired.

"Are you glad I've come home?" asked James.

"Yes; if you won't let me be whipped tomorrow."

"You won't be whipped. You must try to be a good girl," counselled James.

"If I do, I get whipped;" sobbed the child. "They won't believe what I say. Oh, I wish I had my mother back; then I should not be kicked and whipped so. Who made me so?"

"God;" answered James.

"Did God make you?"

"Yes."

"Who made Aunt Abby?"

"God."

"Who made your mother?"

"God."

"Did the same God that made her make me?"

"Yes."

"Well, then, I don't like him."

"Why not?"

"Because he made her white, and me black. Why didn't he make us *both* white?"

"I don't know; try to go to sleep, and you will feel better in the morning," was all the reply he could make to her knotty queries. It was a long time before she fell asleep; and a number of days before James felt in a mood to visit and entertain old associates and friends.

Chapter 5

Departures

Life is a strange avenue of various trees and flowers;
Lightsome at commencement, but darkening to its end in a distant, massy portal.
It beginneth as a little path, edged with the violet and primrose,
A little path of lawny grass and soft to tiny feet.
Soon, spring thistles in the way.[60]

Tupper.

JAMES's[61] visit concluded. Frado had become greatly attached to him, and with sorrow she listened and joined in the farewells which preceded his exit. The remembrance of his kindness cheered her through many a weary month, and an occasional word to her in letters to Jack were like "cold waters to a thirsty soul." Intelligence came that James would soon marry; Frado hoped he would, and remove her from such severe treatment as she was subject to. There had been additional burdens laid on her since his return. She must now *milk* the cows, she had then only to drive. Flocks of sheep had been added to the farm, which daily claimed a portion of her time. In the absence of the men, she must harness the horse for Mary and her mother to ride, go to mill, in short, do the work of a boy, could one be procured to endure the tirades of Mrs. Bellmont. She was first up in the morning, doing what she could towards breakfast. Occasionally, she would utter some funny thing for Jack's benefit, while she was waiting on the table, provoking a sharp look from his mother, or expulsion from the room.

On one such occasion, they found her on the roof of the barn. Some repairs having been necessary, a staging had been erected, and was not wholly removed. Availing herself of ladders, she was mounted in high glee on the topmost board. Mr. Bellmont called sternly for her to come down; poor Jane nearly fainted from fear. Mrs. B. and Mary did not care if she "broke her neck," while Jack and the men laughed at her fearlessness. Strange, one spark of playfulness could remain amid such constant toil; but her natural temperament was in a high degree mirthful, and the encouragement she received from Jack and the hired men, constantly nurtured the inclination. When she

Notes

[60] *"Life is a strange … in the way"* from "Of Life (Second Series)" (1850) by Martin Farquhar Tupper (1810–1889).

[61] *Original reads*: James' [ed.].

had none of the family around to be merry with, she would amuse herself with the animals. Among the sheep was a willful leader, who always persisted in being first served, and many times in his fury he had thrown down Nig, till, provoked, she resolved to punish him. The pasture in which the sheep grazed was bounded on three sides by a wide stream, which flowed on one side at the base of precipitous banks. The first spare moments at her command, she ran to the pasture with a dish in her hand, and mounting the highest point of land nearest the stream, called the flock to their mock repast. Mr Bellmont, with his laborers, were in sight, though unseen by Frado. They paused to see what she was about to do. Should she by any mishap lose her footing, she must roll into the stream, and, without aid, must drown. They thought of shouting; but they feared an unexpected salute might startle her, and thus ensure what they were anxious to prevent. They watched in breathless silence. The willful sheep came furiously leaping and bounding far in advance of the flock. Just as he leaped for the dish, she suddenly jumped one side, when down he rolled into the river, and swimming across, remained alone till night. The men lay down, convulsed with laughter at the trick, and guessed at once its object. Mr. Bellmont talked seriously to the child for exposing herself to such danger; but she hopped about on her toes, and with laughable grimaces replied, she knew she was quick enough to "give him a slide."

But to return. James married a Baltimorean lady of wealthy parentage, an indispensable requisite, his mother had always taught him. He did not marry her wealth, though; he loved *her*, sincerely. She was not unlike his sister Jane, who had a social, gentle, loving nature, rather *too* yielding, her brother thought. His Susan had a firmness which Jane needed to complete her character, but which her ill health may in a measure have failed to produce. Although an invalid, she was not excluded from society. Was it strange *she* should seem a desirable companion, a treasure as a wife?

Two young men seemed desirous of possessing her. One was a neighbor, Henry Reed, a tall, spare young man, with sandy hair, and blue, sinister eyes. He seemed to appreciate her wants, and watch with interest her improvement or decay. His kindness she received, and by it was almost won. Her mother wished her to encourage his attentions. She had counted the acres which were to be transmitted to an only son; she knew there was silver in the purse; she would not have Jane too sentimental.

The eagerness with which he amassed wealth was repulsive to Jane; he did not spare his person or beasts in its pursuit. She felt that to such a man she should be considered an incumbrance; she doubted if he would desire her, if he did not know she would bring a handsome patrimony.[62] Her mother, full in favor with the parents of Henry, commanded her to accept him. She engaged herself, yielding to her mother's wishes, because she had not strength to oppose them; and sometimes, when witness of her mother's and Mary's tyranny, she felt any change would be preferable, even such a one as this. She knew her husband should be the man of her own selecting, one she was conscious of preferring before all others. She could not say this of Henry.

In this dilemma, a visitor came to Aunt Abby's; one of her boy-favorites, George Means, from an adjoining State. Sensible, plain looking, agreeable, talented, he could not long be a stranger to anyone[63] who wished to know him. Jane was accustomed to sit much with Aunt Abby always; her presence now seemed necessary to assist in entertaining this youthful friend. Jane was more pleased with him each day, and silently wished Henry possessed more refinement, and the polished manners of George. She

Notes

[62] *patrimony* dowry.

[63] *Original reads*: any one [ed.].

felt dissatisfied with her relation to him. His calls while George was there, brought their opposing qualities vividly before her, and she found it disagreeable to force herself into those attentions belonging to him. She received him apparently only as a neighbor.

George returned home, and Jane endeavored to stifle the risings of dissatisfaction, and had nearly succeeded, when a letter came which needed but one glance to assure her of its birth-place; and she retired for its perusal. Well was it for her that her mother's suspicion was not aroused, or her curiosity startled to inquire who it came from. After reading it, she glided into Aunt Abby's, and placed it in her hands, who was no stranger to Jane's trials.

George could not rest after his return, he wrote, until he had communicated to Jane the emotions her presence awakened, and his desire to love and possess her as his own. He begged to know if his affections were reciprocated, or could be; if she would permit him to write to her; if she was free from all obligation to another.

"What would mother say?" queried Jane, as she received the letter from her aunt.

"Not much to comfort you."

"Now, aunt, George is just such a man as I could really love, I think, from all I have seen of him; you know I never could say that of Henry" –

"Then don't[64] marry him," interrupted Aunt Abby.

"Mother will make me."

"Your father won't."[65]

"Well, aunt, what can I do? Would you answer the letter, or not?"

"Yes, answer it. Tell him your situation."

"I shall not tell him all my feelings."

Jane answered that she had enjoyed his company much; she had seen nothing offensive in his manner or appearance; that she was under no obligations which forbade her receiving letters from him as a friend and acquaintance. George was puzzled by the reply. He wrote to Aunt Abby, and from her learned all. He could not see Jane thus sacrificed, without making an effort to rescue her. Another visit followed. George heard Jane say she preferred *him*. He then conferred with Henry at his home. It was not a pleasant subject to talk upon. To be thus supplanted was not to be thought of. He would sacrifice everything but his inheritance to secure his betrothed.

"And so you are the cause of her late coldness towards me. Leave! I will talk no more about it; the business is settled between us; there it will remain," said Henry.

"Have you no wish to know the real state of Jane's affections towards you?" asked George.

"No! Go, I say! go!" and Henry opened the door for him to pass out.

He retired to Aunt Abby's. Henry soon followed, and presented his cause to Mrs. Bellmont.

Provoked, surprised, indignant, she summoned Jane to her presence, and after a lengthy tirade upon Nab, and her satanic influence, told her she could not break the bonds which held her to Henry; she should not. George Means was rightly named; he was, truly, mean enough; she knew his family of old; his father had four wives, and five times as many children.

"Go to your room, Miss Jane," she continued. "Don't[66] let me know of your being in Nab's for one while."

Notes

[64] *Original reads*: do n't [ed.].

[65] *Original reads*: wo n't [ed.].

[66] *Original reads*: do n't [ed.].

The storm was now visible to all beholders. Mr. Bellmont sought Jane. She told him her objections to Henry; showed him George's letter; told her answer, the occasion of his visit. He bade her not make herself sick; he would see that she was not compelled to violate her free choice in so important a transaction. He then sought the two young men; told them he could not as a father see his child compelled to an uncongenial union; a free, voluntary choice was of such importance to one of her health. She must be left free to her own choice.

Jane sent Henry a letter of dismission; he her one of a legal bearing, in which he balanced his disappointment by a few hundreds.

To brave her mother's fury, nearly overcame her, but the consolations of a kind father and aunt cheered her on. After a suitable interval she was married to George, and removed to his home in Vermont. Thus another light disappeared from Nig's horizon. Another was soon to follow. Jack was anxious to try his skill in providing for his own support; so a situation as clerk in a store was procured in a Western city, and six months after Jane's departure, was Nig abandoned to the tender mercies of Mary and her mother. As if to remove the last vestige of earthly joy, Mrs. Bellmont sold the companion and pet of Frado, the dog Fido.

Chapter 6

Varieties

"Hard are life's early steps; and but that youth is buoyant, confident,
and strong in hope, men would behold its threshold and despair."[67]

THE sorrow of Frado was very great for her pet, and Mr. Bellmont by great exertion obtained it again, much to the relief of the child. To be thus deprived of all her sources of pleasure was a sure way to exalt their worth, and Fido became, in her estimation, a more valuable presence than the human beings who surrounded her.

James had now been married a number of years, and frequent requests for a visit from the family were at last accepted, and Mrs. Bellmont made great preparations for a fall sojourn in Baltimore. Mary was installed housekeeper[68] – in name merely, for Nig was the only moving power in the house. Although suffering from their joint severity, she felt safer than to be thrown wholly upon an ardent, passionate, unrestrained young lady, whom she always hated and felt it hard to be obliged to obey. The trial she must meet. Were Jack or Jane at home she would have some refuge; one only remained; good Aunt Abby was still in the house.

She saw the fast receding coach which conveyed her master and mistress with regret, and begged for one favor only, that James would send for her when they returned, a hope she had confidently cherished all these five years.

She was now able to do all the washing, ironing, baking, and the common *et cetera* of household duties, though but fourteen. Mary left all for her to do, though she affected great responsibility. She would show herself in the kitchen long enough to relieve herself of some command, better withheld; or insist upon some compliance to

Notes

[67] *"Hard are life's … despair"* from "Success Alone Seen" (1837) by Letitia Elizabeth Landon (1802–1838).

[68] *Original reads*: housekeper [ed.].

her wishes in some department which she was very imperfectly acquainted with, very much less than the person she was addressing; and so impetuous till her orders were obeyed, that to escape the turmoil, Nig would often go contrary to her own knowledge to gain a respite.

Nig was taken sick! What could be done The *work*, certainly, but not by Miss Mary. So Nig would work while she could remain erect, then sink down upon the floor, or a chair, till she could rally for a fresh effort. Mary would look in upon her, chide her for her laziness, threaten to tell mother when she came home, and so forth.

"Nig!" screamed Mary, one of her sickest days, "come here, and sweep these threads from the carpet." She attempted to drag her weary limbs along, using the broom as support. Impatient of delay, she called again, but with a different request. "Bring me some wood, you lazy jade, quick." Nig rested the broom against the wall, and started on the fresh behest.

Too long gone. Flushed with anger, she rose and greeted her with, "What are you gone so long, for? Bring it in quick, I say."

"I am coming as quick as I can," she replied, entering the door.

"Saucy, impudent nigger, you! is this the way you answer me?" and taking a large carving knife from the table, she hurled it, in her rage, at the defenceless girl.

Dodging quickly, it fastened in the ceiling a few inches from where she stood. There rushed on Mary's mental vision a picture of bloodshed, in which she was the perpetrator, and the sad consequences of what was so nearly an actual occurrence.

"Tell anybody of this, if you dare. If you tell Aunt Abby, I'll certainly kill you," said she, terrified. She returned to her room, brushed her threads herself; was for a day or two more guarded, and so escaped deserved and merited penalty.

Oh, how long the weeks seemed which held Nig in subjection to Mary; but they passed like all earth's sorrows and joys. Mr. and Mrs. B. returned delighted with their visit, and laden with rich presents for Mary. No word of hope for Nig. James was quite unwell, and would come home the next spring for a visit.

This, thought Nig, will be my time of release. I shall go back with him.

From early dawn until after all were retired, was she toiling, overworked, disheartened, longing for relief.

Exposure from heat to cold, or the reverse, often destroyed her health for short intervals. She wore no shoes until after frost, and snow even, appeared; and bared her feet again before the last vestige of winter disappeared. These sudden changes she was so illy[69] guarded against, nearly conquered her physical system. Any word of complaint was severely repulsed or cruelly punished.

She was told she had much more than she deserved. So that manual labor was not in reality her only burden; but such an incessant torrent of scolding and boxing and threatening, was enough to deter one of maturer years from remaining within sound of the strife.

It is impossible to give an impression of the manifest enjoyment of Mrs. B. in these kitchen scenes. It was her favorite exercise to enter the apartment[70] noisily, vociferate[71] orders, give a few sudden blows to quicken Nig's pace, then return to the sitting room with *such* a satisfied expression, congratulating herself upon her thorough housekeeping qualities.

Notes

[69] *illy* in an ill manner.

[70] *Original reads*: apartment [ed.].

[71] *vociferate* shout.

She usually rose in the morning at the ringing of the bell for breakfast; if she were heard stirring before that time, Nig knew well there was an extra amount of scolding to be borne.

No one now stood between herself and Frado, but Aunt Abby. And if *she* dared to interfere in the least, she was ordered back to her "own quarters." Nig would creep slyly into her room, learn what she could of her regarding the absent, and thus gain some light in the thick gloom of care and toil and sorrow in which she was immersed.

The first of spring a letter came from James, announcing declining health. He must try northern air as a restorative; so Frado joyfully prepared for this agreeable increase of the family, this addition to her cares.

He arrived feeble, lame, from his disease, so changed Frado wept at his appearance, fearing he would be removed from her forever. He kindly greeted her, took her to the parlor to see his wife and child, and said many things to kindle smiles on her sad face.

Frado felt so happy in his presence, so safe from maltreatment! He was to her a shelter. He observed, silently, the ways of the house a few days; Nig still took her meals in the same manner as formerly, having the same allowance of food. He, one day, bade her not remove the food, but sit down to the table and eat.

"She *will*, mother," said he, calmly, but imperatively; I'm determined; she works hard; I've watched her. Now, while I stay, she is going to sit down *here*, and eat such food as we eat."

A few sparks from the mother's black eyes were the only reply; she feared to oppose where she knew she could not prevail. So Nig's standing attitude and selected diet vanished.

Her clothing was yet poor and scanty; she was not blessed with a Sunday attire; for she was never permitted to attend church with her mistress. "Religion was not meant for niggers," *she* said; when the husband and brothers were absent, she would drive Mrs. B. and Mary there, then return, and go for them at the close of the service, but never remain. Aunt Abby would take her to evening meetings, held in the neighborhood, which Mrs. B. never attended; and impart to her lessons of truth and grace as they walked to the place of prayer.

Many of less piety would scorn to present so doleful a figure; Mrs. B. had shaved her glossy ringlets; and, in her coarse cloth gown and ancient bonnet, she was anything but an enticing object. But Aunt Abby looked within. She saw a soul to save, an immortality of happiness to secure.

These evenings were eagerly anticipated by Nig; it was such a pleasant release from labor.

Such perfect contrast in the melody and prayers of these good people to the harsh tones which fell on her ears during the day.

Soon she had all their sacred songs at command, and enlivened her toil by accompanying it with this melody.

James encouraged his aunt in her efforts. He had found the *Saviour*, he wished to have Frado's desolate heart gladdened, quieted, sustained, by *His* presence. He felt sure there were elements in her heart which, transformed and purified by the gospel, would make her worthy the esteem and friendship of the world. A kind, affectionate heart, native wit, and common sense, and the pertness she sometimes exhibited, he felt if restrained properly, might become useful in originating a self-reliance which would be of service to her in after years.

Yet it was not possible to compass all this, while she remained where she was. He wished to be cautious about pressing too closely her claims on his mother, as it would increase the burdened one he so anxiously wished to relieve. He cheered her on with the hope of returning with his family, when he recovered sufficiently.

Nig seemed awakened to new hopes and aspirations, and realized a longing for the future, hitherto unknown.

To complete Nig's enjoyment, Jack arrived unexpectedly. His greeting was as hearty to herself as to any of the family.

"Where are your curls, Fra?" asked Jack, after the usual salutation.

"Your mother cut them off."

"Thought you were getting handsome, did she? Same old story, is it; knocks and bumps? Better times coming; never fear, Nig."

How different this appellative[72] sounded from him; he said it in such a tone, with such a roguish[73] look!

She laughed, and replied that he had better take her West for a housekeeper.

Jack was pleased with James's innovations of table discipline, and would often tarry in the dining-room, to see Nig in her new place at the family table. As he was thus sitting one day, after the family had finished dinner, Frado seated herself in her mistress' chair, and was just reaching for a clean dessert plate which was on the table, when her mistress entered.

"Put that plate down; you shall not have a clean one; eat from mine," continued she. Nig hesitated. To eat after James, his wife, or Jack, would have been pleasant; but to be commanded to do what was disagreeable by her mistress, *because* it was disagreeable, was trying. Quickly looking about, she took the plate, called Fido to wash it, which he did to the best of his ability; then, wiping her knife and fork on the cloth, she proceeded to eat her dinner.

Nig never looked toward her mistress during the process. She had Jack near; she did not fear her now.

Insulted, full of rage, Mrs. Bellmont rushed to her husband, and commanded him to notice this insult; to whip that child; if he would not do it, James ought.

James came to hear the kitchen version of the affair. Jack was boiling over with laughter. He related all the circumstances to James, and pulling a bright, silver half-dollar from his pocket, he threw it at Nig, saying, "There, take that; 't was worth paying for."

James sought his mother; told her he "would not excuse or palliate Nig's impudence; but she should not be whipped or be punished at all. You have not treated her, mother, so as to gain her love; she is only exhibiting your remissness in this matter."

She only smothered her resentment until a convenient opportunity offered. The first time she was left alone with Nig, she gave her a thorough beating, to bring up arrearages;[74] and threatened, if she ever exposed her to James, she would "cut her tongue out."

James found her, upon his return, sobbing; but fearful of revenge, she dared not answer his queries. He guessed their cause, and longed for returning health to take her under his protection.

Notes

[72] *appellative* name.

[73] *Original reads*: rogueish [ed.].

[74] *arrearages* overdue payments.

Chapter 7

Spiritual Condition of Nig

"What are our joys but dreams? and what our hopes
But goodly shadows in the summer cloud?"[75]
H.K.W.

JAMES did not improve as was hoped. Month after month passed away, and brought no prospect of returning health. He could not walk far from the house for want of strength; but he loved to sit with Aunt Abby in her quiet room, talking of unseen glories, and heart-experiences, while planning for the spiritual benefit of those around them. In these confidential interviews, Frado was never omitted. They would discuss the prevalent opinion of the public, that people of color are really inferior; incapable of cultivation and refinement. They would glance at the qualities of Nig, which promised so much if rightly directed. "I wish you would take her, James, when you are well, home with *you*," said Aunt Abby, in one of these seasons.

"Just what I am longing to do, Aunt Abby. Susan is just of my mind, and we intend to take her; I have been wishing to do so for years."

"She seems much affected by what she hears at the evening meetings, and asks me many questions on serious things; seems to love to read the Bible; I feel hopes of her."

"I hope she *is* thoughtful; no one has a kinder heart, one capable of loving more devotedly. But to think how prejudiced the world are towards her people; that she must be reared in such ignorance as to drown all the finer feelings. When I think of what she might be, of what she will be, I feel like grasping time till opinions change, and thousands like her rise into a noble freedom. I have seen Frado's grief, because she is black, amount to agony. It makes me sick to recall these scenes. Mother pretends to think she don't know enough to sorrow for anything; but if she could see her as I have, when she supposed herself entirely alone, except her little dog Fido, lamenting her loneliness and complexion, I think, if she is not past feeling, she would retract. In the summer I was walking near the barn, and as I stood I heard sobs. 'Oh! oh!' I heard, 'why was I made? why can't I die? Oh, what have I to live for? No one cares for me only to get my work. And I feel sick; who cares for that? Work as long as I can stand, and then fall down and lay there till I can get up. No mother, father, brother or sister to care for me, and then it is, You lazy nigger, lazy nigger – all because I am black! Oh, if I could die!'

"I stepped into the barn, where I could see her. She was crouched down by the hay with her faithful friend Fido, and as she ceased speaking, buried her face in her hands, and cried bitterly; then, patting Fido, she kissed him, saying, 'You love me, Fido, don't you? but we must go work in the field.' She started on her mission; I called her to me, and told her she need not go, the hay was doing well.

"She has such confidence in me that she will do just as I tell her; so we found a seat under a shady tree, and there I took the opportunity to combat the notions she seemed to entertain respecting the loneliness of her condition and want of sympathizing friends. I assured her that mother's views were by no means general; that in our part of the country there were thousands upon thousands who favored the elevation of her

Notes

[75] *"What are our joys … summer cloud"* from "Time, A Poem" by Henry Kirke White (1785–1806).

race, disapproving of oppression in all its forms; that she was not unpitied, friendless, and utterly despised; that she might hope for better things in the future. Having spoken these words of comfort, I rose with the resolution that if I recovered my health I would take her home with me, whether mother was willing or not."

"I don't[76] know what your mother would do without her; still, I wish she was away."

Susan now came for her long absent husband, and they returned home to their room.

The month of November was one of great anxiety on James's account. He was rapidly wasting away.

A celebrated physician was called, and performed a surgical operation, as a last means. Should this fail, there was no hope. Of course he was confined wholly to his room, mostly to his bed. With all his bodily suffering, all his anxiety for his family, whom he might not live to protect, he did not forget Frado. He shielded her from many beatings, and every day imparted religious instructions. No one, but his wife, could move him so easily as Frado; so that in addition to her daily toil she was often deprived of her rest at night.

Yet she insisted on being called; she wished to show her love for one who had been such a friend to her. Her anxiety and grief increased as the probabilities of his recovery became doubtful.

Mrs. Bellmont found her weeping on his account, shut her up, and whipped her with the raw-hide, adding an injunction never to be seen snivelling again because she had a little work to do. She was very careful never to shed tears on his account, in her presence, afterwards.

Chapter 8

Visitor and Departure

"Other cares engross me, and my tired soul with emulative haste,
Looks to its God."[77]

The brother associated with James in business, in Baltimore, was sent for to confer with one who might never be able to see him there.

James began to speak of life as closing; of heaven, as of a place in immediate prospect; of aspirations, which waited for fruition in glory. His brother, Lewis by name, was an especial favorite of sister Mary; more like her in disposition and preferences than James or Jack.

He arrived as soon as possible after the request, and saw with regret the sure indications of fatality in his sick brother, and listened to his admonitions – admonitions to a Christian life – with tears, and uttered some promises of attention to the subject so dear to the heart of James.

How gladly he would have extended healing aid. But, alas! it was not in his power; so, after listening to his wishes and arrangements for his family and business, he decided to return home.

Anxious for company home, he persuaded his father and mother to permit Mary to attend him. She was not at all needed in the sick room; she did not choose to be useful in the kitchen, and then she was fully determined to go.

Notes

[76] *Original reads*: do n't [ed.].

[77] *"Other cares engross me … God"* from "Written in the Prospect of Death" by Henry Kirke White.

So all the trunks were assembled and crammed with the best selections from the wardrobe of herself and mother, where the last-mentioned articles could be appropriated.

"Nig was never so helpful before," Mary remarked, and wondered what had induced such a change in place of former sullenness.

Nig was looking further than the present, and congratulating herself upon some days of peace, for Mary never lost opportunity of informing her mother of Nig's delinquencies[78] were she otherwise ignorant.

Was it strange if she were officious,[79] with such relief in prospect?

The parting from the sick brother was tearful and sad. James prayed in their presence for their renewal in holiness; and urged their immediate attention to eternal realities, and gained a promise that Susan and Charlie should share their kindest regards.

No sooner were they on their way, than Nig slyly crept round to Aunt Abby's room, and tiptoeing and twisting herself into all shapes, she exclaimed –

"She's gone, Aunt Abby, she's gone, fairly gone," and jumped up and down, till Aunt Abby feared she would attract the notice of her mistress by such demonstrations. "Well, she's gone, gone, Aunt Abby. I hope she'll never come back again."

"No! no! Frado, that's wrong! you would be wishing her dead; that won't do."

"Well, I'll bet she'll never come back again; somehow, I feel as though she wouldn't."[80]

"She is James's sister," remonstrated Aunt Abby.

"So is our cross sheep just as much, that I ducked in the river; I'd like to try my hand at curing *her* too."

"But you forget what our good minister told us last week, about doing good to those that hate us."

"Didn't[81] I do good, Aunt Abby, when I washed and ironed and packed her old duds to get rid of her, and helped her pack her trunks, and run here and there for her?"

"Well, well, Frado; you must go finish your work, or your mistress will be after you, and remind you severely of Miss Mary, and some others beside."

Nig went as she was told, and her clear voice was heard as she went, singing in joyous notes the relief she felt at the removal of one of her tormentors.

Day by day the quiet of the sick man's room was increased. He was helpless and nervous; and often wished change of position, thereby hoping to gain momentary relief. The calls upon Frado were consequently more frequent, her nights less tranquil. Her health was impaired by lifting the sick man, and by drudgery in the kitchen. Her ill health she endeavored to conceal from James, fearing he might have less repose if there should be a change of attendants; and Mrs. Bellmont, she well knew, would have no sympathy for her. She was at last so much reduced as to be unable to stand erect for any great length of time. She would *sit* at the table to wash her dishes; if she heard the well-known step of her mistress, she would rise till she returned to her room, and then sink down for further rest. Of course she was longer than usual in completing the services assigned her. This was a subject of complaint to Mrs. Bellmont; and Frado endeavored to throw off all appearance of sickness in her presence.

But it was increasing upon her, and she could no longer hide her indisposition. Her mistress entered one day, and finding her seated, commanded her to go to work.

Notes

[78] *Original reads*: delinquincies [ed.].

[79] *officious* interfering (in this case, overly helpful).

[80] *Original reads*: would n't [ed.].

[81] *Original reads*: Did n't [ed.].

"I am sick," replied Frado, rising and walking slowly to her unfinished task, "and cannot stand long, I feel so bad."

Angry that she should venture a reply to her command, she suddenly inflicted a blow which lay the tottering girl prostrate on the floor. Excited by so much indulgence of a dangerous passion, she seemed left to unrestrained malice; and snatching a towel, stuffed the mouth of the sufferer, and beat her cruelly.

Frado hoped she would end her misery by whipping her to death. She bore it with the hope of a martyr, that her misery would soon close. Though her mouth was muffled, and the sounds much stifled, there was a sensible commotion, which James's[82] quick ear detected.

"Call Frado to come here," he said faintly, "I have not seen her to-day."

Susan retired with the request to the kitchen, where it was evident some brutal scene had just been enacted.

Mrs. Bellmont replied that she had "some work to do just now; when that was done, she might come."

Susan's appearance confirmed her husband's fears, and he requested his father, who sat by the bedside, to go for her. This was a messenger, as James well knew, who could not be denied; and the girl entered the room, sobbing and faint with anguish.

James called her to him, and inquired the cause of her sorrow. She was afraid to expose the cruel author of her misery, lest she should provoke new attacks. But after much entreaty, she told him all, much of which[83] had escaped his watchful ear. Poor James shut his eyes in silence, as if pained to forgetfulness by the recital. Then turning to Susan, he asked her to take Charlie and walk out; "she needed the fresh air," he said. "And say to mother I wish Frado to sit by me till you return. I think you are fading, from staying so long in this sick room." Mr. B. also left, and Frado was thus left alone with her friend. Aunt Abby came in to make her daily visit, and seeing the sick countenance of the attendant, took her home with her to administer some cordial. She soon returned, however, and James kept her with him the rest of the day; and a comfortable night's repose following, she was enabled to continue, as usual, her labors. James insisted on her attending religious meetings in the vicinity with Aunt Abby.

Frado, under the instructions of Aunt Abby and the minister, became a believer in a future existence – one of happiness or misery. Her doubt was, *is* there a heaven for the black? She knew there was one for James, and Aunt Abby, and all good white people; but was there any for blacks? She had listened attentively to all the minister said, and all Aunt Abby had told her; but then it was all for white people.

As James approached that blessed world, she felt a strong desire to follow, and be with one who was such a dear, kind friend to her.

While she was exercised with these desires and aspirations, she attended an evening meeting with Aunt Abby, and the good man urged all, young or old, to accept the offers of mercy, to receive a compassionate Jesus as their Saviour. "Come to Christ," he urged, "all, young or old, white or black, bond or free, come all to Christ for pardon; repent, believe."

This was the message she longed to hear; it seemed to be spoken for her. But he had told them to repent; "what was that?" she asked. She knew she was unfit for any heaven, made for whites or blacks. She would gladly repent, or do anything which would admit her to share the abode of James.

Notes

[82] *Original reads*: James' [ed.].

[83] *Original reads*: much which [ed.].

Her anxiety increased; her countenance bore marks of solicitude unseen before; and though she said nothing of her inward contest, they all observed a change.

James and Aunt Abby hoped it was the springing of good seed sown by the Spirit of God. Her tearful attention at the last meeting encouraged his aunt to hope that her mind was awakened, her conscience aroused. Aunt Abby noticed that she was particularly engaged in reading the Bible; and this strengthened her conviction that a heavenly Messenger was striving with her. The neighbors dropped in to inquire after the sick, and also if Frado was *"serious?"* They noticed she seemed very thoughtful and tearful at the meetings. Mrs. Reed was very inquisitive; but Mrs. Bellmont saw no appearance of change for the better. She did not feel responsible for her spiritual culture, and hardly believed she had a soul.

Nig was in truth suffering much; her feelings were very intense on any subject, when once aroused. She read her Bible carefully, and as often as an opportunity presented, which was when entirely secluded in her own apartment, or by Aunt Abby's side, who kindly directed her to Christ, and instructed her in the way of salvation.

Mrs. Bellmont found her one day quietly reading her Bible. Amazed and half crediting the reports of officious neighbors, she felt it was time to interfere. Here she was, reading and shedding tears over the Bible. She ordered her to put up the book, and go to work, and not be snivelling about the house, or stop to read again.

But there was one little spot seldom penetrated by her mistress' watchful eye: this was her room, uninviting and comfortless; but to herself a safe retreat. Here she would listen to the pleadings of a Saviour, and try to penetrate the veil of doubt and sin which clouded her soul, and long to cast off the fetters of sin, and rise to the communion of saints.

Mrs. Bellmont, as we before said, did not trouble herself about the future destiny of her servant. If she did what she desired for *her* benefit, it was all the responsibility she acknowledged. But she seemed to have great aversion to the notice Nig would attract should she become pious. How could she meet this case? She resolved to make her complaint to John. Strange, when she was always foiled in this direction, she should resort to him. It was time something was done; she had begun to read the Bible openly.

The night of this discovery, as they were retiring, Mrs. Bellmont introduced the conversation, by saying:

"I want your attention to what I am going to say. I have let Nig go out to evening meetings a few times, and, if you will believe it, I found her reading the Bible to-day, just as though she expected to turn pious nigger, and preach to white folks. So now you see what good comes of sending her to school. If she should get converted she would have to go to meeting: at least, as long as James lives. I wish he had not such queer notions about her. It seems to trouble him to know he must die and leave her. He says if he should get well he would take her home with him, or educate her here. Oh, how awful! What can the child mean? So careful, too, of her! He says we shall ruin her health making her work so hard, and sleep in such a place. O, John! do you think he is in his right mind?"

"Yes, yes; she is slender."

"Yes, *yes!*" she repeated sarcastically, "you know these niggers are just like black snakes; you *can't* kill them. If she wasn't tough she would have been killed long ago. There was never one of my girls could do half the work."

"Did they ever try?" interposed her husband. "I think she can do more than all of them together."

"What a man!" said she, peevishly. "But I want to know what is going to be done with her about getting pious?"

"Let her do just as she has a mind to. If it is a comfort to her, let her enjoy the privilege of being good. I see no objection."

"I should think *you* were crazy, sure. Don't[84] you know that every night she will want to go toting off to meeting? and Sundays, too? and you know we have a great deal of company Sundays, and she can't be spared."

"I thought you Christians held to going to church," remarked Mr. B.

"Yes, but who ever thought of having a nigger go, except to drive others there? Why, according to you and James, we should very soon have her in the parlor, as smart as our own girls. It's of no use talking to you or James. If you should go on as you would like, it would not be six months before she would be leaving me; and that won't do. Just think how much profit she was to us last summer. We had no work hired out; she did the work of two girls – "

"And got the whippings for two with it!" remarked Mr. Bellmont.

"I'll beat the money out of her, if I can't[85] get her worth any other way," retorted Mrs. B. sharply. While this scene was passing, Frado was trying to utter the prayer of the publican, "God be merciful to me a sinner."[86]

Chapter 9

Death

We have now
But a small portion of what men call time,
To hold communion.[87]

SPRING opened, and James, instead of rallying, as was hoped, grew worse daily. Aunt Abby and Frado were the constant allies of Susan. Mrs. Bellmont dared not lift him. She was not "strong enough," she said.

It was very offensive to Mrs. B. to have Nab about James so much. She had thrown out many a hint to detain her from so often visiting the sick-room; but Aunt Abby was too well accustomed to her ways to mind them. After various unsuccessful efforts, she resorted to the following expedient. As she heard her cross the entry below, to ascend the stairs, she slipped out and held the latch of the door which led into the upper entry.

"James does not want to see you, or anyone[88] else," she said.

Aunt Abby hesitated, and returned slowly to her own room; wondering if it were really James's[89] wish not to see her. She did not venture again that day, but still felt disturbed and anxious about him. She inquired of Frado, and learned that he was no worse. She asked her if James did not wish her to come and see him; what could it mean?

Quite late next morning, Susan came to see what had become of her aunt.

"Your mother said James did not wish to see me, and I was afraid I tired him."

"Why, aunt, that is a mistake, I *know*. What could mother mean?" asked Susan.

The next time she went to the sitting-room she asked her mother –

"Why does not Aunt Abby visit James as she has done? Where is she?"

"At home. I hope that she will stay there," was the answer.

Notes

[84] *Original reads*: Do n't [ed.].

[85] *Original reads*: ca n't [ed.].

[86] *"God … a sinner"* Luke 18:13.

[87] *"We have now but …"* from "Written in the Prospect of Death" by Henry Kirke White.

[88] *Original reads*: any one [ed.].

[89] *Original reads*: James' [ed.].

"I should think she would come in and see James," continued Susan.

"I told her he did want to see her, and to stay out. You need make no stir about it; remember:" she added, with one of her fiery glances.

Susan kept silence. It was a day or two before James spoke of her absence. The family were at dinner, and Frado was watching beside him. He inquired the cause of her absence, and *she* told him all. After the family returned he sent his wife for her. When she entered, he took her hand, and said, "Come to me often, Aunt. Come any time – I am always glad to see you. I have but a little longer to be with you – come often, Aunt. Now please help lift me up, and see if I can rest a little."

Frado was called in, and Susan and Mrs. B. all attempted; Mrs. B. was too weak; she did not feel able to lift so much. So the three succeeded in relieving the sufferer.

Frado returned to her work. Mrs. B. followed. Seizing Frado, she said she would "cure her of tale-bearing," and, placing the wedge of wood between her teeth, she beat her cruelly with the raw-hide. Aunt Abby heard the blows, and came to see if she could hinder them.

Surprised at her sudden appearance, Mrs. B. suddenly stopped, but forbade her removing the wood till she gave her permission, and commanded Nab to go home.

She was thus tortured when Mr. Bellmont came in, and, making inquiries which she did not, because she could not, answer, approached her; and seeing her situation, quickly removed the instrument of torture, and sought his wife. Their conversation we will omit; suffice it to say, a storm raged which required many days to exhaust its strength.

Frado was becoming seriously ill. She had no relish for food, and was constantly overworked, and then she had such solicitude about the future. She wished to pray for pardon. She did try to pray. Her mistress had told her it would do no good for her to attempt prayer; prayer was for whites, not for blacks. If she minded her mistress, and did what she commanded, it was all that was required of her.

This did not satisfy her, or appease her longings. She knew her instructions did not harmonize with those of the man of God or Aunt Abby's. She resolved to persevere. She said nothing on the subject, unless asked. It was evident to all her mind was deeply exercised. James longed to speak with her alone on the subject. An opportunity presented soon, while the family were at tea. It was usual to summon Aunt Abby to keep company with her, as his death was expected hourly.

As she took her accustomed seat, he asked, "Are you afraid to stay with me alone, Frado?"

"No," she replied, and stepped to the window to conceal her emotion.

"Come here, and sit by me; I wish to talk with you."

She approached him, and, taking her hand, he remarked:

"How poor you are, Frado! I want to tell you that I fear I shall never be able to talk with you again. It is the last time, perhaps, I shall *ever* talk with you. You are old enough to remember my dying words and profit by them. I have been sick a long time; I shall die pretty soon. My Heavenly Father is calling me home. Had it been His[90] will to let me live I should take you to live with me; but, as it is, I shall go and leave you. But, Frado, if you will be a good girl, and love and serve God, it will be but a short time before we are in a *heavenly* home together. There will never be any sickness or sorrow there."

Notes

[90] *Original reads*: his [ed.].

Frado, overcome with grief, sobbed, and buried her face in his pillow. She expected he would die; but to hear him speak of his departure himself was unexpected.

"Bid me good bye, Frado."

She kissed him, and sank on her knees by his bedside; his hand rested on her head; his eyes were closed; his lips moved in prayer for this disconsolate child.

His wife entered, and interpreting the scene, gave him some restoratives, and withdrew for a short time.

It was a great effort for Frado to cease sobbing; but she dared not be seen below in tears; so she choked her grief, and descended to her usual toil. Susan perceived a change in her husband. She felt that death was near.

He tenderly looked on her, and said, "Susan, my wife, our farewells are all spoken. I feel prepared to go. I shall meet you in heaven. Death is indeed creeping fast upon me. Let me see them all once more. Teach Charlie the way to heaven; lead him up as you come."

The family all assembled. He could not talk as he wished to them. He seemed to sink into unconsciousness. They watched him for hours. He had labored hard for breath some time, when he seemed to awake suddenly, and exclaimed, "Hark! do you hear it?"

"Hear what, my son?" asked the father.

"Their call. Look, look, at the shining ones! Oh, let me go and be at rest!"

As if waiting for this petition, the Angel of Death severed the golden thread, and he was in heaven. At midnight the messenger came.

They called Frado to see his last struggle. Sinking on her knees at the foot of his bed, she buried her face in the clothes, and wept like one inconsolable. They led her from the room. She seemed to be too much absorbed to know it was necessary for her to leave. Next day she would steal into the chamber as often as she could, to weep over his remains, and ponder his last words to her. She moved about the house like an automaton.[91] Every duty performed – but an abstraction from all, which shewed her thoughts were busied elsewhere. Susan wished her to attend his burial as one of the family. Lewis and Mary and Jack it was not thought best to send for, as the season would not allow them time for the journey. Susan provided her with a dress for the occasion, which was her first intimation that she would be allowed to mingle her grief with others.

The day of the burial she was attired in her mourning dress; but Susan, in her grief, had forgotten a bonnet.

She hastily ransacked the closets, and found one of Mary's, trimmed with bright pink ribbon.

It was too late to change the ribbon, and she was unwilling to leave Frado at home; she knew it would be the wish of James she should go with her. So tying it on, she said, "Never mind, Frado, you shall see where our dear James is buried." As she passed out, she heard the whispers of the by-standers, "Look there! see there! how that looks – a black dress and a pink ribbon!"

Another time, such remarks would have wounded Frado. She had now a sorrow with which such were small in comparison.

As she saw his body lowered in the grave she wished to share it; but she was not fit to die. She could not go where he was if she did. She did not love God; she did not serve Him[92] or know how to.

She retired at night to mourn over her unfitness for heaven, and gaze out upon the stars, which, she felt, studded the entrance of heaven, above which James reposed in the bosom of Jesus, to which her desires were hastening. She wished she could see

Notes

[91] *automaton* machine.

[92] *Original reads*: him [ed.].

God, and ask Him[93] for eternal life. Aunt Abby had taught her that He was ever looking upon her. Oh, if she could see Him,[94] or hear Him[95] speak words of forgiveness. Her anxiety increased; her health seemed impaired, and she felt constrained to go to aunt Abby and tell her all about her conflicts.

She received her like a returning wanderer; seriously urged her to accept of Christ; explained the way; read to her from the Bible, and remarked upon such passages as applied to her state. She warned her against stifling that voice which was calling her to heaven; echoed the farewell words of James, and told her to come to her with her difficulties, and not to delay a duty so important as attention to the truths of religion, and her soul's interests.

Mrs. Bellmont would occasionally give instruction, though far different. She would tell her she could not go where James was; she need not try. If she should get to heaven at all, she would never be as high up as he.

He was the attraction. Should she "want to go there if she could not see him?"

Mrs. B. seldom mentioned her bereavement, unless in such allusion to Frado. She donned her weeds from custom; kept close her crape veil for so many Sabbaths, and abated nothing of her characteristic harshness.

The clergyman called to minister consolation to the afflicted widow and mother. Aunt Abby seeing him approach the dwelling, knew at once the object of his visit, and followed him to the parlor, unasked by Mrs. B! What a daring affront! The good man dispensed the consolations, of which he was steward, to the apparently grief-smitten mother, who talked like one schooled in a heavenly atmosphere. Such resignation expressed, as might have graced the trial of the holiest. Susan, like a mute sufferer, bared her soul to his sympathy and godly counsel, but only replied to his questions in short syllables. When he offered prayer, Frado stole to the door that she might hear of the heavenly bliss of one who was her friend on earth. The prayer caused profuse weeping, as any tender reminder of the heaven-born was sure to. When the good man's voice ceased, she returned to her toil, carefully removing all trace of sorrow. Her mistress soon followed, irritated by Nab's impudence in presenting herself unasked in the parlor, and upbraided[96] her with indolence, and bade her apply herself more diligently. Stung by unmerited rebuke, weak from sorrow and anxiety, the tears rolled down her dark face, soon followed by sobs, and then, losing all control of herself, she wept aloud. This was an act of disobedience. Her mistress grasping her raw-hide, caused a longer flow of tears, and wounded a spirit that was craving healing mercies.

Chapter 10

Perplexities – Another Death

Neath the billows of the ocean,
Hidden treasures wait the hand,
That again to light shall raise them
With the diver's magic wand.
G.W. Cook.

THE family, gathered by James's[97] decease, returned to their homes. Susan and Charles returned to Baltimore. Letters were received from the absent, expressing their sympathy

Notes

[93] *Original reads*: him [ed.].
[94] *Original reads*: him [ed.].
[95] *Original reads*: him [ed.].
[96] *Original reads*: upraided [ed.].
[97] *Original reads*: James' [ed.].

and grief. The father bowed like a "bruised reed," under the loss of his beloved son. He felt desirous to die the death of the righteous; also, conscious that he was unprepared, he resolved to start on the narrow way, and sometime[98] solicit entrance through the gate which leads to the celestial city. He acknowledged his too ready acquiescence with Mrs. B., in permitting Frado to be deprived of her only religious privileges for weeks together. He accordingly asked his sister to take her to meeting once more, which she was ready at once to do.

At the first[99] opportunity they once more attended meeting together. The minister conversed faithfully with every person present. He was surprised to find the little colored girl so solicitous, and kindly directed her to the flowing fountain[100] where she might wash and be clean. He inquired of the origin of her anxiety, of her progress up to this time, and endeavored to make Christ, instead of James, the attraction of Heaven. He invited her to come to his house, to speak freely her mind to him, to pray much, to read her Bible often.

The neighbors, who were at meeting – among them Mrs. Reed – discussed the opinions Mrs. Bellmont would express on the subject. Mrs. Reed called and informed Mrs. B. that her colored girl "related her experience the other night at the meeting."

"What experience?" asked she, quickly, as if she expected to hear the number of times she had whipped Frado, and the number of lashes set forth in plain Arabic numbers.

"Why, you know she is serious, don't you ? She told the minister about it."

Mrs. B. made no reply, but changed the subject adroitly. Next morning she told Frado she should not go out of the house for one while, except on errands; and if she did not stop trying to be religious, she would whip her to death.

Frado pondered; her mistress was a professor of religion; was *she* going to heaven? then she did not wish to go. If she should be near James, even, she could not be happy with those fiery eyes watching her ascending path. She resolved to give over all thought of the future world, and strove daily to put her anxiety far from her.

Mr. Bellmont found himself unable to do what James or Jack could accomplish for her. He talked with her seriously, told her he had seen her many times punished undeservedly; he did not wish to have her saucy or disrespectful, but when she was *sure* she did not deserve a whipping, to avoid it if she could. "You are looking sick," he added, "you cannot endure beating as you once could."

It was not long before an opportunity offered of profiting by his advice. She was sent for wood, and not returning as soon as Mrs. B. calculated, she followed her, and, snatching from the pile a stick, raised it over her.

"Stop!" shouted Frado, "strike me, and I'll never work a mite more for you"; and throwing down what she had gathered, stood like one who feels the stirring of free and independent thoughts.

By this unexpected demonstration, her mistress, in amazement, dropped her weapon, desisting from her purpose of chastisement. Frado walked towards the house, her mistress following with the wood she herself was sent after. She did not know, before, that she had a power to ward off assaults. Her triumph in seeing her enter the door with *her* burden, repaid her for much of her former suffering.

Notes

[98] *Original reads*: some time [ed.].

[99] *Original reads*: The first [ed.].

[100] *flowing fountain* belief in Christ.

It was characteristic of Mrs. B. never to rise in her majesty, unless she was sure she should be victorious.

This affair never met with an "after clap," like many others.

Thus passed a year. The usual amount of scolding, but fewer whippings. Mrs. B. longed once more for Mary's return, who had been absent over a year; and she wrote imperatively for her to come quickly to her. A letter came in reply, announcing that she would comply as soon as she was sufficiently recovered from an illness which detained her.

No serious apprehensions were cherished by either parent, who constantly looked for notice of her arrival, by mail. Another letter brought tidings that Mary was seriously ill; her mother's presence was solicited.

She started without delay. Before she reached her destination, a letter came to the parents announcing her death.

No sooner was the astounding news received, than Frado rushed into Aunt Abby's, exclaiming:–

"She's dead, Aunt Abby!"

"Who?" she asked, terrified by the unprefaced announcement.

"Mary; they've just had a letter."

As Mrs. B. was away, the brother and sister could freely sympathize, and she sought him in this fresh sorrow, to communicate such solace as she could, and to learn particulars of Mary's untimely death, and assist him in his journey thither.

It seemed a thanksgiving to Frado. Every hour or two she would pop in into Aunt Abby's room with some strange query:

"She got into the *river* again, Aunt Abby, didn't[101] she; the Jordan[102] is a big one to tumble into, anyhow.[103] S'posen she goes to hell, she'll be as black as I am. Wouldn't[104] mistress be mad to see her a nigger!" and others of a similar stamp, not at all acceptable to the pious, sympathetic dame; but she could not evade them.

The family returned from their sorrowful journey, leaving the dead behind. Nig looked for a change in her tyrant; what could subdue her, if the loss of her idol could not?

Never was Mrs. B. known to shed tears so profusely, as when she reiterated to one and another the sad particulars of her darling's sickness and death. There was, indeed, a season of quiet grief; it was the lull of the fiery elements. A few weeks revived the former tempests, and so at variance did they seem with chastisement sanctified, that Frado felt them to be unbearable. She determined to flee. But where? Who would take her? Mrs. B. had always represented her ugly. Perhaps everyone[105] thought her so. Then no one would take her. She was black, no one would love her. She might have to return, and then she would be more in her mistress' power than ever.

She remembered her victory at the wood-pile. She decided to remain to do as well as she could; to assert her rights when they were trampled on; to return once more to her meeting in the evening, which had been prohibited. She had learned how to conquer; she would not abuse the power while Mr. Bellmont was at home.

But had she not better run away? Where? She had never been from the place far enough to decide what course to take. She resolved to speak to Aunt Abby. *She* mapped the dangers of her course, her liability to fail in finding so good friends as John and herself. Frado's mind was busy for days and nights. She contemplated administering poison to her mistress, to rid herself and the house of so detestable a plague.

Notes

[101] *Original reads*: did n't [ed.].

[102] *the Jordan* a river leading to the Biblical promised land (located in the Middle East).

[103] *Original reads*: any how [ed.].

[104] *Original reads*: Would n't [ed.].

[105] *Original reads*: every one [ed.].

But she was restrained by an overruling Providence; and finally decided to stay contentedly through her period of service, which would expire when she was eighteen years of age.

In a few months Jane returned home with her family, to relieve her parents, upon whom years and affliction had left the marks of age. The years intervening since she had left her home had, in some degree, softened the opposition to her unsanctioned marriage with George. The more Mrs. B. had about her, the more energetic seemed her directing capabilities, and her fault-finding propensities. Her own, she had full power over; and Jane, after vain endeavors, became disgusted, weary, and perplexed, and decided that, though her mother might suffer, she could not endure her home. They followed Jack to the West. Thus vanished all hopes of sympathy or relief from this source to Frado. There seemed no one capable of enduring the oppressions of the house but her. She turned to the darkness of the future with the determination previously formed, to remain until she should be eighteen. Jane begged her to follow her so soon as she should be released; but so wearied out was she by her mistress, she felt disposed to flee from any and everyone[106] having her similitude of name or feature.

Chapter 11

Marriage Again

Crucified the hopes that cheered me,
All that to the earth endeared me;
Love of wealth and fame and power,
Love, – all have been crucified.[107]

C.E.

Darkness before day. Jane left, but Jack was now to come again. After Mary's death he visited home, leaving a wife behind. An orphan whose home was with a relative, gentle, loving, the true mate of kind, generous Jack. His mother was a stranger to her, of course, and had perfect right to interrogate:

"Is she good looking, Jack?" asked his mother.

"Looks well to me," was the laconic reply.

"Was her *father* rich?"

"Not worth a copper,[108] as I know of; I never asked him," answered Jack.

"Hadn't she any property? What did you marry her for," asked his mother.

"Oh, she's *worth a million* dollars, mother, though not a cent of it is in money."

"Jack! what do you want to bring such a poor being into the family for? You'd better stay here, at home, and let your wife go. Why couldn't[109] you try to do better, and not disgrace your parents?"

"Don't judge, till you see her," was Jack's reply, and immediately changed the subject. It was no recommendation to his mother, and she did not feel prepared to welcome her cordially now he was to come with his wife. He was indignant at his mother's

Notes

[106] *Original reads*: every one [ed.].

[107] *"Crucified the hopes ... crucified"* from the poem "Crucified" by Carrie Calderwood (C.C., not "C.E."), published in *Godey's Lady's Book* Volume 59 (1859).

[108] *copper* a penny.

[109] *Original reads*: could n't [ed.].

advice to desert her. It rankled bitterly in his soul, the bare suggestion. He had more to bring. He now came with a child also. He decided to leave the West, but not his family.

Upon their arrival, Mrs. B. extended a cold welcome to her new daughter, eyeing her dress with closest scrutiny. Poverty was to her a disgrace, and she could not associate with any thus dishonored. This coldness was felt by Jack's worthy wife, who only strove the harder to recommend herself by her obliging, winning ways.

Mrs. B. could never let Jack be with her alone without complaining of this or that deficiency in his wife.

He cared not so long as the complaints were piercing his own ears. He would not have Jenny disquieted. He passed his time in seeking employment.

A letter came from his brother Lewis, then at the South, soliciting his services. Leaving his wife, he repaired thither.

Mrs. B. felt that great restraint was removed, that Jenny was more in her own power. She wished to make her feel her inferiority; to relieve Jack of his burden if he would not do it himself. She watched her incessantly to catch at some act of Jenny's which might be construed into conjugal unfaithfulness.

Nearby[110] were a family of cousins, one a young man of Jack's age, who, from love to his cousin, proffered all needful courtesy to his stranger relative. Soon news reached Jack that Jenny was deserting her covenant vows, and had formed an illegal intimacy with his cousin. Meantime Jenny was told by her mother-in-law that Jack did not marry her untrammelled.[111] He had another love whom he would be glad, even now, if he could, to marry. It was very doubtful if he ever came for her.

Jenny would feel pained by her unwelcome gossip, and, glancing at her child, she decided, however true it might be, she had a pledge which would enchain him yet. Ere long, the mother's inveterate[112] hate crept out into some neighbor's enclosure, and, caught up hastily, they passed the secret round till it became none, and Lewis was sent for, the brother by whom Jack was employed. The neighbors saw her fade in health and spirits; they found letters never reached their destination when sent by either. Lewis arrived with the joyful news that he had come to take Jenny home with him.

What a relief to her to be freed from the gnawing taunts of her adversary.

Jenny retired to prepare for the journey, and Mrs. B. and Henry[113] had a long interview. Next morning he informed Jenny that new clothes would be necessary, in order to make her presentable to Baltimore society, and he should return without her, and she must stay till she was suitably attired.

Disheartened, she rushed to her room, and, after relief from weeping, wrote to Jack to come; to have pity on her, and take her to him. No answer came. Mrs. Smith, a neighbor, watchful and friendly, suggested that she write away from home, and employ someone[114] to carry it to the office who would elude Mrs. B., who, they very well knew, had intercepted Jenny's letter, and influenced Lewis to leave her behind. She accepted the offer, and Frado succeeded in managing the affair so that Jack soon came to the rescue, angry, wounded, and forever after alienated from his early home and his mother. Many times would Frado steal up into Jenny's room, when she knew she was

Notes

110 *Original reads*: Near by [ed.].

111 *untrammelled* without obligations.

112 *inveterate* engrained.

113 *Henry* A possible mistake by the author, indicating Henry instead of Lewis.

114 *Original reads*: some one [ed.].

tortured by her mistress' malignity, and tell some of her own encounters with her, and tell her she might "be sure it wouldn't[115] kill her, for she should have died long before at the same treatment."

Susan and her child succeeded Jenny as visitors. Frado had merged into womanhood, and, retaining what she had learned, in spite of the few privileges enjoyed formerly, was striving to enrich her mind. Her school-books were her constant companions, and every leisure moment was applied to them. Susan was delighted to witness her progress, and some little book from her was a reward sufficient for any task imposed, however difficult. She had her book always fastened open near her, where she could glance from toil to soul refreshment. The approaching spring would close the term of years which Mrs. B. claimed as the period of her servitude. Often as she passed the way-marks of former years did she pause to ponder on her situation, and wonder if she *could* succeed in providing for her own wants. Her health was delicate, yet she resolved to try.

Soon she counted the time by days which should release her. Mrs. B. felt that she could not well spare one who could so well adapt herself to all departments – man, boy, housekeeper, domestic, etc. She begged Mrs. Smith to talk with her, to show her how ungrateful it would appear to leave a home of such comfort – how wicked it was to be ungrateful! But Frado replied that she had had enough of such comforts; she wanted some new ones; and as it was so wicked to be ungrateful, she would go from temptation; Aunt Abby said "we mustn't[116] put ourselves in the way of temptation."

Poor little Fido! She shed more tears over him than over all beside.

The morning for departure dawned. Frado engaged to work for a family a mile distant. Mrs. Bellmont dismissed her with the assurance that she would soon wish herself back again, and a present of a silver half dollar.

Her wardrobe consisted of one decent dress, without any superfluous accompaniments. A Bible from Susan she felt was her greatest treasure.

Now was she alone in the world. The past year had been one of suffering resulting from a fall, which had left her lame.

The first summer passed pleasantly, and the wages earned were expended in garments necessary for health and cleanliness. Though feeble, she was well satisfied with her progress. Shut up in her room, after her toil was finished, she studied what poor samples of apparel she had, and, for the first time, prepared her own garments.

Mrs. Moore, who employed her, was a kind friend to her, and attempted to heal her wounded spirit by sympathy and advice, burying the past in the prospects of the future. But her failing health was a cloud no kindly human hand could dissipate. A little light work was all she could accomplish. A clergyman, whose family was small, sought her, and she was removed there. Her engagement with Mrs. Moore finished in the fall. Frado was anxious to keep up her reputation for efficiency, and often pressed far beyond prudence. In the winter she entirely gave up work, and confessed herself thoroughly sick. Mrs. Hale, soon overcome by additional cares, was taken sick also, and now it became necessary to adopt some measures for Frado's comfort, as well as to relieve Mrs. Hale. Such dark forebodings as visited her as she lay, solitary and sad, no moans or sighs could relieve.

The family physician pronounced her case one of doubtful issue. Frado hoped it was final. She could not feel relentings that her former home was abandoned,

Notes

[115] *Original reads*: would n't [ed.].

[116] *Original reads*: must n't [ed.].

and yet, should she be in need of succor could she obtain it from one who would now so grudgingly bestow it? The family were applied to, and it was decided to take her there. She was removed to a room built out from the main building, used formerly as a workshop, where cold and rain found unobstructed access, and here she fought with bitter reminiscences and future prospects till she became reckless of her faith and hopes and person, and half wished to end what nature seemed so tardily to take.

Aunt Abby made her frequent visits, and at last had her removed to her own apartment, where she might supply her wants, and minister to her once more in heavenly things.

Then came the family consultation.

"What is to be done with her," asked Mrs. B., "after she is moved there with Nab?"

"Send for the Dr., your brother," Mr. B. replied.

"When?"

"To-night."

"To-night! and for her! Wait till morning," she continued.

"She has waited too long now; I think something should be done soon."

"I doubt if she is much sick," sharply interrupted Mrs. B.

"Well, we'll see what our brother thinks."

His coming was longed for by Frado, who had known him well during her long sojourn in the family; and his praise of her nice butter and cheese, from which his table was supplied, she knew he felt as well as spoke.

"You're sick, very sick," he said, quickly, after a moment's pause. "Take good care of her, Abby, or she'll never get well. All broken down."

"Yes, it was at Mrs. Moore's," said Mrs. B., "all this was done. She did but little the latter part of the time she was here."

"It was commenced longer ago than last summer. Take good care of her; she may never get well," remarked the Dr.

"We sha'n't[117] pay you for doctoring her; you may look to the town for that, sir," said Mrs. B., and abruptly left the room.

"Oh dear! oh dear!" exclaimed Frado, and buried her face in the pillow.

A few kind words of consolation, and she was once more alone in the darkness which enveloped her previous days. Yet she felt sure they owed her a shelter and attention, when disabled, and she resolved to feel patient, and remain till she could help herself. Mrs. B. would not attend her, nor permit her domestic to stay with her at all. Aunt Abby was her sole comforter. Aunt Abby's nursing had the desired effect, and she slowly improved. As soon as she was able to be moved, the kind Mrs. Moore took her to her home again, and completed what Aunt Abby had so well commenced. Not that she was well, or ever would be; but she had recovered so far as rendered it hopeful she might provide for her own wants. The clergyman at whose house she was taken sick, was now seeking someone[118] to watch his sick children, and as soon as he heard of her recovery, again asked for her services.

What seemed so light and easy to others, was too much for Frado; and it became necessary to ask once more where the sick should find an asylum.

All felt that the place where her declining health began should be the place of relief; so they applied once more for a shelter.

Notes

[117] *Original reads*: sha' n't [ed.].

[118] *Original reads*: some one [ed.].

"No," exclaimed the indignant Mrs. B.; "she[119] shall never come under this roof again; never! never!" she repeated, as if each repetition were a bolt to prevent admission.

One only resource; the public must pay the expense. So she was removed to the home of two maidens (old), who had principle enough to be willing to earn the money a charitable public disburses.

Three years of weary sickness wasted her, without extinguishing a life apparently so feeble. Two years had these maidens watched and cared for her, and they began to weary, and finally to request the authorities to remove her.

Mrs. Hoggs was a lover of gold and silver, and she asked the favor of filling her coffers[120] by caring for the sick. The removal caused severe sickness.

By being bolstered in the bed, after a time she could use her hands, and often would ask for sewing to beguile the tedium. She had become very expert with her needle the first year of her release from Mrs. B., and she had forgotten none of her skill. Mrs. H. praised her, and as she improved in health, was anxious to employ her. She told her she could in this way replace her clothes, and as her board would be paid for, she would thus gain something.

Many times her hands wrought when her body was in pain; but the hope that she might yet help herself, impelled her on.

Thus she reckoned her store of means by a few dollars, and was hoping soon to come in possession, when she was startled by the announcement that Mrs. Hoggs had reported her to the physician and town officers as an impostor. That she was, in truth, able to get up and go to work.

This brought on a severe sickness of two weeks, when Mrs. Moore again sought her, and took her to her home. She had formerly had wealth at her command, but misfortune had deprived her of it, and unlocked her heart to sympathies and favors she had never known while it lasted. Her husband, defrauded of his last means by a branch of the Bellmont family, had supported them by manual labor, gone to the West, and left his wife and four young children. But she felt humanity required her to give a shelter to one she knew to be worthy of a hospitable reception. Mrs. Moore's physician was called, and pronounced her a very sick girl, and encouraged Mrs. M. to keep her and care for her, and he would see that the authorities were informed of Frado's helplessness, and pledged assistance.

Here she remained till sufficiently restored to sew again. Then came the old resolution to take care of herself, to cast off the unpleasant charities of the public.

She learned that in some towns in Massachusetts, girls make straw bonnets – that it was easy and profitable. But how should *she*, black, feeble, and poor, find anyone[121] to teach her. But God prepares the way, when human agencies see no path. Here was found a plain, poor, simple woman, who could see merit beneath a dark skin; and when the invalid mulatto told her sorrows, she opened her door and her heart, and took the stranger in. Expert with the needle, Frado soon equalled her instructress; and she sought also to teach her the value of useful books; and while one read aloud to the other of deeds historic and names renowned, Frado experienced a new impulse. She felt herself capable of elevation; she felt that this book information supplied an undefined dissatisfaction she had long felt, but could not express. Every leisure moment was carefully applied to self-improvement, and a devout and Christian exterior invited confidence from the villagers. Thus she passed months of quiet, growing in the confidence of her neighbors and newfound[122] friends.

Notes

[119] *Original reads*: she she [ed.].

[120] *coffers* money chests.

[121] *Original reads*: any one [ed.].

[122] *Original reads*: new found [ed.].

Chapter 12

The Winding Up of the Matter

Nothing new under the sun.
Solomon.[123]

A FEW years ago, within the compass of my narrative, there appeared often in some of our New England villages, professed fugitives from slavery, who recounted their personal experience in homely phrase, and awakened the indignation of non-slaveholders against brother Pro.[124] Such a one appeared in the new home of Frado; and as people of color were rare there, was it strange she should attract her dark brother; that he should inquire her out; succeed in seeing her; feel a strange sensation in his heart towards her; that he should toy with her shining curls, feel proud to provoke her to smile and expose the ivory concealed by thin, ruby lips; that her sparkling eyes should fascinate; that he should propose; that they should marry? A short acquaintance was indeed an objection, but she saw him often, and thought she knew him. He never spoke of his enslavement to her when alone, but she felt that, like her own oppression, it was painful to disturb oftener than was needful.

He was a fine, straight negro, whose back showed no marks of the lash, erect as if it never crouched beneath a burden. There was a silent sympathy which Frado felt attracted her, and she opened her heart to the presence of love – that arbitrary and inexorable tyrant.

She removed to Singleton, her former residence, and there was married. Here were Frado's first feelings of trust and repose on human arm. She realized, for the first time, the relief of looking to another for comfortable support. Occasionally he would leave her to "lecture."

Those tours were prolonged often to weeks. Of course he had little spare money. Frado was again feeling her self-dependence, and was at last compelled to resort alone to that. Samuel was kind to her when at home, but made no provision for his absence, which was at last unprecedented.

He left her to her fate – embarked at sea, with the disclosure that he had never seen the South, and that his illiterate harangues[125] were humbugs for hungry abolitionists. Once more alone! Yet not alone. A still newer companionship would soon force itself upon her. No one wanted her with such prospects. Her self[126] was burden enough; who would have an additional one?

The horrors of her condition nearly prostrated her, and she was again thrown upon the public for sustenance. Then followed the birth of her child. The long absent Samuel unexpectedly returned, and rescued her from charity. Recovering from her expected illness, she once more commenced toil for herself and child, in a room obtained of a poor woman, but with better fortune. One so well known would not be wholly neglected. Kind friends watched her when Samuel was from home, prevented her from suffering, and when the cold weather pinched the warmly clad, a kind friend took them in, and thus preserved them. At last Samuel's business became very engrossing, and after long desertion, news reached his family that he had become a victim of yellow fever, in New Orleans.

Notes

[123] *Solomon* Old Testament King, see Ecclesiastes 1:9.

[124] *brother Pro* those who were proslavery.

[125] *harangues* rants.

[126] *Original reads*: herself [ed.].

So much toil as was necessary to sustain Frado, was more than she could endure. As soon as her babe could be nourished without his mother, she left him in charge of a Mrs. Capon, and procured an agency,[127] hoping to recruit her health, and gain an easier livelihood for herself and child. This afforded her better maintenance than she had yet found. She passed into the various towns of the State she lived in, then into Massachusetts. Strange were some of her adventures. Watched by kidnappers, maltreated by professed abolitionists, who didn't[128] want slaves at the South, nor niggers in their own houses, North. Faugh! to lodge one; to eat with one; to admit one through the front door; to sit next to one;[129] awful!

Traps slyly laid by the vicious to ensnare her, she resolutely avoided. In one of her tours, Providence favored her with a friend who, pitying her cheerless lot, kindly provided her with a valuable recipe, from which she might herself manufacture a useful article for her maintenance. This proved a more agreeable, and an easier way of sustenance.

And thus, to the present time, may you see her busily employed in preparing her merchandise; then sallying forth to encounter many frowns, but some kind friends and purchasers. Nothing turns her from her steadfast purpose of elevating herself. Reposing on God, she has thus far journeyed securely. Still an invalid, she asks your sympathy,[130] gentle reader. Refuse not, because some part of her history is unknown, save by the Omniscient God. Enough has been unrolled to demand your sympathy and aid.

Do you ask the destiny of those connected with her *early* history? A few years only have elapsed since Mr. and Mrs. B. passed into another world. As age increased, Mrs. B. became more irritable, so that no one, even her own children, could remain with her; and she was accompanied by her husband to the home of Lewis, where, after an agony in death unspeakable, she passed away. Only a few months since, Aunt Abby entered heaven. Jack and his wife rest in heaven, disturbed by no intruders; and Susan and her child are yet with the living. Jane has silver locks in place of auburn tresses, but she has the early love of Henry[131] still, and has never regretted her exchange of lovers. Frado has passed from their memories, as Joseph from the butler's,[132] but she will never cease to track them till beyond mortal vision.

1859

Notes

[127] *procured an agency* obtained a job as a traveling agent.

[128] *Original reads*: did n't [ed.].

[129] *Original reads*: sit next one [ed.].

[130] *Original reads*: symyathy [ed.].

[131] *Henry* A possible mistake by the author, indicating Henry instead of George.

[132] *Joseph from the butler's* Genesis 40:23.

Harriet Ann Jacobs (1813–1897)

The heroine of the 1861 book *Incidents in the Life of a Slave Girl. Written by Herself.*, Linda Brent, dramatically proclaims the gendered nature of slavery and racism: "Slavery is terrible for men," she writes, "but it is far more terrible for women. Superadded to the burden common to all, *they* have wrongs, and sufferings, and mortifications peculiarly their own." These peculiar mortifications characterized much of the life of Harriet Ann Jacobs, the author of this book, which also happens to be the first slave narrative written by a woman, and one of the only antebellum texts to describe the sexual exploitation of African American women in the slaveholding South.

Jacobs was born in Edenton, North Carolina, to slaves Elijah Knox and Delilah Horniblow. Despite enslavement, Harriet and her brother, John S. Jacobs, were allowed certain privileges because their grandmother ran a popular store in the community. When her mother died, the six-year-old Jacobs went to live with her mother's mistress, Margaret Horniblow, who taught the girl how to read, write, and sew. But in 1825 Margaret Horniblow died, and Harriet came into the possession of Dr James Norcom, whose sexual predations are recreated through the character of "Dr Flint."

Norcom's relentless sexual harassment became the defining terror of Jacob's youth. She took as her lover a young white neighbor, a lawyer named Samuel Sawyer. Two children resulted from this relationship, Louisa and Joseph, but it still did not protect Jacobs from Norcom's manipulation. Since he had legal ownership of the children, Norcom threatened to sell them if Harriet resisted his sexual advances. This fear for her children's lives urged Jacobs to escape in 1835, hoping that Sawyer would purchase the children from Norcom in her absence. She first hid briefly in a nearby swamp, then in a crawl space above a shack in her grandmother's home. Jacobs remained in the crawl space for seven years. From a hole in the roof she observed her children, and wrote spurious letters to Norcom to confuse him as to her whereabouts.

In 1842, nearly crippled from her years of confinement, Jacobs finally escaped to Philadelphia. By this point, Sawyer had married, and purchased the children. In Philadelphia, antislavery friends helped Jacobs relocate to New York. There she reunited with her daughter Louisa (whom Sawyer had sent to Brooklyn) and her brother John. For the rest of Jacobs's life, she and Louisa worked together as abolitionists, feminists, and companions. They enjoyed a bond that slavery had denied.

Beginning in 1845, Jacobs worked as a nurse in the home of Nathaniel Parker Willis, the highest-paid magazine writer of the day, and founder of the popular *Home Journal*. Although this job afforded her the opportunity to travel to England, her ultimate desire was to cultivate the familial bonds that Dr Norcom had tried to break in North Carolina. In 1846, Jacobs left Willis for Boston, where she lived for the first time with her brother John Jacobs and two children. By this point, John was active in abolitionist circles. He created an antislavery reading room in Rochester, and helped to send Louisa to school in Clinton, New York. While in New York, Harriet Jacobs began a life-long friendship with leading abolitionist and author Amy Post. Encouraged by her brother's political activity and Post's feminism, she began speaking before antislavery audiences in Rochester.

The Wiley Blackwell Anthology of African American Literature: Volume 1, 1746–1920, First Edition.
Edited by Gene Andrew Jarrett.

With the passage of the 1850 Fugitive Slave Law, Harriet Jacobs and her family were separated again when her brother, fearing for his safety, fled to California, and she returned to New York City. In 1852, after her son also relocated to California, Harriet got word that Norcom's son-in-law, Daniel Messmore, was in New York City, plotting to kidnap her. In spite of Harriet's objections to being bought, Nathaniel Willis's new wife, Cornelia Grinnell Willis, intervened and paid Messmore $300 for her freedom. Finally free, Harriet moved to Idlewild, the Willis's mansion on the banks of the Hudson River, where she began work on her autobiography.

Incidents was initially published as a serial in Horace Greeley's *New York Tribune*, but Harriet Jacobs's account of sexual harassment alarmed readers and the newspaper stopped publication. By this point, Harriet Beecher Stowe's 1852 novel *Uncle Tom's Cabin* had changed the world of American literary publishing and increased the popular appeal of slave narratives. Jacobs explored collaborating with Stowe, who was interested in including her story in the 1853 sequel *A Key to Uncle Tom's Cabin*, but they could not come to an agreement. Under the pseudonym of Linda Brent, *Incidents* thus appeared in 1861, with a preface by the author and an introductory note from its editor, the popular abolitionist writer Lydia Maria Child. The book was groundbreaking not only for its frank exposure of slavery's sexual implications, but also for the way Jacobs incorporated the forms of the domestic novel and familial concerns into the slave narrative genre. In this she conformed the nineteenth-century "cult of true womanhood" to the historical realities of African American women.

Jacobs presented the book to the Philadelphia Female Anti-Slavery Society in January of 1862, and sent a copy to the Emancipation Committee in London, where her brother sold it to British reformers under the title *A True Tale of Slavery*. After Lincoln's Emancipation Proclamation went into effect in 1863, Jacobs was unanimously elected to the Woman's Loyal League's Executive Committee, an organization led by Elizabeth Cady Stanton that linked African American emancipation to the Union War effort. Jacobs used the League to solicit support for freed people in Alexandria, Virginia. She and Louisa arrived in Virginia with the New England Freedman's Aid Society in 1862. Two years later they opened the Jacobs Free School in Alexandria.

Like most African Americans working in the trenches of southern Reconstruction, the mother-daughter team were quickly frustrated by southern violence and pervasive racism. In 1866, after a wave of violence swept Savannah, Georgia, where the two women worked under the auspices of the New England Freedman's Aid Society, Harriet and Louisa Jacobs fled to New York. Louisa briefly joined the feminist American Equal Rights Association as a lecturer, sharing the podium with Frances Ellen Watkins Harper and Elizabeth Cady Stanton. But the split between feminists who supported the Fifteenth Amendment to the Constitution, which granted all citizens the right to vote "regardless of race, color, or previous condition of servitude," and those who objected to African American males gaining suffrage over white women led Louisa to leave the organization by the 1870s. Always short of money, Harriet Jacobs settled in Cambridge, Massachusetts, where she operated a boarding house. In the 1880s, she relocated the business to Washington, DC, where she housed African American federal appointees like Blanche K. Bruce and James Monroe Trotter. She died in 1897 and is buried in Cambridge's Mount Auburn Cemetery, under a headstone proclaiming, "Patient in tribulation, fervent in spirit, serving the Lord."

Further reading

Bennett, Michael. *Democratic Discourses: The Radical Abolition Movement and Antebellum American Literature*. New Brunswick: Rutgers University Press, 2005. Ch. 5.

Cox, John D. *Traveling South: Travel Narratives and the Construction of American Identity*. Athens: University of Georgia Press, 2005. Ch. 3.

Gomaa, Sally. "Writing to 'Virtuous' and 'Gentle' Readers: The Problem of Pain in Harriet Jacobs's *Incidents* and Harriet Wilson's *Sketches*." *African American Review* 43.2 (2009): 371–381.

Gould, Philip. "The Economies of the Slave Narrative." *A Companion to African American Literature*. Ed. Gene Andrew Jarrett. Malden, MA: Wiley-Blackwell, 2010. 90–102.

Gruesser, John Cullen. *Confluences: Postcolonialism, African American Literary Studies, and the Black Atlantic*. Athens: University of Georgia Press, 2005. Ch. 4.

Li, Stephanie. "Motherhood as Resistance in Harriet Jacobs's *Incidents in the Life of a Slave Girl*." *Legacy* 23.1 (2006): 14–29.

Moore, Geneva Cobb. "A Freudian Reading of Harriet Jacobs' *Incidents in the Life of a Slave Girl*." *Southern Literary Journal* 38.1 (2005): 3–20.

Perry, Lewis. "Harriet Jacobs and the 'Dear Old Flag.'" *African American Review* 42.3–4 (2008): 595–605.

Smith, Stephanie. "Harriet Jacobs: A Case History of Authentication." *The Cambridge Companion to the African American Slave Narrative*. Ed. Audrey Fisch. New York: Cambridge University Press, 2007. 189–200.

Stewart, Anna. "Revising 'Harriet Jacobs' for 1865." *American Literature: A Journal of Literary History, Criticism, and Bibliography* 82.4 (2010): 701–724.

Tricomi, Albert H. "Harriet Jacobs's Autobiography and the Voice of Lydia Maria Child." *ESQ: A Journal of the American Renaissance* 1.3 (2007): 216–252.

Warner, Anne Bradford. "Harriet Jacobs at Home in *Incidents in the Life of a Slave Girl*." *Southern Quarterly: A Journal of the Arts in the South* 45.3 (2008): 30–47.

Yellin, Jean Fagan. *Harriet Jacobs: A Life*. New York: Basic Civitas Books, 2004.

Yellin, Jean Fagan, ed. *The Harriet Jacobs Family Papers*. 2 vols. Chapel Hill: University of North Carolina Press, 2008.

Incidents in the Life of a Slave Girl. Written by Herself.

Preface by the Author

READER, be assured this narrative is no fiction. I am aware that some of my adventures may seem incredible; but they are, nevertheless, strictly true. I have not exaggerated the wrongs inflicted by Slavery; on the contrary, my descriptions fall far short of the facts. I have concealed the names of places, and given persons fictitious names. I had no motive for secrecy on my own account, but I deemed it kind and considerate towards others to pursue this course.

I wish I were more competent to the task I have undertaken. But I trust my readers will excuse deficiencies in consideration of circumstances. I was born and reared in Slavery; and I remained in a Slave State twenty-seven years. Since I have been in the North, it has been necessary for me to work diligently for my own support, and the education of my children. This has not left me much leisure to make up for the loss of early opportunities to improve myself; and it has compelled me to write these pages at irregular intervals, whenever I could snatch an hour from household duties.

When I first arrived in Philadelphia, Bishop Paine[1] advised me to publish a sketch of my life, but I told him I was altogether incompetent to complete such an undertaking. Though I have improved my mind somewhat since that time, I still remain of the same opinion; but I trust my motives will excuse what might otherwise seem presumptuous. I have not written my experiences in order to attract attention to myself; on the contrary, it would have been more pleasant to me to have been silent

Notes

[1] *Bishop Paine* Daniel A. Payne (1811–1893), American bishop and educator.

about my own history. Neither do I care to excite sympathy for my own sufferings. But I do earnestly desire to arouse the women of the North to a realizing sense of the condition of two millions of women in the South, still in bondage, suffering what I suffered, and most of them far worse. I want to add my testimony to that of abler pens to convince the people of the Free States what Slavery really is. Only by experience can anyone[2] realize how deep, and dark, and foul is that pit of abominations. May the blessing of God rest on this imperfect effort in behalf of my persecuted people!

Linda Brent

Introduction by the Editor

THE author of the following autobiography is personally known to me, and her conversation and manners inspire me with confidence. During the last seventeen years, she has lived the greater part of the time with a distinguished family in New York, and has so deported herself as to be highly esteemed by them. This fact is sufficient, without further credentials of her character. I believe those who know her will not be disposed to doubt her veracity, though some incidents in her story are more romantic than fiction.

At her request, I have revised her manuscript; but such changes as I have made have been mainly for purposes of condensation and orderly arrangement. I have not added anything to the incidents, or changed the import of her very pertinent remarks. With trifling exceptions, both the ideas and the language are her own. I pruned excrescences a little, but otherwise I had no reason for changing her lively and dramatic way of telling her own story. The names of both persons and places are known to me; but for good reasons I suppress them.

It will naturally excite surprise that a woman reared in Slavery should be able to write so well. But circumstances will explain this. In the first place, nature endowed her with quick perceptions. Secondly, the mistress, with whom she lived till she was twelve years old, was a kind, considerate friend, who taught her to read and spell. Thirdly, she was placed in favorable circumstances after she came to the North; having frequent intercourse with intelligent persons, who felt a friendly interest in her welfare, and were disposed to give her opportunities for self-improvement.

I am well aware that many will accuse me of indecorum for presenting these pages to the public; for the experiences of this intelligent and much-injured woman belong to a class which some call delicate subjects, and others indelicate. This peculiar phase of Slavery has generally been kept veiled; but the public ought to be made acquainted with its monstrous features, and I willingly take the responsibility of presenting them with the veil withdrawn. I do this for the sake of my sisters in bondage, who are suffering wrongs so foul, that our ears are too delicate to listen to them. I do it with the hope of arousing conscientious and reflecting women in the North to a sense of their duty in the exertion of moral influence on the question of Slavery, on all possible occasions. I do it with the hope that every man who reads this narrative will swear solemnly before God that, so far as he has power to prevent it, no fugitive from Slavery shall ever be sent back to suffer in that loathsome den of corruption and cruelty.

L. Maria Child[3]

Notes

[2] *Original reads*: any one [ed.].

[3] *L. Maria Child* Lydia Maria Francis Child (1802–1880), American women's rights activist and abolitionist.

Incidents in the Life of a Slave Girl, Seven Years Concealed

Chapter 1

Childhood

I WAS born a slave; but I never knew it till six years of happy childhood had passed away. My father was a carpenter, and considered so intelligent and skilful in his trade, that, when buildings out of the common line were to be erected, he was sent for from long distances, to be head workman. On condition of paying his mistress two hundred dollars a year, and supporting himself, he was allowed to work at his trade, and manage his own affairs. His strongest wish was to purchase his children; but, though he several times offered his hard earnings for that purpose, he never succeeded. In complexion my parents were a light shade of brownish yellow, and were termed mulattoes. They lived together in a comfortable home; and, though we were all slaves, I was so fondly shielded that I never dreamed I was a piece of merchandise, trusted to them for safe keeping, and liable to be demanded of them at any moment. I had one brother, William, who was two years younger than myself – a bright, affectionate child. I had also a great treasure in my maternal grandmother, who was a remarkable woman in many respects. She was the daughter of a planter in South Carolina, who, at his death, left her mother and his three children free, with money to go to St. Augustine, where they had relatives. It was during the Revolutionary War; and they were captured on their passage, carried back, and sold to different purchasers. Such was the story my grandmother used to tell me; but I do not remember all the particulars. She was a little girl when she was captured and sold to the keeper of a large hotel. I have often heard her tell how hard she fared during childhood. But as she grew older she evinced so much intelligence, and was so faithful, that her master and mistress could not help seeing it was for their interest to take care of such a valuable piece of property. She became an indispensable personage in the household, officiating in all capacities, from cook and wet nurse to seamstress. She was much praised for her cooking; and her nice crackers became so famous in the neighborhood that many people were desirous of obtaining them. In consequence of numerous requests of this kind, she asked permission of her mistress to bake crackers at night, after all the household work was done; and she obtained leave to do it, provided she would clothe herself and her children from the profits. Upon these terms, after working hard all day for her mistress, she began her midnight bakings assisted by her two oldest children. The business proved profitable; and each year she laid by a little, which was saved for a fund to purchase her children. Her master died, and the property was divided among his heirs. The widow had her dower in the hotel, which she continued to keep open. My grandmother remained in her service as a slave; but her children were divided among her master's children. As she had five, Benjamin, the youngest one, was sold, in order that each heir might have an equal portion of dollars and cents. There was so little difference in our ages that he seemed more like my brother than my uncle. He was a bright, handsome lad, nearly white; for he inherited the complexion my grandmother had derived from Anglo-Saxon ancestors. Though only ten years old, seven hundred and twenty dollars were paid for him. His sale was a terrible blow to my grandmother; but she was naturally hopeful, and she went to work with renewed energy, trusting in time to be able to purchase some of her children. She had laid up three hundred dollars, which her mistress one day begged as a loan, promising to pay her soon. The reader probably knows that no promise or writing given to a slave is legally binding; for, according to Southern laws, a slave, *being* property, can *hold* no property. When my grandmother lent her hard earnings to her mistress, she trusted solely to her honor. The honor of a slaveholder to a slave!

To this good grandmother I was indebted for many comforts. My brother Willie and I often received portions of the crackers, cakes, and preserves she made to sell; and after we ceased to be children we were indebted to her for many more important services.

Such were the unusually fortunate circumstances of my early childhood. When I was six years old, my mother died; and then, for the first time, I learned, by the talk around me, that I was a slave. My mother's mistress was the daughter of my grandmother's mistress. She was the foster sister of my mother; they were both nourished at my grandmother's breast. In fact, my mother had been weaned at three months old, that the babe of the mistress might obtain sufficient food. They played together as children; and, when they became women, my mother was a most faithful servant to her whiter foster sister. On her death-bed her mistress promised that her children should never suffer for anything;[4] and during her lifetime she kept her word. They all spoke kindly of my dead mother, who had been a slave merely in name, but in nature was noble and womanly. I grieved for her, and my young mind was troubled with the thought of who[5] would now take care of me and my little brother. I was told that my home was now to be with her mistress; and I found it a happy one. No toilsome or disagreeable duties were imposed upon me. My mistress was so kind to me that I was always glad to do her bidding, and proud to labor for her as much as my young years would permit. I would sit by her side for hours, sewing diligently, with a heart as free from care as that of any free-born white child. When she thought I was tired, she would send me out to run and jump; and away I bounded, to gather berries or flowers to decorate her room. Those were happy days – too happy to last. The slave child had no thought for the morrow; but there came that blight, which too surely waits on every human being born to be a chattel.

When I was nearly twelve years old, my kind mistress sickened and died. As I saw the cheek grow paler, and the eye more glassy, how earnestly I prayed in my heart that she might live! I loved her; for she had been almost like a mother to me. My prayers were not answered. She died, and they buried her in the little churchyard, where, day after day, my tears fell upon her grave.

I was sent to spend a week with my grandmother. I was now old enough to begin to think of the future; and again and again I asked myself what they would do with me. I felt sure I should never find another mistress so kind as the one who was gone. She had promised my dying mother that her children should never suffer for anything; and when I remembered that, and recalled her many proofs of attachment to me, I could not help having some hopes that she had left me free. My friends were almost certain it would be so. They thought she would be sure to do it, on account of my mother's love and faithful service. But, alas! we all know that the memory of a faithful slave does not avail much to save her children from the auction block.

After a brief period of suspense, the will of my mistress was read, and we learned that she had bequeathed me to her sister's daughter, a child of five years old. So vanished our hopes. My mistress had taught me the precepts of God's Word: " Thou shalt love thy neighbor as thyself."[6] "Whatsoever ye would that men should do unto you, do ye even so unto them."[7] But I was her slave, and I suppose she did not

Notes

[4] *Original reads*: any thing [ed.].

[5] *Original reads*: the thought who [ed.].

[6] *"Thou shalt love … thyself"* Mark 12:31.

[7] *Whatsoever ye … unto them"* Matthew 7:12.

recognize me as her neighbor. I would give much to blot out from my memory that one great wrong. As a child, I loved my mistress; and, looking back on the happy days I spent with her, I try to think with less bitterness of this act of injustice. While I was with her, she taught me to read and spell; and for this privilege, which so rarely falls to the lot of a slave, I bless her memory.

She possessed but few slaves; and at her death those were all distributed among her relatives. Five of them were my grandmother's children, and had shared the same milk that nourished her mother's children. Notwithstanding my grandmother's long and faithful service to her owners, not one of her children escaped the auction block. These God-breathing machines are no more, in the sight of their masters, than the cotton they plant, or the horses they tend.

Chapter 2

The New Master and Mistress

Dr. Flint, a physician in the neighborhood, had married the sister of my mistress, and I was now the property of their little daughter. It was not without murmuring that I prepared for my new home; and what added to my unhappiness, was the fact that my brother William was purchased by the same family. My father, by his nature, as well as by the habit of transacting business as a skilful mechanic, had more of the feelings of a freeman than is common among slaves. My brother was a spirited boy; and being brought up under such influences, he early detested the name of master and mistress. One day, when his father and his mistress both happened to call him at the same time, he hesitated between the two; being perplexed to know which had the strongest claim upon his obedience. He finally concluded to go to his mistress. When my father reproved him for it, he said, "You both called me, and I didn't know which I ought to go to first."

"You are *my* child," replied our father, "and when I call you, you should come immediately, if you have to pass through fire and water."

Poor Willie! He was now to learn his first lesson of obedience to a master. Grandmother tried to cheer us with hopeful words, and they found an echo in the credulous hearts of youth.

When we entered our new home we encountered cold looks, cold words, and cold treatment. We were glad when the night came. On my narrow bed I moaned and wept, I felt so desolate and alone.

I had been there nearly a year, when a dear little friend of mine was buried. I heard her mother sob, as the clods fell on the coffin of her only child, and I turned away from the grave, feeling thankful that I still had something left to love. I met my grandmother, who said, "Come with me, Linda"; and from her tone I knew that something sad had happened. She led me apart from the people, and then said, "My child, your father is dead." Dead! How could I believe it? He had died so suddenly I had not even heard that he was sick. I went home with my grandmother. My heart rebelled against God, who had taken from me mother, father, mistress, and friend. The good grandmother tried to comfort me. "Who knows the ways of God?" said she. "Perhaps they have been kindly taken from the evil days to come." Years afterwards I often thought of this. She promised to be a mother to her grandchildren, so far as she might be permitted to do so; and strengthened by her love, I returned to my master's. I thought I should be allowed to go to my father's house the next morning; but I was ordered to go for flowers, that my mistress's house might be decorated for an evening party. I spent the day gathering flowers and weaving them into festoons,[8] while the dead body of my father was lying within a mile of me. What cared my owners for that? he was merely a piece of property. Moreover, they thought he had spoiled his children, by teaching them to feel that they were human beings. This was blasphemous doctrine for a slave to teach; presumptuous in him, and dangerous to the masters.

The next day I followed his remains to a humble grave beside that of my dear mother. There were those who knew my father's worth, and respected his memory.

My home now seemed more dreary than ever. The laugh of the little slave-children sounded harsh and cruel. It was selfish to feel so about the joy of others. My brother moved about with a very grave face. I tried to comfort him, by saying, "Take courage, Willie; brighter days will come by and by."

"You don't know anything about it, Linda," he replied. "We shall have to stay here all our days; we shall never be free."

I argued that we were growing older and stronger, and that perhaps we might, before long, be allowed to hire our own time, and then we could earn money to buy our freedom. William declared this was much easier to say than to do; moreover, he did not intend to *buy* his freedom. We held daily controversies upon this subject.

Little attention was paid to the slaves' meals in Dr. Flint's house. If they could catch a bit of food while it was going, well and good. I gave myself no trouble on that score, for on my various errands I passed my grandmother's house, where there was always something to spare for me. I was frequently threatened with punishment if I stopped there; and my grandmother, to avoid detaining me, often stood at the gate with something for my breakfast or dinner. I was indebted to *her* for all my comforts, spiritual or temporal. It was *her* labor that supplied my scanty wardrobe. I have a vivid recollection of the linsey-woolsey[9] dress given me every winter by Mrs. Flint. How I hated it! It was one of the badges of slavery.

While my grandmother was thus helping to support me from her hard earnings, the three hundred dollars she had lent her mistress were never repaid. When her mistress died, her son-in-law, Dr. Flint, was appointed executor. When grandmother applied to him for payment, he said the estate was insolvent, and the law prohibited payment. It did not, however, prohibit him from retaining the silver candelabra, which had been purchased with that money. I presume they will be handed down in the family, from generation to generation.

My grandmother's mistress had always promised her that, at her death, she should be free; and it was said that in her will she made good the promise. But when the estate was settled, Dr. Flint told the faithful old servant that, under existing circumstances, it was necessary she should be sold.

On the appointed day, the customary advertisement was posted up, proclaiming that there would be a "public sale of negroes, horses, &c." Dr. Flint called to tell my grandmother that he was unwilling to wound her feelings by putting her up at auction, and that he would prefer to dispose of her at private sale. My grandmother saw through his hypocrisy; she understood very well that he was ashamed of the job. She was a very spirited woman, and if he was base enough to sell her, when her mistress intended she should be free, she was determined the public should know it. She had for a long time supplied many families with crackers and preserves; consequently, "Aunt Marthy," as she was called, was generally known, and everybody[10] who knew

Notes

[8] *festoons* garlands.

[9] *linsey-woolsey* coarse fabric made of linen and wool scraps.

[10] *Original reads*: every body [ed.].

her respected her intelligence and good character. Her long and faithful service in the family was also well known, and the intention of her mistress to leave her free. When the day of sale came, she took her place among the chattels, and at the first call she sprang upon the auction-block. Many voices called out, "Shame! Shame! Who is going to sell *you*, Aunt[11] Marthy? Don't stand there! That is no place for *you*." Without saying a word, she quietly awaited her fate. No one bid for her. At last, a feeble voice said, "Fifty dollars." It came from a maiden lady, seventy years old, the sister of my grandmother's deceased mistress. She had lived forty years under the same roof with my grandmother; she knew how faithfully she had served her owners, and how cruelly she had been defrauded of her rights; and she resolved to protect her. The auctioneer waited for a higher bid; but her wishes were respected; no one bid above her. She could neither read nor write; and when the bill of sale was made out, she signed it with a cross. But of what consequence[12] was that, when she had a big heart overflowing with human kindness? She gave the old servant her freedom.

At that time, my grandmother was just fifty years old. Laborious years had passed since then; and now my brother and I were slaves to the man who had defrauded her of her money, and tried to defraud her of her freedom. One of my mother's sisters, called Aunt Nancy, was also a slave in his family. She was a kind, good aunt to me; and supplied the place of both housekeeper and waiting maid to her mistress. She was, in fact, at the beginning and end of everything.

Mrs. Flint, like many southern women, was totally deficient in energy. She had not strength to superintend her household affairs; but her nerves were so strong that she could sit in her easy chair and see a woman whipped till the blood trickled from every stroke of the lash. She was a member of the church; but partaking of the Lord's supper did not seem to put her in a Christian frame of mind. If dinner was not served at the exact time on that particular Sunday, she would station herself in the kitchen, and wait till it was dished, and then spit in all the kettles and pans that had been used for cooking. She did this to prevent the cook and her children from eking out their meagre fare with the remains of the gravy and other scrapings. The slaves could get nothing to eat except what she chose to give them. Provisions were weighed out by the pound and ounce, three times a day. I can assure you she gave them no chance to eat wheat bread from her flour barrel. She knew how many biscuits a quart of flour would make, and exactly what size they ought to be.

Dr. Flint was an epicure. The cook never sent a dinner to his table without fear and trembling; for if there happened to be a dish not to his liking, he would either order her to be whipped, or compel her to eat every mouthful of it in his presence. The poor, hungry creature might not have objected to eating it; but she did object to having her master cram it down her throat till she choked.

They had a pet dog that was a nuisance in the house. The cook was ordered to make some Indian mush[13] for him. He refused to eat, and when his head was held over it, the froth flowed from his mouth into the basin. He died a few minutes after. When Dr. Flint came in, he said the mush had not been well cooked, and that was the reason the animal would not eat it. He sent for the cook, and compelled her to eat it. He thought that the woman's stomach was stronger than the dog's; but her sufferings afterwards proved that he was mistaken. This poor woman endured many cruelties from her master and mistress; sometimes she was locked up, away from her nursing baby, for a whole day and night.

Notes

[11] *Original reads*: aunt [ed.].

[12] *Original reads*: But what consequence [ed.].

[13] *Indian mush* corn porridge.

When I had been in the family a few weeks, one of the plantation slaves was brought to town, by order of his master. It was near night when he arrived, and Dr. Flint ordered him to be taken to the work house, and tied up to the joist,[14] so that his feet would just escape the ground. In that situation he was to wait till the doctor had taken his tea. I shall never forget that night. Never before, in my life, had I heard hundreds of blows fall, in succession, on a human being. His piteous groans, and his "O, pray don't, massa," rang in my ear for months afterwards. There were many conjectures as to the cause of this terrible punishment. Some said master accused him of stealing corn; others said the slave had quarrelled with his wife, in presence of the overseer, and had accused his master of being the father of her child. They were both black, and the child was very fair.

I went into the work house next morning, and saw the cowhide[15] still wet with blood, and the boards all covered with gore. The poor man lived, and continued to quarrel with his wife. A few months afterwards Dr. Flint handed them both over to a slave-trader. The guilty man put their value into his pocket, and had the satisfaction of knowing that they were out of sight and hearing. When the mother was delivered into the trader's hands, she said, "You *promised* to treat me well." To which he replied, "You have let your tongue run too far; damn you!" She had forgotten that it was a crime for a slave to tell who was the father of her child.

From others than the master persecution also comes in such cases. I once saw a young slave girl dying soon after the birth of a child nearly white. In her agony she cried out, "O Lord, come and take me! " Her mistress stood by, and mocked at her like an incarnate fiend. "You suffer, do you?" she exclaimed. "I am glad of it. You deserve it all, and more too."

The girl's mother said, "The baby is dead, thank God; and I hope my poor child will soon be in heaven, too."

"Heaven!" retorted the mistress. "There is no such place for the like of her and her bastard."

The poor mother turned away, sobbing. Her dying daughter called her, feebly, and as she bent over her, I heard her say, "Don't grieve so, mother; God knows all about it; and HE will have mercy upon me."

Her sufferings, afterwards, became so intense, that her mistress felt unable to stay; but when she left the room, the scornful smile was still on her lips. Seven children called her mother. The poor black woman had but the one child, whose eyes she saw closing in death, while she thanked God for taking her away from the greater bitterness of life.

Chapter 3

The Slaves' New Year's Day

DR. FLINT owned a fine residence in town, several farms, and about fifty slaves, besides hiring a number by the year.

Hiring-day at the south takes place on the 1st of January. On the 2d, the slaves are expected to go to their new masters. On a farm, they work until the corn and cotton are laid. They then have two holidays. Some masters give them a good dinner under the trees. This over, they work until Christmas Eve.[16] If no heavy charges are meantime brought against them, they are given four or five holidays, whichever the master or overseer may think proper. Then comes New Year's Eve;[17] and they gather

Notes

[14] *joist* support beam.

[15] *cowhide* whip.

[16] *Original reads*: Christmas eve [ed.].

[17] *Original reads*: New Year's eve [ed.].

together their little alls,[18] or more properly speaking, their little nothings, and wait anxiously for the dawning of day. At the appointed hour the grounds are thronged with men, women, and children, waiting, like criminals, to hear their doom pronounced. The slave is sure to know who is the most humane, or cruel master, within forty miles of him.

It is easy to find out, on that day, who clothes and feeds his slaves well; for he is surrounded by a crowd, begging, "Please, massa, hire me this year. I will work *very* hard, massa."

If a slave is unwilling to go with his new master, he is whipped, or locked up in jail, until he consents to go, and promises not to run away during the year. Should he chance to change his mind, thinking it justifiable to violate an extorted promise, woe unto him if he is caught! The whip is used till the blood flows at his feet; and his stiffened limbs are put in chains, to be dragged in the field for days and days!

If he lives until the next year, perhaps the same man will hire him again, without even giving him an opportunity of going to the hiring-ground. After those for hire are disposed of, those for sale are called up.

O, you happy free women, contrast *your* New Year's Day[19] with that of the poor bond-woman! With you it is a pleasant season, and the light of the day is blessed. Friendly wishes meet you everywhere, and gifts are showered upon you. Even hearts that have been estranged from you soften at this season, and lips that have been silent echo back, "I wish you a happy New Year." Children bring their little offerings, and raise their rosy lips for a caress. They are your own, and no hand but that of death can take them from you.

But to the slave mother New Year's Day[20] comes laden with peculiar sorrows. She sits on her cold cabin floor, watching the children who may all be torn from her the next morning; and often does she wish that she and they might die before the day dawns. She may be an ignorant creature, degraded by the system that has brutalized her from childhood; but she has a mother's instincts, and is capable of feeling a mother's agonies.

On one of these sale days, I saw a mother lead seven children to the auction-block. She knew that *some* of them would be taken from her; but they took *all*. The children were sold to a slave-trader, and their mother was bought by a man in her own town. Before night her children were all far away. She begged the trader to tell her where he intended to take them; this he refused to do. How *could* he, when he knew he would sell them, one by one, wherever he could command the highest price? I met that mother in the street, and her wild, haggard face lives to-day in my mind. She wrung her hands in anguish, and exclaimed, "Gone! All gone! Why *don't* God kill me?" I had no words wherewith to comfort her. Instances of this kind are of daily, yea, of hourly occurrence.

Slaveholders have a method, peculiar to their institution, of getting rid of *old* slaves, whose lives have been worn out in their service. I knew an old woman, who for seventy years faithfully served her master. She had become almost helpless, from hard labor and disease. Her owners moved to Alabama, and the old black woman was left to be sold to anybody[21] who would give twenty dollars for her.

Notes

[18] *alls* everything of importance.

[19] *Original reads*: New Year's day [ed.].

[20] *Original reads*: New Year's day [ed.].

[21] *Original reads*: any body [ed.].

Chapter 4

The Slave Who Dared to Feel Like a Man

Two years had passed since I entered Dr. Flint's family, and those years had brought much of the knowledge that comes from experience, though they had afforded little opportunity for any other kinds of knowledge.

My grandmother had, as much as possible, been a mother to her orphan grandchildren. By perseverance and unwearied industry, she was now mistress of a snug little home, surrounded with the necessaries of life. She would have been happy could her children have shared them with her. There remained but three children and two grandchildren, all slaves. Most earnestly did she strive to make us feel that it was the will of God: that He had seen fit to place us under such circumstances; and though it seemed hard, we ought to pray for contentment.

It was a beautiful faith, coming from a mother who could not call her children her own. But I, and Benjamin, her youngest boy, condemned it. We reasoned that it was much more the will of God that we should be situated as she was. We longed for a home like hers. There we always found sweet balsam[22] for our troubles. She was so loving, so sympathizing! She always met us with a smile, and listened with patience to all our sorrows. She spoke so hopefully, that unconsciously the clouds gave place to sunshine. There was a grand big oven there, too, that baked bread and nice things for the town, and we knew there was always a choice bit in store for us.

But, alas! even the charms of the old oven failed to reconcile us to our hard lot. Benjamin was now a tall, handsome lad, strongly and gracefully made, and with a spirit too bold and daring for a slave. My brother William, now twelve years old, had the same aversion to the word master that he had when he was an urchin of seven years. I was his confidante.[23] He came to me with all his troubles. I remember one instance in particular. It was on a lovely spring morning, and when I marked the sunlight dancing here and there, its beauty seemed to mock my sadness. For my master, whose restless, craving, vicious nature roved about day and night, seeking whom to devour, had just left me, with stinging, scorching words; words that scathed ear and brain like fire. O, how I despised him! I thought how glad I should be, if some day when he walked the earth, it would open and swallow him up, and disencumber the world of a plague.

When he told me that I was made for his use, made to obey his command in *everything*;[24] that I was nothing but a slave, whose will must and should surrender to his, never before had my puny arm felt half so strong.

So deeply was I absorbed in painful reflections afterwards, that I neither saw nor heard the entrance of anyone,[25] till the voice of William sounded close beside me. "Linda," said he, "what makes you look so sad? I love you. O, Linda, isn't this a bad world? Everybody[26] seems so cross and unhappy. I wish I had died when poor father did."

I told him that everybody[27] was *not* cross, or unhappy; that those who had pleasant homes, and kind friends, and who were not afraid to love them, were happy. But we, who were slave-children, without father or mother, could not expect to be happy. We must be good; perhaps that would bring us contentment.

Notes

[22] *sweet balsam* healing balm (see Jeremiah 8:22).

[23] *Original reads*: confidant [ed.].

[24] *Original reads*: *every* thing [ed.].

[25] *Original reads*: any one [ed.].

[26] *Original reads*: Every body [ed.].

[27] *Original reads*: every body [ed.].

"Yes," he said, "I try to be good; but what's the use? They are all the time troubling me." Then he proceeded to relate his afternoon's difficulty with young master Nicholas. It seemed that the brother of master Nicholas had pleased himself with making up stories about William. Master Nicholas said he should be flogged, and he would do it. Whereupon he went to work; but William fought bravely, and the young master, finding he was getting the better of him, undertook to tie his hands behind him. He failed in that likewise. By dint of kicking and fisting, William came out of the skirmish none the worse for a few scratches.

He continued to discourse on his young master's *meanness;* how he whipped the *little* boys, but was a perfect coward when a tussle ensued between him and white boys of his own size. On such occasions he always took to his legs. William had other charges to make against him. One was his rubbing up pennies with quicksilver,[28] and passing them off for quarters of a dollar on an old man who kept a fruit stall. William was often sent to buy fruit, and he earnestly inquired of me what he ought to do under such circumstances. I told him it was certainly wrong to deceive the old man, and that it was his duty to tell him of the impositions practised by his young master. I assured him the old man would not be slow to comprehend the whole, and there the matter would end. William thought it might with the old man, but not with *him*. He said he did not mind the smart of the whip, but he did not like the *idea* of being whipped.

While I advised him to be good and forgiving I was not unconscious of the beam in my own eye. It was the very knowledge of my own shortcomings that urged me to retain, if possible, some sparks of my brother's God-given nature. I had not lived fourteen years in slavery for nothing. I had felt, seen, and heard enough, to read the characters, and question the motives, of those around me. The war of my life had begun; and though one of God's most powerless creatures, I resolved never to be conquered. Alas, for me!

If there was one pure, sunny spot for me, I believed it to be in Benjamin's heart, and in another's, whom I loved with all the ardor of a girl's first love. My owner knew of it, and sought in every way to render me miserable. He did not resort to corporal punishment, but to all the petty, tyrannical ways that human ingenuity could devise.

I remember the first time I was punished. It was in the month of February. My grandmother had taken my old shoes, and replaced them with a new pair. I needed them; for several inches of snow had fallen, and it still continued to fall. When I walked through Mrs. Flint's room, their creaking grated harshly on her refined nerves. She called me to her, and asked what I had about me that made such a horrid noise. I told her it was my new shoes. "Take them off," said she; "and if you put them on again, I'll throw them into the fire."

I took them off, and my stockings also. She then sent me a long distance, on an errand. As I went through the snow, my bare feet tingled. That night I was very hoarse; and I went to bed thinking the next day would find me sick, perhaps dead. What was my grief on waking to find myself quite well!

I had imagined if I died, or was laid up for some time, that my mistress would feel a twinge of remorse that she had so hated "the little imp," as she styled me. It was my ignorance of that mistress that gave rise to such extravagant imaginings.

Dr. Flint occasionally had high prices offered for me; but he always said, "She don't belong to me. She is my daughter's property, and I have no right to sell her." Good, honest man! My young mistress was still a child, and I could look for no protection

Notes

[28] *quicksilver* mercury.

from her. I loved her, and she returned my affection. I once heard her father allude to her attachment to me; and his wife promptly replied that it proceeded from fear. This put unpleasant doubts into my mind. Did the child feign what she did not feel? or was her mother jealous of the mite of love she bestowed on me? I concluded it must be the latter. I said to myself, "Surely, little children are true."

One afternoon I sat at my sewing, feeling unusual depression of spirits. My mistress had been accusing me of an offence, of which I assured her I was perfectly innocent; but I saw, by the contemptuous curl of her lip, that she believed I was telling a lie.

I wondered for what wise purpose God was leading me through such thorny paths, and whether still darker days were in store for me. As I sat musing thus, the door opened softly, and William came in. "Well, brother," said I, "what is the matter this time?"

"O Linda, Ben and his master have had a dreadful time!" said he.

My first thought was that Benjamin was killed. "Don't be frightened, Linda," said William; "I will tell you all about it."

It appeared that Benjamin's master had sent for him, and he did not immediately obey the summons. When he did, his master was angry, and began to whip him. He resisted. Master and slave fought, and finally the master was thrown. Benjamin had cause to tremble; for he had thrown to the ground his master – one of the richest men in town. I anxiously awaited the result.

That night I stole to my grandmother's house, and Benjamin also stole thither from his master's. My grandmother had gone to spend a day or two with an old friend living in the country.

"I have come," said Benjamin, "to tell you goodbye.[29] I am going away."

I inquired where.

"To the north," he replied.

I looked at him to see whether he was in earnest. I saw it all in his firm, set mouth. I implored him not to go, but he paid no heed to my words. He said he was no longer a boy, and every day made his yoke more galling. He had raised his hand against his master: and was to be publicly whipped for the offence. I reminded him of the poverty and hardships he must encounter among strangers. I told him he might be caught and brought back; and that was terrible to think of.

He grew vexed, and asked if poverty and hardships with freedom were not preferable to our treatment in slavery. "Linda," he continued, "we are dogs here; foot-balls, cattle, everything[30] that's mean. No, I will not stay. Let them bring me back. We don't die but once."

He was right; but it was hard to give him up. "Go," said I, "and break your mother's heart."

I repented of my words ere they were out.

"Linda," said he, speaking as I had not heard him speak that evening, "how *could* you say that? Poor mother! be kind to her, Linda; and you, too, cousin Fanny."

Cousin Fanny was a friend who had lived some years with us.

Farewells were exchanged, and the bright, kind boy, endeared to us by so many acts of love, vanished from our sight.

It is not necessary to state how he made his escape. Suffice it to say, he was on his way to New York when a violent storm overtook the vessel. The captain said he must put into the nearest port. This alarmed Benjamin, who was aware that he would be

Notes

[29] *Original reads*: good by [ed.].

[30] *Original reads*: every thing [ed.].

advertised in every port near his own town. His embarrassment was noticed by the captain. To port they went. There the advertisement met the captain's eye. Benjamin so exactly answered its description, that the captain laid hold on him, and bound him in chains. The storm passed, and they proceeded to New York. Before reaching that port Benjamin managed to get off his chains and throw them overboard. He escaped from the vessel, but was pursued, captured, and carried back to his master.

When my grandmother returned home and found her youngest child had fled, great was her sorrow; but, with characteristic piety, she said, "God's will be done." Each morning, she inquired if any news had been heard from her boy. Yes, news *was* heard. The master was rejoicing over a letter, announcing the capture of his human chattel.

That day seems but as yesterday, so well do I remember it. I saw him led through the streets in chains, to jail. His face was ghastly pale, yet full of determination. He had begged one of the sailors to go to his mother's house and ask her not to meet him. He said the sight of her distress would take from him all self-control. She yearned to see him, and she went; but she screened herself in the crowd, that it might be as her child had said.

We were not allowed to visit him; but we had known the jailer for years, and he was a kind-hearted man. At midnight he opened the jail door for my grandmother and me[31] to enter, in disguise. When we entered the cell not a sound broke the stillness. "Benjamin, Benjamin!" whispered my grandmother. No answer. "Benjamin!" she again faltered. There was a jingle of chains. The moon had just risen, and cast an uncertain light through the bars of the window. We knelt down and took Benjamin's cold hands in ours. We did not speak. Sobs were heard, and Benjamin's lips were unsealed; for his mother was weeping on his neck. How vividly does memory bring back that sad night! Mother and son talked together. He asked her pardon for the suffering he had caused her. She said she had nothing to forgive; she could not blame his desire for freedom. He told her that when he was captured, he broke away, and was about casting himself into the river, when thoughts of *her* came over him, and he desisted. She asked if he did not also think of God. I fancied I saw his face grow fierce in the moonlight. He answered, "No, I did not think of him. When a man is hunted like a wild beast he forgets there is a God, a heaven. He forgets everything[32] in his struggle to get beyond the reach of the bloodhounds."

"Don't talk so, Benjamin," said she. "Put your trust in God. Be humble, my child, and your master will forgive you."

"Forgive me for *what*, mother? For not letting him treat me like a dog? No! I will never humble myself to him. I have worked for him for nothing all my life, and I am repaid with stripes and imprisonment. Here I will stay till I die, or till he sells me."

The poor mother shuddered at his words. I think he felt it; for when he next spoke, his voice was calmer. "Don't fret about me, mother. I ain't worth it," said he. "I wish I had some of your goodness. You bear everything[33] patiently, just as though you thought it was all right. I wish I could."

She told him she had not always been so; once, she was like him; but when sore troubles came upon her, and she had no arm to lean upon, she learned to call on God, and he lightened her burdens. She besought him to do likewise.

We overstaid our time, and were obliged to hurry from the jail.

Notes

[31] *Original reads*: myself [ed.].

[32] *Original reads*: every thing [ed.].

[33] *Original reads*: every thing [ed.].

Benjamin had been imprisoned three weeks, when my grandmother went to intercede for him with his master. He was immovable. He said Benjamin should serve as an example to the rest of his slaves; he should be kept in jail till he was subdued, or be sold if he got but one dollar for him. However, he afterwards relented in some degree. The chains were taken off, and we were allowed to visit him.

As his food was of the coarsest kind, we carried him as often as possible a warm supper, accompanied with some little luxury for the jailer.

Three months elapsed, and there was no prospect of release or of a purchaser. One day he was heard to sing and laugh. This piece of indecorum was told to his master, and the overseer was ordered to re-chain him. He was now confined in an apartment with other prisoners, who were covered with filthy rags. Benjamin was chained near them, and was soon covered with vermin. He worked at his chains till he succeeded in getting out of them. He passed them through the bars of the window, with a request that they should be taken to his master, and he should be informed that he was covered with vermin.

This audacity was punished with heavier chains, and prohibition of our visits.

My grandmother continued to send him fresh changes of clothes. The old ones were burned up. The last night we saw him in jail his mother still begged him to send for his master, and beg his pardon. Neither persuasion nor argument could turn him[34] from his purpose. He calmly answered, "I am waiting his time."

Those chains were mournful to hear.

Another three months passed, and Benjamin left his prison walls. We that loved him waited to bid him a long and last farewell. A slave-trader had bought him. You remember, I told you what price he brought when ten years of age. Now he was more than twenty years old, and sold for three hundred dollars. The master had been blind to his own interest. Long confinement had made his face too pale, his form too thin; moreover, the trader had heard something of his character, and it did not strike him as suitable for a slave. He said he would give any price if the handsome lad was a girl. We thanked God that he was not.

Could you have seen that mother clinging to her child, when they fastened the irons upon his wrists; could you have heard her heart-rending groans, and seen her bloodshot eyes wander wildly from face to face, vainly pleading for mercy; could you have witnessed that scene as I saw it, you would exclaim, *Slavery is damnable!*

Benjamin, her youngest, her pet, was forever gone! She could not realize it. She had had an interview with the trader for the purpose of ascertaining if Benjamin could be purchased. She was told it was impossible, as he had given bonds not to sell him till he was out of the state. He promised that he would not sell him till he reached New Orleans.

With a strong arm and unvaried trust, my grandmother began her work of love. Benjamin must be free. If she succeeded, she knew they would still be separated; but the sacrifice was not too great. Day and night she labored. The trader's price would treble that he gave; but she was not discouraged.

She employed a lawyer to write to a gentleman, whom she knew, in New Orleans. She begged him to interest himself for Benjamin, and he willingly favored her request. When he saw Benjamin, and stated his business, he thanked him; but said he preferred to wait a while before making the trader an offer. He knew he had tried to obtain a high price for him, and had invariably failed. This encouraged him to make another

Notes

[34] *Original reads*: hin [ed.].

effort for freedom. So one morning, long before day, Benjamin was missing. He was riding over the blue billows, bound for Baltimore.

For once his white face did him a kindly service. They had no suspicion that it belonged to a slave; otherwise, the law would have been followed out to the letter, and the *thing* rendered back to slavery. The brightest skies are often overshadowed by the darkest clouds. Benjamin was taken sick, and compelled to remain in Baltimore three weeks. His strength was slow in returning; and his desire to continue his journey seemed to retard his recovery. How could he get strength without air and exercise? He resolved to venture on a short walk. A by-street was selected, where he thought himself secure of not being met by anyone[35] that knew him; but a voice called out, "Halloo, Ben, my boy! what are you doing *here*?"

His first impulse was to run; but his legs trembled so that he could not stir. He turned to confront his antagonist, and behold, there stood his old master's next door neighbor! He thought it was all over with him now; but it proved otherwise. That man was a miracle. He possessed a goodly number of slaves, and yet was not quite deaf to that mystic clock, whose ticking is rarely heard in the slaveholder's breast.

"Ben, you are sick," said he. "Why, you look like a ghost. I guess I gave you something of a start. Never mind, Ben, I am not going to touch you. You had a pretty tough time of it, and you may go on your way rejoicing for all me. But I would advise you to get out of this place plaguy[36] quick, for there are several gentlemen here from our town." He described the nearest and safest route to New York, and added, "I shall be glad to tell your mother I have seen you. Goodbye,[37] Ben."

Benjamin turned away, filled with gratitude, and surprised that the town he hated contained such a gem – a gem worthy of a purer setting.

This gentleman was a Northerner by birth, and had married a southern lady. On his return, he told my grandmother that he had seen her son, and of the service he had rendered him.

Benjamin reached New York safely, and concluded to stop there until he had gained strength enough to proceed further. It happened that my grandmother's only remaining son had sailed for the same city on business for his mistress. Through God's providence, the brothers met. You may be sure it was a happy meeting. "O Phil," exclaimed Benjamin, "I am here at last." Then he told him how near he came to dying, almost in sight of free land, and how he prayed that he might live to get one breath of free air. He said life was worth something now, and it would be hard to die. In the old jail he had not valued it; once, he was tempted to destroy it; but something, he did not know what, had prevented him; perhaps it was fear. He had heard those who profess to be religious declare there was no heaven for self-murderers; and as his life had been pretty hot here, he did not desire a continuation of the same in another world. "If I die now," he exclaimed, "thank God, I shall die a freeman!"

He begged my Uncle[38] Phillip not to return south; but stay and work with him, till they earned enough to buy those at home. His brother told him it would kill their mother if he deserted her in her trouble. She had pledged her house, and with difficulty had raised money to buy him. Would he be bought?

"No, never!" he replied. "Do you suppose, Phil, when I have got so far out of their clutches, I will give them one red cent? No! And do you suppose I would turn mother out of her home in her old age? That I would let her pay all those hard-earned dollars

Notes

[35] *Original reads*: any one [ed.].

[36] *plaguy* colloquial term for "extremely."

[37] *Original reads*: Good by [ed.].

[38] *Original reads*: uncle [ed.].

for me, and never to see me? For you know she will stay south as long as her other children are slaves. What a good mother! Tell her to buy *you*, Phil. You have been a comfort to her, and I have been a trouble. And Linda, poor Linda; what'll become of her? Phil, you don't know what a life they lead her. She has told me something about it, and I wish old Flint was dead, or a better man. When I was in jail, he asked her if she didn't want *him* to ask my master to forgive me, and take me home again. She told him, No; that I didn't want to go back. He got mad, and said we were all alike. I never despised my own master half as much as I do that man. There is many a worse slave-holder than my master; but for all that I would not be his slave."

While Benjamin was sick, he had parted with nearly all his clothes to pay necessary expenses. But he did not part with a little pin I fastened in his bosom when we parted. It was the most valuable thing I owned, and I thought none more worthy to wear it. He had it still.

His brother furnished him with clothes, and gave him what money he had. They parted with moistened eyes; and as Benjamin turned away, he said, "Phil, I part with all my kindred."

And so it proved. We never heard from him again.

Uncle Phillip came home; and the first words he uttered when he entered the house were, "Mother, Ben is free! I have seen him in New York." She stood looking at him with a bewildered air. "Mother, don't you believe it?" he said, laying his hand softly upon her shoulder. She raised her hands, and exclaimed, "God be praised! Let us thank him." She dropped on her knees, and poured forth her heart in prayer. Then Phillip sat down and repeated[39] to her every word Benjamin had said. He told her all; only he forbore to mention how sick and pale her darling looked. Why should he distress her when she could do him no good?

The brave old woman still toiled on, hoping to rescue some of her other children. After a while she succeeded in buying Phillip. She paid eight hundred dollars, and came home with the precious document[40] that secured his freedom. The happy mother and son sat together by the old hearthstone that night, telling how proud they were of each other, and how they would prove to the world that they could take care of themselves, as they had long taken care of others. We all concluded by saying, "He that is *willing* to be a slave, let him be a slave."

Chapter 5

The Trials of Girlhood

During the first years of my service in Dr. Flint's family, I was accustomed to share some indulgences with the children of my mistress. Though this seemed to me no more than right, I was grateful for it, and tried to merit the kindness by the faithful discharge of my duties. But I now entered on my fifteenth year – a sad epoch in the life of a slave girl. My master began to whisper foul words in my ear. Young as I was, I could not remain ignorant of their import. I tried to treat them with indifference or contempt. The master's age, my extreme youth, and the fear that his conduct would be reported to my grandmother, made him bear this treatment for many months. He was a crafty man, and resorted to many means to accomplish his purposes. Sometimes

Notes

[39] *Original reads*: Then Phillip must sit down and repeat [ed.].

[40] *precious document* a bill of sale.

he had stormy, terrific ways that made his victims tremble; sometimes he assumed a gentleness that he thought must surely subdue. Of the two, I preferred his stormy moods, although they left me trembling. He tried his utmost to corrupt the pure principles my grandmother had instilled. He peopled my young mind with unclean images, such as only a vile monster could think of. I turned from him with disgust and hatred. But he was my master. I was compelled to live under the same roof with him – where I saw a man forty years my senior daily violating the most sacred commandments of nature. He told me I was his property; that I must be subject to his will in all things. My soul revolted against the mean tyranny. But where could I turn for protection? No matter whether the slave girl be as black as ebony or as fair as her mistress. In either case, there is no shadow of law to protect her from insult, from violence, or even from death; all these are inflicted by fiends who bear the shape of men. The mistress, who ought to protect the helpless victim, has no other feelings towards her but those of jealousy and rage. The degradation, the wrongs, the vices that grow out of slavery, are more than I can describe. They are greater than you would willingly believe. Surely, if you credited one half the truths that are told you concerning the helpless millions suffering in this cruel bondage, you at the north would not help to tighten the yoke. You surely would refuse to do for the master; on your own soil, the mean and cruel work which trained bloodhounds and the lowest class of whites to do for him at the south.[41]

Everywhere[42] the years bring to all enough of sin and sorrow; but in slavery the very dawn of life is darkened by these shadows. Even the little child, who is accustomed to wait on her mistress and her children, will learn, before she is twelve years old, why it is that her mistress hates such and such a one among the slaves. Perhaps the child's own mother is among those hated ones. She listens to violent outbreaks of jealous passion, and cannot help understanding what is the cause. She will become prematurely knowing in evil things. Soon she will learn to tremble when she hears her master's footfall. She will be compelled to realize that she is no longer a child. If God has bestowed beauty upon her, it will prove her greatest curse. That which commands admiration in the white woman only hastens the degradation of the female slave. I know that some are too much brutalized by slavery to feel the humiliation of their position; but many slaves feel it most acutely, and shrink from the memory of it. I cannot tell how much I suffered in the presence of these wrongs, nor how I am still pained by the retrospect. My master met me at every turn, reminding me that I belonged to him, and swearing by heaven and earth that he would compel me to submit to him. If I went out for a breath of fresh air, after a day of unwearied toil, his footsteps dogged me. If I knelt by my mother's grave, his dark shadow fell on me even there. The light heart which nature had given me became heavy with sad forebodings. The other slaves in my master's house noticed the change. Many of them pitied me; but none dared to ask the cause. They had no need to inquire. They knew too well the guilty practices under that roof; and they were aware that to speak of them was an offence that never went unpunished.

I longed for someone[43] to confide in. I would have given the world to have laid my head on my grandmother's faithful bosom, and told her all my troubles. But Dr. Flint swore he would kill me, if I was not as silent as the grave. Then, although my grandmother was all in all to me, I feared her as well as loved her. I had been accustomed to look up to her with a respect bordering upon awe. I was very young, and felt

Notes

[41] *Original reads*: the lowest class of whites do for him at the south [ed.].

[42] *Original reads*: Every where [ed.].

[43] *Original reads*: some one [ed.].

shamefaced about telling her such impure things, especially as I knew her to be very strict on such subjects. Moreover, she was a woman of a high spirit. She was usually very quiet in her demeanor; but if her indignation was once roused, it was not very easily quelled. I had been told that she once chased a white gentleman with a loaded pistol, because he insulted one of her daughters. I dreaded the consequences of a violent outbreak; and both pride and fear kept me silent. But though I did not confide in my grandmother, and even evaded her vigilant watchfulness and inquiry, her presence in the neighborhood was some protection to me. Though she had been a slave, Dr. Flint was afraid of her. He dreaded her scorching rebukes. Moreover, she was known and patronized by many people; and he did not wish to have his villany made public. It was lucky for me that I did not live on a distant plantation, but in a town not so large that the inhabitants were ignorant of each other's affairs. Bad as are the laws and customs in a slaveholding community, the doctor, as a professional man, deemed it prudent to keep up some outward show of decency.

O, what days and nights of fear and sorrow that man caused me! Reader, it is not to awaken sympathy for myself that I am telling you truthfully what I suffered in slavery. I do it to kindle a flame of compassion in your hearts for my sisters who are still in bondage, suffering as I once suffered.

I once saw two beautiful children playing together. One was a fair white child; the other was her slave, and also her sister. When I saw them embracing each other, and heard their joyous laughter, I turned sadly away from the lovely sight. I foresaw the inevitable blight that would fall on the little slave's heart. I knew how soon her laughter would be changed to sighs. The fair child grew up to be a still fairer woman. From childhood to womanhood her pathway was blooming with flowers, and overarched by a sunny sky. Scarcely one day of her life had been clouded when the sun rose on her happy bridal morning.

How had those years dealt with her slave sister, the little playmate of her childhood? She, also, was very beautiful; but the flowers and sunshine of love were not for her. She drank the cup of sin, and shame, and misery, whereof her persecuted race are compelled to drink.

In view of these things, why are ye silent, ye free men and women of the north? Why do your tongues falter in maintenance of the right? Would that I had more ability! But my heart is so full, and my pen is so weak! There are noble men and women who plead for us, striving to help those who cannot help themselves. God bless them! God give them strength and courage to go on! God bless those, everywhere,[44] who are laboring to advance the cause of humanity!

Chapter 6

The Jealous Mistress

I WOULD ten thousand times rather that my children should be the half-starved paupers[45] of Ireland than to be the most pampered among the slaves of America. I would rather drudge out my life on a cotton plantation, till the grave opened to give me rest, than to live with an unprincipled master and a jealous mistress. The felon's

Notes

[44] *Original reads*: every where [ed.].

[45] *half-starved paupers* referring to the Irish potato famine of 1845–1849.

home in a penitentiary is preferable. He may repent, and turn from the error of his ways, and so find peace; but it is not so with a favorite slave. She is not allowed to have any pride of character. It is deemed a crime in her to wish to be virtuous.

Mrs. Flint possessed the key to her husband's character before I was born. She might have used this knowledge to counsel and to screen the young and the innocent among her slaves; but for them she had no sympathy. They were the objects of her constant suspicion and malevolence. She watched her husband with unceasing vigilance; but he was well practised in means to evade it. What he could not find opportunity to say in words he manifested in signs. He invented more than were ever thought of in a deaf and dumb asylum. I let them pass, as if I did not understand what he meant; and many were the curses and threats bestowed on me for my stupidity. One day he caught me teaching myself to write. He frowned, as if he was not well pleased; but I suppose he came to the conclusion that such an accomplishment might help to advance his favorite scheme. Before long, notes were often slipped into my hand. I would return them, saying, "I can't read them, sir." "Can't you?" he replied; "then I must read them to you." He always finished the reading by asking, "Do you understand?" Sometimes he would complain of the heat of the tea room, and order his supper to be placed on a small table in the piazza.[46] He would seat himself there with a well-satisfied smile, and tell me to stand by and brush away the flies. He would eat very slowly, pausing between the mouthfuls. These intervals were employed in describing the happiness I was so foolishly throwing away, and in threatening me with the penalty that finally awaited my stubborn disobedience. He boasted much of the forbearance he had exercised towards me, and reminded me that there was a limit to his patience. When I succeeded in avoiding opportunities for him to talk to me at home, I was ordered to come to his office, to do some errand. When there, I was obliged to stand and listen to such language as he saw fit to address to me. Sometimes I so openly expressed my contempt for him that he would become violently enraged, and I wondered why he did not strike me. Circumstanced as he was, he probably thought it was better policy to be forbearing. But the state of things grew worse and worse daily. In desperation I told him that I must and would apply to my grandmother for protection. He threatened me with death, and worse than death, if I made any complaint to her. Strange to say, I did not despair. I was naturally of a buoyant disposition, and always I had a hope of somehow getting out of his clutches. Like many a poor, simple slave before me, I trusted that some threads of joy would yet be woven into my dark destiny.

I had entered my sixteenth year, and every day it became more apparent that my presence was intolerable to Mrs. Flint. Angry words frequently passed between her and her husband. He had never punished me himself, and he would not allow anybody[47] else to punish me. In that respect, she was never satisfied; but, in her angry moods, no terms were too vile for her to bestow upon me. Yet I, whom she detested so bitterly, had far more pity for her than he had, whose duty it was to make her life happy. I never wronged her, or wished to wrong her; and one word of kindness from her would have brought me to her feet.

After repeated quarrels between the doctor and his wife, he announced his intention to take his youngest daughter, then four years old, to sleep in his apartment. It was necessary that a servant should sleep in the same room, to be on hand if the child stirred. I was selected for that office, and informed for what purpose that arrangement had been made. By managing to keep within sight of people, as much as

Notes

[46] *piazza* porch.

[47] *Original reads*: any body [ed.].

possible, during the daytime,[48] I had hitherto succeeded in eluding my master, though a razor was often held to my throat to force me to change this line of policy. At night I slept by the side of my great aunt, where I felt safe. He was too prudent to come into her room. She was an old woman, and had been in the family many years. Moreover, as a married man, and a professional man, he deemed it necessary to save appearances in some degree. But he resolved to remove the obstacle in the way of his scheme; and he thought he had planned it so that he should evade suspicion. He was well aware how much I prized my refuge by the side of my old aunt, and he determined to dispossess me of it. The first night the doctor had the little child in his room alone. The next morning, I was ordered to take my station as nurse the following night. A kind Providence interposed in my favor. During the day, Mrs. Flint heard of this new arrangement, and a storm followed. I rejoiced to hear it rage.

After a while my mistress sent for me to come to her room. Her first question was, "Did you know you were to sleep in the doctor's room?"

"Yes, ma'am."

"Who told you?"

"My master."

"Will you answer truly all the questions I ask?"

"Yes, ma'am."

"Tell me, then, as you hope to be forgiven, are you innocent of what I have accused you?"

"I am."

She handed me a Bible, and said, "Lay your hand on your heart, kiss this holy book, and swear before God that you tell me the truth."

I took the oath she required, and I did it with a clear conscience.

"You have taken God's holy word to testify your innocence," said she. "If you have deceived me, beware! Now take this stool, sit down, look me directly in the face, and tell me all that has passed between your master and you."

I did as she ordered. As I went on with my account her color changed frequently, she wept, and sometimes groaned. She spoke in tones so sad, that I was touched by her grief. The tears came to my eyes; but I was soon convinced that her emotions arose from anger and wounded pride. She felt that her marriage vows were desecrated, her dignity insulted; but she had no compassion for the poor victim of her husband's perfidy.[49] She pitied herself as a martyr; but she was incapable of feeling for the condition of shame and misery in which her unfortunate, helpless slave was placed.

Yet perhaps she had some touch of feeling for me; for when the conference was ended, she spoke kindly, and promised to protect me. I should have been much comforted by this assurance if I could have had confidence in it; but my experiences in slavery had filled me with distrust. She was not a very refined woman, and had not much control over her passions. I was an object of her jealousy, and, consequently, of her hatred; and I knew I could not expect kindness or confidence from her under the circumstances in which I was placed. I could not blame her. Slaveholders' wives feel as other women would under similar circumstances. The fire of her temper kindled from small sparks, and now the flame became so intense that the doctor was obliged to give up his intended arrangement.

I knew I had ignited the torch, and I expected to suffer for it afterwards; but I felt too thankful to my mistress for the timely aid she rendered me to care much about that.

Notes

[48] *Original reads*: day time [ed.].

[49] *perfidy* treachery.

She now took me to sleep in a room adjoining her own. There I was an object of her especial care, though not of her especial comfort, for she spent many a sleepless night to watch over me. Sometimes I woke up, and found her bending over me. At other times she whispered in my ear, as though it was her husband who was speaking to me, and listened to hear what I would answer. If she startled me, on such occasions, she would glide stealthily away; and the next morning she would tell me I had been talking in my sleep, and ask who I was talking to. At last, I began to be fearful for my life. It had been often threatened; and you can imagine, better than I can describe, what an unpleasant sensation it must produce to wake up in the dead of night and find a jealous woman bending over you. Terrible as this experience was, I had fears that it would give place to one more terrible.

My mistress grew weary of her vigils; they did not prove satisfactory. She changed her tactics. She now tried the trick of accusing my master of crime, in my presence, and gave my name as the author of the accusation. To my utter astonishment, he replied, "I don't believe it; but if she did acknowledge it, you tortured her into exposing me." Tortured into exposing him! Truly, Satan had no difficulty in distinguishing the color of his soul! I understood his object in making this false representation. It was to show me that I gained nothing by seeking the protection of my mistress; that the power was still all in his own hands. I pitied Mrs. Flint. She was a second wife, many years the junior of her husband; and the hoary-headed miscreant was enough to try the patience of a wiser and better woman. She was completely foiled, and knew not how to proceed. She would gladly have had me flogged for my supposed false oath; but, as I have already stated, the doctor never allowed anyone[50] to whip me. The old sinner was politic. The application of the lash might have led to remarks that would have exposed him in the eyes of his children and grandchildren. How often did I rejoice that I lived in a town where all the inhabitants knew each other! If I had been on a remote plantation, or lost among the multitude of a crowded city, I should not be a living woman at this day.

The secrets of slavery are concealed like those of the Inquisition.[51] My master was, to my knowledge, the father of eleven slaves. But did the mothers dare to tell who was the father of their children? Did the other slaves dare to allude to it, except in whispers among themselves? No, indeed! They knew too well the terrible consequences.

My grandmother could not avoid seeing things which excited her suspicions. She was uneasy about me, and tried various ways to buy me; but the never-changing answer was always repeated: "Linda does not belong to *me*. She is my daughter's property, and I have no legal right to sell her." The conscientious man! He was too scrupulous to *sell* me; but he had no scruples whatever about committing a much greater wrong against the helpless young girl placed under his guardianship, as his daughter's property. Sometimes my persecutor would ask me whether I would like to be sold. I told him I would rather be sold to anybody[52] than to lead such a life as I did. On such occasions he would assume the air of a very injured individual, and reproach me for my ingratitude. "Did I not take you into the house, and make you the companion of my own children?" he would say. "Have I ever treated you like a negro? I have never allowed you to be punished, not even to please your mistress. And this is the recompense I get, you ungrateful girl!" I answered that he had reasons of his own for

Notes

[50] *Original reads*: any one [ed.].

[51] *the Inquisition* the Spanish Inquisition, infamous for its torture techniques.

[52] *Original reads*: any body [ed.].

screening me from punishment, and that the course he pursued made my mistress hate me and persecute me. If I wept, he would say, "Poor child! Don't cry! don't cry! I will make peace for you with your mistress. Only let me arrange matters in my own way. Poor, foolish girl! you don't know what is for your own good. I would cherish you. I would make a lady of you. Now go, and think of all I have promised you."

I did think of it.

Reader, I draw no imaginary pictures of southern homes. I am telling you the plain truth. Yet when victims make their escape from this wild beast of Slavery, northerners consent to act the part of bloodhounds, and hunt the poor fugitive back into his den, "full of dead men's bones, and all uncleanness."[53] Nay, more, they are not only willing, but proud, to give their daughters in marriage to slaveholders. The poor girls have romantic notions of a sunny clime, and of the flowering vines that all the year round shade a happy home. To what disappointments are they destined! The young wife soon learns that the husband in whose hands she has placed her happiness pays no regard to his marriage vows. Children of every shade of complexion play with her own fair babies, and too well she knows that they are born unto him of his own household. Jealousy and hatred enter the flowery home, and it is ravaged of its loveliness.

Southern women often marry a man knowing that he is the father of many little slaves. They do not trouble themselves about it. They regard such children as property, as marketable as the pigs on the plantation; and it is seldom that they do not make them aware of this by passing them into the slave-trader's hands as soon as possible, and thus getting them out of their sight. I am glad to say there are some honorable exceptions.

I have myself known two southern wives who exhorted their husbands to free those slaves towards whom they stood in a "parental relation"; and their request was granted. These husbands blushed before the superior nobleness of their wives' natures. Though they had only counselled them to do that which it was their duty to do, it commanded their respect, and rendered their conduct more exemplary. Concealment was at an end, and confidence took the place of distrust.

Though this bad institution deadens the moral sense, even in white women, to a fearful extent, it is not altogether extinct. I have heard southern ladies say of Mr. Such a one, "He not only thinks it no disgrace to be the father of those little niggers, but he is not ashamed to call himself their master. I declare, such things ought not to be tolerated in any decent society!"

Chapter 7

The Lover

Why does the slave ever love? Why allow the tendrils of the heart to twine around objects which may at any moment be wrenched away by the hand of violence? When separations come by the hand of death, the pious soul can bow in resignation, and say, "Not my will, but thine be done, O Lord!"[54] But when the ruthless hand of man strikes the blow, regardless of the misery he causes, it is hard to be submissive. I did not reason thus when I was a young girl. Youth will be youth. I loved, and I indulged the hope that

Notes

[53] *"full of dead men's … uncleanness."* Matthew 23:27.

[54] *"Not my will … Lord"* Matthew 26:39.

the dark clouds around me would turn out a bright lining. I forgot that in the land of my birth the shadows are too dense for light to penetrate. A land

"Where laughter is not mirth; nor thought the mind;
Nor words a language; nor e'en men mankind.
Where cries reply to curses, shrieks to blows,
And each is tortured in his separate hell."[55]

There was in the neighborhood a young colored carpenter; a free born man. We had been well acquainted in childhood, and frequently met together afterwards. We became mutually attached, and he proposed to marry me. I loved him with all the ardor of a young girl's first love. But when I reflected that I was a slave, and that the laws gave no sanction to the marriage of such, my heart sank within me.[56] My lover wanted to buy me; but I knew that Dr. Flint was too wilful and arbitrary a man to consent to that arrangement. From him, I was sure of experiencing all sorts of opposition, and I had nothing to hope from my mistress. She would have been delighted to have got rid of me, but not in that way. It would have relieved her mind of a burden if she could have seen me sold to some distant state, but if I was married near home I should be just as much in her husband's power as I had previously been – for the husband of a slave has no power to protect her. Moreover, my mistress, like many others, seemed to think that slaves had no right to any family ties of their own; that they were created merely to wait upon the family of the mistress. I once heard her abuse a young slave girl, who told her that a colored man wanted to make her his wife. "I will have you peeled and pickled,[57] my lady," said she, "if I ever hear you mention that subject again. Do you suppose that I will have you tending *my* children with the children of that nigger?" The girl to whom she said this had a mulatto child, of course not acknowledged by its father. The poor black man who loved her would have been proud to acknowledge his helpless offspring.

Many and anxious were the thoughts I revolved in my mind. I was at a loss what to do. Above all things, I was desirous to spare my lover the insults that had cut so deeply into my own soul. I talked with my grandmother about it, and partly told her my fears. I did not dare to tell her the worst. She had long suspected all was not right, and if I confirmed her suspicions I knew a storm would rise that would prove the overthrow of all my hopes.

This love-dream had been my support through many trials; and I could not bear to run the risk of having it suddenly dissipated. There was a lady in the neighborhood, a particular friend of Dr. Flint's, who often visited the house. I had a great respect for her, and she had always manifested a friendly interest in me. Grandmother thought she would have great influence with the doctor. I went to this lady, and told her my story. I told her I was aware that my lover's being a free-born man would prove a great objection; but he wanted to buy me; and if Dr. Flint would consent to that arrangement, I felt sure he would be willing to pay any reasonable price. She knew that Mrs. Flint disliked me; therefore, I ventured to suggest that perhaps my mistress would approve of my being sold, as that would rid her of me. The lady listened with kindly sympathy,

Notes

[55] *"Where laughter ... hell"* from "The Lament of Tasso" (1817) by Lord Byron (1788–1824).

[56] *But when ... sank within me* Slaves needed their master's consent to marry a free man.

[57] *peeled and pickled* to be whipped and washed with salt water.

and promised to do her utmost to promote my wishes. She had an interview with the doctor, and I believe she pleaded my cause earnestly; but it was all to no purpose.

How I dreaded my master now! Every minute I expected to be summoned to his presence; but the day passed, and I heard nothing from him. The next morning, a message was brought to me: "Master wants you in his study." I found the door ajar, and I stood a moment gazing at the hateful man who claimed a right to rule me, body and soul. I entered, and tried to appear calm. I did not want him to know how my heart was bleeding. He looked fixedly at me, with an expression which seemed to say, "I have half a mind to kill you on the spot." At last he broke the silence, and that was a relief to both of us.

"So you want to be married, do you? " said he, " and to a free nigger."

"Yes, sir."

"Well, I'll soon convince you whether I am your master, or the nigger fellow you honor so highly. If you *must* have a husband, you may take up with one of my slaves."

What a situation I should be in, as the wife of one of *his* slaves, even if my heart had been interested!

I replied, "Don't you suppose, sir, that a slave can have some preference about marrying? Do you suppose that all men are alike to her?"

"Do you love this nigger?" said he, abruptly.

"Yes, sir."

"How dare you tell me so!" he exclaimed, in great wrath. After a slight pause, he added, "I supposed you thought more of yourself; that you felt above the insults of such puppies."

I replied, "If he is a puppy I am a puppy, for we are both of the negro race. It is right and honorable for us to love each other. The man you call a puppy never insulted me, sir; and he would not love me if he did not believe me to be a virtuous woman."[58]

He sprang upon me like a tiger, and gave me a stunning blow. It was the first time he had ever struck me; and fear did not enable me to control my anger. When I had recovered a little from the effects, I exclaimed, "You have struck me for answering you honestly. How I despise you!"

There was silence for some minutes. Perhaps he was deciding what should be my punishment; or, perhaps, he wanted to give me time to reflect on what I had said, and to whom I had said it. Finally, he asked, "Do you know what you have said?"

"Yes, sir; but your treatment drove me to it."

"Do you know that I have a right to do as I like with you – that I can kill you, if I please?"

"You have tried to kill me, and I wish you had; but you have no right to do as you like with me."

"Silence!" he exclaimed, in a thundering voice. "By heavens, girl, you forget yourself too far! Are you mad? If you are, I will soon bring you to your senses. Do you think any other master would bear what I have borne from you this morning? Many masters would have killed you on the spot. How would you like to be sent to jail for your insolence?"

"I know I have been disrespectful, sir," I replied; "but you drove me to it; I couldn't help it. As for the jail, there would be more peace for me there than there is here."

"You deserve to go there," said he, "and to be under such treatment, that you would forget the meaning of the word *peace*. It would do you good. It would take some of

Notes

[58] *virtuous woman* a virgin.

your high notions out of you. But I am not ready to send you there yet, notwithstanding your ingratitude for all my kindness and forbearance. You have been the plague of my life. I have wanted to make you happy, and I have been repaid with the basest ingratitude; but though you have proved yourself incapable of appreciating my kindness, I will be lenient towards you, Linda. I will give you one more chance to redeem your character. If you behave yourself and do as I require, I will forgive you and treat you as I always have done; but if you disobey me, I will punish you as I would the meanest slave on my plantation. Never let me hear that fellow's name mentioned again. If I ever know of your speaking to him, I will cowhide you both; and if I catch him lurking about my premises, I will shoot him as soon as I would a dog. Do you hear what I say? I'll teach you a lesson about marriage and free niggers! Now go, and let this be the last time I have occasion to speak to you on this subject."

Reader, did you ever hate? I hope not. I never did but once; and I trust I never shall again. Somebody has called it "the atmosphere of hell"; and I believe it is so.

For a fortnight[59] the doctor did not speak to me. He thought to mortify me; to make me feel that I had disgraced myself by receiving the honorable addresses of a respectable colored man, in preference to the base proposals of a white man. But though his lips disdained to address me, his eyes were very loquacious. No animal ever watched its prey more narrowly than he watched me. He knew that I could write, though he had failed to make me read his letters; and he was now troubled lest I should exchange letters with another man. After a while he became weary of silence; and I was sorry for it. One morning, as he passed through the hall, to leave the house, he contrived to thrust a note into my hand. I thought I had better read it, and spare myself the vexation of having him read it to me. It expressed regret for the blow he had given me, and reminded me that I myself was wholly to blame for it. He hoped I had become convinced of the injury I was doing myself by incurring his displeasure. He wrote that he had made up his mind to go to Louisiana; that he should take several slaves with him, and intended I should be one of the number. My mistress would remain where she was; therefore I should have nothing to fear from that quarter. If I merited kindness from him, he assured me that it would be lavishly bestowed. He begged me to think over the matter, and answer the following day.

The next morning I was called to carry a pair of scissors to his room. I laid them on the table, with the letter beside them. He thought it was my answer, and did not call me back. I went as usual to attend my young mistress to and from school. He met me in the street, and ordered me to stop at his office on my way back. When I entered, he showed me his letter, and asked me why I had not answered it. I replied, "I am your daughter's property, and it is in your power to send me, or take me, wherever you please." He said he was very glad to find me so willing to go, and that we should start early in the autumn. He had a large practice in the town, and I rather thought he had made up the story merely to frighten me. However that might be, I was determined that I would never go to Louisiana with him.

Summer passed away, and early in the autumn Dr. Flint's eldest son was sent to Louisiana to examine the country, with a view to emigrating. That news did not disturb me. I knew very well that I should not be sent with *him*. That I had not been taken to the plantation before this time was owing to the fact that his son was there. He was jealous of his son; and jealousy of the overseer had kept him from punishing me by sending me

Notes

[59] *fortnight* two weeks.

into the fields to work. Is it strange that I was not proud of these protectors? As for the overseer, he was a man for whom I had less respect than I had for a bloodhound.

Young Mr. Flint did not bring back a favorable report of Louisiana, and I heard no more of that scheme. Soon after this, my lover met me at the corner of the street, and I stopped to speak to him. Looking up, I saw my master watching us from his window. I hurried home, trembling with fear. I was sent for, immediately, to go to his room. He met me with a blow. "When is mistress to be married?" said he, in a sneering tone. A shower of oaths and imprecations followed. How thankful I was that my lover was a free man! that my tyrant had no power to flog him for speaking to me in the street!

Again and again I revolved in my mind how all this would end. There was no hope that the doctor would consent to sell me on any terms. He had an iron will, and was determined to keep me, and to conquer me. My lover was an intelligent and religious man. Even if he could have obtained permission to marry me while I was a slave, the marriage would give him no power to protect me from my master. It would have made him miserable to witness the insults I should have been subjected to. And then, if we had children, I knew they must "follow the condition of the mother."[60] What a terrible blight that would be on the heart of a free, intelligent father! For *his* sake, I felt that I ought not to link his fate with my own unhappy destiny. He was going to Savannah to see about a little property left him by an uncle; and hard as it was to bring my feelings to it, I earnestly entreated him not to come back. I advised him to go to the Free States, where his tongue would not be tied, and where his intelligence would be of more avail to him. He left me, still hoping the day would come when I could be bought. With me the lamp of hope had gone out. The dream of my girlhood was over. I felt lonely and desolate.

Still I was not stripped of all. I still had my good grandmother, and my affectionate brother. When he put his arms round my neck, and looked into my eyes, as if to read there the troubles I dared not tell, I felt that I still had something to love. But even that pleasant emotion was chilled by the reflection that he might be torn from me at any moment, by some sudden freak of my master. If he had known how we loved each other, I think he would have exulted in separating us. We often planned together how we could get to the north. But, as William remarked, such things are easier said than done. My movements were very closely watched, and we had no means of getting any money to defray our expenses. As for grandmother, she was strongly opposed to her children's undertaking any such project. She had not forgotten poor Benjamin's sufferings, and she was afraid that if another child tried to escape, he would have a similar or a worse fate. To me, nothing seemed more dreadful than my present life. I said to myself, "William *must* be free. He shall go to the north, and I will follow him." Many a slave sister has formed the same plans.

Chapter 8

What Slaves Are Taught to Think of the North

Slaveholders pride themselves upon being honorable men; but if you were to hear the enormous lies they tell their slaves, you would have small respect for their veracity. I have spoken plain English. Pardon me. I cannot use a milder term. When they visit

Notes

[60] *"follow the condition of the mother."* Children born to slave women were classified as slaves.

the north, and return home, they tell their slaves of the runaways they have seen, and describe them to be in the most deplorable condition. A slaveholder once told me that he had seen a runaway friend of mine in New York, and that she besought him to take her back to her master, for she was literally dying of starvation; that many days she had only one cold potato to eat, and at other times could get nothing at all. He said he refused to take her, because he knew her master would not thank him for bringing such a miserable wretch to his house. He ended by saying to me, "This is the punishment she brought on herself for running away from a kind master."

This whole story was false. I afterwards staid with that friend in New York, and found her in comfortable circumstances. She had never thought of such a thing as wishing to go back to slavery. Many of the slaves believe such stories, and think it is not worthwhile[61] to exchange slavery for such a hard kind of freedom. It is difficult to persuade such that freedom could make them useful men, and enable them to protect their wives and children. If those heathen in our Christian land had as much teaching as some Hindoos,[62] they would think otherwise. They would know that liberty is more valuable than life. They would begin to understand their own capabilities, and exert themselves to become men and women.

But while the Free States sustain a law which hurls fugitives back into slavery, how can the slaves resolve to become men? There are some who strive to protect wives and daughters from the insults of their masters; but those who have such sentiments have had advantages above the general mass of slaves. They have been partially civilized and Christianized by favorable circumstances. Some are bold enough to *utter* such sentiments to their masters. O, that there were more of them!

Some poor creatures have been so brutalized by the lash that they will sneak out of the way to give their masters free access to their wives and daughters. Do you think this proves the black man to belong to an inferior order of beings? What would *you* be, if you had been born and brought up a slave, with generations of slaves for ancestors? I admit that the black man *is* inferior. But what is it that makes him so? It is the ignorance in which white men compel him to live; it is the torturing whip that lashes manhood out of him; it is the fierce bloodhounds of the South, and the scarcely less cruel human bloodhounds of the north, who enforce the Fugitive Slave Law. *They* do the work.

Southern gentlemen indulge in the most contemptuous expressions about the Yankees, while they, on their part, consent to do the vilest work for them, such as the ferocious bloodhounds and the despised negro-hunters are employed to do at home. When southerners go to the north, they are proud to do them honor; but the northern man is not welcome south of Mason and Dixon's line, unless he suppresses every thought and feeling at variance with their "peculiar institution." Nor is it enough to be silent. The masters are not pleased, unless they obtain a greater degree of subservience than that; and they are generally accommodated.[63] Do they respect the northerner for this? I trow[64] not. Even the slaves despise "a northern man with southern principles"; and that is the class they generally see. When northerners go to the south to reside, they prove very apt scholars. They soon imbibe the sentiments and disposition of their neighbors, and generally go beyond their teachers. Of the two, they are proverbially the hardest masters.

Notes

[61] *Original reads*: worth while [ed.].

[62] *Hindoos* Hindus.

[63] *Original reads*: accomodated [ed.].

[64] *trow* trust.

They seem to satisfy their consciences with the doctrine that God created the Africans to be slaves. What a libel upon the heavenly Father, who "made of one blood all nations of men!" And then who *are* Africans? Who can measure the amount of Anglo-Saxon blood coursing in the veins of American slaves?

I have spoken of the pains slaveholders take to give their slaves a bad opinion of the north; but, notwithstanding this, intelligent slaves are aware that they have many friends in the Free States. Even the most ignorant have some confused notions about it. They knew that I could read; and I was often asked if I had seen anything[65] in the newspapers about white folks over in the big north, who were trying to get their freedom for them. Some believe that the abolitionists have already made them free, and that it is established by law, but that their masters prevent the law from going into effect. One woman begged me to get a newspaper and read it over. She said her husband told her that the black people had sent word to the queen of 'Merica that they were all slaves; that she didn't believe it, and went to Washington city to see the president about it. They quarrelled; she drew her sword upon him, and swore that he should help her to make them all free.

That poor, ignorant woman thought that America was governed by a Queen, to whom the President was subordinate. I wish the President was subordinate to Queen Justice.

Chapter 9

Sketches of Neighboring Slaveholders

THERE was a planter in the country, not far from us, whom I will call Mr. Litch. He was an ill-bred, uneducated man, but very wealthy. He had six hundred slaves, many of whom he did not know by sight. His extensive plantation was managed by well-paid overseers. There was a jail and a whipping post on his grounds; and whatever cruelties were perpetrated there, they passed without comment. He was so effectually screened by his great wealth that he was called to no account for his crimes, not even for murder.

Various were the punishments resorted to. A favorite one was to tie a rope round a man's body, and suspend him from the ground. A fire was kindled over him, from which was suspended a piece of fat pork. As this cooked, the scalding drops of fat continually fell on the bare flesh. On his own plantation, he required very strict obedience to the eighth commandment. But depredations on the neighbors were allowable, provided the culprit managed to evade detection or suspicion. If a neighbor brought a charge of theft against any of his slaves, he was browbeaten by the master, who assured him that his slaves had enough of everything[66] at home, and had no inducement to steal. No sooner was the neighbor's back turned, than the accused was sought out, and whipped for his lack of discretion. If a slave stole from him even a pound of meat or a peck of corn, if detection followed, he was put in chains and imprisoned, and so kept till his form was attenuated by hunger and suffering.

A freshet[67] once bore his wine cellar and meat house miles away from the plantation. Some slaves followed, and secured bits of meat and bottles of wine. Two were detected;

Notes

[65] *Original reads*: any thing [ed.].

[66] *Original reads*: every thing [ed.].

[67] *freshet* flood.

a ham and some liquor being found in their huts. They were summoned by their master. No words were used, but a club felled them to the ground. A rough box was their coffin, and their interment was a dog's burial. Nothing was said.

Murder was so common on his plantation that he feared to be alone after nightfall. He might have believed in ghosts.

His brother, if not equal in wealth, was at least equal in cruelty. His bloodhounds were well trained. Their pen was spacious, and a terror to the slaves. They were let loose on a runaway, and, if they tracked him, they literally tore the flesh from his bones. When this slaveholder died, his shrieks and groans were so frightful that they appalled his own friends. His last words were, "I am going to hell; bury my money with me."

After death his eyes remained open. To press the lids down, silver dollars were laid on them. These were buried with him. From this circumstance, a rumor went abroad that his coffin was filled with money. Three times his grave was opened, and his coffin taken out. The last time, his body was found on the ground, and a flock of buzzards were pecking at it. He was again interred, and a sentinel set over his grave. The perpetrators were never discovered. Cruelty is contagious in uncivilized communities. Mr. Conant, a neighbor of Mr. Litch, returned from town one evening in a partial state of intoxication. His body servant gave him some offence. He was divested of his clothes, except his shirt, whipped, and tied to a large tree in front of the house. It was a stormy night in winter. The wind blew bitterly cold, and the boughs of the old tree crackled under falling sleet. A member of the family, fearing he would freeze to death, begged that he might be taken down; but the master would not relent. He remained there three hours; and, when he was cut down, he was more dead than alive. Another slave, who stole a pig from this master, to appease his hunger, was terribly flogged. In desperation, he tried to run away. But at the end of two miles, he was so faint with loss of blood, he thought he was dying. He had a wife, and he longed to see her once more. Too sick to walk, he crept back that long distance on his hands and knees. When he reached his master's, it was night. He had not strength to rise and open the gate. He moaned, and tried to call for help. I had a friend living in the same family. At last his cry reached her. She went out and found the prostrate man at the gate. She ran back to the house for assistance, and two men returned with her. They carried him in, and laid him on the floor. The back of his shirt was one clot of blood. By means of lard, my friend loosened it from the raw flesh. She bandaged him, gave him a cool drink,[68] and left him to rest. The master said he deserved a hundred more lashes. When his own labor was stolen from him, he had stolen food to appease his hunger. This was his crime.

Another neighbor was a Mrs. Wade. At no hour of the day was there cessation of the lash on her premises. Her labors began with the dawn, and did not cease till long after nightfall. The barn was her particular place of torture. There she lashed the slaves with the might of a man. An old slave of hers once said to me, "It is hell in missis's house. 'Pears I can never get out. Day and night I prays to die."

The mistress died before the old woman, and, when dying, entreated her husband not to permit any one of her slaves to look on her after death. A slave who had nursed her children, and had still a child in her care, watched her chance, and stole with it in her arms to the room where lay her dead mistress. She gazed a while on her, then raised her hand and dealt two blows on her face, saying, as she did so, "The

Notes

[68] *Original reads*: gave him cool drink [ed.].

devil is got you *now!*" She forgot that the child was looking on. She had just begun to talk; and she said to her father, "I did see ma, and mammy did strike ma, so," striking her own face with her little hand. The master was startled. He could not imagine how the nurse could obtain access to the room where the corpse lay; for he kept the door locked. He questioned her. She confessed that what the child had said was true, and told how she had procured the key. She was sold to Georgia.

In my childhood I knew a valuable slave, named Charity, and loved her, as all children did. Her young mistress married, and took her to Louisiana. Her little boy, James, was sold to a good sort of master. He became involved in debt, and James was sold again to a wealthy slaveholder, noted for his cruelty. With this man he grew up to manhood, receiving the treatment of a dog. After a severe whipping, to save himself from further infliction of the lash, with which he was threatened, he took to the woods. He was in a most miserable condition – cut by the cowskin, half naked, half starved, and without the means of procuring a crust of bread.

Some weeks after his escape, he was captured, tied, and carried back to his master's plantation. This man considered punishment in his jail, on bread and water, after receiving hundreds of lashes, too mild for the poor slave's offence. Therefore he decided, after the overseer should have whipped him to his satisfaction, to have him placed between the screws of the cotton gin, to stay as long as he had been in the woods. This wretched creature was cut with the whip from his head to his feet, then washed with strong brine, to prevent the flesh from mortifying, and make it heal sooner than it otherwise would. He was then put into the cotton gin, which was screwed down, only allowing him room to turn on his side when he could not lie on his back. Every morning a slave was sent with a piece of bread and bowl of water, which were placed within reach of the poor fellow. The slave was charged, under penalty of severe punishment, not to speak to him.

Four days passed, and the slave continued to carry the bread and water. On the second morning, he found the bread gone, but the water untouched. When he had been in the press four days and five nights, the slave informed his master that the water had not been used for four mornings, and that a horrible stench came from the gin house. The overseer was sent to examine into it. When the press was unscrewed, the dead body was found partly eaten by rats and vermin. Perhaps the rats that devoured his bread had gnawed him before life was extinct. Poor Charity! Grandmother and I often asked each other how her affectionate heart would bear the news, if she should ever hear of the murder of her son. We had known her husband, and knew that James was like him in manliness and intelligence. These were the qualities that made it so hard for him to be a plantation slave. They put him into a rough box, and buried him with less feeling than would have been manifested for an old house dog. Nobody asked any questions. He was a slave; and the feeling was that the master had a right to do what he pleased with his own property. And what did *he* care for the value of a slave? He had hundreds of them. When they had finished their daily toil, they must hurry to eat their little morsels, and be ready to extinguish their pine knots[69] before nine o'clock, when the overseer went on his patrol rounds.[70] He entered every cabin, to see that men and their wives had gone to bed together, lest the men, from over-fatigue, should fall asleep in the chimney corner, and remain there till the morning horn called them to their daily task. Women are considered of no value, unless they continually increase their owner's stock. They are put on a par with animals. This same master shot a woman

Notes

[69] *pine knots* firewood.

[70] *Original reads*: went his patrol rounds [ed.].

through the head, who had run away and been brought back to him. No one called him to account for it. If a slave resisted being whipped, the bloodhounds were unpacked, and set upon him, to tear his flesh from his bones. The master who did these things was highly educated, and styled a perfect gentleman. He also boasted the name and standing of a Christian, though Satan never had a truer follower.

I could tell of more slaveholders as cruel as those I have described. They are not exceptions to the general rule. I do not say there are no humane slaveholders. Such characters do exist, notwithstanding the hardening influences around them. But they are "like angels' visits – few and far between."

I knew a young lady who was one of these rare specimens. She was an orphan, and inherited as slaves a woman and her six children. Their father was a free man. They had a comfortable home of their own, parents and children living together. The mother and eldest daughter served their mistress during the day, and at night returned to their dwelling, which was on the premises. The young lady was very pious, and there was some reality in her religion. She taught her slaves to lead pure lives, and wished them to enjoy the fruit of their own industry. *Her* religion was not a garb put on for Sunday, and laid aside till Sunday returned again. The eldest daughter of the slave mother was promised in marriage to a free man; and the day before the wedding this good mistress emancipated her, in order that her marriage might have the sanction of *law*.

Report said that this young lady cherished an unrequited affection for a man who had resolved to marry for wealth. In the course of time a rich uncle of hers died. He left six thousand dollars to his two sons by a colored woman, and the remainder of his property to this orphan niece. The metal soon attracted the magnet. The lady and her weighty purse became his. She offered to manumit her slaves – telling them that her marriage might make unexpected changes in their destiny, and she wished to ensure[71] their happiness. They refused to take their freedom, saying that she had always been their best friend, and they could not be so happy anywhere[72] as with her. I was not surprised. I had often seen them in their comfortable home, and thought that the whole town did not contain a happier family. They had never felt slavery; and, when it was too late, they were convinced of its reality.

When the new master claimed this family as his property, the father became furious, and went to his mistress for protection. "I can do nothing for you now, Harry," said she. "I no longer have the power I had a week ago. I have succeeded in obtaining the freedom of your wife; but I cannot obtain it for your children." The unhappy father swore that nobody should take his children from him. He concealed them in the woods for some days; but they were discovered and taken. The father was put in jail, and the two oldest boys sold to Georgia. One little girl, too young to be of service to her master, was left with the wretched mother. The other three were carried to their master's plantation. The eldest soon became a mother; and, when the slaveholder's wife looked at the babe, she wept bitterly. She knew that her own husband had violated the purity she had so carefully inculcated. She had a second child by her master, and then he sold her and his offspring to his brother. She bore two children to the brother, and was sold again. The next sister went crazy. The life she was compelled to lead drove her mad. The third one became the mother of five daughters. Before the birth of the fourth the pious mistress died. To the last, she rendered every kindness to the slaves that her unfortunate circumstances permitted. She passed away peacefully, glad to close her eyes on a life which had been made so wretched by the man she loved.

Notes

[71] *Original reads*: insure [ed.].

[72] *Original reads*: any where [ed.].

This man squandered the fortune he had received, and sought to retrieve his affairs by a second marriage; but, having retired after a night of drunken debauch, he was found dead in the morning. He was called a good master; for he fed and clothed his slaves better than most masters, and the lash was not heard on his plantation so frequently as on many others. Had it not been for slavery, he would have been a better man, and his wife a happier woman.

No pen can give an adequate description of the all-pervading corruption produced by slavery. The slave girl is reared in an atmosphere of licentiousness and fear. The lash and the foul talk of her master and his sons are her teachers. When she is fourteen or fifteen, her owner, or his sons, or the overseer, or perhaps all of them, begin to bribe her with presents. If these fail to accomplish their purpose, she is whipped or starved into submission to their will. She may have had religious principles inculcated by some pious mother or grandmother, or some good mistress; she may have a lover, whose good opinion and peace of mind are dear to her heart; or the profligate men who have power over her may be exceedingly odious to her. But resistance is hopeless.

"The poor worm
Shall prove her contest vain. Life's little day
Shall pass, and she is gone!"

The slaveholder's sons are, of course, vitiated, even while boys, by the unclean influences everywhere[73] around them. Nor do the master's daughters always escape. Severe retributions sometimes come upon him for the wrongs he does to the daughters of the slaves. The white daughters early hear their parents quarrelling about some female slave. Their curiosity is excited, and they soon learn the cause. They are attended by the young slave girls whom their father has corrupted; and they hear such talk as should never meet youthful ears, or any other ears. They know that the women slaves are subject to their father's authority in all things; and in some cases they exercise the same authority over the men slaves. I have myself seen the master of such a household whose head was bowed down in shame; for it was known in the neighborhood that his daughter had selected one of the meanest slaves on his plantation to be the father of his first grandchild. She did not make her advances to her equals, nor even to her father's more intelligent servants. She selected the most brutalized, over whom her authority could be exercised with less fear of exposure. Her father, half frantic with rage, sought to revenge himself on the offending black man; but his daughter, foreseeing the storm that would arise, had given him free papers, and sent him out of the state.

In such cases the infant is smothered, or sent where it is never seen by any who know its history. But if the white parent is the *father*, instead of the mother, the offspring are unblushingly reared for the market. If they are girls, I have indicated plainly enough what will be their inevitable destiny.

You may believe what I say; for I write only that whereof I know. I was twenty-one years in that cage of obscene birds. I can testify, from my own experience and observation, that slavery is a curse to the whites as well as to the blacks. It makes the white fathers cruel and sensual; the sons violent and licentious; it contaminates the daughters, and makes the wives wretched. And as for the colored race, it needs an

Notes

[73] *Original reads*: every where [ed.].

abler pen than mine to describe the extremity of their sufferings, the depth of their degradation.

Yet few slaveholders seem to be aware of the widespread moral ruin occasioned by this wicked system. Their talk is of blighted cotton crops – not of the blight on their children's souls.

If you want to be fully convinced of the abominations of slavery, go on a southern plantation, and call yourself a negro trader. Then there will be no concealment; and you will see and hear things that will seem to you impossible among human beings with immortal souls.

Chapter 10

A Perilous Passage in the Slave Girl's Life

After my lover went away, Dr. Flint contrived a new plan. He seemed to have an idea that my fear of my mistress was his greatest obstacle. In the blandest tones, he told me that he was going to build a small house for me, in a secluded place, four miles away from the town. I shuddered; but I was constrained to listen, while he talked of his intention to give me a home of my own, and to make a lady of me. Hitherto, I had escaped my dreaded fate, by being in the midst of people. My grandmother had already had high words with my master about me. She had told him pretty plainly what she thought of his character, and there was considerable gossip in the neighborhood about our affairs, to which the open-mouthed jealousy of Mrs. Flint contributed not a little. When my master said he was going to build a house for me, and that he could do it with little trouble and expense, I was in hopes something would happen to frustrate his scheme; but I soon heard that the house was actually begun. I vowed before my Maker that I would never enter it. I had rather toil on the plantation from dawn till dark; I had rather live and die in jail, than drag on, from day to day, through such a living death. I was determined that the master, whom I so hated and loathed, who had blighted the prospects of my youth, and made my life a desert, should not, after my long struggle with him, succeed at last in trampling his victim under his feet. I would do anything, everything,[74] for the sake of defeating him. What *could* I do? I thought and thought, till I became desperate, and made a plunge into the abyss.

And now, reader, I come to a period in my unhappy life, which I would gladly forget if I could. The remembrance fills me with sorrow and shame. It pains me to tell you of it; but I have promised to tell you the truth, and I will do it honestly, let it cost me what it may. I will not try to screen myself behind the plea of compulsion from a master; for it was not so. Neither can I plead ignorance or thoughtlessness. For years, my master had done his utmost to pollute my mind with foul images, and to destroy the pure principles inculcated by my grandmother, and the good mistress of my childhood. The influences of slavery had had the same effect on me that they had on other young girls; they had made me prematurely knowing, concerning the evil ways of the world. I knew what I did, and I did it with deliberate calculation.

But, O, ye happy women, whose purity has been sheltered from childhood, who have been free to choose the objects of your affection, whose homes are protected by

Notes

[74] *Original reads*: any thing, every thing [ed.].

law, do not judge the poor desolate slave girl too severely! If slavery had been abolished, I, also, could have married the man of my choice; I could have had a home shielded by the laws; and I should have been spared the painful task of confessing what I am now about to relate; but all my prospects had been blighted by slavery. I wanted to keep myself pure; and, under the most adverse circumstances, I tried hard to preserve my self-respect; but I was struggling alone in the powerful grasp of the demon Slavery; and the monster proved too strong for me. I felt as if I was forsaken by God and man; as if all my efforts must be frustrated; and I became reckless in my despair.

I have told you that Dr. Flint's persecutions and his wife's jealousy had given rise to some gossip in the neighborhood. Among others, it chanced that a white unmarried gentleman had obtained some knowledge of the circumstances in which I was placed. He knew my grandmother, and often spoke to me in the street. He became interested for me, and asked questions about my master, which I answered in part. He expressed a great deal of sympathy, and a wish to aid me. He constantly sought opportunities to see me, and wrote to me frequently. I was a poor slave girl, only fifteen years old.

So much attention from a superior person was, of course, flattering; for human nature is the same in all. I also felt grateful for his sympathy, and encouraged by his kind words. It seemed to me a great thing to have such a friend. By degrees, a more tender feeling crept into my heart. He was an educated and eloquent gentleman; too eloquent, alas, for the poor slave girl who trusted in him. Of course I saw whither all this was tending. I knew the impassable gulf between us; but to be an object of interest to a man who is not married, and who is not her master, is agreeable to the pride and feelings of a slave, if her miserable situation has left her any pride or sentiment. It seems less degrading to give one's self, than to submit to compulsion. There is something akin to freedom in having a lover who has no control over you, except that which he gains by kindness and attachment. A master may treat you as rudely as he pleases, and you dare not speak; moreover, the wrong does not seem so great with an unmarried man, as with one who has a wife to be made unhappy. There may be sophistry in all this; but the condition of a slave confuses all principles of morality, and, in fact, renders the practice of them impossible.

When I found that my master had actually begun to build the lonely cottage, other feelings mixed with those I have described. Revenge, and calculations of interest, were added to flattered vanity and sincere gratitude for kindness. I knew nothing would enrage Dr. Flint so much as to know that I favored another; and it was something to triumph over my tyrant even in that small way. I thought he would revenge himself by selling me, and I was sure my friend, Mr. Sands, would buy me. He was a man of more generosity and feeling than my master, and I thought my freedom could be easily obtained from him. The crisis of my fate now came so near that I was desperate. I shuddered to think of being the mother of children that should be owned by my old tyrant. I knew that as soon as a new fancy took him, his victims were sold far off to get rid of them; especially if they had children. I had seen several women sold, with his babies at the breast. He never allowed his offspring by slaves to remain long in sight of himself and his wife. Of a man who was not my master I could ask to have my children well supported; and in this case, I felt confident I should obtain the boon. I also felt quite sure that they would be made free. With all these thoughts revolving in my mind, and seeing no other way of escaping the doom I so much dreaded, I made a headlong plunge. Pity me, and pardon me, O virtuous reader! You never knew what it is to be a slave; to be entirely unprotected by law or custom; to have the laws reduce you to the condition of a chattel, entirely subject to the will of another. You never exhausted your ingenuity in avoiding the snares, and eluding the power of a hated tyrant; you never shuddered at the sound of his footsteps, and trembled within hearing of his voice. I know I did wrong. No one can feel it more sensibly than I do. The painful and humiliating memory will haunt me to my dying day. Still, in looking back, calmly, on the events of my life, I feel that the slave woman ought not to be judged by the same standard as others.

The months passed on. I had many unhappy hours. I secretly mourned over the sorrow I was bringing on my grandmother, who had so tried to shield me from harm. I knew that I was the greatest comfort of her old age, and that it was a source of pride to her that I had not degraded myself, like most of the slaves. I wanted to confess to her that I was no longer worthy of her love; but I could not utter the dreaded words.

As for Dr. Flint, I had a feeling of satisfaction and triumph in the thought of telling *him*. From time to time he told me of his intended arrangements, and I was silent. At last, he came and told me the cottage was completed, and ordered me to go to it. I told him, I would never enter it. He said, "I have heard enough of such talk as that. You shall go, if you are carried by force; and you shall remain there."

I replied, "I will never go there. In a few months I shall be a mother."

He stood and looked at me in dumb amazement, and left the house without a word. I thought I should be happy in my triumph over him. But now that the truth was out, and my relatives would hear of it, I felt wretched. Humble as were their circumstances, they had pride in my good character. Now, how could I look them in the face? My self-respect was gone! I had resolved that I would be virtuous, though I was a slave. I had said, "Let the storm beat! I will brave it till I die." And now, how humiliated I felt!

I went to my grandmother. My lips moved to make confession, but the words stuck in my throat. I sat down in the shade of a tree at her door and began to sew. I think she saw something unusual was the matter with me. The mother of slaves is very watchful. She knows there is no security for her children. After they have entered their teens she lives in daily expectation of trouble. This leads to many questions. If the girl is of a sensitive nature, timidity keeps her from answering truthfully, and this well-meant course has a tendency to drive her from maternal counsels. Presently, in came my mistress, like a mad woman, and accused me concerning her husband. My grandmother, whose suspicions had been previously awakened, believed what she said. She exclaimed, "O Linda! has it come to this? I had rather see you dead than to see you as you now are. You are a disgrace to your dead mother." She tore from my fingers my mother's wedding ring and her silver thimble. "Go away!" she exclaimed, "and never come to my house, again." Her reproaches fell so hot and heavy, that they left me no chance to answer. Bitter tears, such as the eyes never shed but once, were my only answer. I rose from my seat, but fell back again, sobbing. She did not speak to me; but the tears were running down her furrowed cheeks, and they scorched me like fire. She had always been so kind to me! So kind! How I longed to throw myself at her feet, and tell her all the truth! But she had ordered me to go, and never to come there again. After a few minutes, I mustered strength, and started to obey her. With what feelings did I now close that little gate, which I used to open with such an eager hand in my childhood! It closed upon me with a sound I never heard before.

Where could I go? I was afraid to return to my master's. I walked on recklessly, not caring where I went, or what would become of me. When I had gone four or five miles, fatigue compelled me to stop. I sat down on the stump of an old tree. The stars were shining through the boughs above me. How they mocked me, with their bright, calm light! The hours passed by, and as I sat there alone a chilliness and deadly sickness came over me. I sank on the ground. My mind was full of horrid thoughts. I prayed to die; but the prayer was not answered. At last, with great effort I roused myself, and walked some distance further, to the house of a woman who had been a friend of my mother. When I told her why I was there, she spoke soothingly to me; but I could not be comforted. I thought I could bear my shame if I could only be reconciled to my grandmother. I longed to open my heart to her. I thought if she could know the real state of the case, and all I had been bearing for years, she would perhaps judge me less harshly. My friend advised me to send for her. I did so; but days of agonizing suspense passed before she came. Had she utterly forsaken me? No. She came at last. I knelt before her, and told her the things that had poisoned my life; how long I had been persecuted; that I saw no way of escape; and in an hour of extremity I had become desperate. She listened in silence. I told her I would bear anything[75] and do anything,[76] if in time I had hopes of obtaining her forgiveness. I begged of her to pity me, for my dead mother's sake. And she did pity me. She did not say, "I forgive you"; but she looked at me lovingly, with her eyes full of tears. She laid her old hand gently on my head, and murmured, "Poor child! Poor child!"

Chapter 11

The New Tie to Life

I RETURNED to my good grandmother's house. She had an interview with Mr. Sands. When she asked him why he could not have left her one ewe lamb – whether there were not plenty of slaves who did not care about character – he made no answer; but he spoke kind and encouraging words. He promised to care for my child, and to buy me, be the conditions what they might.

I had not seen Dr. Flint for five days. I had never seen him since I made the avowal to him. He talked of the disgrace I had brought on myself; how I had sinned against my master, and mortified my old grandmother. He intimated that if I had accepted his proposals, he, as a physician, could have saved me from exposure. He even condescended to pity me. Could he have offered wormwood more bitter? He, whose persecutions had been the cause of my sin!

"Linda," said he, "though you have been criminal towards me, I feel for you, and I can pardon you if you obey my wishes. Tell me whether the fellow you wanted to marry is the father of your child. If you deceive me, you shall feel the fires of hell."

I did not feel as proud as I had done. My strongest weapon with him was gone. I was lowered in my own estimation, and had resolved to bear his abuse in silence. But when he spoke contemptuously of the lover who had always treated me honorably; when I remembered that but for *him* I might have been a virtuous, free, and happy wife, I lost my patience. "I have sinned against God and myself," I replied; "but not against you."

He clinched his teeth, and muttered, "Curse you!" He came towards me, with ill-suppressed rage, and exclaimed, "You obstinate girl! I could grind your bones to powder! You have thrown yourself away on some worthless rascal. You are weak-minded, and have been easily persuaded by those who don't care a straw for you. The future will settle accounts between us. You are blinded now; but hereafter you will be convinced that your master was your best friend. My lenity towards you is a proof of it. I might have punished you in many ways. I might have had you whipped till you fell dead under the lash. But I wanted you to live; I would have bettered your condition. Others cannot do it. You are my slave. Your mistress, disgusted by your conduct,

Notes

[75] *Original reads*: any thing [ed.].

[76] *Original reads*: any thing [ed.].

forbids you to return to the house; therefore I leave you here for the present; but I shall see you often. I will call tomorrow."

He came with frowning brows that showed a dissatisfied state of mind. After asking about my health, he inquired whether my board was paid, and who visited me. He then went on to say that he had neglected his duty; that as a physician there were certain things that he ought to have explained to me. Then followed talk such as would have made the most shameless blush. He ordered me to stand up before him. I obeyed. "I command you," said he, "to tell me whether the father of your child is white or black," I hesitated. "Answer me this instant!" he exclaimed. I did answer. He sprang upon me like a wolf, and grabbed my arm as if he would have broken it. "Do you love him?" said he, in a hissing tone.

"I am thankful that I do not despise him," I replied.

He raised his hand to strike me; but it fell again. I don't know what arrested the blow. He sat down, with lips tightly compressed. At last he spoke. "I came here," said he, "to make you a friendly proposition; but your ingratitude chafes me beyond endurance. You turn aside all my good intentions towards you. I don't know what it is that keeps me from killing you." Again he rose, as if he had a mind to strike me.

But he resumed. "On one condition I will forgive your insolence and crime. You must henceforth have no communication of any kind with the father of your child. You must not ask anything[77] from him, or receive anything[78] from him. I will take care of you and your child. You had better promise this at once, and not wait till you are deserted by him. This is the last act of mercy I shall show towards you."

I said something about being unwilling to have my child supported by a man who had cursed it and me also. He rejoined, that a woman who had sunk to my level had no right to expect anything[79] else. He asked, for the last time, would I accept his kindness? I answered that I would not.

"Very well," said he; "then take the consequences of your wayward course. Never look to me for help. You are my slave, and shall always be my slave. I will never sell you; that you may depend upon."

Hope died away in my heart as he closed the door after him. I had calculated that in his rage he would sell me to a slave-trader; and I knew the father of my child was on the watch to buy me.

About this time my Uncle[80] Phillip was expected to return from a voyage. The day before his departure I had officiated as bridesmaid to a young friend. My heart was then ill at ease, but my smiling countenance did not betray it. Only a year had passed; but what fearful changes it had wrought! My heart had grown gray in misery. Lives that flash in sunshine, and lives that are born in tears, receive their hue from circumstances. None of us know what a year may bring forth.

I felt no joy when they told me my uncle had come. He wanted to see me, though he knew what had happened. I shrank from him at first; but at last consented that he should come to my room. He received me as he always had done. O, how my heart smote me when I felt his tears on my burning cheeks! The words of my grandmother came to my mind – "Perhaps your mother and father are taken from the evil days to come." My disappointed heart could now praise God that it was so. But why, thought I, did my relatives ever cherish hopes for me? What was there to save me

Notes

[77] *Original reads*: any thing [ed.].
[78] *Original reads*: any thing [ed.].
[79] *Original reads*: any thing [ed.].
[80] *Original reads*: uncle [ed.].

from the usual fate of slave girls? Many more beautiful and more intelligent than I had experienced a similar fate, or a far worse one. How could they hope that I should escape?

My uncle's stay was short, and I was not sorry for it. I was too ill in mind and body to enjoy my friends as I had done. For some weeks I was unable to leave my bed. I could not have any doctor but my master, and I would not have him sent for. At last, alarmed by my increasing illness, they sent for him. I was very weak and nervous; and as soon as he entered the room, I began to scream. They told him my state was very critical. He had no wish to hasten me out of the world, and he withdrew.

When my babe was born, they said it was premature. It weighed only four pounds; but God let it live. I heard the doctor say I could not survive till morning. I had often prayed for death; but now I did not want to die, unless my child could die too. Many weeks passed before I was able to leave my bed. I was a mere wreck of my former self. For a year there was scarcely a day when I was free from chills and fever. My babe also was sickly. His little limbs were often racked with pain. Dr. Flint continued his visits, to look after my health; and he did not fail to remind me that my child was an addition to his stock of slaves.

I felt too feeble to dispute with him, and listened to his remarks in silence. His visits were less frequent; but his busy spirit could not remain quiet. He employed my brother in his office, and he was made the medium of frequent notes and messages to me. William was a bright lad, and of much use to the doctor. He had learned to put up medicines, to leech, cup, and bleed. He had taught himself to read and spell. I was proud of my brother; and the old doctor suspected as much. One day, when I had not seen him for several weeks, I heard his steps approaching the door. I dreaded the encounter, and hid myself. He inquired for me, of course; but I was nowhere to be found. He went to his office, and despatched William with a note. The color mounted to my brother's face when he gave it to me; and he said, "Don't you hate me, Linda, for bringing you these things?" I told him I could not blame him; he was a slave, and obliged to obey his master's will. The note ordered me to come to his office. I went. He demanded to know where I was when he called. I told him I was at home. He flew into a passion, and said he knew better. Then he launched out upon his usual themes – my crimes against him, and my ingratitude for his forbearance. The laws were laid down to me anew, and I was dismissed. I felt humiliated that my brother should stand by, and listen to such language as would be addressed only to a slave. Poor boy! He was powerless to defend me; but I saw the tears, which he vainly strove to keep back. This manifestation of feeling irritated the doctor. William could do nothing to please him. One morning he did not arrive at the office so early as usual; and that circumstance afforded his master an opportunity to vent his spleen. He was put in jail. The next day my brother sent a trader to the doctor, with a request to be sold. His master was greatly incensed at what he called his insolence. He said he had put him there to reflect upon his bad conduct, and he certainly was not giving any evidence of repentance. For two days he harassed himself to find somebody to do his office work; but everything[81] went wrong without William. He was released, and ordered to take his old stand, with many threats, if he was not careful about his future behavior.

As the months passed on, my boy improved in health. When he was a year old, they called him beautiful. The little vine was taking deep root in my existence, though its clinging fondness excited a mixture of love and pain. When I was most sorely oppressed

Notes

[81] *Original reads*: every thing [ed.].

I found a solace in his smiles. I loved to watch his infant slumbers; but always there was a dark cloud over my enjoyment. I could never forget that he was a slave. Sometimes I wished that he might die in infancy. God tried me. My darling became very ill. The bright eyes grew dull, and the little feet and hands were so icy cold that I thought death had already touched them. I had prayed for his death, but never so earnestly as I now prayed for his life; and my prayer was heard. Alas, what mockery it is for a slave mother to try to pray back her dying child to life! Death is better than slavery. It was a sad thought that I had no name to give my child. His father caressed him and treated him kindly, whenever he had a chance to see him. He was not unwilling that he should bear his name; but he had no legal claim to it; and if I had bestowed it upon him, my master would have regarded it as a new crime, a new piece of insolence, and would, perhaps, revenge it on the boy. O, the serpent of Slavery has many and poisonous fangs!

Chapter 12

Fear of Insurrection

Not far from this time Nat Turner's insurrection broke out; and the news threw our town into great commotion. Strange that they should be alarmed, when their slaves were so "contented and happy"! But so it was.

It was always the custom to have a muster every year. On that occasion every white man shouldered his musket. The citizens and the so-called country gentlemen wore military uniforms. The poor whites took their places in the ranks in every-day dress, some without shoes, some without hats. This grand occasion had already passed; and when the slaves were told there was to be another muster, they were surprised and rejoiced. Poor creatures! They thought it was going to be a holiday. I was informed of the true state of affairs, and imparted it to the few I could trust. Most gladly would I have proclaimed it to every slave; but I dared not. All could not be relied on. Mighty is the power of the torturing lash.

By sunrise, people were pouring in from every quarter within twenty miles of the town. I knew the houses were to be searched; and I expected it would be done by country bullies and the poor whites. I knew nothing annoyed them so much as to see colored people living in comfort and respectability; so I made arrangements for them with especial care. I arranged everything[82] in my grandmother's house as neatly as possible. I put white quilts on the beds, and decorated some of the rooms with flowers. When all was arranged, I sat down at the window to watch. Far as my eye could reach, it rested on a motley crowd of soldiers. Drums and fifes were discoursing martial music. The men were divided into companies of sixteen, each headed by a captain. Orders were given, and the wild scouts rushed in every direction, wherever a colored face was to be found.

It was a grand opportunity for the low whites, who had no negroes of their own to scourge. They exulted in such a chance to exercise a little brief authority, and show their subserviency to the slaveholders; not reflecting that the power which trampled on the colored people also kept themselves in poverty, ignorance, and moral degradation. Those who never witnessed such scenes can hardly believe what I know was inflicted at this time on innocent men, women, and children, against whom there was

Notes

[82] *Original reads*: every thing [ed.].

not the slightest ground for suspicion. Colored people and slaves who lived in remote parts of the town suffered in an especial manner. In some cases the searchers scattered powder and shot among their clothes, and then sent other parties to find them, and bring them forward as proof that they were plotting insurrection. Everywhere[83] men, women, and children were whipped till the blood stood in puddles at their feet. Some received five hundred lashes; others were tied hands and feet, and tortured with a bucking paddle, which blisters the skin terribly. The dwellings of the colored people, unless they happened to be protected by some influential white person, who was nigh at hand, were robbed of clothing and everything[84] else the marauders thought worth carrying away. All day long these unfeeling wretches went round, like a troop of demons, terrifying and tormenting the helpless. At night, they formed themselves into patrol bands, and went wherever they chose among the colored people, acting out their brutal will. Many women hid themselves in woods and swamps, to keep out of their way. If any of the husbands or fathers told of these outrages, they were tied up to the public whipping post, and cruelly scourged for telling lies about white men. The consternation was universal. No two people that had the slightest tinge of color in their faces dared to be seen talking together.

I entertained no positive fears about our household, because we were in the midst of white families who would protect us. We were ready to receive the soldiers whenever they came. It was not long before we heard the tramp of feet and the sound of voices. The door was rudely pushed open; and in they tumbled, like a pack of hungry wolves. They snatched at everything[85] within their reach. Every box, trunk, closet, and corner underwent a thorough examination. A box in one of the drawers containing some silver change was eagerly pounced upon. When I stepped forward to take it from them, one of the soldiers turned and said angrily, "What d'ye foller us fur? D'ye s'pose white folks is come to steal?"

I replied, "You have come to search; but you have searched that box, and I will take it, if you please."

At that moment I saw a white gentleman who was friendly to us; and I called to him, and asked him to have the goodness to come in and stay till the search was over. He readily complied. His entrance into the house brought in the captain of the company, whose business it was to guard the outside of the house, and see that none of the inmates left it. This officer was Mr. Litch, the wealthy slaveholder whom I mentioned, in the account of neighboring planters, as being notorious for his cruelty. He felt above soiling his hands with the search. He merely gave orders; and, if a bit of writing was discovered, it was carried to him by his ignorant followers, who were unable to read.

My grandmother had a large trunk of bedding and table cloths. When that was opened, there was a great shout of surprise; and one exclaimed, "Where'd the damned niggers git all dis sheet an' table clarf?"

My grandmother, emboldened by the presence of our white protector, said, "You may be sure we didn't pilfer 'em from *your* houses."

"Look here, mammy," said a grim-looking fellow without any coat, "you seem to feel mighty gran' 'cause you got all them 'ere fixens. White folks oughter have 'em all."

His remarks were interrupted by a chorus of voices shouting, "We's got 'em! We's got 'em! Dis 'ere yaller gal's got letters!"

Notes

[83] *Original reads*: Every where [ed.].

[84] *Original reads*: every thing [ed.].

[85] *Original reads*: every thing [ed.].

There was a general rush for the supposed letter, which, upon examination, proved to be some verses written to me by a friend. In packing away my things, I had overlooked them. When their captain informed them of their contents, they seemed much disappointed. He inquired of me who wrote them. I told him it was one of my friends. "Can you read them?" he asked. When I told him I could, he swore, and raved, and tore the paper into bits. "Bring me all your letters!" said he, in a commanding tone. I told him I had none. "Don't be afraid," he continued, in an insinuating way. "Bring them all to me. Nobody shall do you any harm." Seeing I did not move to obey him, his pleasant tone changed to oaths and threats. "Who writes to you? half free niggers?" inquired he. I replied, "O, no; most of my letters are from white people. Some request me to burn them after they are read, and some I destroy without reading."

An exclamation of surprise from some of the company put a stop to our conversation. Some silver spoons which ornamented an old-fashioned buffet had just been discovered. My grandmother was in the habit of preserving fruit for many ladies in the town, and of preparing suppers for parties; consequently she had many jars of preserves. The closet that contained these was next invaded, and the contents tasted. One of them, who was helping himself freely, tapped his neighbor on the shoulder, and said, "Wal done! Don't wonder de niggers want to kill all de white folks, when dey live on 'sarves."[86] I stretched out my hand to take the jar, saying, "You were not sent here to search for sweetmeats."

"And what *were* we sent for?" said the captain, bristling up to me. I evaded the question.

The search of the house was completed, and nothing found to condemn us. They next proceeded to the garden, and knocked about every bush and vine, with no better success. The captain called his men together, and, after a short consultation, the order to march was given. As they passed out of the gate, the captain turned back, and pronounced a malediction on the house. He said it ought to be burned to the ground, and each of its inmates receive thirty-nine lashes. We came out of this affair very fortunately; not losing anything[87] except some wearing apparel.

Towards evening the turbulence increased. The soldiers, stimulated by drink, committed still greater cruelties. Shrieks and shouts continually rent the air. Not daring to go to the door, I peeped under the window curtain. I saw a mob dragging along a number of colored people, each white man, with his musket upraised, threatening instant death if they did not stop their shrieks. Among the prisoners was a respectable old colored minister. They had found a few parcels of shot in his house, which his wife had for years used to balance her scales. For this they were going to shoot him on Court House Green. What a spectacle was that for a civilized country! A rabble, staggering under intoxication, assuming to be the administrators of justice!

The better class of the community exerted their influence to save the innocent, persecuted people; and in several instances they succeeded, by keeping them shut up in jail till the excitement abated. At last the white citizens found that their own property was not safe from the lawless rabble they had summoned to protect them. They rallied the drunken swarm, drove them back into the country, and set a guard over the town.

The next day, the town patrols were commissioned to search colored people that lived out of the city; and the most shocking outrages were committed with perfect impunity. Every day for a fortnight, if I looked out, I saw horsemen with some poor

Notes

[86] *'sarves* preserves.

[87] *Original reads*: any thing [ed.].

panting negro tied to their saddles, and compelled by the lash to keep up with their speed, till they arrived at the jail yard. Those who had been whipped too unmercifully to walk were washed with brine, tossed into a cart, and carried to jail. One black man, who had not fortitude to endure scourging, promised to give information about the conspiracy. But it turned out that he knew nothing at all. He had not even heard the name of Nat Turner. The poor fellow had, however, made up a story, which augmented his own sufferings and those of the colored people.

The day patrol continued for some weeks, and at sundown a night guard was substituted. Nothing at all was proved against the colored people, bond or free. The wrath of the slaveholders was somewhat appeased by the capture of Nat Turner. The imprisoned were released. The slaves were sent to their masters, and the free were permitted to return to their ravaged homes. Visiting was strictly forbidden on the plantations. The slaves begged the privilege of again meeting at their little church in the woods, with their burying ground around it. It was built by the colored people, and they had no higher happiness than to meet there and sing hymns together, and pour out their hearts in spontaneous prayer. Their request was denied, and the church was demolished. They were permitted to attend the white churches, a certain portion of the galleries being appropriated to their use. There, when everybody[88] else had partaken of the communion, and the benediction had been pronounced, the minister said, "Come down, now, my colored friends." They obeyed the summons, and partook of the bread and wine, in commemoration of the meek and lowly Jesus, who said, "God is your Father, and all ye are brethren."

Chapter 13

The Church and Slavery

After the alarm caused by Nat Turner's insurrection had subsided, the slaveholders came to the conclusion that it would be well to give the slaves enough of religious instruction to keep them from murdering their masters. The Episcopal clergyman offered to hold a separate service on Sundays for their benefit. His colored members were very few, and also very respectable – a fact which I presume had some weight with him. The difficulty was to decide on a suitable place for them to worship. The Methodist and Baptist churches admitted them in the afternoon; but their carpets and cushions were not so costly as those at the Episcopal church. It was at last decided that they should meet at the house of a free colored man, who was a member.

I was invited to attend, because I could read. Sunday evening came, and, trusting to the cover of night, I ventured out. I rarely ventured out by daylight, for I always went with fear, expecting at every turn to encounter Dr. Flint, who was sure to turn me back, or order me to his office to inquire where I got my bonnet, or some other article of dress. When the Rev. Mr. Pike came, there were some twenty persons present. The reverend gentleman knelt in prayer, then seated himself, and requested all present, who could read, to open their books, while he gave out the portions he wished them to repeat or respond to.

His text was, "Servants, be obedient to them that are your masters according to the flesh, with fear and trembling, in singleness of your heart, as unto Christ."

Notes

[88] *Original reads*: every body [ed.].

Pious Mr. Pike brushed up his hair till it stood upright, and, in deep, solemn tones, began: "Hearken, ye servants! Give strict heed unto my words. You are rebellious sinners. Your hearts are filled with all manner of evil. 'Tis the devil who tempts you. God is angry with you, and will surely punish you, if you don't forsake your wicked ways. You that live in town are eye-servants behind your master's back. Instead of serving your masters faithfully, which is pleasing in the sight of your heavenly Master, you are idle, and shirk your work. God sees you. You tell lies. God hears you. Instead of being engaged in worshipping him, you are hidden away somewhere, feasting on your master's substance; tossing coffee-grounds with some wicked fortuneteller, or cutting cards with another old hag. Your masters may not find you out, but God sees you, and will punish you. O, the depravity of your hearts! When your master's work is done, are you quietly together, thinking of the goodness of God to such sinful creatures? No; you are quarrelling, and tying up little bags of roots to bury under the door-steps to poison each other with. God sees you. You men steal away to every grog shop to sell your master's corn, that you may buy rum to drink. God sees you. You sneak into the back streets, or among the bushes, to pitch coppers. Although your masters may not find you out, God sees you; and he will punish you. You must forsake your sinful ways, and be faithful servants. Obey your old master and your young master – your old mistress and your young mistress. If you disobey your earthly master, you offend your heavenly Master. You must obey God's commandments. When you go from here, don't stop at the corners of the streets to talk, but go directly home, and let your master and mistress see that you have come."

The benediction was pronounced. We went home, highly amused at brother Pike's gospel teaching, and we determined to hear him again. I went the next Sabbath evening, and heard pretty much a repetition of the last discourse. At the close of the meeting, Mr. Pike informed us that he found it very inconvenient to meet at the friend's house, and he should be glad to see us, every Sunday evening, at his own kitchen.

I went home with the feeling that I had heard the Reverend Mr. Pike for the last time. Some of his members repaired to his house, and found that the kitchen sported two tallow candles; the first time, I am sure, since its present occupant owned it, for the servants never had anything[89] but pine knots. It was so long before the reverend gentleman descended from his comfortable parlor that the slaves left, and went to enjoy a Methodist shout. They never seem so happy as when shouting and singing at religious meetings. Many of them are sincere, and nearer to the gate of heaven than sanctimonious Mr. Pike, and other long-faced Christians, who see wounded Samaritans, and pass by on the other side.

The slaves generally compose their own songs and hymns; and they do not trouble their heads much about the measure. They often sing the following verses:

"Old Satan is one busy ole man;
He rolls dem blocks all in my way;
But Jesus is my bosom friend;
He rolls dem blocks away.

If I had died when I was young,
Den how my stam'ring tongue would have sung;
But I am ole, and now I stand
A narrow chance for to tread dat heavenly land."

Notes

[89] *Original reads*: any thing [ed.].

I well remember one occasion when I attended a Methodist class meeting. I went with a burdened spirit, and happened to sit next a poor, bereaved mother, whose heart was still heavier than mine. The class leader was the town constable – a man who bought and sold slaves, who whipped his brethren and sisters of the church at the public whipping post, in jail or out of jail. He was ready to perform that Christian office anywhere[90] for fifty cents. This white-faced, black-hearted brother came near us, and said to the stricken woman, "Sister, can't you tell us how the Lord deals with your soul? Do you love him as you did formerly?"

She rose to her feet, and said, in piteous tones, "My Lord and Master, help me! My load is more than I can bear. God has hid himself from me, and I am left in darkness and misery." Then, striking her breast, she continued, "I can't tell you what is in here! They've got all my children. Last week they took the last one. God only knows where they've sold her. They let me have her sixteen years, and then – O! O! Pray for her brothers and sisters! I've got nothing to live for now. God make my time short!"

She sat down, quivering in every limb. I saw that constable class leader become crimson in the face with suppressed laughter, while he held up his handkerchief, that those who were weeping for the poor woman's calamity might not see his merriment. Then, with assumed gravity, he said to the bereaved mother, "Sister, pray to the Lord that every dispensation of his divine will may be sanctified to the good of your poor needy soul!"

The congregation struck up a hymn, and sang[91] as though they were as free as the birds that warbled round us –

"Ole Satan thought he had a mighty aim;
He missed my soul, and caught my sins.
Cry Amen, cry Amen, cry Amen to God!

He took my sins upon his back;
Went muttering and grumbling down to hell.
Cry Amen, cry Amen, cry Amen to God!

Ole Satan's church is here below.
Up to God's free church I hope to go.
Cry Amen, cry Amen, cry Amen to God!"

Precious are such moments to the poor slaves. If you were to hear them at such times, you might think they were happy. But can that hour of singing and shouting sustain them through the dreary week, toiling without wages, under constant dread of the lash?

The Episcopal clergyman, who, ever since my earliest recollection, had been a sort of god among the slaveholders, concluded, as his family was large, that he must go where money was more abundant. A very different clergyman took his place. The change was very agreeable to the colored people, who said, "God has sent us a good man this time." They loved him, and their children followed him for a smile or a kind word. Even the slaveholders felt his influence. He brought to the rectory five slaves. His wife taught them to read and write, and to be useful to her and themselves. As soon as he was settled, he turned his attention to the needy slaves around him. He

Notes

[90] *Original reads*: any where [ed.].

[91] *Original reads*: sung [ed.].

urged upon his parishioners the duty of having a meeting expressly for them every Sunday, with a sermon adapted to their comprehension. After much argument and importunity, it was finally agreed that they might occupy the gallery of the church on Sunday evenings. Many colored people, hitherto unaccustomed to attend church, now gladly went to hear the gospel preached. The sermons were simple, and they understood them. Moreover, it was the first time they had ever been addressed as human beings. It was not long before his white parishioners began to be dissatisfied. He was accused of preaching better sermons to the negroes than he did to them. He honestly confessed that he bestowed more pains upon those sermons than upon any others; for the slaves were reared in such ignorance that it was a difficult task to adapt himself to their comprehension. Dissensions arose in the parish. Some wanted he should preach to them in the evening, and to the slaves in the afternoon. In the midst of these disputings his wife died, after a very short illness. Her slaves gathered round her dying bed in great sorrow. She said, "I have tried to do you good and promote your happiness; and if I have failed, it has not been for want of interest in your welfare. Do not weep for me; but prepare for the new duties that lie before you. I leave you all free. May we meet in a better world." Her liberated slaves were sent away, with funds to establish them comfortably. The colored people will long bless the memory of that truly Christian woman. Soon after her death her husband preached his farewell sermon, and many tears were shed at his departure.

Several years after, he passed through our town and preached to his former congregation. In his afternoon sermon he addressed the colored people. "My friends," said he, "it affords me great happiness to have an opportunity of speaking to you again. For two years I have been striving to do something for the colored people of my own parish; but nothing is yet accomplished. I have not even preached a sermon to them. Try to live according to the word of God, my friends. Your skin is darker than mine; but God judges men by their hearts, not by the color of their skins." This was strange doctrine from a southern pulpit. It was very offensive to slaveholders. They said he and his wife had made fools of their slaves, and that he preached like a fool to the negroes.

I knew an old black man, whose piety and childlike trust in God were beautiful to witness. At fifty-three years old he joined the Baptist Church.[92] He had a most earnest desire to learn to read. He thought he should know how to serve God better if he could only read the Bible. He came to me, and begged me to teach him. He said he could not pay me, for he had no money; but he would bring me nice fruit when the season for it came. I asked him if he didn't know it was contrary to law; and that slaves were whipped and imprisoned for teaching each other to read. This brought the tears into his eyes. "Don't be troubled, Uncle[93] Fred," said I. "I have no thoughts of refusing to teach you. I only told you of the law, that you might know the danger, and be on your guard." He thought he could plan to come three times a week without its being suspected. I selected a quiet nook, where no intruder was likely to penetrate, and there I taught him his A, B, C. Considering his age, his progress was astonishing. As soon as he could spell in two syllables he wanted to spell out words in the Bible. The happy smile that illuminated his face put joy into my heart. After spelling out a few words, he paused, and said, "Honey, it 'pears when I can read dis good book I shall be nearer to God. White man is got all de sense. He can larn easy. It ain't easy for ole black man like me. I only wants to read dis book, dat I may know how to live; den I hab no fear 'bout dying."

Notes

[92] *Original reads*: church [ed.].

[93] *Original reads*: uncle [ed.].

I tried to encourage him by speaking of the rapid progress he had made. "Hab patience, child," he replied. "I larns slow."

I had no need of patience. His gratitude, and the happiness I imparted, were more than a recompense for all my trouble.

At the end of six months he had read through the New Testament, and could find any text in it. One day, when he had recited unusually well, I said, "Uncle Fred, how do you manage to get your lessons so well?"

"Lord bress you, chile," he replied. "You nebber gibs me a lesson dat I don't pray to God to help me to understan' what I spells and what I reads. And he *does* help me, chile. Bress his holy name!"

There are thousands, who, like good Uncle[94] Fred, are thirsting for the water of life; but the law forbids it, and the churches withhold it. They send the Bible to heathen abroad, and neglect the heathen at home. I am glad that missionaries go out to the dark corners of the earth; but I ask them not to overlook the dark corners at home. Talk to American slaveholders as you talk to savages in Africa. Tell *them* it is wrong to traffic in men. Tell them it is sinful to sell their own children, and atrocious to violate their own daughters. Tell them that all men are brethren, and that man has no right to shut out the light of knowledge from his brother. Tell them they are answerable to God for sealing up the Fountain of Life from souls that are thirsting for it.

There are men who would gladly undertake such missionary work as this; but, alas! their number is small. They are hated by the south, and would be driven from its soil, or dragged to prison to die, as others have been before them. The field is ripe for the harvest, and awaits the reapers. Perhaps the great grandchildren of Uncle[95] Fred may have freely imparted to them the divine treasures, which he sought by stealth, at the risk of the prison and the scourge.

Are doctors of divinity blind, or are they hypocrites? I suppose some are the one, and some the other; but I think if they felt the interest in the poor and the lowly, that they ought to feel, they would not be so *easily* blinded. A clergyman who goes to the south, for the first time, has usually some feeling, however vague, that slavery is wrong. The slaveholder suspects this, and plays his game accordingly. He makes himself as agreeable as possible; talks on theology, and other kindred topics. The reverend gentleman is asked to invoke a blessing on a table loaded with luxuries. After dinner he walks round the premises, and sees the beautiful groves and flowering vines, and the comfortable huts of favored household slaves. The southerner invites him to talk with these slaves. He asks them if they want to be free, and they say, "O, no, massa." This is sufficient to satisfy him. He comes home to publish a "South-Side View of Slavery," and to complain of the exaggerations of abolitionists. He assures people that he has been to the south, and seen slavery for himself; that it is a beautiful "patriarchal institution": that the slaves don't want their freedom; that they have hallelujah meetings, and other religious privileges.

What does *he* know of the half-starved wretches toiling from dawn till dark on the plantations? of mothers shrieking for their children, torn from their arms by slave-traders? of young girls dragged down into moral filth? of pools of blood around the whipping post? of hounds trained to tear human flesh? of men screwed into cotton gins to die? The slaveholder showed him none of these things, and the slaves dared not tell of them if he had asked them.

Notes

[94] *Original reads*: uncle [ed.].

[95] *Original reads*: uncle [ed.].

There is a great difference between Christianity and religion at the south. If a man goes to the communion table, and pays money into the treasury of the church, no matter if it be the price of blood, he is called religious. If a pastor has offspring by a woman not his wife, the church dismisses[96] him, if she is a white woman; but if she is colored, it does not hinder his continuing to be their good shepherd.

When I was told that Dr. Flint had joined the Episcopal Church,[97] I was much surprised. I supposed that religion had a purifying effect on the character of men; but the worst persecutions I endured from him were after he was a communicant. The conversation of the doctor, the day after he had been confirmed, certainly gave *me* no indication that he had "renounced the devil and all his works." In answer to some of his usual talk, I reminded him that he had just joined the church. "Yes, Linda," said he. "It was proper for me to do so. I am getting on in years,[98] and my position in society requires it, and it puts an end to all the damned slang. You would do well to join the church, too, Linda."

"There are sinners enough in it already," rejoined I. "If I could be allowed to live like a Christian, I should be glad."

"You can do what I require; and if you are faithful to me, you will lie as virtuous as my wife," he replied.

I answered that the Bible didn't say so.

His voice became hoarse with rage. "How dare you preach to me about your infernal Bible!" he exclaimed. "What right have you, who are *my* negro, to talk to me about what you would like, and what you wouldn't like? I am your master, and you shall obey me."

No wonder the slaves sing –

"Ole Satan's church is here below;
Up to God's free church I hope to go."

Chapter 14

Another Link to Life

I HAD not returned to my master's house since the birth of my child. The old man raved to have me thus removed from his immediate power; but his wife vowed, by all that was good and great, she would kill me if I came back; and he did not doubt her word. Sometimes he would stay away for a season. Then he would come and renew the old threadbare discourse about his forbearance and my ingratitude. He labored, most unnecessarily, to convince me that I had lowered myself. The venomous old reprobate had no need of descanting on that theme. I felt humiliated enough. My unconscious babe was the ever-present witness of my shame. I listened with silent contempt when he talked about my having forfeited *his* good opinion; but I shed bitter tears that I was no longer worthy of being respected by the good and pure. Alas! slavery still held me in its poisonous grasp. There was no chance for me to be respectable. There was no prospect of being able to lead a better life.

Notes

[96] *Original reads*: dismiss [ed.].

[97] *Original reads*: church [ed.].

[98] *Original reads*: I am getting in years [ed.].

Sometimes, when my master found that I still refused to accept what he called his kind offers, he would threaten to sell my child. "Perhaps that will humble you," said he.

Humble *me!* Was I not already in the dust? But his threat lacerated my heart. I knew the law gave him power to fulfil it; for slaveholders have been cunning enough to enact that "the child shall follow the condition of the *mother*" not of the *father*; thus taking care that licentiousness shall not interfere with avarice. This reflection made me clasp my innocent babe all the more firmly to my heart. Horrid visions passed through my mind when I thought of his liability to fall into the slave-trader's hands. I wept over him, and said, "O my child! perhaps they will leave you in some cold cabin to die, and then throw you into a hole, as if you were a dog."

When Dr. Flint learned that I was again to be a mother, he was exasperated beyond measure. He rushed from the house, and returned with a pair of shears. I had a fine head of hair; and he often railed about my pride of arranging it nicely. He cut every hair close to my head, storming and swearing all the time. I replied to some of his abuse, and he struck me. Some months before, he had pitched me downstairs[99] in a fit of passion; and the injury I received was so serious that I was unable to turn myself in bed for many days. He then said, "Linda, I swear by God I will never raise my hand against you again"; but I knew that he would forget his promise.

After he discovered my situation, he was like a restless spirit from the pit. He came every day; and I was subjected to such insults as no pen can describe. I would not describe them if I could; they were too low, too revolting. I tried to keep them from my grandmother's knowledge as much as I could. I knew she had enough to sadden her life, without having my troubles to bear. When she saw the doctor treat me with violence, and heard him utter oaths terrible enough to palsy a man's tongue, she could not always hold her peace. It was natural and motherlike that she should try to defend me; but it only made matters worse.

When they told me my new-born babe was a girl, my heart was heavier than it had ever been before. Slavery is terrible for men; but it is far more terrible for women. Superadded to the burden common to all, *they* have wrongs, and sufferings, and mortifications peculiarly their own.

Dr. Flint had sworn that he would make me suffer, to my last day, for this new crime against him, as he called it; and as long as he had me in his power, he kept his word. On the fourth day after the birth of my babe, he entered my room suddenly, and commanded me to rise and bring my baby to him. The nurse who took care of me had gone out of the room to prepare some nourishment, and I was alone. There was no alternative. I rose, took up my babe, and crossed the room to where he sat. "Now stand there," said he, "till I tell you to go back!" My child bore a strong resemblance to her father, and to the deceased Mrs. Sands, her grandmother. He noticed this; and while I stood before him, trembling with weakness, he heaped upon me and my little one every vile epithet he could think of. Even the grandmother in her grave did not escape his curses. In the midst of his vituperations I fainted at his feet. This recalled him to his senses. He took the baby from my arms, laid it on the bed, dashed cold water in my face, took me up, and shook me violently, to restore my consciousness before anyone[100] entered the room. Just then my grandmother came in, and he hurried out of the house. I suffered in consequence of this treatment; but I begged my friends to let me die, rather than send for the doctor. There was nothing I dreaded so much as his presence. My life was spared; and I was glad for the sake of my little ones. Had it

Notes

[99] *Original reads*: down stairs [ed.].

[100] *Original reads*: any one [ed.].

not been for these ties to life, I should have been glad to be released by death, though I had lived only nineteen years.

Always it gave me a pang that my children had no lawful claim to a name. Their father offered his; but, if I had wished to accept the offer, I dared not while my master lived. Moreover, I knew it would not be accepted at their baptism. A Christian name they were at least entitled to; and we resolved to call my boy for our dear good Benjamin, who had gone far away from us.

My grandmother belonged to the church; and she was very desirous of having the children christened. I knew Dr. Flint would forbid it, and I did not venture to attempt it. But chance favored me. He was called to visit a patient out of town, and was obliged to be absent during Sunday. "Now is the time," said my grandmother; " we will take the children to church, and have them christened."

When I entered the church, recollections of my mother came over me, and I felt subdued in spirit. There she had presented me for baptism, without any reason to feel ashamed. She had been married, and had such legal rights as slavery allows to a slave. The vows had at least been sacred to *her*, and she had never violated them. I was glad she was not alive, to know under what different circumstances her grandchildren were presented for baptism. Why had my lot been so different from my mother's? *Her* master had died when she was a child; and she remained with her mistress till she married. She was never in the power of any master; and thus she escaped one class of the evils that generally fall upon slaves.

When my baby was about to be christened, the former mistress of my father stepped up to me, and proposed to give it her Christian name. To this I added the surname of my father, who had himself no legal right to it; for my grandfather on the paternal side was a white gentleman. What tangled skeins are the genealogies of slavery! I loved my father; but it mortified me to be obliged to bestow his name on my children.

When we left the church, my father's old mistress invited me to go home with her. She clasped a gold chain round my baby's neck. I thanked her for this kindness; but I did not like the emblem. I wanted no chain to be fastened on my daughter, not even if its links were of gold. How earnestly I prayed that she might never feel the weight of slavery's chain, whose iron entereth into the soul!

Chapter 15

Continued Persecutions

My children grew finely; and Dr. Flint would often say to me, with an exulting smile, "These brats will bring me a handsome sum of money one of these days."

I thought to myself that, God being my helper, they should never pass into his hands. It seemed to me I would rather see them killed than have them given up to his power. The money for the freedom of myself and my children could be obtained; but I derived no advantage from that circumstance. Dr. Flint loved money, but he loved power more. After much discussion, my friends resolved on making another trial. There was a slaveholder about to leave for Texas, and he was commissioned to buy me. He was to begin with nine hundred dollars, and go up to twelve. My master refused his offers. "Sir," said he, "she don't belong to me. She is my daughter's property, and I have no right to sell her. I mistrust that you come from her paramour. If so, you may tell him that he cannot buy her for any money; neither can he buy her children."

The doctor came to see me the next day, and my heart beat quicker as he entered. I never had seen the old man tread with so majestic a step. He seated himself and looked at me with withering scorn. My children had learned to be afraid of him. The little one would shut her eyes and hide her face on my shoulder whenever she saw him; and Benny, who was now nearly five years old, often inquired, "What makes that bad man come here so many times? Does he want to hurt us?" I would clasp the dear boy in my arms, trusting that he would be free before he was old enough to solve the problem. And now, as the doctor sat there so grim and silent, the child left his play and came and nestled up by me. At last my tormentor spoke. "So you are left in disgust, are you?" said he. "It is no more than I expected. You remember I told you years ago that you would be treated so. So he is tired of you? Ha! ha! ha! The virtuous madam don't like to hear about it, does she? Ha! ha! ha!" There was a sting in his calling me virtuous madam. I no longer had the power of answering him as I had formerly done. He continued: "So it seems you are trying to get up another intrigue. Your new paramour came to me, and offered to buy you; but you may be assured you will not succeed. You are mine; and you shall be mine for life. There lives no human being that can take you out of slavery. I would have done it; but you rejected my kind offer."

I told him I did not wish to get up any intrigue; that I had never seen the man who offered to buy me.

"Do you tell me I lie?" exclaimed he, dragging me from my chair. "Will you say again that you never saw that man?"

I answered, "I do say so."

He clinched my arm with a volley of oaths. Ben began to scream, and I told him to go to his grandmother.

"Don't you stir a step, you little wretch!" said he. The child drew nearer to me, and put his arms round me, as if he wanted to protect me. This was too much for my enraged master. He caught him up and hurled him across the room. I thought he was dead, and rushed towards him to take him up.

"Not yet!" exclaimed the doctor. "Let him lie there till he comes to."

"Let me go! Let me go!" I screamed, "or I will raise the whole house." I struggled and got away; but he clinched me again. Somebody opened the door, and he released me. I picked up my insensible child, and when I turned my tormentor was gone. Anxiously I bent over the little form, so pale and still; and when the brown eyes at last opened, I don't know whether I was very happy.

All the doctor's former persecutions were renewed. He came morning, noon, and night. No jealous lover ever watched a rival more closely than he watched me and the unknown slaveholder, with whom he accused me of wishing to get up an intrigue. When my grandmother was out of the way he searched every room to find him.

In one of his visits, he happened to find a young girl, whom he had sold to a trader a few days previous. His statement was that he sold her because she had been too familiar with the overseer. She had had a bitter life with him, and was glad to be sold. She had no mother, and no near ties. She had been torn from all her family years before. A few friends had entered into bonds for her safety, if the trader would allow her to spend with them the time that intervened between her sale and the gathering up of his human stock. Such a favor was rarely granted. It saved the trader the expense of board and jail fees, and though the amount was small, it was a weighty consideration in a slave-trader's mind.

Dr. Flint always had an aversion to meeting slaves after he had sold them. He ordered Rose out of the house; but he was no longer her master, and she took no notice of him. For once the crushed Rose was the conqueror. His gray eyes flashed angrily upon her; but that was the extent of his power. "How came this girl here?" he exclaimed. "What right had you to allow it, when you knew I had sold her?"

I answered "This is my grandmother's house, and Rose came to see her. I have no right to turn anybody[101] out of doors that comes here for honest purposes."

He gave me the blow that would have fallen upon Rose if she had still been his slave. My grandmother's attention had been attracted by loud voices, and she entered in time to see a second blow dealt. She was not a woman to let such an outrage, in her own house, go unrebuked. The doctor undertook to explain that I had been insolent. Her indignant feelings rose higher and higher, and finally boiled over in words. "Get out of my house!" she exclaimed. "Go home, and take care of your wife and children, and you will have enough to do, without watching my family." He threw the birth of my children in her face, and accused her of sanctioning the life I was leading. She told him I was living with her by compulsion of his wife; that he needn't accuse her, for he was the one to blame; he was the one who had caused all the trouble. She grew more and more excited as she went on. "I tell you what, Dr. Flint," said she, "you ain't got many more years to live, and you'd better be saying your prayers. It will take 'em all, and more too, to wash the dirt off your soul."

"Do you know whom you are talking to?" he exclaimed.

She replied, "Yes, I know very well who I am talking to."

He left the house in a great rage. I looked at my grandmother. Our eyes met. Their angry expression had passed away, but she looked sorrowful and weary – weary of incessant strife. I wondered that it did not lessen her love for me; but if it did she never showed it. She was always kind, always ready to sympathize with my troubles. There might have been peace and contentment in that humble home if it had not been for the demon Slavery.

The winter passed undisturbed by the doctor. The beautiful spring came; and when Nature resumes her loveliness, the human soul is apt to revive also. My drooping hopes came to life again with the flowers. I was dreaming of freedom again; more for my children's sake than my own. I planned and I planned. Obstacles hit against plans. There seemed no way of overcoming them; and yet I hoped.

Back came the wily doctor. I was not at home when he called. A friend had invited me to a small party, and to gratify her I went. To my great consternation, a messenger came in haste to say that Dr. Flint was at my grandmother's, and insisted on seeing me. They did not tell him where I was, or he would have come and raised a disturbance in my friend's house. They sent me a dark wrapper;[102] I threw it on and hurried home. My speed did not save me; the doctor had gone away in anger. I dreaded the morning, but I could not delay it; it came, warm and bright. At an early hour the doctor came and asked me where I had been last night. I told him. He did not believe me, and sent to my friend's house to ascertain the facts. He came in the afternoon to assure me he was satisfied that I had spoken the truth. He seemed to be in a facetious mood, and I expected some jeers were coming. "I suppose you need some recreation," said he, "but I am surprised at your being there, among those negroes. It was not the place for *you*. Are you *allowed* to visit such people?"

I understood this covert fling at the white gentleman who was my friend; but I merely replied, "I went to visit my friends, and any company they keep is good enough for me."

Notes

[101] *Original reads*: any body [ed.].

[102] *wrapper* a loose outer garment for women.

He went on to say, "I have seen very little of you of late, but my interest in you is unchanged. When I said I would have no more mercy on you I was rash. I recall my words. Linda, you desire freedom for yourself and your children, and you can obtain it only through me. If you agree to what I am about to propose, you and they shall be free. There must be no communication of any kind between you and their father. I will procure a cottage, where you and the children can live together. Your labor shall be light, such as sewing for my family. Think what is offered you, Linda – a home and freedom! Let the past be forgotten. If I have been harsh with you at times, your wilfulness drove me to it. You know I exact obedience from my own children, and I consider you as yet a child."

He paused for an answer, but I remained silent.

"Why don't you speak?" said he. "What more do you wait for?"

"Nothing, sir."

"Then you accept my offer?"

"No, sir."

His anger was ready to break loose; but he succeeded in curbing it, and replied, "You have answered without thought. But I must let you know there are two sides to my proposition; if you reject the bright side, you will be obliged to take the dark one. You must either accept my offer, or you and your children shall be sent to your young master's plantation, there to remain till your young mistress is married; and your children shall fare like the rest of the negro children. I give you a week to consider of it."

He was shrewd; but I knew he was not to be trusted. I told him I was ready to give my answer now.

"I will not receive it now," he replied. "You act too much from impulse. Remember that you and your children can be free a week from to-day if you choose."

On what a monstrous chance hung the destiny of my children! I knew that my master's offer was a snare, and that if I entered it escape would be impossible. As for his promise, I knew him so well that I was sure if he gave me free papers, they would be so managed as to have no legal value. The alternative was inevitable. I resolved to go to the plantation. But then I thought how completely I should be in his power, and the prospect was appalling.[103] Even if I should kneel before him, and implore him to spare me, for the sake of my children, I knew he would spurn me with his foot, and my weakness would be his triumph.

Before the week expired, I heard that young Mr. Flint was about to be married to a lady of his own stamp. I foresaw the position I should occupy in his establishment. I had once been sent to the plantation for punishment, and fear of the son had induced the father to recall me very soon. My mind was made up; I was resolved that I would foil my master and save my children, or I would perish in the attempt. I kept my plans to myself; I knew that friends would try to dissuade me from them, and I would not wound their feelings by rejecting their advice.

On the decisive day the doctor came, and said he hoped I had made a wise choice.

"I am ready to go to the plantation, sir," I replied.

"Have you thought how important your decision is to your children?" said he.

I told him I had.

"Very well. Go to the plantation, and my curse go with you," he replied. "Your boy shall be put to work, and he shall soon be sold; and your girl shall be raised for the purpose of selling well. Go your own ways!" He left the room with curses, not to be repeated.

Notes

[103] *Original reads*: apalling [ed.].

As I stood rooted to the spot, my grandmother came and said, "Linda, child, what did you tell him?"

I answered that I was going to the plantation.

"*Must* you go?" said she. "Can't something be done to stop it?"

I told her it was useless to try; but she begged me not to give up. She said she would go to the doctor, and remind him how long and how faithfully she had served in the family, and how she had taken her own baby from her breast to nourish his wife. She would tell him I had been out of the family so long they would not miss me; that she would pay them for my time, and the money would procure a woman who had more strength for the situation than I had. I begged her not to go; but she persisted in saying, "He will listen to *me*, Linda." She went, and was treated as I expected. He coolly listened to what she said, but denied her request. He told her that what he did was for my good, that my feelings were entirely above my situation, and that on the plantation I would receive treatment that was suitable to my behavior.

My grandmother was much cast down. I had my secret hopes; but I must fight my battle alone. I had a woman's pride, and a mother's love for my children; and I resolved that out of the darkness of this hour a brighter dawn should rise for them. My master had power and law on his side; I had a determined will. There is might in each.

Chapter 16

Scenes at the Plantation

Early the next morning I left my grandmother's with my youngest child. My boy was ill, and I left him behind. I had many sad thoughts as the old wagon jolted on. Hitherto, I had suffered alone; now, my little one was to be treated as a slave. As we drew near the great house, I thought of the time when I was formerly sent there out of revenge. I wondered for what purpose I was now sent. I could not tell. I resolved to obey orders so far as duty required; but within myself, I determined to make my stay as short as possible. Mr. Flint was waiting to receive us, and told me to follow him up stairs to receive orders for the day. My little Ellen was left below in the kitchen. It was a change for her, who had always been so carefully tended. My young master said she might amuse herself in the yard. This was kind of him, since the child was hateful to his sight. My task was to fit up the house for the reception of the bride. In the midst of sheets, tablecloths, towels, drapery, and carpeting, my head was as busy planning, as were my fingers with the needle. At noon I was allowed to go to Ellen. She had sobbed herself to sleep. I heard Mr. Flint say to a neighbor, "I've got her down here, and I'll soon take the town notions out of her head. My father is partly to blame for her nonsense. He ought to have broke her in long ago." The remark was made within my hearing, and it would have been quite as manly to have made it to my face. He *had* said things to my face which might, or might not, have surprised his neighbor if he had known of them. He was "a chip off the old block."[104]

I resolved to give him no cause to accuse me of being too much of a lady, so far as work was concerned. I worked day and night, with wretchedness before me. When

Notes

[104] *Original reads*: a chip of the old block [ed.].

I lay down beside my child, I felt how much easier it would be to see her die than to see her master beat her about, as I daily saw him beat other little ones. The spirit of the mothers was so crushed by the lash that they stood by, without courage to remonstrate. How much more must I suffer, before I should be "broke in" to that degree?

I wished to appear as contented as possible. Sometimes I had an opportunity to send a few lines home; and this brought up recollections that made it difficult, for a time, to seem calm and indifferent to my lot. Notwithstanding my efforts, I saw that Mr. Flint regarded me with a suspicious eye. Ellen broke down under the trials of her new life. Separated from me, with no one to look after her, she wandered about, and in a few days cried herself sick. One day, she sat under the window where I was at work, crying that weary cry which makes a mother's heart bleed. I was obliged to steel myself to bear it. After a while it ceased. I looked out, and she was gone. As it was near noon, I ventured to go down in search of her. The great house was raised two feet above the ground. I looked under it, and saw her about midway, fast asleep. I crept under and drew her out. As I held her in my arms, I thought how well it would be for her if she never woke up;[105] and I uttered my thought aloud. I was startled to hear someone[106] say, "Did you speak to me?" I looked up, and saw Mr. Flint standing beside me. He said nothing further, but turned, frowning, away. That night he sent Ellen a biscuit and a cup of sweetened milk. This generosity surprised me. I learned afterwards, that in the afternoon he had killed a large snake, which crept from under the house; and I supposed that incident had prompted his unusual kindness.

The next morning the old cart was loaded with shingles for town. I put Ellen into it, and sent her to her grandmother. Mr. Flint said I ought to have asked his permission. I told him the child was sick, and required attention which I had no time to give. He let it pass; for he was aware that I had accomplished much work in a little time.

I had been three weeks on the plantation, when I planned a visit home. It must be at night, after everybody[107] was in bed. I was six miles from town, and the road was very dreary. I was to go with a young man, who, I knew, often stole to town to see his mother. One night, when all was quiet, we started. Fear gave speed to our steps, and we were not long in performing the journey. I arrived at my grandmother's. Her bedroom[108] was on the first floor, and the window was open, the weather being warm. I spoke to her and she awoke. She let me in and closed the window, lest some late passer-by should see me. A light was brought, and the whole household gathered round me, some smiling and some crying. I went to look at my children, and thanked God for their happy sleep. The tears fell as I leaned over them. As I moved to leave, Benny stirred. I turned back, and whispered, "Mother is here." After digging at his eyes with his little fist, they opened, and he sat up in bed, looking at me curiously. Having satisfied himself that it was I, he exclaimed, "O mother! you ain't dead, are you? They didn't cut off your head at the plantation, did they?"

My time was up too soon, and my guide was waiting for me. I laid Benny back in his bed, and dried his tears by a promise to come again soon. Rapidly we retraced our steps back to the plantation. About half way we were met by a company of four patrols. Luckily we heard their horses'[109] hoofs before they came in sight, and we had time to hide behind a large tree. They passed, hallooing and shouting in a manner that indicated a recent carousal. How thankful we were that they had not their dogs with

Notes

[105] *Original reads*: waked up [ed.].

[106] *Original reads*: some one [ed.].

[107] *Original reads*: every body [ed.].

[108] *Original reads*: bed room [ed.].

[109] *Original reads*: horse's [ed.].

them! We hastened our footsteps, and when we arrived on the plantation we heard the sound of the hand-mill. The slaves were grinding their corn. We were safely in the house before the horn summoned them to their labor. I divided my little parcel of food with my guide, knowing that he had lost the chance of grinding his corn, and must toil all day in the field.

Mr. Flint often took an inspection of the house, to see that no one was idle. The entire management of the work was trusted to me, because he knew nothing about it; and rather than hire a superintendent he contented himself with my arrangements. He had often urged upon his father the necessity of having me at the plantation to take charge of his affairs, and make clothes for the slaves; but the old man knew him too well to consent to that arrangement.

When I had been working a month at the plantation, the great aunt of Mr. Flint came to make him a visit. This was the good old lady who paid fifty dollars for my grandmother, for the purpose of making her free, when she stood on the auction block. My grandmother loved this old lady, whom we all called Miss Fanny. She often came to take tea with us. On such occasions the table was spread with a snow-white cloth, and the china cups and silver spoons were taken from the old-fashioned buffet. There were hot muffins, tea rusks, and delicious sweetmeats. My grandmother kept two cows, and the fresh cream was Miss Fanny's delight. She invariably declared that it was the best in town. The old ladies had cozy[110] times together. They would work and chat, and sometimes, while talking over old times, their spectacles would get dim with tears, and would have to be taken off and wiped. When Miss Fanny bade us goodbye,[111] her bag was filled with grandmother's best cakes, and she was urged to come again soon.

There had been a time when Dr. Flint's wife came to take tea with us, and when her children were also sent to have a feast of "Aunt Marthy's" nice cooking. But after I became an object of her jealousy and spite, she was angry with grandmother for giving a shelter to me and my children. She would not even speak to her in the street. This wounded my grandmother's feelings, for she could not retain ill will against the woman whom she had nourished with her milk when a babe. The doctor's wife would gladly have prevented our intercourse with Miss Fanny if she could have done it, but fortunately she was not dependent on the bounty of the Flints. She had enough to be independent; and that is more than can ever be gained from charity, however lavish it may be.

Miss Fanny was endeared to me by many recollections, and I was rejoiced to see her at the plantation. The warmth of her large, loyal heart made the house seem pleasanter while she was in it. She staid a week, and I had many talks with her. She said her principal object in coming was to see how I was treated, and whether anything[112] could be done for me. She inquired whether she could help me in any way. I told her I believed not. She condoled with me in her own peculiar way; saying she wished that I and all my grandmother's family were at rest in our graves, for not until then should she feel any peace about us. The good old soul did not dream that I was planning to bestow peace upon her, with regard to myself and my children; not by death, but by securing our freedom.

Again and again I had traversed those dreary twelve miles, to and from the town; and all the way, I was meditating upon some means of escape for myself and my

Notes

[110] *Original reads*: cosey [ed.].

[111] *Original reads*: good by [ed.].

[112] *Original reads*: any thing [ed.].

children. My friends had made every effort that ingenuity could devise to effect our purchase, but all their plans had proved abortive. Dr. Flint was suspicious, and determined not to loosen his grasp upon us. I could have made my escape alone; but it was more for my helpless children than for myself that I longed for freedom. Though the boon would have been precious to me, above all price, I would not have taken it at the expense of leaving them in slavery. Every trial I endured, every sacrifice I made for their sakes, drew them closer to my heart, and gave me fresh courage to beat back the dark waves that rolled and rolled over me in a seemingly endless night of storms.

The six weeks were nearly completed, when Mr. Flint's bride was expected to take possession of her new home. The arrangements were all completed, and Mr. Flint said I had done well. He expected to leave home on Saturday, and return with his bride the following Wednesday. After receiving various orders from him, I ventured to ask permission to spend Sunday in town. It was granted; for which favor I was thankful. It was the first I had ever asked of him, and I intended it should be the last. It needed more than one night to accomplish the project I had in view; but the whole of Sunday would give me an opportunity. I spent the Sabbath with my grandmother. A calmer, more beautiful day never came down out of heaven. To me it was a day of conflicting emotions. Perhaps it was the last day I should ever spend under that dear, old sheltering roof! Perhaps these were the last talks I should ever have with the faithful old friend of my whole life! Perhaps it was the last time I and my children should be together! Well, better so, I thought, than that they should be slaves. I knew the doom that awaited my fair baby in slavery, and I determined to save her from it, or perish in the attempt. I went to make this vow at the graves of my poor parents, in the burying-ground of the slaves. "There the wicked cease from troubling, and there the weary be at rest. There the prisoners rest together; they hear not the voice of the oppressor; the servant is free from his master."[113] I knelt by the graves of my parents, and thanked God, as I had often done before, that they had not lived to witness my trials, or to mourn over my sins. I had received my mother's blessing when she died; and in many an hour of tribulation I had seemed to hear her voice, sometimes chiding me, sometimes whispering loving words into my wounded heart. I have shed many and bitter tears, to think that when I am gone from my children they cannot remember me with such entire satisfaction as I remembered my mother.

The graveyard was in the woods, and twilight was coming on. Nothing broke the death-like stillness except the occasional twitter of a bird. My spirit was overawed by the solemnity of the scene. For more than ten years I had frequented this spot, but never had it seemed to me so sacred as now. A black stump, at the head of my mother's grave, was all that remained of a tree my father had planted. His grave was marked by a small wooden board, bearing his name, the letters of which were nearly obliterated. I knelt down and kissed them, and poured forth a prayer to God for guidance and support in the perilous step I was about to take. As I passed the wreck of the old meeting house, where, before Nat Turner's time, the slaves had been allowed to meet for worship, I seemed to hear my father's voice come from it, bidding me not to tarry till I reached freedom or the grave. I rushed on with renovated hopes. My trust in God had been strengthened by that prayer among the graves.

Notes

[113] *"There the wicked ... master"* Job 3:17.

My plan was to conceal myself at the house of a friend, and remain there a few weeks till the search was over. My hope was that the doctor would get discouraged, and, for fear of losing my value, and also of subsequently finding my children among the missing, he would consent to sell us; and I knew somebody would buy us. I had done all in my power to make my children comfortable during the time I expected to be separated from them. I was packing my things, when grandmother came into the room, and asked what I was doing. "I am putting my things in order," I replied. I tried to look and speak cheerfully; but her watchful eye detected something beneath the surface. She drew me towards her, and asked me to sit down. She looked earnestly at me, and said, "Linda, do you want to kill your old grandmother? Do you mean to leave your little, helpless children? I am old now, and cannot do for your babies as I once did for you."

I replied that if I went away, perhaps their father would be able to secure their freedom.

"Ah, my child," said she, "don't trust too much to him. Stand by your own children, and suffer with them till death. Nobody respects a mother who forsakes her children; and if you leave them, you will never have a happy moment. If you go, you will make me miserable the short time I have to live. You would be taken and brought back, and your sufferings would be dreadful. Remember poor Benjamin. Do give it up, Linda. Try to bear a little longer. Things may turn out better than we expect."

My courage failed me, in view of the sorrow I should bring[114] on that faithful, loving old heart. I promised that I would try longer, and that I would take nothing out of her house without her knowledge.

Whenever the children climbed on my knee, or laid their heads on my lap, she would say, "Poor little souls! what would you do without a mother? She don't love you as I do." And she would hug them to her own bosom, as if to reproach me for my want of affection; but she knew all the while that I loved them better than my life. I slept with her that night, and it was the last time. The memory of it haunted me for many a year.

On Monday I returned to the plantation, and busied myself with preparations for the important day. Wednesday came. It was a beautiful day, and the faces of the slaves were as bright as the sunshine. The poor creatures were merry. They were expecting little presents from the bride, and hoping for better times under her administration. I had no such hopes for them. I knew that the young wives of slaveholders often thought their authority and importance would be best established and maintained by cruelty; and what I had heard of young Mrs. Flint gave me no reason to expect that her rule over them would be less severe than that of the master and overseer. Truly, the colored race are the most cheerful and forgiving people on the face of the earth. That their masters sleep in safety is owing to their superabundance of heart; and yet they look upon their sufferings with less pity than they would bestow on those of a horse or a dog.

I stood at the door with others to receive the bridegroom and bride. She was a handsome, delicate-looking girl, and her face flushed with emotion at sight of her new home. I thought it likely that visions of a happy future were rising before her. It made me sad; for I knew how soon clouds would come over her sunshine. She examined

Notes

[114] *Original reads*: briug [ed.].

every part of the house, and told me she was delighted with the arrangements I had made. I was afraid old Mrs. Flint had tried to prejudice her against me, and I did my best to please her.

All passed off smoothly for me until dinner time arrived. I did not mind the embarrassment of waiting on a dinner party, for the first time in my life, half so much as I did the meeting with Dr. Flint and his wife, who would be among the guests. It was a mystery[115] to me why Mrs. Flint had not made her appearance at the plantation during all the time I was putting the house in order. I had not met her, face to face, for five years, and I had no wish to see her now. She was a praying woman, and, doubtless, considered my present position a special answer to her prayers. Nothing could please her better than to see me humbled and trampled upon. I was just where she would have me – in the power of a hard, unprincipled master. She did not speak to me when she took her seat at table; but her satisfied, triumphant smile, when I handed her plate, was more eloquent than words. The old doctor was not so quiet in his demonstrations. He ordered me here and there, and spoke with peculiar emphasis when he said "your *mistress*." I was drilled like a disgraced soldier. When all was over, and the last key turned, I sought my pillow, thankful that God had appointed a season of rest for the weary.

The next day my new mistress began her housekeeping. I was not exactly appointed maid of all work; but I was to do whatever I was told. Monday evening came. It was always a busy time. On that night the slaves received their weekly allowance of food. Three pounds of meat, a peck of corn, and perhaps a dozen herring were allowed to each man. Women received a pound and a half of meat, a peck of corn, and the same number of herring. Children over twelve years old had half the allowance of the women. The meat was cut and weighed by the foreman of the field hands, and piled on planks before the meat house. Then the second foreman went behind the building, and when the first foreman called out, "Who takes this piece of meat?" he answered by calling somebody's name. This method was resorted to as a means of preventing partiality in distributing the meat. The young mistress came out to see how things were done on her plantation, and she soon gave a specimen of her character. Among those in waiting for their allowance was a very old slave, who had faithfully served the Flint family through three generations. When he hobbled up to get his bit of meat, the mistress said he was too old to have any allowance; that when niggers were too old to work, they ought to be fed on grass. Poor old man! He suffered much before he found rest in the grave.

My mistress and I got along very well together. At the end of a week, old Mrs. Flint made us another visit, and was closeted a long time with her daughter-in-law. I had my suspicions what was the subject of the conference. The old doctor's wife had been informed that I could leave the plantation on one condition, and she was very desirous to keep me there. If she had trusted me, as I deserved to be trusted by her, she would have had no fears of my accepting that condition. When she entered her carriage to return home, she said to young Mrs. Flint, "Don't neglect to send for them as quick as possible." My heart was on the watch all the time, and I at once concluded that she spoke of my children. The doctor came the next day, and as I entered the room to spread the tea table, I heard him say, "Don't wait any longer. Send for them to-morrow." I saw through the plan. They thought my children's being there would fetter me to

Notes

[115] *mystery* See Mark 4:11, in which God promises to reveal all mysteries to his followers.

the spot, and that it was a good place to break us all in to abject submission to our lot as slaves. After the doctor left, a gentleman called, who had always manifested friendly feelings towards my grandmother and her family. Mr. Flint carried him over the plantation to show him the results of labor performed by men and women who were unpaid, miserably clothed, and half famished. The cotton crop was all they thought of. It was duly admired, and the gentleman returned with specimens to show his friends. I was ordered to carry water to wash his hands. As I did so, he said, "Linda, how do you like your new home?" I told him I liked it as well as I expected. He replied, "They don't think you are contented, and to-morrow they are going to bring your children to be with you. I am sorry for you, Linda. I hope they will treat you kindly." I hurried from the room, unable to thank him. My suspicions were correct. My children were to be brought to the plantation to be "broke in."

To this day I feel grateful to the gentleman who gave me this timely information. It nerved me to immediate action.

Chapter 17

The Flight

Mr. Flint was hard pushed for house servants, and rather than lose me he had restrained his malice. I did my work faithfully, though not, of course, with a willing mind. They were evidently afraid I should leave them. Mr. Flint wished that I should sleep in the great house instead of the servants' quarters. His wife agreed to the proposition, but said I mustn't bring my bed into the house, because it would scatter feathers on her carpet. I knew when I went there that they would never think of such a thing as furnishing a bed of any kind for me and my little one. I therefore carried my own bed, and now I was forbidden to use it. I did as I was ordered. But now that I was certain my children were to be put in their power, in order to give them a stronger hold on me, I resolved to leave them that night. I remembered the grief this step would bring upon my dear old grandmother; and nothing less than the freedom of my children would have induced me to disregard her advice. I went about my evening work with trembling steps. Mr. Flint twice called from his chamber door to inquire why the house was not locked up. I replied that I had not done my work. "You have had time enough to do it," said he. "Take care how you answer me!" I shut all the windows, locked all the doors, and went up to the third story, to wait till midnight. How long those hours seemed, and how fervently I prayed that God would not forsake me in this hour of utmost need! I was about to risk everything[116] on the throw of a die; and if I failed, O what would become of me and my poor children? They would be made to suffer for my fault.

At half past twelve I stole softly downstairs.[117] I stopped on the second floor, thinking I heard a noise. I felt my way down into the parlor, and looked out of the window. The night was so intensely dark that I could see nothing. I raised the window very softly and jumped out. Large drops of rain were falling, and the darkness bewildered me. I dropped on my knees, and breathed a short prayer to God for guidance and protection. I groped my way to the road, and rushed towards the town with almost lightning speed. I arrived at my grandmother s house, but dared not see her. She would say, "Linda, you are killing me"; and I knew that would unnerve me. I tapped softly at the

Notes

[116] *Original reads*: every thing [ed.].

[117] *Original reads*: down stairs [ed.].

window of a room, occupied by a woman, who had lived in the house several years. I knew she was a faithful friend, and could be trusted with my secret. I tapped several times before she heard me. At last she raised the window, and I whispered, "Sally, I have run away. Let me in, quick." She opened the door softly, and said in low tones, "For God's sake, don't. Your grandmother is trying to buy you and de chillern. Mr. Sands was here last week. He tole her he was going away on business, but he wanted her to go ahead about buying you and de chillern, and he would help her all he could. Don't run away, Linda. Your grandmother is all bowed down wid trouble now."

I replied, "Sally, they are going to carry my children to the plantation to-morrow; and they will never sell them to anybody[118] so long as they have me in their power. Now, would you advise me to go back?"

"No, chile, no," answered she. "When dey finds you is gone, dey won't want de plague ob de chillern; but where is you going to hide? Dey knows ebery inch ob dis house."

I told her I had a hiding-place, and that was all it was best for her to know. I asked her to go into my room as soon as it was light, and take all my clothes out of my trunk, and pack them in hers; for I knew Mr. Flint and the constable would be there early to search my room. I feared the sight of my children would be too much for my full heart; but I could not go out into the uncertain future without one last look. I bent over the bed where lay my little Benny and baby Ellen. Poor little ones! fatherless and motherless! Memories of their father came over me. He wanted to be kind to them; but they were not all to him, as they were to my womanly heart. I knelt and prayed for the innocent little sleepers. I kissed them lightly, and turned away.

As I was about to open the street door, Sally laid her hand on my shoulder, and said, "Linda, is you gwine all alone? Let me call your uncle."

"No, Sally," I replied, "I want no one to be brought into trouble on my account."

I went forth into the darkness and rain. I ran on till I came to the house of the friend who was to conceal me.

Early the next morning Mr. Flint was at my grandmother's inquiring for me. She told him she had not seen me, and supposed I was at the plantation. He watched her face narrowly, and said, "Don't you know anything[119] about her running off?" She assured him that she did not. He went on to say, "Last night she ran off without the least provocation. We had treated her very kindly. My wife liked her. She will soon be found and brought back. Are her children with you? "When told that they were, he said, "I am very glad to hear that. If they are here, she cannot be far off. If I find out that any of my niggers have had anything[120] to do with this damned business, I'll give 'em five hundred lashes." As he started to go to his father's, he turned round and added, persuasively, "Let her be brought back, and she shall have her children to live with her."

The tidings made the old doctor rave and storm at a furious rate. It was a busy day for them. My grandmother's house was searched from top to bottom. As my trunk was empty, they concluded I had taken my clothes with me. Before ten o'clock every vessel northward bound was thoroughly examined, and the law against harboring fugitives was read to all on board. At night a watch was set over the town. Knowing how distressed my grandmother would be, I wanted to send her a message; but it could not be done. Everyone[121] who went in or out of her house was closely watched. The doctor said he would take my children, unless she became responsible for them;

Notes

[118] *Original reads*: any body [ed.].

[119] *Original reads*: any thing [ed.].

[120] *Original reads*: any thing [ed.].

[121] *Original reads*: Every one [ed.].

which of course she willingly did. The next day was spent in searching. Before night, the following advertisement was posted at every corner, and in every public place for miles round:–

"$300 Reward! Ran away from the subscriber, an intelligent, bright, mulatto girl, named Linda, 21 years of age. Five feet four inches high. Dark eyes, and black hair inclined to curl; but it can be made straight. Has a decayed spot on a front tooth. She can read and write, and in all probability will try to get to the Free States. All persons are forbidden, under penalty of the law, to harbor or employ said slave. $150 will be given to whoever takes her in the state, and $300 if taken out of the state and delivered to me, or lodged in jail.

Dr. Flint."

Chapter 18

Months of Peril

The search for me was kept up with more perseverance[122] than I had anticipated. I began to think that escape was impossible. I was in great anxiety lest I should implicate the friend who harbored me. I knew the consequences would be frightful; and much as I dreaded being caught, even that seemed better than causing an innocent person to suffer for kindness to me. A week had passed in terrible suspense, when my pursuers came into such close vicinity that I concluded they had tracked me to my hiding-place. I flew out of the house, and concealed myself in a thicket of bushes. There I remained in an agony of fear for two hours. Suddenly, a reptile of some kind seized my leg. In my fright, I struck a blow which loosened its hold, but I could not tell whether I had killed it; it was so dark, I could not see what it was; I only knew it was something cold and slimy. The pain I felt soon indicated that the bite was poisonous. I was compelled to leave my place of concealment, and I groped my way back into the house. The pain had become intense, and my friend was startled by my look of anguish. I asked her to prepare a poultice of warm ashes and vinegar, and I applied it to my leg, which was already much swollen. The application gave me some relief, but the swelling did not abate. The dread of being disabled was greater than the physical pain I endured. My friend asked an old woman, who doctored among the slaves, what was good for the bite of a snake or a lizard. She told her to steep a dozen coppers in vinegar, overnight,[123] and apply the cankered vinegar to the inflamed part.*

I had succeeded[124] in cautiously conveying some messages to my relatives. They were harshly threatened, and despairing of my having a chance to escape, they advised me to return to my master, ask his forgiveness, and let him make an example of me. But such counsel had no influence with me. When I started upon this hazardous undertaking, I had resolved that, come what would, there should be no turning back. "Give me liberty, or give me death," was my motto.[125] When my friend contrived to

Notes

* The poison of a snake is a powerful acid, and is counteracted by powerful alkalies, such as potash, ammonia, &c. The Indians are accustomed to apply wet ashes, or plunge the limb into strong lye [*Original reads*: lie [ed.]]. White men, employed to lay out railroads in snaky places, often carry ammonia with them as an antidote. – Editor.

122 *Original reads*: perseverence [ed.].

123 *Original reads*: over night [ed.].

124 *Original reads*: succeded [ed.].

125 *my motto* from Patrick Henry's famous speech before the Virginia Convention in 1775.

make known to my relatives the painful situation I had been in for twenty-four hours, they said no more about my going back to my master. Something must be done, and that speedily; but where to turn for help, they knew not. God in his mercy raised up "a friend in need."

Among the ladies who were acquainted with my grandmother, was one who had known her from childhood and always been very friendly to her. She had also known my mother and her children, and felt interested for them. At this crisis of affairs she called to see my grandmother, as she not unfrequently did. She observed the sad and troubled expression of her face, and asked if she knew where Linda was, and whether she was safe. My grandmother shook her head, without answering. "Come, Aunt Martha," said the kind lady, "tell me all about it. Perhaps I can do something to help you." The husband of this lady held many slaves, and bought and sold slaves. She also held a number in her own name; but she treated them kindly, and would never allow any of them to be sold. She was unlike the majority of slaveholders' wives. My grandmother looked earnestly at her. Something in the expression of her face said "Trust me!" and she did trust her. She listened attentively to the details of my story, and sat thinking for a while. At last she said, "Aunt Martha, I pity you both. If you think there is any chance of Linda's getting to the Free States, I will conceal her for a time. But first you must solemnly promise that my name shall never be mentioned. If such a thing should become known, it would ruin me and my family. No one in my house must know of it, except the cook. She is so faithful that I would trust my own life with her; and I know she likes Linda. It is a great risk; but I trust no harm will come of it. Get word to Linda to be ready as soon as it is dark, before the patrols are out. I will send the housemaids on errands, and Betty shall go to meet Linda." The place where we were to meet was designated and agreed upon. My grandmother was unable to thank the lady for this noble deed; overcome by her emotions, she sank on her knees and sobbed like a child.

I received a message to leave my friend's house at such an hour, and go to a certain place where a friend would be waiting for me. As a matter of prudence no names were mentioned. I had no means of conjecturing who I was to meet, or where I was going. I did not like to move thus blindfolded, but I had no choice. It would not do for me to remain where I was. I disguised myself, summoned up courage to meet the worst, and went to the appointed place. My friend Betty was there; she was the last person I expected to see. We hurried along in silence. The pain in my leg was so intense that it seemed as if I should drop; but fear gave me strength. We reached the house and entered unobserved. Her first words were: "Honey, now you is safe. Dem devils ain't coming to search *dis* house. When I get you into missis' safe place, I will bring some nice hot supper. I specs you need it after all dis skeering." Betty's vocation led her to think eating the most important thing in life. She did not realize that my heart was too full for me to care much about supper.

The mistress came to meet us, and led me up stairs to a small room over her own sleeping apartment. "You will be safe here, Linda," said she; "I keep this room to store away things that are out of use. The girls are not accustomed to be sent to it, and they will not suspect anything[126] unless they hear some noise. I always keep it locked, and Betty shall take care of the key. But you must be very careful, for my sake as well as your own; and you must never tell my secret; for it would ruin me and my family. I will keep the girls busy in the morning, that Betty may have a chance to bring your

Notes

[126] *Original reads*: any thing [ed.].

breakfast; but it will not do for her to come to you again till night. I will come to see you sometimes. Keep up your courage. I hope this state of things will not last long." Betty came with the "nice hot supper," and the mistress hastened downstairs[127] to keep things straight till she returned. How my heart overflowed with gratitude! Words choked in my throat; but I could have kissed the feet of my benefactress. For that deed of Christian womanhood, may God forever bless her!

I went to sleep that night with the feeling that I was for the present the most fortunate slave in town. Morning came and filled my little cell with light. I thanked the heavenly Father for this safe retreat. Opposite my window was a pile of feather beds. On the top of these I could lie perfectly concealed, and command a view of the street through which Dr. Flint passed to his office. Anxious as I was, I felt a gleam of satisfaction when I saw him. Thus far I had outwitted him, and I triumphed over it. Who can blame slaves for being cunning? They are constantly compelled to resort to it. It is the only weapon of the weak and oppressed against the strength of their tyrants.

I was daily hoping to hear that my master had sold my children; for I knew who was on the watch to buy them. But Dr. Flint cared even more for revenge than he did for money. My brother William, and the good aunt who had served in his family twenty years, and my little Benny, and Ellen, who was a little over two years old, were thrust into jail, as a means of compelling my relatives to give some information about me. He swore my grandmother should never see one of them again till I was brought back. They kept these facts from me for several days. When I heard that my little ones were in a loathsome jail, my first impulse was to go to them. I was encountering dangers for the sake of freeing them, and must I be the cause of their death? The thought was agonizing. My benefactress tried to soothe me by telling me that my aunt would take good care of the children while they remained in jail. But it added to my pain to think that the good old aunt, who had always been so kind to her sister's orphan children, should be shut up in prison for no other crime than loving them. I suppose my friends feared a reckless movement on my part, knowing, as they did, that my life was bound up in my children. I received a note from my brother William. It was scarcely legible, and ran thus: "Wherever you are, dear sister, I beg of you not to come here. We are all much better off than you are. If you come, you will ruin us all. They would force you to tell where you had been, or they would kill you. Take the advice of your friends; if not for the sake of me and your children, at least for the sake of those you would ruin."

Poor William! He also must suffer for being my brother. I took his advice and kept quiet. My aunt was taken out of jail at the end of a month, because Mrs. Flint could not spare her any longer. She was tired of being her own housekeeper. It was quite too fatiguing to order her dinner and eat it too. My children remained in jail, where brother William did all he could for their comfort. Betty went to see them sometimes, and brought me tidings. She was not permitted to enter the jail; but William would hold them up to the grated window while she chatted with them. When she repeated their prattle, and told me how they wanted to see their ma, my tears would flow. Old Betty would exclaim, "Lors, chile! what's you *crying* 'bout? Dem young uns vil kill you dead. Don't be so chick'n hearted! If you does, you vil nebber git thro' dis world."

Good old soul! She had gone through the world childless. She had never had little ones to clasp their arms round her neck; she had never seen their soft eyes looking into hers; no sweet little voices had called her mother; she had never pressed her own infants to her heart, with the feeling that even in fetters there was something to live for.

Notes

[127] *Original reads*: down stairs [ed.].

How could she realize my feelings? Betty's husband loved children dearly, and wondered why God had denied them to him. He expressed great sorrow when he came to Betty with the tidings that Ellen had been taken out of jail and carried to Dr. Flint's. She had the measles a short time before they carried her to jail, and the disease had left her eyes affected. The doctor had taken her home to attend to them. My children had always been afraid of the doctor and his wife. They had never been inside of their house. Poor little Ellen cried all day to be carried back to prison. The instincts of childhood are true. She knew she was loved in the jail. Her screams and sobs annoyed Mrs. Flint. Before night she called one of the slaves, and said, "Here, Bill, carry this brat back to the jail. I can't stand her noise. If she would be quiet I should like to keep the little minx. She would make a handy waiting-maid for my daughter by and by. But if she staid here, with her white face, I suppose I should either kill her or spoil her. I hope the doctor will sell them as far as wind and water can carry them. As for their mother, her ladyship will find out yet what she gets by running away. She hasn't so much feeling for her children as a cow has for its calf. If she had, she would have come back long ago, to get them out of jail, and save all this expense and trouble. The good-for-nothing hussy! When she is caught, she shall stay in jail, in irons, for one six months, and then be sold to a sugar plantation. I shall see her broke in yet. What do you stand there for, Bill? Why don't you go off with the brat? Mind, now, that you don't let any of the niggers speak to her in the street!"

When these remarks were reported to me, I smiled at Mrs. Flint's saying that she should either kill my child or spoil her. I thought to myself there was very little danger of the latter. I have always considered it as one of God's special providences that Ellen screamed till she was carried back to jail.

That same night Dr. Flint was called to a patient, and did not return till near morning. Passing my grandmother's, he saw a light in the house, and thought to himself, "Perhaps this has something to do with Linda." He knocked, and the door was opened. "What calls you up so early?" said he. "I saw your light, and I thought I would just stop and tell you that I have found out where Linda is. I know where to put my hands on her, and I shall have her before twelve o'clock." When he had turned away, my grandmother and my uncle looked anxiously at each other. They did not know whether or not it was merely one of the doctor's tricks to frighten them. In their uncertainty, they thought it was best to have a message conveyed to my friend Betty. Unwilling to alarm her mistress, Betty resolved to dispose of me herself. She came to me, and told me to rise and dress quickly. We hurried downstairs,[128] and across the yard, into the kitchen. She locked the door, and lifted up a plank in the floor. A buffalo skin and a bit of carpet were spread for me to lie on, and a quilt thrown over me. "Stay dar," said she, "till I sees if dey know 'bout you. Dey say dey vil put thar hans on you afore twelve o'clock. If dey *did* know whar you are, dey won't know *now*. Dey'll be disapinted dis time. Dat's all I got to say. If dey comes rummagin 'mong *my* tings, dey'll get one bressed sarssin from dis 'ere nigger." In my shallow bed I had but just room enough to bring my hands to my face to keep the dust out of my eyes; for Betty walked over me twenty times in an hour, passing from the dresser to the fireplace. When she was alone, I could hear her pronouncing anathemas over Dr. Flint and all his tribe, every now and then saying, with a chuckling laugh, "Dis nigger's too cute for 'em dis time." When the housemaids were about, she had sly ways of drawing them out, that I might hear what they would say. She would repeat stories she had heard about my being in this, or that, or the other place. To which

Notes

[128] *Original reads*: down stairs [ed.].

they would answer, that I was not fool enough to be staying round there; that I was in Philadelphia or New York before this time. When all were abed and asleep, Betty raised the plank, and said, "Come out, chile; come out. Dey don't know nottin 'bout you. 'Twas only white folks' lies, to skeer de niggers." Some days after this adventure I had a much worse fright. As I sat very still in my retreat above stairs, cheerful visions floated through my mind. I thought Dr. Flint would soon get discouraged, and would be willing to sell my children, when he lost all hopes of making them the means of my discovery. I knew who was ready to buy them. Suddenly I heard a voice that chilled my blood. The sound was too familiar to me, it had been too dreadful for me not to recognize at once my old master. He was in the house, and I at once concluded he had come to seize me. I looked round in terror. There was no way of escape. The voice receded. I supposed the constable was with him, and they were searching the house. In my alarm I did not forget the trouble I was bringing on my generous benefactress. It seemed as if I were born to bring sorrow on all who befriended me, and that was the bitterest drop in the bitter cup of my life. After a while I heard approaching footsteps; the key was turned in my door. I braced myself against the wall to keep from falling. I ventured to look up, and there stood my kind benefactress alone. I was too much overcome to speak, and sunk down upon the floor.

"I thought you would hear your master's voice," she said; "and knowing you would be terrified, I came to tell you there is nothing to fear. You may even indulge in a laugh at the old gentleman's expense. He is so sure you are in New York, that he came to borrow five hundred dollars to go in pursuit of you. My sister had some money to loan on interest. He has obtained it, and proposes to start for New York to-night. So, for the present, you see you are safe. The doctor will merely lighten his pocket hunting after the bird he has left behind."

Chapter 19

The Children Sold

The doctor came back from New York, of course without accomplishing his purpose. He had expended considerable money, and was rather disheartened. My brother and the children had now been in jail two months, and that also was some expense. My friends thought it was a favorable time to work on his discouraged feelings. Mr. Sands sent a speculator to offer him nine hundred dollars for my brother William, and eight hundred for the two children. These were high prices, as slaves were then selling; but the offer was rejected. If it had been merely a question of money, the doctor would have sold any boy of Benny's age for two hundred dollars; but he could not bear to give up the power of revenge. But he was hard pressed for money, and he revolved the matter in his mind. He knew that if he could keep Ellen till she was fifteen, he could sell her for a high price; but I presume he reflected that she might die, or might be stolen away. At all events, he came to the conclusion that he had better accept the slave-trader's offer. Meeting him in the street, he inquired when he would leave town. "To-day, at ten o'clock," he replied. "Ah, do you go so soon?" said the doctor; "I have been reflecting upon your proposition, and I have concluded to let you have the three negroes if you will say nineteen hundred dollars." After some parley, the trader agreed to his terms. He wanted the bill of sale drawn up and signed immediately, as he had a great deal to attend to during the short time he remained in town. The doctor went to the jail and told William he would take him back into his service if he would promise to behave himself; but he replied that he would rather be sold.

"And you *shall* be sold, you ungrateful rascal!" exclaimed the doctor. In less than an hour the money was paid, the papers were signed, sealed, and delivered, and my brother and children were in the hands of the trader.

It was a hurried transaction; and after it was over, the doctor's characteristic caution returned. He went back to the speculator, and said, "Sir, I have come to lay you under obligations of a thousand dollars not to sell any of those negroes in this state." "You come too late," replied the trader; "our bargain is closed." He had, in fact, already sold them to Mr. Sands, but he did not mention it. The doctor required him to put irons on "that rascal, Bill," and to pass through the back streets when he took his gang out of town. The trader was privately instructed to concede to his wishes. My good old aunt went to the jail to bid the children goodbye,[129] supposing them to be the speculator's property, and that she should never see them again. As she held Benny in her lap, he said, "Aunt Nancy, I want to show you something." He led her to the door and showed her a long row of marks, saying, "Uncle Will taught me to count. I have made a mark for every day I have been here, and it is sixty days. It is a long time; and the speculator is going to take me and Ellen away. He's a bad man. It's wrong for him to take grandmother's children. I want to go to my mother."

My grandmother was told that the children would be restored to her, but she was requested to act as if they were really to be sent away. Accordingly, she made up a bundle of clothes and went to the jail. When she arrived, she found William handcuffed among the gang, and the children in the trader's cart. The scene seemed too much like reality. She was afraid there might have been some deception or mistake. She fainted, and was carried home.

When the wagon stopped at the hotel, several gentlemen came out and proposed to purchase William, but the trader refused their offers, without stating that he was already sold. And now came the trying hour for that drove of human beings, driven away like cattle, to be sold they knew not where. Husbands were torn from wives, parents from children, never to look upon each other again this side the grave. There was wringing of hands and cries of despair.

Dr. Flint had the supreme satisfaction of seeing the wagon leave town, and Mrs. Flint had the gratification of supposing that my children were going "as far as wind and water would carry them." According to agreement, my uncle followed the wagon some miles, until they came to an old farm house. There the trader took the irons from William, and as he did so, he said, "You are a damned clever fellow. I should like to own you myself. Them gentlemen that wanted to buy you said you was a bright, honest chap, and I must git you a good home. I guess your old master will swear tomorrow, and call himself an old fool for selling the children. I reckon he'll never git their mammy back agin. I expect she's made tracks for the north. Goodbye,[130] old boy. Remember, I have done you a good turn. You must thank me by coaxing all the pretty gals to go with me next fall. That's going to be my last trip. This trading in niggers is a bad business for a fellow that's got any heart. Move on, you fellows!" And the gang went on, God alone knows where.

Much as I despise and detest the class of slave-traders, whom I regard as the vilest wretches on earth, I must do this man the justice to say that he seemed to have some feeling. He took a fancy to William in the jail, and wanted to buy him. When he heard the story of my children, he was willing to aid them in getting out of Dr. Flint's power, even without charging the customary fee.

Notes

[129] *Original reads*: good by [ed.].

[130] *Original reads*: Good by [ed.].

My uncle procured a wagon and carried William and the children back to town. Great was the joy in my grandmother's house! The curtains were closed, and the candles lighted. The happy grandmother cuddled the little ones to her bosom. They hugged her, and kissed her, and clapped their hands, and shouted. She knelt down and poured forth one of her heartfelt prayers of thanksgiving to God. The father was present for a while; and though such a "parental relation" as existed between him and my children takes slight hold of the hearts or consciences of slaveholders, it must be that he experienced some moments of pure joy in witnessing the happiness he had imparted.

I had no share in the rejoicings of that evening. The events of the day had not come to my knowledge. And now I will tell you something that happened to me; though you will, perhaps, think it illustrates the superstition of slaves. I sat in my usual place on the floor near the window, where I could hear much that was said in the street without being seen. The family had retired for the night, and all was still. I sat there thinking of my children, when I heard a low strain of music. A band of serenaders were under the window, playing "Home, sweet home."[131] I listened till the sounds did not seem like music, but like the moaning of children. It seemed as if my heart would burst. I rose from my sitting posture, and knelt. A streak of moonlight was on the floor before me, and in the midst of it appeared the forms of my two children. They vanished; but I had seen them distinctly. Some will call it a dream, others a vision. I know not how to account for it, but it made a strong impression on my mind, and I felt certain something had happened to my little ones.

I had not seen Betty since morning. Now I heard her softly turning the key. As soon as she entered, I clung to her, and begged her to let me know whether my children were dead, or whether they were sold; for I had seen their spirits in my room, and I was sure something had happened to them. "Lor, chile," said she, putting her arms round me, "you's got de highsterics. I'll sleep wid you to-night, 'cause you'll make a noise, and ruin missis. Something has stirred you up mightily. When you is done cryin, I'll talk wid you. De chillern is well, and mighty happy. I seed 'em myself. Does dat satisfy you? Dar, chile, be still! Somebody vill hear you." I tried to obey her. She lay down, and was soon sound asleep; but no sleep would come to my eyelids.

At dawn, Betty was up and off to the kitchen. The hours passed on, and the vision of the night kept constantly recurring to my thoughts. After a while I heard the voices of two women in the entry. In one of them I recognized the housemaid. The other said to her, "Did you know Linda Brent's children was sold to the speculator yesterday. They say ole massa Flint was mighty glad to see 'em drove out of town; but they say they've come back agin. I 'spect it's all their daddy's doings. They say he's bought William too. Lor! how it will take hold of ole massa Flint! I'm going roun' to Aunt[132] Marthy's to see 'bout it."

I bit my lips till the blood came to keep from crying out. Were my children with their grandmother, or had the speculator carried them off? The suspense was dreadful. Would Betty *never* come, and tell me the truth about it? At last she came, and I eagerly repeated what I had overheard. Her face was one broad, bright smile. "Lor, you foolish ting!" said she. "I'se gwine to tell you all 'bout it. De gals is eating thar breakfast, and missus tole me to let her tell you; but, poor creeter! t'aint right to keep you waitin', and I'se gwine to tell you. Brudder, chillern, all is bought by de daddy! I'se laugh more dan

Notes

[131] *"Home, sweet home"* from the opera *Clari; or, The Maid of Milan* (1823) by John Payne (1791–1852).

[132] *Original reads*: aunt [ed.].

nuff, tinking 'bout ole massa Flint. Lor, how he *vill* swar! He's got ketched dis time, anyhow;[133] but I must be getting out o' dis, or dem gals vill come and ketch *me*."

Betty went off laughing; and I said to myself, "Can it be true that my children are free? I have not suffered for them in vain. Thank God!"

Great surprise was expressed when it was known that my children had returned to their grandmother's. The news spread through the town, and many a kind word was bestowed on the little ones.

Dr. Flint went to my grandmother's to ascertain who was the owner of my children, and she informed him. "I expected as much," said he. "I am glad to hear it. I have had news from Linda lately, and I shall soon have her. You need never expect to see *her* free. She shall be my slave as long as I live, and when I am dead she shall be the slave of my children. If I ever find out that you or Phillip had anything[134] to do with her running off I'll kill him. And if I meet William in the street, and he presumes to look at me, I'll flog him within an inch of his life. Keep those brats out of my sight!"

As he turned to leave, my grandmother said something to remind him of his own doings. He looked back upon her, as if he would have been glad to strike her to the ground.

I had my season of joy and thanksgiving. It was the first time since my childhood that I had experienced any real happiness. I heard of the old doctor's threats, but they no longer had the same power to trouble me. The darkest cloud that hung over my life had rolled away. Whatever slavery might do to me, it could not shackle my children. If I fell a sacrifice, my little ones were saved. It was well for me that my simple heart believed all that had been promised for their welfare. It is always better to trust than to doubt.

Chapter 20

New Perils

The doctor, more exasperated than ever, again tried to revenge himself on my relatives. He arrested Uncle[135] Phillip on the charge of having aided my flight. He was carried before a court, and swore truly that he knew nothing of my intention to escape, and that he had not seen me since I left my master's plantation. The doctor then demanded that he should give bail for five hundred dollars that he would have nothing to do with me. Several gentlemen offered to be security for him; but Mr. Sands told him he had better go back to jail, and he would see that he came out without giving bail.

The news of his arrest was carried to my grandmother, who conveyed it to Betty. In the kindness of her heart, she again stowed me away under the floor; and as she walked back and forth, in the performance of her culinary duties, she talked apparently to herself, but with the intention that I should hear what was going on. I hoped that my uncle's imprisonment would last but few days; still I was anxious. I thought it likely Dr. Flint would do his utmost to taunt and insult him, and I was afraid my uncle might lose control of himself, and retort in some way that would be construed into a punishable offence; and I was well aware that in court his word would not be taken against any

Notes

[133] *Original reads*: any how [ed.].

[134] *Original reads*: any thing [ed.].

[135] *Original reads*: uncle [ed.].

white man's. The search for me was renewed. Something had excited suspicions that I was in the vicinity. They searched the house I was in. I heard their steps and their voices. At night, when all were asleep, Betty came to release me from my place of confinement. The fright I had undergone, the constrained posture, and the dampness of the ground, made me ill for several days. My uncle was soon after taken out of prison; but the movements of all my relatives, and of all our friends, were very closely watched.

We all saw that I could not remain where I was much longer. I had already staid longer than was intended, and I knew my presence must be a source of perpetual anxiety to my kind benefactress. During this time, my friends had laid many plans for my escape, but the extreme vigilance of my persecutors made it impossible to carry them into effect.

One morning I was much startled by hearing somebody trying to get into my room. Several keys were tried, but none fitted. I instantly conjectured it was one of the housemaids; and I concluded she must either have heard some noise in the room, or have noticed the entrance of Betty. When my friend came, at her usual time, I told her what had happened. "I knows who it was," said she. "'Pend upon it, 'twas dat Jenny. Dat nigger allers got de debble in her." I suggested that she might have seen or heard something that excited her curiosity.

"Tut! tut! chile!" exclaimed Betty, "she ain't seen notin', nor hearn notin'. She only 'spects someting. Dat's all. She wants to fine out who hab cut and make my gownd.[136] But she won't nebber know. Dat's sartin. I'll git missis to fix her."

I reflected a moment, and said, "Betty, I must leave here to-night."

"Do as you tink best, poor chile," she replied. "I'se mighty 'fraid dat 'ere nigger vill pop on you some time."

She reported the incident to her mistress, and received orders to keep Jenny busy in the kitchen till she could see my Uncle[137] Phillip. He told her he would send a friend for me that very evening. She told him she hoped I was going to the north, for it was very dangerous for me to remain anywhere[138] in the vicinity. Alas, it was not an easy thing, for one in my situation, to go to the north. In order to leave the coast quite clear for me, she went into the country to spend the day with her brother, and took Jenny with her. She was afraid to come and bid me goodbye,[139] but she left a kind message with Betty. I heard her carriage roll from the door, and I never again saw her who had so generously befriended the poor, trembling fugitive! Though she was a slaveholder, to this day my heart blesses her!

I had not the slightest idea where I was going. Betty brought me a suit of sailor's clothes – jacket, trowsers, and tarpaulin hat. She gave me a small bundle, saying I might need it where I was going. In cheery tones, she exclaimed, "I'se *so* glad you is gwine to free parts! Don't forget ole Betty. P'raps I'll come 'long by and by."

I tried to tell her how grateful I felt for all her kindness, but she interrupted me. "I don't want no tanks, honey. I'se glad I could help you, and I hope de good Lord vill open de path for you. I'se gwine wid you to de lower gate. Put your hands in your pockets, and walk ricketty, like de sailors."

I performed to her satisfaction. At the gate I found Peter, a young colored man, waiting for me. I had known him for years. He had been an apprentice to my father, and had always borne a good character. I was not afraid to trust to him. Betty bade me a hurried goodbye,[140] and we walked off. "Take courage, Linda," said my friend Peter. "I've got a dagger, and no man shall take you from me, unless he passes over my dead body."

Notes

[136] *who hab cut and make my gownd* what I'm up to.

[137] *Original reads*: uncle [ed.].

[138] *Original reads*: any where [ed.].

[139] *Original reads*: good by [ed.].

[140] *Original reads*: good by [ed.].

It was a long time since I had taken a walk out of doors, and the fresh air revived me. It was also pleasant to hear a human voice speaking to me above a whisper. I passed several people whom I knew, but they did not recognize me in my disguise. I prayed internally that, for Peter's sake, as well as my own, nothing might occur to bring out his dagger. We walked on till we came to the wharf. My Aunt[141] Nancy's husband was a seafaring man, and it had been deemed necessary to let him into our secret. He took me into his boat, rowed out to a vessel not far distant, and hoisted me on board. We three were the only occupants of the vessel. I now ventured to ask what they proposed to do with me. They said I was to remain on board till near dawn, and then they would hide me in Snaky Swamp,[142] till my Uncle[143] Phillip had prepared a place of concealment for me. If the vessel had been bound north, it would have been of no avail to me, for it would certainly have been searched. About four o'clock, we were again seated in the boat, and rowed three miles to the swamp. My fear of snakes had been increased by the venomous bite I had received, and I dreaded to enter this hiding-place. But I was in no situation to choose, and I gratefully accepted the best that my poor, persecuted friends could do for me.

Peter landed first, and with a large knife cut a path through bamboos and briers of all descriptions. He came back, took me in his arms, and carried me to a seat made among the bamboos. Before we reached it, we were covered with hundreds of mosquitos. In an hour's time they had so poisoned my flesh that I was a pitiful sight to behold. As the light increased, I saw snake after snake crawling round us. I had been accustomed to the sight of snakes all my life, but these were larger than any I had ever seen. To this day I shudder when I remember that morning. As evening approached, the number of snakes increased so much that we were continually obliged to thrash them with sticks to keep them from crawling over us. The bamboos were so high and so thick that it was impossible to see beyond a very short distance. Just before it became dark we procured a seat nearer to the entrance of the swamp, being fearful of losing our way back to the boat. It was not long before we heard the paddle of oars, and the low whistle, which had been agreed upon as a signal. We made haste to enter the boat, and were rowed back to the vessel. I passed a wretched night; for the heat of the swamp, the mosquitos, and the constant terror of snakes, had brought on a burning fever. I had just dropped asleep, when they came and told me it was time to go back to that horrid swamp. I could scarcely summon courage to rise. But even those large, venomous snakes were less dreadful to my imagination than the white men in that community called civilized. This time Peter took a quantity of tobacco to burn, to keep off the mosquitos. It produced the desired effect on them, but gave me nausea and severe headache. At dark we returned to the vessel. I had been so sick during the day, that Peter declared I should go home that night, if the devil himself was on patrol. They told me a place of concealment had been provided for me at my grandmother's. I could not imagine how it was possible to hide me in her house, every nook and corner of which was known to the Flint family. They told me to wait and see. We were rowed ashore, and went boldly through the streets, to my grandmother's. I wore my sailor's clothes, and had blackened my face with charcoal. I passed several people

Notes

[141] *Original reads*: aunt [ed.].

[142] *Snaky Swamp* Cabarrus Pocosin, a swamp measuring about 10 miles wide and 30 miles long and running from Virginia to North Carolina.

[143] *Original reads*: uncle [ed.].

whom I knew. The father of my children came so near that I brushed against his arm; but he had no idea who it was.

"You must make the most of this walk," said my friend Peter, "for you may not have another very soon."

I thought his voice sounded sad. It was kind of him to conceal from me what a dismal hole was to be my home for a long, long time.

Chapter 21

The Loophole of Retreat[144]

A SMALL shed had been added to my grandmother's house years ago. Some boards were laid across the joists at the top, and between these boards and the roof was a very small garret,[145] never occupied by anything[146] but rats and mice. It was a pent roof, covered with nothing but shingles, according to the southern custom for such buildings. The garret was only nine feet long and seven wide. The highest part was three feet high, and sloped down abruptly to the loose board floor. There was no admission for either light or air. My Uncle[147] Philip, who was a carpenter, had very skilfully made a concealed trap-door, which communicated with the storeroom. He had been doing this while I was waiting in the swamp. The storeroom opened upon a piazza. To this hole I was conveyed as soon as I entered the house. The air was stifling; the darkness total. A bed had been spread on the floor. I could sleep quite comfortably on one side; but the slope was so sudden that I could not turn on the other without hitting the roof. The rats and mice ran over my bed; but I was weary, and I slept such sleep as the wretched may, when a tempest has passed over them. Morning came. I knew it only by the noises I heard; for in my small den day and night were all the same. I suffered for air even more than for light. But I was not comfortless. I heard the voices of my children. There was joy and there was sadness in the sound. It made my tears flow. How I longed to speak to them! I was eager to look on their faces; but there was no hole, no crack, through which I could peep. This continued darkness was oppressive. It seemed horrible to sit or lie in a cramped position day after day, without one gleam of light. Yet I would have chosen this, rather than my lot as a slave, though white people considered it an easy one; and it was so compared with the fate of others. I was never cruelly overworked; I was never lacerated with the whip from head to foot; I was never so beaten and bruised that I could not turn from one side to the other; I never had my heel-strings cut to prevent my running away; I was never chained to a log and forced to drag it about, while I toiled in the fields from morning till night; I was never branded with hot iron, or torn by bloodhounds. On the contrary, I had always been kindly treated, and tenderly cared for, until I came into the hands of Dr. Flint. I had never wished for freedom till then. But though my life in slavery was comparatively devoid of hardships, God pity the woman who is compelled to lead such a life!

My food was passed up to me through the trap-door my uncle had contrived; and my grandmother, my Uncle[148] Phillip, and Aunt[149] Nancy would seize such opportunities as they could, to mount up there and chat with me at the opening. But of course this was

Notes

[144] *loophole of retreat* a reference to *The Task* (1785) by English poet William Cowper (1731–1800).

[145] *garret* attic.

[146] *Original reads*: any thing [ed.].

[147] *Original reads*: uncle [ed.].

[148] *Original reads*: uncle [ed.].

[149] *Original reads*: aunt [ed.].

not safe in the daytime. It must all be done in darkness. It was impossible for me to move in an erect position, but I crawled about my den for exercise. One day I hit my head against something, and found it was a gimlet.[150] My uncle had left it sticking there when he made the trap-door. I was as rejoiced as Robinson Crusoe[151] could have been at finding such a treasure. It put a lucky thought into my head. I said to myself, "Now I will have some light. Now I will see my children." I did not dare to begin my work during the daytime, for fear of attracting attention. But I groped round; and having found the side next to the street,[152] where I could frequently see my children, I stuck the gimlet in and waited for evening. I bored three rows of holes, one above another; then I bored out the interstices between. I thus succeeded in making one hole about an inch long and an inch broad. I sat by it till late into the night, to enjoy the little whiff of air that floated in. In the morning I watched for my children. The first person I saw in the street was Dr. Flint. I had a shuddering, superstitious feeling that it was a bad omen. Several familiar faces passed by. At last I heard the merry laugh of children, and presently two sweet little faces were looking up at me, as though they knew I was there, and were conscious of the joy they imparted. How I longed to *tell* them I was there!

My condition was now a little improved. But for weeks I was tormented by hundreds of little red insects, fine as a needle's point, that pierced through my skin, and produced an intolerable burning. The good grandmother gave me herb teas and cooling medicines, and finally I got rid of them. The heat of my den was intense, for nothing but thin shingles protected me from the scorching summer's sun. But I had my consolations. Through my peeping-hole I could watch the children, and when they were near enough, I could hear their talk. Aunt Nancy brought me all the news she could hear at Dr. Flint's. From her I learned that the doctor had written to New York to a colored woman, who had been born and raised in our neighborhood, and had breathed his contaminating atmosphere. He offered her a reward if she could find out anything[153] about me. I know not what was the nature of her reply; but he soon after started for New York in haste, saying to his family that he had business of importance to transact. I peeped at him as he passed on his way to the steamboat. It was a satisfaction to have miles of land and water between us, even for a little while; and it was a still greater satisfaction to know that he believed me to be in the Free States. My little den seemed less dreary than it had done. He returned, as he did from his former journey to New York, without obtaining any satisfactory information. When he passed our house next morning, Benny was standing at the gate. He had heard them say that he had gone to find me, and he called out, "Dr. Flint, did you bring my mother home? I want to see her." The doctor stamped his foot at him in a rage, and exclaimed, "Get out of the way, you little damned rascal! If you don't, I'll cut off your head."

Benny ran terrified into the house, saying, "You can't put me in jail again. I don't belong to you now." It was well that the wind carried the words away from the doctor's ear. I told my grandmother of it, when we had our next conference at the trap-door; and begged of her not to allow the children to be impertinent to the irascible[154] old man.

Autumn came, with a pleasant abatement of heat. My eyes had become accustomed to the dim light, and by holding my book or work in a certain position near the aperture I contrived to read and sew. That was a great relief to the tedious monotony of

Notes

[150] *gimlet* a tool used for boring holes.

[151] *Robinson Crusoe* reference to Daniel Defoe's eponymous protagonist and castaway (1719).

[152] *Original reads*: next the street [ed.].

[153] *Original reads*: any thing [ed.].

[154] *irascible* hot-tempered.

my life. But when winter came, the cold penetrated through the thin shingle roof, and I was dreadfully chilled. The winters there are not so long, or so severe, as in northern latitudes; but the houses are not built to shelter from cold, and my little den was peculiarly comfortless. The kind grandmother brought me bed-clothes and warm drinks. Often I was obliged to lie in bed all day to keep comfortable; but with all my precautions, my shoulders and feet were frostbitten. O, those long, gloomy days, with no object for my eye to rest upon, and no thoughts to occupy my mind, except the dreary past and the uncertain future! I was thankful when there came a day sufficiently mild for me to wrap myself up and sit at the loophole to watch the passers-by. Southerners have the habit of stopping and talking in the streets, and I heard many conversations not intended to meet my ears. I heard slave-hunters planning how to catch some poor fugitive. Several times I heard allusions to Dr. Flint, myself, and the history of my children, who, perhaps, were playing near the gate. One would say, "I wouldn't move my little finger to catch her, as old Flint's property." Another would say, "I'll catch *any* nigger for the reward. A man ought to have what belongs to him, if he *is* a damned brute." The opinion was often expressed that I was in the Free States. Very rarely did anyone[155] suggest that I might be in the vicinity. Had the least suspicion rested on my grandmother's house, it would have been burned to the ground. But it was the last place they thought of. Yet there was no place, where slavery existed, that could have afforded me so good a place of concealment.

Dr. Flint and his family repeatedly tried to coax and bribe my children to tell something they had heard said about me. One day the doctor took them into a shop, and offered them some bright little silver pieces and gay handkerchiefs if they would tell where their mother was. Ellen shrank away from him, and would not speak; but Benny spoke up, and said, "Dr. Flint, I don't know where my mother is. I guess she's in New York; and when you go there again, I wish you'd ask her to come home, for I want to see her; but if you put her in jail, or tell her you'll cut her head off, I'll tell her to go right back."

Chapter 22

Christmas Festivities

Christmas was approaching. Grandmother brought me materials, and I busied myself making some new garments and little playthings for my children. Were it not that hiring day is near at hand, and many families are fearfully looking forward to the probability of separation in a few days, Christmas might be a happy season for the poor slaves. Even slave mothers try to gladden the hearts of their little ones on that occasion. Benny and Ellen had their Christmas stockings filled. Their imprisoned mother could not have the privilege of witnessing their surprise and joy. But I had the pleasure of peeping at them as they went into the street with their new suits on. I heard Benny ask a little playmate whether Santa Claus brought him anything.[156] "Yes," replied the boy; "but Santa Claus ain't a real man. It's the children's mothers that put things into the stockings." "No, that can't be," replied Benny, "for Santa Claus brought Ellen and me these new clothes, and my mother has been gone this long time."

Notes

[155] *Original reads*: any one [ed.].

[156] *Original reads*: any thing [ed.].

How I longed to tell him that his mother made those garments, and that many a tear fell on them while she worked!

Every child rises early on Christmas morning to see the Johnkannaus.[157] Without them, Christmas would be shorn of its greatest attraction. They consist of companies of slaves from the plantations, generally of the lower class. Two athletic men, in calico wrappers, have a net thrown over them, covered with all manner of bright-colored stripes. Cows' tails are fastened to their backs, and their heads are decorated with horns. A box, covered with sheepskin, is called the gumbo box. A dozen beat on this, while others strike triangles and jawbones, to which bands of dancers keep time. For a month previous they are composing songs, which are sung on this occasion. These companies, of a hundred each, turn out early in the morning, and are allowed to go round till twelve o'clock, begging for contributions. Not a door is left unvisited where there is the least chance of obtaining a penny or a glass of rum. They do not drink while they are out, but carry the rum home in jugs, to have a carousal.[158] These Christmas donations frequently amount to twenty or thirty dollars. It is seldom that any white man or child refuses to give them a trifle. If he does, they regale his ears with the following song:–

"Poor massa, so dey say;
  Down in de heel, so dey say;
Got no money, so dey say;
  Not one shillin, so dey say;
God A'mighty bress you, so dey say."

Christmas is a day of feasting, both with white and colored people. Slaves who are lucky enough to have a few shillings are sure to spend them for good eating; and many a turkey and pig is captured, without saying, "By your leave, sir." Those who cannot obtain these, cook a 'possum, or a raccoon, from which savory dishes can be made. My grandmother raised poultry and pigs for sale; and it was her established custom to have both a turkey and a pig roasted for Christmas dinner.

On this occasion, I was warned to keep extremely quiet, because two guests had been invited. One was the town constable, and the other was a free colored man, who tried to pass himself off for white, and who was always ready to do any mean work for the sake of currying favor with white people. My grandmother had a motive for inviting them. She managed to take them all over the house. All the rooms on the lower floor were thrown open for them to pass in and out; and after dinner, they were invited upstairs[159] to look at a fine mocking bird my uncle had just brought home. There, too, the rooms were all thrown open, that they might look in. When I heard them talking on the piazza, my heart almost stood still. I knew this colored man had spent many nights hunting for me. Everybody[160] knew he had the blood of a slave father in his veins; but for the sake of passing himself off for white, he was ready to kiss the slaveholders' feet. How I despised him! As for the constable, he wore no false colors. The duties of his office were despicable, but he was superior to his companion, inasmuch as he did not pretend to be what he was not. Any white man, who could raise money enough to buy a slave, would have considered himself degraded by being a constable;

Notes

[157] *Johnkannaus* a West African carnival celebration and masquerade.

[158] *carousal* a drunken party.

[159] *Original reads*: up stairs [ed.].

[160] *Original reads*: Every body [ed.].

but the office enabled its possessor to exercise authority. If he found any slave out after nine o'clock, he could whip him as much as he liked; and that was a privilege to be coveted. When the guests were ready to depart, my grandmother gave each of them some of her nice pudding, as a present for their wives. Through my peep-hole I saw them go out of the gate, and I was glad when it closed after them. So passed the first Christmas in my den.

Chapter 23

Still in Prison

When spring returned, and I took in the little patch of green the aperture commanded, I asked myself how many more summers and winters I must be condemned to spend thus. I longed to draw in a plentiful draught of fresh air, to stretch my cramped limbs, to have room to stand erect, to feel the earth under my feet again. My relatives were constantly on the lookout for a chance of escape; but none offered that seemed practicable, and even tolerably safe. The hot summer came again, and made the turpentine drop from the thin roof over my head.

During the long nights I was restless for want of air, and I had no room to toss and turn. There was but one compensation; the atmosphere was so stifled that even mosquitos would not condescend to buzz in it. With all my detestation of Dr. Flint, I could hardly wish him a worse punishment, either in this world or that which is to come, than to suffer what I suffered in one single summer. Yet the laws allowed *him* to be out in the free air, while I, guiltless of crime, was pent up here, as the only means of avoiding the cruelties the laws allowed him to inflict upon me! I don't know what kept life within me. Again and again, I thought I should die before long; but I saw the leaves of another autumn whirl through the air, and felt the touch of another winter. In summer the most terrible thunder storms were acceptable, for the rain came through the roof, and I rolled up my bed that it might cool the hot boards under it. Later in the season, storms sometimes wet my clothes through and through, and that was not comfortable when the air grew chilly. Moderate storms I could keep out by filling the chinks with oakum.[161]

But uncomfortable as my situation was, I had glimpses of things out of doors, which made me thankful for my wretched hiding-place. One day I saw a slave pass our gate, muttering, "It's his own, and he can kill it if he will." My grandmother told me that woman's history. Her mistress had that day seen her baby for the first time, and in the lineaments of its fair face she saw a likeness to her husband. She turned the bondwoman and her child out of doors, and forbade her ever to return. The slave went to her master, and told him what had happened. He promised to talk with her mistress, and make it all right. The next day she and her baby were sold to a Georgia trader.

Another time I saw a woman rush wildly by, pursued by two men. She was a slave, the wet nurse of her mistress's children. For some trifling offence her mistress ordered her to be stripped and whipped. To escape the degradation and the torture, she rushed to the river, jumped in, and ended her wrongs in death.

Notes

[161] *oakum* hemp fiber coated in tar.

Senator Brown,[162] of Mississippi, could not be ignorant of many such facts as these, for they are of frequent occurrence in every Southern State. Yet he stood up in the Congress of the United States, and declared that slavery was "a great moral, social, and political blessing; a blessing to the master, and a blessing to the slave!"

I suffered much more during the second winter than I did during the first. My limbs were benumbed by inaction, and the cold filled them with cramp. I had a very painful sensation of coldness in my head; even my face and tongue stiffened, and I lost the power of speech. Of course it was impossible, under the circumstances, to summon any physician. My brother William came and did all he could for me. Uncle Phillip also watched tenderly over me; and poor grandmother crept up and down to inquire whether there were any signs of returning life. I was restored to consciousness by the dashing of cold water in my face, and found myself leaning against my brother's arm, while he bent over me with streaming eyes. He afterwards told me he thought I was dying, for I had been in an unconscious state sixteen hours. I next became delirious, and was in great danger of betraying myself and my friends. To prevent this, they stupefied me with drugs. I remained in bed six weeks, weary in body and sick at heart. How to get medical advice was the question. William finally went to a Thompsonian[163] doctor, and described himself as having all my pains and aches. He returned with herbs, roots, and ointment. He was especially charged to rub on the ointment by a fire; but how could a fire be made in my little den? Charcoal in a furnace was tried, but there was no outlet for the gas, and it nearly cost me my life. Afterwards, coals, already kindled, were brought up in an iron pan, and placed on bricks. I was so weak, and it was so long since I had enjoyed the warmth of a fire, that those few coals actually made me weep. I think the medicines did me some good; but my recovery was very slow. Dark thoughts passed through my mind as I lay there day after day. I tried to be thankful for my little cell, dismal as it was, and even to love it, as part of the price I had paid for the redemption of my children. Sometimes I thought God was a compassionate Father, who would forgive my sins for the sake of my sufferings. At other times, it seemed to me there was no justice or mercy in the divine government. I asked why the curse of slavery was permitted to exist, and why I had been so persecuted and wronged from youth upward. These things took the shape of mystery, which is to this day not so clear to my soul as I trust it will be hereafter.

In the midst of my illness, grandmother broke down under the weight of anxiety and toil. The idea of losing her, who had always been my best friend and a mother to my children, was the sorest trial I had yet had. O, how earnestly I prayed that she might recover! How hard it seemed, that I could not tend upon her, who had so long and so tenderly watched over me!

One day the screams of a child nerved me with strength to crawl to my peeping-hole, and I saw my son covered with blood. A fierce dog, usually kept chained, had seized and bitten him. A doctor was sent for, and I heard the groans and screams of my child while the wounds were being sewed up. O, what torture to a mother's heart, to listen to this and be unable to go to him!

But childhood is like a day in spring, alternately shower and sunshine. Before night Benny was bright and lively, threatening the destruction of the dog; and great was his delight when the doctor told him the next day that the dog had bitten another boy and been shot. Benny recovered from his wounds; but it was long before he could walk.

Notes

[162] *Senator Brown* Albert Gallatin Brown (1813–1880), whose speech helped repeal the Missouri Compromise in 1854 and opened land from the Louisiana Purchase up to slavery.

[163] *Thompsonian* alternative, herbalist medicine named after its founder Samuel Thomson (1769–1843).

When my grandmother's illness became known, many ladies, who were her customers, called to bring her some little comforts, and to inquire whether she had everything[164] she wanted. Aunt Nancy one night asked permission to watch with her sick mother, and Mrs. Flint replied, "I don't see any need of your going. I can't spare you." But when she found other ladies in the neighborhood were so attentive, not wishing to be outdone in Christian charity, she also sallied forth, in magnificent condescension, and stood by the bedside of her who had loved her in her infancy, and who had been repaid by such grievous wrongs. She seemed surprised to find her so ill, and scolded Uncle[165] Phillip for not sending for Dr. Flint. She herself sent for him immediately, and he came. Secure as I was in my retreat, I should have been terrified if I had known he was so near me. He pronounced my grandmother in a very critical situation, and said if her attending physician wished it, he would visit her. Nobody wished to have him coming to the house at all hours, and we were not disposed to give him a chance to make out a long bill.

As Mrs. Flint went out, Sally told her the reason Benny was lame was that a dog had bitten him. "I'm glad of it," replied she. "I wish he had killed him. It would be good news to send to his mother. *Her* day will come. The dogs will grab *her* yet." With these Christian words she and her husband departed, and, to my great satisfaction, returned no more.

I heard from Uncle[166] Phillip, with feelings of unspeakable joy and gratitude, that the crisis was passed and grandmother would live. I could now say from my heart, "God is merciful. He has spared me the anguish of feeling that I caused her death."

Chapter 24

The Candidate for Congress

THE summer had nearly ended, when Dr. Flint made a third visit to New York, in search of me. Two candidates were running for Congress, and he returned in season to vote. The father of my children was the Whig candidate. The doctor had hitherto been a stanch Whig; but now he exerted all his energies for the defeat of Mr. Sands. He invited large parties of men to dine in the shade of his trees, and supplied them with plenty of rum and brandy. If any poor fellow drowned his wits in the bowl, and, in the openness of his convivial heart, proclaimed that he did not mean to vote for the Democratic ticket,[167] he was shoved into the street without ceremony.

The doctor expended his liquor in vain. Mr. Sands was elected; an event which occasioned me some anxious thoughts. He had not emancipated my children, and if he should die they would be at the mercy of his heirs. Two little voices, that frequently met my ear, seemed to plead with me not to let their father depart without striving to make their freedom secure. Years had passed since I had spoken to him. I had not even seen him since the night I passed him, unrecognized, in my disguise of a sailor. I supposed he would call before he left, to say something to my grandmother concerning the children, and I resolved what course to take.

The day before his departure for Washington I made arrangements, towards evening, to get from my hiding-place into the storeroom below. I found myself so stiff and clumsy that it was with great difficulty I could hitch from one resting place to another.

Notes

[164] *Original reads*: every thing [ed.].

[165] *Original reads*: uncle [ed.].

[166] *Original reads*: uncle [ed.].

[167] *Original reads*: vote the Democratic ticket [ed.].

When I reached the storeroom my ankles gave way under me, and I sank exhausted on the floor. It seemed as if I could never use my limbs again. But the purpose I had in view roused all the strength I had. I crawled on my hands and knees to the window, and, screened behind a barrel, I waited for his coming. The clock struck nine, and I knew the steamboat would leave between ten and eleven. My hopes were failing. But presently I heard his voice, saying to someone,[168] "Wait for me a moment. I wish to see Aunt[169] Martha." When he came out, as he passed the window, I said, "Stop one moment, and let me speak for my children." He started, hesitated, and then passed on, and went out of the gate. I closed the shutter I had partially opened, and sank down behind the barrel. I had suffered much; but seldom had I experienced a keener pang than I then felt. Had my children, then, become of so little consequence to him? And had he so little feeling for their wretched mother that he would not listen a moment while she pleaded for them? Painful memories were so busy within me, that I forgot I had not hooked the shutter, till I heard someone[170] opening it. I looked up. He had come back. "Who called me?" said he, in a low tone. "I did," I replied. "Oh, Linda," said he, "I knew your voice; but I was afraid to answer, lest my friend should hear me. Why do you come here? Is it possible you risk yourself in this house? They are mad to allow it. I shall expect to hear that you are all ruined." I did not wish to implicate him, by letting him know my place of concealment; so I merely said, "I thought you would come to bid grandmother goodbye,[171] and so I came here to speak a few words to you about emancipating my children. Many changes may take place during the six months you are gone to Washington, and it does not seem right for you to expose them to the risk of such changes. I want nothing for myself; all I ask is that you will free my children, or authorize some friend to do it, before you go."

He promised he would do it, and also expressed a readiness to make any arrangements whereby I could be purchased.

I heard footsteps approaching, and closed the shutter hastily. I wanted to crawl back to my den, without letting the family know what I had done; for I knew they would deem it very imprudent. But he stepped back into the house, to tell my grandmother that he had spoken with me at the storeroom window, and to beg of her not to allow me to remain in the house overnight.[172] He said it was the height of madness for me to be there; that we should certainly all be ruined. Luckily, he was in too much of a hurry to wait for a reply, or the dear old woman would surely have told him all.

I tried to go back to my den, but found it more difficult to go up than I had to come down. Now that my mission was fulfilled, the little strength that had supported me through it was gone, and I sank helpless on the floor. My grandmother, alarmed at the risk I had run, came into the storeroom in the dark, and locked the door behind her. "Linda," she whispered, "where are you?"

"I am here by the window," I replied. "I *couldn't* have him go away without emancipating the children. Who knows what may happen?"

"Come, come, child," said she, "it won't do for you to stay here another minute. You've done wrong; but I can't blame you, poor thing!"

I told her I could not return without assistance, and she must call my uncle. Uncle Phillip came, and pity prevented him from scolding me. He carried me back to my

Notes

[168] *Original reads*: some one [ed.].

[169] *Original reads*: aunt [ed.].

[170] *Original reads*: some one [ed.].

[171] *Original reads*: good by [ed.].

[172] *Original reads*: over night [ed.].

dungeon, laid me tenderly on the bed, gave me some medicine, and asked me if there was anything[173] more he could do. Then he went away, and I was left with my own thoughts – starless as the midnight darkness around me.

My friends feared I should become a cripple for life; and I was so weary of my long imprisonment that, had it not been for the hope of serving my children, I should have been thankful to die; but, for their sakes, I was willing to bear on.

Chapter 25

Competition in Cunning

Dr. Flint had not given me up. Every now and then he would say to my grandmother that I would yet come back, and voluntarily surrender myself; and that when I did, I could be purchased by my relatives, or anyone[174] who wished to buy me. I knew his cunning nature too well not to perceive[175] that this was a trap laid for me; and so all my friends understood it. I resolved to match my cunning against his cunning. In order to make him believe that I was in New York, I resolved to write him a letter dated from that place. I sent for my friend Peter, and asked him if he knew any trustworthy seafaring person, who would carry such a letter to New York, and put it in the post office there. He said he knew one that he would trust with his own life to the ends of the world. I reminded him that it was a hazardous thing for him to undertake. He said he knew it, but he was willing to do anything[176] to help me. I expressed a wish for a New York paper, to ascertain the names of some of the streets. He ran[177] his hand into his pocket, and said, "Here is half a one, that was round a cap I bought of a peddler[178] yesterday." I told him the letter would be ready the next evening. He bade me goodbye,[179] adding, "Keep up your spirits, Linda; brighter days will come by and by."

My Uncle[180] Phillip kept watch over the gate until our brief interview was over. Early the next morning, I seated myself near the little aperture to examine the newspaper. It was a piece of the New York Herald;[181] and, for once, the paper that systematically abuses the colored people was made to render them a service. Having obtained what information I wanted concerning streets and numbers, I wrote two letters, one to my grandmother, the other to Dr. Flint. I reminded him how he, a gray-headed man, had treated a helpless child, who had been placed in his power, and what years of misery he had brought upon her. To my grandmother, I expressed a wish to have my children sent to me at the north, where I could teach them to respect themselves, and set them a virtuous example; which a slave mother was not allowed to do at the south. I asked her to direct her answer to a certain street in Boston, as I did not live in New York, though I went there sometimes. I dated these letters ahead, to allow for the time it would take to carry them, and sent a memorandum of the date to the messenger. When my friend came for the letters, I said, "God bless and reward you, Peter, for this disinterested kindness. Pray be careful. If you are detected, both you and I will have to suffer dreadfully. I have not a relative who would dare to do it for me." He replied, "You may trust to me, Linda. I don't forget that your father was my best friend, and I will be a friend to his children so long as God lets me live."

Notes

173 *Original reads*: any thing [ed.].

174 *Original reads*: any one [ed.].

175 *Original reads*: percieve [ed.].

176 *Original reads*: any thing [ed.].

177 *Original reads*: run [ed.].

178 *Original reads*: pedler [ed.].

179 *Original reads*: good by [ed.].

180 *Original reads*: uncle [ed.].

181 *New York Herald* a daily paper known for its proslavery views.

It was necessary to tell my grandmother what I had done, in order that she might be ready for the letter, and prepared to hear what Dr. Flint might say about my being at the north. She was sadly troubled. She felt sure mischief would come of it. I also told my plan to Aunt[182] Nancy, in order that she might report to us what was said at Dr. Flint's house. I whispered it to her through a crack, and she whispered back, "I hope it will succeed. I shan't mind being a slave all *my* life, if I can only see you and the children free."

I had directed that my letters should be put into the New York post office on the 20th of the month. On the evening of the 24th my aunt came to say that Dr. Flint and his wife had been talking in a low voice about a letter he had received, and that when he went to his office he promised to bring it when he came to tea. So I concluded I should hear my letter read the next morning. I told my grandmother Dr. Flint would be sure to come, and asked her to have him sit near a certain door, and leave it open, that I might hear what he said. The next morning I took my station within sound of that door, and remained motionless as a statue. It was not long before I heard the gate slam, and the well-known footsteps enter the house. He seated himself in the chair that was placed for him, and said, "Well, Martha, I've brought you a letter from Linda. She has sent me a letter, also. I know exactly where to find her; but I don't choose to go to Boston for her. I had rather she would come back of her own accord, in a respectable manner. Her Uncle[183] Phillip is the best person to go for her. With *him*, she would feel perfectly free to act. I am willing to pay his expenses going and returning. She shall be sold to her friends. Her children are free; at least I suppose they are; and when you obtain her freedom, you'll make a happy family. I suppose, Martha, you have no objection to my reading to you the letter Linda has written to you."

He broke the seal, and I heard him read it. The old villain! He had suppressed the letter I wrote to grandmother, and prepared a substitute of his own, the purport of which was as follows:–

"Dear Grandmother: I have long wanted to write to you; but the disgraceful manner in which I left you and my children made me ashamed to do it. If you knew how much I have suffered since I ran away, you would pity and forgive me. I have purchased freedom at a dear rate. If any arrangement could be made for me to return to the south without being a slave, I would gladly come. If not, I beg of you to send my children to the north. I cannot live any longer without them. Let me know in time, and I will meet them in New York or Philadelphia, whichever place best suits my uncle's convenience. Write as soon as possible to your unhappy daughter,

Linda."

"It is very much as I expected it would be," said the old hypocrite, rising to go. "You see the foolish girl has repented of her rashness, and wants to return. We must help her to do it, Martha. Talk with Phillip about it. If he will go for her, she will trust to him, and come back. I should like an answer tomorrow. Good morning, Martha."

As he stepped out on the piazza, he stumbled over my little girl. "Ah, Ellen, is that you?" he said, in his most gracious manner. "I didn't see you. How do you do?"

"Pretty well, sir," she replied. "I heard you tell grandmother that my mother is coming home. I want to see her."

"Yes, Ellen, I am going to bring her home very soon," rejoined he; "and you shall see her as much as you like, you little curly-headed nigger."

Notes

[182] *Original reads*: aunt [ed.].

[183] *Original reads*: uncle [ed.].

This was as good as a comedy to me, who had heard it all; but grandmother was frightened and distressed, because the doctor wanted my uncle to go for me.

The next evening Dr. Flint called to talk the matter over. My uncle told him that from what he had heard of Massachusetts, he judged he should be mobbed if he went there after a runaway slave. "All stuff and nonsense, Phillip!" replied the doctor. "Do you suppose I want you to kick up a row in Boston? The business can all be done quietly. Linda writes that she wants to come back. You are her relative, and she would trust *you*. The case would be different if I went. She might object to coming with *me*; and the damned abolitionists, if they knew I was her master, would not believe me, if I told them she had begged to go back. They would get up a row; and I should not like to see Linda dragged through the streets like a common negro. She has been very ungrateful to me for all my kindness; but I forgive her, and want to act the part of a friend towards her. I have no wish to hold her as my slave. Her friends can buy her as soon as she arrives here."

Finding that his arguments failed to convince my uncle, the doctor "let the cat out of the bag," by saying that he had written to the mayor of Boston, to ascertain whether there was a person of my description at the street and number from which my letter was dated. He had omitted this date in the letter he had made up to read to my grandmother. If I had dated from New York, the old man would probably have made another journey to that city. But even in that dark region, where knowledge is so carefully excluded from the slave, I had heard enough about Massachusetts to come to the conclusion that slaveholders did not consider it a comfortable place to go to in search of a runaway. That was before the Fugitive Slave Law was passed; before Massachusetts had consented to become a "nigger hunter" for the south.

My grandmother, who had become skittish by seeing her family always in danger, came to me with a very distressed countenance, and said, "What will you do if the mayor of Boston lends him word that you haven't been there? Then he will suspect the letter was a trick; and maybe he'll find out something about it, and we shall all get into trouble. O Linda, I wish you had never sent the letters."

"Don't worry yourself, grandmother," said I. "The mayor of Boston won't trouble himself to hunt niggers for Dr. Flint. The letters will do good in the end. I shall get out of this dark hole sometime[184] or other."

"I hope you will, child," replied the good, patient old friend. "You have been here a long time; almost five years; but whenever you do go, it will break your old grandmother's heart. I should be expecting every day to hear that you were brought back in irons and put in jail, God help you, poor child! Let us be thankful that some time or other we shall go "where the wicked cease from troubling, and the weary are at rest."[185] My heart responded, Amen.

The fact that Dr. Flint had written to the mayor of Boston convinced me that he believed my letter to be genuine, and of course that he had no suspicion of my being anywhere[186] in the vicinity. It was a great object to keep up this delusion, for it made me and my friends feel less anxious, and it would be very convenient whenever there was a chance to escape. I resolved, therefore, to continue to write letters from the north from time to time.

Two or three weeks passed, and as no news came from the mayor of Boston, grandmother began to listen to my entreaty to be allowed to leave my cell, sometimes, and

Notes

[184] *Original reads*: some time [ed.].

[185] *"where ... the weary are at rest"* Job 3:17.

[186] *Original reads*: any where [ed.].

exercise my limbs to prevent my becoming a cripple. I was allowed to slip down into the small storeroom, early in the morning, and remain there a little while. The room was all filled up with barrels, except a small open space under my trap-door. This faced the door, the upper part of which was of glass, and purposely left uncurtained, that the curious might look in. The air of this place was close; but it was so much better than the atmosphere of my cell that I dreaded to return. I came down as soon as it was light, and remained till eight o'clock, when people began to be about, and there was danger that someone[187] might come on the piazza. I had tried various applications to bring warmth and feeling into my limbs, but without avail. They were so numb and stiff that it was a painful effort to move; and had my enemies come upon me during the first mornings I tried to exercise them a little in the small unoccupied space of the storeroom, it would have been impossible for me to have escaped.

Chapter 26

Important Era in My Brother's Life

I MISSED the company and kind attentions of my brother William, who had gone to Washington with his master, Mr. Sands. We received several letters from him, written without any allusion to me, but expressed in such a manner that I knew he did not forget me. I disguised my hand, and wrote to him in the same manner. It was a long session; and when it closed, William wrote to inform us that Mr. Sands was going to the north, to be gone some time, and that he was to accompany him. I knew that his master had promised to give him his freedom, but no time had been specified. Would William trust to a slave's chances? I remembered how we used to talk together, in our young days, about obtaining our freedom, and I thought it very doubtful whether he would come back to us.

Grandmother received a letter from Mr. Sands, saying that William had proved a most faithful servant, and he would also say a valued friend; that no mother had ever trained a better boy. He said he had travelled through the Northern States and Canada; and though the abolitionists had tried to decoy him away, they had never succeeded. He ended by saying they should be at home shortly.

We expected letters from William, describing the novelties of his journey, but none came. In time, it was reported that Mr. Sands would return late in the autumn, accompanied by a bride. Still no letters from William. I felt almost sure I should never see him again on southern soil; but had he no word of comfort to send to his friends at home? to the poor captive in her dungeon? My thoughts wandered through the dark past, and over the uncertain future. Alone in my cell, where no eye but God's could see me, I wept bitter tears. How earnestly I prayed to him to restore me to my children, and enable me to be a useful woman and a good mother!

At last the day arrived for the return of the travellers. Grandmother had made loving preparations to welcome her absent boy back to the old hearthstone. When the dinner table was laid, William's plate occupied its old place. The stage coach went by empty. My grandmother waited dinner. She thought perhaps he was necessarily detained by his master. In my prison I listened anxiously, expecting every moment to hear my dear brother's voice and step. In the course of the afternoon a lad was sent by Mr. Sands to tell grandmother that William did not return with him; that the abolitionists

Notes

[187] *Original reads*: some one [ed.].

had decoyed him away. But he begged her not to feel troubled about it, for he felt confident she would see William in a few days. As soon as he had time to reflect he would come back, for he could never expect to be so well off at the north as he had been with him.

If you had seen the tears, and heard the sobs, you would have thought the messenger had brought tidings of death instead of freedom. Poor old grandmother felt that she should never see her darling boy again. And I was selfish. I thought more of what I had lost than of what my brother had gained. A new anxiety began to trouble me. Mr. Sands had expended a good deal of money, and would naturally feel irritated by the loss he had incurred. I greatly feared this might injure the prospects of my children, who were now becoming valuable property. I longed to have their emancipation made certain. The more so, because their master and father was now married. I was too familiar with slavery not to know that promises made to slaves, though with kind intentions, and sincere at the time, depend upon many contingencies for their fulfilment.

Much as I wished William to be free, the step he had taken made me sad and anxious. The following Sabbath was calm and clear; so beautiful that it seemed like a Sabbath in the eternal world. My grandmother brought the children out on the piazza, that I might hear their voices. She thought it would comfort me in my despondency; and it did. They chatted merrily, as only children can. Benny said, "Grandmother, do you think Uncle[188] Will has gone for good? Won't he ever come back again? Maybe[189] he'll find mother. If he does, *won't* she be glad to see him! Why don't you and Uncle[190] Phillip, and all of us, go and live where mother is? I should like it; wouldn't you, Ellen?"

"Yes, I should like it," replied Ellen; "but how could we find her? Do you know the place, grandmother? I don't remember how mother looked – do you, Benny?"

Benny was just beginning to describe me when they were interrupted by an old slave woman, a near neighbor, named Aggie. This poor creature had witnessed the sale of her children, and seen them carried off to parts unknown, without any hopes of ever hearing from them again. She saw that my grandmother had been weeping, and she said, in a sympathizing tone, "What's the matter, Aunt[191] Marthy?"

"O Aggie," she replied, "it seems as if I shouldn't have any of my children or grandchildren left to hand me a drink when I'm dying, and lay my old body in the ground. My boy didn't come back with Mr. Sands. He staid at the north."

Poor old Aggie clapped her hands for joy. "Is *dat* what you's crying fur?" she exclaimed. "Git down on your knees and bress de Lord! I don't know whar my poor chillern is, and I nebber 'spect to know. You don't know whar poor Linda's gone to; but you *do* know whar her brudder is. He's in free parts; and dat's de right place. Don't murmur at de Lord's doings, but git down on your knees and tank him for his goodness."

My selfishness was rebuked by what poor Aggie said. She rejoiced over the escape of one who was merely her fellow-bondman, while his own sister was only thinking what his good fortune might cost her children. I knelt and prayed God to forgive me; and I thanked him from my heart that one of my family was saved from the grasp of slavery.

Notes

188 *Original reads*: uncle [ed.].

189 *Original reads*: May be [ed.].

190 *Original reads*: uncle [ed.].

191 *Original reads*: aunt [ed.].

It was not long before we received a letter from William. He wrote that Mr. Sands had always treated him kindly, and that he had tried to do his duty to him faithfully. But ever since he was a boy, he had longed to be free; and he had already gone through enough to convince him he had better not lose the chance that offered. He concluded by saying, "Don't worry about me, dear grandmother. I shall think of you always; and it will spur me on to work hard and try to do right. When I have earned money enough to give you a home, perhaps you will come to the north, and we can all live happy together."

Mr. Sands told my Uncle[192] Phillip the particulars about William's leaving him. He said, "I trusted him as if he were my own brother, and treated him as kindly. The abolitionists talked to him in several places; but I had no idea they could tempt him. However, I don't blame William. He's young and inconsiderate, and those Northern rascals decoyed him. I must confess the scamp was very bold about it. I met him coming down the steps of the Astor House with his trunk on his shoulder, and I asked him where he was going. He said he was going to change his old trunk. I told him it was rather shabby, and asked if he didn't need some money. He said, No, thanked me, and went off. He did not return so soon as I expected; but I waited patiently. At last I went to see if our trunks were packed, ready for our journey. I found them locked, and a sealed note on the table informed me where I could find the keys. The fellow even tried to be religious. He wrote that he hoped God would always bless me, and reward me for my kindness; that he was not unwilling to serve me; but he wanted to be a free man; and that if I thought he did wrong, he hoped I would forgive him. I intended to give him his freedom in five years. He might have trusted me. He has shown himself ungrateful; but I shall not go for him, or send for him. I feel confident that he will soon return to me."

I afterwards heard an account of the affair from William himself. He had not been urged away by abolitionists. He needed no information they could give him about slavery to stimulate his desire for freedom. He looked at his hands, and remembered that they were once in irons. What security had he that they would not be so again? Mr. Sands was kind to him; but he might indefinitely postpone the promise he had made to give him his freedom. He might come under pecuniary embarrassments, and his property be seized by creditors; or he might die, without making any arrangements in his favor. He had too often known such accidents to happen to slaves who had kind masters, and he wisely resolved to make sure of the present opportunity to own himself. He was scrupulous about taking any money from his master on false pretences; so he sold his best clothes to pay for his passage to Boston. The slaveholders pronounced him a base, ungrateful wretch, for thus requiting his master's indulgence. What would *they* have done under similar circumstances?

When Dr. Flint's family heard that William had deserted Mr. Sands, they chuckled greatly over the news. Mrs. Flint made her usual manifestations of Christian feeling, by saying, "I'm glad of it. I hope he'll never get him again. I like to see people paid back in their own coin. I reckon Linda's children will have to pay for it. I should be glad to see them in the speculator's hands again, for I'm tired of seeing those little niggers march about the streets."

Notes

[192] *Original reads*: uncle [ed.].

Chapter 27

New Destination for the Children

Mrs. Flint proclaimed her intention of informing Mrs. Sands who was the father of my children. She likewise proposed to tell her what an artful devil I was; that I had made a great deal of trouble in her family; that when Mr. Sands was at the north, she didn't doubt I had followed him in disguise, and persuaded William to run away. She had some reason to entertain such an idea; for I had written from the north, from time to time, and I dated my letters from various places. Many of them fell into Dr. Flint's hands, as I expected they would; and he must have come to the conclusion that I travelled about a good deal. He kept a close watch over my children, thinking they would eventually lead to my detection.

A new and unexpected trial was in store for me. One day, when Mr. Sands and his wife were walking in the street, they met Benny. The lady took a fancy to him, and exclaimed, "What a pretty little negro! Whom does he belong to?"

Benny did not hear the answer; but he came home very indignant with the stranger lady, because she had called him a negro.[193] A few days afterwards, Mr. Sands called on my grandmother, and told her he wanted her to take the children to his house. He said he had informed his wife of his relation to them, and told her they were motherless; and she wanted to see them. When he had gone, my grandmother came and asked what I would do. The question seemed a mockery. What *could* I do? They were Mr. Sands's slaves, and their mother was a slave, whom he had represented to be dead. Perhaps he thought I was. I was too much pained and puzzled to come to any decision; and the children were carried without my knowledge.

Mrs. Sands had a sister from Illinois staying with her. This lady, who had no children of her own, was so much pleased with Ellen that she offered to adopt her, and bring her up as she would a daughter. Mrs. Sands wanted to take Benjamin. When grandmother reported this to me, I was tried almost beyond endurance. Was this all I was to gain by what I had suffered for the sake of having my children free? True, the prospect *seemed* fair; but I knew too well how lightly slaveholders held such "parental relations." If pecuniary troubles should come, or if the new wife required more money than could conveniently be spared, my children might be thought of as a convenient means of raising funds. I had no trust in thee, O Slavery! Never should I know peace till my children were emancipated with all due formalities of law.

I was too proud to ask Mr. Sands to do anything[194] for my own benefit; but I could bring myself to become a supplicant for my children. I resolved to remind him of the promise he had made me, and to throw myself upon his honor for the performance of it. I persuaded my grandmother to go to him, and tell him I was not dead, and that I earnestly entreated him to keep the promise he had made me; that I had heard of the recent proposals concerning my children, and did not feel easy to accept them; that he had promised to emancipate them, and it was time for him to redeem his pledge. I knew there was some risk in thus betraying that I was in the vicinity; but what will not a mother do for her children? He received the message with surprise, and said, "The children are free. I have never intended to claim them as slaves. Linda may decide their fate. In my opinion, they had better be sent to the north. I don't

Notes

[193] *"Benny … called him a negro"* Perhaps Joseph was light enough to pass for white.

[194] *Original reads*: any thing [ed.].

think they are quite safe here. Dr. Flint boasts that they are still in his power. He says they were his daughter's property, and as she was not of age when they were sold, the contract is not legally binding."

So, then, after all I had endured for their sakes, my poor children were between two fires; between my old master and their new master! And I was powerless. There was no protecting arm of the law for me to invoke. Mr. Sands proposed that Ellen should go, for the present, to some of his relatives, who had removed to Brooklyn, Long Island. It was promised that she should be well taken care of, and sent to school. I consented to it, as the best arrangement I could make for her. My grandmother, of course, negotiated it all; and Mrs. Sands knew of no other person in the transaction. She proposed that they should take Ellen with them to Washington, and keep her till they had a good chance of sending her, with friends, to Brooklyn. She had an infant daughter. I had had a glimpse of it, as the nurse passed with it in her arms. It was not a pleasant thought to me, that the bondwoman's child should tend her free-born sister; but there was no alternative. Ellen was made ready for the journey. O, how it tried my heart to send her away, so young, alone, among strangers! Without a mother's love to shelter her from the storms of life; almost without memory of a mother! I doubted whether she and Benny would have for me the natural affection that children feel for a parent. I thought to myself that I might perhaps never see my daughter again, and I had a great desire that she should look upon me, before she went, that she might take my image with her in her memory. It seemed to me cruel to have her brought to my dungeon. It was sorrow enough for her young heart to know that her mother was a victim of slavery, without seeing the wretched hiding-place to which it had driven her. I begged permission to pass the last night in one of the open chambers, with my little girl. They thought I was crazy to think of trusting such a young child with my perilous secret. I told them I had watched her character, and I felt sure she would not betray me; that I was determined to have an interview, and if they would not facilitate it, I would take my own way to obtain it. They remonstrated against the rashness of such a proceeding; but finding they could not change my purpose, they yielded. I slipped through the trap-door into the storeroom, and my uncle kept watch at the gate, while I passed into the piazza and went upstairs,[195] to the room I used to occupy. It was more than five years since I had seen it; and how the memories crowded on me! There I had taken shelter when my mistress drove me from her house; there came my old tyrant, to mock, insult, and curse me; there my children were first laid in my arms; there I had watched over them, each day with a deeper and sadder love; there I had knelt to God, in anguish of heart, to forgive the wrong I had done. How vividly it all came back! And after this long, gloomy interval, I stood there such a wreck!

In the midst of these meditations, I heard footsteps on the stairs. The door opened, and my Uncle[196] Phillip came in, leading Ellen by the hand. I put my arms round her, and said, "Ellen, my dear child, I am your mother." She drew back a little, and looked at me; then, with sweet confidence, she laid her cheek against mine, and I folded her to the heart that had been so long desolated. She was the first to speak. Raising her head, she said, inquiringly, "You really *are* my mother?" I told her I really was; that during all the long time she had not seen me, I had loved her most tenderly; and that now she was going away, I wanted to see her and talk with her, that she might remember me. With a sob in her voice, she said, "I'm glad you've come to see me; but why didn't you ever come before? Benny and I have wanted so much to see you! He remembers

Notes

[195] *Original reads*: up stairs [ed.].

[196] *Original reads*: uncle [ed.].

you, and sometimes he tells me about you. Why didn't you come home when Dr. Flint went to bring you?"

I answered, "I couldn't come before, dear. But now that I am with you, tell me whether you like to go away." "I don't know," said she, crying. "Grandmother says I ought not to cry; that I am going to a good place, where I can learn to read and write, and that by and by I can write her a letter. But I shan't have Benny, or grandmother, or Uncle[197] Phillip, or anybody[198] to love me. Can't you go with me? O, *do* go, dear mother!"

I told her I couldn't go now; but sometime I would come to her, and then she and Benny and I would live together, and have happy times. She wanted to run and bring Benny to see me now. I told her he was going to the north, before long, with Uncle[199] Phillip, and then I would come to see him before he went away. I asked if she would like to have me stay all night and sleep with her. "O, yes," she replied. Then, turning to her uncle, she said, pleadingly, "*May* I stay? Please, Uncle![200] She is my own mother." He laid his hand on her head, and said, solemnly, "Ellen, this is the secret you have promised grandmother never to tell. If you ever speak of it to anybody,[201] they will never let you see your grandmother again, and your mother can never come to Brooklyn." "Uncle," she replied, "I will never tell." He told her she might stay with me; and when he had gone, I took her in my arms and told her I was a slave, and that was the reason she must never say she had seen me. I exhorted her to be a good child, to try to please the people where she was going, and that God would raise her up friends. I told her to say her prayers, and remember always to pray for her poor mother, and that God would permit us to meet again. She wept, and I did not check her tears. Perhaps she would never again have a chance to pour her tears into a mother's bosom. All night she nestled in my arms, and I had no inclination to slumber. The moments were too precious to lose any of them. Once, when I thought she was asleep, I kissed her forehead softly, and she said, "I am not asleep, dear mother."

Before dawn they came to take me back to my den. I drew aside the window curtain, to take a last look of my child. The moonlight shone on her face, and I bent over her, as I had done years before, that wretched night when I ran away. I hugged her close to my throbbing heart; and tears, too sad for such young eyes to shed, flowed down her cheeks, as she gave her last kiss, and whispered in my ear, "Mother, I will never tell." And she never did.

When I got back to my den, I threw myself on the bed and wept there alone in the darkness. It seemed as if my heart would burst. When the time for Ellen's departure drew nigh, I could hear neighbors and friends saying to her, "Goodbye,[202] Ellen. I hope your poor mother will find you out. *Won't* you be glad to see her!" She replied, "Yes, ma'am"; and they little dreamed of the weighty secret that weighed down her young heart. She was an affectionate child, but naturally very reserved, except with those she loved, and I felt secure that my secret would be safe with her. I heard the gate close after her, with such feelings as only a slave mother can experience. During the day my meditations were very sad. Sometimes I feared I had been very selfish not to give up all claim to her, and let her go to Illinois, to be adopted by Mrs. Sands's sister. It was my experience of slavery that decided me against it. I feared that circumstances might arise that would cause her to be sent back. I felt confident that I should go to New York myself; and then I should be able to watch over her, and in some degree protect her.

Notes

[197] *Original reads*: uncle [ed.].
[198] *Original reads*: any body [ed.].
[199] *Original reads*: uncle [ed.].
[200] *Original reads*: uncle [ed.].
[201] *Original reads*: any body [ed.].
[202] *Original reads*: Good by [ed.].

Dr. Flint's family knew nothing of the proposed arrangement till after Ellen was gone, and the news displeased them greatly. Mrs. Flint called on Mrs. Sands's sister to inquire into the matter. She expressed her opinion very freely as to the respect Mr. Sands showed for his wife, and for his own character, in acknowledging those "young niggers." And as for sending Ellen away, she pronounced it to be just as much stealing as it would be for him to come and take a piece of furniture out of her parlor. She said her daughter was not of age to sign the bill of sale, and the children were her property; and when she became of age, or was married, she could take them, wherever she could lay hands on them.

Miss Emily Flint, the little girl to whom I had been bequeathed, was now in her sixteenth year. Her mother considered it all right and honorable for her, or her future husband, to steal my children; but she did not understand how anybody[203] could hold up their heads in respectable society, after they had purchased their own children, as Mr. Sands had done. Dr. Flint said very little. Perhaps he thought that Benny would be less likely to be sent away if he kept quiet. One of my letters that fell into his hands was dated from Canada; and he seldom spoke of me now. This state of things enabled me to slip down into the storeroom more frequently, where I could stand upright, and move my limbs more freely.

Days, weeks, and months passed, and there came no news of Ellen. I sent a letter to Brooklyn, written in my grandmother's name, to inquire whether she had arrived there. Answer was returned that she had not. I wrote to her in Washington; but no notice was taken of it. There was one person there who ought to have had some sympathy with the anxiety of the child's friends at home; but the links of such relations as he had formed with me are easily broken and cast away as rubbish. Yet how protectingly and persuasively he once talked to the poor, helpless slave girl! And how entirely I trusted him! But now suspicions darkened my mind. Was my child dead, or had they deceived me, and sold her?

If the secret memoirs of many members of Congress should be published, curious details would be unfolded. I once saw a letter from a member of Congress to a slave, who was the mother of six of his children. He wrote to request that she would send her children away from the great house before his return, as he expected to be accompanied by friends. The woman could not read, and was obliged to employ another to read the letter. The existence of the colored children did not trouble this gentleman, it was only the fear that friends might recognize in their features a resemblance to him.

At the end of six months, a letter came to my grandmother, from Brooklyn. It was written by a young lady in the family, and announced that Ellen had just arrived. It contained the following message from her: "I do try to do just as you told me to, and I pray for you every night and morning." I understood that these words were meant for me; and they were a balsam to my heart. The writer closed her letter by saying, "Ellen is a nice little girl, and we shall like to have her with us. My cousin, Mr. Sands, has given her to me, to be my little waiting maid. I shall send her to school, and I hope someday[204] she will write to you herself." This letter perplexed and troubled me. Had my child's father merely placed her there till she was old enough to support herself? Or had he given her to his cousin, as a piece of property? If the last idea was correct, his cousin might return to the south at any time, and hold Ellen as a slave. I tried to put away from me the painful thought that such a foul wrong could have been done to us. I said to myself, "Surely there must be *some* justice in man"; then I remembered, with

Notes

[203] *Original reads*: any body [ed.].

[204] *Original reads*: some day [ed.].

a sigh, how slavery perverted all the natural feelings of the human heart. It gave me a pang to look on my light-hearted boy. He believed himself free; and to have him brought under the yoke of slavery would be more than I could bear. How I longed to have him safely out of the reach of its power!

Chapter 28

Aunt Nancy

I HAVE mentioned my great aunt, who was a slave in Dr. Flint's family, and who had been my refuge during the shameful persecutions I suffered from him. This aunt had been married at twenty years of age; that is, as far as slaves *can* marry. She had the consent of her master and mistress, and a clergyman performed the ceremony. But it was a mere form, without any legal value. Her master or mistress could annul it any day they pleased. She had always slept on the floor in the entry, near Mrs. Flint's chamber door, that she might be within call. When she was married, she was told she might have the use of a small room in an outhouse. Her mother and her husband furnished it. He was a seafaring man, and was allowed to sleep there when he was at home. But on the wedding evening, the bride was ordered to her old post on the entry floor.

Mrs. Flint, at that time, had no children; but she was expecting to be a mother, and if she should want a drink of water in the night, what could she do without her slave to bring it? So my aunt was compelled to lie at her door, until one midnight she was forced to leave, to give premature birth to a child. In a fortnight she was required to resume her place on the entry floor, because Mrs. Flint's babe needed her attentions. She kept her station there through summer and winter, until she had given premature birth to six children; and all the while she was employed as night-nurse to Mrs. Flint's children. Finally, toiling all day, and being deprived of rest at night, completely broke down her constitution, and Dr. Flint declared it was impossible she could ever become the mother of a living child. The fear of losing so valuable a servant by death, now induced them to allow her to sleep in her little room in the out-house, except when there was sickness in the family. She afterwards had two feeble babes, one of whom died in a few days, and the other in four weeks. I well remember her patient sorrow as she held the last dead baby in her arms. "I wish it could have lived," she said; "it is not the will of God that any of my children should live. But I will try to be fit to meet their little spirits in heaven."

Aunt Nancy was housekeeper and waiting-maid in Dr. Flint's family. Indeed, she was the *factotum*[205] of the household. Nothing went on well without her. She was my mother's twin sister, and, as far as was in her power, she supplied a mother's place to us orphans. I slept with her all the time I lived in my old master's house, and the bond between us was very strong. When my friends tried to discourage me from running away, she always encouraged me. When they thought I had better return and ask my master's pardon, because there was no possibility of escape, she sent me word never to yield. She said if I persevered I might, perhaps, gain the freedom of my children; and even if I perished in doing it, that was better than to leave them to groan under the same persecutions that had blighted my own life. After I was shut up in my dark cell, she stole away, whenever she could, to bring me the news and say something cheering. How often did I kneel down to listen to her words of consolation, whispered through

Notes

[205] *factotum* busybody.

a crack! "I am old, and have not long to live," she used to say; "and I could die happy if I could only see you and the children free. You must pray to God, Linda, as I do for you, that he will lead you out of this darkness." I would beg her not to worry herself on my account; that there was an end of all suffering sooner or later, and that whether I lived in chains or in freedom, I should always remember her as the good friend who had been the comfort of my life. A word from her always strengthened me; and not me only. The whole family relied upon her judgment, and were guided by her advice.

I had been in my cell six years when my grandmother was summoned to the bedside of this, her last remaining daughter. She was very ill, and they said she would die. Grandmother had not entered Dr. Flint's house for several years. They had treated her cruelly, but she thought nothing of that now. She was grateful for permission to watch by the death-bed of her child. They had always been devoted to each other; and now they sat looking into each other's eyes, longing to speak of the secret that had weighed so much on the hearts of both. My aunt had been stricken with paralysis. She lived but two days, and the last day she was speechless. Before she lost the power of utterance, she told her mother not to grieve if she could not speak to her; that she would try to hold up her hand, to let her know that all was well with her. Even the hard-hearted doctor was a little softened when he saw the dying woman try to smile on the aged mother, who was kneeling by her side. His eyes moistened for a moment, as he said she had always been a faithful servant, and they should never be able to supply her place. Mrs. Flint took to her bed, quite overcome by the shock. While my grandmother sat alone with the dead, the doctor came in, leading his youngest son, who had always been a great pet with Aunt[206] Nancy, and was much attached to her. "Martha," said he, "Aunt[207] Nancy loved this child, and when he comes where you are, I hope you will be kind to him, for her sake." She replied, "Your wife was my foster-child, Dr. Flint, the foster-sister of my poor Nancy, and you little know me if you think I can feel anything[208] but good will for her children."

"I wish the past could be forgotten, and that we might never think of it," said he; "and that Linda would come to supply her aunt's place. She would be worth more to us than all the money that could be paid for her. I wish it for your sake also, Martha. Now that Nancy is taken away from you, she would be a great comfort to your old age."

He knew he was touching a tender chord. Almost choking with grief, my grandmother replied, "It was not I that drove Linda away. My grandchildren are gone; and of my nine children only one is left. God help me!"

To me, the death of this kind relative was an inexpressible sorrow. I knew that she had been slowly murdered; and I felt that my troubles had helped to finish the work. After I heard of her illness, I listened constantly to hear what news was brought from the great house; and the thought that I could not go to her made me utterly miserable. At last, as Uncle[209] Phillip came into the house, I heard someone[210] inquire, "How is she?" and he answered, "She is dead." My little cell seemed whirling round, and I knew nothing more till I opened my eyes and found Uncle[211] Phillip bending over me. I had no need to ask any questions. He whispered, "Linda, she died happy." I could not weep. My fixed gaze troubled him. "Don't look *so*," he said. "Don't add to my poor mother's trouble. Remember how much she has to bear, and that we ought to do all we can to

Notes

[206] *Original reads*: aunt [ed.].

[207] *Original reads*: aunt [ed.].

[208] *Original reads*: any thing [ed.].

[209] *Original reads*: uncle [ed.].

[210] *Original reads*: some one [ed.].

[211] *Original reads*: uncle [ed.].

comfort her." Ah, yes, that blessed old grandmother, who for seventy-three years had borne the pelting storms of a slave-mother's life. She did indeed need consolation!

Mrs. Flint had rendered her poor foster-sister childless, apparently without any compunction; and with cruel selfishness had ruined her health by years of incessant, unrequited toil, and broken rest. But now she became very sentimental. I suppose she thought it would be a beautiful illustration of the attachment existing between slaveholder and slave, if the body of her old worn-out servant was buried at her feet. She sent for the clergyman and asked if he had any objection to burying Aunt[212] Nancy in the doctor's family burial-place. No colored person had ever been allowed interment in the white people's burying-ground, and the minister knew that all the deceased of our family reposed together in the old graveyard of the slaves. He therefore replied, "I have no objection to complying with your wish; but perhaps Aunt[213] Nancy's *mother* may have some choice as to where her remains shall be deposited."

It had never occurred to Mrs. Flint that slaves could have any feelings. When my grandmother was consulted, she at once said she wanted Nancy to lie with all the rest of her family, and where her own old body would be buried. Mrs. Flint graciously complied with her wish, though she said it was painful to her to have Nancy buried away from *her*. She might have added with touching pathos, "I was so long *used* to sleep with her lying near me, on the entry floor."

My Uncle[214] Phillip asked permission to bury his sister at his own expense; and slaveholders are always ready to grant *such* favors to slaves and their relatives. The arrangements were very plain, but perfectly respectable. She was buried on the Sabbath, and Mrs. Flint's minister read the funeral service. There was a large concourse[215] of colored people, bond and free, and a few white persons who had always been friendly to our family. Dr. Flint's carriage was in the procession; and when the body was deposited in its humble resting place, the mistress dropped a tear, and returned to her carriage, probably thinking she had performed her duty nobly.

It was talked of by the slaves as a mighty grand funeral. Northern travellers, passing through the place, might have described this tribute of respect to the humble dead as a beautiful feature in the "patriarchal institution"; a touching proof of the attachment between slaveholders and their servants; and tender-hearted Mrs. Flint would have confirmed this impression, with handkerchief at her eyes. *We* could have told them a different story. We could have given them a chapter of wrongs and sufferings that would have touched their hearts, if they *had* any hearts to feel for the colored people. We could have told them how the poor old slave-mother had toiled, year after year, to earn eight hundred dollars to buy her son Phillip's right to his own earnings; and how that same Phillip paid the expenses of the funeral, which they regarded as doing so much credit to the master. We could also have told them of a poor, blighted young creature, shut up in a living grave for years, to avoid the tortures that would be inflicted on her, if she ventured to come out and look on the face of her departed friend.

All this, and much more, I thought of, as I sat at my loophole, waiting for the family to return from the grave; sometimes weeping, sometimes falling asleep, dreaming strange dreams of the dead and the living.

It was sad to witness the grief of my bereaved grandmother. She had always been strong to bear, and now, as ever, religious faith supported her. But her dark life had become still darker, and age and trouble were leaving deep traces on her withered face. She had four places to knock for me to come to the trap-door, and each place had a

Notes

[212] *Original reads*: aunt [ed.].

[213] *Original reads*: aunt [ed.].

[214] *Original reads*: uncle [ed.].

[215] *concourse* crowd.

different meaning. She now came oftener than she had done, and talked to me of her dead daughter, while tears trickled slowly down her furrowed cheeks. I said all I could to comfort her; but it was a sad reflection, that instead of being able to help her, I was a constant source of anxiety and trouble. The poor old back was fitted to its burden. It bent under it, but did not break.

Chapter 29

Preparations for Escape

I HARDLY expect that the reader will credit me, when I affirm that I lived in that little dismal hole, almost deprived of light and air, and with no space to move my limbs, for nearly seven years. But it is a fact; and to me a sad one, even now; for my body still suffers from the effects of that long imprisonment, to say nothing of my soul. Members of my family, now living in New York and Boston, can testify to the truth of what I say.

Countless were the nights that I sat late at the little loophole scarcely large enough to give me a glimpse of one twinkling star. There, I heard the patrols and slave-hunters conferring together about the capture of runaways, well knowing how rejoiced they would be to catch me.

Season after season, year after year, I peeped at my children's faces, and heard their sweet voices, with a heart yearning all the while to say, "Your mother is here." Sometimes it appeared to me as if ages had rolled away since I entered upon that gloomy, monotonous existence. At times, I was stupefied and listless; at other times, I became very impatient to know when these dark years would end, and I should again be allowed to feel the sunshine, and breathe the pure air.

After Ellen left us, this feeling increased. Mr. Sands had agreed that Benny might go to the north whenever his Uncle[216] Phillip could go with him; and I was anxious to be there also, to watch over my children, and protect them so far as I was able. Moreover, I was likely to be drowned out of my den, if I remained much longer; for the slight roof was getting badly out of repair, and Uncle[217] Phillip was afraid to remove the shingles, lest someone[218] should get a glimpse of me. When storms occurred in the night, they spread mats and bits of carpet, which in the morning appeared to have been laid out to dry; but to cover the roof in the daytime might have attracted attention. Consequently, my clothes and bedding were often drenched; a process by which the pains and aches in my cramped and stiffened limbs were greatly increased. I revolved various plans of escape in my mind, which I sometimes imparted to my grandmother, when she came to whisper with me at the trap-door. The kind-hearted old woman had an intense sympathy for runaways. She had known too much of the cruelties inflicted on those who were captured. Her memory always flew back at once to the sufferings of her bright and handsome son, Benjamin, the youngest and dearest of her flock. So, whenever I alluded to the subject, she would groan out, "O, don't think of it, child. You'll break my heart." I had no good old Aunt[219] Nancy now to encourage me; but my brother William and my children were continually beckoning me to the north.

And now I must go back a few months in my story. I have stated that the first of January was the time for selling slaves, or leasing them out to new masters. If time were counted by heart-throbs, the poor slaves might reckon years of suffering during

Notes

[216] *Original reads*: uncle [ed.].

[217] *Original reads*: uncle [ed.].

[218] *Original reads*: some one [ed.].

[219] *Original reads*: aunt [ed.].

that festival so joyous to the free. On the New Year's Day[220] preceding my aunt's death, one of my friends, named Fanny, was to be sold at auction, to pay her master's debts. My thoughts were with her during all the day, and at night I anxiously inquired what had been her fate. I was told that she had been sold to one master, and her four little girls to another master, far distant; that she had escaped from her purchaser, and was not to be found. Her mother was the old Aggie I have spoken of. She lived in a small tenement belonging to my grandmother, and built on the same lot with her own house. Her dwelling was searched and watched, and that brought the patrols so near me that I was obliged to keep very close in my den. The hunters were somehow eluded; and not long afterwards Benny accidentally caught sight of Fanny in her mother's hut. He told his grandmother, who charged him never to speak of it, explaining to him the frightful consequences; and he never betrayed the trust. Aggie little dreamed that my grandmother knew where her daughter was concealed, and that the stooping form of her old neighbor was bending under a similar burden of anxiety and fear; but these dangerous secrets deepened the sympathy between the two old persecuted mothers.

My friend Fanny and I remained many weeks hidden within call of each other; but she was unconscious of the fact. I longed to have her share my den, which seemed a more secure retreat than her own; but I had brought so much trouble on my grandmother, that it seemed wrong to ask her to incur greater risks. My restlessness increased. I had lived too long in bodily pain and anguish of spirit. Always I was in dread that by some accident, or some contrivance, slavery would succeed in snatching my children from me. This thought drove me nearly frantic, and I determined to steer for the North Star at all hazards. At this crisis, Providence opened an unexpected way for me to escape. My friend Peter came one evening, and asked to speak with me. "Your day has come, Linda," said he. "I have found a chance for you to go to the Free States. You have a fortnight to decide." The news seemed too good to be true; but Peter explained his arrangements, and told me all that was necessary was for me to say I would go. I was going to answer him with a joyful yes, when the thought of Benny came to my mind. I told him the temptation was exceedingly strong, but I was terribly afraid of Dr. Flint's alleged power over my child, and that I could not go and leave him behind. Peter remonstrated earnestly. He said such a good chance might never occur again; that Benny was free, and could be sent to me; and that for the sake of my children's welfare I ought not to hesitate a moment. I told him I would consult with Uncle[221] Phillip. My uncle rejoiced in the plan, and bade me go by all means. He promised, if his life was spared, that he would either bring or send my son to me as soon as I reached a place of safety. I resolved to go, but thought nothing had better be said to my grandmother till very near the time of departure. But my uncle thought she would feel it more keenly if I left her so suddenly. "I will reason with her," said he, "and convince her how necessary it is, not only for your sake, but for hers also. You cannot be blind to the fact that she is sinking under her burdens." I was not blind to it. I knew that my concealment was an ever-present source of anxiety, and that the older she grew the more nervously fearful she was of discovery. My uncle talked with her, and finally succeeded in persuading her that it was absolutely necessary for me to seize the chance so unexpectedly offered.

The anticipation of being a free woman proved almost too much for my weak frame. The excitement stimulated me, and at the same time bewildered me. I made

Notes

[220] *Original reads*: New Year's day [ed.].

[221] *Original reads*: uncle [ed.].

busy preparations for my journey, and for my son to follow me. I resolved to have an interview with him before I went, that I might give him cautions and advice, and tell him how anxiously I should be waiting for him at the north. Grandmother stole up to me as often as possible to whisper words of counsel. She insisted upon my writing to Dr. Flint, as soon as I arrived in the Free States, and asking him to sell me to her. She said she would sacrifice her house, and all she had in the world, for the sake of having me safe with my children in any part of the world. If she could only live to know *that* she could die in peace. I promised the dear old faithful friend that I would write to her as soon as I arrived, and put the letter in a safe way to reach her; but in my own mind I resolved that not another cent of her hard earnings should be spent to pay rapacious slaveholders for what they called their property. And even if I had not been unwilling to buy what I had already a right to possess, common humanity would have prevented me from accepting the generous offer, at the expense of turning my aged relative out of house and home, when she was trembling on the brink of the grave.

I was to escape in a vessel; but I forbear to mention any further particulars.[222] I was in readiness, but the vessel was unexpectedly detained several days. Meantime, news came to town of a most horrible murder committed on a fugitive slave, named James. Charity, the mother of this unfortunate young man, had been an old acquaintance of ours. I have told the shocking particulars of his death, in my description of some of the neighboring slaveholders. My grandmother, always nervously sensitive about runaways, was terribly frightened. She felt sure that a similar fate awaited me, if I did not desist from my enterprise. She sobbed, and groaned, and entreated me not to go. Her excessive fear was somewhat contagious, and my heart was not proof against her extreme agony. I was grievously disappointed, but I promised to relinquish my project.

When my friend Peter was apprised of this, he was both disappointed and vexed. He said, that judging from our past experience, it would be a long time before I had such another chance to throw away. I told him it need not be thrown away; that I had a friend concealed nearby,[223] who would be glad enough to take the place that had been provided for me. I told him about poor Fanny, and the kind-hearted, noble fellow, who never turned his back upon anybody[224] in distress, white or black, expressed his readiness to help her. Aggie was much surprised when she found that we knew her secret. She was rejoiced to hear of such a chance for Fanny, and arrangements were made for her to go on board the vessel the next night. They both supposed that I had long been at the north, therefore my name was not mentioned in the transaction. Fanny was carried on board at the appointed time, and stowed away in a very small cabin. This accommodation had been purchased at a price that would pay for a voyage to England. But when one proposes to go to fine old England, they stop to calculate whether they can afford the cost of the pleasure; while in making a bargain to escape from slavery, the trembling victim is ready to say, "Take all I have, only don't betray me!"

The next morning I peeped through my loophole, and saw that it was dark and cloudy. At night I received news that the wind was ahead, and the vessel had not sailed. I was exceedingly anxious about Fanny, and Peter too, who was running a tremendous risk at my instigation. Next day the wind and weather remained the same. Poor Fanny had been half dead with fright when they carried her on board, and I could readily imagine how she must be suffering now. Grandmother came often to my den, to say

Notes

[222] *Original reads*: paticulars [ed.].

[223] *Original reads*: near by [ed.].

[224] *Original reads*: any body [ed.].

how thankful she was I did not go. On the third morning she rapped for me to come down to the storeroom. The poor old sufferer was breaking down under her weight of trouble. She was easily flurried now. I found her in a nervous, excited state, but I was not aware that she had forgotten to lock the door behind her, as usual. She was exceedingly worried about the detention of the vessel. She was afraid all would be discovered, and then Fanny, and Peter, and I, would all be tortured to death, and Phillip would be utterly ruined, and her house would be torn down. Poor Peter! If he should die such a horrible death as the poor slave James had lately done, and all for his kindness in trying to help me, how dreadful it would be for us all! Alas, the thought was familiar to me, and had sent many a sharp pang through my heart. I tried to suppress my own anxiety, and speak soothingly to her. She brought in some allusion to Aunt[225] Nancy, the dear daughter she had recently buried, and then she lost all control of herself. As she stood there, trembling and sobbing, a voice from the piazza called out, "Whar is you, Aunt[226] Marthy?" Grandmother was startled, and in her agitation opened the door, without thinking of me. In stepped Jenny, the mischievous housemaid, who had tried to enter my room when I was concealed in the house of my white benefactress. "I's bin huntin ebery whar for you, Aunt[227] Marthy," said she. "My missis wants you to send her some crackers." I had slunk down behind a barrel, which entirely screened me, but I imagined that Jenny was looking directly at the spot, and my heart beat violently. My grandmother immediately thought what she had done, and went out quickly with Jenny to count the crackers locking the door after her. She returned to me, in a few minutes, the perfect picture of despair. "Poor child!" she exclaimed, "my carelessness has ruined you. The boat ain't gone yet. Get ready immediately, and go with Fanny. I ain't got another word to say against it now; for there's no telling what may happen this day."

Uncle Phillip was sent for, and he agreed with his mother in thinking that Jenny would inform Dr. Flint in less than twenty-four hours. He advised getting me on board the boat, if possible; if not, I had better keep very still in my den, where they could not find me without tearing the house down. He said it would not do for him to move in the matter, because suspicion would be immediately excited; but he promised to communicate with Peter. I felt reluctant to apply to him again, having implicated him too much already; but there seemed to be no alternative. Vexed as Peter had been by my indecision, he was true to his generous nature, and said at once that he would do his best to help me, trusting I should show myself a stronger woman this time.

He immediately proceeded to the wharf, and found that the wind had shifted, and the vessel was slowly beating down stream. On some pretext of urgent necessity, he offered two boatmen a dollar apiece to catch up with her. He was of lighter complexion than the boatmen he hired, and when the captain saw them coming so rapidly, he thought officers were pursuing his vessel in search of the runaway slave he had on board. They hoisted sails, but the boat gained upon them, and the indefatigable Peter sprang on board.

The captain at once recognized him. Peter asked him to go below, to speak about a bad bill he had given him. When he told his errand, the captain replied, "Why, the woman's here already; and I've put her where you or the devil would have a tough job to find her."

"But it is another woman I want to bring," said Peter. "*She* is in great distress, too, and you shall be paid anything[228] within reason, if you'll stop and take her."

Notes

[225] *Original reads*: aunt [ed.].

[226] *Original reads*: aunt [ed.].

[227] *Original reads*: aunt [ed.].

[228] *Original reads*: any thing [ed.].

"What's her name?" inquired the captain.

"Linda," he replied.

"That's the name of the woman already here," rejoined the captain. "By George! I believe you mean to betray me."

"O!" exclaimed Peter, "God knows I wouldn't harm a hair of your head. I am too grateful to you. But there really *is* another woman in great danger. Do have the humanity to stop and take her!"

After a while they came to an understanding. Fanny, not dreaming I was anywhere[229] about in that region, had assumed my name, though she called herself Johnson. "Linda is a common name," said Peter, "and the woman I want to bring is Linda Brent."

The captain agreed to wait at a certain place till evening, being handsomely paid for his detention.

Of course, the day was an anxious one for us all. But we concluded that if Jenny had seen me, she would be too wise to let her mistress know of it; and that she probably would not get a chance to see Dr. Flint's family till evening, for I knew very well what were the rules in that household. I afterwards believed that she did not see me; for nothing ever came of it, and she was one of those base characters that would have jumped to betray a suffering fellow being for the sake of thirty pieces of silver.[230]

I made all my arrangements to go on board as soon as it was dusk. The intervening time I resolved to spend with my son. I had not spoken to him for seven years, though I had been under the same roof, and seen him every day, when I was well enough to sit at the loophole. I did not dare to venture beyond the storeroom; so they brought him there, and locked us up together, in a place concealed from the piazza door. It was an agitating interview for both of us. After we had talked and wept together for a little while, he said, "Mother, I'm glad you're going away. I wish I could go with you. I knew you was here; and I have been *so* afraid they would come and catch you!"

I was greatly surprised, and asked him how he had found it out.

He replied, "I was standing under the eaves, one day, before Ellen went away, and I heard somebody cough up over the wood shed. I don't know what made me think it was you, but I did think so. I missed Ellen, the night before she went away; and grandmother brought her back into the room in the night; and I thought maybe she'd been to see *you*, before she went, for I heard grandmother whisper to her, 'Now go to sleep; and remember never to tell.'"

I asked him if he ever mentioned his suspicions to his sister. He said he never did; but after he heard the cough, if he saw her playing with other children on that side of the house, he always tried to coax her round to the other side, for fear they would hear me cough, too. He said he had kept a close lookout for Dr. Flint, and if he saw him speak to a constable, or a patrol, he always told grandmother. I now recollected that I had seen him manifest uneasiness, when people were on that side of the house, and I had at the time been puzzled to conjecture a motive for his actions. Such prudence may seem extraordinary in a boy of twelve years, but slaves, being surrounded by mysteries, deceptions, and dangers, early learn to be suspicious and watchful, and prematurely cautious and cunning. He had never asked a question of grandmother, or Uncle[231] Phillip, and I had often heard him chime in with other children, when they spoke of my being at the north.

Notes

[229] *Original reads*: any where [ed.].

[230] *thirty pieces of silver* the amount for which Judas Iscariot betrayed Jesus (Matthew 26:14–15).

[231] *Original reads*: uncle [ed.].

I told him I was now really going to the Free States, and if he was a good, honest boy, and a loving child to his dear old grandmother, the Lord would bless him, and bring him to me, and we and Ellen would live together. He began to tell me that grandmother had not eaten anything[232] all day. While he was speaking, the door was unlocked, and she came in with a small bag of money, which she wanted me to take. I begged her to keep a part of it, at least, to pay for Benny's being sent to the north; but she insisted, while her tears were falling fast, that I should take the whole. "You may be sick among strangers," she said, "and they would send you to the poorhouse to die." Ah, that good grandmother!

For the last time I went up to my nook. Its desolate appearance no longer chilled me, for the light of hope had risen in my soul. Yet, even with the blessed prospect of freedom before me, I felt very sad at leaving forever that old homestead, where I had been sheltered so long by the dear old grandmother; where I had dreamed my first young dream of love; and where, after that had faded away, my children came to twine themselves so closely round my desolate heart. As the hour approached for me to leave, I again descended to the storeroom. My grandmother and Benny were there. She took me by the hand, and said, "Linda, let us pray." We knelt down together, with my child pressed to my heart, and my other arm round the faithful, loving old friend I was about to leave forever. On no other occasion has it ever been my lot to listen to so fervent a supplication for mercy and protection. It thrilled through my heart, and inspired me with trust in God.

Peter was waiting for me in the street. I was soon by his side, faint in body, but strong of purpose. I did not look back upon the old place, though I felt that I should never see it again.

Chapter 30

Northward Bound

I NEVER could tell how we reached the wharf. My brain was all of a whirl, and my limbs tottered under me. At an appointed place we met my Uncle[233] Phillip, who had started before us on a different route, that he might reach the wharf first, and give us timely warning if there was any danger. A row-boat was in readiness. As I was about to step in, I felt something pull me gently, and turning round I saw Benny, looking pale and anxious. He whispered in my ear, "I've been peeping into the doctor's window, and he's at home. Goodbye,[234] mother. Don't cry; I'll come." He hastened away. I clasped the hand of my good uncle, to whom I owed so much, and of Peter, the brave, generous friend who had volunteered to run such terrible risks to secure my safety. To this day I remember how his bright face beamed with joy, when he told me he had discovered a safe method for me to escape. Yet that intelligent, enterprising, noble-hearted man was a chattel! liable, by the laws of a country that calls itself civilized, to be sold with horses and pigs! We parted in silence. Our hearts were all too full for words!

Swiftly the boat glided over the water. After a while, one of the sailors said, "Don't be down-hearted, madam. We will take you safely to your husband, in ——." At first I could not imagine what he meant; but I had presence of mind to think that it probably referred to something the captain had told him; so I thanked him, and said I hoped we should have pleasant weather.

Notes

[232] *Original reads*: any thing [ed.].

[233] *Original reads*: uncle [ed.].

[234] *Original reads*: Good by [ed.].

When I entered the vessel the captain came forward to meet me. He was an elderly man, with a pleasant countenance. He showed me to a little box of a cabin, where sat my friend Fanny. She started as if she had seen a spectre. She gazed on me in utter astonishment, and exclaimed, "Linda, can this be *you?* or is it your ghost?" When we were locked in each other's arms, my overwrought feelings could no longer be restrained. My sobs reached the ears of the captain, who came and very kindly reminded us, that for his safety, as well as our own, it would be prudent for us not to attract any attention. He said that when there was a sail in sight he wished us to keep below; but at other times, he had no objection to our being on deck. He assured us that he would keep a good lookout, and if we acted prudently, he thought we should be in no danger. He had represented us as women going to meet our husbands in ——. We thanked him, and promised to observe carefully all the directions he gave us.

Fanny and I now talked by ourselves, low and quietly, in our little cabin. She told me of the sufferings she had gone through in making her escape, and of her terrors while she was concealed in her mother's house. Above all, she dwelt on the agony of separation from all her children on that dreadful auction day. She could scarcely credit me, when I told her of the place where I had passed nearly seven years. "We have the same sorrows," said I. "No," replied she, "you are going to see your children soon, and there is no hope that I shall ever even hear from mine."

The vessel was soon under way, but we made slow progress. The wind was against us. I should not have cared for this, if we had been out of sight of the town; but until there were miles of water between us and our enemies, we were filled with constant apprehensions that the constables would come on board. Neither could I feel quite at ease with the captain and his men. I was an entire stranger to that class of people, and I had heard that sailors were rough, and sometimes cruel. We were so completely in their power, that if they were bad men, our situation would be dreadful. Now that the captain was paid for our passage, might he not be tempted to make more money by giving us up to those who claimed us as property? I was naturally of a confiding disposition, but slavery had made me suspicious of everybody.[235] Fanny did not share my distrust of the captain or his men. She said she was afraid at first, but she had been on board three days while the vessel lay in the dock, and nobody had betrayed her, or treated her otherwise than kindly.

The captain soon came to advise us to go on deck for fresh air. His friendly and respectful manner, combined with Fanny's testimony, reassured me, and we went with him. He placed us in a comfortable seat, and occasionally entered into conversation. He told us he was a Southerner by birth, and had spent the greater part of his life in the Slave States, and that he had recently lost a brother who traded in slaves. "But," said he, "it is a pitiable and degrading business, and I always felt ashamed to acknowledge my brother in connection with it." As we passed Snaky Swamp, he pointed to it, and said, "There is a slave territory that defies all the laws." I thought of the terrible days I had spent there, and though it was not called Dismal Swamp, it made me feel very dismal as I looked at it.

I shall never forget that night. The balmy air of spring was so refreshing! And how shall I describe my sensations when we were fairly sailing on Chesapeake Bay? O, the beautiful sunshine! the exhilarating breeze! and I could enjoy them without fear or restraint. I had never realized what grand things air and sunlight are till I had been deprived of them.

Notes

[235] *Original reads*: every body [ed.].

Ten days after we left land we were approaching Philadelphia. The captain said we should arrive there in the night, but he thought we had better wait till morning, and go on shore in broad daylight, as the best way to avoid suspicion.

I replied, "You know best. But will you stay on board and protect us?"

He saw that I was suspicious, and he said he was sorry, now that he had brought us to the end of our voyage, to find I had so little confidence in him. Ah, if he had ever been a slave he would have known how difficult it was to trust a white man. He assured us that we might sleep through the night without fear; that he would take care we were not left unprotected. Be it said to the honor of this captain, Southerner as he was, that if Fanny and I had been white ladies, and our passage lawfully engaged, he could not have treated us more respectfully. My intelligent friend, Peter, had rightly estimated the character of the man to whose honor he had intrusted us.

The next morning I was on deck as soon as the day dawned. I called Fanny to see the sun rise, for the first time in our lives, on free soil; for such I *then* believed it to be. We watched the reddening sky, and saw the great orb come up slowly out of the water, as it seemed. Soon the waves began to sparkle, and everything[236] caught the beautiful glow. Before us lay the city of strangers.[237] We looked at each other, and the eyes of both were moistened with tears. We had escaped from slavery, and we supposed ourselves to be safe from the hunters. But we were alone in the world, and we had left dear ties behind us; ties cruelly sundered by the demon Slavery.

Chapter 31

Incidents in Philadelphia

I HAD heard that the poor slave had many friends at the north. I trusted we should find some of them. Meantime, we would take it for granted that all were friends, till they proved to the contrary. I sought out the kind captain, thanked him for his attentions, and told him I should never cease to be grateful for the service he had rendered us. I gave him a message to the friends I had left at home, and he promised to deliver it. We were placed in a row-boat, and in about fifteen minutes were landed on a wood wharf in Philadelphia. As I stood looking round, the friendly captain touched me on the shoulder, and said, "There is a respectable-looking colored man behind you. I will speak to him about the New York trains, and tell him you wish to go directly on." I thanked him, and asked him to direct me to some shops where I could buy gloves and veils. He did so, and said he would talk with the colored man till I returned. I made what haste I could. Constant exercise on board the vessel, and frequent rubbing with salt water, had nearly restored the use of my limbs. The noise of the great city confused me, but I found the shops, and bought some double veils and gloves for Fanny and myself. The shopman told me they were so many levies. I had never heard the word before, but I did not tell him so. I thought if he knew I was a stranger he might ask me where I came from. I gave him a gold piece, and when he returned the change, I counted it, and found out how much a levy was: I made my way back to the wharf, where the captain introduced me to the colored man, as the Rev. Jeremiah Durham, minister of Bethel church. He took me by the hand, as if I had been an old friend. He told us we were too late for the morning cars to New York, and must wait until the

Notes

[236] *Original reads*: every thing [ed.].

[237] *city of strangers* a play on Philadelphia's motto: "the City of Brotherly Love."

evening, or the next morning. He invited me to go home with him, assuring me that his wife would give me a cordial welcome; and for my friend he would provide a home with one of his neighbors. I thanked him for so much kindness to strangers, and told him if I must be detained, I should like to hunt up some people who formerly went from our part of the country. Mr. Durham insisted that I should dine with him, and then he would assist me in finding my friends. The sailors came to bid us goodbye.[238] I shook their hardy hands, with tears in my eyes. They had all been kind to us, and they had rendered us a greater service than they could possibly conceive of.

I had never seen so large a city, or been in contact with so many people in the streets. It seemed as if those who passed looked at us with an expression of curiosity. My face was so blistered and peeled, by sitting on deck, in wind and sunshine, that I thought they could not easily decide to what nation I belonged.

Mrs. Durham met me with a kindly welcome, without asking any questions. I was tired, and her friendly manner was a sweet refreshment. God bless her! I was sure that she had comforted other weary hearts, before I received her sympathy. She was surrounded by her husband and children, in a home made sacred by protecting laws. I thought of my own children, and sighed.

After dinner Mr. Durham went with me in quest of the friends I had spoken of. They went from my native town, and I anticipated much pleasure in looking on familiar faces. They were not at home, and we retraced our steps through streets delightfully clean. On the way, Mr. Durham observed that I had spoken to him of a daughter I expected to meet; that he was surprised, for I looked so young he had taken me for a single woman. He was approaching a subject on which I was extremely sensitive. He would ask about my husband next, I thought, and if I answered him truly, what would he think of me? I told him I had two children, one in New York the other at the south. He asked some further questions, and I frankly told him some of the most important events of my life. It was painful for me to do it; but I would not deceive him. If he was desirous of being my friend, I thought he ought to know how far I was worthy of it. "Excuse me, if I have tried your feelings," said he. "I did not question you from idle curiosity. I wanted to understand your situation, in order to know whether I could be of any service to you, or your little girl. Your straight-forward answers do you credit; but don't answer everybody[239] so openly. It might give some heartless people a pretext for treating you with contempt."

That word *contempt* burned me like coals of fire. I replied, "God alone knows how I have suffered; and He, I trust, will forgive me. If I am permitted to have my children, I intend to be a good mother, and to live in such a manner that people cannot treat me with contempt."

"I respect your sentiments," said he. "Place your trust in God, and be governed by good principles, and you will not fail to find friends."

When we reached home, I went to my room, glad to shut out the world for a while. The words he had spoken made an indelible impression upon me. They brought up great shadows from the mournful past. In the midst of my meditations I was startled by a knock at the door. Mrs. Durham entered, her face all beaming with kindness, to say that there was an anti-slavery friend downstairs,[240] who would like to see me. I overcame my dread of encountering strangers, and went with her. Many questions were asked concerning my experiences, and my escape from slavery; but I observed how careful they all were not to say anything[241] that might wound my feelings. How gratifying this

Notes

[238] *Original reads*: good by [ed.].

[239] *Original reads*: every body [ed.].

[240] *Original reads*: down stairs [ed.].

[241] *Original reads*: any thing [ed.].

was can be fully understood only by those who have been accustomed to be treated as if they were not included within the pale of human beings. The anti-slavery friend had come to inquire into my plans, and to offer assistance, if needed. Fanny was comfortably established, for the present, with a friend of Mr. Durham. The Anti-Slavery Society agreed to pay her expenses to New York. The same was offered to me, but I declined to accept it, telling them that my grandmother had given me sufficient to pay my expenses to the end of my journey. We were urged to remain in Philadelphia a few days, until some suitable escort could be found for us. I gladly accepted the proposition, for I had a dread of meeting slaveholders, and some dread also of railroads. I had never entered a railroad car in my life, and it seemed to me quite an important event.

That night I sought my pillow with feelings I had never carried to it before. I verily believed myself to be a free woman. I was wakeful for a long time, and I had no sooner fallen asleep than I was roused by fire-bells. I jumped up, and hurried on my clothes. Where I came from, everybody[242] hastened to dress themselves on such occasions. The white people thought a great fire might be used as a good opportunity for insurrection, and that it was best to be in readiness; and the colored people were ordered out to labor in extinguishing the flames. There was but one engine in our town, and colored women and children were often required to drag it to the river's edge and fill it. Mrs. Durham's daughter slept in the same room with me, and seeing that she slept through all the din, I thought it was my duty to wake her. "What's the matter?" said she, rubbing her eyes.

"They're screaming fire in the streets, and the bells are ringing," I replied.

"What of that?" said she, drowsily. "We are used to it. We never get up, without the fire is very near. What good would it do?"

I was quite surprised that it was not necessary for us to go and help fill the engine. I was an ignorant child, just beginning to learn how things went on in great cities.

At daylight, I heard women crying fresh fish, berries, radishes, and various other things. All this was new to me. I dressed myself at an early hour, and sat at the window to watch that unknown tide of life. Philadelphia seemed to me a wonderfully great place. At the breakfast table, my idea of going out to drag the engine was laughed over, and I joined in the mirth.

I went to see Fanny, and found her so well contented among her new friends that she was in no haste to leave. I was also very happy with my kind hostess. She had had advantages for education, and was vastly my superior. Every day, almost every hour, I was adding to my little stock of knowledge. She took me out to see the city as much as she deemed prudent. One day she took me to an artist's room, and showed me the portraits of some of her children. I had never seen any paintings of colored people before, and they seemed to me beautiful.

At the end of five days, one of Mrs. Durham's friends offered to accompany us to New York the following morning. As I held the hand of my good hostess in a parting clasp, I longed to know whether her husband had repeated to her what I had told him. I supposed he had, but she never made any allusion to it. I presume it was the delicate silence of womanly sympathy.

When Mr. Durham handed us our tickets, he said, "I am afraid you will have a disagreeable ride; but I could not procure tickets for the first-class cars."

Supposing I had not given him money enough, I offered more. "O, no," said he, "they could not be had for any money. They don't allow colored people to go in the first-class cars."

Notes

[242] *Original reads*: every body [ed.].

This was the first chill to my enthusiasm about the Free States. Colored people were allowed to ride in a filthy box, behind white people, at the south, but there they were not required to pay for the privilege. It made me sad to find how the north aped the customs of slavery.

We were stowed away in a large, rough car, with windows on each side, too high for us to look out without standing up. It was crowded with people, apparently of all nations. There were plenty of beds and cradles, containing screaming and kicking babies. Every other man had a cigar or pipe in his mouth, and jugs of whiskey were handed round freely. The fumes of the whiskey and the dense tobacco smoke were sickening to my senses, and my mind was equally nauseated by the coarse jokes and ribald songs around me. It was a very disagreeable ride. Since that time there has been some improvement in these matters.

Chapter 32

The Meeting of Mother and Daughter

WHEN we arrived in New York, I was half crazed by the crowd of coachmen calling out, "Carriage, ma'am?" We bargained with one to take us to Sullivan Street for twelve shillings. A burly Irishman stepped up and said, "I'll tak' ye for sax shillings." The reduction of half the price was an object to us, and we asked if he could take us right away. "Troth an I will, ladies," he replied. I noticed that the hackmen smiled at each other, and I inquired whether his conveyance was decent. "Yes, it's dacent it is, marm. Devil a bit would I be after takin' ladies in a cab that was not dacent." We gave him our checks. He went for the baggage, and soon reappeared, saying, "This way, if you plase, ladies." We followed, and found our trunks on a truck, and we were invited to take our seats on them. We told him that was not what we bargained for, and he must take the trunks off. He swore they should not be touched till we had paid him six shillings. In our situation it was not prudent to attract attention, and I was about to pay him what he required, when a man near by shook his head for me not to do it. After a great ado we got rid of the Irishman, and had our trunks fastened on a hack. We had been recommended to a boarding-house in Sullivan Street, and thither we drove. There Fanny and I separated. The Anti-Slavery Society provided a home for her, and I afterwards heard of her in prosperous circumstances. I sent for an old friend from my part of the country, who had for some time been doing business in New York. He came immediately. I told him I wanted to go to my daughter, and asked him to aid me in procuring an interview.

I cautioned him not to let it be known to the family that I had just arrived from the south, because they supposed I had been at the north seven years. He told me there was a colored woman in Brooklyn who came from the same town I did, and I had better go to her house, and have my daughter meet me there. I accepted the proposition thankfully, and he agreed to escort me to Brooklyn. We crossed on Fulton ferry,[243] went up Myrtle Avenue, and stopped at the house he designated. I was just about to enter, when two girls passed. My friend called my attention to them. I turned, and recognized in the eldest, Sarah, the daughter of a woman who used to live with my grandmother, but who had left the south years ago. Surprised

Notes

[243] *Original reads*: We crossed Fulton ferry [ed.].

and rejoiced at this unexpected meeting, I threw my arms round her, and inquired concerning her mother.

"You take no notice of the other girl," said my friend. I turned, and there stood my Ellen! I pressed her to my heart, then held her away from me to take a look at her. She had changed a good deal in the two years since I parted from her. Signs of neglect could be discerned by eyes less observing than a mother's. My friend invited us all to go into the house; but Ellen said she had been sent on an errand,[244] which she would do as quickly as possible, and go home and ask Mrs. Hobbs to let her come and see me. It was agreed that I should send for her the next day. Her companion, Sarah, hastened to tell her mother of my arrival. When I entered the house, I found the mistress of it absent, and I waited for her return. Before I saw her, I heard her saying, "Where is Linda Brent? I used to know her father and mother." Soon Sarah came with her mother. So there was quite a company of us, all from my grandmother's neighborhood. These friends gathered round me and questioned me eagerly. They laughed, they cried, and they shouted. They thanked God that I had got away from my persecutors and was safe on Long Island. It was a day of great excitement. How different from the silent days I had passed in my dreary den!

The next morning was Sunday. My first waking thoughts were occupied with the note I was to send to Mrs. Hobbs, the lady with whom Ellen lived. That I had recently come into that vicinity was evident; otherwise I should have sooner inquired for my daughter. It would not do to let them know I had just arrived from the south, for that would involve the suspicion of my having been harbored there, and might bring trouble, if not ruin, on several people.

I like a straightforward course, and am always reluctant to resort to subterfuges. So far as my ways have been crooked, I charge them all upon slavery. It was that system of violence and wrong which now left me no alternative but to enact a falsehood. I began my note by stating that I had recently arrived from Canada, and was very desirous to have my daughter come to see me. She came and brought a message from Mrs. Hobbs, inviting me to her house, and assuring me that I need not have any fears. The conversation I had with my child did not leave my mind at ease. When I asked if she was well treated, she answered yes; but there was no heartiness in the tone, and it seemed to me that she said it from an unwillingness to have me troubled on her account. Before she left me, she asked very earnestly, "Mother, when will you take me to live with you?" It made me sad to think that I could not give her a home till I went to work and earned the means; and that might take me a long time. When she was placed with Mrs. Hobbs, the agreement was that she should be sent to school. She had been there two years, and was now nine years old, and she scarcely knew her letters. There was no excuse for this, for there were good public schools in Brooklyn, to which she could have been sent without expense.

She staid with me till dark, and I went home with her. I was received in a friendly manner by the family, and all agreed in saying that Ellen was a useful, good girl. Mrs. Hobbs looked me coolly in the face, and said, "I suppose you know that my cousin, Mr. Sands, has *given* her to my eldest daughter. She will make a nice waiting-maid for her when she grows up." I did not answer a word. How *could* she, who knew by experience the strength of a mother's love, and who was perfectly aware of the relation Mr. Sands bore to my children – how *could* she look me in the face, while she thrust such a dagger into my heart?

Notes

[244] *Original reads*: sent of an errand [ed.].

I was no longer surprised that they had kept her in such a state of ignorance. Mr. Hobbs had formerly been[245] wealthy, but he had failed, and afterwards obtained a subordinate situation in the Custom House. Perhaps they expected to return to the south some day; and Ellen's knowledge was quite sufficient for a slave's condition. I was impatient to go to work and earn money, that I might change the uncertain position of my children. Mr. Sands had not kept his promise to emancipate them. I had also been deceived about Ellen. What security had I with regard to Benjamin? I felt that I had none.

I returned to my friend's house in an uneasy state of mind. In order to protect my children, it was necessary that I should own myself. I called myself free, and sometimes felt so; but I knew I was insecure. I sat down that night and wrote a civil letter to Dr, Flint, asking him to state the lowest terms on which he would sell me; and as I belonged by law to his daughter, I wrote to her also, making a similar request.

Since my arrival at the north I had not been unmindful of my dear brother William. I had made diligent inquiries for him, and having heard of him in Boston, I went thither. When I arrived there, I found he had gone to New Bedford. I wrote to that place, and was informed he had gone on a whaling voyage, and would not return for some months. I went back to New York to get employment near Ellen. I received an answer from Dr. Flint, which gave me no encouragement. He advised me to return and submit myself to my rightful owners, and then any request I might make would be granted. I lent this letter to a friend, who lost it; otherwise I would present a copy to my readers.

Chapter 33

A Home Found

My greatest anxiety now was to obtain employment. My health was greatly improved, though my limbs continued to trouble me with swelling whenever I walked much. The greatest difficulty in my way was that those who employed strangers required a recommendation; and in my peculiar position, I could, of course, obtain no certificates from the families I had so faithfully served.

One day an acquaintance told me of a lady who wanted a nurse for her babe, and I immediately applied for the situation. The lady told me she preferred to have one who had been a mother, and accustomed to the care of infants. I told her I had nursed two babes of my own. She asked me many questions, but, to my great relief, did not require a recommendation from my former employers. She told me she was an English woman, and that was a pleasant circumstance to me, because I had heard they had less prejudice against color than Americans entertained. It was agreed that we should try each other for a week. The trial proved satisfactory to both parties, and I was engaged for a month.

The heavenly Father had been most merciful to me in leading me to this place. Mrs. Bruce was a kind and gentle lady, and proved a true and sympathizing friend. Before the stipulated month expired, the necessity of passing up and down stairs frequently caused my limbs to swell so painfully that I became unable to perform my duties. Many ladies would have thoughtlessly discharged me; but Mrs. Bruce made arrangements to save me steps, and employed a physician to attend upon me. I had not

Notes

[245] *Original reads*: heen [ed.].

yet told her that I was a fugitive slave. She noticed that I was often sad, and kindly inquired the cause. I spoke of being separated from my children, and from relatives who were dear to me; but I did not mention the constant feeling of insecurity which oppressed my spirits. I longed for someone[246] to confide in; but I had been so deceived by white people, that I had lost all confidence in them. If they spoke kind words to me, I thought it was for some selfish purpose. I had entered this family with the distrustful feelings I had brought with me out of slavery; but ere six months had passed, I found that the gentle deportment of Mrs. Bruce and the smiles of her lovely babe were thawing my chilled heart. My narrow mind also began to expand under the influences of her intelligent conversation, and the opportunities for reading, which were gladly allowed me whenever I had leisure from my duties. I gradually became more energetic and more cheerful. The old feeling of insecurity, especially with regard to my children, often threw its dark shadow across my sunshine. Mrs. Bruce offered me a home for Ellen; but pleasant as it would have been, I did not dare to accept it, for fear of offending the Hobbs family. Their knowledge of my precarious situation placed me in their power; and I felt that it was important for me to keep on the right side of them, till, by dint of labor and economy, I could make a home for my children.

I was far from feeling satisfied with Ellen's situation. She was not well cared for. She sometimes came to New York to visit me; but she generally brought a request from Mrs. Hobbs that I would buy her a pair of shoes, or some article of clothing. This was accompanied by a promise of payment when Mr. Hobbs's salary at the Custom House became due; but somehow[247] or other the pay-day never came. Thus many dollars of my earnings were expended to keep my child comfortably clothed. That, however, was a slight trouble, compared with the fear that their pecuniary embarrassments might induce them to sell my precious young daughter. I knew they were in constant communication with Southerners, and had frequent opportunities to do it. I have stated that when Dr. Flint put Ellen in jail, at two years old, she had an inflammation of the eyes, occasioned by measles. This disease still troubled her; and kind Mrs. Bruce proposed that she should come to New York for a while, to be under the care of Dr. Elliott, a well-known oculist. It did not occur to me that there was anything[248] improper in a mother's making such a request; but Mrs. Hobbs was very angry, and refused to let her go. Situated as I was, it was not politic to insist upon it. I made no complaint, but I longed to be entirely free to act a mother's part towards my children. The next time I went over to Brooklyn, Mrs. Hobbs, as if to apologize for her anger, told me she had employed her own physician to attend to Ellen's eyes, and that she had refused my request because she did not consider it safe to trust her in New York. I accepted the explanation in silence; but she had told me that my child *belonged* to her daughter, and I suspected that her real motive was a fear of my conveying her property away from her. Perhaps I did her injustice; but my knowledge of Southerners made it difficult for me to feel otherwise.

Sweet and bitter were mixed in the cup of my life, and I was thankful that it had ceased to be entirely bitter. I loved Mrs. Brace's babe. When it laughed and crowed in my face, and twined its little tender arms confidingly about my neck, it made me think of the time when Benny and Ellen were babies, and my wounded heart was soothed. One bright morning, as I stood at the window, tossing baby in my arms, my attention was attracted by a young man in sailor's dress, who was closely observing every house

Notes

[246] *Original reads*: some one [ed.].

[247] *Original reads*: some how [ed.].

[248] *Original reads*: any thing [ed.].

as he passed. I looked at him earnestly. Could it be my brother William? It *must* be he – and yet, how changed! I placed the baby safely, flew downstairs,[249] opened the front door, beckoned to the sailor, and in less than a minute I was clasped in my brother's arms. How much we had to tell each other! How we laughed, and how we cried, over each other's adventures! I took him to Brooklyn, and again saw him with Ellen, the dear child whom he had loved and tended so carefully, while I was shut up in my miserable den. He staid in New York a week. His old feelings of affection for me and Ellen were as lively as ever. There are no bonds so strong as those which are formed by suffering together.

Chapter 34

The Old Enemy Again

My young mistress, Miss Emily Flint, did not return any answer to my letter requesting her to consent to my being sold. But after a while, I received a reply, which purported to be written by her younger brother. In order rightly to enjoy the contents of this letter, the reader must bear in mind that the Flint family supposed I had been at the north many years. They had no idea that I knew of the doctor's three excursions to New York in search of me; that I had heard his voice, when he came to borrow five hundred dollars for that purpose; and that I had seen him pass on his way to the steamboat. Neither were they aware that all the particulars of Aunt[250] Nancy's death and burial were conveyed to me at the time they occurred. I have kept the letter, of which I herewith subjoin a copy:–

"Your letter to sister was received a few days ago. I gather from it that you are desirous of returning to your native place, among your friends and relatives. We were all gratified with the contents of your letter; and let me assure you that if any members of the family have had any feeling of resentment towards you, they feel it no longer. We all sympathize with you in your unfortunate condition, and are ready to do all in our power to make you contented and happy. It is difficult for you to return home as a free person. If you were purchased by your grandmother, it is doubtful whether you would be permitted to remain, although it would be lawful for you to do so. If a servant should be allowed to purchase herself, after absenting herself so long from her owners, and return free, it would have an injurious effect. From your letter, I think your situation must be hard and uncomfortable. Come home. You have it in your power to be reinstated in our affections. We would receive you with open arms and tears of joy. You need not apprehend any unkind treatment, as we have not put ourselves to any trouble or expense to get you. Had we done so, perhaps we should feel otherwise. You know my sister was always attached to you, and that you were never treated as a slave. You were never put to hard work, nor exposed to field labor. On the contrary, you were taken into the house, and treated as one of us, and almost as free; and we, at least, felt that you were above disgracing yourself by running away. Believing you may be induced to come home voluntarily has induced me to write for my sister. The family will be rejoiced to see you; and your poor old grandmother expressed a great desire to have you come, when she heard your letter read. In her old age she needs the consolation of having her children round her. Doubtless you have heard of the death of your

Notes

[249] *Original reads*: down stairs [ed.].

[250] *Original reads*: aunt [ed.].

aunt. She was a faithful servant, and a faithful member of the Episcopal Church.[251] In her Christian life she taught us how to live – and, O, too high the price of knowledge, she taught us how to die! Could you have seen us round her death bed, with her mother, all mingling our tears in one common stream, you would have thought the same heart-felt tie existed between a master and his servant, as between a mother and her child. But this subject is too painful to dwell upon. I must bring my letter to a close. If you are contented to stay away from your old grandmother, your child, and the friends who love you, stay where you are. We shall never trouble ourselves to apprehend you. But should you prefer to come home, we will do all that we can to make you happy. If you do not wish to remain in the family, I know that father, by our persuasion, will be induced to let you be purchased by any person you may choose in our community. You will please answer this as soon as possible, and let us know your decision. Sister sends much love to you. In the meantime[252] believe me your sincere friend and well-wisher."

This letter was signed by Emily's brother, who was as yet a mere lad. I knew, by the style, that it was not written by a person of his age, and though the writing was disguised, I had been made too unhappy by it, in former years, not to recognize at once the hand of Dr. Flint. O, the hypocrisy of slaveholders! Did the old fox suppose I was goose enough to go into such a trap? Verily, he relied too much on "the stupidity of the African race." I did not return the family of Flints any thanks for their cordial invitation – a remissness for which I was, no doubt, charged with base ingratitude.

Not long afterwards I received a letter from one of my friends at the south, informing me that Dr. Flint was about to visit the north. The letter had been delayed, and I supposed he might be already on the way. Mrs. Bruce did not know I was a fugitive. I told her that important business called me to Boston, where my brother then was, and asked permission to bring a friend to supply my place as nurse, for a fortnight. I started on my journey immediately; and as soon as I arrived, I wrote to my grandmother that if Benny came, he must be sent to Boston. I knew she was only waiting for a good chance to send him north, and, fortunately, she had the legal power to do so, without asking leave of anybody.[253] She was a free woman; and when my children were purchased, Mr. Sands preferred to have the bill of sale drawn up in her name. It was conjectured that he advanced the money, but it was not known. At the south, a gentleman may have a shoal of colored children without any disgrace; but if he is known to purchase them, with the view of setting them free, the example is thought to be dangerous to their "peculiar institution," and he becomes unpopular.

There was a good opportunity to send Benny in a vessel coming directly to New York. He was put on board with a letter to a friend, who was requested to see him off to Boston. Early one morning, there was a loud rap at my door, and in rushed Benjamin, all out of breath. "O mother!" he exclaimed, "here I am! I run all the way; and I come all alone. How d'you do?"

O reader, can you imagine my joy? No, you cannot, unless you have been a slave mother. Benjamin rattled away as fast as his tongue could go. "Mother, why don't you bring Ellen here? I went over to Brooklyn to see her, and she felt very bad when I bid her goodbye.[254] She said, 'O Ben, I wish I was going too.' I thought she'd know ever so much; but she don't know so much as I do; for I can read, and she can't. And, mother, I lost all my clothes coming. What can I do to get some more? I 'spose free boys can get along here at the north as well as white boys."

Notes

[251] *Original reads*: church [ed.].
[252] *Original reads*: mean time [ed.].
[253] *Original reads*: any body [ed.].
[254] *Original reads*: good by [ed.].

I did not like to tell the sanguine, happy little fellow how much he was mistaken. I took him to a tailor, and procured a change of clothes. The rest of the day was spent in mutual asking and answering of questions, with the wish constantly repeated that the good old grandmother was with us, and frequent injunctions from Benny to write to her immediately, and be sure to tell her everything[255] about his voyage, and his journey to Boston.

Dr. Flint made his visit to New York, and made every exertion to call upon me, and invite me to return with him; but not being able to ascertain where I was, his hospitable intentions were frustrated, and the affectionate family, who were waiting for me with "open arms," were doomed to disappointment.

As soon as I knew he was safely at home, I placed Benjamin in the care of my brother William, and returned to Mrs. Bruce. There I remained through the winter and spring, endeavoring to perform my duties faithfully, and finding a good degree of happiness in the attractions of baby Mary, the considerate kindness of her excellent mother, and occasional interviews with my darling daughter.

But when summer came, the old feeling of insecurity haunted me. It was necessary for me to take little Mary out daily, for exercise and fresh air, and the city was swarming with Southerners, some of whom might recognize me. Hot weather brings out snakes and slaveholders, and I like one class of the venomous creatures as little as I do the other. What a comfort it is, to be free to *say* so!

Chapter 35

Prejudice Against Color

It was a relief to my mind to see preparations for leaving the city. We went to Albany in the steamboat Knickerbocker. When the gong sounded for tea, Mrs. Bruce said, "Linda, it is late, and you and baby had better come to the table with me." I replied, "I know it is time baby had her supper, but I had rather not go with you, if you please. I am afraid of being insulted." "O no, not if you are with *me*" she said. I saw several white nurses go with their ladies, and I ventured to do the same. We were at the extreme end of the table. I was no sooner seated, than a gruff voice said, "Get up! You know you are not allowed to sit here." I looked up, and, to my astonishment and indignation, saw that the speaker was a colored man. If his office required him to enforce the by-laws of the boat, he might, at least, have done it politely. I replied, "I shall not get up, unless the captain comes and takes me up." No cup of tea was offered me, but Mrs. Bruce handed me hers and called for another. I looked to see whether the other nurses were treated in a similar manner. They were all properly waited on.

Next morning, when we stopped at Troy for breakfast, everybody[256] was making a rush for the table. Mrs. Bruce said, "Take my arm, Linda, and we'll go in together." The landlord heard her, and said, "Madam, will you allow your nurse and baby to take breakfast with my family?" I knew this was to be attributed to my complexion; but he spoke courteously, and therefore I did not mind it.

At Saratoga we found the United States Hotel crowded, and Mr. Bruce took one of the cottages belonging to the hotel. I had thought, with gladness, of going to the quiet

Notes

[255] *Original reads*: every thing [ed.].

[256] *Original reads*: every body [ed.].

of the country, where I should meet few people, but here I found myself in the midst of a swarm of Southerners. I looked round me with fear and trembling, dreading to see someone[257] who would recognize me. I was rejoiced to find that we were to stay but a short time.

We soon returned to New York, to make arrangements for spending the remainder of the summer at Rockaway. While the laundress was putting the clothes in order, I took an opportunity to go over to Brooklyn to see Ellen. I met her going to a grocery store, and the first words she said, were, "O, mother, don't go to Mrs. Hobbs's. Her brother, Mr. Thorne, has come from the south, and maybe[258] he'll tell where you are." I accepted the warning. I told her I was going away with Mrs. Bruce the next day, and would try to see her when I came back.

Being in servitude to the Anglo-Saxon race, I was not put into a "Jim Crow car," on our way to Rockaway, neither was I invited to ride through the streets on the top of trunks in a truck; but everywhere[259] I found the same manifestations of that cruel prejudice, which so discourages the feelings, and represses the energies of the colored people. We reached Rockaway before dark, and put up at the Pavilion – a large hotel, beautifully situated by the sea-side – a great resort of the fashionable world. Thirty or forty nurses were there, of a great variety of nations. Some of the ladies had colored waiting-maids and coachmen, but I was the only nurse tinged with the blood of Africa. When the tea bell rang, I took little Mary and followed the other nurses. Supper was served in a long hall. A young man, who had the ordering of things, took the circuit of the table two or three times, and finally pointed me to a seat at the lower end of it. As there was but one chair, I sat down and took the child in my lap. Whereupon the young man came to me and said, in the blandest manner possible, "Will you please to seat the little girl in the chair, and stand behind it and feed her? After they have done, you will be shown to the kitchen, where you will have a good supper."

This was the climax! I found it hard to preserve my self-control, when I looked round, and saw women who were nurses, as I was, and only one shade lighter in complexion, eyeing me with a defiant look, as if my presence were a contamination. However, I said nothing. I quietly took the child in my arms, went to our room, and refused to go to the table again. Mr. Bruce ordered meals to be sent to the room for little Mary and I. This answered for a few days; but the waiters of the establishment were white, and they soon began to complain, saying they were not hired to wait on negroes. The landlord requested Mr. Bruce to send me down to my meals, because his servants rebelled against bringing them up, and the colored servants of other boarders were dissatisfied because all were not treated alike.

My answer was that the colored servants ought to be dissatisfied with *themselves*, for not having too much self-respect to submit to such treatment; that there was no difference in the price of board for colored and white servants, and there was no justification for difference of treatment. I staid a month after this, and finding I was resolved to stand up for my rights, they concluded to treat me well. Let every colored man and woman do this, and eventually we shall cease to be trampled under foot by our oppressors.

Notes

[257] *Original reads*: some one [ed.].

[258] *Original reads*: may be [ed.].

[259] *Original reads*: every where [ed.].

Chapter 36

The Hairbreadth Escape

After we returned to New York, I took the earliest opportunity to go and see Ellen. I asked to have her called downstairs;[260] for I supposed Mrs. Hobbs's southern brother might still be there, and I was desirous to avoid seeing him, if possible. But Mrs. Hobbs came to the kitchen, and insisted on my going upstairs.[261] "My brother wants to see you," said she, "and he is sorry you seem to shun him. He knows you are living in New York. He told me to say to you that he owes thanks to good old Aunt[262] Martha for too many little acts of kindness for him to be base enough to betray her grandchild."

This Mr. Thorne had become poor and reckless long before he left the south, and such persons had much rather go to one of the faithful old slaves to borrow a dollar, or get a good dinner, than to go to one whom they consider an equal. It was such acts of kindness as these for which he professed to feel grateful to my grandmother. I wished he had kept at a distance, but as he was here, and knew where I was, I concluded there was nothing to be gained by trying to avoid him; on the contrary, it might be the means of exciting his ill will. I followed his sister up stairs. He met me in a very friendly manner, congratulated me on my escape from slavery, and hoped I had a good place, where I felt happy.

I continued to visit Ellen as often as I could. She, good thoughtful child, never forgot my hazardous situation, but always kept a vigilant lookout for my safety. She never made any complaint about her own inconveniences and troubles; but a mother's observing eye easily perceived that she was not happy. On the occasion of one of my visits I found her unusually serious. When I asked her what was the matter, she said nothing was the matter. But I insisted upon knowing what made her look so very grave. Finally, I ascertained that she felt troubled about the dissipation that was continually going on in the house. She was sent to the store very often for rum and brandy, and she felt ashamed to ask for it so often; and Mr. Hobbs and Mr. Thorne drank a great deal, and their hands trembled so that they had to call her to pour out the liquor for them. "But for all that," said she, "Mr. Hobbs is good to me, and I can't help liking him. I feel sorry for him." I tried to comfort her, by telling her that I had laid up a hundred dollars, and that before long I hoped to be able to give her and Benjamin a home, and send them to school. She was always desirous not to add to my troubles more than she could help, and I did not discover till years afterwards that Mr. Thorne's intemperance was not the only annoyance she suffered from him. Though he professed too much gratitude to my grandmother to injure any of her descendants, he had poured vile language into the ears of her innocent great-grandchild.

I usually went to Brooklyn to spend Sunday afternoon. One Sunday, I found Ellen anxiously waiting for me near the house. "O, mother," said she, "I've been waiting for you this long time. I'm afraid Mr. Thorne has written to tell Dr. Flint where you are. Make haste and come in. Mrs. Hobbs will tell you all about it!"

The story was soon told. While the children were playing in the grape-vine arbor, the day before, Mr. Thorne came out with a letter in his hand, which he tore up and scattered about. Ellen was sweeping the yard at the time, and having her mind full of suspicions of him, she picked up the pieces and carried them to the children, saying, "I wonder who Mr. Thorne has been writing to."

Notes

[260] *Original reads*: down stairs [ed.].

[261] *Original reads*: up stairs [ed.].

[262] *Original reads*: aunt [ed.].

"I'm sure I don't know, and don't care," replied the oldest of the children; "and I don't see how it concerns you."

"But it does concern me," replied Ellen; "for I'm afraid he's been writing to the south about my mother."

They laughed at her, and called her a silly thing, but good-naturedly put the fragments of writing together, in order to read them to her. They were no sooner arranged, than the little girl exclaimed, "I declare, Ellen, I believe you are right."

The contents of Mr. Thorne's letter, as nearly as I can remember, were as follows: "I have seen your slave, Linda, and conversed with her. She can be taken very easily, if you manage prudently. There are enough of us here to swear to her identity as your property. I am a patriot, a lover of my country, and I do this as an act of justice to the laws." He concluded by informing the doctor of the street and number where I lived. The children carried the pieces to Mrs. Hobbs, who immediately went to her brother's room for an explanation. He was not to be found. The servants said they saw him go out with a letter in his hand, and they supposed he had gone to the post office. The natural inference was that he had sent to Dr. Flint a copy of those fragments. When he returned, his sister accused him of it, and he did not deny the charge. He went immediately to his room, and the next morning he was missing. He had gone over to New York, before any of the family were astir.

It was evident that I had no time to lose; and I hastened back to the city with a heavy heart. Again I was to be torn from a comfortable home, and all my plans for the welfare of my children were to be frustrated by that demon Slavery! I now regretted that I never told Mrs. Bruce my story. I had not concealed it merely on account of being a fugitive; that would have made her anxious, but it would have excited sympathy in her kind heart. I valued her good opinion, and I was afraid of losing it, if I told her all the particulars of my sad story. But now I felt that it was necessary for her to know how I was situated. I had once left her abruptly, without explaining the reason, and it would not be proper to do it again. I went home resolved to tell her in the morning. But the sadness of my face attracted her attention, and, in answer to her kind inquiries, I poured out my full heart to her, before bedtime.[263] She listened with true womanly sympathy, and told me she would do all she could to protect me. How my heart blessed her!

Early the next morning, Judge Vanderpool and Lawyer Hopper were consulted. They said I had better leave the city at once, as the risk would be great if the case came to trial. Mrs. Bruce took me in a carriage to the house of one of her friends, where she assured me I should be safe until my brother could arrive, which would be in a few days. In the interval my thoughts were much occupied with Ellen. She was mine by birth, and she was also mine by Southern law, since my grandmother held the bill of sale that made her so. I did not feel that she was safe unless I had her with me. Mrs. Hobbs, who felt badly about her brother's treachery, yielded to my entreaties, on condition that she should return in ten days. I avoided making any promise. She came to me clad in very thin garments, all outgrown, and with a school satchel on her arm, containing a few articles. It was late in October, and I knew the child must suffer; and not daring to go out in the streets to purchase anything,[264] I took off my own flannel skirt and converted it into one for her. Kind Mrs. Bruce came to bid me goodbye,[265] and when she saw that I had taken off my clothing for my child, the tears came to her eyes.

Notes

[263] *Original reads*: bed time [ed.].

[264] *Original reads*: any thing [ed.].

[265] *Original reads*: good by [ed.].

She said, "Wait for me, Linda," and went out. She soon returned with a nice warm shawl and hood for Ellen. Truly, of such souls as hers is[266] the kingdom of heaven.

My brother reached New York on Wednesday. Lawyer Hopper advised us to go to Boston by the Stonington route, as there was less Southern travel in that direction. Mrs. Bruce directed her servants to tell all inquirers that I formerly lived there, but had gone from the city.

We reached the steamboat Rhode Island in safety. That boat employed colored hands, but I knew that colored passengers were not admitted to the cabin. I was very desirous for the seclusion of the cabin, not only on account of exposure to the night air, but also to avoid observation. Lawyer Hopper was waiting on board for us. He spoke to the stewardess, and asked, as a particular favor, that she would treat us well. He said to me, "Go and speak to the captain yourself by and by. Take your little girl with you, and I am sure that he will not let her sleep on deck." With these kind words and a shake of the hand he departed.

The boat was soon on her way, bearing me rapidly from the friendly home where I had hoped to find security and rest. My brother had left me to purchase the tickets, thinking that I might have better success than he would. When the stewardess came to me, I paid what she asked, and she gave me three tickets with clipped corners. In the most unsophisticated manner I said, "You have made a mistake; I asked you for cabin tickets. I cannot possibly consent to sleep on deck with my little daughter." She assured me there was no mistake. She said on some of the routes colored people were allowed to sleep in the cabin, but not on this route, which was much travelled by the wealthy. I asked her to show me to the captain's office, and she said she would after tea. When the time came, I took Ellen by the hand and went to the captain, politely requesting him to change our tickets, as we should be very uncomfortable on deck. He said it was contrary to their custom, but he would see that we had berths below; he would also try to obtain comfortable seats for us in the cars; of that he was not certain, but he would speak to the conductor about it, when the boat arrived. I thanked him, and returned to the ladies' cabin. He came afterwards and told me that the conductor of the cars was on board, that he had spoken to him, and he had promised to take care of us. I was very much surprised at receiving so much kindness. I don't know whether the pleasing face of my little girl had won his heart, or whether the stewardess inferred from Lawyer Hopper's manner that I was a fugitive, and had pleaded with him in my behalf.

When the boat arrived at Stonington, the conductor kept his promise, and showed us to seats in the first car, nearest the engine. He asked us to take seats next the door, but as he passed through, we ventured to move on toward the other end of the car. No incivility was offered us, and we reached Boston in safety.

The day after my arrival was one of the happiest of my life. I felt as if I was beyond the reach of the bloodhounds; and, for the first time during many years, I had both my children together with me. They greatly enjoyed their reunion, and laughed and chatted merrily. I watched them with a swelling heart. Their every motion delighted me.

I could not feel safe in New York, and I accepted the offer of a friend, that we should share expenses and keep house together. I represented to Mrs. Hobbs that Ellen must have some schooling, and must remain with me for that purpose. She felt ashamed of being unable to read or spell at her age, so instead of sending her to school with Benny, I instructed her myself till she was fit[267] to enter an intermediate school. The winter passed pleasantly, while I was busy with my needle, and my children with their books.

Notes

[266] *Original reads*: are [ed.].

[267] *Original reads*: fitted [ed.].

Chapter 37

A Visit to England

In the spring, sad news came to me. Mrs. Bruce was dead. Never again, in this world, should I see her gentle face, or hear her sympathizing voice. I had lost an excellent friend, and little Mary had lost a tender mother. Mr. Bruce wished the child to visit some of her mother's relatives in England, and he was desirous that I should take charge of her. The little motherless one was accustomed to me, and attached to me, and I thought she would be happier in my care than in that of a stranger. I could also earn more in this way than I could by my needle. So I put Benny to a trade, and left Ellen to remain in the house with my friend and go to school.

We sailed from New York, and arrived in Liverpool after a pleasant voyage of twelve days. We proceeded directly to London, and took lodgings at the Adelaide Hotel. The supper seemed to me less luxurious than those I had seen in American hotels; but my situation was indescribably more pleasant. For the first time in my life I was in a place where I was treated according to my deportment, without reference to my complexion. I felt as if a great millstone had been lifted from my breast. Ensconced in a pleasant room, with my dear little charge, I laid my head on my pillow, for the first time, with the delightful consciousness of pure, unadulterated freedom.

As I had constant care of the child, I had little opportunity to see the wonders of that great city; but I watched the tide of life that flowed through the streets, and found it a strange contrast to the stagnation in our Southern towns. Mr. Bruce took his little daughter to spend some days with friends in Oxford Crescent, and of course it was necessary for me to accompany her. I had heard much of the systematic method of English education, and I was very desirous that my dear Mary should steer straight in the midst of so much propriety. I closely observed her little playmates and their nurses, being ready to take any lessons in the science of good management. The children were more rosy than American children, but I did not see that they differed materially in other respects. They were like all children – sometimes docile and sometimes wayward.

We next went to Steventon, in Berkshire. It was a small town, said to be the poorest in the county. I saw men working in the fields for six shillings, and seven shillings, a week, and women for sixpence, and seven-pence, a day, out of which they boarded themselves. Of course they lived in the most primitive manner; it could not be otherwise, where a woman's wages for an entire day were not sufficient to buy a pound of meat. They paid very low rents, and their clothes were made of the cheapest fabrics, though much better than could have been procured in the United States for the same money. I had heard much about the oppression of the poor in Europe. The people I saw around me were, many of them, among the poorest poor. But when I visited them in their little thatched cottages, I felt that the condition of even the meanest and most ignorant among them was vastly superior to the condition of the most favored slaves in America. They labored hard; but they were not ordered out to toil while the stars were in the sky, and driven and slashed by an overseer, through heat and cold, till the stars shone out again. Their homes were very humble; but they were protected by law. No insolent patrols could come, in the dead of night, and flog them at their pleasure. The father, when he closed his cottage door, felt safe with his family around him. No master or overseer could come and take from him his wife, or his daughter. They must separate to earn their living; but the parents knew where their children were going, and could communicate with them by letters. The relations of husband and wife, parent and child, were too sacred for the richest noble in the land to violate with impunity. Much was being done to enlighten these poor people. Schools were established among them, and benevolent societies were active in efforts to ameliorate their condition. There was no law forbidding them to learn to read and write; and if they helped each other in spelling out the Bible, they were in no danger of thirty-nine lashes, as was the case with myself and poor, pious, old Uncle[268] Fred. I repeat that the most ignorant and the most destitute of these peasants was a thousand fold better off than the most pampered American slave.

I do not deny that the poor are oppressed in Europe. I am not disposed to paint their condition so rose-colored as the Hon. Miss Murray[269] paints the condition of the slaves in the United States. A small portion of *my* experience would enable her to read her own pages with anointed eyes. If she were to lay aside her title, and, instead of visiting among the fashionable, become domesticated, as a poor governess, on some plantation in Louisiana or Alabama, she would see and hear things that would make her tell quite a different story.

My visit to England is a memorable event in my life, from the fact of my having there received strong religious impressions. The contemptuous manner in which the communion had been administered to colored people in my native place; the church membership of Dr. Flint, and others like him; and the buying and selling of slaves by professed ministers of the gospel, had given me a prejudice against the Episcopal Church.[270] The whole service seemed to me a mockery and a sham. But my home in Steventon was in the family of a clergyman, who was a true disciple of Jesus. The beauty of his daily life inspired me with faith in the genuineness of Christian professions. Grace entered my heart, and I knelt at the communion table, I trust, in true humility of soul.

I remained abroad ten months, which was much longer than I had anticipated. During all that time, I never saw the slightest symptom of prejudice against color. Indeed, I entirely forgot it, till the time came for us to return to America.

Chapter 38

Renewed Invitations to Go South

We had a tedious winter passage, and from the distance spectres seemed to rise up on the shores of the United States. It is a sad feeling to be afraid of one's native country. We arrived in New York safely, and I hastened to Boston to look after my children. I found Ellen well, and improving at her school; but Benny was not there to welcome me. He had been left at a good place to learn a trade, and for several months everything[271] worked well. He was liked by the master, and was a favorite with his fellow-apprentices; but one day they accidentally discovered a fact they had never before suspected – that he was colored! This at once transformed him into a different being. Some of the apprentices were Americans, others American-born Irish; and it was offensive to their dignity to have a "nigger" among them, after they had been told that he *was* a "nigger." They began by treating him with silent scorn, and finding that he returned the same, they resorted to insults and abuse. He was too spirited a boy to stand that, and he went off. Being desirous to do something to support himself, and having no one to advise him, he shipped for a whaling voyage. When I received these

Notes

[268] *Original reads*: uncle [ed.].

[269] Amelia Matilda Murray (1795–1884), botanist, artist, and advocate for the abolition of slavery; fourth daughter of Anglican cleric Lord George Murray (1761–1803).

[270] *Original reads*: church [ed.].

[271] *Original reads*: every thing [ed.].

tidings I shed many tears, and bitterly reproached myself for having left him so long. But I had done it for the best, and now all I could do was to pray to the heavenly Father to guide and protect him.

Not long after my return, I received the following letter from Miss Emily Flint, now Mrs. Dodge:–

"In this you will recognize the hand of your friend and mistress. Having heard that you had gone with a family to Europe, I have waited to hear of your return to write to you. I should have answered the letter you wrote to me long since, but as I could not then act independently of my father, I knew there could be nothing done satisfactory to you. There were persons here who were willing to buy you and run the risk of getting you. To this I would not consent. I have always been attached to you, and would not like to see you the slave of another, or have unkind treatment. I am married now, and can protect you. My husband expects to move to Virginia this spring, where we think of settling. I am very anxious that you should come and live with me. If you are not willing to come, you may purchase yourself; but I should prefer having you live with me. If you come, you may, if you like, spend a month with your grandmother and friends, then come to me in Norfolk, Virginia. Think this over, and write as soon as possible, and let me know the conclusion. Hoping that your children are well, I remain you friend and mistress."

Of course I did not write to return thanks for this cordial invitation. I felt insulted to be thought stupid enough to be caught by such professions.

"'Come up into my parlor,' said the spider to the fly;
''Tis the prettiest little parlor that ever you did spy.'"

It was plain that Dr. Flint's family were apprised of my movements, since they knew of my voyage to Europe. I expected to have further trouble from them; but having eluded them thus far, I hoped to be as successful in future. The money I had earned, I was desirous to devote to the education of my children, and to secure a home for them. It seemed not only hard, but unjust, to pay for myself. I could not possibly regard myself as a piece of property. Moreover, I had worked many years without wages, and during that time had been obliged to depend on my grandmother for many comforts in food and clothing. My children certainly belonged to me; but though Dr. Flint had incurred no expense for their support, he had received a large sum of money for them. I knew the law would decide that I was his property, and would probably still give his daughter a claim to my children; but I regarded such laws as the regulations of robbers, who had no rights that I was bound to respect.

The Fugitive Slave Law had not then passed. The judges of Massachusetts had not then stooped under chains to enter her courts of justice, so called. I knew my old master was rather skittish of Massachusetts. I relied on her love of freedom, and felt safe on her soil. I am now aware that I honored the old Commonwealth beyond her deserts.

Chapter 39

The Confession

For two years my daughter and I supported ourselves comfortably in Boston. At the end of that time, my brother William offered to send Ellen to a boarding school. It required a great effort for me to consent to part with her, for I had few near ties, and it was her presence that made my two little rooms seem home-like. But my judgment prevailed over my selfish feelings. I made preparations for her departure. During the two years we had lived together I had often resolved to tell her something about her father; but I had never been able to muster sufficient courage. I had a shrinking dread of diminishing my child's love. I knew she must have curiosity on the subject, but she had never asked a question. She was always very careful not to say anything[272] to remind me of my troubles. Now that she was going from me, I thought if I should die before she returned, she might hear my story from someone[273] who did not understand the palliating circumstances; and that if she were entirely ignorant on the subject, her sensitive nature might receive a rude shock.

When we retired for the night, she said, "Mother, it is very hard to leave you alone. I am almost sorry I am going, though I do want to improve myself. But you will write to me often; won't you, mother?"

I did not throw my arms round her. I did not answer her. But in a calm, solemn way, for it cost me great effort, I said, "Listen to me, Ellen; I have something to tell you!" I recounted my early sufferings in slavery, and told her how nearly they had crushed me. I began to tell her how they had driven me into a great sin, when she clasped me in her arms, and exclaimed, "O, don't, mother! Please don't tell me any more."

I said, "But, my child, I want you to know about your father."

"I know all about it, mother," she replied; "I am nothing to my father, and he is nothing to me. All my love is for you. I was with him five months in Washington, and he never cared for me. He never spoke to me as he did to his little Fanny. I knew all the time he was my father, for Fanny's nurse told me so; but she said I must never tell anybody,[274] and I never did. I used to wish he would take me in his arms and kiss me, as he did Fanny; or that he would sometimes smile at me, as he did at her. I thought if he was my own father, he ought to love me. I was a little girl then, and didn't know any better. But now I never think anything[275] about my father. All my love is for you." She hugged me closer as she spoke, and I thanked God that the knowledge I had so much dreaded to impart had not diminished the affection of my child. I had not the slightest idea she knew that portion of my history. If I had, I should have spoken to her long before; for my pent-up feelings had often longed to pour themselves out to someone[276] I could trust. But I loved the dear girl better for the delicacy she had manifested towards her unfortunate mother.

The next morning, she and her uncle started on their journey to the village in New York, where she was to be placed at school. It seemed as if all the sunshine had gone away. My little room was dreadfully lonely. I was thankful when a message came from a lady, accustomed to employ me, requesting me to come and sew in her family for several weeks. On my return, I found a letter from brother William. He thought of opening an anti-slavery reading room in Rochester, and combining with it the sale of some books and stationery; and he wanted me to unite with him. We tried it, but it was not successful. We found warm anti-slavery friends there, but the feeling was not general enough to support such an establishment. I passed nearly a year in the family of Isaac and Amy Post, practical believers in the Christian doctrine of human brotherhood. They measured a man's worth by his character, not by his complexion. The memory of those beloved and honored friends will remain with me to my latest hour.

Notes

[272] *Original reads*: any thing [ed.].

[273] *Original reads*: some one [ed.].

[274] *Original reads*: any body [ed.].

[275] *Original reads*: any thing [ed.].

[276] *Original reads*: some one [ed.].

Chapter 40

The Fugitive Slave Law

My brother, being disappointed in his project, concluded to go to California; and it was agreed that Benjamin should go with him. Ellen liked her school, and was a great favorite there. They did not know her history, and she did not tell it, because she had no desire to make capital out of their sympathy. But when it was accidentally discovered that her mother was a fugitive slave, every method was used to increase her advantages and diminish her expenses.

I was alone again. It was necessary for me to be earning money, and I preferred that it should be among those who knew me. On my return from Rochester, I called at the house of Mr. Bruce, to see Mary, the darling little babe that had thawed my heart, when it was freezing into a cheerless distrust of all my fellow-beings. She was growing a tall girl now, but I loved her always. Mr. Bruce had married again, and it was proposed that I should become nurse to a new infant. I had but one hesitation, and that was my feeling of insecurity in New York, now greatly increased by the passage of the Fugitive Slave Law. However, I resolved to try the experiment. I was again fortunate in my employer. The new Mrs. Bruce was an American, brought up under aristocratic influences, and still living in the midst of them; but if she had any prejudice against color, I was never made aware of it; and as for the system of slavery, she had a most hearty dislike of it. No sophistry of Southerners could blind her to its enormity. She was a person of excellent principles and a noble heart. To me, from that hour to the present, she has been a true and sympathizing friend. Blessings be with her and hers!

About the time that I reentered the Bruce family, an event occurred of disastrous import to the colored people. The slave Hamlin, the first fugitive that came under the new law, was given up by the bloodhounds of the north to the bloodhounds of the south. It was the beginning of a reign of terror to the colored population. The great city rushed on in its whirl of excitement, taking no note of the "short and simple annals of the poor."[277] But while fashionables were listening to the thrilling voice of Jenny Lind in Metropolitan Hall, the thrilling voices of poor hunted colored people went up, in an agony of supplication, to the Lord, from Zion's church. Many families, who had lived in the city for twenty years, fled from it now. Many a poor washerwoman, who, by hard labor, had made herself a comfortable home, was obliged to sacrifice her furniture, bid a hurried farewell to friends, and seek her fortune among strangers in Canada. Many a wife discovered a secret she had never known before – that her husband was a fugitive, and must leave her to ensure[278] his own safety. Worse still, many a husband discovered that his wife had fled from slavery years ago, and as "the child follows the condition of its mother," the children of his love were liable to be seized and carried into slavery. Everywhere,[279] in those humble homes, there was consternation and anguish. But what cared the legislators of the "dominant race" for the blood they were crushing out of trampled hearts?

When my brother William spent his last evening with me, before he went to California, we talked nearly all the time of the distress brought on our oppressed people by the passage of this iniquitous law; and never had I seen him manifest such bitterness of spirit, such stern hostility to our oppressors. He was himself free from the

Notes

[277] *"short and simple annals of the poor."* from "Elegy Written in a Country Churchyard" (1751) by Thomas Gray (1716–1771).

[278] *Original reads*: insure [ed.].

[279] *Original reads*: Every where [ed.].

operation of the law; for he did not run from any Slaveholding State, being brought into the Free States by his master. But I was subject to it; and so were hundreds of intelligent and industrious people all around us. I seldom ventured into the streets; and when it was necessary to do an errand for Mrs. Bruce, or any of the family, I went as much as possible through back streets and by-ways. What a disgrace to a city calling itself free, that inhabitants, guiltless of offence, and seeking to perform their duties conscientiously, should be condemned to live in such incessant fear, and have nowhere to turn for protection! This state of things, of course, gave rise to many impromptu vigilance committees. Every colored person, and every friend of their persecuted race, kept their eyes wide open. Every evening I examined the newspapers carefully, to see what Southerners had put up at the hotels. I did this for my own sake, thinking my young mistress and her husband might be among the list; I wished also to give information to others, if necessary; for if many were "running to and fro," I resolved that "knowledge should be increased."[280]

This brings up one of my Southern reminiscences, which I will here briefly relate. I was somewhat acquainted with a slave named Luke, who belonged to a wealthy man in our vicinity. His master died, leaving a son and daughter heirs to his large fortune. In the division of the slaves, Luke was included in the son's portion. This young man became a prey to the vices growing out of the "patriarchal institution," and when he went to the north, to complete his education, he carried his vices with him. He was brought home, deprived of the use of his limbs, by excessive dissipation. Luke was appointed to wait upon his bed-ridden master, whose despotic habits were greatly increased by exasperation at his own helplessness. He kept a cowhide beside him, and, for the most trivial occurrence, he would order his attendant to bare his back, and kneel beside the couch, while he whipped him till his strength was exhausted. Some days he was not allowed to wear anything[281] but his shirt, in order to be in readiness to be flogged. A day seldom passed without his receiving more or less blows. If the slightest resistance was offered, the town constable was sent for to execute the punishment, and Luke learned from experience how much more the constable's strong arm was to be dreaded than the comparatively feeble one of his master. The arm of his tyrant grew weaker, and was finally palsied; and then the constable's services were in constant requisition. The fact that he was entirely dependent on Luke's care, and was obliged to be tended like an infant, instead of inspiring any gratitude or compassion towards his poor slave, seemed only to increase his irritability and cruelty. As he lay there on his bed, a mere degraded wreck of manhood, he took into his head the strangest freaks of despotism; and if Luke hesitated to submit to his orders, the constable was immediately sent for. Some of these freaks were of a nature too filthy to be repeated. When I fled from the house of bondage, I left poor Luke still chained to the bedside of this cruel and disgusting wretch.

One day, when I had been requested to do an errand for Mrs. Bruce, I was hurrying through back streets, as usual, when I saw a young man approaching, whose face was familiar to me. As he came nearer, I recognized Luke. I always rejoiced to see or hear of anyone[282] who had escaped from the black pit; but, remembering this poor fellow's extreme hardships, I was peculiarly glad to see him on Northern soil, though I no longer called it *free* soil. I well remembered what a desolate feeling it was to be alone among strangers, and I went up to him and greeted him cordially. At first, he did not

Notes

[280] *"running to and fro,"... "knowledge should be increased."* Daniel 12:4.

[281] *Original reads*: any thing [ed.].

[282] *Original reads*: any one [ed.].

know me; but when I mentioned my name, he remembered all about me. I told him of the Fugitive Slave Law, and asked him if he did not know that New York was a city of kidnappers.

He replied, "De risk ain't so bad for me, as 'tis fur you. 'Cause I runned away from de speculator, and you runned away from de massa. Dem speculators vont spen dar money to come here fur a runaway, if dey ain't sartin sure to put dar hans right on him. An I tell you I's tuk good car 'bout dat. I had too hard times down dar, to let 'em ketch dis nigger."

He then told me of the advice he had received, and the plans he had laid. I asked if he had money enough to take him to Canada. "'Pend upon it, I hab," he replied. "I tuk car fur dat. I'd bin workin all my days fur dem cussed whites, an got no pay but kicks and cuffs. So I tought dis nigger had a right to money nuff to bring him to de Free States. Massa Henry he lib till ebery body vish him dead; an ven he did die, I knowed de debbil would hab him, an vouldn't vant him to bring his money 'long too. So I tuk some of his bills, and put 'em in de pocket of his ole trousers. An ven he was buried, dis nigger ask fur dem ole trousers, an dey gub 'em to me." With a low, chuckling laugh, he added, "You see I didn't *steal* it; dey *gub* it to me. I tell you, I had mighty hard time to keep de speculator from findin it; but he didn't git it."

This is a fair specimen of how the moral sense is educated by slavery. When a man has his wages stolen from him, year after year, and the laws sanction and enforce the theft, how can he be expected to have more regard to honesty than has the man who robs him? I have become somewhat enlightened, but I confess that I agree with poor, ignorant, much-abused Luke, in thinking he had a *right* to that money, as a portion of his unpaid wages. He went to Canada forthwith, and I have not since heard from him.

All that winter I lived in a state of anxiety. When I took the children out to breathe the air, I closely observed the countenances of all I met. I dreaded the approach of summer, when snakes and slaveholders make their appearance. I was, in fact, a slave in New York, as subject to slave laws as I had been in a Slave State. Strange incongruity in a State called free!

Spring returned, and I received warning from the south that Dr. Flint knew of my return to my old place, and was making preparations to have me caught. I learned afterwards that my dress, and that of Mrs. Brace's children, had been described to him by some of the Northern tools, which slaveholders employ for their base purposes, and then indulge in sneers at their cupidity and mean servility.

I immediately informed Mrs. Bruce of my danger, and she took prompt measures for my safety. My place as nurse could not be supplied immediately, and this generous, sympathizing lady proposed that I should carry her baby away. It was a comfort to me to have the child with me; for the heart is reluctant to be torn away from every object it loves. But how few mothers would have consented to have one of their own babes become a fugitive, for the sake of a poor, hunted nurse, on whom the legislators of the country had let loose the bloodhounds! When I spoke of the sacrifice she was making, in depriving herself of her dear baby, she replied, "It is better for you to have baby with you, Linda; for if they get on your track, they will be obliged to bring the child to me; and then, if there is a possibility of saving you, you shall be saved."

This lady had a very wealthy relative, a benevolent gentleman in many respects, but aristocratic and pro-slavery. He remonstrated with her for harboring a fugitive slave; told her she was violating the laws of her country; and asked her if she was aware of the penalty. She replied, "I am very well aware of it. It is imprisonment and one thousand dollars fine. Shame on my country that it *is* so! I am ready to incur the penalty. I will go to the state's prison, rather than have any poor victim torn from *my* house, to be carried back to slavery."

The noble heart! The brave heart! The tears are in my eyes while I write of her. May the God of the helpless reward her for her sympathy with my persecuted people!

I was sent into New England, where I was sheltered by the wife of a senator, whom I shall always hold in grateful remembrance. This honorable gentleman would not have voted for the Fugitive Slave Law, as did the senator in "Uncle Tom's Cabin"; on the contrary, he was strongly opposed to it; but he was enough under its influence to be afraid of having me remain in his house many hours. So I was sent into the country, where I remained a month with the baby. When it was supposed that Dr. Flint's emissaries had lost track of me, and given up the pursuit for the present, I returned to New York.

Chapter 41

Free at Last

MRS. BRUCE, and every member of her family, were exceedingly kind to me. I was thankful for the blessings of my lot, yet I could not always wear a cheerful countenance. I was doing harm to no one; on the contrary, I was doing all the good I could in my small way; yet I could never go out to breathe God's free air without trepidation at my heart. This seemed hard; and I could not think it was a right state of things in any civilized country.

From time to time I received news from my good old grandmother. She could not write; but she employed others to write for her. The following is an extract from one of her last letters:–

"Dear Daughter: I cannot hope to see you again on earth; but I pray to God to unite us above, where pain will no more rack this feeble body of mine; where sorrow and parting from my children will be no more.[283] God has promised these things if we are faithful unto the end. My age and feeble health deprive me of going to church now; but God is with me here at home. Thank your brother for his kindness. Give much love to him, and tell him to remember the Creator[284] in the days of his youth, and strive to meet me in the Father's kingdom. Love to Ellen and Benjamin. Don't neglect him. Tell him for me, to be a good boy. Strive, my child, to train them for God's children. May he protect and provide for you, is the prayer of your loving old mother."

These letters both cheered and saddened me. I was always glad to have tidings from the kind, faithful old friend of my unhappy youth; but her messages of love made my heart yearn to see her before she died, and I mourned over the fact that it was impossible. Some months after I returned from my flight to New England, I received a letter from her, in which she wrote, "Dr. Flint is dead. He has left a distressed family. Poor old man! I hope he made his peace with God."

I remembered how he had defrauded my grandmother of the hard earnings she had loaned; how he had tried to cheat her out of the freedom her mistress had promised her, and how he had persecuted her children; and I thought to myself that she was a better Christian than I was, if she could entirely forgive him. I cannot say, with truth, that the news of my old master's death softened my feelings towards him. There are wrongs which even the grave does not bury. The man was odious to me while he lived, and his memory is odious now.

Notes

[283] *"will be no more"* Revelations 21:4.

[284] *"remember the Creator"* Ecclesiastes 12:1.

His departure from this world did not diminish my danger. He had threatened my grandmother that his heirs should hold me in slavery after he was gone; that I never should be free so long as a child of his survived. As for Mrs. Flint, I had seen her in deeper afflictions than I supposed the loss of her husband would be, for she had buried several children; yet I never saw any signs of softening in her heart. The doctor had died in embarrassed circumstances, and had little to will to his heirs, except such property as he was unable to grasp. I was well aware what I had to expect from the family of Flints; and my fears were confirmed by a letter from the south, warning me to be on my guard, because Mrs. Flint openly declared that her daughter could not afford to lose so valuable a slave as I was.

I kept close watch of the newspapers for arrivals; but one Saturday night, being much occupied, I forgot to examine the Evening Express as usual. I went down into the parlor for it, early in the morning, and found the boy about to kindle a fire with it. I took it from him and examined the list of arrivals. Reader, if you have never been a slave, you cannot imagine the acute sensation of suffering at my heart, when I read the names of Mr. and Mrs. Dodge, at a hotel in Courtland Street. It was a third-rate hotel, and that circumstance convinced me of the truth of what I had heard, that they were short of funds and had need of my value, as *they* valued me; and that was by dollars and cents. I hastened with the paper to Mrs. Bruce. Her heart and hand were always open to everyone[285] in distress, and she always warmly sympathized with mine. It was impossible to tell how near the enemy was. He might have passed and repassed the house while we were sleeping. He might at that moment be waiting to pounce upon me if I ventured out of doors. I had never seen the husband of my young mistress, and therefore I could not distinguish him from any other stranger. A carriage was hastily ordered; and, closely veiled, I followed Mrs. Bruce, taking the baby again with me into exile. After various turnings and crossings, and returnings, the carriage stopped at the house of one of Mrs. Bruce's friends, where I was kindly received. Mrs. Bruce returned immediately, to instruct the domestics what to say if anyone[286] came to inquire for me.

It was lucky for me that the evening paper was not burned up before I had a chance to examine the list of arrivals. It was not long after Mrs. Bruce's return to her house, before several people came to inquire for me. One inquired for me, another asked for my daughter Ellen, and another said he had a letter from my grandmother, which he was requested to deliver in person.

They were told, "She *has* lived here, but she has left."

"How long ago?"

"I don't know, sir."

"Do you know where she went?"

"I do not, sir." And the door was closed.

This Mr. Dodge, who claimed me as his property, was originally a Yankee peddler[287] in the south; then he became a merchant, and finally a slaveholder. He managed to get introduced into what was called the first society, and married Miss Emily Flint. A quarrel arose between him and her brother, and the brother cowhided him. This led to a family feud, and he proposed to remove to Virginia. Dr. Flint left him no property, and his own means had become circumscribed, while a wife and children depended upon him for support. Under these circumstances, it was very natural that he should make an effort to put me into his pocket.

Notes

[285] *Original reads*: every one [ed.].

[286] *Original reads*: any one [ed.].

[287] *Original reads*: pedler [ed.].

I had a colored friend, a man from my native place, in whom I had the most implicit confidence. I sent for him, and told him that Mr. and Mrs. Dodge had arrived in New York. I proposed that he should call upon them to make inquiries about his friends at the south, with whom Dr. Flint's family were well acquainted. He thought there was no impropriety in his doing so, and he consented. He went to the hotel, and knocked at the door of Mr. Dodge's room, which was opened by the gentleman himself, who gruffly inquired, "What brought you here? How came you to know I was in the city?"

"Your arrival was published in the evening papers, sir; and I called to ask Mrs. Dodge about my friends at home. I didn't suppose it would give any offence."

"Where's that negro girl, that belongs to my wife?"

"What girl, sir?"

"You know well enough. I mean Linda, that ran away from Dr. Flint's plantation, some years ago. I dare say you've seen her, and know where she is."

"Yes, sir, I've seen her, and know where she is. She is out of your reach, sir."

"Tell me where she is, or bring her to me, and I will give her a chance to buy her freedom."

"I don't think it would be of any use, sir. I have heard her say she would go to the ends of the earth, rather than pay any man or woman for her freedom, because she thinks she has a right to it. Besides, she couldn't do it, if she would, for she has spent her earnings to educate her children."

This made Mr. Dodge very angry, and some high words passed between them. My friend was afraid to come where I was; but in the course of the day I received a note from him. I supposed they had not come from the south, in the winter, for a pleasure excursion; and now the nature of their business was very plain.

Mrs. Bruce came to me and entreated me to leave the city the next morning. She said her house was watched, and it was possible that some clue[288] to me might be obtained. I refused to take her advice. She pleaded with an earnest tenderness, that ought to have moved me; but I was in a bitter, disheartened mood. I was weary of flying from pillar to post. I had been chased during half my life, and it seemed as if the chase was never to end. There I sat, in that great city, guiltless of crime, yet not daring to worship God in any of the churches. I heard the bells ringing for afternoon service, and, with contemptuous sarcasm, I said, "Will the preachers take for their text, 'Proclaim liberty to the captive, and the opening of prison doors to them that are bound'?[289] or will they preach from the text, 'Do unto others as ye would they should do unto you'?"[290] Oppressed Poles and Hungarians could find a safe refuge in that city; John Mitchell[291] was free to proclaim in the City Hall his desire for "a plantation well stocked with slaves"; but there I sat, an oppressed American, not daring to show my face. God forgive the black and bitter thoughts I indulged on that Sabbath day! The Scripture says, "Oppression makes even a wise man mad";[292] and I was not wise.

I had been told that Mr. Dodge said his wife had never signed away her right to my children, and if he could not get me, he would take them. This it was, more than anything[293] else, that roused such a tempest in my soul. Benjamin was with his Uncle[294] William in California, but my innocent young daughter had come to spend a vacation with me. I thought of what I had suffered in slavery at her age, and my heart was like a tiger's when a hunter tries to seize her young.

Notes

[288] *Original reads*: clew [ed.].

[289] *"Proclaim liberty to the captive … bound"* Isaiah 61:1.

[290] *"Do unto others … unto you"* Matthew 7:12.

[291] John Mitchell (1815–1875), proslavery Irish nationalist.

[292] *"Oppression makes … mad"* Ecclesiastes 7:17.

[293] *Original reads*: any thing [ed.].

[294] *Original reads*: uncle [ed.].

Dear Mrs. Bruce! I seem to see the expression of her face, as she turned away discouraged by my obstinate mood. Finding her expostulations unavailing, she sent Ellen to entreat me. When ten o'clock in the evening arrived and Ellen had not returned, this watchful and unwearied friend became anxious. She came to us in a carriage, bringing a well-filled trunk for my journey – trusting that by this time I would listen to reason. I yielded to her, as I ought to have done before.

The next day, baby and I set out in a heavy snow storm, bound for New England again. I received letters from the City of Iniquity, addressed to me under an assumed name. In a few days one came from Mrs. Bruce, informing me that my new master was still searching for me, and that she intended to put an end to this persecution by buying my freedom. I felt grateful for the kindness that prompted this offer, but the idea was not so pleasant to me as might have been expected. The more my mind had become enlightened, the more difficult it was for me to consider myself an article of property; and to pay money to those who had so grievously oppressed me seemed like taking from my sufferings the glory of triumph. I wrote to Mrs. Bruce, thanking her, but saying that being sold from one owner to another seemed too much like slavery; that such a great obligation could not be easily cancelled; and that I preferred to go to my brother in California.

Without my knowledge, Mrs. Bruce employed a gentleman in New York to enter into negotiations with Mr. Dodge. He proposed to pay three hundred dollars down, if Mr. Dodge would sell me, and enter into obligations to relinquish all claim to me or my children forever after. He who called himself my master said he scorned so small an offer for such a valuable servant. The gentleman replied, "You can do as you choose, sir. If you reject this offer you will never get anything;[295] for the woman has friends who will convey her and her children out of the country."

Mr. Dodge concluded that "half a loaf was better than no bread," and he agreed to the proffered terms. By the next mail I received this brief letter from Mrs. Bruce: "I am rejoiced to tell you that the money for your freedom has been paid to Mr. Dodge. Come home to-morrow. I long to see you and my sweet babe."

My brain reeled as I read these lines. A gentleman near me said, "It's true; I have seen the bill of sale." "The bill of sale!" Those words struck me like a blow. So I was *sold* at last! A human being *sold* in the free city of New York! The bill of sale is on record, and future generations will learn from it that women were articles of traffic in New York, late in the nineteenth century of the Christian religion. It may hereafter prove a useful document to antiquaries, who are seeking to measure the progress of civilization in the United States. I well know the value of that bit of paper; but much as I love freedom, I do not like to look upon it. I am deeply grateful to the generous friend who procured it, but I despise the miscreant who demanded payment for what never rightfully belonged to him or his.

I had objected to having my freedom bought, yet I must confess that when it was done I felt as if a heavy load had been lifted from my weary shoulders. When I rode home in the cars I was no longer afraid to unveil my face and look at people as they passed. I should have been glad to have met Daniel Dodge himself; to have had him see me and know me,[296] that he might have mourned over the untoward circumstances which compelled him to sell me for three hundred dollars.

When I reached home, the arms of my benefactress were thrown round me, and our tears mingled. As soon as she could speak, she said, "O Linda, I'm *so* glad it's all

Notes

[295] *Original reads*: any thing [ed.].

[296] *Original reads*: to have had him seen me and known me [ed.].

over! You wrote to me as if you thought you were going to be transferred from one owner to another. But I did not buy you for your services. I should have done just the same if you had been going to sail for California to-morrow. I should, at least, have the satisfaction of knowing that you left me a free woman."

My heart was exceedingly full. I remembered how my poor father had tried to buy me, when I was a small child, and how he had been disappointed. I hoped his spirit was rejoicing over me now. I remembered how my good old grandmother had laid up her earnings to purchase me in later years, and how often her plans had been frustrated. How that faithful, loving old heart would leap for joy if she could look on me and my children now that we were free! My relatives had been foiled in all their efforts, but God had raised me up a friend among strangers, who had bestowed on me the precious, long-desired boon. Friend! It is a common word, often lightly used. Like other good and beautiful things, it may be tarnished by careless handling; but when I speak of Mrs. Bruce as my friend, the word is sacred.

My grandmother lived to rejoice in my freedom; but not long after, a letter came with a black seal. She had gone "where the wicked cease from troubling, and the weary are at rest."[297]

Time passed on, and a paper came to me from the south, containing an obituary notice of my Uncle[298] Phillip. It was the only case I ever knew of such an honor conferred upon a colored person. It was written by one of his friends, and contained these words: "Now that death has laid him low, they call him a good man and a useful citizen; but what are eulogies to the black man, when the world has faded from his vision? It does not require man's praise to obtain rest in God's kingdom." So they called a colored man a *citizen*! Strange words to be uttered in that region!

Reader, my story ends with freedom; not in the usual way, with marriage.[299] I and my children are now free! We are as free from the power of slaveholders as are the white people of the north; and though that, according to my ideas, is not saying a great deal, it is a vast improvement in *my* condition. The dream of my life is not yet realized. I do not sit with my children in a home of my own. I still long for a hearthstone of my own, however humble. I wish it for my children's sake far more than for my own. But God so orders circumstances as to keep me with my friend Mrs. Bruce. Love, duty, gratitude also bind me to her side. It is a privilege to serve her who pities my oppressed people, and who has bestowed the inestimable boon of freedom on me and my children.

It has been painful to me, in many ways, to recall the dreary years I passed in bondage. I would gladly forget them if I could. Yet the retrospection is not altogether without solace; for with those gloomy recollections come tender memories of my good old grandmother, like light, fleecy clouds floating over a dark and troubled sea.

1861

Notes

297 *"where the wicked … are at rest."* Job 3:17.

298 *Original reads*: uncle [ed.].

299 *"Reader, my story ends …"* a possible play on Charlotte Bronte's Victorian novel *Jane Eyre* (1847), in which the conclusion opens with the line "Reader, I married him." Jacobs again asserts black women's exclusion from genteel conventions.

Part Three

The Literatures of Reconstruction, Racial Uplift, and the New Negro

*c.*1865–1920

Introduction

The end of over two centuries of slavery on the North American continent and the ensuing emancipation of four million African Americans promised a radical rethinking of citizenship through Reconstruction in the South. Between 1865 and 1870, the Thirteenth, Fourteenth, and Fifteenth Amendments to the Constitution abolished slavery, guaranteed "equal protection" for citizens under the federal government, and promised that the right to vote would not be infringed upon based on "race, color, or previous condition of servitude." For the first time in the country's history, over one thousand African American men held public office in the same states where they had previously been property. New representative governments, composed of freed people and their white allies, drafted state constitutions that created the first public education system in the South, abolished imprisonment for debt, and expanded suffrage to all men.

Yet white resistance and violence countered the optimism of Radical Reconstruction in the former Confederacy, and escalated sharply after federal troops withdrew from the South in 1877. By 1910, all states in the former Confederacy had passed laws disfranchising, segregating, and subjugating African Americans. Thousands of lynchings – over 3,500 recorded between 1885 and 1910 – mocked the rule of civic law in the South. The North and West also suffered from violent conflict and disappointed promises, as struggles mounted between workers and the monopoly trusts of industrial and corporate capitalism during the Gilded Age.

The railroad was the symbol of the times. In 1862, Congress passed the first of five Pacific Railroad Acts, which granted western land and government bonds to corporations (rather than states) to create rail lines linking the eastern to the western parts of the country. The First Transcontinental Railroad opened in 1869, extending the eastern rail network from Iowa to San Francisco Bay, and bringing resources on the nation's West Coast into the capital's reach on the East Coast. The tides of industry and populations spread westward as railroad track mileage tripled between 1860 and 1880, and doubled again between 1880 and 1918. The rise of the railroads in turn triggered the phenomenal and lucrative expansion of such related industries as coal, oil, and steel. With antitrust law in its infancy, a number of corporations came to establish monopolies that dominated the interests of labor and open markets alike. Single companies, such as John D. Rockefeller's Standard Oil and the Carnegie Steel Company, thus could

The Wiley Blackwell Anthology of African American Literature: Volume 1, 1746–1920, First Edition.
Edited by Gene Andrew Jarrett.

control certain manufactured goods and the industries that they supported. Despite the 1890 Sherman Antitrust Act, at the turn of the century trusts managed steel, oil, sugar, meat, and farm machinery production through vertical enterprise. Profits rose as the cost of production remained low.

Industrial expansion invited massive immigration from southern and eastern Europe. Expansion increased the demand for unskilled labor in manufacturing, construction, and mining. The ensuing demographic shifts caused domestic tensions. Many native-born Protestants were leery of, and outright hostile to, the "new immigrants" who brought their own culture, language, and allegiances to cities in the United States. As the scientific management of Frederick Winslow Taylor became the dominant paradigm, these native-born skilled workers, engineers, and secretaries constituted a new middle class of managers and designers above the unskilled, foreign-born workers tasked with the drudgery of manufacturing.

This was a time of unparalleled innovation and investment. The US government issued 500,000 patents for new inventions between 1860 and 1890, over 10 times the number issued between 1790 and 1860. George Westinghouse's air brakes, Theodore Vail's American Telephone and Telegraph Company, and Thomas Edison's General Electric stimulated industrial production and commercial demand. By 1900, the nation's per capita income was double that of Germany and France, and 50% higher than Great Britain's. Yet such prosperity also bred labor unrest, a consequence of the exploitation of the working class. Workers consistently struck for higher wages and less degrading working conditions. Efforts to unionize and collectively protest often ended in violence and the brutal suppression of unrest. This conflict between labor and capital, along with the twin "problems" of western Native Americans and southern African Americans, colored all aspects of US politics through World War I.

Political tension also marked the Gilded Age. Immigrants populated urban centers, uniting and mobilizing, beholding the promise of power at the voting booth. Urban political machines, like New York City's Tammany Hall, exercised enormous influence, and managed an illicit spoils system that made all political contests a battle over patronage. Grover Cleveland was the only Democratic candidate elected to the Presidency between 1868 and 1912, but the Republican Party's control of the Executive Office did not translate into electoral calm. Economic instability (including crippling depressions in 1873 and 1893) and struggles over monetary policy instead made the era one of partisan strife. The low-tariff, free-market, anti-imperialist Democratic Party, popular among urban immigrants most affected by federal monetary policy, maintained a stranglehold on the former Confederacy that did not loosen until after World War II.

Toward the western part of the United States, Democratic "workingmen" channeled southern-style bigotry to oppose Chinese immigration, leading the call for the country's first anti-immigration law, the 1882 Chinese Exclusion Act. Firmly entrenched in the North, the Republican Party opposed labor rights and endorsed temperance reform, while pursuing land policies and military intervention in the West that devastated Native American holdings. The 1887 Dawes Severalty Act abolished collective tribal rights to land in favor of an inequitable allotment system. Three years later, the Massacre at Wounded Knee crushed any hopes of Indian autonomy. By 1934 Native Americans had lost to white settlers over two-thirds of the 150 million acres of western land that they held in 1887.

Theodore Roosevelt championed rising Progressive ideas in support of stronger federal oversight of trusts and industrial policy, yet he was also instrumental to pushing America toward overseas empire. Following the 1867 Alaska Purchase and the 1893 overthrow of the Kingdom of Hawaii, the Spanish–American War (tenuously justified by the *USS Maine* explosion in 1898) provided the occasion for the United States to compete with Europe in the exercise of colonial power, annexing the Philippines and gaining control over Puerto Rico and Cuba. By the time the Panama Canal was completed in 1915, helping to seal the hegemony of the United States over the broader Americas, the race, ethnic, and class divisions of the Civil War had expanded to include a newly freed yet economically marginalized African American population, an extensive yet economically disadvantaged working class, and a policy of white supremacy that informed federal policy at home and diplomacy abroad.

As American literature was shaped by and reflected these political, economic, and cultural changes between the Civil War and World War I, it also greatly benefited from an increasingly national print culture supported by the technology of mass production. Americans in the late nineteenth and early twentieth centuries enjoyed access to newspapers, magazines, and cheap dime novels that appealed especially to young, working-class readers. One of the most popular dime novelists was Horatio Alger, whose "rags-to-riches" stories tell of impoverished boys rising to middle-class respectability through hard work, ingenuity, and personal integrity – an idealized blueprint of acculturation for immigrant readers. Between 1868 and his death in 1899, Alger published over one hundred short novels – *Ragged Dick* (1868) being the most famous – with titles like *Paul the Peddler; or, The Fortunes of a Young Street Merchant* (1871) and *Mark Mason's Victory; or, The Trials and Triumphs of a Telegraph Boy* (1899). Counter to such popular works was the solidification of a high literary class. Literary magazines such as New York's *Harper's* (founded in 1850), Boston's *The Atlantic Monthly* (1857), and *Scribner's Monthly* (1870) provided a platform for literary realism, which succeeded romanticism and sentimentalism as the dominant genre of the age. Literary magazines had a more lasting impact on American literature than their yearly circulation numbers would suggest. Under William Dean Howells, *The Atlantic Monthly* introduced readers to some of the most significant writers of the era, including Mark Twain and Thomas Wentworth Higginson.

Realism, primarily an urban and northeastern genre concerned with quotidian life and psychological interiority, happened to coexist alongside the rise of regional or "local color" literature, a movement spurred on by a newfound interest in local folkways and dialects – and the fear that they were disappearing, as the railroad and mass production bred national homogeneity. The terms "realism" and "regionalism," though, encoded an elitism sanctioned by powerful literary tastemakers like Howells. "Regionalism" was a label condescendingly applied to literature written by those generally on the margins of society – women, immigrants, African Americans, and Southerners. "Realism," on the other hand, was a moniker for literature written by white men of education, standing, and urban living.

All writers during the era nonetheless were concerned with the relationship between the individual and the increasing technological standardization that permeated all aspects of life in a modern age of mass production and distribution. Thus Sarah Orne Jewett's description of rural Maine in *The Country of the Pointed Firs* (1896) and Jack London's tale of the Alaskan Yukon in *The Call of the Wild* (1903) were technically "local color" texts, even as they addressed themes no less pertinent to modernity than the gender conflict in Henry James's *The Bostonians* (1885) or the psychology of racism in Mark Twain's *The Adventures of Huckleberry Finn* (1885). By century's end, much of the sanguinity of realist and local-color literature shifted into naturalism, a darker genre that reflected pessimism about human agency and progress in a squalid, Darwinian world. Novels by Theodore Dreiser, Frank Norris, and Kate Chopin dwelt on the overwhelming effects of environment and heredity on personal agency.

African American authors like Charles Waddell Chesnutt, Paul Laurence Dunbar, and Pauline Hopkins were equally concerned with realism. Racial violence, disfranchisement, and segregation, after all, had spread in the aftermath of Reconstruction. Yet these and other authors were also faced with a literary culture that sought to pigeonhole them and fellow African Americans as child-like Sambos, promiscuous Jezebels, or lustful brutes. The rise of the so-called plantation tradition in Joel Chandler Harris's *Uncle Remus* stories (published as books during his lifetime, between 1880 and 1907) and Thomas Dixon's virulently racist *The Clansman* (1905) glorified the antebellum South as an idyllic past ruined by the emancipation and enfranchisement of African Americans. This myth resonated with nativist fears of ethnic impurity and with the rhetoric of white supremacy. The sensational popularity of *The Clansman*, for example, culminated in a massively successful and groundbreaking film, D.W. Griffith's *The Birth of a Nation* (1915). In this context, Chesnutt's postbellum conjure tales and Dunbar's dialect poetry subtly yet subversively tried to challenge the racial assumptions held by the white readers of *The Atlantic Monthly*, where both writers happened to earn their national fame.

The majority of African American writers still depended on the national "negro" press. After slavery, the press flourished as Freedman's Bureau-supported schools – 4,000 were built across the South across 1867 and 1877 – educated over a quarter of a million former slaves. Literacy rates rose. The ranks of a small yet noticeable middle class grew as well. By 1895, there were 150 African American newspapers. Some of the writers who gained fame in the black press, like Frances Ellen Watkins Harper, were veterans of the antebellum abolition movement and had written for an already established biracial audience in the urban Northeast. Others were the children of men and women transformed by the Civil War – both Dunbar's father and W.E.B. Du Bois's relatives, for instance, fought for the Union. Regardless of their experiential relationship to slavery, most African American writers used common literary tropes of racial uplift, or symbols of cultural, intellectual, and political refinement, that counteracted the racial stereotypes held by whites, and that shaped the way African Americans perceived themselves. Racial uplift was the theme in Pauline Hopkins's *Contending Forces* (1900), and in her successful literary magazine, *The Colored American* (founded in 1900). It was also the focus of much of Anna Julia Cooper's activism on behalf of African American women.

By the dawn of World War I, Booker T. Washington and W.E.B. Du Bois hotly debated over the best means of racial uplift. Although recent scholarship has complicated commonly held notions about the oppositional nature of Washington and Du Bois's disagreements on how best to "lead the race," the main terms of their basic argument – Washington's accommodation versus Du Bois's agitation – shaped African American thought at the turn of the century. Questions about the role of racial uplift in advocating for civil rights, however, grew only more vexing as the years progressed. Harper's Iola Leroy and James Weldon Johnson's "ex-colored man" both face a dilemma similar to that faced by fin-de-siècle realist characters: how to preserve the self amid a world either indifferent or overtly hostile to individual survival. What Chesnutt called "post-bellum, pre-Harlem" literature indeed concerned itself with uplifting the race, even as it subversively challenged the historical realities that hindered this process. A decade later this dynamic would blossom in Harlem.

Frank J. Webb (1828–1894)

Breaking new ground in its exploration of interracial marriage and passing, Frank J. Webb's 1857 novel *The Garies and Their Friends* is a candid portrait of racial prejudice and rapacity in the antebellum urban Northeast. Unfortunately, Webb's personal history remains difficult to trace. His novellas and essays on racial injustice appeared in the Reconstruction-era African American newspaper *New National Era*, but the biographical trail ends in Galveston, Texas, where he ran his own newspaper and taught school in the 1870s. Only recently have scholars recognized his remarkable contribution to African American literature.

Frank Johnson Webb was born in Philadelphia. His employment and early education are unknown, although evidence suggests that he worked in a clothing business, or possibly in the printing trade, and was well-educated and well-spoken. Webb's wife, Mary, was born in New Bedford, Massachusetts, the daughter of a fugitive slave from Virginia and a wealthy Spanish gentleman. A gifted orator, Mary Webb's public readings gained the attention of leading writers of the day, including Harriet Beecher Stowe and Henry Wadsworth Longfellow. Stowe even dramatized sections of her 1852 novel *Uncle Tom's Cabin* "expressly for the readings of Mrs. Mary E. Webb." When Frank Webb's business failed in 1855, Mary supported the couple by performing Shakespeare and Longfellow's "The Song of Hiawatha" at abolitionist meetings along the East Coast. That same year the Webbs sought to leave Philadelphia so that Frank could take up a position in Rio de Janeiro, but the ship's captain refused to allow them aboard on account of their dark skin color. They were more fortunate the following year, when Mary went on tour in England with letters of introduction to British high society from Stowe and Longfellow. The British sojourn was highly successful. Webb wrote *Garies* and, in 1857, published it in London, where it sold well. But the novel's critical depiction of life and racism in the northeastern United States likely muted the success it might have enjoyed with abolitionists.

Mary's failing health prompted the couple to seek warmer climes. In 1858, he secured a position in the Post Office of Kingston, Jamaica. Thereafter, she died of consumption, but Frank Webb remained in Kingston for a decade, and was married again in 1864 to one Mary Rodgers. By 1869, he was back in the United States with his new wife and four children. He took courses at Howard University Law School in Washington, DC, and worked as a clerk in the Freedmen's Bureau. For a prolific period in the first half of 1870, he wrote for *The New Era*; he contributed two novellas, *Two Wolves and a Lamb* and *Marvin Hayle*, whose autobiographical experimentation cast racially unmarked characters. He left shortly after Frederick Douglass took over the publication and renamed it the *New National Era*. By 1872, Webb was working at a post office in Galveston, Texas, where he edited his own newspaper, the *Republican*, and served as an alternate delegate to the state's Republican convention. Records exist of the lives of his sons in Galveston in the 1890s, but little is known about the last decades of his own life. Frank J. Webb died in 1894.

Further reading

Borgstrom, Michael. *Minority Reports: Identity and Social Knowledge in Nineteenth-Century American Literature*. New York: Palgrave Macmillan, 2010. Ch. 2.

Clymer, Jeffory A. "Family Money: Race and Economic Rights in Antebellum US Law and Fiction." *American Literary History* 21.2 (2009): 211–238.

Duane, Anna Mae. "Remaking Black Motherhood in Frank J. Webb's. *The Garies and Their Friends*" *African American Review* 38.2 (2004): 201–212.

The Wiley Blackwell Anthology of African American Literature: Volume 1, 1746–1920, First Edition.
Edited by Gene Andrew Jarrett.

Gardner, Eric. "'A Gentleman of Superior Cultivation and Refinement': Recovering the Biography of Frank J. Webb." *African American Review* 35.2 (2001): 297–308.

Knadler, Stephen P. "Traumatized Racial Performativity: Passing in Nineteenth-Century African-American Testimonies." *Cultural Critique* 55.1 (2003): 63–100.

Lee, Maurice S. "The 1850s: The First Renaissance of Black Letters." *A Companion to African American Literature*. Ed. Gene Andrew Jarrett. Malden, MA: Wiley-Blackwell, 2010. 103–118.

Nowatzki, Robert. "Blurring the Color Line: Black Freedom, Passing, Abolitionism, and Iris Ethnicity in Frank J. Webb's *The Garies and Their Friends*." *Studies in American Fiction* 33.1 (2005): 29–58.

Otter, Samuel. "Frank Webb's Still Life: Rethinking Literature and Politics through *The Garies and Their Friends*." *American Literary History* 20.4 (2008): 728–752.

Otter, Samuel. *Philadelphia Stories: America's Literature of Race and Freedom*. New York: Oxford University Press, 2010. Ch. 4.

Sollors, Werner. "Frank J. Webb (1828–1894)." *African American Literature beyond Race: An Alternative Reader*. Ed. Gene Andrew Jarrett. New York: New York University Press, 2006: 25–29.

Two Wolves and a Lamb

"Gus, who were those three young ladies to whom you bowed so graciously as we drove through the *Bois de Boulogne*[1] this evening?"

Gus deigned me no reply, but eyed lovingly a morsel of cotelet[2] he held exalted upon the point of his fork, as though he would first thoroughly enjoy the sense of sight ere that of taste was gratified.

"I say, do you hear me, Gus?" I repeated, impatiently.

Gus, who continued to eye the mutton, remarked vaguely:

"'Pon honour, 'tis too bad: this cotelet is decidedly overdone – too brown entirely; it is a burning shame that in an establishment like this a cook should be employed capable of such an atrocity. No, my cook – "

"Hang your cook!" I interrupted, impatiently; "when you are at dinner it seems impossible to get from you a word or idea not associated with the food you are consuming. Did you hear my question?"

"Yes, I did hear you grumbling something about carriage – young ladies – *Bois de Boulogne*. Pass that claret, please. Tut! This is too bad! The wine is as warm as Mississippi water in July, and quite as turbid, too. I declare, that vile *garçon*[3] has been giving it a shake."

At this juncture a look of most ineffable disgust must have overspread my face, for Gus smiled, and resumed:

"Oh, pardon me. You made some inquiry about those girls we met during our drive. Ah, yes, I remember. At present, however, I am much too hungry to be communicative; better wait until we have finished dinner. Here comes the omelette soufflée; there is no time for chat now; an omelette, you know, must be eaten hot. Let us get through it at once like men. There is nothing so calculated to produce serenity of mind as a steady performance of one's duties; and I wish to have nothing to reproach myself with on that score. Besides, I will confide to you in the strictest confidence that I am lion-like in my nature – magnanimous and all that sort of thing – yet with a decided prejudice against being disturbed at my meals. I prefer doing but one thing at a time, especially when that thing is dining. 'Yes', as Johnson said, 'I like to dine.'"

Notes

TWO WOLVES AND A LAMB

[1] *Bois de Boulogne* a large park on the western edge of Paris.

[2] *cotelet* a meat chop.

[3] *garçon* waiter.

Gus was incorrigible. I deemed it prudent for the present to let him alone. It seemed almost unkind to disturb him from what was evidently so near his heart; so I sat quietly whilst he finished his omelette, trifled with a portion of the Charlotte Russe,[4] devoured a large Marie Louise pear, and not until the *garçon* brought in the coffee and we had lighted our cigars did I again venture the question with which I have commenced my story.

We were quite alone in one of the petits salons[5] at Verys, where, after a long drive, we had betaken ourselves for dinner. The smoke from our fragrant panetellas[6] was floating dreamily and cloudlike over our heads, when Gus, arousing himself with an effort, said:

"So you are interested in that singular trio whom the Parisians, with their fondness for *soubriquets*,[7] have named 'the Wolves and the Lamb'. They are countrymen of mine, who have accompanied their venerable father to Paris to dissipate the fortune he has been lucky enough to accumulate."

"Are they sisters?" I inquired.

"The tall girls are twins; the other is their cousin. She is as different from them as it is possible for a woman to be. The twins have ordinary cultivation and acquirements – are excessively brusque in manner and eccentric in disposition. Their cousin is a girl of angelic sweetness of temper; besides she is one of the most accomplished ladies I have ever met. The sole occupation of the Wolves seems to be the invention of torments to inflict upon the Lamb, who endures them with a patience worthy of the name. The present pet weakness of the Wolves is a disgusting penchant for snakes. But, by the way, should you like to know them?"

"Of course, I should; your description has aroused my curiosity. One so fascinating, the others so singular. Let me know them by all means; they will be anything but everyday acquaintances."

"Well, then, so be it," rejoined Gus. "I am pretty certain we shall find them at home this evening. There is no better time than the present – only bear in mind, my good fellow, you are not to fall in love with the Lamb; that amiable creature is already appropriated."

As he concluded he rose lazily and drew on his *paletot*.[8] The dinner paid for and the accustomed *douceur*[9] given to the *garçon*, we departed. Arm in arm we sauntered slowly to the Hotel Wagram, and soon were in our rooms dressing for our visit to the Goffes.

"Don't be surprised," said Gus as we were walking along the Boulevard on our way thither, "at any eccentricity, however gross, the Wolves may be disposed to commit; nor visit your displeasure on my unfortunate head in case they should snub you. Many a man as good as yourself, my dear fellow, has met with shocking treatment at their fair hands. One thing you will have to console you. No matter how much the Wolves may snap and snarl, you will be amply recompensed for any injuries they may inflict in the winning kindness and gentleness of the Lamb."

We found them occupying a splendid suite of apartments in the Rue de ——. When I say splendid, I mean that sort of gorgeousness made up of gilding and French upholstery. The furniture was as costly as money could procure, but each article of it seemed to have been chosen more for its individual value, than with reference to the rest. It had been, seemingly, gathered together without any idea of harmony, or even contrast.

Notes

4 *Charlotte Russe* a decadent French cake.

5 *petits salons* lounges.

6 *panetellas* slender cigars.

7 *soubriquets* nicknames.

8 *paletot* overcoat.

9 *douceur* a tip (literally "sweetness").

I entered leaning on the arm of my friend. Being somewhat nearsighted, I found myself *vis-à-vis* with[10] the twins ere I was aware of it.

Gus introduced me in his blandest manner, producing, however, no other result than a cold nod from the eldest of the twins and an exclamation from the sister of ——.

"Mr. William, I beg you will not introduce me to any more men. I know four now, and I hate them."

My friend's warning had led me to expect that I might not be most graciously received; yet I was quite appalled at this rough, insulting reception. I began to stammer something about venturing to intrude, anxiety to be introduced, and so forth, when I was cut short in my timid utterances by the twin who had honoured me with a nod remarking:

"You can sit down, sir, now that you are here; and do pray dispose of your hat. People who twirl their hats are always bores."

I ventured something about the pleasure I had anticipated in making their acquaintance, when I was again interrupted by her saying:

"Pray, spare us that; I hate conventional compliments."

I was quite demolished by this. Sinking into the vacant chair, I became so nervous and embarrassed that I was about to deposit my hat upon the table, when the lady who rejoiced in her hatred of her four male friends almost shouted at me:

"Be careful, sir, where you place your hat. Do you wish to crush my pet?"

Standing up, I was completely horrified to discover squirming upon the table in all its lithe hideousness, a harmless but disgusting reptile, known in America as the garter snake.

Miss Goffe gave me a reproachful glance as she took it up and placed it in her bosom, where the greater part of it lay concealed in the folds of her dress; whilst its head and neck moved hither and thither caressed by the jeweled hand of its mistress.

I was absorbed and fascinated by this scene, in the same manner and with something of the same feeling, by which we may imagine a bird to be impressed, when it finds itself, despite all its struggles, hopping hopelessly toward the distended jaws of a snake. I was experiencing a feeling akin to this, when the door opened, and the spell was broken by the entrance of a spiritual looking creature into the drawing room.

Gus took her hand as she approached, and turning to me said, "Allow me to present my friend, Mr. Philip Braham."

She smiled sweetly as she extended her hand, rejoining kindly as she did so, "A friend of yours cannot but be a welcome visitor. I am delighted to see you."

A hasty glance impressed me with the value of my friend's admonition "not to fall in love with her." She was just that sort of creature that one might imagine a man would fall in love with at first sight, recklessly, hopelessly. She was most winning and gracious in her manner, with one of those indescribably sweet faces, which at once attracts us without our being able to assign any exact reason why. Her eyes were of dark hazel, and she had a dreamy way of looking out from them that gave you an impression of her being connected with, or attracted to some other, better existence that did not entirely separate her from this. One often hears the expression "a spiritual looking woman." I had, however, never before met anyone who so thoroughly realized the description. I was enchanted with her. I almost forgot the Wolves and began to devote myself to the Lamb.

Notes

[10] *Original reads*: to [ed.].

The Wolves merely looked up as she entered. I observed them exchange a malicious glance. The one who gloried in her hatred of her four male acquaintances exclaimed in a warning tone:

"Mind how you step, my nervous cousin, Mimi is out. I know your ladyship pretends to be afraid of him."

Miss Burrows shuddered. An expression of alarm and disgust flitted across her face as she observed tremulously:

"I am very sorry: had I been aware of it I should not have left my room."

"Oh! it was not on your account I spoke," rejoined the Wolf. "I feared it might get upon the floor and be trodden upon by you, as it was the other day. It is in sister's bosom now. You need not be alarmed for its safety; only pray keep your eyes about you."

Miss Burrows drew back as she observed the object of her horror and detestation so close to her. Gliding across the room she took a seat beside me upon the sofa.

"I have an unconquerable horror of all creeping things," said she in an agitated voice. "I have tried to reason myself out of it without success, being conscious that it must be somehow wrong to hate, or rather detest, anything God has made, and doubtless designed to serve some useful purpose in the economy of nature. A snake, however, I cannot tolerate. It inspires me with indescribable disgust and terror."

"And will not your cousins give it up," I asked. "It is singular they should be disposed to cherish such *outré*[11] pets."

"My cousins are somewhat peculiar in their tastes I must admit," replied she. "Perhaps they are a little spoiled by never having been compelled to sacrifice them to the feelings or wishes of others. That, however, is not their fault. I am sure they do not cherish their pets to annoy others, but to afford pleasure to themselves."

I gazed at the young creature who spoke thus apologetically for her cousins, and felt she was a deal too charitable in her disposition.

I was indeed very much interested in her. In conversations about many things in France and England, of which we cherished reminiscences in common, with discussions upon books, music and the various topics of the day, I found the evening gliding most agreeably away. The Wolf with the snake in her bosom left her seat, where she had evidently been quarrelling with Gus, and took a chair beside the centre table, upon which she deposited her scaly pet, where it lay twisting and coiling its flexile, half torpid length about her hand and arm, in a manner most disgusting to behold.

Although she seemingly concentrated her attention upon her strange pet, there was about her, when narrowly observed, a half watchful, expectant air that would lead to the impression that something else also occupied her mind. She always started with a timid look when the door opened, which look contrasted strongly with her generally assured, almost defiant air. This expectant manner was shared to so great an extent by Miss Burrows that I was led to remark:

"You appear to be expecting somebody or something – which is it? At least I feel assured it is an agreeable anticipation from the delighted, eager manner with which you look up whenever the door is opened."

"Ah, yes," she rejoined, "I am expecting Mr. Walton."

"Happy Mr. Walton," said I with a smile, "to excite so much interest."

"Oh, it is very natural" she replied with an air of most charming naiveté. "Do you not know that Mr. Walton and I are engaged?"

Notes

[11] *outré* unusual, extreme.

I could not help smiling as I looked at her, for this was a sort of acknowledgment that ladies find it very difficult to make, and which they seldom or never volunteer. On the contrary, in most cases, they consider themselves privileged to make all manner of evasions with regard to it, and often tell most ingenious and admirably concocted fibs about the matter. In her, however, it did not appear an exhibition of vanity or a manifestation of forwardness, but a confession quite in harmony with the genuine innocence and simplicity of her character.

As she concluded I looked up and found the Wolf glaring at her with a look of such concentrated, intensified hatred, as fairly made me shudder. "There is no mistaking it," thought I, "these two women are rivals – a spirit of light and a spirit of darkness worshipping at the same shrine; both of their offerings cannot be accepted."

There was something revolting in the glittering snaky look that gleamed from the Wolf. It seemed as if the light that glistened in the eyes of her scaly pet was reflected from her own and rendered terrible by its human association and intelligence. At that moment I felt that it would be preferable to take to my bosom her disgusting pet, with its clammy folds, than to come in contact with its mistress. I shuddered, and after a few moments silence remarked to the Lamb:

"Am I to regard this as a remarkable proof of confidence?"

"Oh, no"; she replied with the same innocent manner. "I thought everyone knew that cousin Walton was engaged to me."

At this juncture the door opened and a delicately formed man of middle height entered the room. Miss Burrows rose and extended both her hands, which he took in his own whilst he looked tenderly at her.

"You have been well?" said he in a quiet tone.

"Yes, only a little nervous at times. I shall, however, quiet myself again, now that you have come. Let me present you to Mr. Braham." He bowed and shook my hand cordially, then crossed the room to where the Wolf sat at the table, ostensibly absorbed in her scaly pet. I could observe, however, from the furtive manner in which she looked up without raising her head, that she was watching his movements. When she arose and extended to him her hand there was more softness in her face than I had ever deemed it capable of expressing.

"Still cultivating my old antipathy," remarked he smilingly, "I have brought you a book I am sure you will revel in – a book of travels in Java[12] – a place that would be a Paradise to you, from the number and variety of snakes it contains. You shall have it bye and bye when I unpack."

"And have you brought me nothing?" enquired the other Wolf.

"Well, no; I am sorry to say I have not. The only thing I saw that I thought would strike your fancy would have been most difficult to procure and inconvenient to transport."

"What was it?" both exclaimed in a breath.

"One of the preserved specimens of antediluvian[13] reptilia, which some geologist with an unpronounceable name has just presented to the Crystal Palace Association.[14] Although being only thirty feet long, it would have been rather difficult to put in my trunk, besides which the directors of that transparent institution might not have been inclined to part with it."

Whilst Mr. Walton had been giving expression to this banter, I had leisure to study his face, and observed how strongly marked his countenance was. You would have

Notes

[12] *Java* an island of Indonesia.

[13] *antediluvian* prehistoric (literally, "before the [biblical] Flood").

[14] *Crystal Palace Association* The Crystal Palace was a building erected in London's Hyde Park for the Great Exhibition of 1851.

imagined him to be about twenty-two, but there were deep lines on his forehead and a thoroughly grave, almost stern expression of face that showed him to be older than a first glance would have suggested. Even whilst uttering these pleasantries the upper half of his face never seemed to smile. The eye, which is most difficult, nay, almost impossible, to school, did not seem to harmonize with his playful banter. The lines on his forehead, the indentations between his eyebrows neither softened nor changed; his thin lips alone smiled and they only for an instant, then relapsed into a severe expression. I do not know that I ever saw a mouth express such inflexible determination as did his in repose. His complexion was feminine in its transparent fairness. His rich auburn hair, parted in the middle, was thrown off his forehead (which was rather narrow and not very high) and hung almost to his shoulders in a mass of rich, wavy curls, which in their glossy luxuriance might have inspired a woman with envy. This, together with his boyish style of dress, gave to his *tout ensemble*[15] that air of adolescence, which would impress one on seeing him for the first time.

About that period all Paris was in a ferment of excitement with regard to a murder which had been recently committed, under circumstances of horrible atrocity. A young lady, in a respectable position amongst the bourgeoisie, had poisoned a lady friend from motives of jealousy. By this terrible crime the lover of the murdered Mad'lle Varigny had been driven to desperation, and to be rid of an existence so full of misery, had drowned himself in the Seine. Our friends had some slight acquaintance with the parties, so the lamentable occurrence naturally became a topic of conversation during the evening. Numberless suggestions had been made as to what would be a fitting punishment for so horrible a crime; none of us were inclined to clemency, or seemed for a moment to think or wish that she should be spared the penalty of death, as the murder was characterized by many revolting features, and was the undoubted result of long premeditation.

Walton, on being appealed to for an opinion, said, "If they wish to punish her, the infliction of death will not effect that object. A woman, who loves with such intensity of passion that she will commit murder to attain the object of her affections, must also be capable of feeling in the keenest manner the pangs of remorse. A woman like that should be made to live and be so environed, that every moment of her existence the evidences of her crime should be kept unavoidably before her. Had the lover of the murdered girl been else than a fool, he would have endeavoured to suppress the evidence he gave which led to her conviction, and held it ever suspended over her like the sword of Damocles.[16] He should have let her live; yet so live as to be each moment face to face with death. I cannot understand why men destroy themselves under such circumstances. Had I been he, I should have spared no effort to save her: and, having accomplished that, she should have lived to have welcomed death in its most appalling form, as the sweetest boon Heaven could bestow upon her."

That man, thought I, as I regarded the vindictive expression that crept over his face as he spoke, is not one to be safely offended.

As Walton ceased speaking he rose, crossed the room, and rang the bell.

"Laura," said he, turning to Miss Burrows, "I wish to hear you execute a piece of music that I have brought with me from London. It was performed by a young lady at one of Dr. Morton's soirees. She has no musical education whatever, and whilst in a

Notes

[15] *tout ensemble* all together.

[16] *sword of Damocles* in Greek legend, a man with a sword hanging over his head by a single thread; suggests imminent danger.

state of clairvoyance she sat at the piano and improvised the most extraordinary melodies to which I ever listened.

"You know I am quick at catching such things. I jotted down the notes, and it was afterwards played over from my manuscript ere the company dispersed, and was pronounced by them all a correct reproduction of the melody note for note. The most singular part of the whole is that the lady herself, in her natural state, was perfectly incapable of playing it from the manuscript, and had not the slightest recollection of ever having performed it."

The servant here made his appearance.

"Bring me," said Walton, "a parcel you will find on my dressing room table.

"I saw at Dr. Morton's some things so mysterious and inexplicable that they have haunted me ever since. You know I have ever been a skeptic with reference to spiritualism, clairvoyance, and kindred mysteries. Had the things I there saw been related to me, I should have been most incredulous. I not only saw much that I cannot explain, but things that made me doubt my own senses. At my particular request, the clairvoyant was transported here. I wish to test the truth of her revelations. Laura, permit me to examine your arm."

At this request Miss Burrows started up and became by turns pale and red. The Wolves also were pale and much agitated. Miss Burrows said, with a forced smile:

"What an odd request. Why should you wish to see my arm?"

I now observed, for the first time, that whilst the twins wore dresses extremely low in the neck, with short sleeves, Miss Burrows wore her sleeves buttoned at the wrist, and the body of her dress half high.

There was an evident indisposition exhibited on her part to comply with Walton's request. I observed the elder of the Wolves give her a deprecating look, and the whole affair began to wear an air of interest. After a few moments of hesitation Miss Burrows rejoined:

"No, no cousin Walton; I cannot show it to you. There is, in fact – "

"Your very hesitation," said Walton, earnestly, "makes me more anxious for a compliance with my request. I do not ask for the gratification of an idle curiosity, but to confirm me either in a belief or disbelief in a subject of more than ordinary interest. "Tell me," continued he almost sternly, "does not your arm bear the marks of violence?"

At this one of the twins grew absolutely livid, whilst the other, starting forward, exclaimed:

"Nonsense, Maria! Why do you look so frightened? Don't be stupid. Can't you see it is all a trick? It is plain enough that someone has been telling cousin Walton of the row you had with Laura."

Walton's lips seemed to grow thinner every moment. There was a wild sparkle in his eye, which seemed to make him look devilish.

"It is true, then, there has been a quarrel," he uttered in a suppressed tone. "Had I believed in the truth of clairvoyance, had I not deemed it all a delusion, I would not have asked questions that have led to this painful *exposé*. Yet, as we have gone thus far," continued he, sneeringly, "if only for the purpose of deciding a question of science, let us investigate this strange affair thoroughly."

As he concluded, he half playfully seized Laura's hand, and raising the sleeve of her dress, disclosed just above the elbow on her delicate and beautifully molded arm the deep imprint of a hand, the nails of which had buried themselves in the flesh.

Walton looked inquiringly from one to the other, as though he would ask some explanation.

"It is nothing, cousin Walton," pleaded Laura, disengaging her arm from him. "I trod most carelessly on Maria's poor little pet, and to save it from being crushed she seized my arm rather more roughly than she intended."

An embarrassing pause here ensued. Walton broke in upon it by sternly remarking:

"I would advise you, Maria, to give up those disgusting pets. I have a fearful presentiment they will occasion some lamentable catastrophe, something that will bring us to sorrow. At all events," he concluded, "I am convinced there is some truth in clairvoyance. I did not, however, expect so painful an evidence of its reality. Let me again warn you, Maria, to give up those horrible pets, for I cannot rid myself of the conviction," repeated he, impressively, "that something terrible will result from cherishing them."

Happily at this moment the servant entered the room bringing with him the music. I immediately proposed it should be played, being thoroughly delighted to find anything to interrupt what had become a painful, embarrassing scene.

Miss Burrows seated herself at the piano. After glancing at the music, she remarked:

"It seems odd and rather difficult in character, better suited, I should say, to the violin-cello[17] than the piano. However, let me try."

It was decidedly original in its character, and differed from any composition to which I had ever listened. It seemed to suggest in a striking degree the sounds of Nature, at one moment like the caroling notes of a bird, the musical dripping of a fountain, or the soft murmur of a brook, recalling, too, the sighing of the night-wind as I have heard it in the tropics whispering through the delicate leaves of the bamboo and mimosa; then again like the music of the waves as they fall in solemn regularity upon the sea-shore; in short, all the harmonies of Nature blended into one soft melody.

I could not but regard the fixed expression of Walton's face as Miss Burrows continued playing. When she concluded, he remarked:

"I have lately felt that I stand upon the brink of some great discovery in myself – that I have within me some latent power soon to be developed. At times I seem endowed with a penetration almost painful to me, and a foreknowledge of events that borders on the supernatural. When I say events, I mean those of an individual character and connected with some particular person. Most singular, too, it is only toward those for whom I cherish regard. People that I dislike, or toward whom I am indifferent, cross my mind only in thought but those I love are as palpable to me in their waking visions as you are now. Do you now remember," continued he, turning toward the Lamb, "that some time since, whilst reading the morning newspaper, a presentiment flashed over me that something terrible had happened at home? You will also recollect how you all endeavoured to ridicule me out of the idea. Then I hesitated to say how deep an impression it had made upon me; nor would I relate with what vivid distinctness I had seen pass in review before me the terrified faces of my mother and sister. Judge my surprise on opening my letters, which awaited me in London, to learn that (allowing for the difference in time that a variation in longitude would produce) at the very hour, aye, the very moment, when those terrified faces passed in review before me they were in the midst of a frightful rail-road accident, from which they narrowly escaped with life."

At this moment Gus, who had been fidgeting in his chair, crossed the room and seating himself beside me, said, in an undertone:

"'Pon my word. I don't believe they are going to have a drop of tea."

Notes

[17] *violin-cello* a cello.

I gave him a look of disgust, for I did not wish to leave. I knew what his whisper indicated, so I pretended to be absorbed in a playful dispute that was going on between the Wolves for the possession of the scaly pet, which, seemingly aroused from its torpor, was writhing and turning its disgusting length first about the arm of one, then another of the sisters; now upon the sofa, then upon the floor, under the cushions, twirling itself about the chair legs, erecting its little scaly head, darting forth its forked tongue, all to the great delight of the twins and the horror and disgust of the rest of the company.

Gus again nudged me. "Come," said he, "do you know it is almost eleven?"

"Don't bother me, it makes no difference to me if it is twelve," I rejoined.

"I shall leave you then to stumble home the best way you can," he threatened.

"Go on," said I coolly. "I believe I have a few francs in my pocket, and can take a *fiacre*[18] if it is necessary."

At this moment of controversy the drawing room door opened, and we heard distinctly the jingling of glasses outside. A sunny smile instantly illumined the hungry visage of my friend, who hastily replaced his gloves in his pocket and wore the appearance of a man who accepted the situation.

Two servants entered. One bore a tray of wine, the other a silver basket containing a variety of light cakes, biscuit, &c.

When Gus saw the kind of refreshments provided, he did not look so happy as before. He helped himself to a couple of macaroons, poured out a glass of wine, and, between the sips, he whispered to me:

"Cousins or not cousins, I shall cut these people; I can't stand this. When they first came to Paris they were more Christian-like and less polished. They then fed the hungry. When you came to see them you were sure of your supper. Nowadays, they are getting entirely too French for my tastes. It strikes me they are improving in the wrong direction. Let us go."

"You can go if you like, Gus, I told you that long ago," I rejoined with an air of dignity; "and what is more, you have my humble permission to stop at every restaurant on the way home and gorge yourself to your heart's content. If you have no money with you, my purse is at your command. I think I have observed no less than four places between here and the hotel where you may comfort and regale yourself. Amongst them all you may find sufficient to satisfy your voracious appetite; but, as I am not hungry, I beg to be permitted to remain where I am."

Gus continued to grumble at intervals; but, as I would not then take my leave, he remained to accompany me home.

Conversation was resumed after the refreshments were disposed of. We entered upon the discussion of spiritual manifestations from the Misses Fox[19] and their rappings down to Hume[20] and his wonderful performances, Brewster on natural magic,[21] Mesmer,[22] Crowe's night-side of nature,[23] and the whole cycle of kindred mysteries. At last we were reduced to the discussion of ghosts and ghost stories, and so ended the evening.

Notes

[18] *fiacre* a four-wheeled carriage for hire.

[19] *Misses Fox* three sisters from upstate New York, instrumental in starting the Spiritualist movement with their claims of occult communication with spirits.

[20] *Hume* David Hume (1711–1776), Scottish philosopher.

[21] *Brewster on natural magic* David Brewster (1781–1868), a Scottish scientist and inventor, who wrote *Letters on Natural Magic* in 1832.

[22] *Mesmer* Franz Anton Mesmer (1734–1815), German physician and proponent of a theory of "animal magnetism."

[23] *Crowe's night-side of nature* Catherine Crowe (1803–1876), English author whose *The Night-side of Nature* (1848) was a collection of ghostly anecdotes and sketches.

After this my first meeting with the Misses Goffe I spent many evenings in their society. By degrees they came to regard me as a person of whom they could not get rid, and whose society they must endure if they could not enjoy. My intimacy with Gus naturally led me frequently to the house, where the attractions of the Lamb alone would have been sufficient to have drawn me.

Being so frequently in their society, I could not but notice in how many ways the Wolf Maria exhibited her fondness for Walton. Close observation detected efforts on her part, which would have been trifling in another woman, yet more remarkable in her as evincing a desire to please Walton – an effort she made for no other human being.

By degrees the aversion, with which they had at first inspired me, gave place to a feeling of toleration, which finally merged into indifference, as far as their eccentricities were concerned. I came to regard them in the light of two women to whom obscurity was misery, not being endowed with those qualities of heart and mind that would have conduced to their celebrity; they chose to be notorious in preference to remaining obscure.

Every day we were more and more together, until at length they began to regard me in the light of a brother. They made me the envy[24] of my male friends by the distinguished consideration with which they treated me.

Each day I deemed the Lamb grew more charming. It was almost happiness to look on her and Walton; they were so loving, so quietly tender to each other. Their two lives seemed bound up together. There was an astonishing similarity of taste between them.

I do not know that I have before mentioned that Walton held the rank of captain in the American army. He was devoted to his profession, the principal object of his visit to Europe being the study of military science.

At that time the Emperor frequently indulged his subjects with those brilliant military spectacles, which his magnificent army enables him to produce. Walton was a constant attendant of these reviews, and a frequent visitor at the many camps scattered throughout France.

About this time a review on the grandest scale was to take place in the vicinity of Lyons. Walton, as usual, prepared to attend.

It was rather cool weather. The evening previous to his departure we were at the Goffes indulging in what few enjoy in Paris, the luxury of a wood fire upon the hearth. I had observed that Walton was rather dull and dreamy in his manner. He remarked to me with a sigh:

"I cannot tell why, but I have a presentiment that I should not go to this review. I have an undefined sense of some o'er-hanging danger that oppresses me and makes me feel gloomy; yet it does not assume any definite shape."

We passed one of these evenings (which the most intimate friends sometimes pass together) in a sort of dull tranquility, productive of a happiness negative in character. Whether it was the sparkling wood fire upon the hearth suggesting reminiscences of far-off homes, drawing our attention from our immediate surroundings, or that the gloomy presentiment expressed by Walton affected us, I cannot tell, but this I know, we all felt strangely subdued.

Even Mimi partook of the general tranquility and lay coiled up in his soft cotton-lined basket, only opening his eyes and giving a lazy wink, when the fitful

Notes

24 *Original reads*: envied [ed.].

flames mounted higher and higher, or the fierce crackling fire scattered sparks upon the hearth stone. At last, on slyly drawing my tiny watch I discovered it was nearly twelve o'clock. We arose to go. With that consideration with which I wish to be treated when I am in love, I inveigled the Lamb toward the window, and pointed out to her attention some object moving in the semi-darkness of the street. I also called Walton to notice it. Then leaving them, I stirred up Mimi vigorously as the most effective way of arresting the attention of the twins, thus to leave Walton and Laura in that position that lovers most desire – alone with each other.

At length the inevitable leave-taking came, and when it was over, Walton (who had arranged to walk home with me) followed with lingering footsteps down into the Boulevard.

We had proceeded but a few yards from the house when he clutched my hand nervously and exclaimed:

"Now I am sure of it. I know who it affects. It is Laura. I must return and warn her." Leaving me bewildered by his abrupt manner, he rushed back into the house.

Ere many moments had elapsed he reappeared, and having joined me, passed his arm through mine, saying calmly: "It would be foolish to disturb her tranquility with what, perhaps, may be after all but phantasy. Warn her against what? I am sure I cannot tell. She is in God's hands."

Walton was habitually grave, but this unwonted seriousness of manners impressed me strongly.

The morning after Walton's departure I called at the Goffes and entered into an arrangement with them for a ride in the *Bois de Boulogne*. Laura was famed as the most graceful and accomplished horsewoman in Paris. All her natural timidity of manner vanished when she was once mounted. She had successfully managed animals that no other horsewoman in Paris was willing to essay to ride. It seemed strange to see that delicate creature, generally so shrinking, so timid, sit upon a restless, spirited horse that it had appeared impossible that she could control.

Walton had presented Laura with a chestnut mare, which was the admiration of Paris; docile and easily managed with no other fault than an inclination to start and shy when unusual objects met her eye.

On the eventful evening to which I refer, on being brought around from the stables (where she had been without exercise for nearly a week) she appeared unusually unquiet and restively inclined.

"The mare is very restive to-day; uncommonly so. I am afraid, George, you have not given her exercise enough," I observed to the groom.

"She has been shut up a little too much lately; besides we met a great horse on our way here, and she didn't like the look of it. She hasn't quite got over it yet, sir. After she has a canter she will come all right again."

Laura stood by prepared to mount. She patted the arched neck of the beautiful creature, who seemed to recognize her, and became comparatively quiet beneath her caresses.

"Just put me up, Mr. Braham. We get on charmingly together as soon as I am mounted. We know each other, don't we Xirifa?"

With the assistance of my hand she sprang lightly into the saddle, rode from beneath the archway into the courtyard, around which she walked the mare a few times, until she had become quite passive under her influence and control.

We rode through the most quiet and unfrequented streets on our way to the *Bois de Boulogne*. We had not proceeded a great distance from home ere I perceived that Miss Goffe had concealed in her bosom her pet snake, Mimi, whose head now and then appeared and disappeared amidst the frill that decorated the front of her riding dress, one or two of the buttons of which had been left unfastened to enable it to move its scaly folds.

"How could you venture on anything so rash as bringing that little torment with you? Suppose it should get about your arms and interfere with the management of your horse?"

"Don't alarm yourself," she said indifferently. "I and Mimi are safe together."

I had been riding on the outside next to Miss Goffe. I turned my horse and then rode between the ladies so as more effectually to shield Laura from contact with or observation of the object of her aversion. We rode on quietly to the woods; then in conversation I forgot my precaution, and changed my position from between them.

Ere long my attention was attracted by a group of familiar faces in the distance, and whilst bowing to someone who had recognized me, I was startled by a sharp, quick cry from Laura, and discovered to my horror on turning round that Mimi, by some means or other, had entwined itself about Laura's arm, and by a contraction of its folds, had drawn the horse's head completely round, and rendered her hands perfectly useless. At the same moment it caught the eye of Xirifa, who, with a wild snort and plunge, threw down her head, almost unseating her rider, then darted furiously forward into the forest.

I was so horror-stricken as to be almost paralyzed. She was many lengths ahead ere I sufficiently recovered my presence of mind to pursue. There were but few riders in the wood, and all seemed incapable of affording the least assistance. When at last by dint of hard spurring, I managed to approach within a short distance of her, the mare, alarmed by something in the pathway, suddenly veered from her courses, shying violently. Then there was a shriek – a crushing noise – and Laura was thrown to the ground. She was breathing when we took her up. She opened her eyes and endeavoured to speak. A little stream of blood trickled from her nostrils, and she fell back in my arms – DEAD.

At first I could not believe in the reality of what had occurred. It seemed I must be labouring under some painful dream. A young army surgeon, who happened to be near, tendered us his assistance. He at length essayed to bleed her; but the attempt was entirely unsuccessful. I at last was constrained to admit the awful truth – Laura was dead.

The agony of Maria Goffe was something terrible to look at. She o'erwhelmed herself with the bitterest reproaches, and threw herself frantically on the ground beside Laura, entreating her in most piteous terms, for the love of God, only to look up – to speak once more – and say she forgave her.

A crowd had now gathered around us. It was suggested that she had better be removed. An elderly gentleman, handing his card, begged we would make use of his carriage to return to Paris. I thankfully accepted his offer. Placing the dead body of poor Laura therein, we drove back to our home.

I cannot describe the horror and consternation that prevailed[25] at the Goffe's. Old Mr. Goffe was distracted by the occurrence. Miss Anne evinced more feeling than I ever believed her capable of exhibiting.

But they seemed most appalled at the thought of what Walton would say; how Walton would hear it. Miss Goffe, wringing her hands, would exclaim bitterly, "He will

Notes

[25] *Original reads*: consternation, which prevailed [ed.].

charge me with murdering her. Why would I not be warned? My own obstinacy has occasioned her death. It is my ruin. He will never bear to look at me. He will hate me forever."

A servant was immediately dispatched to the telegraph office with a message for Walton, and an order that a copy should be transmitted to every hotel in Lyons, until the gentleman was found.

In about two hours our messenger returned with the disagreeable intelligence that the government were engaged in transmitting important dispatches to Algeria, and that the wires could not be placed at the disposal of the general public for fourteen hours.

Soon after we were greatly startled by the sudden appearance of Walton. He was strikingly pale, but his face wore its usual impassable calmness. Until he spoke we did not think he knew what had happened. Maria seemed as though she would sink into the ground with fear. Her characteristic bravado of manner had entirely deserted her.

"Do not tell him; for God's sake do not tell him it was *I*," she whispered to me.

"Walton," said I, "we have terrible news for you."

"The worst you can tell me will not exceed my forebodings – Laura is dying or dead," he replied.

For a second none of us could summon courage to rejoin. At last I said hoarsely, "Yes, Walton, Laura is dead, I cannot here tell you all – how or when she died." He interrupted here by saying, "I know perfectly when she died. How, but indistinctly. This I know: she must have died violently, for she came to me with blood upon her face."

Maria Goffe and her sister seemed appalled by terror and surprise at this startling declaration of Walton's, whilst the author of so much misery exclaimed:

"It was I. Walton, it was all my fault. Is it possible for you to forgive me?"

Walton made no immediate reply, but after looking fixedly at her for a few moments, answered:

"That, Maria, is between you and God."

I was anxious as far as possible to cut short this harrowing scene, so I led Walton from the room.

In a few hours all was over, and sweet Laura rested in her last home, a quiet corner in the *Père Lachaise*.[26] During the interval that elapsed between the return of Walton and the final obsequies, he had not uttered a word concerning her. He never shed a tear at the grave, or evinced the slightest emotion. That he did feel, and feel deeply, it was impossible not to believe. His calmness could only be ascribed to that wonderful mastery of expression he seemed so capable of exercising. I longed to ascertain the cause of his sudden return to Paris, knowing that from the circumstances of the case he could have received no intelligence of the terrible misfortune that had befallen us.[27] He seemed so taciturn, so reserved, that I did not venture to intrude my questions upon him.

Two days succeeding the funeral, Walton and I were alone together in my room at the hotel. I could no longer repress my curiosity to learn whether accident or design had caused his return to Paris.

"You received our telegraphic dispatch?" said I inquiringly.

His face assumed a somewhat gloomy look as he replied:

Notes

[26] *Père Lachaise* a Parisian cemetery.

[27] *Original reads*: the terrible misfortune, which had befallen us [ed.].

"Do you not remember with what reluctance I quitted Paris? The forebodings to which I was subjected? I felt it was a sort of weakness to give way to it, to this undefined apprehension, or I should not have left town. Succeeding, however, in conquering my reluctance, I started. Once out of Paris, my attention arrested by unfamiliar objects, a new train of reflections, more cheerful in character, dissipated the disagreeable presentiments that had so recently overshadowed me. We stopped at D., as usual, for refreshments. On my return to the car I felt somewhat drowsy, much inclined to sleep. It was growing dusk, and with declining day returned, doubled in force, the dismal forebodings, which had so oppressed me in the morning. I endeavoured unsuccessfully to shake them off, and strove to encourage sleep as a resource against them.

"At last I succeeded in falling into a partial slumber, from which I was rudely awakened by a terrible shock, seemingly a blow upon the head. Starting up, my senses bewildered, my perceptions – my vision – obscured for a few moments, I found a difficulty in remembering where I was; but as a full consciousness of my position returned, the objects about me grew more distinct.

"Instantaneously I felt sure something had happened to Laura, for it was toward her that my gloomy thoughts had been constantly tending."

Here Walton's face grew almost livid in its pallor. He stopped and covered it with his hands. In a few seconds he conquered his agitation, and in a subdued tone continued:

"It seems almost incredible, and to one whose strong material nature rendered him incapable of understanding the sympathetic connection between Laura and I, I would not disclose what I now[28] relate to you."

"Many men are too often prone to ridicule what they cannot understand. Dull, gross, and unimpressionable themselves, they deem others superstitious and weak-minded. I should be wary of exposing myself to the ridicule of such people, for even I, cold and impassable as I seem to be, am vulnerable there.

"But, let me resume. The physical effect of the shock I had received, and for which I could not account, had scarcely worn off, when raising my eyes I discovered in the extreme end of the car, through the partial gloom of evening, what I had first imagined to be a shadow was developing itself with fearful distinctness into the form of Laura. Could I be dreaming? Had the unaccountable shock I had received so far upset my nervous system as to render me mad? I started forward, but the spirit, for such it was, preserved the same relative distance between us, yet grew each moment more and more distinct.

"Had it been quite dark and the lamps burning dimly about me, I should have fancied it to be a shadow cast into the compartment by the light outside: a shadow which my excited imagination had tortured into a resemblance to Laura. But just then the setting sun, which had been partially obscured by a cloud, threw a rich flood of golden light upon her. Her face was pale, her hair slightly disheveled, and the expression of her countenance was that of pain mingled with an almost unearthly resignation, whilst her hazel eyes were bent upon me, oh! with *such* a look of tenderness and pity. Just over her temple was a wound from which blood trickled. I saw the form but for a few seconds longer, and as it faded away, such a circle of heavenly radiance played about her head and illuminated her features that I cried, 'Laura has seen her last of earth, Laura is an angel.' Ere I had finished speaking, the form vanished. So convinced was I that Laura was dying or dead that I quitted the cars at the first stopping place and returned to Paris."

Notes

[28] *Original reads*: knew [ed.].

I knew Walton to be imaginative, and but for the strong coincidence would have believed the whole story to be the effect of a diseased imagination. But the utter impossibility of any communication having reached him, coupled with many other extraordinary things about him, caused me to believe implicitly what he said.

Walton soon left Paris. He spoke of the misfortune that had befallen him in the loss of Laura without the slightest appearance of agitation. He acted like one who knew he must become familiar with the constant presence of some almost o'erwhelming misery, and was wisely endeavouring to accustom himself to confront it at once.

The effect of this lamentable accident was more apparent on the Misses Goffe. It seemed to have completely crushed Maria, the boldest, most daring of the two. She moved and spoke like one whom the burden of a great grief had entirely subdued.

"If," said she mournfully, "I had but one year to live, and I know that would be the happiest of my life, I would cheerfully lay it down to give Walton one hour of forgetfulness; for that he feels more keenly than half the world will ever believe, I know too well."

Walton remained in the south of France six months, then returned and entered the gayest society of Paris. The world soon began to comment upon the ease with which Mr. Walton had forgotten a woman to whom, apparently, he had been so devotedly attached.

Walton seemed to wish to remove from the mind of Maria Goffe a sort of dread with which it was evident he inspired her. He paid her those gentle, quiet attentions most acceptable in her peculiar situation. He visited them daily, was the companion of their walks, and endeavoured to inspire them with the cheerfulness that now characterized himself.[29] At first I could not understand it. I attributed his conduct to one of two things: either the great shock he had received was productive of total change in his character, or by his indomitable will he had succeeded in burying a hopeless grief. But the world, the dear thousand and one friends, were greatly scandalized at Mr. Walton's great want of feeling. They never imagined that he could be acting a part, or that to one in his peculiar position solitude would become the parent of insanity, and that only in the activity of the present he could forget the misfortune of the past.

At the expiration of the allotted period of mourning the Goffes appeared in society, the brusquerie of their manner greatly abated, from poor Maria almost gone. If the gay world were scandalized at Walton's early appearance amongst them, still more greatly were they shocked when they learned he had given place in his heart to another love; that the Wolf was cherished where the Lamb had nestled. He was engaged to Maria Goffe. The gossiping world wondered how such a man could marry such a woman. How could they harmonize? What sentiments or tastes could they have in common?

Walton had been seen in gaming saloons. No one could say they knew him to be a loser; but the mercenary regarded it as highly probable that Miss Goffe's large fortune had attracted him.

Disappointed women, whose charms had made no impression on him, pitied him, and expressed regret that one of their sex could stoop to acts which Maria Goffe had been guilty of to win him. The charitable few, who may be found even in what is termed "the best society," believed he was marrying her to show that he could forgive, and that she had accepted his love that she might repair in the future the misfortunes of the past.

Notes

[29] *Original reads*: the cheerfulness, which now characterized himself [ed.].

None of these reasons ever entered my mind, or if they had, they never could have satisfactorily accounted to me for his conduct. I could not credit that the event, terrible as it was in its character, could have wrought such a revolution in his disposition as to enable him to forgive or forget. I did not believe him to be the man to so far overlook a mortal injury, direct or indirect, accidental or premeditated. I grew suspicious, and watched his actions. It was painful to play the spy upon him, but I felt that the motive justified it. I could not divest my mind of the idea that there was some design cherished by him, not apparent upon the surface, in marrying Maria Goffe. I noticed at times that the studied smiles his face wore in society, or when she was regarding him, gave place to an expression of concentrated bitterness and hatred almost diabolic when he did not imagine any one's attention was directed toward him. It shot out from beneath his heavy eyebrows, o'er the fixed smile that wreathed his mouth, like heat lightening over the soft beauty of a summer landscape.

Walton had always been a connoisseur[30] in painting. He now became an art student, and during the time not devoted to military matters, might have been found, palette in hand, in his studio.

I remember on entering there one morning I found him copying from a miniature a full-length likeness of Laura. I was startled into saying as I gazed at it:

"Strange occupation for you, Walton. I thought you had forgotten her."

He looked at me and replied with a sneer:

"And you, too, Braham, then have joined the fools."

I did not like his manner. There was something in it that impressed me strongly. I felt more convinced now than ever that Walton was acting a part. I began to feel myself placed in a most trying and difficult position. I felt sure this union was to be productive of no good, and a sort of nameless terror crept over me whenever I heard it mentioned. My face must have expressed my foreboding, for Walton, after regarding me for a few seconds, continued:

"Don't mind me, Braham. You have sufficient good sense to know that it is the artist painting the features of a beautiful woman, and not the lover reviving remembrance of the lost one. I trust I am too wise to recall the past, if I thought that past would embitter the future."

After a short desultory conversation we parted. I went to the Goffe's. I found Maria alone in the drawing room engaged in some needlework, to her an unwanted occupation. The misfortune, of which she had been the involuntary occasion, and the acknowledged, what she believed, reciprocated love, which had entered her heart, seemed to have strangely subdued and softened her. The wild fiery light, which formerly shone from her eyes, had given place to a tender, almost melancholy, expression. In her whole manner there was something so imploring that I was involuntarily touched.

"Do you go to the Brebilles to-night?" I asked.

"No," she replied "neither sister nor I. Walton does not approve of them."

"And yet you used to be very intimate; and they have been kind to you. I trust you have some good reason for so unceremoniously throwing them over."

"No," she replied quietly, "I have none other than the one I have offered. That seems sufficient."

"To you, perhaps, but it does not seem so to me."

Notes

[30] *Original reads*: had always been connoisseur [ed.].

why not," she rejoined, with a slight flash of the old manner coming over her. …tisfied with what Walton does, for what he does is for the best. If he says do …o that, I do it unquestioningly,[31] because I believe his judgments to be always …nd his motives pure."

… Goffe, pardon me," I responded, "if I suggest that this blind reliance on the will of another is not always likely to produce the most beneficial results. We have every day such instances of the fallibility of human judgments as to render it exceedingly unsafe to trust any mortal to the extent you have just declared your willingness to rely on Mr. Walton. I have heard him censure the recent conduct of Madame de Brebille. As I am convinced he does not know all the circumstances of the case, I feel sure he is governed by his prejudices; not guided by his sense of justice."

"Notwithstanding this homily," replied she coldly, as she rose from her seat as if to terminate the interview, "I cannot but reiterate my unabated reliance on the correctness of Walton's opinion. I will go even further:[32] were the evidence of my own senses opposed to the mere word or opinion of Walton, I would unhesitatingly yield my own conviction to his superior judgment and penetration."

A declaration strong as this, uncalled-for too, in view of the matter under discussion, suggested to my mind that there had been a previous contest in her own with regard to her lover; that a doubt of his sincerity might have crept in, a doubt she had struggled with and vanquished. Feeling there was for herself with regard to Walton, no halfway position, she must[33] either place implicit reliance on him, or cease to trust him at all.

Soon after this I had occasion to observe a marked change in the manner of the Goffes toward me, a sort of cold reserve that had never before characterized their intercourse with me. I naturally concluded that to Walton the change was to be directly or indirectly ascribed. A man of his keenness and penetration could not but observe that I had become suspicious of him, but I knew he was too subtle to say anything to them which they could repeat to me. I was determined, however, to be blind to this, and not to permit anything except positive rudeness to prevent my preserving that same degree of intimacy that I had maintained during my previous visits.

At length the marriage was consummated. I never saw a man apparently in such wild spirits as Walton. I followed Laura to the grave with a far less heavy heart than that I bore at Mrs. Walton's bridal. They departed from Paris amid the congratulations of friends, and as her father blessed her I could not help thinking, "Never woman needed a blessing more."

Some months passed away, during which time I only heard of the newly married pair through the Goffes, until one morning I found amongst my other post letters one from Gus Williams, who thus ran on:

"You will be surprised, my dear fellow, to see this letter dated from Cannes instead of Nice.[34] The fact is, Demelwhof went away, a week ago and took his cook with him, and as Vigior's has closed his café at the latter place and opened another here, Nice had then few charms for me, so I followed in his wake; a man, you know, must eat. Yesterday I went out to fish for St. Pierre, and had the infernal luck to catch none. Judge my surprise on going ashore on one of our little islands, near the mainland, to stumble over Walton. I learned the fellow has actually been here nearly two months whilst I was at Nice, and did not drop me a line. I taxed him with unkindness; he said he did not like to ask me over until he got a decent cook, for if he gave me a bad dinner he would

Notes

[31] *Original reads*: unquestionably [ed.].

[32] *Original reads*: farther [ed.].

[33] *Original reads*: that she must [ed.].

[34] *Cannes … Nice* seaside towns in the south of France.

never hear the last of it. I don't like the fellow's looks; there is a wild sort of glassiness about his eyes, and he has become lean as a razor. I am sure he cannot be all right, for I had one of the whitest French rolls, with such capital crust, and a *real* Bologna sausage – would you believe it, he actually refused to taste it. I was convinced by this that something must be wrong with him. He told me Maria was at a hotel and not very well, that he did not think the air of the mainland agreed with her, and that he was endeavouring to prepare a place for her on the island. I can't say that I was very agreeably impressed by it. It is the reclaimed portion of an old monastery: quite a ruin in fact. Walton always was a fellow with odd tastes: the place is romantic enough, one must confess. It might suit him, but it would not do for me. There was a jolly old doctor with him, who asked me to waive the ceremony of a call, and meet my cousins and a few other friends at his house at dinner in the evening. I found him a brick of an old fellow; he gave us a capital feed. I sat next a Chevalier D'Oyen, who seems to know the house like a book. He pointed out to me just what dishes to eat. I found him a man whose opinions on all subjects relating to grub were not to be despised. A *fricandeau*[35] I particularly remember. I might have enjoyed myself thoroughly but for Cousin Maria's strange behaviour. She is dreadfully altered in her appearance. I would never have dreamed that two months of married life could have made such a change in anyone. To begin with, she refused soup, which was not only rude, but in this case positively unwise; for from the moment the lid was taken from the tureen and the steam wafted toward me, I knew we were to have a treat. She watched Walton, not like a cat watching a mouse, but a mouse watching a cat. When he speaks to her ever so tenderly she starts; you will remember she had a very heavy spice of the devil in her composition, but it does not show now; she appears cowed. I do not believe she ate two mouthfuls, but sat crumbling bread during the whole meal. D'Oyen, who did not know of our relationship, said that she was a patient of Dr. Saddler, and that there was a rumour current in town, to use a Scotch expression, 'she had a bee in her bonnet.' She was fond of snakes and lizards, had them at times for pets; was also fond of dressing herself in all sorts of ridiculous costumes. That her husband, poor fellow, to prevent her appearing in public thus, and creating scandal, used to sit patiently making sketches of her all day long, and that it was said Walton was fitting up a place on the island to remove her from the observation of society.

I made several vain attempts to stop him doing this, but without success. I did not like to embarrass him by saying, "she is my cousin"; for he appeared to be a good natured sort of fellow. I went to see them the next morning. I was shown into his studio. Sure enough, I found Maria most ridiculously got up. She said Walton had taken to painting lately, and was making a series of sketches from Shakespeare – that she was then sitting for one of the witches in Macbeth.

Walton gave a very hasty assent, and suggested to her that she should change her dress. When she left the room to do so, he remarked to me that his wife was growing eccentric, and had recently given him considerable cause for uneasiness; that he thought her mind had received a great shock from the fatal accident to Laura; but that he hoped she would come right in time. He trusted I would not write anything to alarm the family, for that he had taken the house on the island for the purpose of removing her temporarily from society."

A few more lines relating to his favourite topic, and Gus closed his letter.

Notes

[35] *fricandeau* veal braised in its own juices.

Maria, exhibiting symptoms of insanity. Had it been Walton I should not have been surprised. But Maria; that was indeed something strange. I felt it my duty to show the letter to her father and sister. I had not been near them for a week, and was surprised to learn, on calling for that purpose, that they had been absent from town three days. I was in almost as bad position with regard to them as I was with Maria previous to her marriage. The letter would prove nothing with regard to Walton. I could not tell them what fears I myself entertained, which, after all, were[36] but the vaguest suspicion, so I myself determined to visit Cannes to ascertain whether Maria's safety was groundless.[37]

Three days after I was in Provence,[38] and my first inquiry was,[39] of course, for them. I learned at my hotel that they had already removed to the island. My second was for Gus Williams, in which I was more successful. I found he was lodging at the same hotel.

Unluckily for my anxiety I found him at his dinner. I paused before the door to which a servant conducted me. Within there was an ominous silence, broken occasionally by the rattle of knives and forks.

On entering, I discovered Gus seated *vis à vis* with[40] a fat merry-faced gentleman, who with a napkin tucked under his chin, was busily engaged upon the viands[41] before them.

Gus started up on seeing me. Shaking my hand heartily he said:

"Now, old fellow, you know my weakness. D'Oyen, the friend of whom you so often hear me speak, Phil. Braham, you will find him a brick of a fellow, only he does not know what is what as well as you or I, D'Oyen. *Garçon*, bring back that soup. Sit down, Phil. *Garçon*, bring another knife and fork. Now let us resume business. Don't ask me about anybody, Phil; you know I never talk before dessert, and we are only on the third course."

I was, as may be well imagined, all anxiety to make some inquiries about Maria, but D'Oyen and Williams, who were wrapped up in the viands before them, only spoke at intervals to comment on the different dishes. When they got to fruit I ventured to ask Gus how Maria was?

"Oh, just the same as when I wrote; there is but little change in her. I seldom see them now, they are gone to the island."

"And what sort of a physician is this they have in attendance on her?"

"A very good, fatherly sort of a man, who takes a great deal of interest in her. He would bring you triumphantly through a fever, or give you a capital palliative for a cough, but I doubt very much his ability to manage that peculiarly subtle disease, insanity."

"Of course it is too late to visit them to-night," said I. "I will postpone it until I have had an opportunity of seeing the doctor, who can either dispel my fears or confirm them."

I found Dr. Saddler as agreeable and acceptable as Gus had described him to be, and after informing him of the very intimate relation in which I stood to the family, we conversed very unreservedly about Maria.

I inferred from the tone of his conversation in speaking of them, that he was under the impression that the Goffes knew perfectly well of her malady. I further judged from what he said that he believed Walton had written them in the fullest manner concerning her.

Notes

[36] *Original reads*: was [ed.].

[37] *whether Maria's safety was groundless* possibly "whether my fears for Maria's safety were groundless."

[38] *Provence* a region in southeastern France.

[39] *Original reads*: Three days after I was in Provence, my first inquiry was [ed.].

[40] *Original reads*: to [ed.].

[41] *viands* food, provisions.

Here already was something exceedingly strange. It was evident from this that he had been deceiving Dr. Saddler, which afforded another ground for suspicion.

The night seemed exceedingly long to me. I scarcely slept, so much was I interested in the probable events of the morrow. I, having ordered a boat overnight, was on my way to the Waltons' soon after breakfast.

Ere I got there it struck me that I was making a call uncommonly early, absurdly so. What reasonable excuse could I offer for breaking in (even by a friendly visit) upon the privacy of a family at such an hour?

There did not seem to be a living creature about the premises. The whole place had to me a most forbidding aspect – cold, gloomy, isolated. The cloistered ruins, which in the humid atmosphere of England would have grown beautiful in a garniture of moss and ivy, appeared cold and bare in the clear morning light. It was a ruin in the fullest sense of the word; there was nothing to relieve the general aspect of decay and dreary discomfort. At another time, and under other circumstances, I might have in imagination restored it to the period when mailed warriors, half priest half soldier, had peopled its cloisters and sung[42] their battle hymns on their way to Palestine.[43] But now I could only see a long line of dilapidated walls, unenlivened by a single touch of Nature's kindliness.

At one end of the structure an attempt had been made to render a portion of it habitable, but in its raw newness it appeared as bare and comfortless as all the rest.

Had this portion of the building been designed for a jail instead of a pleasure seat, it could not have been more jealously constructed. On the land side, or rather the side toward Cannes, all the windows had been walled up: the only opening visible was a strong cross-barred door of iron, behind which was another of wood, apparently very strong and heavy, and another small door at the extreme end in the wall over the rocky shore. On the upper story, toward the sea, there were three windows like all the rest, securely barred across; on the lower story there was a small door and window, just over the rocks that fringed the seaside, at which a small boat was moored.

I was the more surprised at its appearance when I remembered that it had been chosen for an invalid, one, too, whose mind was said to be affected. The whole aspect of the place seemed better calculated to induce madness than to effect its cure.

There was, however, little or nothing to be gained by a prolonged outward survey of the premises; and as I had serious doubts as to the propriety of disturbing its inmates at so early an hour, I resolved to join some fishermen who were drawing their nets upon the beach some little distance away, and return at a more reasonable time.

The customary salute and "bonjour" paved the way for conversation, which turned upon the island and its vicinity. One old man informed me that it had not been inhabited in his time until an Englishman a few months since had taken a fancy to build upon the ruins. People said his wife was mad, and that he had put her there to keep her out of the way, but that he thought the gentleman the most mad of the two. His wife, who had washed for them when they first came to the ruins, told him Monsieur Walton was always muttering to himself. He could keep no servants any length of time: none would live in the house with a mad woman. Their food was cooked and brought over from the hut at the end of the island each day for the last few weeks. No one had seen the lady; Mr. Walton alone went in and out, looking more dead than alive, with a wild light shining out of his eyes.

Notes

[42] *Original reads*: sang [ed.].

[43] *mailed warriors ... Palestine* a reference to the Crusades, a series of military campaigns by Christian Europe against the Muslim Middle East.

From him I also learned many particulars relative to the general deportment and habits of Walton.

Each morning he sailed off to Capru, Isle Ste. Marguerite,[44] and other not far distant places, remaining absent the greater part of the day, during which time his wife could be seen at the upper windows, pale and thin, more resembling a ghost than a living woman. During his absence none could enter the house. If any one came bringing supplies or letters from Cannes they placed them in a small out-room, where they remained until Walton's return. He informed me that if I was not particularly anxious to speak to Mr. Walton at once, and waited, I would find out that what he said was quite true. I pondered some time over his suggestion, and determined to act in accordance with it. We resumed the conversation:

"Is Monsieur a relative of the gentleman or lady?"

"No, only a particular friend," I replied. "I am intimate with Mr. Walton and the family of his wife."

"If she has a family, or friends, they had better be looking after her. Indeed, they had, Monsieur," he added, as he left me to return to his companions.

Hours passed wearily away. At length, when almost tired of watching and waiting, I saw Walton emerge from the house, unmoor his boat, hoist sail, and bear away for Capru.

I sat watching the boat until it was only a speck upon the broad blue sea, then left my covert[45] and approached the dwelling. I knocked at the door. No answer. Again I knocked, and was answered by a voice from above. I retired from the door, and looking up in the direction from whence the voice proceeded, discerned Maria at the grating of the window.

She gave a glad start of surprise, stretched out her arms between the bars, and exclaimed, "Oh! Thank God. At last someone has come to release me."

"Cannot you come down and let me in?" I asked.

"No, I am a prisoner here. I am alone in this wretched house, bolted, barred in. It is impossible for me to get out of this room. For God's sake save me! Take me from this horrible place, or I *shall* go mad. Aye, mad as Walton is."

I looked about me for some means to effect an entrance. I shook, or tried to shake, the door. I might as well have tried to tear down the walls with my fingernails. I could not move it one hair's breath. I took a heavy log I saw lying nearby and used it as a sort of battering ram, but with no better effect and I was at length reluctantly obliged to confess to her that, without assistance, entrance was impossible.

"Oh, try then and get some help, lose no time. I cannot tell you the horrors of my situation: Walton is mad or else a demon in his man form. I know not which. Go, go. Try and succor[46] me ere he returns, delay may be death to me. Go. Pray go. It is useless to appeal to anyone on the Island, I have done it in vain, all believe me mad."

I was in a most trying situation. I had sent my own boat back to Cannes, with orders to return for me in the evening. Thus I was unable to communicate with the mainland, unless chance threw a boat in my way. I walked up and down the beach, returning from time to time to say an assuring word to Maria, until I was despairing of ever seeing a boat, when at last, to my infinite relief, I saw a small craft standing in toward the shore, heading in such a course as must bring it within sailing distance of the Island.

Notes

[44] *Isle Ste. Marguerite* Île Sainte-Marguerite, an island a half mile off-shore from Cannes, on the French Riviera.

[45] *covert* hiding place.

[46] *succor* aid.

Boat never seemed to sail more slowly: It appeared an age ere they approached; on hailing them, they bore up for the beach, and were at length beside the shore.

To my disappointment it contained but two small boys who were returning from a fishing excursion, and not a single implement that would be of the least assistance in affecting an entrance to the house.

I therefore deemed it best to waste no more time in ineffectual attempts, but to make sail at once for Cannes and obtain efficient assistance.

In my anxiety I had not noticed that a storm was brewing, one of those sudden squalls for which the Mediterranean is so notorious. I began to tremble for our safety in the tiny shell in which we were tossed about by the turbulent water. The wind blew down from the mountains, full in our teeth. We were obliged to beat in at the momentary peril of an upset. At last a gust of extreme violence tore our half furled sail to shreds, and sent the fragments flying over the water. At this we were reduced to a pair of miserable sculls; whilst I was obliged to bail continually to save our now leaking craft from sinking.

Hours were flying by, we seemed driven hopelessly seaward, instead of making headway toward the shore. It was as difficult to turn back to the Island as to go on. This same accident under different circumstances would not have been so disastrous. I felt that Maria's life was in the hands of a madman, that it would be cowardly, aye inhuman, not to run all risks to reach the shore.

The wind veered round a little about nightfall, and we now began to make perceptible headway toward Cannes. I urged the rowers by promises of large rewards, and they strained every nerve to increase our speed. It was long after dark when I landed upon the Quai,[47] cold, wet, exhausted. I hastened to the hotel and found Gus at supper.

"Just in the nick of time, sit down," he cried. "Bouillabaisse, rather heavy for supper but a drop of vin Charteuse after will soon digest it. Why don't you sit down?"

He gave me a second and longer look. I was so completely exhausted by my day's exertion, and famished by my long abstinence, that I could not speak. I poured out a glass of wine and drank it.

"Good Heavens," exclaimed Gus, starting up from the table and laying his hand on my wet coat, "Man: where have you been? Drowned, eh? Why, you are pale as a ghost. What on earth is the matter with you – you've had no dinner, or something like it: sit down. Drink and eat."

"No, No, Gus," I replied. "I cannot, I left Maria Walton in a most dangerous situation. Walton is mad as a March hare and she is exposed to the greatest danger."

"Then there is a pair of them," responded Gus. "I suspected something of the kind was the matter with him, from the day he refused that roll and real Bologna. As for Maria, you remember what I told you about her refusing soup."

"Gus, you are talking nonsense," I said, impatiently. "You seem incapable of receiving the idea into your addled head, disconnected with something to eat. I assure you Maria is in imminent danger, and unless you can render me some assistance in rescuing her, I must seek it elsewhere. It would be murder, worse than murder, to leave her where she is." I then detailed to him, as hurriedly as I could,[48] the events of the day.

Gus was at the conclusion fully roused to the necessity of immediate action. He proposed securing the assistance of D'Oyen, whom he undertook to call, whilst I went to secure Dr. Saddler and a boat, with necessary instruments to force entrance into the

Notes

[47] *Quai* a riverside street.

[48] *Original reads*: I then detailed to him, hurriedly as I could [ed.].

house. The old Dr. got quite into a fright on hearing my statement. He smiled at the idea of Walton being mad, and related instances illustrating the singular acuteness of maniacs, and the success they often achieved in assuming the appearance of sanity; also their proneness to charge others with the very affliction of which they were themselves the victims.

I pointed out to him that I thought Walton was then actually illustrating his statement; that whilst himself insane, he had been only too successful inducing others to believe that it was his wife who was afflicted.

At last he consented to accompany me, and, with the air of a martyr, drew on his overcoat for the expedition. We then sallied out together to procure boat and crew.

The sky was still very towering, occasional heavy gusts of wind indicated a probable return of the squalls.

Reward, entreaty, promises – everything except threats, which would be useless and unavailing – were they freely lavished to procure boatmen willing to put out at once to sea. At last we succeed at[49] this; then we again experienced difficulty in procuring crowbars with which to effect an entrance in case Walton refused us admittance. Thus the night was far spent ere we started. The wind still blew with gusty violence and rendered it dangerous to put up our sail, so we had no recourse[50] but to row the whole distance, which made it nearly daylight ere we reached the shore of the island. I proposed that I should first reconnoiter the premises, to ascertain if an entry could not be secured without force. I thought that if Walton only saw me[51] he might be induced to permit my ingress. I could then be guided by circumstances in opening the way for the rest. I knocked loudly at the grated door several times. At last Walton cried out from one of the windows above:

"Who is there?"

"Philip Braham," I answered.

"Philip Braham, a most unexpected pleasure. You are very early; wait a minute, I will come down and let you in."

Several moments elapsed, still I heard no movement toward the door. I grew impatient; still I did not like to knock again. Five minutes more, still no one came. I walked from the doorway to look up at the window; still no one visible. Overcome by impatience I knocked again, and was startled at hearing a maniacal laugh and cry of "Find her! Find her!" from Walton, who had crept silently out the side door and over the rocks, down which he had glided, entered his boat and pushed out to sea. For a few seconds I was taken aback by the turn affairs had made. I clambered around to the door from which he had emerged, only to find it locked fast.[52] I then hurried to our boat to get the assistance of my companions. We hastened to the house, and called aloud to Maria, without receiving any reply; the silence within was most suspicious and alarming.

We now commenced our endeavours to open the door, which stoutly resisted all our efforts, and we had been a long time to work upon it when we were startled by a piercing scream; a scream replete with agony and terror. It only made my blood curdle.

"Save me! Oh, God! is there no one to save me?" It was Maria's voice.

We plied the pick and crowbar perseveringly, at the same time calling Maria that we would soon reach her.

Notes

[49] *Original reads*: succeed to [ed.].

[50] *Original reads*: resource [ed.].

[51] *Original reads*: myself [ed.].

[52] *Original reads*: fast locked [ed.].

"Come, oh, come!" she cried frantically: "they are upon me. The snakes – the snakes, they twine around me. They sting me. Help, help! or I am lost!"

We worked like giants and at last the doorway was forced open. It was so dark within that at first we found it difficult to grope our way about. We were guided more by Maria's screams than our sight.

At length we discovered at the farther[53] end of the room a flight of steps leading to the chamber above. We swiftly mounted to the upper story, where a sight met our eyes that almost petrified us with horror.

Our progress was here arrested by a heavy oak door in the upper panel of which an iron grating had been set in, through which we gazed at an appalling spectacle.

There stood Maria, her tangled hair hanging in masses over her bare shoulders; eyes starting from her head, whilst she frantically tore from her half-naked form the venomous snakes that darted at and clung to her.

Ere we reached her, terror seemed to have frozen her tongue. She was incapable of speech. With a look of ghastly horror on her face that will haunt me until my dying day, she ceased her efforts, stretched out her arms imploringly to us, then sank upon the ground, amidst the venomous serpents that coiled, twined, and hissed as they writhed over and above her.

In an instant we were at work, beating down the door, and soon succeeded in forcing our entrance into this chamber of horrors.

A sharp, dangerous battle of a few moments, and such of the snakes as did not escape lay dead or disabled about us. We lifted Maria from where she lay. She was now quite insensible, bitten, too, in several places by the venomous reptiles that lay around.

The odour from the snakes was nauseating in the extreme. We carried her to the doorway, where the air was purer. She did not, however, then revive, but gave indications of suffering in heavy groans.

Search discovered to us other rooms well furnished. On a sofa in one of these we placed her.

Dr. Saddler looked at the haggard face, his fingers the while upon her pulse.

"If I could get oil or coffee to give her, either might afford her temporary relief. She may revive, but live, never. She has been bitten in twenty places. Her case is hopeless."

D'Oyen went hastily in search of some coffee or oil. He soon returned with a cup of the latter. Dr. S. forced several spoonfuls down her throat. Gus, assisted by the fisherman I had seen the previous day, who had unexpectedly made his appearance, found and assisted in preparing some coffee.

At length she seemed to revive, and moaned as if in great agony. Opening her eyes she stared wildly about her for a few seconds, then shrieked with pain.

"Oh, can no one relieve me? Can you not give me something to relieve me from this awful agony? The snakes! The snakes! Save me from them! Save me; Oh, this pain. Do something for me." With an effort she started up only to fall back exhausted upon her pillow.

Some hours after this she rallied, but there was plainly written on her face that unmistakable aspect of coming death. We raised her up, and propped her about with pillows, then, after she had rallied, with many a painful effort she told her frightful story.

Notes

[53] *Original reads*: further [ed.].

"Walton was most kind to me until we came to Cannes, then he grew moody and melancholy, exhibiting inequalities of temper that I never knew him to display before. He had strange vagaries too, at least I then thought them so. I committed many extravagancies to humour his uncertain temper, and to prevent others from noticing his conduct toward me. I know now that was part of his plan; that he induced me to misrepresent myself, that I might be thought deranged. I see it all now. Why was I then so blind?

"At last he persuaded me to come to this island to reside in this dreary ruin. He said that he hated society, and that when we were alone together, we should be as happy as before. I came. I did come reluctantly for I had a sort of dread, an undefined apprehension of evil to grow out of it.

"Ah, doctor, do you not remember, you, too, prevailed upon me. Said it would be for his good. He has duped you also. Do not turn away or look so grieved. You did it for the best – I know you did.

"Each day, after he came here, he would go out in the boat – sometimes he took me. He often, however, went alone. Sometimes we would meet others on the water, who, if they spoke to me, did so in a kind, pitying tone that I could not understand. Now I know they thought me mad.

"One day I observed a small vessel lying off the shore, from which they landed, with great care, several boxes. After that no servants would remain at night. They would not tell me why. They slept in the hut at the extreme end of the island. At last they would not stay here at all. Still no reason why.

"One day Walton was upstairs arranging the room in which you found me. He was so long there that I went up to ascertain what kept him. He met me upon the stairway and playfully refused to let me ascend further, saying he had a surprise in store for me. For several days he spent hours there alone, and during these days he revived all the tender gaiety of our honeymoon. On the last evening he was surpassingly kind. When our servant left in the evening (for they had all now left our service except one), he insisted on my taking a glass of Vin Chartreuse.

"After it I remember feeling so drowsy that I could not undress without difficulty. My head scarcely touched my pillow ere I slept. The wine must have been drugged. When I awoke I found myself a prisoner in the room from which you delivered me. Alas! too late. For some moments I was completely bewildered, and sat looking about me. On three sides of the room were cages filled with hissing, writhing[54] snakes, on the fourth, a likeness of Laura, painted by himself, about her arm was coiled a snake. I started up in horror. I endeavoured to open the door. It was fastened. I cried out in terror, no answer. I shouted, screamed; no one came, my heart sank each moment lower and lower, crushed by its burthen of fears, its frightful presentment of coming horrors yet unseen. My fright and agony was augmented by dread of the venomous reptiles that reared their scaly heads, and hissed behind the close network of their cages. I suddenly remembered, I cannot tell why, but it flashed across me just then, the discussion we had in Paris. You recollect Mr. Braham, that murder of Mad'lle[55] Varigney, and Walton's expressed idea of a fitting punishment, or revenge; that of surrounding the murderer with such associations as would keep alive in his memory a remembrance of his guilt, so environ him that he could never for one instant in his waking moments separate himself from a memory of his crime. The snakes, the likeness of Laura, the barred windows, and grated door hurried me to the appalling conclusion,

Notes

[54] *Original reads*: writing [ed.].

[55] *Original reads*: Mad'le [ed.].

that this was the result of a long premeditated plan of revenge upon me, for my involuntary yet fatal agency in the death of Laura. All was now explained. His seeming love was but a ruse to get me completely in his power, to separate me from my family that he might the more easily secure my destruction and minister to his unnatural thirst for vengeance. The jail-like appearance of the chamber, our isolation on this solitary island all too apparent, I gave myself up for lost; and lost I am." Here a paroxysm of pain, more intense than those that had so often silenced the broken voice in which she related her sad story, caused her to stop abruptly. Great beads of water gathered upon her waxen brow. She seemed to be choking.[56] We thought it her last struggle, but she rallied, and in a weak voice continued. "At length Walton made his appearance at the grating, Oh! my God, what malignant joy. What fiendish exultation his face displayed. 'At last,' said he in a tone of concentrated hate. 'At last! I now no longer need wear a mask. Now wretched woman know me as I am. One who never forgets, who "never forgives".'

"'Oh! Walton,' I replied as calmly as I could, in my endeavour to feign a belief in the idea that he was amusing himself with my terror. 'Do let me out. I have been long enough a prisoner.'

"'I never joke,' said he in an awfully calm voice, whilst his eyes fairly scintillated with malice. 'Do not endeavour to deceive yourself. I am terribly earnest. Your presence there is the result of a long-meditated plan for your punishment and to avenge her.' Here he pointed to where hung the likeness of Laura. 'In this room you will live day after day until you die. Be it years, months, or days. I will leave no means untried to keep you where you are. You shall live without one thing to withdraw your remembrance from your crime, of what you term your misfortune. Crime or misfortune, whichever it may be, here is to be the scene of its expiation. You cannot escape. The world believes you mad – ask heaven, as a blessing, that you may soon be really so.'

"'Walton are you human?' I cried. 'Can you immure me here? Tell me that it is but for a little while. That there is some hope.'

"He shook his head gloomily. 'No hope,' he answered – 'no hope! It is just.' He turned away from the grating and descended the stairs.

"You know the superstitious terror with which ignorant peasants regard the insane. He told them I was mad, and they believed him; so they shunned me. Each day Walton brought me my food, and would turn from me without uttering a word, deaf to my frantic entreaties for release. Now and then I saw fishermen among the ruins. I have grown so haggard and wild in appearance that I do not wonder they thought me mad. Walton must have drugged my drink, for I would wake from slumber to find evidences that he had been in my room to feed the venomous torments by which I was surrounded. Thus the days passed hopelessly, wearily away, until you came, and hope once more beamed in upon me. Oh! how miserable I had been – how deeply wretched! Oh! unutterably wretched! Your face inspired me with new life. In the evening, when he returned, with his wonderful penetration he at once discovered that something had occurred to brighten me. My hopes must have been written on my face.

"'Who has been here?' he asked.

"I would not reply.

"'Someone has communicated with you,' he repeated, 'I am sure of that. Tell me who.'

"I denied having spoken to anyone, dreading he should find some means to debar me from succor, place me beyond the help I felt sure you would bring. I heard him leave the

Notes

[56] *Original reads*: She seemed choking [ed.].

house; presently he returned, unlocked the grate and took away my carafe to fill it with water. When he returned he held up a glove before me, simply said, 'Liar!' and turned away. I heard him through the night moving through the house. I could not sleep. I was torn with expectation, with dread and hope. With feverish thirst I drank some water. I soon fell asleep, and woke to find those loathsome horrors writhing and creeping over me. Just then you came. Too late! Too late! God help me – I must die! I feel it – I must die!"

She now spoke with infinite difficulty. She was frightfully swollen. For a while she lay motionless; then, with an expiring effort, she raised herself partially upon her elbow, her eyes glazed with approaching death, and she whispered:[57]

"Do not let them harm him. He must be mad; and, after all, I drove him to it. Do not harm him; only remember how I loved him and how he suffered. Tell him that to the last I loved him."

Her voice died away in an inarticulate murmur; her head sank slowly, one long-drawn sigh, then death.

Search was immediately instituted for Walton. Two weeks after his boat was found, bottom upward, upon the rocks near Capru, and beneath the clear, bright waters his lifeless body.

1870

Marvin Hayle

"Ella, God is love; those whom He loveth He chasteneth."[1] I removed impatiently from my shoulder the hand of Mr. Bryson, my pastor and friend. I fear at that moment my face wore a rebellious expression. I had no faith, found no comfort in his words. I, proud and worldly, felt that I had been singled out by Providence for a heavier visitation of sorrow, an affliction more severe than fell to the common lot. I could discern no future good to emanate from the anguish of that hour; hence his words only inspired me with a feeling of bitter resentment against Providence; and as I stood beside my father's corpse, whilst I clung to those stiffened fingers, clasped that cold, cold hand, that gave back no loving, responsive pressure, I asked myself what had I done to God that He should tear from me the only love that I then dared to claim?

I was indeed very miserable. Heaven had thus suddenly deprived me of the love of my last parent, at a moment that would make the separation most keenly felt; there had been months of coldness between us, to which death had now placed it beyond our reach to change. There was ever more between him and me – the shadow of a pall, a deep grave, a mound of silent earth. These were to be evermore between me and that loving protection, that tender care, to which I owed so much of the happiness of my life.

Ah, yes, I was indeed truly miserable. Besides the pain of his great loss, there was another sorrow that nearly wore out my life. It had been wringing my heart for months, aye, years; I idolized a man, to whom, I feared, I should never be united. But I get on to the end of my story too swiftly. Let me speak of that part of my history so necessary to explain the whole.

Father was extremely wealthy. From humble beginnings, he had, by his talent, probity, and untiring industry, won his way to the front rank of those manufacturing

Notes

[57] *Original reads*: with approaching death, she whispered [ed.].

Marvin Hayle

[1] *"those whom He loveth He chasteneth"* Hebrews 12:6.

princes, who contribute so much to the prosperity of dear old England. He was characterized somewhat by that purse pride and sense of personal importance so frequently perceptible in men who have won their way to golden honours by a successful struggle with "low birth and iron fortune."

Innately a gentleman, he had not allowed himself (as often is the case with men who spend the most of their lives in the pursuit of wealth) to neglect the acquisition of polite knowledge. He was as well known for his liberal patronage of literature and art as for his vast possession.

We lived magnificently. All my earliest associations are connected with scenes of splendor. Father maintained a state more befitting a duke than a commoner; all the luxury that wealth could procure surrounded me from infancy to womanhood. He married late in life, and lost my mother when I was only twelve. I can remember her with great distinctness. Her beautifully molded head covered with golden hair, her soft blue eyes, pale face, and tall, graceful form are to memory as things of yesterday. I have been told she did not love my father; that she had been induced by her parents to sacrifice herself, to bargain away her life-happiness for my father's wealth. There were whisperings, too, of an early attachment smothered by cold, calculating hands, strangled in its fullness of hope by Prudence, at whose shrine her parents were devoted worshippers.

I can believe all this was true from concurring circumstances of which I have a vivid recollection, as they produced a stronger display of feeling than she was accustomed to exhibit.

One of these grew out of a conversation between her and papa respecting the marriage of a young lady friend to an old yet wealthy suitor. My mother was advocating the claims of one (evidently preferred by the lady) who had the fortune to be young, the misfortune to be poor. I well remember the sneering tone in which my father said, "It is evident you give your friend credit for more disinterestedness and less prudence than you yourself possess." Then I did not understand the taunt, yet I could judge from the tone of his voice, his manner, her moistened eyes and quivering lips, that what he had said pained her deeply. Childlike, I nestled closer to her. As she bent over me her tears fell on my face. She took me by the hand and led me to her room. When the door closed upon us, she sat down, and drawing me closer to her, said:

"Come, Ella, I wish to say something to you that you must never forget. When you grow to womanhood you will be the heiress of great wealth. No doubt you will have many to admire you. Some day you will be asked to marry. Your father is ambitious; perhaps he may wish you to wed someone who may have wealth equal to your own, else a noble name. If you love him, darling, marry him; but, oh, my child, if you do not, never, never go before God's altar and make a solemn promise which your heart cannot ratify. By that time, Ella, I shall perhaps be gone. If I live, I shall not fear for your future; but there is something that admonishes me," continued she with quivering lips, "that we shall not be always together. Oh! remember what I tell you now as you would my last words in life. Better, far better, darling, bear all the ills of poverty, the meanest food, the coarsest clothing – aye, child, even rags and hunger are preferable if shared with a manly, honest heart, which has won all your own – than a marble palace, troops of servitors, and gold to waste with an aching heart, starving for love, bearing out its cheerless, weary life[2] 'neath lustrous silks and glittering diamonds, gliding away into the grave with all its tenderest wants unsatisfied."

Notes

[2] *Original reads*: starving for love, out its cheerless, weary life [ed.].

I shall never forget the agony her face displayed. She covered it with her hands, and the tears forcing their way between her jeweled fingers, fell upon my upturned face, baptizing me in a faith from which I never swerved.

As I grew older, father continually pressed upon me the necessity of being on my guard against adventurers.

He urged that I should disregard the professions of those who had not something to offer as an equivalent for my vast wealth. Either high rank or money. Hearts were something he never took into consideration. He could have imagined nothing more preposterous than the offer of a heart for all my possessions. 'Tis true I had many acquaintances and some intimacies amongst my sex; but none of them were calculated to neutralize the effect of my father's teachings.

An accomplished girl, who is the heiress of a vast fortune, whose personal attractions are of a high order, and who is being constantly reminded of it, by the adulation, the deference and the flatteries of those who surround her; cannot fail to become somewhat vain and egotistic. She must be more than woman, and little less than angel, to avoid it.

I was conscious of my own rare beauty. I would at that time have realized the highest conception of the most devoted worshiper of art.

Features of pure Grecian type – eyes of deepest blue – looking out from beneath long black lashes, a forehead not high, but broader than is common with my sex, surmounted with locks black as night, a complexion so dazzlingly fair, that artists have thrown down their brushes in despair at their unavailing efforts to transfer its beauty to canvas.

With the combined attractions of accomplishments, extraordinary beauty, and enormous wealth, of course I was much sought. When I entered society, I became the rage. Men of rank, of wealth and fame, paid homage to me. I had numberless suitors; but none of them touched my heart. I bore in mind the admonition of my mother and rejected them. Father was irritated by my frequent refusals of offers he thought in every way eligible. Perhaps I did injustice to many – yet I could not help feeling that my consols,[3] my bank stock, my estates, were oftener the objects of attraction than myself. At last I became cynical and unhappy. How I longed to be loved for myself alone. How often have I almost cursed that "wall of gold," which seemed destined to exclude me from the happiness accessible to others of my sex. Time after time, I saw my young companions with nothing except their good hearts or personal charms to recommend them, made happy wives and mothers, whilst I felt myself debarred from participation in their happiness by that for which so many envied me – my gold.

A London season of remarkable brilliancy passed by taxing my health severely. I was constantly out, moving hither and thither until I was ennuyée[4] with society, sick of gayeties that bored me, yet without which I could not exist. Autumn found me with a slight cough, which so greatly alarmed my father, that he hurried me off to the south of France, in search of milder air. Here, as at home, we received a great deal of company. Our house soon became the resort of the clever, the witty and distinguished. I was constantly hearing of one Marvin Hayle, an amateur artist; seemingly every visitor had something to say in his praise. Not alone the gay and young, but the learned and grave, seemed to have conspired to speak in the most glowing terms of his acquirement and goodness. Frequently coupled with these praises was the remark "what a pity it is, he is so poor."

Notes

[3] *consols* Consolidated Annuities, Great Britain's government securities.

[4] *ennuyée* weary.

At length my curiosity was aroused concerning a man whom all consented with one accord to praise. I desired Papa to call upon him. He did so. The only result it produced was a card left at our door during our absence – Papa sent him an invitation to dine. To my surprise it was declined. I thought that very strange; people seldom declined invitations to our house. I was sorry for it, for as my health did not then permit me to go out, the prospect of meeting him seemed very remote. A residence of a few months in lovely Provence[5] tended greatly to the re-establishing of my health, and enabled me to go out daily as before. I sometimes attended the charming little church, which the liberality of a wealthy English resident had bestowed upon our sunny watering place. One Sabbath morning as I took my accustomed seat, I observed, nearly opposite to me, a gentleman who had frequently attracted my attention at the Opera in London. He invariably occupied the same stall. I could never look in the direction in which he sat without finding his eyes fixed upon me. Even in the midst of Grisi's[6] most glorious efforts, should I but turn toward him I would discover that I, and not the actress, absorbed his attention. There was something in his gaze that fascinated me.

There was not a shade of impertinence in it; on the contrary, something so winning and gentle. I often thought of inquiring who he was: but as I never saw him in conversation with any of my acquaintances, I had no opportunity to learn. As girls often will, I used to weave in my imagination romantic stories of which he was the hero: but for the two past seasons I had missed him from his accustomed seat, and he had, to a degree, faded from my mind. This unexpected meeting however re-aroused and intensified my curiosity concerning him.

I touched the arm of my companion, Lucy Grant, and whispered to her. "Do you remember the gentleman who I told you used to stare at me so constantly at the Opera?"

"Yes," she answered.

"Well, he is sitting in the pew with Lord G."

Lucy stole a glance in the direction indicated, and then said to me: "That is Marvin Hayle."

Involuntarily I looked up again, and discovered his eyes bent upon me, in the same old, gentle way. I felt the blood rush to my face; holding my book high to screen it, I did not once venture to look again in that direction during service. As we drove home, our carriage overtook Lord G. and Mr. Hayle. The former was intimate at our house, an almost everyday visitor, a most welcome one too, as he brought us all the *on dits*,[7] and chit-chat of the town. As we approached, he turned and held up his hand for us to stop. Mr. Hayle walked on.

I felt piqued at this; it looked like avoidance. To say the least, Mr. Hayle showed a decided disinclination to accept what many manifested anxiety to obtain, the *entreé*[8] of our house. It was the first time, and he, the first person who had ever seemed indifferent toward[9] me. As I have said before, I was piqued at it.

"Your friend," I remarked to Lord G., "seems very retiring, he has not even bestowed a look upon us."

"Insensible fellow, truly an unpardonable offence where there was so much to be seen and admired. By the way, you must however have been at some time or other an object of interest to him. You must have made an impression of some kind upon him

Notes

[5] *Provence* a region in southeastern France.

[6] *Grisi* Giulia Grisi (1811–1869), an Italian opera singer.

[7] *on dits* gossip.

[8] *entreé* entrance.

[9] *Original reads*: towards [ed.].

for there is a face in one of his pictures, a face so startlingly like your own, that one might declare it a portrait.

"It means the same look your face wore when you first came out in London." I blushed at that. "Then he has a Madonna; your face over again, features, eyes, hair, complexion. The expression only is different. It has a more thoughtful, matured look. I have tried several times to inveigle him out of it, but have been compelled to give it up in despair. I am detaining you here, however, to discuss Hayle's pictures, and leaving the man to walk on alone. Good-bye."

The carriage whirled on; the horses grown restive from delay pranced from side to side. They almost touched Mr. Hayle as we passed him. He did not even look up; he only moved a little from the way.

"My face on Marvin Hayle's canvas!" I thought of this nearly all the remainder of that day. I was so abstracted and absorbed as to attract the attention of Papa. I even called Lucy Grant "Mr. Hayle," and was duly teased for it all the rest of the evening.

Lord G. called next day. Somehow or other the conversation turned upon art. Ah! I remember; I had been sketching as I sat at the window. From art to artists the transition was easy; from artists in general to particular artists, and so on quite naturally, until we came to Mr. Hayle. I pronounced him a singular man.

"Yes," Lord G. admitted. "Hayle was, perhaps, peculiar in his ideas, still the most agreeable of men. What do you think?" he added. "Hayle might make a horde of money if he would sell his pictures – he has only a few hundred a year, and yet he will not do it. He entertains some peculiar and eccentric notions about the sanctity of his art, and will not, he declares, degrade it to the level of a trade. He lives by his pen and his small income." Lord G. ran on and praised his friend enthusiastically. He told me of several kind acts Hayle had done; for instance, resigning his right to three hundred a year, that some orphan nieces might be educated with it; also, of his depriving himself for months to spare a sufficient sum to enable a fellow art-student, at Rome, to go home and see his sick mother. "And only the other day he gave to the Abbé de Merriviele that group of Arabs, that sunset scene at the Isle Ste. Marguerite,[10] to assist in relieving a case of destitution. How I wish I had been so fortunate as to become its purchaser. The Dutch minister bought it. I would gladly have paid double the price he gave for it." Thus he ran on talking of Mr. Hayle, sounding his praises in his earnest good-hearted way until my desire to know his friend became almost a longing. At last, just as he was going away, he remembered the principal object of his visit. He had made up a little party for a picnic on the Isle Ste. Marguerite. He wanted Lucy Grant and me to join it. The Beverlys and Wainwrights were going, so were the Rylands – that amusing Chevalier D'Oyen – and a number of others.

I pleaded my cough, fear of its return, unsettled weather, and a number of other objections. Just then Dr. Saddler came in. He agreed with Lord G. that it would be a capital thing for me, a beneficial change; he thought it would be perfectly safe.

"Oh! I forgot to add," said Lord G., "Hayle, too, has consented to lay aside his palette for the day. Do come and make our party complete."

I consented, but not on Mr. Hayle's account, of course not. I quite convinced myself that he had nothing whatever to do with my determination. I do not know why I lay awake so late that night. I was half angry with myself for allowing the simple fact that I was to meet Marvin Hayle, a gentleman to whom I had never spoken, and who, to a degree, avoided me, to excite and absorb me so much.

Notes

10 *group of Arabs* presumably this group is part of the painting of the sunset scene at the Île Sainte-Marguerite.

I had given orders to be awakened very early. As the first streaks of gray made their appearance over the tops of the Estrelles,[11] my maid entered my room.

How severely I taxed her patience that morning. She pronounced me *"très exigeante."*[12] I could not find a dress suited to the occasion, or to me. I was disposed to echo the popular feminine lament of "nothing to wear." Lucy Grant was provokingly ironical, and desired to know if I was arming myself for conquest. She suggested that perhaps I designed sitting for my portrait to a celebrated amateur artist, an acquaintance of hers. Between her banter and my fastidiousness, I succeeded in dressing myself worse than I ever remember to have done before; and went down stairs painfully conscious that I never appeared more dowdyish. Of course I was not on the best of terms with myself when we sallied out for the beach.

There never was a more delicious morning. I felt my ill humour vanish like a dream as I drank in the fresh air that came sweeping down the mountainside, swept with the mingled breath of the cassia, the orange, and the rose, the rose of Provence, sweeter than which blossoms not in the fairest gardens of earth. It was a rare occurrence for us to be up so early. Seemingly a new earth, adorned with novel beauties, had broken upon me. It did not take us long to reach the seaside where we were all to rendezvous before sunrise, that we might be early on the water, and see the first rays of the sun tinge the snowclad summits of the Maritime Alps.[13]

We found but one member of our party had arrived, and that person – Marvin Hayle. He greeted Lucy Grant warmly (they had often met), bowing rather distantly, I thought, when presented to me, and expressed a hope that I had regained my health.

Then, for the first time, did I understand what others meant when they spoke of the agreeable voice of Mr. Hayle. It had something indescribable in its tone – a peculiar charm in the sound, imparting an interest to the most ordinary conversation.

He had simply expressed a wish that I daily heard repeated by scores of acquaintances, without attracting my particular notice. There was something, however, in *his* tone that impressed me with the belief that he meant it.

"I fear our party is to be delayed," he continued. "I learned from Lord G. last night that some trifling accident had befallen the rigging of his yacht; so we will not start for an hour after the appointed time."

"I am extremely sorry for that," I rejoined in a tone of disappointment. "I anticipated so much pleasure from seeing the sun rise upon the Alps. I am told it is exquisitely beautiful. That there is nothing in nature surpassing in loveliness the sun's first kiss upon those Alpine snows."

I was embarrassed by my own speech, and felt somewhat abashed by the extravagance of my expression. Blushing, I looked down, feeling all the while that Mr. Hayle's eyes were bent upon me. When I ventured to look up again I found my surmise correct. A half smile played about his mouth as he asked:

"Are you then such a lover of nature? Are you accustomed to rising this early? I trust for your own sake you are; for there is more health in one rich draught of this morning air, than in all the prescriptions the faculty of Cannes are able to compound."

"Oh! look yonder!" exclaimed Lucy Grant. "How lovely! What a glorious purple hue. Now, Mr. Hayle, if you would immortalize yourself, copy that. Ah! what painter can transfer to canvas, clouds so richly beautiful in all their varied tints as those." As she spoke she pointed to the rose-tinted clouds that overhung the summits of the Estrelles.

Notes

[11] *Estrelles* another mountain range in southern France.

[12] *très exigeante* highly demanding.

[13] *Maritime Alps* a mountain range separating southern France from northern Italy.

"That is an indication," observed Mr. Hayle, "that the sight you have just expressed so great a desire to see, will soon have escaped us for the day."

"I am truly sorry for it," I rejoined in a tone of disappointment. "I have so often heard it spoken of, and with so much enthusiasm. The day promised me but one more pleasure that would compare with it."

"And that was?" asked Mr. Hayle.

"The pleasure of meeting one," I replied, "of whom every friend I have speaks in the warmest terms – his name – Mr. Hayle."

It was now his turn to blush and look down. After a moment's silence he said:

"I will take care you are not disappointed in the first. It will rest with you whether you are in the second."

As he concluded, he drew off his paletot, threw it upon some rocks near at hand, unfastened the chain by which a small boat was moored to the shore, and pushed it into deeper water.

"If Miss Grant and yourself will trust to my nautical skill, I will row you sufficiently far out, if not in time to see the sun's kiss, at least to greet the lingering blush that kiss will leave."

We readily consented, and soon were safely seated in the boat. I should have hesitated to have committed myself to the care of a mere amateur boatman, but there was something in the self-reliant air, the decided manner of Mr. Hayle, that would have made me feel safe under his protection, even in stormy water. But here there was nothing to fear, our boat glided as smoothly over the surface of the sea as a swan upon the bosom of a lake.

As we receded from the shore, the view became enchanting. Terrace after terrace, clothed with the rich verdure of the grape, the white hue of the blossoming orange relieved by the somber green of the olive, rose one above the other until they almost reached the summits of the lower ranges of the Estrelles, which were beginning to reflect the purple tints of the opening morn. Far away to the west, above the dark, tile-covered houses of the old town of Cannes, rose the gray walls of the half-ruined church which, nearly despoiled of all its beauty in the revolutionary fury of the past, still held aloft its spire, which was just catching a reflection of the almost universal blush. The matutinal[14] bell that called together for early prayers the few priests who still clung to the old building, sent its ringing notes far away over the waves, to come back again in sweeter, fainter notes, in seeming harmony with the strokes of the oars upon the water. As we receded further and further from the shore, the rosy peaks of the glacier-clad Alps rose gradually up from behind the hills of deep green, and stood out in clear relief against the dark gray masses of clouds beyond; still, cold, beautiful, animating one with emotions of profound delight.

I had seen the sun set amid the fastnesses of Scottish hills, and watched its last golden rays fade away upon the still waters of Windermere,[15] but this blending of barren eternal snow into harmony with the almost tropical luxuriance and verdant beauty of a Provence landscape, by the prevalence of one universal rosy tint, was to me strikingly unique, and stirred in my bosom emotions to which I was before a stranger. For a moment I could not speak. I was spellbound. At last I bent down my head, for my face was hot and flushed, my eyes suffused with tears. Even Lucy Grant seemed stirred in a manner entirely inconsistent with her usually unemotional habit.

Notes

[14] *matutinal* relating to or occurring in the morning.

[15] *Windermere* the largest lake in England.

What a longing desire I felt to express the profound pleasure, the intense delight that I experienced. Had Lucy and I been alone, something that (like a prayer) mounted to my lips, would have found utterance; but in the presence of a comparative stranger, I could but remain silent. I stole a glance at Mr. Hayle. He, too, seemed impressed in no ordinary degree. There was unusual excitement displayed in his eyes as he gazed with fixed intensity upon the glorious view.

"It is in the presence of scenes like these," said he, "that I most fully realize the religious sentiment with which art may inspire one. A man who could transfer to canvas this glorious sight, in whose bosom a love of nature glowed so strong that he could, tint by tint, line for line, produce a picture so like what is now before us that it would inspire beholders with the emotions that animate us now, and then trade it away for gold, would be worthy of the power he was enabled to wield. I often come here for inspiration, and find it, too. Aye, more. I go away with a heart glowing with thankfulness to Him who made it all for us.

"Art, to me," he continued, "must be ever a solace – never a trade. If I must find bread by labour, let it be rather in compliance with the Divine declaration, 'In the sweat of thy brow shalt thou eat bread.'[16] I would rather work side by side with the humblest who dig and plant upon those hills, than barter away for gold that which draws me so near my God." He concluded with a sigh, and dropping the oars in the water, slowly propelled us to the shore.

"My Father made them all" had trembled on my lips, and he had almost spoken the same words. I silently mused upon it, leaving Mr. Hayle to be amused by the merry chat of Lucy Grant until we reached the shore.

Soon our party began to assemble – a polyglot group of health-seekers, drawn together in search of a day's pleasure in that balmy clime. There was the voluble chevalier,[17] D'Oyen, with his ever merry face, as usual, perpetrating witticisms, first in French, then in German, with here and there a sprinkling of English. Lord G., with his quiet, thoroughly insular air, moving from group to group, courteously welcoming his guests; the wife of a Russian Boyard, with her mellow complexion, dark almond-shaped eyes, enwrapped in her gorgeous cashmere, suggested associations with the far east; an American lady whose over-done toilet[18] more befitted a drawing room than a picnic, linked us with the regions west of the broad Atlantic; whilst the whole picture was warmed and heightened by the brilliant uniforms of the French officers, who were to accompany our party.

At length the yacht made its appearance. We were then soon embarked and glided smoothly over the waters toward the picturesque Isle Ste. Marguerite. How thoroughly I enjoyed the sail. The air was never more fragrant, nor the sky more clear. The intense blue of the Mediterranean seemed more like what a painter would have imagined, than a reality of nature.

There was just wind enough to give full swell to our sails and a gentle ripple to the crater, and after a short time we found ourselves at the landing near the portals of the castle, celebrated as the dreary prison-house of "The Man of the Iron Mask."[19] As we passed onward to the gateway we here and there encountered groups of Arabs. Their mournful countenances, their melancholy demeanour, plead painfully against their captivity,

Notes

[16] *"in the sweat of thy brow ... bread"* God's injunction to Adam and Eve when they sin and are cast out of Eden, cf. Genesis 3:19.

[17] *chevalier* a horseman.

[18] *toilet* dressing up.

[19] *"The Man of the Iron Mask"* an 1847 novel by French author Alexandre Dumas (1802–1870).

and led us to imagine what happiness it would be to them to be again permitted to bestride their coursers, and madly skim over the broad deserts of their native land.

The early rising, fresh air, and morning sail had given us all unwonted appetites; so we attacked with hearty good will the dainty viands which the unapproachable cook of Lord G. had prepared in such luxurious profusion.

How the Chevalier's rotund face glowed over the outspread delicacies!

"Ah!" he exclaimed, "dis is de best part of de entertainment! It is all vare well for dreaming sentimentalists like Monsieur Hayle who feast on de morning sunrises, and slake[20] their thirsts with far-off views of de Alpine snow; but we find greater charm in dis bottle of Chablis and a *pâté aux truffes, suit un mauvais sujet*[21] like me much better, and produce result more substantial and satisfactory."

Soon we were all seated round the table merrily chatting over our plans for the day. Fortune seemed to have decided, for the present at least, Mr. Hayle and I should not be separated, for I found him seated beside me at the table. He ate very sparingly from the dishes nearest him, seemingly without choice. I am afraid I, however, might have earned for myself the title of "the lady with an appetite," for I partook with unusual zest and heartiness of the delicate slices of Reindeer's tongue, which Mr. Hayle carved for me, and was even induced by the Chevalier to share a portion of the pâté aux truffes.

"Notting, Mademoiselle, to make one eat of de breakfast like a sail over de water in dis fresh morning air."

I agreed with him.

After breakfast we broke into small parties, wandering away in different directions over the beautiful island.

Lucy Grant, Lord G., and I stood leaning upon the wall gazing into the still, transparent water beneath. I could not forbear looking back from time to time to see if Marvin Hayle was approaching to join us. I heard a number of footsteps. I felt sure his was amongst them. I must confess a little disappointment when it proved only our French military friends, some of whom knew my dot[22] was large, and were determined to make the most of their advantages.

At last I enquired what had become of him. I learned from Lord G. that he had joined the Rylands, some English friends, with whom he had gone to fish, within hailing distance of the shore. I felt a little piqued, particularly when I discovered he was almost the only beau absent from my side. I had begun to indulge the wish that we would have been companions for the day.

"Who are the Rylands?" I enquired of Lord G. "I have seen their cards upon our table. They called whilst I was so ill. I returned the visit; they were not at home."

"Two of the plainest girls on the list of my acquaintances," he replied; "at home very much addicted to scandal, tract distributing, and tea; and here, to proselyting."

"And no longer with the power to break hearts," added the Chevalier. "Dey have determined to give de rest of their days to de reformation of dem; and dose days, I am fear, is very few. Neder of dem is *poulet*[23] – "

"Oh! shocking! shocking, Chevalier!" exclaimed Lucy Grant; "you are positively cruel. Ladies' ages are sacred – one of those things to be thought upon, not spoken of; besides, I am afraid the Chevalier is a little malicious; they did not invite him to their last party. What do you think, Colonel Damoir?"

Notes

[20] *Original reads*: stake [ed.].

[21] *Chablis … pâté aux truffes, suit un maivais sujet* a Burgundy red wine and truffle pâté, following a bad subject.

[22] *dot* dowry.

[23] *poulet* chicken, implying youth.

"They are quite old, and very plain," said the blunt Colonel, in his best French. *"Elles sont*[24] – "

"That is just like Hayle," here interrupted Lord G. "Just fancy his tramping off with them! Really, he is an odd fellow. It is most amusing to see him at a ball. He is the adored of the wallflowers. It is quite a treat to see the bland air with which he will hand out a blushing girl of forty and whirl her aged limbs about in the giddy mazes of the polka. He says these things exercise a moral influence in their fair bosoms; inspire them with feelings of gratitude, without making himself an object of envy to his own sex."

We amused ourselves in a variety of ways; yet, in spite of everything done to interest me, the acknowledged belle and invalid of the party, it seemed to me a long morning. I even got tired of the Chevalier's wit and *badinage*,[25] and permitted that man of many languages to retire disconsolate, and amuse himself by chatting in Arabic with an old Bedouin sheik,[26] a hoary-headed, intellectual-looking scamp, who, I was shocked to hear (notwithstanding his venerable appearance), was incarcerated in the fortress for crime. Not satisfied with breaking one of the Commandments and coveting his neighbour's wife, this venerable Nomad had gone so far as to burn down the house of the lady's husband over his head, and, after maltreating that unhappy person in the most unwarrantable manner, carried the fair dame away captive, to add to his already numerous harem. Although they have become sufficiently civilized, even in Algeria, to show delicate attention to other people's spouses, it is not regarded as strictly the proper thing, even there, to commit arson in furtherance of one's passion. So the astonished and disconsolate sheik had been sent hither to expiate his offence.

At last Lord G. proposed a dance, which was cheerfully assented to by all present, and particularly welcomed by the Chevalier as something likely to promote an appetite for the coming lunch.

"We shall never be able to get on without Hayle," remarked Lord G. "I must send for him."

In due time Mr. Hayle made his appearance, accompanied by the Rylands, the eldest and plainest of whom he immediately asked to become his partner for the quadrille. Polkas, lancers, and mazurkas[27] followed each other in quick succession. To join in none of which was I invited by Mr. Hayle. Not until the last dance was announced did he come to ask my hand. He was too late; I was engaged to another. I was so provoked and annoyed, that when my partner came I pleaded fatigue, and begged to be absolved from my engagement.

A few of us were invited that evening to Lord G.'s, at dinner; amongst them Mr. Hayle. He did not sit next to me at the table;[28] I sat beside the mother of Lord G., who was very kind to me. Mr. Hayle confined his attention within the limits of the most formal courtesy. I could but contrast his manner then with the comparative freedom that characterized it in the morning. I thought he rather avoided me. During the evening, when the accidents of conversation drew us together, there was exhibited in his manner a sort of restraint that I did not observe in him when addressing others.

To me, the evening passed wearily. Immediately after our return to the drawing room papa reminded me of my weak health and the necessity for returning early – I looked around for Mr. Hayle as we left the room; he was gone. On reaching our carriage I found him standing near it, apparently waiting for us.

Notes

[24] *Elles sont* They are.

[25] *badinage* witty banter.

[26] *Bedouin sheik* sheiks are Arabic leaders, Bedouins a nomadic desert people.

[27] *quadrille. Polkas, lancers, and mazurkas* lively dances.

[28] *Original reads*: He did not sit next me at table [ed.].

Papa lingered in conversation with Lord G. who accompanied us to the door. Mr. Hayle handed me into the carriage.

A cold north wind swept down from the mountains chilling me through. I shivered as I leaned back in the carriage. Mr. Hayle was enwrapped in a scotch plaid, as he saw me shivering with cold, he advised me to draw up the hood of my cloak, and ere I was aware of his intention, he removed his plaid and gently covered my feet with it, saying as he did, "so pardon me this liberty, you must not forget you are delicate and the wind blows keenly to-night, you, who have so many to love you, should take care of yourself, good night." Without even shaking my hand he moved quickly away. Papa soon joined me. The carriage rolled on and I was again at my home. Lucy Grant came after and when she, as usual, entered my room for her nightly chat, I feigned sleep; I did not wish to talk. I wanted to repeat to myself those words he had so sweetly spoken, and add to them – singular, inexplicable Mr. Hayle.

A week passed and he did not call. Day after day I looked for him – hoped to see him amidst our throng of visitors: but only to be disappointed. Father proposed a ball in return for the many civilities we had received at Cannes.

My birth night, which occurred some two weeks after, was fixed upon as the night for the entertainment.

A few days after our invitations were issued (during our absence for a drive) Mr. Hayle and Lord G. called. How provoked I was on my return to find their cards on my table. That evening came an acceptance of our invitation.

With what pleasure I looked forward to that ball, despite my efforts not to do so. I betrayed in many ways my anxiety for his presence. He called again before the ball, at a time when we had many visitors in our drawing room. His conversation was almost monopolized by papa, who also became enthusiastic about him, pronouncing Mr. Hayle in his blunt way a clever, unassuming young man, who he should be always glad to see at his house.

At last the long-expected evening came. I descended to the drawing room in all the consciousness of well-arrayed beauty, my head filled with one thought, one name – Marvin Hayle. I paused to survey myself as I passed the mirror. A feeling of exaltation filled my breast as I gazed on my reflection; for never had I been more charmingly attired, never better satisfied with myself. What will he think sprang spontaneously to my lips – unconsciously I uttered these words aloud. I startled at the sound of my own voice, blushing scarlet as I did so. Pausing, I then asked myself am I giving my heart to a man almost a stranger to me, one, too, who has never said so much as "I love you?" Am I not playing a foolish part to be ever dreaming of this Marvin Hayle, who, perhaps, never thinks of me? Sighing I turned away to welcome some guests, whose names were just announced.

One after another, group after group, they came pouring in. Our rooms promised to be crowded. I began to think he would never make his appearance; at length I discovered he had entered quietly, and was then chatting with a group, conspicuous amidst which were[29] the noisy Chevalier and Lord G.

I found his eyes resting on me in the old way. He bowed smilingly as he met my gaze, advancing at the same time with out-stretched hand.

"I saw you so completely surrounded," said he apologetically, "that I thought I would wait a better opportunity than my entrée afforded, to extend my congratulation, and express the hope that each succeeding birthday may find you happier than to-day."

Notes

[29] *Original reads*: was [ed.].

He was about to say something further, when as usual we were interrupted. A dandified French Lieut. of Artillery (who was my pet aversion) came to claim my hand for the Lancers. I am afraid he found me an indifferent partner. My thoughts were busy with someone else. I gave cold monosyllabic replies to his flutter of compliments. How I detested such butterflies. When the set was over he led me to a seat beside a table at which Mr. Hayle was standing engaged in turning over the leaves of a book that Lucy Grant had been perusing during the day.

"Have you read that book," I enquired.

"Yes, more than that – I knew the author," he answered.

"And is his book like him?" I continued.

"Ah yes! very like. Now that he is dead, I need not hesitate to tell, that under the shield of other names, he has told the story of his own life."

"And what was that?" asked I.

Mr. Hayle looked grave for a moment, and then replied, "The history of a man, in whose bosom pride conquered love, who could break his heart, but could not forfeit his self-respect."

"That to me, Mr. Hayle, is rather enigmatic; tell me more plainly something of the book and its author," I rejoined.

"Well," continued he, "the author was the son of a German nobleman. He was a man of brilliant talent, and honoured name, but like myself, poor as poverty itself.

"I sometimes think that that was one of the links in the chain that united us; similarity of tastes, and harmony of sentiment, draw men together, but companionship in suffering unites them to each other with bonds of steel. He loved a woman worthy of his warm heart, high virtue, and brilliant ability. She alas! was rich, and though he had every reason to believe she reciprocated his affection, he rather chose (as he could not so abate his pride as to rank himself amongst the mercenary horde that encircled her) to smother his love, and break his heart, rather than ask the hand of a woman, on whom he could not bestow a fortune equal to what she would bring. 'A wall of gold,' shut her out from the truest love she ever inspired. Poor fellow, whilst he lived he worshipped her. He died in these arms. His last words were coupled with her name."

"Oh! Mr. Hayle, your story seems more like romance than reality. Do such men ever live?"

"Ah, yes," he answered mournfully, turning his eyes upon me as he spoke, "aye, oftener than we dream. They live and move amongst us. The world has yet immercenary[30] hearts, and God grant you may live to learn the truth of what I utter." As he concluded, he closed the book abruptly and left my side.

Lucy Grant approached, looking very mischievous.

"Is it progressing?" she asked significantly whilst a merry smile played over her face.

"What progressing?" said I with an assumed air of indifference.

"Why, your little affair with Mr. Hayle."

I looked round me, startled, and blushed scarlet. I feared someone had overheard her. "Fie, fie, Lucy," I whispered, "you are a silly girl."

"Oh yes, that sort of a put-off is all very well, but not to the point Ella; with you I am always a silly girl, just when I am nearest the truth. To say the least there is a desperate flirtation going on between you both, else what on earth could have made you look so deeply interested and caused Marvin Hayle to close that book so abruptly, and leave your side with so grave a countenance."

Notes

[30] *immercenary* mercenary.

"Oh, he was simply relating something concerning the author. Indeed he was. Pray, Lucy, don't permit your imagination to run riot as usual, nor let it lead you to jump in your rash way to the conclusion that there is something beyond. You are a famous hand for placing impossible construction on people's conduct."

"No," said Lucy Grant, with an air of mock gravity, "of course not – I would not insinuate such a thing. It is nothing more than a game of battledore and shuttlecock, with hearts for corks.[31] I do not think either of you are experienced players, and the hearts may be lost in the game. You had better both take care. But there is the music again. Lucky me, I have such a charming partner."

As she concluded, she hastened away to meet Lord G., who was advancing toward her from the opposite end of the room. He placed his arm about her waist, and whirled her away amidst the throng of dancers.

What a wonder! Mr. Hayle danced with me three times that night. The air of self-restraint that he so generally exhibited in his manners toward[32] me seemed to have abandoned him entirely. To me he was never more winning, never more gentle. Sometimes in his looks and tones I thought him even tender. I had partly resolved, after my conversation with Lucy Grant, that I would be guarded in my manner toward him; that I would try to suppress any manifestation of the partiality (so evident to myself) that I felt toward him.

Never had the claims of social life hung more irksomely upon me. I could not always dance or talk with Mr. Hayle; yet I desired to do so with none else. Was it chance or was it some indefinable mutual attraction that made us *vis-à-vis* when we could not be partners? Why did my hand tremble when it touched his in the dance, and fall so coldly and quickly from the hand of others? I could not account for my buoyant happiness; yet Marvin Hayle had not spoken one word of love.

As my partner handed me to seat, I was again asked to dance by Mr. Hayle. How delighted I was! How readily I consented. It was the last dance before supper, and he consequently would hand me to the table.

He talked but little as he sat by my side, but showed me all those quiet, little attentions always so acceptable to my sex.

Lord G. sat opposite. During one of those lulls of conversation he remarked:

"Allow me, Hayle, to remind you to comply with the request I made you this evening. You know, my dear old boy, how felicitously you can do these things."

"No, no; not to-night," rejoined Mr. Hayle. "I should make a signal failure. I should neither do justice to myself or my theme. I am not eloquent enough to say all I feel; and, if I could succeed in so doing, I should only show I feel too much."

Then I did not know to what they alluded, but I was struck with the significance of Mr. Hayle's reply. I subsequently learned he had been requested to propose my health.

Lord G. opened his eyes with an appearance of astonishment at Mr. Hayle's words, and the warmth with which they were spoken. Turning toward Lucy Grant, he said something in a quiet tone that caused her to break into a merry laugh and give me one of her naughtiest looks. Mr. Hayle relapsed into a silence that remained unbroken until we left the table.

Despite my efforts to be self-possessed, I felt my hand tremble as I placed my arm in his to return to the drawing room, where he left me, after seeing me seated. Lucy Grant came in soon after. I whispered: "I know it is somewhat rude to leave my guests;[33] but do let us go out on the terrace for a few moments."

Notes

[31] *a game of battledore and shuttlecock, with hearts for corks* tossing a trifling object back and forth.

[32] *Original reads*: towards [ed.].

[33] *Original reads*: guest [ed.].

We glided through the window (which opened to the floor), descended the steps to the terrace beneath, where seating ourselves on the rustic bench, we looked down on the silvery face of the Mediterranean, which lay, seemingly, almost at our feet.

"What a lovely night!" said Lucy Grant. "They call Alexander Smith extravagant, yet are not those lines of his –

'The full-faced moon sits silver on the sea,
The eager waves lift up their heads,
Each shouldering for her smile'[34]

– most appropriate to a scene like this? Scarcely had we ceased to speak when we heard footsteps above us. We had descended to the second terrace, and were consequently entirely hid by the overhanging shrubbery. We expected to be joined by whoever it was approaching; but they halted at the terrace above. Presently we heard Mr. Hayle's voice, he was in earnest conversation with Lord G.

"G.," he exclaimed, "I am a fool – a mad man! I am daily adding to my store of misery. Is it not an act of most consummate folly in me to think of loving Ella C.?"

Lord G. made no reply. Mr. Hayle continued, after a moment's pause:

"I will tell you now what I never dared to confide to anyone. I have been a mad worshipper of that woman for nearly four years. For almost three of them I followed her from place to place, and was near her whenever I could be without attracting her notice. The first time I saw her was at the opera. It was a 'Queen's night.' All that was bright and beautiful of the highest society of London seemed to have been gathered within the walls of the theatre. Even in that dazzling assemblage of beauty, rank, and fashion she shone purest, brightest of them all. I heard several ask, 'Who is she?' None could tell – she seemed a stranger to all near me. She at once riveted my attention, approaching, as she did, nearer my ideal conception of female beauty than any woman I had ever seen. The opera over, I hastened to the crush-room, where I stood watching the corridor from whence she would emerge. I soon had the satisfaction of seeing her approach, leaning on the arm of an elderly gentleman, who proved to be her father. I followed close beside them, feasting my eyes on her rare beauty, which was half disclosed beneath the gorgeous cashmere that enveloped her. I heard the gentleman say, 'To Sir George Jasper's,' to the footman, as the carriage whirled away. I walked up to a circle of friends who were chatting beneath the portico of the theatre, and asked of one, 'Who is Sir George Jasper?' I learned he was a city merchant, of princely wealth, who had just been knighted. My long residence abroad had rendered me a comparative stranger to the fashionable world of London. I was, besides, so much engrossed by my art, that I cared but little for it. I contrived, however, to get an introduction at Lady Jasper's, and though I never met her there, I learned who she was. G., you know my ideas with reference to rich women. Judge, then, my regret when I learned she was one of the wealthiest heiresses in the kingdom – something far above the aspirations of a beggar like myself.

"I have often ridiculed men who have fallen in love at first sight madly and recklessly. I deemed it nonsense. I could not understand how, without a knowledge of a

Notes

[34] *'The full-faced moon ... her smile'* Alexander Smith (1829–1867) was a Scottish poet; these lines are from his 1851 dramatic poem, "A Life-Drama."

woman's disposition, mind and heart, a man could love her. I tried to banish her from my mind, endeavoured to reason myself out of what I deemed an absurd fancy. I knew she was beyond my reach. To want and expect to have her seemed to me almost as ridiculous as a child crying for the moon. I firmly resolved I would never meet her. Yet, with that false reasoning with which one contrives to delude himself, I argued myself into the belief that it need not disturb my peace to see her. I thought I could regard her from a distance with the same eyes that a painter would look upon a *chef d'œuvre*[35] of Raphael, or a divine conception of Canova. Fool that I was – vain, self-deluded fool! I dreamed myself a philosopher, I awoke to find myself a poor, weak man. I still had sense enough to combat my infatuation so far as to forbear seeking an introduction; yet I could not refrain from feasting my eyes upon her loveliness. Every female head I painted about that time has in it something of her beauty – either the excelling sweetness of her mouth, the pure, deep blue of her eyes, or her wondrous regularity of features.

"Day after day, night after night, at concerts, theatre, exhibitions, wherever and whenever I had an opportunity of worshipping her at a distance, I was always to be found."

"If a day or two passed without my seeing her, I was like one bewildered. I endeavoured in every way to banish her from my mind. Once I succeeded for a week, a whole week (which seemed to me an age), in avoiding her. G., imagine in what state of mind I was. G., I have gone down on my very knees and prayed, aye, prayed as earnestly and faithfully to be delivered from the fascinating vision of her beauty, as ever a crime-laden wretch has done, to crave deliverance from the pangs of remorse. She haunted me. I grew pale and haggard. Some thought it ill health. You, G., are the first to learn. I came here to be alone with my misery. For a while I thought I had conquered that which I could not but deem an infatuation. I had begun to flatter myself that after all there was truth in the old proverb, 'That absence conquers love.' Judge, then, my feelings when, one evening, as I was descending the steps of my hotel, I met her father and herself ascending. For a moment I felt as if I would have fallen. I conquered my agitation, and stepped out of sight, within the shadow of a doorway. That night I left the house. I thought they were there *en passant*.[36] I subsequently learned they had come to winter at Cannes.

"For a while I was tempted to fly. I concluded to remain and leave Providence to deal with that which I had not strength to avoid.

"It must have seemed strange to you, G. Indeed, you must have noticed how resolutely I avoided her society. What motive you attributed it to, I know not. Now you are informed of the true one. Like the opium-eater who clings to the fatal drug that he knows will destroy him, yet from which he has not the power to abstain; so have I abandoned myself to a fatal passion as hopeless of fruition, as dangerous to my peace. And this suffering must be intensified by a conviction that has crept slowly o'er me, that she will – perhaps does love me. Not with that devotion I cherish for her – that is impossible. Yet I somehow hope, or dream, she loves me. The effort she sometimes makes to conceal her preference renders it more apparent to me."

"Then why not become a suitor for her hand?" asked Lord G., "doubtless she would marry you."

Notes

[35] *chef d'œuvre of Raphael, or a divine conception of Canova* a masterpiece of Raphael (1483–1520), Italian Renaissance painter; Antonio Canova (1757–1822) was a Venetian sculptor.

[36] *en passant* in passing.

"What! Rank myself amongst the mercenary horde that encircles her. Permit myself to be looked upon as a despicable fortune-hunter! G., you do me great injustice. I trusted you at least knew me better. Had I wealth equal to her own, the case would be different. Even were that so, none except the most liberal-minded would give me credit for disinterestedness. Virtuous, beautiful, accomplished, as she is, few would think but that her gold was the chief attraction. And there is a sentiment in the heart of some men that dominates over love, and that is pride. Ah! unhappy is he in whose bosom a conflict rages betwixt the two. Alas! G., that man am I. But let us go in and talk no more of my folly. I am half mad now."

I heard Mr. Hayle walk hurriedly away. Lord G. followed with slower footsteps, saying, "My poor unhappy friend."

For a few moments I silently stood holding the hand of Lucy Grant. Neither of us had spoken since the first few words Mr. Hayle had uttered. We could not, then, make our presence known. Almost the first words exchanged between them compelled us to become listeners to the rest. I fancied that Mr. Hayle had a decided preference for me, but never dreamed I was to him an object of such intense devotion as his words revealed.

At first I was elated by the discovery I had made. I learned that there existed what I had so longed to find – a man who loved me without one selfish consideration. But in the midst of my joy came the disheartening conviction, that the relations between us could never be altered whilst our circumstances remained unchanged. I felt he would not be the only sufferer; that my misery must likewise be entailed by the conflict he had proclaimed betwixt pride and love. I felt that in a bosom like his, pride would be the conqueror.

I waited until Lord G. had re-entered the drawing room, then passively suffered myself to be led in the same direction.

Almost the first person's gaze I encountered on entering was Marvin Hayle.

I had taken the precaution to go around by the side door, entering in an opposite direction to that in which I left. I was pale and agitated; he calm, impassable as a rock. No one looking at him would have dreamed of what had so recently occurred. His face gave no evidence of what was passing in his bosom.

I sat down beside the mother of Lord G. She looked at me piercingly and remarked, "Your hand is very cold. You are pale, and tremble too. Are you well?"

"Oh yes, quite well," I answered hurriedly. Turning away, I endeavoured to conceal my agitation by engaging in some trifling *badinage* with one of my admirers, who had approached me as I returned to the room.

At this juncture up walked, to my infinite relief, the Chevalier, saying, as he extended his hand, "Two or three of *des fleurs de murrielle*[37] have endeavoured to inveigle me to dance wid dem, but I have save myself for one grand gallop. Listen, the band has commence to play. Come!"

Lady G. protested against my joining in what she called "that furious dance." I was only too ready to go. I feared her questionings if I remained at her side. Leaning on the Chevalier's arm, I soon joined the throng of dancers. As we whirled by the numerous mirrors I now and then caught a glimpse of Marvin Hayle's eyes, bent upon me with a strange half-frightened look. A glance at myself in the mirror, discovered the cause. I was ghastly pale. A giddy, sickening sensation passed over me,

Notes

[37] *des fleurs de murrielle* des fleurs de muraille (French); wallflowers.

a gradual overshadowing – a misty appearance in all surrounding objects. I remember hearing Mr. Hayle exclaim, "Quick! Quick! Chevalier, she is fainting," then all was dark. Beyond that, I have no recollection of anything that passed.

The next morning when I awoke I found my father, Lucy Grant, and Dr. Saddler at my bedside. The latter said I "had had a series of fainting fits," but pronounced me much better – that I "only needed quiet." The excitement attendant on the ball he averred had been too much for me. He was very severe upon those frightfully fast dances; pronounced them only fit for lunatics – sufficient to cause death to robust people, and entirely unsuited to one so delicately constituted as myself. He trusted I would never indulge myself with another.

I was murmuring something about its not being the dance, when a warning look from Lucy Grant stopped me. She bent over and whispered, "Better permit them to imagine it is that, than know the real cause. Do not say anything more. I have something to tell you about Mr. Hayle's strange conduct last night after you fainted."

After strict injunctions about my being kept quiet, Dr. Saddler left the room, accompanied by Papa.

As the door closed upon them I turned and looked at Lucy Grant. She knew what I meant. Taking a seat beside me on the bed, she said:

"Mr. Hayle acted most strangely last night. You know generally he is not the least excitable in manner. Yet when you fainted and nearly fell last night, he seemed like a man distracted. He put everyone aside, and took you from the arms of the Chevalier, as though he had a right to you. He even took the restoratives from the hands of your father and administered them himself. When it was found necessary to bring you up here, he lifted you as tenderly as though you were an infant, and laid you where you now are. I was closer to him and you than the rest. Thrice I heard him murmur softly 'Ella; dear Ella.' Never in my life have I seen a face express so much love, such tender pity, as did his. I heard several remark significantly upon the extreme interest, the active sympathy, Mr. Hayle exhibited. Ah, Ella! they do not know all, or how deep his interest is. Tell me, Ella, do you love him?"

I could not reply. I hid my face in Lucy's bosom and burst into a passionate flood of tears. She soothed and petted me as if I were a child.

One morning during my convalescence I had been sleeping gently upon the sofa, near the window, where I had been looking out upon the beach. The scene of my first meeting with Marvin Hayle.

I had been thinking of all that had passed since that eventful morning – of the change that had come over me since that day. I almost wished we had never met, when I pondered over what I had heard him confide to Lord G. on the terrace. I was sick at heart when I remembered his pride and my own position. I hated that "wall of gold" that seemed destined to separate us forever. Never before was I so fully penetrated with the conviction of utter uselessness of wealth alone, for the production of happiness. Here was I, the heiress of enormous fortune, whom[38] all my wealth could not cure.

I had slept little the night before, and a feeling of weariness crept over me. I fell into a gentle slumber and dreamt of Marvin Hayle. When I awoke I found my father sitting by my side, my hand clasped in his. His face was very grave. I thought a little stern. He looked piercingly at me, and said gently, though firmly: "Ella, my child, you love this Marvin Hayle."

Notes

[38] *Original reads*: which [ed.].

I started up as though to speak. He held up his hand with a deprecating look, and continued: "You never yet deceived me. Tell me, do you love this man? I fear you do. Women do not murmur names in their sleep, as you murmured his, unless that name has for them a more than ordinary charm. What passed between you and Mr. Hayle the night of the ball?"

"Nothing, Father, I assure you, nothing but what you yourself saw."

"Nothing," he repeated, doubtingly.

"No, Father, I assure you, he has never spoken a word to me that he might not have uttered with the world for listeners."

After a moment's pause he continued:

"Ella, this seems to me something like evasion; can you honestly assure me you do not love this man?"

I dared not answer. I covered my face with my hands and turned away. My father started up exclaiming violently: "The mercenary beggar, has he dared thus stealthily to insinuate himself into the affections of my child. The subtle scoundrel, I thought him better than the generality of men. How lamentably have I been deceived. I find him worse than the rest. The – " I could bear no more and cried: "Father, Father, you do him the grossest injustice. A less mercenary, or more unselfish spirit than his does not breathe. He has never uttered to me one word of love." Bursting into tears, I concluded in a despairing tone: "Ah me! greater misery than all is to fear he never will."

Papa gave me a look of contemptuous anger as he asked:

"Can it be possible that my child is so poor for love that she weeps because a beggarly artist has not ventured to honour her with an offer?" He strode up and down the room for some time in violent agitation ere another word was exchanged between us. I had risen from my couch, and stood leaning on the windowsill, looking out upon the water. He paused in his walk, approached, and laid his hand gently on my shoulder. He seemed to have conquered his agitation somewhat. His voice was quite calm, when he said:

"Perhaps I have been rather hasty. Come, Ella, let us sit down and fully understand each other.

"When I wedded your mother, I was already a man of wealth. Wealth accumulated by no ordinary energy, in the face of difficulties that would have appalled a less determined spirit. A year after, when you were placed in my arms, I welcomed you, not perhaps as I would one that could have perpetuated my name, but as something on which I could lavish the fount of love pent up in my heart. A love your mother never strove to win. Since that day I have had no thought, performed no act, cherished no purpose, that had not for its aim and object your aggrandizement and happiness." He continued bitterly. "I am not one of those who believe in the necessity of mutual devotion in man and wife for the production of domestic comfort. I have looked forward to the time when you would wed a man of title, and adorn a rank you seem born to fill. For this end I have bargained, bought and sold; aye, toiled like a galley slave, night and day. Is the cherished object of nearly half a lifetime to be denied me, by the lovesick phantasies of a romantic girl? Shall the wealth I have so laboured to accumulate go to enrich a man without a name, who can offer in exchange for it (added to peerless beauty like your own) nothing but a heart? Perhaps I have done Mr. Hayle injustice. Doubtless, as you aver, he has been honourable enough not to declare the love I feel he cherishes, and which I regret to see so ardently reciprocated.

"Yet," he continued, rising and pointing to the Estrelles, "sooner could those hills be moved from their base, than I be shaken in my determination. My child shall never become the wife of a nameless man, a comparative beggar." As he concluded, he left the room.

That night he was hurriedly summoned to London on important business. Not a word was uttered by either of us with reference to what had passed. He kissed me with his usual tenderness, and bade me be careful of my health during his absence.

Determination and firmness were my father's distinguishing characteristics. Indeed, some thought his firmness bordered upon obstinacy. I never once knew him to say no, and change it to yes. I was appalled at the hopelessness of my position. I felt that between my father's ambitious desires and Marvin Hayle's pride I was destined to become the victim of a hopeless attachment. In vain Lucy Grant endeavoured to inspire hope. I could discern nothing in the dreary future but years of unhappiness. Mr. Hayle sent often to inquire concerning my health. He had obtained an inkling of what had passed through Lord G., from whom, I subsequently discovered, Lucy Grant could keep nothing secret. This couple became active conspirators against my father, to secure my happiness. Yet alas! in vain.

One morning he came in looking very grave. He informed me he had just parted from Mr. Hayle, who was plunged in the deepest distress by the recently received intelligence of the death of his mother. On that eventful night of the ball, whilst he and Lord G. were conversing on the terrace, she had breathed her last. "He is very miserable," said Lord G. "He was a devoted son. I have heard him speak of her in language of the truest affection. I have prevailed on him to come up and live with me. 'Tis better for him than living alone. It seems to me that the greatest lot of unhappiness falls to those men who deserve it least.

"We must not presume, however," concluded he sighing, "to question the inscrutable ways of Providence."

He left me more oppressed than ever. Here was another wave added to that tide of unhappiness already sweeping over him. Pride might enable him to combat love; but it would be powerless against this new, this sudden affliction. Alas! we were both very miserable.

Three weeks passed away, during which I saw nothing of him, save a glimpse I caught whilst he was one day walking with Lord G. upon the seashore, too far distant for me to distinguish his face.

At length came letters from my father urging my immediate return to England. It was now summer, and sufficiently warm to enable me to do so without risk to my health. I felt that I could not go without seeing him once more. I longed to have him tell me that he loved me. I knew he felt that, circumstanced as we were, our love was hopeless. I also firmly believed that his was an affection that would not falter or change. I desired that he should feel and know that he was not the only sufferer. To a man like him, I knew it would be a consolation to know that I appreciated highly the motive that debarred him from offering me his hand. I longed for an opportunity to assure him, that through all times, under all and any circumstances, he alone would possess my heart; that I should love him until we passed beyond the vale of shadows to that happier land where "love becomes immortal."

I desired Lord G. to say that I wished him to come to me. The next day he called.

When he was announced my courage failed me. There seemed something indelicate (not to say unwomanly) in thus endeavouring to extract from a man who seemed so reticent, the avowal that he loved me. I was shocked at the change a few weeks had wrought in his appearance, he was so pale, so haggard. There was a mournful depth in his dark gray eyes that spoke a world of sorrow. He endeavoured to be cheerful, replying with a few simple words of thanks to my condolences with him in his afflictions.

In the course of conversation he asked me how I had been passing the time during the involuntary seclusion my recent illness had rendered necessary.

"As usual," I replied: "principally with books."

In a moment it flashed across me how I might convey to him that assurance I had so longed for an opportunity to give.

"I have recently taken up a poet that hitherto I have never felt a strong inclination to read. I have heard him spoken of as a man who had suffered, and whose poetry had a sad tone. Perhaps 'tis selfish, yet I never could conquer my antipathy to burden my heart with woes of others, even though they might be fictitious, or conveyed in the soft language of poetry. But in looking over this volume," continued I, as I took a copy of Longfellow[39] in my hand, "I have discovered that even sorrow has its fascinations; and there was something there that touched me." As I spoke I pointed to the last three verses of Endymion:

'Oh, weary hearts; ah! slumbering eyes!
O, drooping souls! whose destinies
Are fraught with fear and pain,
Ye shall be loved again!

No one is so accursed by fate,
No one so utterly desolate,
But some heart, though unknown,
Responds unto his own.

Responds – as if with unseen wings
An angel touched its quivering strings,
And whispered in its song,
Where hast thou stayed so long.'

As I placed the book in his hand I turned partially away, and entered into conversation with Lucy Grant. I saw a flush overspread his pale face as he read on. A happy, grateful look beamed from his eyes. His lip quivered slightly as he replaced the book upon the table, saying in a subdued tone:

"To one they are indeed beautiful. I am glad they were pointed out by you to me. They indeed contain a solace."

After a little more conversation on indifferent subjects he rose to go.

"Now comes," said he, "that word hardest of all to speak – I can sincerely say I never uttered it with more regret than now – Good-bye. Providence, in severing one of the dearest ties that bound me to life, has been disposed, perhaps in love, to chasten me. Now comes this parting. True, 'tis not death, yet seemingly something so near akin as to give me infinite pain and sorrow.

"To-morrow I start for Marseilles, en route for Signia,[40] a country I have long desired to see. This, then, must be a long, long good-bye, for we all," said he, extending his hand to me and with the other taking Lucy's in his own, "may never meet again." He pressed mine gently, and with an agitated countenance quitted the apartment. Two weeks after we were again in England.

Two years passed away, bringing to me new scenes, new faces, fresh admirers. The first winter after our departure from Cannes was passed in Paris, where I obtained for myself the sobriquet of "*La chandelle de glace*."[41]

Notes

[39] Henry Wadsworth Longfellow (1807–1882).

[40] *Signia* (Latin) Segni, an Italian town near Rome.

[41] *La chandelle de glace* the ice candle.

I could scarcely tolerate admirers, much less was I disposed to wish for lovers. An heir to an earldom, whose fortune placed him beyond the suspicion of mercenary motives, honoured me with his marked attention. From the first I saw my father was bent upon my accepting him. I was resolutely determined on his rejection. I desired neither rank, title, nor wealth. I felt my heart pledged to a love from which it could never change. I had determined never to tell a lie to God, even to grace my brow with the coronet of a countess.

I strove in every way to repel him. I was, in manner, cold as ice. He was not a sensitive man, and bore seemingly, without notice, that which would have driven forever from me a man like Marvin Hayle. At last he formally proposed. I firmly, yet kindly I trust, rejected him. He was most pertinacious, and would not receive no as an answer, but appealed to my father. I felt that a conflict must necessarily ensue. I had arrived at the determination to take my fate into my own hands, as far as matrimony was concerned, and make this a final and decisive settlement of the question between us. I loved Marvin Hayle; that man would I marry and no other.

The evening of the day I had so decidedly rejected my suitor, father desired my attendance in his library.

"Ella," said he, "I have just received this note from Morland; he informs me you have rejected him. It is now two years since a scene occurred between us sufficiently painful to impress itself upon the memories of us both. You then acknowledged an attachment for a man who, from motives we will at least believe to be honourable, neither ventured to declare his love, nor honoured you," continued he in a somewhat sneering tone, "with an offer of his hand. I deemed the impression he had made upon you to be of so evanescent a character that it might be obliterated by change of scene and associations. I have continued to flatter myself with this supposition, although I have noticed the cold manner in which you have received the attentions of men whose passing notice many superior women would have considered an honour. Until to-day, I have thought it was because you attributed to them motives that would have warranted their rejection. I can, however, no longer delude myself with this idea, when I find you so decidedly declining the addresses of a man almost your equal in wealth, your superior in rank, of unblemished reputation and time-honoured name. Can it be possible that you are still governed by the romantic infatuation that took such tenacious hold upon your young fancy at the time to which I refer? Tell me what objection can you have to urge against so eligible a man as Morland?"

There was a long, painful pause ere I summoned courage to say:

"Papa, I regret to be obliged to declare what I fear will cause you pain and displeasure. I cannot marry Lord Morland. I do not love him. The impressions you have been pleased to characterize as evanescent and romantic have been strengthened and deepened, instead of being obliterated by time. Believe me, Father, I am most willing to make any sacrifice, except the one you demand, to augment your happiness. Willingly I would renounce all claim to your wealth, go forth into the world and earn my bread by the meanest drudgery, the humblest, most labourious occupation; but there is one thing I cannot, dare not do – I dare not tell a lie to God. I will not stand before his altar and utter what neither my heart nor conscience can ratify. One man I love; he I will marry. Oh! Father, dear Father! remember you are old and I am young. You have but little of time, I much, in the future to look forward to. Life has brought to you that which contents the ambitions – wealth and a name. Will it not suffice you? Compare it with the little I crave for myself in the long future perhaps to come. I only anticipate passive endurance, or it may be content. Of happiness I dare not dream. Do not, for the gratification of a few years of worldly ambition, consign me, in the long future, to one endless round of misery. The other day, when you spoke of Mama, you almost in the same breath spoke of your own heart as one lacking love. You remember the courteous smile with which she entertained your guests, the dignity with which she presided at your table, the lavish hospitality with which you gratified her every whim. You think of the beautiful woman, the charm and attraction of your house that glittered in your social world, magnificent in silk and diamonds. But I know that through it all she bore an aching heart more hungry for love than yours has ever been. And would you urge me to a sacrifice that, whilst it gratified your ambition, consigned me to a misery greater than hers? Papa, painful as it will be to live in the endurance of your displeasure, I deem it far preferable than falsely swearing to love and cherish one man whilst my heart is irrevocably given to another."

After a pause, in which I saw my father endeavouring to repress the angry feeling that animated him, he rejoined coldly:

"It is enough, Ella; you may leave me," and, mutually initiated, we parted.

In a few days we returned to England – I to our country home, he to immerse himself deeper still in the toils and cares of a London life.

Time passed on, bringing to me days of repining, regret, and unhappiness. I heard but once of Mr. Hayle – then through a letter of Lord G. to Lucy Grant. He had resigned his consulship, and was traveling in the Holy Land, with a few Arabs as companions and guides. Lucy had returned to her home, soon to become the wife of Lord G. I know Lucy pitied me; yet even she seemed to have grown tired of my society, I had become so morose and irritable.

Each time Papa returned from London he seemed more engrossed in business cares, more cold and distant. The old loving confidence that once existed between us was marred forever. Sometimes I made feeble attempts to reason myself into acquiescence with his wishes; but at each ineffectual effort, it seemed that the reproachful eyes of my dead mother were bent upon me. I imagined I again saw her tearful face – once more heard her sweet lips utter their mournful warning. The struggle between my wish to restore harmony between myself and father, yet, at the same time, to accomplish my own happiness, made my bosom the arena of perpetual conflict.

About this time there came upon the commercial world of London a crisis, sweeping into irreclaimable ruin the fortunes of the little and the great. As it widened and deepened its maelstrom-like influence, it involved in its vortex the prosperity of houses that had existed for over half a century. With them my father's was also tottering.

At the close of each week he came down from the city to pass the Sabbath with me. He was more haggard and gloomy than ever. How miserable we both were. I longed, as in the old time, to throw my arms about him, and tell him how I loved him; but my slightest attempt was met by a coldness that drove me back upon myself, checking all outpouring of the tender feeling that set so strongly toward him.

One Saturday evening, as usual, he went into his library from the dinner table. At midnight he was found sitting before a table strewed with papers – dead!

It was as I stood beside him, forgetful of all but the loving kindness of the past, and my heart appalled by the utter cheerlessness of the future, that Mr. Bryson, my friend and pastor, laid his hand upon me, telling me with his sincere earnestness, that "those whom God loveth He chasteneth."

The investigation into my father's financial affairs that ensued after his death disclosed the fact that the magnificent fortune he had accumulated by the toil of a lifetime had been swept away by the vicissitudes of a few short months. When all demands upon his estate were satisfied, I found myself an orphan with scarcely more than enough to supply the necessary comforts of life, and with nothing to minister to its luxuries. I did not care for the loss of fortune. To me it had never been a source of happiness. I parted from it without one shade of regret.

Unaccustomed anxieties and cares, brought upon me by my father's sudden death, combined with my long unhappiness, again prostrated my health, and compelled me to seek a more congenial atmosphere. I could think of no more attractive place than dear old Cannes – the place where I had experienced the first great joy of a woman's life; which joy, alas! too often terminates in life-long sorrow.

It was late in the season when I arrived there. The winter was unusually severe. For the first time in many years, the Estrelles was covered with snow; the biting frost had nipped the sweet blossom of the orange, and scattered over the half frozen earth the withered leaves of the Provence rose. All seemed changed – changed, too, in melancholy harmony with my own sad fortunes. It was a little after sunset that I drove by the magnificent house we occupied in more prosperous times. The shutters were closed, the alleys choked with weeds and the bleak winds swept down the path I had trod in days gone by with such light, happy footsteps. The surface of the Mediterranean was covered with white-capped angry waves, that broke in a sullen, continuous roar on the rocks near which we had embarked on that eventful morning, when we met for the first time one who I should ever remember – Marvin Hayle.

The Diligence[42] rattled on through the Quartier Anglais[43] and halted before the principal hotel of the old town. Of all the many friends who had feasted at our tables and danced in our halls when I was last there, there was none to greet me except the Chevalier D'Oyen. He tried to assume the merry, jovial air that characterized him of old. My deep mourning and haggard face saddened him. He lifted me from the Diligence as tenderly as if I were a child, then raising his hand he brushed the gathering tears from his eyes. I did not dream he had so soft a heart. With some attempt at joviality, he exclaimed – "Ah, you have tried to steal one march upon us; but G. wrote us you were coming and we are here to meet you." Turning to a gentle-looking little French lady who stood near him, he said: "This is Madame D'Oyen, you must love her vare much for she is to be your sister; she is come to take you to live with us."

I was overpowered by this unexpected kindness. I could not but consent. I had intended to have arranged to live with Dr. Saddler's family during the winter. I could not, however, resist the kind pleadings of the Chevalier and Madame; so I soon found myself seated in their carriage speeding over the road toward their happy home. The Chevalier, on whom saddening influences were happily transient, soon resumed his accustomed liveliness. He was eloquent upon the transcending charms of a "baby" I should find at home. "Madame" he averred, declared it strikingly like him. He admitted that it was undeniable, there were points of resemblance between them; that "baby" was ever ready for laugh, vare fat, and *faim injours*.[44] And he ran on in his old hilarious way, until he conjured upon my wan face the first smile it had worn for many long weeks.

The kindness of the Chevalier, the unceasing attention of Madame, combined with the skill of Dr. Saddler, produced the best results, and soon I felt my good health returning, with equable spirits and content.

There is no chastened like sorrow,[45] and in my sore affection, my trials of the heart, I had felt the want of some higher, purer sustaining power than earthly sympathy, however acute, could ever yield me. I had met others whose burdens in life had been

Notes

[42] *Diligence* a type of four-wheeled enclosed coach.

[43] *Quartier Anglais* English Quarter.

[44] *faim injours* perhaps "faim toujours," always hungry.

[45] Perhaps "Nothing chastened like sorrow …" or "There is nothing chastened like sorrow …"

hard to bear; yet they walked cheerfully over life's rough pathway, smiling as they trod; believing it was in love, not in anger, their Divine Father had tried them.

Soon I asked myself whether I might not secure the same serene tranquility; whether I too could not kiss the rod with which I had been smitten and believe it was in love and in love alone God had laid his afflicting hand upon me. By our earnest prayerful effort I succeeded in acquiring that peace that fadeth not away.

Spring came again with its wealth of orange blossoms. Its violets on the sunny slopes of the Estrelles with its rosebuds, its tender tendrils of the young grape vines, clinging about their old supports making them look fresh and green again. The sky was as blue, the Mediterranean as placid, as if angry foam-capped waves had never ruffled the surface of the one, or leaden hued clouds darkened the face of the other: all nature seemed hopeful in its new lease of life, and I thought, why should I not be also.

I wondered if he would ever come again. I had perfect faith in the depth and enduring tenderness of his love, I felt sure that did he know the 'wall of gold' that so long stood between us and happiness had been removed, he would fly on the wings of the wind to claim me as his own. In this faith I lived, trusting to time, the rectifier and healer of the future.

One day I rose with a feeling of uncommon elation. A tender joy seemed to have crept over my heart for which I could not account. It seemed that I was near the presence of some intangible happiness for whose existence I could not account, yet which pervaded all things about and above me.

That evening I walked out to the beach, to visit the scene of my first meeting with Marvin Hayle. What a tide of memories swept o'er me as I stood on that well remembered spot. I wandered to where a point of rocks jutted far into the sea, where the misty spray leaped up in the golden sunlight filling the air with untold wealth of diamonds. So absorbed was I that I did not hear approaching footsteps. They came nearer – nearer – causing, unconsciously to me, the wild, troubled beating of my heart. I turned and discovered approaching me one who that poor troubled heart knew too well. Marvin Hayle stood before me.

One long, long kiss, a look deep down into each other's eyes, almost told the story of our mutual love and mutual trial; with all its sorrow in the past, all its hopes in the future.

Hand in hand we wandered homeward through the soft twilight, the air redolent with the sweet breath of flowers, with the silent stars coming out one by one, beautified and brightened in our eyes by that foretaste of heaven to those who purely, holily love. We told each other of the pain of the long separation in the past and each grew happier in learning from the other, that from sorrow's lesson each had learned the same – had learned through faith and tears: "That those whom God loveth He chasteneth."

1870

Pauline Elizabeth Hopkins (1859–1930)

Among African American women writers at the turn of the century, Pauline Hopkins is particularly noteworthy for her prolific writing across genres. While still a teenager, she became the first African American woman to write, publish, and perform her own play. She was also the only woman during her era to edit a major literary journal putatively by and for African Americans, a forum highlighting not only the political motivation behind her own publications but also the importance of publishing ventures to the modern development of African American intellectual discourse.

Pauline Elizabeth Hopkins was born in Boston in 1859. Her biological father, Benjamin Northup, was a native of Providence, Rhode Island, whose own father, Cato Northup, was a leader in the city's free African American community. Hopkins's mother was Sarah A. Allen, the daughter of a Boston family of distinguished artists and abolitionists. Her maternal relatives were related by marriage to the abolitionist Thomas Paul, founder of the African Baptist Church on Beacon Hill in Boston (the oldest extant African American church building in the United States). Sarah Allen's uncle was James Monroe Whitfield, a well-known abolitionist poet whose writings appeared in Frederick Douglass's *The North Star*. Annie Pauline Pindell (Hopkins's aunt) was a popular vocalist who toured California as the "Black Nightingale" in 1859. After Sarah Allen and Benjamin Northup's divorce in 1863, Sarah married William Hopkins. A barber, janitor, and dermatologist whose varied career disguised a personal passion for theater and literature, William helped to raise Pauline in Boston's vibrant African American artistic community. She went on to attend Boston Girls High School.

In 1875, Pauline Hopkins made her debut performing in her cousin's choral group, the Progressive Musical Union. Two years later, while performing in local stage productions, she copyrighted, but did not publish, two of her own plays: *Aristocracy* and *Winona*. In 1879, she produced *The Slaves' Escape; or, The Underground Railroad*, the first play written and performed by an African American woman. The play also made use of the leading African American stage performers of the time: the prodigious Hyers Sisters, who toured the country singing opera throughout the 1870s, and Sam Lucas, whom James Weldon Johnson called the "Grand Old Man of the Negro Stage." The success of *The Slaves' Escape* allowed Hopkins to create her own performance company, the Hopkins Colored Troubadours, in 1881. She also completed her first novel, *Hagar's Daughter*, in 1891, but the need to earn a steady income forced her to abandon her stage career for clerical training. In 1892, she became a full-time stenographer in Massachusetts government, which eventually led to a position with the state census bureau. As a stenographer and part-time writer, Hopkins formally entered politics, first in local Republican campaigns, and then as a member of Josephine St Pierre Ruffin's New Era Club. New Era published the first African American women's newspaper, *Woman's Era*, in 1894, and launched the National Association of Colored Women in 1896.

When Hopkins joined *The Colored American* magazine in 1900, she produced a body of work across multiple genres that propelled the monthly to popular acclaim, including serialized versions of *Hagar's Daughter, Of One Blood*, and the novelistic version of *Winona*. (*Contending Forces*, published in 1900, was sold by the Colored Co-operative Publishing Company.) Hopkins also served on the board of directors, and became the

The Wiley Blackwell Anthology of African American Literature: Volume 1, 1746–1920, First Edition.
Edited by Gene Andrew Jarrett.

magazine's literary editor when men dominated the profession. Between 1900 and 1904, *The Colored American* was the most widely distributed African American literary magazine of its time, with subscribers spanning the United States to Canada and the Caribbean. In addition to publishing political articles, literary writings, and Hopkins's famous profiles of African and African American heroes, the magazine also honored the abolitionist past that had such a significant influence on her own writing. One magazine cover featured sketches of Phillis Wheatley and Frederick Douglass, while a 1901 promotional poster featured the image of an African American baby wrapped in an American flag.

Despite its popularity, *The Colored American* was never able to make up for the high cost of its publication. In 1902, supporters of the magazine hired New York businessman John C. Freund to lead a fundraiser, but, almost immediately, Freund and Hopkins clashed over the issues of racial activism and the magazine's political content. Whereas Hopkins saw *The Colored American* as a forum for renewing political zeal, Freund believed that her writing concentrated too much on African Americans as a "proscribed race." In 1904, with help from Booker T. Washington, Freund moved the periodical to New York City. Hopkins resigned. The identity of *The Colored American* changed under Washington. After a period of plummeting sales, the magazine shut down in 1908.

Hopkins's public life did not end with the demise of *The Colored American*. As a leading African American intellectual, she continued to write articles for Jesse Max Barber's Atlanta-based *Voice of the Negro* (1904). With the rise of New Negro literature and politics during World War I, she eventually returned to publishing with Boston's *New Era* magazine in 1916. This magazine reflected Hopkins's increasingly global perspective on race and racism that had emerged with her pan-Africanist serial novel *Of One Blood* in 1902. Writers for *New Era* included local African American intellectuals, but Harvard University's international students of color also provided copy. Plenyono Gbe Wolo, a Liberian student and treasurer of Harvard's Cosmopolitan Club, wrote a series called "A Word from Africa," describing struggles against European colonialism. Future Puerto Rican nationalist Pedro Albizu Campos also wrote anti-imperialist articles for the magazine during his Harvard days. But the venture failed to succeed in proportion to its vision, and ceased publication after two issues.

The last years of Hopkins's life were spent away from the public eye. She continued to work as a stenographer for the Massachusetts Institute of Technology and participated in local civil rights battles. In 1930 she died following a fire at her Cambridge, Massachusetts, home.

Further reading

Beam, Dorri. *Style, Gender, and Fantasy in Nineteenth-Century American Women's Writing*. New York: Cambridge University Press, 2010. Ch. 4.

Brown, Lois. *Pauline Elizabeth Hopkins: Black Daughter of the Revolution*. Chapel Hill: University of North Carolina Press, 2008.

Gillman, Susan. *Blood Talk: American Race Melodrama and the Culture of the Occult*. Chicago: University of Chicago Press, 2003. Ch. 2.

Goyal, Yogita. *Romance, Diaspora, and Black Atlantic Literature*. New York: Cambridge University Press, 2010. Ch. 1.

Knight, Alisha. *Pauline Hopkins and the American Dream: An African American Writer's (Re) Visionary Gospel of Success*. Knoxville: University of Tennessee Press, 2012.

Korobkin, Laura H. "Imagining State and Federal Law in Pauline E. Hopkins's ." *Contending Forces Legacy: A Journal of American Women Writers* 28.1 (2011): 1–23.

Levander, Caroline. *Cradle of Liberty: Race, the Child, and National Belonging from Thomas Jefferson to W.E.B. Du Bois*. Durham: Duke University Press, 2007. Ch 5.

Mitchell, Verner D. and Cynthia Davis. *Literary Sisters: Dorothy West and Her Circle a Biography of the Harlem Renaissance*. New Brunswick: Rutgers University Press, 2011. Ch. 3.

Nurhussein, Nadia. "'The Hand of Mysticism': Ethiopianist Writing in Pauline Hopkins's ." *Of One Blood and the Colored American Magazine*." *Callaloo* 33.1 (2010): 278–289.

O'Brien, Colleen C. "'Blacks in all Quarters of the Globe': Anti-Imperialism, Insurgent Cosmopolitanism, and International Labor in Pauline Hopkins's Literary Journalism." *American Quarterly* 61.2 (2009): 245–270.

Patterson, Martha H. *Beyond the Gibson Girl: Reimagining the American New Woman, 1895–1915*. Urbana: University of Illinois Press, 2005. Ch. 2.

Putzi, Jennifer. "'Raising the Stigma': Black Womanhood and the Marked Body in Pauline Hopkins's." *Contending Forces." College Literature* 31.2 (2004): 1–21.

Rohy, Valerie. "Time Lines: Pauline Hopkins' Literary History." *American Literary Realism* 35.3 (2003): 212–232.

Salvant, Shawn. "Pauline Hopkins and the End of Incest." *African American Review* 42.3–4 (2008): 659–677.

Sawaya, Francesca. *Modern Women, Modern Work: Domesticity, Professionalism, and American Writing, 1890–1950*. Philadelphia: University of Pennsylvania Press, 2003. Ch. 2.

Peculiar Sam, or the Underground Railroad: A Musical Drama in Four Acts

Cast

SAM, [Lucas] *a peculiar fellow (1st Tenor)*
JIM, *overseer (2nd Tenor)*
CAESAR, *station master (Baritone)*
PETE, POMP, *friends to Sam (Tenor, Bass)*
VIRGINIA, *the plantation nightingale (Soprano)*
JUNO, *sister to Sam (Alto)*
MAMMY, *mother to Sam (2nd Soprano)*

Act I

[*Scene, interior of an old cabin. Entrance at back, usual furniture. Time, evening. Unseen chorus sings as curtain rises. At close of chorus, enter* SAM, *followed by* JIM, CAESAR, PETE, *and* POMP, *dressed as field hands.* POMP *with banjo.*]

SAM: Come on boys we'll hab a right smart time hyar, all to ourselves. Mammy and Juno is gone out an' de coast am clar.

PETE: I say Sam, show de boys dat new step you war takin' in de fiel' dis mornin'. [*to rest*] Clar, I neber seed a fellar use his feet as dat Sam kan.

[*laughter*]

SAM: I allers likes to be 'comidatin' to my frien's. Now Pomp you strike up suthin lively an' de res' ob you gimmens take a turn wid de music till you git kin' o' warmed up, an' soon as you's at de right pitch I'll wade in on de new step.

PETE: Jes' so sir.

[POMP *strikes up lively dance, each takes a turn.* SAM *beats time and grows more and more excited.*]

SAM: [*unable to restrain himself longer*] Take kar dar, de spirits a movin' in me, Ise comin'.

[*Rest cease dancing, mark time until he drops, exhausted, into a seat.*]

SAM: I tell you what gimmens, when I gits off on an ole Virginie,[1] I feels jes like an onthoughtful horse, died I does.

Notes

[1] *ole Virginie* a southern folksong and dance.

POMP: [*rising*] I tell you boy, you's a hi ole dancer, you doesn't kno' your own walloo. [*to rest*] Les all go down to uncle Eph's backyard an' hearse dis new step. Clar, I jes tingles to get at it.
ALL: Dat's jes de ting.

[JIM, CAESAR, PETE, *and* POMP *move toward door.*]

SAM: I'll meet you dar, soon as I 'sposes ob some tickler bisness Ise got on han'. [*laughter*]
PETE: 'Spec' boy you'd better look out for Jim; he's got young Marse mighty sweet, an' ole times am pas' since old Marse died. I doesn't like to say it, but Ise might 'fraid you's gwine to lose your gal.
SAM: [*answers* PETE *with solo*]

One night as the moon was beamin'
I lay fas' asleep a dreamin';
That the sun was shinin' bright,
In the middle of the night
And the darkies had assembled to have a little fight.
I woke an' the banjo was soundin'
An' the bones through the air were boundin';
How happy I did seem, I was married in a dream,
In an ole Virginie mudscow[2] floatin down stream.

CHORUS: [JIM, CAESAR, PETE, *and* POMP *sing.*]
SAM: Din I warn all de niggers not to love her

Ef they do it'll cause them to blubber;
Now git out of my way an' member what I say,
I'm gwine to marry her myself some very fine day.

ALL: Kiah! Kiah! Kiah!
PETE: I 'spec' you will Sam, 'spec' you will.

[*Exit* JIM, CAESAR, PETE, *and* POMP.]

SAM: Wonder whar all de folks is. [*thoughtfully*]'Pears like to me nuthin's wrong; I feel it inter my bones dat dars gwine to be a disjointin' hyar soon, an' when I gits dose 'pressions dey's neber wrong.

[*Enter* MAMMY, *excited.*]

MAMMY: [*breathing hard*] For de Lor's sake boy do you kno' what dey's gone an' done up to de big house? Dey's gone an married dat dear chile, dat lamb ob a Jinny, to dat rascal ob an oberseer Jim.
SAM: [*excited, grasps her arm*] Mammy, tell me agin! You don't mean it! Tell me dey haint done dat!
MAMMY: [*astonished*] He yar boy, lef' be my arm. You mean to scrunch me to a jelly? [*He drops her arm.*] Yes, deys bring dat gal up like a lady; she neber done nuthin' but jes wait on Marse fambly an' now ole Marser's dead dey's gone an' married her, their way to Jim an' de gal can't bar de sight ob him. It's de meanes' thing I eber seed.

Notes

[2] *mudscow* a flat mud barge.

SAM: [*dejected*] An' dats' de way they treats dar slabes! An' den they tells how kin' dey is, an' how satisfied we is, 'an' den thar dogs an' horses. [*to* MAMMY] Mammy, when am dat time comin' dat you's tol me 'bout eber since I was knee high to a cricket, when am Moses gwine to lead us forsook niggers fro' de Red Sea?[3] [*covers face with arm, and turns away*]

MAMMY: [*lays hand on his arm*] Poor boy! Poor Sammy! Chile, I didn't kno' you loved dat gal, but I might a knowed it, I might a knowed it. Don't yer gib up nor lose your spirits, for de Lord am comin' on his mighty chariot, drawn by his big white horse, an' de white folks hyar, am a gwine to tremble. Son Ise been waitin' dese twenty-five year, an' I aint guv up yet.

SAM: Yes Mammy, but Ise bibbed dat gal eber sense we made mud pies, down inter de holler, an' I used to steal milk for her out ob de hog tro. [*sorrowfully*] Po' Jinny, po' little gal [*sings*]:

Ah! Jinny is a simple chile,
Wif pretty shinin' curls,
An' white folks love her best, of all
The young mulatto girls;
Tell her to wait a little while,
Tell her in hope to wait,
For I will surely break the chain,
That binds her to the gate.

CHORUS: [*mixed quartet, unseen, sings*]
SAM: Our old cabin stands upon the stream,

In old Mississippi state
And I must quickly hurry on
An' take po' Jinny from de gate.

Ole Marser's dead an' I am sold,
From Mississippi state;
But I can't leave her here alone,
To weep beside the gate;
I cannot tell her we must part,
Alas! Our cruel fate;
And so with patient eyes she'll watch
For me, beside the gate.

CHORUS: [*sings*]
SAM: T'would be wrong for me to leave her 'lone.

In Mississippi state;
But cunning, it will break the chain
That binds her to the gate;
So I'll Marser's gol' an' silver get,
Pray heaven I'm not too late;

Notes

[3] *Moses … Red Sea* Exodus 13:17–14:29. The Israelites escape slavery in Egypt when, led by Moses, they cross through the Red Sea after God parts the waters.

To set my darling Jinny free,
And take her to the gate.

Chorus: [*sings*]

Sam: If you should ever travel to the South.

To Mississippi state;
Don't fail to find this cabin out,
Where Jinny stood at the gate;
Tell her to wait a little while,
Tell her in hope to wait;
For I am he, shall make her free,
An take her from the gate.

Chorus: [*sings*]

[*At close, enter* Virginia *and* Juno, *and* Jim *with bundle*.]

Juno: Mammy, I jes toted Jinny down hyar, for you to use some salvation wif her; talk 'bout dat gal's bein' sof' and easy. She says she's gwine to run 'way tonight.

[Sam *takes* Virginia *by one hand*, Mammy *takes the other*, Juno *makes circuit around them*.]

Virginia: Yes, Mammy, and Sam, I have come to say good-bye, it's hard to leave the place where I was born, but it is better to do this, than to remain here, and become what they wish me to be. To fulfill this so-called marriage.

Juno: Yes, Mammy, orrlies thing they done in de worl' was, Marse he say, "Jim you want to marry Jinny?" Jim he say yes, course Jim say yes. Marse he say, "Jinny you want to marry Jim?" Jinny her say no, like to kno' what Jinny want to igernunt ole Jim. Marse say, "You man an' wife, an Lor' hab mussy on you soul." Dat no kin' ob weddin'.

Sam: Jinny, you isn't 'fraid to trust ol' peculiar Sam, I know, kase you see Ise allers willin' to die fer you. You needn't bid any on us good-bye, kase dis night I 'tends to tote you and Mammy and Juno 'way from hyar. Yas, an' I'll neber drop ye till Ise toted you safe inter Canidy.

Mammy: [*astonished*] Boy what you talkin' 'bout!

Juno: Golly mighty jes hyar dat fellar.

Sam: Yas, we's all gwine to Canidy! Dars been suthin' a growin' an' a growin' inter me, an' it keep sayin', "Run 'way, run away, Sam. Be a man, be a free man." An' Mammy, ef it hadn't been fer you an' de gals I'd been gone long 'go. But Ise prepared myself, in kase ob a 'mergensy.

Mammy: Look hyar boy, what has you been a doin'? I doesn't want you to bring no disrace onter me.

Sam: [*looks carefully around*] See hyar. [*They gather around him as he produces slip of paper from his pocket*.] Dat's a pass for us to go to camp meetin'. Now all ob you kno's dat dars a lot of fellars roun' hyar runnin' off slabes. Dey runs dem to Canidy, an' all 'long de road, de white 'litioners helps 'em deceitfully, an' dey calls dis, de underground railroad. Ef we kin get 'way from hyar inter te nex' state, we kin reach de fus' station oo de road, an' from dar, they'll take charge on us, an' band us safe in Canidy.

Juno: I know whar dat is, dar aint no slabe niggers dar, dey's all tooken care on by Mrs. Queen Victoria,[4] she's de Presidunt ob Canidy.

Notes

[4] Queen Victoria (1819–1901), Queen of England from 1837 until her death.

MAMMY: You hish up gal, an' laf your brudder talk. Day allers tol' me dat boy was pecoolar, but I neber 'spected it would revelop itself in dis way.

SAM: Dars a mullato fellar gwine to start a gang up river to-night, an' Ise gwine to be dat fellar, an' you's gwine to be de gang. Ef we kin 'complish dis we's all right, an' we'll say good-bye to the ole plantation.

JUNO: Sh! Dars somebody comin'. [*runs quickly and seats herself on* VIRGINIA's *bundle. Enter* JIM *as overseer.*]

JIM: I 'spected I'd fin' you hyar Miss Airy but you're my wife now, an' you's got to do as I says. Dars dat hoe cake aint baked for my supper, an' dars my ol' pants wants mendin', an' you's got it to do. [VIRGINIA *shrinks from him.* JIM *follows her.* SAM *follows him.*] You's full o' airs, data what you is, but I'll bring em out o' you, ef I has to tie you up an' gib you a dozen lashes. [*Seizes* VIRGINIA *by her arm,* SAM *seizes him by collar, jerks him, then releases him.*]

SAM: [*shudders with anger*] See hyar, Ise soed you swellin' roun' hyar consid'able, but when you talks 'bout struckin' Jinny, Ise got suthin' to say.

JIM: You's anoder sassy nigger. But you'e fixed long wif de res' ob you 'culiar coons.[5] Marse[6] gwine to sell you all down Red riber to-morrer, den I reckon Miss Jinny will have herself. An meantime I don't want any ob your sass.

[*Women huddle together.*]

MAMMY: [*rocking herself to and fro*] Ef old Marse had libed he'd neber 'low it. O Lor', O Lor'!

SAM: I jes wants you to answer one question, do you 'cider dat Jinny am your wife?

JIM: Yas sar, an' you's only mad kase she aint yourn. [*cracks his whip at* SAM]

SAM: [*leaps upon him, seizes whip*] You's a har sar, dats what you is! You crack your whip at me! [*flourishes whip around* JIM, *then takes it by butt end as if to strike him with it*] You say Jinny's your wife agin an' I'll mash you all up, you mean ol' yank nigger. [*Chases* JIM *around room with whip.* JIM *tries to take it from him.*]

JIM: Ef you strike me, Marse'll skun you.

SAM: [*contemptuously*] Marser's pet! [*throws whip aside*] Come on, you, you lizard hearted coon, we'll hab a set-to, for Ise boun' to take your sass out on your hide. [*They spar with their fists. Two or three times* JIM *butts at* SAM, *but misses him,* SAM *passing over his head in careless manner. Make this set-to as comical as possible.*]

JIM: [*glaring at him*] O, ef I only had you tied to the widder!

SAM: [*edging up to* JIM] This thing is played out; as for havin' a common nigger talkin' 'bout tyin' me up, I isn't gwine to. I wouldn't be such a 'teriated coon as you is for all de Norf. I want you to know dat the ascendant ob seen a 'structible fambly as I is can lick a dozen sech cantankerferous niggers as you is. You can jes look out now Ise done foolin', Ise gwine to hurt you.

[*They stand and glare at each other.* JIM *is off guard, and* SAM *rushes at him head first, strikes him in the stomach,* JIM *staggers across room, doubles up.*]

JIM: [*howls*] O, Ise gone dead, Ise gone dead.

[*Women rush to* SAM, *to hold him.*]

SAM: [*rubs his head*] Jingo, dat nigger's stomick am made ob some kind ob cast of iron, I reckon.

MAMMY: O sonny, sonny, Marse'll kill us all. [*Enter* POMP *and* PETE. PETE *with banjo.* JIM *rises, groaning, limps to door.*]

Notes

[5] *coons* (offensive slang) African Americans.

[6] *Original reads*: Mearse [ed.].

JIM: [*to* SAM] Neber min' my fine genman, you'll be sol' down South, an' I'll take de res' ob it out o' Jinny. [*Exit* JIM *hurriedly, as* SAM *takes two long strides toward him.*]

PETE AND POMP: Why wha's de matter?

JUNO: Sam's been showin' de oberseer how 'culiar he is, dat's all.

VIRGINIA: O, let us leave as soon as possible, who can tell what may happen?

SAM: Dat's jes so Jinny. [*to* PETE *and* POMP] Boys we's gwine to board de train to-night, am you ready?

PETE: Lord boy, Ise been ready for de las' year.

POMP: You kin bet on me, kass my trunk am packed. [*holds up banjo*] An' I allers carries my walables wif me.

SAM: Well den I'll leave you hyar wif Mammy an' de girls while I goes to reconoyster, an' see if de coas' am clar. [*Exit* SAM.]

[MAMMY *and* JUNO *pack up bundles.* JUNO *ties plain handkerchief on her head.*]

VIRGINIA: While we are waiting for Sam let's sing again before we leave our old home. For though we leave it in darkness and sorrow, it is still our home. [*She sings solo, others join in quartet. I should think "Home, Sweet Home" well sung by the soprano might be a decided hit. Reenter* SAM *at close, dressed as gentleman overseer.*]

JUNO: [*not knowing him*] See hyar Marse, you's in de wrong place. De big house am up ce road dar.

SAM: [*flourising whip*] Why, don't you know me?

ALL: Am dat you Sam?

MAMMY: Why, honey, I hardly know'd my own chile.

JUNO: What a peccoliar fellar you is! Look jes like a gemman.

SAM: Am you ready? Now is our safest time. [*They pick up their bundles. Start for door, turn as they reach it and form tableau in door around* VIRGINIA *and* MAMMY.]

MAMMY: [*weeping*] Good-bye ole home, de place whar my chillern war born, an' my ole man am buried. Ise ole now, I may neber see you 'gin, but my chillern's gwine, an' I'm boun' to go too. So Good-bye ole home.

[*Chorus. Curtain.*]

Act 2

Scene 1

[*Time, night. Front of an old hut in the woods. Enter* SAM, VIRGINIA, MAMMY, JUNO, PETE, *and* POMP. *Sing several choruses.*]

CAESAR: [*opens window as they finish*] Whar in de name ob de Lor' did all you stray coons drap down from? Ef you don't go 'way from hyar mislestin' 'spectible people, I'll set de dogs onter you, so you'd better git. [*Closes window.*]

SAM: [*pounds at the door*] Ol' man, ol' man, open de do', it's de delegation from down de riber, don't be 'feard, its' only me, peculiar Sam.

CAESAR: [*opens window slowly*] Aint you gone yet? You needn't tell me you's 'cular Sam, you's one ob dem tricksy m'latter fellars, dat's what you is.

SAM: 'Deed it are me uncle, don't you 'member how I was to come hyar by 'the undergroun'[7] –

Notes

[7] *Original reads*: hyar by the 'the undergroun' [ed.].

CAESAR: [*interrupts him*] You's bin 'tirely mistook, kase dar aint no underhan' nuthin' hyar, done moved up Norf long 'go.

SAM: Now look hyar uncle dar aint no use bein' uppish, kase de black clouds am risin'.

CAESAR: [*astonished*] Wha', wha' dat you say? Finish dat now, say de res' ob it.

JUNO: Say uncle, aint you got a 'possum leg in dar, Ise mos' starved?

MAMMY: You gal hish.

SAM: Uncle dar aint nuthin' in de worl' dat tastes so sweet as a good ole ash cake.

CAESAR: [*excited*] Dats de word! dats to word! ash cake am de word!! How you tink I gwine to kno' you, comin hyar all dressed up dat a way.

MAMMY: [*peers at* CAESAR *from under her hand*] 'Pears like to me Ise seed you befo'; aint you Caesar dat used to lib down on de ol' 'Nolin plantation?

CAESAR: Who dat? In course Ise Caesar. [*looks at her earnestly*] Why Mammy, dat aint you am it? Jes wait til I comes down dar an' takes a look at you. [*disappears from window, reenters from door.* MAMMY *and* CAESAR *laugh and shake hands heartily.*]

MAMMY: Why ol' man thought you war dead an' gone dese ten year!

CAESAR: Why ol' 'ooman, Ise mighty glad to see you, you's lookin' jes as han'som' as eny gal. [*still shake hands*] Why whar's you all gwine?

SAM: We're trablin' to Canidy. 'Deed uncle dey is gittin' so hi on des plantations dat a fellar's got to run 'way ef he's got eny 'spectible feelin's 'tall.

CAESAR: Well children, Ise glad you's foun' de ol' man, an' hope you'll 'scuse my 'seption, but de slabe holders am layin' fer de 'litioners an' I doesn't dar to breaf hard knowin' dat Ise in charge ob one ob dese stations.

SAM: I tell you uncle Ise jes b'ginnin' te feel mysel', an' ef eny man puts his han' onter me to stop me dar's gwine te be trubble, kase Ise foo'ld long nuff. Ef youll jes gib Mammy an' de gals a chance to take breaf an' den put us onto de nex station you'll 'lieve my min'; fer we's had a hard time, de white folks am arter us an' we's been almos' kotched, an' we haint got long to stay hyar.

CHORUS: "Steal Away"[8]

CAESAR: [*at close*] Well son, you stay an' take keer ob de house, while I tote de folks to de car; den I'll come back fer you.

SAM: All right uncle, an' ef eny body cames, I reckon I can gib dem all de defamation dey wants. Now you jez han' ober dat dressum gown an' dat cap an' I'll reguise mysel' inter them. [*places wig and moustache in his pocket, exchanges his coat and hat for* CAESAR'*s*]

CAESAR: [*dons* SAM'*s hat and coat*] 'Member honey dat de black clouds is risin' an' ash cake am de words. [*all, save* SAM, *exit singing*]

SAM: [*calls to* VIRGINIA] Don't git scared Jinny I'll meet you by me by. Now I reckon I'll make a reconoyster, an' den turn in an' take some sleep. [*yawns, looks around carefully, yawns again. Disappears in hut. Enter* JIM.]

JIM: I kno' dey mus' hab come dis way, I'm moz' sho' dis am one ob dem stations. Wonder ef dat do' am fastened. [*tries door, it does not yield, knocks, no answer*] Playin' 'possum. [*knocks louder, no answer*] Wonder ef dar aint no one hyar sho' nuff. [*knocks again*]

SAM: [*faintly, as if half asleep*] Who dar? Wha's de matter?

JIM: [*still pounding*] Ol' man you'd better come down hyar, I wants to see you on a very reportant matter.

SAM: [*appears at window with lighted candle, disguised voice*] What you mean comin' hyar in sech a blunderous manner? Ef you don't go 'way fro' dat do', I'll, I'll, I'll spill suthin' on you, 'deed I will.

Notes

[8] *"Steal Away"* "Steal Away to Jesus," an African American spiritual.

JIM: [*as* SAM *turns to go away*] See hyar uncle, you kno's me, you kno's oberseer Jim; Ise only come to ax you a few questions.

SAM: Well, what you want no how? Kase Ise a gemman ob bisness, I hires my time, I does.

JIM: I doesn't mean no defense uncle, but you sees some ob my nigs is runned away, an' I wants to kno' had you hyard ob dem eny whar?

SAM: [*in scolding voice*] What you doin' lettin' your slabes run 'way? What kin' oberseer is you losin' nigs, an' den runnin' all ober creation an' ebry whar else lookin' fer em. No I haint seed 'em, I jes haint.

JIM: See hyar uncle, dars a 'ward out for dem fellars, an' ef you'll gib me eny reformation, I'll 'garve some o' it fer you.

SAM: Has you got eny idee whar dey is?

JIM: O yas, Marse gib me a hunded dollar; an' I foller de trail up from de plantation, an' jes as I get hyar I lose it. But I reckon de 'litioners am running dem off. But we'll ketch 'em sho. Has you seed enythig' on 'em?

SAM: Come to think ob it I did see some stray coons 'roun'. But Lot', my 'membance am so bad.

JIM: [*excited*] You mus' 'member uncle, whar'd dey go, wha'd dey look like?

SAM: 'Clar, it are clean gone from me. My membance am so bad.

JIM: See hyar uncle, ef you'll tell me anythin' 'bout dem fellars, I'll gib you … [*thoughtfully*] I'll gib you fifty cents.

SAM: Wha's fifty cents side ob a hunded dollars? No, I don't 'member nuthin'.

JIM: Ef you'll 'member anythin' 'bout dem pussons uncle, I'll gib you, yas I'll gib you dollar.

SAM: 'Pears like dar was a tall coon wif de crowd I see, but I isn't sho.

JIM: Yas! Yas! Dem's em! An' a singin' gal, say dar war a singin' gal, an' I gib you … [*pauses*] I'll gib you two whole dollars.

SAM: Lor' child 'taint no use axing on me, kase I jes don' kno' wesfer I 'member dat tickler gal or not.

JIM: Ef you'll jes say she war dar, kase I know'd you seed her, I'll gib you free dollars, dat's all de change Ise got.

SAM: Lay de money onter de do' sill dar, den I'll see ef I can 'member any mo! [JIM *lays money down*.] I reckon de singin' gal war wif dem fellars, reckon you'll fin' her sho nuff, when you kotch 'em.

JIM: Whar'd dey go? Which way'd dey go?

SAM: Down de road a piece, dar's a empty house, an' I reckon deys done gone dar.

JIM: How'd you get at dat house?

SAM: Reckon you'd better take de railroad track on yer right an' de woods onto your lef' an' foller dat paf till you gits to a blasted juniper tree, an' when you git to dat tree you turn ober it, an' foller dat puf till you gits to de house. Ef you don't fin' it, you kin come back an' go 'roun' de tother way.

JIM: [*ready to start*] How long's dey been gone?

SAM: 'Deed it might a bin a hour 'go, an' it might a bin fourteen hour 'go; an' den agin it might a bin longer, an' it mightent a bin so long, it war some whar 'roun' dar. My membance has 'clipses wery bad, but I reckun dat's about de time dey whar hyar. [SAM *disappears from window*.]

JIM: Dat fellar aint foolin' me eny, I hasn't got fer to go to fin' dem coons; I'll kotch him. [*disappears. Enter* SAM *from door*.]

SAM: [*chuckles*] Hope dat fellar'll fin' dat house. [*laughs*] Don't blive dars any sech place on de face ob de earth. [*picks up money*] Dis money come in right smart, it'll be mighty handy up dar in Canidy. 'Clar I wishes I could git dat hunded dollars. [*enter*

JIM, *as ghost, groans*. SAM *turns, startled, and stands shaking in terror.*] Who, who'd you want to see sar? Kase dar aint nobody to home, I don't lib hyar mysel' Ise jes keepin' house till de fambly 'turns. [*ghost groans, extends right arm, moves slowly toward* SAM, *who retreats, followed by ghost, step for step*] O Marse debbil, jes 'low me to satisfy you dat I isn't de fellar you's lookin fer, 'deed I aint, he's done gone 'way five long year 'go. [*ghost draws nearer*] I neber done nuthin' to nobody. I allers says my prayers ebery night, 'deed I does. [*ghost places his hand on* SAM. SAM *falls on his knees.*] I'll 'fess, I'll 'fess. [*his eyes fall on ghost's feet.* SAM *rises to his feet with mouth open in astonishment. Aside*] I know dem feet! 'Course I knows dem feet! [*looks at them again*] Dem's de same pair o'feet. I know dey is, kase dem feet neber growed on no oder fellar but Jim, in de worl'. [*to ghost*] Playin' ghos' am you? Well reckon I'll make you de sickes' ghos' in 'Merica, 'fore I'm done wif you. [*ghost turns to run.* SAM *grapples with him. Overcomes him and has arms behind him.*] Gwine to leab me war you? When you kno's how Mammy an' de gals will 'mire to see a ghos'. [*helps* JIM *to his feet*] You's a pretty lookin' ghos', aint you? You's a disrace to de prefeshun. Now I wants you to hand out dat hunded dollar Marse guv you.

JIM: [*feebly*] It's in my pants pocket.

[SAM *takes out pocket book, opens it disclosing bills. Forgets ghost, sits down on stage floor, begins to count, chuckling to himself.*]

SAM: Dars a five, an' a ten, an' a one, an' a twenty … [JIM *meantime steals along stage to entrance, stumbles in his dress, making noise.* SAM *stops counting, looks up, produces pistol, which he points at ghost.*] Come back hyar sar, ef you moves dat karkass o' yourn de lengf of a 'possum's tail, I'll make a sho nuff ghos' ob you.

JIM: For de Lor's sake Sam don't shoot, Ise only playin' wif you.

SAM: [*rising*] Well I isn't playin', an' ef you tries to git 'way I'll shoot you. 'Taint no harm to shoot ghosts, an' dis pistol got a piece ob silber in it, so you see Ise a peculiar fellar to play wif. Recken I'd better shoot you anyway, don't b'lieve anythin' else will 'bieve my feelin's.

JIM: See hyar Sam you wouldn't hurt an unabled fellar would you?

[*Enter* CAESAR.]

CAESAR: For de good Marser's sake boy, what is you doin', wha's dat you got?

SAM: Dis am a ghos' uncle, dat Ise captivated. He comed powlin' roun' hyar, tryin to do mischief, an' Ise been promisin' him to make a truly ghos' ob him.

CAESAR: [*examines* JIM *curiously. To* SAM] Ghos' hey! 'Pears like to me dat dis am oberseer Jim.

SAM: Dis am dat very same ole snake.

CAESAR: Well chile, I reckon de ol' man'll hab to tot himself to Canidy 'long wif you. It's been gittin' woserer an' woserer, an' now dis fellar has foun' me out, de ol' man'll hab to go.

SAM: Den de sooner we's gone, de better. Ise glad you's gwine uncle. Won't we be happy when we all "git on board."

CHORUS: "Gospel Trail."[9]

[CAESAR *disappears and returns with bundle, while* SAM *strikes up song and is answered by unseen chorus. They take* JIM *between them and exit.*]

Notes

[9] *"Gospel Trail"* an African American spiritual.

Scene 2

[*Scene 2 changes, disclosing interior of cavern, damp fire, table, three or four rude stools. Some of fugitives sitting, some stretched before fire.*]

MAMMY: Wonder whar dat boy ob mine are? I tell you chillern Ise clean tuckered out, trablin' to freedom.

JUNO: [*sorrowfully*] Dar aint no use tryin' to be like white folks, we's jus made fer nuthin' but igerrant slabes, an' I jes b'lieve God don't want nuthin' to do wid us no how.

MAMMY: You Juno, hish, fer we's all His chillren, an He lubs us all.

JUNO: But Mammy dey say angels am all white. How's I gwine to be a angel Mammy? I jes don' 'lieve God wants eny brack angels, 'deed I don', less 'tis to tote things for Him.

MAMMY: Why chile, we's all to be washed in a powerful riber, an' arter that, we'll be all white.

JUNO: What Mammy, white as Marse and Misse?

MAMMY: Yes chile, jes as white as dem clouds Ise ofen showed you ridin' fro' God's blessed sky.

JUNO: Golly! Den I wants to be washed now, so's to be sho.

VIRGINIA: There Juno, don't plague Mammy any more but let's sing some of our old songs, and think we are back on the plantation.

CHORUS: "Rise and Shine"[10]

[*Enter* SAM, JIM, *and* CAESAR *as they finish.*]

SAM: Hyar we is Mammy all back safe, an' we's brought you a kurosiry in de shape ob a ghos'. [*Throws* JIM *on stool. All crowd around him.*]

MAMMY: Why honey, whar'd you git this fellar from?

JUNO: Am dat Jim? Lef me git at him!

VIRGINIA: O Sam! What made you bring him here?

SAM: Neber min' Jinny, he isn't gwine to tech you while Ise 'roun'. You see while I was waitin' for uncle to come back from totin' you, dis gemmun relieved himsel' to me in de shape ob a ghos' an I captivated him; fus' I thought, as he 'joyed playin' ghos', I'd sen' him whar he'd hab plenty ob dat kin' o' company; but I took the secon' thought an' recluded to tote him hyar, an' leave him to inflect on his pas', presunt, an' future kreer. [*shows pistol*] An' hyar's what I captivated him wif.

JUNO: Why Sam dats Marser's gun! Wha'd you git dat gun from?

SAM: Wha' you kno bout dis gun, who tol' you 'twas Marser's gun?

JUNO: Why I kno's all 'bout shootin' dat gun. I used to go up inter Misses room, an' shoot dat ol' gun at de bedstead, an' Marse he, he, Marse an' Misse wonder how dat bedstead kamed full o'holes.

SAM: Well Juno, I want some liable pusson to 'gard dis gemman, 'spose you could take good care o' him.

JUNO: O Sammy, please Sammy, jes lef me 'gard him, O. I take rememse care ob him.

SAM: [*gives her the pistol*] Hyar it are, an' ef he 'tempts to git off dat stool, shoot him. [*thoughtfully*] Yas shoot him in de mos' convenient place. [*to his mother*] Now Mammy jes git dem bundles ready, kase we's got no time to tarry.

JUNO: [*walks around* JIM, *and plays at shooting him.* JIM *rolls his eyes in terror.*] Ef you move one har, yas ef you wink, I'll shoot dem feet clean off ob you. [*keep this by-play through remainder of this scene*]

SAM: [*to* CAESAR] Whar's dem 'rections?

Notes

10 *"Rise and Shine"* an African American spiritual.

CAESAR: Dey's right hyar son in de post office. [*removes stone from one side of cavern, takes out paper, gives it to* SAM] Dar honey, I neber war no great at readin'; you see what dey says.

SAM: [*reads slowly, sometimes stopping to spell*] Ef de party am large [*spells*] d-i, di, v-i, divide, yas dats it. Inter two parties. Some one by s-e, se, c-r-e-t, secret road, an' one by public road, an' when you gits on de oder shore you'll be teckon care on.

CAESAR: [*admiring* SAM] Why boy yous eddicated, dat's wha' you is. You doesn't kno' you're wally. Now 'cordin' to orders, you take one lot en' I'll tote de other wid de gal, kase she's de one dat would make trouble for us. In de oder side ob dis cave, you'll fin' a heap o'tings dat you'll kno' what to do wif.

SAM: All right uncle, be ready to start when I comes back. [*exit*]

CHORUS: "Way Over in Jordan"[11]

JUNO: [*stops singing, points pistol at* JIM] I thought I hyard you wink. Kase ef I did ise gwine to shoot you right froom dem feet.

[*Reenter* SAM *dresssed as old man.*]

MAMMY: [*stares at him*] Why boy, I hardly knowed you!

VIRGINIA: What should we do without Sam?

SAM: [*in disguised voice*] Ise ole uncle Ned, ladies an' gemmen, an' Ise trablin' to freedom, won't you lef de ole man go 'long wif you?

[*Sings old man character songs, "Old Man Jake."*[12] *At close they divide into two parties,* VIRGINIA *goes with* CAESAR *and* PETE; SAM *with* MAMMY, JUNO, *and* POMP. *They leave* JIM, *and exit singing.*]

JUNO: Now min', Ise commin' back to see ef you wink, an' ef you do! [*points pistol at his feet ominously, backs out.* JIM *moves himself, and begins to rise to his feet.* JUNO *returns.*] I jes corned back to take a las' look at you, ef you dare to move or even breaf hard. I'll shoot de top ob dat ugly black head o' yourn clean off, 'deed I will.

MAMMY: [*outside*] You Juno, you gal, come hyar, an' stop playin' yer tricks.

JUNO: You'd better min' kase one ob dese days, I'll drap on you, an' spile de beauty ob dem understanders o' yourn. [*still threatening, she exits*]

[*Curtain*]

Act 3

[*Time, night. Banks of a river. River at back. Trees and shrubbery along banks. Enter party led by* SAM.]

SAM: [*looks around*] See hyar Mammy, I hope nuthin' aint happened to Jinny, kase when I was on de top ob dat las' hill we crossed 'pears like I seed a lot ob white folks comin'.

MAMMY: It's only through de blessin' ob de Lor', we haint been tooken long 'go. I don't neber see wha's got inter Marser's dogs.

SAM: Mammy dar aint a dog widin' ten mile roun' Marser's place, dat aint so sick he kan't hol' his head up. 'Deed Mammy a chile could play wif 'em.

MAMMY: [*holds up her hands in astonishment*] Wha! Wha' you been doin' to Marser's dogs? Why boy hell kill us.

Notes

[11] *"Way Over in Jordan"* an African American spiritual.

[12] *"Old Man Jake"* a minstrel song.

SAM: He will sho nuff Mammy ef he ketches us. Marse he hab plenty ob money an' I thought I'd done nuff to 'sarve some ob it, an' I jes helped mysel' to a pocket full. An' wif some ob it I bought de stuff wha' fixed dem dogs; 'deed I did, kase dis chile am no fool.

MAMMY: [*more surprised*] Been stealin' too. [*groans*] I neber 'spected dat ob you Sam.

SAM: No use Mammy, we mus' hab money, de 'litioners am good frien's to us, but money's ebery man's frien', an'll neber 'tray eben a forsook coon.

JUNO: [*has been looking anxiously up the road*] Dey's comin Mammy! Here's Jinny Sam.

[*All rush to look up road.* VIRGINIA *sings solo, all join in chorus. At close enter* CAESAR, VIRGINIA, *and* PETE, *throw down bundles, embrace.*]

CAESAR: Well my chillern, we's almos' free de dark valley, le's sing one mo' hymn 'fo' we bids good-bye to de sunny Souf.

CHORUS: "Old Kentucky Home"[13]

SAM: [*as they close picks up bundle*] Come on Mammy, come on Jinny, le's git on board de raf'. I tell you chillern I feels so happy I doesn't kno' mysel'. Jes feel dis air, it smells like freedom; jes see dose trees, dey look like freedom. [*points across river*] An' look ober yonder chillern, look dar good, dat ar am ol' freedom himsel'. [*gets happy, begins to sing*] "Dar's only one mo' riber to cross."

[*All join in song, shake hands, laugh and shout, exit. Singing grows fainter, but louder as raft shoots into sight.* JIM *rushes panting on the stage, peers after raft. Tableau, music growing fainter.*]

[*Curtain.*]

Act 4

[*The time is after the war in Canada. The place is an old fashioned kitchen with a fireplace. There is a door at back and a window at the right with closed inside blinds.* MAMMY *sits at table knitting,* CAESAR, *her husband now, sits before fireplace.*]

CAESAR: Ol' 'ooman it are a long time sense we an' de chillern lef' de ol' home, seems to me de Lor' has blessed us all. Hyars you an' me married, Jinny a singist, Juno a school marm; an' las' but not leas', dat boy, dat pecoolar Sam, eddicated an' gwine to de United States Congress. I tell you ol' 'ooman de ways ob de Lor' am pas' findin' out.

MAMMY: Yas ol' man, an' hyar we is dis blessed Christmas evenin', a settin' hyar like kings an' queens, waitin', fer dat blessed boy o' ours to come home to us. Tell you ol' man, it's 'mazin' how dat boy has 'scaped de gins an' sneers ob de worl', an' to-day am runnin' fer Congress dar in Cincinattie, it am 'mazin. D' ye s'pose he'll git it ol' man?

CAESAR: I don't spec' nothin' else, kase dat boy allers gits what he goes fer. But it's 'mos' time fer de train, wonder whar dem gals is.

[*Song by* VIRGINIA, *behind scenes, after style of "Swanee River."*[14]]

MAMMY: [*at close*] Ol' man, Ise totable 'tented hyar till I hears dat dear chile sing dem ol' songs, in dat angel voice ob hers, an' den I feels so bad, kase dey carries me way bact to dem good ol' times dat'll neber return. De ol' plantation, an' Mistis an' ol' Marser, an' de dear little lily chillern; thar I kin seem to see de fiel's ob cotton, an' I kin seem to smell de orange blossoms dat growed on de trees down de carriage drive. [*wipes her eyes*] Ise been totable 'tented hyar, but I boun' to trabble back 'gin 'fo' I die.

Notes

[13] *"Old Kentucky Home"* a popular minstrel song by American composer Stephen Foster (1826–1864).

[14] *"Swanee River"* a popular minstrel song by American composer Stephen Foster (1826–1864).

CAESAR: [*wiping his eyes*] An' ol' 'ooman, ef de ol' man dies firs', bury me at ol' Marser's feet, under de 'Nolin tree.[15]

[*Clocks strikes seven. Enter* VIRGINIA *and* JUNO.]

VIRGINIA: O, Mammy isn't it time for the train yet? It seems as if the hours would never pass. [*Throws open the blinds, disclosing moonlight on the snow. She stands looking out.*]

JUNO: Virginia you're not the only anxious one. How I do long to see my dear old fellow, my own old Sam. I tell you Mammy I could dance. [*places her hands in her apron pockets, and takes two or three steps of a jig*]

MAMMY: [*interrupts her*] Quit dat, you Juno, quit dat. 'Deed I neber seed sech a crazy head as you has got.

CAESAR: Mammy do lef' dat gal 'lone, let her 'joy herself, fer I does like to see young people spirited.

JUNO: Of course you do Poppy. [*hugs him with one arm around the neck*] And just to think, if Sam's elected you'll be poppy to a representative, and Mammy'll be mother to one, and I'll be sister to one. [*to* VIRGINIA] And what'll you be to him, Jinny?

VIRGINIA: Don't talk about that Juno; there can be nothing done until Jim is found. [*turns to come from window*]

MAMMY: [*listens*] Shh! I thought I hyard sleigh bells!

[*All listen. Tableau. Sleigh bells outside.*]

SAM: [*outside*] Whoa!

ALL: It's Sam! [*rush to door. Enter* SAM, *all surround him, and advance to footlights followed by* PETE *and* POMP.]

SAM: [*throws off wraps,* JUNO *carries them off, returns immediately.*] Yes, it is I, and I cannot tell you how happy I am to be at home once more.

PETE: Jes tell us one thing cap'n, 'fore you goes eny farther, is you 'lected?

VIRGINIA: Yes, Sam, do relieve our anxiety.

SAM: I think you may safely congratulate me, on a successful election. My friends in Cincinnati have stood by me nobly.

MAMMY: Praise de Lord! Chillern I hasn't nuthin' lef' to lib fer.

PETE: [*he and* POMP *shake hands with* SAM *in congratulation*] Ol' fellar Ise glad of it. Now I'll jes step out an' put up dat annimal, an' then return. [*exit door*]

CAESAR: [*goes up to* SAM] Lef' me look at you, I wants to see ef you's changed eny. [*shakes his head solemnly*] No, you's all dar jes de same. [*to* MAMMY] Ol' 'ooman, I allers knowed dat boy neber growed dat high fer nuthin'.

[*Reenter* PETE. *Company seat themselves.*]

JUNO: If things don't stop happening I shall have to get someone to hold me. Virginia, imagine you and me at Washington leading the colored bong tongs. O my! [*fans herself, laughter*]

SAM: [*to* VIRGINIA] Haven't you one word for me, Virginia?

VIRGINIA: Find Jim, and we will be happy.

SAM: Well, then sing for me. Surely you cannot refuse this request.

[*Solos, quartets, and chorus.* MR. [SAM] LUCAS *introduces any of his songs that have not been sung elsewhere. At close loud knocking at door.*]

Notes

[15] *'Nolin tree* Nolin is a lake in Kentucky.

MAMMY: Wonder who dat is? [*all rise*]

SAM: [*hurries to door, opens it.* JIM *rushes past him into room.*] Whom do you wish to see sir? I think you have made a mistake.

CAESAR: [*aside*] 'Pears like I know dat fellar.

JIM: [*looks smilingly around*] Don't you know me? Well I don't reckon you do, bein's Ise changed so. There's my card. [*gives immense card to* SAM]

SAM: [*reads*] "Mr. James Peters, Esq., D.D., attorney at law, at the Massachusetts bar, and declined overseer of the Magnolia plantation." [*all astonished,* VIRGINIA *shrinks behind* MAMMY]

JIM: [*bows profoundly*] Dat's me. Declined overseer ob de 'Nolia plantation.

JUNO: Overseer JIM, as I live, turned monkey! [*exits hurriedly*]

SAM: If you have come here to create a disturbance, sir, I warn you to go out the way you came in, or I'll throw you out.

JUNO: [*reenters on a run, with pistol; rushes at* JIM] Did you wink, did you dare to wink?

JIM: [*frightened, stumbles over two or three chairs. Groans*] O Lord no! [*to company*] Don't let her shoot me, Ise oly called hyar to 'stantiate myself an' be frien's 'long wif you.

[JUNO *lays pistol aside, laughing.*]

SAM: Well sir, state your business, and be quick about it.

JIM: [*goes toward* VIRGINIA *followed by* SAM] Virginie, you needn't be 'fraid on me, kase I isn't hyar to mislest you. Chilc, I kno's dat warnt no weddin', de law wouldn't 'low it nohow. [*to all*] An' den you see, I has no free distution ob mysel' at all, kase Ise got a truly wife, an' Ise got twins, a boy an' gal; one's nam'd Jinny an' de tother on Sam. [*laughter*]

SAM: Mr. Peters I congratulate you, you have certainly made the most of your freedom.

JIM: [*strutting up and down*] Fac'! An' you's all hyar. Mammy and Caesar, an' the Virginie rose-bird, an' Juno, and Pete, and Pomp. [*slaps* SAM *on arm*] Ol' ol' Sam himself. [SAM *shrinks*] O, I know you feel big, but I can't forgit dem ol' times, an' what a chase I had after you, an' then jes missed of you.

MAMMY: Well tell us Jim, wha' ol' Marse done, when he foun' we was gone? [*all gather around* JIM]

JIM: Fus' place you see, I had to walk clean back home, kase dat pecoolar rascal thar, stole all my money. [*laughter*] An' when I had done got back, Marse he nigh took all de skin off this ol' back o' mine; an' I declar, I wished I'd gone 'long wif you. Well arter that ol' Lincoln sent his sogers down dar, an' Marse he runned 'way an' seein' he didn't stop for his valuables, I propitiated[16] 'em to my private uses. Then I started North, got as far as Massatoosetts, found the eddicational devantages were 'ery perfectible, an' hyar I is, one ob de pillows ob de Massatoosetts bar.

SAM: Well Jim, I forgive you freely for all that's past, and here's my hand on it. [JIM *shakes hands all around to* VIRGINIA.] And now Virginia I await your answer, when shall our wedding take place?

MAMMY: Gals neber know nothin' 'bout sech things; an' seein's tomorror's Christmas, we'll celebrate it wif a weddin', whether Jinny's willin' or not. What dyo say ol' man?

CAESAR: Den is jes' my senimens ol' 'ooman, we'll has a weddin'.

Notes

[16] *propitiated* a partial malapropism; "to propitiate" is to win or regain the favor of someone.

[SAM *and* VIRGINIA *talk at one side.*]

JUNO: Somebody hold me, or I shall bust. I'm so full. [*to company*] Come on boys and girls, let's have an ol' Virginia, it's the only safe exit for surplus steam.

CAESAR: [*rising*] Dat's jes the thing, I feel mysel' growin' twenty-five years younger dis blessed minute, aint dat so ol' 'ooman?

MAMMY: Dat's jes so ol' man.

JUNO: But Lor', I forgot, we can't dance anything but high-toned[17] dances, we must remember that ther's the dignity of an M.C.[18] to be upheld. But anyhow, you fellows have out the chairs and things, an' we'll have a quadrille.[19] [*Stage cleared. Lively music. Each one selects partner,* PETE *with* JUNO, JIM *with* POMP. SAM *as caller. Go through three or four figures lively,* JUNO, MAMMY, *and* CAESAR *begin to get happy. Suddenly* SAM *stops calling, rushes to footlights.*]

SAM: Ladies and gentlemen, I hope you will excuse me for laying aside the dignity of an elected M.C., and allow me to appear before you once more as peculiar Sam of the old underground railroad.

[*Plantation chorus,* SAM *dancing to "Golden Slippers,"*[20] *remainder happy.*]

[*Curtain.*]

1879

Notes

[17] *high-toned* elegant.

[18] *M.C.* Member of Congress.

[19] *quadrille* a square dance performed by four couples.

[20] *"Golden Slippers"* or "Oh Dem Golden Slippers," another popular minstrel song.

Charles Waddell Chesnutt (1858–1932)

In 1880, Charles Waddell Chesnutt confided in his diary his goal of becoming an author. "The object of my writings would not be so much the elevation of the colored people as the elevation of the whites," he wrote, "for I consider the unjust spirit of caste which is so insidious as to pervade a whole nation, and so powerful as to subject a whole race and all connected with it to scorn and social ostracism … a barrier to the moral progress of the American people; and I would be one of the first to head a determined, organized crusade against it." As one of the preeminent authors at the turn of the century, Chesnutt stayed true to this vow, writing novels and short stories that indicted the racism of the New South. By the time Oscar Micheaux adapted his 1901 novel, *The House Behind the Cedars*, for a film in 1924, Chesnutt was a living relic of an era he ruefully called "Post-Bellum – Pre-Harlem," respected but eclipsed by writers of the New Negro Renaissance. Nevertheless, Chesnutt's large body of work, spanning four decades and various genres, displayed a talent rivaled during his time only by Paul Laurence Dunbar for its craft, satirical humor, and use of southern dialect.

Charles Waddell Chesnutt was born in Cleveland, Ohio, but his roots lay in Fayetteville, North Carolina, in the free African American community of his parents, Andrew Jackson Chesnutt and Anna Maria (Sampson) Chesnutt. Anna Maria secretly taught enslaved children how to read, while Andrew was recognized and assisted by his wealthy white father, Waddell Cade. However, the Chesnutts left Fayetteville for Ohio prior to the Civil War, as North Carolina increased restrictions on its free people of color. Before settling in Cleveland, they lived briefly in Oberlin. There, Andrew Chesnutt was arrested for his participation in the famed Oberlin–Wellington rescue in which townspeople resisted slave catchers' attempts to arrest local fugitives. In 1866, after serving as a teamster for the Union Army, Andrew Chesnutt moved the family back to Fayetteville, where his father helped him open a grocery.

Charles spent the next 15 years of his life in his family's hometown, but his intellect, ambition, and fair skin isolated him from the community. He found an ally in the principal of the Howard Normal School, Robert Harris, who hired Charles as a teacher when his father considered withdrawing him from the school to work on the family farm. Charles taught and studied intensively in the early 1870s. He became Assistant Principal of the State Colored Normal School in Fayetteville for African American schoolteachers in 1877. After marrying a fellow teacher, Susan Perry, in 1878, he set his sights on the North.

While looking for work in New York City and Washington, DC, Chesnutt studied Goethe and Shakespeare, read contemporary authors like Albion Tourgée and Mark Twain, and wrote poetry and short stories in his spare time. By 1883, he had resigned from the Normal School, working briefly as a reporter for the Dow, Jones and Company news agency in New York City before settling in Cleveland, where he would live for the rest of his life. His first short story, "Uncle Peter's House," was sold to the S.S. McClure syndicate in 1885 while he worked as a stenographer and studied law under a local judge. Additional short stories appeared in popular magazines such as *Family Fiction*, *Tid-Bits*, and *Puck*, where he developed his distinctive

The Wiley Blackwell Anthology of African American Literature: Volume 1, 1746–1920, First Edition.
Edited by Gene Andrew Jarrett.

blend of local color and literary realism. By the time "The Goophered Grapevine" (1887) became the first piece of African American fiction published in *The Atlantic Monthly*, Chesnutt had adapted to his multiple occupations as legal stenographer, author, cultural critic, and father. That same year, he passed the Ohio bar examination with the highest grade in his group.

Chesnutt's short stories for *The Atlantic* (in which "Po' Sandy" appeared in 1888) led to a professional and personal relationship with the exiled Louisiana writer George Washington Cable, who offered him a job as his personal secretary in Northampton, Massachusetts. Chesnutt declined, but the friendship led Cable to invite Chesnutt to join his "Open Letter Club," a forum designed to circulate letters and essays on race. Although Chesnutt's 1891 proposal for a short story collection was rejected by Houghton Mifflin, his involvement in progressive intellectual circles like the Open Letter Club allowed him to publish steadily throughout the 1890s. By the time his two separate short story collections were published by Houghton Mifflin in 1899 – *The Conjure Woman* and *The Wife of His Youth and Other Stories of the Color Line* – Chesnutt had earned a reputation as a leading intellectual of his day. His stories sounded the moral and psychological dilemmas of life around the color line, while articles like "What is a White Man?" – published in the May 30, 1889, issue of the *Independent* – pushed the boundaries of America's binary definitions of race.

By 1900, Chesnutt closed his successful court reporting business to pursue literary endeavors full time. He set up a literary office out of his Cleveland home, and began writing a biography of Frederick Douglass for M.A. DeWolfe Howe's prestigious Beacon Biographies of Eminent Americans. Chesnutt's most famous novels, *The House Behind the Cedars* (1900) and *The Marrow of Tradition* (1901), appeared when his fame as a public intellectual was on the rise, even as his fiction received a lukewarm reception from the public. *The House Behind the Cedars* was a modest success, but *The Marrow of Tradition*, which depicted the 1898 race riot in his erstwhile home of North Carolina, suffered from low sales. He continued to publish short stories, essays, and reviews, but his other novels – *Mandy Oxendine* (1897), *The Rainbow Chasers* (1900), and *Evelyn's Husband* (c.1902) – failed to find a publisher. By the time *The Colonel's Dream* was published by Doubleday, Page, & Company in 1905, Chesnutt had recognized that his novel writing would never adequately provide for his family. He decided to reopen his court reporting business.

During this time Chesnutt was very politically active, even as his partisanship remained highly nuanced. After Chesnutt's favorable review of his *The Future of the American Negro*, Booker T. Washington invited him to Tuskegee during his southern tour in 1901. In a sign of his reputation as a leading racial theorist of the day, Chesnutt's article "The Disfranchisement of the Negro" appeared alongside writings by Washington and W.E.B. Du Bois in the 1903 volume *The Negro Problem: A Series of Articles by Representative American Negroes of Today*. He remained close to Washington, serving on the educator's Committee of Twelve in 1905, but he also lectured the same year before the anti-Washington Boston Historical and Literary Association on "Race Prejudice: Its Causes and Its Cure." In 1908, he gave a searing public speech, "The Courts and the Negro," that criticized a series of Supreme Court rulings weakening federal civil rights legislation. And he attended the 1910 National Negro Committee, which led to the formation of the National Association of Advanced Colored People. Still,he refused to support Du Bois's public criticism of Booker T. Washington's political conservatism.

Still, by the time Chesnutt's short story "The Doll" appeared in Du Bois's 1912 edition of *Crisis*, Chesnutt's civil rights activism was less apologetic. From his lobbying of Newton Baker, the mayor of Cleveland, to defeat a bill that would have outlawed interracial marriage, to his creation of that city's Playhouse Settlement, to his successful protests against D.W. Griffith's 1915 silent film *Birth of a Nation*, Chesnutt's involvement in civil rights took public precedence over his creative writing in the final decades of his life. For his political activism Chesnutt was awarded an honorary LLD from Wilberforce University in 1913, and a Spingarn Medal from the National Association for the Advancement of Colored People in 1928. He continued to write essays, short stories, and novels until his death in 1932. Two of his novels, *Paul Marchand, F.M.C.* (1921) and *The Quarry* (1928), were published posthumously.

Further reading

Bentley, Nancy. "The Strange Career of Love and Slavery: Chesnutt, Engels, Masoch." *American Literary History* 17.3 (2005): 460–485.

Glass, Ernestine Pickens and Susan Prothro Wright, eds. *Passing in the Works of Charles W. Chesnutt*. Jackson: University Press of Mississippi, 2010.

Gleason, William A. *Sites Unseen: Architecture, Race, and American Literature*. New York: New York University Press, 2011. Ch. 2.

Hewitt, Elizabeth. "Charles Chesnutt's Capitalist Conjurings." *ELH* 76.4 (2009): 931–962.

Izzo, David Garrett and Maria Orban, eds. *Charles Chesnutt Reappraised: Essays on the First Major African American Fiction Writer*. Jefferson, NC: McFarland & Co., 2009.

Jarrett, Gene Andrew. "The Dialect of New Negro Literature." *A Companion to African American Literature*. Ed. Gene Andrew Jarrett. Malden, MA: Wiley-Blackwell, 2010. 169–184.

Margolis, Stacey. *The Public Life of Privacy in Nineteenth-Century American Literature*. Durham: Duke University Press, 2005. Ch. 4

Matheson, Neill. "History and Survival: Charles Chesnutt and the Time of Conjure." *American Literary Realism* 43.1 (2010): 1–22.

McWilliams, Dean. *Charles W. Chesnutt and the Fictions of Race*. Athens: University of Georgia Press, 2002.

Simmons, Ryan. *Chesnutt and Realism: A Study of the Novels*. Tuscaloosa: University of Alabama Press, 2006.

Toth, Margaret. "Staged Bodies: Passing, Performance, and Masquerade in Charles W. Chesnutt's *The House Behind the Cedars*." *MELUS: Multi-Ethnic Literature of the U.S.* 37.4 (2012): 69–91.

Williams, Andreá N. "African American Literary Realism, 1865–1914." *A Companion to African American Literature*. Ed. Gene Andrew Jarrett. Malden, MA: Wiley-Blackwell, 2010. 185–199.

Wilson, Matthew. *Whiteness in the Novels of Charles W. Chesnutt*. Jackson: University Press of Mississippi, 2004.

Wonham, Henry B. "What Is a Black Author? A Review of Recent Charles Chesnutt Studies." *American Literary History* 18.4 (2006): 829–835.

Worden, Daniel. "Birth in the Briar Patch: Charles W. Chesnutt and the Problem of Racial Identity." *Southern Literary Journal* 41.2 (2009): 1–20.

What Is a White Man?

The fiat[1] having gone forth from the wise men of the South that the "all-pervading, all-conquering Anglo-Saxon race" must continue forever to exercise exclusive control and direction of the government of this so-called Republic, it becomes important to every citizen who values his birthright to know who are included in this grandiloquent term. It is of course perfectly obvious that the writer or speaker who used this expression – perhaps Mr. Grady of Georgia[2] – did not say what he meant. It is not probable that he meant to exclude from full citizenship the Celts and Teutons and Gauls and Slavs[3] who make up so large a proportion of our population; he hardly meant to exclude the Jews, for even the most ardent fire-eater would hardly venture to advocate

Notes

What Is a White Man?

[1] *fiat* order.

[2] *Mr. Grady of Georgia* Henry Grady (1850–1889), southern journalist and orator.

[3] *Celts and Teutons and Gauls and Slavs* Irish, Germans, French, Eastern Europeans; the "whiteness" of these ethnic groups was hotly contested in America in the 1880s.

the disfranchisement of the thrifty race whose mortgages cover so large a portion of Southern soil. What the eloquent gentleman really meant by this high-sounding phrase was simply the white race; and the substance of the argument of that school of Southern writers to which he belongs, is simply that for the good of the country the Negro should have no voice in directing the government or public policy of the Southern States or of the nation.

But it is evident that where the intermingling of the races has made such progress as it has in this country, the line which separates the races must in many instances have been practically obliterated. And there has arisen in the United States a very large class of the population who are certainly not Negroes in an ethnological sense, and whose children will be no nearer Negroes than themselves. In view, therefore, of the very positive ground taken by the white leaders of the South, where most of these people reside, it becomes in the highest degree important to them to know what race they belong to. It ought to be also a matter of serious concern to the Southern white people; for if their zeal for good government is so great that they contemplate the practical overthrow of the Constitution and laws of the United States to secure it, they ought at least to be sure that no man entitled to it by their own argument, is robbed of a right so precious as that of free citizenship; the "all-pervading, all conquering Anglo-Saxon" ought to set as high a value on American citizenship as the all-conquering Roman placed upon the franchise of his State two thousand years ago. This discussion would of course be of little interest to the genuine Negro, who is entirely outside of the charmed circle, and must content himself with the acquisition of wealth, the pursuit of learning and such other privileges as his "best friends" may find it consistent with the welfare of the nation to allow him; but to every other good citizen the inquiry ought to be a momentous one, What is a white man?

In spite of the virulence and universality of race prejudice in the United States, the human intellect long ago revolted at the manifest absurdity of classifying men fifteen-sixteenths white as black men; and hence there grew up a number of laws in different states of the Union defining the limit which separated the white and colored races, which was, when these laws took their rise, and is now to a large extent, the line which separated freedom and opportunity from slavery or hopeless degradation. Some of these laws are of legislative origin; others are judge-made laws, brought out by the exigencies of special cases which came before the courts for determination. Someday[4] they will, perhaps, become mere curiosities of jurisprudence; the "black laws" will be bracketed with the "blue laws,"[5] and will be at best but landmarks by which to measure the progress of the nation. But today these laws are in active operation, and they are, therefore, worthy of attention; for every good citizen ought to know the law, and, if possible, to respect it; and if not worthy of respect, it should be changed by the authority which enacted it. Whether any of the laws referred to here have been in any manner changed by very recent legislation the writer cannot say, but they are certainly embodied in the latest editions of the revised statutes of the states referred to.

The colored people were divided, in most of the Southern States, into two classes, designated by law as Negroes and mulattoes respectively. The term Negro was used in its ethnological sense, and needed no definition; but the term "mulatto" was held by legislative enactment to embrace all persons of color not Negroes. The words

Notes

[4] *Original reads*: Some day [ed.].

[5] *"blue laws"* colonial laws which enforce religious standards (most are now obsolete).

"quadroon"[6] and "mestizo"[7] are employed in some of the law books, tho' not defined; but the term "octoroon," as indicating a person having one-eighth of Negro blood, is not used at all, so far as the writer has been able to observe.

The states vary slightly in regard to what constitutes a mulatto or person of color, and as to what proportion of white blood should be sufficient to remove the disability of color. As a general rule, less than one-fourth of Negro blood left the individual white – in theory; race questions being, however, regulated very differently in practice. In Missouri, by the code of 1855, still in operation, so far as not inconsistent with the Federal Constitution and laws, "any person other than a Negro, any one of whose grandmothers or grandfathers is or shall have been a Negro, tho' all of his or her progenitors except those descended from the Negro may have been white persons, shall be deemed a mulatto." Thus the color-line is drawn at one-fourth of Negro blood, and persons with only one-eighth are white.

By the Mississippi code of 1880, the color-line is drawn at one-fourth of Negro blood, all persons having less being theoretically white.

Under the *code noir* of Louisiana, the descendant of a white and a quadroon is white, thus drawing the line at one-eighth of Negro blood. The code of 1876 abolished all distinctions of color; as to whether they have been re-enacted since the Republican Party went out of power in that state the writer is not informed.

Jumping to the extreme North, persons are white within the meaning of the Constitution of Michigan who have less than one-fourth of Negro blood.

In Ohio the rule, as established by numerous decisions of the Supreme Court, was that a preponderance[8] of white blood constituted a person a white man in the eye of the law, and entitled him to the exercise of all the civil rights of a white man. By a retrogressive step the color-line was extended in 1861 in the case of marriage, which by statute was forbidden between a person of pure white blood and one having a visible admixture of African blood. But by act of legislature, passed in the spring of 1887, all laws establishing or permitting distinctions of color were repealed. In many parts of the state these laws were always ignored, and they would doubtless have been repealed long ago but for the sentiment of the southern counties, separated only by the width of the Ohio River from a former slave-holding state. There was a bill introduced in the legislature during the last session to re-enact the "black laws," but it was hopelessly defeated; the member who introduced it evidently mistook his latitude; he ought to be a member of the Georgia legislature.

But the state which, for several reasons, one might expect to have the strictest laws in regard to the relations of the races, has really the loosest. Two extracts from decisions of the Supreme Court of South Carolina will make clear the law of that state in regard to the color-line.

> The definition of the term mulatto, as understood in this state, seems to be vague, signifying generally a person of mixed white or European and Negro parentage, in whatever proportions the blood of the two races may be mingled in the individual. But it is not invariably applicable to every admixture of African blood with the European, nor is one having all the features of a white to be

Notes

6 *quadroon* one who has one-fourth African ancestry.

7 *mestizo* Spanish term for one who is both Spanish and American Indian.

8 *preponderance* majority.

> ranked with the degraded class designated by the laws of this state as persons of color, because of some remote taint of the Negro race. The line of distinction, however, is not ascertained by any rule of law.... Juries would probably be justified in holding a person to be white in whom the admixture of African blood did not exceed the proportion of one-eighth. But it is in all cases a question for the jury, to be determined by them upon the evidence of features and complexion afforded by inspection, the evidence of reputation as to parentage, and the evidence of the rank and station in society occupied by the party. The only rule which can be laid down by the courts is that where there is a distinct and visible admixture of Negro blood, the individual is to be denominated a mulatto or person of color.

In a later case the court held:

> The question whether persons are colored or white, where color or feature are doubtful, is for the jury to decide by reputation, by reception into society, and by their exercise of the privileges of the white man, as well as by admixture of blood.

It is an interesting question why such should have been, and should still be, for that matter, the law of South Carolina, and why there should exist in that state a condition of public opinion which would accept such a law. Perhaps it may be attributed to the fact that the colored population of South Carolina always outnumbered the white population, and the eagerness of the latter to recruit their ranks was sufficient to overcome in some measure their prejudice against the Negro blood. It is certainly true that the color-line is, in practice as in law, more loosely drawn in South Carolina than in any other Southern State, and that no inconsiderable element of the population of that state consists of these legal white persons, who were either born in the state; or, attracted thither by this feature of the laws, have come in from surrounding states, and, forsaking home and kindred, have taken their social position as white people. A reasonable degree of reticence in regard to one's antecedents is, however, usual in such cases.

Before the War the color-line, as fixed by law, regulated in theory the civil and political status of persons of color. What that status was, was expressed in the Dred Scott decision.[9] But since the War, or rather since the enfranchisement of the colored people, these laws have been mainly confined – in theory, be it always remembered – to the regulation of the intercourse of the races in schools and in the marriage relation. The extension of the color-line to places of public entertainment and resort, to inns and public highways, is in most states entirely a matter of custom. A colored man can sue in the courts of any Southern State for the violation of his common-law rights, and recover damages of say fifty cents without costs. A colored minister who sued a Baltimore steamboat company a few weeks ago for refusing him first-class accommodation, he having paid first-class fare, did not even meet with that measure of success: the learned judge, a Federal judge by the way, held that the plaintiff's rights had been invaded, and that he had suffered humiliation at the hands of the defendant company, but that "the humiliation was not sufficient to entitle him to damages." And the learned judge dismissed the action without costs to either party.

Notes

[9] *Dred Scott decision* the Supreme Court ruled in the *Dred Scott v. Sandford* (1857) case that free Negroes were not United States citizens.

Having thus ascertained what constitutes a white man, the good citizen may be curious to know what steps have been taken to preserve the purity of the white race, Nature, by some unaccountable oversight having to some extent neglected a matter so important to the future prosperity and progress of mankind. The marriage laws referred to here are in active operation, and cases under them are by no means infrequent. Indeed, instead of being behind the age, the marriage laws in the Southern States are in advance of public opinion; for very rarely will a Southern community stop to figure on the pedigree of the contracting parties to a marriage where one is white and the other is known to have any strain of Negro blood.

In Virginia, under the title "Offenses against Morality," the law provides that "any white person who shall intermarry with a Negro shall be confined in jail not more than one year and fined not exceeding one hundred dollars." In a marginal note on the statute-book, attention is called to the fact that "a similar penalty is not imposed on the Negro" – a stretch of magnanimity to which the laws of other states are strangers. A person who performs the ceremony of marriage in such a case is fined two hundred dollars, one-half of which goes to the informer.

In Maryland, a minister who performs the ceremony of marriage between a Negro and a white person is liable to a fine of one hundred dollars.

In Mississippi, code of 1880, it is provided that "the marriage of a white person to a Negro or mulatto or person who shall have one-fourth or more of Negro blood, shall be unlawful"; and as this prohibition does not seem sufficiently emphatic, it is further declared to be "incestuous and void," and is punished by the same penalty prescribed for marriage within the forbidden degrees of consanguinity.

But it is Georgia, the *alma genetrix*[10] of the chain-gang, which merits the questionable distinction of having the harshest set of color laws. By the law of Georgia the term "person of color" is defined to mean "all such as have an admixture of Negro blood, and the term 'Negro,' includes mulattoes." This definition is perhaps restricted somewhat by another provision, by which "all Negroes, mestizoes, and their descendants, having one-eighth of Negro or mulatto blood in their veins, shall be known in this State as persons of color." A colored minister is permitted to perform the ceremony of marriage between colored persons only; the white ministers are not forbidden to join persons of color in wedlock. It is further provided that "the marriage relation between white persons and persons of African descent is forever prohibited, and such marriages shall be null and void." This is a very sweeping provision; it will be noticed that the term "persons of color," previously defined, is not employed, the expression "persons of African descent" being used instead. A court which was so inclined would find no difficulty in extending this provision of the law to the remotest strain of African blood. The marriage relation is forever prohibited. Forever is a long time. There is a colored woman in Georgia said to be worth $300,000 – an immense fortune in the poverty stricken South. With a few hundred such women in that state, possessing a fair degree of good looks, the color-line would shrivel up like a scroll in the heat of competition for their hands in marriage. The penalty for the violation of the law against intermarriage is the same sought to be imposed by the defunct Glenn Bill[11] for violation of its provisions; *i.e.*, a fine not to exceed one thousand dollars, and imprisonment not to exceed six months, or twelve months in the chain-gang.

Notes

[10] *alma genetrix* fostering progenitor.

[11] *Glenn Bill* 1887 Georgia bill that penalized administrators who did not segregate their schools (while the bill passed in the House of Representatives, it failed in the Senate).

Whatever the wisdom or justice of these laws, there is one objection to them which is not given sufficient prominence in the consideration of the subject, even where it is discussed at all; they make mixed blood a *prima-facie*[12] proof of illegitimacy. It is a fact that at present, in the United States, a colored man or woman whose complexion is white or nearly white is presumed in the absence of any knowledge of his or her antecedents, to be the offspring of a union not sanctified by law. And by a curious but not uncommon process, such persons are not held in the same low estimation as white people in the same position. The sins of their fathers[13] are not visited upon the children, in that regard at least, and their mothers' lapses from virtue are regarded at least as misfortunes or as faults excusable under the circumstances. But in spite of all this, illegitimacy is not a desirable distinction, and is likely to become less so as these people of mixed blood advance in wealth and social standing. This presumption of illegitimacy was once, perhaps, true of the majority of such persons; but the times have changed. More than half of the colored people of the United States are of mixed blood; they marry and are given in marriage, and they beget children of complexions similar to their own. Whether or not, therefore, laws which stamp these children as illegitimate, and which by indirection establish a lower standard of morality for a large part of the population than the remaining part is judged by, are wise laws; and whether or not the purity of the white race could not be as well preserved by the exercise of virtue, and the operation of those natural laws which are so often quoted by Southern writers as the justification of all sorts of Southern "policies" – are questions which the good citizen may at least turn over in his mind occasionally, pending the settlement of other complications which have grown out of the presence of the Negro on this continent.

1889

Notes

[12] *prima-facie* at first appearance.

[13] *The sins of their fathers* Exodus 34:6–7.

The Marrow of Tradition

Chapter 1

At Break of Day

"Stay here beside her, major. I shall not be needed for an hour yet. Meanwhile I'll go downstairs and snatch a bit of sleep, or talk to old Jane."

The night was hot and sultry. Though the windows of the chamber were wide open, and the muslin[1] curtains looped back, not a breath of air was stirring. Only the shrill chirp of the cicada and the muffled croaking of the frogs in some distant marsh broke the night silence. The heavy scent of magnolias, overpowering even the strong smell of drugs in the sickroom, suggested death and funeral wreaths, sorrow and tears, the long home, the last sleep. The major shivered with apprehension as the slender hand which he held in his own contracted nervously and in a spasm of pain clutched his fingers with a viselike grip.

Major Carteret, though dressed in brown linen, had thrown off his coat for greater comfort. The stifling heat, in spite of the palm-leaf fan which he plied mechanically, was scarcely less oppressive than his own thoughts. Long ago, while yet a mere boy in years, he had come back from Appomattox[2] to find his family, one of the oldest and proudest in the state, hopelessly impoverished by the war – even their ancestral home swallowed up in the common ruin. His elder brother had sacrificed his life on the bloody altar of the lost cause, and his father, broken and chagrined, died not many years later, leaving the major the last of his line. He had tried in various pursuits to gain a foothold in the new life, but with indifferent success until he won the hand of Olivia Merkell, whom he had seen grow from a small girl to glorious womanhood. With her money he had founded the Morning Chronicle, which he had made the leading organ of his party and the most influential paper in the State. The fine old house in which they lived was hers. In this very room she had first drawn the breath of life; it had been their nuptial chamber; and here, too, within a few hours, she might die, for it seemed impossible that one could long endure such frightful agony and live.

One cloud alone had marred the otherwise perfect serenity of their happiness. Olivia was childless. To have children to perpetuate the name of which he was so proud, to write it still higher on the roll of honor, had been his dearest hope. His disappointment had been proportionately keen. A few months ago this dead hope had revived, and altered the whole aspect of their lives. But as time went on, his wife's age had begun to tell upon her, until even Dr. Price, the most cheerful and optimistic of physicians, had warned him, while hoping for the best, to be prepared for the worst. To add to the danger, Mrs. Carteret had only this day suffered from a nervous shock, which, it was feared, had hastened by several weeks the expected event.

Dr. Price went downstairs to the library, where a dim light was burning. An old black woman, dressed in a gingham frock, with a red bandana handkerchief coiled around her head by way of turban, was seated by an open window. She rose and curtsied as the doctor entered and dropped into a willow rocking-chair near her own.

Notes

The Marrow of Tradition

[1] *muslin* thin white cloth.

[2] *Appomattox* the last battle of the Civil War (where Confederate General Robert E. Lee surrendered to Union General Ulysses Grant), in Appomattox, Virginia.

"How did this happen, Jane?" he asked in a subdued voice, adding, with assumed severity, "You ought to have taken better care of your mistress."

"Now look a-hyuh, Doctuh Price," returned the old woman in an unctuous[3] whisper, "you don' wanter come talkin' none er yo' foolishness 'bout my not takin' keer er Mis' 'Livy. *She* never would 'a' said sech a thing! Seven er eight mont's ago, w'en she sent fer me, I says ter her, says I:–

"'Lawd, Lawd, honey! You don' tell me dat after all dese long w'ary years er waitin' de good Lawd is done heared yo' prayer an' is gwine ter sen' you de chile you be'n wantin' so long an' so bad? Bless his holy name! Will I come an' nuss yo' baby? Why, honey, I nussed you, an' nussed yo' mammy thoo her las' sickness, an' laid her out w'en she died. I wouldn'[4] *let* nobody e'se nuss yo' baby; an' mo'over, I'm gwine ter come an' nuss you too. You're young side er me, Mis' 'Livy, but you're ove'ly ole ter be havin' yo' fus' baby, an' you'll need somebody roun', honey, w'at knows all 'bout de fam'ly, an' deir ways an' deir weaknesses, an' I don' know who dat'd be ef it wa'n't me.'

"''Deed, Mammy Jane,' says she, 'dere ain' nobody e'se I'd have but you. You kin come ez soon ez you wanter an' stay ez long ez you mineter.'[5]

"An hyuh I is, an' hyuh I'm gwine ter stay. Fer Mis' 'Livy is my ole mist'ess's daughter, an' my ole mist'ess wuz good ter me, an' dey ain' none er her folks gwine ter suffer ef ole Jane kin he'p it."

"Your loyalty does you credit, Jane," observed the doctor; "but you haven't[6] told me yet what happened to Mrs. Carteret to-day. Did the horse run away, or did she see something that frightened her?"

"No, suh, de hoss didn'[7] git skeered at nothin', but Mis' 'Livy did see somethin', er somebody; an' it wa'n't no fault er mine ner her'n neither – it goes fu'ther back, suh, fu'ther dan dis day er dis year. Does you 'member de time w'en my ole mist'ess, Mis' 'Livy upstairs's mammy, died? No? Well, you wuz prob'ly 'way ter school den, studyin' ter be a doctuh. But I'll tell you all erbout it.

"W'en my ole mist'ess, Mis' 'Liz'beth Merkell – an' a good mist'ess she wuz – tuck sick fer de las' time, her sister Polly – ole Mis' Polly Ochiltree w'at is now – come ter de house ter he'p nuss her. Mis' 'Livy upstairs yander wuz erbout six years ole den, de sweetes' little angel you ever laid eyes on; an' on her dyin' bed Mis' 'Liz'beth ax' Mis' Polly fer ter stay hyuh an' take keer er her chile, an' Mis' Polly she promise'. She wuz a widder fer de secon' time, an' didn'[8] have no child'en, an' could jes' as well come as not.

"But dere wuz trouble after de fune'al, an' it happen' right hyuh in dis lib'ary. Mars Sam wuz settin' by de table, w'en Mis' Polly come downstairs, slow an' solemn, an' stood dere in de middle er de flo', all in black, till Mars Sam sot a cheer fer her.

"'Well, Samuel,' says she, 'now dat we've done all we can fer po' 'Liz'beth, it only 'mains fer us ter consider Olivia's future.'

"Mars Sam nodded his head, but didn'[9] say nothin'.

"'I don' need ter tell you,' says she, 'dat I am willin' ter carry out de wishes er my dead sister, an' sac'ifice my own comfo't, an' make myse'f yo' housekeeper an' yo' child's nuss, fer my dear sister's sake. It wuz her dyin' wish, an' on it I will ac', ef it is also yo'n.'

Notes

[3] *unctuous* excessively flattering.

[4] *Original reads*: would n' [ed.].

[5] *mineter* have a mind to.

[6] *Original reads*: have n't [ed.].

[7] *Original reads*: did n' [ed.].

[8] *Original reads*: did n' [ed.].

[9] *Original reads*: did n' [ed.].

"Mars Sam didn'[10] want Mis' Polly ter come, suh; fur he didn'[11] like Mis' Polly. He wuz skeered er Miss Polly."

"I don't wonder," yawned the doctor, "if she was anything like she is now."

"Wuss, suh, fer she wuz younger, an' stronger. She always would have her say, no matter 'bout what, an' her own way, no matter who 'posed her. She had already be'n in de house fer a week, an' Mars Sam knowed ef she once come ter stay, she'd be de mist'ess of eve'ybody in it an' him too. But w'at could he do but say yas?

"'Den it is unde'stood, is it,' says Mis' Polly, w'en he had spoke, 'dat I am ter take cha'ge er de house?'

"'All right, Polly,' says Mars Sam, wid a deep sigh.

"Mis' Polly 'lowed he wuz sighin' fer my po' dead mist'ess, fer she didn'[12] have no idee er his feelin's to'ds her – she alluz did 'low dat all de gent'emen wuz in love wid 'er.

"'You won' fin' much ter do,' Mars Sam went on, 'fer Julia is a good housekeeper, an' kin ten' ter mos' eve'ything, under yo' d'rections.'

"Mis' Polly stiffen' up like a ramrod. 'It mus' be unde'stood, Samuel,' says she, 'dat w'en I 'sumes cha'ge er yo' house, dere ain' gwine ter be no 'vided 'sponsibility; an' as fer dis Julia, me an' her couldn'[13] git 'long tergether nohow. Ef I stays, Julia goes.'

"W'en Mars Sam heared dat, he felt better, an' 'mence' ter pick up his courage. Mis' Polly had showed her han' too plain. My mist'ess hadn'[14] got col' yit, an' Mis' Polly, who'd be'n a widder fer two years dis las' time, wuz already fig'rin' on takin' her place fer good, an' she didn'[15] want no other woman roun' de house dat Mars Sam might take a' intrus' in.

"'My dear Polly,' says Mars Sam, quite determine', 'I couldn'[16] possibly sen' Julia 'way. Fac' is, I couldn'[17] git 'long widout Julia. She'd be'n runnin' dis house like clockwo'k befo' you come, an' I likes her ways. My dear, dead 'Liz'beth sot a heap er sto' by Julia, an' I'm gwine ter keep her here fer 'Liz'beth's sake.'

"Mis' Polly's eyes flash' fire.

"'Ah,' says she, 'I see – I see! You perfers her housekeepin' ter mine, indeed! Dat is a fine way ter talk ter a lady! An' a heap er rispec' you is got fer de mem'ry er my po' dead sister!'

"Mars Sam knowed w'at she 'lowed she seed wa'n't so[18]; but he didn'[19] let on, fer it only made him de safer. He wuz willin' fer her ter 'magine w'at she please', jes' so long ez she kep' out er his house an' let him alone.

"'No, Polly,' says he, gittin' bolder ez she got madder, 'dere ain' no use talkin'. Nothin' in de worl' would make me part wid Julia.'

"Mis' Polly she r'ared an' she pitch', but Mars Sam helt on like grim death. Mis' Polly wouldn'[20] give in neither, an' so she fin'lly went away. Dey made some kind er 'rangement afterwa'ds, an' Miss Polly tuck Mis' 'Livy ter her own house. Mars Sam paid her bo'd an' 'lowed Mis' Polly somethin' fer takin' keer er her."

"And Julia stayed?"

Notes

[10] *Original reads*: did n' [ed.].

[11] *Original reads*: did n' [ed.].

[12] *Original reads*: did n' [ed.].

[13] *Original reads*: could n' [ed.].

[14] *Original reads*: had n' [ed.].

[15] *Original reads*: did n' [ed.].

[16] *Original reads*: could n' [ed.].

[17] *Original reads*: could n' [ed.].

[18] *"w'at she 'lowed she seed wa'n't so"* that Sam and Julia are having a sexual relationship.

[19] *Original reads*: did n' [ed.].

[20] *Original reads*: would n' [ed.].

"Julia stayed, suh, an' a couple er years later her chile wuz bawn, right here in dis house."

"But you said," observed the doctor, "that Mrs. Ochiltree was in error about Julia."

"Yas, suh, so she wuz, w'en my ole mist'ess died. But dis wuz two years after – an' w'at has ter be has ter be. Julia had a easy time; she had a black gal ter wait on her, a buggy to ride in, an' eve'ything she wanted. Eve'ybody s'posed Mars Sam would give her a house an' lot, er leave her somethin' in his will. But he died suddenly, and didn'[21] leave no will, an' Mis' Polly got herse'f 'pinted gyardeen ter young Mis' 'Livy, an' driv Julia an' her young un out er de house, an' lived here in dis house wid Mis' 'Livy till Mis' 'Livy ma'ied Majah Carteret."

"And what became of Julia?" asked Dr. Price.

Such relations, the doctor knew very well, had been all too common in the old slavery days, and not a few of them had been projected into the new era. Sins, like snakes, die hard. The habits and customs of a people were not to be changed in a day, nor by the stroke of a pen. As family physician, and father confessor by brevet,[22] Dr. Price had looked upon more than one hidden skeleton; and no one in town had had better opportunities than old Jane for learning the undercurrents in the lives of the old families.

"Well," resumed Jane, "eve'ybody s'posed, after w'at had happen', dat Julia'd keep on livin' easy, fer she wuz young an' good-lookin'. But she did n'. She tried ter make a livin' sewin', but Mis' Polly wouldn'[23] let de bes' w'ite folks hire her. Den she tuck up washin', but didn'[24] do no better at dat; an' bimeby she got so discourage' dat she ma'ied a shif'less yaller[25] man, an' died er consumption soon after – an' wuz 'bout ez well off, fer dis man couldn'[26] hardly feed her nohow."

"And the child?"

"One er de No'the'n w'ite lady teachers at de mission school tuck a likin' ter little Janet, an' put her thoo school, an' den sent her off ter de No'th fer ter study ter be a school teacher. W'en she come back, 'stead er teachin' she ma'ied ole Adam Miller's son."

"The rich stevedore's[27] son, Dr. Miller?"

"Yas, suh, dat's de man – you knows 'im. Dis yer boy wuz jes' gwine 'way fer ter study ter be a doctuh, an' he ma'ied dis Janet, an' tuck her 'way wid 'im. Dey went off ter Europe, er Irope, er Orope, er somewhere er 'nother, 'way off yander, an' come back here las' year an' sta'ted dis yer horspital an' school fer ter train de black gals fer nusses."

"He's a very good doctor, Jane, and is doing a useful work. Your chapter of family history is quite interesting – I knew part of it before, in a general way; but you haven't yet told me what brought on Mrs. Carteret's trouble."

"I'm jes' comin' ter dat dis minute, suh – w'at I be'n tellin' you is all a part of it. Dis yer Janet, w'at's Mis' 'Livy's half-sister, is ez much like her ez ef dey wuz twins. Folks sometimes takes 'em fer one ernudder – I s'pose it tickles Janet mos' ter death, but it do make Mis' 'Livy rippin'.[28] An'den 'way back yander jes' after de wah, w'en de ole Carteret mansion had ter be sol', Adam Miller bought it, an' dis yer Janet an' her husban' is be'n

Notes

[21] *Original reads*: did n' [ed.].
[22] *brevet* unofficial commission.
[23] *Original reads*: would n' [ed.].
[24] *Original reads*: did n' [ed.].
[25] *yaller* yellow (mixed-race).
[26] *Original reads*: could n' [ed.].
[27] *stevedore* dockworker.
[28] *rippin'* furious.

livin' in it ever sence ole Adam died, 'bout a year ago; an' dat makes de majah mad, 'ca'se he don' wanter see cullud folks livin' in de ole fam'ly mansion w'at he wuz bawn in. An' mo'over, an' dat's de wust of all, w'iles Mis' 'Livy ain' had no child'en befo', dis yer sister er her'n is got a fine-lookin' little yaller boy, w'at favors de fam'ly so dat ef Mis' 'Livy'd see de chile anywhere, it'd mos' break her heart fer ter think 'bout her not havin' no child'en herse'f. So ter-day, w'en Mis' 'Livy wuz out ridin' an' met dis yer Janet wid her boy, an' w'en Mis' 'Livy got ter studyin' 'bout her own chances, an' how she mought not come thoo safe, she jes' had a fit er hysterics right dere in de buggy. She wuz mos' home, an' William got her here, an' you knows de res'."

Major Carteret, from the head of the stairs, called the doctor anxiously.

"You had better come along up now, Jane," said the doctor.

For two long hours they fought back the grim spectre that stood by the bedside. The child was born at dawn. Both mother and child, the doctor said, would live.

"Bless its 'ittle hea't!" exclaimed Mammy Jane, as she held up the tiny mite, which bore as much resemblance to mature humanity as might be expected of an infant which had for only a few minutes drawn the breath of life. "Bless its 'ittle hea't! it's de ve'y spit an' image er its pappy!"

The doctor smiled. The major laughed aloud. Jane's unconscious witticism, or conscious flattery, whichever it might be, was a welcome diversion from the tense strain of the last few hours.

"Be that as it may," said Dr. Price cheerfully, "and I'll not dispute it, the child is a very fine boy – a very fine boy, indeed! Take care of it, major," he added with a touch of solemnity, "for your wife can never bear another."

With the child's first cry a refreshing breeze from the distant ocean cooled the hot air of the chamber; the heavy odor of the magnolias, with its mortuary suggestiveness, gave place to the scent of rose and lilac and honeysuckle. The birds in the garden were singing lustily.

All these sweet and pleasant things found an echo in the major's heart. He stood by the window, and looking toward the rising sun, breathed a silent prayer of thanksgiving. All nature seemed to rejoice in sympathy with his happiness at the fruition of this long-deferred hope, and to predict for this wonderful child a bright and glorious future.

Old Mammy Jane, however, was not entirely at ease concerning the child. She had discovered, under its left ear, a small mole, which led her to fear that the child was born for bad luck. Had the baby been black, or yellow, or poor-white, Jane would unhesitatingly have named, as his ultimate fate, a not uncommon form of taking off, usually resultant upon the infraction of certain laws, or, in these swift modern days, upon too violent a departure from established social customs. It was manifestly impossible that a child of such high quality as the grandson of her old mistress should die by judicial strangulation; but nevertheless the warning was a serious thing, and not to be lightly disregarded.

Not wishing to be considered as a prophet of evil omen, Jane kept her own counsel in regard to this significant discovery. But later, after the child was several days old, she filled a small vial with water in which the infant had been washed, and took it to a certain wise old black woman, who lived on the farther edge of the town and was well known to be versed in witchcraft and conjuration. The conjure woman added to the contents of the bottle a bit of calamus root, and one of the cervical vertebræ from the skeleton of a black cat, with several other mysterious ingredients, the nature of which she did not disclose. Following instructions given her, Aunt Jane buried the bottle in Carteret's back yard, one night during the full moon, as a good-luck charm to ward off evil from the little grandson of her dear mistress, so long since dead and gone to heaven.

Chapter 2

The Christening Party

THEY named the Carteret baby Theodore Felix. Theodore was a family name, and had been borne by the eldest son for several generations, the major himself being a second son. Having thus given the child two beautiful names, replete with religious and sentimental significance, they called him – "Dodie."

The baby was christened some six weeks after its birth, by which time Mrs. Carteret was able to be out. Old Mammy Jane, who had been brought up in the church, but who, like some better informed people in all ages, found religion not inconsistent with a strong vein of superstition, felt her fears for the baby's future much relieved when the rector had made the sign of the cross and sprinkled little Dodie with the water from the carved marble font, which had come from England in the reign of King Charles the Martyr, as the ill-fated son of James I. was known to St. Andrew's. Upon this special occasion Mammy Jane had been provided with a seat downstairs among the white people, to her own intense satisfaction, and to the secret envy of a small colored attendance in the gallery, to whom she was ostentatiously pointed out by her grandson Jerry, porter at the Morning Chronicle office, who sat among them in the front row.

On the following Monday evening the major gave a christening party in honor of this important event. Owing to Mrs. Carteret's still delicate health, only a small number of intimate friends and family connections were invited to attend. These were the rector of St. Andrew's; old Mrs. Polly Ochiltree, the godmother; old Mr. Delamere, a distant relative and also one of the sponsors; and his grandson, Tom Delamere. The major had also invited Lee Ellis, his young city editor, for whom he had a great liking apart from his business value, and who was a frequent visitor at the house. These, with the family itself, which consisted of the major, his wife, and his half-sister, Clara Pemberton, a young woman of about eighteen, made up the eight persons for whom covers were laid.

Ellis was the first to arrive, a tall, loose-limbed young man, with a slightly freckled face, hair verging on auburn, a firm chin, and honest gray eyes. He had come half an hour early, and was left alone for a few minutes in the parlor, a spacious, high-ceilinged room, with large windows, and fitted up in excellent taste, with stately reminiscences of a past generation. The walls were hung with figured paper. The ceiling was whitewashed, and decorated in the middle with a plaster centre-piece, from which hung a massive chandelier sparkling with prismatic rays from a hundred crystal pendants. There was a handsome mantel, set with terra-cotta tiles, on which fauns and satyrs, nymphs and dryads, disported themselves in idyllic abandon. The furniture was old, and in keeping with the room.

At seven o'clock a carriage drove up, from which alighted an elderly gentleman, with white hair and mustache, and bowed somewhat with years. Short of breath and painfully weak in the legs, he was assisted from the carriage by a colored man, apparently about forty years old, to whom short side-whiskers and spectacles imparted an air of sobriety. This attendant gave his arm respectfully to the old gentleman, who leaned upon it heavily, but with as little appearance of dependence as possible. The servant, assuming a similar unconsciousness of the weight resting upon his arm, assisted the old gentleman carefully up the steps.

"I'm all right now, Sandy," whispered the gentleman as soon as his feet were planted firmly on the piazza.[29] "You may come back for me at nine o'clock."

Notes

[29] *piazza* porch.

Having taken his hand from his servant's arm, he advanced to meet a lady who stood in the door awaiting him, a tall, elderly woman, gaunt and angular of frame, with a mottled face, and high cheekbones partially covered by bands of hair entirely too black and abundant for a person of her age, if one might judge from the lines of her mouth, which are rarely deceptive in such matters.

"Perhaps you'd better not send your man away, Mr. Delamere," observed the lady, in a high shrill voice, which grated upon the old gentleman's ears. He was slightly hard of hearing, but, like most deaf people, resented being screamed at. "You might need him before nine o'clock. One never knows what may happen after one has had the second stroke. And moreover, our butler has fallen down the back steps – negroes are so careless! – and sprained his ankle so that he can't stand. I'd like to have Sandy stay and wait on the table in Peter's place, if you don't mind."

"I thank you, Mrs. Ochiltree, for your solicitude," replied Mr. Delamere, with a shade of annoyance in his voice, "but my health is very good just at present, and I do not anticipate any catastrophe which will require my servant's presence before I am ready to go home. But I have no doubt, madam," he continued, with a courteous inclination, "that Sandy will be pleased to serve you, if you desire it, to the best of his poor knowledge."

"I shill be honored, ma'am," assented Sandy, with a bow even deeper than his master's, "only I'm 'feared I ain't rightly dressed fer ter wait on table. I wuz only goin' ter pra'r-meetin', an' so I didn'[30] put on my bes' clo's. Ef Mis' Ochiltree ain' gwine ter need me fer de nex' fifteen minutes, I kin ride back home in de ca'ige an' dress myse'f suitable fer de occasion, suh."

"If you think you'll wait on the table any better," said Mrs. Ochiltree, "you may go along and change your clothes; but hurry back, for it is seven now, and dinner will soon be served."

Sandy retired with a bow. While descending the steps to the carriage, which had waited for him, he came face to face with a young man just entering the house.

"Am I in time for dinner, Sandy?" asked the newcomer.

"Yas, Mistuh Tom, you're in plenty er time. Dinner won't be ready till *I* git back, which won' be fer fifteen minutes er so yit."

Throwing away the cigarette which he held between his fingers, the young man crossed the piazza with a light step, and after a preliminary knock, for an answer to which he did not wait, entered the house with the air of one thoroughly at home. The lights in the parlor had been lit, and Ellis, who sat talking to Major Carteret when the newcomer entered, covered him with a jealous glance.

Slender and of medium height, with a small head of almost perfect contour, a symmetrical face, dark almost to swarthiness, black eyes, which moved somewhat restlessly, curly hair of raven tint, a slight mustache, small hands and feet, and fashionable attire, Tom Delamere, the grandson of the old gentleman who had already arrived, was easily the handsomest young man in Wellington. But no discriminating observer would have characterized his beauty as manly. It conveyed no impression of strength, but did possess a certain element, feline rather than feminine, which subtly negatived the idea of manliness.

He gave his hand to the major, nodded curtly to Ellis, saluted his grandfather respectfully, and inquired for the ladies.

Notes

[30] *Original reads*: did n' [ed.].

"Olivia is dressing for dinner," replied the major; "Mrs. Ochiltree is in the kitchen, struggling with the servants. Clara – Ah, here she comes now!"

Ellis, whose senses were preternaturally acute where Clara was concerned, was already looking toward the hall and was the first to see her. Clad in an evening gown of simple white, to the close-fitting corsage of which she had fastened a bunch of pink roses, she was to Ellis a dazzling apparition. To him her erect and well-moulded form was the embodiment of symmetry, her voice sweet music, her movements the perfection of grace; and it scarcely needed a lover's imagination to read in her fair countenance a pure heart and a high spirit – the truthfulness that scorns a lie, the pride which is not haughtiness. There were suggestive depths of tenderness, too, in the curl of her lip, the droop of her long lashes, the glance of her blue eyes – depths that Ellis had long since divined, though he had never yet explored them. She gave Ellis a friendly nod as she came in, but for the smile with which she greeted Delamere, Ellis would have given all that he possessed – not a great deal, it is true, but what could a man do more?

"You are the last one, Tom," she said reproachfully. "Mr. Ellis has been here half an hour."

Delamere threw a glance at Ellis which was not exactly friendly. Why should this fellow always be on hand to emphasize his own shortcomings?

"The rector is not here," answered Tom triumphantly. "You see I am not the last."

"The rector," replied Clara, "was called out of town at six o'clock this evening, to visit a dying man, and so cannot be here. You are the last, Tom, and Mr. Ellis was the first."

Ellis was ruefully aware that this comparison in his favor was the only visible advantage that he had gained from his early arrival. He had not seen Miss Pemberton a moment sooner by reason of it. There had been a certain satisfaction in being in the same house with her, but Delamere had arrived in time to share or, more correctly, to monopolize, the sunshine of her presence.

Delamere gave a plausible excuse which won Clara's pardon and another enchanting smile, which pierced Ellis like a dagger. He knew very well that Delamere's excuse was a lie. Ellis himself had been ready as early as six o'clock, but judging this to be too early, had stopped in at the Clarendon Club for half an hour, to look over the magazines. While coming out he had glanced into the card-room, where he had seen his rival deep in a game of cards, from which Delamere had evidently not been able to tear himself until the last moment. He had accounted for his lateness by a story quite inconsistent with these facts.

The two young people walked over to a window on the opposite side of the large room, where they stood talking to one another in low tones. The major had left the room for a moment. Old Mr. Delamere, who was watching his grandson and Clara with an indulgent smile, proceeded to rub salt into Ellis's wounds.

"They make a handsome couple," he observed. "I remember well when her mother, in her youth an ideally beautiful woman, of an excellent family, married Daniel Pemberton, who was not of so good a family, but had made money. The major, who was only a very young man then, disapproved of the match; he considered that his mother, although a widow and nearly forty, was marrying beneath her. But he has been a good brother to Clara, and a careful guardian of her estate. Ah, young gentleman, you cannot appreciate, except in imagination, what it means, to one standing on the brink of eternity, to feel sure that he will live on in his children and his children's children!"

Ellis was appreciating at that moment what it meant, in cold blood, with no effort of the imagination, to see the girl whom he loved absorbed completely in another man. She had looked at him only once since Tom Delamere had entered the room, and then merely to use him as a spur with which to prick his favored rival.

"Yes, sir," he returned mechanically, "Miss Clara is a beautiful young lady."

"And Tom is a good boy – a fine boy," returned the old gentleman. "I am very well pleased with Tom, and shall be entirely happy when I see them married."

Ellis could not echo this sentiment. The very thought of this marriage made him miserable. He had always understood that the engagement was merely tentative, a sort of family understanding, subject to confirmation after Delamere should have attained his majority, which was still a year off, and when the major should think Clara old enough to marry. Ellis saw Delamere with the eye of a jealous rival, and judged him mercilessly – whether correctly or not the sequel will show. He did not at all believe that Tom Delamere would make a fit husband for Clara Pemberton; but his opinion would have had no weight – he could hardly have expressed it without showing his own interest. Moreover, there was no element of the sneak in Lee Ellis's make-up. The very fact that he might profit by the other's discomfiture left Delamere secure, so far as he could be affected by anything that Ellis might say. But Ellis did not shrink from a fair fight, and though in this one the odds were heavily against him, yet so long as this engagement remained indefinite, so long, indeed, as the object of his love was still unwed, he would not cease to hope. Such a sacrifice as this marriage clearly belonged in the catalogue of impossibilities. Ellis had not lived long enough to learn that impossibilities are merely things of which we have not learned, or which we do not wish to happen.

Sandy returned at the end of a quarter of an hour, and dinner was announced. Mr. Delamere led the way to the dining-room with Mrs. Ochiltree. Tom followed with Clara. The major went to the head of the stairs and came down with Mrs. Carteret upon his arm, her beauty rendered more delicate by the pallor of her countenance and more complete by the happiness with which it glowed. Ellis went in alone. In the rector's absence it was practically a family party which sat down, with the exception of Ellis, who, as we have seen, would willingly have placed himself in the same category.

The table was tastefully decorated with flowers, which grew about the house in lavish profusion. In warm climates nature adorns herself with true feminine vanity.

"What a beautiful table!" exclaimed Tom, before they were seated.

"The decorations are mine," said Clara proudly. "I cut the flowers and arranged them all myself."

"Which accounts for the admirable effect," rejoined Tom with a bow, before Ellis, to whom the same thought had occurred, was able to express himself. He had always counted himself the least envious of men, but for this occasion he coveted Tom Delamere's readiness.

"The beauty of the flowers," observed old Mr. Delamere, with sententious[31] gallantry, "is reflected upon all around them. It is a handsome company."

Mrs. Ochiltree beamed upon the table with a dry smile.

"I don't perceive any effect that it has upon you or me," she said. "And as for the young people, 'Handsome is as handsome does.' If Tom here, for instance, were as good as he looks" –

"You flatter me, Aunt Polly," Tom broke in hastily, anticipating the crack of the whip; he was familiar with his aunt's conversational idiosyncrasies.

"If you are as good as you look," continued the old lady, with a cunning but indulgent smile, "someone[32] has been slandering you."

Notes

[31] *sentenious* pompous.

[32] *Original reads*: some one [ed.].

"Thanks, Aunt Polly! Now you don't flatter me."

"There is Mr. Ellis," Mrs. Ochiltree went on, "who is not half so good-looking, but is steady as a clock, I dare say."

"Now, Aunt Polly," interposed Mrs. Carteret, "let the gentlemen alone."

"She doesn't[33] mean half what she says," continued Mrs. Carteret apologetically, "and only talks that way to people whom she likes."

Tom threw Mrs. Carteret a grateful glance. He had been apprehensive, with the sensitiveness of youth, lest his old great-aunt should make a fool of him before Clara's family. Nor had he relished the comparison with Ellis, who was out of place, anyway, in this family party. He had never liked the fellow, who was too much of a plodder and a prig to make a suitable associate for a whole-souled, generous-hearted young gentleman. He tolerated him as a visitor at Carteret's and as a member of the Clarendon Club, but that was all.

"Mrs. Ochiltree has a characteristic way of disguising her feelings," observed old Mr. Delamere, with a touch of sarcasm.

Ellis had merely flushed and felt uncomfortable at the reference to himself. The compliment to his character hardly offset the reflection upon his looks. He knew he was not exactly handsome, but it was not pleasant to have the fact emphasized in the presence of the girl he loved; he would like at least fair play, and judgment upon the subject left to the young lady.

Mrs. Ochiltree was quietly enjoying herself. In early life she had been accustomed to impale fools on epigrams, like flies on pins, to see them wriggle. But with advancing years she had lost in some measure the faculty of nice discrimination – it was pleasant to see her victims squirm, whether they were fools or friends. Even one's friends, she argued, were not always wise, and were sometimes the better for being told the truth. At her niece's table she felt at liberty to speak her mind, which she invariably did, with a frankness that sometimes bordered on brutality. She had long ago outgrown the period where ambition or passion, or its partners, envy and hatred, were springs of action in her life, and simply retained a mild enjoyment in the exercise of an old habit, with no active malice whatever. The ruling passion merely grew stronger as the restraining faculties decreased in vigor.

A diversion was created at this point by the appearance of old Mammy Jane, dressed in a calico[34] frock, with clean white neckerchief and apron, carrying the wonderful baby in honor of whose naming this feast had been given. Though only six weeks old, the little Theodore had grown rapidly, and Mammy Jane declared was already quite large for his age, and displayed signs of an unusually precocious intelligence. He was passed around the table and duly admired. Clara thought his hair was fine. Ellis inquired about his teeth. Tom put his finger in the baby's fist to test his grip. Old Mr. Delamere was unable to decide as yet whether he favored most his father or his mother. The object of these attentions endured them patiently for several minutes, and then protested with a vocal vigor which led to his being taken promptly back upstairs. Whatever fate might be in store for him, he manifested no sign of weak lungs.

"Sandy," said Mrs. Carteret when the baby had retired, "pass that tray standing upon the side table, so that we may all see the presents."

Notes

[33] *Original reads*: does n't [ed.].

[34] *calico* cheap cotton fabric.

Mr. Delamere had brought a silver spoon, and Tom a napkin ring. Ellis had sent a silver watch; it was a little premature, he admitted, but the boy would grow to it, and could use it to play with in the meantime. It had a glass back, so that he might see the wheels go round. Mrs. Ochiltree's present was an old and yellow ivory rattle, with a handle which the child could bite while teething, and a knob screwed on at the end to prevent the handle from slipping through the baby's hand.

"I saw that in your cedar chest, Aunt Polly," said Clara, "when I was a little girl, and you used to pull the chest out from under your bed to get me a dime."

"You kept the rattle in the right-hand corner of the chest," said Tom, "in the box with the red silk purse, from which you took the gold piece you gave me every Christmas."

A smile shone on Mrs. Ochiltree's severe features at this appreciation, like a ray of sunlight on a snowbank.

"Aunt Polly's chest is like the widow's cruse,"[35] said Mrs. Carteret, "which was never empty."

"Or Fortunatus's[36] purse, which was always full," added old Mr. Delamere, who read the Latin poets, and whose allusions were apt to be classical rather than scriptural.

"It will last me while I live," said Mrs. Ochiltree, adding cautiously, "but there'll not be a great deal left. It won't take much to support an old woman for twenty years."

Mr. Delamere's man Sandy had been waiting upon the table with the decorum of a trained butler, and a gravity all his own. He had changed his suit of plain gray for a long blue coat with brass buttons, which dated back to the fashion of a former generation, with which he wore a pair of plaid trousers of strikingly modern cut and pattern. With his whiskers, his spectacles, and his solemn air of responsibility, he would have presented, to one unfamiliar with the negro type, an amusingly impressive appearance. But there was nothing incongruous about Sandy to this company, except perhaps to Tom Delamere, who possessed a keen eye for contrasts and always regarded Sandy, in that particular rig, as a very comical darkey.

"Is it quite prudent, Mrs. Ochiltree," suggested the major at a moment when Sandy, having set down the tray, had left the room for a little while, "to mention, in the presence of the servants, that you keep money in the house?"

"I beg your pardon, major," observed old Mr. Delamere, with a touch of stiffness. "The only servant in hearing of the conversation has been my own; and Sandy is as honest as any man in Wellington."

"You mean, sir," replied Carteret, with a smile, "as honest as any *negro* in Wellington."

"I make no exceptions, major," returned the old gentleman, with emphasis. "I would trust Sandy with my life – he saved it once at the risk of his own."

"No doubt," mused the major, "the negro is capable of a certain doglike fidelity – I make the comparison in a kindly sense – a certain personal devotion which is admirable in itself, and fits him eminently for a servile career. I should imagine, however, that one could more safely trust his life with a negro than his portable property."

"Very clever, major! I read your paper, and know that your feeling is hostile toward the negro, but" –

The major made a gesture of dissent, but remained courteously silent until Mr. Delamere had finished.

Notes

[35] *widow's cruse* reference to the miracle in I Kings 17, in which a widow's jug of oil was always full during a famine.

[36] *Fortunatus's purse* medieval legend of a purse that is never empty.

"For my part," the old gentleman went on, "I think they have done very well, considering what they started from, and their limited opportunities. There was Adam Miller, for instance, who left a comfortable estate. His son George carries on the business, and the younger boy, William, is a good doctor and stands well with his profession. His hospital is a good thing, and if my estate were clear, I should like to do something for it."

"You are mistaken, sir, in imagining me hostile to the negro," explained Carteret. "On the contrary, I am friendly to his best interests. I give him employment; I pay taxes for schools to educate him, and for court-houses and jails to keep him in order. I merely object to being governed by an inferior and servile race."

Mrs. Carteret's face wore a tired expression. This question was her husband's hobby, and therefore her own nightmare. Moreover, she had her personal grievance against the negro race, and the names mentioned by old Mr. Delamere had brought it vividly before her mind. She had no desire to mar the harmony of the occasion by the discussion of a distasteful subject.

Mr. Delamere, glancing at his hostess, read something of this thought, and refused the challenge to further argument.

"I do not believe, major," he said, "that Olivia relishes the topic. I merely wish to say that Sandy is an exception to any rule which you may formulate in derogation of the negro. Sandy is a gentleman in ebony!"

Tom could scarcely preserve his gravity at this characterization of old Sandy, with his ridiculous air of importance, his long blue coat, and his loud plaid trousers. That suit would make a great costume for a masquerade. He would borrow it sometime – there was nothing in the world like it.

"Well, Mr. Delamere," returned the major good-humoredly, "no doubt Sandy is an exceptionally good negro – he might well be, for he has had the benefit of your example all his life – and we know that he is a faithful servant. But nevertheless, if I were Mrs. Ochiltree, I should put my money in the bank. Not all negroes are as honest as Sandy, and an elderly lady might not prove a match for a burly black burglar."

"Thank you, major," retorted Mrs. Ochiltree, with spirit, "I'm not yet too old to take care of myself. That cedar chest has been my bank for forty years, and I shall not change my habits at my age."

At this moment Sandy reentered the room. Carteret made a warning gesture, which Mrs. Ochiltree chose not to notice.

"I've proved a match for two husbands, and am not afraid of any man that walks the earth, black or white, by day or night. I have a revolver, and know how to use it. Whoever attempts to rob me will do so at his peril."

After dinner Clara played the piano and sang duets with Tom Delamere. At nine o'clock Mr. Delamere's carriage came for him, and he went away accompanied by Sandy. Under cover of the darkness the old gentleman leaned on his servant's arm with frank dependence, and Sandy lifted him into the carriage with every mark of devotion.

Ellis had already excused himself to go to the office and look over the late proofs for the morning paper. Tom remained a few minutes longer than his grandfather, and upon taking his leave went round to the Clarendon Club, where he spent an hour or two in the card-room with a couple of congenial friends. Luck seemed to favor him, and he went home at mid-night with a comfortable balance of winnings. He was fond of excitement, and found a great deal of it in cards. To lose was only less exciting than to win. Of late he had developed into a very successful player – so successful, indeed, that several members of the club generally found excuses to avoid participating in a game where he made one.

Chapter 3

The Editor at Work

To go back a little, for several days after his child's birth Major Carteret's chief interest in life had been confined to the four walls of the chamber where his pale wife lay upon her bed of pain, and those of the adjoining room where an old black woman crooned lovingly over a little white infant. A new element had been added to the major's consciousness, broadening the scope and deepening the strength of his affections. He did not love Olivia the less, for maternity had crowned her wifehood with an added glory; but side by side with this old and tried attachment was a new passion, stirring up dormant hopes and kindling new desires. His regret had been more than personal at the thought that with himself an old name should be lost to the State; and now all the old pride of race, class, and family welled up anew, and swelled and quickened the current of his life.

Upon the major's first appearance at the office, which took place the second day after the child's birth, he opened a box of cigars in honor of the event. The word had been passed around by Ellis, and the whole office force, including reporters, compositors, and pressmen, came in to congratulate the major and smoke at his expense. Even Jerry, the colored porter – Mammy Jane's grandson and therefore a protégé of the family – presented himself among the rest, or rather, after the rest. The major shook hands with them all except Jerry, though he acknowledged the porter's congratulations with a kind nod and put a good cigar into his outstretched palm, for which Jerry thanked him without manifesting any consciousness of the omission. He was quite aware that under ordinary circumstances the major would not have shaken hands with white workingmen, to say nothing of negroes; and he had merely hoped that in the pleasurable distraction of the moment the major might also overlook the distinction of color. Jerry's hope had been shattered, though not rudely; for the major had spoken pleasantly and the cigar was a good one. Mr. Ellis had once shaken hands with Jerry – but Mr. Ellis was a young man, whose Quaker father had never owned any slaves, and he could not be expected to have as much pride as one of the best "quality," whose families had possessed land and negroes for time out of mind. On the whole, Jerry preferred the careless nod of the editor-in-chief to the more familiar greeting of the subaltern.[37]

Having finished this pleasant ceremony, which left him with a comfortable sense of his new dignity, the major turned to his desk. It had been much neglected during the week, and more than one matter claimed his attention; but as typical of the new trend of his thoughts, the first subject he took up was one bearing upon the future of his son. Quite obviously the career of a Carteret must not be left to chance – it must be planned and worked out with a due sense of the value of good blood.

There lay upon his desk a letter from a well-known promoter, offering the major an investment which promised large returns, though several years must elapse before the enterprise could be put upon a paying basis. The element of time, however, was not immediately important. The Morning Chronicle provided him an ample income. The money available for this investment was part of his wife's patrimony. It was invested in a local cotton mill, which was paying ten per cent., but this was a beggarly return

Notes

[37] *subaltern* subordinate.

compared with the immense profits promised by the offered investment – profits which would enable his son, upon reaching manhood, to take a place in the world commensurate with the dignity of his ancestors, one of whom, only a few generations removed, had owned an estate of ninety thousand acres of land and six thousand slaves.

This letter having been disposed of by an answer accepting the offer, the major took up his pen to write an editorial. Public affairs in the state were not going to his satisfaction. At the last state election his own party, after an almost unbroken rule of twenty years, had been defeated by the so-called "Fusion" ticket, a combination of Republicans and Populists. A clean sweep had been made of the offices in the state, which were now filled by new men. Many of the smaller places had gone to colored men, their people having voted almost solidly for the Fusion ticket. In spite of the fact that the population of Wellington was two thirds colored, this state of things was gall and wormwood to the defeated party, of which the Morning Chronicle was the acknowledged organ. Major Carteret shared this feeling. Only this very morning, while passing the city hall, on his way to the office, he had seen the steps of that noble building disfigured by a fringe of job-hunting negroes, for all the world – to use a local simile – like a string of buzzards sitting on a rail, awaiting their opportunity to batten upon the helpless corpse of a moribund city.

Taking for his theme the unfitness of the negro to participate in government – an unfitness due to his limited education, his lack of experience, his criminal tendencies, and more especially to his hopeless mental and physical inferiority to the white race – the major had demonstrated, it seemed to him clearly enough, that the ballot in the hands of the negro was a menace to the commonwealth. He had argued, with entire conviction, that the white and black races could never attain social and political harmony by commingling their blood; he had proved by several historical parallels that no two unassimilable races could ever live together except in the relation of superior and inferior; and he was just dipping his gold pen into the ink to indite his conclusions from the premises thus established, when Jerry, the porter, announced two visitors.

"Gin'l Belmont an' Cap'n McBane would like ter see you, suh."

"Show them in, Jerry."

The man who entered first upon this invitation was a dapper little gentleman with light-blue eyes and a Vandyke beard. He wore a frock coat, patent leather shoes, and a Panama hat. There were crow's-feet about his eyes, which twinkled with a hard and, at times, humorous shrewdness. He had sloping shoulders, small hands and feet, and walked with the leisurely step characteristic of those who have been reared under hot suns.

Carteret gave his hand cordially to the gentleman thus described.

"How do you do, Captain McBane," he said, turning to the second visitor.

The individual thus addressed was strikingly different in appearance from his companion. His broad shoulders, burly form, square jaw, and heavy chin betokened strength, energy, and unscrupulousness. With the exception of a small, bristling mustache, his face was clean shaven, with here and there a speck of dried blood due to a carelessly or unskillfully handled razor. A single deep-set gray eye was shadowed by a beetling brow, over which a crop of coarse black hair, slightly streaked with gray, fell almost low enough to mingle with his black, bushy eyebrows. His coat had not been brushed for several days, if one might judge from the accumulation of dandruff upon the collar, and his shirt-front, in the middle of which blazed a showy diamond, was plentifully stained with tobacco juice. He wore a large slouch hat, which, upon entering the office, he removed and held in his hand.

Having greeted this person with an unconscious but quite perceptible diminution of the warmth with which he had welcomed the other, the major looked around the room for seats for his visitors, and perceiving only one chair, piled with exchanges, and a broken stool propped against the wall, pushed a button, which rang a bell in the hall, summoning the colored porter to his presence.

"Jerry," said the editor when his servant appeared, "bring a couple of chairs for these gentlemen."

While they stood waiting, the visitors congratulated the major on the birth of his child, which had been announced in the Morning Chronicle, and which the prominence of the family made in some degree a matter of public interest.

"And now that you have a son, major," remarked the gentleman first described, as he lit one of the major's cigars, "you'll be all the more interested in doing something to make this town fit to live in, which is what we came up to talk about. Things are in an awful condition! A negro justice of the peace has opened an office on Market Street, and only yesterday summoned a white man to appear before him. Negro lawyers get most of the business in the criminal court. Last evening a group of young white ladies, going quietly along the street arm-in-arm, were forced off the sidewalk by a crowd of negro girls. Coming down the street just now, I saw a spectacle of social equality and negro domination that made my blood boil with indignation – a white and a black convict, chained together, crossing the city in the charge of[38] a negro officer! We cannot stand that sort of thing, Carteret – it is the last straw! Something must be done, and that quickly!"

The major thrilled with responsive emotion. There was something prophetic in this opportune visit. The matter was not only in his own thoughts, but in the air; it was the spontaneous revulsion of white men against the rule of an inferior race. These were the very men, above all others in the town, to join him in a movement to change these degrading conditions.

General Belmont, the smaller of the two, was a man of good family, a lawyer by profession, and took an active part in state and local politics. Aristocratic by birth and instinct, and a former owner of slaves, his conception of the obligations and rights of his caste was nevertheless somewhat lower than that of the narrower but more sincere Carteret. In serious affairs Carteret desired the approval of his conscience, even if he had to trick that docile organ into acquiescence. This was not difficult to do in politics, for he believed in the divine right of white men and gentlemen, as his ancestors had believed in and died for the divine right of kings. General Belmont was not without a gentleman's distaste for meanness, but he permitted no fine scruples to stand in the way of success. He had once been minister, under a Democratic administration, to a small Central American state. Political rivals had characterized him as a tricky demagogue, which may of course have been a libel. He had an amiable disposition, possessed the gift of eloquence, and was a prime social favorite.

Captain George McBane had sprung from the poor-white class, to which, even more than to the slaves, the abolition of slavery had opened the door of opportunity. No longer overshadowed by a slaveholding caste, some of this class had rapidly pushed themselves forward. Some had made honorable records. Others, foremost in negro-baiting and election frauds, had done the dirty work of politics, as their fathers had done that of slavery, seeking their reward at first in minor offices – for which men of gentler breeding did not care – until their ambition began to reach out for higher honors.

Notes

[38] *Original reads*: in charge of [ed.].

Of this class McBane – whose captaincy, by the way, was merely a polite fiction – had been one of the most successful. He had held, until recently, as the reward of questionable political services, a contract with the State for its convict labor, from which in a few years he had realized a fortune. But the methods which made his contract profitable had not commended themselves to humane people, and charges of cruelty and worse had been preferred against him. He was rich enough to escape serious consequences from the investigation which followed, but when the Fusion ticket carried the state he lost his contract, and the system of convict labor was abolished. Since then McBane had devoted himself to politics: he was ambitious for greater wealth, for office, and for social recognition. A man of few words and self-engrossed, he seldom spoke of his aspirations except where speech might favor them, preferring to seek his ends by secret "deals" and combinations rather than to challenge criticism and provoke rivalry by more open methods.

At sight, therefore, of these two men, with whose careers and characters he was entirely familiar, Carteret felt sweep over his mind the conviction that now was the time and these the instruments with which to undertake the redemption of the state from the evil fate which had befallen it.

Jerry, the porter, who had gone downstairs to the counting-room to find two whole chairs, now entered with one in each hand. He set a chair for the general, who gave him an amiable nod, to which Jerry responded with a bow and a scrape. Captain McBane made no acknowledgment, but fixed Jerry so fiercely with his single eye that upon placing the chair Jerry made his escape from the room as rapidly as possible.

"I don' like dat Cap'n McBane," he muttered, upon reaching the hall. "Dey says he got dat eye knock' out tryin' ter whip a cullud 'oman, when he wuz a boy, an' dat he ain' never had no use fer niggers sence – 'cep'n' fer what he could make outen 'em wid his convic' labor contrac's. His daddy wuz a' overseer befo' 'im, an' it come nachul fer him ter be a nigger-driver. I don' want dat one eye er his'n restin' on me no longer 'n I kin he'p, an' I don' know how I'm gwine ter like dis job ef he's gwine ter be comin' roun' here. He ain' nothin' but po' w'ite trash nohow; but Lawd! Lawd! look at de money he's got – livin' at de hotel, wearin' di'mon's, an' colloguin' wid de bes' quality er dis town! 'Pears ter me de bottom rail is gittin' mighty close ter de top. Well, I s'pose it all comes f'm bein' w'ite. I wush ter Gawd I wuz w'ite!"

After this fervent aspiration, having nothing else to do for the time being, except to remain within call, and having caught a few words of the conversation as he went in with the chairs, Jerry, who possessed a certain amount of curiosity, placed close to the wall the broken stool upon which he sat while waiting in the hall, and applied his ear to a hole in the plastering of the hallway. There was a similar defect in the inner wall, between the same two pieces of studding, and while this inner opening was not exactly opposite the outer, Jerry was enabled, through the two, to catch in a more or less fragmentary way what was going on within.

He could hear the major, now and then, use the word "negro," and McBane's deep voice was quite audible when he referred, it seemed to Jerry with alarming frequency, to "the damned niggers," while the general's suave tones now and then pronounced the word "niggro" – a sort of compromise between ethnology and the vernacular. That the gentlemen were talking politics seemed quite likely, for gentlemen generally talked politics when they met at the Chronicle office. Jerry could hear the words "vote," "franchise," "eliminate," "constitution," and other expressions which marked the general tenor of the talk, though he could not follow it all – partly because he could not hear everything distinctly, and partly because of certain limitations which nature had placed in the way of Jerry's understanding anything very difficult or abstruse.

He had gathered enough, however, to realize, in a vague way, that something serious was on foot, involving his own race, when a bell sounded over his head, at which he sprang up hastily and entered the room where the gentlemen were talking.

"Jerry," said the major, "wait on Captain McBane."

"Yas, suh," responded Jerry, turning toward the captain, whose eye he carefully avoided meeting directly.

"Take that half a dollar, boy," ordered McBane, "an' go 'cross the street to Mr. Sykes's, and tell him to send me three whiskies. Bring back the change, and make has'e."

The captain tossed the half dollar at Jerry, who, looking to one side, of course missed it. He picked the money up, however, and backed out of the room. Jerry did not like Captain McBane, to begin with, and it was clear that the captain was no gentleman, or he would not have thrown the money at him. Considering the source, Jerry might have overlooked this discourtesy had it not been coupled with the remark about the change, which seemed to him in very poor taste.

Returning in a few minutes with three glasses on a tray, he passed them round, handed Captain McBane his change, and retired to the hall.

"Gentlemen," exclaimed the captain, lifting his glass, "I propose a toast: 'No nigger domination.'"

"Amen!" said the others, and three glasses were solemnly drained.

"Major," observed the general, smacking his lips, "I should like to use Jerry for a moment, if you will permit me."

Jerry appeared promptly at the sound of the bell. He had remained conveniently near – calls of this sort were apt to come in sequence.

"Jerry," said the general, handing Jerry half a dollar, "go over to Mr. Brown's – I get my liquor there – and tell them to send me three glasses of my special mixture. And, Jerry – you may keep the change!"

"Thank y', gin'l, thank y', marster," replied Jerry, with unctuous gratitude, bending almost double as he backed out of the room.

"Dat's a gent'eman, a rale ole time gent'eman," he said to himself when he had closed the door. "But dere's somethin' gwine on in dere – dere sho' is! 'No nigger damnation!' Dat soun's all right – I'm sho' dere ain' no nigger I knows w'at wants damnation, do' dere's lots of 'em w'at deserves it; but ef dat one-eyed Cap'n McBane got anything ter do wid it, w'atever it is, it don' mean no good fer de niggers – damnation 'd be better fer 'em dan dat Cap'n McBane! He looks at a nigger lack he could jes' eat 'im alive."

"This mixture, gentlemen," observed the general when Jerry had returned with the glasses, "was originally compounded by no less a person than the great John C. Calhoun himself, who confided the recipe to my father over the convivial board. In this nectar of the gods, gentlemen, I drink with you to 'White Supremacy!'"

"White Supremacy everywhere!" added McBane with fervor.

"Now and forever!" concluded Carteret solemnly.

When the visitors, half an hour later, had taken their departure, Carteret, inspired by the theme, and in less degree by the famous mixture of the immortal Calhoun,[39] turned to his desk and finished, at a white heat, his famous editorial in which he sounded the tocsin[40] of a new crusade.

Notes

[39] John C. Calhoun (1782–1850), southern politician, secessionist, and slavery apologist.

[40] *tocsin* alarm bell.

At noon, when the editor, having laid down his pen, was leaving the office, he passed Jerry in the hall without a word or a nod. The major wore a rapt look, which Jerry observed with a vague uneasiness.

"He looks jes' lack he wuz walkin' in his sleep," muttered Jerry uneasily. "Dere's somethin' up, sho's you bawn! 'No nigger damnation!' Anybody'd 'low dey wuz all gwine ter heaven; but I knows better! W'en a passel er w'ite folks gits ter talkin' 'bout de niggers lack dem in yander, it's mo' lackly dey're gwine ter ketch somethin' e'se dan heaven! I got ter keep my eyes open an' keep up wid w'at's happenin'. Ef dere's gwine ter be anudder flood 'roun' here, I wants ter git in de ark wid de w'ite folks – I may haf ter be anudder Ham,[41] an' sta't de cullud race all over ag'in."

Chapter 4

Theodore Felix

THE young heir of the Carterets had thriven apace, and at six months old was, according to Mammy Jane, whose experience qualified her to speak with authority, the largest, finest, smartest, and altogether most remarkable baby that had ever lived in Wellington. Mammy Jane had recently suffered from an attack of inflammatory rheumatism, as the result of which she had returned to her own home. She nevertheless came now and then to see Mrs. Carteret. A younger nurse had been procured to take her place, but it was understood that Jane would come whenever she might be needed.

"You really mean that about Dodie, do you, Mammy Jane?" asked the delighted mother, who never tired of hearing her own opinion confirmed concerning this wonderful child, which had come to her like an angel from heaven.

"Does I mean it!" exclaimed Mammy Jane, with a tone and an expression which spoke volumes of reproach. "Now, Mis' 'Livy, what is I ever uttered er said er spoke er done dat would make you s'pose I could tell you a lie 'bout yo' own chile?"

"No, Mammy Jane, I'm sure you wouldn't."

"'Deed, ma'am, I'm tellin' you de Lawd's truf. I don' haf ter tell no lies ner strain no p'ints 'bout my ole mist'ess's gran'chile. Dis yer boy is de ve'y spit an' image er yo' brother, young Mars Alick, w'at died w'en he wuz 'bout eight mont's ole, w'iles I wuz laid off havin' a baby er my own, an' couldn'[42] be roun' ter look after 'im. An' dis chile is a rale quality chile, he is – I never seed a baby wid sech fine hair fer his age, ner sech blue eyes, ner sech a grip, ner sech a heft. W'y, dat chile mus' weigh 'bout twenty-fo' poun's, an' he not but six mont's ole. Does dat gal w'at does de nussin' w'iles I'm gone ten' ter dis chile right, Mis' 'Livy?"

"She does fairly well, Mammy Jane, but I could hardly expect her to love the baby as you do. There's no one like you, Mammy Jane."

"'Deed dere ain't, honey; you is talkin' de gospel truf now! None er dese yer young folks ain' got de trainin' my ole mist'ess give me. Dese yer new-fangle' schools don' l'arn 'em nothin' ter compare wid it. I'm jes' gwine ter give dat gal a piece er my min', befo' I go, so she'll ten' ter dis chile right."

The nurse came in shortly afterwards, a neat-looking brown girl, dressed in a clean calico gown, with a nurse's cap and apron.

Notes

[41] *Ham* the son of Noah who is cursed to serve his brothers, interpreted as the beginning of slavery (Genesis 9:25–27).

[42] *Original reads*: could n' [ed.].

"Look a-here, gal," said Mammy Jane sternly, "I wants you ter understan' dat you got ter take good keer er dis chile; fer I nussed his mammy dere, an' his gran'mammy befo' 'im, an' you is got a priv'lege dat mos' lackly you don' 'preciate. I wants you to 'member, in yo' incomin's an' outgoin's, dat I got my eye on you, an' am gwine ter see dat you does yo' wo'k right."

"Do you need me for anything, ma'am?" asked the young nurse, who had stood before Mrs. Carteret, giving Mammy Jane a mere passing glance, and listening impassively to her harangue. The nurse belonged to the younger generation of colored people. She had graduated from the mission school, and had received some instruction in Dr. Miller's class for nurses. Standing, like most young people of her race, on the border line between two irreconcilable states of life, she had neither the picturesqueness of the slave, nor the unconscious dignity of those of whom freedom has been the immemorial birthright; she was in what might be called the chip-on-the-shoulder stage, through which races as well as individuals must pass in climbing the ladder of life – not an interesting, at least not an agreeable stage, but an inevitable one, and for that reason entitled to a paragraph in a story of Southern life, which, with its as yet imperfect blending of old with new, of race with race, of slavery with freedom, is like no other life under the sun.

Had this old woman, who had no authority over her, been a little more polite, or a little less offensive, the nurse might have returned her a pleasant answer. These old-time negroes, she said to herself, made her sick with their slavering over the white folks, who, she supposed, favored them and made much of them because they had once belonged to them – much the same reason why they fondled their cats and dogs. For her own part, they gave her nothing but her wages, and small wages at that, and she owed them nothing more than equivalent service. It was purely a matter of business; she sold her time for their money. There was no question of love between them.

Receiving a negative answer from Mrs. Carteret, she left the room without a word, ignoring Mammy Jane completely, and leaving that venerable relic of ante-bellum times gasping in helpless astonishment.

"Well, I nevuh!" she ejaculated, as soon as she could get her breath, "ef dat ain' de beatinis' pe'fo'mance I ever seed er heared of! Dese yer young niggers ain' got de manners dey wuz bawned wid! I don' know w'at dey're comin' to, w'en dey ain' got no mo' rispec' fer ole age – I don' know – I don' know!"

"Now what are you croaking about, Jane?" asked Major Carteret, who came into the room and took the child into his arms.

Mammy Jane hobbled to her feet and bobbed a curtsy. She was never lacking in respect to white people of proper quality; but Major Carteret, the quintessence of aristocracy, called out all her reserves of deference. The major was always kind and considerate to these old family retainers, brought up in the feudal atmosphere now so rapidly passing away. Mammy Jane loved Mrs. Carteret; toward the major she entertained a feeling bordering upon awe.

"Well, Jane," returned the major sadly, when the old nurse had related her grievance, "the old times have vanished, the old ties have been ruptured. The old relations of dependence and loyal obedience on the part of the colored people, the responsibility of protection and kindness upon that of the whites, have passed away forever. The young negroes are too self-assertive. Education is spoiling them, Jane; they have been badly taught. They are not content with their station in life. Some time they will overstep the mark. The white people are patient, but there is a limit to their endurance.

"Dat's w'at I tells dese young niggers," groaned Mammy Jane, with a portentous shake of her tur-baned head, "w'en I hears 'em gwine on wid deir foolishniss; but dey don' min' me. Dey 'lows dey knows mo' d'n I does, 'ca'se dey be'n l'arnt ter look in a book. But, pshuh! my ole mist'ess showed me mo' d'n dem niggers'll l'arn in a thousan' years! I's fetch' my gran'son' Jerry up ter be 'umble, an' keep in 'is place. An' I tells dese other niggers dat ef dey'd do de same, an' not crowd de w'ite folks, dey'd git ernuff ter eat, an' live out deir days in peace an' comfo't. But dey don' min' me – dey don' min' me!"

"If all the colored people were like you and Jerry, Jane," rejoined the major kindly, "there would never be any trouble. You have friends upon whom, in time of need, you can rely implicitly for protection and succor. You served your mistress faithfully before the war; you remained by her when the other negroes were running hither and thither like sheep without a shepherd; and you have transferred your allegiance to my wife and her child. We think a great deal of you, Jane."

"Yes, indeed, Mammy Jane," assented Mrs. Carteret, with sincere affection, glancing with moist eyes from the child in her husband's arms to the old nurse, whose dark face was glowing with happiness at these expressions of appreciation, "you shall never want so long as we have anything. We would share our last crust with you."

"Thank y', Mis' 'Livy," said Jane with reciprocal emotion, "I knows who my frien's is, an' I ain' gwine ter let nothin' worry me. But fer de Lawd's sake, Mars Philip, gimme dat chile, an' lemme pat 'im on de back, er he'll choke hisse'f ter death!"

The old nurse had been the first to observe that little Dodie, for some reason, was gasping for breath. Catching the child from the major's arms, she patted it on the back, and shook it gently. After a moment of this treatment, the child ceased to gasp, but still breathed heavily, with a strange, whistling noise.

"Oh, my child!" exclaimed the mother, in great alarm, taking the baby in her own arms, "what can be the matter with him, Mammy Jane?"

"Fer de Lawd's sake, ma'am, I don' know, 'less he's swallered somethin'; an' he ain' had nothin' in his han's but de rattle Mis' Polly give 'im."

Mrs. Carteret caught up the ivory rattle, which hung suspended by a ribbon from the baby's neck.

"He has swallowed the little piece off the end of the handle," she cried, turning pale with fear, "and it has lodged in his throat. Telephone Dr. Price to come immediately, Philip, before my baby chokes to death! Oh, my baby, my precious baby!"

An anxious half hour passed, during which the child lay quiet, except for its labored breathing. The suspense was relieved by the arrival of Dr. Price, who examined the child carefully.

"It's a curious accident," he announced at the close of his inspection. "So far as I can discover, the piece of ivory has been drawn into the trachea, or windpipe, and has lodged in the mouth of the right bronchus. I'll try to get it out without an operation, but I can't guarantee the result."

At the end of another half hour Dr. Price announced his inability to remove the obstruction without resorting to more serious measures.

"I do not see," he declared, "how an operation can be avoided."

"Will it be dangerous?" inquired the major anxiously, while Mrs. Carteret shivered at the thought.

"It will be necessary to cut into his throat from the outside. All such operations are more or less dangerous, especially on small children. If this were some other child, I might undertake the operation unassisted; but I know how you value this one, major, and I should prefer to share the responsibility with a specialist."

"Is there one in town?" asked the major.

"No, but we can get one from out of town."

"Send for the best one in the country," said the major, "who can be got here in time. Spare no expense, Dr. Price. We value this child above any earthly thing."

"The best is the safest," replied Dr. Price. "I will send for Dr. Burns, of Philadelphia, the best surgeon in that line in America. If he can start at once, he can reach here in sixteen or eighteen hours, and the case can wait even longer, if inflammation does not set in."

The message was dispatched forthwith. By rare good fortune the eminent specialist was able to start within an hour or two after the receipt of Dr. Price's telegram. Meanwhile the baby remained restless and uneasy, the doctor spending most of his time by its side. Mrs. Carteret, who had never been quite strong since the child's birth, was a prey to the most agonizing apprehensions.

Mammy Jane, while not presuming to question the opinion of Dr. Price, and not wishing to add to her mistress's distress, was secretly oppressed by forebodings which she was unable to shake off. The child was born for bad luck. The mole under its ear, just at the point where the hangman's knot would strike, had foreshadowed dire misfortune. She had already observed several little things which had rendered her vaguely anxious.

For instance, upon one occasion, on entering the room where the baby had been left alone, asleep in his crib, she had met a strange cat hurrying from the nursery, and, upon examining closely the pillow upon which the child lay, had found a depression which had undoubtedly been due to the weight of the cat's body. The child was restless and uneasy, and Jane had ever since believed that the cat had been sucking little Dodie's breath, with what might have been fatal results had she not appeared just in the nick of time.

This untimely accident of the rattle, a fatality for which no one could be held responsible, had confirmed the unlucky omen. Jane's duties in the nursery did not permit her to visit her friend the conjure woman; but she did find time to go out in the back yard at dusk, and to dig up the charm which she had planted there. It had protected the child so far; but perhaps its potency had become exhausted. She picked up the bottle, shook it vigorously, and then laid it back, with the other side up. Refilling the hole, she made a cross over the top with the thumb of her left hand, and walked three times around it.

What this strange symbolism meant, or whence it derived its origin, Aunt Jane did not know. The cross was there, and the Trinity, though Jane was scarcely conscious of these, at this moment, as religious emblems. But she hoped, on general principles, that this performance would strengthen the charm and restore little Dodie's luck. It certainly had its moral effect upon Jane's own mind, for she was able to sleep better, and contrived to impress Mrs. Carteret with her own hopefulness.

Chapter 5

A Journey Southward

As the south-bound train was leaving the station at Philadelphia, a gentleman took his seat in the single sleeping-car attached to the train, and proceeded to make himself comfortable. He hung up his hat and opened his newspaper, in which he remained absorbed for a quarter of an hour. When the train had left the city behind, he threw the paper aside, and looked around at the other occupants of the car. One of these, who had been on the car since it had left New York, rose from his seat upon perceiving the other's glance, and came down the aisle.

"How do you do, Dr. Burns?" he said, stopping beside the seat of the Philadelphia passenger.

The gentleman looked up at the speaker with an air of surprise, which, after the first keen, incisive glance, gave place to an expression of cordial recognition.

"Why, it's Miller!" he exclaimed, rising and giving the other his hand, "William Miller – Dr. Miller, of course. Sit down, Miller, and tell me all about yourself – what you're doing, where you've been, and where you're going. I'm delighted to meet you, and to see you looking so well – and so prosperous."

"I deserve no credit for either, sir," returned the other, as he took the proffered seat, "for I inherited both health and prosperity. It is a fortunate chance that permits me to meet you."

The two acquaintances, thus opportunely thrown together so that they might while away in conversation the tedium of their journey, represented very different and yet very similar types of manhood. A celebrated traveler, after many years spent in barbarous or savage lands, has said that among all varieties of mankind the similarities are vastly more important and fundamental than the differences. Looking at these two men with the American eye, the differences would perhaps be the more striking, or at least the more immediately apparent, for the first was white and the second black, or, more correctly speaking, brown; it was even a light brown, but both his swarthy complexion and his curly hair revealed what has been described in the laws of some of our states as a "visible admixture" of African blood.

Having disposed of this difference, and having observed that the white man was perhaps fifty years of age and the other not more than thirty, it may be said that they were both tall and sturdy, both well dressed, the white man with perhaps a little more distinction; both seemed from their faces and their manners to be men of culture and accustomed to the society of cultivated people. They were both handsome men, the elder representing a fine type of Anglo-Saxon, as the term is used in speaking of our composite white population; while the mulatto's erect form, broad shoulders, clear eyes, fine teeth, and pleasingly moulded features showed nowhere any sign of that degeneration which the pessimist so sadly maintains is the inevitable heritage of mixed races.

As to their personal relations, it has already appeared that they were members of the same profession. In past years they had been teacher and pupil. Dr. Alvin Burns was professor in the famous medical college where Miller had attended lectures. The professor had taken an interest in his only colored pupil, to whom he had been attracted by his earnestness of purpose, his evident talent, and his excellent manners and fine physique. It was in part due to Dr. Burns's friendship that Miller had won a scholarship which had enabled him, without drawing too heavily upon his father's resources, to spend in Europe, studying in the hospitals of Paris and Vienna, the two most delightful years of his life. The same influence had strengthened his natural inclination toward operative surgery, in which Dr. Burns was a distinguished specialist of national reputation.

Miller's father, Adam Miller, had been a thrifty colored man, the son of a slave, who, in the olden time, had bought himself with money which he had earned and saved, over and above what he had paid his master for his time. Adam Miller had inherited his father's thrift, as well as his trade, which was that of a stevedore, or contractor for the loading and unloading of vessels at the port of Wellington. In the flush turpentine days following a few years after the civil war, he had made money. His savings, shrewdly invested, had by constant accessions become a competence. He had brought up his eldest son to the trade; the other he had given a professional education, in the proud hope that his children or his grandchildren might be gentlemen in the town where their ancestors had once been slaves.

Upon his father's death, shortly after Dr. Miller's return from Europe, and a year or two before the date at which this story opens, he had promptly spent part of his inheritance in founding a hospital, to which was to be added a training school for nurses, and in time perhaps a medical college and a school of pharmacy. He had been strongly tempted to leave the South, and seek a home for his family and a career for himself in the freer North, where race antagonism was less keen, or at least less oppressive, or in Europe, where he had never found his color work to his disadvantage. But his people had needed him, and he had wished to help them, and had sought by means of this institution to contribute to their uplifting. As he now informed Dr. Burns, he was returning from New York, where he had been in order to purchase equipment for his new hospital, which would soon be ready for the reception of patients.

"How much I can accomplish I do not know," said Miller, "but I'll do what I can. There are eight or nine million of us, and it will take a great deal of learning of all kinds to leaven that lump."

"It is a great problem, Miller, the future of your race," returned the other, "a tremendously interesting problem. It is a serial story which we are all reading, and which grows in vital interest with each successive installment. It is not only your problem, but ours. Your race must come up or drag ours down."

"We shall come up," declared Miller; "slowly and painfully, perhaps, but we shall win our way. If our race had made as much progress everywhere as they have made in Wellington, the problem would be well on the way toward solution."

"Wellington?" exclaimed Dr. Burns. "That's where I'm going. A Dr. Price, of Wellington, has sent for me to perform an operation on a child's throat. Do you know Dr. Price?"

"Quite well," replied Miller, "he is a friend of mine."

"So much the better. I shall want you to assist me. I read in the Medical Gazette, the other day, an account of a very interesting operation of yours. I felt proud to number you among my pupils. It was a remarkable case – a rare case. I must certainly have you with me in this one."

"I shall be delighted, sir," returned Miller, "if it is agreeable to all concerned."

Several hours were passed in pleasant conversation while the train sped rapidly southward. They were already far down in Virginia, and had stopped at a station beyond Richmond, when the conductor entered the car.

"All passengers," he announced, "will please transfer to the day coaches ahead. The sleeper has a hot box, and must be switched off here."

Dr. Burns and Miller obeyed the order, the former leading the way into the coach immediately in front of the sleeping-car.

"Let's sit here, Miller," he said, having selected a seat near the rear of the car and deposited his suitcase in a rack. "It's on the shady side."

Miller stood a moment hesitatingly, but finally took the seat indicated, and a few minutes later the journey was again resumed.

When the train conductor made his round after leaving the station, he paused at the seat occupied by the two doctors, glanced interrogatively at Miller, and then spoke to Dr. Burns, who sat in the end of the seat nearest the aisle.

"This man is with you?" he asked, indicating Miller with a slight side movement of his head, and a keen glance in his direction.

"Certainly," replied Dr. Burns curtly, and with some surprise. "Don't you see that he is?"

The conductor passed on. Miller paid no apparent attention to this little interlude, though no syllable had escaped him. He resumed the conversation where it had been broken off, but nevertheless followed with his eyes the conductor, who stopped at a seat near the forward end of the car, and engaged in conversation with a man whom Miller had not hitherto noticed.

As this passenger turned his head and looked back toward Miller, the latter saw a broad-shouldered, burly white man, and recognized in his square-cut jaw, his coarse, firm mouth, and the single gray eye with which he swept Miller for an instant with a scornful glance, a well-known character of Wellington, with whom the reader has already made acquaintance in these pages. Captain McBane wore a frock coat and a slouch hat; several buttons of his vest were unbuttoned, and his solitaire diamond blazed in his soiled shirt-front like the headlight of a locomotive.

The conductor in his turn looked back at Miller, and retraced his steps. Miller braced himself for what he feared was coming, though he had hoped, on account of his friend's presence, that it might be avoided.

"Excuse me, sir," said the conductor, addressing Dr. Burns, "but did I understand you to say that this man was your servant?"

"No, indeed!" replied Dr. Burns indignantly. "The gentleman is not my servant, nor anybody's servant, but is my friend. But, by the way, since we are on the subject, may I ask what affair it is of yours?"

"It's very much my affair," returned the conductor, somewhat nettled at this questioning of his authority. "I'm sorry to part *friends*, but the law of Virginia does not permit colored passengers to ride in the white cars. You'll have to go forward to the next coach," he added, addressing Miller this time.

"I have paid my fare on the sleeping-car, where the separate-car law does not apply," remonstrated Miller.

"I can't help that. You can doubtless get your money back from the sleeping-car company. But this is a day coach, and is distinctly marked 'White,' as you must have seen before you sat down here. The sign is put there for that purpose."

He indicated a large card neatly framed and hung at the end of the car, containing the legend, "White," in letters about a foot long, painted in white upon a dark background, typical, one might suppose, of the distinction thereby indicated.

"You shall not stir a step, Miller," exclaimed Dr. Burns wrathfully. "This is an outrage upon a citizen of a free country. You shall stay right here."

"I'm sorry to discommode you," returned the conductor, "but there's no use kicking. It's the law of Virginia, and I am bound by it as well as you. I have already come near losing my place because of not enforcing it, and I can take no more such chances, since I have a family to support."

"And my friend has his rights to maintain," returned Dr. Burns with determination. "There is a vital principle at stake in the matter."

"Really, sir," argued the conductor, who was a man of peace and not fond of controversy, "there's no use talking – he absolutely cannot ride in this car."

"How can you prevent it?" asked Dr. Burns, lapsing into the argumentative stage.

"The law gives me the right to remove him by force. I can call on the train crew to assist me, or on the other passengers. If I should choose to put him off the train entirely, in the middle of a swamp, he would have no redress – the law so provides. If I did not wish to use force, I could simply switch this car off at the next siding, transfer the white passengers to another, and leave you and your friend in possession until you were arrested and fined or imprisoned."

"What he says is absolutely true, doctor," interposed Miller at this point. "It is the law, and we are powerless to resist it. If we made any trouble, it would merely delay your journey and imperil a life at the other end. I'll go into the other car."

"You shall not go alone," said Dr. Burns stoutly, rising in his turn. "A place that is too good for you is not good enough for me. I will sit wherever you do."

"I'm sorry again," said the conductor, who had quite recovered his equanimity, and calmly conscious of his power, could scarcely restrain an amused smile; "I dislike to interfere, but white passengers are not permitted to ride in the colored car."

"This is an outrage," declared Dr. Burns, "a d——d outrage! You are curtailing the rights, not only of colored people, but of white men as well. I shall sit where I please!"

"I warn you, sir," rejoined the conductor, hardening again, "that the law will be enforced. The beauty of the system lies in its strict impartiality – it applies to both races alike."

"And is equally infamous in both cases," declared Dr. Burns. "I shall immediately take steps" –

"Never mind, doctor," interrupted Miller, soothingly, "it's only for a little while. I'll reach my destination just as surely in the other car, and we can't help it, anyway. I'll see you again at Wellington."

Dr. Burns, finding resistance futile, at length acquiesced and made way for Miller to pass him.

The colored doctor took up his valise and crossed the platform to the car ahead. It was an old car, with faded upholstery, from which the stuffing projected here and there through torn places. Apparently the floor had not been swept for several days. The dust lay thick upon the window sills, and the water-cooler, from which he essayed to get a drink, was filled with stale water which had made no recent acquaintance with ice. There was no other passenger in the car, and Miller occupied himself in making a rough calculation of what it would cost the Southern railroads to haul a whole car for every colored passenger. It was expensive, to say the least; it would be cheaper, and quite as considerate of their feelings, to make the negroes walk.

The car was conspicuously labeled at either end with large cards, similar to those in the other car, except that they bore the word "Colored" in black letters upon a white background. The author of this piece of legislation had contrived, with an ingenuity worthy of a better cause, that not merely should the passengers be separated by the color line, but that the reason for this division should be kept constantly in mind. Lest a white man should forget that he was white – not a very likely contingency – these cards would keep him constantly admonished of the fact; should a colored person endeavor, for a moment, to lose sight of his disability, these staring signs would remind him continually that between him and the rest of mankind not of his own color, there was by law a great gulf fixed.

Having composed himself, Miller had opened a newspaper, and was deep in an editorial which set forth in glowing language the inestimable advantages which would follow to certain recently acquired islands by the introduction of American liberty, when the rear door of the car opened to give entrance to Captain George McBane, who took a seat near the door and lit a cigar. Miller knew him quite well by sight and by reputation, and detested him as heartily. He represented the aggressive, offensive element among the white people of the New South, who made it hard for a negro to maintain his self-respect or to enjoy even the rights conceded to colored men by Southern laws. McBane had undoubtedly identified him to the conductor in the other car. Miller had no desire to thrust himself upon the society of white people, which, indeed, to one who had traveled so much and so far, was no novelty; but he very naturally resented being at this late day – the law had been in operation only a few months – branded and tagged and set apart from the rest of mankind upon the public highways, like an unclean thing. Nevertheless, he preferred even this to the exclusive society of Captain George McBane.

"Porter," he demanded of the colored train attaché who passed through the car a moment later, "is this a smoking car for white men?"

"No, suh," replied the porter, "but they comes in here sometimes, when they ain' no cullud ladies on the kyar."

"Well, I have paid first-class fare, and I object to that man's smoking in here. You tell him to go out."

"I'll tell the conductor, suh," returned the porter in a low tone. "I'd jus' as soon talk ter the devil as ter that man."

The white man had spread himself over two seats, and was smoking vigorously, from time to time spitting carelessly in the aisle, when the conductor entered the compartment.

"Captain," said Miller, "this car is plainly marked 'Colored.' I have paid first-class fare, and I object to riding in a smoking car."

"All right," returned the conductor, frowning irritably. "I'll speak to him."

He walked over to the white passenger, with whom he was evidently acquainted, since he addressed[43] him by name.

"Captain McBane," he said, "it's against the law for you to ride in the nigger car."

"Who are you talkin' to?" returned the other. "I'll ride where I damn please."

"Yes, sir, but the colored passenger objects. I'm afraid I'll have to ask you to go into the smoking-car."

"The hell you say!" rejoined McBane. "I'll leave this car when I get good and ready, and that won't be till I've finished this cigar. See?"

He was as good as his word. The conductor escaped from the car before Miller had time for further expostulation. Finally McBane, having thrown the stump of his cigar into the aisle and added to the floor a finishing touch in the way of expectoration,[44] rose and went back into the white car.

Left alone in his questionable glory, Miller buried himself again in his newspaper, from which he did not look up until the engine stopped at a tank station to take water.

As the train came to a standstill, a huge negro, covered thickly with dust, crawled off one of the rear trucks unobserved, and ran round the rear end of the car to a watering-trough by a neighboring well. Moved either by extreme thirst or by the fear that his time might be too short to permit him to draw a bucket of water, he threw himself down by the trough, drank long and deep, and plunging his head into the water, shook himself like a wet dog, and crept furtively back to his dangerous perch.

Miller, who had seen this man from the car window, had noticed a very singular thing. As the dusty tramp passed the rear coach, he cast toward it a glance of intense ferocity. Up to that moment the man's face, which Miller had recognized under its grimy coating, had been that of an ordinarily good-natured, somewhat reckless, pleasure-loving negro, at present rather the worse for wear. The change that now came over it suggested a concentrated hatred almost uncanny in its murderousness. With awakened curiosity Miller followed the direction of the negro's glance, and saw that it rested upon a window where Captain McBane sat looking out. When Miller looked back, the negro had disappeared.

At the next station a Chinaman, of the ordinary laundry type, boarded the train, and took his seat in the white car without objection. At another point a colored nurse found a place with her mistress.

"White people," said Miller to himself, who had seen these passengers from the window, "do not object to the negro as a servant. As the traditional negro – the servant – he is welcomed; as an equal, he is repudiated."

Notes

[43] *Original reads*: adressed [ed.].

[44] *expectoration* spitting.

Miller was something of a philosopher. He had long ago had the conclusion forced upon him that an educated man of his race, in order to live comfortably in the United States, must be either a philosopher or a fool; and since he wished to be happy, and was not exactly a fool, he had cultivated philosophy. By and by he saw a white man, with a dog, enter the rear coach. Miller wondered whether the dog would be allowed to ride with his master, and if not, what disposition would be made of him. He was a handsome dog, and Miller, who was fond of animals, would not have objected to the company of a dog, as a dog. He was nevertheless conscious of a queer sensation when he saw the porter take the dog by the collar and start in his own direction, and felt consciously relieved when the canine passenger was taken on past him into the baggage-car ahead. Miller's hand was hanging over the arm of his seat, and the dog, an intelligent shepherd, licked it as he passed. Miller was not entirely sure that he would not have liked the porter to leave the dog there; he was a friendly dog, and seemed inclined to be sociable.

Toward evening the train drew up at a station where quite a party of farm laborers, fresh from their daily toil, swarmed out from the conspicuously labeled colored waiting-room, and into the car with Miller. They were a jolly, good-natured crowd, and, free from the embarrassing presence of white people, proceeded to enjoy themselves after their own fashion. Here an amorous fellow sat with his arm around a buxom girl's waist. A musically inclined individual – his talents did not go far beyond inclination – produced a mouth-organ and struck up a tune, to which a limber-legged boy danced in the aisle. They were noisy, loquacious, happy, dirty, and malodorous. For a while Miller was amused and pleased. They were his people, and he felt a certain expansive warmth toward them in spite of their obvious shortcomings. By and by, however, the air became too close, and he went out upon the platform. For the sake of the democratic ideal, which meant so much to his race, he might have endured the affliction. He could easily imagine that people of refinement, with the power in their hands, might be tempted to strain the democratic ideal in order to avoid such contact; but personally, and apart from the mere matter of racial sympathy, these people were just as offensive to him as to the whites in the other end of the train. Surely, if a classification of passengers on trains was at all desirable, it might be made upon some more logical and considerate basis than a mere arbitrary, tactless, and, by the very nature of things, brutal drawing of a color line. It was a veritable bed of Procrustes,[45] this standard which the whites had set for the negroes. Those who grew above it must have their heads cut off, figuratively speaking – must be forced back to the level assigned to their race; those who fell beneath the standard set had their necks stretched, literally enough, as the ghastly record in the daily papers gave conclusive evidence.

Miller breathed more freely when the lively crowd got off at the next station, after a short ride. Moreover, he had a light heart, a conscience void of offense, and was only thirty years old. His philosophy had become somewhat jaded on this journey, but he pulled it together for a final effort. Was it not, after all, a wise provision of nature that had given to a race, destined to a long servitude and a slow emergence therefrom, a cheerfulness of spirit which enabled them to catch pleasure on the wing, and endure with equanimity the ills that seemed inevitable? The ability to live and thrive under adverse circumstances is the surest guaranty of the future. The race which at the last shall inherit the earth – the residuary legatee of civilization – will be the race which

Notes

[45] *bed of Procrustes* referring to arbitrary and unfair standards (in Greek mythology, Procrustes would chop or stretch people's limbs to fit onto his metal bed; he was eventually defeated by Theseus).

remains longest upon it. The negro was here before the Anglo-Saxon was evolved, and his thick lips and heavy-lidded eyes looked out from the inscrutable face of the Sphinx across the sands of Egypt while yet the ancestors of those who now oppress him were living in caves, practicing human sacrifice, and painting themselves with woad – and the negro is here yet.

"'Blessed are the meek,'"[46] quoted Miller at the end of these consoling reflections, "'for they shall inherit the earth.' If this be true, the negro may yet come into his estate, for meekness seems to be set apart as his portion."

The journey came to an end just as the sun had sunk into the west.

Simultaneously with Miller's exit from the train, a great black figure crawled off the trucks of the rear car, on the side opposite the station platform. Stretching and shaking himself with a free gesture, the black man, seeing himself unobserved, moved somewhat stiffly round the end of the car to the station platform.

"'Fo de Lawd!" he muttered, "ef I hadn'[47] had a cha'm' life, I'd 'a' never got here on dat ticket, an' dat's a fac' – it sho' am! I kind er 'lowed I wuz gone a dozen times, ez it wuz. But I got my job ter do in dis worl', an' I knows I ain' gwine ter die 'tel I've complished it. I jes' want one mo' look at dat man, an' den I'll haf ter git somethin' ter eat; fer two raw turnips in twelve hours is slim pickin's fer a man er my size!"

Chapter 6

Janet

As the train drew up at the station platform, Dr. Price came forward from the white waiting-room, and stood expectantly by the door of the white coach. Miller, having left his car, came down the platform in time to intercept Burns as he left the train, and to introduce him to Dr. Price.

"My carriage is in waiting," said Dr. Price. "I should have liked to have you at my own house, but my wife is out of town. We have a good hotel, however, and you will doubtless find it more convenient."

"You are very kind, Dr. Price. Miller, won't you come up and dine with me?"

"Thank you, no," said Miller, "I am expected at home. My wife and child are waiting for me in the buggy yonder by the platform."

"Oh, very well; of course you must go; but don't forget our appointment. Let's see, Dr. Price, I can eat and get ready in half an hour – that will make it" –

"I have asked several of the local physicians to be present at eight o'clock," said Dr. Price. "The case can safely wait until then."

"Very well, Miller, be on hand at eight. I shall expect you without fail. Where shall he come, Dr. Price?"

"To the residence of Major Philip Carteret, on Vine Street."

"I have invited Dr. Miller to be present and assist in the operation," Dr. Burns continued, as they drove toward the hotel. "He was a favorite pupil of mine, and is a credit to the profession. I presume you saw his article in the Medical Gazette?"

Notes

[46] *"Blessed are the meek ... earth"* from Jesus's Sermon on the Mount (Matthew 5:5).

[47] *Original reads*: had n' [ed.].

"Yes, and I assisted him in the case," returned Dr. Price. "It was a colored lad, one of his patients, and he called me in to help him. He is a capable man, and very much liked by the white physicians."

Miller's wife and child were waiting for him in fluttering anticipation. He kissed them both as he climbed into the buggy.

"We came at four o'clock," said Mrs. Miller, a handsome young woman, who might be anywhere between twenty-five and thirty, and whose complexion, in the twilight, was not distinguishable from that of a white person, "but the train was late two hours, they said. We came back at six, and have been waiting ever since."

"Yes, papa," piped the child, a little boy of six or seven, who sat between them, "and I am very hungry."

Miller felt very much elated as he drove homeward through the twilight. By his side sat the two persons whom he loved best in all the world. His affairs were prosperous. Upon opening his office in the city, he had been received by the members of his own profession with a cordiality generally frank, and in no case much reserved. The colored population of the city was large, but in the main poor, and the white physicians were not unwilling to share this unprofitable practice with a colored doctor worthy of confidence. In the intervals of the work upon his hospital, he had built up a considerable practice among his own people; but except in the case of some poor unfortunate whose pride had been lost in poverty or sin, no white patient had ever called upon him for treatment. He knew very well the measure of his powers – a liberal education had given him opportunity to compare himself with other men – and was secretly conscious that in point of skill and knowledge he did not suffer by comparison with any other physician in the town. He liked to believe that the race antagonism which hampered his progress and that of his people was a mere temporary thing, the outcome of former conditions, and bound to disappear in time, and that when a colored man should demonstrate to the community in which he lived that he possessed character and power, that community would find a way in which to enlist his services for the public good.

He had already made himself useful, and had received many kind words and other marks of appreciation. He was now offered a further confirmation of his theory: having recognized his skill, the white people were now ready to take advantage of it. Any lurking doubt he may have felt when first invited by Dr. Burns to participate in the operation had been dispelled by Dr. Price's prompt acquiescence.

On the way homeward Miller told his wife of this appointment. She was greatly interested; she was herself a mother, with an only child. Moreover, there was a stronger impulse than mere humanity to draw her toward the stricken mother. Janet had a tender heart, and could have loved this white sister, her sole living relative of whom she knew. All her life long she had yearned for a kind word, a nod, a smile, the least thing that imagination might have twisted into a recognition of the tie between them. But it had never come.

And yet Janet was not angry. She was of a forgiving temper; she could never bear malice. She was educated, had read many books, and appreciated to the full the social forces arrayed against any such recognition as she had dreamed of. Of the two barriers between them a man might have forgiven the one; a woman would not be likely to overlook either the bar sinister or the difference of race, even to the slight extent of a silent recognition. Blood is thicker than water, but, if it flows[48] too far from conventional

Notes

[48] *Original reads*: if it flow [ed.].

channels, may turn to gall and wormwood. Nevertheless, when the heart speaks, reason falls into the background, and Janet would have worshiped this sister, even afar off, had she received even the slightest encouragement. So strong was this weakness that she had been angry with herself for her lack of pride, or even of a decent self-respect. It was, she sometimes thought, the heritage of her mother's race, and she was ashamed of it as part of the taint of slavery. She had never acknowledged, even to her husband, from whom she concealed nothing else, her secret thoughts upon this lifelong sorrow. This silent grief was nature's penalty, or society's revenge, for whatever heritage of beauty or intellect or personal charm had come to her with her father's blood. For she had received no other inheritance. Her sister was rich by right of her birth; if Janet had been fortunate, her good fortune had not been due to any provision made for her by her white father.

She knew quite well how passionately, for many years, her proud sister had longed and prayed in vain for the child which had at length brought joy into her household, and she could feel, by sympathy, all the sickening suspense with which the child's parents must await the result of this dangerous operation.

"O Will," she adjured her husband anxiously, when he had told her of the engagement, "you must be very careful. Think of the child's poor mother! Think of our own dear child, and what it would mean to lose him!"

Chapter 7

The Operation

Dr. Price was not entirely at ease in his mind as the two doctors drove rapidly from the hotel to Major Carteret's. Himself a liberal man, from his point of view, he saw no reason why a colored doctor might not operate upon a white male child – there are fine distinctions in the application of the color line – but several other physicians had been invited, some of whom were men of old-fashioned notions, who might not relish such an innovation.

This, however, was but a small difficulty compared with what might be feared from Major Carteret himself. For he knew Carteret's unrelenting hostility to anything that savored of recognition of the negro as the equal of white men. It was traditional in Wellington that no colored person had ever entered the front door of the Carteret residence, and that the luckless individual who once presented himself there upon alleged business and resented being ordered to the back door had been unceremoniously thrown over the piazza railing into a rather thorny clump of rosebushes below. If Miller were going as a servant, to hold a basin or a sponge, there would be no difficulty; but as a surgeon – well, he wouldn't borrow trouble. Under the circumstances the major might yield a point.

But as they neared the house the major's unyielding disposition loomed up formidably. Perhaps if the matter were properly presented to Dr. Burns, he might consent to withdraw the invitation. It was not yet too late to send Miller a note.

"By the way, Dr. Burns," he said, "I'm very friendly to Dr. Miller, and should personally like to have him with us to-night. But – I ought to have told you this before, but I couldn't[49] very well do so, on such short notice, in Miller's presence – we are a

Notes

[49] *Original reads*: could n't [ed.].

conservative people, and our local customs are not very flexible. We jog along in much the same old way our fathers did. I'm not at all sure that Major Carteret or the other gentlemen would consent to the presence of a negro doctor."

"I think you misjudge your own people," returned Dr. Burns, "they are broader than you think. We have our prejudices against the negro at the North, but we do not let them stand in the way of anything that we want. At any rate, it is too late now, and I will accept the responsibility. If the question is raised, I will attend to it. When I am performing an operation I must be *aut Caesar, aut nullus*."[50]

Dr. Price was not reassured, but he had done his duty and felt the reward of virtue. If there should be trouble, he would not be responsible. Moreover, there was a large fee at stake, and Dr. Burns was not likely to prove too obdurate.

They were soon at Carteret's, where they found assembled the several physicians invited by Dr. Price. These were successively introduced as Drs. Dudley, Hooper, and Ashe, all of whom were gentlemen of good standing, socially and in their profession, and considered it a high privilege to witness so delicate an operation at the hands of so eminent a member of their profession.

Major Carteret entered the room and was duly presented to the famous specialist. Carteret's anxious look lightened somewhat at sight of the array of talent present. It suggested, of course, the gravity of the impending event, but gave assurance of all the skill and care which science could afford.

Dr. Burns was shown to the nursery, from which he returned in five minutes.

"The case is ready," he announced. "Are the gentlemen all present?"

"I believe so," answered Dr. Price quickly.

Miller had not yet arrived. Perhaps, thought Dr. Price, a happy accident, or some imperative call, had detained him. This would be fortunate indeed. Dr. Burns's square jaw had a very determined look. It would be a pity if any acrimonious discussion should arise on the eve of a delicate operation. If the clock on the mantel would only move faster, the question might never come up.

"I don't see Dr. Miller," observed Dr. Burns, looking around the room. "I asked him to come at eight. There are ten minutes yet."

Major Carteret looked up with a sudden frown.

"May I ask to whom you refer?" he inquired, in an ominous tone.

The other gentlemen showed signs of interest, not to say emotion. Dr. Price smiled quizzically.

"Dr. Miller, of your city. He was one of my favorite pupils. He is also a graduate of the Vienna hospitals, and a surgeon of unusual skill. I have asked him to assist in the operation."

Every eye was turned toward Carteret, whose crimsoned face had set in a look of grim determination.

"The person to whom you refer is a negro, I believe?" he said.

"He is a colored man, certainly," returned Dr. Burns, "though one would never think of his color after knowing him well."

"I do not know, sir," returned Carteret, with an effort at self-control, "what the customs of Philadelphia or Vienna may be; but in the South we do not call negro doctors to attend white patients. I could not permit a negro to enter my house upon such an errand."

Notes

[50] *aut Caesar, aut nullus* (Latin) either Caesar or nobody.

"I am here, sir," replied Dr. Burns with spirit, "to perform a certain operation. Since I assume the responsibility, the case must be under my entire control. Otherwise I cannot operate."

"Gentlemen," interposed Dr. Price, smoothly, "I beg of you both – this is a matter for calm discussion, and any asperity is to be deplored. The life at stake here should not be imperiled by any consideration of minor importance."

"Your humanity does you credit, sir," retorted Dr. Burns. "But other matters, too, are important. I have invited this gentleman here. My professional honor is involved, and I merely invoke my rights to maintain it. It is a matter of principle, which ought not to give way to a mere prejudice."

"That also states the case for Major Carteret," rejoined Dr. Price, suavely. "He has certain principles – call them prejudices, if you like – certain inflexible rules of conduct by which he regulates his life. One of these, which he shares with us all in some degree, forbids the recognition of the negro as a social equal."

"I do not know what Miller's social value may be," replied Dr. Burns, stoutly, "or whether you gain or lose by your attitude toward him. I have invited him here in a strictly professional capacity, with which his color is not at all concerned."

"Dr. Burns does not quite appreciate Major Carteret's point of view," said Dr. Price. "This is not with him an unimportant matter, or a mere question of prejudice, or even of personal taste. It is a sacred principle, lying at the very root of our social order, involving the purity and prestige of our race. You Northern gentlemen do not quite appreciate our situation; if you lived here a year or two you would act as we do. Of course," he added, diplomatically, "if there were no alternative – if Dr. Burns were willing to put Dr. Miller's presence on the ground of imperative necessity" –

"I do nothing of the kind, sir," retorted Dr. Burns with some heat. "I have not come all the way from Philadelphia to undertake an operation which I cannot perform without the aid of some particular physician. I merely stand upon my professional rights."

Carteret was deeply agitated. The operation must not be deferred; his child's life might be endangered by delay. If the negro's presence were indispensable he would even submit to it, though in order to avoid so painful a necessity, he would rather humble himself to the Northern doctor. The latter course involved merely a personal sacrifice – the former a vital principle. Perhaps there was another way of escape. Miller's presence could not but be distasteful to Mrs. Carteret for other reasons. Miller's wife was the living evidence of a painful episode in Mrs. Carteret's family, which the doctor's presence would inevitably recall. Once before, Mrs. Carteret's life had been endangered by encountering, at a time of great nervous strain, this ill-born sister and her child. She was even now upon the verge of collapse at the prospect of her child's suffering, and should be protected from the intrusion of any idea which might add to her distress.

"Dr. Burns," he said, with the suave courtesy which was part of his inheritance, "I beg your pardon for my heat, and throw myself upon your magnanimity, as between white men" –

"I am a gentleman, sir, before I am a white man," interposed Dr. Burns, slightly mollified, however, by Carteret's change of manner.

"The terms should be synonymous," Carteret could not refrain from saying. "As between white men, and gentlemen, I say to you, frankly, that there are vital, personal reasons, apart from Dr. Miller's color, why his presence in this house would be distasteful. With this statement, sir, I throw myself upon your mercy. My child's life is worth more to me than any earthly thing, and I must be governed by your decision."

Dr. Burns was plainly wavering. The clock moved with provoking slowness. Miller would be there in five minutes.

"May I speak with you privately a moment, doctor?" asked Dr. Price.

They withdrew from the room and were engaged in conversation for a few moments. Dr. Burns finally yielded.

"I shall nevertheless feel humiliated when I meet Miller again," he said, "but of course if there is a personal question involved, that alters the situation. Had it been merely a matter of color, I should have maintained my position. As things stand, I wash my hands of the whole affair, so far as Miller is concerned, like Pontius Pilate[51] – yes, indeed, sir, I feel very much like that individual."

"I'll explain the matter to Miller," returned Dr. Price, amiably, "and make it all right with him. We Southern people understand the negroes better than you do, sir. Why should we not? They have been constantly under our interested observation for several hundred years. You feel this vastly more than Miller will. He knows the feeling of the white people, and is accustomed to it. He wishes to live and do business here, and is quite too shrewd to antagonize his neighbors or come where he is not wanted. He is in fact too much of a gentleman to do so."

"I shall leave the explanation to you entirely," rejoined Dr. Burns, as they reentered the other room.

Carteret led the way to the nursery, where the operation was to take place. Dr. Price lingered for a moment. Miller was not likely to be behind the hour, if he came at all, and it would be well to head him off before the operation began.

Scarcely had the rest left the room when the doorbell sounded, and a servant announced Dr. Miller.

Dr. Price stepped into the hall and met Miller face to face.

He had meant to state the situation to Miller frankly, but now that the moment had come he wavered. He was a fine physician, but he shrank from strenuous responsibilities. It had been easy to theorize about the negro; it was more difficult to look this man in the eyes – whom at this moment he felt to be as essentially a gentleman as himself – and tell him the humiliating truth.

As a physician his method was to ease pain – he would rather take the risk of losing a patient from the use of an anaesthetic than from the shock of an operation. He liked Miller, wished him well, and would not wittingly wound his feelings. He really thought him too much of a gentleman for the town, in view of the restrictions with which he must inevitably be hampered. There was something melancholy, to a cultivated mind, about a sensitive, educated man who happened to be off color. Such a person was a sort of social misfit, an odd quantity, educated out of his own class, with no possible hope of entrance into that above it. He felt quite sure that if he had been in Miller's place, he would never have settled in the South – he would have moved to Europe, or to the West Indies, or some Central or South American state where questions of color were not regarded as vitally important.

Dr. Price did not like to lie, even to a negro. To a man of his own caste, his word was his bond. If it were painful to lie, it would be humiliating to be found out. The principle of *noblesse oblige*[52] was also involved in the matter. His claim of superiority to the colored doctor rested fundamentally upon the fact that he was white and Miller was not; and yet this superiority, for which he could claim no credit, since he had not made himself, was the very breath of his nostrils – he would not have changed places with the other for wealth untold; and as a gentleman, he would not care to have another

Notes

[51] *Pontius Pilate* judge who absolved himself of any complicity in Jesus's crucifixion (Matthew 27:24).

[52] *noblesse oblige* the obligation of honorable behavior from those of high rank.

gentleman, even a colored man, catch him in a lie. Of this, however, there was scarcely any danger. A word to the other surgeons would insure their corroboration of whatever he might tell Miller. No one of them would willingly wound Dr. Miller or embarrass Dr. Price; indeed, they need not know that Miller had come in time for the operation.

"I'm sorry, Miller," he said with apparent regret, "but we were here ahead of time, and the case took a turn which would admit of no delay, so the gentlemen went in. Dr. Burns is with the patient now, and asked me to explain why we did not wait for you."

"I'm sorry too," returned Miller, regretfully, but nothing doubting. He was well aware that in such cases danger might attend upon delay. He had lost his chance, through no fault of his own or of anyone[53] else.

"I hope that all is well?" he said, hesitatingly, not sure whether he would be asked to remain.

"All is well, so far. Step round to my office in the morning, Miller, or come in when you're passing, and I'll tell you the details."

This was tantamount to a dismissal, so Miller took his leave. Descending the doorsteps, he stood for a moment, undecided whether to return home or to go to the hotel and await the return of Dr. Burns, when he heard his name called from the house in a low tone.

"Oh, doctuh!"

He stepped back toward the door, outside of which stood the colored servant who had just let him out.

"Dat's all a lie, doctuh," he whispered, "'bout de operation bein' already pe'fo'med. Dey-all had jes' gone in de minute befo' you come – Doctuh Price hadn'[54] even got out 'n de room. Dey be'n quollin' 'bout you fer de las' ha'f hour. Majah Ca'te'et say he wouldn'[55] have you, an' de No'then doctuh say he wouldn't[56] do nothin' widout you, an' Doctuh Price he j'ined in on bofe sides, an' dey had it hot an' heavy, nip an' tuck, till bimeby Majah Ca'te'et up an' say it wa'n't altogether yo' color he objected to, an' wid dat de No'then doctuh give in. He's a fine man, suh, but dey wuz too much fer 'im!"

"Thank you, Sam, I'm much obliged," returned Miller mechanically. "One likes to know the truth."

Truth, it has been said, is mighty, and must prevail; but it sometimes leaves a bad taste in the mouth. In the ordinary course of events Miller would not have anticipated such an invitation, and for that reason had appreciated it all the more. The rebuff came with a corresponding shock. He had the heart of a man, the sensibilities of a cultivated gentleman; the one was sore, the other deeply wounded. He was not altogether sure, upon reflection, whether he blamed Dr. Price very much for the amiable lie, which had been meant to spare his feelings, or thanked Sam a great deal for the unpalatable truth.

Janet met him at the door. "How is the baby?" she asked excitedly.

"Dr. Price says he is doing well."

"What is the matter, Will, and why are you back so soon?"

He would have spared her the story, but she was a woman, and would have it. He was wounded, too, and wanted sympathy, of which Janet was an exhaustless fountain. So he told her what had happened. She comforted him after the manner of a loving woman, and felt righteously indignant toward her sister's husband, who had thus been

Notes

[53] *Original reads*: any one [ed.].

[54] *Original reads*: had n' [ed.].

[55] *Original reads*: would n' [ed.].

[56] *Original reads*: would n't [ed.].

instrumental in the humiliation of her own. Her anger did not embrace her sister, and yet she felt obscurely that their unacknowledged relationship had been the malignant force which had given her husband pain, and defeated his honorable ambition.

When Dr. Price entered the nursery, Dr. Burns was leaning attentively over the operating table. The implements needed for the operation were all in readiness – the knives, the basin, the sponge, the materials for dressing the wound – all the ghastly paraphernalia of vivisection.

Mrs. Carteret had been banished to another room, where Clara vainly attempted to soothe her. Old Mammy Jane, still burdened by her fears, fervently prayed the good Lord to spare the life of the sweet little grandson of her dear old mistress.

Dr. Burns had placed his ear to the child's chest, which had been bared for the incision. Dr. Price stood ready to administer the anaesthetic. Little Dodie looked up with a faint expression of wonder, as if dimly conscious of some unusual event. The major shivered at the thought of what the child must undergo.

"There's a change in his breathing," said Dr. Burns, lifting his head. "The whistling noise is less pronounced, and he breathes easier. The obstruction seems to have shifted."

Applying his ear again to the child's throat, he listened for a moment intently, and then picking the baby up from the table, gave it a couple of sharp claps between the shoulders. Simultaneously a small object shot out from the child's mouth, struck Dr. Price in the neighborhood of his waistband, and then rattled lightly against the floor. Whereupon the baby, as though conscious of his narrow escape, smiled and gurgled, and reaching upward clutched the doctor's whiskers with his little hand, which, according to old Jane, had a stronger grip than any other infant's in Wellington.

Chapter 8

The Campaign Drags

THE campaign for white supremacy was dragging. Carteret had set out, in the columns of the Morning Chronicle, all the reasons why this movement, inaugurated by the three men who had met, six months before, at the office of the Chronicle, should be supported by the white public. Negro citizenship was a grotesque farce – Sambo and Dinah[57] raised from the kitchen to the cabinet were a spectacle to make the gods laugh. The laws by which it had been sought to put the negroes on a level with the whites must be swept away in theory, as they had failed in fact. If it were impossible, without a further education of public opinion, to secure the repeal of the fifteenth amendment,[58] it was at least the solemn duty of the state to endeavor, through its own constitution, to escape from the domination of a weak and incompetent electorate and confine the negro to that inferior condition for which nature had evidently designed him.

In spite of the force and intelligence with which Carteret had expressed these and similar views, they had not met the immediate response anticipated. There were thoughtful men, willing to let well enough alone, who saw no necessity for such a movement. They believed that peace, prosperity, and popular education offered a surer

Notes

[57] *Sambo and Dinah* stereotypical names for African Americans.

[58] *fifteenth amendment* passed in 1870, the Fifteenth Amendment granted all citizens the right to vote regardless of race.

remedy for social ills than the reopening of issues supposed to have been settled. There were timid men who shrank from civic strife. There were busy men, who had something else to do. There were a few fair men, prepared to admit, privately, that a class constituting half to two thirds of the population were fairly entitled to some representation in the law-making bodies. Perhaps there might have been found, somewhere in the state, a single white man ready to concede that all men were entitled to equal rights before the law.

That there were some white men who had learned little and forgotten nothing goes without saying, for knowledge and wisdom are not impartially distributed among even the most favored race. There were ignorant and vicious negroes, and they had a monopoly of neither ignorance nor crime, for there were prosperous negroes and poverty-stricken whites. Until Carteret and his committee began their baleful campaign the people of the state were living in peace and harmony. The anti-negro legislation in more southern states, with large negro majorities, had awakened scarcely an echo in this state, with a population two thirds white. Even the triumph of the Fusion party had not been regarded as a race issue. It remained for Carteret and his friends to discover, with inspiration from whatever supernatural source the discriminating reader may elect, that the darker race, docile by instinct, humble by training, patiently waiting upon its as yet uncertain destiny, was an incubus, a corpse chained to the body politic, and that the negro vote was a source of danger to the state, no matter how cast or by whom directed.

To discuss means for counteracting this apathy, a meeting of the "Big Three," as they had begun to designate themselves jocularly, was held at the office of the "Morning Chronicle," on the next day but one after little Dodie's fortunate escape from the knife.

"It seems," said General Belmont, opening the discussion, "as though we had undertaken more than we can carry through. It is clear that we must reckon on opposition, both at home and abroad. If we are to hope for success, we must extend the lines of our campaign. The North, as well as our own people, must be convinced that we have right upon our side. We are conscious of the purity of our motives, but we should avoid even the appearance of evil."

McBane was tapping the floor impatiently with his foot during this harangue.

"I don't see the use," he interrupted, "of so much beating about the bush. We may as well be honest about this thing. We are going to put the niggers down because we want to, and think we can; so why waste our time in mere pretense? I'm no hypocrite myself – if I want a thing I take it, provided I'm strong enough."

"My dear captain," resumed the general, with biting suavity, "your frankness does you credit – 'an honest man's the noblest work of God'[59] – but we cannot carry on politics in these degenerate times without a certain amount of diplomacy. In the good old days when your father was alive, and perhaps nowadays in the discipline of convicts, direct and simple methods might be safely resorted to; but this is a modern age, and in dealing with so fundamental a right as the suffrage we must profess a decent regard for the opinions of even that misguided portion of mankind which may not agree with us. This is the age of crowds, and we must have the crowd with us."

Notes

[59] *"an honest man … God"* quotation from Alexander Pope, English satirical poet (1688–1744).

The captain flushed at the allusion to his father's calling, at which he took more offense than at the mention of his own. He knew perfectly well that these old aristocrats, while reaping the profits of slavery, had despised the instruments by which they were attained – the poor-white overseer only less than the black slave. McBane was rich; he lived in Wellington, but he had never been invited to the home of either General Belmont or Major Carteret, nor asked to join the club of which they were members. His face, therefore, wore a distinct scowl, and his single eye glowed ominously. He would help these fellows carry the state for white supremacy, and then he would have his innings – he would have more to say than they dreamed, as to who should fill the offices under the new deal. Men of no better birth or breeding than he had represented Southern states in Congress since the war. Why should he not run for governor, representative, whatever he chose? He had money enough to buy out half a dozen of these broken-down aristocrats, and money was all-powerful.

"You see, captain," the general went on, looking McBane smilingly and unflinchingly in the eye, "we need white immigration – we need Northern capital. 'A good name is better than great riches,' and we must prove our cause a righteous one."

"We must be armed at all points," added Carteret, "and prepared for defense as well as for attack – we must make our campaign a national one."

"For instance," resumed the general, "you, Carteret, represent the Associated Press. Through your hands passes all the news of the state. What more powerful medium for the propagation of an idea? The man who would govern a nation by writing its songs was a blethering idiot beside the fellow who can edit its news dispatches. The negroes are playing into our hands – every crime that one of them commits is reported by us. With the latitude they have had in this state they are growing more impudent and self-assertive every day. A yellow demagogue in New York made a speech only a few days ago, in which he deliberately, and in cold blood, advised negroes to defend themselves to the death when attacked by white people! I remember well the time when it was death for a negro to strike a white man."

"It's death now, if he strikes the right one," interjected McBane, restored to better humor by this mention of a congenial subject.

The general smiled a fine smile. He had heard the story of how McBane had lost his other eye.

"The local negro paper is quite outspoken, too," continued the general, "if not impudent. We must keep track of that; it may furnish us some good campaign material."

"Yes," returned Carteret, "we must see to that. I threw a copy into the waste-basket this morning, without looking at it. Here it is now!"

Chapter 9

A White Man's "Nigger"

Carteret fished from the depths of the waste-basket and handed to the general an eighteen by twenty-four sheet, poorly printed on cheap paper, with a "patent" inside, a number of advertisements of proprietary medicines, quack doctors, and fortune-tellers, and two or three columns of editorial and local news. Candor compels the admission that it was not an impressive sheet in any respect, except when regarded as the first local effort of a struggling people to make public expression of their life and aspirations. From this point of view it did not speak at all badly for a class to whom, a generation before, newspapers, books, and learning had been forbidden fruit.

"It's an elegant specimen of journalism, isn't[60] it?" laughed the general, airily. "Listen to this 'ad':–

"'Kinky, curly hair made straight by one application of our specific. Our face bleach will turn the skin of a black or brown person four or five shades lighter, and of a mulatto perfectly white. When you get the color you wish, stop using the preparation.'

"Just look at those heads! – 'Before using' and 'After using.' We'd better hurry, or there'll be no negroes to disfranchise! If they don't stop till they get the color they desire, and the stuff works according to contract, they'll all be white. Ah! what have we here? This looks as though it might be serious."

Opening the sheet the general read aloud an editorial article, to which Carteret listened intently, his indignation increasing in strength from the first word to the last, while McBane's face grew darkly purple with anger.

The article was a frank and somewhat bold discussion of lynching and its causes. It denied that most lynchings were for the offense most generally charged as their justification, and declared that, even of those seemingly traced to this cause, many were not for crimes at all, but for voluntary acts which might naturally be expected to follow from the miscegenation laws by which it was sought, in all the Southern States, to destroy liberty of contract, and, for the purpose of maintaining a fanciful purity of race, to make crimes of marriages to which neither nature nor religion nor the laws of other states interposed any insurmountable barrier. Such an article in a Northern newspaper would have attracted no special attention, and might merely have furnished food to an occasional reader for serious thought upon a subject not exactly agreeable; but coming from a colored man, in a Southern city, it was an indictment of the laws and social system of the South that could not fail of creating a profound sensation.

"Infamous – infamous!" exclaimed Carteret, his voice trembling with emotion. "The paper should be suppressed immediately."

"The impudent nigger ought to be horsewhipped and run out of town," growled McBane.

"Gentlemen," said the general soothingly, after the first burst of indignation had subsided, "I believe we can find a more effective use for this article, which, by the way, will not bear too close analysis – there's some truth in it, at least there's an argument."

"That is not the point," interrupted Carteret.

"No," interjected McBane with an oath, "that ain't at all the point. Truth or not, no damn nigger has any right to say it."

"This article," said Carteret, "violates an unwritten law of the South. If we are to tolerate this race of weaklings among us, until they are eliminated by the stress of competition, it must be upon terms which we lay down. One of our conditions is violated by this article, in which our wisdom is assailed, and our women made the subject of offensive comment. We must make known our disapproval."

"I say lynch the nigger, break up the press, and burn down the newspaper office," McBane responded promptly.

"Gentlemen," interposed the general, "would you mind suspending the discussion for a moment, while I send Jerry across the street? I think I can then suggest a better plan."

Notes

[60] *Original reads*: is n't [ed.].

Carteret rang the bell for Jerry, who answered promptly. He had been expecting such a call ever since the gentlemen had gone in.

"Jerry," said the general, "step across to Brown's and tell him to send me three Calhoun cocktails. Wait for them – here's the money."

"Yas, suh," replied Jerry, taking the proffered coin.

"And make has'e, charcoal," added McBane, "for we're gettin' damn dry."

A momentary cloud of annoyance darkened Carteret's brow. McBane had always grated upon his aristocratic susceptibilities. The captain was an upstart, a product of the democratic idea operating upon the poor white man, the descendant of the indentured bondservant and the socially unfit. He had wealth and energy, however, and it was necessary to make use of him; but the example of such men was a strong incentive to Carteret in his campaign against the negro. It was distasteful enough to rub elbows with an illiterate and vulgar white man of no ancestry – the risk of similar contact with negroes was to be avoided at any cost. He could hardly expect McBane to be a gentleman, but when among men of that class he might at least try to imitate their manners. A gentleman did not order his own servants around offensively, to say nothing of another's.

The general had observed Carteret's annoyance, and remarked pleasantly while they waited for the servant's return:–

"Jerry, now, is a very good negro. He's not one of your new negroes, who think themselves as good as white men, and want to run the government. Jerry knows his place – he is respectful, humble, obedient, and content with the face and place assigned to him by nature."

"Yes, he's one of the best of 'em," sneered McBane. "He'll call any man 'master' for a quarter, or 'God' for half a dollar; for a dollar he'll grovel at your feet, and for a cast off coat you can buy an option on his immortal soul – if he has one! I've handled niggers for ten years, and I know 'em from the ground up. They're all alike – they're a scrub race, an affliction to the country, and the quicker we're rid of 'em all the better."

Carteret had nothing to say by way of dissent. McBane's sentiments, in their last analysis, were much the same as his, though he would have expressed them less brutally.

"The negro," observed the general, daintily flicking the ash from his cigar, "is all right in his place and very useful to the community. We lived on his labor for quite a long time, and lived very well. Nevertheless we are better off without slavery, for we can get more out of the free negro, and with less responsibility. I really do not see how we could get along without the negroes. If they were all like Jerry, we'd have no trouble with them."

Having procured the drinks, Jerry, the momentary subject of the race discussion which goes on eternally in the South, was making his way back across the street, somewhat disturbed in mind.

"O Lawd!" he groaned, "I never troubles trouble till trouble troubles me; but w'en I got dem drinks befo', Gin'l Belmont gimme half a dollar an' tol' me ter keep de change. Dis time he didn'[61] say nothin' 'bout de change. I s'pose he jes' fergot erbout it, but w'at is a po' nigger gwine ter do w'en he has ter conten' wid w'ite folks's fergitfulniss? I don' see no way but ter do some fergittin' myse'f. I'll jes' stan' outside de do' here till dey

Notes

[61] *Original reads*: did n' [ed.].

gits so wrop' up in deir talk dat dey won' 'member nothin' e'se, an' den at de right minute I'll han' de glasses 'roun, an' mos' lackly de gin'l'll fergit all 'bout de change."

While Jerry stood outside, the conversation within was plainly audible, and some inkling of its purport filtered through his mind.

"Now, gentlemen," the general was saying, "here's my plan. That editorial in the negro newspaper is good campaign matter, but we should reserve it until it will be most effective. Suppose we just stick it in a pigeon-hole, and let the editor – what's his name?"

"The nigger's name is Barber," replied McBane. "I'd like to have him under me for a month or two; he'd write no more editorials."

"Let Barber have all the rope he wants," resumed the general, "and he'll be sure to hang himself. In the mean time we will continue to work up public opinion – we can use this letter privately for that purpose – and when the state campaign opens we'll print the editorial, with suitable comment, scatter it broadcast throughout the state, fire the Southern heart, organize the white people on the color line, have a little demonstration with red shirts and shot-guns, scare the negroes into fits, win the state for white supremacy, and teach our colored fellow citizens that we are tired of negro domination and have put an end to it forever. The Afro-American Banner will doubtless die about the same time."

"And so will the editor!" exclaimed McBane ferociously; "I'll see to that. But I wonder where that nigger is with them cocktails? I'm so thirsty I could swallow blue blazes."

"Here's yo' drinks, gin'l," announced Jerry, entering with the glasses on a tray.

The gentlemen exchanged compliments and imbibed – McBane at a gulp, Carteret with more deliberation, leaving about half the contents of his glass.

The general drank slowly, with every sign of appreciation. "If the illustrious statesman," he observed, "whose name this mixture bears, had done nothing more than invent it, his fame would still deserve to go thundering down the endless ages."

"It ain't bad liquor," assented McBane, smacking his lips.

Jerry received the empty glasses on the tray and left the room. He had scarcely gained the hall when the general called him back.

"O Lawd!" groaned Jerry, "he's gwine ter ax me fer de change. Yas, suh, yas, suh; comin', gin'l, comin', suh!"

"You may keep the change, Jerry," said the general.

Jerry's face grew radiant at this announcement. "Yas, suh, gin'l; thank y', suh; much obleedzed, suh. I wuz jus' gwine ter fetch it in, suh, w'en I had put de tray down. Thank y', suh, truly, suh!"

Jerry backed and bowed himself out into the hall.

"Dat wuz a close shave," he muttered, as he swallowed the remaining contents of Major Carteret's glass. "I 'lowed dem twenty cents wuz gone dat time – an' whar I wuz gwine ter git de money ter take my gal ter de chu'ch festibal ter-night, de Lawd only knows! – 'less'n I borried it off'n Mr. Ellis, an' I owes him sixty cents a'ready. But I wonduh w'at dem w'ite folks in dere is up ter? Dere's one thing sho' – dey're gwine ter git after de niggers some way er 'nuther, an' w'en dey does, what is Jerry gwine ter be? Dat's de mos' impo'tantes' question. I'm gwine ter look at dat newspaper dey be'n talkin' 'bout, an' 'less'n my min' changes might'ly, I'm gwine ter keep my mouf shet an' stan' in wid de Angry-Saxon race – ez dey calls deyse'ves nowadays – an' keep on de right side er my bread an' meat. W'at nigger ever give me twenty cents in all my bawn days?"

"By the way, major," said the general, who lingered behind McBane as they were leaving, "is Miss Clara's marriage definitely settled upon?"

"Well, general, not exactly; but it's the understanding that they will marry when they are old enough."

"I was merely thinking," the general went on, "that if I were you I'd speak to Tom about cards and liquor. He gives more time to both than a young man can afford. I'm speaking in his interest and in Miss Clara's – we of the old families ought to stand together."

"Thank you, general, for the hint. I'll act upon it."

This political conference was fruitful in results. Acting upon the plans there laid out, McBane traveled extensively through the state, working up sentiment in favor of the new movement. He possessed a certain forceful eloquence; and white supremacy was so obviously the divine intention that he had merely to affirm the doctrine in order to secure adherents.

General Belmont, whose business required him to spend much of the winter in Washington and New York, lost no opportunity to get the ear of lawmakers, editors, and other leaders of national opinion, and to impress upon them, with persuasive eloquence, the impossibility of maintaining existing conditions, and the tremendous blunder which had been made in conferring the franchise upon the emancipated race.

Carteret conducted the press campaign, and held out to the Republicans of the North the glittering hope that, with the elimination of the negro vote, and a proper deference to Southern feeling, a strong white Republican party might be built up in the New South. How well the bait took is a matter of history – but the promised result is still in the future. The disfranchisement of the negro has merely changed the form of the same old problem. The negro had no vote before the rebellion, and few other rights, and yet the negro question was, for a century, the pivot of American politics. It plunged the nation into a bloody war, and it will trouble the American government and the American conscience until a sustained attempt is made to settle it upon principles of justice and equity.

The personal ambitions entertained by the leaders of this movement are but slightly involved in this story. McBane's aims have been touched upon elsewhere. The general would have accepted the nomination for governor of the state, with a vision of a senatorship in the future. Carteret hoped to vindicate the supremacy of his race, and make the state fit for his son to live in, and, incidentally, he would not refuse any office, worthy of his dignity, which a grateful people might thrust upon him.

So powerful a combination of bigot, self-seeking demagogue, and astute politician was fraught with grave menace to the peace of the state and the liberties of the people – by which is meant the whole people, and not any one class, sought to be built up at the expense of another.

Chapter 10

Delamere Plays A Trump

Carteret did not forget what General Belmont had said in regard to Tom. The major himself had been young, not so very long ago, and was inclined toward indulgence for the foibles of youth. A young gentleman should have a certain knowledge of life – but there were limits. Clara's future happiness must not be imperiled.

The opportunity to carry out this purpose was not long delayed. Old Mr. Delamere wished to sell some timber which had been cut at Belleview, and sent Tom down to the Chronicle office to leave an advertisement. The major saw him at the desk, invited him into his sanctum, and delivered him a mild lecture. The major was kind, and talked in a fatherly way about the danger of extremes, the beauty of moderation, and the value of discretion as a rule of conduct. He mentioned collaterally the unblemished honor of a fine old family, its contemplated alliance with his own, and dwelt upon the sweet simplicity of Clara's character. The major was a man of feeling and of tact, and could not have put the subject in a way less calculated to wound the *amour propre*[62] of a very young man.

Delamere had turned red with anger while the major was speaking. He was impulsive, and an effort was required to keep back the retort that sprang once or twice to his lips; but his conscience was not clear, and he could not afford hard words with Clara's guardian and his grandfather's friend. Clara was rich, and the most beautiful girl in town; they were engaged; he loved her as well as he could love anything of which he seemed sure; and he did not mean that anyone[63] else should have her. The major's mild censure disturbed slightly his sense of security; and while the major's manner did not indicate that he knew anything definite against him, it would be best to let well enough alone.

"Thank you, major," he said, with well-simulated frankness. "I realize that I may have been a little careless, more from thoughtlessness than anything else; but my heart is all right, sir, and I am glad that my conduct has been brought to your attention, for what you have said enables me to see it in a different light. I will be more careful of my company hereafter; for I love Clara, and mean to try to be worthy of her. Do you know whether she will be at home this evening?"

"I have heard nothing to the contrary," replied the major warmly. "Call her up by telephone and ask – or come up and see. You're always welcome, my boy."

Upon leaving the office, which was on the second floor, Tom met Ellis coming up the stairs. It had several times of late occurred to Tom that Ellis had a sneaking fondness for Clara. Panoplied[64] in his own engagement, Tom had heretofore rather enjoyed the idea of a hopeless rival. Ellis was such a solemn prig, and took life so seriously, that it was a pleasure to see him sit around sighing for the unattainable. That he should be giving pain to Ellis added a certain zest to his own enjoyment.

But this interview with the major had so disquieted him that upon meeting Ellis upon the stairs he was struck by a sudden suspicion. He knew that Major Carteret seldom went to the Clarendon Club, and that he must have got his information from someone[65] else. Ellis was a member of the club, and a frequent visitor. Who more likely than he to try to poison Clara's mind, or the minds of her friends, against her accepted lover? Tom did not think that the world was using him well of late; bad luck had pursued him, in cards and other things, and despite his assumption of humility, Carteret's lecture had left him in an ugly mood. He nodded curtly to Ellis without relaxing the scowl that disfigured his handsome features.

"That's the damned sneak who's been giving me away," he muttered. "I'll get even with him yet for this."

Delamere's suspicions with regard to Ellis's feelings were not, as we have seen, entirely without foundation. Indeed, he had underestimated the strength of this rivalry and its chances of success. Ellis had been watching Delamere for a year. There had been nothing surreptitious about it, but his interest in Clara had led him to note things about his favored rival which might have escaped the attention of others less concerned.

Notes

[62] *amour propre* (French) self-love.

[63] *Original reads*: any one [ed.].

[64] *Panoplied* securely equipped.

[65] *Original reads*: some one [ed.].

Ellis was an excellent judge of character, and had formed a very decided opinion of Tom Delamere. To Ellis, unbiased by ancestral traditions, biased perhaps by jealousy, Tom Delamere was a type of the degenerate aristocrat. If, as he had often heard, it took three or four generations to make a gentleman, and as many more to complete the curve and return to the base from which it started, Tom Delamere belonged somewhere on the downward slant, with large possibilities of further decline. Old Mr. Delamere, who might be taken as the apex of an ideal aristocratic development, had been distinguished, during his active life, as Ellis had learned, for courage and strength of will, courtliness of bearing, deference to his superiors, of whom there had been few, courtesy to his equals, kindness and consideration for those less highly favored, and above all, a scrupulous sense of honor; his grandson Tom was merely the shadow without the substance, the empty husk without the grain. Of grace he had plenty. In manners he could be perfect, when he so chose. Courage and strength he had none. Ellis had seen this fellow, who boasted of his descent from a line of cavaliers, turn pale with fright and spring from a buggy to which was harnessed a fractious horse, which a negro stable-boy drove fearlessly. A valiant carpet-knight, skilled in all parlor exercises, great at whist or euchre, a dream of a dancer, unexcelled in cakewalk[66] or "coon" impersonations, for which he was in large social demand, Ellis had seen him kick an inoffensive negro out of his path and treat a poor-white man with scant courtesy. He suspected Delamere of cheating at cards, and knew that others entertained the same suspicion. For while regular in his own habits – his poverty would not have permitted him any considerable extravagance – Ellis's position as a newspaper man kept him in touch with what was going on about town. He was a member, proposed by Carteret, of the Clarendon Club, where cards were indulged in within reasonable limits, and a certain set were known to bet dollars in terms of dimes.

Delamere was careless, too, about money matters. He had a habit of borrowing, right and left, small sums which might be conveniently forgotten by the borrower, and for which the lender would dislike to ask. Ellis had a strain of thrift, derived from a Scotch ancestry, and a tenacious memory for financial details. Indeed, he had never had so much money that he could lose track of it. He never saw Delamere without being distinctly conscious that Delamere owed him four dollars, which he had lent at a time when he could ill afford to spare it. It was a prerogative of aristocracy, Ellis reflected, to live upon others, and the last privilege which aristocracy in decay would willingly relinquish. Neither did the aristocratic memory seem able to retain the sordid details of a small pecuniary transaction.

No doubt the knowledge that Delamere was the favored lover of Miss Pemberton lent a touch of bitterness to Ellis's reflections upon his rival. Ellis had no grievance against the "aristocracy" of Wellington. The "best people" had received him cordially, though his father had not been of their caste; but Ellis hated a hypocrite, and despised a coward, and he felt sure that Delamere was both. Otherwise he would have struggled against his love for Clara Pemberton. His passion for her had grown with his appreciation of Delamere's unworthiness. As a friend of the family, he knew the nature and terms of the engagement, and that if the marriage took place at all, it would not be for at least a year. This was a long time – many things might happen in a year, especially to a man like Tom Delamere. If for any reason Delamere lost his chance, Ellis meant

Notes

[66] *cakewalk* lively dance competition (the winning couple would receive a large cake).

to be next in the field. He had not made love to Clara, but he had missed no opportunity of meeting her and making himself quietly and unobtrusively agreeable.

On the day after this encounter with Delamere on the stairs of the Chronicle office, Ellis, while walking down Vine Street, met old Mrs. Ochiltree. She was seated in her own buggy, which was of ancient build and pattern, driven by her colored coachman and man of all work.

"Mr. Ellis," she called in a shrill voice, having directed her coachman to draw up at the curb as she saw the young man approaching, "come here. I want to speak to you."

Ellis came up to the buggy and stood uncovered beside it.

"People are saying," said Mrs. Ochiltree, "that Tom Delamere is drinking hard, and has to be carried home intoxicated, two or three times a week, by old Mr. Delamere's man Sandy. Is there any truth in the story?"

"My dear Mrs. Ochiltree, I am not Tom Delamere's keeper. Sandy could tell you better than I."

"You are dodging my question, Mr. Ellis. Sandy wouldn't[67] tell me the truth, and I know that you wouldn't[68] lie – you don't look like a liar. They say Tom is gambling scandalously. What do you know about that?"

"You must excuse me, Mrs. Ochiltree. A great deal of what we hear is mere idle gossip, and the truth is often grossly exaggerated. I'm a member of the same club with Delamere, and gentlemen who belong to the same club are not in the habit of talking about one another. As long as a man retains his club membership, he's presumed to be a gentleman. I wouldn't say anything against Delamere if I could."

"You don't need to," replied the old lady, shaking her finger at him with a cunning smile. "You are a very open young man, Mr. Ellis, and I can read you like a book. You are much smarter than you look, but you can't fool me. Good-morning."

Mrs. Ochiltree drove immediately to her niece's, where she found Mrs. Carteret and Clara at home. Clara was very fond of the baby, and was holding him in her arms. He was a fine baby, and bade fair to realize the bright hopes built upon him.

"You hold a baby very naturally, Clara," chuckled the old lady. "I suppose you are in training. But you ought to talk to Tom. I have just learned from Mr. Ellis that Tom is carried home drunk two or three times a week, and that he is gambling in the most reckless manner imaginable."

Clara's eyes flashed indignantly. Ere she could speak, Mrs. Carteret exclaimed:–

"Why, Aunt Polly! did Mr. Ellis say that?"

"I got it from Dinah," she replied, "who heard it from her husband, who learned it from a waiter at the club. And" –

"Pshaw!" said Mrs. Carteret, "mere servants' gossip."

"No, it isn't, Olivia. I met Mr. Ellis on the street, and asked him point blank, and he didn't deny it. He's a member of the club, and ought to know."

"Well, Aunt Polly, it can't be true. Tom is here every other night, and how could he carry on so without showing the signs of it? and where would he get the money? You know he has only a moderate allowance."

"He may win it at cards – it's better to be born lucky than rich," returned Mrs. Ochiltree. "Then he has expectations, and can get credit. There's no doubt that Tom is going on shamefully."

Notes

[67] *Original reads*: would n't [ed.].

[68] *Original reads*: would n't [ed.].

Clara's indignation had not yet found vent in speech; Olivia had said all that was necessary, but she had been thinking rapidly. Even if all this had been true, why should Mr. Ellis have said it? Or, if he had not stated it directly, he had left the inference to be drawn. It seemed a most unfair and ungentlemanly thing. What motive could Ellis have for such an act?

She was not long in reaching a conclusion which was not flattering to Ellis. Mr. Ellis came often to the house, and she had enjoyed his society in a friendly way. That he had found her pleasant company had been very evident. She had never taken his attentions seriously, however, or regarded his visits as made especially to her, nor had the rest of the family treated them from that point of view. Her engagement to Tom Delamere, though not yet formally ratified, was so well understood by the world of Wellington that Mr. Ellis would scarcely have presumed to think of her as anything more than a friend.

This revelation of her aunt's, however, put a different face upon his conduct. Certain looks and sighs and enigmatical remarks of Ellis, to which she had paid but casual attention and attached no particular significance, now recurred to her memory with a new meaning. He had now evidently tried, in a roundabout way, to besmirch Tom's character and undermine him in her regard. While loving Tom, she had liked Ellis well enough, as a friend; but he had abused the privileges of friendship, and she would teach him a needed lesson.

Nevertheless, Mrs. Ochiltree's story had given Clara food for thought. She was uneasily conscious, after all, that there might be a grain of truth in what had been said, enough, at least, to justify her in warning Tom to be careful, lest his enemies should distort some amiable weakness into a serious crime.

She put this view of the case to Tom at their next meeting, assuring him, at the same time, of her unbounded faith and confidence. She did not mention Ellis's name, lest Tom, in righteous indignation, might do something rash, which he might thereafter regret. If any subtler or more obscure motive kept her silent as to Ellis, she was not aware of it; for Clara's views of life were still in the objective stage, and she had not yet fathomed the deepest recesses of her own consciousness.

Delamere had the cunning of weakness. He knew, too, better than anyone[69] else could know, how much truth there was in the rumors concerning him, and whether or not they could be verified too easily for him to make an indignant denial. After a little rapid reflection, he decided upon a different course.

"Clara," he said with a sigh, taking the hand which she generously yielded to soften any suggestion of reproach which he may have read into her solicitude, "you are my guardian angel. I do not know, of course, who has told you this pack of lies – for I can see that you have heard more than you have told me – but I think I could guess the man they came from. I am not perfect, Clara, though I have done nothing of which a gentleman should be ashamed. There is one sure way to stop the tongue of calumny.[70] My home life is not ideal – grandfather is an old, weak man, and the house needs the refining and softening influence of a lady's presence. I do not love club life; its ideals are not elevating. With you by my side, dearest, I should be preserved from every influence except the purest and the best. Don't you think, dearest, that the major might be induced to shorten our weary term of waiting?"

Notes

[69] *Original reads*: any one [ed.].

[70] *calumny* slander.

"Oh, Tom," she demurred blushingly, "I shall be young enough at eighteen; and you are barely twenty-one."

But Tom proved an eloquent pleader, and love a still more persuasive advocate. Clara spoke to the major the same evening, who looked grave at the suggestion, and said he would think about it. They were both very young; but where both parties were of good family, in good health and good circumstances, an early marriage might not be undesirable. Tom was perhaps a little unsettled, but blood would tell in the long run, and marriage always exercised a steadying influence.

The only return, therefore, which Ellis received for his well-meant effort to ward off Mrs. Ochiltree's embarrassing inquiries was that he did not see Clara upon his next visit, which was made one afternoon while he was on night duty at the office. In conversation with Mrs. Carteret he learned that Clara's marriage had been definitely agreed upon, and the date fixed – it was to take place in about six months. Meeting Miss Pemberton on the street the following day, he received the slightest of nods. When he called again at the house, after a week of misery, she treated him with a sarcastic coolness which chilled his heart.

"How have I offended you, Miss Clara?" he demanded desperately, when they were left alone for a moment.

"Offended me?" she replied, lifting her eyebrows with an air of puzzled surprise. "Why, Mr. Ellis! What could have put such a notion into your head? Oh dear, I think I hear Dodie – I know you'll excuse me, Mr. Ellis, won't you? Sister Olivia will be back in a moment; and we're expecting Aunt Polly this afternoon – if you'll stay awhile she'll be glad to talk to you! You can tell her all the interesting news about your friends!"

Chapter 11

The Baby and the Bird

When Ellis, after this rebuff, had disconsolately taken his leave, Clara, much elated at the righteous punishment she had inflicted upon the slanderer, ran upstairs to the nursery, and, snatching Dodie from Mammy Jane's arms, began dancing gayly with him round the room.

"Look a-hyuh, honey," said Mammy Jane, "you better be keerful wid dat chile, an' don' drap 'im on de flo'. You might let him fall on his head an' break his neck. My, my! but you two does make a pretty pictur'! You'll be wantin' ole Jane ter come an' nuss yo' child'en some er dese days," she chuckled unctuously.

Mammy Jane had been very much disturbed by the recent dangers through which little Dodie had passed; and his escape from strangulation, in the first place, and then from the knife had impressed her as little less than miraculous. She was not certain whether this result had been brought about by her manipulation of the buried charm, or by the prayers which had been offered for the child, but was inclined to believe that both had cooperated to avert the threatened calamity. The favorable outcome of this particular incident had not, however, altered the general situation. Prayers and charms, after all, were merely temporary things, which must be constantly renewed, and might be forgotten or overlooked; while the mole, on the contrary, neither faded nor went away. If its malign influence might for a time seem to disappear, it was merely lying dormant, like the germs of some deadly disease, awaiting its opportunity to strike at an unguarded spot.

Clara and the baby were laughing in great glee, when a mockingbird, perched on the topmost bough of a small tree opposite the nursery window, burst suddenly into song, with many a trill and quaver. Clara, with the child in her arms, sprang to the open window.

"Sister Olivia," she cried, turning her face toward Mrs. Carteret, who at that moment entered the room, "come and look at Dodie."

The baby was listening intently to the music, meanwhile gurgling with delight, and reaching his chubby hands toward the source of this pleasing sound. It seemed as though the mockingbird were aware of his appreciative audience, for he ran through the songs of a dozen different birds, selecting, with the discrimination of a connoisseur and entire confidence in his own powers, those which were most difficult and most alluring.

Mrs. Carteret approached the window, followed by Mammy Jane, who waddled over to join the admiring party. So absorbed were the three women in the baby and the bird that neither one of them observed a neat top buggy, drawn by a sleek sorrel pony, passing slowly along the street before the house. In the buggy was seated a lady, and beside her a little boy, dressed in a child's sailor suit and a straw hat. The lady, with a wistful expression, was looking toward the party grouped in the open window.

Mrs. Carteret, chancing to lower her eyes for an instant, caught the other woman's look directed toward her and her child. With a glance of cold aversion she turned away from the window.

Old Mammy Jane had observed this movement, and had divined the reason for it. She stood beside Clara, watching the retreating buggy.

"Uhhuh!" she said to herself, "it's huh sister Janet! She ma'ied a doctuh, an' all dat, an' she lives in a big house, an' she's be'n roun' de worl' an de Lawd knows where e'se: but Mis' 'Livy don' liko de sight er her, an' never will, ez long ez de sun rises an' sets. Dey ce't'nly does favor one anudder – anybody mought 'low dey wuz twins, ef dey didn'[71] know better. Well, well! Fo'ty yeahs ago who'd 'a' ever expected ter see a nigger gal ridin' in her own buggy? My, my! but I don' know – I don' know! It don' look right, an' it ain' gwine ter las'! – you can't make me b'lieve!"

Meantime Janet, stung by Mrs. Carteret's look – the nearest approach she had ever made to a recognition of her sister's existence – had turned away with hardening face. She had struck her pony sharply with the whip, much to the gentle creature's surprise, when the little boy, who was still looking back, caught his mother's sleeve and exclaimed excitedly:–

"Look, look mamma! The baby – the baby!" Janet turned instantly, and with a mother's instinct gave an involuntary cry of alarm.

At the moment when Mrs. Carteret had turned away from the window, and while Mammy Jane was watching Janet, Clara had taken a step forward, and was leaning against the window-sill. The baby, convulsed with delight, had given a spasmodic spring and slipped from Clara's arms. Instinctively the young woman gripped the long skirt as it slipped through her hands, and held it tenaciously, though too frightened for an instant to do more. Mammy Jane, ashen with sudden dread, uttered an inarticulate scream, but retained self-possession enough to reach down and draw up the child, which hung dangerously suspended, head downward, over the brick pavement below.

"Oh, Clara, Clara, how could you!" exclaimed Mrs. Carteret reproachfully; "you might have killed my child!"

Notes

[71] *Original reads*: did n' [ed.].

She had snatched the child from Jane's arms, and was holding him closely to her own breast. Struck by a sudden thought, she drew near the window and looked out. Twice within a few weeks her child had been in serious danger, and upon each occasion a member of the Miller family had been involved, for she had heard of Dr. Miller's presumption in trying to force himself where he must have known he would be unwelcome.

Janet was just turning her head away as the buggy moved slowly off. Olivia felt a violent wave of antipathy sweep over her toward this baseborn sister who had thus thrust herself beneath her eyes. If she had not cast her brazen glance toward the window, she herself would not have turned away and lost sight of her child. To this shameless intrusion, linked with Clara's carelessness, had been due the catastrophe, so narrowly averted, which might have darkened her own life forever. She took to her bed for several days, and for a long time was cold toward Clara, and did not permit her to touch the child.

Mammy Jane entertained a theory of her own about the accident, by which the blame was placed, in another way, exactly where Mrs. Carteret had laid it. Julia's daughter, Janet, had been looking intently toward the window just before little Dodie had sprung from Clara's arms. Might she not have cast the evil eye upon the baby, and sought thereby to draw him out of the window? One would not ordinarily expect so young a woman to possess such a power, but she might have acquired it, for this very purpose, from some more experienced person. By the same reasoning, the mocking-bird might have been a familiar[72] of the witch, and the two might have conspired to lure the infant to destruction. Whether this were so or not, the transaction at least wore a peculiar look. There was no use telling Mis' 'Livy about it, for she didn't[73] believe, or pretended not to believe, in witchcraft and conjuration. But one could not be too careful. The child was certainly born to be exposed to great dangers – the mole behind the left ear was an unfailing sign – and no precaution should be omitted to counteract its baleful influence.

While adjusting the baby's crib, a few days later, Mrs. Carteret found fastened under one of the slats a small bag of cotton cloth, about half an inch long and tied with a black thread, upon opening which she found a few small roots or fibres and a pinch of dried and crumpled herbs. It was a good-luck charm which Mammy Jane had placed there to ward off the threatened evil from the grandchild of her dear old mistress. Mrs. Carteret's first impulse was to throw the bag into the fire, but on second thoughts she let it remain. To remove it would give unnecessary pain to the old nurse. Of course these old negro superstitions were absurd – but if the charm did no good, it at least would do no harm.

Chapter 12

Another Southern Product

One morning shortly after the opening of the hospital, while Dr. Miller was making his early rounds, a new patient walked in with a smile on his face and a broken arm hanging limply by his side. Miller recognized in him a black giant by the name of Josh Green, who for many years had worked on the docks for Miller's father – and simultaneously identified him as the dust-begrimed negro who had stolen a ride to Wellington on the trucks of a passenger car.

Notes

[72] *familiar* a spirit who aids a witch.

[73] *Original reads*: did n't [ed.].

"Well, Josh," asked the doctor, as he examined the fracture, "how did you get this? Been fighting again?"

"No, suh, I don' s'pose you could ha'dly call it a fight. One er dem dagoes[74] off'n a Souf American boat gimme some er his jaw, an' I give 'im a back answer, an' here I is wid a broken arm. He got holt er a belayin'-pin befo' I could hit 'im."

"What became of the other man?" demanded Miller suspiciously. He perceived, from the indifference with which Josh bore the manipulation of the fractured limb, that such an accident need not have interfered seriously with the use of the remaining arm, and he knew that Josh had a reputation for absolute fearlessness.

"Lemme see," said Josh reflectively, "ef I kin 'member w'at *did* become er him! Oh, yes, I'member now! Dey tuck him ter de Marine Horspittle in de amberlance, 'cause his leg wuz broke, an' I reckon somethin' must 'a' accident'ly hit 'im in de jaw, fer he wuz scatt'rin' teeth all de way 'long de street. I didn'[75] wan' ter kill de man, fer he might have somebody dependin' on 'im, an' I knows how dat 'd be ter dem. But no man kin call me a damn' low-down nigger and keep on enjoyin' good health right along."

"It was considerate of you to spare his life," said Miller dryly, "but you'll hit the wrong man someday.[76] These are bad times for bad negroes. You'll get into a quarrel with a white man, and at the end of it there'll be a lynching, or a funeral. You'd better be peaceable and endure a little injustice, rather than run the risk of a sudden and violent death."

"I expec's ter die a vi'lent death in a quarrel wid a w'ite man," replied Josh, in a matter-of-fact tone, "an' fu'thermo', he's gwine ter die at the same time, er a little befo'. I be'n takin' my own time 'bout killin' 'im; I ain' be'n crowdin' de man, but I'll be ready after a w'ile, an' den he kin look out!"

"And I suppose you're merely keeping in practice on these other fellows who come your way. When I get your arm dressed, you'd better leave town till that fellow's boat sails; it may save you the expense of a trial and three months in the chain-gang. But this talk about killing a man is all nonsense. What has any man in this town done to you, that you should thirst for his blood?"

"No, suh, it ain' nonsense – it's straight, solem' fac'. I'm gwine ter kill dat man as sho' as I'm settin' in dis cheer; an' dey ain' nobody kin say I ain' got a right ter kill 'im. Does you 'member de Ku-Klux?"

"Yes, but I was a child at the time, and recollect very little about them. It is a page of history which most people are glad to forget."

"Yas, suh; I was a chile, too, but I wuz right in it, an' so I 'members mo' erbout it'n you does. My mammy an' daddy lived 'bout ten miles f'm here, up de river. One night a crowd er w'ite men come ter ou' house an' tuck my daddy out an' shot 'im ter death, an' skeered my mammy so she ain' be'n herse'f f'm dat day ter dis. I wa'n't mo' 'n ten years ole at de time, an' w'en my mammy seed de w'ite men comin', she tol' me ter run. I hid in de bushes an' seen de whole thing, an' it wuz branded on my mem'ry, suh, like a red-hot iron bran's de skin. De w'ite folks had masks on, but one of 'em fell off – he wuz de boss, he wuz de head man, an' tol' de res' w'at ter do – an' I seen his face. It wuz a easy face ter 'member; an' I swo den, 'way down deep in my hea't, little ez I wuz, dat someday[77] er 'nother I'd kill dat man. I ain't never had no doubt erbout it; it's jus' w'at I'm livin' fer, an' I know I ain' gwine ter die till I've done it. Some lives fer one thing an'

Notes

[74] *dagoes* derogatory term for Italians or Spaniards.

[75] *Original reads*: did n' [ed.].

[76] *Original reads*: some day [ed.].

[77] *Original reads*: some day [ed.].

some fer another, but dat's my job. I ain' be'n in no has'e, fer I'm not ole yit, an' dat man is in good health. I'd like ter see a little er de worl' befo' I takes chances on leavin' it sudden; an', mo'over, somebody's got ter take keer er de ole 'oman. But her time'll come some er dese days, an den *his* time'll be come – an' prob'ly mine. But I ain' keerin' 'bout myse'f: w'en I git thoo wid him, it won' make no diff'ence 'bout me."

Josh was evidently in dead earnest. Miller recalled, very vividly, the expression he had seen twice on his patient's face, during the journey to Wellington. He had often seen Josh's mother, old Aunt Milly – "Silly Milly," the children called her – wandering aimlessly about the street, muttering to herself incoherently. He had felt a certain childish awe at the sight of one of God's creatures who had lost the light of reason, and he had always vaguely understood that she was the victim of human cruelty, though he had dated it farther back into the past. This was his first knowledge of the real facts of the case.

He realized, too, for a moment, the continuity of life, how inseparably the present is woven with the past, how certainly the future will be but the outcome of the present. He had supposed this old wound healed. The negroes were not a vindictive people. If, swayed by passion or emotion, they sometimes gave way to gusts of rage, these were of brief duration. Absorbed in the contemplation of their doubtful present and their uncertain future, they gave little thought to the past – it was a dark story, which they would willingly forget. He knew the timeworn explanation that the Ku-Klux movement, in the main, was merely an ebullition of boyish spirits, begun to amuse young white men by playing upon the fears and superstitions of ignorant negroes. Here, however, was its tragic side – the old wound still bleeding, the fruit of one tragedy, the seed of another. He could not approve of Josh's application of the Mosaic law of revenge,[78] and yet the incident was not without significance. Here was a negro who could remember an injury, who could shape his life to a definite purpose, if not a high or holy one. When his race reached the point where they would resent a wrong, there was hope that they might soon attain the stage where they would try, and, if need be, die, to defend a right. This man, too, had a purpose in life, and was willing to die that he might accomplish it. Miller was willing to give up his life to a cause. Would he be equally willing, he asked himself, to die for it? Miller had no prophetic instinct to tell him how soon he would have the opportunity to answer his own question. But he could not encourage Josh to carry out this dark and revengeful purpose. Every worthy consideration required him to dissuade his patient from such a desperate course.

"You had better put away these murderous fancies, Josh," he said seriously. "The Bible says that we should 'forgive our enemies, bless them that curse us, and do good to them that despitefully use us.'"[79]

"Yas, suh, I've l'arnt all dat in Sunday-school, an' I've heared de preachers say it time an' time ag'in. But it 'pears ter me dat dis fergitfulniss an' fergivniss is mighty one-sided. De w'ite folks don' fergive nothin' de niggers does. Dey got up de Ku-Klux, dey said, on 'count er de kyarpit-baggers. Dey be'n talkin' 'bout de kyarpit-baggers ever sence, an' dey 'pears ter fergot all 'bout de Ku-Klux. But I ain' fergot. De niggers is be'n train' ter fergiveniss; an' fer fear dey might fergit how ter fergive, de w'ite folks gives 'em somethin' new ev'y now an' den, ter practice on. A w'ite man kin do w'at he wants ter a nigger, but de minute de nigger gits back at 'im, up goes de nigger, an' don' come down tell somebody cuts 'im down. If a nigger gits a' office, er de race 'pears ter be

Notes

[78] *Mosaic law of revenge* Exodus 21:23–25 (i.e., "an eye for an eye").

[79] *"forgive our enemies ... use us."* Matthew 5:44.

prosperin' too much, de w'ite folks up an' kills a few, so dat de res' kin keep on fergivin' an' bein' thankful dat dey're lef' alive. Don' talk ter me 'bout dese w'ite folks – I knows 'em, I does! Ef a nigger wants ter git down on his marrow-bones, an' eat dirt, an' call 'em 'marster,' *he's* a good nigger, dere's room fer *him*. But I ain' no w'ite folks' nigger, I ain'. I don' call no man 'marster.' I don' wan' nothin' but w'at I wo'k fer, but I wants all er dat. I never moles's no w'ite man, 'less 'n he moles's me fus'. But w'en de ole 'oman dies, doctuh, an' I gits a good chance at dat w'ite man – dere ain' no use talkin', suh! – dere's gwine ter be a mix-up, an' a fune'al, er two fune'als – er may be mo', ef anybody is keerliss enough to git in de way."

"Josh," said the doctor, laying a cool hand on the other's brow, "you're feverish, and don't know what you're talking about. I shouldn't[80] let my mind dwell on such things, and you must keep quiet until this arm is well, or you may never be able to hit anyone[81] with it again."

Miller determined that when Josh got better he would talk to him seriously and dissuade him from this dangerous design. He had not asked the name of Josh's enemy, but the look of murderous hate which the dust-begrimed tramp of the railway journey had cast at Captain George McBane rendered any such question superfluous. McBane was probably deserving of any evil fate which might befall him; but such a revenge would do no good, would right no wrong; while every such crime, committed by a colored man, would be imputed to the race, which was already staggering under a load of obloquy because, in the eyes of a prejudiced and undiscriminating public, it must answer as a whole for the offenses of each separate individual. To die in defense of the right was heroic. To kill another for revenge was pitifully human and weak: "Vengeance is mine, I will repay,"[82] saith the Lord.

Chapter 13

The Cakewalk

Old Mr. Delamere's servant, Sandy Campbell, was in deep trouble.

A party of Northern visitors had been staying for several days at the St. James Hotel. The gentlemen of the party were concerned in a projected cotton mill, while the ladies were much interested in the study of social conditions, and especially in the negro problem. As soon as their desire for information became known, they were taken courteously under the wing of prominent citizens and their wives, who gave them, at elaborate luncheons, the Southern white man's views of the negro, sighing sentimentally over the disappearance of the good old negro of before the war, and gravely deploring the degeneracy of his descendants. They enlarged upon the amount of money the Southern whites had spent for the education of the negro, and shook their heads over the inadequate results accruing from this unexampled generosity. It was sad, they said, to witness this spectacle of a dying race, unable to withstand the competition of a superior type. The severe reprisals taken by white people for certain crimes committed by negroes were of course not the acts of the best people, who deplored them; but still a certain charity should be extended towards those who in the intense and righteous anger of the moment should take the law into their own hands

Notes

[80] *Original reads*: should n't [ed.].

[81] *Original reads*: any one [ed.].

[82] *"Vengeance is mine … repay"* Romans 12:19.

and deal out rough but still substantial justice; for no negro was ever lynched without incontestable proof of his guilt. In order to be perfectly fair, and give their visitors an opportunity to see both sides of the question, they accompanied the Northern visitors to a colored church where they might hear a colored preacher, who had won a jocular popularity throughout the whole country by an oft-repeated sermon intended to demonstrate that the earth was flat like a pancake. This celebrated divine could always draw a white audience, except on the days when his no less distinguished white rival in the field of sensationalism preached his equally famous sermon to prove that hell was exactly one half mile, linear measure, from the city limits of Wellington. Whether accidentally or not, the Northern visitors had no opportunity to meet or talk alone with any colored person in the city except the servants at the hotel. When one of the party suggested a visit to the colored mission school, a Southern friend kindly volunteered to accompany them.

The visitors were naturally much impressed by what they learned from their courteous hosts, and felt inclined to sympathize with the Southern people, for the negro is not counted as a Southerner, except to fix the basis of congressional representation. There might of course be things to criticise here and there, certain customs for which they did not exactly see the necessity, and which seemed in conflict with the highest ideals of liberty but surely these courteous, soft-spoken ladies and gentlemen, entirely familiar with local conditions, who descanted so earnestly and at times pathetically upon the grave problems confronting them, must know more about it than people in the distant North, without their means of information. The negroes who waited on them at the hotel seemed happy enough, and the teachers whom they had met at the mission school had been well-dressed, well-mannered, and apparently content with their position in life. Surely a people who made no complaints could not be very much oppressed.

In order to give the visitors, ere they left Wellington, a pleasing impression of Southern customs, and particularly of the joyous, happy-go-lucky disposition of the Southern darky and his entire contentment with existing conditions, it was decided by the hotel management to treat them, on the last night of their visit, to a little diversion, in the shape of a genuine negro cakewalk.

On the afternoon of this same day Tom Delamere strolled into the hotel, and soon gravitated to the bar, where he was a frequent visitor. Young men of leisure spent much of their time around the hotel, and no small part of it in the bar. Delamere had been to the club, but had avoided the card-room. Time hanging heavy on his hands, he had sought the hotel in the hope that some form of distraction might present itself.

"Have you heard the latest, Mr. Delamere?" asked the bartender, as he mixed a cocktail for his customer.

"No, Billy; what is it?"

"There's to be a big cakewalk upstairs to-night. The No'the'n gentlemen an' ladies who are down here to see about the new cotton fact'ry want to study the nigger some more, and the boss has got up a cakewalk for 'em, 'mongst the waiters and chambermaids, with a little outside talent."

"Is it to be public?" asked Delamere.

"Oh, no, not generally, but friends of the house won't be barred out. The clerk'll fix it for you. Ransom, the head waiter, will be floor manager."

Delamere was struck with a brilliant idea. The more he considered it, the brighter it seemed. Another cocktail imparted additional brilliancy to the conception. He had been trying, after a feeble fashion, to keep his promise to Clara, and was really suffering from lack of excitement.

He left the bar-room, found the head waiter, held with him a short conversation, and left in his intelligent and itching palm a piece of money.

The cakewalk was a great success. The most brilliant performer was a late arrival, who made his appearance just as the performance was about to commence. The newcomer was dressed strikingly, the conspicuous features of his attire being a long blue coat with brass buttons and a pair of plaid trousers. He was older, too, than the other participants, which made his agility the more remarkable. His partner was a new chambermaid, who had just come to town, and whom the head waiter introduced to the newcomer upon his arrival. The cake was awarded to this couple by a unanimous vote. The man presented it to his partner with a grandiloquent flourish, and returned thanks in a speech which sent the Northern visitors into spasms of delight at the quaintness of the darky dialect and the darky wit. To cap the climax, the winner danced a buck dance[83] with a skill and agility that brought a shower of complimentary silver, which he gathered up and passed to the head waiter.

Ellis was off duty for the evening. Not having ventured to put in an appearance at Carteret's since his last rebuff, he found himself burdened with a superfluity of leisure, from which he essayed to find relief by dropping into the hotel office at about nine o'clock. He was invited up to see the cakewalk, which he rather enjoyed, for there was some graceful dancing and posturing. But the grotesque contortions of one participant had struck him as somewhat overdone, even for the comical type of negro. He recognized the fellow, after a few minutes' scrutiny, as the body-servant of old Mr. Delamere. The man's present occupation, or choice of diversion, seemed out of keeping with his employment as attendant upon an invalid old gentleman, and strangely inconsistent with the gravity and decorum which had been so noticeable when this agile cakewalker had served as butler at Major Carteret's table, upon the occasion of the christening dinner. There was a vague suggestion of unreality about this performance, too, which Ellis did not attempt to analyze, but which recurred vividly to his memory upon a subsequent occasion.

Ellis had never pretended to that intimate knowledge of negro thought and character by which some of his acquaintances claimed the ability to fathom every motive of a negro's conduct, and predict in advance what anyone[84] of the darker race would do under a given set of circumstances. He would not have believed that a white man could possess two so widely varying phases of character; but as to negroes, they were as yet a crude and undeveloped race, and it was not safe to make predictions concerning them. No one could tell at what moment the thin veneer of civilization might peel off and reveal the underlying savage.

The champion cakewalker, much to the surprise of his sable companions, who were about equally swayed by admiration and jealousy, disappeared immediately after the close of the performance. Anyone[85] watching him on his way home through the quiet streets to old Mr. Delamere's would have seen him now and then shaking with laughter. It had been excellent fun. Nevertheless, as he neared home, a certain aspect of the affair, hitherto unconsidered, occurred to him, and it was in a rather serious frame of mind that he cautiously entered the house and sought his own room.

The cakewalk had results which to Sandy were very serious. The following week he was summoned before the disciplinary committee of his church and charged with unchristian conduct, in the following particulars, to wit: dancing, and participating in

Notes

[83] *buck dance* clog dance or jig.

[84] *Original reads*: any one [ed.].

[85] *Original reads*: any one [ed.].

a sinful diversion called a cakewalk, which was calculated to bring the church into disrepute and make it the mockery of sinners.

Sandy protested his innocence vehemently, but in vain. The proof was overwhelming. He was positively identified by Sister 'Manda Patterson, the hotel cook, who had watched the whole performance from the hotel corridor for the sole, single, solitary, and only purpose, she averred, of seeing how far human wickedness could be carried by a professing Christian. The whole thing had been shocking and offensive to her, and only a stern sense of duty had sustained her in looking on, that she might be qualified to bear witness against the offender. She had recognized his face, his clothes, his voice, his walk – there could be no shadow of doubt that it was Brother Sandy. This testimony was confirmed by one of the deacons, whose son, a waiter at the hotel, had also seen Sandy at the cakewalk.

Sandy stoutly insisted that he was at home the whole evening; that he had not been near the hotel for three months; that he had never in his life taken part in a cakewalk, and that he did not know how to dance. It was replied that wickedness, like everything else, must have a beginning; that dancing was an art that could be acquired in secret, and came natural to some people. In the face of positive proof, Sandy's protestations were of no avail; he was found guilty, and suspended from church fellowship until he should have repented and made full confession.

Sturdily refusing to confess a fault of which he claimed to be innocent, Sandy remained in contumacy,[86] thereby falling somewhat into disrepute among the members of his church, the largest in the city. The effect of a bad reputation being subjective as well as objective, and poor human nature arguing that one may as well have the game as the name, Sandy insensibly glided into habits of which the church would not have approved, though he took care that they should not interfere with his duties to Mr. Delamere. The consolation thus afforded, however, followed as it was by remorse of conscience, did not compensate him for the loss of standing in the church, which to him was a social club as well as a religious temple. At times, in conversation with young Delamere, he would lament his hard fate.

Tom laughed until he cried at the comical idea which Sandy's plaint always brought up, of half-a-dozen negro preachers sitting in solemn judgment upon that cakewalk – it had certainly been a good cakewalk! – and sending poor Sandy to spiritual Coventry.[87]

"Cheer up, Sandy, cheer up!" he would say when Sandy seemed most depressed. "Go into my room and get yourself a good drink of liquor. The devil's church has a bigger congregation than theirs, and we have the consolation of knowing that when we die, we'll meet all our friends on the other side. Brace up, Sandy, and be a man, or, if you can't be a man, be as near a man as you can!"

Hoping to revive his drooping spirits, Sandy too often accepted the proffered remedy.

Chapter 14

The Maunderings of Old Mrs. Ochiltree

When Mrs. Carteret had fully recovered from the shock attendant upon the accident at the window, where little Dodie had so narrowly escaped death or serious injury, she ordered her carriage one afternoon and directed the coachman to drive her to Mrs. Ochiltree's.

Notes

[86] *contumacy* a state of disobedience.

[87] *sending poor Sandy to spiritual Coventry* To "send to Coventry" is to ostracize someone.

Mrs. Carteret had discharged her young nurse only the day before, and had sent for Mammy Jane, who was now recovered from her rheumatism, to stay until she could find another girl. The nurse had been ordered not to take the child to negroes' houses. Yesterday, in driving past the old homestead of her husband's family, now occupied by Dr. Miller and his family, Mrs. Carteret had seen her own baby's carriage standing in the yard.

When the nurse returned home, she was immediately discharged. She offered some sort of explanation, to the effect that her sister worked for Mrs. Miller, and that some family matter had rendered it necessary for her to see her sister. The explanation only aggravated the offense: if Mrs. Carteret could have overlooked the disobedience, she would by no means have retained in her employment a servant whose sister worked for the Miller woman.

Old Mrs. Ochiltree had within a few months begun to show signs of breaking up. She was over seventy years old, and had been of late, by various afflictions, confined to the house much of the time. More than once within the year, Mrs. Carteret had asked her aunt to come and live with her; but Mrs. Ochiltree, who would have regarded such a step as an acknowledgment of weakness, preferred her lonely independence. She resided in a small, old-fashioned house, standing back in the middle of a garden on a quiet street. Two old servants made up her modest household.

This refusal to live with her niece had been lightly borne, for Mrs. Ochiltree was a woman of strong individuality, whose comments upon her acquaintance, present or absent, were marked by a frankness at times no less than startling. This characteristic caused her to be more or less avoided. Mrs. Ochiltree was aware of this sentiment on the part of her acquaintance, and rather exulted in it. She hated fools. Only fools ran away from her, and that because they were afraid she would expose their folly. If most people were fools, it was no fault of hers, and she was not obliged to indulge them by pretending to believe that they knew anything. She had once owned considerable property, but was reticent about her affairs, and told no one how much she was worth, though it was supposed that she had considerable ready money, besides her house and some other real estate. Mrs. Carteret was her nearest living relative, though her grand-nephew Tom Delamere had been a great favorite with her. If she did not spare him her tongue-lashings, it was nevertheless expected in the family that she would leave him something handsome in her will.

Mrs. Ochiltree had shared in the general rejoicing upon the advent of the Carteret baby. She had been one of his godmothers, and had hinted at certain intentions held by her concerning him. During Mammy Jane's administration she had tried the old nurse's patience more or less by her dictatorial interference. Since her partial confinement to the house, she had gone, when her health and the weather would permit, to see the child, and at other times had insisted that it be sent to her in the charge of[88] the nurse at least every other day.

Mrs. Ochiltree's faculties had shared insensibly in the decline of her health. This weakness manifested itself by fits of absent-mindedness, in which she would seemingly lose connection with the present, and live over again, in imagination, the earlier years of her life. She had buried two husbands, had tried in vain to secure a third, and had never borne any children. Long ago she had petrified into a character which nothing under heaven could change, and which, if death is to take us as it finds us, and the

Notes

[88] *Original reads*: in charge of [ed.].

future life to keep us as it takes us, promised anything but eternal felicity to those with whom she might associate after this life. Tom Delamere had been heard to say, profanely, that if his Aunt Polly went to heaven, he would let his mansion in the skies on a long lease, at a low figure.

When the carriage drove up with Mrs. Carteret, her aunt was seated on the little front piazza, with her wrinkled hands folded in her lap, dozing the afternoon away in fitful slumber.

"Tie the horse, William," said Mrs. Carteret, "and then go in and wake Aunt Polly, and tell her I want her to come and drive with me."

Mrs. Ochiltree had not observed her niece's approach, nor did she look up when William drew near. Her eyes were closed, and she would let her head sink slowly forward, recovering it now and then with a spasmodic jerk.

"Colonel Ochiltree," she muttered, "was shot at the battle of Culpepper Court House,[89] and left me a widow for the second time. But I would not have married any man on earth after him."

"Mis' Ochiltree!" cried William, raising his voice, "oh, Mis' Ochiltree!"

"If I had found a man – a real man – I might have married again. I did not care for weaklings. I could have married John Delamere if I had wanted him. But pshaw! I could have wound him round" –

"Go round to the kitchen, William," interrupted Mrs. Carteret impatiently, "and tell Aunt Dinah to come and wake her up."

William returned in a few moments with a fat, comfortable looking black woman, who curtsied to Mrs. Carteret at the gate, and then going up to her mistress seized her by the shoulder and shook her vigorously.

"Wake up dere, Mis' Polly," she screamed, as harshly as her mellow voice would permit. "Mis' 'Livy wants you ter go drivin' wid 'er!"

"Dinah," exclaimed the old lady, sitting suddenly upright with a defiant assumption of wakefulness, "why do you take so long to come when I call? Bring me my bonnet and shawl. Don't you see my niece waiting for me at the gate?"

"Hyuh dey is, hyuh dey is!" returned Dinah, producing the bonnet and shawl, and assisting Mrs. Ochiltree to put them on.

Leaning on William's arm, the old lady went slowly down the walk, and was handed to the rear seat with Mrs. Carteret.

"How's the baby to-day, Olivia, and why didn't you bring him?"

"He has a cold to-day, and is a little hoarse," replied Mrs. Carteret, "so I thought it best not to bring him out. Drive out the Weldon road, William, and back by Pine Street."

The drive led past an eminence crowned by a handsome brick building of modern construction, evidently an institution of some kind, surrounded on three sides by a grove of venerable oaks.

"Hugh Poindexter," Mrs. Ochiltree exclaimed explosively, after a considerable silence, "has been building a new house, in place of the old family mansion burned during the war."

"It isn't Mr. Poindexter's house, Aunt Polly. That is the new colored hospital built by the colored doctor."

Notes

[89] *battle of Culpepper Court House* Civil War battle fought in 1863.

"The new colored hospital, indeed, and the colored doctor! Before the war the negroes were all healthy, and when they got sick we took care of them ourselves! Hugh Poindexter has sold the graves of his ancestors to a negro – I should have starved first!"

"He had his grandfather's grave opened, and there was nothing to remove, except a few bits of heart-pine from the coffin. All the rest had crumbled into dust."

"And he sold the dust to a negro! The world is upside down."

"He had the tombstone transferred to the white cemetery, Aunt Polly, and he has moved away."

"Esau sold his birthright for a mess of pottage.[90] When I die, if you outlive me, Olivia, which is not likely, I shall leave my house and land to this child! He is a Carteret – he would never sell them to a negro. I can't trust Tom Delamere, I'm afraid."

The carriage had skirted the hill, passing to the rear of the new building.

"Turn to the right, William," ordered Mrs. Carteret, addressing the coachman, "and come back past the other side of the hospital."

A turn to the right into another road soon brought them to the front of the building, which stood slightly back from the street, with no intervening fence or inclosure. A sorrel pony in a light buggy was fastened to a hitching-post near the entrance. As they drove past, a lady came out of the front door and descended the steps, holding by the hand a very pretty child about six years old.

"Who is that woman, Olivia?" asked Mrs. Ochiltree abruptly, with signs of agitation.

The lady coming down the steps darted at the approaching carriage a look which lingered involuntarily.

Mrs. Carteret, perceiving this glance, turned away coldly.

With a sudden hardening of her own features the other woman lifted the little boy into the buggy and drove sharply away in the direction opposite to that taken by Mrs. Carteret's carriage.

"Who is that woman, Olivia?" repeated Mrs. Ochiltree, with marked emotion.

"I have not the honor of her acquaintance," returned Mrs. Carteret sharply. "Drive faster, William."

"I want to know who that woman is," persisted Mrs. Ochiltree querulously. "William," she cried shrilly, poking the coachman in the back with the end of her cane, "who is that woman?"

"Dat's Mis' Miller, ma'am," returned the coachman, touching his hat; "Doctuh Miller's wife."

"What was her mother's name?"

"Her mother's name wuz Julia Brown. She's be'n dead dese twenty years er mo'. Why, you knowed Julia, Mis' Polly! – she used ter b'long ter yo' own father befo' de wah; an' after de wah she kep' house fer" –

"Look to your horses, William!" exclaimed Mrs. Carteret sharply.

"It's that hussy's child," said Mrs. Ochiltree, turning to her niece with great excitement. "When your father died, I turned the mother and the child out into the street. The mother died and went to – the place provided for such as she. If I hadn't been just in time, Olivia, they would have turned you out. I saved the property for you and your son! You can thank me for it all!"

Notes

90 *"Esau sold his birthright … pottage"* Genesis 25:29–34.

"Hush, Aunt Polly, for goodness' sake! William will hear you. Tell me about it when you get home."

Mrs. Ochiltree was silent, except for a few incoherent mumblings. What she might say, what distressing family secret she might repeat in William's hearing, should she take another talkative turn, was beyond conjecture.

Olivia looked anxiously around for something to distract her aunt's attention, and caught sight of a colored man, dressed in sober gray, who was coming toward the carriage.

"There's Mr. Delamere's Sandy!" exclaimed Mrs. Carteret, touching her aunt on the arm. "I wonder how his master is? Sandy, oh, Sandy!"

Sandy approached the carriage, lifting his hat with a slight exaggeration of Chesterfieldian[91] elegance. Sandy, no less than his master, was a survival of an interesting type. He had inherited the feudal deference for his superiors in position, joined to a certain self-respect which saved him from sycophancy. His manners had been formed upon those of old Mr. Delamere, and were not a bad imitation; for in the man, as in the master, they were the harmonious reflection of a mental state.

"How is Mr. Delamere, Sandy?" asked Mrs. Carteret, acknowledging Sandy's salutation with a nod and a smile.

"He ain't ez peart ez he has be'n, ma'am," replied Sandy, "but he's doin' tol'able well. De doctuh say he's good fer a dozen years yit, ef he'll jes' take good keer of hisse'f an' keep f'm gittin' excited; fer sence dat secon' stroke, excitement is dange'ous fer 'im."

"I'm sure you take the best care of him," returned Mrs. Carteret kindly.

"You can't do anything for him, Sandy," interposed old Mrs. Ochiltree, shaking her head slowly to emphasize her dissent. "All the doctors in creation couldn't keep him alive another year. I shall outlive him by twenty years, though we are not far from the same age."

"Lawd, ma'am!" exclaimed Sandy, lifting his hands in affected amazement – his study of gentle manners had been more than superficial – "whoever would 'a' s'picion' dat you an' Mars John wuz nigh de same age? I'd 'a' 'lowed you wuz ten years younger 'n him, easy, ef you wuz a day!"

"Give my compliments to the poor old gentleman," returned Mrs. Ochiltree, with a simper of senile vanity, though her back was weakening under the strain of the effort to sit erect that she might maintain this illusion of comparative youthfulness. "Bring him to see me someday[92] when he is able to walk."

"Yas'm, I will," rejoined Sandy. "He's gwine out ter Belleview nex' week, fer ter stay a mont' er so, but I'll fetch him 'roun' w'en he comes back. I'll tell 'im dat you ladies 'quired fer 'im."

Sandy made another deep bow, and held his hat in his hand until the carriage had moved away. He had not condescended to notice the coachman at all, who was one of the young negroes of the new generation; while Sandy regarded himself as belonging to the quality, and seldom stooped to notice those beneath him. It would not have been becoming in him, either, while conversing with white ladies, to have noticed a colored servant. Moreover, the coachman was a Baptist, while Sandy was a Methodist, though under a cloud, and considered a Methodist in poor standing as better than a Baptist of any degree of sanctity.

Notes

[91] *Chesterfieldian* named after the fourth Earl of Chesterfield (1694–1773), known for his etiquette.

[92] *Original reads*: some day [ed.].

"Lawd, Lawd!" chuckled Sandy, after the carriage had departed, "I never seed nothin' lack de way dat ole lady do keep up her temper! Wid one foot in de grave, an' de other hov'rin' on de edge, she talks 'bout my ole marster lack he wuz in his secon' chil'hood. But I'm jes' willin' ter bet dat he'll out-las' her! She ain't half de woman she wuz dat night I waited on de table at de christenin' pa'ty, w'en she 'lowed she wuzn'[93] feared er no man livin'."

Chapter 15

Mrs. Carteret Seeks an Explanation

As a stone dropped into a pool of water sets in motion a series of concentric circles which disturb the whole mass in varying degree, so Mrs. Ochiltree's enigmatical remark had started in her niece's mind a disturbing train of thought. Had her words, Mrs. Carteret asked herself, any serious meaning, or were they the mere empty babblings of a clouded intellect?

"William," she said to the coachman when they reached Mrs. Ochiltree's house, "you may tie the horse and help us out. I shall be here a little while."

William helped the ladies down, assisted Mrs. Ochiltree into the house, and then went round to the kitchen. Dinah was an excellent hand at potato-pone and other culinary delicacies dear to the Southern heart, and William was a welcome visitor in her domain.

"Now, Aunt Polly," said Mrs. Carteret resolutely, as soon as they were alone, "I want to know what you meant by what you said about my father and Julia, and this – this child of hers?"

The old woman smiled cunningly, but her expression soon changed to one more grave.

"Why do you want to know?" she asked suspiciously. "You've got the land, the houses, and the money. You've nothing to complain of. Enjoy yourself, and be thankful!"

"I'm thankful to God," returned Olivia, "for all his good gifts – and He has blessed me abundantly – but why should I be thankful to *you* for the property my father left me?"

"Why should you be thankful to me?" rejoined Mrs. Ochiltree with querulous indignation. "You'd better ask why *shouldn't*[94] you be thankful to me. What have I not done for you?"

"Yes, Aunt Polly, I know you've done a great deal. You reared me in your own house when I had been cast out of my father's; you have been a second mother to me, and I am very grateful – you can never say that I have not shown my gratitude. But if you have done anything else for me, I wish to know it. Why should I thank you for my inheritance?"

"Why should you thank me? Well, because I drove that woman and her brat away."

"But she had no right to stay, Aunt Polly, after father died. Of course she had no moral right before, but it was his house, and he could keep her there if he chose. But after his death she surely had no right."

Notes

[93] *Original reads*: wuz n' [ed.].

[94] *Original reads*: *should n't* [ed.].

"Perhaps not so surely as you think – if she had not been a negro. Had she been white, there might have been a difference. When I told her to go, she said" –

"What did she say, Aunt Polly," demanded Olivia eagerly.

It seemed for a moment as though Mrs. Ochiltree would speak no further: but her once strong will, now weakened by her bodily infirmities, yielded to the influence of her niece's imperious demand.

"I'll tell you the whole story," she said, "and then you'll know what I did for you and yours."

Mrs. Ochiltree's eyes assumed an introspective expression, and her story, as it advanced, became as keenly dramatic as though memory had thrown aside the veil of intervening years and carried her back directly to the events which she now described.

"Your father," she said, "while living with that woman, left home one morning the picture of health. Five minutes later he tottered into the house groaning with pain, stricken unto death by the hand of a just God, as a punishment for his sins."

Olivia gave a start of indignation, but restrained herself.

"I was at once informed of what had happened, for I had means of knowing all that took place in the household. Old Jane – she was younger then – had come with you to my house; but her daughter remained, and through her I learned all that went on.

"I hastened immediately to the house, entered without knocking, and approached Mr. Merkell's bedroom, which was on the lower floor and opened into the hall. The door was ajar, and as I stood there for a moment I heard your father's voice.

"'Listen, Julia,' he was saying. 'I shall not live until the doctor comes. But I wish you to know, *dear* Julia!' – he called her 'dear Julia!' – 'before I die, that I have kept my promise. You did me one great service, Julia – you saved me from Polly Ochiltree!' Yes, Olivia, that is what he said! 'You have served me faithfully and well, and I owe you a great deal, which I have tried to pay.'

"'Oh, Mr. Merkell, dear Mr. Merkell,' cried the hypocritical hussy, falling to her knees by his bedside, and shedding her crocodile tears, 'you owe me nothing. You have done more for me than I could ever repay. You will not die and leave me – no, no, it cannot be!'

"'Yes, I am going to die – I am dying now, Julia. But listen – compose yourself and listen, for this is a more important matter. Take the keys from under my pillow, open the desk in the next room, look in the second drawer on the right, and you will find an envelope containing three papers: one of them is yours, one is the paper I promised to make, and the third is a letter which I wrote last night. As soon as the breath has left my body, deliver the envelope to the address indorsed upon it. Do not delay one moment, or you may live to regret it. Say nothing until you have delivered the package, and then be guided by the advice which you receive – it will come from a friend of mine who will not see you wronged.'

"I slipped away from the door without making my presence known and entered, by a door from the hall, the room adjoining the one where Mr. Merkell lay. A moment later there was a loud scream. Returning quickly to the hall, I entered Mr. Merkell's room as though just arrived.

"'How is Mr. Merkell?' I demanded, as I crossed the threshold.

"'He is dead,' sobbed the woman, without lifting her head – she had fallen on her knees by the bedside. She had good cause to weep, for my time had come.

"'Get up,' I said. 'You have no right here. You pollute Mr. Merkell's dead body by your touch. Leave the house immediately – your day is over!'

"'I will not!' she cried, rising to her feet and facing me with brazen-faced impudence. 'I have a right to stay – he has given me the right!'

"'Ha, ha!' I laughed. 'Mr. Merkell is dead, and I am mistress here henceforth. Go, and go at once – do you hear?'

"'I hear, but I shall not heed. I can prove my rights! I shall not leave!'

"'Very well,' I replied, 'we shall see. The law will decide.'

"I left the room, but did not leave the house. On the contrary, I concealed myself where I could see what took place in the room adjoining the death-chamber.

"She entered the room a moment later, with her child on one arm and the keys in the other hand. Placing the child on the floor, she put the key in the lock, and seemed surprised to find the desk already unfastened. She opened the desk, picked up a roll of money and a ladies' watch, which first caught her eye, and was reaching toward the drawer upon the right, when I interrupted her:–

"'Well, thief, are you trying to strip the house before you leave it?'

"She gave an involuntary cry, clasped one hand to her bosom and with the other caught up her child, and stood like a wild beast at bay.

"'I am not a thief,' she panted. 'The things are mine!'

"'You lie,' I replied. 'You have no right to them – no more right than you have to remain in this house!'

"'I have a right,' she persisted, 'and I can prove it!'

"She turned toward the desk, seized the drawer, and drew it open. Never shall I forget her look – never shall I forget that moment; it was the happiest of my life. The drawer was empty!

"Pale as death she turned and faced me.

"'The papers!' she shrieked, 'the papers! *You* have stolen them!'

"'Papers?' I laughed, 'what papers? Do you take me for a thief, like yourself?'

"'There were papers here,' she cried, 'only a minute since. They are mine – give them back to me!'

"'Listen, woman,' I said sternly, 'you are lying – or dreaming. My brother-in-law's papers are doubtless in his safe at his office, where they ought to be. As for the rest – you are a thief.'

"'I am not,' she screamed; 'I am his wife. He married me, and the papers that were in the desk will prove it.'

"'Listen,' I exclaimed, when she had finished – 'listen carefully, and take heed to what I say. You are a liar. You have no proofs – there never were any proofs of what you say, because it never happened – it is absurd upon the face of it. Not one person in Wellington would believe it. Why should he marry you? He did not need to! You are merely lying – you are not even self-deceived. If he had really married you, you would have made it known long ago. That you did not is proof that your story is false.'

"She was hit so hard that she trembled and sank into a chair. But I had no mercy – she had saved your father from *me* – 'dear Julia,' indeed!

"'Stand up,' I ordered. 'Do not dare to sit down in my presence. I have you on the hip, my lady, and will teach you your place.'

"She struggled to her feet, and stood supporting herself with one hand on the chair. I could have killed her, Olivia! She had been my father's slave; if it had been before the war, I would have had her whipped to death.

"'You are a thief,' I said, 'and of that there *are* proofs. I have caught you in the act. The watch in your bosom is my own, the money belongs to Mr. Merkell's estate, which belongs to my niece, his daughter Olivia. I saw you steal them. My word is worth yours a hundred times over, for I am a lady, and you are – what? And now hear me: if ever you breathe to a living soul one word of this preposterous story, I will charge you with the theft, and have you sent to the penitentiary. Your child will be taken from you, and you shall never see it again. I will give you now just ten minutes to take your brat and your rags out of this house forever. But before you go, put down your plunder there upon the desk!'

"She laid down the money and the watch, and a few minutes later left the house with the child in her arms.

"And now, Olivia, you know how I saved your estate, and why you should be grateful to me."

Olivia had listened to her aunt's story with intense interest. Having perceived the old woman's mood, and fearful lest any interruption might break the flow of her narrative, she had with an effort kept back the one question which had been hovering upon her lips, but which could now no longer be withheld.

"What became of the papers, Aunt Polly?"

"Ha, ha!" chuckled Mrs. Ochiltree with a cunning look, "did I not tell you that she found no papers?"

A change had come over Mrs. Ochiltree's face, marking the reaction from her burst of energy. Her eyes were half closed, and she was muttering incoherently. Olivia made some slight effort to arouse her, but in vain, and realizing the futility of any further attempt to extract information from her aunt at this time, she called William and drove homeward.

Chapter 16

Ellis Takes a Trick

LATE one afternoon a handsome trap,[95] drawn by two spirited bays, drove up to Carteret's gate. Three places were taken by Mrs. Carteret, Clara, and the major, leaving the fourth seat vacant.

"I've asked Ellis to drive out with us," said the major, as he took the lines from the colored man who had the trap in charge. "We'll go by the office and pick him up."

Clara frowned, but perceiving Mrs. Carteret's eye fixed upon her, restrained any further expression of annoyance.

The major's liking for Ellis had increased within the year. The young man was not only a good journalist, but possessed sufficient cleverness and tact to make him excellent company. The major was fond of argument, but extremely tenacious of his own opinions. Ellis handled the foils of discussion with just the requisite skill to draw out the major, permitting himself to be vanquished, not too easily, but, as it were, inevitably, by the major's incontrovertible arguments.

Olivia had long suspected Ellis of feeling a more than friendly interest in Clara. Herself partial to Tom, she had more than once thought it hardly fair to Delamere, or even to Clara, who was young and impressionable, to have another young man constantly about the house. True, there had seemed to be no great danger, for Ellis had neither the family nor the means to make him a suitable match for the major's sister; nor had Clara made any secret of her dislike for Ellis, or of her resentment for his supposed depreciation of Delamere. Mrs. Carteret was inclined to a more just and reasonable view of Ellis's conduct in this matter, but nevertheless did not deem it wise to undeceive Clara. Dislike was a stout barrier, which remorse might have broken down. The major, absorbed in schemes of empire and dreams of his child's future, had not become cognizant of the affair. His wife, out of friendship for Tom, had refrained from mentioning it; while the major, with a delicate regard for Clara's feelings, had said nothing at home in regard to his interview with her lover.

Notes

[95] *trap* two-wheeled horse-drawn carriage.

At the Chronicle office Ellis took the front seat beside the major. After leaving the city pavements, they bowled along merrily over an excellent toll-road, built of oyster shells from the neighboring sound, stopping at intervals to pay toll to the gate-keepers, most of whom were white women with tallow complexions and snuff-stained lips – the traditional "poor-white." For part of the way the road was bordered with a growth of scrub oak and pine, interspersed with stretches of cleared land, white with the opening cotton or yellow with ripening corn. To the right, along the distant river-bank, were visible here and there groups of turpentine pines, though most of this growth had for some years been exhausted. Twenty years before, Wellington had been the world's greatest shipping port for naval stores. But as the turpentine industry had moved southward, leaving a trail of devastated forests in its rear, the city had fallen to a poor fifth or sixth place in this trade, relying now almost entirely upon cotton for its export business.

Occasionally our party passed a person, or a group of persons – mostly negroes approximating the pure type, for those of lighter color grew noticeably scarcer as the town was left behind. Now and then one of these would salute the party respectfully, while others glanced at them indifferently or turned away. There would have seemed, to a stranger, a lack of spontaneous friendliness between the people of these two races, as though each felt that it had no part or lot in the other's life. At one point the carriage drew near a party of colored folks who were laughing and jesting among themselves with great glee. Paying no attention to the white people, they continued to laugh and shout boisterously as the carriage swept by.

Major Carteret's countenance wore an angry look.

"The negroes around this town are becoming absolutely insufferable," he averred. "They are sadly in need of a lesson in manners."

Half an hour later they neared another group, who were also making merry. As the carriage approached, they became mute and silent as the grave until the major's party had passed.

"The negroes are a sullen race," remarked the major thoughtfully. "They will learn their lesson in a rude school, and perhaps much sooner than they dream. By the way," he added, turning to the ladies, "what was the arrangement with Tom? Was he to come out this evening?"

"He came out early in the afternoon," replied Clara, "to go a-fishing. He is to join us at the hotel."

After an hour's drive they reached the hotel, in front of which stretched the beach, white and inviting, along the shallow sound. Mrs. Carteret and Clara found seats on the veranda. Having turned the trap over to a hostler, the major joined a group of gentlemen, among whom was General Belmont, and was soon deep in the discussion of the standing problem of how best to keep the negroes down.

Ellis remained by the ladies. Clara seemed restless and ill at ease. Half an hour elapsed and Delamere had not appeared.

"I wonder where Tom is," said Mrs. Carteret.

"I guess he hasn't[96] come in yet from fishing," said Clara. "I wish he would come. It's lonesome here. Mr. Ellis, would you mind looking about the hotel and seeing if there's anyone[97] here that we know?"

Notes

[96] *Original reads*: has n't [ed.].

[97] *Original reads*: any one [ed.].

For Ellis the party was already one too large. He had accepted this invitation eagerly, hoping to make friends with Clara during the evening. He had never been able to learn definitely the reason of her coldness, but had dated it from his meeting with old Mrs. Ochiltree, with which he felt it was obscurely connected. He had noticed Delamere's scowling look, too, at their last meeting. Clara's injustice, whatever its cause, he felt keenly. To Delamere's scowl he had paid little attention – he despised Tom so much that, but for his engagement to Clara, he would have held his opinions in utter contempt.

He had even wished that Clara might make some charge against him – he would have preferred that to her attitude of studied indifference, the only redeeming feature about which was that it *was* studied, showing that she, at least, had him in mind. The next best thing, he reasoned, to having a woman love you, is to have her dislike you violently – the main point is that you should be kept in mind, and made the subject of strong emotions. He thought of the story of Hall Caine's,[98] where the woman, after years of persecution at the hands of an unwelcome suitor, is on the point of yielding, out of sheer irresistible admiration for the man's strength and persistency, when the lover, unaware of his victory and despairing of success, seizes her in his arms and, springing into the sea, finds a watery grave for both. The analogy of this case with his own was, of course, not strong. He did not anticipate any tragedy in their relations; but he was glad to be thought of upon almost any terms. He would not have done a mean thing to make her think of him; but if she did so because of a misconception, which he was given no opportunity to clear up, while at the same time his conscience absolved him from evil and gave him the compensating glow of martyrdom, it was at least better than nothing.

He would, of course, have preferred to be upon a different footing. It had been a pleasure to have her speak to him during the drive – they had exchanged a few trivial remarks in the general conversation. It was a greater pleasure to have her ask a favor of him – a pleasure which, in this instance, was partly offset when he interpreted her request to mean that he was to look for Tom Delamere. He accepted the situation gracefully, however, and left the ladies alone.

Knowing Delamere's habits, he first went directly to the bar-room – the atmosphere would be congenial, even if he were not drinking. Delamere was not there. Stepping next into the office, he asked the clerk if young Mr. Delamere had been at the hotel.

"Yes, sir," returned the man at the desk, "he was here at luncheon, and then went out fishing in a boat with several other gentlemen. I think they came back about three o'clock. I'll find out for you."

He rang the bell, to which a colored boy responded.

"Front," said the clerk, "see if young Mr. Delamere's upstairs. Look in 255 or 256, and let me know at once."

The bell-boy returned in a moment.

"Yas, suh," he reported, with a suppressed grin, "he's in 256, suh. De do' was open, an' I seed 'im from de hall, suh."

"I wish you'd go up and tell him," said Ellis, "that – What are you grinning about?" he asked suddenly, noticing the waiter's expression.

"Nothin', suh, nothin' at all, suh," responded the negro, lapsing into the stolidity of a wooden Indian. "What shall I tell Mr. Delamere, suh?"

Notes

[98] Hall Caine (1853–1931), popular British novelist.

"Tell him," resumed Ellis, still watching the boy suspiciously – "no, I'll tell him myself."

He ascended the broad stair to the second floor. There was an upper balcony and a parlor, with a piano for the musically inclined. To reach these one had to pass along the hall upon which the room mentioned by the bell-boy opened. Ellis was quite familiar with the hotel. He could imagine circumstances under which he would not care to speak to Delamere; he would merely pass through the hall and glance into the room casually, as anyone[99] else might do, and see what the darky downstairs might have meant by his impudence.

It required but a moment to reach the room. The door was not wide open, but far enough ajar for him to see what was going on within.

Two young men, members of the fast set at the Clarendon Club, were playing cards at a small table, near which stood another, decorated with an array of empty bottles and glasses. Sprawling on a lounge, with flushed face and disheveled hair, his collar unfastened, his vest buttoned awry, lay Tom Delamere, breathing stertorously, in what seemed a drunken sleep. Lest there should be any doubt of the cause of his condition, the fingers of his right hand had remained clasped mechanically around the neck of a bottle which lay across his bosom.

Ellis turned away in disgust, and went slowly back to the ladies.

"There seems to be no one here yet," he reported. "We came a little early for the evening crowd. The clerk says Tom Delamere was here to luncheon, but he hasn't seen him for several hours."

"He's not a very gallant cavalier," said Mrs. Carteret severely. "He ought to have been waiting for us."

Clara was clearly disappointed, and made no effort to conceal her displeasure, leaving Ellis in doubt as to whether or not he were its object. Perhaps she suspected him of not having made a very thorough search. Her next remark might have borne such a construction.

"Sister Olivia," she said pettishly, "let's go up to the parlor. I can play the piano anyway, if there's no one to talk to."

"I find it very comfortable here, Clara," replied her sister placidly. "Mr. Ellis will go with you. You'll probably find someone[100] in the parlor, or they'll come when you begin to play."

Clara's expression was not cordial, but she rose as if to go. Ellis was in a quandary. If she went through the hall, the chances were at least even that she would see Delamere. He did not care a rap for Delamere – if he chose to make a public exhibition of himself, it was his own affair; but to see him would surely spoil Miss Pemberton's evening, and, in her frame of mind, might lead to the suspicion that Ellis had prearranged the exposure. Even if she should not harbor this unjust thought, she would not love the witness of her discomfiture. We had rather not meet the persons who have seen, even though they never mention, the skeletons in our closets. Delamere had disposed of himself for the evening. Ellis would have a fairer field with Delamere out of sight and unaccounted for, than with Delamere in evidence in his present condition.

"Wouldn't you rather take a stroll on the beach, Miss Clara?" he asked, in the hope of creating a diversion.

Notes

[99] *Original reads*: any one [ed.].

[100] *Original reads*: some one [ed.].

"No, I'm going to the parlor. *You* needn't[101] come, Mr. Ellis, if you'd rather go down to the beach. I can quite as well go alone."

"I'd rather go with you," he said meekly.

They were moving toward the door opening into the hall, from which the broad staircase ascended. Ellis, whose thoughts did not always respond quickly to a sudden emergency, was puzzling his brain as to how he should save her from any risk of seeing Delamere. Through the side door leading from the hall into the office, he saw the bell-boy to whom he had spoken seated on the bench provided for the servants.

"Won't you wait for me just a moment, Miss Clara, while I step into the office? I'll be with you in an instant."

Clara hesitated.

"Oh, certainly," she replied nonchalantly.

Ellis went direct to the bell-boy. "Sit right where you are," he said, "and don't move a hair. What is the lady in the hall doing?"

"She's got her back tu'ned this way, suh. I 'spec' she's lookin' at the picture on the opposite wall, suh."

"All right," whispered Ellis, pressing a coin into the servant's hand. "I'm going up to the parlor with the lady. You go up ahead of us, and keep in front of us along the hall. Don't dare to look back. I shall keep on talking to the lady, so that you can tell by my voice where we are. When you get to room 256, go in and shut the door behind you: pretend that you were called – ask the gentlemen what they want – tell any kind of a lie you like – but keep the door shut until you're sure we've got by. Do you hear?"

"Yes, suh," replied the negro intelligently.

The plan worked without a hitch. Ellis talked steadily, about the hotel, the furnishings, all sorts of irrelevant subjects, to which Miss Pemberton paid little attention. She was angry with Delamere, and took no pains to conceal her feelings. The bell-boy entered room 256 just before they reached the door. Ellis had heard loud talking as they approached, and as they were passing there was a crash of broken glass, as though some object had been thrown at the door.

"What is the matter there?" exclaimed Clara, quickening her footsteps and instinctively drawing closer to Ellis.

"Someone[102] dropped a glass, I presume," replied Ellis calmly.

Miss Pemberton glanced at him suspiciously. She was in a decidedly perverse mood. Seating herself at the piano, she played brilliantly for a quarter of an hour. Quite a number of couples strolled up to the parlor, but Delamere was not among them.

"Oh dear!" exclaimed Miss Pemberton, as she let her fingers fall upon the keys with a discordant crash, after the last note, "I don't see why we came out here to-night. Let's go back downstairs."

Ellis felt despondent. He had done his utmost to serve and to please Miss Pemberton, but was not likely, he foresaw, to derive much benefit from his opportunity. Delamere was evidently as much or more in her thoughts by reason of his absence than if he had been present. If the door should have been opened, and she should see him from the hall upon their return, Ellis could not help it. He took the side next to the door, however, meaning to hurry past the room so that she might not recognize Delamere.

Fortunately the door was closed and all quiet within the room. On the stairway they met the bell-boy, rubbing his head with one hand and holding a bottle of seltzer upon

Notes

[101] *Original reads*: need n't [ed.].

[102] *Original reads*: some one [ed.].

a tray in the other. The boy was well enough trained to give no sign of recognition, though Ellis guessed the destination of the bottle.

Ellis hardly knew whether to feel pleased or disappointed at the success of his manœuvres. He had spared Miss Pemberton some mortification, but he had saved Tom Delamere from merited exposure. Clara ought to know the truth, for her own sake.

On the beach, a few rods[103] away, fires were burning, around which several merry groups had gathered. The smoke went mostly to one side, but a slight whiff came now and then to where Mrs. Carteret sat awaiting them.

"They're roasting oysters," said Mrs. Carteret. "I wish you'd bring me some, Mr. Ellis."

Ellis strolled down to the beach. A large iron plate, with a turned-up rim like a great baking-pan, supported by legs which held it off the ground, was set over a fire built upon the sand. This primitive oven was heaped with small oysters in the shell, taken from the neighboring sound, and hauled up to the hotel by a negro whose pony cart stood near by. A wet coffee-sack of burlaps was spread over the oysters, which, when steamed sufficiently, were opened by a colored man and served gratis to all who cared for them.

Ellis secured a couple of plates of oysters, which he brought to Mrs. Carteret and Clara; they were small, but finely flavored.

Meanwhile Delamere, who possessed a remarkable faculty of recuperation from the effects of drink, had waked from his sleep, and remembering his engagement, had exerted himself to overcome the ravages of the afternoon's debauch. A dash of cold water braced him up somewhat. A bottle of seltzer and a big cup of strong coffee still further strengthened his nerves.

When Ellis returned to the veranda, after having taken away the plates, Delamere had joined the ladies and was explaining the cause of his absence.

He had been overcome by the heat, he said, while out fishing, and had been lying down ever since. Perhaps he ought to have sent for a doctor, but the fellows had looked after him. He hadn't[104] sent word to his friends because he hadn't[105] wished to spoil their evening.

"That was very considerate of you, Tom," said Mrs. Carteret dryly, "but you ought to have let us know. We have been worrying about you very much. Clara has found the evening dreadfully dull."

"Indeed, no, sister Olivia," said the young lady cheerfully, "I've been having a lovely time. Mr. Ellis and I have been up in the parlor; I played the piano; and we've been eating oysters and having a most delightful time. Won't you take me down there to the beach, Mr. Ellis? I want to see the fires. Come on."

"Can't I go?" asked Tom jealously.

"No, indeed, you mustn't stir a foot! You must not overtax yourself so soon; it might do you serious injury. Stay here with sister Olivia."

She took Ellis's arm with exaggerated cordiality. Delamere glared after them angrily. Ellis did not stop to question her motives, but took the goods the gods provided. With no very great apparent effort, Miss Pemberton became quite friendly, and they strolled along the beach, in sight of the hotel, for nearly half an hour. As they were coming up she asked him abruptly –

Notes

[103] *rod* a unit of measurement; one rod is equal to 16.5 feet.

[104] *Original reads*: had n't [ed.].

[105] *Original reads*: had n't [ed.].

"Mr. Ellis, did you know Tom was in the hotel?"

Ellis was looking across the sound, at the lights of a distant steamer which was making her way toward the harbor.

"I wonder," he said musingly, as though he had not heard her question, "if that is the Ocean Belle?"

"And was he really sick?" she demanded.

"She's later than usual this trip," continued Ellis, pursuing his thought. "She was due about five o'clock."

Miss Pemberton, under cover of the darkness, smiled a fine smile, which foreboded ill for someone.[106] When they joined the party on the piazza, the major had come up and was saying that it was time to go. He had been engaged in conversation, for most of the evening, with General Belmont and several other gentlemen.

"Here comes the general now. Let me see. There are five of us. The general has offered me a seat in his buggy, and Tom can go with you-all."

The general came up and spoke to the ladies. Tom murmured his thanks; it would enable him to make up a part of the delightful evening he had missed.

When Mrs. Carteret had taken the rear seat, Clara promptly took the place beside her. Ellis and Delamere sat in front. When Delamere, who had offered to drive, took the reins, Ellis saw that his hands were shaking.

"Give me the lines," he whispered. "Your nerves are unsteady and the road is not well lighted."

Delamere prudently yielded the reins. He did not like Ellis's tone, which seemed sneering rather than expressive of sympathy with one who had been suffering. He wondered if the beggar knew anything about his illness. Clara had been acting strangely. It would have been just like Ellis to have slandered him. The upstart had no business with Clara anyway. He would cheerfully have strangled Ellis, if he could have done so with safety to himself and no chance of discovery.

The drive homeward through the night was almost a silent journey. Mrs. Carteret was anxious about her baby. Clara did not speak, except now and then to Ellis with reference to some object in or near the road. Occasionally they passed a vehicle in the darkness, sometimes barely avoiding a collision. Far to the north the sky was lit up with the glow of a forest fire. The breeze from the Sound was deliciously cool. Soon the last toll-gate was passed and the lights of the town appeared.

Ellis threw the lines to William, who was waiting, and hastened to help the ladies out.

"Good-night, Mr. Ellis," said Clara sweetly, as she gave Ellis her hand. "Thank you for a very pleasant evening. Come up and see us soon."

She ran into the house without a word to Tom.

Chapter 17

The Social Aspirations of Captain Mcbane

It was only eleven o'clock, and Delamere, not being at all sleepy, and feeling somewhat out of sorts as the combined results of his afternoon's debauch and the snubbing he had received at Clara's hands, directed the major's coachman, who had taken charge of

Notes

[106] *Original reads*: some one [ed.].

the trap upon its arrival, to drive him to the St. James Hotel before returning the horses to the stable. First, however, the coachman left Ellis at his boarding-house, which was near by. The two young men parted with as scant courtesy as was possible without an open rupture.

Delamere hoped to find at the hotel some form of distraction to fill in an hour or two before going home. Ill fortune favored him by placing in his way the burly form of Captain George McBane, who was sitting in an armchair alone, smoking a midnight cigar, under the hotel balcony. Upon Delamere's making known his desire for amusement, the captain proposed a small game of poker in his own room.

McBane had been waiting for some such convenient opportunity. We have already seen that the captain was desirous of social recognition, which he had not yet obtained beyond the superficial acquaintance acquired by association with men about town. He had determined to assault society in its citadel by seeking membership in the Clarendon Club of which most gentlemen of the best families of the city were members.

The Clarendon Club was a historic institution, and its membership a social cult, the temple of which was located just off the main street of the city, in a dignified old colonial mansion which had housed it for the nearly one hundred years during which it had maintained its existence unbroken. There had grown up around it many traditions and special usages. Membership in the Clarendon was the *sine qua non*[107] of high social standing, and was conditional upon two of three things – birth, wealth, and breeding. Breeding was the prime essential, but, with rare exceptions, must be backed by either birth or money.

Having decided, therefore, to seek admission into this social arcanum, the captain, who had either not quite appreciated the standard of the Clarendon's membership, or had failed to see that he fell beneath it, looked about for an intermediary through whom to approach the object of his desire. He had already thought of Tom Delamere in this connection, having with him such an acquaintance as one forms around a hotel, and having long ago discovered that Delamere was a young man of superficially amiable disposition, vicious instincts, lax principles, and a weak will, and, which was quite as much to the purpose, a member of the Clarendon Club. Possessing mental characteristics almost entirely opposite, Delamere and the captain had certain tastes in common, and had smoked, drunk, and played cards together more than once.

Still more to his purpose, McBane had detected Delamere trying to cheat him at cards. He had said nothing about this discovery, but had merely noted it as something which at some future time might prove useful. The captain had not suffered by Delamere's deviation from the straight line of honor, for while Tom was as clever with the cards as might be expected of a young man who had devoted most of his leisure for several years to handling them, McBane was past master in their manipulation. During a stormy career he had touched more or less pitch, and had escaped few sorts of defilement.

The appearance of Delamere at a late hour, unaccompanied, and wearing upon his countenance an expression in which the captain read aright the craving for mental and physical excitement, gave him the opportunity for which he had been looking. McBane was not the man to lose an opportunity, nor did Delamere require a second invitation. Neither was it necessary, during the progress of the game, for the captain to press upon his guest the contents of the decanter which stood upon the table within convenient reach.

Notes

[107] *sine qua non* essential element.

The captain permitted Delamere to win from him several small amounts, after which he gradually increased the stakes and turned the tables.

Delamere, with every instinct of a gamester, was no more a match for McBane in self-control than in skill. When the young man had lost all his money, the captain expressed his entire willingness to accept notes of hand, for which he happened to have convenient blanks in his apartment.

When Delamere, flushed with excitement and wine, rose from the gaming table at two o'clock, he was vaguely conscious that he owed McBane a considerable sum, but could not have stated how much. His opponent, who was entirely cool and collected, ran his eye carelessly over the bits of paper to which Delamere had attached his signature.

"Just one thousand dollars even," he remarked.

The announcement of this total had as sobering an effect upon Delamere as though he had been suddenly deluged with a shower of cold water. For a moment he caught his breath. He had not a dollar in the world with which to pay this sum. His only source of income was an allowance from his grandfather, the monthly installment of which, drawn that very day, he had just lost to McBane, before starting in upon the notes of hand.

"I'll give you your revenge another time," said McBane, as they rose. "Luck is against you to-night, and I'm unwilling to take advantage of a clever young fellow like you. Meantime," he added, tossing the notes of hand carelessly on a bureau, "don't worry about these bits of paper. Such small matters shouldn't[108] cut any figure between friends; but if you are around the hotel to-morrow, I should like to speak to you upon another subject."

"Very well, captain," returned Tom somewhat ungraciously.

Delamere had been completely beaten with his own weapons. He had tried desperately to cheat McBane. He knew perfectly well that McBane had discovered his efforts and had cheated him in turn, for the captain's play had clearly been gauged to meet his own. The biter had been bit, and could not complain of the outcome.

The following afternoon McBane met Delamere at the hotel, and bluntly requested the latter to propose him for membership in the Clarendon Club.

Delamere was annoyed at this request. His aristocratic gorge rose at the presumption of this son of an overseer and ex-driver of convicts. McBane was good enough to win money from, or even to lose money to, but not good enough to be recognized as a social equal. He would instinctively have blackballed McBane had he been proposed by someone[109] else; with what grace could he put himself forward as the sponsor for this impossible social aspirant? Moreover, it was clearly a vulgar, cold-blooded attempt on McBane's part to use his power over him for a personal advantage.

"Well, now, Captain McBane," returned Delamere diplomatically, "I've never put anyone[110] up yet, and it's not regarded as good form for so young a member as myself to propose candidates. I'd much rather you'd ask some older man."

"Oh, well," replied McBane, "just as you say, only I thought you had cut your eye teeth."[111]

Delamere was not pleased with McBane's tone. His remark was not acquiescent, though couched in terms of assent. There was a sneering savagery about it, too, that

Notes

[108] *Original reads*: should n't [ed.].

[109] *Original reads*: some one [ed.].

[110] *Original reads*: any one [ed.].

[111] *cut your eye teeth* to have experience of something.

left Delamere uneasy. He was, in a measure, in McBane's power. He could not pay the thousand dollars, unless it fell from heaven, or he could win it from someone[112] else. He would not dare go to his grandfather for help. Mr. Delamere did not even know that his grandson gambled. He might not have objected, perhaps, to a gentleman's game, with moderate stakes, but he would certainly, Tom knew very well, have looked upon a thousand dollars as a preposterous sum to be lost at cards by a man who had nothing with which to pay it. It was part of Mr. Delamere's creed that a gentleman should not make debts that he was not reasonably able to pay.

There was still another difficulty. If he had lost the money to a gentleman, and it had been his first serious departure from Mr. Delamere's perfectly well understood standard of honor, Tom might have risked a confession and thrown himself on his grandfather's mercy; but he owed other sums here and there, which, to his just now much disturbed imagination, loomed up in alarming number and amount. He had recently observed signs of coldness, too, on the part of certain members of the club. Moreover, like most men with one commanding vice, he was addicted to several subsidiary forms of iniquity, which in case of a scandal were more than likely to come to light. He was clearly and most disagreeably caught in the net of his own hypocrisy. His grandfather believed him a model of integrity, a pattern of honor; he could not afford to have his grandfather undeceived.

He thought of old Mrs. Ochiltree. If she were a liberal soul, she could give him a thousand dollars now, when he needed it, instead of making him wait until she died, which might not be for ten years or more, for a legacy which was steadily growing less and might be entirely exhausted if she lived long enough – some old people were very tenacious of life! She was a careless old woman, too, he reflected, and very foolishly kept her money in the house. Latterly she had been growing weak and childish. Someday[113] she might be robbed, and then his prospective inheritance from that source would vanish into thin air!

With regard to this debt to McBane, if he could not pay it, he could at least gain a long respite by proposing the captain at the club. True, he would undoubtedly be blackballed, but before this inevitable event his name must remain posted for several weeks, during which interval McBane would be conciliatory. On the other hand, to propose McBane would arouse suspicion of his own motives; it might reach his grandfather's ears, and lead to a demand for an explanation, which it would be difficult to make. Clearly, the better plan would be to temporize with McBane, with the hope that something might intervene to remove this cursed obligation.

"Suppose, captain," he said affably, "we leave the matter open for a few days. This is a thing that can't be rushed. I'll feel the pulse of my friends and yours, and when we get the lay of the land, the affair can be accomplished much more easily."

"Well, that's better," returned McBane, somewhat mollified – "*if* you'll do that."

"To be sure I will," replied Tom easily, too much relieved to resent, if not too preoccupied to perceive, the implied doubt of his veracity.

McBane ordered and paid for more drinks, and they parted on amicable terms.

"We'll let these notes stand for the time being, Tom," said McBane, with significant emphasis, when they separated.

Delamere winced at the familiarity. He had reached that degree of moral deterioration where, while principles were of little moment, the externals of social intercourse

Notes

[112] *Original reads*: some one [ed.].

[113] *Original reads*: Some day [ed.].

possessed an exaggerated importance. McBane had never before been so personal. He had addressed the young aristocrat first as "Mr. Delamere," then, as their acquaintance advanced, as "Delamere." He had now reached the abbreviated Christian name stage of familiarity. There was no lower depth to which Tom could sink, unless McBane should invent a nickname by which to address him.

He did not like McBane's manner – it was characterized by a veiled insolence which was exceedingly offensive. He would go over to the club and try his luck with some honest player – perhaps something might turn up to relieve him from his embarrassment.

He put his hand in his pocket mechanically – and found it empty! In the present state of his credit, he could hardly play without money.

A thought struck him. Leaving the hotel, he hastened home, where he found Sandy dusting his famous suit of clothes on the back piazza. Mr. Delamere was not at home, having departed for Belleview about two o'clock, leaving Sandy to follow him in the morning.

"Hello, Sandy," exclaimed Tom, with an assumed jocularity which he was very far from feeling, "what are you doing with those gorgeous garments?"

"I'm a-dustin' of 'em, Mistuh Tom, dat's w'at I'm a-doin'. Dere's somethin' wrong 'bout dese clo's er mine – I don' never seem ter be able ter keep 'em clean no mo'. Ef I b'lieved in dem ole-timey sayin's, I'd 'low dere wuz a witch come here eve'y night an' tuk 'em out an' wo' 'em, er tuk me out an' rid me in 'em. Dere wuz somethin' wrong 'bout dat cakewalk business, too, dat I ain' never unde'stood an' don' know how ter 'count fer, 'less dere wuz some kin' er dev'lishness goin' on dat don' show on de su'face."

"Sandy," asked Tom irrelevantly, "have you any money in the house?"

"Yas, suh, I got de money Mars John give me ter git dem things ter take out ter Belleview in de mawnin'."

"I mean money of your own."

"I got a qua'ter ter buy terbacker wid," returned Sandy cautiously.

"Is that all? Haven't[114] you some saved up?"

"Well, yas, Mistuh Tom," returned Sandy, with evident reluctance, "dere's a few dollahs put away in my bureau drawer fer a rainy day – not much, suh."

"I'm a little short this afternoon. Sandy, and need some money right away. Grandfather isn't[115] here, so I can't get any from him. Let me take what you have for a day or two, Sandy, and I'll return it with good interest."

"Now, Mistuh Tom," said Sandy seriously, "I don' min' lettin' you take my money, but I hopes you ain' gwine ter use it fer none er dem rakehelly gwines-on er yo'n – gamblin' an' bettin' an' so fo'th. Yo' grandaddy 'll fin' out 'bout you yit, ef you don' min' yo' P's an' Q's. I does my bes' ter keep yo' misdoin's f'm 'im, an' sense I b'en tu'ned out er de chu'ch – thoo no fault er my own, God knows! – I've tol' lies 'nuff 'bout you ter sink a ship. But it ain't right, Mistuh Tom, it ain't right! an' I only does it fer de sake er de fam'ly honuh, dat Mars John sets so much sto' by, an' ter save his fee-lin's; fer de doctuh says he mus'n'[116] git ixcited 'bout nothin', er it mought bring on another stroke."

Notes

[114] *Original reads*: have n't [ed.].

[115] *Original reads*: is n't [ed.].

[116] *Original reads*: mus' n' [ed.].

"That's right, Sandy," replied Tom approvingly; "but the family honor is as safe in my hands as in grandfather's own, and I'm going to use the money for an excellent purpose, in fact to relieve a case of genuine distress; and I'll hand it back to you in a day or two – perhaps to-morrow. Fetch me the money, Sandy – that's a good darky!"

"All right, Mistuh Tom, you shill have de money; but I wants ter tell you, suh, dat in all de yeahs I has wo'ked fer yo' gran'daddy, he has never called me a 'darky' ter my face, suh. Co'se I knows dere's w'ite folks an' black folks – but dere's manners, suh, dere's manners, an' gent'emen oughter be de ones ter use em, suh, ef dey ain't ter be fergot enti'ely!"

"There, there, Sandy," returned Tom in a conciliatory tone, "I beg your pardon! I've been associating with some Northern white folks at the hotel, and picked up the word from them. You're a high-toned colored gentleman, Sandy – the finest one on the footstool."

Still muttering to himself, Sandy retired to his own room, which was in the house, so that he might be always near his master. He soon returned with a time-stained leather pocket-book and a coarse-knit cotton sock, from which two receptacles he painfully extracted a number of bills and coins.

"You count dat, Mistuh Tom, so I'll know how much I'm lettin' you have."

"This isn't[117] worth anything," said Tom, pushing aside one roll of bills. "It's Confederate money."

"So it is, suh. It ain't wuth nothin' now; but it has be'n money, an' who kin tell but what it mought be money agin? De rest er dem bills is greenbacks – dey'll pass all right, I reckon."

The good money amounted to about fifty dollars, which Delamere thrust eagerly into his pocket.

"You won't say anything to grandfather about this, will you, Sandy," he said, as he turned away.

"No, suh, co'se I won't! Does I ever tell 'im 'bout yo' gwines-on? Ef I did," he added to himself, as the young man disappeared down the street, "I wouldn'[118] have time ter do nothin' e'se ha'dly. I don' know whether I'll ever see dat money agin er no, do' I 'magine de ole gent'eman wouldn'[119] lemme lose it ef he knowed. But I ain' gwine ter tell him, whether I git my money back er no, fer he is jes' so wrop' up in dat boy dat I b'lieve it'd jes' break his hea't ter fin' out how he's be'n gwine on. Doctuh Price has tol' me not ter let de ole gent'eman git ixcited, er e'se dere's no tellin' w'at mought happen. He's be'n good ter me, he has, an' I'm gwine ter take keer er him – dat's w'at I is, ez long ez I has de chance."

Delamere went directly to the club, and soon lounged into the card-room, where several of the members were engaged in play. He sauntered here and there, too much absorbed in his own thoughts to notice that the greetings he received were less cordial than those usually exchanged between the members of a small and select social club. Finally, when Augustus, commonly and more appropriately called "Gus," Davidson came into the room, Tom stepped toward him.

"Will you take a hand in a game, Gus?"

"Don't care if I do," said the other. "Let's sit over here."

Notes

[117] *Original reads*: is n't [ed.].

[118] *Original reads*: would n' [ed.].

[119] *Original reads*: would n' [ed.].

Davidson led the way to a table near the fireplace, near which stood a tall screen, which at times occupied various places in the room. Davidson took the seat opposite the fireplace, leaving Delamere with his back to the screen.

Delamere staked half of Sandy's money, and lost. He staked the rest, and determined to win, because he could not afford to lose. He had just reached out his hand to gather in the stakes, when he was charged with cheating at cards, of which two members, who had quietly entered the room and posted themselves behind the screen, had secured specific proof.

A meeting of the membership committee was hastily summoned, it being an hour at which most of them might be found at the club. To avoid a scandal, and to save the feelings of a prominent family, Delamere was given an opportunity to resign quietly from the club, on condition that he paid all his gambling debts within three days, and took an oath never to play cards again for money. This latter condition was made at the suggestion of an elderly member, who apparently believed that a man who would cheat at cards would stick at perjury.

Delamere acquiesced very promptly. The taking of the oath was easy. The payment of some fifteen hundred dollars of debts was a different matter. He went away from the club thoughtfully, and it may be said, in full justice to a past which was far from immaculate, that in his present thoughts he touched a depth of scoundrelism far beyond anything of which he had as yet deemed himself capable. When a man of good position, of whom much is expected, takes to evil courses, his progress is apt to resemble that of a well-bred woman who has started on the downward path – the pace is all the swifter because of the distance which must be traversed to reach the bottom. Delamere had made rapid headway; having hitherto played with sin, his servant had now become his master, and held him in an iron grip.

Chapter 18

Sandy Sees His Own Ha'nt

Having finished cleaning his clothes, Sandy went out to the kitchen for supper, after which he found himself with nothing to do. Mr. Delamere's absence relieved him from attendance at the house during the evening. He might have smoked his pipe tranquilly in the kitchen until bedtime, had not the cook intimated, rather pointedly, that she expected other company. To a man of Sandy's tact a word was sufficient, and he resigned himself to seeking companionship elsewhere.

Under normal circumstances, Sandy would have attended prayer-meeting on this particular evening of the week; but being still in contumacy, and cherishing what he considered the just resentment of a man falsely accused, he stifled the inclination which by long habit led him toward the church, and set out for the house of a friend with whom it occurred to him that he might spend the evening pleasantly. Unfortunately, his friend proved to be not at home, so Sandy turned his footsteps toward the lower part of the town, where the streets were well lighted, and on pleasant evenings quite animated. On the way he met Josh Green, whom he had known for many years, though their paths did not often cross. In his loneliness Sandy accepted an invitation to go with Josh and have a drink – a single drink.

When Sandy was going home about eleven o'clock, three sheets in the wind, such was the potent effect of the single drink and those which had followed it, he was scared almost into soberness by a remarkable apparition. As it seemed to Sandy, he saw himself hurrying along in front of himself toward the house. Possibly the muddled condition of

Sandy's intellect had so affected his judgment as to vitiate any conclusion he might draw, but Sandy was quite sober enough to perceive that the figure ahead of him wore his best clothes and looked exactly like him, but seemed to be in something more of a hurry, a discrepancy which Sandy at once corrected by quickening his own pace so as to maintain as nearly as possible an equal distance between himself and his double. The situation was certainly an incomprehensible one, and savored of the supernatural.

"Ef dat's me gwine 'long in front," mused Sandy, in vinous perplexity, "den who is dis behin' here? Dere ain' but one er me, an' my ha'nt wouldn'[120] leave my body 'tel I wuz dead. Ef dat's me in front, den I mus' be my own ha'nt; an' whichever one of us is de ha'nt, de yuther must be dead an' don' know it. I don' know what ter make er no sech gwines-on, I don't. Maybe it ain' me after all, but it certainly do look lack me."

When the apparition disappeared in the house by the side door, Sandy stood in the yard for several minutes, under the shade of an elm-tree, before he could make up his mind to enter the house. He took courage, however, upon the reflection that perhaps, after all, it was only the bad liquor he had drunk. Bad liquor often made people see double.

He entered the house. It was dark, except for a light in Tom Delamere's room. Sandy tapped softly at the door.

"Who's there?" came Delamere's voice, in a somewhat startled tone, after a momentary silence.

"It's me, suh; Sandy."

They both spoke softly. It was the rule of the house when Mr. Delamere had retired, and though he was not at home, habit held its wonted sway.

"Just a moment, Sandy."

Sandy waited patiently in the hall until the door was opened. If the room showed any signs of haste or disorder, Sandy was too full of his own thoughts – and other things – to notice them.

"What do you want, Sandy," asked Tom.

"Mistuh Tom," asked Sandy solemnly, "ef I wuz in yo'place, an' you wuz in my place, an' we wuz bofe in de same place, whar would I be?"

Tom looked at Sandy keenly, with a touch of apprehension. Did Sandy mean anything in particular by this enigmatical inquiry, and if so, what? But Sandy's face clearly indicated a state of mind in which consecutive thought was improbable; and after a brief glance Delamere breathed more freely.

"I give it up, Sandy," he responded lightly. "That's too deep for me."

"'Scuse me, Mistuh Tom, but is you heared er seed anybody er anything come in de house fer de las' ten minutes?"

"Why, no, Sandy, I haven't[121] heard anyone.[122] I came from the club an hour ago. I had forgotten my key, and Sally got up and let me in, and then went back to bed. I've been sitting here reading ever since. I should have heard anyone[123] who came in."

"Mistuh Tom," inquired Sandy anxiously, "would you 'low dat I'd be'n drinkin' too much?"

"No, Sandy, I should say you were sober enough, though of course you may have had a few drinks. Perhaps you'd like another? I've got something good here."

Notes

[120] *Original reads*: would n' [ed.].

[121] *Original reads*: have n't [ed.].

[122] *Original reads*: any one [ed.].

[123] *Original reads*: any one [ed.].

"No, suh, Mistuh Tom, no, suh! No mo' liquor fer me, suh, never! When liquor kin make a man see his own ha'nt, it's 'bout time fer dat man ter quit drinkin', it sho' is! Good-night, Mistuh Tom."

As Sandy turned to go, Delamere was struck by a sudden and daring thought. The creature of impulse, he acted upon it immediately.

"By the way, Sandy," he exclaimed carelessly, "I can pay you back that money you were good enough to lend me this afternoon. I think I'll sleep better if I have the debt off my mind, and I shouldn't wonder if you would. You don't mind having it in gold, do you?"

"No, indeed, suh," replied Sandy. "I ain' seen no gol' fer so long dat de sight er it'd be good fer my eyes."

Tom counted out ten five-dollar gold pieces upon the table at his elbow.

"And here's another, Sandy," he said, adding an eleventh, "as interest for the use of it."

"Thank y', Mistuh Tom. I didn't[124] spec' no intrus', but I don' never 'fuse gol' w'en I kin git it."

"And here," added Delamere, reaching carelessly into a bureau drawer, "is a little old silk purse that I've had since I was a boy. I'll put the gold in it, Sandy; it will hold it very nicely."

"Thank y', Mistuh Tom. You're a gentleman, suh, an' wo'thy er de fam'ly name. Good-night, suh, an' I hope yo' dreams'll be pleasanter 'n mine. Ef it wa'n't fer dis gol' kinder takin' my min' off'n dat ha'nt, I don' s'pose I'd be able to do much sleepin' ter-night. Good-night, suh."

"Good-night, Sandy."

Whether or not Delamere slept soundly, or was troubled by dreams, pleasant or unpleasant, it is nevertheless true that he locked his door, and sat up an hour later, looking through the drawers of his bureau, and burning several articles in the little iron stove which constituted part of the bedroom furniture.

It is also true that he rose very early, before the household was stirring. The cook slept in a room off the kitchen, which was in an outhouse in the back yard. She was just stretching herself, preparatory to getting up, when Tom came to her window and said that he was going off fishing, to be gone all day, and that he would not wait for breakfast.

Chapter 19

A Midnight Walk

Ellis left the office of the Morning Chronicle about eleven o'clock the same evening and set out to walk home. His boarding-house was only a short distance beyond old Mr. Delamere's residence, and while he might have saved time and labor by a slightly shorter route, he generally selected this one because it led also by Major Carteret's house. Sometimes there would be a ray of light from Clara's room, which was on one of the front corners; and at any rate he would have the pleasure of gazing at the outside of the casket that enshrined the jewel of his heart. It was true that this purely sentimental pleasure was sometimes dashed with bitterness at the thought of his

Notes

[124] *Original reads*: did n't [ed.].

rival; but one in love must take the bitter with the sweet, and who would say that a spice of jealousy does not add a certain zest to love? On this particular evening, however, he was in a hopeful mood. At the Clarendon Club, where he had gone, a couple of hours before, to verify a certain news item for the morning paper, he had heard a story about Tom Delamere which, he imagined, would spike that gentleman's guns for all time, so far as Miss Pemberton was concerned. So grave an affair as cheating at cards could never be kept secret – it was certain to reach her ears; and Ellis was morally certain that Clara would never marry a man who had been proved dishonorable. In all probability there would be no great sensation about the matter. Delamere was too well connected; too many prominent people would be involved – even Clara, and the editor himself, of whom Delamere was a distant cousin. The reputation of the club was also to be considered. Ellis was not the man to feel a malicious delight in the misfortunes of another, nor was he a pessimist who welcomed scandal and disgrace with open arms, as confirming a gloomy theory of human life. But, with the best intentions in the world, it was no more than human nature that he should feel a certain elation in the thought that his rival had been practically disposed of, and the field left clear; especially since this good situation had been brought about merely by the unmasking of a hypocrite, who had held him at an unfair disadvantage in the race for Clara's favor.

The night was quiet, except for the faint sound of distant music now and then, or the mellow laughter of some group of revelers. Ellis met but few pedestrians, but as he neared old Mr. Delamere's, he saw two men walking in the same direction as his own, on the opposite side of the street. He had observed that they kept at about an equal distance apart, and that the second, from the stealthy manner in which he was making his way, was anxious to keep the first in sight, without disclosing his own presence. This aroused Ellis's curiosity, which was satisfied in some degree when the man in advance stopped beneath a lamp-post and stood for a moment looking across the street, with his face plainly visible in the yellow circle of light. It was a dark face, and Ellis recognized it instantly as that of old Mr. Delamere's body servant, whose personal appearance had been very vividly impressed upon Ellis at the christening dinner at Major Carteret's. He had seen Sandy once since, too, at the hotel cakewalk. The negro had a small bundle in his hand, the nature of which Ellis could not make out.

When Sandy had stopped beneath the lamp-post, the man who was following him had dodged behind a tree-trunk. When Sandy moved on, Ellis, who had stopped in turn, saw the man in hiding come out and follow Sandy. When this second man came in range of the light, Ellis wondered that there should be two men so much alike. The first of the two had undoubtedly been Sandy. Ellis had recognized the peculiar, old-fashioned coat that Sandy had worn upon the two occasions when he had noticed him. Barring this difference, and the somewhat unsteady gait of the second man, the two were as much alike as twin brothers.

When they had entered Mr. Delamere's house, one after the other – in the stillness of the night Ellis could perceive that each of them tried to make as little noise as possible – Ellis supposed that they were probably relatives, both employed as servants, or that some younger negro, taking Sandy for a model, was trying to pattern himself after his superior. Why all this mystery, of course he could not imagine, unless the younger man had been out without permission and was trying to avoid the accusing eye of Sandy. Ellis was vaguely conscious that he had seen the other negro somewhere, but he could not for the moment place him – there were so many negroes, nearly three negroes to one white man in the city of Wellington!

The subject, however, while curious, was not important as compared with the thoughts of his sweetheart which drove it from his mind. Clara had been kind to him the night before – whatever her motive, she had been kind, and could not consistently return to her attitude of coldness. With Delamere hopelessly discredited, Ellis hoped to have at least fair play – with fair play, he would take his chances of the outcome.

Chapter 20

A Shocking Crime

ON Friday morning, when old Mrs. Ochiltree's cook Dinah went to wake her mistress, she was confronted with a sight that well-nigh blanched her ebony cheek and caused her eyes almost to start from her head with horror. As soon as she could command her trembling limbs sufficiently to make them carry her, she rushed out of the house and down the street, bareheaded, covering in an incredibly short time the few blocks that separated Mrs. Ochiltree's residence from that of her niece.

She hastened around the house, and finding the back door open and the servants stirring, ran into the house and up the stairs with the familiarity of an old servant, not stopping until she reached the door of Mrs. Carteret's chamber, at which she knocked in great agitation.

Entering in response to Mrs. Carteret's invitation, she found the lady, dressed in a simple wrapper, superintending the morning toilet of little Dodie, who was a wakeful child, and insisted upon rising with the birds, for whose music he still showed a great fondness, in spite of his narrow escape while listening to the mockingbird.

"What is it, Dinah?" asked Mrs. Carteret, alarmed at the frightened face of her aunt's old servitor.

"O my Lawd, Mis' 'Livy, my Lawd, my Lawd! My legs is trim'lin' so dat I can't ha'dly hol' my han's stiddy 'nough ter say w'at I got ter say! O Lawd have mussy on us po' sinners! W'atever is gwine ter happen in dis worl' er sin an' sorrer!"

"What in the world is the matter, Dinah?" demanded Mrs. Carteret, whose own excitement had increased with the length of this preamble. "Has anything happened to Aunt Polly?"

"Somebody done broke in de house las' night, Mis' 'Livy, an' kill' Mis' Polly, an' lef' her layin' dead on de flo', in her own blood, wid her cedar chis' broke' open, an' eve'thing scattered roun' de flo'! O my Lawd, my Lawd, my Lawd, my Lawd!"

Mrs. Carteret was shocked beyond expression. Perhaps the spectacle of Dinah's unrestrained terror aided her to retain a greater measure of self-control than she might otherwise have been capable of. Giving the nurse some directions in regard to the child, she hastily descended the stairs, and seizing a hat and jacket from the rack in the hall, ran immediately with Dinah to the scene of the tragedy. Before the thought of this violent death all her aunt's faults faded into insignificance, and only her good qualities were remembered. She had reared Olivia; she had stood up for the memory of Olivia's mother when others had seemed to forget what was due to it. To her niece she had been a second mother, and had never been lacking in affection.

More than one motive, however, lent wings to Mrs. Carteret's feet. Her aunt's incomplete disclosures on the day of the drive past the hospital had been weighing upon Mrs. Carteret's mind, and she had intended to make another effort this very day, to get an answer to her question about the papers which the woman had claimed were in existence. Suppose her aunt had really found such papers – papers which would seem to prove the preposterous claim made by her father's mulatto mistress? Suppose that, with the fatuity which generally leads human beings to keep compromising documents, her aunt had preserved these papers? If they should be found there in the house, there might be a scandal, if nothing worse, and this was to be avoided at all hazards.

Guided by some fortunate instinct, Dinah had as yet informed no one but Mrs. Carteret of her discovery. If they could reach the house before the murder became known to any third person, she might be the first to secure access to the remaining contents of the cedar chest, which would be likely to be held as evidence in case the officers of the law forestalled her own arrival.

They found the house wrapped in the silence of death. Mrs. Carteret entered the chamber of the dead woman. Upon the floor, where it had fallen, lay the body in a pool of blood, the strongly marked countenance scarcely more grim in the rigidity of death than it had been in life. A gaping wound in the head accounted easily for the death. The cedar chest stood open, its strong fastenings having been broken by a steel bar which still lay beside it. Near it were scattered pieces of old lace, antiquated jewelry, tarnished silverware – the various mute souvenirs of the joys and sorrows of a long and active life.

Kneeling by the open chest, Mrs. Carteret glanced hurriedly through its contents. There were no papers there except a few old deeds and letters. She had risen with a sigh of relief, when she perceived the end of a paper projecting from beneath the edge of a rug which had been carelessly rumpled, probably by the burglar in his hasty search for plunder. This paper, or sealed envelope as it proved to be, which evidently contained some inclosure, she seized, and at the sound of approaching footsteps thrust hastily into her own bosom.

The sight of two agitated women rushing through the quiet streets at so early an hour in the morning had attracted attention and aroused curiosity, and the story of the murder, having once become known, spread with the customary rapidity of bad news. Very soon a policeman, and a little later a sheriff's officer, arrived at the house and took charge of the remains to await the arrival of the coroner.

By nine o'clock a coroner's jury had been summoned, who, after brief deliberation, returned a verdict of willful murder at the hands of some person or persons unknown, while engaged in the commission of a burglary.

No sooner was the verdict announced than the community, or at least the white third of it, resolved itself spontaneously into a committee of the whole to discover the perpetrator of this dastardly crime, which, at this stage of the affair, seemed merely one of robbery and murder.

Suspicion was at once directed toward the negroes, as it always is when an unexplained crime is committed in a Southern community. The suspicion was not entirely an illogical one. Having been, for generations, trained up to thriftlessness, theft, and immorality, against which only thirty years of very limited opportunity can be offset, during which brief period they have been denied in large measure the healthful social stimulus and sympathy which holds most men in the path of rectitude, colored people might reasonably be expected to commit at least a share of crime proportionate to their numbers. The population of the town was at least two thirds colored. The chances were, therefore, in the absence of evidence, at least two to one that a man of color had committed the crime. The Southern tendency to charge the negroes with all the crime and immorality of that region, unjust and exaggerated as the claim may be, was therefore not without a logical basis to the extent above indicated.

It must not be imagined that any logic was needed, or any reasoning consciously worked out. The mere suggestion that the crime had been committed by a negro was equivalent to proof against any negro that might be suspected and could not prove his innocence. A committee of white men was hastily formed. Acting independently of the police force, which was practically ignored as likely to favor the negroes, this committee set to work to discover the murderer.

The spontaneous activity of the whites was accompanied by a visible shrinkage of the colored population. This could not be taken as any indication of guilt, but was merely a recognition of the palpable fact that the American habit of lynching had so whetted the thirst for black blood that a negro suspected of crime had to face at least the possibility of a short shrift and a long rope, not to mention more gruesome horrors, without the intervention of judge or jury. Since to have a black face at such a time was to challenge suspicion, and since there was neither the martyr's glory nor the saint's renown in being killed for someone[125] else's crime, and very little hope of successful resistance in case of an attempt at lynching, it was obviously the part of prudence for those thus marked to seek immunity in a temporary disappearance from public view.

Chapter 21

The Necessity of an Example

About ten o'clock on the morning of the discovery of the murder, Captain McBane and General Belmont, as though moved by a common impulse, found themselves at the office of the Morning Chronicle. Carteret was expecting them, though there had been no appointment made. These three resourceful and energetic minds, representing no organized body, and clothed with no legal authority, had so completely arrogated to themselves the leadership of white public sentiment as to come together instinctively when an event happened which concerned the public, and, as this murder presumably did, involved the matter of race.

"Well, gentlemen," demanded McBane impatiently, "what are we going to do with the scoundrel when we catch him?"

"They've got the murderer," announced a reporter, entering the room.

"Who is he?" they demanded in a breath.

"A nigger by the name of Sandy Campbell, a servant of old Mr. Delamere."

"How did they catch him?"

"Our Jerry saw him last night, going toward Mrs. Ochiltree's house, and a white man saw him coming away, half an hour later."

"Has he confessed?"

"No, but he might as well. When the posse went to arrest him, they found him cleaning the clothes he had worn last night, and discovered in his room a part of the plunder. He denies it strenuously, but it seems a clear case."

"There can be no doubt," said Ellis, who had come into the room behind the reporter. "I saw the negro last night, at twelve o'clock, going into Mr. Delamere's yard, with a bundle in his hand."

"He is the last negro I should have suspected," said Carteret. "Mr. Delamere had implicit confidence in him."

"All niggers are alike," remarked McBane sententiously. "The only way to keep them from stealing is not to give them the chance. A nigger will steal a cent off a dead man's eye. He has assaulted and murdered a white woman – an example should be made of him."

Notes

[125] *Original reads*: some one [ed.].

Carteret recalled very distinctly the presence of this negro at his own residence on the occasion of little Theodore's christening dinner. He remembered having questioned the prudence of letting a servant know that Mrs. Ochiltree kept money in the house. Mr. Delamere had insisted strenuously upon the honesty of this particular negro. The whole race, in the major's opinion, was morally undeveloped, and only held within bounds by the restraining influence of the white people. Under Mr. Delamere's thumb this Sandy had been a model servant – faithful, docile, respectful, and self-respecting; but Mr. Delamere had grown old, and had probably lost in a measure his moral influence over his servant. Left to his own degraded ancestral instincts, Sandy had begun to deteriorate, and a rapid decline had culminated in this robbery and murder – and who knew what other horror? The criminal was a negro, the victim a white woman – it was only reasonable to expect the worst.

"He'll swing for it," observed the general.

Ellis went into another room, where his duty called him.

"He should burn for it," averred McBane. "I say, burn the nigger."

"This," said Carteret, "is something more than an ordinary crime, to be dealt with by the ordinary processes of law. It is a murderous and fatal assault upon a woman of our race – upon our race in the person of its womanhood, its crown and flower. If such crimes are not punished with swift and terrible directness, the whole white womanhood of the South is in danger."

"Burn the nigger," repeated McBane automatically.

"Neither is this a mere sporadic crime," Carteret went on. "It is symptomatic; it is the logical and inevitable result of the conditions which have prevailed in this town for the past year. It is the last straw."

"Burn the nigger," reiterated McBane. "We seem to have the right nigger, but whether we have or not, burn *a* nigger. It is an assault upon the white race, in the person of old Mrs. Ochiltree, committed by the black race, in the person of some nigger. It would justify the white people in burning *any* nigger. The example would be all the more powerful if we got the wrong one. It would serve notice on the niggers that we shall hold the whole race responsible for the misdeeds of each individual."

"In ancient Rome," said the general, "when a master was killed by a slave, all his slaves were put to the sword."

"We couldn't afford that before the war," said McBane, "but the niggers don't belong to anybody now, and there's nothing to prevent our doing as we please with them. A dead nigger is no loss to any white man. I say, burn the nigger."

"I do not believe," said Carteret, who had gone to the window and was looking out, "I do not believe that we need trouble ourselves personally about his punishment. I should judge, from the commotion in the street, that the public will take the matter into its own hands. I, for one, would prefer that any violence, however justifiable, should take place without my active intervention."

"It won't take place without mine, if I know it," exclaimed McBane, starting for the door.

"Hold on a minute, captain," exclaimed Carteret.

"There's more at stake in this matter than the life of a black scoundrel. Wellington is in the hands of negroes and scalawags.[126] What better time to rescue it?"

Notes

[126] *scalawags* southern white men who allied themselves with African Americans and the Republican Party following the Civil War.

"It's a trifle premature," replied the general. "I should have preferred to have this take place, if it was to happen, say three months hence, on the eve of the election – but discussion always provokes thirst with me; I wonder if I could get Jerry to bring us some drinks?"

Carteret summoned the porter. Jerry's usual manner had taken on an element of self-importance, resulting in what one might describe as a sort of condescending obsequiousness. Though still a porter, he was also a hero, and wore his aureole.[127]

"Jerry," said the general kindly, "the white people are very much pleased with the assistance you have given them in apprehending this scoundrel Campbell. You have rendered a great public service, Jerry, and we wish you to know that it is appreciated."

"Thank y', gin'l, thank y', suh! I alluz tries ter do my duty, suh, an' stan' by dem dat stan's by me. Dat low-down nigger oughter be lynch', suh, don't you think, er e'se bu'nt? Dere ain' nothin' too bad ter happen ter 'im."

"No doubt he will be punished as he deserves, Jerry," returned the general, "and we will see that you are suitably rewarded. Go across the street and get me three Calhoun cocktails. I seem to have nothing less than a two-dollar bill, but you may keep the change, Jerry – all the change."

Jerry was very happy. He had distinguished himself in the public view, for to Jerry, as to the white people themselves, the white people were the public. He had won the goodwill of the best people, and had already begun to reap a tangible reward. It is true that several strange white men looked at him with lowering brows as he crossed the street, which was curiously empty of colored people; but he nevertheless went firmly forward, panoplied in the consciousness of his own rectitude, and serenely confident of the protection of the major and the major's friends.

"Jerry is about the only negro I have seen since nine o'clock," observed the general when the porter had gone. "If this were election day, where would the negro vote be?"

"In hiding, where most of the negro population is to-day," answered McBane. "It's a pity, if old Mrs. Ochiltree had to go this way, that it couldn't have been deferred a month or six weeks."

Carteret frowned at this remark, which, coming from McBane, seemed lacking in human feeling, as well as in respect to his wife's dead relative.

"But," resumed the general, "if this negro is lynched, as he well deserves to be, it will not be without its effect. We still have in reserve for the election a weapon which this affair will only render more effective. What became of the piece in the negro paper?"

"I have it here," answered Carteret. "I was just about to use it as the text for an editorial."

"Save it awhile longer," responded the general.

"This crime itself will give you text enough for a four-volume work."

When this conference ended, Carteret immediately put into press an extra edition of the Morning Chronicle, which was soon upon the streets, giving details of the crime, which was characterized as an atrocious assault upon a defenseless old lady, whose age and sex would have protected her from harm at the hands of anyone[128] but a brute in the lowest human form. This event, the Chronicle suggested, had only

Notes

[127] *aureole* halo.

[128] *Original reads*: any one [ed.].

confirmed the opinion, which had been of late growing upon the white people, that drastic efforts were necessary to protect the white women of the South against brutal, lascivious, and murderous assaults at the hands of negro men. It was only another significant example of the results which might have been foreseen from the application of a false and pernicious political theory, by which ignorance, clothed in a little brief authority, was sought to be exalted over knowledge, vice over virtue, an inferior and degraded race above the heaven-crowned Anglo-Saxon. If an outraged people, justly infuriated, and impatient of the slow processes of the courts, should assert their inherent sovereignty, which the law after all was merely intended to embody, and should choose, in obedience to the higher law, to set aside, temporarily, the ordinary judicial procedure, it would serve as a warning and an example to the vicious elements of the community, of the swift and terrible punishment which would fall, like the judgment of God, upon anyone[129] who laid sacrilegious hands upon white womanhood.

Chapter 22

How Not to Prevent a Lynching

Dr. Miller, who had sat up late the night before with a difficult case at the hospital, was roused, about eleven o'clock, from a deep and dreamless sleep. Struggling back into consciousness, he was informed by his wife, who stood by his bedside, that Mr. Watson, the colored lawyer, wished to see him upon a matter of great importance.

"Nothing but a matter of life and death would make me get up just now," he said with a portentous yawn.

"This *is* a matter of life and death," replied Janet. "Old Mrs. Polly Ochiltree was robbed and murdered last night, and Sandy Campbell has been arrested for the crime – and they are going to lynch him!"

"Tell Watson to come right up," exclaimed Miller, springing out of bed. "We can talk while I'm dressing."

While Miller made a hasty toilet Watson explained the situation. Campbell had been arrested on the charge of murder. He had been seen, during the night, in the neighborhood of the scene of the crime, by two different persons, a negro and a white man, and had been identified later while entering Mr. Delamere's house, where he lived, and where damning proofs of his guilt had been discovered; the most important item of which was an old-fashioned knit silk purse, recognized as Mrs. Ochiltree's, and several gold pieces of early coinage, of which the murdered woman was known to have a number. Watson brought with him one of the first copies procurable of the extra edition of the Chronicle, which contained these facts and further information.

They were still talking when Mrs. Miller, knocking at the door, announced that big Josh Green wished to see the doctor about Sandy Campbell. Miller took his collar and necktie in his hand and went downstairs, where Josh sat waiting.

"Doctuh," said Green, "de w'ite folks is talkin' 'bout lynchin' Sandy Campbell fer killin' ole Mis' Ochiltree. He never done it, an' dey oughtn'[130] ter be 'lowed ter lynch 'im."

"They ought not to lynch him, even if he committed the crime," returned Miller, "but still less if he didn't. What do you know about it?"

Notes

[129] *Original reads*: any one [ed.].

[130] *Original reads*: ought n' [ed.].

"I know he was wid me, suh, las' night, at de time when dey say ole Mis' Ochiltree wuz killed. We wuz down ter Sam Taylor's place, havin' a little game of kyards an' a little liquor. Den we lef dere an' went up ez fur ez de corner er Main an' Vine Streets, where we pa'ted, an' Sandy went 'long to'ds home. Mo'over, dey say he had on check' britches an' a blue coat. When Sandy wuz wid me he had on gray clo's, an' when we sep'rated he wa'n't in no shape ter be changin' his clo's, let 'lone robbin' er killin' anybody."

"Your testimony ought to prove an alibi for him," declared Miller.

"Dere ain' gwine ter be no chance ter prove nothin', 'less'n we kin do it mighty quick! Dey say dey're gwine ter lynch 'im ter-night – some on 'em is talkin' 'bout burnin' 'im. My idee is ter hunt up de niggers an' git 'em ter stan' tergether an' gyard de jail."

"Why shouldn't we go to the principal white people of the town and tell them Josh's story, and appeal to them to stop this thing until Campbell can have a hearing?"

"It wouldn't do any good," said Watson despondently; "their blood is up. It seems that some colored man attacked Mrs. Ochiltree – and he was a murderous villain, whoever he may be. To quote Josh would destroy the effect of his story – we know he never harmed anyone[131] but himself" –

"An' a few keerliss people w'at got in my way," corrected Josh.

"He has been in court several times for fighting – and that's against him. To have been at Sam Taylor's place is against Sandy, too, rather than in his favor. No, Josh, the white people would believe that you were trying to shield Sandy, and you would probably be arrested as an accomplice."

"But look a-here, Mr. Watson – Dr. Miller, is we-all jes' got ter set down here, widout openin' ou' mouths, an' let dese w'ite folks hang er bu'n a man w'at we *know* ain' guilty? Dat ain't no law, ner jestice, ner nothin'! Ef you-all won't he'p, I'll do somethin' myse'f! Dere's two niggers ter one white man in dis town, an' I'm sho' I kin fin' fifty of 'em w'at 'll fight, ef dey kin fin' anybody ter lead 'em."

"Now hold on, Josh," argued Miller; "what is to be gained by fighting? Suppose you got your crowd together and surrounded the jail – what then?"

"There'd be a clash," declared Watson, "and instead of one dead negro there'd be fifty. The white people are claiming now that Campbell didn't stop with robbery and murder. A special edition of the Morning Chronicle, just out, suggests a further purpose, and has all the old shopworn cant about race purity and supremacy and imperative necessity, which always comes to the front whenever it is sought to justify some outrage on the colored folks. The blood of the whites is up, I tell you!"

"Is there anything to that suggestion?" asked Miller incredulously.

"It doesn't matter whether there is or not," returned Watson. "Merely to suggest it proves it. Nothing was said about this feature until the paper came out – and even its statement is vague and indefinite – but now the claim is in every mouth. I met only black looks as I came down the street. White men with whom I have long been on friendly terms passed me without a word. A negro has been arrested on suspicion – the entire race is condemned on general principles."

"The whole thing is profoundly discouraging," said Miller sadly. "Try as we may to build up the race in the essentials of good citizenship and win the good opinion of the best people, some black scoundrel comes along, and by a single criminal act, committed in the twinkling of an eye, neutralizes the effect of a whole year's work."

Notes

[131] *Original reads*: any one [ed.].

"It's mighty easy neut'alize', er whatever you call it," said Josh sullenly. "De w'ite folks don' want too good an opinion er de niggers – ef dey had a good opinion of 'em, dey wouldn'[132] have no excuse fer 'busin' an' hangin' an' burnin' 'em. But ef dey can't keep from doin' it, let 'em git de right man! Dis way er pickin' up de fus' nigger dey comes across, an' stringin' 'im up rega'dliss, ought ter be stop', an' stop' right now!"

"Yes, that's the worst of lynch law," said Watson; "but we are wasting valuable time – it's hardly worthwhile for us to discuss a subject we are all agreed upon. One of our race, accused of certain acts, is about to be put to death without judge or jury, ostensibly because he committed a crime – really because he is a negro, for if he were white he would not be lynched. It is thus made a race issue, on the one side as well as on the other. What can we do to protect him?"

"We kin fight, ef we haf ter," replied Josh resolutely.

"Well, now, let us see. Suppose the colored people armed themselves? Messages would at once be sent to every town and county in the neighborhood. White men from all over the state, armed to the teeth, would at the slightest word pour into town on every railroad train, and extras would be run for their benefit."

"They're already coming in," said Watson.

"We might go to the sheriff," suggested Miller, "and demand that he telegraph the governor to call out the militia."

"I spoke to the sheriff an hour ago," replied Watson. "He has a white face and a whiter liver. He does not dare call out the militia to protect a negro charged with such a brutal crime – and if he did, the militia are white men, and who can say that their efforts would not be directed to keeping the negroes out of the way, in order that the white devils might do their worst? The whole machinery of the state is in the hands of white men, elected partly by our votes. When the color line is drawn, if they choose to stand together with the rest of their race against us, or to remain passive and let the others work their will, we are helpless – our cause is hopeless."

"We might call on the general government," said Miller. "Surely the President would intervene."

"Such a demand would be of no avail," returned Watson. "The government can only intervene under certain conditions, of which it must be informed through designated channels. It never sees anything that is not officially called to its attention. The whole negro population of the South might be slaughtered before the necessary red tape could be spun out to inform the President that a state of anarchy prevailed. There's no hope there."

"Den w'at we gwine ter do?" demanded Josh indignantly; "jes' set here an' let 'em hang Sandy, er bu'n 'im?"

"God knows!" exclaimed Miller. "The outlook is dark, but we should at least try to do something. There must be some white men in the town who would stand for law and order – there's no possible chance for Sandy to escape hanging by due process of law, if he is guilty. We might at least try half a dozen gentlemen."

"We'd better leave Josh here," said Watson. "He's too truculent. If he went on the street he'd make trouble, and if he accompanied us he'd do more harm than good. Wait for us here, Josh, until we've seen what we can do. We'll be back in half an hour."

In half an hour they had both returned.

Notes

[132] *Original reads*: would n' [ed.].

"It's no use," reported Watson gloomily. "I called at the mayor's office and found it locked. He is doubtless afraid on his own account, and would not dream of asserting his authority. I then looked up Judge Everton, who has always seemed to be fair. My reception was cold. He admitted that lynching was, as a rule, unjustifiable, but maintained that there were exceptions to all rules – that laws were made, after all, to express the will of the people in regard to the ordinary administration of justice, but that in an emergency the sovereign people might assert itself and take the law into its own hands – the creature was not greater than the creator. He laughed at my suggestion that Sandy was innocent. 'If he is innocent,' he said, 'then produce the real criminal. You negroes are standing in your own light when you try to protect such dastardly scoundrels as this Campbell, who is an enemy of society and not fit to live. I shall not move in the matter. If a negro wants the protection of the law, let him obey the law.' A wise judge – a second Daniel come to judgment! If this were the law, there would be no need of judges or juries."

"I called on Dr. Price," said Miller, "my good friend Dr. Price, who would rather lie than hurt my feelings. 'Miller,' he declared, 'this is no affair of mine, or yours. I have too much respect for myself and my profession to interfere in such a matter, and you will accomplish nothing, and only lessen your own influence, by having anything to say.' 'But the man may be innocent,' I replied; 'there is every reason to believe that he is.' He shook his head pityingly. 'You are self-deceived, Miller; your prejudice has warped your judgment. The proof is overwhelming that he robbed this old lady, laid violent hands upon her, and left her dead. If he did no more, he has violated the written and unwritten law of the Southern States. I could not save him if I would, Miller, and frankly, I would not if I could. If he is innocent, his people can console themselves with the reflection that Mrs. Ochiltree was also innocent, and balance one crime against the other, the white against the black. Of course I shall take no part in whatever may be done – but it is not my affair, nor yours. Take my advice, Miller, and keep out of it.'

"That is the situation," added Miller, summing up. "Their friendship for us, a slender stream at the best, dries up entirely when it strikes their prejudices. There is seemingly not one white man in Wellington who will speak a word for law, order, decency, or humanity. Those who do not participate will stand idly by and see an untried man deliberately and brutally murdered. Race prejudice is the devil unchained."

"Well, den, suh," said Josh, "where does we stan' now? W'at is we gwine ter do? I wouldn'[133] min' fightin', fer my time ain't come yit – I feels dat in my bones. W'at we gwine ter do, dat's w'at I wanter know."

"What does old Mr. Delamere have to say about the matter?" asked Miller suddenly. "Why haven't we thought of him before? Has he been seen?"

"No," replied Watson gloomily, "and for a good reason – he is not in town. I came by the house just now, and learned that he went out to his country place yesterday afternoon, to remain a week. Sandy was to have followed him out there this morning – it's a pity he didn't go yesterday. The old gentleman has probably heard nothing about the matter."

"How about young Delamere?"

"He went away early this morning, down the river, to fish. He'll probably not hear of it before night, and he's only a boy anyway, and could very likely do nothing," said Watson.

Miller looked at his watch.

Notes

[133] *Original reads*: would n' [ed.].

"Belleview is ten miles away," he said. "It is now eleven o'clock. I can drive out there in an hour and a half at the farthest. I'll go and see Mr. Delamere – he can do more than any living man, if he is able to do anything at all. There's never been a lynching here, and one good white man, if he choose, may stem the flood long enough to give justice a chance. Keep track of the white people while I'm gone, Watson; and you, Josh, learn what the colored folks are saying, and do nothing rash until I return. In the meantime, do all that you can to find out who did commit this most atrocious murder."

Chapter 23

Belleview

MILLER did not reach his destination without interruption. At one point a considerable stretch of the road was under repair, which made it necessary for him to travel slowly. His horse cast a shoe, and threatened to go lame; but in the course of time he arrived at the entrance gate of Belleview, entering which he struck into a private road, bordered by massive oaks, whose multitudinous branches, hung with long streamers of trailing moss, formed for much of the way a thick canopy above his head. It took him only a few minutes to traverse the quarter of a mile that lay between the entrance gate and the house itself.

This old colonial plantation, rich in legendary lore and replete with historic distinction, had been in the Delamere family for nearly two hundred years. Along the bank of the river which skirted its domain the famous pirate Blackbeard had held high carnival, and was reputed to have buried much treasure, vague traditions of which still lingered among the negroes and poor-whites of the country roundabout. The beautiful residence, rising white and stately in a grove of ancient oaks, dated from 1750, and was built of brick which had been brought from England. Enlarged and improved from generation to generation, it stood, like a baronial castle, upon a slight eminence from which could be surveyed the large demesne still belonging to the estate, which had shrunk greatly from its colonial dimensions. While still embracing several thousand acres, part forest and part cleared land, it had not of late years been profitable; in spite of which Mr. Delamere, with the conservatism of his age and caste, had never been able to make up his mind to part with any considerable portion of it. His grandson, he imagined, could make the estate pay and yet preserve it in its integrity. Here, in pleasant weather, surrounded by the scenes which he loved, old Mr. Delamere spent much of the time during his declining years.

Dr. Miller had once passed a day at Belleview, upon Mr. Delamere's invitation. For this old-fashioned gentleman, whose ideals not even slavery had been able to spoil, regarded himself as a trustee for the great public, which ought, in his opinion, to take as much pride as he in the contemplation of this historic landmark. In earlier years Mr. Delamere had been a practicing lawyer, and had numbered Miller's father among his clients. He had always been regarded as friendly to the colored people, and, until age and ill health had driven him from active life, had taken a lively interest in their advancement since the abolition of slavery. Upon the public opening of Miller's new hospital, he had made an effort to be present, and had made a little speech of approval and encouragement which had manifested his kindliness and given Miller much pleasure.

It was with the consciousness, therefore, that he was approaching a friend, as well as Sandy's master, that Miller's mind was chiefly occupied as his tired horse, scenting the end of his efforts, bore him with a final burst of speed along the last few rods of the journey; for the urgency of Miller's errand, involving as it did the issues of life and death, did not permit him to enjoy the charm of mossy oak or forest reaches, or even to appreciate the noble front of Belleview House when it at last loomed up before him.

"Well, William," said Mr. Delamere, as he gave his hand to Miller from the armchair in which he was seated under the broad and stately portico, "I didn't expect to see you out here. You'll excuse my not rising – I'm none too firm on my legs. Did you see anything of my man Sandy back there on the road? He ought to have been here by nine o'clock, and it's now one. Sandy is punctuality itself, and I don't know how to account for his delay."

Clearly there need be no time wasted in preliminaries. Mr. Delamere had gone directly to the subject in hand.

"He will not be here to-day, sir," replied Miller. "I have come to you on his account."

In a few words Miller stated the situation.

"Preposterous!" exclaimed the old gentleman, with more vigor than Miller had supposed him to possess. "Sandy is absolutely incapable of such a crime as robbery, to say nothing of murder; and as for the rest, that is absurd upon the face of it! And so the poor old woman is dead! Well, well, well! she could not have lived much longer anyway; but Sandy did not kill her – it's simply impossible! Why, *I* raised that boy! He was born on my place. I'd as soon believe such a thing of my own grandson as of Sandy! No negro raised by a Delamere would ever commit such a crime. I really believe, William, that Sandy has the family honor of the Delameres quite as much at heart as I have. Just tell them I say Sandy is innocent, and it will be all right."

"I'm afraid, sir," rejoined Miller, who kept his voice up so that the old gentleman could understand without having it suggested that Miller knew he was hard of hearing, "that you don't quite appreciate the situation. I believe Sandy innocent; you believe him innocent; but there are suspicious circumstances which do not explain themselves, and the white people of the city believe him guilty, and are going to lynch him before he has a chance to clear himself."

"Why doesn't he explain the suspicious circumstances?" asked Mr. Delamere. "Sandy is truthful and can be believed. I would take Sandy's word as quickly as another man's oath."

"He has no chance to explain," said Miller. "The case is prejudged. A crime has been committed. Sandy is charged with it. He is black, and therefore he is guilty. No colored lawyer would be allowed in the jail, if one should dare to go there. No white lawyer will intervene. He'll be lynched to-night, without judge, jury, or preacher, unless we can stave the thing off for a day or two."

"Have you seen my grandson?" asked the old gentleman. "Is he not looking after Sandy?"

"No, sir. It seems he went down the river this morning to fish, before the murder was discovered; no one knows just where he has gone, or at what hour he will return."

"Well, then," said Mr. Delamere, rising from his chair with surprising vigor, "I shall have to go myself. No faithful servant of mine shall be hanged for a crime he didn't commit, so long as I have a voice to speak or a dollar to spend. There'll be no trouble after I get there, William. The people are naturally wrought up at such a crime. A fine old woman – she had some detestable traits, and I was always afraid she wanted to marry me, but she was of an excellent family and had many good points – an old woman of one of the best families, struck down by the hand of a murderer! You must remember, William, that blood is thicker than water, and that the provocation is extreme, and that a few hotheads might easily lose sight of the great principles involved and seek immediate vengeance, without too much discrimination. But they are good people, William, and when I have spoken, and they have an opportunity for the sober second thought, they will do nothing rashly, but will wait for the operation of the law, which will, of course, clear Sandy."

"I'm sure I hope so," returned Miller. "Shall I try to drive you back, sir, or will you order your own carriage?"

"My horses are fresher, William, and I'll have them brought around. You can take the reins, if you will – I'm rather old to drive – and my man will come behind with your buggy."

In a few minutes they set out along the sandy road. Having two fresh horses, they made better headway than Miller had made coming out, and reached Wellington easily by three o'clock.

"I think, William," said Mr. Delamere, as they drove into the town, "that I had first better talk with Sandy. He may be able to explain away the things that seem to connect him with this atrocious affair; and that will put me in a better position to talk to other people about it."

Miller drove directly to the county jail. Thirty or forty white men, who seemed to be casually gathered near the door, closed up when the carriage approached. The sheriff, who had seen them from the inside, came to the outer door and spoke to the visitor through a grated wicket.[134]

"Mr. Wemyss," said Mr. Delamere, when he had made his way to the entrance with the aid of his cane, "I wish to see my servant, Sandy Campbell, who is said to be in your custody."

The sheriff hesitated. Meantime there was some parleying in low tones among the crowd outside. No one interfered, however, and in a moment the door opened sufficiently to give entrance to the old gentleman, after which it closed quickly and clangorously behind him.

Feeling no desire to linger in the locality, Miller, having seen his companion enter the jail, drove the carriage round to Mr. Delamere's house, and leaving it in the charge of[135] a servant with instructions to return for his master in a quarter of an hour, hastened to his own home to meet Watson and Josh and report the result of his efforts.

Chapter 24

Two Southern Gentlemen

THE iron bolt rattled in the lock, the door of a cell swung open, and when Mr. Delamere had entered was quickly closed again.

"Well, Sandy!"

"Oh, Mars John! Is you fell from hebben ter he'p me out er here? I prayed de Lawd ter sen' you, an' He answered my prayer, an' here you is, Mars John – here you is! Oh, Mars John, git me out er dis place!"

"Tut, tut, Sandy!" answered his master; "of course I'll get you out. That's what I've come for. How in the world did such a mistake ever happen? You would no more commit such a crime than I would!"

Notes

[134] *wicket* a small window.

[135] *Original reads*: in charge of [ed.].

"No, suh, 'deed I would n', an' you know I would n'! I wouldn'[136] want ter bring no disgrace on de fam'ly dat raise' me, ner ter make no trouble fer you, suh; but here I is, suh, lock' up in jail, an' folks talkin' 'bout hangin' me fer somethin' dat never entered my min', suh. I swea' ter God I never thought er sech a thing!"

"Of course you didn't, Sandy," returned Mr. Delamere soothingly; "and now the next thing, and the simplest thing, is to get you out of this. I'll speak to the officers, and at the preliminary hearing to-morrow I'll tell them all about you, and they will let you go. You won't mind spending one night in jail for your sins."

"No, suh, ef I wuz sho' I'd be 'lowed ter spen' it here. But dey say dey're gwine ter lynch me ter-night – I kin hear 'em talkin' f'm de winders er de cell, suh."

"Well, *I* say, Sandy, that they shall do no such thing! Lynch a man brought up by a Delamere, for a crime of which he is innocent? Preposterous! I'll speak to the authorities and see that you are properly protected until this mystery is unraveled. If Tom had been here, he would have had you out before now, Sandy. My grandson is a genuine Delamere, is he not, Sandy?"

"Yas, suh, yas, suh," returned Sandy, with a lack of enthusiasm which he tried to conceal from his master. "An' I s'pose ef he hadn'[137] gone fishin' so soon dis mawnin', he'd 'a' be'n lookin' after me, suh."

"It has been my love for him and your care of me, Sandy," said the old gentleman tremulously, "that have kept me alive so long; but now explain to me everything concerning this distressing matter, and I shall then be able to state your case to better advantage."

"Well, suh," returned Sandy, "I mought's well tell de whole tale an' not hol' nothin' back. I wuz kind er lonesome las' night, an' sence I be'n tu'ned outen de chu'ch on account er dat cakewalk I didn'[138] go ter, so he'p me God! I didn'[139] feel like gwine ter prayer-meetin', so I went roun' ter see Solomon Williams, an' he wa'n't home, an' den I walk' down street an' met Josh Green, an' he ax' me inter Sam Taylor's place, an' I sot roun' dere wid Josh till 'bout 'leven o'clock, w'en I sta'ted back home. I went straight ter de house, suh, an' went ter bed an' ter sleep widout sayin' a wo'd ter a single soul excep' Mistuh Tom, who wuz settin' up readin' a book w'en I come in. I wish I may drap dead in my tracks, suh, ef dat ain't de God's truf, suh, eve'y wo'd of it!"

"I believe every word of it, Sandy; now tell me about the clothes that you are said to have been found cleaning, and the suspicious articles that were found in your room?"

"Dat's w'at beats me, Mars John," replied Sandy, shaking his head mournfully. "W'en I lef' home las' night after supper, my clo's wuz all put erway in de closet in my room, folded up on de she'f ter keep de moths out. Dey wuz my good clo's – de blue coat dat you wo' ter de weddin' fo'ty years ago, an' dem dere plaid pants I gun Mistuh Cohen fo' dollars fer three years ago; an' w'en I looked in my closet dis mawnin', suh, befo' I got ready ter sta't fer Belleview, dere wuz my clo's layin' on de flo', all muddy an' crumple' up, des lack somebody had wo' 'em in a fight! Somebody e'se had wo' my clo's – er e'se dere'd be'n some witchcraf', er some sort er devilment gwine on dat I can't make out, suh, ter save my soul!"

"There was no witchcraft, Sandy, but that there was some deviltry might well be. Now, what other negro, who might have been mistaken for you, could have taken your clothes? Surely no one about the house?"

Notes

[136] *Original reads*: I would n'! I would n' [ed.].

[137] *Original reads*: had n' [ed.].

[138] *Original reads*: did n' [ed.].

[139] *Original reads*: did n' [ed.].

"No, suh, no, suh. It couldn't 'a' be'n Jeff, fer he wuz at Belleview wid you; an' it couldn't 'a' be'n Billy, fer he wuz too little ter wear my clo's; an' it couldn't 'a' be'n Sally, fer she's a 'oman. It's a myst'ry ter me, suh!"

"Have you no enemies? Is there anyone[140] in Wellington whom you imagine would like to do you an injury?"

"Not a livin' soul dat I knows of, suh. I've be'n tu'ned out'n de chu'ch, but I don' know who my enemy is dere, er ef it wuz all a mistake, like dis yer jailin' is; but de Debbil is in dis somewhar, Mars John – an' I got my reasons fer sayin' so."

"What do you mean, Sandy?"

Sandy related his experience of the preceding evening: how he had seen the apparition preceding him to the house, and how he had questioned Tom upon the subject.

"There's some mystery here, Sandy," said Mr. Delamere reflectively. "Have you told me all, now, upon your honor? I am trying to save your life, Sandy, and I must be able to trust your word implicitly. You must tell me every circumstance; a very little and seemingly unimportant bit of evidence may sometimes determine the issue of a great lawsuit. There is one thing especially, Sandy: where did you get the gold which was found in your trunk?"

Sandy's face lit up with hopefulness.

"Why, Mars John, I kin 'splain dat part easy. Dat wuz money I had lent out, an' I got back f'm – But no, suh, I promise' not ter tell."

"Circumstances absolve you from your promise, Sandy. Your life is of more value to you than any other thing. If you will explain where you got the gold, and the silk purse that contained it, which is said to be Mrs. Ochiltree's, you will be back home before night."

Old Mr. Delamere's faculties, which had been waning somewhat in sympathy with his health, were stirred to unusual acuteness by his servant's danger. He was watching Sandy with all the awakened instincts of the trial lawyer. He could see clearly enough that, in beginning to account for the possession of the gold, Sandy had started off with his explanation in all sincerity. At the mention of the silk purse, however, his face had blanched to an ashen gray, and the words had frozen upon his lips.

A less discerning observer might have taken these things as signs of guilt, but not so Mr. Delamere.

"Well, Sandy," said his master encouragingly, "go on. You got the gold from" –

Sandy remained silent. He had had a great shock, and had taken a great resolution.

"Mars John," he asked dreamily, "you don' b'lieve dat I done dis thing?"

"Certainly not, Sandy, else why should I be here?"

"An' nothin' wouldn'[141] make you b'lieve it, suh?"

"No, Sandy – I could not believe it of you. I've known you too long and too well."

"An' you wouldn'[142] b'lieve it, not even ef I wouldn'[143] say one wo'd mo' about it?"

"No, Sandy, I believe you no more capable of this crime than I would be – or my grandson, Tom. I wish Tom were here, that he might help me overcome your stubbornness; but you'll not be so foolish, so absurdly foolish, Sandy, as to keep silent and risk your life merely to shield someone[144] else, when by speaking you might clear up this mystery and be restored at once to liberty. Just tell me where you got the gold," added the old gentleman persuasively. "Come, now, Sandy, that's a good fellow!"

Notes

[140] *Original reads*: any one [ed.].

[141] *Original reads*: would n' [ed.].

[142] *Original reads*: would n' [ed.].

[143] *Original reads*: would n' [ed.].

[144] *Original reads*: some one [ed.].

"Mars John," asked Sandy softly, "w'en my daddy, 'way back yander befo' de wah, wuz about ter be sol' away f'm his wife an' child'en, you bought him an' dem, an' kep' us all on yo' place tergether, didn't[145] you, suh?"

"Yes, Sandy, and he was a faithful servant, and proved worthy of all I did for him."

"And w'en he had wo'ked fer you ten years, suh, you sot 'im free?"

"Yes, Sandy, he had earned his freedom."

"An' w'en de wah broke out, an' my folks wuz scattered, an' I didn'[146] have nothin' ter do ner nowhar ter go, you kep' me on yo' place, and tuck me ter wait on you, suh, didn't[147] you?"

"Yes, Sandy, and you have been a good servant and a good friend; but tell me now about this gold, and I'll go and get you out of this, right away, for I need you, Sandy, and you 'll not be of any use to me shut up here!"

"Jes' hol' on a minute befo' you go, Mars John; fer ef dem people outside should git holt er me befo' you *does* git me out er here, I may never see you no mo', suh, in dis worl'. W'en Mars Billy McLean shot me by mistake, w'ile we wuz out huntin' dat day, who wuz it boun' up my woun's an' kep' me from bleedin' ter def, an' kyar'ed me two miles on his own shoulders ter a doctuh?"

"Yes, Sandy, and when black Sally ran away with your young mistress and Tom, when Tom was a baby, who stopped the runaway, and saved their lives at the risk of his own?"

"Dat wa'n't nothin', suh; anybody could 'a' done dat, w'at wuz strong ernuff an' swif' ernuff. You is be'n good ter me, suh, all dese years, an' I've tried ter do my duty by you, suh, an' by Mistuh Tom, who wuz yo' own gran'son, an' de las' one er de fam'ly."

"Yes, you have, Sandy, and when I am gone, which will not be very long, Tom will take care of you, and see that you never want. But we are wasting valuable time, Sandy, in these old reminiscences. Let us get back to the present. Tell me about the gold, now, so that I may at once look after your safety. It may not even be necessary for you to remain here all night."

"Jes' one wo'd mo', Mars John, befo' you go! I know you're gwine ter do de bes' you kin fer me, an' I'm sorry I can't he'p you no mo' wid it; but ef dere should be any accident, er ef you *can't* git me out er here, don' bother yo' min' 'bout it no mo', suh, an' don' git yo'se'f ixcited, fer you know de doctuh says, suh, dat you can't stan' ixcitement; but jes' leave me in de han's er de Lawd, suh – *He'll* look after me, here er hereafter. I know I've fell f'm grace mo' d'n once, but I've done made my peace wid Him in dis here jail-house, suh, an' I ain't 'feared ter die – ef I haf ter. I ain' got no wife ner child'n ter mo'n fer me, an' I'll die knowin' dat I've done my duty ter dem dat hi'ed me, an' trusted me, an' had claims on me. Fer I wuz raise' by a Delamere, suh, an' all de ole Delameres wuz gent'emen, an' deir principles spread ter de niggers 'round 'em, suh; an' ef I has ter die fer somethin' I didn'[148] do – I kin die, suh, like a gent'eman! But ez fer dat gol', suh, I ain' gwine ter say one wo'd mo' 'bout it ter nobody in dis worl'!"

Nothing could shake Sandy's determination. Mr. Delamere argued, expostulated, but all in vain. Sandy would not speak.

More and more confident of some mystery, which would come out in time, if properly investigated, Mr. Delamere, strangely beset by a vague sense of discomfort over

Notes

[145] *Original reads*: did n't [ed.].

[146] *Original reads*: did n' [ed.].

[147] *Original reads*: did n't [ed.].

[148] *Original reads*: did n' [ed.].

and beyond that occasioned by his servant's danger, hurried away upon his errand of mercy. He felt less confident of the outcome than when he had entered the jail, but was quite as much resolved that no effort should be spared to secure protection for Sandy until there had been full opportunity for the truth to become known.

"Take good care of your prisoner, sheriff," he said sternly, as he was conducted to the door. "He will not be long in your custody, and I shall see that you are held strictly accountable for his safety."

"I'll do what I can, sir," replied the sheriff in an even tone and seemingly not greatly impressed by this warning. "If the prisoner is taken from me, it will be because the force that comes for him is too strong for resistance."

"There should be no force too strong for an honest man in your position to resist – whether successfully or not is beyond the question. The officer who is intimidated by threats, or by his own fears, is recreant to his duty, and no better than the mob which threatens him. But you will have no such test, Mr. Wemyss! I shall see to it myself that there is no violence!"

Chapter 25

The Honor of a Family

Mr. Delamere's coachman, who, in accordance with instructions left by Miller, had brought the carriage around to the jail and was waiting anxiously at the nearest corner, drove up with some trepidation as he saw his master emerge from the prison. The old gentleman entered the carriage and gave the order to be driven to the office of the Morning Chronicle. According to Jerry, the porter, whom he encountered at the door, Carteret was in his office, and Mr. Delamere, with the aid of his servant, climbed the stairs painfully and found the editor at his desk.

"Carteret," exclaimed Mr. Delamere, "what is all this talk about lynching my man for murder and robbery and criminal assault? It's perfectly absurd! The man was raised by me; he has lived in my house forty years. He has been honest, faithful, and trustworthy. He would no more be capable of this crime than you would, or my grandson Tom. Sandy has too much respect for the family to do anything that would reflect disgrace upon it."

"My dear Mr. Delamere," asked Carteret, with an indulgent smile, "how could a negro possibly reflect discredit upon a white family? I should really like to know."

"How, sir? A white family raised him. Like all the negroes, he has been clay in the hands of the white people. They are what we have made them, or permitted them to become."

"We are not God, Mr. Delamere! We do not claim to have created these – masterpieces."

"No; but we thought to overrule God's laws, and we enslaved these people for our greed, and sought to escape the manstealer's curse by laying to our souls the flattering unction that we were making of barbarous negroes civilized and Christian men. If we did not, if instead of making them Christians we have made some of them brutes, we have only ourselves to blame, and if these prey upon society, it is our just punishment! But my negroes, Carteret, were well raised and well behaved. This man is innocent of this offense, I solemnly affirm, and I want your aid to secure his safety until a fair trial can be had."

"On your bare word, sir?" asked Carteret, not at all moved by this outburst.

Old Mr. Delamere trembled with anger, and his withered cheek flushed darkly, but he restrained his feelings, and answered with an attempt at calmness:–

"Time was, sir, when the word of a Delamere was held as good as his bond, and those who questioned it were forced to maintain their skepticism upon the field of honor. Time was, sir, when the law was enforced in this state in a manner to command the respect of the world! Our lawyers, our judges, our courts, were a credit to humanity and civilization. I fear I have outlasted my epoch – I have lived to hear of white men, the most favored of races, the heirs of civilization, the conservators of liberty, howling like red Indians around a human being slowly roasting at the stake."

"My dear sir," said Carteret soothingly, "you should undeceive yourself. This man is no longer your property. The negroes are no longer under our control, and with their emancipation ceased our responsibility. Their insolence and disregard for law have reached a point where they must be sternly rebuked."

"The law," retorted Mr. Delamere, "furnishes a sufficient penalty for any crime, however heinous, and our code is by no means lenient. To my old-fashioned notions, death would seem an adequate punishment for any crime, and torture has been abolished in civilized countries for a hundred years. It would be better to let a crime go entirely unpunished, than to use it as a pretext for turning the whole white population into a mob of primitive savages, dancing in hellish glee around the mangled body of a man who has never been tried for a crime. All this, however, is apart from my errand, which is to secure your assistance in heading off this mob until Sandy can have a fair hearing and an opportunity to prove his innocence."

"How can I do that, Mr. Delamere?"

"You are editor of the Morning Chronicle. The Chronicle is the leading newspaper of the city. This morning's issue practically suggested the mob; the same means will stop it. I will pay the expense of an extra edition, calling off the mob, on the ground that newly discovered evidence has shown the prisoner's innocence."

"But where is the evidence?" asked Carteret.

Again Mr. Delamere flushed and trembled. "*My* evidence, sir! I say the negro was morally incapable of the crime. A man of forty-five does not change his nature overnight. He is no more capable of a disgraceful deed than my grandson would be!"

Carteret smiled sadly.

"I am sorry, Mr. Delamere," he said, "that you should permit yourself to be so exercised about a worthless scoundrel who has forfeited his right to live. The proof against him is overwhelming. As to his capability of crime, we will apply your own test. You have been kept in the dark too long, Mr. Delamere – indeed, we all have – about others as well as this negro. Listen, sir: last night, at the Clarendon Club, Tom Delamere was caught cheating outrageously at cards. He had been suspected for some time; a trap was laid for him, and he fell into it. Out of regard for you and for my family, he has been permitted to resign quietly, with the understanding that he first pay off his debts, which are considerable."

Mr. Delamere's face, which had taken on some color in the excitement of the interview, had gradually paled to a chalky white while Carteret was speaking. His head sunk forward; already an old man, he seemed to have aged ten years in but little more than as many seconds.

"Can this be true?" he demanded in a hoarse whisper. "Is it – entirely authentic?"

"True as gospel; true as it is that Mrs. Ochiltree has been murdered, and that this negro killed her. Ellis was at the club a few minutes after the affair happened, and learned the facts from one of the participants. Tom made no attempt at denial. We have kept the matter out of the other papers, and I would have spared your feelings – I surely would not wish to wound them – but the temptation proved too strong for me, and it seemed the only way to convince you: it was your own test. If a gentleman of a distinguished name and an honorable ancestry, with all the restraining forces of social position surrounding him, to hold him in check, can stoop to dishonor, what is the improbability of an illiterate negro's being at least *capable* of crime?"

"Enough, sir," said the old gentleman. "You have proved enough. My grandson may be a scoundrel – I can see, in the light of this revelation, how he might be; and he seems not to have denied it. I maintain, nevertheless, that my man Sandy is innocent of the charge against him. He *has* denied it, and it has not been proved. Carteret, I owe that negro my life; he, and his father before him, have served me and mine faithfully and well. I cannot see him killed like a dog, without judge or jury – no, not even if he were guilty, which I do not believe!"

Carteret felt a twinge of remorse for the pain he had inflicted upon this fine old man, this ideal gentleman of the ideal past – the past which he himself so much admired and regretted. He would like to spare his old friend any further agitation; he was in a state of health where too great excitement might prove fatal. But how could he? The negro was guilty, and sure to die sooner or later. He had not meant to interfere, and his intervention might be fruitless.

"Mr. Delamere," he said gently, "there is but one way to gain time. You say the negro is innocent. Appearances are against him. The only way to clear him is to produce the real criminal, or prove an alibi. If you, or some other white man of equal standing, could swear that the negro was in your presence last night at any hour when this crime could have taken place, it might be barely possible to prevent the lynching for the present; and when he is tried, which will probably be not later than next week, he will have every opportunity to defend himself, with you to see that he gets no less than justice. I think it can be managed, though there is still a doubt. I will do my best, for your sake, Mr. Delamere – solely for your sake, be it understood, and not for that of the negro, in whom you are entirely deceived."

"I shall not examine your motives, Carteret," replied the other, "if you can bring about what I desire."

"Whatever is done," added Carteret, "must be done quickly. It is now four o'clock; no one can answer for what may happen after seven. If he can prove an alibi, there may yet be time to save him. White men might lynch a negro on suspicion; they would not kill a man who was proven, by the word of white men, to be entirely innocent."

"I do not know," returned Mr. Delamere, shaking his head sadly. "After what you have told me, it is no longer safe to assume what white men will or will not do – what I have learned here has shaken my faith in humanity. I am going away, but shall return in a short time. Shall I find you here?"

"I will await your return," said Carteret.

He watched Mr. Delamere pityingly as the old man moved away on the arm of the coachman waiting in the hall. He did not believe that Mr. Delamere could prove an alibi for his servant, and without some positive proof the negro would surely die – as he well deserved to die.

Chapter 26

The Discomfort of Ellis

Mr. Ellis was vaguely uncomfortable. In the first excitement following the discovery of the crime, he had given his bit of evidence, and had shared the universal indignation against the murderer. When public feeling took definite shape in the intention to lynch the prisoner, Ellis felt a sudden sense of responsibility growing upon himself. When he learned, an hour later, that it was proposed to burn the negro, his part in the affair assumed a still graver aspect; for his had been the final word to fix the prisoner's guilt.

Ellis did not believe in lynch law. He had argued against it, more than once, in private conversation, and had written several editorials against the practice, while in charge of the Morning Chronicle during Major Carteret's absence. A young man, however, and merely representing another, he had not set up as a reformer, taking rather the view that this summary method of punishing crime, with all its possibilities of error, to say nothing of the resulting disrespect of the law and contempt for the time-honored methods of establishing guilt, was a mere temporary symptom of the unrest caused by the unsettled relations of the two races at the South. There had never before been any special need for any vigorous opposition to lynch law, so far as the community was concerned, for there had not been a lynching in Wellington since Ellis had come there, eight years before, from a smaller town, to seek a place for himself in the world of action. Twenty years before, indeed, there had been wild doings, during the brief Ku-Klux outbreak, but that was before Ellis's time – or at least when he was but a child. He had come of a Quaker family – the modified Quakers of the South – and while sharing in a general way the Southern prejudice against the negro, his prejudices had been tempered by the peaceful tenets of his father's sect. His father had been a Whig, and a non-slaveholder; and while he had gone with the South in the civil war so far as a man of peace could go, he had not done so for love of slavery.

As the day wore on, Ellis's personal responsibility for the intended *auto-da-fé*[149] bore more heavily upon him. Suppose he had been wrong? He had seen the accused negro; he had recognized him by his clothes, his whiskers, his spectacles, and his walk; but he had also seen another man, who resembled Sandy so closely that but for the difference in their clothes, he was forced to acknowledge, he could not have told them apart. Had he not seen the first man, he would have sworn with even greater confidence that the second was Sandy. There had been, he recalled, about one of the men – he had not been then nor was he now able to tell which – something vaguely familiar, and yet seemingly discordant to whichever of the two it was, or, as it seemed to him now, to any man of that race. His mind reverted to the place where he had last seen Sandy, and then a sudden wave of illumination swept over him, and filled him with a thrill of horror. The cakewalk – the dancing – the speech – they were not Sandy's at all, nor any negro's! It was a white man who had stood in the light of the street lamp, so that the casual passer-by might see and recognize in him old Mr. Delamere's servant. The scheme was a dastardly one, and worthy of a heart that was something worse than weak and vicious.

Ellis resolved that the negro should not, if he could prevent it, die for another's crime; but what proof had he himself to offer in support of his theory? Then again, if he denounced Tom Delamere as the murderer, it would involve, in all probability, the destruction of his own hopes with regard to Clara. Of course she could not marry Delamere after the disclosure – the disgraceful episode at the club would have been enough to make that reasonably certain; it had put a nail in Delamere's coffin, but this crime had driven it in to the head and clinched it. On the other hand, would Miss Pemberton ever speak again to the man who had been the instrument of bringing disgrace upon the family? Spies, detectives, police officers, may be useful citizens, but they are rarely pleasant company for other people. We fee the executioner, but we do

Notes

[149] *auto-da-fé* execution.

not touch his bloody hand. We might feel a certain tragic admiration for Brutus[150] condemning his sons to death, but we would scarcely invite Brutus to dinner after the event. It would harrow our feelings too much.

Perhaps, thought Ellis, there might be a way out of the dilemma. It might be possible to save this innocent negro without, for the time being, involving Delamere. He believed that murder will out, but it need not be through his initiative. He determined to go to the jail and interview the prisoner, who might give such an account of himself as would establish his innocence beyond a doubt. If so, Ellis would exert himself to stem the tide of popular fury. If, as a last resort, he could save Sandy only by denouncing Delamere, he would do his duty, let it cost him what it might.

The gravity of his errand was not lessened by what he saw and heard on the way to the jail. The anger of the people was at a white heat. A white woman had been assaulted and murdered by a brutal negro. Neither advanced age, nor high social standing, had been able to protect her from the ferocity of a black savage. Her sex, which should have been her shield and buckler, had made her an easy mark for the villainy of a black brute. To take the time to try him would be a criminal waste of public money. To hang him would be too slight a punishment for so dastardly a crime. An example must be made.

Already the preparations were under way for the impending execution. A T-rail from the railroad yard had been procured, and men were burying it in the square before the jail. Others were bringing chains, and a load of pine wood was piled in convenient proximity. Some enterprising individual had begun the erection of seats from which, for a pecuniary consideration, the spectacle might be the more easily and comfortably viewed.

Ellis was stopped once or twice by persons of his acquaintance. From one he learned that the railroads would run excursions from the neighboring towns in order to bring spectators to the scene; from another that the burning was to take place early in the evening, so that the children might not be kept up beyond their usual bedtime. In one group that he passed he heard several young men discussing the question of which portions of the negro's body they would prefer for souvenirs. Ellis shuddered and hastened forward. Whatever was to be done must be done quickly, or it would be too late. He saw that already it would require a strong case in favor of the accused to overcome the popular verdict.

Going up the steps of the jail, he met Mr. Delamere, who was just coming out, after a fruitless interview with Sandy.

"Mr. Ellis," said the old gentleman, who seemed greatly agitated, "this is monstrous!"

"It is indeed, sir!" returned the younger man. "I mean to stop it if I can. The negro did not kill Mrs. Ochiltree."

Mr. Delamere looked at Ellis keenly, and, as Ellis recalled afterwards, there was death in his eyes. Unable to draw a syllable from Sandy, he had found his servant's silence more eloquent than words. Ellis felt a presentiment that this affair, however it might terminate, would be fatal to this fine old man, whom the city could ill spare, in spite of his age and infirmities.

"Mr. Ellis," asked Mr. Delamere, in a voice which trembled with ill-suppressed emotion, "do you know who killed her?"

Ellis felt a surging pity for his old friend; but every step that he had taken toward the jail had confirmed and strengthened his own resolution that this contemplated crime,

Notes

150 *Brutus* Lucius Junius Brutus, the founder of the Roman Republic, ordered his sons to be executed after their failed attempt to overthrow the republic.

which he dimly felt to be far more atrocious than that of which Sandy was accused, in that it involved a whole community rather than one vicious man, should be stopped at any cost. Deplorable enough had the negro been guilty, it became, in view of his certain innocence, an unspeakable horror, which for all time would cover the city with infamy.

"Mr. Delamere," he replied, looking the elder man squarely in the eyes, "I think I do – and I am very sorry."

"And who was it, Mr. Ellis?"

He put the question hopelessly, as though the answer were a foregone conclusion.

"I do not wish to say at present," replied Ellis, with a remorseful pang, "unless it becomes absolutely necessary, to save the negro's life. Accusations are dangerous – as this case proves – unless the proof be certain."

For a moment it seemed as though Mr. Delamere would collapse upon the spot. Rallying almost instantly, however, he took the arm which Ellis involuntarily offered, and said with an effort:–

"Mr. Ellis, you are a gentleman whom it is an honor to know. If you have time, I wish you would go with me to my house – I can hardly trust myself alone – and thence to the Chronicle office. This thing shall be stopped, and you will help me stop it."

It required but a few minutes to cover the half mile that lay between the prison and Mr. Delamere's residence.

Chapter 27

The Vagaries of the Higher Law

Mr. Delamere went immediately to his grandson's room, which he entered alone, closing and locking the door behind him. He had requested Ellis to wait in the carriage.

The bed had been made, and the room was apparently in perfect order. There was a bureau in the room, through which Mr. Delamere proceeded to look thoroughly. Finding one of the drawers locked, he tried it with a key of his own, and being unable to unlock it, took a poker from beside the stove and broke it ruthlessly open.

The contents served to confirm what he had heard concerning his grandson's character. Thrown together in disorderly confusion were bottles of wine and whiskey; soiled packs of cards; a dice-box with dice; a box of poker chips, several revolvers, and a number of photographs and paper-covered books at which the old gentleman merely glanced to ascertain their nature.

So far, while his suspicion had been strengthened, he had found nothing to confirm it. He searched the room more carefully, and found, in the wood-box by the small heating-stove which stood in the room, a torn and crumpled bit of paper. Stooping to pick this up, his eye caught a gleam of something yellow beneath the bureau, which lay directly in his line of vision.

First he smoothed out the paper. It was apparently the lower half of a label, or part of the cover of a small box, torn diagonally from corner to corner. From the business card at the bottom, which gave the name of a firm of manufacturers of theatrical supplies in a Northern city, and from the letters remaining upon the upper and narrower half, the bit of paper had plainly formed part of the wrapper of a package of burnt cork.[151]

Notes

[151] *burnt cork* used to artificially blacken one's face.

Closing his fingers spasmodically over this damning piece of evidence, Mr. Delamere knelt painfully, and with the aid of his cane drew out from under the bureau the yellow object which had attracted his attention. It was a five-dollar gold piece of a date back toward the beginning of the century.

To make assurance doubly sure, Mr. Delamere summoned the cook from the kitchen in the back yard. In answer to her master's questions, Sally averred that Mr. Tom had got up very early, had knocked at her window – she slept in a room off the kitchen in the yard – and had told her that she need not bother about breakfast for him, as he had had a cold bite from the pantry; that he was going hunting and fishing, and would be gone all day. According to Sally, Mr. Tom had come in about ten o'clock the night before. He had forgotten his night-key, Sandy was out, and she had admitted him with her own key. He had said that he was very tired and was going immediately to bed.

Mr. Delamere seemed perplexed; the crime had been committed later in the evening than ten o'clock. The cook cleared up the mystery.

"I reckon he must 'a' be'n dead ti'ed, suh, fer I went back ter his room fifteen er twenty minutes after he come in fer ter fin' out w'at he wanted fer breakfus'; an' I knock' two or three times, rale ha'd, an' Mistuh Tom didn'[152] wake up no mo' d'n de dead. He sho'ly had a good sleep, er he'd never 'a' got up so ea'ly."

"Thank you, Sally," said Mr. Delamere, when the woman had finished, "that will do."

"Will you be home ter suppah, suh?" asked the cook.

"Yes."

It was a matter of the supremest indifference to Mr. Delamere whether he should ever eat again, but he would not betray his feelings to a servant. In a few minutes he was driving rapidly with Ellis toward the office of the Morning Chronicle. Ellis could see that Mr. Delamere had discovered something of tragic import. Neither spoke. Ellis gave all his attention to the horses, and Mr. Delamere remained wrapped in his own sombre reflections.

When they reached the office, they were informed by Jerry that Major Carteret was engaged with General Belmont and Captain McBane. Mr. Delamere knocked peremptorily at the door of the inner office, which was opened by Carteret in person.

"Oh, it is you, Mr. Delamere."

"Carteret," exclaimed Mr. Delamere, "I must speak to you immediately, and alone."

"Excuse me a moment, gentlemen," said Carteret, turning to those within the room. "I'll be back in a moment – don't go away."

Ellis had left the room, closing the door behind him. Mr. Delamere and Carteret were quite alone.

"Carteret," declared the old gentleman, "this murder must not take place."

"'Murder' is a hard word," replied the editor, frowning slightly.

"It is the right word," rejoined Mr. Delamere, decidedly. "It would be a foul and most unnatural murder, for Sandy did not kill Mrs. Ochiltree."

Carteret with difficulty restrained a smile of pity. His old friend was very much excited, as the tremor in his voice gave proof. The criminal was his trusted servant, who had proved unworthy of confidence. No one could question Mr. Delamere's motives; but he was old, his judgment was no longer to be relied upon. It was a great pity that he should so excite and overstrain himself about a worthless negro, who had

Notes

[152] *Original reads*: did n' [ed.].

forfeited his life for a dastardly crime. Mr. Delamere had had two paralytic strokes, and a third might prove fatal. He must be dealt with gently.

"Mr. Delamere," he said, with patient tolerance, "I think you are deceived. There is but one sure way to stop this execution. If your servant is innocent, you must produce the real criminal. If the negro, with such overwhelming proofs against him, is not guilty, who is?"

"I will tell you who is," replied Mr. Delamere. "The murderer is" – the words came with a note of anguish, as though torn from his very heart – "the murderer is Tom Delamere, my own grandson!"

"Impossible, sir!" exclaimed Carteret, starting back involuntarily. "That could not be! The man was seen leaving the house, and he was black!"

"All cats are gray in the dark, Carteret; and, moreover, nothing is easier than for a white man to black his face. God alone knows how many crimes have been done in this guise! Tom Delamere, to get the money to pay his gambling debts, committed this foul murder, and then tried to fasten it upon as honest and faithful a soul as ever trod the earth."

Carteret, though at first overwhelmed by this announcement, perceived with quick intuition that it might easily be true. It was but a step from fraud to crime, and in Delamere's need of money there lay a palpable motive for robbery – the murder may have been an afterthought. Delamere knew as much about the cedar chest as the negro could have known, and more.

But a white man must not be condemned without proof positive.

"What foundation is there, sir," he asked, "for this astounding charge?"

Mr. Delamere related all that had taken place since he had left Belleview a couple of hours before, and as he proceeded, step by step, every word carried conviction to Carteret. Tom Delamere's skill as a mimic and a negro impersonator was well known; he had himself laughed at more than one of his performances. There had been a powerful motive, and Mr. Delamere's discoveries had made clear the means. Tom's unusual departure, before breakfast, on a fishing expedition was a suspicious circumstance. There was a certain devilish ingenuity about the affair which he would hardly have expected of Tom Delamere, but for which the reason was clear enough. One might have thought that Tom would have been satisfied with merely blacking his face, and leaving to chance the identification of the negro who might be apprehended. He would hardly have implicated, out of pure malignity, his grandfather's old servant, who had been his own care-taker for many years. Here, however, Carteret could see where Tom's own desperate position operated to furnish a probable motive for the crime. The surest way to head off suspicion from himself was to direct it strongly toward some particular person, and this he had been able to do conclusively by his access to Sandy's clothes, his skill in making up to resemble him, and by the episode of the silk purse. By placing himself beyond reach during the next day, he would not be called upon to corroborate or deny any inculpating statements which Sandy might make, and in the very probable case that the crime should be summarily avenged, any such statements on Sandy's part would be regarded as mere desperate subterfuges of the murderer to save his own life. It was a bad affair.

"The case seems clear," said Carteret reluctantly but conclusively. "And now, what shall we do about it?"

"I want you to print a handbill," said Mr. Delamere, "and circulate it through the town, stating that Sandy Campbell is innocent and Tom Delamere guilty of this crime. If this is not done, I will go myself and declare it to all who will listen, and I will publicly disown the villain who is no more grandson of mine. There is no deeper sink of iniquity into which he could fall."

Carteret's thoughts were chasing one another tumultuously. There could be no doubt that the negro was innocent, from the present aspect of affairs, and he must not be lynched; but in what sort of position would the white people be placed, if Mr. Delamere carried out his Spartan purpose of making the true facts known? The white people of the city had raised the issue of their own superior morality, and had themselves made this crime a race question.

The success of the impending "revolution," for which he and his *confrères*[153] had labored so long, depended in large measure upon the maintenance of their race prestige, which would be injured in the eyes of the world by such a fiasco. While they might yet win by sheer force, their cause would suffer in the court of morals, where they might stand convicted as pirates, instead of being applauded as patriots. Even the negroes would have the laugh on them – the people whom they hoped to make approve and justify their own despoilment. To be laughed at by the negroes was a calamity only less terrible than failure or death.

Such an outcome of an event which had already been heralded to the four corners of the earth would throw a cloud of suspicion upon the stories of outrage which had gone up from the South for so many years, and had done so much to win the sympathy of the North for the white South and to alienate it from the colored people. The reputation of the race was threatened. They must not lynch the negro, and yet, for the credit of the town, its aristocracy, and the race, the truth of this ghastly story must not see the light – at least not yet.

"Mr. Delamere," he exclaimed, "I am shocked and humiliated. The negro must be saved, of course, but – consider the family honor."

"Tom is no longer a member of my family. I disown him. He has covered the family name – my name, sir – with infamy. We have no longer a family honor. I wish never to hear his name spoken again!"

For several minutes Carteret argued with his old friend. Then he went into the other room and consulted with General Belmont.

As a result of these conferences, and of certain urgent messages sent out, within half an hour thirty or forty of the leading citizens of Wellington were gathered in the Morning Chronicle office. Several other curious persons, observing that there was something in the wind, and supposing correctly that it referred to the projected event of the evening, crowded in with those who had been invited.

Carteret was in another room, still arguing with Mr. Delamere. "It's a mere formality, sir," he was saying suavely, "accompanied by a mental reservation. We know the facts; but this must be done to justify us, in the eyes of the mob, in calling them off before they accomplish their purpose."

"Carteret," said the old man, in a voice eloquent of the struggle through which he had passed, "I would not perjure myself to prolong my own miserable existence another day, but God will forgive a sin committed to save another's life. Upon your head be it, Carteret, and not on mine!"

"Gentlemen," said Carteret, entering with Mr. Delamere the room where the men were gathered, and raising his hand for silence, "the people of Wellington were on the point of wreaking vengeance upon a negro who was supposed to have been guilty of a terrible crime. The white men of this city, impelled by the highest and holiest sentiments, were about to take steps to defend their hearthstones and maintain the purity

Notes

[153] *confrères* colleagues.

and ascendency of their race. Your purpose sprung from hearts wounded in their tenderest susceptibilities."

"'Rah, 'rah!" shouted a tipsy sailor, who had edged in with the crowd.

"But this same sense of justice," continued Carteret oratorically, "which would lead you to visit swift and terrible punishment upon the guilty, would not permit you to slay an innocent man. Even a negro, as long as he behaves himself and keeps in his place, is entitled to the protection of the law. We may be stern and unbending in the punishment of crime, as befits our masterful race, but we hold the scales of justice with even and impartial hand."

"'Rah f' 'mpa'tial han'!" cried the tipsy sailor, who was immediately ejected with slight ceremony.

"We have discovered, beyond a doubt, that the negro Sandy Campbell, now in custody, did not commit this robbery and murder, but that it was perpetrated by some unknown man, who has fled from the city. Our venerable and distinguished fellow townsman, Mr. Delamere, in whose employment this Campbell has been for many years, will vouch for his character, and states, furthermore, that Campbell was with him all last night, covering any hour at which this crime could have been committed."

"If Mr. Delamere will swear to that," said someone[154] in the crowd, "the negro should not be lynched."

There were murmurs of dissent. The preparations had all been made. There would be great disappointment if the lynching did not occur.

"Let Mr. Delamere swear, if he wants to save the nigger," came again from the crowd.

"Certainly," assented Carteret. "Mr. Delamere can have no possible objection to taking the oath. Is there a notary public present, or a justice of the peace?"

A man stepped forward. "I am a justice of the peace," he announced.

"Very well, Mr. Smith," said Carteret, recognizing the speaker. "With your permission, I will formulate the oath, and Mr. Delamere may repeat it after me, if he will. I solemnly swear" –

"I solemnly swear" –

Mr. Delamere's voice might have come from the tomb, so hollow and unnatural did it sound.

"So help me God" –

"So help me God" –

"That the negro Sandy Campbell, now in jail on the charge of murder, robbery, and assault, was in my presence last night between the hours of eight and two o'clock."

Mr. Delamere repeated this statement in a firm voice; but to Ellis, who was in the secret, his words fell upon the ear like clods dropping upon the coffin in an open grave.

"I wish to add," said General Belmont, stepping forward, "that it is not our intention to interfere, by anything which may be done at this meeting, with the orderly process of the law, or to advise the prisoner's immediate release. The prisoner will remain in custody, Mr. Delamere, Major Carteret, and I guaranteeing that he will be proved entirely innocent at the preliminary hearing to-morrow morning."

Several of those present looked relieved; others were plainly disappointed; but when the meeting ended, the news went out that the lynching had been given up. Carteret immediately wrote and had struck off a handbill giving a brief statement of the proceedings, and sent out a dozen boys to distribute copies among the people in the

Notes

[154] *Original reads*: some one [ed.].

streets. That no precaution might be omitted, a call was issued to the Wellington Grays, the crack independent military company of the city, who in an incredibly short time were on guard at the jail.

Thus a slight change in the point of view had demonstrated the entire ability of the leading citizens to maintain the dignified and orderly processes of the law whenever they saw fit to do so.

The night passed without disorder, beyond the somewhat rough handling of two or three careless negroes that came in the way of small parties of the disappointed who had sought alcoholic consolation.

At ten o'clock the next morning, a preliminary hearing of the charge against Campbell was had before a magistrate. Mr. Delamere, perceptibly older and more wizened than he had seemed the day before, and leaning heavily on the arm of a servant, repeated his statement of the evening before. Only one or two witnesses were called, among whom was Mr. Ellis, who swore positively that in his opinion the prisoner was not the man whom he had seen and at first supposed to be Campbell. The most sensational piece of testimony was that of Dr. Price, who had examined the body, and who swore that the wound in the head was not necessarily fatal, and might have been due to a fall – that she had more than likely died of shock attendant upon the robbery, she being of advanced age and feeble health. There was no evidence, he said, of any other personal violence.

Sandy was not even bound over to the grand jury, but was discharged upon the ground that there was not sufficient evidence upon which to hold him. Upon his release he received the congratulations of many present, some of whom would cheerfully have done him to death a few hours before. With the childish fickleness of a mob, they now experienced a satisfaction almost as great as, though less exciting than, that attendant upon taking life. We speak of the mysteries of inanimate nature. The workings of the human heart are the profoundest mystery of the universe. One moment they make us despair of our kind, and the next we see in them the reflection of the divine image. Sandy, having thus escaped from the Mr. Hyde of the mob, now received the benediction of its Dr. Jekyll.[155] Being no cynical philosopher, and realizing how nearly the jaws of death had closed upon him, he was profoundly grateful for his escape, and felt not the slightest desire to investigate or criticise any man's motives.

With the testimony of Dr. Price, the worst feature of the affair came to an end. The murder eliminated or rendered doubtful, the crime became a mere vulgar robbery, the extent of which no one could estimate, since no living soul knew how much money Mrs. Ochiltree had had in the cedar chest. The absurdity of the remaining charge became more fully apparent in the light of the reaction from the excitement of the day before.

Nothing further was ever done about the case; but though the crime went unpunished, it carried evil in its train. As we have seen, the charge against Campbell had been made against the whole colored race. All over the United States the Associated Press had flashed the report of another dastardly outrage by a burly black brute – all black brutes it seems are burly – and of the impending lynching with its prospective horrors. This news, being highly sensational in its character, had been displayed in large black type on the front pages of the daily papers. The dispatch that followed, to the effect that the accused had been found innocent and the lynching frustrated, received slight attention, if any, in a fine-print paragraph on an inside page. The facts of the case never

Notes

[155] *Mr. Hyde … Dr. Jekyll* from Robert Louis Stevenson's *The Strange Case of Dr. Jekyll and Mr. Hyde* (1886).

came out at all. The family honor of the Delameres was preserved, and the prestige of the white race in Wellington was not seriously impaired.

Upon leaving the preliminary hearing, old Mr. Delamere had requested General Belmont to call at his house during the day upon professional business. This the general did in the course of the afternoon.

"Belmont," said Mr. Delamere, "I wish to make my will. I should have drawn it with my own hand; but you know my motives, and can testify to my soundness of mind and memory."

He thereupon dictated a will, by the terms of which he left to his servant, Sandy Campbell, three thousand dollars, as a mark of the testator's appreciation of services rendered and sufferings endured by Sandy on behalf of his master. After some minor dispositions, the whole remainder of the estate was devised to Dr. William Miller, in trust for the uses of his hospital and training-school for nurses, on condition that the institution be incorporated and placed under the management of competent trustees. Tom Delamere was not mentioned in the will.

"There, Belmont," he said, "that load is off my mind. Now, if you will call in some witnesses – most of my people can write – I shall feel entirely at ease."

The will was signed by Mr. Delamere, and witnessed by Jeff and Billy, two servants in the house, neither of whom received any information as to its contents, beyond the statement that they were witnessing their master's will.

"I wish to leave that with you for safe keeping, Belmont," said Mr. Delamere, after the witnesses had retired. "Lock it up in your safe until I die, which will not be very long, since I have no further desire to live."

An hour later Mr. Delamere suffered a third paralytic stroke, from which he died two days afterwards, without having in the meantime recovered the power of speech.

The will was never produced. The servants stated, and General Belmont admitted, that Mr. Delamere had made a will a few days before his death; but since it was not discoverable, it seemed probable that the testator had destroyed it. This was all the more likely, the general was inclined to think, because the will had been of a most unusual character. What the contents of the will were, he of course did not state, it having been made under the seal of professional secrecy.

This suppression was justified by the usual race argument: Miller's hospital was already well established, and, like most negro institutions, could no doubt rely upon Northern philanthropy for any further support it might need. Mr. Delamere's property belonged of right to the white race, and by the higher law should remain in the possession of white people. Loyalty to one's race was a more sacred principle than deference to a weak old man's whims.

Having reached this conclusion, General Belmont's first impulse was to destroy the will; on second thoughts he locked it carefully away in his safe. He would hold it awhile. It might some time be advisable to talk the matter over with young Delamere, who was of a fickle disposition and might wish to change his legal adviser.

Chapter 28

In Season and Out

Wellington soon resumed its wonted calm, and in a few weeks the intended lynching was only a memory. The robbery and assault, however, still remained a mystery to all but a chosen few. The affair had been dropped as absolutely as though it had never occurred. No colored man ever learned the reason of this sudden change of front, and Sandy Campbell's loyalty to his old employer's memory kept him silent. Tom Delamere did not offer to retain Sandy in his service, though he presented him with most of the old gentleman's wardrobe. It is only justice to Tom to state that up to this time he had not been informed of the contents of his grandfather's latest will. Major Carteret gave Sandy employment as butler, thus making a sort of vicarious atonement, on the part of the white race, of which the major felt himself in a way the embodiment, for the risk to which Sandy had been subjected.

Shortly after these events Sandy was restored to the bosom of the church, and, enfolded by its sheltering arms, was no longer tempted to stray from the path of rectitude, but became even a more rigid Methodist than before his recent troubles.

Tom Delamere did not call upon Clara again in the character of a lover. Of course they could not help meeting, from time to time, but he never dared presume upon their former relations. Indeed, the social atmosphere of Wellington remained so frigid toward Delamere that he left town, and did not return for several months.

Ellis was aware that Delamere had been thrown over, but a certain delicacy restrained him from following up immediately the advantage which the absence of his former rival gave him. It seemed to him, with the quixotry of a clean, pure mind, that Clara would pass through a period of mourning for her lost illusion, and that it would be indelicate, for the time being, to approach her with a lover's attentions. The work of the office had been unusually heavy of late. The major, deeply absorbed in politics, left the detail work of the paper to Ellis. Into the intimate counsels of the revolutionary committee Ellis had not been admitted, nor would he have desired to be. He knew, of course, in a general way, the results that it was sought to achieve; and while he did not see their necessity, he deferred to the views of older men, and was satisfied to remain in ignorance of anything of which he might disapprove.[156] Moreover, his own personal affairs occupied his mind to an extent that made politics or any other subject a matter of minor importance.

As for Dr. Miller, he never learned of Mr. Delamere's good intentions toward his institution, but regretted the old gentleman's death as the loss of a sincere friend and well-wisher of his race in their unequal struggle.

Despite the untiring zeal of Carteret and his associates, the campaign for the restriction of the suffrage, which was to form the basis of a permanent white supremacy, had seemed to languish for a while after the Ochiltree affair. The lull, however, was only temporary, and more apparent than real, for the forces adverse to the negro were merely gathering strength for a more vigorous assault. While little was said in Wellington, public sentiment all over the country became every day more favorable to the views of the conspirators. The nation was rushing forward with giant strides toward colossal wealth and world-dominion, before the exigencies of which mere abstract ethical theories must not be permitted to stand. The same argument that justified the conquest of an inferior nation could not be denied to those who sought the suppression of an inferior race. In the South, an obscure jealousy of the negro's progress, an obscure fear of the very equality so contemptuously denied, furnished a rich soil for successful agitation. Statistics of crime, ingeniously manipulated, were made to present a fearful showing against the negro. Vital statistics were made to prove that he had degenerated from an imaginary standard of physical excellence which had

Notes

[156] *Original reads*: of anything which he might disapprove [ed.].

existed under the benign influence of slavery. Constant lynchings emphasized his impotence, and bred everywhere a growing contempt for his rights.

At the North, a new Pharaoh[157] had risen, who knew not Israel – a new generation, who knew little of the fierce passions which had played around the negro in a past epoch, and derived their opinions of him from the "coon song" and the police reports. Those of his old friends who survived were disappointed that he had not flown with clipped wings; that he had not in one generation of limited opportunity attained the level of the whites. The whole race question seemed to have reached a sort of *impasse*, a blind alley, of which no one could see the outlet. The negro had become a target at which anyone[158] might try a shot. Schoolboys gravely debated the question as to whether or not the negro should exercise the franchise. The pessimist gave him up in despair; while the optimist, smilingly confident that everything would come out all right in the end, also turned aside and went his buoyant way to more pleasing themes.

For a time there were white men in the state who opposed any reactionary step unless it were of general application. They were conscientious men, who had learned the Ten Commandments and wished to do right; but this class was a small minority, and their objections were soon silenced by the all-powerful race argument. Selfishness is the most constant of human motives. Patriotism, humanity, or the love of God may lead to sporadic outbursts which sweep away the heaped-up wrongs of centuries; but they languish at times, while the love of self works on ceaselessly, unwearyingly, burrowing always at the very roots of life, and heaping up fresh wrongs for other centuries to sweep away. The state was at the mercy of venal and self-seeking politicians, bent upon regaining their ascendency at any cost, stultifying their own minds by vague sophistries and high-sounding phrases, which deceived none but those who wished to be deceived, and these but imperfectly; and dulling the public conscience by a loud clamor in which the calm voice of truth was for the moment silenced. So the cause went on.

Carteret, as spokesman of the campaign, and sincerest of all its leaders, performed prodigies of labor. The Morning Chronicle proclaimed, in season and out, the doctrine of "White Supremacy." Leaving the paper in the charge of[159] Ellis, the major made a tour of the state, rousing the white people of the better class to an appreciation of the terrible danger which confronted them in the possibility that a few negroes might hold a few offices or dictate the terms upon which white men should fill them. Difficulties were explained away. The provisions of the Federal Constitution, it was maintained, must yield to the "higher law," and if the Constitution could neither be altered nor bent to this end, means must be found to circumvent it.

The device finally hit upon for disfranchising the colored people in this particular state was the notorious "grandfather clause." After providing various restrictions of the suffrage, based upon education, character, and property, which it was deemed would in effect disfranchise the colored race, an exception was made in favor of all citizens whose fathers or grandfathers had been entitled to vote prior to 1867. Since none but white men could vote prior to 1867, this exception obviously took in the poor and ignorant whites, while the same class of negroes were excluded.

It was ingenious, but it was not fair. In due time a constitutional convention was called, in which the above scheme was adopted and submitted to a vote of the people

Notes

[157] *a new Pharaoh* Exodus 1:8.

[158] *Original reads*: any one [ed.].

[159] *Original reads*: in charge of [ed.].

for ratification. The campaign was fought on the color line. Many white Republicans, deluded with the hope that by the elimination of the negro vote their party might receive accessions from the Democratic ranks, went over to the white party. By fraud in one place, by terrorism in another, and everywhere by the resistless moral force of the united whites, the negroes were reduced to the apathy of despair, their few white allies demoralized, and the amendment adopted by a large majority. The negroes were taught that this is a white man's country, and that the sooner they made up their minds to this fact, the better for all concerned. The white people would be good to them so long as they behaved themselves and kept their place. As theoretical equals – practical equality being forever out of the question, either by nature or by law – there could have been nothing but strife between them, in which the weaker party would invariably have suffered most.

Some colored men accepted the situation thus outlined, if not as desirable, at least as inevitable. Most of them, however, had little faith in this condescending friendliness which was to take the place of constitutional rights. They knew they had been treated unfairly; that their enemies had prevailed against them; that their whilom[160] friends had stood passively by and seen them undone. Many of the most enterprising and progressive left the state, and those who remain still labor under a sense of wrong and outrage which renders them distinctly less valuable as citizens.

The great steal was made, but the thieves did not turn honest – the scheme still shows the mark of the burglar's tools. Sins, like chickens, come home to roost. The South paid a fearful price for the wrong of negro slavery; in some form or other it will doubtless reap the fruits of this later iniquity.

Drastic as were these "reforms," the results of which we have anticipated somewhat, since the new Constitution was not to take effect immediately, they moved all too slowly for the little coterie of Wellington conspirators, whose ambitions and needs urged them to prompt action. Under the new Constitution it would be two full years before the "nigger amendment" became effective, and meanwhile the Wellington district would remain hopelessly Republican. The committee decided, about two months before the fall election, that an active local campaign must be carried on, with a view to discourage the negroes from attending the polls on election day.

The question came up for discussion one forenoon in a meeting at the office of the Morning Chronicle, at which all of the "Big Three" were present.

"Something must be done," declared McBane, "and that damn quick. Too many white people are saying that it will be better to wait until the amendment goes into effect. That would mean to leave the niggers in charge of this town for two years after the state has declared for white supremacy! I'm opposed to leaving it in their hands one hour – them's my sentiments!"

This proved to be the general opinion, and the discussion turned to the subject of ways and means.

"What became of that editorial in the nigger paper?" inquired the general in his blandest tones, cleverly directing a smoke ring toward the ceiling. "It lost some of its point back there, when we came near lynching that nigger; but now that that has blown over, why wouldn't it be a good thing to bring into play at the present juncture? Let's read it over again."

Notes

[160] *whilom* former.

Carteret extracted the paper from the pigeon-hole where he had placed it some months before. The article was read aloud with emphasis and discussed phrase by phrase. Of its wording there could be little criticism – it was temperately and even cautiously phrased. As suggested by the general, the Ochiltree affair had proved that it was not devoid of truth. Its great offensiveness lay in its boldness: that a negro should publish in a newspaper what white people would scarcely acknowledge to themselves in secret was much as though a Russian *moujik*[161] or a German peasant should rush into print to question the divine right of the Lord's Anointed. The article was racial *lèse-majesté*[162] in the most aggravated form. A peg was needed upon which to hang a *coup d'état*, and this editorial offered the requisite opportunity. It was unanimously decided to republish the obnoxious article, with comment adapted to fire the inflammable Southern heart and rouse it against any further self-assertion of the negroes in politics or elsewhere.

"The time is ripe!" exclaimed McBane. "In a month we can have the niggers so scared that they won't dare stick their heads out of doors on 'lection day."

"I wonder," observed the general thoughtfully, after this conclusion had been reached, "if we couldn't have Jerry fetch us some liquor?"

Jerry appeared in response to the usual summons. The general gave him the money, and ordered three Calhoun cocktails. When Jerry returned with the glasses on a tray, the general observed him with pointed curiosity.

"What in h——ll is the matter with you, Jerry? Your black face is splotched with brown and yellow patches, and your hair shines as though you had fallen head-foremost into a firkin[163] of butter. What's the matter with you?"

Jerry seemed much embarrassed by this inquiry. "Nothin', suh, nothin'," he stammered. "It's – it's jes' somethin' I be'n puttin' on my hair, suh, ter improve de quality, suh."

"Jerry," returned the general, bending a solemn look upon the porter, "you have been playing with edged tools, and your days are numbered. You have been reading the Afro-American Banner."

He shook open the paper, which he had retained in his hand, and read from one of the advertisements:–

"'Kinky, curly hair made straight in two applications. Dark skins lightened two shades; mulattoes turned perfectly white.'

"This stuff is rank poison, Jerry," continued the general with a mock solemnity which did not impose upon Jerry, who nevertheless listened with an air of great alarm. He suspected that the general was making fun of him; but he also knew that the general would like to think that Jerry believed him in earnest; and to please the white folks was Jerry's consistent aim in life. "I can see the signs of decay in your face, and your hair will all fall out in a week or two at the latest – mark my words!"

McBane had listened to this pleasantry with a sardonic sneer. It was a waste of valuable time. To Carteret it seemed in doubtful taste. These grotesque advertisements had their tragic side. They were proof that the negroes had read the handwriting on the wall. These pitiful attempts to change their physical characteristics were an acknowledgment, on their own part, that the negro was doomed, and that the white man was to inherit the earth and hold all other races under his heel. For, as the months

Notes

[161] *moujik* peasant.

[162] *lèse-majesté* crime against the ruler.

[163] *firkin* a cask measuring a quarter of a barrel.

had passed, Carteret's thoughts centring more and more upon the negro, had led him farther and farther, until now he was firmly convinced that there was no permanent place for the negro in the United States, if indeed anywhere in the world, except under the ground. More pathetic even than Jerry's efforts to escape from the universal doom of his race was his ignorance that even if he could, by some strange alchemy, bleach his skin and straighten his hair, there would still remain, underneath it all, only the unbleached darky – the ass in the lion's skin.[164]

When the general had finished his facetious lecture, Jerry backed out of the room shamefacedly, though affecting a greater confusion than he really felt. Jerry had not reasoned so closely as Carteret, but he had realized that it was a distinct advantage to be white – an advantage which white people had utilized to secure all the best things in the world; and he had entertained the vague hope that by changing his complexion he might share this prerogative. While he suspected the general's sincerity, he nevertheless felt a little apprehensive lest the general's prediction about the effects of the face-bleach and other preparations might prove true – the general was a white gentleman and ought to know – and decided to abandon their use.

This purpose was strengthened by his next interview with the major. When Carteret summoned him, an hour later, after the other gentlemen had taken their leave, Jerry had washed his head thoroughly and there remained no trace of the pomade. An attempt to darken the lighter spots in his cuticle by the application of printer's ink had not proved equally successfull – the retouching left the spots as much too dark as they had formerly been too light.

"Jerry," said Carteret sternly, "when I hired you to work for the Chronicle, you were black. The word 'negro' means 'black.' The best negro is a black negro, of the pure type, as it came from the hand of God. If you wish to get along well with the white people, the blacker you are the better – white people do not like negroes who want to be white. A man should be content to remain as God made him and where God placed him. So no more of this nonsense. Are you going to vote at the next election?"

"What would you 'vise me ter do, suh?" asked Jerry cautiously.

"I do not advise you. You ought to have sense enough to see where your own interests lie. I put it to you whether you cannot trust yourself more safely in the hands of white gentlemen, who are your true friends, than in the hands of ignorant and purchasable negroes and unscrupulous white scoundrels?"

"Dere's no doubt about it, suh," assented Jerry, with a vehemence proportioned to his desire to get back into favor. "I ain' gwine ter have nothin' ter do wid de 'lection, suh! Ef I don' vote, I kin keep my job, can't I, suh?"

The major eyed Jerry with an air of supreme disgust. What could be expected of a race so utterly devoid of tact? It seemed as though this negro thought a white gentleman might want to bribe him to remain away from the polls; and the negro's willingness to accept the imaginary bribe demonstrated the venal nature of the colored race – its entire lack of moral principle!

"You will retain your place, Jerry," he said severely, "so long as you perform your duties to my satisfaction and behave yourself properly."

With this grandiloquent subterfuge Carteret turned to his next article on white supremacy. Jerry did not delude himself with any fine-spun sophistry. He knew

Notes

[164] *ass in the lion's skin* from one of Aesop's fables.

perfectly well that he held his job upon the condition that he stayed away from the polls at the approaching election. Jerry was a fool –

"The world of fools hath such a store,
That he who would not see an ass,
Must stay at home and shut his door
And break his looking-glass."[165]

But while no one may be entirely wise, there are degrees of folly, and Jerry was not all kinds of a fool.

Chapter 29

Mutterings of the Storm

EVENTS moved rapidly during the next few days. The reproduction, in the Chronicle, of the article from the Afro-American Banner, with Carteret's inflammatory comment, took immediate effect. It touched the Southern white man in his most sensitive spot. To him such an article was an insult to white womanhood, and must be resented by some active steps – mere words would be no answer at all. To meet words with words upon such a subject would be to acknowledge the equality of the negro and his right to discuss or criticise the conduct of the white people.

The colored people became alarmed at the murmurings of the whites, which seemed to presage a coming storm. A number of them sought to arm themselves, but ascertained, upon inquiring at the stores, that no white merchant would sell a negro firearms. Since all the dealers in this sort of merchandise were white men, the negroes had to be satisfied with oiling up the old army muskets which some of them possessed, and the few revolvers with which a small rowdy element generally managed to keep themselves supplied. Upon an effort being made to purchase firearms from a Northern city, the express company, controlled by local men, refused to accept the consignment. The white people, on the other hand, procured both arms and ammunition in large quantities, and the Wellington Grays drilled with great assiduity at their armory.

All this went on without any public disturbance of the town's tranquillity. A stranger would have seen nothing to excite his curiosity. The white people did their talking among themselves, and merely grew more distant in their manner toward the colored folks, who instinctively closed their ranks as the whites drew away. With each day that passed the feeling grew more tense. The editor of the Afro-American Banner, whose office had been quietly garrisoned for several nights by armed negroes, became frightened, and disappeared from the town between two suns.

The conspirators were jubilant at the complete success of their plans. It only remained for them to so direct this aroused public feeling that it might completely accomplish the desired end – to change the political complexion of the city government and assure the ascendency of the whites until the amendment should go into effect. A revolution, and not a riot, was contemplated.

Notes

[165] *"The world of fools ... looking-glass."* witticism attributed to French lawyer and writer Bernard de la Monnoye (1641–1728).

With this end in view, another meeting was called at Carteret's office.

"We are now ready," announced General Belmont, "for the final act of this drama. We must decide promptly, or events may run away from us."

"What do you suggest?" asked Carteret.

"Down in the American tropics," continued the general, "they have a way of doing things. I was in Nicaragua, ten years ago, when Paterno's revolution[166] drove out Igorroto's government. It was as easy as falling off a log. Paterno had the arms and the best men. Igorroto was not looking for trouble, and the guns were at his breast before he knew it. We have the guns. The negroes are not expecting trouble, and are easy to manage compared with the fiery mixture that flourishes in the tropics."

"I should not advocate murder," returned Carteret. "We are animated by high and holy principles. We wish to right a wrong, to remedy an abuse, to save our state from anarchy and our race from humiliation. I don't object to frightening the negroes, but I am opposed to unnecessary bloodshed."

"I'm not quite so particular," struck in Mc Bane. "They need to be taught a lesson, and a nigger more or less wouldn't be missed. There's too many of 'em now."

"Of course," continued Carteret, "if we should decide upon a certain mode of procedure, and the negroes should resist, a different reasoning might apply; but I will have no premeditated murder."

"In Central and South America," observed the general reflectively, "none are hurt except those who get in the way."

"There'll be no niggers hurt," said McBane contemptuously, "unless they strain themselves running. One white man can chase a hundred of 'em. I've managed five hundred at a time. I'll pay for burying all the niggers that are killed."

The conference resulted in a well-defined plan, to be put into operation the following day, by which the city government was to be wrested from the Republicans and their negro allies.

"And now," said General Belmont, "while we are cleansing the Augean stables,[167] we may as well remove the cause as the effect. There are several negroes too many in this town, which will be much the better without them. There's that yellow lawyer, Watson. He's altogether too mouthy, and has too much business. Every nigger that gets into trouble sends for Watson, and white lawyers, with families to support and social positions to keep up, are deprived of their legitimate source of income."

"There's that damn nigger real estate agent," blurted out McBane. "Billy Kitchen used to get most of the nigger business, but this darky has almost driven him to the poorhouse. A white business man is entitled to a living in his own profession and his own home. That nigger don't belong here nohow. He came from the North a year or two ago, and is hand in glove with Barber, the nigger editor, which is enough of itself to damn him. *He'll* have to go!"

"How about the collector of the port?"

"We'd better not touch him. It would bring the government down upon us, which we want to avoid. We don't need to worry about the nigger preachers either. They want to stay here, where the loaves and the fishes[168] are. We can make 'em write letters to the newspapers justifying our course, as a condition of their remaining."

Notes

[166] *Paterno's revolution* this is fictitious.

[167] *cleansing the Augean stables* one of Hercules's legendary labors, the Augean stables housed over 3,000 oxen.

[168] *loaves and fishes* Matthew 14:13–21.

"What about Billings?" asked McBane. Billings was the white Republican mayor. "Is that skunk to be allowed to stay in town?"

"No," returned the general, "every white Republican office-holder ought to be made to go. This town is only big enough for Democrats, and negroes who can be taught to keep their place."

"What about the colored doctor," queried McBane, "with the hospital, and the diamond ring, and the carriage, and the other fallals?"[169]

"I shouldn't[170] interfere with Miller," replied the general decisively. "He's a very good sort of a negro, doesn't meddle with politics, nor tread on anyone[171] else's toes. His father was a good citizen, which counts in his favor. He's spending money in the community too, and contributes to its prosperity."

"That sort of nigger, though, sets a bad example," retorted McBane. "They make it all the harder to keep the rest of 'em down."

"'One swallow does not make a summer,'" quoted the general. "When we get things arranged, there'll be no trouble. A stream cannot rise higher than its fountain, and a smart nigger without a constituency will no longer be an object of fear. I say, let the doctor alone."

"He'll have to keep mighty quiet, though," muttered McBane discontentedly. "I don't like smart niggers. I've had to shoot several of them, in the course of my life."

"Personally, I dislike the man," interposed Carteret, "and if I consulted my own inclinations, would say expel him with the rest; but my grievance is a personal one, and to gratify it in that way would be a loss to the community. I wish to be strictly impartial in this matter, and to take no step which cannot be entirely justified by a wise regard for the public welfare."

"What's the use of all this hypocrisy, gentlemen?" sneered McBane. "Every last one of us has an axe to grind! The major may as well put an edge on his. We'll never get a better chance to have things our way. If this nigger doctor annoys the major, we'll run him out with the rest. This is a white man's country, and a white man's city, and no nigger has any business here when a white man wants him gone!"

Carteret frowned darkly at this brutal characterization of their motives. It robbed the enterprise of all its poetry, and put a solemn act of revolution upon the plane of a mere vulgar theft of power. Even the general winced.

"I would not consent," he said irritably, "to Miller's being disturbed."

McBane made no further objection.

There was a discreet knock at the door.

"Come in," said Carteret.

Jerry entered. "Mistuh Ellis wants ter speak ter you a minute, suh," he said.

Carteret excused himself and left the room.

"Jerry," said the general, "you lump of ebony, the sight of you reminds me! If your master doesn't want you for a minute, step across to Mr. Brown's and tell him to send me three cocktails."

"Yas, suh," responded Jerry, hesitating. The general had said nothing about paying.

"And tell him, Jerry, to charge them. I'm short of change to-day."

"Yas, suh; yas, suh," replied Jerry, as he backed out of the presence, adding, when he had reached the hall: "Dere ain' no change fer Jerry dis time, sho': I'll jes' make dat *fo'*

Notes

[169] *fallals* showy ornaments.

[170] *Original reads*: should n't [ed.].

[171] *Original reads*: any one [ed.].

cocktails, an' de gin'l won't never know de diffe'nce. I ain' gwine 'cross de road fer nothin', not ef I knows it."

Half an hour later, the conspirators dispersed. They had fixed the hour of the proposed revolution, the course to be pursued, the results to be obtained; but in stating their equation they had overlooked one factor – God, or Fate, or whatever one may choose to call the Power that holds the destinies of man in the hollow of his hand.

Chapter 30

The Missing Papers

Mrs. Carteret was very much disturbed. It was supposed that the shock of her aunt's death had affected her health, for since that event she had fallen into a nervous condition which gave the major grave concern. Much to the general surprise, Mrs. Ochiltree had left no will, and no property of any considerable value except her homestead, which descended to Mrs. Carteret as the natural heir. Whatever she may have had on hand in the way of ready money had undoubtedly been abstracted from the cedar chest by the midnight marauder, to whose visit her death was immediately due. Her niece's grief was held to mark a deep-seated affection for the grim old woman who had reared her.

Mrs. Carteret's present state of mind, of which her nervousness was a sufficiently accurate reflection, did in truth date from her aunt's death, and also in part from the time of the conversation with Mrs. Ochiltree, one afternoon, during and after the drive past Miller's new hospital. Mrs. Ochiltree had grown steadily more and more childish after that time, and her niece had never succeeded in making her pick up the thread of thought where it had been dropped. At any rate, Mrs. Ochiltree had made no further disclosure upon the subject.

An examination, not long after her aunt's death, of the papers found near the cedar chest on the morning after the murder had contributed to Mrs. Carteret's enlightenment, but had not promoted her peace of mind.

When Mrs. Carteret reached home, after her hurried exploration of the cedar chest, she thrust into a bureau drawer the envelope she had found. So fully was her mind occupied, for several days, with the funeral, and with the excitement attending the arrest of Sandy Campbell, that she deferred the examination of the contents of the envelope until near the end of the week.

One morning, while alone in her chamber, she drew the envelope from the drawer, and was holding it in her hand, hesitating as to whether or not she should open it, when the baby in the next room began to cry.

The child's cry seemed like a warning, and yielding to a vague uneasiness, she put the paper back.

"Phil," she said to her husband at luncheon, "Aunt Polly said some strange things to me one day before she died – I don't know whether she was quite in her right mind or not; but suppose that my father had left a will by which it was provided that half his property should go to that woman and her child?"

"It would never have gone by such a will," replied the major easily. "Your Aunt Polly was in her dotage, and merely dreaming. Your father would never have been such a fool; but even if he had, no such will could have stood the test of the courts. It would clearly have been due to the improper influence of a designing woman."

"So that legally, as well as morally," said Mrs. Carteret, "the will would have been of no effect?"

"Not the slightest. A jury would soon have broken down the legal claim. As for any moral obligation, there would have been nothing moral about the affair. The only possible consideration for such a gift was an immoral one. I don't wish to speak harshly of your father, my dear, but his conduct was gravely reprehensible. The woman herself had no right or claim whatever; she would have been whipped and expelled from the town, if justice – blind, bleeding justice, then prostrate at the feet of slaves and aliens – could have had her way!"

"But the child" –

"The child was in the same category. Who was she, to have inherited the estate of your ancestors, of which, a few years before, she would herself have formed a part? The child of shame, it was hers to pay the penalty. But the discussion is all in the air, Olivia. Your father never did and never would have left such a will."

This conversation relieved Mrs. Carteret's uneasiness. Going to her room shortly afterwards, she took the envelope from her bureau drawer and drew out a bulky paper. The haunting fear that it might be such a will as her aunt had suggested was now removed; for such an instrument, in the light of what her husband had said confirming her own intuitions, would be of no valid effect. It might be just as well, she thought, to throw the paper in the fire without looking at it. She wished to think as well as might be of her father, and she felt that her respect for his memory would not be strengthened by the knowledge that he had meant to leave his estate away from her; for her aunt's words had been open to the construction that she was to have been left destitute. Curiosity strongly prompted her to read the paper. Perhaps the will contained no such provision as she had feared, and it might convey some request or direction which ought properly to be complied with.

She had been standing in front of the bureau while these thoughts passed through her mind, and now, dropping the envelope back into the drawer mechanically, she unfolded the document. It was written on legal paper, in her father's own hand.

Mrs. Carteret was not familiar with legal verbiage, and there were several expressions of which she did not perhaps appreciate the full effect; but a very hasty glance enabled her to ascertain the purport of the paper. It was a will, by which, in one item, her father devised to his daughter Janet, the child of the woman known as Julia Brown, the sum of ten thousand dollars, and a certain plantation or tract of land a short distance from the town of Wellington. The rest and residue of his estate, after deducting all legal charges and expenses, was bequeathed to his beloved daughter, Olivia Merkell.

Mrs. Carteret breathed a sigh of relief. Her father had not preferred another to her, but had left to his lawful daughter the bulk of his estate. She felt at the same time a growing indignation at the thought that that woman should so have wrought upon her father's weakness as to induce him to think of leaving so much valuable property to her bastard – property which by right should go, and now would go, to her own son, to whom by every rule of law and decency it ought to descend.

A fire was burning in the next room, on account of the baby – there had been a light frost the night before, and the air was somewhat chilly. For the moment the room was empty. Mrs. Carteret came out from her chamber and threw the offending paper into the fire, and watched it slowly burn. When it had been consumed, the carbon residue of one sheet still retained its form, and she could read the words on the charred portion. A sentence, which had escaped her eye in her rapid reading, stood out in ghostly black upon the gray background:–

"All the rest and residue of my estate I devise and bequeath to my daughter Olivia Merkell, the child of my beloved first wife."

Mrs. Carteret had not before observed the word "first." Instinctively she stretched toward the fire the poker which she held in her hand, and at its touch the shadowy remnant fell to pieces, and nothing but ashes remained upon the hearth.

Not until the next morning did she think again of the envelope which had contained the paper she had burned. Opening the drawer where it lay, the oblong blue envelope confronted her. The sight of it was distasteful. The indorsed side lay uppermost, and the words seemed like a mute reproach:–

"The Last Will and Testament of Samuel Merkell."

Snatching up the envelope, she glanced into it mechanically as she moved toward the next room, and perceived a thin folded paper which had heretofore escaped her notice. When opened, it proved to be a certificate of marriage, in due form, between Samuel Merkell and Julia Brown. It was dated from a county in South Carolina, about two years before her father's death.

For a moment Mrs. Carteret stood gazing blankly at this faded slip of paper. Her father *had* married this woman! – at least he had gone through the form of marriage with her, for to him it had surely been no more than an empty formality. The marriage of white and colored persons was forbidden by law. Only recently she had read of a case where both the parties to such a crime, a colored man and a white woman, had been sentenced to long terms in the penitentiary. She even recalled the circumstances. The couple had been living together unlawfully – they were very low people, whose private lives were beneath the public notice – but influenced by a religious movement pervading the community, had sought, they said at the trial, to secure the blessing of God upon their union. The higher law, which imperiously demanded that the purity and prestige of the white race be preserved at any cost, had intervened at this point.

Mechanically she moved toward the fireplace, so dazed by this discovery as to be scarcely conscious of her own actions. She surely had not formed any definite intention of destroying this piece of paper when her fingers relaxed unconsciously and let go their hold upon it. The draught swept it toward the fireplace. Ere scarcely touching the flames it caught, blazed fiercely, and shot upward with the current of air. A moment later the record of poor Julia's marriage was scattered to the four winds of heaven, as her poor body had long since mingled with the dust of earth.

The letter remained unread. In her agitation at the discovery of the marriage certificate, Olivia had almost forgotten the existence of the letter. It was addressed to "John Delamere, Esq., as Executor of my Last Will and Testament," while the lower left-hand corner bore the direction: "To be delivered only after my death, with seal unbroken."

The seal was broken already; Mr. Delamere was dead; the letter could never be delivered. Mrs. Carteret unfolded it and read:–

My Dear Delamere, I have taken the liberty of naming you as executor of my last will, because you are my friend, and the only man of my acquaintance whom I feel that I can trust to carry out my wishes, appreciate my motives, and preserve the silence I desire.

I have, first, a confession to make. Inclosed in this letter you will find a certificate of marriage between my child Janet's mother and myself. While I have never exactly repented of this marriage, I have never had the courage to acknowledge it openly. If I had not married Julia, I fear Polly Ochiltree would have married me by main force – as she would marry you or any other gentleman unfortunate enough to fall in the way of this twice-widowed man-hunter. When my wife died, three years ago, her sister Polly offered to keep house for me and the child. I would sooner have had the devil in the house, and yet I trembled with alarm – there seemed no way of escape – it was so clearly and obviously the proper thing.

But she herself gave me my opportunity. I was on the point of consenting, when she demanded, as a condition of her coming, that I discharge Julia, my late wife's maid. She was laboring under a misapprehension in regard to the girl, but I grasped at the straw, and did everything to foster her delusion. I declared solemnly that nothing under heaven would induce me to part with Julia. The controversy resulted in my permitting Polly to take the child, while I retained the maid.

Before Polly put this idea into my head, I had scarcely looked at Julia, but this outbreak turned my attention toward her. She was a handsome girl, and, as I soon found out, a good girl. My wife, who raised her, was a Christian woman, and had taught her modesty and virtue. She was free. The air was full of liberty, and equal rights, and all the abolition claptrap, and she made marriage a condition of her remaining longer in the house. In a moment of weakness I took her away to a place where we were not known, and married her. If she had left me, I should have fallen a victim to Polly Ochiltree – to which any fate was preferable.

And then, old friend, my weakness kept to the fore. I was ashamed of this marriage, and my new wife saw it. Moreover, she loved me – too well, indeed, to wish to make me unhappy. The ceremony had satisfied her conscience, had set her right, she said, with God; for the opinions of men she did not care, since I loved her – she only wanted to compensate me, as best she could, for the great honor I had done my handmaiden – for she had read her Bible, and I was the Abraham to her Hagar,[172] compared with whom she considered herself at a great advantage. It was her own proposition that nothing be said of this marriage. If any shame should fall on her, it would fall lightly, for it would be undeserved. When the child came, she still kept silence. No one, she argued, could blame an innocent child for the accident of birth, and in the sight of God this child had every right to exist; while among her own people illegitimacy would involve but little stigma.

I need not say that I was easily persuaded to accept this sacrifice; but touched by her fidelity, I swore to provide handsomely for them both. This I have tried to do by the will of which I ask you to act as executor. Had I left the child more, it might serve as a ground for attacking the will; my acknowledgment of the tie of blood is sufficient to justify a reasonable bequest.

I have taken this course for the sake of my daughter Olivia, who is dear to me, and whom I would not wish to make ashamed; and in deference to public opinion, which it is not easy to defy. If, after my death, Julia should choose to make our secret known, I shall of course be beyond the reach of hard words; but loyalty to my memory will probably keep her silent. A strong man would long since have acknowledged her before the world and taken the consequences; but, alas! I am only myself, and the atmosphere I live in does not encourage moral heroism. I should like to be different, but it is God who hath made us, and not we ourselves![173]

Nevertheless, old friend, I will ask of you one favor. If in the future this child of Julia's and of mine should grow to womanhood; if she should prove to have her mother's gentleness and love of virtue; if, in the new era which is opening up for her mother's race, to which, unfortunately, she must belong, she should become, in time, an educated woman; and if the time should ever come when, by virtue of her education or the development of her people, it would be to her a source of shame or

Notes

[172] *Abraham to her Hagar* Hagar was the slave and concubine of Abraham (Genesis 16:1–16).

[173] *"it is God who hath made us … ourselves!"* Psalms 100:3.

unhappiness that she was an illegitimate child – if you are still alive, old friend, and have the means of knowing or divining this thing, go to her and tell her, for me, that she is my lawful child, and ask her to forgive her father's weakness.

When this letter comes to you, I shall have passed to – the Beyond; but I am confident that you will accept this trust, for which I thank you now, in advance, most heartily.

The letter was signed with her father's name, the same signature which had been attached to the will.

Having firmly convinced herself of the illegality of the papers, and of her own right to destroy them, Mrs. Carteret ought to have felt relieved that she had thus removed all traces of her dead father's folly. True, the other daughter remained – she had seen her on the street only the day before. The sight of this person she had always found offensive, and now, she felt, in view of what she had just learned, it must be even more so. Never, while this woman lived in the town, would she be able to throw the veil of forgetfulness over this blot upon her father's memory.

As the day wore on, Mrs. Carteret grew still less at ease. To herself, marriage was a serious thing – to a right-thinking woman the most serious concern of life. A marriage certificate, rightfully procured, was scarcely less solemn, so far as it went, than the Bible itself. Her own she cherished as the apple of her eye. It was the evidence of her wifehood, the seal of her child's legitimacy, her patent of nobility – the token of her own and her child's claim to social place and consideration. She had burned this pretended marriage certificate because it meant nothing. Nevertheless, she could not ignore the knowledge of another such marriage, of which everyone in the town knew – a celebrated case, indeed, where a white man, of a family quite as prominent as her father's, had married a colored woman during the military occupation of the state just after the civil war. The legality of the marriage had never been questioned. It had been fully consummated by twenty years of subsequent cohabitation. No amount of social persecution had ever shaken the position of the husband. With an iron will he had stayed on in the town, a living protest against the established customs of the South, so rudely interrupted for a few short years; and, though his children were negroes, though he had never appeared in public with his wife, no one had ever questioned the validity of his marriage or the legitimacy of his offspring.

The marriage certificate which Mrs. Carteret had burned dated from the period of the military occupation. Hence Mrs. Carteret, who was a good woman, and would not have done a dishonest thing, felt decidedly uncomfortable. She had destroyed the marriage certificate, but its ghost still haunted her.

Major Carteret, having just eaten a good dinner, was in a very agreeable humor when, that same evening, his wife brought up again the subject of their previous discussion.

"Phil," she asked, "Aunt Polly told me that once, long before my father died, when she went to remonstrate with him for keeping that woman in the house, he threatened to marry Julia if Aunt Polly ever said another word to him about the matter. Suppose he *had* married her, and had *then* left a will – would the marriage have made any difference, so far as the will was concerned?"

Major Carteret laughed. "Your Aunt Polly," he said, "was a remarkable woman, with a wonderful imagination, which seems to have grown more vivid as her memory and judgment weakened. Why should your father marry his negro housemaid? Mr. Merkell was never rated as a fool – he had one of the clearest heads in Wellington. I saw him only a day or two before he died, and I could swear before any court in Christendom that he was of sound mind and memory to the last. These notions of your aunt were mere delusions. Your father was never capable of such a folly."

"Of course I am only supposing a case," returned Olivia. "Imagining such a case, just for the argument, would the marriage have been legal?"

"That would depend. If he had married her during the military occupation, or over in South Carolina, the marriage would have been legally valid, though morally and socially outrageous."

"And if he had died afterwards, leaving a will?"

"The will would have controlled the disposition of his estate, in all probability."

"Suppose he had left no will?"

"You are getting the matter down pretty fine, my dear! The woman would have taken one third of the real estate for life, and could have lived in the homestead until she died. She would also have had half the other property – the money and goods and furniture, everything except the land – and the negro child would have shared with you the balance of the estate. That, I believe, is according to the law of descent and distribution."

Mrs. Carteret lapsed into a troubled silence. Her father *had* married the woman. In her heart she had no doubt of the validity of the marriage, so far as the law was concerned; if one marriage of such a kind would stand, another contracted under similar conditions was equally as good. If the marriage had been valid, Julia's child had been legitimate. The will she had burned gave this sister of hers – she shuddered at the word – but a small part of the estate. Under the law, which intervened now that there was no will, the property should have been equally divided. If the woman had been white – but the woman had *not* been white, and the same rule of moral conduct did not, *could* not, in the very nature of things, apply, as between white people! For, if this were not so, slavery had been, not merely an economic mistake, but a great crime against humanity. If it had been such a crime, as for a moment she dimly perceived it might have been, then through the long centuries there had been piled up a catalogue of wrong and outrage which, if the law of compensation be a law of nature, must sometime, somewhere, in some way, be atoned for. She herself had not escaped the penalty, of which, she realized, this burden placed upon her conscience was but another installment.

If she should make known the facts she had learned, it would mean what? – a division of her father's estate, a recognition of the legality of her father's relations with Julia. Such a stain upon her father's memory would be infinitely worse than if he had not married her. To have lived with her without marriage was a social misdemeanor, at which society in the old days had winked, or at most had frowned. To have married her was to have committed the unpardonable social sin. Such a scandal Mrs. Carteret could not have endured. Should she seek to make restitution, it would necessarily involve the disclosure of at least some of the facts. Had she not destroyed the will, she might have compromised with her conscience by producing it and acting upon its terms, which had been so stated as not to disclose the marriage. This was now rendered impossible by her own impulsive act; she could not mention the will at all, without admitting that she had destroyed it.

Mrs. Carteret found herself in what might be called, vulgarly, a moral "pocket." She could, of course, remain silent. Mrs. Carteret was a good woman, according to her lights, with a cultivated conscience, to which she had always looked as her mentor and infallible guide.

Hence Mrs. Carteret, after this painful discovery, remained for a long time ill at ease – so disturbed, indeed, that her mind reacted upon her nerves, which had never been strong; and her nervousness affected her strength, which had never been great, until Carteret, whose love for her had been deepened and strengthened by the advent of his son, became alarmed for her health, and spoke very seriously to Dr. Price concerning it.

Chapter 31

The Shadow of a Dream

Mrs. Carteret awoke, with a start, from a troubled dream. She had been sailing across a sunlit sea, in a beautiful boat, her child lying on a bright-colored cushion at her feet. Overhead the swelling sail served as an awning to keep off the sun's rays, which far ahead were reflected with dazzling brilliancy from the shores of a golden island. Her son, she dreamed, was a fairy prince, and yonder lay his kingdom, to which he was being borne, lying there at her feet, in this beautiful boat, across the sunlit sea.

Suddenly and without warning the sky was overcast. A squall struck the boat and tore away the sail. In the distance a huge billow – a great white wall of water – came sweeping toward their frail craft, threatening it with instant destruction. She clasped her child to her bosom, and a moment later found herself struggling in the sea, holding the child's head above the water. As she floated there, as though sustained by some unseen force, she saw in the distance a small boat approaching over the storm-tossed waves. Straight toward her it came, and she had reached out her hand to grasp its side, when the rower looked back, and she saw that it was her sister. The recognition had been mutual. With a sharp movement of one oar the boat glided by, leaving her clutching at the empty air.

She felt her strength begin to fail. Despairingly she signaled with her disengaged hand; but the rower, after one mute, reproachful glance, rowed on. Mrs. Carteret's strength grew less and less. The child became heavy as lead. Herself floating in the water, as though it were her native element, she could no longer support the child. Lower and lower it sank – she was powerless to save it or to accompany it – until, gasping wildly for breath, it threw up its little hands and sank, the cruel water gurgling over its head – when she awoke with a start and a chill, and lay there trembling for several minutes before she heard little Dodie in his crib, breathing heavily.

She rose softly, went to the crib, and changed the child's position to an easier one. He breathed more freely, and she went back to bed, but not to sleep.

She had tried to put aside the distressing questions raised by the discovery of her father's will and the papers accompanying it. Why should she be burdened with such a responsibility, at this late day, when the touch of time had well-nigh healed these old sores? Surely, God had put his curse not alone upon the slave, but upon the stealer of men! With other good people she had thanked Him that slavery was no more, and that those who once had borne its burden upon their consciences could stand erect and feel that they themselves were free. The weed had been cut down, but its roots remained, deeply imbedded in the soil, to spring up and trouble a new generation. Upon her weak shoulders was placed the burden of her father's weakness, her father's folly. It was left to her to acknowledge or not this shameful marriage and her sister's rights in their father's estate.

Balancing one consideration against another, she had almost decided that she might ignore this tie. To herself, Olivia Merkell – Olivia Carteret – the stigma of base birth would have meant social ostracism, social ruin, the averted face, the finger of pity or of scorn. All the traditional weight of public disapproval would have fallen upon her as the unhappy fruit of an unblessed union. To this other woman it could have had no such significance – it had been the lot of her race. To them, twenty-five years before, sexual sin had never been imputed as more than a fault. She had lost nothing by her supposed illegitimacy; she would gain nothing by the acknowledgment of her mother's marriage.

On the other hand, what would be the effect of this revelation upon Mrs. Carteret herself? To have it known that her father had married a negress would only be less dreadful than to have it appear that he had committed some terrible crime. It was a crime now, by the laws of every Southern State, for white and colored persons to intermarry. She shuddered before the possibility that at some time in the future some person, none too well informed, might learn that her father had married a colored woman, and might assume that she, Olivia Carteret, or her child, had sprung from this shocking *mésalliance*[174] – a fate to which she would willingly have preferred death. No, this marriage must never be made known; the secret should remain buried forever in her own heart!

But there still remained the question of her father's property and her father's will. This woman was her father's child – of that there could be no doubt, it was written in her features no less than in her father's will. As his lawful child – of which, alas! there could also be no question – she was entitled by law to half his estate. Mrs. Carteret's problem had sunk from the realm of sentiment to that of material things, which, curiously enough, she found much more difficult. For, while the negro, by the traditions of her people, was barred from the world of sentiment, his rights of property were recognized. The question had become, with Mrs. Carteret, a question of *meum* and *tuum*.[175] Had the girl Janet been poor, ignorant, or degraded, as might well have been her fate, Mrs. Carteret might have felt a vicarious remorse for her aunt's suppression of the papers; but fate had compensated Janet for the loss; she had been educated, she had married well; she had not suffered for lack of the money of which she had been defrauded, and did not need it now. She had a child, it is true, but this child's career would be so circumscribed by the accident of color that too much wealth would only be a source of unhappiness; to her own child, on the contrary, it would open every door of life.

It would be too lengthy a task to follow the mind and conscience of this much-tried lady in their intricate workings upon this difficult problem; for she had a mind as logical as any woman's, and conscience which she wished to keep void of offense. She had to confront a situation involving the element of race, upon which the moral standards of her people were hopelessly confused. Mrs. Carteret reached the conclusion, ere daylight dawned, that she would be silent upon the subject of her father's second marriage. Neither party had wished it known – neither Julia nor her father – and she would respect her father's wishes. To act otherwise would be to defeat his will, to make known what he had carefully concealed, and to give Janet a claim of title to one half her father's estate, while he had only meant her to have the ten thousand dollars named in the will.

By the same reasoning, she must carry out her father's will in respect to this bequest. Here there was another difficulty. The mining investment into which they had entered shortly after the birth of little Dodie had tied up so much of her property that it would have been difficult to procure ten thousand dollars immediately; while a demand for half the property at once would mean bankruptcy and ruin. Moreover, upon what ground could she offer her sister any sum of money whatever? So sudden a change of heart, after so many years of silence, would raise the presumption of some right on the part of Janet in her father's estate. Suspicion once aroused, it might be possible to trace this hidden marriage, and establish it by legal proof. The marriage once verified, the claim for half the estate could not be denied. She could not plead her father's will to the contrary, for this would be to acknowledge the suppression of the will, in itself a criminal act.

Notes

[174] *mésalliance* misalliance.

[175] *meum and tuum* mine and yours.

There was, however, a way of escape. This hospital which had recently been opened was the personal property of her sister's husband. Some time in the future, when their investments matured, she would present to the hospital a sum of money equal to the amount her father had meant his colored daughter to have. Thus indirectly both her father's will and her own conscience would be satisfied.

Mrs. Carteret had reached this comfortable conclusion, and was falling asleep, when her attention was again drawn by her child's breathing. She took it in her own arms and soon fell asleep.

"By the way, Olivia," said the major, when leaving the house next morning for the office, "if you have any business down town to-day, transact it this forenoon. Under no circumstances must you or Clara or the baby leave the house after midday."

"Why, what's the matter, Phil?"

"Nothing to alarm you, except that there may be a little political demonstration which may render the streets unsafe. You are not to say anything about it where the servants might hear."

"Will there be any danger for you, Phil?" she demanded with alarm.

"Not the slightest, Olivia dear. No one will be harmed; but it is best for ladies and children to stay indoors."

Mrs. Carteret's nerves were still more or less unstrung from her mental struggles of the night, and the memory of her dream came to her like a dim foreboding of misfortune. As though in sympathy with its mother's feelings, the baby did not seem as well as usual. The new nurse was by no means an ideal nurse – Mammy Jane understood the child much better. If there should be any trouble with the negroes, toward which her husband's remark seemed to point – she knew the general political situation, though not informed in regard to her husband's plans – she would like to have Mammy Jane near her, where the old nurse might be protected from danger or alarm.

With this end in view she dispatched the nurse, shortly after breakfast, to Mammy Jane's house in the negro settlement on the other side of the town, with a message asking the old woman to come immediately to Mrs. Carteret's. Unfortunately, Mammy Jane had gone to visit a sick woman in the country, and was not expected to return for several hours.

Chapter 32

The Storm Breaks

The Wellington riot began at three o'clock in the afternoon of a day as fair as was ever selected for a deed of darkness. The sky was clear, except for a few light clouds that floated, white and feathery, high in air, like distant islands in a sapphire sea. A salt-laden breeze from the ocean a few miles away lent a crisp sparkle to the air.

At three o'clock sharp the streets were filled, as if by magic, with armed white men. The negroes, going about, had noted, with uneasy curiosity, that the stores and places of business, many of which closed at noon, were unduly late in opening for the afternoon, though no one suspected the reason for the delay; but at three o'clock every passing colored man was ordered, by the first white man he met, to throw up his hands. If he complied, he was searched, more or less roughly, for firearms, and then warned to get off the street. When he met another group of white men the scene was repeated. The man thus summarily held up seldom encountered more than two groups before disappearing across lots to his own home or some convenient hiding-place. If he resisted any demand of those who halted him – But the records of the day are historical; they may be found in the newspapers of the following date, but they are more firmly engraved upon the hearts and memories of the people of Wellington. For many months there were negro families in the town whose children screamed with fear and ran to their mothers for protection at the mere sight of a white man.

Dr. Miller had received a call, about one o'clock, to attend a case at the house of a well-to-do colored farmer, who lived some three or four miles from the town, upon the very road, by the way, along which Miller had driven so furiously a few weeks before, in the few hours that intervened before Sandy Campbell would probably have been burned at the stake. The drive to his patient's home, the necessary inquiries, the filling of the prescription from his own medicine-case, which he carried along with him, the little friendly conversation about the weather and the crops, and, the farmer being an intelligent and thinking man, the inevitable subject of the future of their race – these, added to the return journey, occupied at least two hours of Miller's time.

As he neared the town on his way back, he saw ahead of him half a dozen men and women approaching, with fear written in their faces, in every degree from apprehension to terror. Women were weeping and children crying, and all were going as fast as seemingly lay in their power, looking behind now and then as if pursued by some deadly enemy. At sight of Miller's buggy they made a dash for cover, disappearing, like a covey of frightened partridges, in the underbrush along the road.

Miller pulled up his horse and looked after them in startled wonder.

"What on earth can be the matter?" he muttered, struck with a vague feeling of alarm. A psychologist, seeking to trace the effects of slavery upon the human mind, might find in the South many a curious illustration of this curse, abiding long after the actual physical bondage had terminated. In the olden time the white South labored under the constant fear of negro insurrections. Knowing that they themselves, if in the negroes' place, would have risen in the effort to throw off the yoke, all their reiterated theories of negro subordination and inferiority could not remove that lurking fear, founded upon the obscure consciousness that the slaves ought to have risen. Conscience, it has been said, makes cowards of us all. There was never, on the continent of America, a successful slave revolt, nor one which lasted more than a few hours, or resulted in the loss of more than a few white lives; yet never was the planter quite free from the fear that there might be one.

On the other hand, the slave had before his eyes always the fear of the master. There were good men, according to their lights – according to their training and environment – among the Southern slaveholders, who treated their slaves kindly, as slaves, from principle, because they recognized the claims of humanity, even under the dark skin of a human chattel. There was many a one who protected or pampered his negroes, as the case might be, just as a man fondles his dog – because they were his; they were a part of his estate, an integral part of the entity of property and person which made up the aristocrat; but with all this kindness, there was always present, in the consciousness of the lowest slave, the knowledge that he was in his master's power, and that he could make no effectual protest against the abuse of that authority. There was also the knowledge, among those who could think at all, that the best of masters was himself a slave to a system, which hampered his movements but scarcely less than those of his bondmen.

When, therefore, Miller saw these men and women scampering into the bushes, he divined, with this slumbering race consciousness which years of culture had not obliterated, that there was some race trouble on foot. His intuition did not long remain unsupported. A black head was cautiously protruded from the shrubbery, and a black voice – if such a description be allowable – addressed him:–

"Is dat you, Doctuh Miller?"

"Yes. Who are you, and what's the trouble?"

"What's de trouble, suh? Why, all hell's broke loose in town yonduh. De w'ite folks is riz 'gins' de niggers, an' say dey're gwine ter kill eve'y nigger dey kin lay han's on."

Miller's heart leaped to his throat, as he thought of his wife and child. This story was preposterous; it could not be true, and yet there must be something in it. He tried to question his informant, but the man was so overcome with excitement and fear that Miller saw clearly that he must go farther for information. He had read in the Morning Chronicle, a few days before, the obnoxious editorial quoted from the Afro-American Banner, and had noted the comment upon it by the white editor. He had felt, as at the time of its first publication, that the editorial was ill-advised. It could do no good, and was calculated to arouse the animosity of those whose friendship, whose tolerance, at least, was necessary and almost indispensable to the colored people. They were living, at the best, in a sort of armed neutrality with the whites; such a publication, however serviceable elsewhere, could have no other effect in Wellington than to endanger this truce and defeat the hope of a possible future friendship. The right of free speech entitled Barber to publish it; a larger measure of common-sense would have made him withhold it. Whether it was the republication of this article that had stirred up anew the sleeping dogs of race prejudice and whetted their thirst for blood, he could not yet tell; but at any rate, there was mischief on foot.

"Fer God's sake, doctuh, don' go no closeter ter dat town," pleaded his informant, "er you'll be killt sho'. Come on wid us, suh, an' tek keer er yo'se'f. We're gwine ter hide in de swamps till dis thing is over!"

"God, man!" exclaimed Miller, urging his horse forward, "my wife and child are in the town!"

Fortunately, he reflected, there were no patients confined in the hospital – if there should be anything in this preposterous story. To one unfamiliar with Southern life, it might have seemed impossible that these good Christian people, who thronged the churches on Sunday, and wept over the sufferings of the lowly Nazarene, and sent missionaries to the heathen, could be hungering and thirsting for the blood of their fellow men; but Miller cherished no such delusion. He knew the history of his country; he had the threatened lynching of Sandy Campbell vividly in mind; and he was fully persuaded that to race prejudice, once roused, any horror was possible. That women or children would be molested of set purpose he did not believe, but that they might suffer by accident was more than likely.

As he neared the town, dashing forward at the top of his horse's speed, he heard his voice called in a loud and agitated tone, and, glancing around him, saw a familiar form standing by the roadside, gesticulating vehemently.

He drew up the horse with a suddenness that threw the faithful and obedient animal back upon its haunches. The colored lawyer, Watson, came up to the buggy. That he was laboring under great and unusual excitement was quite apparent from his pale face and frightened air.

"What's the matter, Watson?" demanded Miller, hoping now to obtain some reliable information.

"Matter!" exclaimed the other. "Everything's the matter! The white people are up in arms. They have disarmed the colored people, killing half a dozen in the process, and wounding as many more. They have forced the mayor and aldermen to resign, have formed a provisional city government *á la française*,[176] and have ordered me and half a

Notes

[176] *á la française* like the French (during the French Revolution of 1848).

dozen other fellows to leave town in forty-eight hours, under pain of sudden death. As they seem to mean it, I shall not stay so long. Fortunately, my wife and children are away. I knew you were out here, however, and I thought I'd come out and wait for you, so that we might talk the matter over. I don't imagine they mean you any harm, personally, because you tread on nobody's toes; but you're too valuable a man for the race to lose, so I thought I'd give you warning. I shall want to sell you my property, too, at a bargain. For I'm worth too much to my family to dream of ever attempting to live here again."

"Have you seen anything of my wife and child?" asked Miller, intent upon the danger to which they might be exposed.

"No; I didn't[177] go to the house. I inquired at the drugstore and found out where you had gone. You needn't[178] fear for them – it is not a war on women and children."

"War of any kind is always hardest on the women and children," returned Miller; "I must hurry on and see that mine are safe."

"They'll not carry the war so far into Africa as that," returned Watson; "but I never saw anything like it. Yesterday I had a hundred white friends in the town, or thought I had – men who spoke pleasantly to me on the street, and sometimes gave me their hands to shake. Not one of them said to me today: 'Watson, stay at home this afternoon.' I might have been killed, like any one of half a dozen others who have bit the dust, for any word that one of my 'friends' had said to warn me. When the race cry is started in this neck of the woods, friendship, religion, humanity, reason, all shrivel up like dry leaves in a raging furnace."

The buggy, into which Watson had climbed, was meanwhile rapidly nearing the town.

"I think I'll leave you here, Miller," said Watson, as they approached the outskirts, "and make my way home by a roundabout path, as I should like to get there unmolested. Home! – a beautiful word that, isn't[179] it, for an exiled wanderer? It might not be well, either, for us to be seen together. If you put the hood of your buggy down, and sit well back in the shadow, you may be able to reach home without interruption; but avoid the main streets. I'll see you again this evening, if we're both alive, and I can reach you; for my time is short. A committee are to call in the morning to escort me to the train. I am to be dismissed from the community with public honors."

Watson was climbing down from the buggy, when a small party of men were seen approaching, and big Josh Green, followed by several other resolute-looking colored men, came up and addressed them.

"Dr. Miller," cried Green, "Mr. Watson – we're lookin' fer a leader. De w'ite folks are killin' de niggers, an' we ain' gwine ter stan' up an' be shot down like dogs. We're gwine ter defen' ou' lives, an' we ain' gwine ter run away f'm no place where we've got a right ter be; an' woe be ter de w'ite man w'at lays han's on us! Dere's two niggers in dis town ter eve'y w'ite man, an' ef we've got ter be killt, we'll take some w'ite folks 'long wid us, ez sho' ez dere's a God in heaven – ez I s'pose dere is, dough He mus' be 'sleep, er busy somewhar e'se ter-day. Will you-all come an' lead us?"

"Gentlemen," said Watson, "what is the use? The negroes will not back you up. They haven't[180] the arms, nor the moral courage, nor the leadership."

"We'll git de arms, an' we'll git de courage, ef you'll come an' lead us! We wants leaders – dat's w'y we come ter you!"

Notes

[177] *Original reads*: did n't [ed.].

[178] *Original reads*: need n't [ed.].

[179] *Original reads*: is n't [ed.].

[180] *Original reads*: have n't [ed.].

"What's the use?" returned Watson despairingly. "The odds are too heavy. I've been ordered out of town; if I stayed, I'd be shot on sight, unless I had a body-guard around me."

"We'll be yo' body-guard!" shouted half a dozen voices.

"And when my body-guard was shot, what then? I have a wife and children. It is my duty to live for them. If I died, I should get no glory and no reward, and my family would be reduced to beggary – to which they'll soon be near enough as it is. This affair will blow over in a day or two. The white people will be ashamed of themselves to-morrow, and apprehensive of the consequences for some time to come. Keep quiet, boys, and trust in God. You won't gain anything by resistance."

"'God he'ps dem dat he'ps demselves,'" returned Josh stoutly. "Ef Mr. Watson won't lead us, will you, Dr. Miller?" said the spokesman, turning to the doctor.

For Miller it was an agonizing moment. He was no coward, morally or physically. Every manly instinct urged him to go forward and take up the cause of these leaderless people, and, if need be, to defend their lives and their rights with his own – but to what end?

"Listen, men," he said. "We would only be throwing our lives away. Suppose we made a determined stand and won a temporary victory. By morning every train, every boat, every road leading into Wellington, would be crowded with white men – as they probably will be anyway – with arms in their hands, curses on their lips, and vengeance in their hearts. In the minds of those who make and administer the laws, we have no standing in the court of conscience. They would kill us in the fight, or they would hang us afterwards – one way or another, we should be doomed. I should like to lead you; I should like to arm every colored man in this town, and have them stand firmly in line, not for attack, but for defense; but if I attempted it, and they should stand by me, which is questionable – for I have met them fleeing from the town – my life would pay the forfeit. Alive, I may be of some use to you, and you are welcome to my life in that way – I am giving it freely. Dead, I should be a mere lump of carrion. Who remembers even the names of those who have been done to death in the Southern States for the past twenty years?"

"I 'members de name er one of 'em," said Josh, "an' I 'members de name er de man dat killt 'im, an' I s'pec' his time is mighty nigh come."

"My advice is not heroic, but I think it is wise. In this riot we are placed as we should be in a war: we have no territory, no base of supplies, no organization, no outside sympathy – we stand in the position of a race, in a case like this, without money and without friends. Our time will come – the time when we can command respect for our rights; but it is not yet in sight. Give it up, boys, and wait. Good may come of this, after all."

Several of the men wavered, and looked irresolute.

"I reckon that's all so, doctuh," returned Josh, "an', de way you put it, I don' blame you ner Mr. Watson; but all dem reasons ain' got no weight wid me. I'm gwine in dat town, an' ef any w'ite man 'sturbs me, dere'll be trouble – dere'll be double trouble – I feels it in my bones!"

"Remember your old mother, Josh," said Miller.

"Yas, suh, I'll 'member her; dat's all I kin do now. I don' need ter wait fer her no mo', fer she died dis mo'nin'. I'd lack ter see her buried, suh, but I may not have de chance. Ef I gits killt, will you do me a favor?"

"Yes, Josh; what is it?"

"Ef I should git laid out in dis commotion dat's gwine on, will you collec' my wages f'm yo' brother, and see dat de ole 'oman is put away right?"

"Yes, of course."

"Wid a nice coffin, an' a nice fune'al, an' a head-bo'd an' a foot-bo'd?"

"Yes."

"All right, suh! Ef I don' live ter do it, I'll know it'll be 'tended ter right. Now we're gwine out ter de cotton compress, an' git a lot er colored men tergether, an' ef de w'ite folks 'sturbs me, I shouldn't[181] be s'prise' ef dere'd be a mix-up – an' ef dere is, me an *one* w'ite man'll stan' befo' de jedgment th'one er God dis day; an' it won't be me w'at'll be 'feared er de jedgment. Come along, boys! Dese gentlemen may have somethin' ter live fer; but ez fer my pa't, I'd ruther be a dead nigger any day dan a live dog!"

Chapter 33

Into the Lion's Jaws

THE party under Josh's leadership moved off down the road. Miller, while entirely convinced that he had acted wisely in declining to accompany them, was yet conscious of a distinct feeling of shame and envy that he, too, did not feel impelled to throw away his life in a hopeless struggle.

Watson left the buggy and disappeared by a path at the roadside. Miller drove rapidly forward. After entering the town, he passed several small parties of white men, but escaped scrutiny by sitting well back in his buggy, the presumption being that a well-dressed man with a good horse and buggy was white. Torn with anxiety, he reached home at about four o'clock. Driving the horse into the yard, he sprang down from the buggy and hastened to the house, which he found locked, front and rear.

A repeated rapping brought no response. At length he broke a window, and entered the house like a thief.

"Janet, Janet!" he called in alarm, "where are you? It is only I – Will!"

There was no reply. He ran from room to room, only to find them all empty. Again he called his wife's name, and was about rushing from the house, when a muffled voice came faintly to his ear –

"Is dat you, Doctuh Miller?"

"Yes. Who are you, and where are my wife and child?"

He was looking around in perplexity, when the door of a low closet under the kitchen sink was opened from within, and a woolly head was cautiously protruded.

"Are you *sho'* dat's you, doctuh?"

"Yes, Sally; where are" –

"An' not some w'ite man come ter bu'n down de house an' kill all de niggers?"

"No, Sally, it's me all right. Where is my wife? Where is my child?"

"Dey went over ter see Mis' Butler 'long 'bout two o'clock, befo' dis fuss broke out, suh. Oh, Lawdy, Lawdy, suh! Is all de cullud folks be'n killt 'cep'n' me an' you, suh? Fer de Lawd's sake, suh, you won' let 'em kill me, will you, suh? I'll wuk fer you fer nuthin', suh, all my bawn days, ef you'll save my life, suh!"

"Calm yourself, Sally. You'll be safe enough if you stay right here, I've no doubt. They'll not harm women – of that I'm sure enough, although I haven't yet got the bearings of this deplorable affair. Stay here and look after the house. I must find my wife and child!"

Notes

[181] *Original reads*: should n't [ed.].

The distance across the city to the home of the Mrs. Butler whom his wife had gone to visit was exactly one mile. Though Miller had a good horse in front of him, he was two hours in reaching his destination. Never will the picture of that ride fade from his memory. In his dreams he repeats it night after night, and sees the sights that wounded his eyes, and feels the thoughts – the haunting spirits of the thoughts – that tore his heart as he rode through hell to find those whom he was seeking.

For a short distance he saw nothing, and made rapid progress. As he turned the first corner, his horse shied at the dead body of a negro, lying huddled up in the collapse which marks sudden death. What Miller shuddered at was not so much the thought of death, to the sight of which his profession had accustomed him, as the suggestion of what it signified. He had taken with allowance the wild statement of the fleeing fugitives. Watson, too, had been greatly excited, and Josh Green's group were desperate men, as much liable to be misled by their courage as the others by their fears; but here was proof that murder had been done – and his wife and children were in the town. Distant shouts, and the sound of firearms, increased his alarm. He struck his horse with the whip, and dashed on toward the heart of the city, which he must traverse in order to reach Janet and the child.

At the next corner lay the body of another man, with the red blood oozing from a ghastly wound in the forehead. The negroes seemed to have been killed, as the band plays in circus parades, at the street intersections, where the example would be most effective. Miller, with a wild leap of the heart, had barely passed this gruesome spectacle, when a sharp voice commanded him to halt, and emphasized the order by covering him with a revolver. Forgetting the prudence he had preached to others, he had raised his whip to strike the horse, when several hands seized the bridle.

"Come down, you damn fool," growled an authoritative voice. "Don't you see we're in earnest? Do you want to get killed?"

"Why should I come down?" asked Miller.

"Because we've ordered you to come down! This is the white people's day, and when they order, a nigger must obey. We're going to search you for weapons."

"Search away. You'll find nothing but a case of surgeon's tools, which I'm more than likely to need before this day is over, from all indications."

"No matter; we'll make sure of it! That's what we're here for. Come down, if you don't want to be pulled down!"

Miller stepped down from his buggy. His interlocutor, who made no effort at disguise, was a clerk in a dry-goods store where Miller bought most of his family and hospital supplies. He made no sign of recognition, however, and Miller claimed no acquaintance. This man, who had for several years emptied Miller's pockets in the course of more or less legitimate trade, now went through them, aided by another man, more rapidly than ever before, the searchers convincing themselves that Miller carried no deadly weapon upon his person. Meanwhile, a third ransacked the buggy with like result. Miller recognized several others of the party, who made not the slightest attempt at disguise, though no names were called by anyone.[182]

"Where are you going?" demanded the leader.

"I am looking for my wife and child," replied Miller.

Notes

[182] *Original reads*: any one [ed.].

"Well, run along, and keep them out of the streets when you find them; and keep your hands out of this affair, if you wish to live in this town, which from now on will be a white man's town, as you niggers will be pretty firmly convinced before night."

Miller drove on as swiftly as might be.

At the next corner he was stopped again. In the white man who held him up, Miller recognized a neighbor of his own. After a short detention and a perfunctory search, the white man remarked apologetically:–

"Sorry to have had to trouble you, doctuh, but them's the o'ders. It ain't men like you that we're after, but the vicious and criminal class of niggers."

Miller smiled bitterly as he urged his horse forward. He was quite well aware that the virtuous citizen who had stopped him had only a few weeks before finished a term in the penitentiary, to which he had been sentenced for stealing. Miller knew that he could have bought all the man owned for fifty dollars, and his soul for as much more.

A few rods farther on, he came near running over the body of a wounded man who lay groaning by the wayside. Every professional instinct urged him to stop and offer aid to the sufferer; but the uncertainty concerning his wife and child proved a stronger motive and urged him resistlessly forward. Here and there the ominous sound of firearms was audible. He might have thought this merely a part of the show, like the "powder play" of the Arabs, but for the bloody confirmation of its earnestness which had already assailed his vision. Somewhere in this seething caldron of unrestrained passions were his wife and child, and he must hurry on.

His progress was painfully slow. Three times he was stopped and searched. More than once his way was barred, and he was ordered to turn back, each such occasion requiring a detour which consumed many minutes. The man who last stopped him was a well-known Jewish merchant. A Jew – God of Moses! – had so far forgotten twenty centuries of history as to join in the persecution of another oppressed race! When almost reduced to despair by these innumerable delays, he perceived, coming toward him, Mr. Ellis, the sub-editor of the Morning Chronicle. Miller had just been stopped and questioned again, and Ellis came up as he was starting once more upon his endless ride.

"Dr. Miller," said Ellis kindly, "it is dangerous for you on the streets. Why tempt the danger?"

"I am looking for my wife and child," returned Miller in desperation. "They are somewhere in this town – I don't know where – and I must find them."

Ellis had been horror-stricken by the tragedy of the afternoon, the wholly superfluous slaughter of a harmless people, whom a show of force would have been quite sufficient to overawe. Elaborate explanations were afterwards given for these murders, which were said, perhaps truthfully, not to have been premeditated, and many regrets were expressed. The young man had been surprised, quite as much as the negroes themselves, at the ferocity displayed. His own thoughts and feelings were attuned to anything but slaughter. Only that morning he had received a perfumed note, calling his attention to what the writer described as a very noble deed of his, and requesting him to call that evening and receive the writer's thanks. Had he known that Miss Pemberton, several weeks after their visit to the Sound, had driven out again to the hotel and made some inquiries among the servants, he might have understood better the meaning of this missive. When Miller spoke of his wife and child, some subtle thread of suggestion coupled the note with Miller's plight.

"I'll go with you, Dr. Miller," he said, "if you'll permit me. In my company you will not be disturbed."

He took a seat in Miller's buggy, after which it was not molested.

Neither of them spoke. Miller was sick at heart; he could have wept with grief, even had the welfare of his own dear ones not been involved in this regrettable affair. With prophetic instinct he foresaw the hatreds to which this day would give birth; the long years of constraint and distrust which would still further widen the breach between two peoples whom fate had thrown together in one community.

There was nothing for Ellis to say. In his heart he could not defend the deeds of this day. The petty annoyances which the whites had felt at the spectacle of a few negroes in office; the not unnatural resentment of a proud people at what had seemed to them a presumptuous freedom of speech and lack of deference on the part of their inferiors – these things, which he knew were to be made the excuse for overturning the city government, he realized full well were no sort of justification for the wholesale murder or other horrors which might well ensue before the day was done. He could not approve the acts of his own people; neither could he, to a negro, condemn them. Hence he was silent.

"Thank you, Mr. Ellis," exclaimed Miller, when they had reached the house where he expected to find his wife. "This is the place where I was going. I am – under a great obligation to you."

"Not at all, Dr. Miller. I need not tell you how much I regret this deplorable affair."

Ellis went back down the street. Fastening his horse to the fence, Miller sprang forward to find his wife and child. They would certainly be there, for no colored woman would be foolhardy enough to venture on the streets after the riot had broken out.

As he drew nearer, he felt a sudden apprehension. The house seemed strangely silent and deserted. The doors were closed, and the venetian blinds shut tightly. Even a dog which had appeared slunk timidly back under the house, instead of barking vociferously according to the usual habit of his kind.

Chapter 34

The Valley of the Shadow

MILLER knocked at the door. There was no response. He went round to the rear of the house. The dog had slunk behind the woodpile. Miller knocked again, at the back door, and, receiving no reply, called aloud.

"Mrs. Butler! It is I, Dr. Miller. Is my wife here?"

The slats of a nearby blind opened cautiously.

"Is it really you, Dr. Miller?"

"Yes, Mrs. Butler. I am looking for my wife and child – are they here?"

"No, sir; she became alarmed about you, soon after the shooting commenced, and I could not keep her. She left for home half an hour ago. It is coming on dusk, and she and the child are so near white that she did not expect to be molested."

"Which way did she go?"

"She meant to go by the main street. She thought it would be less dangerous than the back streets. I tried to get her to stay here, but she was frantic about you, and nothing I could say would keep her. Is the riot almost over, Dr. Miller? Do you think they will murder us all, and burn down our houses?"

"God knows," replied Miller, with a groan. "But I must find her, if I lose my own life in the attempt."

Surely, he thought, Janet would be safe. The white people of Wellington were not savages; or at least their temporary reversion to savagery would not go as far as to include violence to delicate women and children. Then there flashed into his mind Josh Green's story of his "silly" mother, who for twenty years had walked the earth as a child, as the result of one night's terror, and his heart sank within him.

Miller realized that his buggy, by attracting attention, had been a hindrance rather than a help in his progress across the city. In order to follow his wife, he must practically retrace his steps over the very route he had come. Night was falling. It would be easier to cross the town on foot. In the dusk his own color, slight in the daytime, would not attract attention, and by dodging in the shadows he might avoid those who might wish to intercept him. But he must reach Janet and the boy at any risk. He had not been willing to throw his life away hopelessly, but he would cheerfully have sacrificed it for those whom he loved.

He had gone but a short distance, and had not yet reached the centre of mob activity, when he intercepted a band of negro laborers from the cotton compress, with big Josh Green at their head.

"Hello, doctuh!" cried Josh, "does you wan' ter jine us?"

"I'm looking for my wife and child, Josh. They're somewhere in this den of murderers. Have any of you seen them?"

No one had seen them.

"You men are running a great risk," said Miller. "You are rushing on to certain death."

"Well, suh, maybe we is; but we're gwine ter die fightin'. Dey say de w'ite folks is gwine ter bu'n all de cullud schools an' chu'ches, an' kill all de niggers dey kin ketch. Dey're gwine ter bu'n yo' new hospittle, ef somebody don' stop 'em."

"Josh – men – you are throwing your lives away. It is a fever; it will wear off to-morrow, or to-night. They'll not burn the schoolhouses, nor the hospital – they are not such fools, for they benefit the community; and they'll only kill the colored people who resist them. Every one of you with a gun or a pistol carries his death warrant in his own hand. I'd rather see the hospital burn than have one of you lose his life. Resistance only makes the matter worse – the odds against you are too long."

"Things can't be any wuss, doctuh," replied one of the crowd sturdily. "A gun is mo' dange'ous ter de man in front of it dan ter de man behin' it. Dey're gwine ter kill us anyhow; an' we're tired – we read de newspapers – an' we're tired er bein' shot down like dogs, widout jedge er jury. We'd ruther die fightin' dan be stuck like pigs in a pen!"

"God help you!" said Miller. "As for me, I must find my wife and child."

"Good-by, doctuh," cried Josh, brandishing a huge knife. "'Member 'bout de ole 'oman, ef you lives thoo dis. Don' fergit de headbo'd an' de footbo'd, an' a silver plate on de coffin, ef dere's money ernuff."

They went their way, and Miller hurried on. They might resist attack; he thought it extremely unlikely that they would begin it; but he knew perfectly well that the mere knowledge that some of the negroes contemplated resistance would only further inflame the infuriated whites. The colored men might win a momentary victory, though it was extremely doubtful; and they would as surely reap the harvest later on. The qualities which in a white man would win the applause of the world would in a negro be taken as the marks of savagery. So thoroughly diseased was public opinion in matters of race that the negro who died for the common rights of humanity might look for no need[183] of admiration or glory. At such a time, in the white man's eyes, a negro's courage would be mere desperation; his love of liberty, a mere animal dislike of restraint. Every finer human instinct would be interpreted in terms of savagery. Or, if forced to admire, they would none the less repress. They would applaud his courage

Notes

[183] *Original reads*: meed [ed.].

while they stretched his neck, or carried off the fragments of his mangled body as souvenirs, in much the same way that savages preserve the scalps or eat the hearts of their enemies.

But concern for the fate of Josh and his friends occupied only a secondary place in Miller's mind for the moment. His wife and child were somewhere ahead of him. He pushed on. He had covered about a quarter of a mile more, and far down the street could see the signs of greater animation, when he came upon the body of a woman lying upon the sidewalk. In the dusk he had almost stumbled over it, and his heart came up in his mouth. A second glance revealed that it could not be his wife. It was a fearful portent, however, of what her fate might be. The "war" had reached the women and children. Yielding to a professional instinct, he stooped, and saw that the prostrate form was that of old Aunt Jane Letlow. She was not yet quite dead, and as Miller, with a tender touch, placed her head in a more comfortable position, her lips moved with a last lingering flicker of consciousness:–

"Comin', missis, comin'!"

Mammy Jane had gone to join the old mistress upon whose memory her heart was fixed; and yet not all her reverence for her old mistress, nor all her deference to the whites, nor all their friendship for her, had been able to save her from this raging devil of race hatred which momentarily possessed the town.

Perceiving that he could do no good, Miller hastened onward, sick at heart. Whenever he saw a party of white men approaching – these brave reformers never went singly – he sought concealment in the shadow of a tree or the shrubbery in some yard until they had passed. He had covered about two thirds of the distance homeward, when his eyes fell upon a group beneath a lamp-post, at sight of which he turned pale with horror, and rushed forward with a terrible cry.

Chapter 35

"Mine Enemy, O Mine Enemy!"

The proceedings of the day – planned originally as a "demonstration," dignified subsequently as a "revolution," under any name the culmination of the conspiracy formed by Carteret and his colleagues – had by seven o'clock in the afternoon developed into a murderous riot. Crowds of white men and half-grown boys, drunk with whiskey or with license, raged through the streets, beating, chasing, or killing any negro so unfortunate as to fall into their hands. Why any particular negro was assailed, no one stopped to inquire; it was merely a white mob thirsting for black blood, with no more conscience or discrimination than would be exercised by a wolf in a sheepfold. It was race against race, the whites against the negroes; and it was a one-sided affair, for until Josh Green got together his body of armed men, no effective resistance had been made by any colored person, and the individuals who had been killed had so far left no marks upon the enemy by which they might be remembered.

"Kill the niggers!" rang out now and then through the dusk, and far down the street and along the intersecting thoroughfares distant voices took up the ominous refrain – "Kill the niggers! Kill the damned niggers!"

Now, not a dark face had been seen on the street for half an hour, until the group of men headed by Josh made their appearance in the negro quarter. Armed with guns and axes, they presented quite a formidable appearance as they made their way toward the new hospital, near which stood a schoolhouse and a large church, both used by the colored people. They did not reach their destination without having met a number of white men, singly or in twos or threes; and the rumor spread with incredible swiftness that the negroes in turn were up in arms, determined to massacre all the whites and burn the town. Some of the whites became alarmed, and recognizing the power of the negroes, if armed and conscious of their strength, were impressed by the immediate necessity of overpowering and overawing them. Others, with appetites already whetted by slaughter, saw a chance, welcome rather than not, of shedding more black blood. Spontaneously the white mob flocked toward the hospital, where rumor had it that a large body of desperate negroes, breathing threats of blood and fire, had taken a determined stand.

It had been Josh's plan merely to remain quietly and peaceably in the neighborhood of the little group of public institutions, molesting no one, unless first attacked, and merely letting the white people see that they meant to protect their own; but so rapidly did the rumor spread, and so promptly did the white people act, that by the time Josh and his supporters had reached the top of the rising ground where the hospital stood, a crowd of white men much more numerous than their own party were following them at a short distance.

Josh, with the eye of a general, perceived that some of his party were becoming a little nervous, and decided that they would feel safer behind shelter.

"I reckon we better go inside de hospittle, boys," he exclaimed. "Den we'll be behind brick walls, an' dem other fellows'll be outside, an' ef dere's any fightin', we'll have de bes' show. We ain' gwine ter do no shootin' till we're pestered, an' dey'll be less likely ter pester us ef dey can't git at us widout runnin' some resk. Come along in! Be men! De gov'ner er de President is gwine ter sen' soldiers ter stop dese gwines-on, an' meantime we kin keep dem white devils f'm bu'nin' down our hospittles an' chu'ch-houses. W'en dey comes an' fin's out dat we jes' means ter pertect ou' prope'ty, dey'll go 'long 'bout deir own business. Er, ef dey wants a scrap, dey kin have it! Come erlong, boys!"

Jerry Letlow, who had kept out of sight during the day, had started out, after night had set in, to find Major Carteret. Jerry was very much afraid. The events of the day had filled him with terror. Whatever the limitations of Jerry's mind or character may have been, Jerry had a keen appreciation of the danger to the negroes when they came in conflict with the whites, and he had no desire to imperil his own skin. He valued his life for his own sake, and not for any altruistic theory that it might be of service to others. In other words, Jerry was something of a coward. He had kept in hiding all day, but finding, toward evening, that the riot did not abate, and fearing, from the rumors which came to his ears, that all the negroes would be exterminated, he had set out, somewhat desperately, to try to find his white patron and protector. He had been cautious to avoid meeting any white men, and, anticipating no danger from those of his own race, went toward the party which he saw approaching, whose path would cross his own. When they were only a few yards apart, Josh took a step forward and caught Jerry by the arm.

"Come along, Jerry, we need you! Here's another man, boys. Come on now, and fight fer yo' race!"

In vain Jerry protested. "I don' wan' ter fight," he howled. "De w'ite folks ain' gwine ter pester me; dey're my frien's. Tu'n me loose – tu'n me loose, er we all gwine ter git killed!"

The party paid no attention to Jerry's protestations. Indeed, with the crowd of whites following behind, they were simply considering the question of a position from which they could most effectively defend themselves and the building which they imagined to be threatened. If Josh had released his grip of Jerry, that worthy could easily have escaped from the crowd; but Josh maintained his hold almost mechanically, and, in the confusion, Jerry found himself swept with the rest into the hospital, the doors of which were promptly barricaded with the heavier pieces of furniture, and the windows manned by several men each, Josh, with the instinct of a born commander, posting his forces so that they could cover with their guns all the approaches to the building. Jerry still continuing to make himself troublesome, Josh, in a moment of impatience, gave him a terrific box on the ear, which stretched him out upon the floor unconscious.

"Shet up," he said; "ef you can't stan' up like a man, keep still, and don't interfere wid men w'at will fight!"

The hospital, when Josh and his men took possession, had been found deserted. Fortunately there were no patients for that day, except one or two convalescents, and these, with the attendants, had joined the exodus of the colored people from the town.

A white man advanced from the crowd without toward the main entrance to the hospital. Big Josh, looking out from a window, grasped his gun more firmly, as his eyes fell upon the man who had murdered his father and darkened his mother's life. Mechanically he raised his rifle, but lowered it as the white man lifted up his hand as a sign that he wished to speak.

"You niggers," called Captain McBane loudly – it was that worthy – "you niggers are courtin' death, an' you won't have to court her but a minute er two mo' befo' she'll have you. If you surrender and give up your arms, you'll be dealt with leniently – you may get off with the chain-gang or the penitentiary. If you resist, you'll be shot like dogs."

"Dat's no news, Mr. White Man," replied Josh, appearing boldly at the window. "We're use' ter bein' treated like dogs by men like you. If you w'ite people will go 'long an' ten' ter yo' own business an' let us alone, we'll ten' ter ou'n. You've got guns, an' we've got jest as much right ter carry 'em as you have. Lay down yo'n, an' we'll lay down ou'n – we didn'[184] take 'em up fust; but we ain' gwine ter let you bu'n down ou' chu'ches an' school'ouses, er dis hospittle, an' we ain' comin' out er dis house, where we ain' disturbin' nobody, fer you ter shoot us down er sen' us ter jail. You hear me!"

"All right," responded McBane. "You've had fair warning. Your blood be on your" –

His speech was interrupted by a shot from the crowd, which splintered the window-casing close to Josh's head. This was followed by half a dozen other shots, which were replied to, almost simultaneously, by a volley from within, by which one of the attacking party was killed and another wounded.

This roused the mob to frenzy.

"Vengeance! vengeance!" they yelled. "Kill the niggers!"

A negro had killed a white man – the unpardonable sin, admitting neither excuse, justification, nor extenuation. From time immemorial it had been bred in the Southern white consciousness, and in the negro consciousness also, for that matter, that the person of a white man was sacred from the touch of a negro, no matter what the provocation. A dozen colored men lay dead in the streets of Wellington, inoffensive people, slain in cold blood because they had been bold enough to question the authority of those who had assailed them, or frightened enough to flee when they had been ordered to stand still; but their lives counted nothing against that of a riotous white man, who had courted death by attacking a body of armed men.

The crowd, too, surrounding the hospital, had changed somewhat in character. The men who had acted as leaders in the early afternoon, having accomplished their

Notes

[184] *Original reads*: did n' [ed.].

purpose of overturning the local administration and establishing a provisional government of their own, had withdrawn from active participation in the rioting, deeming the negroes already sufficiently overawed to render unlikely any further trouble from that source. Several of the ringleaders had indeed begun to exert themselves to prevent further disorder, or any loss of property, the possibility of which had become apparent; but those who set in motion the forces of evil cannot always control them afterwards. The baser element of the white population, recruited from the wharves and the saloons, was now predominant.

Captain McBane was the only one of the revolutionary committee who had remained with the mob, not with any purpose to restore or preserve order, but because he found the company and the occasion entirely congenial. He had had no opportunity, at least no tenable excuse, to kill or maim a negro since the termination of his contract with the state for convicts, and this occasion had awakened a dormant appetite for these diversions. We are all puppets in the hands of Fate, and seldom see the strings that move us. McBane had lived a life of violence and cruelty. As a man sows, so shall he reap. In works of fiction, such men are sometimes converted. More often, in real life, they do not change their natures until they are converted into dust. One does well to distrust a tamed tiger.

On the outskirts of the crowd a few of the better class, or at least of the better clad, were looking on. The double volley described had already been fired, when the number of these was augmented by the arrival of Major Carteret and Mr. Ellis, who had just come from the Chronicle office, where the next day's paper had been in hasty preparation. They pushed their way towards the front of the crowd.

"This must be stopped, Ellis," said Carteret. "They are burning houses and killing women and children. Old Jane, good old Mammy Jane, who nursed my wife at her bosom, and has waited on her and my child within a few weeks, was killed only a few rods from my house, to which she was evidently fleeing for protection. It must have been by accident – I cannot believe that any white man in town would be dastard enough to commit such a deed intentionally! I would have defended her with my own life! We must try to stop this thing!"

"Easier said than done," returned Ellis. "It is in the fever stage, and must burn itself out. We shall be lucky if it does not burn the town out. Suppose the negroes should also take a hand at the burning? We have advised the people to put the negroes down, and they are doing the job thoroughly."

"My God!" replied the other, with a gesture of impatience, as he continued to elbow his way through the crowd; "I meant to keep them in their places – I did not intend wholesale murder and arson."

Carteret, having reached the front of the mob, made an effort to gain their attention.

"Gentlemen!" he cried in his loudest tones. His voice, unfortunately, was neither loud nor piercing.

"Kill the niggers!" clamored the mob.

"Gentlemen, I implore you" –

The crash of a dozen windows, broken by stones and pistol shots, drowned his voice.

"Gentlemen!" he shouted; "this is murder, it is madness; it is a disgrace to our city, to our state, to our civilization!"

"That's right!" replied several voices. The mob had recognized the speaker. "It *is* a disgrace, and we'll not put up with it a moment longer. Burn 'em out! Hurrah for Major Carteret, the champion of 'white supremacy'! Three cheers for the Morning Chronicle and 'no nigger domination'!"

"Hurrah, hurrah, hurrah!" yelled the crowd.

In vain the baffled orator gesticulated and shrieked in the effort to correct the misapprehension. Their oracle had spoken; not hearing what he said, they assumed it to mean encouragement and cooperation. Their present course was but the logical outcome of the crusade which the Morning Chronicle had preached, in season and out of season, for many months. When Carteret had spoken, and the crowd had cheered him, they felt that they had done all that courtesy required, and he was good-naturedly elbowed aside while they proceeded with the work in hand, which was now to drive out the negroes from the hospital and avenge the killing of their comrade.

Some brought hay, some kerosene, and others wood from a pile which had been thrown into a vacant lot near by. Several safe ways of approach to the building were discovered, and the combustibles placed and fired. The flames, soon gaining a foothold, leaped upward, catching here and there at the exposed woodwork, and licking the walls hungrily with long tongues of flame.

Meanwhile a desultory firing was kept up from the outside, which was replied to scatteringly from within the hospital. Those inside were either not good marksmen, or excitement had spoiled their aim. If a face appeared at a window, a dozen pistol shots from the crowd sought the spot immediately.

Higher and higher leaped the flames. Suddenly from one of the windows sprang a black figure, waving a white handkerchief. It was Jerry Letlow. Regaining consciousness after the effect of Josh's blow had subsided, Jerry had kept quiet and watched his opportunity. From a safe vantage-ground he had scanned the crowd without, in search of some white friend. When he saw Major Carteret moving disconsolately away after his futile effort to stem the torrent, Jerry made a dash for the window. He sprang forth, and, waving his handkerchief as a flag of truce, ran toward Major Carteret, shouting frantically:–

"Majah Carteret – *O* majah! It's me, suh, Jerry, suh! I didn'[185] go in dere myse'f, suh – I wuz drag' in dere! I wouldn'[186] do nothin' 'g'inst de w'ite folks, suh – no, 'ndeed, I would n', suh!"

Jerry's cries were drowned in a roar of rage and a volley of shots from the mob. Carteret, who had turned away with Ellis, did not even hear his servant's voice. Jerry's poor flag of truce, his explanations, his reliance upon his white friends, all failed him in the moment of supreme need. In that hour, as in any hour when the depths of race hatred are stirred, a negro was no more than a brute beast, set upon by other brute beasts whose only instinct was to kill and destroy.

"Let us leave this inferno, Ellis," said Carteret, sick with anger and disgust. He had just become aware that a negro was being killed, though he did not know whom. "We can do nothing. The negroes have themselves to blame – they tempted us beyond endurance. I counseled firmness, and firm measures were taken, and our purpose was accomplished. I am not responsible for these subsequent horrors – I wash my hands of them. Let us go!"

The flames gained headway and gradually enveloped the burning building, until it became evident to those within as well as those without that the position of the defenders was no longer tenable. Would they die in the flames, or would they be driven out? The uncertainty soon came to an end.

The besieged had been willing to fight, so long as there seemed a hope of successfully defending themselves and their property; for their purpose was purely one of

Notes

[185] *Original reads*: did n' [ed.].

[186] *Original reads*: would n' [ed.].

defense. When they saw the case was hopeless, inspired by Josh Green's reckless courage, they were still willing to sell their lives dearly. One or two of them had already been killed, and as many more disabled. The fate of Jerry Letlow had struck terror to the hearts of several others, who could scarcely hide their fear. After the building had been fired, Josh's exhortations were no longer able to keep them in the hospital. They preferred to fight and be killed in the open, rather than to be smothered like rats in a hole.

"Boys!" exclaimed Josh – "men! – fer nobody but men would do w'at you have done – the day has gone 'g'inst us. We kin see ou' finish; but fer my part, I ain' gwine ter leave dis worl' widout takin' a w'ite man 'long wid me, an' I sees my man right out yonder waitin' – I be'n waitin' fer him twenty years, but he won' have ter wait fer me mo' 'n 'bout twenty seconds. Eve'y one er you pick yo' man! We'll open de do', an' we'll give some w'ite men a chance ter be sorry dey ever started dis fuss!"

The door was thrown open suddenly, and through it rushed a dozen or more black figures, armed with knives, pistols, or clubbed muskets. Taken by sudden surprise, the white people stood motionless for a moment, but the approaching negroes had scarcely covered half the distance to which the heat of the flames had driven back the mob, before they were greeted with a volley that laid them all low but two. One of these, dazed by the fate of his companions, turned instinctively to flee, but had scarcely faced around before he fell, pierced in the back by a dozen bullets.

Josh Green, the tallest and biggest of them all, had not apparently been touched. Some of the crowd paused in involuntary admiration of this black giant, famed on the wharves for his strength, sweeping down upon them, a smile upon his face, his eyes lit up with a rapt expression which seemed to take him out of mortal ken. This impression was heightened by his apparent immunity from the shower of lead which less susceptible persons had continued to pour at him.

Armed with a huge bowie-knife, a relic of the civil war, which he had carried on his person for many years for a definite purpose, and which he had kept sharpened to a razor edge, he reached the line of the crowd. All but the bravest shrank back. Like a wedge he dashed through the mob, which parted instinctively before him, and all oblivious of the rain of lead which fell around him, reached the point where Captain McBane, the bravest man in the party, stood waiting to meet him. A pistol-flame flashed in his face, but he went on, and raising his powerful right arm, buried his knife to the hilt in the heart of his enemy. When the crowd dashed forward to wreak vengeance on his dead body, they found him with a smile still upon his face.

One of the two died as the fool dieth. Which was it, or was it both? "Vengeance is mine,"[187] saith the Lord, and it had not been left to Him. But they that do violence must expect to suffer violence. McBane's death was merciful, compared with the nameless horrors he had heaped upon the hundreds of helpless mortals who had fallen into his hands during his career as a contractor of convict labor.

Sobered by this culminating tragedy, the mob shortly afterwards dispersed. The flames soon completed their work, and this handsome structure, the fruit of old Adam Miller's industry, the monument of his son's philanthropy, a promise of good things for the future of the city, lay smouldering in ruins, a melancholy witness to the fact that our boasted civilization is but a thin veneer, which cracks and scales off at the first impact of primal passions.

Notes

[187] *"Vengeance is mine"* Romans 12:19.

Chapter 36

Fiat Justitia[188]

By the light of the burning building, which illuminated the street for several blocks, Major Carteret and Ellis made their way rapidly until they turned into the street where the major lived. Reaching the house, Carteret tried the door and found it locked. A vigorous ring at the bell brought no immediate response. Carteret had begun to pound impatiently upon the door, when it was cautiously opened by Miss Pemberton, who was pale, and trembled with excitement.

"Where is Olivia?" asked the major.

"She is upstairs, with Dodie and Mrs. Albright's hospital nurse. Dodie has the croup.[189] Virgie ran away after the riot broke out. Sister Olivia had sent for Mammy Jane, but she did not come. Mrs. Albright let her white nurse come over."

"I'll go up at once," said the major anxiously. "Wait for me, Ellis – I'll be down in a few minutes."

"Oh, Mr. Ellis," exclaimed Clara, coming toward him with both hands extended, "can nothing be done to stop this terrible affair?"

"I wish I could do something," he murmured fervently, taking both her trembling hands in his own broad palms, where they rested with a surrendering trustfulness which he has never since had occasion to doubt. "It has gone too far, already, and the end, I fear, is not yet; but it cannot grow much worse."

The editor hurried upstairs. Mrs. Carteret, wearing a worried and haggard look, met him at the threshold of the nursery.

"Dodie is ill," she said. "At three o'clock, when the trouble began, I was over at Mrs. Albright's – I had left Virgie with the baby. When I came back, she and all the other servants had gone. They had heard that the white people were going to kill all the negroes, and fled to seek safety. I found Dodie lying in a draught, before an open window, gasping for breath. I ran back to Mrs. Albright's – I had found her much better to-day – and she let her nurse come over. The nurse says that Dodie is threatened with membranous croup."

"Have you sent for Dr. Price?"

"There was no one to send – the servants were gone, and the nurse was afraid to venture out into the street. I telephoned for Dr. Price, and found that he was out of town; that he had gone up the river this morning to attend a patient, and would not be back until to-morrow. Mrs. Price thought that he had anticipated some kind of trouble in the town to-day, and had preferred to be where he could not be called upon to assume any responsibility."

"I suppose you tried Dr. Ashe?"

"I could not get him, nor anyone[190] else, after that first call. The telephone service is disorganized on account of the riot. We need medicine and ice. The drugstores are all closed on account of the riot, and for the same reason we couldn't[191] get any ice."

Major Carteret stood beside the brass bedstead upon which his child was lying – his only child, around whose curly head clustered all his hopes; upon whom all his life for the past year had been centred. He stooped over the bed, beside which the nurse had

Notes

[188] *Fiat Justitia* (Latin) let justice be done.

[189] *croup* infection of the larynx.

[190] *Original reads*: any one [ed.].

[191] *Original reads*: could n't [ed.].

stationed herself. She was wiping the child's face, which was red and swollen and covered with moisture, the nostrils working rapidly, and the little patient vainly endeavoring at intervals to cough up the obstruction to his breathing.

"Is it serious?" he inquired anxiously. He had always thought of the croup as a childish ailment that yielded readily to proper treatment; but the child's evident distress impressed him with sudden fear.

"Dangerous," replied the young woman laconically. "You came none too soon. If a doctor isn't[192] got at once, the child will die – and it must be a good doctor."

"Whom can I call?" he asked. "You know them all, I suppose. Dr. Price, our family physician, is out of town."

"Dr. Ashe has charge of his cases when he is away," replied the nurse. "If you can't find him, try Dr. Hooper. The child is growing worse every minute. On your way back you'd better get some ice, if possible."

The major hastened downstairs.

"Don't wait for me, Ellis," he said. "I shall be needed here for a while. I'll get to the office as soon as possible. Make up the paper, and leave another stick out for me to the last minute, but fill it up in case I'm not on hand by twelve. We must get the paper out early in the morning."

Nothing but a matter of the most vital importance would have kept Major Carteret away from his office this night. Upon the presentation to the outer world of the story of this riot would depend the attitude of the great civilized public toward the events of the last ten hours. The Chronicle was the source from which the first word would be expected; it would give the people of Wellington their cue as to the position which they must take in regard to this distressful affair, which had so far transcended in ferocity the most extreme measures which the conspirators had anticipated. The burden of his own responsibility weighed heavily upon him, and could not be shaken off; but he must do first the duty nearest to him – he must first attend to his child.

Carteret hastened from the house, and traversed rapidly the short distance to Dr. Ashe's office. Far down the street he could see the glow of the burning hospital, and he had scarcely left his own house when the fusillade of shots, fired when the colored men emerged from the burning building, was audible. Carteret would have hastened back to the scene of the riot, to see what was now going on, and to make another effort to stem the tide of bloodshed; but before the dread of losing his child, all other interests fell into the background. Not all the negroes in Wellington could weigh in the balance for one instant against the life of the feeble child now gasping for breath in the house behind him.

Reaching the house, a vigorous ring brought the doctor's wife to the door.

"Good-evening, Mrs. Ashe. Is the doctor at home?"

"No, Major Carteret. He was called to attend Mrs. Wells, who was taken suddenly ill, as a result of the trouble this afternoon. He will be there all night, no doubt."

"My child is very ill, and I must find someone."[193]

"Try Dr. Yates. His house is only four doors away."

A ring at Dr. Yates's door brought out a young man.

"Is Dr. Yates in?"

"Yes, sir."

"Can I see him?"

Notes

[192] *Original reads*: is n't [ed.].

[193] *Original reads*: some one [ed.].

"You might see him, sir, but that would be all. His horse was frightened by the shooting on the streets, and ran away and threw the doctor, and broke his right arm. I have just set it; he will not be able to attend any patients for several weeks. He is old and nervous, and the shock was great."

"Are you not a physician?" asked Carteret, looking at the young man keenly. He was a serious, gentlemanly looking young fellow, whose word might probably be trusted.

"Yes, I am Dr. Evans, Dr. Yates's assistant. I'm really little more than a student, but I'll do what I can."

"My only child is sick with the croup, and requires immediate attention."

"I ought to be able to handle a case of the croup," answered Dr. Evans, "at least in the first stages. I'll go with you, and stay by the child, and if the case is beyond me, I may keep it in check until another physician comes."

He stepped back into another room, and returning immediately with his hat, accompanied Carteret homeward. The riot had subsided; even the glow from the smouldering hospital was no longer visible. It seemed that the city, appalled at the tragedy, had suddenly awakened to a sense of its own crime. Here and there a dark face, emerging cautiously from some hiding-place, peered from behind fence or tree, but shrank hastily away at the sight of a white face. The negroes of Wellington, with the exception of Josh Green and his party, had not behaved bravely on this critical day in their history; but those who had fought were dead, to the last man; those who had sought safety in flight or concealment were alive to tell the tale.

"We pass right by Dr. Thompson's," said Dr. Evans. "If you haven't spoken to him, it might be well to call him for consultation, in case the child should be very bad."

"Go on ahead," said Carteret, "and I'll get him."

Evans hastened on, while Carteret sounded the old-fashioned knocker upon the doctor's door. A gray-haired negro servant, clad in a dress suit and wearing a white tie, came to the door.

"De doctuh, suh," he replied politely to Carteret's question, "has gone ter ampitate de ahm er a gent'eman who got one er his bones smashed wid a pistol bullet in de – fightin' dis atternoon, suh. He's jes' gone, suh, an' lef' wo'd dat he'd be gone a' hour er mo', suh."

Carteret hastened homeward. He could think of no other available physician. Perhaps no other would be needed, but if so, he could find out from Evans whom it was best to call.

When he reached the child's room, the young doctor was bending anxiously over the little frame. The little lips had become livid, the little nails, lying against the white sheet, were blue. The child's efforts to breathe were most distressing, and each gasp cut the father like a knife. Mrs. Carteret was weeping hysterically.

"How is he, doctor?" asked the major.

"He is very low," replied the young man. "Nothing short of tracheotomy – an operation to open the windpipe – will relieve him. Without it, in half or three quarters of an hour he will be unable to breathe. It is a delicate operation, a mistake in which would be as fatal as the disease. I have neither the knowledge nor the experience to attempt it, and your child's life is too valuable for a student to practice upon. Neither have I the instruments here."

"What shall we do?" demanded Carteret. "We have called all the best doctors, and none are available."

The young doctor's brow was wrinkled with thought. He knew a doctor who could perform the operation. He had heard, also, of a certain event at Carteret's house some months before, when an unwelcome physician had been excluded from a consultation – but it was the last chance.

"There is but one other doctor in town who has performed the operation, so far as I know," he declared, "and that is Dr. Miller. If you can get him, he can save your child's life."

Carteret hesitated involuntarily. All the incidents, all the arguments, of the occasion when he had refused to admit the colored doctor to his house, came up vividly before his memory. He had acted in accordance with his lifelong beliefs, and had carried his point; but the present situation was different – this was a case of imperative necessity, and every other interest or consideration must give way before the imminence of his child's peril. That the doctor would refuse the call, he did not imagine: it would be too great an honor for a negro to decline – unless some bitterness might have grown out of the proceedings of the afternoon. That this doctor was a man of some education he knew; and he had been told that he was a man of fine feeling – for a negro – and might easily have taken to heart the day's events. Nevertheless, he could hardly refuse a professional call – professional ethics would require him to respond. Carteret had no reason to suppose that Miller had ever learned of what had occurred at the house during Dr. Burns's visit to Wellington. The major himself had never mentioned the controversy, and no doubt the other gentlemen had been equally silent.

"I'll go for him myself," said Dr. Evans, noting Carteret's hesitation and suspecting its cause. "I can do nothing here alone, for a little while, and I may be able to bring the doctor back with me. He likes a difficult operation."

It seemed an age ere the young doctor returned, though it was really only a few minutes. The nurse did what she could to relieve the child's sufferings, which grew visibly more and more acute. The mother, upon the other side of the bed, held one of the baby's hands in her own, and controlled her feelings as best she might. Carteret paced the floor anxiously, going every few seconds to the head of the stairs to listen for Evans's footsteps on the piazza without. At last the welcome sound was audible, and a few strides took him to the door.

"Dr. Miller is at home, sir," reported Evans, as he came in. "He says that he was called to your house once before, by a third person who claimed authority to act, and that he was refused admittance. He declares that he will not consider such a call unless it come from you personally."

"That is true, quite true," replied Carteret. "His position is a just one. I will go at once. Will – will – my child live until I can get Miller here?"

"He can live for half an hour without an operation. Beyond that I could give you little hope."

Seizing his hat, Carteret dashed out of the yard and ran rapidly to Miller's house; ordinarily a walk of six or seven minutes, Carteret covered it in three, and was almost out of breath when he rang the bell of Miller's front door.

The ring was answered by the doctor in person.

"Dr. Miller, I believe?" asked Carteret.

"Yes, sir."

"I am Major Carteret. My child is seriously ill, and you are the only available doctor who can perform the necessary operation."

"Ah! You have tried all the others – and then you come to me!"

"Yes, I do not deny it," admitted the major, biting his lip. He had not counted on professional jealousy as an obstacle to be met. "But I *have* come to you, as a physician, to engage your professional services for my child – my only child. I have confidence in your skill, or I should not have come to you. I request – nay, I implore you to lose no more time, but come with me at once! My child's life is hanging by a thread, and you can save it!"

"Ah!" replied the other, "as a father whose only child's life is in danger, you implore *me*, of all men in the world, to come and save it!"

There was a strained intensity in the doctor's low voice that struck Carteret, in spite of his own preoccupation. He thought he heard, too, from the adjoining room, the sound of someone[194] sobbing softly. There was some mystery here which he could not fathom unaided.

Miller turned to the door behind him and threw it open. On the white cover of a low cot lay a childish form in the rigidity of death, and by it knelt, with her back to the door, a woman whose shoulders were shaken by the violence of her sobs. Absorbed in her grief, she did not turn, or give any sign that she had recognized the intrusion.

"There, Major Carteret!" exclaimed Miller, with the tragic eloquence of despair, "there lies a specimen of your handiwork! There lies *my* only child, laid low by a stray bullet in this riot which you and your paper have fomented; struck down as much by your hand as though you had held the weapon with which his life was taken!"

"My God!" exclaimed Carteret, struck with horror. "Is the child dead?"

"There he lies," continued the other, "an innocent child – there he lies dead, his little life snuffed out like a candle, because you and a handful of your friends thought you must override the laws and run this town at any cost! – and there kneels his mother, overcome by grief. We are alone in the house. It is not safe to leave her unattended. My duty calls me here, by the side of my dead child and my suffering wife! I cannot go with you. There is a just God in heaven! – as you have sown, so may you reap!"[195]

Carteret possessed a narrow, but a logical mind, and except when confused or blinded by his prejudices, had always tried to be a just man. In the agony of his own predicament – in the horror of the situation at Miller's house – for a moment the veil of race prejudice was rent in twain, and he saw things as they were, in their correct proportions and relations – saw clearly and convincingly that he had no standing here, in the presence of death, in the home of this stricken family. Miller's refusal to go with him was pure, elemental justice; he could not blame the doctor for his stand. He was indeed conscious of a certain involuntary admiration for a man who held in his hands the power of life and death, and could use it, with strict justice, to avenge his own wrongs. In Dr. Miller's place he would have done the same thing. Miller had spoken the truth – as he had sown, so must he reap! He could not expect, could not ask, this father to leave his own household at such a moment.

Pressing his lips together with grim courage, and bowing mechanically, as though to Fate rather than the physician, Carteret turned and left the house. At a rapid pace he soon reached home. There was yet a chance for his child: perhaps someone[196] of the other doctors had come; perhaps, after all, the disease had taken a favorable turn – Evans was but a young doctor, and might have been mistaken. Surely, with doctors all around him, his child would not be permitted to die for lack of medical attention! He found the mother, the doctor, and the nurse still grouped, as he had left them, around the suffering child.

"How is he now?" he asked, in a voice that sounded like a groan.

"No better," replied the doctor; "steadily growing worse. He can go on probably for twenty minutes longer without an operation."

"Where is the doctor?" demanded Mrs. Carteret, looking eagerly toward the door. "You should have brought him right upstairs. There's not a minute to spare! Phil, Phil, our child will die!"

Notes

194 *Original reads*: some one [ed.].

195 *"As you have sown … reap!"* Galatians 6:7.

196 *Original reads*: some one [ed.].

Carteret's heart swelled almost to bursting with an intense pity. Even his own great sorrow became of secondary importance beside the grief which his wife must soon feel at the inevitable loss of her only child. And it was his fault! Would that he could risk his own life to spare her and to save the child!

Briefly, and as gently as might be, he stated the result of his errand. The doctor had refused to come, for a good reason. He could not ask him again.

Young Evans felt the logic of the situation, which Carteret had explained sufficiently. To the nurse it was even clearer. If she or any other woman had been in the doctor's place, she would have given the same answer.

Mrs. Carteret did not stop to reason. In such a crisis a mother's heart usurps the place of intellect. For her, at that moment, there were but two facts in all the world. Her child lay dying. There was within the town, and within reach, a man who could save him. With an agonized cry she rushed wildly from the room.

Carteret sought to follow her, but she flew down the long stairs like a wild thing. The least misstep might have precipitated her to the bottom; but ere Carteret, with a remonstrance on his lips, had scarcely reached the uppermost step, she had thrown open the front door and fled precipitately out into the night.

Chapter 37

The Sisters

MILLER's doorbell rang loudly, insistently, as though demanding a response. Absorbed in his own grief, into which he had relapsed upon Carteret's departure, the sound was an unwelcome intrusion. Surely the man could not be coming back! If it were someone[197] else – What else might happen to the doomed town concerned him not. His child was dead – his distracted wife could not be left alone.

The doorbell rang – clamorously – appealingly. Through the long hall and the closed door of the room where he sat, he could hear someone[198] knocking, and a faint voice calling.

"Open, for God's sake, open!"

It was a woman's voice – the voice of a woman in distress. Slowly Miller rose and went to the door, which he opened mechanically.

A lady stood there, so near the image of his own wife, whom he had just left, that for a moment he was well-nigh startled. A little older, perhaps, a little fairer of complexion, but with the same form, the same features, marked by the same wild grief. She wore a loose wrapper, which clothed her like the drapery of a statue. Her long dark hair, the counterpart of his wife's, had fallen down, and hung disheveled about her shoulders. There was blood upon her knuckles, where she had beaten with them upon the door.

"Dr. Miller," she panted, breathless from her flight and laying her hand upon his arm appealingly – when he shrank from the contact she still held it there – "Dr. Miller, you will come and save my child? You know what it is to lose a child! I am so sorry about your little boy! You will come to mine!"

"Your sorrow comes too late, madam," he said harshly. "My child is dead. I charged your husband with his murder, and he could not deny it. Why should I save your husband's child?"

Notes

[197] *Original reads*: some one [ed.].

[198] *Original reads*: some one [ed.].

"Ah, Dr. Miller!" she cried, with his wife's voice – she never knew how much, in that dark hour, she owed to that resemblance – "it is *my* child, and I have never injured you. It is my child, Dr. Miller, my only child. I brought it into the world at the risk of my own life! I have nursed it, I have watched over it, I have prayed for it – and it now lies dying! Oh, Dr. Miller, dear Dr. Miller, if you have a heart, come and save my child!"

"Madam," he answered more gently, moved in spite of himself, "my heart is broken. My people lie dead upon the streets, at the hands of yours. The work of my life is in ashes – and, yonder, stretched out in death, lies my own child! God! woman, you ask too much of human nature! Love, duty, sorrow, *justice* call me here. I cannot go!"

She rose to her full height. "Then you are a murderer," she cried wildly. "His blood be on your head, and a mother's curse beside!"

The next moment, with a sudden revulsion of feeling, she had thrown herself at his feet – at the feet of a negro, this proud white woman – and was clasping his knees wildly.

"O God!" she prayed, in tones which quivered with anguish, "pardon my husband's sins, and my own, and move this man's hard heart, by the blood of thy Son, who died to save us all!"

It was the last appeal of poor humanity. When the pride of intellect and caste is broken; when we grovel in the dust of humiliation; when sickness and sorrow come, and the shadow of death falls upon us, and there is no hope elsewhere – we turn to God, who sometimes swallows the insult, and answers the appeal.

Miller raised the lady to her feet. He had been deeply moved – but he had been more deeply injured. This was his wife's sister – ah, yes! but a sister who had scorned and slighted and ignored the existence of his wife for all her life. Only Miller, of all the world, could have guessed what this had meant to Janet, and he had merely divined it through the clairvoyant sympathy of love. This woman could have no claim upon him because of this unacknowledged relationship. Yet, after all, she *was* his wife's sister, his child's kinswoman. She was a fellow creature, too, and in distress.

"Rise, madam," he said, with a sudden inspiration, lifting her gently. "I will listen to you on one condition. My child lies dead in the adjoining room, his mother by his side. Go in there, and make your request of her. I will abide by her decision."

The two women stood confronting each other across the body of the dead child, mute witness of this first meeting between two children of the same father. Standing thus face to face, each under the stress of the deepest emotions, the resemblance between them was even more striking than it had seemed to Miller when he had admitted Mrs. Carteret to the house. But Death, the great leveler, striking upon the one hand and threatening upon the other, had wrought a marvelous transformation in the bearing of the two women. The sad-eyed Janet towered erect, with menacing aspect, like an avenging goddess. The other, whose pride had been her life, stood in the attitude of a trembling suppliant.

"*You* have come here," cried Janet, pointing with a tragic gesture to the dead child – "*you*, to gloat over your husband's work. All my life you have hated and scorned and despised me. Your presence here insults me and my dead. What are you doing here?"

"Mrs. Miller," returned Mrs. Carteret tremulously, dazed for a moment by this outburst, and clasping her hands with an imploring gesture, "my child, my only child, is dying, and your husband alone can save his life. Ah, let me have my child," she moaned, heart-rendingly. "It is my only one – my sweet child – my ewe lamb!"

"This was *my* only child!" replied the other mother; "and yours is no better to die than mine!"

"You are young," said Mrs. Carteret, "and may yet have many children – this is my only hope! If you have a human heart, tell your husband to come with me. He leaves it to you; he will do as you command."

"Ah," cried Janet, "I have a human heart, and therefore I will not let him go. *My* child is dead – O God, my child, my child!"

She threw herself down by the bedside, sobbing hysterically. The other woman knelt beside her, and put her arm about her neck. For a moment Janet, absorbed in her grief, did not repulse her.

"Listen," pleaded Mrs. Carteret. "You will not let my baby die? You are my sister – the child is your own near kin!"

"My child was nearer," returned Janet, rising again to her feet and shaking off the other woman's arm. "He was my son, and I have seen him die. I have been your sister for twenty-five years, and you have only now, for the first time, called me so!"

"Listen – sister," returned Mrs. Carteret. Was there no way to move this woman? Her child lay dying, if he were not dead already. She would tell everything, and leave the rest to God. If it would save her child, she would shrink at no sacrifice. Whether the truth would still further incense Janet, or move her to mercy, she could not tell; she would leave the issue to God.

"Listen, sister!" she said. "I have a confession to make. You *are* my lawful sister. My father was married to your mother. You are entitled to his name, and to half his estate."

Janet's eyes flashed with bitter scorn.

"And you have robbed me all these years, and now tell me that as a reason why I should forgive the murder of my child?"

"No, no!" cried the other wildly, fearing the worst. "I have known of it only a few weeks – since my Aunt Polly's death. I had not meant to rob you – I had meant to make restitution. Sister! for our father's sake, who did you no wrong, give me my child's life!"

Janet's eyes slowly filled with tears – bitter tears – burning tears. For a moment even her grief at her child's loss dropped to second place in her thoughts. This, then, was the recognition for which, all her life, she had longed in secret. It had come, after many days, and in larger measure than she had dreamed; but it had come, not with frank kindliness and sisterly love, but in a storm of blood and tears; not freely given, from an open heart, but extorted from a reluctant conscience by the agony of a mother's fears. Janet had obtained her heart's desire, and now that it was at her lips, found it but apples of Sodom,[199] filled with dust and ashes!

"Listen!" she cried, dashing her tears aside. "I have but one word for you – one last word – and then I hope never to see your face again! My mother died of want, and I was brought up by the hand of charity. Now, when I have married a man who can supply my needs, you offer me back the money which you and your friends have robbed me of! You imagined that the shame of being a negro swallowed up every other ignominy – and in your eyes I am a negro, though I am your sister, and you are white, and people have taken me for you on the streets – and you, therefore, left me nameless all my life! Now, when an honest man has given me a name of which I can be proud, you offer me the one of which you robbed me, and of which I can make no use. For twenty-five years I, poor, despicable fool, would have kissed your feet for a word, a nod, a smile. Now, when this tardy recognition comes, for which I have waited so long, it is tainted with fraud and crime and blood, and I must pay for it with my child's life!"

Notes

[199] *apples of Sodom* Medieval mythology held that these apples were beautiful externally but, once picked, turned to ashes and smoke.

"And I must forfeit that of mine, it seems, for withholding it so long," sobbed the other, as, tottering, she turned to go. "It is but just."

"Stay – do not go yet!" commanded Janet imperiously, her pride still keeping back her tears. "I have not done. I throw you back your father's name, your father's wealth, your sisterly recognition. I want none of them – they are bought too dear! ah, God, they are bought too dear! But that you may know that a woman may be foully wronged, and yet may have a heart to feel, even for one who has injured her, you may have your child's life, if my husband can save it! Will," she said, throwing open the door into the next room, "go with her!"

"God will bless you for a noble woman!" exclaimed Mrs. Carteret. "You do not mean all the cruel things you have said – ah, no! I will see you again, and make you take them back; I cannot thank you now! Oh, doctor, let us go! I pray God we may not be too late!"

Together they went out into the night. Mrs. Carteret tottered under the stress of her emotions, and would have fallen, had not Miller caught and sustained her with his arm until they reached the house, where he turned over her fainting form to Carteret at the door.

"Is the child still alive?" asked Miller.

"Yes, thank God," answered the father, "but nearly gone."

"Come on up, Dr. Miller," called Evans from the head of the stairs. "There's time enough, but none to spare."

1901

Frances Ellen Watkins Harper (1825–1911)

France Ellen Watkins Harper's adherence to Judeo-Christian themes of deliverance and redemption, and her ability to turn abolitionist moral suasion into a lyrical appeal on behalf of the enslaved, made her a popular African American poet of the nineteenth century. Harper's writing found a wide audience in the radical abolitionist and reform press, even as its very existence challenged dominant perceptions of race and gender. As an educated, intellectually gifted African American, she was often forced to prove her authenticity in a world that saw "intellectual" and "African" as mutually exclusive. At one lecture in Ohio, the crowd, evidently unable to accept a woman of African descent "speaking so well," accused her of being a white woman with painted skin. As a woman who earned her own income prior to her marriage, then continued lecturing and writing as a single mother after her husband's death, Harper flouted racially exclusive notions of a woman's sphere that denied the claim of African American women to feminine virtue. Simply by speaking to predominantly white crowds, Harper forced her audience to face the inherent contradictions of a country founded on republican notions of citizenship and equality yet committed to enforcing arbitrary constructions of race. One white reformer remarked, after having witnessed Harper speak in Philadelphia: "As I listened to her, there swept over me ... the realization that this noble woman, had she not been rescued from her mother's condition, might have been sold on the auction block, to the higher bidder – her intellect, fancy, eloquence, the flashing wit, that might make the delight of a Parisian saloon, and her pure, Christian character all thrown in." By the time Frances Harper published her novel, *Iola Leroy, or Shadows Uplifted*, in 1892, she was almost 70 years old, with a national reputation that continued to challenge both racial notions of intellect and gendered notions of political activism.

Frances Ellen Watkins was born free in Baltimore, Maryland, in 1825. Although she was orphaned by the age of three, her family's position within the city protected her from the type of poverty and racial isolation that haunted the childhood of fellow novelist Harriet E. Wilson. She attended her uncle's school, the William Watkins Academy for Negro Youth, which stressed biblical and classical study, elocution, and social service. Her cousin William J. Watkins, meanwhile, was a leading advocate of African American emigration to Canada. Frances Watkins flourished in this politically and intellectually active climate, publishing her first book of poetry, *Forest Leaves*, in 1845 (of which no copies are known to survive). In 1850, she left her family for Ohio, where she became the first female teacher at Union Seminary, a precursor to Wilberforce University. Like Harriet Jacobs, Frances Watkins also worked as a seamstress, supplementing her meager income babysitting for owners of a local bookstore.

Frances Watkins's renown as a gifted speaker and writer, combined with her position at Union Seminary, allowed her to escape the abject poverty that afflicted many free African American women. By 1853, she was unable to return home, as Maryland had passed a law prohibiting freed slaves from entering the state on penalty of imprisonment or bondage. Enraged and pledged to the fight against slavery, she moved

The Wiley Blackwell Anthology of African American Literature: Volume 1, 1746–1920, First Edition.
Edited by Gene Andrew Jarrett.

to Philadelphia, where she lived with abolitionist and Underground Railroad conductor William Still. As part of the African American abolitionist community in Philadelphia, Frances Watkins was able to channel her literary gifts and energy into fighting for racial and gender equality. Her poems and essays appeared in antislavery periodicals across the Northeast, including *Frederick Douglass' Paper*, William Lloyd Garrison's *The Liberator*, and the African Methodist Episcopal Church's *The Christian Recorder*.

In 1854, Frances Watkins's first major collection, *Poems on Miscellaneous Subjects*, was published in Boston and Philadelphia. Selling over 10,000 copies in three years and going through multiple reprints, *Poems* solidified her reputation as the leading African American woman writer of her day. That same year, after lecturing before abolitionist crowds in New Bedford, Massachusetts, the Maine Anti-Slavery Society hired her to lecture across New England, Canada, Ohio, and Michigan. She became increasingly militant prior to the Civil War, and was a vocal supporter of John Brown. Soon her reputation as an orator, and her writings for the abolitionist press, made her one of the first African American writers to earn a living from her craft.

In 1859, Frances Watkins published in the *Anglo-African Magazine* "The Two Offers," considered one of the first short stories by an African American. The story suggests that marriage is not the only option that strong women have. Nevertheless, the following year she married Fenton Harper, a widower with three children. In another display of unusual female independence, she used the money earned from *Poems on Miscellaneous Subjects* to purchase a family farm outside of Columbus, Ohio. The couple had one daughter, Mary, but when Fenton died suddenly and creditors claimed her farm in 1864, Frances Harper returned to the lecture circuit to support her family – and to write, lecture, and organize on behalf of former slaves. Much like the title character in *Iola Leroy*, Harper traveled across the North and through every state of the former Confederacy, rallying support around the Thirteenth, Fourteenth, and Fifteenth Amendments to the Constitution, which respectively outlawed slavery, accorded citizenship to Americans of African descent, and granted all citizens (except women) the right to vote. She also raised money to support freed people's education. Her work among former slaves informed her fiction that appeared in reform newspapers, including the serial novellas *Minnie's Sacrifice* (1869) and *Sowing and Reaping* (1870), as well as a poetry collection, *Sketches of Southern Life* (1872). Another poetic publication, *Moses: A Story of the Nile* (1869), consisted of 700 lines of free verse.

Harper's public career continued long after she stopped campaigning on behalf of Radical Reconstruction. She attended meetings and spoke before gatherings of the American Equal Rights Association (AERA), which sought to maintain the radical abolitionist vision of gender and racial equality as the Federal government battled over suffrage and citizenship. Harper's associates, Elizabeth Cady Stanton and Susan B. Anthony, separated from the AERA to form the National Women's Rights Association (NWRA) in protest against the Fifteenth constitutional amendment's exclusion of women. But Harper remained committed to gender equality while supporting African American male suffrage. Throughout the 1870s and 1880s, she continued to challenge feminist notions of race. She spoke before the NWRA as well as Lucy Stone's less racially divisive American Woman Suffrage Association. Her main organizational affiliation was with the Women's Christian Temperance Union. In 1883, after serving as superintendent of the Colored Section of the Philadelphia and Pennsylvania Women's Christian Temperance Union for 10 years, she became national superintendent of temperance work among the colored people. She maintained her position as one of the founding voices of African American feminism by joining the National Association of Colored Women in 1896, and writing for the reform press until her death in 1911.

Further reading

Fisher, Rebecka Rutledge. "Remnants of Memory: Testimony and Being in Frances E.W. Harper's *Sketches of Southern Life*." *ESQ: A Journal of the American Renaissance* 54.1 (2008): 55–74.

Fulton, DoVeanna S. "Sowing Seeds in an Untilled Field: Temperance and Race, Indeterminacy and Recovery in Frances E.W. Harper's *Sowing and Reaping*." *Legacy* 24.2 (2007): 207–224.

James, Jennifer C. *A Freedom Bought with Blood: African American War Literature from the Civil War to World War II*. Chapel Hill: University of North Carolina Press, 2007. Ch. 2.

Johnson, Sherita L. "'In the Sunny South': Reconstructing Frances Harper as Southern." *Southern Quarterly: A Journal of the Arts in the South* 45.3 (2008): 70–85.

McGill, Meredith. "Frances Ellen Watkins Harper and the Circuits of Abolitionist Poetry." *Early African American Print Culture*. Eds. Lara Langer Cohen and Jordan Alexander Stein. Philadelphia: University of Pennsylvania Press, 2012. 53–74.

O'Brien, C.C. "'The White Women All Go for Sex': Frances Harper on Suffrage, Citizenship, and the Reconstruction South." *African American Review* 43.4 (2009): 605–620.

Palmer-Mehta, Valerie. "'We Are All Bound Up Together': Frances Harper and Feminist Theory." *Black Women's Intellectual Traditions: Speaking Their Minds*. Eds. Kristin Waters and Carol B. Conaway. Burlington: University of Vermont Press; Hanover: University Press of New England, 2007. 192–215.

Petrino, Elizabeth A. "'We Are Rising as a People': Frances Harper's Radical Views on Class and Racial Equality in *Sketches of Southern Life*." *American Transcendental Quarterly* 19.2 (2005): 133–153.

Robbins, Sarah. *Managing Literacy, Mothering America: Women's Narratives on Reading and Writing in the Nineteenth Century*. Pittsburgh: University of Pittsburgh Press, 2004. Ch. 5.

Rutkowski, Alice. "Leaving the Good Mother: Frances E.W. Harper, Lydia Maria Child, and the Literary Politics of Reconstruction." *Legacy* 25.1 (2008): 83–104.

Sanborn, Geoffrey. "Mother's Milk: Frances Harper and the Circulation of Blood." ELH 72.3 (2005): 691–715.

Williams, Andreá N. "African American Literary Realism, 1865–1914." *A Companion to African American Literature*. Ed. Gene Andrew Jarrett. Malden, MA: Wiley-Blackwell, 2010. 185–199.

Zackodnik, Teresa C. *The Mulatta and the Politics of Race*. Jackson: University Press of Mississippi, 2004. Ch. 3.

Aunt Chloe

From *Sketches of Southern Life*

I remember, well remember,
That dark and dreadful day,
When they whispered to me, "Chloe,
Your children's sold away!"

It seemed as if a bullet
Had shot me through and through,
And I felt as if my heart-strings
Was breaking right in two.

And I says to cousin Milly,
"There must be some mistake;
Where's Mistus?"[1] "In the great house crying –
Crying like her heart would break.

Notes

AUNT CHLOE

[1] *Mistus* Mistress.

"And the lawyer's there with Mistus;
Says he's come to 'ministrate,
'Cause when master died he just left
Heap of debt on the estate.

"And I thought 'twould do you good
To bid your boys goodbye –
To kiss them both and shake their hands
And have a hearty cry.

"Oh! Chloe, I knows how you feel,
'Cause I'se been through it all;
I thought my poor old heart would break
When master sold my Saul."

Just then I heard the footsteps
Of my children at the door,
And I rose right up to meet them.
But I fell upon the floor.

And I heard poor Jakey saying,
"Oh, mammy, don't you cry!"
And I felt my children kiss me
And bid me, both, good-bye.

Then I had a mighty sorrow,
Though I nursed it all alone;
But I wasted to a shadow,
And turned to skin and bone.

But one day dear Uncle[2] Jacob
(In heaven he's now a saint)
Said, "Your poor heart is in the fire,
But child you must not faint."

Then I said to Uncle[3] Jacob,
If I was good like you,
When the heavy trouble dashed me
I'd know just what to do.

Then he said to me, "Poor Chloe,
The way is open wide:"
And he told me of the Saviour,
And the fountain in His side.[4]

Notes

[2] *Original reads*: uncle [ed.].

[3] *Original reads*: uncle [ed.].

[4] *fountain in His side* Christ's healing blood.

Then he said, "Just take your burden
   To the blessed Master's[5] feet;
I takes all my troubles, Chloe,
   Right unto the mercy-seat."

His words waked up my courage,
   And I began to pray,
And I felt my heavy burden
   Rolling like a stone away.

And a something seemed to tell me,
   You will see your boys again –
And that hope was like a poultice[6]
   Spread upon a dreadful pain.

And it often seemed to whisper,
   Chloe, trust and never fear;
You'll get justice in the kingdom,
   If you do not get it here.

The Deliverance

From *Sketches of Southern Life*

Master only left old Mistus
   One bright and handsome boy;
But she fairly doted on him,
   He was her pride and joy.

We all liked Mister Thomas,
   He was so kind at heart;
And when the young folkes got in scrapes,
   He always took their part.

He kept right on that very way
   Till he got big and tall,
And old Mistus used to chide him,
   And say he'd spile[1] us all.

But somehow the farm did prosper
   When he took things in hand;
And though all the servants liked him,
   He made them understand.

Notes

[5] *blessed Master* Christ.
[6] *poultice* bandage.

The Deliverance
[1] *spile* spoil.

One evening Mister Thomas said,
"Just bring my easy shoes:
I am going to sit by mother,
And read her up the news."

Soon I heard him tell old Mistus
"We're bound to have a fight;
But we'll whip the Yankees, mother,
We'll whip them sure as night!"

Then I saw old Mistus tremble;
She gasped and held her breath;
And she looked on Mister Thomas
With a face as pale as death.

"They are firing on Fort Sumpter;
Oh! I wish that I was there! –
Why, dear mother! what's the matter?
You're the picture of despair."

"I was thinking, dearest Thomas,
'Twould break my very heart
If a fierce and dreadful battle
Should tear our lives apart."

"None but cowards, dearest mother,
Would skulk[2] unto the rear,
When the tyrant's hand is shaking
All the heart is holding dear."

I felt sorry for old Mistus;
She got too full to speak;
But I saw the great big tear-drops
A running down her cheek.

Mister Thomas too was troubled
With choosing on that night,
Betwixt staying with his mother
And joining in the fight.

Soon down into the village came
A call for volunteers;
Mistus gave up Mister Thomas,
With many sighs and tears.

His uniform was real handsome;
He looked so brave and strong;

Notes

[2] *skulk* creep.

But somehow I couldn't help thinking
His fighting must be wrong.

Though the house was very lonesome,
I thought 'twould all come right,
For I felt somehow or other
We was mixed up in that fight.

And I said to Uncle Jacob,
"Now old Mistus feels the sting,
For this parting with your children
Is a mighty dreadful thing."

"Never mind," said Uncle Jacob,
"Just wait and watch and pray,
For I feel right sure and certain,
Slavery's bound to pass away;

"Because I asked the Spirit,
If God is good and just,
How it happened that the masters
Did grind us to the dust.

"And something reasoned right inside,
Such should not always be;
And you could not beat it out my head,
The Spirit spoke to me."

And his dear old eyes would brighten,
And his lips put on a smile,
Saying, "Pick up faith and courage,
And just wait a little while."

Mistus prayed up in the parlor
That the Secesh[3] all might win;
We were praying in the cabins,
Wanting freedom to begin.

Mister Thomas wrote to Mistus,
Telling 'bout the Bull's Run fight,[4]
That his troops had whipped the Yankees,
And put them all to flight.

Mistus' eyes did fairly glisten;
She laughed and praised the South,

Notes

[3] *Secesh* secessionists (Confederates).

[4] *Bull's Run fight* the First Battle of Bull Run, fought on July 21, 1861.

But I thought some day she'd laugh
   On tother side her mouth.

I used to watch old Mistus' face,
   And when it looked quite long
I would say to Cousin Milly,
   The battle's going wrong;

Not for us, but for the Rebels. –
   My heart 'would fairly skip,
When Uncle Jacob used to say,
   "The North is bound to whip."

And let the fight go as it would –
   Let North or South prevail –
He always kept his courage up,
   And never let it fail.

And he often used to tell us,
   "Children, don't forget to pray;
For the darkest time of morning
   Is just 'fore the break of day."

Well, one morning bright and early
   We heard the fife and drum,
And the booming of the cannon –
   The Yankee troops had come.

When the word ran through the village,
   The colored folks are free –
In the kitchens and the cabins
   We held a jubilee.[5]

When they told us Mister Lincoln
   Said that slavery was dead,
We just poured our prayers and blessings
   Upon his precious head.

We just laughed, and danced, and shouted,
   And prayed, and sang, and cried,
And we thought dear Uncle Jacob
   Would fairly crack his side.

But when old Mistus heard it,
   She groaned and hardly spoke;
When she had to lose her servants,
   Her heart was almost broke.

Notes

[5] *jubilee* celebration.

'Twas a sight to see our people
  Going out, the troops to meet,
Almost dancing to the music,
  And marching down the street.

After years of pain and parting,
  Our chains was broke in two,
And we was so mighty happy,
  We did'nt know what to do.

But we soon got used to freedom,
  Though the way at first was rough;
But we weathered through the tempest,
  For slavery made us tough.

But we had one awful sorrow,
  It almost turned my head,
When a mean and wicked cretur[6]
  Shot Mister Lincoln dead.

'Twas a dreadful solemn morning,
I just staggered on my feet;
And the women they were crying
  And screaming in the street.

But if many prayers and blessings
  Could bear him to the throne,
I should think when Mister Lincoln died,
  That heaven just got its own.

Then we had another President[7] –
  What do you call his name?
Well, if the colored folks forget him
  They would'nt be much to blame.

We thought he'd be the Moses
  Of all the colored race;
But when the Rebels pressed us hard
  He never showed his face.

But something must have happened him,
  Right curi's I'll be bound,
'Cause I heard 'em talking 'bout a circle
  That he was swinging round.

Notes

[6] *cretur* John Wilkes Booth.

[7] *another President* Andrew Johnson.

But everything will pass away –
   He went like time and tide –
And when the next election came
   They let poor Andy slide.

But now we have a President,[8]
   And if I was a man
I'd vote for him for breaking up
   The wicked Ku-Klux Klan.

And if any man should ask me
   If I would sell my vote,
I'd tell him I was not the one
   To change and turn my coat;

If freedom seem'd a little rough
   I'd weather through the gale;
And as to buying up my vote,
   I hadn't it for sale.

I do not think I'd ever be
   As slack as Jonas Handy;
Because I heard he sold his vote
   For just three sticks of candy.

But when John Thomas Reeder brought
   His wife some flour and meat,
And told her he had sold his vote
   For something good to eat,

You ought to seen Aunt Kitty raise,
   And heard her blaze away;
She gave the meat and flour a toss,
   And said they should not stay.

And I should think he felt quite cheap
   For voting the wrong side;
And when Aunt Kitty scolded him,
   He just stood up and cried.

But the worst fooled man I ever saw
   Was when poor David Rand
Sold out for flour and sugar;
   The sugar was mixed with sand.

Notes

[8] *a President* Ulysses S. Grant.

I'll tell you how the thing got out;
  His wife had company,
And she thought the sand was sugar,
  And served it up for tea.

When David sipped and sipped the tea,
  Somehow it did'nt taste right;
I guess when he found he was sipping sand,
  He was mad enough to fight.

The sugar looked so nice and white –
  It was spread some inches deep –
But underneath was a lot of sand;
  Such sugar is mighty cheap.

You'd laughed to seen Lucinda Grange
  Upon her husband's track;
When he sold his vote for rations
  She made him take 'em back.

Day after day did Milly Green
  Just follow after Joe,
And told him if he voted wrong
  To take his rags and go.

I think that Curnel Johnson said
  His side had won the day,
Had not we women radicals
  Just got right in the way.

And yet I would not have you think
  That all our men are shabby;
But 'tis said in every flock of sheep
  There will be one that's scabby.

I've heard, before election came
  They tried to buy John Slade;
But he gave them all to understand
  That he wasn't in that trade.

And we've got lots of other men
  Who rally round the cause,
And go for holding up the hands
  That gave us equal laws.

Who know their freedom cost too much
  Of blood and pain and treasure,
For them to fool away their votes
  For profit or for pleasure.

Aunt Chloe's Politics

From *Sketches of Southern Life*

Of course, I don't know very much
  About these politics,
But I think that some who run 'em
  Do mighty ugly tricks.

I've seen 'em honey-fugle[1] round,
  And talk so awful sweet,
That you'd think them full of kindness,
  As an egg is full of meat.

Now I don't believe in looking
  Honest people in the face,
And saying when you're doing wrong,
  That "I haven't sold my race."

When we want to school our children,
  If the money isn't there,
Whether black or white have took it,
  The loss we all must share.

And this buying up each other[2]
  Is something worse than mean,
Though I thinks a heap of voting,
  I go for voting clean.

Learning to Read

From *Sketches of Southern Life*

Very soon the Yankee teachers
  Came down and set up school;
But, oh! how the Rebs[1] did hate it –
  It was agin'[2] their rule.

Our masters always tried to hide
  Book learning from our eyes;
Knowledge did'nt agree with slavery –
  'Twould make us all too wise.

Notes

Aunt Chloe's Politics

1 *honey-fugle* honeyfuggle, or deceive by flattery.

2 *buying up each other* buying votes.

Learning to Read

1 *the Rebs* the Confederates.

2 *agin'* against.

But some of us would try to steal
A little from the book,
And put the words together,
And learn by hook or crook.

I remember Uncle Caldwell,
Who took pot-liquor[3] fat
And greased the pages of his book,
And hid it in his hat.

And had his master ever seen
The leaves upon his head,
He'd have thought them greasy papers,[4]
But nothing to be read.

And there was Mr. Turner's Ben,
Who heard the children spell,
And picked the words right up by heart,
And learned to read 'em well.

Well, the Northern folks kept sending
The Yankee teachers down;
And they stood right up and helped us,
Though Rebs did sneer and frown.

And, I longed to read my Bible,
For precious words it said;
But when I begun to learn it,
Folks just shook their heads,

And said there is no use trying,
Oh! Chloe, you're too late;
But as I was rising sixty,
I had no time to wait.

So I got a pair of glasses,
And straight to work I went,
And never stopped till I could read
The hymns and Testament.[5]

Then I got a little cabin –
A place to call my own –
And I felt as independent
As the queen upon her throne.

Notes

[3] *pot-liquor* fatty broth from stewing meat.

[4] *greasy papers* see Chapter 6 of *Iola Leroy*.

[5] *Testament* the Bible.

Church Building

From *Sketches of Southern Life*

Uncle Jacob often told us,
Since freedom blessed our race
We ought all to come together
And build a meeting place.

So we pinched, and scraped, and spared,
A little here and there;
Though our wages was but scanty,
The church did get a share.[1]

And, when the house was finished,
Uncle Jacob came to pray;
He was looking mighty feeble,
And his head was awful grey

But his voice rang like a trumpet;
His eyes looked bright and young;
And it seemed a mighty power
Was resting on his tongue.

And he gave us all his blessing –
'Twas parting words he said,
For soon we got the message
The dear old man was dead.

But I believe he's in the kingdom,
For when we shook his hand
He said, "Children, you must meet me
Right in the promised land;

"For when I'm done a moiling[2]
And toiling here below,
Through the gate into the city[3]
Straightway I hope to go."

The Reunion

From *Sketches of Southern Life*

Well, one morning real early
I was going down the street,

Notes

Church Building

[1] *a share* tithing.

[2] *moiling* working hard.

[3] *gate into the city* Heaven's gate.

And I heard a stranger asking
  For Missis Chloe Fleet.

There was a something in his voice
  That made me feel quite shaky,
And when I looked right in his face,
  Who should it be but Jakey!

I grasped him tight, and took him home –
  What gladness filled my cup!
And I laughed, and just rolled over,
  And laughed, and just give up.

"Where have you been? O Jakey, dear!
  Why did'nt you come before?
Oh! when you children went away
  My heart was awful sore."

"Why, mammy, I've been on your hunt
  Since ever I've been free,
And I have heard from brother Ben –
  He's down in Tennessee.

"He wrote me that he had a wife."
  "And children?" "Yes, he's three."
"You married, too?" "Oh no, indeed,
  I thought I'd first get free."

"Then, Jakey, you will stay with me,
  And comfort my poor heart;
Old Mistus got no power now
  To tear us both apart.

"I'm richer now than Mistus,
  Because I have got my son;
And Mister Thomas he is dead,
  And she's got 'nary one.

"You must write to brother Benny
  That he must come this fall,
And we'll make the cabin bigger,
  And that will hold us all.

"Tell him I want to see 'em all
  Before my life do cease:
And then, like good old Simeon,[1]
  I hope to die in peace."

1891

Notes

The Reunion

[1] *Simeon* see Luke 2:25–35; Simeon was promised by the Holy Spirit that he would not die until he had seen Christ.

Iola Leroy, or Shadows Uplifted

Chapter 1

Mystery of Market Speech and Prayer-Meeting

"GOOD mornin', Bob; how's butter dis mornin'?"

"Fresh; just as fresh, as fresh can be."

"Oh, glory!" said the questioner, whom we shall call Thomas Anderson, although he was known among his acquaintances as Marster Anderson's Tom.

His informant regarding the condition of the market was Robert Johnson, who had been separated from his mother in his childhood and reared by his mistress as a favorite slave. She had fondled him as a pet animal, and even taught him to read. Notwithstanding their relation as mistress and slave, they had strong personal likings for each other.

Tom Anderson was the servant of a wealthy planter, who lived in the city of C——, North Carolina. This planter was quite advanced in life, but in his earlier days he had spent much of his time in talking politics in his State and National capitals in winter, and in visiting pleasure resorts and watering places in summer. His plantations were left to the care of overseers who, in their turn, employed negro drivers to aid them in the work of cultivation and discipline. But as the infirmities of age were pressing upon him he had withdrawn from active life, and given the management of his affairs into the hands of his sons. As Robert Johnson and Thomas Anderson passed homeward from the market, having bought provisions for their respective homes, they seemed to be very light-hearted and careless, chatting and joking with each other; but every now and then, after looking furtively around, one would drop into the ears of the other some news of the battle then raging between the North and South which, like two great millstones, were grinding slavery to powder. As they passed along, they were met by another servant, who said in hurried tones, but with a glad accent in his voice:–

"Did you see de fish in de market dis mornin'? Oh, but dey war splendid, jis' as fresh, as fresh kin be."

"That's the ticket," said Robert, as a broad smile overspread his face. "I'll see you later."

"Good mornin', boys," said another servant on his way to market. "How's eggs dis mornin'?"

"Fust rate, fust rate," said Tom Anderson. "Bob's got it down fine."

"I thought so; mighty long faces at de pos'-office dis mornin'; but I'd better move 'long," and with a bright smile lighting up his face he passed on with a quickened tread.

There seemed to be an unusual interest manifested by these men in the state of the produce market, and a unanimous report of its good condition. Surely there was nothing in the primeness of the butter or the freshness of the eggs to change careless looking faces into such expressions of gratification, or to light dull eyes with such gladness. What did it mean?

During the dark days of the Rebellion, when the bondman was turning his eyes to the American flag, and learning to hail it as an ensign of deliverance, some of the shrewder slaves, coming in contact with their masters and overhearing their conversations, invented a phraseology to convey in the most unsuspected manner news to each other from the battle-field. Fragile women and helpless children were left on the plantations while their natural protectors were at the front, and yet these bondmen refrained from violence. Freedom was coming in the wake of the Union army, and while numbers deserted to join their forces, others remained at home, slept in their cabins by night and attended to their work by day; but under this apparently careless exterior there was an undercurrent of thought which escaped the cognizance of their masters. In conveying tidings of the war, if they wished to announce a victory of the Union army, they said the butter was fresh, or that the fish and eggs were in good condition. If defeat befell them, then the butter and other produce were rancid or stale.

Entering his home, Robert set his basket down. In one arm he held a bundle of papers which he had obtained from the train to sell to the boarders, who were all anxious to hear from the seat of battle. He slipped one copy out and, looking cautiously around, said to Linda, the cook, in a low voice:–

"Splendid news in the papers. Secesh routed. Yankees whipped 'em out of their boots. Papers full of it. I tell you the eggs and the butter's mighty fresh this morning."

"Oh, sho, chile," said Linda, " I can't read de newspapers, but ole Missus' face is newspaper nuff for me. I looks at her ebery mornin' wen she comes inter dis kitchen. Ef her face is long an' she walks kine o' droopy den I thinks things is gwine wrong for dem. But ef she comes out yere looking mighty pleased, an' larffin all ober her face, an' steppin' so frisky, den I knows de Secesh is gittin' de bes' ob de Yankees. Robby, honey, does you really b'lieve for good and righty dat dem Yankees is got horns?"

"Of course not."

"Well, I yered so."

"Well, you heard a mighty big whopper."

"Anyhow, Bobby, things goes mighty contrary in dis house. Ole Miss is in de parlor prayin' for de Secesh to gain de day, and we's prayin' in de cabins and kitchens for de Yankees to get de bes' ob it. But wasn't Miss Nancy glad wen dem Yankees run'd away at Bull's Run.[1] It was nuffin but Bull's Run an' run away Yankees. How she did larff and skip 'bout de house. An' den me thinks to myself you'd better not holler till you gits out ob de woods. I specs 'fore dem Yankees gits froo you'll be larffin tother side ob your mouf. While you was gone to market ole Miss com'd out yere, her face looking as long as my arm, tellin' us all 'bout de war and saying dem Yankees whipped our folks all to pieces. And she was 'fraid dey'd all be down yere soon. I thought they couldn't come too soon for we. But I didn't tell her so."

"No, I don't expect you did."

"No, I didn't; ef you buys me for a fool you loses your money shore. She said when dey com'd down yere she wanted all de men to hide, for dey'd kill all de men, but dey wouldn't tech de women."

"It's no such thing. She's put it all wrong. Why them Yankees are our best friends."

"Dat's jis' what I thinks. Ole Miss was jis' tryin to skeer a body. An' when she war done she jis' set down and sniffled an' cried, an' I war so glad I didn't know what to do. But I had to hole in. An' I made out I war orful sorry. An' Jinny said, 'O Miss Nancy, I hope dey won't come yere.' An' she said, 'I'se jis' 'fraid dey will come down yere and gobble up eberything dey can lay dere hands on.' An' she jis' looked as ef her heart war mos' broke, an' den she went inter de house. An' when she war gone, we jis' broke loose. Jake turned somersets, and said he warnt 'fraid ob dem Yankees; he know'd which side his brad was buttered on. Dat Jake is a cuter. When he goes down ter git de letters he cuts up all kines ob shines and capers. An' to look at him skylarking dere while de folks is waitin' for dere letters, an' talkin' bout de war, yer wouldn't think dat boy had a thimbleful of sense. But Jake's listenin' all de time wid his eyes and his mouf wide open, an' ketchin' eberything he kin, an' a heap ob news he gits dat way. As to

Notes

Iola Leroy, or Shadows Uplifted

[1] *Bull's Run* the First Battle of Bull Run, fought on July 21, 1861.

Jinny, she jis' capered and danced all ober de flore. An' I jis' had to put my han' ober her mouf to keep ole Miss from yereing her. Oh, but we did hab a good time. Boy, yer oughter been yere."

"And, Aunt Linda, what did you do?"

"Oh, honey, I war jis' ready to crack my sides larffin, jis' to see what a long face Jinny puts on wen ole Miss is talkin', an' den to see dat face wen missus' back is turned, why it's good as a circus. It's nuff to make a horse larff."

"Why, Aunt Linda, you never saw a circus?"

"No, but I'se hearn tell ob dem, and I thinks dey mus' be mighty funny. An' I know it's orful funny to see how straight Jinny's face looks wen she's almos' ready to bust, while ole Miss is frettin' and fumin' 'bout dem Yankees an' de war. But, somehow, Robby, I ralely b'lieves dat we cullud folks is mixed up in dis fight. I seed it all in a vision. An' soon as dey fired on dat fort, Uncle Dan'el says to me: 'Linda, we's gwine to git our freedom.' An' I says: 'Wat makes you think so?' An' he says: 'Dey've fired on Fort Sumter, an' de Norf is boun' to whip.'"

"I hope so," said Robert. "I think that we have a heap of friends up there."

"Well, I'm jis' gwine to keep on prayin' an' b'lievin'."

Just then the bell rang, and Robert, answering, found Mrs. Johnson suffering from a severe headache, which he thought was occasioned by her worrying over the late defeat of the Confederates. She sent him on an errand, which he executed with his usual dispatch, and returned to some work which he had to do in the kitchen. Robert was quite a favorite with Aunt Linda, and they often had confidential chats together.

"Bobby," she said, when he returned, "I thinks we ort ter hab a prayer-meetin' putty soon."

"I am in for that. Where will you have it?"

"Lem me see. Las' Sunday we had it in Gibson's woods; Sunday 'fore las', in de old cypress swamp; an' nex' Sunday we'el hab one in McCullough's woods. Las' Sunday we had a good time. I war jis' chock full an' runnin' ober. Aunt Milly's daughter's bin monin all summer, an' she's jis' come throo. We had a powerful time. Eberythin' on dat groun' was jis' alive. I tell yer, dere was a shout in de camp."

"Well, you had better look out, and not shout too much, and pray and sing too loud, because, 'fore you know, the patrollers[2] will be on your track and break up your meetin' in a mighty big hurry, before you can say 'Jack Robinson.'"

"Oh, we looks out for dat. We's got a nice big pot, dat got cracked las' winter, but it will hole a lot o' water, an' we puts it whar we can tell it eberything. We has our own good times. An' I want you to come Sunday night an' tell all 'bout the good eggs, fish, and butter. Mark my words, Bobby, we's all gwine to git free. I seed it all in a vision, as plain as de nose on yer face."

"Well, I hope your vision will come out all right, and that the eggs will keep and the butter be fresh till we have our next meetin'."

"Now, Bob, you sen' word to Uncle Dan'el, Tom Anderson, an' de rest ob dem, to come to McCullough's woods nex' Sunday night. I want to hab a sin-killin' an' debildribin' time. But, boy, you'd better git out er yere. Ole Miss'll be down on yer like a scratch cat."

Although the slaves were denied unrestricted travel, and the holding of meetings without the surveillance of a white man, yet they contrived to meet by stealth and hold gatherings where they could mingle their prayers and tears, and lay plans for

Notes

[2] *patrollers* white policers of slaves.

escaping to the Union army. Outwitting the vigilance of the patrollers and home guards, they established these meetings miles apart, extending into several States.

Sometimes their hope of deliverance was cruelly blighted by hearing of some adventurous soul who, having escaped to the Union army, had been pursued and returned again to bondage. Yet hope survived all these disasters which gathered around the fate of their unfortunate brethren, who were remanded to slavery through the undiscerning folly of those who were strengthening the hands which were dealing their deadliest blows at the heart of the Nation. But slavery had cast such a glamour[3] over the Nation, and so warped the consciences of men, that they failed to read aright the legible transcript of Divine retribution which was written upon the shuddering earth, where the blood of God's poor children had been as water freely spilled.

Chapter 2

Contraband of War

A FEW evenings after this conversation between Robert and Linda, a prayer-meeting was held. Under the cover of night a few dusky figures met by stealth in McCullough's woods.

"Howdy," said Robert, approaching Uncle Daniel, the leader of the prayer-meeting, who had preceded him but a few minutes.

"Thanks and praise; I'se all right. How is you, chile?"

"Oh, I'm all right," said Robert, smiling, and grasping Uncle Daniel's hand.

"What's de news?" exclaimed several, as they turned their faces eagerly towards Robert.

"I hear," said Robert, "that they are done sending the runaways back to their masters."

"Is dat so?" said a half dozen earnest voices. "How did you yere it?"

"I read it in the papers. And Tom told me he heard them talking about it last night, at his house. How did you hear it, Tom? Come, tell us all about it."

Tom Anderson hesitated a moment, and then said:–

"Now, boys, I'll tell you all 'bout it. But you's got to be mighty mum 'bout it. It won't do to let de cat outer de bag."

"Dat's so! But tell us wat you yered. We ain't gwine to say nuffin to nobody."

"Well," said Tom, "las' night ole Marster had company. Two big ginerals, and dey was hoppin' mad. One ob dem looked like a turkey gobbler, his face war so red. An' he sed one ob dem Yankee ginerals, I thinks dey called him Beas' Butler, sed dat de slaves dat runned away war some big name – I don't know what he called it. But it meant dat all ob we who com'd to de Yankees should be free."

"Contraband of war," said Robert, who enjoyed the distinction of being a good reader, and was pretty well posted about the war. Mrs. Johnson had taught him to read on the same principle she would have taught a pet animal amusing tricks. She had never imagined the time would come when he would use the machinery she had put in his hands to help overthrow the institution to which she was so ardently attached.

"What does it mean? Is it somethin' good for us?"

"I think," said Robert, a little vain of his superior knowledge, "it is the best kind of good. It means if two armies are fighting and the horses of one run away, the other has a right to take them. And it is just the same if a slave runs away from the Secesh to the

Notes

[3] *glamour* spell.

Union lines. He is called a contraband, just the same as if he were an ox or a horse. They wouldn't send the horses back, and they won't send us back."

"Is dat so?" said Uncle Daniel, a dear old father, with a look of saintly patience on his face. "Well, chillen, what do you mean to do?"

"Go, jis' as soon as we kin git to de army," said Tom Anderson.

"What else did the generals say? And how did you come to hear them, Tom?" asked Robert Johnson.

"Well, yer see, Marster's too ole and feeble to go to de war, but his' heart's in it. An' it makes him feel good all ober when dem big ginerals comes an' tells him all 'bout it. Well, I war laying out on de porch fas' asleep an' snorin' drefful hard. Oh, I war so soun' asleep dat wen Marster wanted some ice-water he had to shake me drefful hard to wake me up. An' all de time I war wide 'wake as he war."

"What did they say?" asked Robert, who was always on the lookout for news from the battle-field.

"One ob dem said, dem Yankees war talkin' of puttin' guns in our han's and settin' us all free. An' de oder said, 'Oh, sho! ef dey puts guns in dere hands dey'll soon be in our'n; and ef dey sets em free dey wouldn't know how to take keer ob demselves.'"

"Only let 'em try it," chorused a half dozen voices, "an' dey'll soon see who'll git de bes' ob de guns; an' as to taking keer ob ourselves, I specs we kin take keer ob ourselves as well as take keer ob dem."

"Yes," said Tom, "who plants de cotton and raises all de crops?"

"'They eat the meat and give us the bones,
Eat the cherries and give us the stones,'

And I'm getting tired of the whole business," said Robert.

"But, Bob," said Uncle Daniel, "you've got a good owner. You don't hab to run away from bad times and wuss a comin'."

"It isn't so good, but it might be better. I ain't got nothing 'gainst my ole Miss, except she sold my mother from me. And a boy ain't nothin' without his mother. I forgive her, but I never forget her, and never expect to. But if she were the best woman on earth I would rather have my freedom than belong to her. Well, boys, here's a chance for us just as soon as the Union army gets in sight. What will you do?"

"I'se a goin," said Tom Anderson, "jis' as soon as dem Linkum soldiers gits in sight."

"An' I'se a gwine wid you, Tom," said another. "I specs my ole Marster'll feel right smart lonesome when I'se gone, but I don't keer 'bout stayin' for company's sake."

"My ole Marster's room's a heap better'n his company," said Tom Anderson, "an' I'se a goner too. Dis yer freedom's too good to be lef' behind, wen you's got a chance to git it. I won't stop to bid ole Marse good bye."

"What do you think," said Robert, turning to Uncle Daniel; "won't you go with us?"

"No, chillen, I don't blame you for gwine; but I'se gwine to stay. Slavery's done got all de marrow out ob dese poor ole bones. Ef freedom comes it won't do me much good; we ole ones[4] will die out, but it will set you youngsters all up."

"But, Uncle Daniel, you're not too old to want your freedom?"

"I knows dat. I lubs de bery name of freedom. I'se been praying and hoping for it dese many years. An' ef I warn't boun', I would go wid you ter-morrer. I won't put a

Notes

[4] *Original reads*: one's [ed.].

straw in your way. You boys go, and my prayers will go wid you. I can't go, it's no use. I'se gwine to stay on de ole place till Marse Robert comes back, or is brought back."

"But, Uncle Daniel," said Robert, "what's the use of praying for a thing if, when it comes, you won't take it? As much as you have been praying and talking about freedom, I thought that when the chance came you would have been one of the first to take it. Now, do tell us why you won't go with us. Ain't you willing?"

"Why, Robbie, my whole heart is wid you. But when Marse Robert went to de war, he called me into his room and said to me, 'Uncle Dan'el, I'se gwine to de war, an' I want you to look arter my wife an' chillen, an' see dat eberything goes right on de place. An' I promised him I'd do it, an' I mus' be as good as my word. 'Cept de overseer, dere isn't a white man on de plantation, an' I hear he has to report ter-morrer or be treated as a deserter. An' der's nobody here to look arter Miss Mary an' de chillen, but myself, an' to see dat eberything goes right. I promised Marse Robert I would do it, an' I mus' be as good as my word."

"Well, what should you keer?" said Tom Anderson. "Who looked arter you when you war sole from your farder and mudder, an' neber seed dem any more, and wouldn't know dem to-day ef you met dem in your dish?"

"Well, dats neither yere nor dere. Marse Robert couldn't help what his father did. He war an orful mean man. But he's dead now, and gone to see 'bout it. But his wife war the nicest, sweetest lady dat eber I did see. She war no more like him dan chalk's like cheese. She used to visit de cabins, an' listen to de pore women when de overseer used to cruelize dem so bad, an' drive dem to work late and early. An' she used to sen' dem nice things when they war sick, and hab der cabins whitewashed an' lookin' like new pins, an' look arter dere chillen. Sometimes she'd try to git ole Marse to take dere part when de oberseer got too mean. But she might as well a sung hymns to a dead horse. All her putty talk war like porin water on a goose's back. He'd jis' bluff her off, an' tell her she didn't run dat plantation, and not for her to bring him any nigger news. I never thought ole Marster war good to her. I often ketched her crying, an' she'd say she had de headache, but I thought it war de heartache. 'Fore ole Marster died, she got so thin an' peaked I war 'fraid she war gwine to die; but she seed him out. He war killed by a tree fallin' on him, an' ef eber de debil got his own he got him. I seed him in a vision arter he war gone. He war hangin' up in a pit, sayin' 'Oh! oh!' wid no close on. He war allers blusterin', cussin', and swearin' at somebody. Marse Robert ain't a bit like him. He takes right arter his mother. Bad as ole Marster war, I think she jis' lob'd de groun' he walked on. Well, women's mighty curious kind of folks anyhow. I sometimes thinks de wuss you treats dem de better dey likes you."

"Well," said Tom, a little impatiently, "what's yer gwine to do? Is yer gwine wid us, ef yer gits a chance?"

"Now, jes' you hole on till I gits a chance to tell yer why I'se gwine to stay."

"Well, Uncle Daniel, let's hear it," said Robert.

"I Was jes' gwine to tell yer when Tom put me out. Ole Marster died when Marse Robert war two years ole, and his pore mother when he war four. When he died, Miss Anna used to keep me 'bout her jes' like I war her shadder. I used to nuss Marse Robert jes' de same as ef I were his own fadder. I used to fix his milk, rock him to sleep, ride him on my back, an' nothin' pleased him better'n fer Uncle Dan'el to ride him piggy-back."

"Well, Uncle Daniel," said Robert, "what has that got to do with your going with us and getting your freedom?"

"Now, jes' wait a bit, and don't frustrate my mine. I seed day arter day Miss Anna war gettin' weaker and thinner, an' she looked so sweet and talked so putty, I thinks to myself, 'you ain't long for dis worl'.' And she said to me one day, 'Uncle Dan'el, when

Ise gone, I want you to be good to your Marster Robert.' An' she looked so pale and weak I war almost ready to cry. I couldn't help it. She hed allers bin mighty good to me. An' I beliebs in praisin' de bridge dat carries me ober. She said, 'Uncle Dan'el, I wish you war free. Ef I had my way you shouldn't serve anyone[5] when I'm gone; but Mr. Thurston had eberything in his power when he made his will. I war tied hand and foot, and I couldn't help it.' In a little while she war gone – jis' faded away like a flower. I belieb ef dere's a saint in glory, Miss Anna's dere."

"Oh, I don't take much stock in white folks' religion," said Robert, laughing carelessly.

"The way," said Tom Anderson, "dat some of dese folks cut their cards yere, I think dey'll be as sceece in hebben as hen's teeth. I think wen some of dem preachers brings de Bible 'round an' tells us 'bout mindin our marsters and not stealin' dere tings, dat dey preach to please de white folks, an' dey frows coleness ober de meetin'."

"An' I," said Aunt Linda, "neber did belieb in dem Bible preachers. I yered one ob dem sayin' wen he war dyin', it war all dark wid him. An' de way he treated his house-girl, pore thing, I don't wonder dat it war dark wid him."

"O, I guess," said Robert, "that the Bible is all right, but some of these church folks don't get the right hang of it"

"May be dat's so," said Aunt Linda. "But I allers wanted to learn how to read. I once had a book, and tried to make out what war in it, but ebery time my mistus caught me wid a book in my hand, she used to whip my fingers. An' I couldn't see ef it war good for white folks, why it warn't good for cullud folks."

"Well," said Tom Anderson, "I belieb in de good ole-time religion. But arter dese white folks is done fussin' and beatin' de cullud folks, I don't want 'em to come talking religion to me. We used to hab on our place a real Guinea man, an' once he made ole Marse mad, an' he had him whipped. Old Marse war trying to break him in, but dat fellow war spunk to de backbone, an' when he 'gin talkin' to him 'bout savin' his soul an' gittin' to hebbin, he tole him ef he went to hebbin an' foun' he war dare, he wouldn't go in. He wouldn't stay wid any such rascal as he war."

"What became of him?" asked Robert.

"Oh, he died. But he had some quare notions 'bout religion. He thought dat when he died he would go back to his ole country. He allers kep' his ole Guinea name."

"What was it?"

"Potobombra. Do you know what he wanted Marster to do 'fore he died?" continued Anderson.

"No."

"He wanted him to gib him his free papers."

"Did he do it?"

"Ob course he did. As de poor fellow war dying an' he couldn't sell him in de oder world, he jis' wrote him de papers to yumor him. He didn't want to go back to Africa a slave. He thought if he did, his people would look down on him, an' he wanted to go back a free man. He war orful weak when Marster brought him de free papers. He jis' ris up in de bed, clutched dem in his han's, smiled, an' gasped out, 'I'se free at las'; an' fell back on de pillar, an' he war gone. Oh, but he war spunky. De oberseers, arter dey foun' out who he war, gin'rally gabe him a wide birth. I specs his father war some ole Guinea king."

Notes

[5] *Original reads*: any one [ed.].

"Well, chillen," said Uncle Daniel, "we's kept up dis meeting long enough. We'd better go home, and not all go one way, cause de patrollers might git us all inter trouble, an' we must try to slip home by hook or crook."

"An' when we meet again, Uncle Daniel can finish his story, an' be ready to go with us," said Robert.

"I wish," said Tom Anderson, "he would go wid us, de wuss kind."

Chapter 3

Uncle Daniel's Story

THE Union had snapped asunder because it lacked the cohesion of justice, and the Nation was destined to pass through the crucible of disaster and defeat, till she was ready to clasp hands with the negro and march abreast with him to freedom and victory.

The Union army was encamping a few miles from C——, in North Carolina. Robert, being well posted on the condition of affairs, had stealthily contrived to call a meeting in Uncle Daniel's cabin. Uncle Daniel's wife had gone to bed as a sick sister, and they held a prayer-meeting by her bedside. It was a little risky, but as Mr. Thurston did not encourage the visits of the patrollers, and heartily detested having them prying into his cabins, there was not much danger of molestation.

"Well, Uncle Daniel, we want to hear your story, and see if you have made up your mind to go with us," said Robert, after he had been seated a few minutes in Uncle Daniel's cabin.

"No, chillen, I've no objection to finishin' my story, but I ain't made up my mind to leave the place till Marse Robert gits back."

"You were telling us about Marse Robert's mother. How did you get along after she died?"

"Arter she war gone, ole Marster's folks come to look arter things. But eberything war lef to Marse Robert, an' he wouldn't do widout me. Dat chile war allers at my heels. I couldn't stir widout him, an' when he missed me, he'd fret an' cry so I had ter stay wid him; an' wen he went to school, I had ter carry him in de mornin' and bring him home in de ebenin'. An' I learned him to hunt squirrels, an' rabbits, an' ketch fish, an' set traps for birds. I beliebs he lob'd me better dan any ob his kin'. An' he showed me how to read."

"Well," said Tom, "ef he lob'd you so much, why didn't he set you free?"

"Marse Robert tole me, ef he died fust he war gwine ter leave me free – dat I should neber sarve anyone[6] else."

"Oh, sho!" said Tom, "promises, like pie crusts, is made to be broken. I don't trust none ob dem. I'se been yere dese fifteen years, an' I'se neber foun' any troof in dem. An' I'se gwine wid dem North men soon's I gits a chance. An' ef you knowed what's good fer you, you'd go, too."

"No, Tom; I can't go. When Marster Robert went to de front, he called me to him an' said: 'Uncle Daniel,' an' he was drefful pale when he said it, 'I are gwine to de war, an' I want yer to take keer of my wife an' chillen, jis' like yer used to take keer of me wen yer called me your little boy.' Well, dat jis' got to me, an' I couldn't help cryin', to save my life."

Notes

[6] *Original reads*: any one [ed.].

"I specs," said Tom, "your tear bags must lie mighty close to your eyes. I wouldn't cry ef dem Yankees would make ebery one ob dem go to de front, an' stay dere foreber. Dey'd only be gittin' back what dey's been a doin' to us."

"Marster Robert war nebber bad to me. An' I beliebs in stannin' by dem dat stans by you. Arter Miss Anna died, I had great 'sponsibilities on my shoulders; but I war orful lonesome, an' thought I'd like to git a wife. But dere warn't a gal on de plantation, an' nowhere's roun', dat filled de bill. So I jis' waited, an' 'tended to Marse Robert till he war ole 'nough to go to college. Wen he went, he allers 'membered me in de letters he used to write his grandma. Wen he war gone, I war lonesomer dan eber. But, one day, I jis' seed de gal dat took de rag off de bush. Gundover had jis' brought her from de up-country. She war putty as a picture!" he exclaimed, looking fondly at his wife, who still bore traces of great beauty. "She had putty hair, putty eyes, putty mouth. She war putty all over; an' she know'd how to put on style."

"O, Daniel," said Aunt Katie, half chidingly, "how you do talk."

"Why, it's true. I 'member when you war de puttiest gal in dese diggins; when nobody could top your cotton."

"I don't," said Aunt Katie.

"Well, I do. Now, let me go on wid my story. De fust time I seed her, I sez to myself, 'Dat's de gal for me, an' I means to hab her ef I kin git her.' So I scraped 'quaintance wid her, and axed her ef she would hab me ef our marsters would let us. I warn't 'fraid 'bout Marse Robert, but I warn't quite shore 'bout Gundover. So when Marse Robert com'd home, I axed him, an' he larf'd an' said, 'All right,' an' dat he would speak to ole Gundover 'bout it.' He didn't relish it bery much, but he didn't like to 'fuse Marse Robert. He wouldn't sell her, for she tended his dairy, an' war mighty handy 'bout de house. He said, I mought marry her an' come to see her wheneber Marse Robert would gib me a pass. I wanted him to sell her, but he wouldn't hear to it, so I had to put up wid what I could git. Marse Robert war mighty good to me, but ole Gundover's wife war de meanest woman dat I eber did see. She used to go out on de plantation an' boss things like a man. Arter I war married, I had a baby. It war de dearest, cutest little thing you eber did see; but, pore thing, it got sick and died. It died 'bout three o'clock; and in de mornin', Katie, habbin her cows to milk, lef her dead baby in de cabin. When she com'd back from milkin' her thirty cows, an' went to look for her pore little baby, someone[7] had been to her cabin an' took'd de pore chile away an' put it in de groun'. Pore Katie, she didn't eben hab a chance to kiss her baby 'fore it war buried. Ole Gundover's wife has been dead thirty years, an' she didn't die a day too soon. An' my little baby has gone to glory, an' is wingin' wid the angels an' a lookin' out for us. One ob de las' things ole Gundover's wife did 'fore she died war to order a woman whipped 'cause she com'd to de field a little late when her husband war sick, an' she had stopped to tend him. Dat mornin' she war taken sick wid de fever, an' in a few days she war gone out like de snuff ob a candle. She lef several sons, an' I specs she would almos' turn ober in her grave ef she know'd she had ten culled granchillen somewhar down in de lower kentry."

"Isn't it funny," said Robert, "how these white folks look down on colored people, an' then mix up with them?"

"Marster war away when Miss 'Liza treated my Katie so mean, an' when I tole him 'bout it, he war tearin' mad, an' went ober an' saw ole Gundover, an' foun' out he war

Notes

[7] *Original reads*: some one [ed.].

hard up for money, an' he bought Katie and brought her home to lib wid me, and we's been a libin in clover eber sence. Marster Robert has been mighty good to me. He stood by me in my troubles, an' now his trouble's come, I'm a gwine to stan' by him. I used to think Gundover's wife war jealous ob my Katie. She war so much puttier. Gundover's wife couldn't tech my Katie wid a ten foot pole."

"But, Aunt Katie, you have had your trials," said Robert, now that Daniel had finished his story; "don't you feel bitter towards these people who are fighting to keep you in slavery?"

Aunt Katie turned her face towards the speaker. It was a thoughtful, intelligent face, saintly and calm. A face which expressed the idea of a soul which had been fearfully tempest tossed, but had passed through suffering into peace. Very touching was the look of resignation and hope which overspread her features as she replied, with the simple child-like faith which she had learned in the darkest hour, "The Lord says, we must forgive." And with her that thought, as coming from the lips of Divine Love, was enough to settle the whole question of forgiveness of injuries and love to enemies.

"Well," said Thomas Anderson, turning to Uncle Daniel, "we can't count on yer to go wid us?"

"Boys," said Uncle Daniel, and there was grief in his voice, "I'se mighty glad you hab a chance for your freedom; but, ez I tole yer, I promised Marse Robert I would stay, an' I mus' be as good as my word. Don't you youngsters stay for an ole stager like me. I'm ole an' mos' worn out. Freedom wouldn't do much for me, but I want you all to be as free as the birds; so, you chillen, take your freedom when you kin get it."

"But, Uncle Dan'el, you won't say nothin' 'bout our going, will you?" said the youngest of the company.

Uncle Daniel slowly arose. There was a mournful flash in his eye, a tremor of emotion in his voice, as he said, "Look yere, boys, de boy dat axed dat question war a new comer on dis plantation, but some ob you's bin here all ob your lives; did you eber know ob Uncle Dan'el gittin' any ob you inter trouble?"

"No, no," exclaimed a chorus of voices, "but many's de time you've held off de blows wen de oberseer got too mean, an' cruelized us too much, wen Marse Robert war away. An' wen he got back, you made him settle de oberseer's hash."

"Well, boys," said Uncle Daniel, with an air of mournful dignity, "I'se de same Uncle Dan'el I eber war. Ef any ob you wants to go, I habben't a word to say agin it. I specs dem Yankees be all right, but I knows Marse Robert, an' I don't know dem, an' I ain't a gwine ter throw away dirty water 'til I gits clean."

"Well, Uncle Ben," said Robert, addressing a stalwart man whose towering form and darkly flashing eye told that slavery had failed to put the crouch in his shoulders or general abjectness into his demeanor, "you will go with us, for sure, won't you?"

"Yes," spoke up Tom Anderson, "'cause de trader's done took your wife, an' got her for his'n now."

As Ben Tunnel looked at the speaker, a spasm of agony and anger darkened his face and distorted his features, as if the blood of some strong race were stirring with sudden vigor through his veins. He clutched his hands together, as if he were struggling with an invisible foe, and for a moment he remained silent. Then suddenly raising his head, he exclaimed, "Boys, there's not one of you loves freedom more than I do, but__"

"But what?" said Tom. "Do you think white folks is your bes' friends?"

"I'll think so when I lose my senses."

"Well, now, I don't belieb you're 'fraid, not de way I yeard you talkin' to de oberseer wen he war threatnin' to hit your mudder. He saw you meant business, an' he let her alone. But, what's to hinder you from gwine wid us?"

"My mother," he replied, in a low, firm voice. "That is the only thing that keeps me from going. If it had not been for her, I would have gone long ago. She's all I've got, an' I'm all she's got."

It was touching to see the sorrow on the strong face, to detect the pathos and indignation in his voice, as he said, "I used to love Mirandy as I love my life. I thought the sun rose and set in her. I never saw a handsomer woman than she was. But she fooled me all over the face and eyes, and took up with that hell-hound of a trader, Lukens; an' he gave her a chance to live easy, to wear fine clothes, an' be waited on like a lady. I thought at first I would go crazy, but my poor mammy did all she could to comfort me. She would tell me there were as good fish in the sea as were ever caught out of it. Many a time I've laid my poor head on her lap, when it seemed as if my brain was on fire and my heart was almost ready to burst. But in course of time I got over the worst of it; an' Mirandy is the first an' last woman that ever fooled me. But that dear old mammy of mine, I mean to stick by her as long as there is a piece of her. I can't go over to the army an' leave her behind, for if I did, an' anything should happen, I would never forgive myself."

"But couldn't you take her with you," said Robert, "the soldiers said we could bring our women."

"It isn't that. The Union army is several miles from here, an' my poor mammy is so skeery that, if I were trying to get her away and any of them Secesh would overtake us, an' begin to question us, she would get skeered almost to death, an' break down an' begin to cry, an' then the fat would be in the fire. So, while I love freedom more than a child loves its mother's milk, I've made up my mind to stay on the plantation. I wish, from the bottom of my heart, I could go. But I can't take her along with me, an' I don't want to be free and leave her behind in slavery. I was only five years old when my master and, as I believe, father, sold us both here to this lower country, an' we've been here ever since. It's no use talking, I won't leave her to be run over by everybody."

A few evenings after this interview, the Union soldiers entered the town of C——, and established their headquarters near the home of Thomas Anderson.

Out of the little company, almost everyone deserted to the Union army, leaving Uncle Daniel faithful to his trust, and Ben Tunnel hushing his heart's deep aspirations for freedom in a passionate devotion to his timid and affectionate mother.

Chapter 4

Arrival of the Union Army

A FEW evenings before the stampede of Robert and his friends to the army, and as he sat alone in his room reading the latest news from the paper he had secreted, he heard a cautious tread and a low tap at his window. He opened the door quietly and whispered:–

"Anything new, Tom?"

"Yes."

"What is it? Come in."

"Well, I'se done bin seen dem Yankees, an' dere ain't a bit of troof in dem stories I'se bin yerin 'bout 'em."

"Where did you see 'em?"

"Down in de woods whar Marster tole us to hide. Yesterday ole Marse sent for me to come in de settin'-room. An' what do you think? Instead ob makin' me stan' wid my hat in my han' while he went froo a whole rigamarole, he axed me to sit down, an' he tole me he 'spected de Yankees would want us to go inter de army, an' dey would put us in front whar we'd all git killed; an' I tole him I didn't want to go, I didn't want to git all momached up. An' den he said we'd better go down in de woods an' hide. Massa Tom and Frank said we'd better go as quick as eber we could. Dey said dem Yankees would put us in dere wagons and make us haul like we war mules. Marse Tom ain't libin' at de great house jis' now. He's keepin' bachelor's hall."

"Didn't he go to the battle?"

"No; he foun' a pore white man who war hard up for money, an' he got him to go."

"But, Tom, you didn't believe these stories about the Yankees. Tom and Frank can lie as fast as horses can trot. They wanted to scare you, and keep you from going to the Union army."

"I knows dat now, but I didn't 'spect so den."

"Well, when did you see the soldiers? Where are they? And what did they say to you?"

"Dey's right down in Gundover's woods. An' de Gineral's got his headquarters almos' next door to our house."

"That near? Oh, you don't say so!"

"Yes, I do. An', oh, golly, ain't I so glad! I jis' stole yere to told you all 'bout it. Yesterday mornin' I war splittin' some wood to git my breakfas', an' I met one ob dem Yankee sogers.[8] Well, I war so skeered, my heart flew right up in my mouf, but I made my manners to him and said, 'Good mornin', Massa.' He said, 'Good mornin'; but don't call me "massa."' Dat war de fust white man I eber seed dat didn't want ter be called 'massa,' eben ef he war as pore as Job's turkey.[9] Den I begin to feel right sheepish, an' he axed me ef my marster war at home, an' ef he war a Reb. I tole him he hadn't gone to de war, but he war Secesh all froo, inside and outside. He war too ole to go to de war, but dat he war all de time gruntin' an' groanin', an' I 'spected he'd grunt hisself to death."

"What did he say?"

"He said he specs he'll grunt worser dan dat fore dey get froo wid him. Den he axed me ef I would hab some breakfas', an' I said, 'No, t'ank you, sir.' An' I war jis' as hungry as a dorg, but I war 'feared to eat. I war 'feared he war gwine to pizen me."

"Poison you! don't you know the Yankees are our best friends?"

"Well, ef dat's so, I'se mighty glad, cause de woods is full ob dem."

"Now, Tom, I thought you had cut your eye-teeth long enough not to let them Anderson boys fool you. Tom, you must not think because a white man says a thing, it must be so, and that a colored man's word is no account 'longside of his. Tom, if ever we get our freedom, we've got to learn to trust each other and stick together if we would be a people. Somebody else can read the papers as well as Marse Tom and Frank. My ole Miss knows I can read the papers, an' she never tries to scare me with big whoppers 'bout the Yankees. She knows she can't catch ole birds with chaff, so she is just as sweet as a peach to her Bobby. But as soon as I get a chance I will play her a trick the devil never did."

"What's that?"

"I'll leave her. I ain't forgot how she sold my mother from me. Many a night I have cried myself to sleep, thinking about her, and when I get free I mean to hunt her up."

"Well, I ain't tole you all. De gemman said he war 'cruiting for de army; dat Massa Linkum hab set us all free, an' dat he wanted some more sogers to put down dem

Notes

[8] *sogers* soldiers.

[9] *poor as Job's turkey* extremely destitute; a reference to the Old Testament story of Job, a man who lost all of his worldly possessions.

Secesh; dat we should all hab our freedom, our wages, an' some kind ob money. I couldn't call it like he did."

"Bounty money," said Robert.

"Yes, dat's jis' what he called it, bounty money. An' I said dat I war in for dat, teeth and toe-nails."

Robert Johnson's heart gave a great bound. Was that so? Had that army, with freedom emblazoned on its banners, come at last to offer them deliverance if they would accept it? Was it a bright, beautiful dream, or a blessed reality soon to be grasped by his willing hands? His heart grew buoyant with hope; the lightness of his heart gave elasticity to his step and sent the blood rejoicingly through his veins. Freedom was almost in his grasp, and the future was growing rose-tinted and rainbow-hued. All the ties which bound him to his home were as ropes of sand, now that freedom had come so near.

When the army was afar off, he had appeared to be light-hearted and content with his lot. If asked if he desired his freedom, he would have answered, very naively, that he was eating his white bread and believed in letting well enough alone; he had no intention of jumping from the frying-pan into the fire. But in the depths of his soul the love of freedom was an all-absorbing passion; only danger had taught him caution. He had heard of terrible vengeance being heaped upon the heads of some who had sought their freedom and failed in the attempt. Robert knew that he might abandon hope if he incurred the wrath of men whose overthrow was only a question of time. It would have been madness and folly for him to have attempted an insurrection against slavery, with the words of McClellan ringing in his ears: "If you rise I shall put you down with an iron hand," and with the home guards ready to quench his aspirations for freedom with bayonets and blood. What could a set of unarmed and undisciplined men do against the fearful odds which beset their path?

Robert waited eagerly and hopefully his chance to join the Union army; and was ready and willing to do anything required of him by which he could earn his freedom and prove his manhood. He conducted his plans with the greatest secrecy. A few faithful and trusted friends stood ready to desert with him when the Union army came within hailing distance. When it came, there was a stampede to its ranks of men ready to serve in any capacity, to labor in the tents, fight on the fields, or act as scouts. It was a strange sight to see these black men rallying around the Stars and Stripes, when white men were trampling them under foot and riddling them with bullets.

Chapter 5

The Release of Iola Leroy

"WELL, boys," said Robert to his trusted friends, as they gathered together at a meeting in Gundover's woods, almost under the shadow of the Union army, "how many of you are ready to join the army and fight for your freedom."

"All ob us."

"The soldiers," continued Robert, " are camped right at the edge of the town. The General has his headquarters in the heart of the town, and one of the officers told me yesterday that the President had set us all free, and that as many as wanted to join the army could come along to the camp. So I thought, boys, that I would come and tell you. Now, you can take your bag and baggage, and get out of here as soon as you choose."

"We'll be ready by daylight," said Tom. "It won't take me long to pack up," looking down at his seedy clothes, with a laugh. "I specs ole Marse'll be real lonesome when I'm gone. An' won't he be hoppin' mad when he finds I'm a goner? I specs he'll hate it like pizen."

"O, well," said Robert, "the best of friends must part. Don't let it grieve you."

"I'se gwine to take my wife an' chillen," said one of the company.

"I'se got nobody but myself," said Tom; "but dere's a mighty putty young gal dere at Marse Tom's. I wish I could git her away. Dey tells me dey's been sellin' her all ober de kentry; but dat she's a reg'lar spitfire; dey can't lead nor dribe her."

"Do you think she would go with us?" said Robert.

"I think she's jis' dying to go. Dey say dey can't do nuffin wid her. Marse Tom's got his match dis time, and I'se glad ob it. I jis' glories in her spunk."

"How did she come there?"

"Oh, Marse bought her ob de trader to keep house for him. But ef you seed dem putty white han's ob hern you'd never tink she kept her own house, let 'lone anybody else's."

"Do you think you can get her away?"

"I don't know; 'cause Marse Tom keeps her mighty close. My! but she's putty. Beautiful long hair comes way down her back; putty blue eyes, an' jis' ez white ez anybody's in dis place. I'd jis' wish you could see her yoresef. I heerd Marse Tom talkin' 'bout her las' night to his brudder; tellin' him she war mighty airish,[10] but he meant to break her in."

An angry curse rose to the lips of Robert, but he repressed it and muttered to himself, "Graceless scamp, he ought to have his neck stretched." Then turning to Tom, said:–

"Get her, if you possibly can, but you must be mighty mum about it."

"Trus' me for dat," said Tom.

Tom was very anxious to get word to the beautiful but intractable girl who was held in durance[11] vile by her reckless and selfish master, who had tried in vain to drag her down to his own low level of sin and shame. But all Tom's efforts were in vain. Finally he applied to the Commander of the post, who immediately gave orders for her release. The next day Tom had the satisfaction of knowing that Iola Leroy had been taken as a trembling dove from the gory vulture's nest and given a place of security. She was taken immediately to the General's headquarters. The General was much impressed by her modest demeanor, and surprised to see the refinement and beauty she possessed. Could it be possible that this young and beautiful girl had been a chattel, with no power to protect herself from the highest insults that lawless brutality could inflict upon innocent and defenseless womanhood? Could he ever again glory in his American citizenship, when any white man, no matter how coarse, cruel, or brutal, could buy or sell her for the basest purposes? Was it not true that the cause of a hapless people had become entangled with the lightnings of heaven, and dragged down retribution upon the land?

The field hospital was needing gentle, womanly ministrations, and Iola Leroy, released from the hands of her tormentors, was given a place as nurse; a position to which she adapted herself with a deep sense of relief. Tom was doubly gratified at the success of his endeavors, which had resulted in the rescue of the beautiful young girl and the discomfiture of his young master who, in the words of Tom, "was mad enough to bite his head off" (a rather difficult physical feat).

Notes

[10] *airish* proud.

[11] *held in durance* restrained.

Iola, freed from her master's clutches, applied herself readily to her appointed tasks. The beautiful, girlish face was full of tender earnestness. The fresh, young voice was strangely sympathetic, as if some great sorrow had bound her heart in loving compassion to every sufferer who needed her gentle ministrations.

Tom Anderson was a man of herculean strength and remarkable courage. But, on account of physical defects, instead of enlisting as a soldier, he was forced to remain a servant, although he felt as if every nerve in his right arm was tingling to strike a blow for freedom. He was well versed in the lay of the country, having often driven his master's cotton to market when he was a field hand. After he became a coachman, he had become acquainted with the different roads and localities of the country. Besides, he had often accompanied his young masters on their hunting and fishing expeditions. Although he could not fight in the army, he proved an invaluable helper. When tents were to be pitched, none were more ready to help than he. When burdens were to be borne, none were more willing to bend beneath them than Thomas Anderson. When the battle-field was to be searched for the wounded and dying, no hand was more tender in its ministrations of kindness than his. As a general factotum[12] in the army, he was ever ready and willing to serve anywhere and at any time, and to gather information from every possible source which could be of any service to the Union army. As a Pagan might worship a distant star and wish to call it his own, so he loved Iola. And he never thought he could do too much for the soldiers who had rescued her and were bringing deliverance to his race.

"What do you think of Miss Iola?" Robert asked him one day, as they were talking together.

"I jis' think dat she's splendid. Las' week I had to take some of our pore boys to de hospital, an' she war dere, lookin' sweet an' putty ez an angel, a nussin' dem pore boys, an' ez good to one ez de oder. It looks to me ez ef dey ralely lob'd her shadder. She sits by 'em so patient, an' writes 'em sech nice letters to der frens, an' yit she looks so heart-broke an' pitiful, it jis' gits to me, an' makes me mos' ready to cry. I'm so glad dat Marse Tom had to gib her up. He war too mean to eat good victuals."

"He ought," said Robert, "to be made to live on herrings' heads and cold potatoes. It makes my blood boil just to think that he was going to have that lovely looking young girl whipped for his devilment. He ought to be ashamed to hold up his head among respectable people."

"I tell you, Bob, de debil will neber git his own till he gits him. When I seed how he war treating her I neber rested till I got her away. He buyed her, he said, for his housekeeper; as many gals as dere war on de plantation, why didn't he git one ob dem to keep house, an' not dat nice lookin' young lady? Her han's look ez ef she neber did a day's work in her life. One day when he com'd down to breakfas', he chucked her under de chin, an' tried to put his arm roun' her waist. But she jis' frew it off like a chunk ob fire. She looked like a snake had bit her. Her eyes fairly spit fire. Her face got red ez blood, an' den she turned so pale I thought she war gwine to faint, but she didn't, an' I yered her say, 'I'll die fust.' I war mad 'nough to stan' on my head. I could hab tore'd him all to pieces wen he said he'd hab her whipped."

"Did he do it?"

"I don't know. But he's mean 'nough to do enythin'. Why, dey say she war sole seben times in six weeks, 'cause she's so putty, but dat she war game[13] to de las'."

Notes

[12] *factotum* servant, assistant.

[13] *game* brave.

"Well, Tom," said Robert, "getting that girl away was one of the best things you ever did in your life."

"I think so, too. Not dat I specs enytin' ob it. I don't spose she would think ob an ugly chap like me; but it does me good to know dat Marse Tom ain't got her."

Chapter 6

Robert Johnson's Promotion and Religion

Robert Johnson, being able to meet the army requirements, was enlisted as a substitute to help fill out the quota of a Northern regiment. With his intelligence, courage, and prompt obedience, he rose from the ranks and became lieutenant of a colored company. He was daring, without being rash; prompt, but not thoughtless; firm, without being harsh. Kind and devoted to the company he drilled, he soon won the respect of his superior officers and the love of his comrades.

"Johnson," said a young officer, Captain Sybil, of Maine, who had become attached to Robert, "what is the use of your saying you're a colored man, when you are as white as I am, and as brave a man as there is among us. Why not quit this company, and take your place in the army just the same as a white man? I know your chances for promotion would be better."

"Captain, you may doubt my word, but to-day I would rather be a lieutenant in my company than a captain in yours."

"I don't understand you."

"Well, Captain, when a man's been colored all his life it comes a little hard for him to get white all at once. Were I to try it, I would feel like a cat in a strange garret.[14] Captain, I think my place is where I am most needed. You do not need me in your ranks, and my company does. They are excellent fighters, but they need a leader. To silence a battery, to capture a flag, to take a fortification, they will rush into the jaws of death."

"Yes, I have often wondered at their bravery."

"Captain, these battles put them on their mettle. They have been so long taught that they are nothing and nobody, that they seem glad to prove they are something and somebody."

"But, Johnson, you do not look like them, you do not talk like them. It is a burning shame to have held such a man as you in slavery."

"I don't think it was any worse to have held me in slavery than the blackest man in the South."

"You are right, Johnson. The color of a man's skin has nothing to do with the possession of his rights."

"Now, there is Tom Anderson," said Robert, "he is just as black as black can be. He has been bought and sold like a beast, and yet there is not a braver man in all the company. I know him well. He is a noble-hearted fellow. True as steel. I love him like a brother. And I believe Tom would risk his life for me any day. He don't know anything about his father or mother. He was sold from them before he could remember. He can read a little. He used to take lessons from a white gardener in Virginia. He would go between the hours of 9 P.M. and 4 A.M. He got a book of his own, tore it up,

Notes

[14] *garret* attic.

greased the pages, and hid them in his hat. Then if his master had ever knocked his hat off he would have thought them greasy papers, and not that Tom was carrying his library on his head. I had another friend who lived near us. When he was nineteen years old he did not know how many letters there were in the A B C's. One night, when his work was done, his boss came into his cabin and saw him with a book in his hand. He threatened to give him five hundred lashes if he caught him again with a book, and said he hadn't work enough to do. He was getting out logs, and his task was ten logs a day. His employer threatened to increase it to twelve. He said it just harassed him; it set him on fire. He thought there must be something good in that book if the white man didn't want him to learn. One day he had an errand in the kitchen, and he heard one of the colored girls going over the A B C's. Here was the key to the forbidden knowledge. She had heard the white children saying them, and picked them up by heart, but did not know them by sight. He was not content with that, but sold his cap for a book and wore a cloth on his head instead. He got the sounds of the letters by heart, then cut off the bark of a tree, carved the letters on the smooth inside, and learned them. He wanted to learn how to write. He had charge of a warehouse where he had a chance to see the size and form of letters. He made the beach of the river his copy-book, and thus he learned to write. Tom never got very far with his learning, but I used to get the papers and tell him all I knew about the war."

"How did you get the papers?"

"I used to have very good privileges for a slave. All of our owners were not alike. Some of them were quite clever, and others were worse than git out. I used to get the morning papers to sell to the boarders and others, and when I got them I would contrive to hide a paper, and let some of the fellow-servants know how things were going on. And our owners thought we cared nothing about what was going on."

"How was that? I thought you were not allowed to hold meetings unless a white man were present."

"That was so. But we contrived to hold secret meetings in spite of their caution. We knew whom we could trust. My ole Miss wasn't mean like some of them. She never wanted the patrollers around prowling in our cabins, and poking their noses into our business. Her husband was an awful drunkard. He ran through every cent he could lay his hands on, and she was forced to do something to keep the wolf from the door, so she set up a boarding-house. But she didn't take in Tom, Dick, and Harry. Nobody but the big bugs stopped with her. She taught me to read and write, and to cast up accounts. It was so handy for her to have someone[15] who could figure up her accounts, and read or write a note, if she were from home and wanted the like done. She once told her cousin how I could write and figure up. And what do you think her cousin said?"

"'Pleased,' I suppose, 'to hear it.'"

"Not a bit of it. She said, if I belonged to her, she would cut off my thumbs; her husband said, 'Oh, then he couldn't pick cotton.' As to my poor thumbs, it did not seem to be taken into account what it would cost me to lose them. My ole Miss used to have a lot of books. She would let me read any one of them except a novel. She wanted to take care of my soul, but she wasn't taking care of her own."

"Wasn't she religious?"

"She went for it. I suppose she was as good as most of them. She said her prayers and went to church, but I don't know that that made her any better. I never did take much stock in white folks' religion."

Notes

[15] *Original reads*: some one [ed.].

"Why, Robert, I'm afraid you are something of an infidel."

"No, Captain, I believe in the real, genuine religion. I ain't got much myself, but I respect them that have. We had on our place a dear, old saint, named Aunt Kizzy. She was a happy soul. She had seen hard times, but was what I call a living epistle. I've heard her tell how her only child had been sold from her, when the man who bought herself did not want to buy her child. Poor little fellow! he was only two years old. I asked her one day how she felt when her child was taken away. 'I felt,' she said, 'as if I was going to my grave. But I knew if I couldn't get justice here, I could get it in another world.'"

"That was faith," said Captain Sybil, as if speaking to himself, "a patient waiting for death to redress the wrongs of life."

"Many a time," continued Robert, "have I heard her humming to herself in the kitchen and saying, 'I has my trials, ups and downs, but it won't allers be so. I specs one day to wing and wing wid de angels, Hallelujah! Den I specs to hear a voice sayin', "Poor ole Kizzy, she's done de bes' she kin. Go down, Gabriel, an' tote her in." Den I specs to put on my golden slippers, my long white robe, an' my starry crown, an' walk dem golden streets, Hallelujah!' I've known that dear, old soul to travel going on two miles, after her work was done, to have someone[16] read to her. Her favorite chapter began with, 'Let not your heart be troubled, ye believe in God, believe also in Me.'"

"I have been deeply impressed," said Captain Sybil, "with the child-like faith of some of these people. I do not mean to say that they are consistent Christians, but I do think that this faith has in a measure underlain the life of the race. It has been a golden thread woven amid the sombre tissues of their lives. A ray of light shimmering amid the gloom of their condition. And what would they have been without it?"

"I don't know. But I know what she was with it. And I believe if there are any saints in glory, Aunt Kizzy is one of them."

"She is dead, then?"

"Yes, went all right, singing and rejoicing until the the last, 'Troubles over, troubles over, and den my troubles will be over. We'll walk de golden streets all 'roun' in de New Jerusalem.' Now, Captain, that's the kind of religion that I want. Not that kind which could ride to church on Sundays, and talk so solemn with the minister about heaven and good things, then come home and light down on the servants like a thousand of bricks. I have no use for it. I don't believe in it. I never did and I never will. If any man wants to save my soul he ain't got to beat my body. That ain't the kind of religion I'm looking for. I ain't got a bit of use for it. Now, Captain, ain't I right?"

"Well, yes, Robert, I think you are more than half right. You ought to know my dear, old mother who lives in Maine. We have had colored company at our house, and I never saw her show the least difference between her colored and white guests. She is a Quaker preacher, and don't believe in war, but when the rest of the young men went to the front, I wanted to go also. So I thought it all over, and there seemed to be no way out of slavery except through the war. I had been taught to hate war and detest slavery. Now the time had come when I could not help the war, but I could strike a blow for freedom. So I told my mother I was going to the front, that I expected to be killed, but I went to free the slave. It went hard with her. But I thought that I ought to come, and I believe my mother's prayers are following me."

"Captain," said Robert, rising, "I am glad that I have heard your story. I think that some of these Northern soldiers do two things – hate slavery and hate niggers."

Notes

[16] *Original reads*: some one [ed.].

"I am afraid that is so with some of them. They would rather be whipped by Rebels than conquer with negroes. Oh, I heard a soldier," said Captain Sybil, "say, when the colored men were being enlisted, that he would break his sword and resign. But he didn't do either. After Colonel Shaw[17] led his charge at Fort Wagner, and died in the conflict, he got bravely over his prejudices. The conduct of the colored troops there and elsewhere has done much to turn public opinion in their favor. I suppose any white soldier would rather have his black substitute receive the bullets than himself."

Chapter 7

Tom Anderson's Death

"WHERE is Tom?" asked Captain Sybil; "I have not seen him for several hours."

"He's gone down the sound with some of the soldiers," replied Robert. "They wanted Tom to row them."

"I am afraid those boys will get into trouble, and the Rebs will pick them off," responded Sybil.

"O, I hope not," answered Robert.

"I hope not, too; but those boys are too venturesome."

"Tom knows the lay of the land better than any of us," said Robert. "He is the most wide-awake and gamiest man I know. I reckon when the war is over Tom will be a preacher. Did you ever hear him pray?"

"No; is he good at that?"

"First-rate," continued Robert. "It would do you good to hear him. He don't allow any cursing and swearing when he's around. And what he says is law and gospel with the boys. But he's *so* good-natured; and they *can't* get mad at him."

"Yes, Robert, there is not a man in our regiment I would sooner trust than Tom. Last night, when he brought in that wounded scout, he couldn't have been more tender if he had been a woman. How gratefully the poor fellow looked in Tom's face as he laid him down so carefully and staunched the blood which had been spurting out of him. Tom seemed to know it was an artery which had been cut, and he did just the right thing to stop the bleeding. He knew there wasn't a moment to be lost. He wasn't going to wait for the doctor. I have often heard that colored people are ungrateful, but I don't think Tom's worst enemy would say that about him."

"Captain," said Robert, with a tone of bitterness in his voice, "what had we to be grateful for? For ages of poverty, ignorance, and slavery? I think if anybody should be grateful, it is the people who have enslaved us and lived off our labor for generations. Captain, I used to know a poor old woman who couldn't bear to hear anyone[18] play on the piano."

"Is that so? Why, I always heard that colored people were a musical race."

"So we are; but that poor woman's daughter was sold, and her mistress took the money to buy a piano. Her mother could never bear to hear a sound from it."

"Poor woman!" exclaimed Captain Sybil, sympathetically; "I suppose it seemed as if the wail of her daughter was blending with the tones of the instrument. I think, Robert, there is a great deal more in the colored people than we give them credit for. Did you know Captain Sellers?"

Notes

[17] *Colonel Shaw* Robert Gould Shaw (1837–1863), commander of the black Fifty-Fourth regiment in the Civil War.

[18] *Original reads*: any one [ed.].

"The officer who escaped from prison and got back to our lines?" asked Robert.

"Yes. Well, he had quite an experience in trying to escape. He came to an aged couple, who hid him in their cabin and shared their humble food with him. They gave him some corn-bread, bacon, and coffee which he thought was made of scorched bran. But he said that he never ate a meal that he relished more than the one he took with them. Just before he went they knelt down and prayed with him. It seemed as if his very hair stood on his head, their prayer was so solemn. As he was going away the man took some shingles and nailed them on his shoes to throw the blood-hounds off his track. I don't think he will ever cease to feel kindly towards colored people. I do wonder what has become of the boys? What can keep them so long?"

Just as Captain Sybil and Robert were wondering at the delay of Tom and the soldiers they heard the measured tread of men who were slowly bearing a burden. They were carrying Tom Anderson to the hospital, fearfully wounded, and nigh to death. His face was distorted, and the blood was streaming from his wounds. His respiration was faint, his pulse hurried, as if life were trembling on its frailest cords.

Robert and Captain Sybil hastened at once towards the wounded man. On Robert's face was a look of intense anguish, as he bent pityingly over his friend.

"O, this is dreadful! How did it happen? "cried Robert.

Captain Sybil, pressing anxiously forward, repeated Robert's question.

"Captain," said one of the young soldiers, advancing and saluting his superior officer, "we were all in the boat when it struck against a mud bank, and there was not strength enough among us to shove her back into the water. Just then the Rebels opened fire upon us. For a while[19] we lay down in the boat, but still they kept firing. Tom took in the whole situation, and said: 'Someone[20] must die to get us out of this. I mought's well be me[21] as any. You are soldiers and can fight. If they kill me, it is nuthin'.' So Tom leaped out to shove the boat into the water. Just then the Rebel bullets began to rain around him. He received seven or eight of them, and I'm afraid there is no hope for him."

"O, Tom, I wish you hadn't gone. O, Tom! Tom!" cried Robert, in tones of agony.

A gleam of grateful recognition passed over the drawn features of Tom, as the wail of his friend fell on his ear. He attempted to speak, but the words died upon his lips, and he became unconscious.

"Well," said Captain Sybil, "put him in one of the best wards. Give him into Miss Leroy's care. If good nursing can win him back to life, he shall not want for any care or pains that she can bestow. Send immediately for Dr. Gresham."

Robert followed his friend into the hospital, tenderly and carefully helped to lay him down, and remained awhile, gazing in silent grief upon the sufferer. Then he turned to go, leaving him in the hands of Iola, but hoping against hope that his wounds would not be fatal.

With tender devotion Iola watched her faithful friend. He recognized her when restored to consciousness, and her presence was as balm to his wounds. He smiled faintly, took her hand in his, stroked it tenderly, looked wistfully into her face, and said, "Miss Iola, I ain't long fer dis! I'se 'most home!"

"Oh, no," said Iola, "I hope that you will soon get over this trouble, and live many long and happy days."

Notes

[19] *Original reads*: awhile [ed.].

[20] *Original reads*: Some one [ed.].

[21] *Original reads*: him [ed.].

"No, Miss Iola, it's all ober wid me. I'se gwine to glory; gwine to glory; gwine to ring dem charmin' bells. Tell all de boys to meet me in heben; dat dey mus' 'list in de hebenly war."

"O, Mr. Tom," said Iola, tenderly, "do not talk of leaving me. You are the best friend I have had since I was torn from my mother. I should be so lonely without you."

"Dere's a frien' dat sticks closer dan a brudder. He will be wid yer in de sixt' trial, an' in de sebbent' he'll not fo'sake yer."

"Yes," answered Iola, "I know that. He is all our dependence. But I can't help grieving when I see you suffering so. But, dear friend, be quiet, and try to go to sleep."

"I'll do enythin' fer yer, Miss Iola."

Tom closed his eyes and lay quiet. Tenderly and anxiously Iola watched over him as the hours waned away. The doctor came, shook his head gravely, and, turning to Iola, said, "There is no hope, but do what you can to alleviate his sufferings."

As Iola gazed upon the kind but homely features of Tom, she saw his eyes open and an unexpressed desire upon his face.

Tenderly and sadly bending over him, with tears in her dark, luminous eyes, she said, "Is there anything I can do for you?"

"Yes," said Tom, with laboring breath; "let me hole yore han', an' sing 'Ober Jordan inter glory' an' 'We'll anchor bye and bye.'"

Iola laid her hand gently in the rough palm of the dying man, and, with a tremulous voice, sang the parting hymns.

Tenderly she wiped the death damps from his dusky brow, and imprinted upon it a farewell kiss. Gratitude and affection lit up the dying eye, which seemed to be gazing into the eternities. Just then Robert entered the room, and, seating himself quietly by Tom's bedside, read the death signs in his face.

"Good-bye, Robert," said Tom, "meet me in de kingdom." Suddenly a look of recognition and rapture lit up his face, and he murmured, "Angels, bright angels, all's well, all's well!"

Slowly his hand released its pressure, a peaceful calm overspread his countenance, and without a sigh or murmur Thomas Anderson, Iola's faithful and devoted friend, passed away, leaving the world so much poorer for her than it was before. Just then Dr. Gresham, the hospital physician, came to the bedside, felt for the pulse which would never throb again, and sat down in silence by the cot.

"What do you think, Doctor," said Iola, "has he fainted?"

"No," said the doctor, "poor fellow! he is dead."

Iola bowed her head in silent sorrow, and then relieved the anguish of her heart by a flood of tears. Robert rose, and sorrowfully left the room.

Iola, with tearful eyes and aching heart, clasped the cold hands over the still breast, closed the waxen lid over the eye which had once beamed with kindness or flashed with courage, and then went back, after the burial, to her daily round of duties, feeling the sad missing of something from her life.

Chapter 8

The Mystified Doctor

"COLONEL," said Dr. Gresham to Col. Robinson, the commander of the post, "I am perfectly mystified by Miss Leroy."

"What is the matter with her?" asked Col. Robinson. "Is she not faithful to her duties and obedient to your directions?"

"Faithful is not the word to express her tireless energy and devotion to her work," responded Dr. Gresham. "She must have been a born nurse to put such enthusiasm into her work."

"Why, Doctor, what is the matter with you? You talk like a lover."

A faint flush rose to the cheek of Dr. Gresham as he smiled, and said, "Oh! come now, Colonel, can't a man praise a woman without being in love with her?"

"Of course he can," said Col. Robinson; "but I know where such admiration is apt to lead. I've been there myself. But, Doctor, had you not better defer your love-making till you're out of the woods?"

"I assure you, Colonel, I am not thinking of love or courtship. That is the business of the drawing-room, and not of the camp. But she did mystify me last night."

"How so?" asked Col. Robinson.

"When Tom was dying," responded the doctor, "I saw that beautiful and refined young lady bend over and kiss him. When she found that he was dead, she just cried as if her heart was breaking. Well, that was a new thing to me. I can eat with colored people, walk, talk, and fight with them, but kissing them is something I don't hanker after."

"And yet you saw Miss Leroy do it?"

"Yes; and that puzzles me. She is one of the most refined and lady-like women I ever saw. I hear she is a refugee, but she does not look like the other refugees who have come to our camp. Her accent is slightly Southern; but her manner is Northern. She is self-respecting without being supercilious;[22] quiet, without being dull. Her voice is low and sweet, yet at times there are tones of such passionate tenderness in it that you would think some great sorrow has darkened and overshadowed her life. Without being the least gloomy, her face at times is pervaded by an air of inexpressible sadness. I sometimes watch her when she is not aware that I am looking at her, and it seems as if a whole volume was depicted on her countenance. When she smiles, there is a longing in her eyes which is never satisfied. I cannot understand how a Southern lady, whose education and manners stamp her as a woman of fine culture and good breeding, could consent to occupy the position she so faithfully holds. It is a mystery I cannot solve. Can you?"

"I think I can," answered Col. Robinson.

"Will you tell me?" queried the doctor.

"Yes, on one condition."

"What is it?"

"Everlasting silence."

"I promise," said the doctor. "The secret between us shall be as deep as the sea."

"She has not requested secrecy, but at present, for her sake, I do not wish the secret revealed. Miss Leroy was a slave."

"Oh, no," said Dr. Gresham, starting to his feet, "it can't be so! A woman as white as she a slave?"

"Yes, it is so," continued the colonel. "In these States the child follows the condition of its mother. This beautiful and accomplished girl was held by one of the worst Rebels in town. Tom told me of it and I issued orders for her release."

"Well, well! Is that so?" said Dr. Gresham, thoughtfully stroking his beard. "Wonders will never cease. Why, I was just beginning to think seriously of her."

"What's to hinder your continuing to think?" asked Col. Robinson.

Notes

[22] *supercilious* arrogant.

"What you tell me changes the whole complexion of affairs," replied the doctor. "If that be so I am glad I told you before you got head over heels in love."

"Yes," said Dr. Gresham, absently.

Dr. Gresham was a member of a wealthy and aristocratic family, proud of its lineage, which it could trace through generations of good blood to its ancestral isle. He had become deeply interested in Iola before he had heard her story, but after it had been revealed to him he tried to banish her from his mind; but his constant observation of her only increased his interest and admiration. The deep pathos of her story, the tenderness of her ministrations, bestowed alike on black and white, and the sad loneliness of her condition, awakened within him a desire to defend and protect her all through her future life. The fierce clashing of war had not taken all the romance out of his nature. In Iola he saw realized his ideal of the woman whom he was willing to marry. A woman, tender, strong, and courageous, and rescued only by the strong arm of his Government from a fate worse than death. She was young in years, but old in sorrow; one whom a sad destiny had changed from a light-hearted girl to a heroic woman. As he observed her, he detected an undertone of sorrow in her most cheerful words, and observed a quick flushing and sudden paling of her cheek, as if she were living over scenes that were thrilling her soul with indignation or chilling her heart with horror. As nurse and physician, Iola and Dr. Gresham were constantly thrown together. His friends sent him magazines and books, which he gladly shared with her. The hospital was a sad place. Mangled forms, stricken down in the flush of their prime and energy; pale young corpses, sacrificed on the altar of slavery, constantly drained on her sympathies. Dr. Gresham was glad to have some reading matter which might divert her mind from the memories of her mournful past, and also furnish them both with interesting themes of conversation in their moments of relaxation from the harrowing scenes through which they were constantly passing. Without any effort or consciousness on her part, his friendship ripened into love. To him her presence was a pleasure, her absence a privation; and her loneliness drew deeply upon his sympathy. He would have merited his own self-contempt if, by word or deed, he had done anything to take advantage of her situation. All the manhood and chivalry of his nature rose in her behalf, and, after carefully revolving the matter, he resolved to win her for his bride, bury her secret in his Northern home, and hide from his aristocratic relations all knowledge of her mournful past. One day he said to Iola:–

"This hospital life is telling on you. Your strength is failing, and although you possess a wonderful amount of physical endurance, you must not forget that saints have bodies and dwell in tabernacles of clay, just the same as we common mortals."

"Compliments aside," she said, smiling; "what are you driving at, Doctor?"

"I mean," he replied, "that you are running down, and if you do not quit and take some rest you will be our patient instead of our nurse. You'd better take a furlough, go North, and return after the first frost."

"Doctor, if that is your only remedy," replied Iola, "I am afraid that I am destined to die at my post. I have no special friends in the North, and no home but this in the South. I am homeless and alone."

There was something so sad, almost despairing in her tones, in the drooping of her head, and the quivering of her lip, that they stirred Dr. Gresham's heart with sudden pity, and, drawing nearer to her, he said, "Miss Leroy, you need not be all alone. Let me claim the privilege of making your life bright and happy. Iola, I have loved you ever since I have seen your devotion to our poor, sick boys. How faithfully you, a young and gracious girl, have stood at your post and performed your duties. And now I ask, will you not permit me to clasp hands with you for life? I do not ask for a hasty reply. Give yourself time to think over what I have proposed."

Chapter 9

Eugene Leroy and Alfred Lorraine

NEARLY twenty years before the war, two young men, of French and Spanish descent, sat conversing on a large verandah which surrounded an ancient home on the Mississippi River. It was French in its style of architecture, large and rambling, with no hint of modern improvements.

The owner of the house was the only heir of a Creole[23] planter. He had come into possession of an inheritance consisting of vast baronial estates, bank stock, and a large number of slaves. Eugene Leroy, being deprived of his parents, was left, at an early age, to the care of a distant relative, who had sent him to school and college, and who occasionally invited him to spend his vacations at his home. But Eugene generally declined his invitations, as he preferred spending his vacations at the watering places in the North, with their fashionable and not always innocent gayeties. Young, vivacious, impulsive, and undisciplined, without the restraining influence of a mother's love or the guidance of a father's hand, Leroy found himself, when his college days were over, in the dangerous position of a young man with vast possessions, abundant leisure, unsettled principles, and uncontrolled desires. He had no other object than to extract from life its most seductive draughts of ease and pleasure. His companion, who sat opposite him on the verandah, quietly smoking a cigar, was a remote cousin, a few years older than himself, the warmth of whose Southern temperament had been modified by an infusion of Northern blood.

Eugene was careless, liberal, and impatient of details, while his companion and cousin, Alfred Lorraine, was selfish, eager, keen, and alert; also hard, cold, methodical, and ever ready to grasp the main chance. Yet, notwithstanding the difference between them, they had formed a warm friendship for each other.

"Alfred," said Eugene, "I am going to be married."

Lorraine opened his eyes with sudden wonder, and exclaimed: "Well, that's the latest thing out! Who is the fortunate lady who has bound you with her silken fetters? Is it one of those beautiful Creole girls who were visiting Augustine's plantation last winter? I watched you during our visit there and thought that you could not be proof against their attractions. Which is your choice? It would puzzle me to judge between the two. They had splendid eyes, dark, luminous, and languishing; lovely complexions and magnificent hair. Both were delightful in their manners, refined and cultured, with an air of vivacity mingled with their repose of manner which was perfectly charming. As the law only allows us one, which is your choice? Miss Annette has more force than her sister, and if I could afford the luxury of a wife she would be my choice."

"Ah, Alf," said Eugene, "I see that you are a practical business man. In marrying you want a wife to assist you as an efficient plantation mistress. One who would tolerate no waste in the kitchen and no disorder in the parlor."

"Exactly so," responded Lorraine; "I am too poor to marry a mere parlor ornament. You can afford to do it; I cannot."

"Nonsense, if I were as poor as a church mouse I would marry the woman I love."

"Very fine sentiments," said Lorraine, "and were I as rich as you I would indulge in them also. You know, when my father died I had great expectations. We had always lived in good style, and I never thought for a moment he was not a rich man, but when his estate was settled I found it was greatly involved, and I was forced to face an uncertain

Notes

[23] *Creole* someone of French and Spanish descent.

future, with scarcely a dollar to call my own. Land, negroes, cattle, and horses all went under the hammer. The only thing I retained was the education I received at the North; that was my father's best investment, and all my stock in trade. With that only as an outfit, it would be madness for me to think of marrying one of those lovely girls. They remind me of beautiful canary birds, charming and pretty, but not fitted for the wear and tear of plantation life. Well, which is your choice?"

"Neither," replied Eugene.

"Then, is it that magnificent looking widow from New Orleans, whom we met before you had that terrible spell of sickness and to whom you appeared so devoted?"

"Not at all. I have not heard from her since that summer. She was fascinating and handsome, but fearfully high strung."

"Were you afraid of her?"

"No; but I valued my happiness too much to trust it in her hands."

"Sour grapes!" said Lorraine.

"No! but I think that slavery and the lack of outside interests are beginning to tell on the lives of our women. They lean too much on their slaves, have too much irresponsible power in their hands, are narrowed and compressed by the routine of plantation life and the lack of intellectual stimulus."

"Yes, Eugene, when I see what other women are doing in the fields of literature and art, I cannot help thinking an amount of brain power has been held in check among us. Yet I cannot abide those Northern women, with their suffrage views and abolition cant. They just shock me."

"But your mother was a Northern woman," said Eugene.

"Yes; but she got bravely over her Northern ideas. As I remember her, she was just as much a Southerner as if she had been to the manor born. She came here as a schoolteacher, but soon after she came she married my father. He was easy and indulgent with his servants, and held them with a very loose rein. But my mother was firm and energetic. She made the niggers move around. No shirking nor dawdling with her. When my father died, she took matters in hand, but she only outlived him a few months. If she had lived I believe that she would have retrieved our fortune. I know that she had more executive ability than my father. He was very squeamish about selling his servants, but she would have put every one of them in her pocket before permitting them to eat her out of house and home. But whom *are* you going to marry?"

"A young lady who graduates from a Northern seminary next week," responded Eugene.

"I think you are very selfish," said Lorraine. "You might have invited a fellow to go with you to be your best man."

"The wedding is to be strictly private. The lady whom I am to marry has negro blood in her veins."

"The devil she has!" exclaimed Lorraine, starting to his feet, and looking incredulously on the face of Leroy. "Are you in earnest? Surely you must be jesting."

"I am certainly in earnest," answered Eugene Leroy. "I mean every word I say."

"Oh, it can't be possible! Are you mad?" exclaimed Lorraine.

"Never was saner in my life."

"What under heaven could have possessed you to do such a foolish thing? Where did she come from."

"Right here, on this plantation. But I have educated and manumitted[24] her, and I intend marrying her."

Notes

[24] *manumitted* freed.

"Why, Eugene, it is impossible that you can have an idea of marrying one of your slaves. Why, man, she is your property, to have and to hold to all intents and purposes. Are you not satisfied with the power and possession the law gives you?"

"No. Although the law makes her helpless in my hands, to me her defenselessness is her best defense."

"Eugene, we have known each other all of our lives, and, although I have always regarded you as eccentric, I never saw you so completely off your balance before. The idea of you, with your proud family name, your vast wealth in land and negroes, intending to marry one of them, is a mystery I cannot solve. Do explain to me why you are going to take this extremely strange and foolish step."

"You never saw Marie?"

"No; and I don't want to."

"She is very beautiful. In the North no one would suspect that she has one drop of negro blood in her veins, but here, where I am known, to marry her is to lose caste.[25] I could live with her, and not incur much if any social opprobrium.[26] Society would wink at the transgression, even if after she had become the mother of my children I should cast her off and send her and them to the auction block."

"Men," replied Lorraine, " would merely shrug their shoulders; women would say you had been sowing your wild oats. Your money, like charity, would cover a multitude of faults."

"But if I make her my lawful wife and recognize her children as my legitimate heirs, I subject myself to social ostracism and a senseless persecution. We Americans boast of freedom, and yet here is a woman whom I love as I never loved any other human being, but both law and public opinion debar me from following the inclination of my heart. She is beautiful, faithful, and pure, and yet all that society will tolerate is what I would scorn to do."

"But has not society the right to guard the purity of its blood by the rigid exclusion of an alien race?"

"Excluding it! How?" asked Eugene.

"By debarring it from social intercourse."

"Perhaps it has," continued Eugene, " but should not society have a greater ban for those who, by consorting with an alien race, rob their offspring of a right to their names and to an inheritance in their property, and who fix their social status among an enslaved and outcast race? Don't eye me so curiously; I am not losing my senses."

"I think you have done that already," said Lorraine. "Don't you know that if she is as fair as a lily, beautiful as a houri,[27] and chaste as ice, that still she is a negro?"

"Oh, come now; she isn't much of a negro."

"It doesn't matter, however. One drop of negro blood in her veins curses all the rest."

"I know it," said Eugene, sadly, " but I have weighed the consequences, and am prepared to take them."

"Well, Eugene, your course is *so* singular! I do wish that you would tell me why you take this unprecedented step?"

Eugene laid aside his cigar, looked thoughtfully at Lorraine, and said, "Well, Alfred, as we are kinsmen and life-long friends, I will not resent your asking my reason for

Notes

[25] *caste* social rank.

[26] *opprobrium* criticism.

[27] *houri* a beautiful woman, from the Islamic tradition.

doing that which seems to you the climax of absurdity, and if you will have the patience to listen I will tell you."

"Proceed, I am all attention."

"My father died," said Eugene, "as you know, when I was too young to know his loss or feel his care and, being an only child, I was petted and spoiled. I grew up to be wayward, self-indulgent, proud, and imperious. I went from home and made many friends both at college and in foreign lands. I was well supplied with money and, never having been forced to earn it, was ignorant of its value and careless of its use. My lavish expenditures and liberal benefactions attracted to me a number of parasites, and men older than myself led me into the paths of vice, and taught me how to gather the flowers of sin which blossom around the borders of hell. In a word, I left my home unwarned and unarmed against the seductions of vice. I returned an initiated devotee to debasing pleasures. Years of my life were passed in foreign lands; years in which my soul slumbered and seemed pervaded with a moral paralysis; years, the memory of which fills my soul with sorrow and shame. I went to the capitals of the old world to see life, but in seeing life I became acquainted with death, the death of true manliness and self-respect. You look astonished; but I tell you, Alf, there is many a poor clodhopper, on whom are the dust and grime of unremitting toil, who feels more self-respect and true manliness than many of us with our family prestige, social position, and proud ancestral halls. After I had lived abroad for years, I returned a broken-down young man, prematurely old, my constitution a perfect wreck. A life of folly and dissipation was telling fearfully upon me. My friends shrank from me in dismay. I was sick nigh unto death, and had it not been for Marie's care I am certain that I should have died. She followed me down to the borders of the grave, and won me back to life and health. I was slow in recovering and, during the time, I had ample space for reflection, and the past unrolled itself before me. I resolved, over the wreck and ruin of my past life, to build a better and brighter future. Marie had a voice of remarkable sweetness, although it lacked culture. Often when I was nervous and restless I would have her sing some of those weird and plaintive melodies which she had learned from the plantation negroes. Sometimes I encouraged her to talk, and I was surprised at the native vigor of her intellect. By degrees I became acquainted with her history. She was all alone in the world. She had no recollection of her father, but remembered being torn from her mother while clinging to her dress. The trader who bought her mother did not wish to buy her. She remembered having a brother, with whom she used to play, but she had been separated from him also, and since then had lost all trace of them. After she was sold from her mother she became the property of an excellent old lady, who seems to have been very careful to imbue her mind with good principles; a woman who loved purity, not only for her own daughters, but also for the defenseless girls in her home. I believe it was the lady's intention to have freed Marie at her death, but she died suddenly, and, the estate being involved, she was sold with it and fell into the hands of my agent. I became deeply interested in her when I heard her story, and began to pity her."

"And I suppose love sprang from pity."

"I not only pitied her, but I learned to respect her. I had met with beautiful women in the halls of wealth and fashion, both at home and abroad, but there was something in her different from all my experience of womanhood."

"I should think so," said Lorraine, with a sneer; "but I should like to know what it was."

"It was something such as I have seen in old cathedrals, lighting up the beauty of a saintly face. A light which the poet tells was never seen on land or sea. I thought of this beautiful and defenseless girl adrift in the power of a reckless man, who, with all the advantages of wealth and education, had trailed his manhood in the dust, and she, with simple, child like faith in the Unseen, seemed to be so good and pure that she commanded my respect and won my heart. In her presence every base and unholy passion died, subdued by the supremacy of her virtue."

"Why, Eugene, what has come over you? Talking of the virtue of these quadroon girls! You have lived so long in the North and abroad, that you seem to have lost the cue of our Southern life. Don't you know that these beautiful girls have been the curse of our homes? You have no idea of the hearts which are wrung by their presence."

"But, Alfred, suppose it is so. Are they to blame for it? What can any woman do when she is placed in the hands of an irresponsible master; when she knows that resistance is vain? Yes, Alfred, I agree with you, these women are the bane of our Southern civilization; but they are the victims and we are the criminals."

"I think from the airs that some of them put on when they get a chance, that they are very willing victims."

"So much the worse for our institution. If it is cruel to debase a hapless victim, it is an increase of cruelty to make her contented with her degradation. Let me tell you, Alf, you cannot wrong or degrade a woman without wronging or degrading yourself."

"What is the matter with you, Eugene? Are you thinking of taking priest's orders?"

"No, Alf," said Eugene, rising and rapidly pacing the floor, "you may defend the system as much as you please, but you cannot deny that the circumstances it creates, and the temptations it affords, are sapping our strength and undermining our character."

"That may be true," said Lorraine, somewhat irritably, "but you had better be careful how you air your Northern notions in public."

"Why so?"

"Because public opinion is too sensitive to tolerate any such discussions."

"And is not that a proof that we are at fault with respect to our institutions?"

"I don't know. I only know we are living in the midst of a magazine[28] of powder, and it is not safe to enter it with a lighted candle."

"Let me proceed with my story," continued Eugene. "During the long months in which I was convalescing, I was left almost entirely to the companionship of Marie. In my library I found a Bible, which I began to read from curiosity, but my curiosity deepened into interest when I saw the rapt expression on Marie's face. I saw in it a loving response to sentiments to which I was a stranger. In the meantime my conscience was awakened, and I scorned to take advantage of her defenselessness. I felt that I owed my life to her faithful care, and I resolved to take her North, manumit, educate, and marry her. I sent her to a Northern academy, but as soon as some of the pupils found that she was colored, objections were raised, and the principal was compelled to dismiss her. During my search for a school I heard of one where three girls of mixed blood were pursuing their studies, every one of whom would have been ignominiously dismissed had their connection with the negro race been known. But I determined to run no risks. I found a school where her connection with the negro race would be no bar to her advancement. She graduates next week, and I intend to marry her before I return home. She was faithful when others were faithless, stood by me when others deserted me to die in loneliness and neglect, and now I am about to reward her care with all the love and devotion it is in my power to bestow. That is why

Notes

[28] *magazine* a place to store firearms.

I am about to marry my faithful and devoted nurse, who snatched me from the jaws of death. Now that I have told you my story, what say you?"

"Madness and folly inconceivable!" exclaimed Lorraine.

"What to you is madness and folly is perfect sanity with me. After all, Alf, is there not an amount of unreason in our prejudices?"

"That may be true; but I wasn't reasoned into it, and I do not expect to be reasoned out of it."

"Will you accompany me North?"

"No; except to put you in an insane asylum. You are the greatest crank out," said Lorraine, thoroughly disgusted.

"No, thank you; I'm all right. I expect to start North to-morrow. You had better come and go."

"I would rather follow you to your grave," replied Lorraine, hotly, while an expression of ineffable scorn passed over his cold, proud face.

Chapter 10

Shadows in the Home

On the next morning after this conversation Leroy left for the North, to attend the commencement and witness the graduation of his ward. Arriving in Ohio, he immediately repaired to the academy and inquired for the principal. He was shown into the reception-room, and in a few moments the principal entered.

"Good morning," said Leroy, rising and advancing towards him; "how is my ward this morning?"

"She is well, and has been expecting you. I am glad you came in time for the commencement. She stands among the foremost in her class."

"I am glad to hear it. Will you send her this?" said Leroy, handing the principal a card. The principal took the card and immediately left the room.

Very soon Leroy heard a light step, and looking up he saw a radiantly beautiful woman approaching him.

"Good morning, Marie," he said, greeting her cordially, and gazing upon her with unfeigned admiration. "You are looking very handsome this morning."

"Do you think so?" she asked, smiling and blushing. "I am glad you are not disappointed; that you do not feel your money has been spent in vain."

"Oh, no, what I have spent on your education has been the best investment I ever made."

"I hope," said Marie, "you may always find it so. But Mas – "

"Hush!" said Leroy, laying his hand playfully on her lips; "you are free. I don't want the dialect of slavery to linger on your lips. You must not call me that name again."

"Why not?"

"Because I have a nearer and dearer one by which I wish to be called."

Leroy drew her nearer, and whispered in her ear a single word. She started, trembled with emotion, grew pale, and blushed painfully. An awkward silence ensued, when Leroy, pressing her hand, exclaimed: "This is the hand that plucked me from the grave, and I am going to retain it as mine; mine to guard with my care until death us do part."

Leroy looked earnestly into her eyes, which fell beneath his ardent gaze. With admirable self-control, while a great joy was thrilling her heart, she bowed her beautiful head and softly repeated, "Until death us do part."

Leroy knew Southern society too well to expect it to condone his offense against its social customs, or give the least recognition to his wife, however cultured, refined, and charming she might be, if it were known that she had the least infusion of negro blood in her veins. But he was brave enough to face the consequences of his alliance, and marry the woman who was the choice of his heart, and on whom his affections were centred.

After Leroy had left the room, Marie sat awhile thinking of the wonderful change that had come over her. Instead of being a lonely slave girl, with the fatal dower of beauty, liable to be bought and sold, exchanged, and bartered, she was to be the wife of a wealthy planter; a man in whose honor she could confide, and on whose love she could lean.

Very interesting and pleasant were the commencement exercises in which Marie bore an important part. To enlist sympathy for her enslaved race, and appear to advantage before Leroy, had aroused all of her energies. The stimulus of hope, the manly love which was environing her life, brightened her eye and lit up the wonderful beauty of her countenance. During her stay in the North she had constantly been brought in contact with anti-slavery people. She was not aware that there was so much kindness among the white people of the country until she had tested it in the North. From the anti-slavery people in private life she had learned some of the noblest lessons of freedom and justice, and had become imbued with their sentiments. Her theme was "American Civilization, its Lights and Shadows."

Graphically she portrayed the lights, faithfully she showed the shadows of our American civilization. Earnestly and feelingly she spoke of the blind Sampson[29] in our land, who might yet shake the pillars of our great Commonwealth. Leroy listened attentively. At times a shadow of annoyance would overspread his face, but it was soon lost in the admiration her earnestness and zeal inspired. Like Esther[30] pleading for the lives of her people in the Oriental courts of a despotic king, she stood before the audience, pleading for those whose lips were sealed, but whose condition appealed to the mercy and justice of the Nation. Strong men wiped the moisture from their eyes, and women's hearts throbbed in unison with the strong, brave words that were uttered in behalf of freedom for all and chains for none. Generous applause was freely bestowed, and beautiful bouquets were showered upon her. When it was known that she was to be the wife of her guardian, warm congratulations were given, and earnest hopes expressed for the welfare of the lonely girl, who, nearly all her life, had been deprived of a parent's love and care. On the eve of starting South Leroy procured a license, and united his destiny with the young lady whose devotion in the darkest hour had won his love and gratitude.

In a few days Marie returned as mistress to the plantation from which she had gone as a slave. But as unholy alliances were common in those days between masters and slaves, no one took especial notice that Marie shared Leroy's life as mistress of his home, and that the family silver and jewelry were in her possession. But Leroy, happy in his choice, attended to the interests of his plantation, and found companionship in his books and in the society of his wife. A few male companions visited him occasionally, admired the magnificent beauty of his wife, shook their heads, and spoke of him as being very eccentric, but thought his marriage the great mistake of his life. But none of his female friends ever entered his doors, when it became known that Marie held

Notes

[29] *Sampson* Old Testament Israelite who destroyed the Philistines' temple (Judges 13–16).

[30] *Esther* Old Testament Jewish queen who convinced her Persian husband not to murder her people.

the position of mistress of his mansion, and presided at his table. But she, sheltered in the warm clasp of loving arms, found her life like a joyous dream.

Into that quiet and beautiful home three children were born, unconscious of the doom suspended over their heads.

"Oh, how glad I am," Marie would often say, "that these children are free." I could never understand how a cultured white man could have his own children enslaved. I can understand how savages, fighting with each other, could doom their vanquished foes to slavery, but it has always been a puzzle to me how a civilized man could drag his own children, bone of his bone, flesh of his flesh, down to the position of social outcasts, abject slaves, and political pariahs."

"But, Marie," said Eugene, "all men do not treat their illegitimate children in the manner you describe. The last time I was in New Orleans I met Henri Augustine at the depot, with two beautiful young girls. At first I thought that they were his own children, they resembled him so closely. But afterwards I noticed that they addressed him as 'Mister.' Before we parted he told me that his wife had taken such a dislike to their mother that she could not bear to see them on the place. At last, weary of her dissatisfaction, he had promised to bring them to New Orleans and sell them. Instead, he was going to Ohio to give them their freedom, and make provision for their future."

"What a wrong!" said Marie.

"Who was wronged?" said Leroy, in astonishment.

"Everyone in the whole transaction," answered Marie. "Your friend wronged himself by sinning against his own soul. He wronged his wife by arousing her hatred and jealousy through his unfaithfulness. He wronged those children by giving them the *status* of slaves and outcasts. He wronged their mother by imposing upon her the burdens and cares of maternity without the rights and privileges of a wife. He made her crown of motherhood a circlet of shame. Under other circumstances she might have been an honored wife and happy mother. And I do think such men wrong their own legitimate children by transmitting to them a weakened moral fibre."

"Oh, Marie, you have such an uncomfortable way of putting things. You make me feel that we have done those things which we ought not to have done, and have left undone those things which we ought to have done."

"If it annoys you," said Marie, " I will stop talking."

"Oh, no, go on," said Leroy, carelessly; and then he continued more thoughtfully, "I know a number of men who have sent such children North, and manumitted, educated, and left them valuable legacies. We are all liable to err, and, having done wrong, all we can do is to make reparation."

"My dear husband, this is a wrong where reparation is impossible. Neither wealth nor education can repair the wrong of a dishonored birth. There are a number of slaves in this section who are servants to their own brothers and sisters; whose fathers have robbed them not simply of liberty but of the right of being well born. Do you think these things will last forever?"

"I suppose not. There are some prophets of evil who tell us that the Union is going to dissolve. But I know it would puzzle their brains to tell where the crack will begin. I reckon we'll continue to jog along as usual. 'Cotton fights, and cotton conquers for American slavery.'"

Even while Leroy dreamed of safety the earthquake was cradling its fire; the ground was growing hollow beneath his tread; but his ear was too dull to catch the sound; his vision too blurred to read the signs of the times.

"Marie," said Leroy, taking up the thread of the discourse, "slavery is a sword that cuts both ways. If it wrongs the negro, it also curses the white man. But we are in it, and what can we do?"

"Get out of it as quickly as possible."

"That is easier said than done. I would willingly free every slave on my plantation if I could do so without expatriating them. Some of them have wives and children on other plantations, and to free them is to separate them from their kith[31] and kin. To let them remain here as a free people is out of the question. My hands are tied by law and custom."

"Who tied them?" asked Marie.

"A public opinion, whose meshes I cannot break. If the negro is the thrall of his master, we are just as much the thralls of public opinion."

"Why do you not battle against public opinion, if you think it is wrong?"

"Because I have neither the courage of a martyr, nor the faith of a saint; and so I drift along, trying to make the condition of our slaves as comfortable as I possibly can. I believe there are slaves on this plantation whom the most flattering offers of freedom would not entice away."

"I do not think," said Marie, "that some of you planters understand your own slaves. Lying is said to be the vice of slaves. The more intelligent of them have so learned to veil their feelings that you do not see the undercurrent of discontent beneath their apparent good humor and jollity. The more discontented they are, the more I respect them. To me a contented slave is an abject creature. I hope that I shall see the day when there will not be a slave in the land. I hate the whole thing from the bottom of my heart."

"Marie, your Northern education has unfitted you for Southern life. You are free, yourself, and so are our children. Why not let well enough alone?"

"Because I love liberty, not only for myself but for every human being. Think how dear these children are to me; and then for the thought to be forever haunting me, that if you were dead they could be turned out of doors and divided among your relatives. I sometimes lie awake at night thinking of how there might be a screw loose somewhere, and, after all, the children and I might be reduced to slavery."

"Marie, what in the world is the matter with you? Have you had a presentiment of my death, or, as Uncle Jack says, 'hab you seed it in a vision?'"

"No, but I have had such sad forebodings that they almost set me wild. One night I dreamt that you were dead; that the lawyers entered the house, seized our property, and remanded us to slavery. I never can be satisfied in the South with such a possibility hanging over my head."

"Marie, dear, you are growing nervous. Your imagination is too active. You are left too much alone on this plantation. I hope that for your own and the children's sake I will be enabled to arrange our affairs so as to find a home for you where you will not be doomed to the social isolation and ostracism that surround you here."

"I don't mind the isolation for myself, but the children. You have enjoined silence on me with respect to their connection with the negro race, but I do not think we can conceal it from them very long. It will not be long before Iola will notice the offishness of girls of her own age, and the scornful glances which, even now, I think, are leveled at her. Yesterday Harry came crying to me, and told me that one of the neighbor's boys had called him 'nigger.'"

A shadow flitted over Leroy's face, as he answered, somewhat soberly, "Oh, Marie, do not meet trouble half way. I have manumitted you, and the children will follow your condition. I have made you all legatees of my will. Except my cousin, Alfred Lorraine, I have only distant relatives, whom I scarcely know and who hardly know me."

Notes

[31] *kith* friends.

"Your cousin Lorraine? Are you sure our interests would be safe in his hands?"

"I think so; I don't think Alfred would do anything dishonorable."

"He might not with his equals. But how many men would be bound by a sense of honor where the rights of a colored woman are in question? Your cousin was bitterly opposed to our marriage, and I would not trust any important interests in his hands. I do hope that in providing for our future you will make assurance doubly sure."

"I certainly will, and all that human foresight can do shall be done for you and our children."

"Oh," said Marie, pressing to her heart a beautiful child of six summers, "I think it would almost make me turn over in my grave to know that every grace and charm which this child possesses would only be so much added to her value as an article of merchandise."

As Marie released the child from her arms she looked wonderingly into her mother's face and clung closely to her, as if to find refuge from some unseen evil. Leroy noticed this, and sighed unconsciously, as an expression of pain flitted over his face.

"Now, Marie," he continued, "stop tormenting yourself with useless fears. Although, with all her faults, I still love the South, I will make arrangements either to live North or go to France. There life will be brighter for us all. Now, Marie, seat yourself at the piano and sing:–

'Sing me the songs that to me were so dear,
Long, long ago.
Sing me the songs I delighted to hear,
Long, long ago.'"

As Marie sang the anxiety faded from her face, a sense of security stole over her, and she sat among her loved ones a happy wife and mother. What if no one recognized her on that lonely plantation! Her world was, nevertheless, there. The love and devotion of her husband brightened every avenue of her life, while her children filled her home with music, mirth, and sunshine.

Marie had undertaken their education, but she could not give them the culture which comes from the attrition of thought, and from contact with the ideas of others. Since her school-days she had read extensively and thought much, and in solitude her thoughts had ripened. But for her children there were no companions except the young slaves of the plantation, and she dreaded the effect of such intercourse upon their lives and characters.

Leroy had always been especially careful to conceal from his children the knowledge of their connection with the negro race. To Marie this silence was oppressive.

One day she said to him, "I see no other way of finishing the education of these children than by sending them to some Northern school."

"I have come," said Leroy, "to the same conclusion. We had better take Iola and Harry North and make arrangements for them to spend several years in being educated. Riches take wings to themselves and fly away, but a good education is an investment on which the law can place no attachment. As there is a possibility of their origin being discovered, I will find a teacher to whom I can confide our story, and upon whom I can enjoin secrecy. I want them well fitted for any emergency in life. When I discover for what they have the most aptitude I will give them especial training in that direction."

A troubled look passed over the face of Marie, as she hesitatingly said: "I am so afraid that you will regret our marriage when you fully realize the complications it brings."

"No, no," said Leroy, tenderly, "it is not that I regret our marriage, or feel the least disdain for our children on account of the blood in their veins; but I do not wish them to grow up under the contracting influence of this race prejudice. I do not wish them to feel that they have been born under a proscription from which no valor can redeem them, nor that any social advancement or individual development can wipe off the ban which clings to them. No, Marie, let them go North, learn all they can, aspire all they may. The painful knowledge will come all too soon. Do not forestall it. I want them simply to grow up as other children; not being patronized by friends nor disdained by foes."

"My dear husband, you may be perfectly right, but are you not preparing our children for a fearful awakening? Are you not acting on the plan, 'After me the deluge?'"

"Not at all, Marie. I want our children to grow up without having their self-respect crushed in the bud. You know that the North is not free from racial prejudice."

"I know it," said Marie, sadly, "and I think one of the great mistakes of our civilization is that which makes color, and not character, a social test."

"I think so, too," said Leroy. "The strongest men and women of a down-trodden race may bare their bosoms to an adverse fate and develop courage in the midst of opposition, but we have no right to subject our children to such crucial tests before their characters are formed. For years, when I lived abroad, I had an opportunity to see and hear of men of African descent who had distinguished themselves and obtained a recognition in European circles, which they never could have gained in this country. I now recall the name of Ira Aldridge, a colored man from New York City, who was covered with princely honors as a successful tragedian. Alexander Dumas was not forced to conceal his origin to succeed as a novelist. When I was in St. Petersburg I was shown the works of Alexander Sergevitch, a Russian poet, who was spoken of as the Byron of Russian literature, and reckoned one of the finest poets that Russia has produced in this century. He was also a prominent figure in fashionable society, and yet he was of African lineage. One of his paternal ancestors was a negro who had been ennobled by Peter the Great. I can't help contrasting the recognition which these men had received with the treatment which has been given to Frederick Douglass and other intelligent colored men in this country. With me the wonder is not that they have achieved so little, but that they have accomplished so much. No, Marie, we will have our children educated without being subjected to the depressing influences of caste feeling. Perhaps by the time their education is finished I will be ready to wind up my affairs and take them abroad, where merit and ability will give them entrance into the best circles of art, literature, and science."

After this conversation Leroy and his wife went North, and succeeded in finding a good school for their children. In a private interview he confided to the principal the story of the cross in their blood, and, finding him apparently free from racial prejudice, he gladly left the children in his care. Gracie, the youngest child, remained at home, and her mother spared no pains to fit her for the seminary against the time her sister should have finished her education.

Chapter 11

The Plague and the Law

YEARS passed, bringing no special change to the life of Leroy and his wife. Shut out from the busy world, its social cares and anxieties, Marie's life flowed peacefully on. Although removed by the protecting care of Leroy from the condition of servitude, she still retained a deep sympathy for the enslaved, and was ever ready to devise plans to ameliorate their condition.

Leroy, although in the midst of slavery, did not believe in the rightfulness of the institution. He was in favor of gradual emancipation, which would prepare both master and slave for a moral adaptation to the new conditions of freedom. While he was willing to have the old rivets taken out of slavery, politicians and planters were devising plans to put in new screws. He was desirous of having it ended in the States; they were clamorous to have it established in the Territories.

But so strong was the force of habit, combined with the feebleness of his moral resistance and the nature of his environment that instead of being an athlete, armed for a glorious strife, he had learned to drift where he should have steered, to float with the current instead of nobly breasting the tide. He conducted his plantation with as much lenity as it was possible to infuse into a system darkened with the shadow of a million crimes.

Leroy had always been especially careful not to allow his children to spend their vacations at home. He and Marie generally spent that time with them at some summer resort.

"I would like," said Marie, one day, "to have our children spend their vacations at home. Those summer resorts are pleasant, yet, after all, there is no place like home. But," and her voice became tremulous, "our children would now notice their social isolation and inquire the cause." A faint sigh arose to the lips of Leroy, as she added: "Man is a social being; I've known it to my sorrow."

There was a tone of sadness in Leroy's voice, as he replied: "Yes, Marie, let them stay North. We seem to be entering on a period fraught with great danger. I cannot help thinking and fearing that we are on the eve of a civil war."

"A civil war!" exclaimed Marie, with an air of astonishment. "A civil war about what?"

"Why, Marie, the thing looks to me so wild and foolish I hardly know how to explain. But some of our leading men have come to the conclusion that North and South had better separate, and instead of having one to have two independent governments. The spirit of secession is rampant in the land. I do not know what the result will be, and I fear it will bode no good to the country. Between the fire-eating Southerners and the meddling Abolitionists we are about to be plunged into a great deal of trouble. I fear there are breakers ahead. The South is dissatisfied with the state of public opinion in the North. We are realizing that we are two peoples in the midst of one nation. William H. Seward[32] has proclaimed that the conflict between freedom and slavery is irrepressible, and that the country cannot remain half free and half slave."

"How will *you* go?" asked Marie.

"My heart is with the Union. I don't believe in secession. There has been no cause sufficient to justify a rupture. The North has met us time and again in the spirit of concession and compromise. When we wanted the continuance of the African slave trade the North conceded that we should have twenty years of slave-trading for the benefit of our plantations. When we wanted more territory she conceded to our desires and gave us land enough to carve out four States, and there yet remains enough for four more. When we wanted power to recapture our slaves when they fled North for refuge, Daniel Webster[33] told Northerners to conquer their prejudices, and they

Notes

[32] William H. Seward (1801–1872), US Senator and Lincoln's Secretary of State.

[33] Daniel Webster (1782–1852), US Senator, orator, and nationalist.

gave us the whole Northern States as a hunting ground for our slaves. The Presidential chair has been filled the greater number of years by Southerners, and the majority of offices has been shared by our men. We wanted representation in Congress on a basis which would include our slaves, and the North, whose suffrage represents only men, gave us a three-fifths representation for our slaves, whom we count as property. I think the step will be suicidal. There are extremists in both sections, but I hope, between them both, wise counsels and measures will prevail."

Just then Alfred Lorraine was ushered into the room. Occasionally he visited Leroy, but he always came alone. His wife was the only daughter of an enterprising slave-trader, who had left her a large amount of property. Her social training was deficient, her education limited, but she was too proud of being a pure white woman to enter the home of Leroy, with Marie as its presiding genius. Lorraine tolerated Marie's presence as a necessary evil, while to her he always seemed like a presentiment of trouble. With his coming a shadow fell upon her home, hushing its music and darkening its sunshine. A sense of dread oppressed her. There came into her soul an intuitive feeling that somehow his coming was fraught with danger. When not peering around she would often catch his eyes bent on her with a baleful expression.

Leroy and his cousin immediately fell into a discussion on the condition of the country. Lorraine was a rank Secessionist, ready to adopt the most extreme measures of the leaders of the movement, even to the reopening of the slave trade. Leroy thought a dissolution of the Union would involve a fearful expenditure of blood and treasure for which, before the eyes of the world, there could be no justification. The debate lasted late into the night, leaving both Lorraine and Leroy just as set in their opinions as they were before they began. Marie listened attentively awhile, then excused herself and withdrew.

After Lorraine had gone Marie said: "There is something about your cousin that fills me with nameless dread. I always feel when he enters the room as if someone[34] were walking over my grave. I do wish he would stay at home."

"I wish so, too, since he disturbs you. But, Marie, you are growing nervous. How cold your hands are. Don't you feel well?"

"Oh, yes; I am only a little faint. I wish he would never come. But, as he does, I must make the best of it."

"Yes, Marie, treat him well for my sake. He is the only relative I have who ever darkens our doors."

"I have no faith in his friendship for either myself or my children. I feel that while he makes himself agreeable to you he hates me from the bottom of his heart, and would do anything to get me out of the way. Oh, I am *so* glad I am your lawful wife, and that you married me before you brought me back to this State! I believe that if you were gone he wouldn't have the least scruple against trying to prove our marriage invalid and remanding us to slavery."

Leroy looked anxiously and soberly at his wife, and said: "Marie, I do not think so. Your life is too lonely here. Write your orders to New Orleans, get what you need for the journey, and let us spend the summer somewhere in the North."

Just then Marie's attention was drawn to some household matters, and it was a short time before she returned.

"Tom," continued Leroy, "has just brought the mail, and here is a letter from Iola."

Marie noticed that he looked quite sober as he read, and that an expression of vexation was lingering on his lips.

Notes

[34] *Original reads*: some one [ed.].

"What is the matter?" asked Marie.

"Nothing much; only a tempest in a teapot. The presence of a colored girl in Mr. Galen's school has caused a breeze of excitement. You know Mr. Galen is quite an Abolitionist, and, being true to his principles, he could not consistently refuse when a colored woman applied for her daughter's admission. Of course, when he took her he was compelled to treat her as any other pupil. In so doing he has given mortal offense to the mother of two Southern boys. She has threatened to take them away if the colored girl remains."

"What will he do about it?" asked Marie, thoughtfully.

"Oh, it is a bitter pill, but I think he will have to swallow it. He is between two fires. He cannot dismiss her from the school and be true to his Abolition principles; yet if he retains her he will lose his Southern customers, and I know he cannot afford to do that."

"What does Iola say?"

"He has found another boarding place for her, but she is to remain in the school. He had to throw that sop to the whale."

"Does she take sides against the girl?"

"No, I don't think she does. She says she feels sorry for her, and that she would hate to be colored. 'It is so hard to be looked down on for what one can't help.'"

"Poor child! I wish we could leave the country. I never would consent to her marrying anyone[35] without first revealing to him her connection with the negro race. This is a subject on which I am not willing to run any risks."

"My dear Marie, when you shall have read Iola's letter you will see it is more than a figment of my imagination that has made me so loth to have our children know the paralyzing power of caste."

Leroy, always liberal with his wife and children, spared neither pains nor expense to have them prepared for their summer outing. Iola was to graduate in a few days. Harry was attending a school in the State of Maine, and his father had written to him, apprising him of his intention to come North that season. In a few days Leroy and his wife started North, but before they reached Vicksburg they were met by the intelligence that the yellow fever was spreading in the Delta, and that pestilence was breathing its bane upon the morning air and distilling its poison upon the midnight dews.

"Let us return home," said Marie.

"It is useless," answered Leroy. "It is nearly two days since we left home. The fever is spreading south of us with fearful rapidity. To return home is to walk into the jaws of death. It was my intention to have stopped at Vicksburg, but now I will go on as soon as I can make the connections."

Early next morning Leroy and his wife started again on their journey. The cars were filled with terror-stricken people who were fleeing from death, when death was everywhere. They fled from the city only to meet the dreaded apparition in the country. As they journeyed on Leroy grew restless and feverish. He tried to brace himself against the infection which was creeping slowly but insidiously into his life, dulling his brain, fevering his blood, and prostrating his strength. But vain were all his efforts. He had no armor strong enough to repel the invasion of death. They stopped at a small town on the way and obtained the best medical skill and most careful nursing, but neither skill nor art availed. On the third day death claimed Leroy as a victim, and Marie wept in hopeless agony over the grave of her devoted husband, whose sad lot it was to die from home and be buried among strangers.

Notes

[35] *Original reads*: any one [ed.].

But before he died he placed his will in Marie's hands, saying: "I have left you well provided for. Kiss the children for me and bid them good-bye."

He tried to say a parting word to Gracie, but his voice failed, and he fainted into the stillness of death. A mortal paleness overspread his countenance, on which had already gathered the shadows that never deceive. In speechless agony Marie held his hand until it released its pressure in death, and then she stood alone beside her dead, with all the bright sunshine of her life fading into the shadows of the grave! Heart-broken and full of fearful forebodings, Marie left her cherished dead in the quiet village of H—— and returned to her death-darkened home.

It was a lovely day in June, birds were singing their sweetest songs, flowers were breathing their fragrance on the air, when Mam Liza, sitting at her cabin-door, talking with some of the house servants, saw a carriage approaching, and wondered who was coming.

"I wonder," she said, excitedly, "whose comin' to de house when de folks is done gone."

But her surprise was soon changed to painful amazement, when she saw Marie, robed in black, alighting from the carnage, and holding Gracie by the hand. She caught sight of the drooping head and grief-stricken face, and rushed to her, exclaiming:–

"Whar's Marse Eugene?"

"Dead," said Marie, falling into Mammy Liza's arms, sobbing out, "dead! *he died* of yellow fever."

A wild burst of sorrow came from the lips of the servants, who had drawn near.

"Where is he?" said Mam Liza, speaking like one suddenly bewildered.

"He is buried in H——. I could not bring him home," said Marie.

"My pore baby," said Mam Liza, with broken sobs. "I'se drefful sorry. My heart's most broke into two." Then, controlling herself, she dismissed the servants who stood around, weeping, and led Marie to her room.

"Come, honey, lie down an' lem'me git yer a cup ob tea."

"Oh, no; I don't want anything," said Marie, wringing her hands in bitter agony.

"Oh, honey," said Mam Liza, "yer musn't gib up. Yer knows whar to put yer trus'. Yer can't lean on de arm of flesh in dis tryin' time." Kneeling by the side of her mistress she breathed out a prayer full of tenderness, hope, and trust.

Marie grew calmer. It seemed as if that earnest, trustful prayer had breathed into her soul a feeling of resignation.

Gracie stood wonderingly by, vainly trying to comprehend the great sorrow which was overwhelming the life of her mother.

After the first great burst of sorrow was over, Marie sat down to her desk and wrote a letter to Iola, informing her of her father's death. By the time she had finished it she grew dizzy and faint, and fell into a swoon. Mammy Liza tenderly laid her on the bed, and helped restore her to consciousness.

Lorraine, having heard of his cousin's death, came immediately to see Marie. She was too ill to have an interview with him, but he picked up the letter she had written and obtained Iola's address.

Lorraine made a careful investigation of the case, to ascertain whether Marie's marriage was valid. To his delight he found there was a flaw in the marriage and an informality in the manumission. He then determined to invalidate Marie's claim, and divide the inheritance among Leroy's white relations. In a short time, strangers, distant relatives of her husband, became frequent visitors at the plantation, and made themselves offensively familiar. At length the dreadful storm burst.

Alfred Lorraine entered suit for his cousin's estate, and for the remanding of his wife and children to slavery. In a short time he came armed with legal authority, and said to Marie:–

"I have come to take possession of these premises."

"By what authority?" she gasped, turning deathly pale. He hesitated a moment, as if his words were arrested by a sense of shame.

"By what authority?" she again demanded.

"By the authority of the law," answered Lorraine, "which has decided that Leroy's legal heirs are his white blood relations, and that your marriage is null and void."

"But," exclaimed Marie, "I have our marriage certificate. I was Leroy's lawful wife."

"Your marriage certificate is not worth the paper it is written on."

"Oh, you must be jesting, cruelly jesting. It can't be so."

"Yes; it is so. Judge Starkins has decided that your manumission is unlawful; your marriage a bad precedent, and inimical[36] to the welfare of society; and that you and your children are remanded to slavery."

Marie stood as one petrified. She seemed a statue of fear and despair. She tried to speak, reached out her hand as if she were groping in the dark, turned pale as death as if all the blood in her veins had receded to her heart, and, with one heart-rending cry of bitter agony, she fell senseless to the floor. Her servants, to whom she had been so kind in her days of prosperity, bent pityingly over her, chafed her cold hands, and did what they could to restore her to consciousness. For a while[37] she was stricken with brain fever, and her life seemed trembling on its frailest cord.

Gracie was like one perfectly dazed. When not watching by her mother's bedside she wandered aimlessly about the house, growing thinner day by day. A slow fever was consuming her life. Faithfully and carefully Mammy Liza watched over her, and did all she could to bring smiles to her lips and light to her fading eyes, but all in vain. Her only interest in life was to sit where she could watch her mother as she tossed to and fro in delirium, and to wonder what had brought the change in her once happy home. Finally she, too, was stricken with brain fever, which intervened as a mercy between her and the great sorrow that was overshadowing her young life. Tears would fill the servants' eyes as they saw the dear child drifting from them like a lovely vision, too bright for earth's dull cares and weary, wasting pain.

Chapter 12

School-Girl Notions

During Iola's stay in the North she found a strong tide of opposition against slavery. Arguments against the institution had entered the Church and made legislative halls the arenas of fierce debate. The subject had become part of the social converse of the fireside, and had enlisted the best brain and heart of the country. Anti-slavery discussions were pervading the strongest literature and claiming a place on the most popular platforms.

Iola, being a Southern girl and a slave-holder's daughter, always defended slavery when it was under discussion.

"Slavery can't be wrong," she would say, "for my father is a slave-holder, and my mother is as good to our servants as she can be. My father often tells her that she spoils them, and lets them run over her. I never saw my father strike one of them. I love my mammy as much as I do my own mother, and I believe she loves us just as if we were

Notes

[36] *inimical* hostile.

[37] *Original reads*: awhile [ed.].

her own children. When we are sick I am sure that she could not do anything more for us than she does."

"But, Iola," responded one of her school friends, "after all, they are not free. Would you be satisfied to have the most beautiful home, the costliest jewels, or the most elegant wardrobe if you were a slave?"

"Oh, the cases are not parallel. Our slaves do not want their freedom. They would not take it if we gave it to them."

"That is not the case with them all. My father has seen men who have encountered almost incredible hardships to get their freedom. Iola, did you ever attend an anti-slavery meeting?"

"No; I don't think these Abolitionists have any right to meddle in our affairs. I believe they are prejudiced against us, and want to get our property. I read about them in the papers when I was at home. I don't want to hear my part of the country run down. My father says the slaves would be very well contented if no one put wrong notions in their heads."

"I don't know," was the response of her friend, "but I do not think that that slave mother[38] who took her four children, crossed the Ohio River on the ice, killed one of the children and attempted the lives of the other two, was a contented slave. And that other one,[39] who, running away and finding herself pursued, threw herself over the Long Bridge into the Potomac, was evidently not satisfied. I do not think the numbers who are coming North on the Underground Railroad can be very contented. It is not natural for people to run away from happiness, and if they are so happy and contented, why did Congress pass the Fugitive Slave Bill?"

"Well, I don't think," answered Iola, "any of our slaves would run away. I know mamma don't like slavery very much. I have often heard her say that she hoped the time would come when there would not be a slave in the land. My father does not think as she does. He thinks slavery is not wrong if you treat them well and don't sell them from their families. I intend, after I have graduated, to persuade pa to buy a house in New Orleans, and spend the winter there. You know this will be my first season out, and I hope that you will come and spend the winter with me. We will have such gay times, and you will so fall in love with our sunny South that you will never want to come back to shiver amid the snows and cold of the North. I think one winter in the South would cure you of your Abolitionism."

"Have you seen her yet?"

This question was asked by Louis Bastine, an attorney who had come North in the interests of Lorraine. The scene was the New England village where Mr. Galen's academy was located, and which Iola was attending. This question was addressed to Camille Lecroix, Bastine's intimate friend, who had lately come North. He was the son of a planter who lived near Leroy's plantation, and was familiar with Iola's family history. Since his arrival North, Bastine had met him and communicated to him his intentions.

"Yes; just caught a glimpse of her this morning as she was going down the street," was Camille's reply.

"She is a most beautiful creature," said Louis Bastine. "She has the proud poise of Leroy, the most splendid eyes I ever saw in a woman's head, lovely complexion, and a glorious wealth of hair. She would bring $2000 any day in a New Orleans market."

Notes

[38] *slave mother* see Harper's 1854 poem "Eliza Harris."

[39] *other one* Margaret Garner. Harper also wrote about Garner in her 1859 "Slave Mother: A Tale of Ohio."

"I always feel sorry," said Camille, "when I see one of those Creole girls brought to the auction block. I have known fathers who were deeply devoted to their daughters, but who through some reverse of fortune were forced to part with them, and I always think the blow has been equally terrible on both sides. I had a friend who had two beautiful daughters whom he had educated in the North. They were cultured, and really belles in society. They were entirely ignorant of their lineage, but when their father died it was discovered that their mother had been a slave. It was a fearful blow. They would have faced poverty, but the knowledge of their tainted blood was more than they could bear."

"What became of them?"

"They both died, poor girls. I believe they were as much killed by the blow as if they had been shot. To tell you the truth, Bastine, I feel sorry for this girl. I don't believe she has the least idea of her negro blood."

"No, Leroy has been careful to conceal it from her," replied Bastine.

"Is that so?" queried Camille. "Then he has made a great mistake."

"I can't help that," said Bastine; "business is business."

"How can you get her away?" asked Camille. "You will have to be very cautious, because if these pesky Abolitionists get an inkling of what you're doing they will balk your game double quick. And when you come to look at it, isn't it a shame to attempt to reduce that girl to slavery? She is just as white as we are, as good as any girl in the land, and better educated than thousands of white girls. A girl with her apparent refinement and magnificent beauty, were it not for the cross in her blood, I would be proud to introduce to our set. She would be the sensation of the season. I believe to-day it would be easier for me to go to the slums and take a young girl from there, and have her introduced as my wife, than to have society condone the offense if I married that lovely girl. There is not a social circle in the South that would not take it as a gross insult to have her introduced into it."

"Well," said Bastine, "my plan is settled. Leroy has never allowed her to spend her vacations at home. I understand she is now very anxious to get home, and, as Lorraine's attorney, I have come on his account to take her home."

"How will you do it?"

"I shall tell her her father is dangerously ill, and desires her to come as quickly as possible."

"And what then?"

"Have her inventoried with the rest of the property."

"Don't she know that her father is dead?"

"I think not," said Bastine. "She is not in mourning, but appeared very light-hearted this morning, laughing and talking with two other girls. I was struck with her great beauty, and asked a gentleman who she was. He said, 'Miss Leroy, of Mississippi.' I think Lorraine has managed the affair so as to keep her in perfect ignorance of her father's death. I don't like the job, but I never let sentiment interfere with my work."

Poor Iola! When she said slavery was not a bad thing, little did she think that she was destined to drink to its bitter dregs the cup she was so ready to press to the lips of others.

"How do you think she will take to her situation?" asked Camille.

"O, I guess," said Bastine, "she will sulk and take it pretty hard at first; but if she is managed right she will soon get over it. Give her plenty of jewelry, fine clothes, and an easy time."

"All this business must be conducted with the utmost secrecy and speed. Her mother could not have written to her, for she has been suffering with brain fever and nervous prostration since Leroy's death. Lorraine knows her market value too well, and is too shrewd to let so much property pass out of his hands without making an effort to retain it."

"Has she any brothers or sisters?"

"Yes, a brother," replied Bastine; "but he is at another school, and I have no orders from Lorraine in reference to him. If I can get the girl I am willing to let well enough alone. I dread the interview with the principal more than anything else. I am afraid he will hem and haw, and have his doubts. Perhaps, when he sees my letters and hears my story, I can pull the wool over his eyes."

"But, Louis, this is a pitiful piece of business. I should hate to be engaged in it."

A deep flush of shame overspread for a moment the face of Lorraine's attorney, as he replied: "I don't like the job, but I have undertaken it, and must go through with it."

"I see no '*must*' about it. Were I in your place I would wash my hands of the whole business."

"I can't afford it," was Bastine's hard, business-like reply. On the next morning after this conversation between these two young men, Louis Bastine presented himself to the principal of the academy, with the request that Iola be permitted to leave immediately to attend the sick-bed of her father, who was dangerously ill. The principal hesitated, but while he was deliberating, a telegram, purporting to come from Iola's mother, summoned Iola to her father's bedside without delay. The principal, set at rest in regard to the truthfulness of the dispatch, not only permitted but expedited her departure.

Iola and Bastine took the earliest train, and traveled without pausing until they reached a large hotel in a Southern city. There they were obliged to wait a few hours until they could resume their journey, the train having failed to make connection. Iola sat in a large, lonely parlor, waiting for the servant to show her to a private room. She had never known a great sorrow. Never before had the shadows of death mingled with the sunshine of her life.

Anxious, travel-worn, and heavy-hearted, she sat in an easy chair, with nothing to divert her from the grief and anxiety which rendered every delay a source of painful anxiety.

"Oh, I hope that he will be alive and growing better!" was the thought which kept constantly revolving in her mind, until she fell asleep. In her dreams she was at home, encircled in the warm clasp of her father's arms, feeling her mother's kisses lingering on her lips, and hearing the joyous greetings of the servants and Mammy Liza's glad welcome as she folded her to her heart. From this dream of bliss she was awakened by a burning kiss pressed on her lips, and a strong arm encircling her. Gazing around and taking in the whole situation, she sprang from her seat, her eyes flashing with rage and scorn, her face flushed to the roots of her hair, her voice shaken with excitement, and every nerve trembling with angry emotion.

"How dare you do such a thing! Don't you know if my father were here he would crush you to the earth?"

"Not so fast, my lovely tigress," said Bastine, "your father knew what he was doing when he placed you in my charge."

"My father made a great mistake, if he thought he had put me in charge of a gentleman."

"I am your guardian for the present," replied Bastine. "I am to see you safe home, and then my commission ends."

"I wish it were ended now," she exclaimed, trembling with anger and mortification. Her voice was choked by emotion, and broken by smothered sobs. Louis Bastine thought to himself, "she is a real spitfire, but beautiful even in her wrath."

During the rest of her journey Iola preserved a most freezing reserve towards Bastine. At length the journey was ended. Pale and anxious she rode up the avenue which led to her home.

A strange silence pervaded the place. The servants moved sadly from place to place, and spoke in subdued tones. The windows were heavily draped with crape, and a funeral air pervaded the house.

Mammy Liza met her at the door, and, with streaming eyes and convulsive sobs, folded her to her heart, as Iola exclaimed, in tones of hopeless anguish:–

"Oh, papa's dead!"

"Oh, my pore baby!" said mammy, "ain't you hearn tell 'bout it? Yore par's dead, an' your mar's bin dreffül sick. She's better now."

Mam Liza stepped lightly into Mrs. Leroy's room, and gently apprised her of Iola's arrival. In a darkened room lay the stricken mother, almost distracted by her late bereavement.

"Oh, Iola," she exclaimed, as her daughter entered, "is this you? I am so sorry you came."

Then, burying her head in Iola's bosom, she wept convulsively. "Much as I love you," she continued, between her sobs, "and much as I longed to see you, I am sorry you came."

"Why, mother," replied Iola, astonished, "I received your telegram last Wednesday, and I took the earliest train I could get."

"My dear child, I never sent you a telegram. It was a trick to bring you down South and reduce you to slavery."

Iola eyed her mother curiously. What did she mean? Had grief dethroned her reason? Yet her eye was clear, her manner perfectly rational.

Marie saw the astounded look on Iola's face, and nerving herself to the task, said: "Iola, I must tell you what your father always enjoined me to be silent about. I did not think it was the wisest thing, but I yielded to his desires. I have negro blood in my veins. I was your father's slave before I married him. His relatives have set aside his will. The courts have declared our marriage null and void and my manumission illegal, and we are all to be remanded to slavery." An expression of horror and anguish swept over Iola's face, and, turning deathly pale, she exclaimed, "Oh, mother, it can't be so! you must be dreaming!"

"No, my child; it is a terrible reality."

Almost wild with agony, Iola paced the floor, as the fearful truth broke in crushing anguish upon her mind.

Then bursting into a paroxysm of tears succeeded by peals of hysterical laughter, said:–

"I used to say that slavery is right. I didn't know what I was talking about." Then growing calmer, she said, "Mother, who is at the bottom of this downright robbery?"

"Alfred Lorraine; I have always dreaded that man, and what I feared has come to pass. Your father had faith in him; I never had."

"But, mother, could we not contest his claim. You have your marriage certificate and papa's will."

"Yes, my dear child, but Judge Starkins has decided that we have no standing in the court, and no testimony according to law."

"Oh, mother, what can I do?"

"Nothing, my child, unless you can escape to the North."

"And leave you?"

"Yes."

"Mother, I will never desert you in your hour of trial. But can nothing be done? Had father no friends who would assist us?"

"None that I know of. I do not think he had an acquaintance who approved of our marriage. The neighboring planters have stood so aloof from me that I do not know where to turn for either help or sympathy. I believe it was Lorraine who sent the telegram. I wrote to you as soon as I could after your father's death, but fainted just as I finished directing the letter. I do not think he knows where your brother is, and, if possible, he must not know. If you can by any means, *do* send a letter to Harry and warn him not to attempt to come home. I don't know how you will succeed, for Lorraine has us all under surveillance. But it is according to law."

"What law, mother?"

"The law of the strong against the weak."

"Oh, mother, it seems like a dreadful dream, a fearful nightmare! But I cannot shake it off. Where is Gracie?"

"The dear child has been running down ever since her papa's death. She clung to me night and day while I had the brain fever, and could not be persuaded to leave me. She hardly ate anything for more than a week. She has been dangerously ill for several days, and the doctor says she cannot live. The fever has exhausted all her rallying power, and yet, dear as she is to me, I would rather consign her to the deepest grave than see her forced to be a slave."

"So would I. I wish I could die myself."

"Oh, Iola, do not talk so. Strive to be a Christian, to have faith in the darkest hour. Were it not for my hope of heaven I couldn't stand all this trouble."

"Mother, are these people Christians who made these laws which are robbing us of our inheritance and reducing us to slavery? If this is Christianity I hate and despise it. Would the most cruel heathen do worse?"

"My dear child, I have not learned my Christianity from them. I have learned it at the foot of the cross, and from this book," she said, placing a New Testament in Iola's hands. "Some of the most beautiful lessons of faith and trust I have ever learned were from among our lowly people in their humble cabins."

"Mamma!" called a faint voice from the adjoining room. Marie immediately arose and went to the bedside of her sick child, where Mammy Liza was holding her faithful vigils. The child had just awakened from a fitful sleep.

"I thought," she said, "that I heard Iola's voice. Has she come?"

"Yes, darling; do you want to see her?"

"Oh, yes," she said, as a bright smile broke over her dying features.

Iola passed quickly into the room. Gracie reached out her thin, bloodless hand, clasped Iola's palm in hers, and said: "I am so glad you have come. Dear Iola, stand by mother. You and Harry are all she has. It is not hard to die. You and mother and Harry must meet me in heaven."

Swiftly the tidings went through the house that Gracie was dying. The servants gathered around her with tearful eyes, as she bade them all good-bye. When she had finished, and Mammy had lowered the pillow, an unwonted radiance lit up her eye, and an expression of ineffable gladness overspread her face, as she murmured: "It is beautiful, so beautiful!" Fainter and fainter grew her voice, until, without a struggle or sigh, she passed away beyond the power of oppression and prejudice.

Chapter 13

A Rejected Suitor

Very unexpected was Dr. Gresham's proposal to Iola. She had heartily enjoyed his society and highly valued his friendship, but he had never been associated in her mind with either love or marriage. As he held her hand in his a tell-tale flush rose to her cheek, a look of grateful surprise beamed from her eye, but it was almost immediately succeeded by an air of inexpressible sadness, a drooping of her eyelids, and an increasing pallor of her cheek. She withdrew her hand from his, shook her head sadly, and said:–

"No, Doctor; that can never be. I am very grateful to you for your kindness. I value your friendship, but neither gratitude nor friendship is love, and I have nothing more than those to give."

"Not at present," said Dr. Gresham; "but may I not hope your friendship will ripen into love?"

"Doctor, I could not promise. I do not think that I should. There are barriers between us that I cannot pass. Were you to know them I think you would say the same."

Just then the ambulance brought in a wounded scout, and Iola found relief from the wounds of her own heart in attending to his.

Dr. Gresham knew the barrier that lay between them. It was one which his love had surmounted. But he was too noble and generous to take advantage of her loneliness to press his suit. He had lived in a part of the country where he had scarcely ever seen a colored person, and around the race their misfortunes had thrown a halo of romance. To him the negro was a picturesque being, over whose woes he had wept when a child, and whose wrongs he was ready to redress when a man. But when he saw the lovely girl who had been rescued by the commander of the post from the clutches of slavery, all the manhood and chivalry in his nature arose in her behalf, and he was ready to lay on the altar of her heart his first grand and overmastering love. Not discouraged by her refusal, but determined to overcome her objections, Dr. Gresham resolved that he would bide[40] his time.

Iola was not indifferent to Dr. Gresham. She admired his manliness and respected his character. He was tall and handsome, a fine specimen of the best brain and heart of New England. He had been nurtured under grand and ennobling influences. His father was a devoted Abolitionist. His mother was kindhearted, but somewhat exclusive and aristocratic. She would have looked upon his marriage with Iola as a mistake and feared that such an alliance would hurt the prospects of her daughters.

During Iola's stay in the North, she had learned enough of the racial feeling to influence her decision in reference to Dr. Gresham's offer. Iola, like other girls, had had her beautiful day-dreams before she was rudely awakened by the fate which had dragged her into the depths of slavery. In the chambers of her imagery were pictures of noble deeds; of high, heroic men, knightly, tender, true, and brave. In Dr. Gresham she saw the ideal of her soul exemplified. But in her lonely condition, with all its background of terrible sorrow and deep abasement, she had never for a moment thought of giving or receiving love from one of that race who had been so lately associated in her mind with horror, aversion, and disgust. His kindness to her had been a new experience. His companionship was an unexpected pleasure. She had learned to enjoy his presence and to miss him when absent, and when she began to question her heart she found that unconsciously it was entwining around him.

"Yes," she said to herself, "I do like him; but I can never marry him. To the man I marry my heart must be as open as the flowers to the sun. I could not accept his hand and hide from him the secret of my birth; and I could not consent to choose the happiest lot on earth without first finding my poor heart-stricken and desolate mother. Perhaps someday[41] I may have the courage to tell him my sad story, and then make my

Notes

[40] *Original reads*: abide [ed.].

[41] *Original reads*: some day [ed.].

heart the sepulchre in which to bury all the love which might have gladdened and brightened my whole life."

During the sad and weary months which ensued while the war dragged its slow length along, Dr. Gresham and Iola often met by the bedsides of the wounded and dying, and sometimes he would drop a few words at which her heart would beat quicker and her cheek flush more vividly. But he was so kind, tender, and respectful, that Iola had no idea he knew her race affiliations. She knew from unmistakable signs that Dr. Gresham had learned to love her, and that he had power to call forth the warmest affection of her soul; but she fought with her own heart and repressed its rising love. She felt that it was best for his sake that they should not marry. When she saw the evidences of his increasing love she regretted that she had not informed him at the first of the barrier that lay between them; it might have saved him unnecessary suffering. Thinking thus, Iola resolved, at whatever cost of pain it might be to herself, to explain to Dr. Gresham what she meant by the insurmountable barrier. Iola, after a continuous strain upon her nervous system for months, began to suffer from general debility and nervous depression. Dr. Gresham saw the increasing pallor on Iola's cheek and the loss of buoyancy in her step. One morning, as she turned from the bed of a young soldier for whom she had just written a letter to his mother, there was such a look of pity and sorrow on her face that Dr. Gresham's whole heart went out in sympathy for her, and he resolved to break the silence he had imposed upon himself.

"Iola," he said, and there was a depth of passionate tenderness in his voice, a volume of unexpressed affection in his face, "you are wronging yourself. You are sinking beneath burdens too heavy for you to bear. It seems to me that besides the constant drain upon your sympathies there is some great sorrow preying upon your life; some burden that ought to be shared." He gazed upon her so ardently that each cord of her heart seemed to vibrate, and unbidden tears sprang to her lustrous eyes, as she said, sadly:–

"Doctor, you are right."

"Iola, my heart is longing to lift those burdens from your life. Love, like faith, laughs at impossibilities. I can conceive of no barrier too high for my love to surmount. Consent to be mine, as nothing else on earth is mine." "Doctor, you know not what you ask," replied Iola. "Instead of coming into this hospital a self-sacrificing woman, laying her every gift and advantage upon the altar of her country, I came as a rescued slave, glad to find a refuge from a fate more cruel than death; a fate from which I was rescued by the intervention of my dear dead friend, Thomas Anderson. I was born on a lonely plantation on the Mississippi River, where the white population was very sparse. We had no neighbors who ever visited us; no young white girls with whom I ever played in my childhood; but, never having enjoyed such companionship, I was unconscious of any sense of privation. Our parents spared no pains to make the lives of their children (we were three) as bright and pleasant as they could. Our home was so happy. We had a large number of servants, who were devoted to us. I never had the faintest suspicion that there was any wrongfulness in slavery, and I never dreamed of the dreadful fate which broke in a storm of fearful anguish over our devoted heads. Papa used to take us to New Orleans to see the Mardi Gras, and while there we visited the theatres and other places of amusement and interest. At home we had books, papers, and magazines to beguile our time. Perfectly ignorant of my racial connection, I was sent to a Northern academy, and soon made many friends among my fellow-students. Companionship with girls of my own age was a new experience, which I thoroughly enjoyed. I spent several years in New England, and was busily preparing for my commencement exercises when my father was snatched away – died of yellow fever on his way North to witness my graduation. Through a stratagem, I was brought hurriedly from the North, and found that my father was dead; that his nearest kinsman had taken possession of our property; that my mother's marriage had been declared illegal, because of an imperceptible infusion of negro blood in her veins; and that she and her children had been remanded to slavery. I was torn from my mother, sold as a slave, and subjected to cruel indignities, from which I was rescued and a place given to me in this hospital. Doctor, I did not choose my lot in life, but I have no other alternative than to accept it. The intense horror and agony I felt when I was first told the story are over. Thoughts and purposes have come to me in the shadow I should never have learned in the sunshine. I am constantly rousing myself up to suffer and be strong. I intend, when this conflict is over, to cast my lot with the freed people as a helper, teacher, and friend. I have passed through a fiery ordeal, but this ministry of suffering will not be in vain. I feel that my mind has matured beyond my years. I am a wonder to myself. It seems as if years had been compressed into a few short months. In telling you this, do you not, can you not, see that there is an insurmountable barrier between us?"

"No, I do not," replied Dr. Gresham. "I love you for your own sake. And with this the disadvantages of birth have nothing to do."

"You say so now, and I believe that you are perfectly sincere. To-day your friendship springs from compassion, but, when that subsides, might you not look on me as an inferior?"

"Iola, you do not understand me. You think too meanly of me. You must not judge me by the worst of my race. Surely our country has produced a higher type of manhood than the men by whom you were tried and tempted."

"Tried, but not tempted," said Iola, as a deep flush overspread her face; "I was never tempted. I was sold from State to State as an article of merchandise. I had outrages heaped on me which might well crimson the cheek of honest womanhood with shame, but I never fell into the clutches of an owner for whom I did not feel the utmost loathing and intensest horror. I have heard men talk glibly of the degradation of the negro, but there is a vast difference between abasement of condition and degradation of character. I was abased, but the men who trampled on me were the degraded ones."

"But, Iola, you must not blame all for what a few have done."

"A few have done? Did not the whole nation consent to our abasement?" asked Iola, bitterly.

"No, Miss Iola, we did not all consent to it. Slavery drew a line of cleavage in this country. Although we were under one government we were farther apart in our sentiments than if we had been divided by lofty mountains and separated by wide seas. And had not Northern sentiment been brought to bear against the institution, slavery would have been intact until to-day."

"But, Doctor, the negro is under a social ban both North and South. Our enemies have the ear of the world, and they can depict us just as they please."

"That is true; but the negro has no other alternative than to make friends of his calamities. Other men have plead his cause, but out of the race must come its own defenders. With them the pen must be mightier than the sword. It is the weapon of civilization, and they must use it in their own defense. We cannot tell what is in them until they express themselves."

"Yes, and I think there is a large amount of latent and undeveloped ability in the race, which they will learn to use for their own benefit. This my hospital experience has taught me."

"But," said Dr. Gresham, "they must learn to struggle, labor, and achieve. By facts, not theories, they will be judged in the future. The Anglo-Saxon race is proud, domineering, aggressive, and impatient of a rival, and, as I think, has more capacity for dragging down a weaker race than uplifting it. They have been a conquering and achieving people, marvelous in their triumphs of mind over matter. They have manifested the traits of character which are developed by success and victory."

"And yet," said Iola, earnestly, "I believe the time will come when the civilization of the negro will assume a better phase than you Anglo-Saxons possess. You will prove unworthy of your high vantage ground if you only use your superior ability to victimize feebler races and minister to a selfish greed of gold and a love of domination."

"But, Iola," said Dr. Gresham, a little impatiently, "what has all this to do with our marriage? Your complexion is as fair as mine. What is to hinder you from sharing my Northern home, from having my mother to be your mother? "The tones of his voice grew tender, as he raised his eyes to Iola's face and anxiously awaited her reply.

"Dr. Gresham," said Iola, sadly, "should the story of my life be revealed to your family, would they be willing to ignore all the traditions of my blood, forget all the terrible humiliations through which I have passed? I have too much self-respect to enter your home under a veil of concealment. I have lived in New England. I love the sunshine of her homes and the freedom of her institutions. But New England is not free from racial prejudice, and I would never enter a family where I would be an unwelcome member."

"Iola, dear, you have nothing to fear in that direction."

"Doctor," she said, and a faint flush rose to her cheek, "suppose we should marry, and little children in after years should nestle in our arms, and one of them show unmistakable signs of color, would you be satisfied?"

She looked steadfastly into his eyes, which fell beneath her truth-seeking gaze. His face flushed as if the question had suddenly perplexed him. Iola saw the irresolution on his face, and framed her answer accordingly.

"Ah, I see," she said, "that you are puzzled. You had not taken into account what might result from such a marriage. I will relieve you from all embarrassment by simply saying I cannot be your wife. When the war is over I intend to search the country for my mother. Doctor, were you to give me a palace-like home, with velvet carpets to hush my tread, and magnificence to surround my way, I should miss her voice amid all other tones, her presence amid every scene. Oh, you do not know how hungry my heart is for my mother! Were I to marry you I would carry an aching heart into your home and dim its brightness. I have resolved never to marry until I have found my mother. The hope of finding her has colored all my life since I regained my freedom. It has helped sustain me in the hour of fearful trial. When I see her I want to have the proud consciousness that I bring her back a heart just as loving, faithful, and devoted as the last hour we parted."

"And is this your final answer?"

"It is. I have pledged my life to that resolve, and I believe time and patience will reward me."

There was a deep shadow of sorrow and disappointment on the face of Dr. Gresham as he rose to leave. For a moment he held her hand as it lay limp in his own. If she wavered in her determination it was only for a moment. No quivering of her lip or paling of her cheek betrayed any struggle of her heart. Her resolve was made, and his words were powerless to swerve her from the purpose of her soul.

After Dr. Gresham had gone Iola went to her room and sat buried in thought. It seemed as if the fate of Tantalus was hers, without his crimes. Here she was lonely and heart-stricken, and unto her was presented the offer of love, home, happiness, and social position; the heart and hand of a man too noble and generous to refuse her companionship for life on account of the blood in her veins. Why should she refuse these desirable boons? But, mingling with these beautiful visions of manly love and protecting care she saw the anguish of her heart-stricken mother and the pale, sweet face of her dying sister, as with her latest breath she had said, "Iola, stand by mamma!" "No, no," she said to herself; "I was right to refuse Dr. Gresham. How dare I dream of happiness when my poor mamma's heart may be slowly breaking? I should be ashamed to live and ashamed to die were I to choose a happy lot for myself and leave poor mamma to struggle alone. I will never be satisfied till I get tidings of her. And when I have found her I will do all I can to cheer and brighten the remnant of her life."

Chapter 14

Harry Leroy

It was several weeks after Iola had written to her brother that her letter reached him. The trusty servant to whom she delivered it watched his opportunity to mail it. At last he succeeded in slipping it into Lorraine's mail and dropping them all into the post-office together. Harry was studying at a boys' academy in Maine. His father had given that State the preference because, while on a visit there, he had been favorably impressed with the kindness and hospitality of the people. He had sent his son a large sum of money, and given him permission to spend a while[42] with some school-chums till he was ready to bring the family North, where they could all spend the summer together. Harry had returned from his visit, and was looking for letters and remittances from home, when a letter, all crumpled, was handed him by the principal of the academy. He recognized his sister's handwriting and eagerly opened the letter. As he read, he turned very pale; then a deep flush overspread his face and an angry light flashed from his eyes. As he read on, his face became still paler; he gasped for breath and fell into a swoon. Appalled at the sudden change which had swept over him like a deadly sirocco,[43] the principal rushed to the fallen boy, picked up the missive that lay beside him, and immediately rang for help and dispatched for the doctor. The doctor came at once and was greatly puzzled. Less than an hour before, he had seen him with a crowd of merry, laughter-loving boys, apparently as light-hearted and joyous as any of them; now he lay with features drawn and pinched, his face deadly pale, as if some terrible suffering had sent all the blood in his veins to stagnate around his heart. Harry opened his eyes, shuddered, and relapsed into silence. The doctor, all at sea in regard to the cause of the sudden attack, did all that he could to restore him to consciousness and quiet the perturbation of his spirit. He succeeded, but found he was strangely silent. A terrible shock had sent a tremor through every nerve, and the doctor watched with painful apprehension its effect upon his reason. Giving him an opiate and enjoining that he should be kept perfectly quiet, the doctor left the room, sought the principal, and said:–

"Mr. Bascom, here is a case that baffles my skill. I saw that boy pass by my window not more than half an hour ago, full of animation, and now he lies hovering between life and death. I have great apprehension for his reason. Can you throw any light on the subject?"

Mr. Bascom hesitated.

"I am not asking you as a matter of idle curiosity, but as a physician. I must have all the light I can get in making my diagnosis of the case."

Notes

[42] *Original reads*: awhile [ed.].

[43] *sirocco* a hot, powerful wind.

The principal arose, went to his desk, took out the letter which he had picked up from the floor, and laid it in the physician's hand. As the doctor read, a look of indignant horror swept over his face. Then he said: "Can it be possible! I never suspected such a thing. It must be a cruel, senseless hoax."

"Doctor," said Mr. Bascom, "I have been a life-long Abolitionist and have often read of the cruelties and crimes of American slavery, but never before did I realize the low moral tone of the social life under which such shameless cruelties could be practiced on a defenseless widow and her orphaned children. Let me read the letter again. Just look at it, all tear-blotted and written with a trembling hand:–

'Dear Brother:– I have dreadful news for you and I hardly know how to tell it. Papa and Gracie are both dead. He died of yellow fever. Mamma is almost distracted. Papa's cousin has taken possession of our property, and instead of heirs we are chattels. Mamma has explained the whole situation to me. She was papa's slave before she married. He loved her, manumitted, educated, and married her. When he died Mr. Lorraine entered suit for his property and Judge Starkins has decided in his favor. The decree of the court has made their marriage invalid, robbed us of our inheritance, and remanded us all to slavery. Mamma is too wretched to attempt to write herself, but told me to entreat you not to attempt to come home. You can do us no good, and that mean, cruel Lorraine may do you much harm. Don't attempt, I beseech you, to come home. Show this letter to Mr. Bascom and let him advise you what to do. But don't, for our sake, attempt to come home.

Your heart-broken sister,
Iola Leroy.'"

"This," said the doctor, "is a very awkward affair. The boy is too ill to be removed. It is doubtful if the nerves which have trembled with such fearful excitement will ever recover their normal condition. It is simply a work of mercy to watch over him with the tenderest care."

Fortunately for Harry he had fallen into good hands, and the most tender care and nursing were bestowed upon him. For a while[44] Harry was strangely silent, never referring to the terrible misfortune which had so suddenly overshadowed his life. It seemed as if the past were suddenly blotted out of his memory. But he was young and of an excellent constitution, and in a few months he was slowly recovering.

"Doctor," said he one day, as the physician sat at his bedside, "I seem to have had a dreadful dream, and to have dreamt that my father was dead, and my mother and sister were in terrible trouble, but I could not help them. Doctor, was it a dream, or was it a reality? It could not have been a dream, for when I fell asleep the grass was green and the birds were singing, but now the winds are howling and the frost is on the ground. Doctor, tell me how it is? How long have I been here?"

Sitting by his bedside, and taking his emaciated hand in his, the doctor said, in a kind, fatherly tone: "My dear boy, you have been very ill, and everything depends on your keeping quiet, very quiet."

As soon as he was strong enough the principal gave him his letter to read.

"But, Mr. Bascom," Harry said, "I do not understand this. It says my mother and father were legally married. How could her marriage be set aside and her children robbed of their inheritance? This is not a heathen country. I hardly think barbarians would have done any worse; yet this is called a Christian country."

Notes

[44] *Original reads*: awhile [ed.].

"Christian in name," answered the principal. "When your father left you in my care, knowing that I was an Abolitionist, he confided his secret to me. He said that life was full of vicissitudes,[45] and he wished you to have a good education. He wanted you and your sister to be prepared for any emergency. He did not wish you to know that you had negro blood in your veins. He knew that the spirit of caste pervaded the nation, North and South, and he was very anxious to have his children freed from its depressing influences. He did not intend to stay South after you had finished your education."

"But," said Harry, "I cannot understand. If my mother was lawfully married, how could they deprive her of her marital rights?"

"When Lorraine," continued Mr. Bascom, "knew your father was dead, all he had to do was to find a flaw in her manumission, and, of course, the marriage became illegal. She could not then inherit property nor maintain her freedom; and her children followed her condition."

Harry listened attentively. Things which had puzzled him once now became perfectly clear. He sighed heavily, and, turning to the principal, said: "I see things in a new light. Now I remember that none of the planters' wives ever visited my mother; and we never went to church except when my father took us to the Cathedral in New Orleans. My father was a Catholic, but I don't think mamma is."

"Now, Harry," said the principal, "life is before you. If you wish to stay North, I will interest friends in your behalf, and try to get you a situation. Going South is out of the question. It is probable that by this time your mother and sister are removed from their home. You are powerless to fight against the law that enslaved them. Should you fall into the clutches of Lorraine, he might give you a great deal of trouble. You would be pressed[46] into the Confederate service to help them throw up barricades, dig trenches, and add to the strength of those who enslaved your mother and sister."

"Never! never!" cried Harry. "I would rather die than do it! I should despise myself forever if I did."

"Numbers of our young men," said Mr. Bascom, "have gone to the war which is now raging between North and South. You have been sick for several months, and much has taken place of which you are unaware. Would you like to enlist?"

"I certainly would; not so much for the sake of fighting for the Government, as with the hope of finding my mother and sister, and avenging their wrongs. I should like to meet Lorraine on the battle-field."

"What kind of a regiment would you prefer, white or colored?"

Harry winced when the question was asked. He felt the reality of his situation as he had not done before. It was as if two paths had suddenly opened before him, and he was forced to choose between them. On one side were strength, courage, enterprise, power of achievement, and memories of a wonderful past. On the other side were weakness, ignorance, poverty, and the proud world's social scorn. He knew nothing of colored people except as slaves, and his whole soul shrank from equalizing himself with them. He was fair enough to pass unchallenged among the fairest in the land, and yet a Christless prejudice had decreed that he should be a social pariah. He sat, thoughtful and undecided, as if a great struggle were going on in his mind. Finally the principal said, "I do not think that you should be assigned to a colored regiment because of

Notes

[45] *vicissitudes* changes.

[46] *pressed* Slaves were commandeered into public service through the act of impressment.

the blood in your veins, but you will have, in such a regiment, better facilities for finding your mother and sister."

"You are right, Mr. Bascom. To find my mother and sister I call no task too heavy, no sacrifice too great."

Since Harry had come North he had learned to feel profound pity for the slave. But there is a difference between looking on a man as an object of pity and protecting him as such, and being identified with him and forced to share his lot. To take his place with them on the arena of life was the test of his life, but love was stronger than pride.

His father was dead. His mother and sister were enslaved by a mockery of justice. It was more than a matter of choice where he should stand on the racial question. He felt that he must stand where he could strike the most effective blow for their freedom. With that thought strong in his mind, and as soon as he recovered, he went westward to find a colored regiment. He told the recruiting officer that he wished to be assigned to a colored regiment.

"Why do you wish that," said the officer, looking at Harry with an air of astonishment.

"Because I am a colored man."

The officer look puzzled. It was a new experience. He had seen colored men with fair complexions anxious to lose their identity with the colored race and pose as white men, but here was a man in the flush of his early manhood, to whom could come dreams of promotion from a simple private to a successful general, deliberately turning his back upon every gilded hope and dazzling opportunity, to cast his lot with the despised and hated negro.

"I do not understand you," said the officer. "Surely you are a white man, and, as such, I will enlist you in a white regiment."

"No," said Harry, firmly, "I am a colored man, and unless I can be assigned to a colored regiment I am not willing to enter the army."

"Well," said the officer, "you are the d——d'st fool I ever saw – a man as white as you are turning his back upon his chances of promotion! But you can take your choice."

So Harry was permitted to enter the army. By his promptness and valor he soon won the hearts of his superior officers, and was made drill sergeant. Having nearly all of his life been used to colored people, and being taught by his mother to be kind and respectful to them, he was soon able to gain their esteem. He continued in the regiment until Grant began the task of opening the Mississippi. After weeks of fruitless effort, Grant marched his army down the west side of the river, while the gunboats undertook the perilous task of running the batteries.[47] Men were found for the hour. The volunteers offered themselves in such numbers that lots were cast to determine who should have the opportunity to enlist in an enterprise so fraught with danger. Harry was one on whom the lot fell. Grant crossed the river below, coiled his forces around Vicksburg like a boa-constrictor, and held it in his grasp. After forty-seven days of endurance the city surrendered to him. Port Hudson,[48] after the surrender of Vicksburg,[49] gave up the unequal contest, and the Mississippi was open to the Gulf.

Notes

[47] *gunboats ... running the batteries* naval warcraft carried guns and other supplies past the other side's artillery.

[48] *Port Hudson* the concurrent Siege of Port Hudson (May 22 to July 9, 1863) opened up the Union's naval route down the Mississippi on the western arena of the Civil War.

[49] *surrender of Vicksburg* the Siege of Vicksburg, Misssissippi (May 18 to July 4, 1863) was a decisive victory for the Union troops.

Chapter 15

Robert and His Company

"GOOD morning, gentlemen," said Robert Johnson, as he approached Colonel Robinson, the commander of the post, who was standing at the door of his tent, talking with Captain Sybil.

"Good morning," responded Colonel Robinson, "I am glad you have come. I was just about to send for you. How is your company getting on?"

"First rate, sir," replied Robert.

"In good health?"

"Excellent. They are all in good health and spirits. Our boys are used to hardship and exposure, and the hope of getting their freedom puts new snap into them."

"I am glad of it," said Colonel Robinson. "They make good fighters and very useful allies. Last night we received very valuable intelligence from some fugitives who had escaped through the Rebel lines. I do not think many of the Northern people realize the service they have been to us in bringing information and helping our boys when escaping from Rebel prisons. I never knew a full-blooded negro to betray us. A month ago, when we were encamped near the Rebel lines, a colored woman managed admirably to keep us posted as to the intended movements of the enemy. She was engaged in laundry work, and by means of hanging her sheets in different ways gave us the right signals."

"I hope," said Captain Sybil, "that the time will come when some faithful historian will chronicle all the deeds of daring and service these people have performed during this struggle, and give them due credit therefor."

"Our great mistake," said Colonel Robinson, "was our long delay in granting them their freedom, and even what we have done is only partial. The border States still retain their slaves. We ought to have made a clean sweep of the whole affair. Slavery is a serpent which we nourished in its weakness, and now it is stinging us in its strength."

"I think so, too," said Captain Sybil. "But in making his proclamation of freedom, perhaps Mr. Lincoln went as far as he thought public opinion would let him."

"It is remarkable," said Colonel Robinson, "how these Secesh hold out. It surprises me to see how poor white men, who, like the negroes, are victims of slavery, rally around the Stripes and Bars. These men, I believe, have been looked down on by the aristocratic slaveholders, and despised by the well-fed and comfortable slaves, yet they follow their leaders into the very jaws of death; face hunger, cold, disease, and danger; and all for what? What, under heaven, are they fighting for? Now, the negro, ignorant as he is, has learned to regard our flag as a banner of freedom, and to look forward to his deliverance as a consequence of the overthrow of the Rebellion."

"I think," said Captain Sybil "that these ignorant white men have been awfully deceived. They have had presented to their imaginations utterly false ideas of the results of Secession, and have been taught that its success would bring them advantages which they had never enjoyed in the Union."

"And I think," said Colonel Robinson, "that the women and ministers have largely fed and fanned the fires of this Rebellion, and have helped to create a public opinion which has swept numbers of benighted men into the conflict. Well might one of their own men say, 'This is a rich man's war and a poor man's fight.' They were led into it through their ignorance, and held in it by their fears."

"I think," said Captain Sybil, "that if the public school had been common through the South this war would never have occurred. Now things have reached such a pass that able-bodied men must report at headquarters, or be treated as deserters. Their leaders are desperate men, of whom it has been said: 'They have robbed the cradle and the grave.'"

"They are fighting against fearful odds," said Colonel Robinson, "and their defeat is only a question of time."

"As soon," said Robert, "as they fired on Fort Sumter, Uncle Daniel, a dear old father who had been praying and hoping for freedom, said to me: 'Dey's fired on Fort Sumter, an' mark my words, Bob, de Norf's boun' ter whip.'"

"Had we freed the slaves at the outset," said Captain Sybil, "we wouldn't have given the Rebels so much opportunity to strengthen themselves by means of slave labor in raising their crops, throwing up their entrenchments, and building their fortifications. Slavery was a deadly cancer eating into the life of the nation; but, somehow, it had cast such a glamour[50] over us that we have acted somewhat as if our national safety were better preserved by sparing the cancer than by cutting it out."

"Political and racial questions have sadly complicated this matter," said Colonel Robinson. "The North is not wholly made up of anti-slavery people. At the beginning of this war we were not permeated with justice, and so were not ripe for victory. The battle of Bull Run inaugurated the war by a failure. Instead of glory we gathered shame, and defeat in place of victory."

"We have been slow," said Captain Sybil, "to see our danger and to do our duty. Our delay has cost us thousands of lives and millions of dollars. Yet it may be it is all for the best. Our national wound was too deep to be lightly healed. When the President issued his Emancipation Proclamation my heart overflowed with joy, and I said: 'This is the first bright rift in the war cloud.'"

"And did you really think that they would accept the terms of freedom and lay down their arms?" asked Robert.

"I hardly thought they would," continued Captain Sybil. "I did not think that their leaders would permit it. I believe the rank and file of their army are largely composed of a mass of ignorance, led, manipulated, and moulded by educated and ambitious wickedness. In attempting to overthrow the Union, a despotism and reign of terror were created which encompassed them as fetters of iron, and they will not accept the conditions until they have reached the last extremity. I hardly think they are yet willing to confess that such extremity has been reached."

"Captain," said Robert, as they left Colonel Robinson's tent, "I have lived all my life where I have had a chance to hear the 'Secesh' talk, and when they left their papers around I used to read everything I could lay my hands on. It seemed to me that the big white men not only ruled over the poor whites and made laws for them, but over the whole nation."

"That was so," replied Captain Sybil. "The North was strong but forbearing. It was busy in trade and commerce, and permitted them to make the Northern States hunting-grounds for their slaves. When we sent back Simms and Burns[51] from beneath the shadow of Bunker Hill Monument and Faneuil Hall,[52] they mistook us; looked upon us as a lot of money-grabbers, who would be willing to purchase peace at any price. I do

Notes

50 *glamour* spell.

51 *Simms and Burns* two runaway slaves who were both captured and tried in Boston after the passage of the Fugitive Slave Act (1850), inciting great outrage amongst abolitionists.

52 *Bunker Hill Monument and Faneuil Hall* two famous Boston landmarks.

not believe when they fired on the 'Star of the West'[53] that they had the least apprehension of the fearful results which were to follow their madness and folly."

"Well, Captain," asked Robert, "if the free North would submit to be called on to help them catch their slaves, what could be expected of us, who all our lives had known no other condition than that of slavery? How much braver would you have been, if your first recollections had been those of seeing your mother maltreated, your father cruelly beaten, or your fellow-servants brutally murdered? I wonder why they never enslaved the Indians!"

"You are mistaken, Robert, if you think the Indians were never enslaved. I have read that the Spaniards who visited the coasts of America kidnapped thousands of Indians, whom they sent to Europe and the West Indies as slaves. Columbus himself, we are informed, captured five hundred natives, and sent them to Spain. The Indian had the lesser power of endurance, and Las Cassas[54] suggested the enslavement of the negro, because he seemed to possess greater breadth of physical organization and stronger power of endurance. Slavery was an old world's crime which, I have heard, the Indians never practiced among themselves. Perhaps it would have been harder to reduce them to slavery and hold them in bondage when they had a vast continent before them, where they could hide in the fastnesses of its mountains or the seclusion of its forests, than it was for white men to visit the coasts of Africa and, with their superior knowledge, obtain cargoes of slaves, bring them across the ocean, hem them in on the plantations, and surround them with a pall of dense ignorance."

"I remember," said Robert, "in reading a history I once came across at our house, that when the Africans first came to this country they did not all speak one language. Some had only met as mutual enemies. They were not all one color, their complexions ranging from tawny yellow to deep black."

"Yes," said Captain Sybil, "and in dealing with the negro we wanted his labor; in dealing with the Indian we wanted his lands. For one we had weapons of war; for the other we had real and invisible chains, the coercion of force, and the terror of the unseen world."

"That's exactly so, Captain! When I was a boy I used to hear the old folks tell what would happen to bad people in another world; about the devil pouring hot lead down people's throats and stirring them up with a pitch-fork; and I used to get so scared that I would be afraid to go to bed at night. I don't suppose the Indians ever heard of such things, or, if they had, I never heard of them being willing to give away all their lands on earth, and quietly wait for a home in heaven."

"But, surely, Robert, you do not think religion has degraded the negro?"

"Oh, I wouldn't say that. But a man is in a tight fix when he takes his part, like Nat Turner or Denmark Vesey,[55] and is made to fear that he will be hanged in this world and be burned in the next. And, since I come to think of it, we colored folks used to get mightily mixed up about our religion. Mr. Gundover had on his plantation a real smart man. He was religious, but he would steal."

"Oh, Robert," queried Sybil, "how could he be religious and steal?"

Notes

[53] *Star of the West* the ship fired upon by the seceded South Carolina troops at Fort Sumter, leading to the Civil War.

[54] *Las Cassas* Bartolomé de las Casas (1484?–1566), Spanish historian who wrote about the atrocities perpetuated upon the indigenous West Indians by the Spaniard colonizers.

[55] Nat Turner and Denmark Vesey were the instigators of two slave uprisings (Vesey's plot was put down before it began); both were hanged. *Original reads*: Veasy [ed.].

"He didn't think," retorted Robert, "it was any harm to steal from his master. I guess he thought it was right to get from his master all he could. He would have thought it wrong to steal from his fellow-servants. He thought that downright mean, but I wouldn't have insured the lives of Gundover's pigs and chickens, if Uncle Jack got them in a tight place. One day there was a minister stopping with Mr. Gundover. As a matter of course, in speaking of his servants, he gave Jack's sins an airing. He would much rather confess Jack's sins than his own. Now Gundover wanted to do two things, save his pigs and poultry, and save Jack's soul. He told the minister that Jack was a liar and a thief, and gave the minister a chance to talk with Uncle Jack about the state of his soul. Uncle Jack listened very quietly, and when taxed with stealing his master's wheat he was ready with an answer. 'Now Massa Parker,' said Jack, 'lem'me tell yer jis' how it war 'bout dat wheat. Wen ole Jack com'd down yere, dis place war all growed up in woods. He go ter work, clared up de groun' an' plowed, an' planted, an' riz a crap, an' den wen it war all done, he hadn't a dollar to buy his ole woman a gown; an' he jis' took a bag ob wheat.'"

"What did Mr. Parker say?" asked Sybil.

"I don't know, though I reckon he didn't think it was a bad steal after all, but I don't suppose he told Jack so. When he came to the next point, about Jack's lying, I suppose he thought he had a clear case; but Jack was equal to the occasion."

"How did he clear up that charge?" interrogated Captain Sybil.

"Finely. I think if he had been educated he would have made a first-rate lawyer. He said, 'Marse Parker, dere's old Joe. His wife don't lib on dis plantation. Old Joe go ober ter see her, but he stayed too long, an' didn't git back in time fer his work. Massa's oberseer kotched him an' cut him all up. When de oberseer went inter de house, pore old Joe war all tired an' beat up, an' so he lay down by de fence corner and go ter sleep. Bimeby Massa oberseer com'd an' axed, "all bin a workin' libely?" I say "Yes, Massa." Then said Mr. Parker, 'You were lying, Joe had been sleeping, not working.' 'I know's dat, but ef I tole on Joe, Massa oberseer cut him all up again, and Massa Jesus says, "Blessed am de Peacemaker."'[56] I heard, continued Robert, that Mr. Parker said to Gundover, 'You seem to me like a man standing in a stream where the blood of Jesus can reach you, but you are standing between it and your slaves. How will you answer that in the Day of Judgment?'"

"What did Gundover say?" asked Captain Sybil.

"He turned pale, and said, 'For God's sake don't speak of the Day of Judgment in connection with slavery.'"

Just then a messenger brought a communication to Captain Sybil. He read it attentively, and, turning to Robert, said, "Here are orders for an engagement at Five Forks[57] to-morrow. Oh, this wasting of life and scattering of treasure might have been saved had we only been wiser. But the time is passing. Look after your company, and see that everything is in readiness as soon as possible."

Carefully Robert superintended the arrangements for the coming battle of a strife which for years had thrown its crimson shadows over the land. The Rebels fought with a valor worthy of a better cause. The disaster of Bull Run had been retrieved. Sherman had made his famous march to the sea. Fighting Joe Hooker[58] had scaled the stronghold of the storm king and won a victory in the palace chamber of the clouds; the Union

Notes

[56] *"Blessed am de Peacemaker"* from Jesus's Sermon on the Mount (Matthew 5:3–10).

[57] *Five Forks* the Battle of Five Forks in Virginia (April 1, 1865).

[58] *Joe Hooker* Joseph Hooker (1814–1879), Union general who secured a victory at the Battle of Lookout Mountain in Georgia (November 1863).

soldiers had captured Columbia, replanted the Stars and Stripes in Charleston, and changed that old sepulchre of slavery into the cradle of a new-born freedom. Farragut had been as triumphant on water as the other generals had been victorious on land, and New Orleans had been wrenched from the hands of the Confederacy. The Rebel leaders were obstinate. Misguided hordes had followed them to defeat and death. Grant was firm and determined to fight it out if it took all summer. The closing battles were fought with desperate courage and firm resistance, but at last the South was forced to succumb. On the ninth day of April, 1865, General Lee surrendered to General Grant. The lost cause went down in blood and tears, and on the brows of a ransomed people God poured the chrism[59] of a new era, and they stood a race newly anointed with freedom.

Chapter 16

After the Battle

Very sad and heart-rending were the scenes with which Iola came in constant contact. Well may Christian men and women labor and pray for the time when nations shall learn war no more; when, instead of bloody conflicts, there shall be peaceful arbitration. The battle in which Robert fought, after his last conversation with Captain Sybil, was one of the decisive struggles of the closing conflict. The mills of doom and fate had ground out a fearful grist of agony and death,

> "And lives of men and souls of States
> Were thrown like chaff beyond the gates."[60]

Numbers were taken prisoners. Pale, young corpses strewed the earth; manhood was stricken down in the flush of its energy and prime. The ambulances brought in the wounded and dying. Captain Sybil laid down his life on the altar of freedom. His prediction was fulfilled. Robert was brought into the hospital, wounded, but not dangerously. Iola remembered him as being the friend of Tom Anderson, and her heart was drawn instinctively towards him. For awhile he was delirious, but her presence had a soothing effect upon him. He sometimes imagined that she was his mother, and he would tell her how he had missed her; and then at times he would call her sister. Iola, tender and compassionate, humored his fancies, and would sing to him in low, sweet tones some of the hymns she had learned in her old home in Mississippi. One day she sang a few verses of the hymn beginning with the words –

> "Drooping souls no longer grieve,
> Heaven is propitious;
> If on Christ you do believe,
> You will find Him precious."

"That," said he, looking earnestly into Iola's face, "was my mother's hymn. I have not heard it for years. Where did you learn it?"

Notes

[59] *chrism* a consecrated oil used in religious rites.

[60] *"And lives of men … the gates"* from "The Mills of God" (1865), a poem by Augustine Joseph Hickey Duganne (1823–1884), a Union officer and author.

Iola gazed inquiringly upon the face of her patient, and saw, by his clear gaze and the expression of his face, that his reason had returned.

"In my home, in Mississippi, from my own dear mother," was Iola's reply.

"Do you know where she learned it?" asked Robert.

"When she was a little girl she heard her mother sing it. Years after, a Methodist preacher came to our house, sang this hymn, and left the book behind him. My father was a Catholic, but my mother never went to any church. I did not understand it then, but I do now. We used to sing together, and read the Bible when we were alone."

"Do you remember where she came from, and who was her mother?" asked Robert, anxiously.

"My dear friend, you must be quiet. The fever has left you, but I will not answer for the consequences if you get excited."

Robert lay quiet and thoughtful for awhile and, seeing he was wakeful, Iola said, "Have you any friends to whom you would like to send a letter?" A pathetic expression flitted over his face, as he sadly replied, "I haven't, to my knowledge, a single relation in the world. When I was about ten years old my mother and sister were sold from me. It is more than twenty years since I have heard from them. But that hymn which you were singing reminded me so much of my mother! She used to sing it when I was a child. Please sing it again."

Iola's voice rose soft and clear by his bedside, till he fell into a quiet slumber. She remembered that her mother had spoken of her brother before they had parted, and her interest and curiosity were awakened by Robert's story. While he slept, she closely scrutinized Robert's features, and detected a striking resemblance between him and her mother.

"Oh, I *do* wonder if he can be my mother's brother, from whom she has been separated so many years!"

Anxious as she was to ascertain if there was any relationship between Robert and her mother, she forebore to question him on the subject which lay so near her heart. But one day, when he was so far recovered as to be able to walk around, he met Iola on the hospital grounds, and said to her:–

"Miss Iola, you remind me so much of my mother and sister that I cannot help wondering if you are the daughter of my long-lost sister."

"Do you think," asked Iola, "if you saw the likeness of your sister you would recognize her?"

"I am afraid not. But there is one thing I can remember about her: she used to have a mole on her cheek, which mother used to tell her was her beauty spot."

"Look at this," said Iola, handing him a locket which contained her mother's picture.

Robert grasped the locket eagerly, scanned the features attentively, then, handing it back, said: "I have only a faint remembrance of my sister's features; but I never could recognize in that beautiful woman the dear little sister with whom I used to play. Oh, the cruelty of slavery! How it wrenched and tore us apart! Where is *your* mother now?"

"Oh, I cannot tell," answered Iola. "I left her in Mississippi. My father was a wealthy Creole planter, who fell in love with my mother. She was his slave, but he educated her in the North, freed, and married her. My father was very careful to have the fact of our negro blood concealed from us. I had not the slightest suspicion of it. When he was dead the secret was revealed. His white relations set aside my father's will, had his marriage declared invalid, and my mother and her children were remanded to slavery." Iola shuddered as she pronounced the horrid word, and grew deadly pale; but, regaining her self-possession, continued: "Now, that freedom has come, I intend to search for my mother until I find her."

"I do not wonder," said Robert, "that we had this war. The nation had sinned enough to suffer."

"Yes," said Iola, "if national sins bring down national judgments, then the nation is only reaping what it sowed."

"What are your plans for the future, or have you any? "asked Robert.

"I intend offering myself as a teacher in one of the schools which are being opened in different parts of the country," replied Iola. "As soon as I am able I will begin my search for my dear mother. I will advertise for her in the papers, hunt for her in the churches, and use all the means in my power to get some tidings of her and my brother Harry. What a cruel thing it was to separate us!"

Chapter 17

Flames in the School-Room

"Good morning," said Dr. Gresham, approaching Robert and Iola. "How are you both? You have mended rapidly," turning to Robert, "but then it was only a flesh wound. Your general health being good, and your blood in excellent condition, it was not hard for you to rally."

"Where have you been, Doctor? I have a faint recollection of having seen you on the morning I was brought in from the field, but not since."

"I have been on a furlough. I was running down through exhaustion and overwork, and I was compelled to go home for a few weeks' rest. But now, as they are about to close the hospital, I shall be permanently relieved. I am glad that this cruel strife is over. It seemed as if I had lived through ages during these last few years. In the early part of the war I lost my arm by a stray shot, and my armless sleeve is one of the mementos of battle I shall carry with me through life. Miss Leroy," he continued, turning respectfully to Iola, "would you permit me to ask you, as I would have someone[61] ask my sister under the same circumstances, if you have matured any plans for the future, or if I can be of the least service to you? If so, I would be pleased to render you any service in my power."

"My purpose," replied Iola, " is to hunt for my mother, and to find her if she is alive. I am willing to go anywhere and do anything to find her. But I will need a standpoint from whence I can send out lines of inquiry. It must take time, in the disordered state of affairs, even to get a clue by which I may discover her whereabouts."

"How would you like to teach? "asked the Doctor. "Schools are being opened all around us. Numbers of excellent and superior women are coming from the North to engage as teachers of the freed people. Would you be willing to take a school among these people? I think it will be uphill work. I believe it will take generations to get over the duncery of slavery. Some of these poor fellows who came into our camp did not know their right hands from their left, nor their ages, nor even the days of the month. It took me some time, in a number of cases, to understand their language. It saddened my heart to see such ignorance. One day I asked one a question, and he answered, 'I no shum.'"

"What did he mean?" asked Iola."

"That he did not see it," replied the doctor. "Of course, this does not apply to all of them. Some of them are wide-awake and sharp as steel traps. I think some of that class may be used in helping others."

Notes

[61] *Original reads*: some one [ed.].

"I should be very glad to have an opportunity to teach," said Iola. "I used to be a great favorite among the colored children on my father's plantation."

In a few days after this conversation the hospital was closed. The sick and convalescent were removed, and Iola obtained a position as a teacher. Very soon Iola realized that while she was heartily appreciated by the freedmen, she was an object of suspicion and dislike to their former owners. The North had conquered by the supremacy of the sword, and the South had bowed to the inevitable. But here was a new army that had come with an invasion of ideas, that had come to supplant ignorance with knowledge, and it was natural that its members should be unwelcome to those who had made it a crime to teach their slaves to read the name of the ever blessed Christ. But Iola had found her work, and the freedmen their friend.

When Iola opened her school she took pains to get acquainted with the parents of the children, and she gained their confidence and co-operation. Her face was a passport to their hearts. Ignorant of books, human faces were the scrolls from which they had been reading for ages. They had been the sunshine and shadow of their lives.

Iola had found a school-room in the basement of a colored church, where the doors were willingly opened to her. Her pupils came from miles around, ready and anxious to get some "book larnin'." Some of the old folks were eager to learn, and it was touching to see the eyes which had grown dim under the shadows of slavery, donning spectacles and trying to make out the words. As Iola had nearly all of her life been accustomed to colored children she had no physical repulsions to overcome, no prejudices to conquer in dealing with parents and children. In their simple childish fashion they would bring her fruits and flowers, and gladden her lonely heart with little tokens of affection.

One day a gentleman came to the school and wished to address the children. Iola suspended the regular order of the school, and the gentleman essayed to talk to them on the achievements of the white race, such as building steamboats and carrying on business. Finally, he asked how they did it?

"They've got money," chorused the children.

"But how did they get it?"

"They took it from us," chimed the youngsters. Iola smiled, and the gentleman was nonplussed;[62] but he could not deny that one of the powers of knowledge is the power of the strong to oppress the weak.

The school was soon overcrowded with applicants, and Iola was forced to refuse numbers, because their quarters were too cramped. The school was beginning to lift up the home, for Iola was not satisfied to teach her children only the rudiments of knowledge. She had tried to lay the foundation of good character. But the elements of evil burst upon her loved and cherished work. One night the heavens were lighted with lurid flames, and Iola beheld the school, the pride and joy of her pupils and their parents, a smouldering ruin. Iola gazed with sorrowful dismay on what seemed the cruel work of an incendiary's torch. While she sat, mournfully contemplating the work of destruction, her children formed a procession, and, passing by the wreck of their school, sang:–

"Oh, do not be discouraged,
For Jesus is your friend."[63]

Notes

[62] *nonplussed* perplexed.

[63] *"Oh, do not be discouraged … friend"* a devotional hymn.

As they sang, the tears sprang to Iola's eyes, and she said to herself, "I am not despondent of the future of my people; there is too much elasticity in their spirits, too much hope in their hearts, to be crushed out by unreasoning malice."

Chapter 18

Searching for Lost Ones

To BIND anew the ties which slavery had broken and gather together the remnants of his scattered family became the earnest purpose of Robert's life. Iola, hopeful that in Robert she had found her mother's brother, was glad to know she was not alone in *her* search. Having sent out lines of inquiry in different directions, she was led to hope, from some of the replies she had received, that her mother was living somewhere in Georgia.

Hearing that a Methodist conference was to convene in that State, and being acquainted with the bishop of that district, she made arrangements to accompany him thither. She hoped to gather some tidings of her mother through the ministers gathered from different parts of that State.

From her brother she had heard nothing since her father's death. On his way to the conference, the bishop had an engagement to dedicate a church, near the city of C——, in North Carolina. Iola was quite willing to stop there a few days, hoping to hear something of Robert Johnson's mother. Soon after she had seated herself in the cars she was approached by a gentleman, who reached out his hand to her, and greeted her with great cordiality. Iola looked up, and recognized him immediately as one of her last patients at the hospital. It was none other than Robert Johnson.

"I am so glad to meet you," he said. "I am on my way to C—— in search of my mother. I want to see the person who sold her last, and, if possible, get some clue[64] to the direction in which she went."

"And I," said Iola, "am in search of *my* mother. I am convinced that when we find those for whom we are searching they will prove to be very nearly related. Mamma said, before we were parted, that her brother had a red spot on his temple. If I could see that spot I should rest assured that my mother is your sister."

"Then," said Robert, "I can give you that assurance," and smilingly he lifted his hair from his temple, on which was a large, red spot.

"I am satisfied," exclaimed Iola, fixing her eyes, beaming with hope and confidence, on Robert. "Oh, I am so glad that I can, without the least hesitation, accept your services to join with me in the further search. What are your plans?"

"To stop for a while[65] in C——," said Robert, "and gather all the information possible from those who sold and bought my mother. I intend to leave no stone unturned in searching for her."

"Oh, I *do* hope that you will succeed. I expect to stop over there a few days, and I shall be *so* glad if, before I leave, I hear your search has been crowned with success, or, a least, that you have been put on the right track. Although I was born and raised in the midst of slavery, I had not the least idea of its barbarous selfishness till I was forced to pass through it. But we lived so much alone I had no opportunity to study it, except on

Notes

[64] *Original reads*: clew [ed.].

[65] *Original reads*: awhile [ed.].

our own plantation. My father and mother were very kind to their slaves. But it was slavery, all the same, and I hate it, root and branch."

Just then the conductor called out the station.

"We stop here," said Robert. "I am going to see Mrs. Johnson, and hunt up some of my old acquaintances. Where do you stop?"

"I don't know," replied Iola. "I expect that friends will be here to meet us. Bishop B——, permit me to introduce you to Mr. Robert Johnson, whom I have every reason to believe is my mother's brother. Like myself, he is engaged in hunting up his lost relatives."

"And I," said Robert, "am very much pleased to know that we are not without favorable clues."

"Bishop," said Iola, "Mr. Johnson wishes to know where I am to stop. He is going on an exploring expedition, and wishes to let me know the result."

"We stop at Mrs. Allston's, 313 New Street," said the bishop. "If I can be of any use to you, I am at your service."

"Thank you," said Robert, lifting his hat, as he left them to pursue his inquiries about his long-lost mother.

Quickly he trod the old familiar streets which led to his former home. He found Mrs. Johnson, but she had aged very fast since the war. She was no longer the lithe, active woman, with her proud manner and resolute bearing. Her eye had lost its brightness, her step its elasticity, and her whole appearance indicated that she was slowly sinking beneath a weight of sorrow which was far heavier than[66] her weight of years. When she heard that Robert had called to see her she was going to receive him in the hall, as she would have done any of her former slaves, but her mind immediately changed when she saw him. He was not the light-hearted, careless, mischief-loving Robby of former days, but a handsome man, with heavy moustache, dark, earnest eyes, and proud military bearing. He smiled, and reached out his hand to her. She hardly knew how to address him. To her colored people were either boys and girls, or "aunties and uncles." She had never in her life addressed a colored person as "Mr. or Mrs." To do so now was to violate the social customs of the place. It would be like learning a new language in her old age. Robert immediately set her at ease by addressing her under the old familiar name of "Miss Nancy." This immediately relieved her of all embarrassment. She invited him into the sitting-room, and gave him a warm welcome.

"Well, Robby," she said, " I once thought that you would have been the last one to leave me. You know I never ill-treated you, and I gave you everything you needed. People said that I was spoiling you. I thought you were as happy as the days were long. When I heard of other people's servants leaving them I used to say to myself, 'I can trust my Bobby; he will stick to me to the last.' But I fooled myself that time. Soon as the Yankee soldiers got in sight you left me without saying a word. That morning I came down into the kitchen and asked Linda, 'Where's Robert? Why hasn't he set the table?' She said she hadn't seen you since the night before. I thought maybe you were sick, and I went to see, but you were not in your room. I couldn't believe at first that you were gone. Wasn't I always good to you?"

"Oh, Miss Nancy," replied Robert; "you were good, but freedom was better."

"Yes," she said, musingly, "I suppose I would have done the same. But, Robby, it did go hard with me at first. However, I soon found out that my neighbors had been

Notes

[66] *Original reads*: heavier far than [ed.].

going through the same thing. But it's[67] all over now. Let by-gones be by-gones. What are you doing now, and where are you living?"

"I am living in the city of P——. have opened a hardware store there. But just now I am in search of my mother and sister."

"I hope that you may find them."

"How long," asked Robert, "do you think it has been since they left here?"

"Let me see; it must have been nearly thirty years. You got my letter?"

"Yes, ma'am; thank you."

"There have been great changes since you left here," Mrs. Johnson said. "Gundover died, and a number of colored men have banded together, bought his plantation, and divided it among themselves. And I hear they have a very nice settlement out there. I hope, since the Government has set them free, that they will succeed."

After Robert's interview with Mrs. Johnson he thought he would visit the settlement and hunt up his old friends. He easily found the place. It was on a clearing in Gundover's woods, where Robert and Uncle Daniel had held their last prayer-meeting. Now the gloomy silence of those woods was broken by the hum of industry, the murmur of cheerful voices, and the merry laughter of happy children. Where they had trodden with fear and misgiving, freedmen walked with light and bounding hearts. The school-house had taken the place of the slave-pen and auction-block.

"How is yer, ole boy?" asked one laborer of another.

"Everything is lobly," replied the other. The blue sky arching overhead and the beauty of the scenery justified the expression.

Gundover had died soon after the surrender. Frank Anderson had grown reckless and drank himself to death. His brother Tom had been killed in battle. Their mother, who was Gundover's daughter, had died insane. Their father had also passed away. The defeat of the Confederates, the loss of his sons, and the emancipation of his slaves, were blows from which he never recovered. As Robert passed leisurely along, delighted with the evidences of thrift and industry which constantly met his eye, he stopped to admire a garden filled with beautiful flowers, clambering vines, and rustic adornments.

On the porch sat an elderly woman darning stockings, the very embodiment of content and good humor. Robert looked inquiringly at her. On seeing him, she almost immediately exclaimed, "Shore as I'se born, dat's Robert! Look yere, honey, whar did yer come from? I'll gib my head fer a choppin' block ef dat ain't Miss Nancy's Bob. Ain't yer our Bobby? Shore yer is."

"Of course I am," responded Robert. "It isn't anybody else. How did you know me?"

"How did I know yer? By dem mischeebous eyes, ob course. I'd a knowed yer if I had seed yer in Europe."

"In Europe, Aunt Linda? Where's that?"

"I don't know. I specs its some big city, somewhar. But yer looks jis' splendid. Yer looks good 'nuff ter kiss."

"Oh, Aunt Linda, don't say that. You make me blush."

"Oh you go 'long wid yer. I specs yer's got a nice little wife up dar whar yer comes from, dat kisses yer ebery day, an' Sunday, too."

"Is that the way your old man does you?"

Notes

[67] *Original reads*: its [ed.].

"Oh, no, not a bit. He isn't one ob de kissin' kine. But sit down," she said, handing Robert a chair. "Won't yer hab a glass ob milk? Boy, I'se a libin' in clover. Neber 'spected ter see sich good times in all my born days."

"Well, Aunt Linda," said Robert, seating himself near her, and drinking the glass of milk which she had handed him, "how goes the battle? How have you been getting on since freedom?"

"Oh, fust rate, fust rate! Wen freedom com'd I jist lit out ob Miss Johnson's kitchen soon as I could. I wanted ter re'lize I war free, an' I couldn't, tell I got out er de sight and soun' ob ole Miss. When de war war ober an' de sogers war still stopping' yere, I made pies an' cakes, sole em to de sogers, an' jist made money han' ober fist. An' I kep' on a workin' an' a savin' till my ole man got back from de war wid his wages and his bounty money. I felt right set up an' mighty big wen we counted all dat money. We had neber seen so much money in our lives befo', let alone hab it fer ourselbs. An' I sez, 'John, you take dis money an' git a nice place wid it.' An' he sez, 'Dere's no use tryin', kase dey don't want ter sell us any lan'.' Ole Gundover said, 'fore he died, dat he would let de lan' grow up in trees 'fore he'd sell it to us. An' dere war Mr. Brayton; he buyed some lan' and sole it to some cullud folks, an' his ole frien's got so mad wid him dat dey wouldn't speak ter him, an' he war borned down yere. I tole ole Miss Anderson's daughter dat we wanted ter git some homes ob our ownselbs. She sez, 'Den you won't want ter work for us?' Jis' de same as ef we could eat an' drink our houses. I tell yer, Robby, dese white folks don't know eberything."

"That's a fact, Aunt Linda."

"Den I sez ter John, 'wen one door shuts anoder opens.' An' shore 'nough, ole Gundover died, an' his place war all in debt, an' had to be sole. Some Jews bought it, but dey didn't want to farm it, so dey gib us a chance to buy it. Dem Jews hez been right helpful to cullud people wen dey hab lan' to sell. I reckon dey don't keer who buys it so long as dey gits de money. Well, John didn't gib in at fust; didn't want to let on his wife knowed more dan he did, an' dat he war ruled ober by a woman. Yer know he is an' ole Firginian, an' some ob dem ole Firginians do so lub to rule a woman. But I kep' naggin at him, till I specs he got tired of my tongue, an' he went and buyed dis piece ob lan'. Dis house war on it, an' war all gwine to wrack. It used to belong to John's ole marster. His wife died right in dis house, an' arter dat her husband went right to de dorgs; an' now he's in de pore-house. My! but ain't dem tables turned. When we knowed it war our own, warn't my ole man proud! I seed it in him, but he wouldn't let on. Ain't you men powerful 'ceitful?"

"Oh, Aunt Linda, don't put me in with the rest!"

"I don't know 'bout dat. Put you all in de bag for 'ceitfulness, an' I don't know which would git out fust."

"Well, Aunt Linda, I suppose by this time you know how to read and write?"

"No, chile, sence freedom's com'd I'se bin scratchin' too hard to get a libin' to put my head down to de book."

"But, Aunt Linda, it would be such company when your husband is away, to take a book. Do you never get lonesome?"

"Chile, I ain't got no time ter get lonesome. Ef you had eber so many chickens to feed, an' pigs squealin' fer somethin' ter eat, an' yore ducks an' geese squakin' 'roun' yer, yer wouldn't hab. time ter git lonesome."

"But, Aunt Linda, you might be sick for months, and think what a comfort it would be if you could read your Bible."

"Oh, I could hab prayin' and singin'. Dese people is mighty good 'bout prayin' by de sick. Why, Robby, I think it would gib me de hysterics ef I war to try to git book larnin' froo my pore ole head. How long is yer gwine to stay? An' whar is yer stoppin?"

"I got here to-day," said Robert, "but I expect to stay several days."

"Well, I wants yer to meet my ole man, an' talk 'bout ole times. Couldn't yer come an' stop wid me, or isn't my house sniptious 'nuff?"

"Yes, thank you; but there is a young lady in town whom I think is my niece, my sister's daughter, and I want to be with her all I can."

"Your niece! Whar did you git any niece from?"

"Don't you remember," asked Robert, "that my mother had a little daughter, when Mrs. Johnson sold her? Well, I believe this young lady is that daughter's child."

"Laws a marcy!" exclaimed Aunt Linda, "yer don't tell me so! Whar did yer ketch up wid her?"

"I met her first," said Robert, "at the hospital here, when our poor Tom was dying; and when I was wounded at Five Forks she attended me in the field hospital there. She was just as good as gold."

"Well, did I eber! You jis' fotch dat chile to see me, ef she ain't too fine. I'se pore, but I'se clean, an' I ain't forgot how ter git up good dinners. Now, I wants ter hab a good talk 'bout our feller-sarvants."

"Yes, and I," said Robert, "want to hear all about Uncle Daniel, and Jennie, and Uncle Ben Tunnel."

"Well, I'se got lots an' gobs ter tell yer. I'se kep' track ob dem all. Aunt Katie died an' went ter hebben in a blaze ob glory. Uncle Dan'el stayed on de place till Marse Robert com'd back. When de war war ober he war smashed all ter pieces. I did pity him from de bottom ob my heart. When he went ter de war he looked so brave an' han'some; an' wen he com'd back he looked orful. 'Fore he went he gib Uncle Dan'el a bag full ob money ter take kere ob. An' wen he com'd back Uncle Dan'el gibed him ebery cent ob it. It warn't ebery white pusson he could hab trusted wid it. 'Cause yer know, Bobby, money's a mighty temptin' thing. Dey tells me dat Marster Robert los' a heap ob property by de war; but Marse Robert war always mighty good ter Uncle Dan'el and Aunt Katie. He war wid her wen she war dyin' an' she got holt his han' an' made him promise dat he would meet her in glory. I neber seed anybody so happy in my life. She singed an' prayed ter de last. I tell you dis ole time religion is good 'nuff fer me. Mr. Robert didn't stay yere long arter her, but I beliebs he went all right. But 'fore he went he looked out fer Uncle Dan'el. Did you see dat nice little cabin down dere wid de green shutters an' nice little garden in front? Well, 'fore Marse Robert died he gib Uncle Dan'el dat place, an' Miss Mary and de chillen looks arter him yet; an' he libs jis' as snug as a bug in a rug. I'se gwine ter axe him ter take supper wid you. He'll be powerful glad ter see you."

"Do you ever go to see old Miss?" asked Robert.

"Oh, yes; I goes ebery now and den. But she's jis' fell froo. Ole Johnson jis' drunk hisself to death. He war de biggest guzzler I eber seed in my life. Why, dat man he drunk up ebery thing he could lay his han's on. Sometimes he would go 'roun' tryin' to borrer money from pore cullud folks. 'Twas rale drefful de way dat pore feller did frow hisself away. But drink did it all. I tell you, Bobby, dat drink's a drefful thing wen it gits de upper han' ob you. You'd better steer clar ob it."

"That's so," assented Robert.

"I know'd Miss Nancy's fadder and mudder. Dey war mighty rich. Some ob de real big bugs. Marse Jim used to know dem, an' come ober ter de plantation, an' eat an' drink wen he got ready, an' stay as long as he choose. Ole Cousins used to have wine at dere table ebery day, an' Marse Jim war mighty fon' ob dat wine, an' sometimes he would drink till he got quite boozy. Ole Cousins liked him bery well, till he foun' out he wanted his darter, an' den he didn't want him fer rags nor patches. But Miss Nancy war mighty headstrong, an' allers liked to hab her own way; an' dis time she got it. But didn't she step her foot inter it? Ole Johnson war mighty han'some, but when dat war said all war said. She run'd off an' got married, but wen she got down she war too spunkey to axe her pa for anything. Wen you war wid her, yer know she only took big bugs. But wen de war com'd 'roun' it tore her all ter pieces, an' now she's as pore as Job's turkey. I feel's right sorry fer her. Well, Robby, things is turned 'roun' mighty quare. Ole Mistus war up den, an' I war down; now, she's down, an' I'se up. But I pities her, 'cause she warn't so bad arter all. De wuss thing she eber did war to sell your mudder, an' she wouldn't hab done dat but she snatched de whip out ob her han' an gib her a lickin'. Now I belieb in my heart she war 'fraid ob your mudder arter dat. But we women had ter keep 'em from whippin' us, er dey'd all de time been libin' on our bones. She had no man ter whip us 'cept dat ole drunken husband ob hern, an' he war allers too drunk ter whip hisself. He jis' wandered off, an' I reckon he died in somebody's pore-house. He warn't no 'count nohow you fix it. Weneber I goes to town I carries her some garden sass, er a little milk an' butter. An' she's mighty glad ter git it. I ain't got nothin' agin her. She neber struck me a lick in her life, an' I belieb in praising de bridge dat carries me ober. Dem Yankees set me free, an' I thinks a powerful heap ob dem. But it does rile me ter see dese mean white men comin' down yere an' settin' up dere grog-shops, tryin' to fedder dere nests sellin' licker to pore culled people. Deys de bery kine ob men dat used ter keep dorgs to ketch de runaways. I'd be chokin' fer a drink 'fore I'd eber spen' a cent wid dem, a spreadin' dere traps to git de black folks' money. You jis' go down town 'fore sun up to-morrer mornin' an' you see ef dey don't hab dem bars open to sell dere drams to dem hard workin' culled people 'fore dey goes ter work. I thinks some niggers is mighty big fools."

"Oh, Aunt Linda, don't run down your race. Leave that for the white people."

"I ain't runnin' down my people. But a fool's a fool, wether he's white or black. An' I think de nigger who will spen' his hard-earned money in dese yere new grogshops is de biggest kine ob a fool, an' I sticks ter dat. You know we didn't hab all dese low places in slave times. An' what is dey fer, but to get the people's money. An' its a shame how dey do sling de licker 'bout 'lection times."

"But don't the temperance people want the colored people to vote the temperance ticket?"

"Yes, but some ob de culled people gits mighty skittish ef dey tries to git em to vote dare ticket 'lection time, an' keeps dem at a proper distance wen de 'lection's ober. Some ob dem say dere's a trick behine it, an' don't want to tech it. Dese white folks could do a heap wid de culled folks ef dey'd only treat em right."

"When our people say there is a trick behind it," said Robert, "I only wish they could see the trick before it – the trick of worse than wasting their money, and of keeping themselves and families poorer and more ignorant than there is any need for them to be."

"Well, Bobby, I beliebs we might be a people ef it warn't for dat mizzable drink. An' Robby, I jis' tells yer what I wants; I wants some libe man to come down yere an' splain things ter dese people. I don't mean a politic man, but a man who'll larn dese people how to bring up dere chillen, to keep our gals straight, an' our boys from runnin' in de saloons an' gamblin' dens."

"Don't your preachers do that?" asked Robert.

"Well, some ob dem does, an' some ob dem doesn't. An' wen dey preaches, I want dem to practice wat dey preach. Some ob dem says dey's called, but I jis' thinks laziness called some ob dem. An' I thinks since freedom come deres some mighty pore sticks set up for preachers. Now dere's John Anderson, Tom's brudder; you 'member Tom."

"Yes; as brave a fellow and as honest as ever stepped in shoe leather."

"Well, his brudder war mighty diff'rent. He war down in de lower kentry wen de war war ober. He war mighty smart, an' had a good head-piece, an' a orful glib tongue. He set up store an' sole whisky, an' made a lot ob money. Den he wanted ter go to de legislatur. Now what should he do but make out he'd got 'ligion, an' war called to preach. He had no more 'ligion dan my ole dorg. But he had money an' built a meetin' house, whar he could hole meeting, an' hab funerals; an' you know cullud folks is mighty great on funerals. Well dat jis' tuck wid de people, an' he got 'lected to de legislatur. Den he got a fine house, an' his ole wife warn't good 'nuff for him. Den dere war a young school-teacher, an' he begun cuttin' his eyes at her. But she war as deep in de mud as he war in de mire, an' he jis' gib up his ole wife and married her, a fusty thing. He war a mean ole hypocrit, an' I wouldn't sen' fer him to bury my cat. Robby, I'se down on dese kine ob preachers like a thousand bricks."

"Well, Aunt Linda, all the preachers are not like him."

"No; I knows dat; not by a jug full. We's got some mighty good men down yere, an' we's glad when dey comes, an' orful sorry when dey goes 'way. De las preacher we had war a mighty good man. He didn't like too much hollerin'."

"Perhaps," said Robert, "he thought it were best for only one to speak at a time."

"I specs so. His wife war de nicest and sweetest lady dat eber I did see. None ob yer airish, stuck up folks, like a tarrapin carryin' eberything on its back. She used ter hab meetins fer de mudders, an' larn us how to raise our chillen, an' talk so putty to de chillen. I sartinly did lub dat woman."

"Where is she now?"asked Robert.

"De Conference moved dem 'bout thirty miles from yere. Deys gwine to hab a big meetin' ober dere next Sunday. Don't you 'member dem meetins we used to hab in de woods? We don't hab to hide like we did den. But it don't seem as ef de people had de same good 'ligion we had den. 'Pears like folks is took up wid makin' money an' politics."

"Well, Aunt Linda, don't you wish those good old days would come back?"

"No, chile; neber! neber! Wat fer you take me? I'd ruther lib in a corn-crib. Freedom needn't keep me outer heben; an' ef I'se sich a fool as ter lose my 'ligion cause I'se free, I oughtn' ter git dere."

"But, Aunt Linda, if old Miss were able to take care of you, wouldn't you just as leave be back again?"

There was a faint quiver of indignation in Aunt Linda's voice, as she replied:–

"Don't yer want yer freedom? Well I wants ter pat my free foot. Halleluyah! But, Robby, I wants yer ter go ter dat big meetin' de wuss kine."

"How will I get there?" asked Robert.

"Oh, dat's all right. My ole man's got two ob de nicest mules you eber set yer eyes on. It'll jis' do yer good ter look at dem. I 'spect you'll see some ob yer ole frens dere. Dere's a nice settlemen' of cullud folks ober dere, an' I wants yer to come an' bring dat young lady. I wants dem folks to see wat nice folks I kin bring to de meetin'. I hope's yer didn't lose all your 'ligion in de army."

"Oh, I hope not," replied Robert.

"Oh, chile, yer mus' be shore 'bout dat. I don't want yer to ride hope's hoss down to torment. Now be shore an' come to-morrer an' bring dat young lady, an' take supper wid me. I'se all on nettles to see dat chile."

Chapter 19

Striking Contrasts

THE next day, Robert, accompanied by Iola, went to the settlement to take supper with Aunt Linda, and a very luscious affair it was. Her fingers had not lost their skill since she had tasted the sweets of freedom. Her biscuits were just as light and flaky as ever. Her jelly was as bright as amber, and her preserves were perfectly delicious. After she had set the table she stood looking in silent admiration, chuckling to herself: "Ole Mistus can't set sich a table as dat. She ought'er be yere to see it. Specs 'twould make her mouf water. Well, I mus' let by-gonesbe by-gones. But dis yere freedom's mighty good."

Aunt Linda had invited Uncle Daniel, and, wishing to give him a pleasant surprise, she had refrained from telling him that Robert Johnson was the one she wished him to meet.

"Do you know dis gemmen?" said Aunt Linda to Uncle Daniel, when the latter arrived.

"Well, I can't say's I do. My eyes is gittin dim, an I disremembers him."

"Now jis' you look right good at him. Don't yer 'member him?"

Uncle Daniel looked puzzled and, slowly scanning Robert's features, said: "He do look like somebody I used ter know, but I can't make him out ter save my life. I don't know whar to place him. Who is de gemmen, ennyhow?"

"Why, Uncle Dan'el," replied Aunt Linda, "dis is Robby; Miss Nancy's bad, mischeebous Robby, dat war allers playin' tricks on me."

"Well, shore's I'se born, ef dis ain't our ole Bobby!" exclaimed Uncle Daniel, delightedly. "Why, chile, whar did yer come from? Thought you war dead an' buried long 'go."

"Why, Uncle Daniel, did you send anybody to kill me?" asked Robert, laughingly.

"Oh, no'n 'deed, chile! but I yeard dat you war killed in de battle, an' I never 'spected ter see you agin."

"Well, here I am," replied Robert, "large as life, and just as natural. And this young lady, Uncle Daniel, I believe is my niece." As he spoke he turned to Iola.

"Do you remember my mother?"

"Oh, yes," said Uncle Daniel, looking intently at Iola as she stepped forward and cordially gave him her hand.

"Well, I firmly believe," continued Robert, "that this is the daughter of the little girl whom Miss Nancy sold away with my mother."

"Well, I'se rale glad ter see her. She puts me mighty much in mine ob dem days wen we war all young togedder; wen Miss Nancy sed Harriet war too high fer her. It jis' seems like yisterday wen I yeard Miss Nancy say no house could flourish whar dere war two mistresses.[68] Well, Mr. Robert – "

"Oh, no, no, Uncle Daniel," interrupted Robert, "don't say that! Call me Robby or Bob, just as you used to."

"Well, Bobby, I'se glad klar from de bottom of my heart ter see yer."

"Even if you wouldn't go with us when we left?"

"Oh, Bobby, dem war mighty tryin' times. You boys didn't know it, but Marster Robert hab giben me a bag ob money ter take keer ob, an' I promised him I'd do it an' I had ter be ez good ez my word."

"Oh, Uncle Daniel, why didn't you tell us boys all about it? We could have helped you take care of it."

"Now, wouldn't dat hab bin smart ter let on ter you chaps, an' hab you huntin' fer it from Dan ter Barsheba?[69] I specs some ob you would bin a rootin' fer it yit!"

Notes

[68] *Original reads*: Miss Nancy sed 'Harriet war too high fer her.' It jis' seems like yisterday wen I yeard Miss Nancy say 'No house could flourish whar dere war two mistresses.' [ed.].

[69] *from Dan ter Barsheba* a great distance; from the Biblical phrase, "from Dan to Beersheba," which describes the territories of the Tribes of Israel (see Judges 20:1).

"Well, Uncle Daniel, we were young then; I can't tell what we would have done if we had found it. But we are older now."

"Yes, yer older, but I wouldn't put it pas' yer eben now, ef yer foun' out whar it war."

"Yes," said Iola, laughing, "they say 'caution is the parent of safety.'"

"Money's a mighty tempting thing," said Robert, smiling.

"But, Robby, dere's nothin' like a klar conscience; a klar conscience, Robby!"

Just then Aunt Linda, who had been completing the preparations for her supper, entered the room with her husband, and said, "Salters, let me interdoos you ter my fren', Mr. Robert Johnson, an' his niece, Miss Leroy."

"Why, is it possible," exclaimed Robert, rising, and shaking hands, "that you are Aunt Linda's husband?"

"Dat's what de parson sed," replied Salters.

"I thought," pursued Robert, "that your name was John Andrews. It was such when you were in my company."

"All de use I'se got fer dat name is ter git my money wid it; an' wen dat's done, all's done. Got 'nuff ob my ole Marster in slave times, widout wearin' his name in freedom. Wen I got done wid him, I got done wid his name. Wen I 'listed, I war John Andrews; and wen I gits my pension, I'se John Andrews; but now Salters is my name, an' I likes it better."

"But how came you to be Aunt Linda's husband? Did you get married since the war?"

"Lindy an' me war married long 'fore de war. But my ole Marster sole me away from her an' our little gal, an' den sole her chile ter somebody else. Arter freedom, I hunted up our little gal, an' foun' her. She war a big woman den. Den I com'd right back ter dis place an' foun' Lindy. She hedn't married agin, nuther hed I; so we jis' let de parson marry us out er de book; an' we war mighty glad ter git togedder agin, an' feel hitched togedder fer life."

"Well, Uncle Daniel," said Robert, turning the conversation toward him, "you and Uncle Ben wouldn't go with us, but you came out all right at last."

"Yes, indeed," said Aunt Linda, "Ben got inter a stream of luck. Arter freedom com'd, de people had a heap of fath in Ben; an' wen dey wanted someone[70] to go ter Congress dey jist voted for Ben ter go. An' he went, too. An' wen Salters went to Washin'ton to git his pension, who should he see dere wid dem big men but our Ben, lookin' jist as big as any ob dem."

"An' it did my ole eyes good jist ter see it," broke in Salters; "if I couldn't go dere myself, I war mighty glad to see someone[71] ob my people dat could. I felt like de boy who, wen somebody said he war gwine to slap off his face, said, 'Yer kin slap off my face, but I'se got a big brudder, an' you can't slap off his face.' I went to see him 'fore I lef, and he war jist de same as he war wen we war boys togedder. He hadn't got de big head a bit."

"I reckon Mirandy war mighty sorry she didn't stay wid him. I know I should be," said Aunt Linda.

"Uncle Daniel," asked Robert, "are you still preaching?"

"Yes, chile, I'se still firing off de Gospel gun."

"I hear some of the Northern folks are down here teaching theology, that is, teaching young men how to preach. Why don't you study theology?"

Notes

[70] *Original reads*: some one [ed.].

[71] *Original reads*: some one [ed.].

"Look a yere, boy, I'se been a preach in' dese thirty years, an' you come yere a tellin' me 'bout studying yore ologies. I larn'd my 'ology at de foot ob de cross. You bin dar?"

"Dear Uncle Daniel," said Iola, "the moral aspect of the nation would be changed if it would learn at the same cross to subordinate the spirit of caste to the spirit of Christ."

"Does yer 'member Miss Nancy's Harriet," asked Aunt Linda, "dat she sole away kase she wouldn't let her whip her? Well, we think dis is Harriet's gran'chile. She war sole away from her mar, an' now she's a lookin' fer her."

"Well, I hopes she may fine her," replied Salters. "I war sole 'way from my mammy wen I war eighteen mont's ole, an' I wouldn't know her now from a bunch ob turnips."

"I," said Iola, "am on my way South seeking for my mother, and I shall not give up until I find her."

"Come," said Aunt Linda, "we mustn't stan' yer talkin', or de grub'll git cole. Come, frens, sit down, an' eat some ob my pore supper."

Aunt Linda sat at the table in such a flutter of excitement that she could hardly eat, but she gazed with intense satisfaction on her guests. Robert sat on her right hand, contrasting Aunt Linda's pleasant situation with the old days in Mrs. Johnson's kitchen, where he had played his pranks upon her, and told her the news of the war.

Over Iola there stole a spirit of restfulness. There was something so motherly in Aunt Linda's manner that it seemed to recall the bright, sunshiny days when she used to nestle in Mam Liza's arms, in her own happy home. The conversation was full of army reminiscences and recollections of the days of slavery. Uncle Daniel was much interested, and, as they rose from the table, exclaimed:–

"Robby, seein' yer an' hearin' yer talk, almos' puts new springs inter me. I feel 'mos' like I war gittin' younger."

After the supper, Salters and his guests returned to the front room, which Aunt Linda regarded with so much pride, and on which she bestowed so much care.

"Well, Captin," said Salters, "I neber 'spected ter see you agin. Do you know de las' time I seed yer? Well, you war on a stretcher, an' four ob us war carryin' you ter de hospital. War you much hurt?

"No," replied Robert, "it was only a flesh wound; and this young lady nursed me so carefully that I soon got over it."

"Is dat de way you foun' her?"

"Yes, Andrews," –

"Salters, ef you please," interrupted Salters. I'se only Andrews wen I gits my money."

"Well, Salters," continued Robert, "our freedom was a costly thing. Did you know that Captain Sybil was killed in one of the last battles of the war? These young chaps, who are taking it so easy, don't know the hardships through which we older ones passed. But all the battles are not fought, nor all the victories won. The colored man has escaped from one slavery, and I don't want him to fall into another. I want the young folks to keep their brains clear, and their right arms strong, to fight the battles of life manfully, and take their places alongside of every other people in this country. And I cannot see what is to hinder them if they get a chance."

"I don't nuther," said Salters. "I don't see dat dey drinks any more dan anybody else, nor dat dere is any meanness or debilment dat a black man kin do dat a white man can't keep step wid him."

"Yes," assented Robert, "but while a white man is stealing a thousand dollars, a black man is getting into trouble taking a few chickens."

"All that may be true," said Iola, "but there are some things a white man can do that we cannot afford to do."

"I beliebs eberybody, Norf and Souf, is lookin' at us; an' some ob dem ain't got no good blood fer us, nohow you fix it," said Salters.

"I specs cullud folks mus' hab done something" interposed Aunt Linda.

"O, nonsense," said Robert. "I don't think they are any worse than the white people. I don't believe, if we had the power, we would do any more lynching, burning, and murdering than they do."

"Dat's so," said Aunt Linda, "it's ralely orful how our folks hab been murdered sence de war. But I don't think dese young folks is goin' ter take things as we's allers done."

"We war cowed down from the beginnin'," said Uncle Daniel, "but dese young folks ain't comin' up dat way."

"No," said Salters, "fer one night arter some ob our pore people had been killed, an' some ob our women had run'd away 'bout seventeen miles, my gran'son, looking me squar in de face, said: 'Ain't you got five fingers? Can't you pull a trigger as well as a white man?' I tell yer, Cap, dat jis' got to me, an' I made up my mine dat my boy should neber call me a coward."

"It is not to be expected," said Robert, "that these young people are going to put up with things as we did, when we weren't permitted to hold a meeting by ourselves, or to own a club or learn to read."

"I tried," said Salters, "to git a little out'er de book wen I war in de army. On Sundays I sometimes takes a book an' tries to make out de words, but my eyes is gittin' dim an' de letters all run togedder, an' I gits sleepy, an' ef yer wants to put me to sleep jis' put a book in my han'. But wen it comes to gittin' out a stan' ob cotton, an' plantin' corn, I'se dere all de time. But dat gran'son ob mine is smart as a steel trap. I specs he'll be a preacher."

Salters looked admiringly at his grandson, who sat grinning in the corner, munching a pear he had brought from the table.

"Yes," said Aunt Linda, "his fadder war killed by the Secesh, one night, comin' home from a politic meetin', an' his pore mudder died a few weeks arter, an' we mean to make a man ob him."

"He's got to larn to work fust," said Salters, "an' den ef he's right smart I'se gwine ter sen' him ter college. An' ef he can't get a libin' one way, he kin de oder."

"Yes," said Iola, "I hope he will turn out an excellent young man, for the greatest need of the race is noble, earnest men, and true women."

"Job," said Salters, turning to his grandson, "tell Jake ter hitch up de mules, an' you stay dere an' help him. We's all gwine ter de big meetin'. Yore grandma hab set her heart on goin', an' it'll be de same as a spell ob sickness ef she don't hab a chance to show her bes' bib an' tucker. That ole gal's as proud as a peacock."

"Now, John Salters," exclaimed Aunt Linda, "ain't you 'shamed ob yourself? Allers tryin' to poke fun at yer pore wife. Never mine; wait till I'se gone, an' you'll miss me."

"Ef I war single," said Salters, "I could git a putty young gal, but it wouldn't be so easy wid you."

"Why not?" said Iola, smiling.

"'Cause young men don't want ole hens, an' ole men want young pullets," was Salter's reply.

"Robby, honey," said Aunt Linda, "when you gits a wife, don't treat her like dat man treats me."

"Oh, his head's level," answered Robert; "at least it was in the army."

"Dat's jis' de way; you see dat, Miss Iola? One man takin' up for de oder. But I'll be eben wid you bof. I must go now an' git ready."

Iola laughed. The homely enjoyment of that evening was very welcome to her after the trying scenes through which she had passed. Further conversation was interrupted by the appearance of the wagon, drawn by two fine mules. John Salters stopped joking his wife to admire his mules.

"Jis' look at dem," he said. "Ain't dey beauties? I bought 'em out ob my bounty-money. Arter de war war ober I had a little money, an' I war gwine ter rent a plantation on sheers an' git out a good stan' ob cotton. Cotton war bringin' orful high prices den, but Lindy said to me, 'Now, John, you'se got a lot ob money, an' you'd better salt it down. I'd ruther lib on a little piece ob lan' ob my own dan a big piece ob somebody else's. Well, I says to Lindy, I dun know nuthin' 'bout buyin' lan', an' I'se 'fraid arter I'se done buyed it an' put all de marrer ob dese bones in it, dat somebody's far-off cousin will come an' say de title ain't good, an' I'll lose it all."

"You're right thar, John," said Uncle Daniel. "White man's so unsartain, black man's nebber safe."

"But somehow," continued Salters, "Lindy warn't satisfied wid rentin', so I buyed a piece ob lan', an' I'se glad now I'se got it. Lindy's got a lot ob gumption; knows most as much as a man. She ain't got dat long head fer nuffin. She's got lots ob sense, but I don't like to tell her so."

"Why not?" asked Iola. "Do you think it would make her feel too happy?"

"Well, it don't do ter tell you women how much we thinks ob you. It sets you up too much. Ole Gundover's overseer war my marster, an' he used ter lib in dis bery house. I'se fixed it up sence I'se got it. Now I'se better off dan he is, 'cause he tuck to drink, an' all his frens is gone, an' he's in de pore-house."

Just then Linda came to the door with her baskets.

"Now, Lindy, ain't you ready yet? Do hurry up."

"Yes, I'se ready, but things wouldn't go right ef you didn't hurry me."

"Well, put your chicken fixins an' cake right in yere. Captin, you'll ride wid me, an' de young lady an' my ole woman'll take de back seat. Uncle Dan'el, dere's room for you ef you'll go."

"No, I thank you. It's time fer ole folks to go to bed. Good night! An', Bobby, I hopes to see you agin'."

Chapter 20

A Revelation

It was a lovely evening for the journey. The air was soft and balmy. The fields and hedges were redolent with flowers. Not a single cloud obscured the brightness of the moon or the splendor of the stars. The ancient trees were festooned with moss, which hung like graceful draperies. Ever and anon a startled hare glided over the path, and whip-poor-wills and crickets broke the restful silence of the night. Robert rode quietly along, quaffing the beauty of the scene and thinking of his boyish days, when he gathered nuts and wild plums in those woods; he also indulged pleasant reminiscences of later years, when, with Uncle Daniel and Tom Anderson, he attended the secret prayer-meetings. Iola rode along, conversing with Aunt Linda, amused and interested at the quaintness of her speech and the shrewdness of her intellect. To her the ride was delightful.

"Does yer know dis place, Robby," asked Aunt Linda, as they passed an old resort.

"I should think I did," replied Robert. "It is the place where we held our last prayer-meeting."

"An' dere's dat ole broken pot we used, ter tell 'bout de war. But warn't ole Miss hoppin' wen she foun' out you war goin' to de war! I thought she'd go almos' wile. Now, own up, Robby, didn't you feel kine ob mean to go off widout eben biddin' her good bye? An' I ralely think ole Miss war fon' ob yer. Now, own up, honey, didn't yer feel a little down in de mouf wen yer lef' her."

"Not much," responded Robert. "I only thought she was getting paid back for selling my mother."

"Dat's so, Robby! yore mudder war a likely[72] gal, wid long black hair, an' kine ob ginger-bread color. An' you neber hearn tell ob her sence dey sole her to Georgia?"

"Never," replied Robert, "but I would give everything I have on earth to see her once more. I *do* hope, if she is living, that I may meet her before I die."

"You's right, boy, cause she lub'd you as she lub'd her own life. Many a time hes she set in my ole cabin an' cried 'bout yer wen you war fas' asleep. It's all ober now, but I'se gwine to hole up fer dem Yankees dat gib me my freedom, an' sent dem nice ladies from de Norf to gib us some sense. Some ob dese folks calls em nigger teachers, an' won't hab nuffin to do wid 'em, but I jis' thinks dey's splendid. But dere's some triflin' niggers down yere who'll sell der votes for almost nuffin. Does you 'member Jake Williams an' Gundover's Tom? Well dem two niggers is de las' ob pea-time. Dey's mighty small pertaters an' few in a hill."

"Oh, Aunt Linda," said Robert, "don't call them niggers. They are our own people."

"Dey ain't my kine ob people. I jis' calls em niggers, an' niggers I means; an' de bigges' kine ob niggers. An' if my John war sich a nigger I'd whip him an' leave him."

"An' what would I be a doin'," queried John, suddenly rousing up at the mention of his name.

"Standing still and taking it, I suppose," said Iola, who had been quietly listening to and enjoying the conversation.

"Yes, an' I'd ketch myself stan'in' still an' takin' it," was John's plucky response.

"Well, you oughter, ef you's mean enough to wote dat ticket ter put me back inter slavery," was Aunt Linda's parting shot. "Robby," she continued, "you 'member Miss Nancy's Jinnie?"

"Of course I do," said Robert.

"She married Mr. Gundover's Dick. Well, dere warn't much git up an' go 'bout him. So, wen 'lection time com'd, de man he war workin' fer tole him ef he woted de radical ticket he'd turn him off. Well, Jinnie war so 'fraid he'd do it, dat she jis' follered him fer days."

"Poor fellow!" exclaimed Robert. "How did he come out?"

"He certainly was between two fires," interposed Iola.

"Oh, Jinnie gained de day. She jis' got her back up, and said, 'Now ef yer wote dat ticket ter put me back inter slavery, you take yore rags an' go.' An' Dick jis' woted de radical ticket. Jake Williams went on de Secesh side, woted whar he thought he'd git his taters, but he got fooled es slick es greese."

"How was that?" asked Robert.

"Some ob dem folks, dat I 'spects buyed his wote, sent him some flour an' sugar. So one night his wife hab company ter tea. Dey made a big spread, an' put a lot ob sugar on de table fer supper, an' Tom jis' went fer dat sugar. He put a lot in his tea. But somehow it didn't tase right, an' wen dey come ter fine out what war de matter, dey hab sent him a barrel ob san' wid some sugar on top, an' wen de sugar war all gone de san' war dare. Wen I yeard it, I jis' split my sides a larfin. It war too good to keep; an' wen it got roun', Jake war as mad as a March hare.[73] But it sarved him right."

"Well, Aunt Linda, you musn't be too hard on Uncle Jake; you know he's getting old."

Notes

[72] *likely* attractive.

[73] *mad as a March hare* exhibiting erratic behavior like that of the hare observed during the spring mating season.

"Well he ain't too ole ter do right. He ain't no older dan Uncle Dan'el. An' I yered dey offered him $500 ef he'd go on dere side. An' Uncle Dan'el wouldn't tech it. An' dere's Uncle Job's wife; why didn't she go dat way? She war down on Job's meanness."

"What did she do?"

"Wen 'lection time 'rived, he com'd home bringing some flour an' meat; an' he says ter Aunt Polly, 'Ole woman, I got dis fer de wote.' She jis' picked up dat meat an' flour an' sent it sailin' outer doors, an' den com'd back an' gib him a good tongue-lashin'. 'Oder people,' she said, 'a wotin' ter lib good, an' you a sellin' yore wote! Ain't you got 'nuff ob ole Marster, an' ole Marster bin cuttin' you up? It shan't stay yere.' An' so she wouldn't let de things stay in de house."

"What did Uncle Job do?"

"He jis' stood dere an' cried."

"And didn't you feel sorry for him?" asked Iola.

"Not a bit! he hedn't no business ter be so shabby."

"But, Aunt Linda," pursued Iola, "if it were shabby for an ignorant colored man to sell his vote, wasn't it shabbier for an intelligent white man to buy it?"

"You see," added Robert, "all the shabbiness is not on our side."

"I knows dat," said Aunt Linda, "but I can't help it. I wants my people to wote right, an' to think somethin' ob demselves."

"Well, Aunt Linda, they say in every flock of sheep there will be one that's scabby," observed Iola.

"Dats so! But I ain't got no use fer scabby sheep."[74]

"Lindy," cried John, "we's most dar! Don't you yere dat singin'? Dey's begun a'ready."

"Neber mine," said Aunt Linda, "sometimes de las' ob de wine is de bes'."

Thus discoursing they had beguiled the long hours of the night and made their long journey appear short.

Very soon they reached the church, a neat, commodious, frame building, with a blue ceiling, white walls within and without, and large windows with mahogany-colored facings. It was a sight full of pathetic interest to see that group which gathered from miles around. They had come to break bread with each other, relate their experiences, and tell of their hopes of heaven. In that meeting were remnants of broken families – mothers who had been separated from their children before the war, husbands who had not met their wives for years. After the bread had been distributed and the handshaking was nearly over, Robert raised the hymn which Iola had sung for him when he was recovering from his wounds, and Iola, with her clear, sweet tones, caught up the words and joined him in the strain. When the hymn was finished a dear old mother rose from her seat. Her voice was quite strong. With still a lingering light and fire in her eye, she said:–

"I rise, bredren an' sisters, to say I'm on my solemn march to glory."

"Amen!" "Glory!" came from a number of voices.

"I'se had my trials an' temptations, my ups an' downs; but I feels I'll soon be in one ob de many mansions.[75] If it hadn't been for dat hope I 'spects I would have broken down long ago. I'se bin through de deep waters, but dey didn't overflow me; I'se bin in de fire, but de smell ob it isn't on my garments. Bredren an' sisters, it war a drefful time when I war tored away from my pore little chillen."

Notes

[74] *scabby sheep* a sheep with an infectious pox called scab-mouth.

[75] *mansions* places in Heaven.

"Dat's so!" exclaimed a chorus of voices. Some of her hearers moaned, others rocked to and fro, as thoughts of similar scenes in their own lives arose before them.

"When my little girl," continued the speaker, "took hole ob my dress an' begged me ter let her go wid me, an' I couldn't do it, it mos' broke my heart. I had a little boy, an' wen my mistus sole me she kep' him. She carried on a boardin' house. Many's the time I hab stole out at night an' seen dat chile an' sleep'd wid him in my arms tell mos' day. Bimeby de people I libed wid got hard up fer money, an' dey sole me one way an' my pore little gal de oder; an' I neber laid my eyes on my pore chillen sence den. But, honeys, let de wind blow high or low, I 'spects to outwedder de storm an' anchor by'm bye in bright glory. But I'se bin a prayin' fer one thing, an' I beliebs I'll git it; an' dat is dat I may see my chillen 'fore I die. Pray fer me dat I may hole out an' hole on, an' neber make a shipwrack ob faith, an' at las' fine my way from earth to glory."

Having finished her speech, she sat down and wiped away the tears that flowed all the more copiously as she remembered her lost children. When she rose to speak her voice and manner instantly arrested Robert's attention. He found his mind reverting to the scenes of his childhood. As she proceeded his attention became riveted on her. Unbidden tears filled his eyes and great sobs shook his frame. He trembled in every limb. Could it be possible that after years of patient search through churches, papers, and inquiring friends, he had accidentally stumbled on his mother – the mother who, long years ago, had pillowed his head upon her bosom and left her parting kiss upon his lips? How should he reveal himself to her? Might not sudden joy do what years of sorrow had failed to accomplish? Controlling his feelings as best he could, he rose to tell his experience. He referred to the days when they used to hold their meetings in the lonely woods and gloomy swamps. How they had prayed for freedom and plotted to desert to the Union army; and continuing, he said: "Since then, brethren and sisters, I have had my crosses and trials, but I try to look at the mercies. Just think what it was then and what it is now! How many of us, since freedom has come, have been looking up our scattered relatives. I have just been over to visit my old mistress, Nancy Johnson, and to see if I could get some clue to my long-lost mother, who was sold from me nearly thirty years ago."

Again there was a chorus of moans.

On resuming, Robert's voice was still fuller of pathos.

"When," he said, "I heard that dear old mother tell her experience it seemed as if someone[76] had risen from the dead. She made me think of my own dear mother, who used to steal out at night to see me, fold me in her arms, and then steal back again to her work. After she was sold away I never saw her face again by daylight. I have been looking for her ever since the war, and I think at last I have got on the right track. If Mrs. Johnson, who kept the boarding-house in C——, is the one who sold that dear old mother from her son, then she is the one I am looking for, and I am the son she has been praying for."

The dear old mother raised her eyes. They were clear and tearless. An expression of wonder, hope, and love flitted over her face. It seemed as if her youth were suddenly renewed and, bounding from her seat, she rushed to the speaker in a paroxysm of joy. "Oh, Robby! Robby! is dis you? Is dat my pore, dear boy I'se been prayin' 'bout all dese years? Oh, glory! glory!" And overflowing with joyous excitement she threw her arms

Notes

[76] *Original reads*: some one [ed.].

around him, looking the very impersonation of rapturous content. It was a happy time. Mothers whose children had been torn from them in the days of slavery knew how to rejoice in her joy. The young people caught the infection of the general happiness and rejoiced with them that rejoiced. There were songs of rejoicing and shouts of praise. The undertone of sadness which had so often mingled with their songs gave place to strains of exultation; and tears of tender sympathy flowed from eyes which had often been blurred by anguish. The child of many prayers and tears was restored to his mother.

Iola stood by the mother's side, smiling, and weeping tears of joy. When Robert's mother observed Iola, she said to Robert, "Is dis yore wife?"

"Oh, no," replied Robert, "but I believe she is your grandchild, the daughter of the little girl who was sold away from you so long ago. She is on her way to the farther South in search of her mother."

"Is she? Dear chile! I hope she'll fine her! She puts me in mine ob my pore little Marie. Well, I'se got one chile, an' I means to keep on prayin' tell I fine my daughter. I'm *so* happy! I feel's like a new woman!"

"My dear mother," said Robert, "now that I have found you, I mean to hold you fast just as long as you live. Ever since the war I have been trying to find out if you were living, but all efforts failed. At last, I thought I would come and hunt you myself and, now that I have found you, I am going to take you home to live with me, and to be as happy as the days are long. I am living in the North, and doing a good business there. I want you to see joy according to all the days wherein you have seen sorrow. I do hope this young lady will find *her* ma and that, when found, she will prove to be your daughter!"

"Yes, pore, dear chile! I specs her mudder's heart's mighty hungry fer her. I does hope she's my gran'chile."

Tenderly and caressingly Iola bent over the happy mother, with her heart filled with mournful memories of her own mother.

Aunt Linda was induced to stay until the next morning, and then gladly assisted Robert's mother in arranging for her journey northward. The friends who had given her a shelter in their hospitable home, learned to value her so much that it was with great reluctance they resigned her to the care of her son. Aunt Linda was full of bustling activity, and her spirits overflowed with good humor.

"Now, Harriet," she said, as they rode along on their return journey, "you mus' jis' thank me fer finin' yore chile, 'cause I got him to come to dat big meetin' wid me."

"Oh, Lindy," she cried, "I'se glad from de bottom ob my heart ter see you's all. I com'd out dere ter git a blessin', an' I'se got a double po'tion. De frens I war libin' wid war mighty good ter me. Dey lib'd wid me in de lower kentry, an' arter de war war ober I stopped wid 'em and helped take keer ob de chillen; an' when dey com'd up yere dey brought me wid 'em. I'se com'd a way I didn't know, but I'se mighty glad I'se com'd."

"Does you know dis place?" asked Aunt Linda, as they approached the settlement.

"No'n 'deed I don't. It's all new ter me."

"Well, dis is whar I libs. Ain't you mighty tired? I feels a little stiffish. Dese bones is gittin' ole."

"Dat's so! But I'se mighty glad I'se lib'd to see my boy 'fore I crossed ober de riber. An' now I feel like ole Simeon."[77]

Notes

[77] *Simeon* see Luke 2:25–35; Simeon was promised by the Holy Spirit that he would not die until he had seen Christ.

"But, mother," said Robert, "if you are ready to go, I am not willing to let you. I want you to stay ever so long where I can see you."

A bright smile overspread her face. Robert's words reassured and gladdened her heart. She was well satisfied to have a pleasant aftermath from life on this side of the river.

After arriving home Linda's first thought was to prepare dinner for her guests. But, before she began her work of preparation, she went to the cupboard to get a cup of home-made wine.

"Here," she said, filling three glasses, "is some wine I made myself from dat grape-vine out dere. Don't it look nice and clar? Jist taste it. It's fus'-rate."

"No, thank you," said Robert. "I'm a temperance man, and never take anything which has alcohol in it."

"Oh, dis ain't got a bit ob alcohol in it. I made it myself."

"But, Aunt Linda, you didn't make the law which ferments grape-juice and makes it alcohol."

"But, Robby, ef alcohol's so bad, w'at made de Lord put it here?"

"Aunt Lindy," said Iola, "I heard a lady say that there were two things the Lord didn't make. One is sin, and the other alcohol."

"Why, Aunt Linda," said Robert, "there are numbers of things the Lord has made that I wouldn't touch with a pair of tongs."

"What are they?"

"Rattlesnakes, scorpions, and moccasins."

"Oh, sho!"

"Aunt Linda," said Iola, "the Bible says that the wine at last will bite like a serpent[78] and sting like an adder."

"And, Aunt Linda," added Robert, "as I wouldn't wind a serpent around my throat, I don't want to put something inside of it which will bite like a serpent and sting as an adder."

"I reckon Robby's right," said his mother, setting down her glass and leaving the wine unfinished. "You young folks knows a heap more dan we ole folks."

"Well," declared Aunt Linda, "you all is temp'rence to de backbone. But what could I do wid my wine ef we didn't drink it?"

"Let it turn to vinegar, and sign the temperance pledge," replied Robert.

"I don't keer 'bout it myself, but I don't 'spect John would be willin' ter let it go, 'cause he likes it a heap."

"Then you must give it up for his sake and Job's," said Robert. "They may learn to like it too well."

"You know, Aunt Linda," said Iola, "people don't get to be drunkards all at once. And you wouldn't like to feel, if Job should learn to drink, that you helped form his appetite."

"Dat' so! I beliebs I'll let dis turn to winegar, an' not make any more."

"That's right, Aunt Linda. I hope you'll hold to it," said Robert, encouragingly.

Very soon Aunt Linda had an excellent dinner prepared. After it was over Robert went with Iola to C——, where her friend, the bishop, was awaiting her return. She told him the wonderful story of Robert's finding his mother, and of her sweet, childlike faith.

Notes

[78] *the wine … will bite like a serpent* Proverbs 23:32.

The bishop, a kind, fatherly man, said, "Miss Iola, I hope that such happiness is in store for you. My dear child, still continue to pray and trust. I am old-fashioned enough to believe in prayer. I knew an old lady living in Illinois, who was a slave. Her son got a chance to come North and beg money to buy his mother. The mother was badly treated, and made up her mind to run away. But before she started she thought she would kneel down to pray. And something, she said, reasoned within her, and whispered, 'Stand still and see what I am going to do for you.' So real was it to her that she unpacked her bundle and desisted from her flight. Strange as it may appear to you, her son returned, bringing with him money enough to purchase her freedom, and she was redeemed from bondage. Had she persisted in running away she might have been lost in the woods and have died, exhausted by starvation. But she believed, she trusted, and was delivered. Her son took her North, where she could find a resting place for the soles of her feet."

That night Iola and the bishop left for the South.

Chapter 21

A Home for Mother

AFTER Iola had left the settlement, accompanied by Robert as far as the town, it was a pleasant satisfaction for the two old friends to settle themselves down, and talk of times past, departed friends, and long-forgotten scenes.

"What," said Mrs. Johnson, as we shall call Robert's mother, "hab become ob Miss Nancy's husband? Is he still a libin'?"

"Oh, he drunk hisself to death," responded Aunt Linda.

"He used ter be mighty handsome."

"Yes, but drink war his ruination."

"An' how's Miss Nancy?"

"Oh, she's com'd down migh'ly. She's pore as a church mouse. I thought 'twould com'd home ter her wen she sole yer 'way from yore chillen. Dere's nuffin goes ober de debil's back dat don't come under his belly. Do yo 'member Miss Nancy's fardder?"

"Ob course I does!"

"Well," said Aunt Linda, "he war a nice ole gemmen. Wen he died, I said de las' gemmen's dead, an' dere's noboddy ter step in his shoes."

"Pore Miss Nancy!" exclaimed Robert's mother. "I ain't nothin' agin her. But I wouldn't swap places wid her, 'cause I'se got my son; an' I beliebs he'll do a good part by me."

"Mother," said Robert, as he entered the room, "I've brought an old friend to see you. Do you remember Uncle Daniel?"

Uncle Daniel threw back his head, reached out his hand, and manifested his joy with "Well, Haryet! is dis you? I neber 'spected to see you in dese lower grouns! How does yer do? an' whar hab you bin all dis time?"

"O, I'se been tossin' roun' 'bout; but it's all com'd right at las'. I'se lib'd to see my boy 'fore I died."

"My wife an' boys is in glory," said Uncle Daniel. "But I 'spects to see 'em 'fore long. 'Cause I'se tryin' to dig deep, build sure, an' make my way from earth ter glory."

"Dat's de right kine ob talk, Dan'el. We ole folks ain't got long ter stay yere."

They chatted together until Job and Salters came home for supper. After they had eaten, Uncle Daniel said:–

"We'll hab a word ob prayer."

There, in that peaceful habitation, they knelt down, and mingled their prayers together, as they had done in bygone days, when they had met by stealth in lonely swamps or silent forests.

The next morning Robert and his mother started northward. They were well supplied with a bountiful luncheon by Aunt Linda, who had so thoroughly enjoyed their sojourn with her. On the next day he arrived in the city of P——, and took his mother to his boarding-house, until he could find a suitable home into which to install her. He soon came across one which just suited his taste, but when the agent discovered that Robert's mother was colored, he told him that the house had been previously engaged. In company with his mother he looked at several other houses in desirable neighborhoods, but they were constantly met with the answer, "The house is engaged," or, "We do not rent to colored people."

At length Robert went alone, and, finding a desirable house, engaged it, and moved into it. In a short time it was discovered that he was colored, and, at the behest of the local sentiment of the place, the landlord used his utmost endeavors to oust him, simply because he belonged to an unfashionable and unpopular race. At last he came across a landlord who was broad enough to rent him a good house, and he found a quiet resting place among a set of well-to-do and well-disposed people.

Chapter 22

Further Lifting of the Veil

In one of those fearful conflicts by which the Mississippi was freed from Rebel intrusion and opened to commerce, Harry was severely wounded, and forced to leave his place in the ranks for a bed in the hospital.

One day, as he lay in his bed, thinking of his former home in Mississippi and wondering if the chances of war would ever restore him to his loved ones, he fell into a quiet slumber. When he awoke he found a lady bending over him, holding in her hands some fruit and flowers. As she tenderly bent over Harry's bed their eyes met, and with a thrill of gladness they recognized each other.

"Oh, my son, my son!" cried Marie, trying to repress her emotion, as she took his wasted hand in hers, and kissed the pale cheeks that sickness and suffering had blanched. Harry was very weak, but her presence was a call to life. He returned the pressure of her hand, kissed it, and his eyes grew full of sudden light, as he murmured faintly, but joyfully:–

"Mamma; oh, mamma! have I found you at last?"

The effort was too much, and he immediately became unconscious.

Anxious, yet hopeful, Marie sat by the bedside of her son till consciousness was restored. Caressingly she bent over his couch, murmuring in her happiness the tenderest, sweetest words of motherly love. In Harry's veins flowed new life and vigor, calming the restlessness of his nerves.

As soon as possible Harry was carried to his mother's home; a home brought into the light of freedom by the victories of General Grant. Nursed by his mother's tender, loving care, he rapidly recovered, but, being too disabled to re-enter the army, he was honorably discharged.

Lorraine had taken Marie to Vicksburg, and there allowed her to engage in confectionery and preserving for the wealthy ladies of the city. He had at first attempted to refugee with her in Texas, but, being foiled in the attempt, he was compelled to enlist in the Confederate Army, and met his fate by being killed just before the surrender of Vicksburg.

"My dear son," Marie would say, as she bent fondly over him, "I am deeply sorry that you are wounded, but I am glad that the fortunes of war have brought us together. Poor Iola! I *do* wonder, what has become of her? Just as soon as this war is over I want you to search the country all over. Poor child! How my heart has ached for her!"

Time passed on. Harry and his mother searched and inquired for Iola, but no tidings of her reached them.

Having fully recovered his health, and seeing the great need of education for the colored people, Harry turned his attention toward them, and joined the new army of Northern teachers.

He still continued his inquiries for his sister, not knowing whether or not she had succumbed to the cruel change in her life. He thought she might have passed into the white basis for the sake of bettering her fortunes. Hope deferred, which had sickened his mother's heart, had only roused him to renewed diligence.

A school was offered him in Georgia, and thither he repaired, taking his mother with him. They were soon established in the city of A——. In hope of finding Iola he visited all the conferences of the Methodist Church, but for a long time his search was in vain.

"Mamma," said Harry, one day during his vacation, "there is to be a Methodist Conference in this State in the city of S——, about one hundred and fifty miles from here. I intend to go and renew my search for Iola."

"Poor child!" burst out Marie, as the tears gathered in her eyes, "I wonder if she is living."

"I think so," said Harry, kissing the pale cheek of his mother; "I don't feel that Iola is dead. I believe we will find her before long."

"It seems to me my heart would burst with joy to see my dear child just once more. I am glad that you are going. When will you leave?"

"To-morrow morning."

"Well, my son, go, and my prayers will go with you," was Marie's tender parting wish.

Early next morning Harry started for the conference, and reached the church before the morning session was over. Near him sat two ladies, one fair, the other considerably darker. There was something in the fairer one that reminded him forcibly of his sister, but she was much older and graver than he imagined his sister to be. Instantly he dismissed the thought that had forced itself into his mind, and began to listen attentively to the proceedings of the conference.

When the regular business of the morning session was over the bishop arose and said:–

"I have an interesting duty to perform. I wish to introduce a young lady to the conference, who was the daughter of a Mississippi planter. She is now in search of her mother and brother, from whom she was sold a few months before the war. Her father married her mother in Ohio, where he had taken her to be educated. After his death they were robbed of their inheritance and enslaved by a distant relative named Lorraine. Miss Iola Leroy is the young lady's name. If anyone[79] can give the least information respecting the objects of her search it will be thankfully received."

Notes

[79] *Original reads*: any one [ed.].

"I can," exclaimed a young man, rising in the midst of the audience, and pressing eagerly, almost impetuously, forward. "I am her brother, and I came here to look for her."

Iola raised her eyes to his face, so flushed and bright with the glow of recognition, rushed to him, threw her arms around his neck, kissed him again and again, crying: "O, Harry!" Then she fainted from excitement. The women gathered around her with expressions of tender sympathy, and gave her all the care she needed. They called her the "dear child," for without any effort on her part she had slidden into their hearts and found a ready welcome in each sympathizing bosom.

Harry at once telegraphed the glad tidings to his mother, who waited their coming with joyful anticipation. Long before the cars reached the city, Mrs. Leroy was at the depot, restlessly walking the platform or eagerly peering into the darkness to catch the first glimpse of the train which was bearing her treasures.

At length the cars arrived, and, as Harry and Iola alighted, Marie rushed forward, clasped Iola in her arms and sobbed out her joy in broken words.

Very happy was the little family that sat together around the supper-table for the first time for years. They partook of that supper with thankful hearts and with eyes overflowing with tears of joy. Very touching were the prayers the mother uttered, when she knelt with her children that night to return thanks for their happy reunion, and to seek protection through the slumbers of the night.

The next morning, as they sat at the breakfast-table, Marie said:–

"My dear child, you are so changed I do not think I would have known you if I had met you in the street!"

"And I," said Harry, "can hardly realize that you are our own Iola, whom I recognized as sister a half dozen years ago."

"Am I so changed?" asked Iola, as a faint sigh escaped her lips.

"Why, Iola," said Harry, "you used to be the most harum-scarum girl I ever knew – laughing, dancing, and singing from morning until night."

"Yes, I remember," said Iola. "It all comes back to me like a dream. Oh, mamma! I have passed through a fiery ordeal of suffering since then. But it is useless," and as she continued her face assumed a brighter look, "to brood over the past. Let us be happy in the present. Let me tell you something which will please you. Do you remember telling me about your mother and brother?"

"Yes," said Marie, in a questioning tone.

"Well," continued Iola, with eyes full of gladness, "I think I have found them."

"Can it be possible!" exclaimed Marie, in astonishment. "It is more than thirty years since we parted. I fear you are mistaken."

"No, mamma; I have drawn my conclusions, from good circumstantial evidence. After I was taken from you, I passed through a fearful siege of suffering, which would only harrow up your soul to hear. I often shudder at the remembrance. The last man in whose clutches I found myself was mean, brutal, and cruel. I was in his power when the Union army came into C——, where I was living. A number of colored men stampeded to the Union ranks, with a gentleman as a leader, whom I think is your brother. A friend of his reported my case to the commander of the post, who instantly gave orders for my release. A place was given me as nurse in the hospital. I attended that friend in his last illness. Poor fellow! he was the best friend I had in all the time I have been tossing about. The gentleman whom I think is your brother appeared to be very anxious about his friend's recovery, and was deeply affected by his death. In one of the last terrible battles of the war, that of Five Forks, he was wounded and put into the hospital ward where I was an attendant.

For a while[80] he was delirious, and in his delirium he would sometimes think that I was his mother and at other times his sister. I humored his fancies, would often sing to him when he was restless, and my voice almost invariably soothed him to sleep. One day I sang to him that old hymn we used to sing on the plantation:–

'Drooping souls no longer grieve,
Heaven is propitious;
If on Christ you do believe,
You will find Him precious.'"

"I remember," said Marie, with a sigh, as memories of the past swept over her.

"After I had finished the hymn," continued Iola, "he looked earnestly and inquiringly into my face, and asked, 'Where did you learn that hymn? I have heard my mother sing it when I was a boy, but I have never heard it since.' I think, mamma, the words, 'I was lost but now I'm found; glory! glory! glory!' had imprinted themselves on his memory, and that his mind was assuming a higher state of intellectuality. He asked me to sing it again, which I did, until he fell asleep. Then I noticed a marked resemblance between him and Harry, and I thought, 'Suppose he should prove to be your long-lost brother?' During his convalescence we found that we had a common ground of sympathy. We were anxious to be reunited to our severed relations. We had both been separated from our mothers. He told me of his little sister, with whom he used to play. She had a mole on her cheek which he called her beauty spot. He had the red spot on his forehead which you told me of."

Chapter 23

Delightful Reunions

VERY bright and happy was the home where Marie and her children were gathered under one roof. Mrs. Leroy's neighbors said she looked ten years younger. Into that peaceful home came no fearful forebodings of cruel separations. Harry and Iola were passionately devoted to their mother, and did all they could to flood her life with sunshine.

"Iola, dear," said Harry, one morning at the breakfast-table, "I have a new pleasure in store for you."

"What is it, brother mine?" asked Iola, assuming an air of interest.

"There is a young lady living in this city to whom I wish to introduce you. She is one of the most remarkable women I have ever met."

"Do tell me all about her," said Iola. "Is she young and handsome, brilliant and witty?

"She," replied Harry, "is more than handsome, she is lovely; more than witty, she is wise; more than brilliant, she is excellent."

"Well, Harry," said Mrs. Leroy, smiling, "if you keep on that way I shall begin to fear that I shall soon be supplanted by a new daughter."

"Oh, no, mamma," replied Harry, looking slightly confused, "I did not mean that."

"Well, Harry," said Iola, amused, "go on with your description; I am becoming interested. Tax your powers of description to give me her likeness."

Notes

[80] *Original reads*: awhile [ed.].

"Well, in the first place," continued Harry, "I suppose she is about twenty-five years old."

"Oh, the idea," interrupted Iola, "of a gentleman talking of a lady's age. That is a tabooed subject."

"Why, Iola, that adds to the interest of my picture. It is her combination of earnestness and youthfulness which enhances her in my estimation."

"Pardon the interruption," said Iola; "I am anxious to hear more about her."

"Well, she is of medium height, somewhat slender, and well formed, with dark, expressive eyes, full of thought and feeling. Neither hair nor complexion show the least hint of blood admixture."

"I am glad of it," said Iola. "Every person of unmixed blood who succeeds in any department of literature, art, or science is a living argument for the capability which is in the race."

"Yes," responded Harry, "for it is not the white blood which is on trial before the world. Well, I will bring her around this evening."

In the evening Harry brought Miss Delany to call on his sister and mother. They were much pleased with their visitor. Her manner was a combination of suavity and dignity. During the course of the evening they learned that she was a graduate of the University of A——. One day she saw in the newspapers that colored women were becoming unfit to be servants for white people. She then thought that if they are not fit to be servants for white people, they are unfit to be mothers to their own children, and she conceived the idea of opening a school to train future wives and mothers. She began on a small scale, in a humble building, and her work was soon crowned with gratifying success. She had enlarged her quarters, increased her teaching force, and had erected a large and commodious school-house through her own exertions and the help of others.

Marie cordially invited her to call again, saying, as she rose to go: "I am very glad to have met you. Young women like you always fill my heart with hope for the future of our race. In you I see reflected some of the blessed possibilities which lie within us."

"Thank you," said Miss Delany, "I want to be classed among those of whom it is said, 'She has done what she could.'"[81]

Very pleasant was the acquaintance which sprang up between Miss Delany and Iola. Although she was older than Iola, their tastes were so congenial, their views of life and duty in such unison, that their acquaintance soon ripened into strong and lasting friendship. There were no foolish rivalries and jealousies between them. Their lives were too full of zeal and earnestness for them to waste in selfishness their power to be moral and spiritual forces among a people who so much needed their helping hands. Miss Delany gave Iola a situation[82] in her school; but before the term was quite over she was forced[83] to resign, her health having been so undermined by the fearful strain through which she had passed, that she was quite unequal to the task. She remained at home, and did what her strength would allow in assisting her mother in the work of canning and preserving fruits.

In the meantime, Iola had been corresponding with Robert. She had told him of her success in finding her mother and brother, and had received an answer congratulating her on the glad fruition of her hopes. He also said that his business was flourishing, that his mother was keeping house for him, and, to use her own expression, was as

Notes

[81] *'She has done what she could'* Mark 14:8.

[82] *a situation* a position.

[83] *Original reads*: force [ed.].

happy as the days are long. She was firmly persuaded that Marie was her daughter, and she wanted to see her before she died.

"There is one thing," continued the letter, "that your mother may remember her by. It was a little handkerchief on which were a number of cats' heads. She gave one to each of us."

"I remember it well," said Marie, "she must, indeed, be my mother. Now, all that is needed to complete my happiness is her presence, and my brother's. And I intend, if I live long enough, to see them both."

Iola wrote Robert that her mother remembered the incident of the handkerchief, and was anxious to see them.

In the early fall Robert started for the South in order to clear up all doubts with respect to their relationship. He found Iola, Harry, and their mother living cosily together. Harry was teaching and was a leader among the rising young men of the State. His Northern education and later experience had done much toward adapting him to the work of the new era which had dawned upon the South.

Marie was very glad to welcome Robert to her home, but it was almost impossible to recognize her brother in that tall, handsome man, with dark-brown eyes and wealth of chestnut-colored hair, which he readily lifted to show the crimson spot which lay beneath it.

But as they sat together, and recalled the long-forgotten scenes of their childhood, they concluded that they were brother and sister.

"Marie," said Robert, "how would you like to leave the South?"

"I should like to go North, but I hate to leave Harry. He's a splendid young fellow, although I say it myself. He is so fearless and outspoken that I am constantly anxious about him, especially at election time."

Harry then entered the room, and, being introduced to Robert, gave him a cordial welcome. He had just returned from school.

"We were talking of you, my son," said Marie.

"What were you saying? Nothing of the absent but good?" asked Harry.

"I was telling your uncle, who wants me to come North, that I would go, but I am afraid that you will get into trouble and be murdered, as many others have been."

"Oh, well, mother, I shall not die till my time comes. And if I die helping the poor and needy, I shall die at my post. Could a man choose a better place to die?"

"Were you aware of the virulence of caste prejudice and the disabilities which surround the colored people when you cast your lot with them?" asked Robert.

"Not fully," replied Harry; "but after I found out that I was colored, I consulted the principal of the school, where I was studying, in reference to the future. He said that if I stayed in the North, he had friends whom he believed would give me any situation I could fill, and I could simply take my place in the rank of workers, the same as any other man. Then he told me of the army, and I made up my mind to enter it, actuated by a desire to find my mother and sister; and at any rate I wanted to avenge their wrongs. I do not feel so now. Since I have seen the fearful ravages of war, I have learned to pity and forgive. The principal said he thought I would be more apt to find my family if I joined a colored regiment in the West than if I joined one of the Maine companies. I confess at first I felt a shrinking from taking the step, but love for my mother overcame all repugnance on my part. Now that I have linked my fortunes to the race I intend to do all I can for its elevation."

As he spoke Robert gazed admiringly on the young face, lit up by noble purposes and lofty enthusiasm.

"You are right, Harry. I think it would be treason, not only to the race, but to humanity, to have you ignoring your kindred and masquerading as a white man."

"I think so, too," said Marie.

"But, sister, I am anxious for you all to come North. If Harry feels that the place of danger is the post of duty, let him stay, and he can spend his vacations with us. I think both you and Iola need rest and change. Mother longs to see you before she dies. She feels that we have been the children of many prayers and tears, and I want to make her last days as happy as possible. The South has not been a paradise to you all the time, and I should think you would be willing to leave it."

"Yes, that is so. Iola needs rest and change, and she would be such a comfort to mother. I suppose, for her sake, I will consent to have her go back with you, at least for a while."

In a few days, with many prayers and tears, Marie, half reluctantly, permitted Iola to start for the North in company with Robert Johnson, intending to follow as soon as she could settle her business and see Harry in a good boarding place.

Very joyful was the greeting of the dear grandmother. Iola soon nestled in her heart and lent additional sunshine to her once checkered life, and Robert, who had so long been robbed of kith and kin, was delighted with the new accession to his home life.

Chapter 24

Northern Experience

"UNCLE ROBERT," said Iola, after she had been North several weeks, "I have a theory that every woman ought to know how to earn her own living. I believe that a great amount of sin and misery springs from the weakness and inefficiency of women."

"Perhaps that's so, but what are you going to do about it?"

"I am going to join the great rank of bread-winners. Mr. Waterman has advertised for a number of saleswomen, and I intend to make application."

"When he advertises for help he means white women," said Robert.

"He said nothing about color," responded Iola.

"I don't suppose he did. He doesn't expect any colored girl to apply."

"Well, I think I could fill the place. At least I should like to try. And I do not think when I apply that I am in duty bound to tell him my great-grandmother was a negro."

"Well, child, there is no necessity for you to go out to work. You are perfectly welcome here, and I hope that you feel so."

"Oh, I certainly do. But still I would rather earn my own living."

That morning Iola applied for the situation, and, being prepossessing in her appearance, she obtained it. For a while[84] everything went as pleasantly as a marriage bell. But one day a young colored lady, well-dressed and well-bred in her manner, entered the store. It was an acquaintance which Iola had formed in the colored church which she attended. Iola gave her a few words of cordial greeting, and spent a few moments chatting with her. The attention of the girls who sold at the same counter was attracted, and their suspicion awakened. Iola was a stranger in that city. Who was she, and who were her people? At last it was decided that one of the girls should act as a spy, and bring what information she could concerning Iola.

The spy was successful. She found out that Iola was living in a good neighborhood, but that none of the neighbors knew her. The man of the house was very fair, but

Notes

[84] *Original reads*: awhile [ed.].

there was an old woman whom Iola called "Grandma," and she was unmistakably colored. The story was sufficient. If that were true, Iola must be colored, and she should be treated accordingly.

Without knowing the cause, Iola noticed a chill in the social atmosphere of the store, which communicated itself to the cash-boys, and they treated her so insolently that her situation became very uncomfortable. She saw the proprietor, resigned her position, and asked for and obtained a letter of recommendation to another merchant who had advertised for a saleswoman.

In applying for the place, she took the precaution to inform her employer that she was colored. It made no difference to him; but he said:–

"Don't say anything about it to the girls. They might not be willing to work with you."

Iola smiled, did not promise, and accepted the situation. She entered upon her duties, and proved quite acceptable as a saleswoman.

One day, during an interval in business, the girls began to talk of their respective churches, and the question was put to Iola:–

"Where do you go to church?"

"I go," she replied, "to Rev. River's church, corner of Eighth and L Streets."

"Oh, no; you must be mistaken. There is no church there except a colored one."

"That is where I go."

"Why do you go there?"

"Because I liked it when I came here, and joined it."

"A member of a colored church? What under heaven possessed you to do such a thing?"

"Because I wished to be with my own people."

Here the interrogator stopped, and looked surprised and pained, and almost instinctively moved a little farther from her. After the store was closed, the girls had an animated discussion, which resulted in the information being sent to Mr. Cohen that Iola was a colored girl, and that they protested against her being continued in his employ. Mr. Cohen yielded to the pressure, and informed Iola that her services were no longer needed.

When Robert came home in the evening, he found that Iola had lost her situation, and was looking somewhat discouraged.

"Well, uncle," she said, "I feel out of heart. It seems as if the prejudice pursues us through every avenue of life, and assigns us the lowest places."

"That is so," replied Robert, thoughtfully.

"And yet I am determined," said Iola, "to win for myself a place in the fields of labor. I have heard of a place in New England, and I mean to try for it, even if I only stay a few months."

"Well, if you *will* go, say nothing about your color."

"Uncle Robert, I see no necessity for proclaiming that fact on the house-top. Yet I am resolved that nothing shall tempt me to deny it. The best blood in my veins is African blood, and I am not ashamed of it."

"Hurrah for you!" exclaimed Robert, laughing heartily.

As Iola wished to try the world for herself, and so be prepared for any emergency, her uncle and grandmother were content to have her go to New England. The town to which she journeyed was only a few hours' ride from the city of P——, and Robert, knowing that there is no teacher like experience, was willing that Iola should have the benefit of her teaching.

Iola, on arriving in H——, sought the firm, and was informed that her services were needed. She found it a pleasant and lucrative position. There was only one drawback – her boarding place was too far from her work. There was an institution conducted by professed Christian women, which was for the special use of respectable young working girls. This was in such a desirable location that she called at the house to engage board.

The matron conducted her over the house, and grew so friendly in the interview that she put her arm around her, and seemed to look upon Iola as a desirable accession to the home. But, just as Iola was leaving, she said to the matron: "I must be honest with you; I am a colored woman."

Swift as light a change passed over the face of the matron. She withdrew her arm from Iola, and said: "I must see the board of managers about it."

When the board met, Iola's case was put before them, but they decided not to receive her. And these women, professors of a religion which taught, "If ye have respect to persons ye commit sin,"[85] virtually shut the door in her face because of the outcast blood in her veins.

Considerable feeling was aroused by the action of these women, who, to say the least, had not put their religion in the most favorable light.

Iola continued to work for the firm until she received letters from her mother and uncle, which informed her that her mother, having arranged her affairs in the South, was ready to come North. She then resolved to return to the city of P—— to be ready to welcome her mother on her arrival.

Iola arrived in time to see that everything was in order for her mother's reception. Her room was furnished neatly, but with those touches of beauty that womanly hands are such adepts in giving. A few charming pictures adorned the walls, and an easy chair stood waiting to receive the travel-worn mother. Robert and Iola met her at the depot; and grandma was on her feet at the first sound of the bell, opened the door, clasped Marie to her heart, and nearly fainted for joy.

"Can it be possible dat dis is my little Marie?" she exclaimed.

It did seem almost impossible to realize that this faded woman, with pale cheeks and prematurely whitened hair, was the rosy-cheeked child from whom she had been parted more than thirty years.

"Well," said Robert, after the first joyous greeting was over, "love is a very good thing, but Marie has had a long journey and needs something that will stick by the ribs. How about dinner, mother?"

"It's all ready," said Mrs. Johnson.

After Marie had gone to her room and changed her dress, she came down and partook of the delicious repast which her mother and Iola had prepared for her.

In a few days Marie was settled in the home, and was well pleased with the change. The only drawback to her happiness was the absence of her son, and she expected him to come North after the closing of his school.

"Uncle Robert," said Iola, after her mother had been with them several weeks, "I am tired of being idle."

"What's the matter now?" asked Robert. "You are surely not going East again, and leave your mother?"

"Oh, I hope not," said Marie, anxiously. "I have been so long without you."

"No, mamma, I am not going East. I can get suitable employment here in the city of P——."

Notes

[85] *"If ye have respect to persons … sin"* James 2:9.

"But, Iola," said Robert, "you have tried, and been defeated. Why subject yourself to the same experience again?"

"Uncle Robert, I think that every woman should have some skill or art which would insure her at least a comfortable support. I believe there would be less unhappy marriages if labor were more honored among women."

"Well, Iola," said her mother, "what is your skill?"

"Nursing. I was very young when I went into the hospital, but I succeeded so well that the doctor said I must have been a born nurse. Now, I see by the papers, that a gentleman who has an invalid daughter wants someone[86] who can be a nurse and companion for her, and I mean to apply for the situation. I do not think, if I do my part well in that position, that the blood in my veins will be any bar to my success."

A troubled look stole over Marie's face. She sighed faintly, but made no remonstrance. And so it was decided that Iola should apply for the situation.

Iola made application, and was readily accepted. Her patient was a frail girl of fifteen summers, who was ill with a low fever. Iola nursed her carefully, and soon had the satisfaction of seeing her restored to health. During her stay, Mr. Cloten, the father of the invalid, had learned some of the particulars of Iola's Northern experience as a bread-winner, and he resolved to give her employment in his store when her services were no longer needed in the house. As soon as a vacancy occurred he gave Iola a place in his store.

The morning she entered on her work he called his employs together, and told them that Miss Iola had colored blood in her veins, but that he was going to employ her and give her a desk. If anyone[87] objected to working with her, he or she could step to the cashier's desk and receive what was due. Not a man remonstrated, not a woman demurred; and Iola at last found a place in the great army of bread-winners, which the traditions of her blood could not affect.

"How did you succeed?" asked Mrs. Cloten of her husband, when he returned to dinner.

"Admirably! 'Everything is lovely and the goose hangs high.' I gave my employes to understand that they could leave if they did not wish to work with Miss Leroy. Not one of them left, or showed any disposition to rebel."

"I am very glad," said Mrs Cloten. "I am ashamed of the way she has been treated in our city, when seeking to do her share in the world's work. I am glad that you were brave enough to face this cruel prejudice, and give her a situation."

"Well, my dear, do not make me a hero for a single act. I am grateful for the care Miss Leroy gave our Daisy. Money can buy services, but it cannot purchase tender, loving sympathy. I was also determined to let my employées[88] know that I, not they, commanded my business. So, do not crown me a hero until I have won a niche in the temple of fame. In dealing with Southern prejudice against the negro, we Northerners could do it with better grace if we divested ourselves of our own. We irritate the South by our criticisms, and, while I confess that there is much that is reprehensible in their treatment of colored people, yet if our Northern civilization is higher than theirs we should 'criticise by creation.' We should stamp ourselves on the South, and not let the South stamp itself on us. When we have learned to treat men according to the complexion of their souls, and not the color of their skins, we will have given our best contribution towards the solution of the negro problem."

Notes

[86] *Original reads*: some one [ed.].

[87] *Original reads*: any one [ed.].

[88] *Original reads*: employés [ed.].

"I feel, my dear," said Mrs. Cloten, "that what you have done is a right step in the right direction, and I hope that other merchants will do the same. We have numbers of businessmen, rich enough to afford themselves the luxury of a good conscience."

Chapter 25

An Old Friend

"GOOD-MORNING, Miss Leroy," said a cheery voice in tones of glad surprise, and, intercepting her path, Dr. Gresham stood before Iola, smiling, and reaching out his hand.

"Why, Dr. Gresham, is this you?" said Iola, lifting her eyes to that well-remembered face. "It has been several years since we met. How have you been all this time, and where?"

"I have been sick, and am just now recovering from malaria and nervous prostration. I am attending a medical convention in this city, and hope that I shall have the pleasure of seeing you again."

Iola hesitated, and then replied: "I should be pleased to have you call."

"It would give me great pleasure. Where shall I call?"

"My home is 1006 South Street, but I am only at home in the evenings."

They walked together a short distance till they reached Mr. Cloten's store; then, bidding the doctor good morning, Iola left him repeating to himself the words of his favorite poet:–

> "Thou art too lovely and precious a gem
> To be bound to their burdens and sullied by them."[89]

No one noticed the deep flush on Iola's face as she entered the store, nor the subdued, quiet manner with which she applied herself to her tasks. She was living over again the past, with its tender, sad, and thrilling reminiscences.

In the evening Dr. Gresham called on Iola. She met him with a pleasant welcome. Dr. Gresham gazed upon her with unfeigned admiration, and thought that the years, instead of detracting from, had only intensified, her loveliness. He had thought her very beautiful in the hospital, in her gray dress and white collar, with her glorious wealth of hair drawn over her ears. But now, when he saw her with that hair artistically arranged, and her finely-proportioned form arrayed in a dark crimson dress, relieved by a shimmer of lace and a bow of white ribbon at her throat, he thought her superbly handsome. The lines which care had written upon her young face had faded away. There was no undertone of sorrow in her voice as she stood up before him in the calm loveliness of her ripened womanhood, radiant in beauty and gifted in intellect. Time and failing health had left their traces upon Dr. Gresham. His step was less bounding, his cheek a trifle paler, his manner somewhat graver than it was when he had parted from Iola in the hospital, but his meeting with her had thrilled his heart with unexpected pleasure. Hopes and sentiments

Notes

[89] *"thou art too lovely ... them"* from the poem "The Yankee Girl" by John Greenleaf Whittier (1807–1892).

which long had slept awoke at the touch of her hand and the tones of her voice, and Dr. Gresham found himself turning to the past, with its sad memories and disappointed hopes. No other face had displaced her image in his mind; no other love had woven itself around every tendril of his soul. His heart and hand were just as free as they were the hour they had parted.

"To see you again," said Dr. Gresham, "is a great and unexpected pleasure."

"You had not forgotten me, then?" said Iola, smiling.

"Forget you! I would just as soon forget my own existence. I do not think that time will ever efface the impressions of those days in which we met so often. When last we met you were intending to search for your mother. Have you been successful?"

"More than successful," said Iola, with a joyous ring in her voice. "I have found my mother, brother, grandmother, and uncle, and, except my brother, we are all living together, and we are so happy. Excuse me a few minutes," she said, and left the room. Iola soon returned, bringing with her her mother and grandmother.

"These," said Iola, introducing her mother and grandmother, "are the once-severed branches of our family; and this gentleman you have seen before," continued Iola, as Robert entered the room.

Dr. Gresham looked scrutinizingly at him and said: "Your face looks familiar, but I saw so many faces at the hospital that I cannot just now recall your name."

"Doctor," said Robert Johnson, "I was one of your last patients, and I was with Tom Anderson when he died."

"Oh, yes," replied Dr. Gresham; "it all comes back to me. You were wounded at the battle of Five Forks, were you not?"

"Yes," said Robert.

"I saw you when you were recovering. You told me that you thought you had a clue to your lost relatives, from whom you had been so long separated. How have you succeeded?"

"Admirably! I have been fortunate in finding my mother, my sister, and her children."

"Ah, indeed! I am delighted to hear it. Where are they?"

"They are right here. This is my mother," said Robert, bending fondly over her, as she returned his recognition with an expression of intense satisfaction; "and this," he continued, "is my sister, and Miss Leroy is my niece."

"Is it possible! I am very glad to hear it. It has been said that every cloud has its silver lining, and the silver lining of our war cloud is the redemption of a race and the reunion of severed hearts. War is a dreadful thing; but worse than the war was the slavery which preceded it."

"Slavery," said Iola, "was a fearful cancer eating into the nation's heart, sapping its vitality, and undermining its life."

"And war," said Dr. Gresham, "was the dreadful surgery by which the disease was eradicated. The cancer has been removed, but for years to come I fear that we will have to deal with the effects of the disease. But I believe that we have vitality enough to outgrow those effects."

"I think, Doctor," said Iola, "that there is but one remedy by which our nation can recover from the evil entailed upon her by slavery."

"What is that?" asked Robert.

"A fuller comprehension of the claims of the Gospel of Jesus Christ, and their application to our national life."

"Yes," said Robert; "while politicians are stumbling on the barren mountains of fretful controversy, and asking what shall we do with the negro, I hold that Jesus answered that question nearly two thousand years ago, when he said, 'Whatsoever ye would that men should do to you, do ye even so to them.'"[90]

"Yes." said Dr. Gresham; "the application of that rule in dealing with the negro would solve the whole problem."

"Slavery," said Mrs. Leroy, "is dead, but the spirit which animated it still lives; and I think that a reckless disregard for human life is more the outgrowth of slavery than any actual hatred of the negro."

"The problem of the nation," continued Dr. Gresham, "is not what men will do with the negro, but what will they do with the reckless, lawless white men who murder, lynch, and burn their fellow-citizens. To me these lynchings and burnings are perfectly alarming. Both races have reacted on each other – men fettered the slave, and cramped their own souls; denied him knowledge, and darkened their spiritual insight; subdued him to the pliancy of submission, and in their turn became the thralls of public opinion. The negro came here from the heathenism of Africa; but the young colonies could not take into their early civilization a stream of barbaric blood without being affected by its influence, and the negro, poor and despised as he is, has laid his hands on our Southern civilization and helped mould its character."

"Yes," said Mrs. Leroy; "the colored nurse could not nestle her master's child in her arms, hold up his baby footsteps on their floors, and walk with him through the impressible and formative period of his young life without leaving upon him the impress of her hand."

"I am glad," said Robert, "for the whole nation's sake, that slavery has been destroyed."

"And our work," said Dr. Gresham, "is to build over the desolations of the past a better and brighter future. The great distinction between savagery and civilization is the creation and maintenance of law. A people cannot habitually trample on law and justice without retrograding toward barbarism. But I am hopeful that time will bring us changes for the better; that, as we get farther away from the war, we will outgrow the animosities and prejudices engendered by slavery. The short-sightedness of our fathers linked the negro's destiny to ours. We are feeling the friction of the ligatures which bind us together, but I hope that the time will speedily come when the best members of both races will unite for the maintenance of law and order and the progress and prosperity of the country, and that the intelligence and virtue of the South will be strong to grapple effectually with its ignorance and vice."

"I hope that time will speedily come," said Marie. "My son is in the South, and I am always anxious for his safety. He is not only a teacher, but a leading young man in the community where he lives."

"Yes," said Robert, "and when I see the splendid work he is doing in the South, I am glad that, instead of trying to pass for a white man, he has cast his lot with us."

"But," answered Dr. Gresham, "he would possess advantages as a white man which he could not if he were known to be colored."

"Doctor," said Iola, decidedly, "he has greater advantages as a colored man."

"I do not understand you," said Dr. Gresham, looking somewhat puzzled.

"Doctor," continued Iola, "I do not think life's highest advantages are those that we can see with our eyes or grasp with our hands. To whom to-day is the world most indebted – to its millionaires or to its martyrs?"

"Taking it from the ideal standpoint," replied the doctor, "I should say its martyrs."

Notes

[90] *"Whatsoever ye would ... to them."* Matthew 7:12.

"To be," continued Iola, "the leader of a race to higher planes of thought and action, to teach men clearer views of life and duty, and to inspire their souls with loftier aims, is a far greater privilege than it is to open the gates of material prosperity and fill every home with sensuous enjoyment."

"And I," said Mrs. Leroy, her face aglow with fervid feeling, "would rather – ten thousand times rather – see Harry the friend and helper of the poor and ignorant than the companion of men who, under the cover of night, mask their faces and ride the country on lawless raids."[91]

"Dr. Gresham," said Robert, "we ought to be the leading nation of the earth, whose influence and example should give light to the world."

"Not simply," said Iola, "a nation building up a great material prosperity, founding magnificent cities, grasping the commerce of the world, or excelling in literature, art, and science, but a nation wearing sobriety as a crown and righteousness as the girdle of her loins."

Dr. Gresham gazed admiringly upon Iola. A glow of enthusiasm overspread her beautiful, expressive face. There was a rapt and far-off look in her eye, as if she were looking beyond the present pain to a brighter future for the race with which she was identified, and felt the grandeur of a divine commission to labor for its uplifting.

As Dr. Gresham was parting with Robert, he said: "This meeting has been a very unexpected pleasure. I have spent a delightful evening. I only regret that I had not others to share it with me. A doctor from the South, a regular Bourbon,[92] is stopping at the hotel. I wish he could have been here to-night. Come down to the Concordia, Mr. Johnson, to-morrow night. If you know any colored man who is a strong champion of equal rights, bring him along. Good-night. I shall look for you," said the doctor, as he left the door.

When Robert returned to the parlor he said to Iola: "Dr. Gresham has invited me to come to his hotel tomorrow night, and to bring some wide-awake colored man with me. There is a Southerner whom he wishes me to meet. I suppose he wants to discuss the negro problem, as they call it. He wants someone[93] who can do justice to the subject. I wonder whom I can take with me?"

"I will tell you who, I think, will be a capital one to take with you, and I believe he would go," said Iola.

"Who?" asked Robert.

"Rev. Carmicle, your pastor."

"He is just the one," said Robert, "courteous in his manner and very scholarly in his attainments. He is a man whom if everybody hated him no one could despise him."

Chapter 26

Open Questions

In the evening Robert and Rev. Carmicle called on Dr. Gresham, and found Dr. Latrobe, the Southerner, and a young doctor by the name of Latimer, already there. Dr. Gresham introduced Dr. Latrobe, but it was a new experience to receive colored men socially. His wits, however, did not forsake him, and he received the introduction and survived it.

Notes

[91] *men who … lawless raids* the Ku Klux Klan.

[92] *a regular Bourbon* a Kentuckian.

[93] *Original reads*: some one [ed.].

"Permit me, now," said Dr. Gresham, "to introduce you to my friend, Dr. Latimer, who is attending our convention. He expects to go South and labor among the colored people. Don't you think that there is a large field of usefulness before him?"

"Yes," replied Dr. Latrobe, "if he will let politics alone."

"And why let politics alone?" asked Dr. Gresham.

"Because," replied Dr. Latrobe, "we Southerners will never submit to negro supremacy. We will never abandon our Caucasian civilization to an inferior race."

"Have you any reason," inquired Rev. Carmicle, "to dread that a race which has behind it the heathenism of Africa and the slavery of America, with its inheritance of ignorance and poverty, will be able, in less than one generation, to domineer over a race which has behind it ages of dominion, freedom, educ ation, and Christianity?"

A slight shade of vexation and astonishment passed over the face of Dr. Latrobe. He hesitated a moment, then replied:–

"I am not afraid of the negro as he stands alone, but what I dread is that in some closely-contested election ambitious men will use him to hold the balance of power and make him an element of danger. He is ignorant, poor, and clannish, and they may impact him as their policy would direct."

"Any more," asked Robert, "than the leaders of the Rebellion did the ignorant, poor whites during our late conflict?"

"Ignorance, poverty, and clannishness," said Dr. Gresham, "are more social than racial conditions, which may be outgrown."

"And I think," said Rev. Carmicle, "that we are outgrowing them as fast as any other people would have done under the same conditions."

"The negro," replied Dr. Latrobe, "always has been and always will be an element of discord in our country."

"What, then, is your remedy?" asked Dr. Gresham.

"I would eliminate him from the politics of the country."

"As disfranchisement is a punishment for crime, is it just to punish a man before he transgresses the law?" asked Dr. Gresham.

"If," said Dr. Latimer, "the negro is ignorant, poor, and clannish, let us remember that in part of our land it was once a crime to teach him to read. If he is poor, for ages he was forced to bend to unrequited toil. If he is clannish, society has segregated him to himself."

"And even," said Robert, "has given him a negro pew in your churches and a negro seat at your communion table."

"Wisely, or unwisely," said Dr. Gresham, "the Government has put the ballot in his hands. It is better to teach him to use that ballot aright than to intimidate him by violence or vitiate his vote by fraud."

"To-day," said Dr. Latimer, "the negro is not plotting in beer-saloons against the peace and order of society. His fingers are not dripping with dynamite, neither is he spitting upon your flag, nor flaunting the red banner of anarchy in your face."

"Power," said Dr. Gresham, "naturally gravitates into the strongest hands. The class who have the best brain and most wealth can strike with the heaviest hand. I have too much faith in the inherent power of the white race to dread the competition of any other people under heaven."

"I think you Northerners fail to do us justice," said Dr. Latrobe. "The men into whose hands you put the ballot were our slaves, and we would rather die than submit to them. Look at the carpet-bag governments the wicked policy of the Government inflicted upon us. It was only done to humiliate us."

"Oh, no!" said Dr. Gresham, flushing, and rising to his feet. "We had no other alternative than putting the ballot in their hands."

"I will not deny," said Rev. Carmicle, "that we have made woeful mistakes, but with our antecedents it would have been miraculous if we had never committed any mistakes or made any blunders."

"They were allies in war," continued Dr. Gresham, "and I am sorry that we have not done more to protect them in peace."

"Protect them in peace!" said Robert, bitterly. "What protection does the colored man receive from the hands of the Government? I know of no civilized country outside of America where men are still burned for real or supposed crimes."

"Johnson," said Dr. Gresham, compassionately, "it is impossible to have a policeman at the back of each colored man's chair, and a squad of soldiers at each crossroad, to detect with certainty, and punish with celerity,[94] each invasion of his rights. We tried provisional governments and found them a failure. It seemed like leaving our former allies to be mocked with the name of freedom and tortured with the essence of slavery. The ballot is our weapon of defense, and we gave it to them for theirs."

"And there," said Dr. Latrobe, emphatically, "is where you signally failed. We are numerically stronger in Congress to-day than when we went out. You made the law, but the administration of it is in our hands, and we are a unit."

"But, Doctor," said Rev. Carmicle, "you cannot willfully deprive the negro of a single right as a citizen without sending demoralization through your own ranks."

"I think," said Dr. Latrobe, "that we are right in suppressing the negro's vote. This is a white man's government, and a white man's country. We own nineteen-twentieths of the land, and have about the same ratio of intelligence. I am a white man, and, right or wrong, I go with my race."

"But, Doctor," said Rev. Carmicle, "there are rights more sacred than the rights of property and superior intelligence."

"What are they?" asked Dr. Latrobe.

"The rights of life and liberty," replied Rev. Carmicle.

"That is true," said Dr. Gresham; "and your Southern civilization will be inferior until you shall have placed protection to those rights at its base, not in theory but in fact."

"But, Dr. Gresham, we have to live with these people, and the North is constantly irritating us by its criticisms."

"The world," said Dr. Gresham, "is fast becoming a vast whispering gallery, and lips once sealed can now state their own grievances and appeal to the conscience of the nation, and, as long as a sense of justice and mercy retains a hold upon the heart of our nation, you cannot practice violence and injustice without rousing a spirit of remonstrance. And if it were not so I would be ashamed of my country and of my race."

"You speak," said Dr. Latrobe, "as if we had wronged the negro by enslaving him and being unwilling to share citizenship with him. I think that slavery has been of incalculable value to the negro. It has lifted him out of barbarism and fetich worship,[95] given him a language of civilization, and introduced him to the world's best religion. Think what he was in Africa and what he is in America!"

"The negro," said Dr. Gresham, thoughtfully, "is not the only branch of the human race which has been low down in the scale of civilization and freedom, and which has outgrown the measure of his chains. Slavery, polygamy, and human sacrifices have been practiced among Europeans in bygone days; and when Tyndall[96] tells us that

Notes

[94] *celerity* speed.

[95] *fetich worship* the worship of fetishes or idols.

[96] John Tyndall (1820–1893), Irish physician whose 1874 Belfast Address explored evolutionary development in humankind.

out of savages unable to count to the number of their fingers and speaking only a language of nouns and verbs, arise at length our Newtons and Shakspeares, I do not see that the negro could not have learned our language and received our religion without the intervention of ages of slavery."

"If," said Rev. Carmicle, "Mohammedanism,[97] with its imperfect creed, is successful in gathering large numbers of negroes beneath the Crescent, could not a legitimate commerce and the teachings of a pure Christianity have done as much to plant the standard of the Cross over the ramparts of sin and idolatry in Africa? Surely we cannot concede that the light of the Crescent is greater than the glory of the Cross, that there is less constraining power in the Christ of Calvary than in the Prophet of Arabia? I do not think that I underrate the difficulties in your way when I say that you young men are holding in your hands golden opportunities which it would be madness and folly to throw away. It is your grand opportunity to help build up a new South, not on the shifting sands of policy and expediency, but on the broad basis of equal justice and universal freedom. Do this and you will be blessed, and will make your life a blessing."

After Robert and Rev. Carmicle had left the hotel, Drs. Latimer, Gresham, and Latrobe sat silent and thoughtful awhile, when Dr. Gresham broke the silence by asking Dr. Latrobe how he had enjoyed the evening.

"Very pleasantly," he replied. "I was quite interested in that parson. Where was he educated?"

"In Oxford, I believe. I was pleased to hear him say that he had no white blood in his veins."

"I should think not," replied Dr. Latrobe, "from his looks. But one swallow does not make a summer. It is the exceptions which prove the rule."

"Don't you think," asked Dr. Gresham, "that we have been too hasty in our judgment of the negro? He has come handicapped into life, and is now on trial before the world. But it is not fair to subject him to the same tests that you would a white man. I believe that there are possibilities of growth in the race which we have never comprehended."

"The negro," said Dr. Latrobe, "is perfectly comprehensible to me. The only way to get along with him is to let him know his place, and make him keep it."

"I think," replied Dr. Gresham, "every man's place is the one he is best fitted for."

"Why," asked Dr. Latimer, "should any place be assigned to the negro more than to the French, Irish, or German?"

"Oh," replied Dr. Latrobe, "they are all Caucasians."

"Well," said Dr. Gresham, "is all excellence summed up in that branch of the human race?"

"I think," said Dr. Latrobe, proudly, "that we belong to the highest race on earth and the negro to the lowest."

"And yet," said Dr. Latimer, "you have consorted with them till you have bleached their faces to the whiteness of your own. Your children nestle in their bosoms; they are around you as body servants, and yet if one of them should attempt to associate with you your bitterest scorn and indignation would be visited upon them."

"I think," said Dr. Latrobe, "that feeling grows out of our Anglo-Saxon regard for the marriage relation. These white negroes are of illegitimate origin, and we would scorn to share our social life with them. Their blood is tainted."

"Who tainted it?" asked Dr. Latimer, bitterly. "You give absolution to the fathers, and visit the misfortunes of the mothers upon the children."

Notes

[97] *Mohammedanism* Islam.

"But, Doctor, what kind of society would we have if we put down the bars and admitted everybody to social equality?"

"This idea of social equality," said Dr. Latimer, "is only a bugbear[98] which frightens well-meaning people from dealing justly with the negro. I know of no place on earth where there is perfect social equality, and I doubt if there is such a thing in heaven. The sinner who repents on his death-bed cannot be the equal of St. Paul or the Beloved Disciple."[99]

"Doctor," said Dr. Gresham, "I sometimes think that the final solution of this question will be the absorption of the negro into our race."

"Never! never!" exclaimed Dr. Latrobe, vehemently. "It would be a death blow to American civilization."

"Why, Doctor," said Dr. Latimer, "you Southerners began this absorption before the war. I understand that in one decade the mixed bloods rose from one-ninth to one-eighth of the population, and that as early as 1663 a law was passed in Maryland to prevent English women from intermarrying with slaves; and, even now, your laws against miscegenation presuppose that you apprehend danger from that source."

"Doctor, it is no use talking," replied Dr. Latrobe, wearily. "There are niggers who are as white as I am, but the taint of blood is there and we always exclude it."

"How do you know it is there?" asked Dr. Gresham.

"Oh, there are tricks of blood which always betray them. My eyes are more practiced than yours. I can always tell them. Now, that Johnson is as white as any man; but I knew he was a nigger the moment I saw him. I saw it in his eye."

Dr. Latimer smiled at Dr. Latrobe's assertion, but did not attempt to refute it; and bade him good-night.

"I think," said Dr. Latrobe, "that our war was the great mistake of the nineteenth century. It has left us very serious complications. We cannot amalgamate with the negroes. We cannot expatriate them. Now, what are we to do with them?"

"Deal justly with them," said Dr. Gresham, "and let them alone. Try to create a moral sentiment in the nation, which will consider a wrong done to the weakest of them as a wrong done to the whole community. Whenever you find ministers too righteous to be faithless, cowardly, and time serving; women too Christly to be scornful; and public men too noble to be tricky and too honest to pander to the prejudices of the people, stand by them and give them your moral support."

"Doctor," said Latrobe, "with your views you ought to be a preacher striving to usher in the millennium."

"It can't come too soon," replied Dr. Gresham.

Chapter 27

Diverging Paths

On the eve of his departure from the city of P——, Dr. Gresham called on Iola, and found her alone. They talked awhile of reminiscences of the war and hospital life, when Dr. Gresham, approaching Iola, said:–

"Miss Leroy, I am glad the great object of your life is accomplished, and that you have found all your relatives. Years have passed since we parted, years in which I have vainly tried to get a trace of you and have been baffled, but I have found you at last!" Clasping her hand in his, he continued, "I would it were so that I should never lose you again! Iola, will

Notes

[98] *bugbear* boogeyman.

[99] *the Beloved Disciple* John (see John 21:24).

you not grant me the privilege of holding this hand as mine all through the future of our lives? Your search for your mother is ended. She is well cared for. Are you not free at last to share with me my Northern home, free to be mine as nothing else on earth is mine?" Dr. Gresham looked eagerly on Iola's face, and tried to read its varying expression. "Iola, I learned to love you in the hospital. I have tried to forget you, but it has been all in vain. Your image is just as deeply engraven on my heart as it was the day we parted."

"Doctor," she replied, sadly, but firmly, as she withdrew her hand from his, "I feel now as I felt then, that there is an insurmountable barrier between us."

"What is it, Iola?" asked Dr. Gresham, anxiously.

"It is the public opinion which assigns me a place with the colored people."

"But what right has public opinion to interfere with our marriage relations? Why should we yield to its behests?"

"Because it is stronger than we are, and we cannot run counter to it without suffering its penalties."

"And what are they, Iola? Shadows that you merely dread?"

"No! no! the penalties of social ostracism North and South, except here and there some grand and noble exceptions. I do not think that you fully realize how much prejudice against colored people permeates society, lowers the tone of our religion, and reacts upon the life of the nation. After freedom came, mamma was living in the city of A——, and wanted to unite with a Christian church there. She made application for membership. She passed her examination as a candidate, and was received as a church member. When she was about to make her first communion, she unintentionally took her seat at the head of the column. The elder who was administering the communion gave her the bread in the order in which she sat, but before he gave her the wine someone[100] touched him on the shoulder and whispered a word in his ear. He then passed mamma by, gave the cup to others, and then returned to her. From that rite connected with the holiest memories of earth, my poor mother returned humiliated and depressed."

"What a shame!" exclaimed Dr. Gresham, indignantly.

"I have seen," continued Iola, "the same spirit manifested in the North. Mamma once attempted to do missionary work in this city. One day she found an outcast colored girl, whom she wished to rescue. She took her to an asylum for fallen women and made an application for her, but was refused. Colored girls were not received there. Soon after mamma found among the colored people an outcast white girl. Mamma's sympathies, unfettered by class distinction, were aroused in her behalf, and, in company with two white ladies, she went with the girl to that same refuge. For her the door was freely opened and admittance readily granted. It was as if two women were sinking in the quicksands, and on the solid land stood other women with life-lines in their hands, seeing the deadly sands slowly creeping up around the hapless victims. To one they readily threw the lines of deliverance, but for the other there was not one strand of salvation. Sometime since, to the same asylum, came a poor fallen girl who had escaped from the clutches of a wicked woman. For her the door would have been opened, had not the vile woman from whom she was escaping followed her to that place of refuge and revealed the fact that she belonged to the colored race. That fact was enough to close the door upon her, and to send her back to sin and to suffer, and perhaps to die as a wretched outcast. And yet in this city where a number of charities are advertised, I do not think there is one of them which, in appealing to the public, talks more religion than the managers of this asylum. This prejudice against the colored race environs our lives and mocks our aspirations."

Notes

[100] *Original reads*: some one [ed.].

"Iola, I see no use in your persisting that you are colored when your eyes are as blue and complexion as white as mine."

"Doctor, were I your wife, are there not people who would caress me as a white woman who would shrink from me in scorn if they knew I had one drop of negro blood in my veins? When mistaken for a white woman I should hear things alleged against the race at which my blood would boil. No, Doctor, I am not willing to live under a shadow of concealment which I thoroughly hate as if the blood in my veins were an undetected crime of my soul."

"Iola, dear, surely you paint the picture too darkly."

"Doctor, I have painted it with my heart's blood. It is easier to outgrow the dishonor of crime than the disabilities of color. You have created in this country an aristocracy of color wide enough to include the South with its treason and Utah with its abominations, but too narrow to include the best and bravest colored man who bared his breast to the bullets of the enemy during your fratricidal strife. Is not the most arrant Rebel to-day more acceptable to you than the most faithful colored man?"

"No! no!" exclaimed Dr. Gresham, vehemently. "You are wrong. I belong to the Grand Army of the Republic. We have no separate State Posts for the colored people, and, were such a thing proposed, the majority of our members, I believe, would be against it. In Congress colored men have the same seats as white men, and the color line is slowly fading out in our public institutions."

"But how is it in the Church?" asked Iola.

"The Church is naturally conservative. It preserves old truths, even if it is somewhat slow in embracing new ideas. It has its social as well as its spiritual side. Society is woman's realm. The majority of church members are women, who are said to be the aristocratic element of our country. I fear that one of the last strongholds of this racial prejudice will be found beneath the shadow of some of our churches. I think, on account of this social question, that large bodies of Christian temperance women and other reformers, in trying to reach the colored people even for their own good, will be quicker to form separate associations than our National Grand Army, whose ranks are open to black and white, liberals and conservatives, saints and agnostics. But, Iola, we have drifted far away from the question. No one has a right to interfere with our marriage if we do not infringe on the rights of others."

"Doctor," she replied, gently, "I feel that our paths must diverge. My life-work is planned. I intend spending my future among the colored people of the South."

"My dear friend," he replied, anxiously, "I am afraid that you are destined to sad disappointment. When the novelty wears off you will be disillusioned, and, I fear, when the time comes that you can no longer serve them they will forget your services and remember only your failings."

"But, Doctor, they need me; and I am sure when I taught among them they were very grateful for my services."

"I think," he replied, "these people are more thankful than grateful."

"I do not think so; and if I did it would not hinder me from doing all in my power to help them. I do not expect all the finest traits of character to spring from the hot-beds of slavery and caste. What matters it if they do forget the singer, so they don't forget the song? No, Doctor, I don't think that I could best serve my race by forsaking them and marrying you."

"Iola," he exclaimed, passionately, "if you love your race, as you call it, work for it, live for it, suffer for it, and, if need be, die for it; but don't marry for it. Your education has unfitted you for social life among them."

"It was," replied Iola, "through their unrequited toil that I was educated, while they were compelled to live in ignorance. I am indebted to them for the power I have to serve them. I wish other Southern women felt as I do. I think they could do so much to help the colored people at their doors if they would look at their opportunities in the light of the face of Jesus Christ. Nor am I wholly unselfish in allying myself with the colored people. All the rest of my family have done so. My dear grandmother is one of the excellent of the earth, and we all love her too much to ignore our relationship with her. I did not choose my lot in life, and the simplest thing I can do is to accept the situation and do the best I can."

"And is this your settled purpose?" he asked, sadly.

"It is, Doctor," she replied, tenderly but firmly. "I see no other. I must serve the race which needs me most."

"Perhaps you are right," he replied; "but I cannot help feeling sad that our paths, which met so pleasantly, should diverge so painfully. And yet, not only the freedmen, but the whole country, need such helpful, self-sacrificing teachers as you will prove; and if earnest prayers and holy wishes can brighten your path, your lines will fall in the pleasantest places."

As he rose to go, sympathy, love, and admiration were blended in the parting look he gave her; but he felt it was useless to attempt to divert her from her purpose. He knew that for the true reconstruction of the country something more was needed than bayonets and bullets, or the schemes of selfish politicians or plotting demagogues. He knew that the South needed the surrender of the best brain and heart of the country to build, above the wastes of war, more stately temples of thought and action.

Chapter 28

Dr. Latrobe's Mistake

On the morning previous to their departure for their respective homes, Dr. Gresham met Dr. Latrobe in the parlor of the Concordia.

"How," asked Dr. Gresham, "did you like Dr. Latimer's paper?"

"Very much, indeed. It was excellent. He is a very talented young man. He sits next to me at lunch and I have conversed with him several times. He is very genial and attractive, only he seems to be rather cranky on the negro question. I hope if he comes South that he will not make the mistake of mixing up with the negroes. It would be throwing away his influence and ruining his prospects. He seems to be well versed in science and literature and would make a very delightful accession to our social life."

"I think," replied Dr. Gresham, "that he is an honor to our profession. He is one of the finest specimens of our young manhood."

Just then Dr. Latimer entered the room. Dr. Latrobe arose and, greeting him cordially, said: "I was delighted with your paper; it was full of thought and suggestion."

"Thank you," answered Dr. Latimer, "it was my aim to make it so."

"And you succeeded admirably," replied Dr. Latrobe. "I could not help thinking how much we owe to heredity and environment."

"Yes," said Dr. Gresham. "Continental Europe yearly sends to our shores subjects to be developed into citizens. Emancipation has given us millions of new citizens, and to them our influence and example should be a blessing and not a curse."

"Well," said Dr. Latimer, "I intend to go South, and help those who so much need helpers from their own ranks."

"I hope," answered Dr. Latrobe, "that if you go South you will only sustain business relations with the negroes, and not commit the folly of equalizing yourself with them."

"Why not?" asked Dr. Latimer, steadily looking him in the eye.

"Because in equalizing yourself with them you drag us down; and our social customs must be kept intact."

"You have been associating with me at the convention for several days; I do not see that the contact has dragged you down, has it?"

"You! What has that got to do with associating with niggers?" asked Dr. Latrobe, curtly.

"The blood of that race is coursing through my veins. I am one of them," replied Dr. Latimer, proudly raising his head.

"You!" exclaimed Dr. Latrobe, with an air of profound astonishment and crimsoning face.

"Yes," interposed Dr. Gresham, laughing heartily at Dr. Latrobe's discomfiture. "He belongs to that negro race both by blood and choice. His father's mother made overtures to receive him as her grandson and heir, but he has nobly refused to forsake his mother's people and has cast his lot with them."

"And I," said Dr. Latimer, "would have despised myself if I had done otherwise."

"Well, well," said Dr. Latrobe, rising, "I was never so deceived before. Good morning!"

Dr. Latrobe had thought he was clear-sighted enough to detect the presence of negro blood when all physical traces had disappeared. But he had associated with Dr. Latimer for several days, and admired his talent, without suspecting for one moment his racial connection. He could not help feeling a sense of vexation at the signal mistake he had made.

Dr. Frank Latimer was the natural grandson of a Southern lady, in whose family his mother had been a slave. The blood of a proud aristocratic ancestry was flowing through his veins, and generations of blood admixture had effaced all trace of his negro lineage. His complexion was blonde, his eye bright and piercing, his lips firm and well moulded; his manner very affable; his intellect active and well stored with information. He was a man capable of winning in life through his rich gifts of inheritance and acquirements. When freedom came, his mother, like Hagar of old, went out into the wide world to seek a living for herself and child. Through years of poverty she labored to educate her child, and saw the glad fruition of her hopes when her son graduated as an M.D. from the University of P——.

After his graduation he met his father's mother, who recognized him by his resemblance to her dear, departed son. All the mother love in her lonely heart awoke, and she was willing to overlook "the missing link of matrimony," and adopt him as her heir, if he would ignore his identity with the colored race.

Before him loomed all the possibilities which only birth and blood can give a white man in our Democratic country. But he was a man of too much sterling worth of character to be willing to forsake his mother's race for the richest advantages his grandmother could bestow.

Dr. Gresham had met Dr. Latimer at the beginning of the convention, and had been attracted to him by his frank and genial manner. One morning, when conversing with him, Dr. Gresham had learned some of the salient points of his history, which, instead of repelling him, had only deepened his admiration for the young doctor. He was much amused when he saw the pleasant acquaintanceship between him and Dr. Latrobe, but they agreed to be silent about his racial connection until the time came when they were ready to divulge it; and they were hugely delighted at his signal blunder.

Chapter 29

Visitors from the South

"MAMMA is not well," said Iola to Robert. "I spoke to her about sending for a doctor, but she objected and I did not insist."

"I will ask Dr. Latimer, whom I met at the Concordia, to step in. He is a splendid young fellow. I wish we had thousands like him."

In the evening the doctor called. Without appearing to make a professional visit he engaged Marie in conversation, watched her carefully, and came to the conclusion that her failing health proceeded more from mental than physical causes.

"I am so uneasy about Harry," said Mrs. Leroy. He is so fearless and outspoken. I do wish the attention of the whole nation could be turned to the cruel barbarisms which are a national disgrace. I think the term 'bloody shirt'[101] is one of the most heartless phrases ever invented to divert attention from cruel wrongs and dreadful outrages."

Just then Iola came in and was introduced by her uncle to Dr. Latimer, to whom the introduction was a sudden and unexpected pleasure.

After an interchange of courtesies, Marie resumed the conversation, saying: "Harry wrote me only last week that a young friend of his had lost his situation because he refused to have his pupils strew flowers on the streets through which Jefferson Davis was to pass."

"I think," said Dr. Latimer, indignantly, "that the Israelites had just as much right to scatter flowers over the bodies of the Egyptians, when the waves threw back their corpses on the shores of the Red Sea, as these children had to strew the path of Jefferson Davis with flowers. We want our boys to grow up manly citizens, and not cringing sycophants. When do you expect your son, Mrs. Leroy?"

"Some time next week," answered Marie.

"And his presence will do you more good than all the medicine in my chest."

"I hope, Doctor," said Mrs. Leroy, "that we will not lose sight of you, now that your professional visit is ended; for I believe your visit was the result of a conspiracy between Iola and her uncle."

Dr. Latimer laughed, as he answered, "Ah, Mrs. Leroy, I see you have found us all out."

"Oh, Doctor," exclaimed Iola, with pleasing excitement, "there is a young lady coming here to visit me next week. Her name is Miss Lucille Delany, and she is my ideal woman. She is grand, brave, intellectual, and religious."

"Is that so? She would make some man an excellent wife," replied Dr. Latimer.

"Now isn't that perfectly manlike," answered Iola, smiling. "Mamma, what do you think of that? Did any of you gentlemen ever see a young woman of much ability that you did not look upon as a flotsam all adrift until some man had appropriated her?"

"I think, Miss Leroy, that the world's work, if shared, is better done than when it is performed alone. Don't you think your life-work will be better done if someone[102] shares it with you?" asked Dr. Latimer, slowly, and with a smile in his eyes.

"That would depend on the person who shared it," said Iola, faintly blushing.

"Here," said Robert, a few evenings after this conversation, as he handed Iola a couple of letters, "is something which will please you."

Notes

[101] *'bloody shirt'* waving the bloody shirt; to draw attention away from other atrocities.

[102] *Original reads*: some one [ed.].

Iola took the letters, and, after reading one of them, said: "Miss Delany and Harry will be here on Wednesday; and this one is an invitation which also adds to my enjoyment."

"What is it?" asked Marie; "an invitation to a hop or a german?"

"No; but something which I value far more. We are all invited to Mr. Stillman's to a *conversazione*."[103]

"What is the object?"

"His object is to gather some of the thinkers and leaders of the race to consult on subjects of vital interest to our welfare. He has invited Dr. Latimer, Professor Gradnor, of North Carolina, Mr. Forest, of New York, Hon. Dugdale, Revs. Carmicle, Cantnor, Tunster, Professor Langhorne, of Georgia, and a few ladies, Mrs. Watson, Miss Brown, and others."

"I am glad that it is neither a hop nor a german," said Iola, "but something for which I have been longing."

"Why, Iola," asked Robert, "don't you believe in young people having a good time?"

"Oh, yes," answered Iola, seriously, "I believe in young people having amusements and recreations; but the times are too serious for us to attempt to make our lives a long holiday."

"Well, Iola," answered Robert, "this is the first holiday we have had in two hundred and fifty years, and you shouldn't be too exacting."

"Yes," replied Marie, "human beings naturally crave enjoyment, and if not furnished with good amusements they are apt to gravitate to low pleasures."

"Someone,"[104] said Robert, "has said that the Indian belongs to an old race and looks gloomily back to the past, and that the negro belongs to a young race and looks hopefully towards the future."

"If that be so," replied Marie, "our race-life corresponds more to the follies of youth than the faults of maturer years."

On Dr. Latimer's next visit he was much pleased to see a great change in Marie's appearance. Her eye had grown brighter, her step more elastic, and the anxiety had faded from her face. Harry had arrived, and with him came Miss Delany.

"Good evening, Dr. Latimer," said Iola, cheerily, as she entered the room with Miss Lucille Delany. "This is my friend, Miss Delany, from Georgia. Were she not present I would say she is one of the grandest women in America."

"I am very much pleased to meet you," said Dr. Latimer, cordially; "I have heard Miss Leroy speak of you. We were expecting you," he added, with a smile.

Just then Harry entered the room, and Iola presented him to Dr. Latimer, saying, "This is my brother, about whom mamma was so anxious."

"Had you a pleasant journey?" asked Dr. Latimer, after the first greetings were over.

"Not especially," answered Miss Delany. "Southern roads are not always very pleasant to travel. When Mr. Leroy entered the cars at A——, where he was known, had he taken his seat among the white people he would have been remanded to the colored car."

"But after a while,"[105] said Harry, "as Miss Delany and myself were sitting together, laughing and chatting, a colored man entered the car, and, mistaking me for a white man, asked the conductor to have me removed, and I had to insist that I was colored in order to be permitted to remain. It would be ludicrous, if it were not vexatious, to be too white to be black, and too black to be white."

Notes

[103] *conversazione* a meeting.

[104] *Original reads*: Some one [ed.].

[105] *Original reads*: awhile [ed.].

"Caste plays such fantastic tricks in this country," said Dr. Latimer.

"I tell Mr. Leroy," said Miss Delany, "that when he returns he must put a label on himself, saying, 'I am a colored man,' to prevent annoyance."

Chapter 30

Friends in Council

On the following Friday evening, Mr. Stillman's pleasant, spacious parlors were filled to overflowing with a select company of earnest men and women deeply interested in the welfare of the race.

Bishop Tunster had prepared a paper on "Negro Emigration." Dr. Latimer opened the discussion by speaking favorably of some of the salient points, but said:–

"I do not believe self-exilement is the true remedy for the wrongs of the negro. Where should he go if he left this country?"

"Go to Africa," replied Bishop Tunster, in his bluff, hearty tones. "I believe that Africa is to be redeemed to civilization, and that the negro is to be gathered into the family of nations and recognized as a man and a brother."

"Go to Africa?" repeated Professor Langhorne, of Georgia. "Does the United States own one foot of African soil? And have we not been investing our blood in the country for ages?"

"I am in favor of missionary efforts," said Professor Gradnor, of North Carolina, "for the redemption of Africa, but I see no reason for expatriating ourselves because some persons do not admire the color of our skins."

"I do not believe," said Mr. Stillman, "in emptying on the shores of Africa a horde of ignorant, poverty-stricken people, as missionaries of civilization or Christianity. And while I am in favor of missionary efforts, there is need here for the best heart and brain to work in unison for justice and righteousness."

"America," said Miss Delany, "is the best field for human development. God has not heaped up our mountains with such grandeur, flooded our rivers with such majesty, crowned our valleys with such fertility, enriched our mines with such wealth, that they should only minister to grasping greed and sensuous enjoyment."

"Climate, soil, and physical environments," said Professor Gradnor, "have much to do with shaping national characteristics. If in Africa, under a tropical sun, the negro has lagged behind other races in the march of civilization, at least for once in his history he has, in this country, the privilege of using climatic advantages and developing under new conditions."

"Yes," replied Dr. Latimer, "and I do not wish our people to become restless and unsettled before they have tried one generation of freedom."

"I am always glad," said Mr. Forest, a tall, distinguished-looking gentleman from New York, "when I hear of people who are ill treated in one section of the country emigrating to another. Men who are deaf to the claims of mercy, and oblivious to the demands of justice, can feel when money is slipping from their pockets."

"The negro," said Hon. Dugdale, "does not present to my mind the picture of an effete and exhausted people, destined to die out before a stronger race. Gilbert Haven once saw a statue which suggested this thought, 'I am black but comely; the sun has looked down upon me, but I will teach you who despise me to feel that I am your superior.' The men who are acquiring property and building up homes in the South show us what energy and determination may do even in that part of the country. I believe such men can do more to conquer prejudice than if they spent all their lives in shouting for their rights and ignoring their duties. No! as there are millions of us in this country, I think it best to settle down and work out our own salvation here."

"How many of us to-day," asked Professor Langhorne, "would be teaching in the South, if every field of labor in the North was as accessible to us as to the whites? It has been estimated that a million young white men have left the South since the war, and, had our chances been equal to theirs, would we have been any more willing to stay in the South with those who need us than they? But this prejudice, by impacting us together, gives us a common cause and brings our intellect in contact with the less favored of our race."

"I do not believe," said Miss Delany, "that the Southern white people themselves desire any wholesale exodus of the colored from their labor fields. It would be suicidal to attempt their expatriation."

"History," said Professor Langhorne, "tells that Spain was once the place where barbarian Europe came to light her lamp. Seven hundred years before there was a public lamp in London you might have gone through the streets of Cordova amid ten miles of lighted lamps, and stood there on solidly paved land, when hundreds of years afterwards, in Paris, on a rainy day you would have sunk to your ankles in the mud. But she who bore the name of the 'Terror of Nations,' and the 'Queen of the Ocean,' was not strong enough to dash herself against God's law of retribution and escape unscathed. She inaugurated a crusade of horror[106] against a million of her best laborers and artisans. Vainly she expected the blessing of God to crown her work of violence. Instead of seeing the fruition of her hopes in the increased prosperity of her land, depression and paralysis settled on her trade and business. A fearful blow was struck at her agriculture; decay settled on her manufactories; money became too scarce to pay the necessary expenses of the king's exchequer; and that once mighty empire became a fallen kingdom, pierced by her crimes and dragged down by her transgressions."

"We did not," said Iola, "place the bounds of our habitation. And I believe we are to be fixtures in this country. But beyond the shadows I see the coruscation of a brighter day; and we can help usher it in, not by answering hate with hate, or giving scorn for scorn, but by striving to be more generous, noble, and just. It seems as if all creation travels to respond to the song of the Herald angels, 'Peace on earth, good-will toward men.'"

The next paper was on "Patriotism," by Rev. Cantnor. It was a paper in which the white man was extolled as the master race, and spoke as if it were a privilege for the colored man to be linked to his destiny and to live beneath the shadow of his power. He asserted that the white race of this country is the broadest, most Christian, and humane of that branch of the human family.

Dr. Latimer took exception to his position. "Law," he said, "is the pivot on which the whole universe turns; and obedience to law is the gauge by which a nation's strength or weakness is tried. We have had two evils by which our obedience to law has been tested – slavery and the liquor traffic. How have we dealt with them both? We have been weighed in the balance and found wanting. Millions of slaves and serfs have been liberated during this century, but not even in semi-barbaric Russia, heathen Japan, or Catholic Spain has slavery been abolished through such a fearful conflict as it was in the United States. The liquor traffic still sends its floods of ruin and shame to the habitations of men, and no political party has been found with enough moral power and numerical strength to stay the tide of death."

Notes

[106] *a crusade of horror* the Spanish Inquisition.

"I think," said Professor Gradnor, "that what our country needs is truth more than flattery. I do not think that our moral life keeps pace with our mental development and material progress. I know of no civilized country on the globe, Catholic, Protestant, or Mohammedan, where life is less secure than it is in the South. Nearly eighteen hundred years ago the life of a Roman citizen in Palestine was in danger from mob violence. That pagan government threw around him a wall of living clay, consisting of four hundred and seventy men, when more than forty Jews had bound themselves with an oath that they would neither eat nor drink until they had taken the life of the Apostle Paul. Does not true patriotism demand that citizenship should be as much protected in Christian America as it was in heathen Rome?"

"I would have our people," said Miss Delany, "more interested in politics. Instead of forgetting the past, I would have them hold in everlasting remembrance our great deliverance. Hitherto we have never had a country with tender, precious memories to fill our eyes with tears, or glad reminiscences to thrill our hearts with pride and joy. We have been aliens and outcasts in the land of our birth. But I want my pupils to do all in their power to make this country worthy of their deepest devotion and loftiest patriotism. I want them to feel that its glory is their glory, its dishonor their shame."

"Our esteemed friend, Mrs. Watson," said Iola, "sends regrets that she cannot come, but has kindly favored us with a poem, called the "Rallying Cry." In her letter she says that, although she is no longer young, she feels that in the conflict for the right there's room for young as well as old. She hopes that we will here unite the enthusiasm of youth with the experience of age, and that we will have a pleasant and profitable conference. Is it your pleasure that the poem be read at this stage of our proceedings, or later on?"

"Let us have it now," answered Harry, "and I move that Miss Delany be chosen to lend to the poem the charm of her voice."

"I second the motion," said Iola, smiling, and handing the poem to Miss Delany.

Miss Delany took the poem and read it with fine effect. The spirit of the poem had entered her soul.

A RALLYING CRY

Oh, children of the tropics,
Amid our pain and wrong
Have you no other mission
Than music, dance, and song?

When through the weary ages
Our dripping tears still fall,
Is this a time to dally
With pleasure's silken thrall?

Go, muffle all your viols;
As heroes learn to stand,
With faith in God's great justice
Nerve every heart and hand.

Dream not of ease nor pleasure,
Nor honor, wealth, nor fame,
Till from the dust you've lifted
Our long-dishonored name;

And crowned that name with glory
By deeds of holy worth,
To shine with light emblazoned,
The noblest name on earth.

Count life a dismal failure,
Unblessing and unblest,
That seeks 'mid ease inglorious
For pleasure or for rest.

With courage, strength, and valor
Your lives and actions brace;
Shrink not from toil or hardship,
And dangers bravely face.

Engrave upon your banners,
In words of golden light,
That honor, truth, and justice
Are more than godless might.

Above earth's pain and sorrow
Christ's dying face I see;
I hear the cry of anguish:–
"Why hast thou forsaken me?"

In the pallor of that anguish
I see the only light,
To flood with peace and gladness
Earth's sorrow, pain, and night.

Arrayed in Christly armor
'Gainst error, crime, and sin,
The victory can't be doubtful,
For God is sure to win.

The next paper was by Miss Iola Leroy, on the "Education of Mothers."

"I agree," said Rev. Eustace, of St. Mary's parish, "with the paper. The great need of the race is enlightened mothers."

"And enlightened fathers, too," added Miss Delany, quickly. "If there is anything I chafe to see it is a strong, hearty man shirking his burdens, putting them on the shoulders of his wife, and taking life easy for himself."

"I always pity such mothers," interposed Iola, tenderly.

"I think," said Miss Delany, with a flash in her eye and a ring of decision in her voice, "that such men ought to be drummed out of town!" As she spoke, there was an expression which seemed to say, "And I would like to help do it!"

Harry smiled, and gave her a quick glance of admiration.

"I do not think," said Mrs. Stillman, "that we can begin too early to teach our boys to be manly and self-respecting, and our girls to be useful and self-reliant."

"You know," said Mrs. Leroy, "that after the war we were thrown upon the nation a homeless race to be gathered into homes, and a legally unmarried race to be taught the sacredness of the marriage relation. We must instill into our young people that the true strength of a race means purity in women and uprightness in men; who can say, with Sir Galahad:–

> 'My strength is the strength of ten,
> Because my heart is pure.'[107]

And where this is wanting neither wealth nor culture can make up the deficiency."

"There is a field of Christian endeavor which lies between the school-house and the pulpit, which needs the hand of a woman more in private than in public," said Miss Delany.

"Yes, I have often felt the need of such work in my own parish. We need a union of women with the warmest hearts and clearest brains to help in the moral education of the race," said Rev. Eustace.

"Yes," said Iola, "if we would have the prisons empty we must make the homes more attractive."

"In civilized society," replied Dr. Latimer, "there must be restraint either within or without. If parents fail to teach restraint within, society has her check-reins without in the form of chain-gangs, prisons, and the gallows."

The closing paper was on the "Moral Progress of the Race," by Hon. Dugdale. He said: "The moral progress of the race was not all he could desire, yet he could not help feeling that, compared with other races, the outlook was not hopeless. I am so sorry to see, however, that in some States there is an undue proportion of colored people in prisons."

"I think," answered Professor Langhorne, of Georgia, "that this is owing to a partial administration of law in meting out punishment to colored offenders. I know red-handed murderers who walk in this Republic unwhipped of justice, and I have seen a colored woman sentenced to prison for weeks for stealing twenty-five cents. I knew a colored girl who was executed for murder when only a child in years. And it was through the intervention of a friend of mine, one of the bravest young men of the South, that a boy of fifteen was saved from the gallows."

"When I look," said Mr. Forest, "at the slow growth of modern civilization – the ages which have been consumed in reaching our present altitude, and see how we have outgrown slavery, feudalism, and religious persecutions, I cannot despair of the future of the race."

"Just now," said Dr. Latimer, "we have the fearful grinding and friction which comes in the course of an adjustment of the new machinery of freedom in the old ruts of slavery. But I am optimistic enough to believe that there will yet be a far higher and better Christian civilization than our country has ever known."

"And in that civilization I believe the negro is to be an important factor," said Rev. Cantnor.

"I believe it also," said Miss Delany, hopefully, "and this thought has been a blessed inspiration to my life. When I come in contact with Christless prejudices, I feel that my life is too much a part of the Divine plan, and invested with too much intrinsic worth, for me to be the least humiliated by indignities that beggarly souls can inflict. I feel more pitiful than resentful to those who do not know how much they miss by living mean, ignoble lives."

Notes

107 *"My strength … is pure"* from "Sir Galahad" (1842), a poem by Alfred, Lord Tennyson (1809–1892).

"My heart," said Iola, "is full of hope for the future. Pain and suffering are the crucibles out of which come gold more fine than the pavements of heaven, and gems more precious than the foundations of the Holy City."

"If," said Mrs. Leroy, "pain and suffering are factors in human development, surely we have not been counted too worthless to suffer."

"And is there," continued Iola, "a path which we have trodden in this country, unless it be the path of sin, into which Jesus Christ has not put His feet and left it luminous with the light of His steps? Has the negro been poor and homeless? The birds of the air had nests and the foxes had holes, but the Son of man had not where to lay His head. Has our name been a synonym for contempt? 'He shall be called a Nazarene.'[108] Have we been despised and trodden under foot? Christ was despised and rejected of men. Have we been ignorant and unlearned? It was said of Jesus Christ, 'How knoweth this man letters, never having learned?' Have we been beaten and bruised in the prison-house of bondage? 'They took Jesus and scourged Him.'[109] Have we been slaughtered, our bones scattered at the graves' mouth? He was spit upon by the mob, smitten and mocked by the rabble, and died as died Rome's meanest criminal slave. To-day that cross of shame is a throne of power. Those robes of scorn have changed to habiliments of light, and that crown of mockery to a diadem of glory. And never, while the agony of Gethsemane and the sufferings of Calvary have their hold upon my heart, will I recognize any religion as His which despises the least of His brethren."

As Iola finished, there was a ring of triumph in her voice, as if she were reviewing a path she had trodden with bleeding feet, and seen it change to lines of living light. Her soul seemed to be flashing through the rare loveliness of her face and etherealizing its beauty.

Everyone was spell-bound. Dr. Latimer was entranced, and, turning to Hon. Dugdale, said, in a low voice and with deep-drawn breath, "She is angelic!"

Hon. Dugdale turned, gave a questioning look, then replied, "She is strangely beautiful! Do you know her?"

"Yes; I have met her several times. I accompanied her here to-night. The tones of her voice are like benedictions of peace; her words a call to higher service and nobler life."

Just then Rev. Carmicle was announced. He had been on a Southern tour, and had just returned.

"Oh, Doctor," exclaimed Mrs. Stillman, "I am delighted to see you. We were about to adjourn, but we will postpone action to hear from you."

"Thank you," replied Rev. Carmicle. "I have not the cue to the meeting, and will listen while I take breath."

"Pardon me," answered Mrs. Stillman. "I should have been more thoughtful than to press so welcome a guest into service before I had given him time for rest and refreshment; but if the courtesy failed on my lips it did not fail in my heart. I wanted our young folks to see one of our thinkers who had won distinction before the war."

"My dear friend," said Rev. Carmicle, smiling, "some of these young folks will look on me as a back number. You know the cry has already gone forth, 'Young men to the front.'"[110]

"But we need old men for counsel," interposed Mr. Forest, of New York.

Notes

[108] *'He shall be called a Nazarene'* Matthew 2:23; the verse seems to refer to Jesus's humble beginnings.

[109] *'They took Jesus and scourged Him'* John 19:1.

[110] *"Young men to the front"* the title of an essay by Richard T. Greener (1844–1902), the first African American to graduate from Harvard.

"Of course," said Rev. Carmicle, "we older men would rather retire gracefully than be relegated or hustled to a back seat. But I am pleased to see doors open to you which were closed to us, and opportunities which were denied us embraced by you."

"How," asked Hon. Dugdale, "do you feel in reference to our people's condition in the South?"

"Very hopeful, although at times I cannot help feeling anxious about their future. I was delighted with my visits to various institutions of learning, and surprised at the desire manifested among the young people to obtain an education. Where toil-worn mothers bent beneath their heavy burdens their more favored daughters are enjoying the privileges of education. Young people are making recitations in Greek and Latin where it was once a crime to teach their parents to read. I also became acquainted with colored professors and presidents of colleges. Saw young ladies who had graduated as doctors. Comfortable homes have succeeded old cabins of slavery. Vast crops have been raised by free labor. I read with interest and pleasure a number of papers edited by colored men. I saw it estimated that two millions of our people had learned to read, and I feel deeply grateful to the people who have supplied us with teachers who have stood their ground so nobly among our people."

"But," asked Mr. Forest, "you expressed fears about the future of our race. From whence do your fears arise?"

"From the unfortunate conditions which slavery has entailed upon that section of our country. I dread the results of that racial feeling which ever and anon breaks out into restlessness and crime. Also, I am concerned about the lack of home training for those for whom the discipline of the plantation has been exchanged for the penalties of prisons and chain-gangs. I am sorry to see numbers of our young men growing away from the influence of the church and drifting into prisons. I also fear that in some sections, as colored men increase in wealth and intelligence, there will be an increase of race rivalry and jealousy. It is said that savages, by putting their ears to the ground, can hear a far-off tread. So, to-day, I fear that there are savage elements in our civilization which hear the advancing tread of the negro and would retard his coming. It is the incarnation of these elements that I dread. It is their elimination I do so earnestly desire. Whether it be outgrown or not is our unsolved problem. Time alone will tell whether or not the virus of slavery and injustice has too fully permeated our Southern civilization for a complete recovery. Nations, honey-combed by vice, have fallen beneath the weight of their iniquities. Justice is always uncompromising in its claims and inexorable in its demands. The laws of the universe are never repealed to accommodate our follies."

"Surely," said Bishop Tunster, "the negro has a higher mission than that of aimlessly drifting through life and patiently waiting for death."

"We may not," answered Rev. Carmicle, "have the same dash, courage, and aggressiveness of other races, accustomed to struggle, achievement, and dominion, but surely the world needs something better than the results of arrogance, aggressiveness, and indomitable power. For the evils of society there are no solvents as potent as love and justice, and our greatest need is not more wealth and learning, but a religion replete with life and glowing with love. Let this be the impelling force in the race and it cannot fail to rise in the scale of character and condition."

"And," said Dr. Latimer," instead of narrowing our sympathies to mere racial questions, let us broaden them to humanity's wider issues."

"Let us," replied Rev. Carmicle, "pass it along the lines, that to be willfully ignorant is to be shamefully criminal. Let us teach our people not to love pleasure or to fear death, but to learn the true value of life, and to do their part to eliminate the paganism of caste from our holy religion and the lawlessness of savagery from our civilization."

"How did you enjoy the evening, Marie?" asked Robert, as they walked homeward.

"I was interested and deeply pleased," answered Marie.

"I," said Robert, "was thinking of the wonderful changes that have come to us since the war. When I sat in those well-lighted, beautifully-furnished rooms, I was thinking of the meetings we used to have in by-gone days. How we used to go by stealth into lonely woods and gloomy swamps, to tell of our hopes and fears, sorrows and trials. I hope that we will have many more of these gatherings. Let us have the next one here."

"I am sure," said Marie, "I would gladly welcome such a conference at any time. I think such meetings would be so helpful to our young people."

Chapter 31

Dawning Affections

"DOCTOR," said Iola, as they walked home from the *conversazione*, "I wish I could do something more for our people than I am doing. I taught in the South till failing health compelled me to change my employment. But, now that I am well and strong, I would like to do something of lasting service for the race."

"Why not," asked Dr. Latimer, "write a good, strong book which would be helpful to them? I think there is an amount of dormant talent among us, and a large field from which to gather materials for such a book."

"I would do it, willingly, if I could; but one needs both leisure and money to make a successful book. There is material among us for the broadest comedies and the deepest tragedies, but, besides money and leisure, it needs patience, perseverance, courage, and the hand of an artist to weave it into the literature of the country."

"Miss Leroy, you have a large and rich experience; you possess a vivid imagination and glowing fancy. Write, out of the fullness of your heart, a book to inspire men and women with a deeper sense of justice and humanity."

"Doctor," replied Iola, "I would do it if I could, not for the money it might bring, but for the good it might do. But who believes any good can come out of the black Nazareth?"[III]

"Miss Leroy, out of the race must come its own thinkers and writers. Authors belonging to the white race have written good racial books, for which I am deeply grateful, but it seems to be almost impossible for a white man to put himself completely in our place. No man can feel the iron which enters another man's soul."

"Well, Doctor, when I write a book I shall take you for the hero of my story."

"Why, what have I done," asked Dr. Latimer, in a surprised tone, "that you should impale me on your pen?"

"You have done nobly," answered Iola, "in refusing your grandmother's offer."

"I only did my duty," he modestly replied.

"But," said Iola, "when others are trying to slip out from the race and pass into the white basis, I cannot help admiring one who acts as if he felt that the weaker the race is the closer he would cling to it."

"My mother," replied Dr. Latimer, "faithful and true, belongs to that race. Where else should I be? But I know a young lady who could have cast her lot with the favored race, yet

Notes

[III] *black Nazareth* Matthew 2:23; the verse seems to refer to Jesus's humble beginnings.

chose to take her place with the freed people, as their teacher, friend, and adviser. This young lady was alone in the world. She had been fearfully wronged, and to her stricken heart came a brilliant offer of love, home, and social position. But she bound her heart to the mast of duty, closed her ears to the syren song, and could not be lured from her purpose."

A startled look stole over Iola's face, and, lifting her eyes to his, she faltered:–

"Do you know her?"

"Yes, I know her and admire her; and she ought to be made the subject of a soul-inspiring story. Do you know of whom I speak?"

"How should I, Doctor? I am sure you have not made me your confidante," she responded, demurely; then she quickly turned and tripped up the steps of her home, which she had just reached.

After this conversation Dr. Latimer became a frequent visitor at Iola's home, and a firm friend of her brother. Harry was at that age when, for the young and inexperienced, vice puts on her fairest guise and most seductive smiles. Dr. Latimer's wider knowledge and larger experience made his friendship for Harry very valuable, and the service he rendered him made him a favorite and ever-welcome guest in the family.

"Are you all alone," asked Robert, one night, as he entered the cosy little parlor where Iola sat reading. "Where are the rest of the folks?"

"Mamma and grandma have gone to bed," answered Iola. "Harry and Lucille are at the concert. They are passionately fond of music, and find facilities here that they do not have in the South. They wouldn't go to hear a seraph[112] where they must take a negro seat. I was too tired to go. Besides, 'two's company and three's a crowd,'" she added, significantly.

"I reckon you struck the nail on the head that time," said Robert, laughing. "But you have not been alone all the time. Just as I reached the comer I saw Dr. Latimer leaving the door. I see he still continues his visits. Who is his patient now?"

"Oh, Uncle Robert," said Iola, smiling and flushing, "he is out with Harry and Lucille part of the time, and drops in now and then to see us all."

"Well," said Robert, "I suppose the case is now an affair of the heart. But I cannot blame him for it," he added, looking fondly on the beautiful face of his niece, which sorrow had touched only to chisel into more loveliness. "How do you like him?"

"I must have within me," answered Iola, with unaffected truthfulness, "a large amount of hero worship. The characters of the Old Testament I most admire are Moses and Nehemiah.[113] They were willing to put aside their own advantages for their race and country. Dr. Latimer comes up to my ideal of a high, heroic manhood."

"I think," answered Robert, smiling archly, "he would be delighted to hear your opinion of him."

"I tell him," continued Iola, "that he belongs to the days of chivalry. But he smiles and says he only belongs to the days of hard-pan service."

"Someone,"[114] said Robert, "was saying to-day that he stood in his own light when he refused his grandmother's offer to receive him as her son."

"I think," said Iola, "it was the grandest hour of his life when he made that decision. I have admired him ever since I heard his story."

"But, Iola, think of the advantages he set aside. It was no sacrifice for me to remain colored, with my lack of education and race sympathies, but Dr. Latimer had doors open to

Notes

[112] *seraph* angel.

[113] *Moses and Nehemiah* two Jewish prophets who held positions of privilege (Moses was raised by the Egyptian pharaoh's daughter; Nehemiah was the cupbearer to the king).

[114] *Original reads*: Some one [ed.].

him as a white man which are forever closed to a colored man. To be born white in this country is to be born to an inheritance of privileges, to hold in your hands the keys that open before you the doors of every occupation, advantage, opportunity, and achievement."

"I know that, uncle," answered Iola; "but even these advantages are too dearly bought if they mean loss of honor, true manliness, and self-respect. He could not have retained these had he ignored his mother and lived under a veil of concealment, constantly haunted by a dread of detection. The gain would not have been worth the cost. It were better that he should walk the ruggedest paths of life a true man than tread the softest carpets a moral cripple."

"I am afraid," said Robert, laying his hand caressingly upon her head, "that we are destined to lose the light of our home."

"Oh, uncle, how you talk! I never dreamed of what you are thinking," answered Iola, half reproachfully.

"And how," asked Robert, "do you know what I am thinking about?"

"My dear uncle, I'm not blind."

"Neither am I," replied Robert, significantly, as he left the room.

Iola's admiration for Dr. Latimer was not a one-sided affair. Day after day she was filling a larger place in his heart. The touch of her hand thrilled him with emotion. Her lightest words were an entrancing melody to his ear. Her noblest sentiments found a response in his heart. In their desire to help the race their hearts beat in loving unison. One grand and noble purpose was giving tone and color to their lives and strengthening the bonds of affection between them.

Chapter 32

Wooing and Wedding

HARRY's vacation had been very pleasant. Miss Delany, with her fine conversational powers and ready wit, had added much to his enjoyment. Robert had given his mother the pleasantest room in the house, and in the evening the family would gather around her, tell her the news of the day, read to her from the Bible, join with her in thanksgiving for mercies received and in prayer for protection through the night. Harry was very grateful to Dr. Latimer for the kindly interest he had shown in accompanying Miss Delany and himself to places of interest and amusement. He was grateful, too, that in the city of P—— doors were open to them which were barred against them in the South.

The bright, beautiful days of summer were gliding into autumn, with its glorious wealth of foliage, and the time was approaching for the departure of Harry and Miss Delany to their respective schools, when Dr. Latimer received several letters from North Carolina, urging him to come South, as physicians were greatly needed there. Although his practice was lucrative in the city of P——, he resolved he would go where his services were most needed.

A few evenings before he started he called at the house, and made an engagement to drive Iola to the park.

At the time appointed he drove up to the door in his fine equipage.[115] Iola stepped gracefully in and sat quietly by his side to enjoy the loveliness of the scenery and the gorgeous grandeur of the setting sun.

Notes

[115] *equipage* a horse-drawn carriage.

"I expect to go South," said Dr. Latimer, as he drove slowly along.

"Ah, indeed," said Iola, assuming an air of interest, while a shadow flitted over her face. "Where do you expect to pitch your tent?"

"In the city of C——, North Carolina," he answered.

"Oh, I wish," she exclaimed, "that you were going to Georgia, where you could take care of that high-spirited brother of mine."

"I suppose if he were to hear you he would laugh, and say that he could take care of himself. But I know a better plan than that."

"What is it?" asked Iola, innocently.

"That you will commit yourself, instead of your brother, to my care."

"Oh, dear," replied Iola, drawing a long breath. "What would mamma say?"

"That she would willingly resign you, I hope."

"And what would grandma and Uncle Robert say?" again asked Iola.

"That they would cheerfully acquiesce. Now, what would I say if they all consent?"

"I don't know," modestly responded Iola.

"Well," replied Dr. Latimer, "I would say:–

'Could deeds my love discover,
Could valor gain thy charms,
To prove myself thy lover
I'd face a world in arms.'"

"And prove a good soldier," added Iola, smiling, "when there is no battle to fight."

"Iola, I am in earnest," said Dr. Latimer, passionately. "In the work to which I am devoted every burden will be lighter, every path smoother, if brightened and blessed with your companionship."

A sober expression swept over Iola's face, and, dropping her eyes, she said: "I must have time to think."

Quietly they rode along the river bank until Dr. Latimer broke the silence by saying:–

"Miss Iola, I think that you brood too much over the condition of our people."

"Perhaps I do," she replied, "but they never burn a man in the South that they do not kindle a fire around my soul."

"I am afraid," replied Dr. Latimer, "that you will grow morbid and nervous. Most of our people take life easily – why shouldn't you?"

"Because," she answered, "I can see breakers ahead which they do not."

"Oh, give yourself no uneasiness. They will catch the fret and fever of the nineteenth century soon enough. I have heard several of our ministers say that it is chiefly men of disreputable characters who are made the subjects of violence and lynch-law."

"Suppose it is so," responded Iola, feelingly. "If these men believe in eternal punishment they ought to feel a greater concern for the wretched sinner who is hurried out of time with all his sins upon his head, than for the godly man who passes through violence to endless rest."

"That is true; and I am not counseling you to be selfish; but, Miss Iola, had you not better look out for yourself?"

"Thank you, Doctor, I am feeling quite well."

"I know it, but your devotion to study and work is too intense," he replied.

"I am preparing to teach, and must spend my leisure time in study. Mr. Cloten is an excellent employer, and treats his employes as if they had hearts as well as hands. But to be an expert accountant is not the best use to which I can put my life."

"As a teacher you will need strong health and calm nerves. You had better let me prescribe for you. You need," he added, with a merry twinkle in his eyes, "change of air, change of scene, and change of name."

"Well, Doctor," said Iola, laughing, "that is the newest nostrum[116] out. Had you not better apply for a patent?"

"Oh," replied Dr. Latimer, with affected gravity, "you know you must have unlimited faith in your physician."

"So you wish me to try the faith cure?" asked Iola, laughing.

"Yes, faith in me," responded Dr. Latimer, seriously.

"Oh, here we are at home!" exclaimed Iola. "This has been a glorious evening, Doctor. I am indebted to you for a great pleasure. I am extremely grateful."

"You are perfectly welcome," replied Dr. Latimer. "The pleasure has been mutual, I assure you."

"Will you not come in?" asked Iola.

Tying his horse, he accompanied Iola into the parlor. Seating himself near her, he poured into her ears words eloquent with love and tenderness.

"Iola," he said, "I am not an adept in courtly phrases. I am a plain man, who believes in love and truth. In asking you to share my lot, I am not inviting you to a life of ease and luxury, for year after year I may have to struggle to keep the wolf from the door, but your presence would make my home one of the brightest spots on earth, and one of the fairest types of heaven. Am I presumptuous in hoping that your love will become the crowning joy of my life?"

His words were more than a tender strain wooing her to love and happiness, they were a clarion call to a life of high and holy worth, a call which found a response in her heart. Her hand lay limp in his. She did not withdraw it, but, raising her lustrous eyes to his, she softly answered: "Frank, I love you."

After he had gone, Iola sat by the window, gazing at the splendid stars, her heart quietly throbbing with a delicious sense of joy and love. She had admired Dr. Gresham and, had there been no barrier in her way, she might have learned to love him; but Dr. Latimer had grown irresistibly upon her heart. There were depths in her nature that Dr. Gresham had never fathomed; aspirations in her soul with which he had never mingled. But as the waves leap up to the strand, so her soul went out to Dr. Latimer. Between their lives were no impeding barriers, no inclination impelling one way and duty compelling another. Kindred hopes and tastes had knit their hearts; grand and noble purposes were lighting up their lives; and they esteemed it a blessed privilege to stand on the threshold of a new era and labor for those who had passed from the old oligarchy of slavery into the new commonwealth of freedom.

On the next evening, Dr. Latimer rang the bell and was answered by Harry, who ushered him into the parlor, and then came back to the sitting-room, saying, "Iola, Dr. Latimer has called to see you."

"Has he?" answered Iola, a glad light coming into her eyes. "Come, Lucille, let us go into the parlor."

"Oh, no," interposed Harry, shrugging his shoulders and catching Lucille's hand. "He didn't ask for you. When we went to the concert we were told three's a crowd. And I say one good turn deserves another."

"Oh, Harry, you are so full of nonsense. Let Lucille go!" said Iola.

Notes

[116] *nostrum* questionable medicine.

"Indeed I will not. I want to have a good time as well as you," said Harry.

"Oh, you're the most nonsensical man I know," interposed Miss Delany. Yet she stayed with Harry.

"You're looking very bright and happy," said Dr. Latimer to Iola, as she entered.

"My ride in the park was so refreshing! I enjoyed it so much! The day was so lovely, the air delicious, the birds sang so sweetly, and the sunset was so magnificent."

"I am glad of it. Why, Iola, your home is so happy your heart should be as light as a school-girl's."

"Doctor," she replied, "I must be prematurely old. I have scarcely known what it is to be light-hearted since my father's death."

"I know it, darling," he answered, seating himself beside her, and drawing her to him. "You have been tried in the fire, but are you not better for the crucial test?"

"Doctor," she replied, "as we rode along yesterday, mingling with the sunshine of the present came the shadows of the past. I was thinking of the bright, joyous days of my girlhood, when I defended slavery, and of how the cup that I would have pressed to the lips of others was forced to my own. Yet, in looking over the mournful past, I would not change the Iola of then for the Iola of now."

"Yes," responded Dr. Latimer, musingly,

'Darkness shows us worlds of light
We never saw by day.'"[117]

"Oh, Doctor, you cannot conceive what it must have been to be hurled from a home of love and light into the dark abyss of slavery; to be compelled to take your place among a people you have learned to look upon as inferiors and social outcasts; to be in the power of men whose presence would fill you with horror and loathing, and to know that there is no earthly power to protect you from the highest insults which brutal cowardice could shower upon you. I am so glad that no other woman of my race will suffer as I have done."

The flush deepened on her face, a mournful splendor beamed from her beautiful eyes, into which the tears had slowly gathered.

"Darling," he said, his voice vibrating with mingled feelings of tenderness and resentment, "you must forget the sad past. You are like a tender lamb snatched from the jaws of a hungry wolf, but who still needs protecting, loving care. But it must have been terrible," he added, in a painful tone.

"It was indeed! For a while[118] I was like one dazed. I tried to pray, but the heavens seemed brass over my head. I was wild with agony, and had I not been placed under conditions which roused all the resistance of my soul, I would have lost my reason."

"Was it not a mistake to have kept you ignorant of your colored blood?"

"It was the great mistake of my father's life, but dear papa knew something of the cruel, crushing power of caste; and he tried to shield us from it."

"Yes, yes," replied Dr. Latimer, thoughtfully, "in trying to shield you from pain he plunged you into deeper suffering."

"I never blame him, because I know he did it for the best. Had he lived he would have taken us to France, where I should have had a life of careless ease and pleasure.

Notes

[117] *"Darkness shows us ... by day"* from the poem "O Thou Who Dry'st The Mourner's Tear" by Thomas Moore (1779–1852).

[118] *Original reads*: awhile [ed.].

But now my life has a much grander significance than it would have had under such conditions. Fearful as the awakening was, it was better than to have slept through life."

"Best for you and best for me," said Dr. Latimer. "There are souls that never awaken; but if they miss the deepest pain they also lose the highest joy."

Dr. Latimer went South, after his engagement, and through his medical skill and agreeable manners became very successful in his practice. In the following summer, he built a cosy home for the reception of his bride, and came North, where, with Harry and Miss Delany as attendants, he was married to Iola, amid a pleasant gathering of friends, by Rev. Carmicle.

Chapter 33

Conclusion

It was late in the summer when Dr. Latimer and his bride reached their home in North Carolina. Over the cottage porch were morning-glories to greet the first flushes of the rising day, and roses and jasmines to distill their fragrance on the evening air. Aunt Linda, who had been apprised of their coming, was patiently awaiting their arrival, and Uncle Daniel was pleased to know that "dat sweet young lady who had sich putty manners war comin' to lib wid dem."

As soon as they arrived, Aunt Linda rushed up to Iola, folded her in her arms, and joyfully exclaimed: "How'dy, honey! Ise so glad you's come. I seed it in a vision dat somebody fair war comin' to help us. An' wen I yered it war you, I larffed and jist rolled ober, and larffed and jist gib up."

"But, Aunt Linda, I am not very fair," replied Mrs. Latimer.

"Well, chile, you's fair to me. How's all yore folks in de up kentry?"

"All well. I expect them down soon to live here."

"What, Har'yet, and Robby, an' yer ma? Oh, dat is too good. I allers said Robby had san' in his craw, and war born for good luck. He war a mighty nice boy. Har'yet's in clover now. Well, ebery dorg has its day, and de cat has Sunday. I allers tole Har'yet ter keep a stiff upper lip; dat it war a long road dat had no turn."

Dr. Latimer was much gratified by the tender care Aunt Linda bestowed on Iola.

"I ain't goin' to let her do nuffin till she gits seasoned. She looks as sweet as a peach. I allers wanted some nice lady to come down yere and larn our gals some sense. I can't read myself, but I likes ter yere dem dat can."

"Well, Aunt Linda, I am going to teach in the Sunday-school, help in the church, hold mothers' meetings to help these boys and girls to grow up to be good men and women. Won't you get a pair of spectacles and learn to read?"

"Oh, yer can't git dat book froo my head, no way you fix it. I knows nuff to git to hebben, and dats all I wants to know." Aunt Linda was kind and obliging, but there was one place where she drew the line, and that was at learning to read.

Harry and Miss Delany accompanied Iola as far as her new home, and remained several days. The evening before their departure, Harry took Miss Delany a drive of several miles through the pine barrens.

"This thing is getting very monotonous," Harry broke out, when they had gone some distance.

"Oh, I enjoy it!" replied Miss Delany. "These stately pines look so grand and solemn, they remind me of a procession of hooded monks."

"What in the world are you talking about, Lucille?" asked Harry, looking puzzled.

"About those pine-trees," replied Miss Delany, in a tone of surprise.

"Pshaw, I wasn't thinking about them. I'm thinking about Iola and Frank."

"What about them?" asked Lucille.

"Why, when I was in P——, Dr. Latimer used to be first-rate company, but now it is nothing but what Iola wants, and what Iola says, and what Iola likes. I don't believe that there is a subject I could name to him, from spinning a top to circumnavigating the globe, that he wouldn't somehow contrive to bring Iola in. And I don't believe you could talk ten minutes to Iola on any subject, from dressing a doll to the latest discovery in science, that she wouldn't manage to lug in Frank."

"Oh, you absurd creature!" responded Lucille, "this is their honeymoon, and they are deeply in love with each other. Wait till you get in love with someone."[119]

"I am in love now," replied Harry, with a serious air.

"With whom?" asked Lucille, archly.

"With you," answered Harry, trying to take her hand.

"Oh, Harry!" she exclaimed, playfully resisting. "Don't be so nonsensical! Don't you think the bride looked lovely, with that dress of spotless white and with those orange blossoms in her hair?"

"Yes, she did; that's a fact," responded Harry. "But, Lucille, I think there is a great deal of misplaced sentiment at weddings," he added, more seriously.

"How so?"

"Oh, here are a couple just married, and who are as happy as happy can be; and people will crowd around them wishing much joy; but who thinks of wishing joy to the forlorn old bachelors and restless old maids?"

"Well, Harry, if you want people to wish you much happiness, why don't you do as the doctor has done, get yourself a wife?"

"I will," he replied, soberly, "when you say so."

"Oh, Harry, don't be so absurd."

"Indeed there isn't a bit of absurdity about what I say. I am in earnest." There was something in the expression of Harry's face and the tone of his voice which arrested the banter on Lucille's lips.

"I think it was Charles Lamb,"[120] replied Lucille, "who once said that school-teachers are uncomfortable people, and, Harry, I would not like to make you uncomfortable by marrying you."

"You will make me uncomfortable by not marrying me."

"But," replied Lucille, "your mother may not prefer me for a daughter. You know, Harry, complexional prejudices are not confined to white people."

"My mother," replied Harry, with an air of confidence, "is too noble to indulge in such sentiments."

"And Iola, would she be satisfied?"

"Why, it would add to her satisfaction. She is not one who can't be white and won't be black."

"Well, then," replied Lucille, "I will take the question of your comfort into consideration."

The above promise was thoughtfully remembered by Lucille till a bridal ring and happy marriage were the result.

Soon after Iola had settled in C—— she quietly took her place in the Sunday-school as a teacher, and in the church as a helper. She was welcomed by the young pastor, who found in her a strong and faithful ally. Together they planned meetings for the especial

Notes

[119] *Original reads*: some one [ed.].

[120] Charles Lamb (1775–1834), English essayist.

benefit of mothers and children. When the dens of vice are spreading their snares for the feet of the tempted and inexperienced her doors are freely opened for the instruction of the children before their feet have wandered and gone far astray. She has no carpets too fine for the tread of their little feet. She thinks it is better to have stains on her carpet than stains on their souls through any neglect of hers. In lowly homes and windowless cabins her visits are always welcome. Little children love her. Old age turns to her for comfort, young girls for guidance, and mothers for counsel. Her life is full of blessedness.

Doctor Latimer by his kindness and skill has won the name of the "Good Doctor." But he is more than a successful doctor; he is a true patriot and a good citizen. Honest, just, and discriminating, he endeavors by precept and example to instill into the minds of others sentiments of good citizenship. He is a leader in every reform movement for the benefit of the community; but his patriotism is not confined to race lines. "The world is his country, and mankind his countrymen."[121] While he abhors their deeds of violence, he pities the short-sighted and besotted men who seem madly intent upon laying magazines of powder under the cradles of unborn generations. He has great faith in the possibilities of the negro, and believes that, enlightened and Christianized, he will sink the old animosities of slavery into the new community of interests arising from freedom; and that his influence upon the South will be as the influence of the sun upon the earth. As when the sun passes from Capricorn to Cancer, beauty, greenness, and harmony spring up in his path, so he hopes that the future career of the negro will be a greater influence for freedom and social advancement than it was in the days of yore for slavery and its inferior civilization.

Harry and Lucille are at the head of a large and flourishing school. Lucille gives her ripening experience to her chosen work, to which she was too devoted to resign. And through the school they are lifting up the homes of the people. Some have pitied, others blamed, Harry for casting his lot with the colored people, but he knows that life's highest and best advantages do not depend on the color of the skin or texture of the hair. He has his reward in the improved condition of his pupils and the superb manhood and noble life which he has developed in his much needed work.

Uncle Daniel still lingers on the shores of time, a cheery, lovable old man, loved and respected by all; a welcome guest in every home. Soon after Iola's marriage, Robert sold out his business and moved with his mother and sister to North Carolina. He bought a large plantation near C——, which he divided into small homesteads, and sold to poor but thrifty laborers, and his heart has been gladdened by their increased prosperity and progress. He has seen the one-roomed cabins change to comfortable cottages, in which cleanliness and order have supplanted the prolific causes of disease and death. Kind and generous, he often remembers Mrs. Johnson and sends her timely aid.

Marie's pale, spiritual face still bears traces of the beauty which was her youthful dower, but its bloom has been succeeded by an air of sweetness and dignity. Though frail in health, she is always ready to lend a helping hand wherever and whenever she can.

Grandmother Johnson was glad to return South and spend the remnant of her days with the remaining friends of her early life. Although feeble, she is in full sympathy with her children for the uplifting of the race. Marie and her mother are enjoying their

Notes

[121] *"The world … countrymen."* quotation by John Smithson (1765–1829), founder of the Smithsonian Institute.

aftermath of life, one by rendering to others all the service in her power, while the other, with her face turned toward the celestial city, is

"Only waiting till the angels
Open wide the mystic gate."[122]

The shadows have been lifted from all their lives; and peace, like bright dew, has descended upon their paths. Blessed themselves, their lives are a blessing to others.

Note

FROM threads of fact and fiction I have woven a story whose mission will not be in vain if it awaken in the hearts of our countrymen a stronger sense of justice and a more Christlike humanity in behalf of those whom the fortunes of war threw, homeless, ignorant and poor, upon the threshold of a new era. Nor will it be in vain if it inspire the children of those upon whose brows God has poured the chrism of that new era to determine that they will embrace every opportunity, develop every faculty, and use every power God has given them to rise in the scale of character and condition, and to add their quota of good citizenship to the best welfare of the nation. There are scattered among us materials for mournful tragedies and mirth-provoking comedies, which some hand may yet bring into the literature of the country, glowing with the fervor of the tropics and enriched by the luxuriance of the Orient, and thus add to the solution of our unsolved American problem.

The race has not had very long to straighten its hands from the hoe, to grasp the pen and wield it as a power for good, and to erect above the ruined auction-block and slave-pen institutions of learning, but

There is light beyond the darkness,
Joy beyond the present pain;
There is hope in God's great justice
And the negro's rising brain.

Though the morning seems to linger
O'er the hill-tops far away,
Yet the shadows bear the promise
Of a brighter coming day.

1892

Notes

[122] *"Only waiting till the angels … gate."* from the poem "Only Waiting" by Frances Laughton Mace (1836–1899).

Anna Julia Cooper (1858–1964)

One of the first African American women to receive a doctoral degree, Anna Julia Cooper spent her life pursuing racial and gender equality through intellectual engagement, even as discrimination and ideological conflicts with her colleagues interfered with her public success. Her 1892 proto-feminist treatise, *A Voice from the South by a Black Woman of the South*, captured the special role African American women played in racial uplift with the famous words, "Not the boys less, but the girls more."

Anna Julia Cooper was born in Raleigh, North Carolina, to a slave woman, Hannah Stanley Haywood, and her white master, George Washington Haywood. After the Civil War, her auspicious scholarly career began at age nine with a scholarship to St Augustine's Normal School and Collegiate Institute, where she insisted on taking an academically rigorous gentleman's course. Through her studies she met and married, in 1877, a teacher and candidate for the Episcopal ministry named George Cooper. Upon his death just two years later, her status as a widow freed her to pursue a teaching career, something often denied to married women in the nineteenth century. Following Fanny Jackson Coppin and Mary Church Terrell, she enrolled at Oberlin College in 1881, and graduated three years later. She also received a master's degree from Oberlin in mathematics, making her one of the most educated African Americans of her time. These credentials earned her a position at the prestigious Preparatory High School for Colored Youth in Washington, DC – later known as the M Street High School.

A Voice from the South solidified Cooper's role as a public intellectual. Her lectures and writing elevated her to a speaking role before the World's Congress of Representative Women in 1893, and a place at the first Pan-African Conference in London in 1900. At both venues, she stood out from the crowd. At the World's Congress in 1893, she was one of only four African Americans; at the Pan-African Conference in 1900, she was one of only a handful of women. Cooper's commitment to intellectual pursuit and higher education for African American students persisted even as Booker T. Washington's promotion of vocational or industrial training was continuing to gain popularity. When she became principal of the newly named M Street High School in 1902, Cooper helped the school gain accreditation by Harvard University. Under her leadership, many M Street graduates went on to prestigious colleges like Yale University, Harvard University, and Oberlin College. Nevertheless, Cooper's white supervisor, Percy Hughes, tried to steer the school's curriculum toward Washington's idea of vocational training. The conflict between Cooper, Hughes, and some members of Washington, DC's African American leadership led, in 1906, to the all-male school board firing her in controversial fashion. The official charges against her included adopting unauthorized textbooks and failing to discipline students properly. Regardless of race, men intensely disliked her also because she permitted a single man, John Love, to board in her home. Later, Cooper taught at Lincoln University in Jefferson City, Missouri, but in 1910 she was invited back to M Street as a Latin teacher.

In 1914, she began courses for her doctorate at Columbia University, studying in the summers at the Sorbonne in Paris. In 1915, she was forced to postpone her studies to care for her orphaned nieces and nephews. She eventually transferred to the University of Paris, where she successfully defended her dissertation in 1925, at the age of

The Wiley Blackwell Anthology of African American Literature: Volume 1, 1746–1920, First Edition.
Edited by Gene Andrew Jarrett.

67. Cooper continued to publish and to promote educational activism into her nineties. She died in her sleep in 1964, in Washington, DC.

Further reading

Baker-Fletcher, Karen. "A Singing Something: Womanist Reflections on Anna Julia Cooper." Black Women's Intellectual Traditions: Speaking Their Minds. Eds. Kristin Waters and Carol B. Conaway. Burlington: University of Vermont Press; Hanover: University Press of New England, 2007. 269–286.

Guy-Sheftall, Beverly. "Black Feminist Studies: The Case of Anna Julia Cooper." *African American Review* 43.1 (2009): 11–15.

Johnson, Karen A. "'In Service for the Common Good': Anna Julia Cooper and Adult Education." *African American Review* 43.1 (2009): 45–56.

Maguire, Roberta S. "Kate Chopin and Anna Julia Cooper: Critiquing Kentucky and the South." *The Southern Literary Journal* 35.1 (2002): 123–137.

May, Vivian M. "'It Is Never a Question of the Slaves': Anna Julia Cooper's Challenge to History's Silences in Her 1925 Sorbonne Thesis." *Callaloo* 31.3 (2008): 903–918.

May, Vivian M. and Beverly Guy-Sheftall. Anna Julia Cooper, Visionary Black Feminist: A Critical Introduction. New York: Routledge, 2007.

McCaskill, Barbara. "Anna Julia Cooper, Pauline Elizbeth Hopkins, and the African American Feminization of Du Bois's Discourse." The Souls of Black Folk One Hundred Years Later. Ed. Dolan Hubbard. Columbia: University of Missouri Press, 2003. 70–84.

Moody-Turner, Shirley. "A Voice beyond the South: Resituating the Locus of Cultural Representation in the Later Writings of Anna Julia Cooper." *African American Review* 43.1 (2009): 57–67.

Ross, Marlon B. "Racial Uplift and the Literature of the New Negro." A Companion to African American Literature. Ed. Gene Andrew Jarrett. Malden, MA: Wiley-Blackwell, 2010. 151–168.

Vogel, Todd. Rewriting White: Race, Class, and Cultural Capital in Nineteenth-Century America. New Brunswick: Rutgers University Press, 2004. Ch. 4.

Washington, Mary Helen. "Anna Julia Cooper: *A Voice from the South.*" Black 'Women's Intellectual Traditions: Speaking Their Minds. Eds. Kristin Waters and Carol B. Conaway. Burlington: University of Vermont Press; Hanover: University Press of New England, 2007. 249–268.

Extract from A Voice from the South

Womanhood: A Vital Element in the Regeneration and Progress of a Race*

The two sources from which, perhaps, modern civilization has derived its noble and ennobling ideal of woman are Christianity and the Feudal System.

In Oriental countries woman has been uniformly devoted to a life of ignorance, infamy, and complete stagnation. The Chinese shoe[1] of to-day does not more entirely dwarf, cramp, and destroy her physical powers, than have the customs, laws, and social instincts, which from remotest ages have governed our Sister of the East, enervated and blighted her mental and moral life.

Mahomet makes no account of woman whatever in his polity. The Koran, which, unlike our Bible, was a product and not a growth, tried to address itself to the needs of Arabian civilization as Mahomet with his circumscribed powers saw them. The Arab was a nomad. Home to him meant his present camping place. That deity who, according to our western ideals, makes and sanctifies the home, was to him a transient bauble to be toyed with so long as it gave pleasure and then to be thrown aside for a new one. As a personality, an individual soul, capable of eternal growth and unlimited development, and destined to mould and shape the civilization of the future to an incalculable extent, Mahomet did not know woman. There was no hereafter, no paradise for her. The heaven

Notes

* Read before the convocation of colored clergy of the Protestant Episcopal Church at Washington, DC, 1886.

[1] *Chinese shoe* a reference to the old Chinese practice of foot binding, or tightly binding and crushing the feet of young girls to prevent growth.

of the Mussulman[2] is peopled and made gladsome not by the departed wife, or sister, or mother, but by *houri*[3] – a figment of Mahomet's brain, partaking of the ethereal qualities of angels, yet imbued with all the vices and inanity of Oriental women. The harem here, and dust to dust" hereafter, this was the hope, the inspiration, the *summum bonum*[4] of the Eastern woman's life! With what result on the life of the nation, the "Unspeakable Turk," the "sick man" of modern Europe, can to-day exemplify?

Says a certain writer: "The private life of the Turk is vilest of the vile, unprogressive, unambitious, and inconceivably low." And yet Turkey is not without her great men. She has produced most brilliant minds; men skilled in all the intricacies of diplomacy and statesmanship; men whose intellects could grapple with the deep problems of empire and manipulate the subtle agencies which check-mate kings. But these minds were not the normal outgrowth of a healthy trunk. They seemed rather ephemeral excrescencies which shoot far out with all the vigor and promise, apparently, of strong branches; but soon alas fall into decay and ugliness because there is no soundness in the root, no life-giving sap, permeating, strengthening, and perpetuating the whole. There is a worm at the core! The homelife is impure! and when we look for fruit, like apples of Sodom,[5] it crumbles within our grasp into dust and ashes.

It is pleasing to turn from this effete and immobile civilization to a society still fresh and vigorous, whose seed is in itself, and whose very name is synonymous with all that is progressive, elevating, and inspiring, viz., the European bud and the American flower of modern civilization.

And here let me say parenthetically that our satisfaction in American institutions rests not on the fruition we now enjoy, but springs rather from the possibilities and promise that are inherent in the system, though as yet, perhaps, far in the future.

"Happiness," says Madame de Stael,[6] "consists not in perfections attained, but in a sense of progress, the result of our own endeavor under conspiring circumstances *toward* a goal which continually advances and broadens and deepens till it is swallowed up in the Infinite." Such conditions in embryo are all that we claim for the land of the West. We have not yet reached our ideal in American civilization. The pessimists even declare that we are not marching in that direction. But there can be no doubt that here in America is the arena in which the next triumph of civilization is to be won; and here too we find promise abundant and possibilities infinite.

Now let us see on what basis this hope for our country primarily and fundamentally rests. Can anyone doubt that it is chiefly on the homelife and on the influence of good women in those homes? Says Macaulay:[7] "You may judge a nation's rank in the scale of civilization from the way they treat their women." And Emerson,[8] "I have thought that a sufficient measure of civilization is the influence of good women." Now this high regard for woman, this germ of a prolific idea which in our own day is bearing such rich and varied fruit, was ingrafted into European civilization, we have said, from two sources, the Christian Church and the Feudal System. For although the Feudal System can in no sense be said to have originated the idea, yet there can be no doubt that the habits of life and modes of thought to which Feudalism gave rise, materially fostered

Notes

[2] *Mussulman* (archaic) a Muslim.

[3] *houri* virgin nymphs promised to the faithful in paradise.

[4] *summum bonum* (Latin) the highest good.

[5] *Sodom* a city in Genesis destroyed by God for its depravity.

[6] *Madame de Stael* Anna Louise Germaine de Staël-Holstein (1766–1817), a French woman of letters renowned for her intellectual and cultural activity.

[7] Thomas Babington Macaulay (1800–859), British historian and politician.

[8] Ralph Waldo Emerson (1803–882), American lecturer and essayist.

and developed it; for they gave us chivalry, than which no institution has more sensibly magnified and elevated woman's position in society.

Tacitus[9] dwells on the tender regard for woman entertained by these rugged barbarians before they left their northern homes to overrun Europe. Old Norse legends too, and primitive poems, all breathe the same spirit of love of home and veneration for the pure and noble influence there presiding – the wife, the sister, the mother.

And when later on we see the settled life of the Middle Ages "oozing out," as M. Guizot[10] expresses it, from the plundering and pillaging life of barbarism and crystallizing into the Feudal System, the tiger of the field is brought once more within the charmed circle of the goddesses of his castle, and his imagination weaves around them a halo whose reflection possibly has not yet altogether vanished.

It is true the spirit of Christianity had not yet put the seal of catholicity on this sentiment. Chivalry, according to Bascom,[11] was but the toning down and softening of a rough and lawless period. It gave a roseate glow to a bitter winter's day. Those who looked out from castle windows revelled in its "amethyst tints." But God's poor, the weak, the unlovely, the commonplace were still freezing and starving none the less in unpitied, unrelieved loneliness.

Respect for woman, the much lauded chivalry of the Middle Ages, meant what I fear it still means to some men in our own day – respect for the elect few among whom they expect to consort.

The idea of the radical amelioration of womankind, reverence for woman as woman regardless of rank, wealth, or culture, was to come from that rich and bounteous fountain from which flow all our liberal and universal ideas – the Gospel of Jesus Christ.

And yet the Christian Church at the time of which we have been speaking would seem to have been doing even less to protect and elevate woman than the little done by secular society. The Church as an organization committed a double offense against woman in the Middle Ages. Making of marriage a sacrament and at the same time insisting on the celibacy of the clergy and other religious orders, she gave an inferior if not an impure character to the marriage relation, especially fitted to reflect discredit on woman. Would this were all or the worst! but the Church by the licentiousness of its chosen servants invaded the household and established too often as vicious connections those relations which it forbade to assume openly and in good faith. "Thus," to use the words of our authority, "the religious corps became as numerous, as searching, and as unclean as the frogs of Egypt,[12] which penetrated into all quarters, into the ovens and kneading troughs, leaving their filthy trail wherever they went." Says Chaucer with characteristic satire, speaking of the Friars:

> "Women may now go safely up and doun,
> In every bush, and under every tree,
> Ther is non other incubus but he,
> And he ne will don hem no dishonour."[13]

Henry, Bishop of Liege, could unblushingly boast the birth of twenty-two children in fourteen years.*

Notes

* Bascom.

[9] Tacitus (56–117), Roman historian and senator.

[10] Francois Guizot (1787–1874), French historian and statesman.

[11] Henry Bidleman Bascom (1796–1850), Methodist bishop.

[12] *frogs of Egypt* the second Biblical Plague, in Exodus 7:25–8:11.

[13] *"Women may now go … no dishonour"* from the "Wife of Bath's Tale" in *The Canterbury Tales* by English poet Geoffrey Chaucer (1343–1400).

It may help us under some of the perplexities which beset our way in "the one Catholic and Apostolic Church" to-day, to recall some of the corruptions and incongruities against which the Bride of Christ has had to struggle in her past history and in spite of which she has kept, through many vicissitudes, the faith once delivered to the saints. Individuals, organizations, whole sections of the Church militant may outrage the Christ whom they profess, may ruthlessly trample under foot both the spirit and the letter of his precepts, yet not till we hear the voices audibly saying "Come let us depart hence," shall we cease to believe and cling to the promise, *"I am with you to the end of the world."*[14]

"Yet saints their watch are keeping,
The cry goes up 'How long!'
And soon the night of weeping
Shall be the morn of song."[15]

However much then the facts of any particular period of history may seem to deny it, I for one do not doubt that the source of the vitalizing principle of woman's development and amelioration is the Christian Church, so far as that church is coincident with Christianity.

Christ gave ideals not formulae. The Gospel is a germ requiring millennia for its growth and ripening. It needs, and at the same time helps, to form around itself a soil enriched in civilization, and perfected in culture and insight without which the embryo can be neither unfolded nor comprehended.[16] With all the strides our civilization has made from the first to the nineteenth century, we can boast not an idea, not a principle of action, not a progressive social force but was already mutely foreshadowed, or directly enjoined in that simple tale of a meek and lowly life. The quiet face of the Nazarene[17] is ever seen a little way ahead, never too far to come down to and touch the life of the lowest in days the darkest, yet ever leading onward, still onward, the tottering childish feet of our strangely boastful civilization.

By laying down for woman the same code of morality, the same standard of purity, as for man; by refusing to countenance the shameless and equally guilty monsters who were gloating over her fall – graciously stooping in all the majesty of his own spotlessness to wipe away the filth and grime of her guilty past and bid her go in peace and sin no more; and again in the moments of his own careworn and footsore dejection, turning trustfully and lovingly, away from the heartless snubbing and sneers, away from the cruel malignity of mobs and prelates in the dusty marts of Jerusalem to the ready sympathy, loving appreciation, and unfaltering friendship of that quiet home at Bethany; and even at the last, by his dying bequest to the disciple whom he loved, signifying the protection and tender regard to be extended to that sorrowing mother and ever afterward to the sex she represented – throughout his life and in his death he has given to men a rule and guide for the estimation of woman as an equal, as a helper, as a friend, and as a sacred charge to be sheltered and cared for with a brother's love and sympathy, lessons which nineteen centuries' gigantic strides in knowledge, arts, and sciences, in social and ethical principles have not been able to probe to their depth or to exhaust in practice.

Notes

[14] *"I am with you to the end of the world"* Matthew 28:20.

[15] *"Yet saints … morn of song."* "The Church's One Foundation," a popular hymn by Samuel John Stone.

[16] *Original reads*: can neither be unfolded or comprehended [ed.].

[17] *Nazarene* i.e., Jesus of Nazareth.

It seems not too much to say then of the vitalizing, regenerating, and progressive influence of womanhood on the civilization of today, that, while it was foreshadowed among Germanic nations in the far away dawn of their history as a narrow, sickly, and stunted growth, it yet owes its catholicity and power, the deepening of its roots and broadening of its branches to Christianity.

The union of these two forces, the Barbaric and the Christian, was not long delayed after the Fall of the Empire. The Church, which fell with Rome, finding herself in danger of being swallowed up by barbarism, with characteristic vigor and fertility of resources, addressed herself immediately to the task of conquering her conquerors.[18] The means chosen does credit to her power of penetration and adaptability, as well as to her profound, unerring, all-compassing diplomacy; and makes us even now wonder if aught human can successfully and ultimately withstand her far-seeing designs and brilliant policy, or gainsay her well-earned claim to the word *Catholic*.

She saw the barbarian, little more developed than a wild beast. She forbore to antagonize and mystify his warlike nature by a full blaze of the heartsearching and humanizing tenets of her great Head. She said little of the rule "If thy brother smite thee on one cheek, turn to him the other also";[19] but thought it sufficient for the needs of those times, to establish the so-called "Truce of God" under which men were bound to abstain from butchering one another for three days of each week and on Church festivals. In other words, she respected their individuality: non-resistance pure and simple being for them an utter impossibility, she contented herself with less radical measures calculated to lead up finally to the full measure of the benevolence of Christ.

Next she took advantage of the barbarian's sensuous love of gaudy display and put all her magnificent garments on. She could not capture him by physical force; she would dazzle him by gorgeous spectacles. It is said that Romanism gained more in pomp and ritual during this trying period of the Dark Ages than throughout all her former history.

The result was she carried her point. Once more Rome laid her ambitious hand on the temporal power, and allied with Charlemagne,[20] aspired to rule the world through a civilization dominated by Christianity and permeated by the traditions and instincts of those sturdy barbarians.

Here was the confluence of the two streams we have been tracing, which, united now, stretch before us as a broad majestic river.

In regard to woman it was the meeting of two noble and ennobling forces, two kindred ideas the resultant of which, we doubt not, is destined to be a potent force in the betterment of the world.

Now, after our appeal to history comparing nations destitute of this force and so destitute also of the principle of progress, with other nations among whom the influence of woman is prominent coupled with a brisk, progressive, satisfying civilization, if in addition we find this strong presumptive evidence corroborated by reason and experience, we may conclude that these two equally varying concomitants are linked as cause and effect; in other words, that the position of woman in society determines the vital elements of its regeneration and progress.

Now, that this is so on *a priori* grounds all must admit. And this not because woman is better or stronger or wiser than man, but from the nature of the case, because it is she who must first form the man by directing the earliest impulses of his character.

Notes

[18] *Original reads*: conquerers [ed.].

[19] *"If thy brother smite thee … the other also"* Matthew 5:39.

[20] Charlemagne (AD 742–814), king of the Franks (modern-day France) and first Holy Roman Emperor.

Byron and Wordsworth[21] were both geniuses and would have stamped themselves on the thought of their age under any circumstances; and yet we find the one a savor of life unto life, the other of death unto death. "Byron, like a rocket, shot his way upward with scorn and repulsion, flamed out in wild, explosive, brilliant excesses and disappeared in darkness made all the more palpable."*

Wordsworth lent of his gifts to reinforce that "power in the Universe which makes for righteousness" by taking the harp handed him from Heaven and using it to swell the strains of angelic choirs. Two locomotives equally mighty stand facing opposite tracks; the one to rush headlong to destruction with all its precious freight, the other to toil grandly and gloriously up the steep embattlements to Heaven and to God. Who – who can say what a world of consequences hung on the first placing and starting of these enormous forces!

Woman, Mother, your responsibility is one that might make angels tremble and fear to take hold! To trifle with it, to ignore or misuse it, is to treat lightly the most sacred and solemn trust ever confided by God to human kind. The training of children is a task on which an infinity of weal or woe depends. Who does not covet it? Yet who does not stand awe-struck before its momentous issues! It is a matter of small moment, it seems to me, whether that lovely girl in whose accomplishments you take such pride and delight, can enter the gay and crowded salon with the ease and elegance of this or that French or English gentlewoman, compared with the decision as to whether her individuality is going to reinforce the good or the evil elements of the world. The lace and the diamonds, the dance and the theater, gain a new significance when scanned in their bearings on such issues. Their influence on the individual personality, and through her on the society and civilization which she vitalizes and inspires – all this and more must be weighed in the balance before the jury can return a just and intelligent verdict as to the innocence or banefulness of these apparently simple amusements.

Now the fact of woman's influence on society being granted, what are its practical bearings on the work which brought together this conference of colored clergy and laymen in Washington? "We come not here to talk." Life is too busy, too pregnant with meaning and far reaching consequences to allow you to come this far for mere intellectual entertainment.

The vital agency of womanhood in the regeneration and progress of a race, as a general question, is conceded almost before it is fairly stated. I confess one of the difficulties for me in the subject assigned lay in its obviousness. The plea is taken away by the opposite attorney's granting the whole question.

"Woman's influence on social progress" – who in Christendom doubts or questions it? One may as well be called on to prove that the sun is the source of light and heat and energy to this many-sided little world.

Nor, on the other hand, could it have been intended that I should apply the position when taken and proven, to the needs and responsibilities of the women of our race in the South. For is it not written, "Cursed is he that cometh after the king"? And has not the King already preceded me in "The Black Woman of the South"?†

They have had both Moses and the Prophets in Dr. Crummell and if they hear not him, neither would they be persuaded though one came up from the South.[22]

Notes

* Bascom's Eng. Lit, p. 253.

† Pamphlet published by Dr. Alexander Crummell.

[21] *Byron and Wordsworth* Lord George Gordon Byron (1788–1824) and William Wordsworth (1770–1850), English Romantic poets.

I would beg, however, with the Doctor's permission, to add my plea for the *Colored Girls* of the South – that large, bright, promising, fatally beautiful class that stand shivering like a delicate plantlet before the fury of tempestuous elements, so full of promise and possibilities, yet so sure of destruction; often without a father to whom they dare apply the loving term, often without a stronger brother to espouse their cause and defend their honor with his life's blood; in the midst of pitfalls and snares, waylaid by the lower classes of white men, with no shelter, no protection nearer than the great blue vault above, which half conceals and half reveals the one Care-Taker they know so little of. Oh, save them, help them, shield, train, develop, teach, inspire them! Snatch them, in God's name, as brands from the burning! There is material in them well worth your while, the hope in germ of a staunch, helpful, regenerating womanhood on which, primarily, rests the foundation stones of our future as a race.

It is absurd to quote statistics showing the Negro's bank account and rent rolls, to point to the hundreds of newspapers edited by colored men and lists of lawyers, doctors, professors, D.D's, LLD's, etc., etc., etc., while the source from which the life-blood of the race is to flow is subject to taint and corruption in the enemy's camp.

True progress is never made by spasms. Real progress is growth. It must begin in the seed. Then, "first the blade, then the ear, after that the full corn in the ear." There is something to encourage and inspire us in the advancement of individuals since their emancipation from slavery. It at least proves that there is nothing irretrievably wrong in the shape of the black man's skull, and that under given circumstances his development, downward or upward, will be similar to that of other average human beings.

But there is no time to be wasted in mere felicitation. That the Negro has his niche in the infinite purposes of the Eternal, no one who has studied the history of the last fifty years in America will deny. That much depends on his own right comprehension of his responsibility and rising to the demands of the hour, it will be good for him to see; and how best to use his present so that the structure of the future shall be stronger and higher and brighter and nobler and holier than that of the past, is a question to be decided each day by every one of us.

The race is just twenty-one years removed from the conception and experience of a chattel, just at the age of ruddy manhood. It is well enough to pause a moment for retrospection, introspection, and prospection. We look back, not to become inflated with conceit because of the depths from which we have arisen, but that we may learn wisdom from experience. We look within that we may gather together once more our forces, and, by improved and more practical methods, address ourselves to the tasks before us. We look forward with hope and trust that the same God whose guiding hand led our fathers through and out of the gall and bitterness of oppression, will still lead and direct their children, to the honor of His name, and for their ultimate salvation.

But this survey of the failures or achievements[23] of the past, the difficulties and embarrassments of the present, and the mingled hopes and fears for the future, must not degenerate into mere dreaming nor consume the time which belongs to the

Notes

[22] *"They have had both Moses and the Prophets … from the South."* a play on Luke 16:31, "If they hear not Moses and the Prophets, neither will they be persuaded though one rose from the dead."

[23] *Original reads*: achievments [ed.].

practical and effective handling of the crucial questions of the hour; and there can be no issue more vital and momentous than this of the womanhood of the race.

Here is the vulnerable point, not in the heel, but at the heart of the young Achilles;[24] and here must the defenses be strengthened and the watch redoubled.

We are the heirs of a past which was not of our fathers' moulding.[25] "Every man the arbiter of his own destiny" was not true for the American Negro of the past: and it is no fault of his that he finds himself to-day the inheritor of a manhood and womanhood impoverished and debased by two centuries and more of compression and degradation.

But weaknesses and malformations, which to-day are attributable to a vicious schoolmaster and a pernicious system, will a century hence be rightly regarded as proofs of innate corruptness and radical incurability.

Now the fundamental agency under God in the regeneration, the re-training of the race, as well as the groundwork and starting point of its progress upward, must be the *black woman*.

With all the wrongs and neglects of her past, with all the weakness, the debasement, the moral thralldom of her present, the black woman of to-day stands mute and wondering at the Herculean task devolving upon her. But the cycles wait for her. No other hand can move the lever. She must be loosed from her bands and set to work.

Our meager and superficial results from past efforts prove their futility; and every attempt to elevate the Negro, whether undertaken by himself or through the philanthropy of others, cannot but prove abortive unless so directed as to utilize the indispensable agency of an elevated and trained womanhood.

A race cannot be purified from without. Preachers and teachers are helps, and stimulants and conditions as necessary as the gracious rain and sunshine are to plant growth. But what are rain and dew and sunshine and cloud if there be no life in the plant germ? We must go to the root and see that that is sound and healthy and vigorous; and not deceive ourselves with waxen flowers and painted leaves of mock chlorophyll.[26]

We too often mistake individuals' honor for race development and so are ready to substitute pretty accomplishments for sound sense and earnest purpose.

A stream cannot rise higher than its source. The atmosphere of homes is no rarer and purer and sweeter than are the mothers in those homes. A race is but a total of families. The nation is the aggregate of its homes. As the whole is sum of all its parts, so the character of the parts will determine the characteristics of the whole. These are all axioms and so evident that it seems gratuitous to remark it; and yet, unless I am greatly mistaken, most of the unsatisfaction from our past results arises from just such a radical and palpable error, as much almost on our own part as on that of our benevolent white friends.

The Negro is constitutionally hopeful and proverbially irrepressible; and naturally stands in danger of being dazzled by the shimmer and tinsel of superficials. We often mistake foliage for fruit and overestimate or wrongly estimate brilliant results.

The late Martin R. Delany,[27] who was an unadulterated black man, used to say when honors of state fell upon him, that when he entered the council of kings the black race entered with him; meaning, I suppose, that there was no discounting his race identity

Notes

[24] *not in the heel ... of young Achilles* in Greek mythology, the warrior Achilles was invulnerable except for his heel.

[25] *Original reads*: not our fathers' moulding [ed.].

[26] *chlorophyll* the pigment that makes plants green.

[27] Martin R. Delany (1812–1885), author, physician and activist.

and attributing his achievements to some admixture of Saxon blood. But our present record of eminent men, when placed beside the actual status of the race in America to-day, proves that no man can represent the race. Whatever the attainments of the individual may be, unless his home has moved on *pari passu*,[28] he can never be regarded as identical with or representative of the whole.

Not by pointing to sun-bathed mountain tops do we prove that Phoebus[29] warms the valleys. We must point to homes, average homes, homes of the rank and file of horny-handed toiling men and women of the South (where the masses are) lighted and cheered by the good, the beautiful, and the true – then and not till then will the whole plateau be lifted into the sunlight.

Only the Black Woman can say "when and where I enter, in the quiet, undisputed dignity of my womanhood, without violence and without suing or special patronage, then and there the whole *Negro race enters with me*." Is it not evident then that as individual workers for this race we must address ourselves with no half-hearted zeal to this feature of our mission? The need is felt and must be recognized by all. There is a call for workers, for missionaries, for men and women with the double consecration of a fundamental love of humanity and a desire for its melioration through the Gospel; but superadded to this we demand an intelligent and sympathetic comprehension of the interests and special needs of the Negro.

I see not why there should not be an organized effort for the protection and elevation of our girls such as the White Cross League in England.[30] English women are strengthened and protected by more than twelve centuries of Christian influences, freedom and civilization; English girls are dispirited and crushed down by no such all-levelling prejudice as that supercilious caste spirit in America which cynically assumes "A Negro woman cannot be a lady." English womanhood is beset by no such snares and traps as betray the unprotected, untrained colored girl of the South, whose only crime and dire destruction often is her unconscious and marvelous beauty. Surely then if English indignation is aroused and English manhood thrilled under the leadership of a Bishop of the English church to build up bulwarks around their wronged sisters, Negro sentiment cannot remain callous and Negro effort nerveless in view of the imminent peril of the mothers of the next generation. *"I am my Sister's keeper!"*[31] should be the hearty response of every man and woman of the race, and this conviction should purify and exalt the narrow, selfish, and petty personal aims of life into a noble and sacred purpose.

We need men who can let their interest and gallantry extend outside the circle of their æsthetic appreciation; men who can be a father, a brother, a friend to every weak, struggling, unshielded girl. We need women who are so sure of their own social footing that they need not fear leaning to lend a hand to a fallen or falling sister. We need men and women who do not exhaust their genius splitting hairs on aristocratic distinctions and thanking God they are not as others; but earnest, unselfish souls, who can go into the highways and byways, lifting up and leading, advising and encouraging with the truly catholic benevolence of the Gospel of Christ.

As Church workers we must confess our path of duty is less obvious; or rather our ability to adapt our machinery to our conception of the peculiar exigencies of this work, as taught by experience and our own consciousness of the needs of the Negro,

Notes

[28] *pari passu* (Latin) on equal footing.

[29] *Phoebus* (Greek Mythology) the personification of the sun.

[30] *White Cross League in England* a late nineteenth century moral reform movement in the Church of England.

[31] *"I am my Sister's keeper!"* an inversion of Cain's retort to God in Genesis 4:9 when asked about his (murdered) brother Abel.

is as yet not demonstrable. Flexibility and aggressiveness are not such strong characteristics of the Church to-day as in the Dark Ages.

As a Mission field for the Church, the Southern Negro is in some aspects most promising; in others, perplexing. Aliens neither in language and customs, nor in associations and sympathies, naturally of deeply rooted religious instincts and taking most readily and kindly to the worship and teachings of the Church, surely the task of proselytizing the American Negro is infinitely less formidable than that which confronted the Church in the Barbarians of Europe. Besides, this people already look to the Church as the hope of their race. Thinking colored men almost uniformly admit that the Protestant Episcopal Church with its quiet, chaste dignity and decorous solemnity, its instructive and elevating ritual, its bright chanting and joyous hymning, is eminently fitted to correct the peculiar faults of worship – the rank exuberance and often ludicrous demonstrativeness of their people. Yet, strange to say, the Church, claiming to be missionary and Catholic, urging that schism is sin and denominationalism inexcusable, has made in all these years almost no inroads upon this semi-civilized religionism.

Harvests from this over ripe field of home missions have been gathered in by Methodists, Baptists, and not least by Congregationalists, who were unknown to the Freedmen before their emancipation.

Our clergy numbers less than two dozen* priests of Negro blood and we have hardly more than one self-supporting colored congregation in the entire Southland. While the organization known as the A.M.E. Church has 14,063 ministers, itinerant and local, 4,069 self-supporting churches, 4,275 Sunday-schools, with property valued at $7,772,284, raising yearly for church purposes $1,427,000.

Stranger and more significant than all, the leading men of this race (I do not mean demagogues and politicians, but men of intellect, heart, and race devotion, men to whom the elevation of their people means more than personal ambition and sordid gain – and the men of that stamp have not all died yet), the Christian workers for the race, of younger and more cultured growth, are noticeably drifting into sectarian churches, many of them declaring all the time that they acknowledge the historic claims of the Church, believe her apostolicity, and would experience greater personal comfort, spiritual and intellectual, in her revered communion. It is a fact which any one may verify for himself, that representative colored men, professing that in their heart of hearts they are Episcopalians, are actually working in Methodist and Baptist pulpits; while the ranks of the Episcopal clergy are left to be filled largely by men who certainly suggest the propriety of a "*perpetual* Diaconate"[32] if they cannot be said to have created the necessity for it.

Now where is the trouble? Something must be wrong. What is it?

A certain Southern Bishop of our Church reviewing the situation, whether in Godly anxiety or in "Gothic antipathy" I know not, deprecates the fact that the colored people do not seem *drawn* to the Episcopal Church, and comes to the sage conclusion that the Church is not adapted to the rude untutored minds of the Freedmen, and that they may be left to go to the Methodists and Baptists whither their racial proclivities undeniably tend. How the good Bishop can agree that all-foreseeing Wisdom, and Catholic Love would have framed his Church as typified in his seamless garment and unbroken

Notes

* The published report of 1891 shows 26 priests for the entire country, including one not engaged in work and one a professor in a non-sectarian school, since made Dean of an Episcopal Annex to Howard University known as King Hall.

[32] *Diaconate* the office of deacon, subordinate to priests or ministers.

body, and yet not leave it broad enough and deep enough and loving enough to seek and save and hold seven millions of God's poor, I cannot see.

But the doctors, while discussing their scientifically conclusive diagnosis of the disease, will perhaps not think it presumptuous in the patient if he dares to suggest where at least the pain is. If this be allowed a *Black woman of the South* would beg to point out two possible oversights in this southern work which may indicate in part both a cause and a remedy for some failure. The first is *not calculating for the Black man's personality;* not having respect, if I may so express it, to his manhood or deferring at all to his conceptions of the needs of his people. When colored persons have been employed it was too often as machines or as manikins. There has been no disposition, generally, to get the black man's ideal or to let his individuality work by its own gravity, as it were. A conference of earnest Christian men has[33] met at regular intervals for some years past to discuss the best methods of promoting the welfare and development of colored people in this country. Yet, strange as it may seem, they have never invited a colored man or even intimated that one would be welcome to take part in their deliberations. Their remedial contrivances are purely theoretical or empirical, therefore, and the whole machinery devoid of soul.

The second important oversight in my judgment is closely allied to this and probably grows out of it, and that is not developing Negro womanhood as an essential fundamental for the elevation of the race, and utilizing this agency in extending the work of the Church.

Of the first I have possibly already presumed to say too much since it does not strictly come within the province of my subject. However, Macaulay somewhere criticises the Church of England as not knowing how to use fanatics, and declares that had Ignatius Loyola[34] been in the Anglican instead of the Roman communion, the Jesuits would have been schismatics instead of Catholics; and if the religious awakenings of the Wesleys[35] had been in Rome, she would have shaven their heads, tied ropes around their waists, and sent them out under her own banner and blessing. Whether this be true or not, there is certainly a vast amount of force potential for Negro evangelization rendered latent, or worse, antagonistic by the halting, uncertain, I had almost said, *trimming* policy of the Church in the South. This may sound both presumptuous and ungrateful. It is mortifying, I know, to benevolent wisdom, after having spent itself in the execution of well conned theories for the ideal development of a particular work, to hear perhaps the weakest and humblest element of that work asking "what doest thou?"

Yet so it will be in life. The "thus far and no farther" pattern cannot be fitted to any growth in God's kingdom. The universal law of development is "onward and upward." It is God-given and inviolable. From the unfolding of the germ in the acorn to reach the sturdy oak, to the growth of a human soul into the full knowledge and likeness of its Creator, the breadth and scope of the movement in each and all are too grand, too mysterious, too like God himself, to be encompassed and locked down in human moulds.[36]

After all, the Southern slave owners were right: either the very alphabet of intellectual growth must be forbidden and the Negro dealt with absolutely as a chattel having

Notes

[33] *Original reads*: have [ed.].

[34] Ignatius Loyola (1491–1556), a Spanish nobleman who founded the Society of Jesus (or Jesuits), an order of Catholic priests.

[35] *awakenings of the Wesleys* John Wesley (1703–1791) and Charles Wesley (1707–1788) were central to the founding of Methodism and the American religious revivals known as the "Great Awakenings" in the eighteenth and nineteenth centuries.

[36] *Original reads*: molds [ed.].

neither rights nor sensibilities; or else the clamps and irons of mental and moral, as well as civil, compression must be riven asunder and the truly enfranchised soul led to the entrance of that boundless vista through which it is to toil upwards to its beckoning God as the buried seed germ to meet the sun.

A perpetual colored diaconate, carefully and kindly superintended by the white clergy; congregations of shiny faced peasants with their clean white aprons and sunbonnets catechised at regular intervals and taught to recite the creed, the Lord's prayer, and the ten commandments – duty towards God and duty towards neighbor – surely such well-tended sheep ought to be grateful to their shepherds and content in that station of life to which it pleased God to call them. True, like the old professor lecturing to his solitary student, we make no provision here for irregularities. "Questions must be kept till after class," or dispensed with altogether. That some do ask questions and insist on answers, in class too, must be both impertinent and annoying. Let not our spiritual pastors and masters however be grieved at such self-assertion as merely signifies we have a destiny to fulfill and as men and women we must *be about our Father's business*.[37]

It is a mistake to suppose that the Negro is prejudiced against a white ministry. Naturally there is not a more kindly and implicit follower of a white man's guidance than the average colored peasant. What would to others be an ordinary act of friendly or pastoral interest he would be more inclined to regard gratefully as a condescension. And he never forgets such kindness. Could the Negro be brought near to his white priest or bishop, he is not suspicious. He is not only willing but often longs to unburden his soul to this intelligent guide. There are no reservations when he is convinced that you are his friend. It is a saddening satire on American history and manners that it takes something to convince him.

That our people are not "drawn" to a church whose chief dignitaries they see only in the chancel,[38] and whom they reverence as they would a painting or an angel, whose life never comes down to and touches theirs with the inspiration of an objective reality, may be "perplexing" truly (American caste and American Christianity both being facts) but it need not be surprising. There must be something of human nature in it, the same as that which brought about that "the Word was made flesh and dwelt among us" that He might "draw" us towards God.

Men are not "drawn" by abstractions. Only sympathy and love can draw, and until our Church in America realizes this and provides a clergy that can come in touch with our life and have a fellow feeling for our woes, without being imbedded and frozen up in their "Gothic antipathies," the good bishops are likely to continue "perplexed" by the sparsity of colored Episcopalians.

A colored priest of my acquaintance recently related to me, with tears in his eyes, how his reverend Father in God, the Bishop who had ordained him, had met him on the cars on his way to the diocesan convention and warned him, not unkindly, not to take a seat in the body of the convention with the white clergy. To avoid disturbance of their godly placidity he would of course[39] please sit back and somewhat apart. I do not imagine that that clergyman had very much heart for the Christly (!) deliberations of that convention.

To return, however, it is not on this broader view of Church work, which I mentioned as a primary cause of its halting progress with the colored people, that I am to

Notes

[37] *we must be about our Father's business* Luke 2:49; "Did you not know that I must be about my Father's business?"

[38] *chancel* the part of the church near the altar.

[39] *Original reads*: cource [ed.].

speak. My proper theme is the second oversight of which, in my judgment, our Christian propagandists have been guilty: or, the necessity of church training, protecting, and uplifting our colored womanhood as indispensable to the evangelization of the race.

Apelles[40] did not disdain even that criticism of his lofty art which came from an uncouth cobbler; and may I not hope that the writer's oneness with her subject both in feeling and in being may palliate undue obtrusiveness of opinions here. That the race cannot be effectually lifted up till its women are truly elevated we take as proven. It is not for us to dwell on the needs, the neglects, and the ways of succor, pertaining to the black woman of the South. The ground has been ably discussed and an admirable and practical plan proposed by the oldest Negro priest in America, advising and urging that special organizations such as Church Sisterhoods and industrial schools be devised to meet her pressing needs in the Southland. That some such movements are vital to the life of this people, and the extension of the Church among them, is not hard to see. Yet the pamphlet fell still-born from the press. So far as I am informed the Church has made no motion towards carrying out Dr. Crummell's suggestion.

The denomination which comes next to our[41] own in opposing the proverbial emotionalism of Negro worship in the South, and which in consequence, like ours, receives the cold shoulder from the old heads, resting as we do under the charge of not "having religion" and not believing in conversion – the Congregationalists – have quietly gone to work on the young, have established industrial and training schools, and now almost every community in the South is yearly enriched by a fresh infusion of vigorous young hearts, cultivated heads, and helpful hands that have been trained at Fisk, at Hampton, in Atlanta University, and in Tuskegee, Alabama.[42]

These young people are missionaries actual or virtual both here and in Africa. They have learned to love the methods and doctrines of the Church which trained and educated them; and so Congregationalism surely and steadily progresses.

Need I compare these well-known facts with results shown by the Church in the same field and during the same or even a longer time?

The institution of the Church in the South to which she mainly looks for the training of her colored clergy and for the help of the "Black Woman" and "Colored Girl" of the South, has graduated since the year 1868, when the school was founded, *five young women;** and while yearly numerous young men have been kept and trained for the ministry by the charities of the Church, the number of indigent females who have here been supported, sheltered, and trained, is phenomenally small. Indeed, to my mind, the attitude of the Church toward this feature of her work is as if the solution of the problem of Negro missions depended solely on sending a quota of deacons and priests into the field, girls being a sort of *tertium quid*[43] whose development may be promoted if they can pay their way and fall in with the plans mapped out for the training of the other sex.

Now I would ask in all earnestness, does not this force potential deserve by education and stimulus to be made dynamic? Is it not a solemn duty incumbent on all colored churchmen to make it so? Will not the aid of the Church be given to prepare our girls

Notes

* Five have been graduated since 1886, two in 1891, two in 1892.

[40] Apelles of Kos (fourth century BC), a famed painter of ancient Greece.

[41] *Original reads*: next our [ed.].

[42] *Fisk, at Hampton, in Atlanta University, and in Tuskegee, Alabama* African American institutions of learning.

[43] *tertium quid* (Latin) third thing.

in head, heart, and hand for the duties and responsibilities that await the intelligent wife, the Christian mother, the earnest, virtuous, helpful woman, at once both the lever and the fulcrum for uplifting the race?

As Negroes and churchmen we cannot be indifferent to these questions. They touch us most vitally on both sides. We believe in the Holy Catholic Church. We believe that however gigantic and apparently remote the consummation, the Church will go on conquering and to conquer till the kingdoms of this world, not excepting the black man and the black woman of the South, shall have become the kingdoms of the Lord and of his Christ.

That past work in this direction has been unsatisfactory we must admit. That without a change of policy results in the future will be as meagre, we greatly fear. Our life as a race is at stake. The dearest interests of our hearts are in the scales. We must either break away from dear old landmarks and plunge out in any line and every line that enables us to meet the pressing need of our people, or we must ask the Church to allow and help us, untrammelled by the prejudices and theories of individuals, to work aggressively[44] under her direction as we alone can, with God's help, for the salvation of our people.

The time is ripe for action. Self-seeking and ambition must be laid on the altar. The battle is one of sacrifice and hardship, but our duty is plain. We have been recipients of missionary bounty in some sort for twenty-one years. Not even the senseless vegetable is content to be a mere reservoir. Receiving without giving is an anomaly in nature. Nature's cells are all little workshops for manufacturing sunbeams, the product to be *given out* to earth's inhabitants in warmth, energy, thought, action. Inanimate creation always pays back an equivalent.

Now, *How much owest thou my Lord?* Will his account be overdrawn if he call for singleness of purpose and self-sacrificing labor for your brethren? Having passed through your drill school, will you refuse a general's commission even if it entails[45] responsibility, risk and anxiety, with possibly some adverse criticism? Is it too much to ask you to step forward and direct the work for your race along those lines which you know to be of first and vital importance?

Will you allow these words of Ralph Waldo Emerson? "In ordinary," says he, "we have a snappish criticism which watches and contradicts the opposite party. We want the will which advances and dictates [acts]. Nature has made up her mind that what cannot defend itself, shall not be defended. Complaining never so loud and with never so much reason, is of no use. What cannot stand must fall; *and the measure of our sincerity and therefore of the respect of men is the amount of health and wealth we will hazard in the defense of our right.*"[46]

1892

Notes

[44] *Original reads*: agressively [ed.].

[45] *Original reads*: entail [ed.].

[46] *"In ordinary ... of our right"* from "Courage," a chapter in Ralph Waldo Emerson's *Society and Solitude* (1870).

Paul Laurence Dunbar (1872–1906)

When Paul Laurence Dunbar wrote "We wear the mask that grins and lies, / It hides our cheeks and shades our eyes" in his poem "We Wear the Mask," included in his 1895 collection *Majors and Minors*, he eloquently describes the racial disguise that many African Americans don to survive in a society whose racial prejudice and discrimination systematically degrade their humanity. And his 1902 novel *The Sport of the Gods* alludes to romantic images of the plantation South, only to develop a tragic tale of African American moral decline following forced migration to the urban North: "Fiction has said so much in regret of the old days when there were plantations and overseers and masters and slaves, that it was good to come upon such a household as Berry Hamilton's, if for no other reason than that it afforded a relief from the monotony of tiresome iteration." From his poetry and essays to his short stories and novels, Dunbar displayed a versatility too often overlooked by contemporaries who reduced his talent, particularly his dialect literature, to mere expressions of racial authenticity. In his introduction to *Lyrics of Lowly Life* (1896), novelist and critic William Dean Howells proclaims Dunbar "the first instance of an American negro who had evinced innate distinction in literature," a condescension illustrative of the misperceptions that Dunbar's work elicited. To literary critics like Howells, Dunbar was remarkable because his poetry confirmed their prejudicial racial and literary assumptions. In contrast, African Americans expressed pride in the person they called, in Booker T. Washington's words, "the Poet Laureate of the Negro race." Immensely talented and prolific, his complex work proved that African American literature could be more than what either his white critics or his African American supporters deemed possible.

Dunbar was born in Dayton, Ohio, in 1872, the son of two former Kentucky slaves. His father, Joshua Dunbar, had fled to Canada and then joined the Fifty-Fifth Massachusetts Infantry and the Fifth Massachusetts Cavalry during the Civil War. His mother, Matilda Murphy, worked as a washerwoman for part of her early life. Although his parents divorced in 1874, young Paul learned from both of his parents the stories and oral traditions of slave culture. He wrote his first poem at age six, and gave his first public reading when he was nine. Although the family was poor, Paul was raised in an environment conducive to intellectual pursuits. One of his mother's employers was the Wright family, who encouraged Dunbar's talent (and whose sons, Orville and Wilbur, attended Dayton's Central High School with Dunbar before they rose to fame as the inventors of the airplane). The only student of color in his school, Dunbar excelled academically. He was elected class president and head of the literary society, and delivered a poem at his class graduation. Despite his talents, discrimination made it difficult for Dunbar to find employment in keeping with his skills. After high school he worked as an elevator operator in Dayton's Callahan Building while writing poetry in his spare time. His friendship with the Wright brothers was fruitful, however. They helped print his newspaper, *The Tattler*, in 1890. Dunbar's first publishing venture lasted only six weeks, but by 1892 he had enough poems to submit a manuscript to the

The Wiley Blackwell Anthology of African American Literature: Volume 1, 1746–1920, First Edition.
Edited by Gene Andrew Jarrett.

United Brethren Publishing House, which was published as *Oak and Ivy* (1893). Dunbar had taken out a loan to subsidize its publication, and he sold copies for a dollar to his elevator passengers. Known locally as the "elevator poet," he was invited to present his work at the Chicago World's Fair that same year, where he gained the patronage of Frederick Douglass.

Also in 1892, Dunbar gave the welcoming address at a Dayton meeting of the Western Association of Writers, after a former teacher arranged to distribute his poems at the event. There, he attracted the attention of Illinois poet James Newton Matthews, who wrote a letter praising Dunbar's poetry that appeared in newspapers across the country. Through Matthews, Dunbar met and collaborated with popular dialect poet James Whitcomb Riley. In 1895, as his fame expanded across the Midwest, Dunbar published his second book of poetry, *Majors and Minors*, which brought him national attention after William Dean Howells praised the collection in *The Atlantic Monthly*. With Howells's assistance, *Oak and Ivy* and *Majors and Minors* were combined into the volume *Lyrics of Lowly Life* in 1896. The collection brought Dunbar international fame, allowing him to leave Ohio for Washington, DC, after a successful tour of England. On this tour he met Afro-British composer Samuel Coleridge-Taylor, who set some of Dunbar's poems to music.

As his literary career gained momentum, Dunbar began a correspondence with New Orleans author Alice Ruth Moore, a college-educated member of Louisiana's creoles of color. After Moore's collection *Violets and Other Tales* was published in 1895, she moved to New York, where she co-founded Brooklyn's White Rose Mission for African American migrants. Dunbar and Moore's romance blossomed after he moved to Washington, DC, and enrolled at Howard University. The two were married in 1898 over her parents' objections. Sadly, the marriage was marred by Dunbar's ill health and consequent alcoholism, Moore's purported lesbianism, and domestic violence. The two separated in 1902.

Despite Dunbar's tumultuous personal life, which included a diagnosis of tuberculosis in 1900, he wrote a prodigious number of short stories, poems, and essays that appeared in major literary magazines. Between 1898 and 1904 he published four collections of short stories and four novels, not to mention several volumes of poetry. His stories frequently appeared in popular periodicals such as *Lippincott's*, *Harper's Weekly*, and *The Saturday Evening Post*. Three of his novels – *The Uncalled* (1898), *The Love of Landry* (1900), and *The Fanatics* (1901) – featured white protagonists in stories of redemption and morality that challenged the popular conception of Dunbar as a dialect poet, even as they left him open to charges of catering to a white mainstream audience. At a time when the plantation stories of Joel Chandler Harris and Thomas Nelson Page popularized "coon" and "darkey" stories, only *The Sport of the Gods* (1902), with its African American protagonists, was popular with critics and audiences.

As the first African American writer to gain popular and critical attention from both African American and mainstream white audiences, Dunbar struggled to maintain his integrity at the same time that he advanced his career. One of his last projects was the 1903 Broadway musical *In Dahomey*, the first full-length Broadway musical written and performed by an African American cast. Dunbar wrote the lyrics to the immensely successful production, which toured England and the United States. Meanwhile, Dunbar, on account of his failing health, had moved back to Dayton in 1904 to live with his mother. He succumbed to tuberculosis in 1906, a few months shy of his thirty-fourth birthday.

Further reading

Daigle, Jonathan. "Paul Laurence Dunbar and the Marshall Circle: Racial Representation from Blackface to Black Naturalism." *African American Review* 43.4 (2009): 633–654.

Fishkin, Shelley Fisher. "Race and the Politics of Memory: Mark Twain and Paul Lawrence Dunbar." *Journal of American Studies* 40.2 (2006): 283–309.

Fishkin, Shelley Fisher, Gavin Jones, Meta DuEwa Jones, Arnold Rampersad, and Richard Yarborough, eds. *Paul Laurence Dunbar*. Special issue of *African American Review* 41.2 (2007): 200–401.

Harrell, Jr, Willie J. ed. *We Wear the Mask: Paul Laurence Dunbar and the Politics of Representative Reality*. Kent: Kent State University Press, 2010.

James, Jennifer C. *A Freedom Bought with Blood: African American War Literature from the Civil War to World War II*. Chapel Hill: University of North Carolina Press, 2007. Ch. 2.

Jarrett, Gene Andrew. *Deans and Truants: Race and Realism in African American Literature*. Philadelphia: University of Pennsylvania Press, 2007. Chs. 1 and 2.

Jarrett, Gene Andrew. "The Dialect of New Negro Literature." *A Companion to African American Literature*. Ed. Gene Andrew Jarrett. Malden, MA: Wiley-Blackwell, 2010. 169–184.

Moody-Turner, Shirley. "Folklore and African American Literature in the Post-Reconstruction Era." *A Companion to African American Literature*. Ed. Gene Andrew Jarrett. Malden, MA: Wiley-Blackwell, 2010. 200–211.

Morgan, Thomas L. "The City as Refuge: Constructing Urban Blackness in Paul Laurence Dunbar's *The Sport of the Gods* and James Weldon Johnson's *The Autobiography of an Ex-Colored Man*." *African American Review* 38.2 (2004): 213–237.

Nurhussein, Nadia. "'On Flow'ry Beds of Ease': Paul Laurence Dunbar and the Cultivation of Dialect Poetry in the *Century*." *American Periodicals: A Journal of History, Criticism, and Bibliography* 20.1 (2010): 46–67.

Ronda, Margaret. "'Work and Wait Unwearying': Dunbar's Georgics." *PMLA: Publications of the Modern Language Association of America* 127.4 (2012): 863–878.

Tsemo, Bridget Harris. "The Politics of Self-Identity in Paul Laurence Dunbar's *The Sport of the Gods*." *The Southern Literary Journal* 41.2 (2009): 21–37.

Williams, Andreá N. "African American Literary Realism, 1865–1914." *A Companion to African American Literature*. Ed. Gene Andrew Jarrett. Malden, MA: Wiley-Blackwell, 2010. 185–199.

Wolosky, Shira. *Poetry and Public Discourse in Nineteenth-Century America*. New York: Palgrave Macmillan, 2010. Ch. 11.

Wooley, Christine A. "'We Are Not in the Old Days Now': Paul Laurence Dunbar and the Problem of Sympathy." *African American Review* 43.2–3 (2009): 359–370.

The Poet and His Song

From *Lyrics of Lowly Life*

A SONG is but a little thing,
And yet what joy it is to sing!
In hours of toil it gives me zest,
And when at eve I long for rest;
When cows come home along the bars,
  And in the fold I hear the bell,
As Night, the shepherd, herds his stars,
  I sing my song, and all is well.

There are no ears to hear my lays,[1]
No lips to lift a word of praise;
But still, with faith unfaltering,
I live and laugh and love and sing.
What matters yon unheeding throng?
  They cannot feel my spirit's spell,
Since life is sweet and love is long,
  I sing my song, and all is well.

Notes

THE POET AND HIS SONG

[1] *lays* ballads (colloq.).

My days are never days of ease;
I till my ground and prune my trees.
When ripened gold is all the plain,
I put my sickle to the grain.
I labor hard, and toil and sweat,
  While others dream within the dell;
But even while my brow is wet,
  I sing my song, and all is well.

Sometimes the sun, unkindly hot,
My garden makes a desert spot;
Sometimes a blight upon the tree
Takes all my fruit away from me;
And then with throes of bitter pain
  Rebellious passions rise and swell;
But – life is more than fruit or grain,
  And so I sing, and all is well.

Accountability

From *Lyrics of Lowly Life*

FOLKS ain't got no right to censuah othah folks about dey habits;
Him dat giv' de squir'ls de bush-tails made de bobtails fu' de rabbits.
Him dat built de gread big mountains hollered out de little valleys,
Him dat made de streets an' driveways wasn't shamed to make de alleys.

We is all constructed diff'ent, d'ain't no two of us de same;
We cain't he'p ouah likes an' dislikes, ef we'se bad we ain't to blame.
Ef we'se[1] good, we needn't[2] show off, case you bet it ain't ouah doin'
We gits into su'ttain channels dat we jes' cain't he'p pu'suin'.

But we all fits into places dat no othah ones could fill,
An' we does the things we has to, big er little, good er ill.
John cain't tek de place o' Henry, Su an' Sally ain't alike;
Bass ain't nuthin' like a suckah, chub ain't nuthin' like a pike.

When you come to think about it, how it's all planned out it's splendid.
Nuthin's done er evah happens, 'dout hit's somefin' dat's intended;
Don't keer whut you does, you has to, an' hit sholy beats de dickens –
Viney, go put on de kittle, I got one o' mastah's chickens.

Notes

ACCOUNTABILITY
[1] *Original reads*: we 'se [ed.].
[2] *Original reads*: need n't [ed.].

Frederick Douglass

From *Lyrics of Lowly Life*

A HUSH is over all the teeming lists,
And there is pause, a breath-space in the strife;
A spirit brave has passed beyond the mists
And vapors that obscure the sun of life.
And Ethiopia, with bosom torn,
Laments the passing of her noblest born.

She weeps for him a mother's burning tears –
She loved him with a mother's deepest love.
He was her champion thro' direful years,
And held her weal[1] all other ends above.
When Bondage held her bleeding in the dust,
He raised her up and whispered, "Hope and Trust."

For her his voice, a fearless clarion,[2] rung
That broke in warning on the ears of men;
For her the strong bow of his power he strung,
And sent his arrows to the very den
Where grim Oppression held his bloody place
And gloated o'er the mis'ries of a race.

And he was no soft-tongued apologist;
He spoke straightforward, fearlessly uncowed;
The sunlight of his truth dispelled the mist,
And set in bold relief each dark hued cloud;
To sin and crime he gave their proper hue,
And hurled at evil what was evil's due.

Through good and ill report he cleaved his way
Right onward, with his face set toward the heights,
Nor feared to face the foeman's dread array –
The lash of scorn, the sting of petty spites.
He dared the lightning in the lightning's track,
And answered thunder with his thunder back.

When men maligned him, and their torrent wrath
In furious imprecations o'er him broke,
He kept his counsel as he kept his path;
'Twas[3] for his race, not for himself he spoke.
He knew the import of his Master's call,
And felt himself too mighty to be small.

Notes

FREDERICK DOUGLASS
[1] *weal* well-being.
[2] *clarion* a war trumpet.
[3] *Original reads*: 'T was [ed.].

No miser in the good he held was he –
  His kindness followed his horizon's rim.
His heart, his talents, and his hands were free
  To all who truly needed aught of him.
Where poverty and ignorance were rife,
He gave his bounty as he gave his life.

The place and cause that first aroused his might
  Still proved its power until his latest day.
In Freedom's lists and for the aid of Right
  Still in the foremost rank he waged the fray;
Wrong lived; his occupation was not gone.
He died in action with his armor on!

We weep for him, but we have touched his hand,
  And felt the magic of his presence nigh,
The current that he sent throughout the land,
  The kindling spirit of his battle-cry.
O'er all that holds us we shall triumph yet,
And place our banner where his hopes were set!

Oh, Douglass, thou hast passed beyond the shore,
  But still thy voice is ringing o'er the gale!
Thou'st[4] taught thy race how high her hopes may soar,
  And bade her seek the heights, nor faint, nor fail.
She will not fail, she heeds thy stirring cry,
She knows thy guardian spirit will be nigh,
And, rising from beneath the chast'ning rod,
She stretches out her bleeding hands to God!

A Prayer

From *Lyrics of Lowly Life*

O Lord, the hard-won miles
  Have worn my stumbling feet:
Oh, soothe me with thy smiles,
  And make my life complete.

The thorns were thick and keen
  Where'er I trembling trod;
The way was long between
  My wounded feet and God.

Notes

[4] *Original reads*: Thou 'st [ed.].

Where healing waters flow
Do thou my footsteps lead.
My heart is aching so;
Thy gracious balm I need.

Passion and Love

From *Lyrics of Lowly Life*

A MAIDEN wept and, as a comforter,
Came one who cried, "I love thee," and he seized
Her in his arms and kissed her with hot breath,
That dried the tears upon her flaming cheeks.
While evermore his boldly blazing eye
Burned into hers; but she uncomforted
Shrank from his arms and only wept the more.

Then one came and gazed mutely in her face
With wide and wistful eyes; but still aloof
He held himself; as with a reverent fear,
As one who knows some sacred presence nigh.
And as she wept he mingled tear with tear,
That cheered her soul like dew a dusty flower –
Until she smiled, approached, and touched his hand!

An Ante-Bellum Sermon

From *Lyrics of Lowly Life*

WE is gathahed hyeah, my brothahs,
In dis howlin' wildaness,
Fu' to speak some words of comfo't
To each othah in distress.
An' we chooses fu' ouah subjic'
Dis – we'll[1] 'splain it by an' by;
"An' de Lawd said, 'Moses, Moses,'
An' de man said, 'Hyeah am I.'"

Now ole Pher'oh, down in Egypt,
Was de wuss man evah bo'n,
An' he had de Hebrew chillun
Down dah wukin' in his co'n;

Notes

AN ANTE-BELLUM SERMON

[1] *Original reads*: we 'll [ed.].

[2] *Original reads*: 'T well [ed.].

'Twell[2] de Lawd got tiahed o' his foolin',
  An' sez he: "I'll let him know–
Look hyeah, Moses, go tell Pher'oh
  Fu' to let dem chillun go."

"An' ef he refuse to do it,
  I will make him rue de houah,
Fu' I'll[3] empty down on Egypt
  All de vials of my powah."
Yes, he did – an' Pher'oh's ahmy
  Wasn't[4] wuth a ha'f a dime;
Fu' de Lawd will he'p his chillun,
  You kin trust him evah time.

An' yo' enemies may 'sail you
  In de back an' in de front;
But de Lawd is all aroun' you,
  Fu' to ba' de battle's brunt.
Dey kin fo'ge yo' chains an' shackles
  F'om de mountains to de sea;
But de Lawd will sen' some Moses
  Fu' to set his chillun free.

An' de lan' shall hyeah his thundah,
  Lak a blas' f'om Gab'el's[5] ho'n,
Fu' de Lawd of hosts is mighty
  When he girds his ahmor on.
But fu' feah someone[6] mistakes me,
  I will pause right hyeah to say,
Dat I'm[7] still a-preachin' ancient,
  I ain't talkin' 'bout to-day.

But I tell you, fellah christuns,
  Things'll[8] happen mighty strange;
Now, de Lawd done dis fu' Isrul,
  An' his ways don't nevah change,
An' de love he showed to Isrul
  Wasn't[9] all on Isrul spent;
Now don't run an' tell yo' mastahs
  Dat I's[10] preachin' discontent.

Notes

3 *Original reads*: I 'll [ed.].

4 *Original reads*: Was n't [ed.].

5 *Gab'el* the archangel Gabriel.

6 *Original reads*: some one [ed.].

7 *Original reads*: I 'm [ed.].

8 *Original reads*: Things 'll [ed.].

9 *Original reads*: Was n't [ed.].

10 *Original reads*: I 's [ed.].

'Cause I isn't;[11] I'se[12] a-judgin'
    Bible people by deir ac's;
I'se[13] a-givin' you de Scriptuah,
    I'se[14] a-handin' you de fac's.
Cose ole Pher'oh b'lieved in slav'ry,
    But de Lawd he let him see,
Dat de people he put bref in –
    Evah mothah's son was free.

An' dahs othahs thinks lak Pher'oh,
    But dey calls de Scriptuah liar,
Fu' de Bible says "a servant
    Is a-worthy of his hire."
An' you cain't git roun' nor thoo dat,
    An' you cain't git ovah it,
Fu' whatevah place you git in,
    Dis hyeah Bible too'll[15] fit.

So you see de Lawd's intention,
    Evah sence de worl' began,
Was dat His almighty freedom
    Should belong to evah man,
But I think it would be bettah,
    Ef I'd[16] pause agin to say,
Dat I'm[17] talkin' 'bout ouah freedom
    In a Bibleistic way.

But de Moses is a-comin',
    An' he's comin', suah and fas'
We kin hyeah his feet a-trompin',
    We kin hyeah his trumpit blas'.
But I want to wa'n you people,
    Don't you git too brigity;
An' don't you git to braggin'
    'Bout dese things, you wait an' see.

But when Moses wif his powah
    Comes an' sets us chillun free,
We will praise de gracious Mastah
    Dat has gin us liberty;
An' we'll[18] shout ouah halleluyahs,
    On dat mighty reck'nin' day,
When we'se[19] reco'nised ez citiz' –
    Huh uh! Chillun, let us pray!

Notes

[11] *Original reads*: Is n't [ed.].
[12] *Original reads*: I 'se [ed.].
[13] *Original reads*: I 'se [ed.].
[14] *Original reads*: I 'se [ed.].
[15] *Original reads*: too 'll [ed.].
[16] *Original reads*: I 'd [ed.].
[17] *Original reads*: I 'm [ed.].
[18] *Original reads*: we 'll [ed.].
[19] *Original reads*: we 'se [ed.].

Ode to Ethiopia

From *Lyrics of Lowly Life*

O Mother Race! to thee I bring
This pledge of faith unwavering,
This tribute to thy glory.
I know the pangs which thou didst feel,
When Slavery crushed thee with its heel,
With thy dear blood all gory.

Sad days were those – ah, sad indeed!
But through the land the fruitful seed
Of better times was growing.
The plant of freedom upward sprung,
And spread its leaves so fresh and young –
Its blossoms now are blowing.

On every hand in this fair land,
Proud Ethiope's swarthy children stand
Beside their fairer neighbor;
The forests flee before their stroke,
Their hammers ring, their forges smoke –
They stir in honest labour.

They tread the fields where honour calls;
Their voices sound through senate halls
In majesty and power.
To right they cling; the hymns they sing
Up to the skies in beauty ring,
And bolder grow each hour.

Be proud, my Race, in mind and soul;
Thy name is writ on Glory's scroll
In characters of fire.
High 'mid the clouds of Fame's bright sky
Thy banner's blazoned folds now fly,
And truth shall lift them higher.

Thou hast the right to noble pride,
Whose spotless robes were purified
By blood's severe baptism.
Upon thy brow the cross was laid,
And labour's painful sweat-beads made
A consecrating chrism.[1]

Notes

Ode to Ethiopia

[1] *chrism* sacramental oil.

No other race, or white or black,
When bound as thou wert, to the rack,
So seldom stooped to grieving;
No other race, when free again,
Forgot the past and proved them men
So noble in forgiving.

Go on and up! Our souls and eyes
Shall follow thy continuous rise;
Our ears shall list thy story
From bards who from thy root shall spring,
And proudly tune their lyres to sing
Of Ethiopia's glory.

Whittier[1]

From *Lyrics of Lowly Life*

Not o'er thy dust let there be spent
The gush of maudlin sentiment;
Such drift as that is not for thee,
Whose life and deeds and songs agree,
Sublime in their simplicity.

Nor shall the sorrowing tear be shed.
O singer sweet, thou art not dead!
In spite of time's malignant chill,
With living fire thy songs shall thrill,
And men shall say, "He liveth still!"

Great poets never die, for Earth
Doth count their lives of too great worth
To lose them from her treasured store;
So shalt thou live for evermore –
Though far thy form from mortal ken –
Deep in the hearts and minds of men.

A Banjo Song

From *Lyrics of Lowly Life*

Oh, dere's[1] lots o' keer an' trouble
  In dis world to swaller down;
An' ol' Sorrer's purty lively

Notes

Whittier
[1] John Greenleaf Whittier (1807–1892), American poet and abolitionist.

A Banjo Song
[1] *Original reads*: dere 's [ed.].

In her way o' gittin' roun'.
Yet dere's[2] times when I furgit em –
Aches an' pains an' troubles all –
An' it's when I tek at ebenin'
My ol' banjo f'om de wall.

'Bout de time dat night is fallin'
An' my daily wu'k is done,
An' above de shady hilltops
I kin see de settin' sun;
When de quiet, restful shadders
Is beginnin' jes' to fall –
Den I take de little banjo
F'om its place upon de wall.

Den my fam'ly gadders roun' me
In de fadin' o' de light,
Ez I strike de strings to try 'em
Ef dey all is tuned er-right.
An' it seems we're[3] so nigh heaben
We kin hyeah de angels sing
When de music o' dat banjo
Sets my cabin all er-ring.

An' my wife an' all de othahs –
Male an' female, small an' big –
Even up to gray-haired granny,
Seem jes' boun' to do a jig;
'Twell I change de style o' music,
Change de movement an' de time,
An' de ringin' little banjo
Plays an ol' hea't-feelin' hime.

An' somehow my th'oat gits choky,
An' a lump keeps tryin' to rise
Lak it wan'ed to ketch de water
Dat was flowin' to my eyes;
An' I feel dat I could sorter
Knock de socks clean off o' sin
Ez I hyeah my po' ol' granny
Wif huh tremblin' voice jine in.

Den we all th'ow in our voices
Fu' to he'p de chune out too,
Lak a big camp-meetin' choiry
Tryin' to sing a mou'nah th'oo.
An' our th'oahts let out de music,

Notes

[2] *Original reads*: dere 's [ed.].

[3] *Original reads*: we 're [ed.].

Sweet an' solemn, loud an' free,
'Twell de raftahs o' my cabin
Echo wif de melody.

Oh, de music o' de banjo,
Quick an' deb'lish, solemn, slow,
Is de greates' joy an' solace
Dat a weary slave kin know!
So jes' let me hyeah it ringin',
Dough de chune be po' an' rough,
It's a pleasure; an' de pleasures
O' dis life is few enough.

Now, de blessed little angels
Up in heaben, we are told.
Don't do nothin' all dere lifetime
'Ceptin' play on ha'ps o' gold.
Now I think heaben'd be mo' homelike
Ef we'd hyeah some music fall
F'om a real ol'-fashioned banjo,
Like dat one upon de wall.

To Louise

From *Lyrics of Lowly Life*

Oh, the poets may sing of their Lady Irenes,
And may rave in their rhymes about wonderful queens;
But I throw my poetical wings to the breeze,
And soar in a song to my Lady Louise.
A sweet little maid, who is dearer, I ween,
Than any fair duchess, or even a queen.
When speaking of her I can't plod in my prose,
For she's the wee lassie who gave me a rose.

Since poets, from seeing a lady's lip curled,
Have written fair verse that has sweetened the world;
Why, then, should not I give the space of an hour
To making a song in return for a flower?
I have found in my life – it has not been so long –
There are too few of flowers – too little of song.
So out of that blossom, this lay of mine grows,
For the dear little lady who gave me the rose.

I thank God for innocence, dearer than Art,
That lights on a by-way which leads to the heart,
And led by an impulse no less than divine,
Walks into the temple and sits at the shrine.
I would rather pluck daisies that grow in the wild,
Or take one simple rose from the hand of a child,

Then to breathe the rich fragrance of flowers that bide
In the gardens of luxury, passion, and pride.

I know not, my wee one, how came you to know
Which way to my heart was the right way to go;
Unless in your purity, soul-clean and clear,
God whispers his messages into your ear.
You have now had my song, let me end with a prayer
That your life may be always sweet, happy, and fair;
That your joys may be many, and absent your woes,
O dear little lady who gave me the rose!

Alice

From *Lyrics of Lowly Life*

KNOW you, winds that blow your course
  Down the verdant valleys,
That somewhere you must, perforce,
  Kiss the brow of Alice?
When her gentle face you find,
Kiss it softly, naughty wind.

Roses waving fair and sweet
  Thro' the garden alleys,
Grow into a glory meet
  For the eye of Alice;
Let the wind your offering bear
Of sweet perfume, faint and rare.

Lily holding crystal dew
  In your pure white chalice,
Nature kind hath fashioned you
  Like the soul of Alice;
It of purest white is wrought,
Filled with gems of crystal thought.

After the Quarrel

From *Lyrics of Lowly Life*

So we, who've[1] supped the self-same cup,
  To-night must lay our friendship by;
Your wrath has burned your judgment up,

Notes

AFTER THE QUARREL
[1] *Original reads*: who 've [ed.].

Hot breath has blown the ashes high.
You say that you are wronged – ah, well,
I count that friendship poor, at best
A bauble, a mere bagatelle,[2]
That cannot stand so slight a test.

I fain would still have been your friend,
And talked and laughed and loved with you;
But since it must, why, let it end;
The false but dies, 'tis[3] not the true.
So we are favored, you and I,
Who only want the living truth.
It was not good to nurse the lie;
'Tis[4] well it died in harmless youth.

I go from you to-night to sleep.
Why, what's the odds? why should I grieve?
I have no fund of tears to weep
For happenings that undeceive.
The days shall come, the days shall go
Just as they came and went before.
The sun shall shine, the streams shall flow
Though you and I are friends no more.

And in the volume of my years,
Where all my thoughts and acts shall be,
The page whereon your name appears
Shall be forever sealed to me.
Not that I hate you over-much,
'Tis[5] less of hate than love defied;
Howe'er, our hands no more shall touch,
We'll[6] go our ways, the world is wide.

Beyond the Years

From Lyrics of Lowly Life

Beyond the years the answer lies, I
Beyond where brood the grieving skies
And Night drops tears.
Where Faith rod-chastened smiles to rise
And doff its fears,
And carping Sorrow pines and dies –
Beyond the years.

Notes

[2] *bagatelle* a trifle.
[3] *Original reads*: 't is [ed.].
[4] *Original reads*: 'T is [ed.].
[5] *Original reads*: 'T is [ed.].
[6] *Original reads*: We 'll [ed.].

Beyond the years the prayer for rest II
Shall beat no more within the breast;
The darkness clears,
And Morn perched on the mountain's crest
Her form uprears –
The day that is to come is best,
Beyond the years.

Beyond the years the soul shall find III
That endless peace for which it pined,
For light appears,
And to the eyes that still were blind
With blood and tears,
Their sight shall come all unconfined
Beyond the years.

The Spellin'-Bee

From *Lyrics of Lowly Life*

I NEVER shall furgit that night when father hitched up Dobbin,[1]
An' all us youngsters clambered in an' down the road went bobbin'
To school where we was kep' at work in every kind o' weather,
But where that night a spellin'-bee was callin' us together.
'Twas one o' Heaven's banner nights, the stars was all a glitter,
The moon was shinin' like the hand o' God had jest then lit her.
The ground was white with spotless snow, the blast was sort o' stingin';
But underneath our round-abouts, you bet our hearts was singin'.
That spellin'-bee had be'n the talk o' many a precious moment,
The youngsters all was wild to see jes' what the precious show meant,
An' we whose years was in their teens was little less desirous
O' gittin' to the meetin' so's[2] our sweethearts could admire us.
So on we went so anxious fur to satisfy our mission
That father had to box our ears, to smother our ambition.
But boxin' ears was too short work to hinder our arrivin',
He jest turned roun' an' smacked us all, an' kep' right on a-drivin'.
Well, soon the schoolhouse hove in sight, the winders beamin' brightly;
The sound o' talkin' reached our ears, and voices laffin' lightly.
It puffed us up so full an' big 'at I'll jest bet a dollar,
There wa'n't a feller there but felt the strain upon his collar.
So down we jumped an' in we went ez sprightly ez you make 'em,
But somethin' grabbed us by the knees an' straight began to shake 'em.
Fur once within that lighted room, our feelin's took a canter,
An' scurried to the zero mark ez quick ez Tam O'Shanter.[3]
'Cause there was crowds o' people there, both sexes an' all stations;

Notes

THE SPELLIN'-BEE
[1] *Dobbin* colloquial name for a farm horse.
[2] *Original reads*: so 's [ed.].
[3] *Tam O'Shanter* a Scottish woolen cap.

It looked like all the town had come an' brought all their relations.
The first I saw was Nettie Gray, I thought that girl was dearer
'N' gold; an' when I got a chance, you bet I aidged up near her.
An' Farmer Dobbs's girl was there, the one 'at Jim was sweet on,
An' Cyrus Jones an' Mandy Smith an' Faith an' Patience Deaton.
Then Parson Brown an' Lawyer Jones were present – all attention,
An' piles on piles of other folks too numerous to mention.
The master rose an' briefly said: "Good friends, dear brother Crawford,
To spur the pupils' minds along, a little prize has offered.
To him who spells the best to-night – or't[4] may be 'her' – no tellin' –
He offers ez a jest reward, this precious work on spellin'."
A little blue-backed spellin'-book with fancy scarlet trimmin';
We boys devoured it with our eyes – so did the girls an' women.
He held it up where all could see, then on the table set it,
An' ev'ry speller in the house felt mortal bound to get it.
At his command we fell in line, prepared to do our dooty,
Outspell the rest an' set 'em down, an' carry home the booty.
'Twas[5] then the merry times began, the blunders, an' the laffin',
The nudges an' the nods an' winks an' stale good-natured chaffin'.
Ole Uncle Hiram Dane was there, the clostest man a-livin',
Whose only bugbear seemed to be the dreadful fear o' givin'.
His beard was long, his hair uncut, his clothes all bare an' dingy;
It wasn't[6] 'cause the man was pore, but jest so mortal stingy;
An' there he sot by Sally Riggs a-smilin' an' a-smirkin',
An' all his children lef' to home a diggin' an' a-workin'.
A widower he was, an' Sal was thinkin' 'at she'd wing him;
I reckon he was wond'rin' what them rings o' hern would bring him.
An' when the spellin'-test commenced, he up an' took his station,
A-spellin' with the best o' them to beat the very nation.
An' when he'd spell some youngster down, he'd turn to look at Sally,
An' say: "The teachin' nowadays can't be o' no great vally."
But true enough the adage says, "Pride walks in slipp'ry places,"
Fur soon a thing occurred that put a smile on all our faces.
The laffter jest kep' ripplin' 'roun' an' teacher couldn't[7] quell it,
Fur when he give out "charity" ole Hiram couldn't[8] spell it.
But laffin' 's ketchin' an' it throwed some others off their bases,
An' folks 'u'd miss the very word that seemed to fit their cases.
Why, fickle little Jessie Lee come near the house upsettin'
By puttin' in a double "kay" to spell the word "coquettin'."[9]
An' when it come to Cyrus Jones, it tickled me all over –
Him settin' up to Mandy Smith an' got sot down on "lover."
But Lawyer Jones of all gone men did shorely look the gonest,
When he found out that he'd furgot to put the "h" in "honest."
An' Parson Brown, whose sermons were too long fur toleration,
Caused lots o' smiles by missin' when they give out "condensation."

Notes

[4] *Original reads*: or 't [ed.].

[5] *Original reads*: 'T was is [ed.].

[6] *Original reads*: was n't [ed.].

[7] *Original reads*: could n't [ed.].

[8] *Original reads*: could n't [ed.].

[9] *coquettin'* flirting.

So one by one they giv' it up – the big words kep' a-landin',
Till me an' Nettie Gray was left, the only ones a-standin',
An' then my inward strife began – I guess my mind was petty –
I did so want that spellin'-book; but then to spell down Nettie
Jest sort o' went ag'in my grain – I somehow couldn't[10] do it,
An' when I git a notion fixed, I'm great on stickin' to it.
So when they giv' the next word out – I hadn't[11] orter tell it,
But then 'twas[12] all fur Nettie's sake – I missed so's she could spell it.
She spelt the word, then looked at me so lovin'-like an' mello',
I tell you 't sent a hunderd pins a shootin' through a fello'.
O' course I had to stand the jokes an' chaffin' of the fello's,
But when they handed her the book I vow I wasn't[13] jealous.
We sung a hymn, an' Parson Brown dismissed us like he orter,
Fur, la! he'd learned a thing er two an' made his blessin' shorter.
'Twas late an' cold when we got out, but Nettie liked cold weather,
An' so did I, so we agreed we'd jest walk home together.
We both wuz silent, fur of words we nuther had a surplus,
'Till she spoke out quite sudden like, "You missed that word on purpose."
Well, I declare it frightened me; at first I tried denyin',
But Nettie, she jest smiled an' smiled, she knowed that I was lyin'.
Sez she: "That book is yourn by right;" sez I: "It never could be –
I – I – you – ah –" an' there I stuck, an' well she understood me.
So we agreed that later on when age had giv' us tether,
We'd jine our lots an' settle down to own that book together.

A Negro Love Song

From *Lyrics of Lowly Life*

Seen my lady home las' night,
Jump back, honey, jump back.
Hel' huh han' an' sque'z it tight,
Jump back, honey, jump back.
Hyeahd huh sigh a little sigh,
Seen a light gleam f'om huh eye,
An' a smile go flittin' by –
Jump back, honey, jump back.

Hyeahd de win' blow thoo de pine,
Jump back, honey, jump back.
Mockin'-bird was singin' fine,
Jump back, honey, jump back.
An' my hea't was beatin' so,
When I reached my lady's do',

Notes

[10] *Original reads*: could n't [ed.].
[11] *Original reads*: had n't [ed.].
[12] *Original reads*: 't was [ed.].
[13] *Original reads*: was n't [ed.].

Dat I couldn't[1] ba' to go –
Jump back, honey, jump back.

Put my ahm aroun' huh wais',
Jump back, honey, jump back.
Raised huh lips an' took a tase,
Jump back, honey, jump back.
Love me, honey, love me true?
Love me well ez I love you?
An' she answe'd, "'Cose I do" –
Jump back, honey, jump back.

The Colored Soldiers

From *Lyrics of Lowly Life*

If the muse were mine to tempt it
And my feeble voice were strong,
If my tongue were trained to measures,
I would sing a stirring song.
I would sing a song heroic
Of those noble sons of Ham,[1]
Of the gallant colored soldiers
Who fought for Uncle Sam!

In the early days you scorned them,
And with many a flip and flout
Said "These battles are the white man's,
And the whites will fight them out."
Up the hills you fought and faltered,
In the vales you strove and bled,
While your ears still heard the thunder
Of the foes' advancing tread.

Then distress fell on the nation,
And the flag was drooping low;
Should the dust pollute your banner?
No! the nation shouted, No!
So when War, in savage triumph,
Spread abroad his funeral pall –
Then you called the colored soldiers,
And they answered to your call.

Notes

A Negro Love Song

[1] *Original reads*: could n't [ed.].

The Colored Soldiers

[1] *Ham* a son of Noah in the Bible, the traditional ancestor of Africans.

And like hounds unleashed and eager
  For the life blood of the prey,
Sprung they forth and bore them bravely
  In the thickest of the fray.
And where'er the fight was hottest,
  Where the bullets fastest fell,
There they pressed unblanched and fearless
  At the very mouth of hell.

Ah, they rallied to the standard
  To uphold it by their might;
None were stronger in the labors,
  None were braver in the fight.
From the blazing breach of Wagner[2]
  To the plains of Olustee,[3]
They were foremost in the fight
  Of the battles of the free.

And at Pillow![4] God have mercy
  On the deeds committed there,
And the souls of those poor victims
  Sent to Thee without a prayer.
Let the fulness of Thy pity
  O'er the hot wrought spirits sway
Of the gallant colored soldiers
  Who fell fighting on that day!

Yes, the Blacks enjoy their freedom,
  And they won it dearly, too;
For the life blood of their thousands
  Did the southern fields bedew.
In the darkness of their bondage,
  In the depths of slavery's night,
Their muskets flashed the dawning,
  And they fought their way to light.

They were comrades then and brothers,
  Are they more or less to-day?
They were good to stop a bullet
  And to front the fearful fray.
They were citizens and soldiers,
  When rebellion raised its head;
And the traits that made them worthy –
  Ah! those virtues are not dead.

Notes

[2] *Wagner* Fort Wagner (South Carolina), where a black regiment led an unsuccessful attack on July 18, 1863.

[3] *Olustee* the Battle of Olustee, Florida (February 20, 1864), where three black regiments fought valiantly.

[4] *Pillow* Fort Pillow (Tennessee), where hundreds of black soldiers were massacred after surrendering to Confederate forces on April 12, 1864.

They have shared your nightly vigils,
  They have shared your daily toil;
And their blood with yours commingling
  Has enriched the Southern soil.
They have slept and marched and suffered
  'Neath the same dark skies as you,
They have met as fierce a foeman,
  And have been as brave and true.

And their deeds shall find a record
  In the registry of Fame;
For their blood has cleansed completely
  Every blot of Slavery's shame.
So all honor and all glory
  To those noble sons of Ham –
The gallant colored soldiers
  Who fought for Uncle Sam!

Nature and Art

To my friend Charles Booth Nettleton

From *Lyrics of Lowly Life*

I

THE young queen Nature, ever sweet and fair,
  Once on a time fell upon evil days.
  From hearing oft herself discussed with praise,
There grew within her heart the longing rare
To see herself; and every passing air
  The warm desire fanned into lusty blaze.
  Full oft she sought this end by devious ways,
But sought in vain, so fell she in despair.
For none within her train nor by her side
  Could solve the task or give the envied boon.[1]
  So day and night, beneath the sun and moon,
She wandered to and fro unsatisfied,
  Till Art came by, a blithe inventive elf,
  And made a glass wherein she saw herself.

II

Enrapt, the queen gazed on her glorious self,
  Then trembling with the thrill of sudden thought,
  Commanded that the skilful wight be brought
That she might dower him with lands and pelf.
Then out upon the silent sea-lapt shelf
  And up the hills and on the downs they sought
  Him who so well and wondrously had wrought;

Notes

NATURE AND ART
[1] *boon* a helpful thing, a favor.

And with much search found and brought home the elf.
But he put by all gifts with sad replies,
And from his lips these words flowed forth like wine:
"O queen, I want no gift but thee," he said.
She heard and looked on him with love-lit eyes,
Gave him her hand, low murmuring, "I am thine,"
And at the morrow's dawning they were wed.

When de Co'n Pone's Hot

From *Lyrics of Lowly Life*

Dey is times in life when Nature
Seems to slip a cog an' go,
Jes' a-rattlin' down creation,
Lak an ocean's overflow;
When de worl' jes' stahts a-spinnin'
Lak a picaninny's[1] top,
An' yo' cup o' joy is brimmin'
'Twell it seems about to slop,
An' you feel jes' lak a racah,[2]
Dat is trainin' fu' to trot –
When yo' mammy says de blessin'
An' de co'n pone's[3] hot.

When you set down at de table,
Kin' o' weary lak an' sad,
An' you'se[4] jes' a little tiahed
An' purhaps a little mad;
How yo' gloom tu'ns into gladness,
How yo' joy drives out de doubt
When de oven do' is opened,
An' de smell comes po'in' out;
Why, de 'lectric light o' Heaven
Seems to settle on de spot,
When yo' mammy says de blessin'
An' de co'n pone's[5] hot.

When de cabbage pot is steamin'
An' de bacon good an' fat,
When de chittlins is a-sputter'n'
So's[6] to show you whah dey's[7] at;
Tek away yo' sody biscuit,

Notes

When de Co'n Pone's Hot

[1] *picaninny* a small black child (offensive).

[2] *racah* racer.

[3] *Original reads*: pone 's [ed.].

[4] *Original reads*: you 'se [ed.].

[5] *Original reads*: pone 's [ed.].

[6] *Original reads*: So 's [ed.].

[7] *Original reads*: dey 's [ed.].

Tek away yo' cake an' pie,
Fu' de glory time is comin',
An' it's[8] 'proachin' mighty nigh,
An' you want to jump an' hollah,
Dough you know you'd bettah not,
When yo' mammy says de blessin'
An' de co'n pone's[9] hot.

I have hyeahd o' lots o' sermons,
An' I've hyeahd o' lots o' prayers,
An' I've listened to some singin'
Dat has tuck me up de stairs
Of de Glory-Lan' an' set me
Jes' below de Mastah's th'one,
An' have lef' my hea't a-singin'
In a happy aftah tone;
But dem wu'ds so sweetly murmured
Seem to tech de softes' spot,
When my mammy says de blessin',
An' de co'n pone's[10] hot.

The Deserted Plantation

From *Lyrics of Lowly Life*

Oh, de grubbin'-hoe's[1] a-rustin' in de co'nah,
An' de plow's[2] a-tumblin' down in de fiel',
While de whippo'will's[3] a-wailin' lak a mou'nah
When his stubbo'n hea't is tryin' ha'd to yiel'.

In de furrers[4] whah de co'n was allus wavin',
Now de weeds is growin' green an' rank an' tall;
An' de swallers roun' de whole place is a-bravin'
Lak dey thought deir folks had allus owned it all.

An' de big house stan's all quiet lak an' solemn,
Not a blessed soul in pa'lor, po'ch, er lawn;
Not a guest, ner not a ca'iage lef' to haul 'em,
Fu' de ones dat tu'ned de latch-string out air gone.

An' de banjo's voice is silent in de qua'ters,
D' ain't a hymn ner co'n-song ringin' in de air;

Notes

8 *Original reads*: it 's [ed.].

9 *Original reads*: pone 's [ed.].

10 *Original reads*: pone 's [ed.].

The Deserted Plantation

1 *Original reads*: grubbin'-hoe 's [ed.].

2 *Original reads*: plow 's [ed.].

3 *Original reads*: whippo'will 's [ed.].

4 *furrers* furrows.

But de murmur of a branch's passin' waters
  Is de only soun' dat breks de stillness dere.

Whah's[5] de da'kies, dem dat used to be a-dancin'
  Evry night befo' de ole cabin do'?
Whah's[6] de chillun, dem dat used to be a-prancin'
  Er a-rollin' in de san' er on de flo'?

Whah's[7] ole Uncle Mordecai an' Uncle Aaron?
  Whah's[8] Aunt Doshy, Sam, an' Kit, an' all de res'?
Whah's[9] ole Tom de da'ky fiddlah, how's he farin'?
  Whah's[10] de gals dat used to sing an' dance de bes'?

Gone! not one o' dem is lef' to tell de story;
  Dey have lef' de deah ole place to fall away.
Couldn't[11] one o' dem dat seed it in its glory
  Stay to watch it in de hour of decay?

Dey have lef' de ole plantation to de swallers,
  But it hol's in me a lover till de las';
Fu' I fin' hyeah in de memory dat follers
  All dat loved me an' dat I loved in de pas'.

So I'll[12] stay an' watch de deah ole place an' tend it
  Ez I used to in de happy days gone by.
'Twell de othah Mastah thinks it's time to end it,
  An' calls me to my qua'ters in de sky.

We Wear the Mask

From *Lyrics of Lowly Life*

We wear the mask that grins and lies,
It hides our cheeks and shades our eyes –
This debt we pay to human guile;
With torn and bleeding hearts we smile,
And mouth with myriad subtleties.

Why should the world be overwise,
In counting all our tears and sighs?
Nay, let them only see us, while
  We wear the mask.

Notes

[5] *Original reads*: Whah 's [ed.].
[6] *Original reads*: Whah 's [ed.].
[7] *Original reads*: Whah 's [ed.].
[8] *Original reads*: Whah 's [ed.].
[9] *Original reads*: Whah 's [ed.].
[10] *Original reads*: Whah 's [ed.].
[11] *Original reads*: could 'nt [ed.].
[12] *Original reads*: I 'll [ed.].

We smile, but, O great Christ, our cries
To thee from tortured souls arise.
We sing, but oh the clay is vile
Beneath our feet, and long the mile;
But let the world dream otherwise,
  We wear the mask!

Phyllis

From *Lyrics of Lowly Life*

PHYLLIS, ah, Phyllis, my life is a gray day,
  Few are my years, but my griefs are not few,
Ever to youth should each day be a May-day,
  Warm wind and rose-breath and diamonded dew –
Phyllis, ah, Phyllis, my life is a gray day.

Oh for the sunlight that shines on a May-day!
  Only the cloud hangeth over my life.
Love that should bring me youth's happiest heyday
  Brings me but seasons of sorrow and strife;
Phyllis, ah, Phyllis, my life is a gray day.

Sunshine or shadow, or gold day or gray day,
  Life must be lived as our destinies rule;
Leisure or labor or work day or play day –
  Feasts for the famous and fun for the fool;
Phyllis, ah, Phyllis, my life is a gray day.

When Malindy Sings

From *Lyrics of Lowly Life*

G'WAY an' quit dat noise, Miss Lucy –
  Put dat music book away;
What's de use to keep on tryin'?
  Ef you practise twell you're[1] gray,
You cain't sta't no notes a-flyin'
  Lak de ones dat rants and rings
F'om de kitchen to be big woods
  When Malindy sings.

You ain't got de nachel o'gans
  Fu' to make de soun' come right,

Notes

WHEN MALINDY SINGS

1 *Original reads*: you 're [ed.].

You ain't got de tu'ns an' twistin's
  Fu' to make it sweet an' light.
Tell you one thing now, Miss Lucy,
  An' I'm tellin' you fu' true,
When hit comes to raal right singin',
  'Tain't[2] no easy thing to do.

Easy 'nough fu' folks to hollah,
  Lookin' at de lines an' dots,
When dey ain't no one kin sence it,
  An' de chune comes in, in spots;
But fu' real melojous music,
  Dat jes' strikes yo' hea't and clings,
Jes' you stan' an' listen wif me
  When Malindy sings.

Ain't you nevah hyeahd Malindy?
  Blessed soul, tek up de cross!
Look hyeah, ain't you jokin', honey?
  Well, you don't know whut you los'.
Y' ought to hyeah dat gal a-wa'b-lin',
  Robins, la'ks, an' all dem things,
Heish dey moufs an' hides dey faces
  When Malindy sings.

Fiddlin' man jes' stop his fiddlin',
  Lay his fiddle on de she'f;
Mockin'-bird quit tryin' to whistle,
  'Cause he jes' so shamed hisse'f.
Folks a-playin' on de banjo
  Draps dey fingahs on de strings –
Bless yo' soul – fu'gits to move em,
  When Malindy sings.

She jes' spreads huh mouf and hollahs,
  "Come to Jesus," twell you hyeah
Sinnahs' tremblin' steps and voices,
  Timid-lak a-drawin' neah;
Den she tu'ns to "Rock of Ages,"
  Simply to de cross she clings,
An' you fin' yo' teahs a-drappin'
  When Malindy sings.

Who dat says dat humble praises
  Wif de Master nevah counts?
Heish yo' mouf, I hyeah dat music,
  Ez hit rises up an' mounts –

Notes

[2] *Original reads*: 'T ain't [ed.].

Floatin' by de hills an' valleys,
Way above dis buryin' sod,
Ez hit makes its way in glory
To de very gates of God!

Oh, hit's sweetah dan de music
Of an edicated band;
An' hit's dearah dan de battle's
Song o' triumph in de lan'.
It seems holier dan evenin'
When de solemn chu'ch bell rings,
Ez I sit an' ca'mly listen
While Malindy sings.

Towsah, stop dat ba'kin', hyeah me!
Mandy, mek dat chile keep still;
Don't you hyeah de echoes callin'
F'om de valley to de hill?
Let me listen, I can hyeah it,
Th'oo de bresh of angels' wings,
Sof' an' sweet, "Swing Low, Sweet Chariot,"
Ez Malindy sings.

1896

Extract from The Heart of Happy Hollow

The Lynching of Jube Benson

GORDON FAIRFAX'S LIBRARY held but three men, but the air was dense with clouds of smoke. The talk had drifted from one topic to another much as the smoke wreaths had puffed, floated, and thinned away. Then Handon Gay, who was an ambitious young reporter, spoke of a lynching story in a recent magazine, and the matter of punishment without trial put new life into the conversation.

"I should like to see a real lynching," said Gay rather callously.

"Well, I should hardly express it that way," said Fairfax, "but if a real, live lynching were to come my way, I should not avoid it."

"I should," spoke the other from the depths of his chair, where he had been puffing in moody silence. Judged by his hair, which was freely sprinkled with gray, the speaker might have been a man of forty-five or fifty, but his face, though lined and serious, was youthful, the face of a man hardly past thirty.

"What, you, Dr. Melville? Why, I thought that you physicians wouldn't weaken at anything."

"I have seen one such affair," said the doctor gravely, "in fact, I took a prominent part in it."

"Tell us about it," said the reporter, feeling for his pencil and note-book, which he was, nevertheless, careful to hide from the speaker.

The men drew their chairs eagerly up to the doctor's, but for a minute he did not seem to see them, but sat gazing abstractedly into the fire, then he took a long draw upon his cigar and began:

"I can see it all very vividly now. It was in the summer time and about seven years ago. I was practising at the time down in the little town of Bradford. It was a small and primitive place, just the location for an impecunious medical man, recently out of college.

"In lieu of a regular office, I attended to business in the first of two rooms which I rented from Hiram Daly, one of the more prosperous of the townsmen. Here I boarded and here also came my patients – white and black – whites from every section, and blacks from 'nigger town,' as the west portion of the place was called.

"The people about me were most of them coarse and rough, but they were simple and generous, and as time passed on I had about abandoned my intention of seeking distinction in wider fields and determined to settle into the place of a modest country doctor. This was rather a strange conclusion for a young man to arrive at, and I will not deny that the presence in the house of my host's beautiful young daughter, Annie, had something to do with my decision. She was a beautiful young girl of seventeen or eighteen, and very far superior to her surroundings. She had a native grace and a pleasing way about her that made everybody that came under her spell her abject slave. White and black who knew her loved her, and none, I thought, more deeply and respectfully than Jube Benson, the black man of all work about the place.

"He was a fellow whom everybody trusted; an apparently steady-going, grinning sort, as we used to call him. Well, he was completely under Miss Annie's thumb, and would fetch and carry for her like a faithful dog. As soon as he saw that I began to care for Annie, and anybody could see that, he transferred some of his allegiance to me and became my faithful servitor also. Never did a man have a more devoted adherent in his wooing than did I, and many a one of Annie's tasks which he volunteered to do gave her an extra hour with me. You can imagine that I liked the boy and you need not wonder any more that as both wooing and my practice waxed apace, I was content to give up my great ambitions and stay just where I was.

"It wasn't a very pleasant thing, then, to have an epidemic of typhoid break out in the town that kept me going so that I hardly had time for the courting that a fellow wants to carry on with his sweetheart while he is still young enough to call her his girl. I fumed, but duty was duty, and I kept to my work night and day. It was now that Jube proved how invaluable he was as a coadjutor. He not only took messages to Annie, but brought sometimes little ones from her to me, and he would tell me little secret things that he had overheard her say that made me throb with joy and swear at him for repeating his mistress' conversation. But best of all, Jube was a perfect Cerberus, and no one on earth could have been more effective in keeping away or deluding the other young fellows who visited the Dalys. He would tell me of it afterwards, chuckling softly to himself. 'An', Doctah, I say to Mistah Hemp Stevens, "'Scuse us, Mistah Stevens, but Miss Annie, she des gone out," an' den he go outer de gate lookin' moughty lonesome. When Sam Elkins come, I say, "Sh, Mistah Elkins, Miss Annie, she done tuk down," an' he say, "What, Jube, you don' reckon hit de –" Den he stop an' look skeert, an' I say, "I feared hit is, Mistah Elkins," an' sheks my haid ez solemn. He goes outer de gate lookin' lak his bes' frien' done daid, an' all de time Miss Annie behine de cu'tain ovah de po'ch des' a laffin' fit to kill.'

"Jube was a most admirable liar, but what could I do? He knew that I was a young fool of a hypocrite, and when I would rebuke him for these deceptions, he would give way and roll on the floor in an excess of delighted laughter until from very contagion I had to join him – and, well, there was no need of my preaching when there had been no beginning to his repentance and when there must ensue a continuance of his wrong-doing.

"This thing went on for over three months, and then, pouf! I was down like a shot. My patients were nearly all up, but the reaction from overwork made me an easy victim of the lurking germs. Then Jube loomed up as a nurse. He put everyone else aside, and with the doctor, a friend of mine from a neighbouring town, took entire charge of me. Even Annie herself was put aside, and I was cared for as tenderly as a baby. Tom, that was my physician and friend, told me all about it afterward with tears in his eyes. Only he was a big, blunt man and his expressions did not convey all that he meant. He told me how my nigger had nursed me as if I were a sick kitten and he my mother. Of how fiercely he guarded his right to be the sole one to 'do' for me, as he called it, and how, when the crisis came, he hovered, weeping, but hopeful, at my bedside, until it was safely passed, when they drove him, weak and exhausted, from the room. As for me, I knew little about it at the time, and cared less. I was too busy in my fight with death. To my chimerical vision there was only a black but gentle demon that came and went, alternating with a white fairy, who would insist on coming in on her head, growing larger and larger and then dissolving. But the pathos and devotion in the story lost nothing in my blunt friend's telling.

"It was during the period of a long convalescence, however, that I came to know my humble ally as he really was, devoted to the point of abjectness. There were times when for very shame at his goodness to me, I would beg him to go away, to do something else. He would go, but before I had time to realise that I was not being ministered to, he would be back at my side, grinning and pottering just the same. He manufactured duties for the joy of performing them. He pretended to see desires in me that I never had, because he liked to pander to them, and when I became entirely exasperated, and ripped out a good round oath, he chuckled with the remark, 'Dah, now, you sholy is gittin' well. Nevah did hyeah a man anywhaih nigh Jo'dan's sho' cuss lak dat.'

"Why, I grew to love him, love him, oh, yes, I loved him as well – oh, what am I saying? All human love and gratitude are damned poor things; excuse me, gentlemen, this isn't a pleasant story. The truth is usually a nasty thing to stand.

"It was not six months after that that my friendship to Jube, which he had been at such great pains to win, was put to too severe a test.

"It was in the summer time again, and as business was slack, I had ridden over to see my friend, Dr. Tom. I had spent a good part of the day there, and it was past four o'clock when I rode leisurely into Bradford. I was in a particularly joyous mood and no premonition of the impending catastrophe oppressed me. No sense of sorrow, present or to come, forced itself upon me, even when I saw men hurrying through the almost deserted streets. When I got within sight of my home and saw a crowd surrounding it, I was only interested sufficiently to spur my horse into a jog trot, which brought me up to the throng, when something in the sullen, settled horror in the men's faces gave me a sudden, sick thrill. They whispered a word to me, and without a thought, save for Annie, the girl who had been so surely growing into my heart, I leaped from the saddle and tore my way through the people to the house.

"It was Annie, poor girl, bruised and bleeding, her face and dress torn from struggling. They were gathered round her with white faces, and, oh, with what terrible patience they were trying to gain from her fluttering lips the name of her murderer. They made way for me and I knelt at her side. She was beyond my skill, and my will merged with theirs. One thought was in our minds.

"'Who?' I asked.

"Her eyes half opened, 'That black——' She fell back into my arms dead.

"We turned and looked at each other. The mother had broken down and was weeping, but the face of the father was like iron.

"'It is enough,' he said; 'Jube has disappeared.' He went to the door and said to the expectant crowd, 'She is dead.'

"I heard the angry roar without swelling up like the noise of a flood, and then I heard the sudden movement of many feet as the men separated into searching parties, and laying the dead girl back upon her couch, I took my rifle and went out to join them.

"As if by intuition the knowledge had passed among the men that Jube Benson had disappeared, and he, by common consent, was to be the object of our search. Fully a dozen of the citizens had seen him hastening toward the woods and noted his skulking air, but as he had grinned in his old good-natured way they had, at the time, thought nothing of it. Now, however, the diabolical reason of his slyness was apparent. He had been shrewd enough to disarm suspicion, and by now was far away. Even Mrs. Daly, who was visiting with a neighbour, had seen him stepping out by a back way, and had said with a laugh, 'I reckon that black rascal's a-running off somewhere.' Oh, if she had only known.

"'To the woods! To the woods!' that was the cry, and away we went, each with the determination not to shoot, but to bring the culprit alive into town, and then to deal with him as his crime deserved.

"I cannot describe the feelings I experienced as I went out that night to beat the woods for this human tiger. My heart smouldered within me like a coal, and I went forward under the impulse of a will that was half my own, half some more malignant power's. My throat throbbed drily, but water nor whiskey would not have quenched my thirst. The thought has come to me since that now I could interpret the panther's desire for blood and sympathise with it, but then I thought nothing. I simply went forward, and watched, watched with burning eyes for a familiar form that I had looked for as often before with such different emotions.

"Luck or ill-luck, which you will, was with our party, and just as dawn was graying the sky, we came upon our quarry crouched in the corner of a fence. It was only half light, and we might have passed, but my eyes had caught sight of him, and I raised the cry. We levelled our guns and he rose and came toward us.

"'I t'ought you wa'n't gwine see me,' he said sullenly, 'I didn't mean no harm.'

"'Harm!'

"Some of the men took the word up with oaths, others were ominously silent.

"We gathered around him like hungry beasts, and I began to see terror dawning in his eyes. He turned to me, 'I's moughty glad you's hyeah, doc,' he said, 'you ain't gwine let 'em whup me.'

"'Whip you, you hound,' I said, 'I'm going to see you hanged,' and in the excess of my passion I struck him full on the mouth. He made a motion as if to resent the blow against even such great odds, but controlled himself.

"'W'y, doctah,' he exclaimed in the saddest voice I have ever heard, 'w'y, doctah! I ain't stole nuffin' o' yo'n, an' I was comin' back. I only run off to see my gal, Lucy, ovah to de Centah.'

"'You lie!' I said, and my hands were busy helping the others bind him upon a horse. Why did I do it? I don't know. A false education, I reckon, one false from the beginning. I saw his black face glooming there in the half light, and I could only think of him as a monster. It's tradition. At first I was told that the black man would catch me, and when

I got over that, they taught me that the devil was black, and when I had recovered from the sickness of that belief, here were Jube and his fellows with faces of menacing blackness. There was only one conclusion: This black man stood for all the powers of evil, the result of whose machinations had been gathering in my mind from childhood up. But this has nothing to do with what happened.

"After firing a few shots to announce our capture, we rode back into town with Jube. The ingathering parties from all directions met us as we made our way up to the house. All was very quiet and orderly. There was no doubt that it was as the papers would have said, a gathering of the best citizens. It was a gathering of stern, determined men, bent on a terrible vengeance.

"We took Jube into the house, into the room where the corpse lay. At sight of it, he gave a scream like an animal's and his face went the colour of storm-blown water. This was enough to condemn him. We divined, rather than heard, his cry of 'Miss Ann, Miss Ann, oh, my God, doc, you don't t'ink I done it?'

"Hungry hands were ready. We hurried him out into the yard. A rope was ready. A tree was at hand. Well, that part was the least of it, save that Hiram Daly stepped aside to let me be the first to pull upon the rope. It was lax at first. Then it tightened, and I felt the quivering soft weight resist my muscles. Other hands joined, and Jube swung off his feet.

"No one was masked. We knew each other. Not even the culprit's face was covered, and the last I remember of him as he went into the air was a look of sad reproach that will remain with me until I meet him face to face again.

"We were tying the end of the rope to a tree, where the dead man might hang as a warning to his fellows, when a terrible cry chilled us to the marrow.

"'Cut 'im down, cut 'im down, he ain't guilty. We got de one. Cut him down, fu' Gawd's sake. Here's de man, we foun' him hidin' in de barn!'

"Jube's brother, Ben, and another Negro, came rushing toward us, half dragging, half carrying a miserable-looking wretch between them. Someone cut the rope and Jube dropped lifeless to the ground.

"'Oh, my Gawd, he's daid, he's daid!' wailed the brother, but with blazing eyes he brought his captive into the centre of the group, and we saw in the full light the scratched face of Tom Skinner – the worst white ruffian in the town – but the face we saw was not as we were accustomed to see it, merely smeared with dirt. It was blackened to imitate a Negro's.

"God forgive me; I could not wait to try to resuscitate Jube. I knew he was already past help, so I rushed into the house and to the dead girl's side. In the excitement they had not yet washed or laid her out. Carefully, carefully, I searched underneath her broken finger nails. There was skin there. I took it out, the little curled pieces, and went with it to my office.

"There, determinedly, I examined it under a powerful glass, and read my own doom. It was the skin of a white man, and in it were embedded strands of short, brown hair or beard.

"How I went out to tell the waiting crowd I do not know, for something kept crying in my ears, 'Blood guilty! Blood guilty!'

"The men went away stricken into silence and awe. The new prisoner attempted neither denial nor plea. When they were gone I would have helped Ben carry his brother in, but he waved me away fiercely, 'You he'ped murder my brothah, you dat was *his* frien', go 'way, go 'way! I'll tek him home myse'f.' I could only respect his wish, and he and his comrade took up the dead man and between them bore him up the street on which the sun was now shining full.

"I saw the few men who had not skulked indoors uncover as they passed, and I – I – stood there between the two murdered ones, while all the while something in my ears kept crying, 'Blood guilty! Blood guilty!'"

The doctor's head dropped into his hands and he sat for some time in silence, which was broken by neither of the men, then he rose, saying, "Gentlemen, that was my last lynching."

1904

Booker T. Washington (1856–1915)

When Booker T. Washington gave his famous speech before the Cotton States and International Exposition in Atlanta on September 18, 1895, he was immediately hailed as successor to Frederick Douglass, who coincidentally had passed away earlier that year. The principal and founder of the Tuskegee Normal and Industrial Institute, Washington was the most innovative African American educator and successful politician of his time, and Tuskegee was the most famous African American institution in the United States. As the first African American to eat dinner with the President of the United States at the White House, Washington espoused the conservative rhetoric that, for African Americans, thrift, hard work, and social usefulness were more important than political agitation for racial equality. Founding the National Negro Business League in 1900, he won the admiration and gratitude of African American entrepreneurs long excluded from predominantly white business organizations. Yet, as W.E.B. Du Bois had pointed out, Booker T. Washington's "paradox" lay in his position as a servant of two opposing constituencies: recently emancipated southern African Americans, and the moneyed white establishment that sought their continued subjugation. Doomed to juggle the demands of these two constituencies, Washington struck compromises that were controversial, if not contentious, given the egalitarian promises of Reconstruction.

Booker Taliafarro Washington was born a slave in southwestern Virginia five years before the Civil War. His mother was an enslaved woman named Jane Ferguson, who took her children to West Virginia to reunite with her husband, Washington Ferguson, after the war ended. Although his biological father was a white man, probably his mother's master, Washington took his stepfather's first name as his own. Raised in profound poverty, Washington worked in the salt furnaces and coal mines of West Virginia throughout his childhood, an education in physical toil that informed his future commitment to manual and industrial training. He attended school at night. In 1872, he walked 200 miles to the Hampton Institute in eastern Virginia in pursuit of further education. Founded under the auspices of the American Missionary Association to educate African Americans and Native Americans in the early days of Reconstruction, Hampton introduced Washington to Samuel Chapman Armstrong, a Union Army general who believed that industrial education provided the best preparation for ex-slaves entering the Gilded Age economy. At Hampton, with Armstrong as his mentor, Washington worked as a janitor to pay his room and board, and graduated with honors in 1875. He briefly attended Wayland Seminary in Washington, DC, but by the late 1870s had returned to serve on the faculty at Hampton. His life underwent a momentous change when General Armstrong recommended him as leader of a new normal school, modeled on Hampton, in Tuskegee, Alabama. When Washington founded the school in 1881, it consisted of a barn, a plot of land, and $2,000 to pay for teachers, books, and equipment. By his death in 1915, Washington's leadership had transformed the school into a sprawling campus with dormitories, classrooms, libraries, and an endowment of $1.5 million.

As southern states reduced funding for African American education in the aftermath of Reconstruction, schools like Tuskegee relied

The Wiley Blackwell Anthology of African American Literature: Volume 1, 1746–1920, First Edition.
Edited by Gene Andrew Jarrett.

increasingly on private donations. Washington vigorously courted philanthropists across the country, gaining personal relationships with Andrew Carnegie, Julius Rosenwald, and other Gilded Age industrialists. In courting wealthy white patrons, Washington espoused laissez-faire capitalism and middle-class values while eschewing political agitation or racial integration. At the Atlanta Exposition in 1895, Washington assured his segregated white audience: "In all things that are purely social we can be as separate as the fingers yet one as the hand in all things essential to mutual progress."

As Du Bois and other critics argued, Washington's statement condoned racial segregation and discrimination. He allowed whites to benefit from African American "uplift," and ignored the role that institutionalized racism played in creating a permanent, disfranchised underclass. Ironically, beneath his public pose of accommodation to white supremacy, Washington used his powerful Tuskegee machine to quietly challenge segregation in US courts and support the legal fortunes of southern African Americans. Despite the cunning and political realism at work in his rhetoric, many aspects of Washington – his statements that slavery was beneficial to African Americans, the blind eye he turned to southern disenfranchisement and lynching, his bullying control over African American newspapers – warranted criticism.

Washington's desire to build his public empire (and monopolize white philanthropy) led him to write or (have ghostwritten on his behalf) a number of non-fiction treatises that bolstered his conservative ideology. Foremost among these is his best-selling 1901 autobiography *Up from Slavery*, with its emphasis on hard work and self-determination. Honorary degrees from 'larvard University in 1896 and Dartmouth 'llege in 1901 sealed his reputation as the 'g educator and racial theorist of his time. 'uent works – *The Future of the American* '00), *The Story of the Negro* (1909), *'ger Education* (1911), to name a few – kept his political platform prominent in the national consciousness. But with the founding of the National Association for the Advancement of Colored People in 1910, Washington's control over African American dissent began to wane. The persistence of the "Negro Problem," despite his assurances that accommodation would fix it, urged a new generation of civil rights activists to challenge his conservative program before and after his death in 1915.

Further reading

Ashton, Susanna. "Entitles: Booker T. Washington's Signs of Play." *Southern Literary Journal* 39.2 (2007): 1–23.

Bieze, Michael. Booker *T. Washington and the Art of Self-Representation*. New York: Peter Lang, 2008.

Hicks, Scott. "W.E.B. Du Bois, Booker T. Washington, and Richard Wright: Toward an Ecocriticism of Color." *Callaloo* 29.1 (2006): 202–222.

Kowalski, Philip J. "No Excuses for Our Dirt: Booker T. Washington and a 'New Negro' Middle Class." *Post-Bellum, Pre-Harlem: African American Literature and Culture*. Eds. Barbara McCaskill and Caroline Gebhard. New York: New York University Press, 2006. 181–196.

Menson-Furr, Ladrica. "Booker T. Washington, August Wilson, and the Shadows in the Garden." *Mosaic: A Journal for the Interdisciplinary Study of Literature* 38.4 (2005): 175–190.

Norrell, Robert J. *Up from History: The Life of Booker T. Washington*. Cambridge, MA: Belknap, 2009.

Pochmara, Anna. *The Making of the New Negro: Black Authorship, Masculinity, and Sexuality in the Harlem Renaissance*. Amsterdam, Netherlands: Amsterdam University Press, 2011. Ch. 1.

Ross, Marlon B. "Racial Uplift and the Literature of the New Negro Renaissance." *A Companion to African American Literature*. Ed. Gene Andrew Jarrett. Malden, MA: Wiley-Blackwell, 2010. 151–168.

Totten, Gary. "Southernizing Travel in the Black Atlantic: Booker T. Washington's *The Man Farthest Down*." *MELUS: The Journal of the Society for the Study of the Multi-Ethnic Literature of the United States* 32.2 (2007): 107–131.

Valelly, Richard M. "Recognizing the True Greatness of Booker T. Washington." *Journal of Policy History* 22.1 (2010): 110–117.

Vivian, Bradford J. "Up from Memory: Epideictic Forgetting in Booker T. Washington's Cotton States Exposition Address." *Philosophy and Rhetoric* 45.2 (2012): 189–212.

West, Michael Rudolph. *The Education of Booker T. Washington: American Democracy and the Idea of Race Relations*. New York: Columbia University Press, 2006.

Zimmerman, Andrew. *Alabama in Africa: Booker T. Washington, the German Empire, and the Globalization of the New South*. Princeton: Princeton University Press, 2010.

Extract from Up from Slavery

Chapter 14

The Atlanta Exposition Address

The Atlanta Exposition, at which I had been asked to make an address as a representative of the Negro race, as stated in the last chapter,[1] was opened with a short address from Governor Bullock.[2] After other interesting exercises, including an invocation from Bishop Nelson,[3] of Georgia, a dedicatory ode by Albert Howell, Jr.,[4] and addresses by the President of the Exposition and Mrs. Joseph Thompson, the President of the Woman's Board, Governor Bullock introduced me with the words, "We have with us to-day a representative of Negro enterprise and Negro civilization."

When I arose to speak, there was considerable cheering, especially from the coloured people. As I remember it now, the thing that was uppermost in my mind was the desire to say something that would cement the friendship of the races and bring about hearty cooperation between them. So far as my outward surroundings were concerned, the only thing that I recall distinctly now is that when I got up, I saw thousands of eyes looking intently into my face. The following is the address which I delivered:–

Mr. President and Gentlemen of the Board of Directors and Citizens.

One-third of the population of the South is of the Negro race. No enterprise seeking the material, civil, or moral welfare of this section can disregard this element of our population and reach the highest success. I but convey to you, Mr. President and Directors, the sentiment of the masses of my race when I say that in no way have the value and manhood of the American Negro been more fittingly and generously recognized than by the managers of this magnificent Exposition at every stage of its progress. It is a recognition that will do more to cement the friendship of the two races than any occurrence since the dawn of our freedom.

Not only this, but the opportunity here afforded will awaken among us a new era of industrial progress. Ignorant and inexperienced, it is not strange that in the first years of our

Notes

1 The previous chapter, "Chapter 13: Two Thousand Miles for a Five-Minute Speech," states: "As the day for the opening of the Exposition drew near, the Board of Directors began preparing the programme for the opening exercises. In the discussion from day to day of the various features of this programme, the question came up as to the advisability of putting a member of the Negro race on for one of the opening addresses, since the Negroes had been asked to take such a prominent part in the Exposition. It was argued, further, that such recognition would mark the good feeling prevailing between the two races. Of course there were those who were opposed to any such recognition of the rights of the Negro, but the Board of Directors, composed of men who represented the best and most progressive element in the South, had their way, and voted to invite a black man to speak on the opening day. The next thing was to decide upon the person who was thus to represent the Negro race. After the question had been canvassed for several days, the directors voted unanimously to ask me to deliver one of the opening-day addresses, and in a few days after that I received the official invitation."

2 *Governor Bullock* Rufus Bullock (1834–1907), governor of Georgia during Reconstruction (1868–1871).

3 *Bishop Nelson* Cleland Kinloch Nelson (1852–1917), Episcopal bishop of Georgia.

4 Albert Howell, Jr. (1863–1936), the brother of Atlanta journalist, editor, and politician Clark Howell.

new life we began at the top instead of at the bottom; that a seat in Congress or the state legislature was more sought than real estate or industrial skill; that the political convention or stump speaking had more attractions than starting a dairy farm or truck garden.

A ship lost at sea for many days suddenly sighted a friendly vessel. From the mast of the unfortunate vessel was seen a signal, "Water, water; we die of thirst!" The answer from the friendly vessel at once came back, "Cast down your bucket where you are." A second time the signal, "Water, water; send us water!" ran up from the distressed vessel, and was answered, "Cast down your bucket where you are." And a third and fourth signal for water was answered, "Cast down your bucket where you are." The captain of the distressed vessel, at last heeding the injunction, cast down his bucket, and it came up full of fresh, sparkling water from the mouth of the Amazon River. To those of my race who depend on bettering their condition in a foreign land or who underestimate the importance of cultivating friendly relations with the Southern white man, who is their next-door neighbour, I would say: "Cast down your bucket where you are" – cast it down in making friends in every manly way of the people of all races by whom we are surrounded.

Cast it down in agriculture, mechanics, in commerce, in domestic service, and in the professions. And in this connection it is well to bear in mind that whatever other sins the South may be called to bear, when it comes to business, pure and simple, it is in the South that the Negro is given a man's chance in the commercial world, and in nothing is this Exposition more eloquent than in emphasizing this chance. Our greatest danger is that in the great leap from slavery to freedom we may overlook the fact that the masses of us are to live by the productions of our hands, and fail to keep in mind that we shall prosper in proportion as we learn to dignify and glorify common labour and put brains and skill into the common occupations of life; shall prosper in proportion as we learn to draw the line between the superficial and the substantial, the ornamental gewgaws of life and the useful. No race can prosper till it learns that there is as much dignity in tilling a field as in writing a poem. It is at the bottom of life we must begin, and not at the top. Nor should we permit our grievances to overshadow our opportunities.

To those of the white race who look to the incoming of those of foreign birth and strange tongue and habits for the prosperity of the South, were I permitted I would repeat what I say to my own race, "Cast down your bucket where you are." Cast it down among the eight millions of Negroes whose habits you know, whose fidelity and love you have tested in days when to have proved treacherous meant the ruin of your firesides. Cast down your bucket among these people who have, without strikes and labour wars, tilled your fields, cleared your forests, builded your railroads and cities, and brought forth treasures from the bowels of the earth, and helped make possible this magnificent representation of the progress of the South. Casting down your bucket among my people, helping and encouraging them as you are doing on these grounds, and to education of head, hand, and heart, you will find that they will buy your surplus land, make blossom the waste places in your fields, and run your factories. While doing this, you can be sure in the future, as in the past, that you and your families will be surrounded by the most patient, faithful, law-abiding, and unresentful people that the world has seen. As we have proved our loyalty to you in the past, in nursing your children, watching by the sick-bed of your mothers and fathers, and often following them with tear-dimmed eyes to their graves, so in the future, in our humble vay, we shall stand by you with a devotion that no foreigner can approach, ready to lay wn our lives, if need be, in defence of yours, interlacing our industrial, commercial, and religious life with yours in a way that shall make the interests of both races all things that are purely social we can be as separate as the fingers, yet one as in all things essential to mutual progress.

There is no defence or security for any of us except in the highest intelligence and development of all. If anywhere there are efforts tending to curtail the fullest growth of the Negro, let these efforts be turned into stimulating, encouraging, and making him the most useful and intelligent citizen. Effort or means so invested will pay a thousand per cent interest. These efforts will be twice blessed – "blessing him that gives and him that takes."

There is no escape through law of man or God from the inevitable:–

> The laws of changeless justice bind
> Oppressor with oppressed;
> And close as sin and suffering joined
> We march to fate abreast.[5]

Nearly sixteen millions of hands will aid you in pulling the load upward, or they will pull against you the load downward. We shall constitute one-third and more of the ignorance and crime of the South, or one-third its intelligence and progress; we shall contribute one-third to the business and industrial prosperity of the South, or we shall prove a veritable body of death, stagnating, depressing, retarding every effort to advance the body politic.

Gentlemen of the Exposition, as we present to you our humble effort at an exhibition of our progress, you must not expect overmuch. Starting thirty years ago with ownership here and there in a few quilts and pumpkins and chickens (gathered from miscellaneous sources), remember the path that has led from these to the inventions and production of agricultural implements, buggies, steam-engines, newspapers, books, statuary, carving, paintings, the management of drug-stores and banks, has not been trodden without contact with thorns and thistles. While we take pride in what we exhibit as a result of our independent efforts, we do not for a moment forget that our part in this exhibition would fall far short of your expectations but for the constant help that has come to our educational life, not only from the Southern states, but especially from Northern philanthropists, who have made their gifts a constant stream of blessing and encouragement.

The wisest among my race understand that the agitation of questions of social equality is the extremest folly, and that progress in the enjoyment of all the privileges that will come to us must be the result of severe and constant struggle rather than of artificial forcing. No race that has anything to contribute to the markets of the world is long in any degree ostracized. It is important and right that all privileges of the law be ours, but it is vastly more important that we be prepared for the exercises of these privileges. The opportunity to earn a dollar in a factory just now is worth infinitely more than the opportunity to spend a dollar in an opera-house.

In conclusion, may I repeat that nothing in thirty years has given us more hope and encouragement, and drawn us so near to you of the white race, as this opportunity offered by the Exposition; and here bending, as it were, over the altar that represents the results of the struggles of your race and mine, both starting practically empty-handed three decades ago, I pledge that in your effort to work out the great and intricate problem which God has laid at the doors of the South, you shall have at all times the patient, sympathetic help of my race; only let this be constantly in mind, that, while from representations in these buildings of the product of field, of forest, of mine, of factory, letters, and

Notes

[5] *The laws of changeless ... fate abreast* lines from John Greenleaf Whittier's "Song of the Negro Boatmen" (1862).

art, much good will come, yet far above and beyond material benefits will be that higher good, that, let us pray God, will come, in a blotting out of sectional differences and racial animosities and suspicions, in a determination to administer absolute justice, in a willing obedience among all classes to the mandates of law. This, this, coupled with our material prosperity, will bring into our beloved South a new heaven and a new earth.

The first thing that I remember, after I had finished speaking, was that Governor Bullock rushed across the platform and took me by the hand, and that others did the same. I received so many and such hearty congratulations that I found it difficult to get out of the building. I did not appreciate to any degree, however, the impression which my address seemed to have made, until the next morning, when I went into the business part of the city. As soon as I was recognized, I was surprised to find myself pointed out and surrounded by a crowd of men who wished to shake hands with me. This was kept up on every street on to which I went, to an extent which embarrassed me so much that I went back to my boarding-place. The next morning I returned to Tuskegee. At the station in Atlanta, and at almost all of the stations at which the train stopped between that city and Tuskegee, I found a crowd of people anxious to shake hands with me.

The papers in all parts of the United States published the address in full, and for months afterward there were complimentary editorial references to it. Mr. Clark Howell, the editor of the Atlanta *Constitution*, telegraphed to a New York paper, among other words, the following, "I do not exaggerate when I say that Professor Booker T. Washington's address yesterday was one of the most notable speeches, both as to character and as to the warmth of its reception, ever delivered to a Southern audience. The address was a revelation. The whole speech is a platform upon which blacks and whites can stand with full justice to each other."

The Boston *Transcript* said editorially: "The speech of Booker T. Washington at the Atlanta Exposition, this week, seems to have dwarfed all the other proceedings and the Exposition itself. The sensation that it has caused in the press has never been equalled."

I very soon began receiving all kinds of propositions from lecture bureaus, and editors of magazines and papers, to take the lecture platform, and to write articles. One lecture bureau offered me fifty thousand dollars, or two hundred dollars a night and expenses, if I would place my services at its disposal for a given period. To all these communications I replied that my life-work was at Tuskegee; and that whenever I spoke it must be in the interests of the Tuskegee school and my race, and that I would enter into no arrangements that seemed to place a mere commercial value upon my services.

Some days after its delivery I sent a copy of my address to the President of the United States, the Hon. Grover Cleveland.[6] I received from him the following autograph reply:–

Gray Gables, Buzzard's Bay, Mass.,
October 6, 1895.

Booker T. Washington, Esq.:

My Dear Sir: I thank you for sending me a copy of your address delivered at the Atlanta Exposition.

I thank you with much enthusiasm for making the address. I have read it with intense interest, and I think the Exposition would be fully justified if it did not do more than furnish the opportunity for its delivery. Your words cannot fail to delight and

---

Cleveland (1837–1908), the 22nd and 24th United States (1885–1889 and 1893–1897).

encourage all who wish well for your race; and if our coloured fellow-citizens do not from your utterances gather new hope and form new determinations to gain every valuable advantage offered them by their citizenship, it will be strange indeed.

Yours very truly,
Grover Cleveland.

Later I met Mr. Cleveland, for the first time, when, as President, he visited the Atlanta Exposition. At the request of myself and others he consented to spend an hour in the Negro Building, for the purpose of inspecting the Negro exhibit and of giving the coloured people in attendance an opportunity to shake hands with him. As soon as I met Mr. Cleveland I became impressed with his simplicity, greatness, and rugged honesty. I have met him many times since then, both at public functions and at his private residence in Princeton, and the more I see of him the more I admire him. When he visited the Negro Building in Atlanta he seemed to give himself up wholly, for that hour, to the coloured people. He seemed to be as careful to shake hands with some old coloured "auntie" clad partially in rags, and to take as much pleasure in doing so, as if he were greeting some millionaire.[7] Many of the coloured people took advantage of the occasion to get him to write his name in a book or on a slip of paper. He was as careful and patient in doing this as if he were putting his signature to some great state document.

Mr. Cleveland has not only shown his friendship for me in many personal ways, but has always consented to do anything I have asked of him for our school. This he has done, whether it was to make a personal donation or to use his influence in securing the donations of others. Judging from my personal acquaintance with Mr. Cleveland, I do not believe that he is conscious of possessing any colour prejudice. He is too great for that. In my contact with people I find that, as a rule, it is only the little, narrow people who live for themselves, who never read good books, who do not travel, who never open up their souls in a way to permit them to come into contact with other souls – with the great outside world. No man whose vision is bounded by colour can come into contact with what is highest and best in the world. In meeting men, in many places, I have found that the happiest people are those who do the most for others; the most miserable are those who do the least. I have also found that few things, if any, are capable of making one so blind and narrow as race prejudice. I often say to our students, in the course of my talks to them on Sunday evenings in the chapel, that the longer I live and the more experience I have of the world, the more I am convinced that, after all, the one thing that is most worth living for – and dying for, if need be – is the opportunity of making someone else more happy and more useful.

The coloured people and the coloured newspapers at first seemed to be greatly pleased with the character of my Atlanta address, as well as with its reception. But after the first burst of enthusiasm began to die away, and the coloured people began reading the speech in cold type, some of them seemed to feel that they had been hypnotized. They seemed to feel that I had been too liberal in my remarks toward the Southern whites, and that I had not spoken out strongly enough for what they termed the "rights" of the race. For a while there was a reaction, so far as a certain element of my own race was concerned, but later these reactionary ones seemed to have been won over to my way of believing and acting.

While speaking of changes in public sentiment, I recall that about ten years after the school at Tuskegee was established, I had an experience that I shall never forget.

Notes

[7] *Original reads*: millionnaire [ed.].

Dr. Lyman Abbott,[8] then the pastor of Plymouth Church, and also editor of the *Outlook* (then the *Christian Union*), asked me to write a letter for his paper giving my opinion of the exact condition, mental and moral, of the coloured ministers in the South, as based upon my observations. I wrote the letter, giving the exact facts as I conceived them to be. The picture painted was a rather black one – or, since I am black, shall I say "white"? It could not be otherwise with a race but a few years out of slavery, a race which had not had time or opportunity to produce a competent ministry.

What I said soon reached every Negro minister in the country, I think, and the letters of condemnation which I received from them were not few. I think that for a year after the publication of this article every association and every conference or religious body of any kind, of my race, that met, did not fail before adjourning to pass a resolution condemning me, or calling upon me to retract or modify what I had said. Many of these organizations went so far in their resolutions as to advise parents to cease sending their children to Tuskegee. One association even appointed a "missionary" whose duty it was to warn the people against sending their children to Tuskegee. This missionary had a son in the school, and I noticed that, whatever the "missionary" might have said or done with regard to others, he was careful not to take his son away from the institution. Many of the coloured papers, especially those that were the organs of religious bodies, joined in the general chorus of condemnation or demands for retraction.

During the whole time of the excitement, and through all the criticism, I did not utter a word of explanation or retraction. I knew that I was right, and that time and the sober second thought of the people would vindicate me. It was not long before the bishops and other church leaders began to make a careful investigation of the conditions of the ministry, and they found out that I was right. In fact, the oldest and most influential bishop in one branch of the Methodist Church said that my words were far too mild. Very soon public sentiment began making itself felt, in demanding a purifying of the ministry. While this is not yet complete by any means, I think I may say, without egotism, and I have been told by many of our most influential ministers, that my words had much to do with starting a demand for the placing of a higher type of men in the pulpit. I have had the satisfaction of having many who once condemned me thank me heartily for my frank words.

The change of the attitude of the Negro ministry, so far as regards myself, is so complete that at the present time I have no warmer friends among any class than I have among the clergymen. The improvement in the character and life of the Negro ministers is one of the most gratifying evidences of the progress of the race. My experience with them, as well as other events in my life, convinces[9] me that the thing to do, when one feels sure that he has said or done the right thing, and is condemned, is to stand still and keep quiet. If he is right, time will show it.

In the midst of the discussion which was going on concerning my Atlanta speech, I received the letter which I give below, from Dr. Gilman,[10] the President of Johns Hopkins University, who had been made chairman of the judges of award in connection with the Atlanta Exposition:–

Johns Hopkins University, Baltimore,
President's Office, September 30, 1895.

Notes

[8] Dr Lyman Abbott (1835–1922), American Congregationalist minister and publisher.

[9] *Original reads*: convince [ed.].

[10] *Dr. Gilman* Daniel Coit Gilman (1831–1908), academic and longtime president of Johns Hopkins University.

Dear Mr. Washington: Would it be agreeable to you to be one of the Judges of Award in the Department of Education at Atlanta? If so, I shall be glad to place your name upon the list. A line by telegraph will be welcomed.

Yours very truly,
D. C. Gilman.

I think I was even more surprised to receive this invitation than I had been to receive the invitation to speak at the opening of the Exposition. It was to be a part of my duty, as one of the jurors, to pass not only upon the exhibits of the coloured schools, but also upon those of the white schools. I accepted the position, and spent a month in Atlanta in performance of the duties which it entailed. The board of jurors was a large one, consisting in all of sixty members. It was about equally divided between Southern white people and Northern white people. Among them were college presidents, leading scientists and men of letters, and specialists in many subjects. When the group of jurors to which I was assigned met for organization, Mr. Thomas Nelson Page,[11] who was one of the number, moved that I be made secretary of that division, and the motion was unanimously adopted. Nearly half of our division were Southern people. In performing my duties in the inspection of the exhibits of white schools I was in every case treated with respect, and at the close of our labours I parted from my associates with regret.

I am often asked to express myself more freely than I do upon the political condition and the political future of my race. These recollections of my experience in Atlanta give me the opportunity to do so briefly. My own belief is, although I have never before said so in so many words, that the time will come when the Negro in the South will be accorded all the political rights which his ability, character, and material possessions entitle him to. I think, though, that the opportunity to freely exercise such political rights will not come in any large degree through outside or artificial forcing, but will be accorded to the Negro by the Southern white people themselves, and that they will protect him in the exercise of those rights. Just as soon as the South gets over the old feeling that it is being forced by "foreigners," or "aliens," to do something which it does not want to do, I believe that the change in the direction that I have indicated is going to begin. In fact, there are indications that it is already beginning in a slight degree.

Let me illustrate my meaning. Suppose that some months before the opening of the Atlanta Exposition there had been a general demand from the press and public platform outside the South that a Negro be given a place on the opening programme, and that a Negro be placed upon the board of jurors of award. Would any such recognition of the race have taken place? I do not think so. The Atlanta officials went as far as they did because they felt it to be a pleasure, as well as a duty, to reward what they considered merit in the Negro race. Say what we will, there is something in human nature which we cannot blot out, which makes one man, in the end, recognize and reward merit in another, regardless of colour or race.

I believe it is the duty of the Negro – as the greater part of the race is already doing – to deport himself modestly in regard to political claims, depending upon the slow but sure influences that proceed from the possession of property, intelligence, and high character for the full recognition of his political rights. I think that the according of the

Notes

[11] Thomas Nelson Page (1853–1922), American ambassador and writer of southern nostalgic/racist fiction.

full exercise of political rights is going to be a matter of natural, slow growth, not an over-night, gourd-vine affair. I do not believe that the Negro should cease voting, for a man cannot learn the exercise of self-government by ceasing to vote, any more than a boy can learn to swim by keeping out of the water, but I do believe that in his voting he should more and more be influenced by those of intelligence and character who are his next-door neighbours.

I know coloured men who, through the encouragement, help, and advice of Southern white people, have accumulated thousands of dollars' worth of property, but who, at the same time, would never think of going to those same persons for advice concerning the casting of their ballots. This, it seems to me, is unwise and unreasonable, and should cease. In saying this I do not mean that the Negro should truckle,[12] or not vote from principle, for the instant he ceases to vote from principle he loses the confidence and respect of the Southern white man even.

I do not believe that any state should make a law that permits an ignorant and poverty-stricken white man to vote, and prevents a black man in the same condition from voting. Such a law is not only unjust, but it will react, as all unjust laws do, in time; for the effect of such a law is to encourage the Negro to secure education and property, and at the same time it encourages the white man to remain in ignorance and poverty. I believe that in time, through the operation of intelligence and friendly race relations, all cheating at the ballot-box in the South will cease. It will become apparent that the white man who begins by cheating a Negro out of his ballot soon learns to cheat a white man out of his, and that the man who does this ends his career of dishonesty by the theft of property or by some equally serious crime. In my opinion, the time will come when the South will encourage all of its citizens to vote. It will see that it pays better, from every standpoint, to have healthy, vigorous life than to have that political stagnation which always results when one-half of the population has no share and no interest in the Government.

As a rule, I believe in universal, free suffrage, but I believe that in the South we are confronted with peculiar conditions that justify the protection of the ballot in many of the states, for a while at least, either by an educational test, a property test, or by both combined; but whatever tests are required, they should be made to apply with equal and exact justice to both races.

1901

Notes

[12] *truckle* to act obsequiously.

William Edward Burghardt Du Bois (1868–1963)

When *The Souls of Black Folk* appeared in 1903, W.E.B. Du Bois had already established himself as one of the most prolific and intellectually formidable African Americans in the United States. He had, by dint of hard work and enormous talent, risen from obscurity in the predominantly white Massachusetts Berkshires to a position of educational and political leadership. Du Bois's rapid emergence as a dominant figure in politics and scholarship is without parallel in the history of African American leadership. At perhaps the nadir of post-Reconstruction race relations, Du Bois intertwined academic, literary, and political careers to steer the discourse and politics of race and civil rights in the twentieth century. Long before his death in 1963 at the age of 94, Du Bois had secured his reputation as perhaps the most influential and erudite intellectual of his time. In 1934 the Board of the National Association for the Advancement of Colored People (NAACP) spoke true when it said, upon Du Bois's resignation, that, nonetheless, "many who have never read a word of his writings are his spiritual disciples and descendants."

Born in 1868 in Great Barrington, Massachusetts, William Edward Burghardt Du Bois was the only child of Mary Sylvina Burghardt and Alfred Du Bois. On his mother's side, the Burghardts were some of the oldest citizens of Great Barrington, having lived there since the mid-eighteenth century; his father was an itinerant who abandoned his family within a year of his birth. Though lacking a father figure, the young William benefited from the maternal attention he received in his family. Du Bois later wrote that "[a]ll the way back in these dim distances it is the mothers and mothers of mothers who seem to count, while fathers are shadowy memories." Nevertheless, he was a happy child in an environment that, if not idyllic, was remarkably free of racial discrimination. The town's African American population was relatively small – Du Bois attended a predominantly white secondary school and worshipped in the white First Congregational Church of Great Barrington. He graduated in 1884 with high honors, the first African American graduate of his high school, and immediately went to work to save money for college. In March of 1885, Mary Sylvina Du Bois died unexpectedly, leaving her son impoverished. The local white community came to his aid; his neighbors and the Congregational Church donated scholarship funds. The ambitious Du Bois hoped to attend Harvard University, but it was beyond his means. Instead, he enrolled at Fisk University in Nashville, Tennessee.

Leaving the sheltered environs of Great Barrington in 1885, Du Bois descended into a South still seething with resentment over its defeat in the Civil War and the federally imposed measures of Reconstruction. "No one but a Negro going into the South without previous experience of color caste can have any conception of its barbarism," Du Bois later wrote. His experiences in the South sharpened his urge to be involved in the politics of race at the turn of the century. At the same time, he was thrilled to be in an academic milieu where his color and ambition were the rule rather than the exception. While at Fisk, Du Bois spent several summers teaching at a small school roughly 50 miles outside of Nashville. The first summer he taught in rural Tennessee marked only the second time

The Wiley Blackwell Anthology of African American Literature: Volume 1, 1746–1920, First Edition.
Edited by Gene Andrew Jarrett.

since Reconstruction that public instruction was offered during the summer to the African American citizens. For the first time in his life, Du Bois witnessed their overwhelming poverty and lack of opportunities.

Before graduating from Fisk in 1888, Du Bois applied to Harvard. On the basis of his stellar grades and recommendations, he gained admittance and a stipend that covered most of his expenses. Despite having already earned a BA, Du Bois entered Harvard as a junior undergraduate, a common practice at the time for students coming from less prestigious institutions. Du Bois regularly mentioned throughout his life that he was a Harvard man in name only. He benefitted from the teaching, but lived a life of social isolation. Still, he excelled at Harvard; he studied and thrived under William James, George Santayana, and William Ellery Channing. He graduated in 1890 with a concentration in philosophy. Since he deemed employment opportunities to be limited for African Americans in this discipline, he elected to pursue history in his graduate studies. While working toward a doctorate at Harvard, he received a fellowship in 1892 to continue his studies at the University of Berlin, focusing on sociology and economics. His time in Berlin prepared him for his future sociological work, while also providing him with a much-welcomed opportunity to experience new cultures. Du Bois wrote a thesis on agricultural economics in the South and hoped to complete a PhD in economics in Berlin, but was unable to do so for lack of funds.

Du Bois returned to America in 1894 and quickly began to advance his phenomenal career. He secured a position teaching classics at Wilberforce University in Ohio. The following year, he became the first person of African descent to receive a PhD from Harvard upon the acceptance of his dissertation, *The Suppression of the African Slave-Trade to the United States of America, 1638–1870*, which was published in 1896 as the first volume of the Harvard Historical Monograph Series. He also married Nina Gomer, a student at Wilberforce, in spring of that year. In the fall, he left Wilberforce to undertake a sociological study of an African American section of Philadelphia on behalf of the University of Pennsylvania. In spite of having little money and no office or assistance, Du Bois published in 1899 *The Philadelphia Negro*, the first sociological study on an African American community to be published in the United States.

In fall 1897, Du Bois accepted a professorship at Atlanta University. He taught economics, history, and sociology. With Alexander Crummell and other African American scholars, he founded the American Negro Academy, the first historically black institute of arts and letters in the world. He also became director of the "Atlanta Conferences," annual conventions that generated precise scientific research regarding the living conditions of Negroes in America. Du Bois edited the results of these conferences and published them in a 16-volume monograph series between 1898 and 1914. His intention was to collect and analyze socioeconomic data on all aspects of African American life in the United States.

Even as he pursued these scholarly ventures, Du Bois was looking for forums beyond the academy: the increase of racial violence and legal entrenchment of racial segregation in the 1896 *Plessy v. Ferguson* Supreme Court decision compelled him to use any means at his disposal. Between 1897 and 1903, Du Bois became one of the most widely published authors in the United States. His essays of cultural criticism appeared in prominent publications such as *The Atlantic Monthly*, *Harper's Weekly*, *World's Work*, and *The Dial*. He likewise launched two short-lived magazines of his own, *Moon* and *The Horizon*. Without a doubt, the finest result of this new direction in his writing was his seminal essay collection *The Souls of Black Folk* (1903). A masterpiece of sociology, history, and creative writing, the book represented a direct challenge to the immensely powerful Booker T. Washington, founder of the Tuskegee Institute, whose theories of laissez-faire economics and political accommodation had established him as the preeminent African American leader upon Frederick Douglass's death in 1895.

At stake in the Du Bois versus Washington debate were questions of education. Du Bois advocated a classical education against Washington's tenets of limited "industrial education" for African Americans. In "The Evolution of Negro Leadership," Du Bois points to a portion of Washington's autobiography in which he decries "the absurdity of a black boy studying a French grammar in the midst of weeds and dirt." Du Bois retorts, "Among the Negroes, Mr. Washington is still far from a popular leader." Instead, Du Bois places himself among African Americans represented by "Dunbar, Tanner, Chesnutt, Miller, and the Grimkes" who "believe in self-assertion and ambition; and they believe in the right of suffrage for blacks on the same terms with whites." Du Bois would amplify these ideas in chapter three of *The Souls of Black Folk*, "Of Mr. Booker T. Washington and Others." This ideological chasm in African American leadership persisted until Washington's death in 1915.

Two of the most famous insights that Du Bois offers in *The Souls of Black Folk* are his premonition that, for America, "the problem of the Twentieth Century is the problem of the color-line," and his powerful description of the double-consciousness of the Negro: "It is a peculiar sensation, this double-consciousness, this sense of always looking at one's self through the eyes of others, of measuring one's soul by the tape of a world that looks on in amused contempt and pity. One ever feels his two-ness – an American, a Negro; two souls, two thoughts, two unreconciled strivings; two warring ideals in one dark body, whose dogged strength alone keeps it from being torn asunder." Each chapter of *Souls* starts with an epigraph consisting of an excerpt from a famous work in Western letters along with a bar of musical notes representing a section of a spiritual. Thus *Souls* fashions itself as both Western and African American, structurally embodying the process of double-consciousness. Between these worlds is the Veil, a metaphor Du Bois introduces in the "Forethought" of *Souls.* In stepping within the Veil, he promises to see and to report the truth of a divided nation. As one who speaks authentically from behind the Veil – "And, finally, need I add that I who speak here am bone of the bone and flesh of the flesh of them that live within the Veil?" – Du Bois presents himself as prophet of his people. By 1903, when *Souls* appeared, the 35-year-old Du Bois could not only count himself among the most widely read, broadly traveled, and impeccably educated of men. As a widely published African American essayist, Du Bois was the public written "voice" of the African American intellectual, as worthy an heir to Frederick Douglass as Booker T. Washington was perceived to be.

Two years after the publication of *The Souls of Black Folk*, Du Bois co-founded the Niagara Movement, a further direct challenge to Washington. The association met annually from 1905 until 1909. Although debilitated by opposing pro-Washington groups and by internal organizational problems, the Niagara Movement eventually led to the establishment in 1909 of the NAACP, in which Du Bois again was a creative participant. He left his position at Atlanta University, which he had held since 1897, and moved to New York to lead the NAACP's division of research and edit its magazine, *The Crisis*, from 1910 until 1934.

Du Bois also continued to use literary means to promote racial equality during the New Negro Renaissance. In "A Litany of Atlanta" (1907), he composed a prose poem in the wake of a 1906 bloody race riot incited by whites. After writing a biography of John Brown in 1909, he published *The Quest of the Silver Fleece* (1911), a novel about African Americans and the cotton industry in the South. His vision for *The Crisis* was not only to combat racism but also to foster a cultural and intellectual renaissance. This vision became a reality in the early 1920s, when (under the editorship of Jessie Fauset) the magazine promoted the early poetry of Langston Hughes, Jean Toomer, and Countée Cullen.

Over the years, Du Bois's intellectual scope panned outward from the African American experience to encompass the African diaspora, the economics and politics of international societies, and the nature of Western imperialism. In 1915 he wrote *The Negro*, an analysis of the African diaspora, and four years later he helped organize the Pan-African Congress in Paris. In later years, Du Bois would become increasingly socialist and radical in his leanings, and more deeply embittered by the political and racial failures of the United States. He remained an active and ambitious scholar well into the last decade of his life, a time when he was battling the US government, and emigrated to Ghana shortly before his death in 1963.

Further reading

Bass, Amy. *Those About Him Remained Silent: The Battle Over W.E.B. Du Bois.* Minneapolis: University of Minnesota Press, 2009.

Blum, Edward J. *W.E.B. Du Bois: American Prophet.* Philadelphia: University of Pennsylvania Press, 2007.

Flatley, Jonathan. *Affective Mapping: Melancholia and the Politics of Modernism.* Cambridge: Harvard University Press, 2008. Ch. 4.

Gilman, Susan and Alys Eve Weinbaum, eds. *Next to the Color Line: Gender, Sexuality, and W.E.B. Du Bois.* Minneapolis: University of Minnesota Press, 2007.

Gooding-Williams, Robert and Dwight A. McBride, eds. "100 Years of *The Souls of Black Folk*: A Celebration of W.E.B. Du Bois." *Special issue of Public Culture* 17.2 (2005): 203–338.

Hartnell, Anna. "W.E.B. Du Bois, William Faulkner, and the Dialectic of Black and White: In Search of Exodus for a Postcolonial American South." *Callaloo* 33.2 (2010): 521–536.

Hubbard, Dolan, ed. *The Souls of Black Folk One Hundred Years Later.* Columbia: University of Missouri Press, 2003.

Judy, Ronald A.T., ed. "Sociology Hesitant: Thinking with W.E.B. Du Bois." *Special issue of boundary 2* 27.3 (2000): 1–286.

Kahn, Jonathon S. *Divine Discontent: The Religious Imagination of W.E.B. Du Bois.* New York: Oxford University Press, 2009.

Lewis, David Levering. *W.E.B. Du Bois, 1868–1919: Biography of a Race.* New York: Holt, 1993.

Oliver, Lawrence J. "W.E.B. Du Bois' *The Quest of the Silver Fleece* and Contract Realism." *American Literary Realism* 38.1 (2005): 32–46.

Rabaka, Reiland. *Against Epistemic Apartheid: W.E.B. Du Bois and the Disciplinary Decadence of Sociology.* New York: Lexington, 2010.

Ross, Marlon B. "Racial Uplift and the Literature of the New Negro." *A Companion to African American Literature.* Ed. Gene Andrew Jarrett. Malden, MA: Wiley-Blackwell, 2010. 151–168.

Smith, Shawn Michelle. *Photography on the Color Line: W.E.B. Du Bois, Race, and Visual Culture.* Durham: Duke University Press, 2004.

Van Wienen, Mark W. *American Socialist Triptych: The Literary Political Work of Charlotte Perkins Gilman, Upton Sinclair, and W.E.B. Du Bois.* Ann Arbor: University of Michigan Press, 2012. Ch. 4.

Wolters, Raymond. *Du Bois and His Rivals.* Columbia: University of Missouri Press, 2002.

Zamir, Shamoon, ed. *The Cambridge Companion to W.E.B. Du Bois.* New York: Cambridge University Press, 2008.

The Souls of Black Folk

The Forethought

Herein lie buried many things which if read with patience may show the strange meaning of being black here in the dawning of the Twentieth Century. This meaning is not without interest to you, Gentle Reader; for the problem of the Twentieth Century is the problem of the color-line.

I pray you, then, receive my little book in all charity, studying my words with me, forgiving mistake and foible for sake of the faith and passion that is in me, and seeking the grain of truth hidden there.

I have sought here to sketch, in vague, uncertain outline, the spiritual world in which ten thousand thousand Americans live and strive. First, in two chapters I have tried to show what Emancipation meant to them, and what was its aftermath. In a third chapter I have pointed out the slow rise of personal leadership, and criticised candidly the leader who bears the chief burden of his race to-day. Then, in two other chapters I have sketched in swift outline the two worlds within and without the Veil, and thus have come to the central problem of training men for life. Venturing now into deeper detail, I have in two chapters studied the struggles of the massed millions of the black peasantry, and in another have sought to make clear the present relations of the sons of master and man.

Leaving, then, the world of the white man, I have stepped within the Veil, raising it that you may view faintly its deeper recesses – the meaning of its religion, the passion of its human sorrow, and the struggle of its greater souls. All this I have ended with a tale twice told but seldom written.

Some of these thoughts of mine have seen the light before in other guises.[1] For kindly consenting to their republication here, in altered and extended form, I must thank the publishers of *The Atlantic Monthly, The World's Work, The Dial, The New World*, and the *Annals of the American Academy of Political and Social Science*.

Before each chapter, as now printed, stands a bar of the Sorrow Songs[2] – some echo of haunting melody from the only American music which welled up from black souls in the dark past. And, finally, need I add that I who speak here am bone of the bone and flesh of the flesh of them that live within the Veil?

W.E.B. Du B.

Atlanta, Ga., Feb. 1, 1903.

Chapter 1

Of Our Spiritual Strivings

O water, voice of my heart, crying in the sand,
  All night long crying with a mournful cry,
As I lie and listen, and cannot understand
    The voice of my heart in my side or the voice of the sea,
O water, crying for rest, is it I, is it I?
    All night long the water is crying to me.

Unresting water, there shall never be rest
  Till the last moon droop and the last tide fail,
And the fire of the end begin to burn in the west;
    And the heart shall be weary and wonder and cry like the sea,
  All life long crying without avail,
    As the water all night long is crying to me.

Arthur Symons.[3]

Notes

[1] *Original reads*: guise [ed.].

[2] *Sorrow Songs* African American spirituals.

[3] Arthur Symons (1865–1945), English poet; the lines quoted come from "The Crying of Water" (1903).

Between me and the other world there is ever an unasked question: unasked by some through feelings of delicacy; by others through the difficulty of rightly framing it. All, nevertheless, flutter round it. They approach me in a half-hesitant sort of way, eye me curiously or compassionately, and then, instead of saying directly, How does it feel to be a problem? they say, I know an excellent colored man in my town; or, I fought at Mechanicsville;[4] or, Do not these Southern outrages make your blood boil? At these I smile, or am interested, or reduce the boiling to a simmer, as the occasion may require. To the real question, How does it feel to be a problem? I answer seldom a word.

And yet, being a problem is a strange experience – peculiar even for one who has never been anything else, save perhaps in babyhood and in Europe. It is in the early days of rollicking boyhood that the revelation first bursts upon one, all in a day, as it were. I remember well when the shadow swept across me. I was a little thing, away up in the hills of New England, where the dark Housatonic[5] winds between Hoosac and Taghkanic to the sea. In a wee wooden school-house, something put it into the boys' and girls' heads to buy gorgeous visiting-cards – ten cents a package – and exchange. The exchange was merry, till one girl, a tall newcomer, refused my card – refused it peremptorily, with a glance. Then it dawned upon me with a certain suddenness that I was different from the others; or like, mayhap, in heart and life and longing, but shut out from their world by a vast veil. I had thereafter no desire to tear down that veil, to creep through; I held all beyond it in common contempt, and lived above it in a region of blue sky and great wandering shadows. That sky was bluest when I could beat my mates at examination-time, or beat them at a foot-race, or even beat their stringy heads. Alas, with the years all this fine contempt began to fade; for the worlds I longed for, and all their dazzling opportunities, were theirs, not mine. But they should not keep these prizes, I said; some, all, I would wrest from them. Just how I would do it I could never decide: by reading law, by healing the sick, by telling the wonderful tales that swam in my head – some way. With other black boys the strife was not so fiercely sunny: their youth shrunk into tasteless sycophancy, or into silent hatred of the pale world about them and mocking distrust of everything white; or wasted itself in a bitter cry, Why did God make me an outcast and a stranger in mine own house? The shades of the prison-house closed round about us all: walls strait and stubborn to the whitest, but relentlessly narrow, tall, and unscalable to sons of night who must plod darkly on in resignation, or beat unavailing palms against the stone, or steadily, half hopelessly, watch the streak of blue above.

After the Egyptian and Indian, the Greek and Roman, the Teuton and Mongolian, the Negro is a sort of seventh son, born with a veil, and gifted with second-sight in this American world – a world which yields him no true self-consciousness, but only lets him see himself through the revelation of the other world. It is a peculiar sensation, this double-consciousness, this sense of always looking at one's self through the eyes of others, of measuring one's soul by the tape of a world that looks on in amused contempt and pity. One ever feels his two-ness – an American, a Negro; two souls, two thoughts, two unreconciled strivings; two warring ideals in one dark body, whose dogged strength alone keeps it from being torn asunder.

The history of the American Negro is the history of this strife – this longing to attain self-conscious manhood, to merge his double self into a better and truer self. In this merging he wishes neither of the older selves to be lost. He would not Africanize America, for America has too much to teach the world and Africa. He would not

Notes

[4] *Mechanicsville* a Civil War battle in Virginia.

[5] *Housatonic* a Massachusetts river.

bleach his Negro soul in a flood of white Americanism, for he knows that Negro blood has a message for the world. He simply wishes to make it possible for a man to be both a Negro and an American, without being cursed and spit upon by his fellows, without having the doors of Opportunity closed roughly in his face.

This, then, is the end of his striving: to be a co-worker in the kingdom of culture, to escape both death and isolation, to husband and use his best powers and his latent genius. These powers of body and mind have in the past been strangely wasted, dispersed, or forgotten. The shadow of a mighty Negro past flits through the tale of Ethiopia the Shadowy and of Egypt the Sphinx. Throughout history, the powers of single black men flash here and there like falling stars, and die sometimes before the world has rightly gauged their brightness. Here in America, in the few days since Emancipation, the black man's turning hither and thither in hesitant and doubtful striving has often made his very strength to lose effectiveness, to seem like absence of power, like weakness. And yet it is not weakness – it is the contradiction of double aims. The double-aimed struggle of the black artisan – on the one hand to escape white contempt for a nation of mere hewers of wood and drawers of water, and on the other hand to plough and nail and dig for a poverty-stricken horde – could only result in making him a poor craftsman, for he had but half a heart in either cause. By the poverty and ignorance of his people, the Negro minister or doctor was tempted toward quackery and demagogy; and by the criticism of the other world, toward ideals that made him ashamed of his lowly tasks. The would-be black *savant* was confronted by the paradox that the knowledge his people needed was a twice-told tale to his white neighbors, while the knowledge which would teach the white world was Greek to his own flesh and blood. The innate love of harmony and beauty that set the ruder souls of his people a-dancing and a-singing raised but confusion and doubt in the soul of the black artist; for the beauty revealed to him was the soul-beauty of a race which his larger audience despised, and he could not articulate the message of another people. This waste of double aims, this seeking to satisfy two unreconciled ideals, has wrought sad havoc with the courage and faith and deeds of ten thousand thousand people – has sent them often wooing false gods and invoking false means of salvation, and at times has even seemed about to make them ashamed of themselves.

Away back in the days of bondage they thought to see in one divine event the end of all doubt and disappointment; few men ever worshipped Freedom with half such unquestioning faith as did the American Negro for two centuries. To him, so far as he thought and dreamed, slavery was indeed the sum of all villainies, the cause of all sorrow, the root of all prejudice; Emancipation was the key to a promised land of sweeter beauty than ever stretched before the eyes of wearied Israelites. In song and exhortation swelled one refrain – Liberty; in his tears and curses the God he implored had Freedom in his right hand. At last it came – suddenly, fearfully, like a dream. With one wild carnival of blood and passion came the message in his own plaintive cadences:–

> "Shout, O children!
> Shout, you're free!
> For God has bought your liberty!"[6]

Notes

[6] *"Shout, O Children! ... liberty!"* the refrain of a Negro spiritual.

Years have passed away since then – ten, twenty, forty; forty years of national life, forty years of renewal and development, and yet the swarthy spectre sits in its accustomed seat at the Nation's feast. In vain do we cry to this our vastest social problem:–

> "Take any shape but that, and my firm nerves
> Shall never tremble!"[7]

The Nation has not yet found peace from its sins; the freedman has not yet found in freedom his promised land. Whatever of good may have come in these years of change, the shadow of a deep disappointment rests upon the Negro people – a disappointment all the more bitter because the unattained ideal was unbounded save by the simple ignorance of a lowly people.

The first decade was merely a prolongation of the vain search for freedom, the boon that seemed ever barely to elude their grasp – like a tantalizing will-o'-the-wisp,[8] maddening and misleading the headless host. The holocaust of war, the terrors of the Ku-Klux Klan, the lies of carpet-baggers,[9] the disorganization of industry, and the contradictory advice of friends and foes, left the bewildered serf with no new watchword beyond the old cry for freedom. As the time flew, however, he began to grasp a new idea. The ideal of liberty demanded for its attainment powerful means, and these the Fifteenth Amendment[10] gave him. The ballot, which before he had looked upon as a visible sign of freedom, he now regarded as the chief means of gaining and perfecting the liberty with which war had partially endowed him. And why not? Had not votes made war and emancipated millions? Had not votes enfranchised the freedmen? Was anything impossible to a power that had done all this? A million black men started with renewed zeal to vote themselves into the kingdom. So the decade flew away, the revolution of 1876[11] came, and left the half-free serf weary, wondering, but still inspired. Slowly but steadily, in the following years, a new vision began gradually to replace the dream of political power – a powerful movement, the rise of another ideal to guide the unguided, another pillar of fire by night after a clouded day. It was the ideal of "book-learning"; the curiosity, born of compulsory ignorance, to know and test the power of the cabalistic letters of the white man, the longing to know. Here at last seemed to have been discovered the mountain path to Canaan;[12] longer than the highway of Emancipation and law, steep and rugged, but straight, leading to heights high enough to overlook life.

Up the new path the advance guard toiled, slowly, heavily, doggedly; only those who have watched and guided the faltering feet, the misty minds, the dull understandings, of the dark pupils of these schools know how faithfully, how piteously, this people strove to learn. It was weary work. The cold statistician wrote down the inches of progress here and there, noted also where here and there a foot had slipped or someone had fallen. To the tired climbers, the horizon was ever dark, the mists were often cold, the Canaan was always dim and far away. If, however, the vistas disclosed as yet no goal, no resting-place, little but flattery and criticism, the journey at least gave leisure for reflection and self-examination; it changed the child of Emancipation to the youth with dawning self-consciousness, self-realization, self-respect. In those sombre

Notes

7 *"Take any shape … never tremble"* Shakespeare, *Macbeth* 3.2.99.

8 *will-o'-the-wisp* illusory hope.

9 *carpet-baggers* northerners who moved to the South to profit from Reconstruction.

10 The Fifteenth Amendment (1870) secured African American men the right to vote.

11 *the revolution of 1876* backlash against the Reconstruction.

12 *Canaan* the Biblical "Promised Land."

forests of his striving his own soul rose before him, and he saw himself – darkly as through a veil; and yet he saw in himself some faint revelation of his power, of his mission. He began to have a dim feeling that, to attain his place in the world, he must be himself, and not another. For the first time he sought to analyze the burden he bore upon his back, that dead-weight of social degradation partially masked behind a half-named Negro problem. He felt his poverty; without a cent, without a home, without land, tools, or savings, he had entered into competition with rich, landed, skilled neighbors. To be a poor man is hard, but to be a poor race in a land of dollars is the very bottom of hardships. He felt the weight of his ignorance – not simply of letters, but of life, of business, of the humanities; the accumulated sloth and shirking and awkwardness of decades and centuries shackled his hands and feet. Nor was his burden all poverty and ignorance. The red stain of bastardy, which two centuries of systematic legal defilement of Negro women had stamped upon his race, meant not only the loss of ancient African chastity, but also the hereditary weight of a mass of corruption from white adulterers, threatening almost the obliteration of the Negro home.

A people thus handicapped ought not to be asked to race with the world, but rather allowed to give all its time and thought to its own social problems. But alas! while sociologists gleefully count his bastards and his prostitutes, the very soul of the toiling, sweating black man is darkened by the shadow of a vast despair. Men call the shadow prejudice, and learnedly explain it as the natural defence of culture against barbarism, learning against ignorance, purity against crime, the "higher" against the "lower" races. To which the Negro cries Amen! and swears that to so much of this strange prejudice as is founded on just homage to civilization, culture, righteousness, and progress, he humbly bows and meekly does obeisance.[13] But before that nameless prejudice that leaps beyond all this he stands helpless, dismayed, and well-nigh speechless; before that personal disrespect and mockery, the ridicule and systematic humiliation, the distortion of fact and wanton license of fancy, the cynical ignoring of the better and the boisterous welcoming of the worse, the all-pervading desire to inculcate disdain for everything black, from Toussaint[14] to the devil – before this there rises a sickening despair that would disarm and discourage any nation save that black host to whom "discouragement" is an unwritten word.

But the facing of so vast a prejudice could not but bring the inevitable self-questioning, self-disparagement, and lowering of ideals which ever accompany repression and breed in an atmosphere of contempt and hate. Whisperings and portents came borne upon the four winds: Lo! we are diseased and dying, cried the dark hosts; we cannot write, our voting is vain; what need of education, since we must always cook and serve? And the Nation echoed and enforced this self-criticism, saying: Be content to be servants, and nothing more; what need of higher culture for half-men? Away with the black man's ballot, by force or fraud – and behold the suicide of a race! Nevertheless, out of the evil came something of good – the more careful adjustment of education to real life, the clearer perception of the Negroes' social responsibilities, and the sobering realization of the meaning of progress.

So dawned the time of *Sturm und Drang*:[15] storm and stress to-day rocks our little boat on the mad waters of the world-sea; there is within and without the sound of conflict, the burning of body and rending of soul; inspiration strives with doubt, and

Notes

[13] *obeisance* bows.

[14] *Toussaint* Toussaint L'Ouverture (1743–1803), hero of the Haitian revolution.

[15] *Sturm und Drang* (German) storm and stress.

faith with vain questionings. The bright ideals of the past – physical freedom, political power, the training of brains and the training of hands – all these in turn have waxed and waned, until even the last grows dim and overcast. Are they all wrong – all false? No, not that, but each alone was over-simple and incomplete – the dreams of a credulous race-childhood, or the fond imaginings of the other world which does not know and does not want to know our power. To be really true, all these ideals must be melted and welded into one. The training of the schools we need to-day more than ever – the training of deft hands, quick eyes and ears, and above all the broader, deeper, higher culture of gifted minds and pure hearts. The power of the ballot we need in sheer self-defence – else what shall save us from a second slavery? Freedom, too, the long-sought, we still seek – the freedom of life and limb, the freedom to work and think, the freedom to love and aspire. Work, culture, liberty – all these we need, not singly but together, not successively but together, each growing and aiding each, and all striving toward that vaster ideal that swims before the Negro people, the ideal of human brotherhood, gained through the unifying ideal of Race; the ideal of fostering and developing the traits and talents of the Negro, not in opposition to or contempt for other races, but rather in large conformity to the greater ideals of the American Republic, in order that someday on American soil two world-races may give each to each those characteristics both so sadly lack. We the darker ones come even now not altogether empty-handed: there are to-day no truer exponents of the pure human spirit of the Declaration of Independence than the American Negroes; there is no true American music but the wild sweet melodies of the Negro slave; the American fairy tales and folk-lore are Indian and African; and, all in all, we black men seem the sole oasis of simple faith and reverence in a dusty desert of dollars and smartness. Will America be poorer if she replace her brutal dyspeptic blundering with light-hearted but determined Negro humility? or her coarse and cruel wit with loving jovial good-humor? or her vulgar music with the soul of the Sorrow Songs?

Merely a concrete test of the underlying principles of the great republic is the Negro Problem, and the spiritual striving of the freedmen's sons is the travail of souls whose burden is almost beyond the measure of their strength, but who bear it in the name of an historic race, in the name of this the land of their fathers' fathers, and in the name of human opportunity.

* * *

And now what I have briefly sketched in large outline let me on coming pages tell again in many ways, with loving emphasis and deeper detail, that men may listen to the striving in the souls of black folk.

Chapter 2

Of the Dawn of Freedom

Careless seems the great Avenger;
History's lessons but record
One death-grapple in the darkness
'Twixt old systems and the Word;
Truth forever on the scaffold,
Wrong forever on the throne;
Yet that scaffold sways the future,

And behind the dim unknown
Standeth God within the shadow
Keeping watch above His own.
Lowell.[16]

The problem of the twentieth century is the problem of the color-line – the relation of the darker to the lighter races of men in Asia and Africa, in America and the islands of the sea. It was a phase of this problem that caused the Civil War; and however much they who marched South and North in 1861 may have fixed on the technical points of union and local autonomy as a shibboleth, all nevertheless knew, as we know, that the question of Negro slavery was the real cause of the conflict. Curious it was, too, how this deeper question ever forced itself to the surface despite effort and disclaimer. No sooner had Northern armies touched Southern soil than this old question, newly guised, sprang from the earth – What shall be done with Negroes? Peremptory military commands, this way and that, could not answer the query; the Emancipation Proclamation seemed but to broaden and intensify the difficulties; and the War Amendments[17] made the Negro problems of to-day.

It is the aim of this essay to study the period of history from 1861 to 1872 so far as it relates to the American Negro. In effect, this tale of the dawn of Freedom is an account of that government of men called the Freedmen's Bureau[18] – one of the most singular and interesting of the attempts made by a great nation to grapple with vast problems of race and social condition.

The war has naught to do with slaves, cried Congress, the President, and the Nation; and yet no sooner had the armies, East and West, penetrated Virginia and Tennessee than fugitive slaves appeared within their lines. They came at night, when the flickering camp-fires shone like vast unsteady stars along the black horizon: old men and thin, with gray and tufted hair; women, with frightened eyes, dragging whimpering hungry children; men and girls, stalwart and gaunt – a horde of starving vagabonds, homeless, helpless, and pitiable, in their dark distress. Two methods of treating these newcomers seemed equally logical to opposite sorts of minds. Ben Butler,[19] in Virginia, quickly declared slave property contraband of war, and put the fugitives to work; while Fremont,[20] in Missouri, declared the slaves free under martial law. Butler's action was approved, but Fremont's was hastily countermanded, and his successor, Halleck,[21]

Notes

[16] James Russell Lowell (1819–1891); the lines come from his poem "The Present Crisis" (1844).

[17] *War Amendments* the Thirteenth Amendment (1865) abolished slavery; the Fourteenth Amendment (1866) granted former slaves "equal protection under the law"; the Fifteenth Amendment (1870) granted African American males the right to vote.

[18] *Freedmen's Bureau* the Bureau of Refugees, Freedmen, and Abandoned Lands (1865–1872) was the primary organ of Reconstruction in the South.

[19] *Ben Butler* Benjamin F. Butler (1818–1893), politician and Civil War general from Massachusetts.

[20] *Fremont* John C. Fremont (1813–1880), Civil War general.

[21] *Halleck* Henry H. Halleck (1815–1872), Civil War general.

saw things differently. "Hereafter," he commanded, "no slaves should be allowed to come into your lines at all; if any come without your knowledge, when owners call for them deliver them." Such a policy was difficult to enforce; some of the black refugees declared themselves freemen, others showed that their masters had deserted them, and still others were captured with forts and plantations. Evidently, too, slaves were a source of strength to the Confederacy, and were being used as laborers and producers. "They constitute a military resource," wrote Secretary Cameron,[22] late in 1861; "and being such, that they should not be turned over to the enemy is too plain to discuss." So gradually the tone of the army chiefs changed; Congress forbade the rendition of fugitives, and Butler's "contrabands" were welcomed as military laborers. This complicated rather than solved the problem, for now the scattering fugitives became a steady stream, which flowed faster as the armies marched.

Then the long-headed man with care-chiselled face who sat in the White House saw the inevitable, and emancipated the slaves of rebels on New Year's, 1863. A month later Congress called earnestly for the Negro soldiers whom the act of July, 1862, had half grudgingly allowed to enlist. Thus the barriers were levelled and the deed was done. The stream of fugitives swelled to a flood, and anxious army officers kept inquiring: "What must be done with slaves, arriving almost daily? Are we to find food and shelter for women and children?"

It was a Pierce of Boston[23] who pointed out the way, and thus became in a sense the founder of the Freedmen's Bureau. He was a firm friend of Secretary Chase; and when, in 1861, the care of slaves and abandoned lands devolved upon the Treasury officials, Pierce was specially detailed from the ranks to study the conditions. First, he cared for the refugees at Fortress Monroe; and then, after Sherman had captured Hilton Head, Pierce was sent there to found his Port Royal experiment[24] of making free workingmen out of slaves. Before his experiment was barely started, however, the problem of the fugitives had assumed such proportions that it was taken from the hands of the over-burdened Treasury Department and given to the army officials. Already centres of massed freedmen were forming at Fortress Monroe, Washington, New Orleans, Vicksburg and Corinth, Columbus, Ky., and Cairo, III., as well as at Port Royal. Army chaplains found here new and fruitful fields; "superintendents of contrabands" multiplied, and some attempt at systematic work was made by enlisting the able-bodied men and giving work to the others.

Then came the Freedmen's Aid societies, born of the touching appeals from Pierce and from these other centres of distress. There was the American Missionary Association, sprung from the *Amistad*,[25] and now full-grown for work; the various church organizations, the National Freedmen's Relief Association, the American Freedmen's Union, the Western Freedmen's Aid Commission – in all fifty or more active organizations, which sent clothes, money, schoolbooks, and teachers southward. All they did was needed, for the destitution of the freedmen was often reported as "too appalling for belief," and the situation was daily growing worse rather than better.

Notes

[22] *Secretary Cameron* Simon L. Cameron (1799–1889), secretary of war under President Lincoln.

[23] *Pierce of Boston* Edward Lillie Pierce (1829–1897), abolitionist and worker for the Freedmen's Bureau.

[24] *Secretary Chase... Port Royal experiment* Salmon P. Chase (1808–1873), secretary of the treasury during the Civil War; the Port Royal experiment was a program he headed in South Carolina during the Civil War in which freed slaves were hired to work land abandoned by plantation owners.

[25] *Amistad* a slave ship on which African captives successfully mutinied in 1839; they were subsequently captured and their case was heard before the Supreme Court in *United States vs. Amistad*, which ruled in their favor in 1841.

And daily, too, it seemed more plain that this was no ordinary matter of temporary relief, but a national crisis; for here loomed a labor problem of vast dimensions. Masses of Negroes stood idle, or, if they worked spasmodically, were never sure of pay; and if perchance they received pay, squandered the new thing thoughtlessly. In these and other ways were camp-life and the new liberty demoralizing the freedmen. The broader economic organization thus clearly demanded sprang up here and there as accident and local conditions determined. Here it was that Pierce's Port Royal plan of leased plantations and guided workmen pointed out the tough way. In Washington the military governor, at the urgent appeal of the superintendent, opened confiscated estates to the cultivation of the fugitives, and there in the shadow of the dome gathered black farm villages. General Dix[26] gave over estates to the freedmen of Fortress Monroe, and so on, South and West. The government and benevolent societies furnished the means of cultivation, and the Negro turned again slowly to work. The systems of control, thus started, rapidly grew, here and there, into strange little governments, like that of General Banks[27] in Louisiana, with its ninety thousand black subjects, its fifty thousand guided laborers, and its annual budget of one hundred thousand dollars and more. It made out four thousand pay-rolls a year, registered all freedmen, inquired into grievances and redressed them, laid and collected taxes, and established a system of public schools. So, too, Colonel Eaton,[28] the superintendent of Tennessee and Arkansas, ruled over one hundred thousand freedmen, leased and cultivated seven thousand acres of cotton land, and fed ten thousand paupers a year. In South Carolina was[29] General Saxton, with his deep interest in black folk. He succeeded Pierce and the Treasury officials, and sold forfeited estates, leased abandoned plantations, encouraged schools, and received from Sherman, after that terribly picturesque march to the sea, thousands of the wretched camp followers.

Three characteristic things one might have seen in Sherman's raid through Georgia, which threw the new situation in shadowy relief: the Conqueror, the Conquered, and the Negro. Some see all significance in the grim front of the destroyer, and some in the bitter sufferers of the Lost Cause. But to me neither soldier nor fugitive speaks with so deep a meaning as that dark human cloud that clung like remorse on the rear of those swift columns, swelling at times to half their size, almost engulfing and choking them. In vain were they ordered back, in vain were bridges hewn from beneath their feet; on they trudged and writhed and surged, until they rolled into Savannah, a starved and naked horde of tens of thousands. There too came the characteristic military remedy: "The islands from Charleston south, the abandoned rice-fields along the rivers for thirty miles back from the sea, and the country bordering the St. John's River, Florida, are reserved and set apart for the settlement of Negroes now made free by act of war." So read the celebrated "Field-order Number Fifteen."

All these experiments, orders, and systems were bound to attract and perplex the government and the nation. Directly after the Emancipation Proclamation, Representative Eliot had introduced a bill creating a Bureau of Emancipation; but it was never reported. The following June a committee of inquiry, appointed by the Secretary of War, reported in favor of a temporary bureau for the "improvement, protection, and employment of refugee freedmen," on much the same lines as were

Notes

[26] *General Dix* John A. Dix (1798–1879), Civil War general who oversaw freedmen's affairs.

[27] *General Banks* Nathaniel P. Banks (1816–1894), Civil War general.

[28] *Colonel Eaton* John Eaton, Jr. (1829–1906), Civil War general and US Commissioner of Education.

[29] *General Saxton* Rufus Saxton, Jr. (1824–1908), Civil War general.

afterwards followed. Petitions came in to President Lincoln from distinguished citizens and organizations, strongly urging a comprehensive and unified plan of dealing with the freedmen, under a bureau which should be "charged with the study of plans and execution of measures for easily guiding, and in every way judiciously and humanely aiding, the passage of our emancipated and yet to be emancipated blacks from the old condition of forced labor to their new state of voluntary industry."

Some half-hearted steps were taken to accomplish this, in part, by putting the whole matter again in charge of the special Treasury agents. Laws of 1863 and 1864 directed them to take charge of and lease abandoned lands for periods not exceeding twelve months, and to "provide in such leases, or otherwise, for the employment and general welfare" of the freedmen. Most of the army officers greeted this as a welcome relief from perplexing "Negro affairs," and Secretary Fessenden,[30] July 29, 1864, issued an excellent system of regulations, which were afterward closely followed by General Howard.[31] Under Treasury agents, large quantities of land were leased in the Mississippi Valley, and many Negroes were employed; but in August, 1864, the new regulations were suspended for reasons of "public policy," and the army was again in control.

Meanwhile Congress had turned its attention to the subject; and in March the House passed a bill by a majority of two establishing a Bureau for Freedmen in the War Department. Charles Sumner, who had charge of the bill in the Senate, argued that freedmen and abandoned lands ought to be under the same department, and reported a substitute for the House bill attaching the Bureau to the Treasury Department. This bill passed, but too late for action by the House. The debates wandered over the whole policy of the administration and the general question of slavery, without touching very closely the specific merits of the measure in hand. Then the national election took place; and the administration, with a vote of renewed confidence from the country, addressed itself to the matter more seriously. A conference between the two branches of Congress agreed upon a carefully drawn measure which contained the chief provisions of Sumner's bill, but made the proposed organization a department independent of both the War and the Treasury officials. The bill was conservative, giving the new department "general superintendence of all freedmen." Its purpose was to "establish regulations" for them, protect them, lease them lands, adjust their wages, and appear in civil and military courts as their "next friend." There were many limitations attached to the powers thus granted, and the organization was made permanent. Nevertheless, the Senate defeated the bill, and a new conference committee was appointed. This committee reported a new bill, February 28, which was whirled through just as the session closed, and became the act of 1865 establishing in the War Department a "Bureau of Refugees, Freedmen, and Abandoned Lands."

This last compromise was a hasty bit of legislation, vague and uncertain in outline. A Bureau was created, "to continue during the present War of Rebellion, and for one year thereafter," to which was given "the supervision and management of all abandoned lands and the control of all subjects relating to refugees and freedmen," under "such rules and regulations as may be presented by the head of the Bureau and approved by the President." A Commissioner, appointed by the President and Senate, was to control the Bureau, with an office force not exceeding ten clerks. The President might also appoint assistant commissioners in the seceded States, and to all these

Notes

[30] *Secretary Fessenden* William P. Fessenden (1806–1869), politician and Secretary of the Treasury under President Lincoln.

[31] *General Howard* Oliver Otis Howard (1830–1909), Civil War general and Reconstruction commissioner.

offices military officials might be detailed at regular pay. The Secretary of War could issue rations, clothing, and fuel to the destitute, and all abandoned property was placed in the hands of the Bureau for eventual lease and sale to ex-slaves in forty-acre parcels.

Thus did the United States government definitely assume charge of the emancipated Negro as the ward of the nation. It was a tremendous undertaking. Here at a stroke of the pen was erected a government of millions of men – and not ordinary men either, but black men emasculated by a peculiarly complete system of slavery, centuries old; and now, suddenly, violently, they come into a new birthright, at a time of war and passion, in the midst of the stricken and embittered population of their former masters. Any man might well have hesitated to assume charge of such a work, with vast responsibilities, indefinite powers, and limited resources. Probably no one but a soldier would have answered such a call promptly; and, indeed, no one but a soldier could be called, for Congress had appropriated no money for salaries and expenses.

Less than a month after the weary Emancipator passed to his rest, his successor assigned Major-Gen. Oliver O. Howard to duty as Commissioner of the new Bureau. He was a Maine man, then only thirty-five years of age. He had marched with Sherman to the sea,[32] had fought well at Gettysburg, and but the year before had been assigned to the command of the Department of Tennessee. An honest man, with too much faith in human nature, little aptitude for business and intricate detail, he had had large opportunity of becoming acquainted at first hand with much of the work before him. And of that work it has been truly said that "no approximately correct history of civilization can ever be written which does not throw out in bold relief, as one of the great landmarks of political and social progress, the organization and administration of the Freedmen's Bureau."

On May 12, 1865, Howard was appointed; and he assumed the duties of his office promptly on the 15th, and began examining the field of work. A curious mess he looked upon: little despotisms, communistic experiments, slavery, peonage, business speculations, organized charity, unorganized alms-giving – all reeling on under the guise of helping the freedmen, and all enshrined in the smoke and blood of war and the cursing and silence of angry men. On May 19 the new government – for a government it really was – issued its constitution; commissioners were to be appointed in each of the seceded States, who were to take charge of "all subjects relating to refugees and freedmen," and all relief and rations were to be given by their consent alone. The Bureau invited continued cooperation with benevolent societies, and declared: "It will be the object of all commissioners to introduce practicable systems of compensated labor," and to establish schools. Forthwith nine assistant commissioners were appointed. They were to hasten to their fields of work; seek gradually to close relief establishments, and make the destitute self-supporting; act as courts of law where there were no courts, or where Negroes were not recognized in them as free; establish the institution of marriage among ex-slaves, and keep records; see that freedmen were free to choose their employers, and help in making fair contracts for them; and finally, the circular said: "Simple good faith, for which we hope on all hands for

Notes

[32] *Howard … had marched with Sherman to the sea* the 1864 Savannah Campaign of Gen. William Tecumseh Sherman (1820–1891), in which he sacked Atlanta and laid waste to Georgia.

those concerned in the passing away of slavery, will especially relieve the assistant commissioners in the discharge of their duties toward the freedmen, as well as promote the general welfare."

No sooner was the work thus started, and the general system and local organization in some measure begun, than two grave difficulties appeared which changed largely the theory and outcome of Bureau work. First, there were the abandoned lands of the South. It had long been the more or less definitely expressed theory of the North that all the chief problems of Emancipation might be settled by establishing the slaves on the forfeited lands of their masters – a sort of poetic justice, said some. But this poetry done into solemn prose meant either wholesale confiscation of private property in the South, or vast appropriations. Now Congress had not appropriated a cent, and no sooner did the proclamations of general amnesty appear than the eight hundred thousand acres of abandoned lands in the hands of the Freedmen's Bureau melted quickly away. The second difficulty lay in perfecting the local organization of the Bureau throughout the wide field of work. Making a new machine and sending out officials of duly ascertained fitness for a great work of social reform is no child's task; but this task was even harder, for a new central organization had to be fitted on a heterogeneous and confused but already existing system of relief and control of ex-slaves; and the agents available for this work must be sought for in an army still busy with war operations – men in the very nature of the case ill fitted for delicate social work – or among the questionable camp followers of an invading host. Thus, after a year's work, vigorously as it was pushed, the problem looked even more difficult to grasp and solve than at the beginning. Nevertheless, three things that year's work did, well worth the doing: it relieved a vast amount of physical suffering; it transported seven thousand fugitives from congested centres back to the farm; and, best of all, it inaugurated the crusade of the New England school-ma'am.

The annals of this Ninth Crusade are yet to be written – the tale of a mission that seemed to our age far more quixotic than the quest of St. Louis seemed to his. Behind the mists of ruin and rapine waved the calico dresses of women who dared, and after the hoarse mouthings of the field guns rang the rhythm of the alphabet. Rich and poor they were, serious and curious. Bereaved now of a father, now of a brother, now of more than these, they came seeking a life work in planting New England schoolhouses among the white and black of the South. They did their work well. In that first year they taught one hundred thousand souls, and more.

Evidently, Congress must soon legislate again on the hastily organized Bureau, which had so quickly grown into wide significance and vast possibilities. An institution such as that was well-nigh as difficult to end as to begin. Early in 1866 Congress took up the matter, when Senator Trumbull,[33] of Illinois, introduced a bill to extend the Bureau and enlarge its powers. This measure received, at the hands of Congress, far more thorough discussion and attention than its predecessor. The war cloud had thinned enough to allow a clearer conception of the work of Emancipation. The champions of the bill argued that the strengthening of the Freedmen's Bureau was still a military necessity; that it was needed for the proper carrying out of the Thirteenth Amendment, and was a work of sheer justice to the ex-slave, at a trifling cost to the government. The opponents of the measure declared that the war was over, and the necessity for war measures past; that the Bureau, by reason of its extraordinary

Notes

[33] *Senator Trumbull* Lyman Trumbull (1813–1896), Illinois senator who co-authored the Thirteenth Amendment.

powers, was clearly unconstitutional in time of peace, and was destined to irritate the South and pauperize the freedmen, at a final cost of possibly hundreds of millions. These two arguments were unanswered, and indeed unanswerable: the one that the extraordinary powers of the Bureau threatened the civil rights of all citizens; and the other that the government must have power to do what manifestly must be done, and that present abandonment of the freedmen meant their practical re-enslavement. The bill which finally passed enlarged and made permanent the Freedmen's Bureau. It was promptly vetoed by President Johnson[34] as "unconstitutional," "unnecessary," and "extrajudicial," and failed of passage over the veto. Meantime, however, the breach between Congress and the President began to broaden, and a modified form of the lost bill was finally passed over the President's second veto, July 16.

The act of 1866 gave the Freedmen's Bureau its final form – the form by which it will be known to posterity and judged of men. It extended the existence of the Bureau to July, 1868; it authorized additional assistant commissioners, the retention of army officers mustered out of regular service, the sale of certain forfeited lands to freedmen on nominal terms, the sale of Confederate public property for Negro schools, and a wider field of judicial interpretation and cognizance. The government of the unreconstructed South was thus put very largely in the hands of the Freedmen's Bureau, especially as in many cases the departmental military commander was now made also assistant commissioner. It was thus that the Freedmen's Bureau became a full-fledged government of men. It made laws, executed them and interpreted them; it laid and collected taxes, defined and punished crime, maintained and used military force, and dictated such measures as it thought necessary and proper for the accomplishment of its varied ends. Naturally, all these powers were not exercised continuously nor to their fullest extent; and yet, as General Howard has said, "scarcely any subject that has to be legislated upon in civil society failed, at one time or another, to demand the action of this singular Bureau."

To understand and criticise intelligently so vast a work, one must not forget an instant the drift of things in the later sixties. Lee had surrendered, Lincoln was dead, and Johnson and Congress were at loggerheads; the Thirteenth Amendment was adopted, the Fourteenth pending, and the Fifteenth declared in force in 1870. Guerrilla raiding, the ever-present flickering after-flame of war, was spending its force against the Negroes, and all the Southern land was awakening as from some wild dream to poverty and social revolution. In a time of perfect calm, amid willing neighbors and streaming wealth, the social uplifting of four million slaves to an assured and self-sustaining place in the body politic and economic would have been a herculean task; but when to the inherent difficulties of so delicate and nice a social operation were added the spite and hate of conflict, the hell of war; when suspicion and cruelty were rife, and gaunt Hunger wept beside Bereavement – in such a case, the work of any instrument of social regeneration was in large part foredoomed to failure. The very name of the Bureau stood for a thing in the South which for two centuries and better men had refused even to argue[35] – that life amid free Negroes was simply unthinkable, the maddest of experiments.

Notes

[34] *President Johnson* Andrew Johnson (1808–1875), who served as President from 1865 to 1869 after the assassination of Abraham Lincoln.

[35] *"which for two centuries and better men"* Although so phrased in the original March 1901 *The Atlantic Monthly* essay "The Freedmen's Bureau," its revision as "which for two centuries better men" is possible.

The agents that the Bureau could command varied all the way from unselfish philanthropists to narrow-minded busybodies and thieves; and even though it be true that the average was far better than the worst, it was the occasional fly that helped spoil the ointment.

Then amid all crouched the freed slave, bewildered between friend and foe. He had emerged from slavery – not the worst slavery in the world, not a slavery that made all life unbearable, rather a slavery that had here and there something of kindliness, fidelity, and happiness – but withal slavery, which, so far as human aspiration and desert were concerned, classed the black man and the ox together. And the Negro knew full well that, whatever their deeper convictions may have been, Southern men had fought with desperate energy to perpetuate this slavery under which the black masses, with half-articulate thought, had writhed and shivered. They welcomed freedom with a cry. They shrank from the master who still strove for their chains; they fled to the friends that had freed them, even though those friends stood ready to use them as a club for driving the recalcitrant South back into loyalty. So the cleft between the white and black South grew. Idle to say it never should have been; it was as inevitable as its results were pitiable. Curiously incongruous elements were left arrayed against each other – the North, the government, the carpet-bagger, and the slave, here; and there, all the South that was white, whether gentleman or vagabond, honest man or rascal, lawless murderer or martyr to duty.

Thus it is doubly difficult to write of this period calmly, so intense was the feeling, so mighty the human passions that swayed and blinded men. Amid it all, two figures ever stand to typify that day to coming ages – the one, a gray-haired gentleman, whose fathers had quit themselves like men, whose sons lay in nameless graves; who bowed to the evil of slavery because its abolition threatened untold ill to all; who stood at last, in the evening of life, a blighted, ruined form, with hate in his eyes – and the other, a form hovering dark and mother-like, her awful face black with the mists of centuries, had aforetime quailed at that white master's command, had bent in love over the cradles of his sons and daughters, and closed in death the sunken eyes of his wife – aye, too, at his behest had laid herself low to his lust, and borne a tawny man-child to the world, only to see her dark boy's limbs scattered to the winds by midnight marauders riding after "cursed Niggers." These were the saddest sights of that woeful[36] day; and no man clasped the hands of these two passing figures of the present-past; but, hating, they went to their long home, and, hating, their children's children live to-day.

Here, then, was the field of work for the Freedmen's Bureau; and since, with some hesitation, it was continued by the act of 1868 until 1869, let us look upon four years of its work as a whole. There were, in 1868, nine hundred Bureau officials scattered from Washington to Texas, ruling, directly and indirectly, many millions of men. The deeds of these rulers fall mainly under seven heads: the relief of physical suffering, the overseeing of the beginnings of free labor, the buying and selling of land, the establishment of schools, the paying of bounties, the administration of justice, and the financiering of all these activities.

Up to June, 1869, over half a million patients had been treated by Bureau physicians and surgeons, and sixty hospitals and asylums had been in operation. In fifty months twenty-one million free rations were distributed at a cost of over four million dollars. Next came the difficult question of labor. First, thirty thousand black men were transported from the refuges and relief stations back to the farms, back to the critical trial

Notes

[36] *Original reads*: woful [ed.].

of a new way of working. Plain instructions went out from Washington: the laborers must be free to choose their employers, no fixed rate of wages was prescribed, and there was to be no peonage or forced labor. So far, so good; but where local agents differed *toto cœlo*[37] in capacity and character, where the *personnel* was continually changing, the outcome was necessarily varied. The largest element of success lay in the fact that the majority of the freedmen were willing, even eager, to work. So labor contracts were written – fifty thousand in a single State – laborers advised, wages guaranteed, and employers supplied. In truth, the organization became a vast labor bureau – not perfect, indeed, notably defective here and there, but on the whole successful beyond the dreams of thoughtful men. The two great obstacles which confronted the officials were the tyrant and the idler – the slaveholder who was determined to perpetuate slavery under another name; and the freedman who regarded freedom as perpetual rest – the Devil and the Deep Sea.[38]

In the work of establishing the Negroes as peasant proprietors, the Bureau was from the first handicapped and at last absolutely checked. Something was done, and larger things were planned; abandoned lands were leased so long as they remained in the hands of the Bureau, and a total revenue of nearly half a million dollars derived from black tenants. Some other lands to which the nation had gained title were sold on easy terms, and public lands were opened for settlement to the very few freedmen who had tools and capital. But the vision of "forty acres and a mule" – the righteous and reasonable ambition to become a landholder, which the nation had all but categorically promised the freedmen – was destined in most cases to bitter disappointment. And those men of marvellous hindsight who are today seeking to preach the Negro back to the present peonage of the soil know well, or ought to know, that the opportunity of binding the Negro peasant willingly to the soil was lost on that day when the Commissioner of the Freedmen's Bureau had to go to South Carolina and tell the weeping freedmen, after their years of toil, that their land was not theirs, that there was a mistake – somewhere. If by 1874 the Georgia Negro alone owned three hundred and fifty thousand acres of land, it was by grace of his thrift rather than by bounty of the government.

The greatest success of the Freedmen's Bureau lay in the planting of the free school among Negroes, and the idea of free elementary education among all classes in the South. It not only called the schoolmistresses through the benevolent agencies and built them schoolhouses, but it helped discover and support such apostles of human culture as Edmund Ware, Samuel Armstrong, and Erastus Cravath. The opposition to Negro education in the South was at first bitter, and showed itself in ashes, insult, and blood; for the South believed an educated Negro to be a dangerous Negro. And the South was not wholly wrong; for education among all kinds of men always has had, and always will have, an element of danger and revolution, of dissatisfaction and discontent. Nevertheless, men strive to know. Perhaps some inkling of this paradox, even in the unquiet days of the Bureau, helped the bayonets allay an opposition to human training which still to-day lies smouldering in the South, but not flaming. Fisk, Atlanta, Howard, and Hampton were founded in these days, and six million dollars were expended for educational work, seven hundred and fifty thousand dollars of which the freedmen themselves gave of their poverty.

Notes

[37] *toto cœlo* by the whole extent of the heavens; i.e., totally.

[38] *the Devil and the Deep Sea* caught between two fearful situations.

Such contributions, together with the buying of land and various other enterprises, showed that the ex-slave was handling some free capital already. The chief initial source of this was labor in the army, and his pay and bounty as a soldier. Payments to Negro soldiers were at first complicated by the ignorance of the recipients, and the fact that the quotas of colored regiments from Northern States were largely filled by recruits from the South, unknown to their fellow soldiers. Consequently, payments were accompanied by such frauds that Congress, by joint resolution in 1867, put the whole matter in the hands of the Freedmen's Bureau. In two years six million dollars was thus distributed to five thousand claimants, and in the end the sum exceeded eight million dollars. Even in this system fraud was frequent; but still the work put needed capital in the hands of practical paupers, and some, at least, was well spent.

The most perplexing and least successful part of the Bureau's work lay in the exercise of its judicial functions. The regular Bureau court consisted of one representative of the employer, one of the Negro, and one of the Bureau. If the Bureau could have maintained a perfectly judicial attitude, this arrangement would have been ideal, and must in time have gained confidence; but the nature of its other activities and the character of its *personnel* prejudiced the Bureau in favor of the black litigants, and led without doubt to much injustice and annoyance. On the other hand, to leave the Negro in the hands of Southern courts was impossible. In a distracted land where slavery had hardly fallen, to keep the strong from wanton abuse of the weak, and the weak from gloating insolently over the half-shorn strength of the strong, was a thankless, hopeless task. The former masters of the land were peremptorily ordered about, seized, and imprisoned, and punished over and again, with scant courtesy from army officers. The former slaves were intimidated, beaten, raped, and butchered by angry and revengeful men. Bureau courts tended to become centres simply for punishing whites, while the regular civil courts tended to become solely institutions for perpetuating the slavery of blacks. Almost every law and method ingenuity could devise was employed by the legislatures to reduce the Negroes to serfdom – to make them the slaves of the State, if not of individual owners; while the Bureau officials too often were found striving to put the "bottom rail on top," and give the freedmen a power and independence which they could not yet use. It is all well enough for us of another generation to wax wise with advice to those who bore the burden in the heat of the day. It is full easy now to see that the man who lost home, fortune, and family at a stroke, and saw his land ruled by "mules and niggers," was really benefited by the passing of slavery. It is not difficult now to say to the young freedman, cheated and cuffed about, who has seen his father's head beaten to a jelly and his own mother namelessly assaulted, that the meek shall inherit the earth. Above all, nothing is more convenient than to heap on the Freedmen's Bureau all the evils of that evil day, and damn it utterly for every mistake and blunder that was made.

All this is easy, but it is neither sensible nor just. Someone had blundered, but that was long before Oliver Howard was born; there was criminal aggression and heedless neglect, but without some system of control there would have been far more than there was. Had that control been from within, the Negro would have been re-enslaved, to all intents and purposes. Coming as the control did from without, perfect men and methods would have bettered all things; and even with imperfect agents and questionable methods, the work accomplished was not undeserving of commendation.

Such was the dawn of Freedom; such was the work of the Freedmen's Bureau, which, summed up in brief, may be epitomized thus: For some fifteen million dollars, beside the sums spent before 1865, and the dole of benevolent societies, this Bureau set going a system of free labor, established a beginning of peasant proprietorship, secured the recognition of black freedmen before courts of law, and founded the free common school in the South. On the other hand, it failed to begin the establishment of goodwill between ex-masters and freedmen, to guard its work wholly from paternalistic methods which discouraged self-reliance, and to carry out to any considerable extent its implied promises to furnish the freedmen with land. Its successes were the result of hard work, supplemented by the aid of philanthropists and the eager striving of black men. Its failures were the result of bad local agents, the inherent difficulties of the work, and national neglect.

Such an institution, from its wide powers, great responsibilities, large control of moneys, and generally conspicuous position, was naturally open to repeated and bitter attack. It sustained a searching Congressional investigation at the instance of Fernando Wood[39] in 1870. Its archives and few remaining functions were with blunt discourtesy transferred from Howard's control, in his absence, to the supervision of Secretary of War Belknap[40] in 1872, on the Secretary's recommendation. Finally, in consequence of grave intimations of wrong-doing made by the Secretary and his subordinates, General Howard was court-martialed in 1874. In both of these trials the Commissioner of the Freedmen's Bureau was officially exonerated from any wilful misdoing, and his work commended. Nevertheless, many unpleasant things were brought to light – the methods of transacting the business of the Bureau were faulty; several cases of defalcation were proved, and other frauds strongly suspected; there were some business transactions which savored of dangerous speculation, if not dishonesty; and around it all lay the smirch of the Freedmen's Bank.

Morally and practically, the Freedmen's Bank was part of the Freedmen's Bureau, although it had no legal connection with it. With the prestige of the government back of it, and a directing board of unusual respectability and national reputation, this banking institution had made a remarkable start in the development of that thrift among black folk which slavery had kept them from knowing. Then in one sad day came the crash – all the hard-earned dollars of the freedmen disappeared; but that was the least of the loss – all the faith in saving went too, and much of the faith in men; and that was a loss that a Nation which to-day sneers at Negro shiftlessness has never yet made good. Not even ten additional years of slavery could have done so much to throttle the thrift of the freedmen as the mismanagement and bankruptcy of the series of savings banks chartered by the Nation for their especial aid. Where all the blame should rest, it is hard to say; whether the Bureau and the Bank died chiefly by reason of the blows of its selfish friends or the dark machinations of its foes, perhaps even time will never reveal, for here lies unwritten history.

Of the foes without the Bureau, the bitterest were those who attacked not so much its conduct or policy under the law as the necessity for any such institution at all. Such attacks came primarily from the Border States and the South; and they were summed up by Senator Davis, of Kentucky, when he moved to entitle the act of 1866 a bill "to promote strife and conflict between the white and black races … by a grant of unconstitutional power." The argument gathered tremendous strength South and North; but its very strength was its weakness. For, argued the plain commonsense of the nation, if it is unconstitutional, unpractical, and futile for the nation to stand guardian over its helpless wards, then there is left but one alternative – to make those wards their own guardians by arming them with the ballot. Moreover, the path of the practical politician

Notes

[39] Fernando Wood (1812–1884), New York politician.

[40] *Secretary of War Belknap* William W. Belknap (1829–1890), Major General and Secretary of War under Ulysses S. Grant.

pointed the same way; for, argued this opportunist, if we cannot peacefully reconstruct the South with white votes, we certainly can with black votes. So justice and force joined hands.

The alternative thus offered the nation was not between full and restricted Negro suffrage; else every sensible man, black and white, would easily have chosen the latter. It was rather a choice between suffrage and slavery, after endless blood and gold had flowed to sweep human bondage away. Not a single Southern legislature stood ready to admit a Negro, under any conditions, to the polls; not a single Southern legislature believed free Negro labor was possible without a system of restrictions that took all its freedom away; there was scarcely a white man in the South who did not honestly regard Emancipation as a crime, and its practical nullification as a duty. In such a situation, the granting of the ballot to the black man was a necessity, the very least a guilty nation could grant a wronged race, and the only method of compelling the South to accept the results of the war. Thus Negro suffrage ended a civil war by beginning a race feud. And some felt gratitude toward the race thus sacrificed in its swaddling clothes on the altar of national integrity; and some felt and feel only indifference and contempt.

Had political exigencies been less pressing, the opposition to government guardianship of Negroes less bitter, and the attachment to the slave system less strong, the social seer can well imagine a far better policy – a permanent Freedmen's Bureau, with a national system of Negro schools; a carefully supervised employment and labor office; a system of impartial protection before the regular courts; and such institutions for social betterment as savings-banks, land and building associations, and social settlements. All this vast expenditure of money and brains might have formed a great school of prospective citizenship, and solved in a way we have not yet solved the most perplexing and persistent of the Negro problems.

That such an institution was unthinkable in 1870 was due in part to certain acts of the Freedmen's Bureau itself. It came to regard its work as merely temporary, and Negro suffrage as a final answer to all present perplexities. The political ambition of many of its agents and *protégés* led it far afield into questionable activities, until the South, nursing its own deep prejudices, came easily to ignore all the good deeds of the Bureau and hate its very name with perfect hatred. So the Freedmen's Bureau died, and its child was the Fifteenth Amendment.

The passing of a great human institution before its work is done, like the untimely passing of a single soul, but leaves a legacy of striving for other men. The legacy of the Freedmen's Bureau is the heavy heritage of this generation. Today, when new and vaster problems are destined to strain every fibre of the national mind and soul, would it not be well to count this legacy honestly and carefully? For this much all men know: despite compromise, war, and struggle, the Negro is not free. In the backwoods of the Gulf States, for miles and miles, he may not leave the plantation of his birth; in well-nigh the whole rural South the black farmers are peons, bound by law and custom to an economic slavery, from which the only escape is death or the penitentiary. In the most cultured sections and cities of the South the Negroes are a segregated servile caste, with restricted rights and privileges. Before the courts, both in law and custom, they stand on a different and peculiar basis. Taxation without representation is the rule of their political life. And the result of all this is, and in nature must have been, lawlessness and crime. That is the large legacy of the Freedmen's Bureau, the work it did not do because it could not.

* * *

I have seen a land right merry with the sun, where children sing, and rolling hills lie like passioned women wanton with harvest. And there in the King's Highway sat and sits a figure veiled and bowed, by which the traveller's footsteps hasten as they go. On the tainted air broods fear. Three centuries' thought has been the raising and unveiling of that bowed human heart, and now behold a century new for the duty and the deed. The problem of the Twentieth Century is the problem of the color-line.

Chapter 3

Of Mr. Booker T. Washington and Others

From birth till death enslaved; in word, in deed, unmanned!
. . . .
Hereditary bondsmen! Know ye not
Who would be free themselves must strike the blow?[41]

Byron.

Easily the most striking thing in the history of the American Negro since 1876 is the ascendancy of Mr. Booker T. Washington. It began at the time when war memories and ideals were rapidly passing; a day of astonishing commercial development was dawning; a sense of doubt and hesitation overtook the freedmen's sons – then it was that his leading began. Mr. Washington came, with a simple definite programme, at the psychological moment when the nation was a little ashamed of having bestowed so much sentiment on Negroes, and was concentrating its energies on Dollars. His programme of industrial education, conciliation of the South, and submission and silence as to civil and political rights, was not wholly original; the Free Negroes from 1830 up to wartime had striven to build industrial schools, and the American Missionary Association had from the first taught various trades; and Price[42] and others had sought a way of honorable alliance with the best of the Southerners. But Mr. Washington first indissolubly linked these things; he put enthusiasm, unlimited energy, and perfect faith into this programme, and changed it from a by-path into a veritable Way of Life. And the tale of the methods by which he did this is a fascinating study of human life.

It startled the nation to hear a Negro advocating such a programme after many decades of bitter complaint; it startled and won the applause of the South, it interested and won the admiration of the North; and after a confused murmur of protest, it silenced if it did not convert the Negroes themselves.

Notes

[41] *"From birth ... strike the blow?"* from *Childe Harold's Pilgrimage* (1812), a long poem by English poet Lord Byron (1788–1824).

[42] *Price* Joseph Charles Price (1854–1893), southern educator and orator.

To gain the sympathy and cooperation of the various elements comprising the white South was Mr. Washington's first task; and this, at the time Tuskegee[43] was founded, seemed, for a black man, well-nigh impossible. And yet ten years later it was done in the word spoken at Atlanta: "In all things purely social we can be as separate as the five fingers, and yet one as the hand in all things essential to mutual progress." This "Atlanta Compromise" is by all odds the most notable thing in Mr. Washington's career. The South interpreted it in different ways: the radicals received it as a complete surrender of the demand for civil and political equality; the conservatives, as a generously conceived working basis for mutual understanding. So both approved it, and to-day its author is certainly the most distinguished Southerner since Jefferson Davis,[44] and the one with the largest personal following.

Next to this achievement comes Mr. Washington's work in gaining place and consideration in the North. Others less shrewd and tactful had formerly essayed to sit on these two stools and had fallen between them; but as Mr. Washington knew the heart of the South from birth and training, so by singular insight he intuitively grasped the spirit of the age which was dominating the North. And so thoroughly did he learn the speech and thought of triumphant commercialism, and the ideals of material prosperity, that the picture of a lone black boy poring over a French grammar amid the weeds and dirt of a neglected home soon seemed to him the acme of absurdities. One wonders what Socrates[45] and St. Francis of Assisi[46] would say to this.

And yet this very singleness of vision and thorough oneness with his age is a mark of the successful man. It is as though Nature must needs make men narrow in order to give them force. So Mr. Washington's cult has gained unquestioning followers, his work has wonderfully prospered, his friends are legion, and his enemies are confounded. To-day he stands as the one recognized spokesman of his ten million fellows, and one of the most notable figures in a nation of seventy millions. One hesitates, therefore, to criticise a life which, beginning with so little, has done so much. And yet the time is come when one may speak in all sincerity and utter courtesy of the mistakes and shortcomings of Mr. Washington's career, as well as of his triumphs, without being thought captious or envious, and without forgetting that it is easier to do ill than well in the world.

The criticism that has hitherto met Mr. Washington has not always been of this broad character. In the South especially has he had to walk warily to avoid the harshest judgments – and naturally so, for he is dealing with the one subject of deepest sensitiveness to that section. Twice – once when at the Chicago celebration of the Spanish–American War he alluded to the color-prejudice that is "eating away the vitals of the South," and once when he dined with President Roosevelt[47] – has the resulting Southern criticism been violent enough to threaten seriously his popularity. In the North the feeling has several times forced itself into words, that Mr. Washington's counsels of submission overlooked certain elements of true manhood, and that his educational programme was unnecessarily narrow. Usually, however, such criticism has not found open expression, although, too, the spiritual sons of the Abolitionists have not been prepared to acknowledge that the schools founded before Tuskegee, by

Notes

[43] *Tuskegee* Tuskegee Normal and Industrial Institute, founded by Booker T. Washington in 1881 as a vocational school for African Americans.

[44] Jefferson Davis (1808–1889), president of the Confederate States of America during the Civil War.

[45] Socrates (*c.*470–399 BC), Athenian philosopher.

[46] St. Francis of Assisi (*c.*1181–1226), Italian religious figure and founder of the Franciscan order.

[47] *President Roosevelt* Theodore Roosevelt (1858–1919), president of the United States (1901–1909).

men of broad ideals and self-sacrificing spirit, were wholly failures or worthy of ridicule. While, then, criticism has not failed to follow Mr. Washington, yet the prevailing public opinion of the land has been but too willing to deliver the solution of a wearisome problem into his hands, and say, "If that is all you and your race ask, take it."

Among his own people, however, Mr. Washington has encountered the strongest and most lasting opposition, amounting at times to bitterness, and even to-day continuing strong and insistent even though largely silenced in outward expression by the public opinion of the nation. Some of this opposition is, of course, mere envy; the disappointment of displaced demagogues and the spite of narrow minds. But aside from this, there is among educated and thoughtful colored men in all parts of the land a feeling of deep regret, sorrow, and apprehension at the wide currency and ascendancy which some of Mr. Washington's theories have gained. These same men admire his sincerity of purpose, and are willing to forgive much to honest endeavor which is doing something worth the doing. They cooperate with Mr. Washington as far as they conscientiously can; and, indeed, it is no ordinary tribute to this man's tact and power that, steering as he must between so many diverse interests and opinions, he so largely retains the respect of all.

But the hushing of the criticism of honest opponents is a dangerous thing. It leads some of the best of the critics to unfortunate silence and paralysis of effort, and others to burst into speech so passionately and intemperately as to lose listeners. Honest and earnest criticism from those whose interests are most nearly touched – criticism of writers by readers, of government by those governed, of leaders by those led – this is the soul of democracy and the safeguard of modern society. If the best of the American Negroes receive by outer pressure a leader whom they had not recognized before, manifestly there is here a certain palpable gain. Yet there is also irreparable loss – a loss of that peculiarly valuable education which a group receives when by search and criticism it finds and commissions its own leaders. The way in which this is done is at once the most elementary and the nicest problem of social growth. History is but the record of such group-leadership; and yet how infinitely changeful is its type and character! And of all types and kinds, what can be more instructive than the leadership of a group within a group? – that curious double movement where real progress may be negative and actual advance be relative retrogression. All this is the social student's inspiration and despair.

Now in the past the American Negro has had instructive experience in the choosing of group leaders, founding thus a peculiar dynasty which in the light of present conditions is worth while studying. When sticks and stones and beasts form the sole environment of a people, their attitude is largely one of determined opposition to and conquest of natural forces. But when to earth and brute is added an environment of men and ideas, then the attitude of the imprisoned group may take three main forms – a feeling of revolt and revenge; an attempt to adjust all thought and action to the will of the greater group; or, finally, a determined effort at self-realization and self-development despite environing opinion. The influence of all of these attitudes at various times can be traced in the history of the American Negro, and in the evolution of his successive leaders.

Before 1750, while the fire of African freedom still burned in the veins of the slaves, there was in all leadership or attempted leadership but the one motive of revolt and revenge – typified in the terrible Maroons, the Danish blacks, and Cato of Stono,[48] and veiling all the Americas in fear of insurrection. The liberalizing tendencies of the latter

Notes

[48] *Maroons, Danish blacks, and Cato of Stono* "Maroons" were fugitive slave communities in the South; "Danish blacks" were slaves who rebelled in 1723 in the Danish West Indies (the present-day Virgin Islands); Cato led the 1739 Stono Rebellion of slaves in South Carolina.

half of the eighteenth century brought, along with kindlier relations between black and white, thoughts of ultimate adjustment and assimilation. Such aspiration was especially voiced in the earnest songs of Phyllis,[49] in the martyrdom of Attucks,[50] the fighting of Salem and Poor,[51] the intellectual accomplishments of Banneker and Derham,[52] and the political demands of the Cuffes.[53]

Stern financial and social stress after the war cooled much of the previous humanitarian ardor. The disappointment and impatience of the Negroes at the persistence of slavery and serfdom voiced itself in two movements. The slaves in the South, aroused undoubtedly by vague rumors of the Haytian[54] revolt, made three fierce attempts at insurrection – in 1800 under Gabriel in Virginia,[55] in 1822 under Vesey[56] in Carolina, and in 1831 again in Virginia under the terrible Nat Turner.[57] In the Free States, on the other hand, a new and curious attempt at self-development was made. In Philadelphia and New York color-prescription led to a withdrawal of Negro communicants from white churches and the formation of a peculiar socio-religious institution among the Negroes known as the African Church – an organization still living and controlling in its various branches over a million of men.

Walker's wild appeal[58] against the trend of the times showed how the world was changing after the coming of the cotton-gin. By 1830 slavery seemed hopelessly fastened on the South, and the slaves thoroughly cowed into submission. The free Negroes of the North, inspired by the mulatto immigrants from the West Indies, began to change the basis of their demands; they recognized the slavery of slaves, but insisted that they themselves were freemen, and sought assimilation and amalgamation with the nation on the same terms with other men. Thus, Forten and Purvis[59] of Philadelphia, Shad of Wilmington,[60] Du Bois of New Haven,[61] Barbadoes of Boston,[62] and others, strove singly and together as men, they said, not as slaves; as "people of color," not as "Negroes." The trend of the times, however, refused them recognition save in individual and exceptional cases, considered them as one with all the despised blacks, and they soon found themselves striving to keep even the rights they formerly had of voting and working and moving as freemen. Schemes of migration and colonization arose among them; but these they refused to entertain, and they eventually turned to the Abolition movement as a final refuge.

Here, led by Remond,[63] Nell,[64] Wells-Brown,[65] and Douglass, a new period of self-assertion and self-development dawned. To be sure, ultimate freedom and assimilation

Notes

[49] *Phyllis* Phillis Wheatley (*c.*1753–1784), African American poet.

[50] *Attucks* Crispus Attucks (*c.*1723–1770), enslaved merchant and seaman killed in the Boston Massacre.

[51] *Salem and Poor* Peter Salem (1750–1816) and Salem Poor (1747–1802), acclaimed soldiers in the American Revolutionary War.

[52] *Banneker and Derham* Benjamin Banneker (1731–1806) and James Durham (*c.*1757–1802), African American surveyor and physician, respectively.

[53] *the Cuffes* Paul Cuffe (1759–1817), a Quaker businessman and abolitionist who, with his brother John, protested in Massachusetts for black suffrage.

[54] *Haytian* Haitian.

[55] *Gabriel in Virginia* Gabriel Prosser (1775–1800), enslaved blacksmith who planned slave insurrection in Richmond, Virginia, in 1800.

[56] *Vesey in Carolina* Denmark Vesey (*c.*1767–1822), slave who planned slave insurrection in Charleston, South Carolina, in 1822.

[57] Nat Turner (1800–1831), organizer of 1831 slave insurrection in Virginia.

[58] *Walker's wild appeal* David Walker (1785–1830), radical abolitionist who in 1829 issued *David Walker's Appeal to the Colored Citizens of the World.*

[59] *Forten and Purvis of Philadelphia* James Forten, Sr. (1766–1842) and Robert Purvis, Sr. (1810–1893), wealthy businessmen and activists.

[60] *Shad of Wilmington* Mary Ann Shadd (1823–1893), antislavery activist and publisher.

[61] *Du Bois of New Haven* Alexander Du Bois, the author's grandfather.

[62] *Barbadoes of Boston* James G. Barbadoes (*c.*1796–1841), a barber and abolitionist.

[63] Charles Lenox Remond (1810–1873), a lecturer and abolitionist.

[64] William C. Nell (1816–1874), journalist and Underground Railroad supporter.

[65] William Wells Brown (*c.*1814–1884), abolitionist lecturer, novelist, and fugitive slave.

was the ideal before the leaders, but the assertion of the manhood rights of the Negro by himself was the main reliance, and John Brown's raid was the extreme of its logic. After the war and emancipation, the great form of Frederick Douglass, the greatest of American Negro leaders, still led the host. Self-assertion, especially in political lines, was the main programme, and behind Douglass came Elliot,[66] Bruce,[67] and Langston,[68] and the Reconstruction politicians, and, less conspicuous but of greater social significance, Alexander Crummell[69] and Bishop Daniel Payne. [70]

Then came the Revolution of 1876, the suppression of the Negro votes, the changing and shifting of ideals, and the seeking of new lights in the great night. Douglass, in his old age, still bravely stood for the ideals of his early manhood – ultimate assimilation *through* self-assertion, and on no other terms. For a time Price arose as a new leader, destined, it seemed, not to give up, but to re-state the old ideals in a form less repugnant to the white South. But he passed away in his prime. Then came the new leader. Nearly all the former ones had become leaders by the silent suffrage of their fellows, had sought to lead their own people alone, and were usually, save Douglass, little known outside their race. But Booker T. Washington arose as essentially the leader not of one race but of two – a compromiser between the South, the North, and the Negro. Naturally the Negroes resented, at first bitterly, signs of compromise which surrendered their civil and political rights, even though this was to be exchanged for larger chances of economic development. The rich and dominating North, however, was not only weary of the race problem, but was investing largely in Southern enterprises, and welcomed any method of peaceful cooperation. Thus, by national opinion, the Negroes began to recognize Mr. Washington's leadership; and the voice of criticism was hushed.

Mr. Washington represents in Negro thought the old attitude of adjustment and submission; but adjustment at such a peculiar time as to make his programme unique. This is an age of unusual economic development, and Mr. Washington's programme naturally takes an economic cast, becoming a gospel of Work and Money to such an extent as apparently almost completely to overshadow the higher aims of life. Moreover, this is an age when the more advanced races are coming in closer contact with the less developed races, and the race-feeling is therefore intensified; and Mr. Washington's programme practically accepts the alleged inferiority of the Negro races. Again, in our own land, the reaction from the sentiment of war time has given impetus to race-prejudice against Negroes, and Mr. Washington withdraws many of the high demands of Negroes as men and American citizens. In other periods of intensified prejudice all the Negro's tendency to self-assertion has been called forth; at this period a policy of submission is advocated. In the history of nearly all other races and peoples the doctrine preached at such crises has been that manly self-respect is worth more than lands and houses, and that a people who voluntarily surrender such respect, or cease striving for it, are not worth civilizing.

In answer to this, it has been claimed that the Negro can survive only through submission. Mr. Washington distinctly asks that black people give up, at least for the present, three things–

Notes

[66] Robert Brown Elliott (1842–1884), South Carolina congressman.

[67] Blanche Kelso Bruce (1841–1898), Mississippi senator.

[68] John Mercer Langston (1829–1897), Virginia congressman.

[69] Alexander Crummell (1819–1898), an African American Episcopal priest and African nationalist.

[70] Bishop Daniel Payne (1811–1893), a leader in the African Methodist Episcopal Church.

First, political power,
Second, insistence on civil rights,
Third, higher education of Negro youth–

and concentrate all their energies on industrial education, the accumulation of wealth, and the conciliation of the South. This policy has been courageously and insistently advocated for over fifteen years, and has been triumphant for perhaps ten years. As a result of this tender of the palm-branch, what has been the return? In these years there have occurred:

1. The disfranchisement of the Negro.
2. The legal creation of a distinct status of civil inferiority for the Negro.
3. The steady withdrawal of aid from institutions for the higher training of the Negro.

These movements are not, to be sure, direct results of Mr. Washington's teachings; but his propaganda has, without a shadow of doubt, helped their speedier accomplishment. The question then comes: Is it possible, and probable, that nine millions of men can make effective progress in economic lines if they are deprived of political rights, made a servile caste, and allowed only the most meagre chance for developing their exceptional men? If history and reason give any distinct answer to these questions, it is an emphatic *No*. And Mr. Washington thus faces the triple paradox of his career:

1. He is striving nobly to make Negro artisans businessmen and property-owners; but it is utterly impossible, under modern competitive methods, for workingmen and property-owners to defend their rights and exist without the right of suffrage.
2. He insists on thrift and self-respect, but at the same time counsels a silent submission to civic inferiority such as is bound to sap the manhood of any race in the long run.
3. He advocates common-school[71] and industrial training, and depreciates institutions of higher learning; but neither the Negro common-schools, nor Tuskegee itself, could remain open a day were it not for teachers trained in Negro colleges, or trained by their graduates.

This triple paradox in Mr. Washington's position is the object of criticism by two classes of colored Americans. One class is spiritually descended from Toussaint the Savior, through Gabriel, Vesey, and Turner, and they represent the attitude of revolt and revenge; they hate the white South blindly and distrust the white race generally, and so far as they agree on definite action, think that the Negro's only hope lies in emigration beyond the borders of the United States. And yet, by the irony of fate, nothing has more effectually made this programme seem hopeless than the recent course of the United States toward weaker and darker peoples in the West Indies, Hawaii, and the Philippines – for where in the world may we go and be safe from lying and brute force?

The other class of Negroes who cannot agree with Mr. Washington has hitherto said little aloud. They deprecate the sight of scattered counsels, of internal disagreement;

Notes

[71] *Common-school* public elementary education.

and especially they dislike making their just criticism of a useful and earnest man an excuse for a general discharge of venom from small-minded opponents. Nevertheless, the questions involved are so fundamental and serious that it is difficult to see how men like the Grimkes,[72] Kelly Miller,[73] J.W.E. Bowen,[74] and other representatives of this group, can much longer be silent. Such men feel in conscience bound to ask of this nation three things:

1. The right to vote.
2. Civic equality.
3. The education of youth according to ability.

They acknowledge Mr. Washington's invaluable service in counselling patience and courtesy in such demands; they do not ask that ignorant black men vote when ignorant whites are debarred, or that any reasonable restrictions in the suffrage should not be applied; they know that the low social level of the mass of the race is responsible for much discrimination against it, but they also know, and the nation knows, that relentless color-prejudice is more often a cause than a result of the Negro's degradation; they seek the abatement of this relic of barbarism, and not its systematic encouragement and pampering by all agencies of social power from the Associated Press to the Church of Christ. They advocate, with Mr. Washington, a broad system of Negro common schools supplemented by thorough industrial training; but they are surprised that a man of Mr. Washington's insight cannot see that no such educational system ever has rested or can rest on any other basis than that of the well-equipped college and university, and they insist that there is a demand for a few such institutions throughout the South to train the best of the Negro youth as teachers, professional men, and leaders.

This group of men honor Mr. Washington for his attitude of conciliation toward the white South; they accept the "Atlanta Compromise" in its broadest interpretation; they recognize, with him, many signs of promise, many men of high purpose and fair judgment, in this section; they know that no easy task has been laid upon a region already tottering under heavy burdens. But, nevertheless, they insist that the way to truth and right lies in straightforward honesty, not in indiscriminate flattery; in praising those of the South who do well and criticising uncompromisingly those who do ill; in taking advantage of the opportunities at hand and urging their fellows to do the same, but at the same time in remembering that only a firm adherence to their higher ideals and aspirations will ever keep those ideals within the realm of possibility. They do not expect that the free right to vote, to enjoy civic rights, and to be educated, will come in a moment; they do not expect to see the bias and prejudices of years disappear at the blast of a trumpet; but they are absolutely certain that the way for a people to gain their reasonable rights is not by voluntarily throwing them away and insisting that they do not want them; that the way for a people to gain respect is not by continually belittling and ridiculing themselves; that, on the contrary, Negroes must insist continually, in season and out of season, that voting is necessary to modern manhood, that color discrimination is barbarism, and that black boys need education as well as white boys.

Notes

[72] *The Grimkes* Archibald H. Grimké (1849–1930) and Francis J. Grimké (1850–1937), civil rights activists.

[73] Kelly Miller (1863–1939), a professor at Howard University.

[74] John Wesley Edward Bowen (1855–1933), lecturer and Methodist minister.

In failing thus to state plainly and unequivocally the legitimate demands of their people, even at the cost of opposing an honored leader, the thinking classes of American Negroes would shirk a heavy responsibility – a responsibility to themselves, a responsibility to the struggling masses, a responsibility to the darker races of men whose future depends so largely on this American experiment, but especially a responsibility to this nation – this common Fatherland. It is wrong to encourage a man or a people in evil-doing; it is wrong to aid and abet a national crime simply because it is unpopular not to do so. The growing spirit of kindliness and reconciliation between the North and South after the frightful differences of a generation ago ought to be a source of deep congratulation to all, and especially to those whose mistreatment caused the war; but if that reconciliation is to be marked by the industrial slavery and civic death of those same black men, with permanent legislation into a position of inferiority, then those black men, if they are really men, are called upon by every consideration of patriotism and loyalty to oppose such a course by all civilized methods, even though such opposition involves disagreement with Mr. Booker T. Washington. We have no right to sit silently by while the inevitable seeds are sown for a harvest of disaster to our children, black and white.

First, it is the duty of black men to judge the South discriminatingly. The present generation of Southerners are not responsible for the past, and they should not be blindly hated or blamed for it. Furthermore, to no class is the indiscriminate endorsement of the recent course of the South toward Negroes more nauseating than to the best thought of the South. The South is not "solid"; it is a land in the ferment of social change, wherein forces of all kinds are fighting for supremacy; and to praise the ill the South is to-day perpetrating is just as wrong as to condemn the good. Discriminating and broad-minded criticism is what the South needs – needs it for the sake of her own white sons and daughters, and for the insurance of robust, healthy mental and moral development.

To-day even the attitude of the Southern whites toward the blacks is not, as so many assume, in all cases the same; the ignorant Southerner hates the Negro, the workingmen fear his competition, the money-makers wish to use him as a laborer, some of the educated see a menace in his upward development, while others – usually the sons of the masters – wish to help him to rise. National opinion has enabled this last class to maintain the Negro common schools, and to protect the Negro partially in property, life, and limb. Through the pressure of the money-makers, the Negro is in danger of being reduced to semi-slavery, especially in the country districts; the workingmen, and those of the educated who fear the Negro, have united to disfranchise him, and some have urged his deportation; while the passions of the ignorant are easily aroused to lynch and abuse any black man. To praise this intricate whirl of thought and prejudice is nonsense; to inveigh indiscriminately against "the South" is unjust; but to use the same breath in praising Governor Aycock,[75] exposing Senator Morgan,[76] arguing with Mr. Thomas Nelson Page,[77] and denouncing Senator Ben Tillman,[78] is not only sane, but the imperative duty of thinking black men.

Notes

[75] *Governor Aycock* Charles Brantley Aycock (1859–1912), North Carolina reformist governor.

[76] *Senator Morgan* John Tyler Morgan (1824–1907), white supremacist Alabama senator.

[77] Thomas Nelson Page (1853–1922), American ambassador and writer of fiction nostalgic for the antebellum South.

[78] *Senator Ben Tillman* Benjamin Ryan Tillman (1847–1918), white supremacist South Carolina governor and senator.

It would be unjust to Mr. Washington not to acknowledge that in several instances he has opposed movements in the South which were unjust to the Negro; he sent memorials to the Louisiana and Alabama constitutional conventions, he has spoken against lynching, and in other ways has openly or silently set his influence against sinister schemes and unfortunate happenings. Notwithstanding this, it is equally true to assert that on the whole the distinct impression left by Mr. Washington's propaganda is, first, that the South is justified in its present attitude toward the Negro because of the Negro's degradation; secondly, that the prime cause of the Negro's failure to rise more quickly is his wrong education in the past; and, thirdly, that his future rise depends primarily on his own efforts. Each of these propositions is a dangerous half-truth. The supplementary truths must never be lost sight of: first, slavery and race-prejudice are potent if not sufficient causes of the Negro's position; second, industrial and common-school training were necessarily slow in planting because they had to await the black teachers trained by higher institutions – it being extremely doubtful if any essentially different development was possible, and certainly a Tuskegee was unthinkable before 1880; and, third, while it is a great truth to say that the Negro must strive and strive mightily to help himself, it is equally true that unless his striving be not simply seconded, but rather aroused and encouraged, by the initiative of the richer and wiser environing group, he cannot hope for great success.

In his failure to realize and impress this last point, Mr. Washington is especially to be criticised. His doctrine has tended to make the whites, North and South, shift the burden of the Negro problem to the Negro's shoulders and stand aside as critical and rather pessimistic spectators; when in fact the burden belongs to the nation, and the hands of none of us are clean if we bend not our energies to righting these great wrongs.

The South ought to be led, by candid and honest criticism, to assert her better self and do her full duty to the race she has cruelly wronged and is still wronging. The North – her co-partner in guilt – cannot salve her conscience by plastering it with gold. We cannot settle this problem by diplomacy and suaveness, by "policy" alone. If worse come to worst, can the moral fibre of this country survive the slow throttling and murder of nine millions of men?

The black men of America have a duty to perform, a duty stern and delicate – a forward movement to oppose a part of the work of their greatest leader. So far as Mr. Washington preaches Thrift, Patience, and Industrial Training for the masses, we must hold up his hands and strive with him, rejoicing in his honors and glorying in the strength of this Joshua[79] called of God and of man to lead the headless host. But so far as Mr. Washington apologizes for injustice, North or South, does not rightly value the privilege and duty of voting, belittles the emasculating effects of caste distinctions, and opposes the higher training and ambition of our brighter minds – so far as he, the South, or the Nation, does this – we must unceasingly and firmly oppose them. By every civilized and peaceful method we must strive for the rights which the world accords to men, clinging unwaveringly to those great words which the sons of the Fathers would fain forget: "We hold these truths to be self-evident: That all men are created equal; that they are endowed by their Creator with certain unalienable rights; that among these are life, liberty, and the pursuit of happiness."

Notes

[79] *Joshua* biblical figure who, after the death of Moses, led the Israelites into the Promised Land.

Chapter 4

Of the Meaning of Progress

Willst Du Deine Macht verkünden,
Wähle sie die frei von Sünden,
Steh'n in Deinem ew'gen Haus!
Deine Geister sende aus!
Die Unsterblichen, die Reinen,
Die nicht fühlen, die nicht weinen!
Nicht die zarte Jungfrau wähle,
Nicht der Hirtin weiche Seele!

Schiller.[80]

Once upon a time I taught school in the hills of Tennessee, where the broad dark vale of the Mississippi begins to roll and crumple to greet the Alleghanies. I was a Fisk student then, and all Fisk men thought that Tennessee – beyond the Veil – was theirs alone, and in vacation time they sallied forth in lusty bands to meet the county school-commissioners. Young and happy, I too went, and I shall not soon forget that summer, seventeen years ago.

First, there was a Teachers' Institute at the county-seat; and there distinguished guests of the superintendent taught the teachers fractions and spelling and other mysteries – white teachers in the morning, Negroes at night. A picnic now and then, and a supper, and the rough world was softened by laughter and song. I remember how – But I wander.

There came a day when all the teachers left the Institute and began the hunt for schools. I learn from hearsay (for my mother was mortally afraid of fire-arms) that the hunting of ducks and bears and men is wonderfully interesting, but I am sure that the man who has never hunted a country school has something to learn of the pleasures of the chase. I see now the white, hot roads lazily rise and fall and wind before me under the burning July sun; I feel the deep weariness of heart and limb as ten, eight, six miles stretch relentlessly ahead; I feel my heart sink heavily as I hear again and again, "Got a teacher? Yes." So I walked on and on – horses were too expensive – until I had wandered beyond railways, beyond stage lines, to a land of "varmints" and rattlesnakes, where the coming of a stranger was an event, and men lived and died in the shadow of one blue hill.

Sprinkled over hill and dale lay cabins and farmhouses, shut out from the world by the forests and the rolling hills toward the east. There I found at last a little school. Josie told me of it; she was a thin, homely girl of twenty, with a dark-brown face and thick, hard hair. I had crossed the stream at Watertown,[81] and rested under the great willows;

Notes

[80] Friedrich von Schiller (1759–1805), German poet. The lines come from "The Maid of Orleans" (1801).

[81] *Watertown* a town in eastern Tennessee.

then I had gone to the little cabin in the lot where Josie was resting on her way to town. The gaunt farmer made me welcome, and Josie, hearing my errand, told me anxiously that they wanted a school over the hill; that but once since the war had a teacher been there; that she herself longed to learn – and thus she ran on, talking fast and loud, with much earnestness and energy.

Next morning I crossed the tall round hill, lingered to look at the blue and yellow mountains stretching toward the Carolinas, then plunged into the wood, and came out at Josie's home. It was a dull frame cottage with four rooms, perched just below the brow of the hill, amid peach-trees. The father was a quiet, simple soul, calmly ignorant, with no touch of vulgarity. The mother was different – strong, bustling, and energetic, with a quick, restless tongue, and an ambition to live "like folks." There was a crowd of children. Two boys had gone away. There remained two growing girls; a shy midget of eight; John, tall, awkward, and eighteen; Jim, younger, quicker, and better looking; and two babies of indefinite age. Then there was Josie herself. She seemed to be the centre of the family: always busy at service, or at home, or berry-picking; a little nervous and inclined to scold, like her mother, yet faithful, too, like her father. She had about her a certain fineness, the shadow of an unconscious moral heroism that would willingly give all of life to make life broader, deeper, and fuller for her and hers. I saw much of this family afterwards, and grew to love them for their honest efforts to be decent and comfortable, and for their knowledge of their own ignorance. There was with them no affectation. The mother would scold the father for being so "easy"; Josie would roundly berate the boys for carelessness; and all knew that it was a hard thing to dig a living out of a rocky side-hill.

I secured the school. I remember the day I rode horseback out to the commissioner's house with a pleasant young white fellow who wanted the white school. The road ran down the bed of a stream; the sun laughed and the water jingled, and we rode on. "Come in," said the commissioner – "come in. Have a seat. Yes, that certificate will do. Stay to dinner. What do you want a month?" "Oh," thought I, "this is lucky"; but even then fell the awful shadow of the Veil, for they ate first, then I – alone.

The schoolhouse was a log hut, where Colonel Wheeler used to shelter his corn. It sat in a lot behind a rail fence and thorn bushes, near the sweetest of springs. There was an entrance where a door once was, and within, a massive rickety fireplace; great chinks between the logs served as windows. Furniture was scarce. A pale blackboard crouched in the corner. My desk was made of three boards, reinforced at critical points, and my chair, borrowed from the landlady, had to be returned every night. Seats for the children – these puzzled me much. I was haunted by a New England vision of neat little desks and chairs, but, alas! the reality was rough plank benches without backs, and at times without legs. They had the one virtue of making naps dangerous – possibly fatal, for the floor was not to be trusted.

It was a hot morning late in July when the school opened. I trembled when I heard the patter of little feet down the dusty road, and saw the growing row of dark solemn faces and bright eager eyes facing me. First came Josie and her brothers and sisters. The longing to know, to be a student in the great school at Nashville, hovered like a star above this child-woman amid her work and worry, and she studied doggedly. There were the Dowells from their farm over toward Alexandria – Fanny, with her smooth black face and wondering eyes; Martha, brown and dull; the pretty girl-wife of a brother, and the younger brood.

There were the Burkes – two brown and yellow lads, and a tiny haughty-eyed girl. Fat Reuben's little chubby girl came, with golden face and old-gold hair, faithful and solemn. 'Thenie was on hand early – a jolly, ugly, good-hearted girl, who slyly dipped snuff[82] and looked after her little bow-legged brother. When her mother could spare her, 'Tildy came – a midnight beauty, with starry eyes and tapering limbs; and her brother, correspondingly homely. And then the big boys – the hulking Lawrences; the lazy Neills, unfathered sons of mother and daughter; Hickman, with a stoop in his shoulders; and the rest.

There they sat, nearly thirty of them, on the rough benches, their faces shading from a pale cream to a deep brown, the little feet bare and swinging, the eyes full of expectation, with here and there a twinkle of mischief, and the hands grasping Webster's blue-back spelling-book.[83] I loved my school, and the fine faith the children had in the wisdom of their teacher was truly marvellous. We read and spelled together, wrote a little, picked flowers, sang, and listened to stories of the world beyond the hill. At times the school would dwindle away, and I would start out. I would visit Mun Eddings, who lived in two very dirty rooms, and ask why little Lugene, whose flaming face seemed ever ablaze with the dark-red hair uncombed, was absent all last week, or why I missed so often the inimitable rags of Mack and Ed. Then the father, who worked Colonel Wheeler's farm on shares, would tell me how the crops needed the boys; and the thin, slovenly mother, whose face was pretty when washed, assured me that Lugene must mind the baby. "But we'll start them again next week." When the Lawrences stopped, I knew that the doubts of the old folks about book-learning had conquered again, and so, toiling up the hill, and getting as far into the cabin as possible, I put Cicero "pro Archia Poeta"[84] into the simplest English with local applications, and usually convinced them – for a week or so.

On Friday nights I often went home with some of the children – sometimes to Doc Burke's farm. He was a great, loud, thin Black, ever working, and trying to buy the seventy-five acres of hill and dale where he lived; but people said that he would surely fail, and the "white folks would get it all." His wife was a magnificent Amazon,[85] with saffron face and shining hair, uncorseted and barefooted, and the children were strong and beautiful. They lived in a one-and-a-half-room cabin in the hollow of the farm, near the spring. The front room was full of great fat white beds, scrupulously neat; and there were bad chromos[86] on the walls, and a tired centre-table. In the tiny back kitchen I was often invited to "take out and help" myself to fried chicken and wheat biscuit, "meat" and corn pone, string-beans and berries. At first I used to be a little alarmed at the approach of bedtime in the one lone bedroom, but embarrassment was very deftly avoided. First, all the children nodded and slept, and were stowed away in one great pile of goose feathers; next, the mother and the father discreetly slipped away to the kitchen while I went to bed; then, blowing out the dim light, they retired in the dark. In the morning all were up and away before I thought of awaking. Across the road, where fat Reuben lived, they all went outdoors while the teacher retired, because they did not boast the luxury of a kitchen.

I liked to stay with the Dowells, for they had four rooms and plenty of good country fare. Uncle Bird had a small, rough farm, all woods and hills, miles from the big road; but he was full of tales – he preached now and then – and with his children, berries, horses, and wheat he was happy and prosperous. Often, to keep the peace, I must go

Notes

82 *snuff* powdered tobacco.

83 *Webster's blue-black spelling-book* Noah Webster (1758–1843) was an American lexicographer instrumental in systematizing language and scholarship in the United States; his *Spelling* book first appeared in 1783.

84 *Cicero "pro Archia Poeta"* Marcus Tullius Cicero (106–43 BC) was a Roman statesman and orator.

85 *Amazon* tall and strong woman.

86 *chromos* lithograph pictures.

where life was less lovely; for instance, 'Tildy's mother was incorrigibly dirty, Reuben's larder was limited seriously, and herds of untamed insects wandered over the Eddingses' beds. Best of all I loved to go to Josie's, and sit on the porch, eating peaches, while the mother bustled and talked: how Josie had bought the sewing-machine; how Josie worked at service in winter, but that four dollars a month was "mighty little" wages; how Josie longed to go away to school, but that it "looked like" they never could get far enough ahead to let her; how the crops failed and the well was yet unfinished; and, finally, how "mean" some of the white folks were.

For two summers I lived in this little world; it was dull and humdrum. The girls looked at the hill in wistful longing, and the boys fretted and haunted Alexandria. Alexandria was "town" – a straggling, lazy village of houses, churches, and shops, and an aristocracy of Toms, Dicks, and Captains. Cuddled on the hill to the north was the village of the colored folks, who lived in three- or four-room unpainted cottages, some neat and homelike, and some dirty. The dwellings were scattered rather aimlessly, but they centred about the twin temples of the hamlet, the Methodist, and the Hard-Shell Baptist churches. These, in turn, leaned gingerly on a sad-colored schoolhouse. Hither my little world wended its crooked way on Sunday to meet other worlds, and gossip, and wonder, and make the weekly sacrifice with frenzied priest at the altar of the "old-time religion." Then the soft melody and mighty cadences of Negro song fluttered and thundered.

I have called my tiny community a world, and so its isolation made it; and yet there was among us but a half-awakened common consciousness, sprung from common joy and grief, at burial, birth, or wedding; from a common hardship in poverty, poor land, and low wages; and, above all, from the sight of the Veil that hung between us and Opportunity. All this caused us to think some thoughts together; but these, when ripe for speech, were spoken in various languages. Those whose eyes twenty-five and more years before had seen "the glory of the coming of the Lord,"[87] saw in every present hindrance or help a dark fatalism bound to bring all things right in His own good time. The mass of those to whom slavery was a dim recollection of childhood found the world a puzzling thing: it asked little of them, and they answered with little, and yet it ridiculed their offering. Such a paradox they could not understand, and therefore sank into listless indifference, or shiftlessness, or reckless bravado. There were, however, some – such as Josie, Jim, and Ben – to whom War, Hell, and Slavery were but childhood tales, whose young appetites had been whetted to an edge by school and story and half-awakened thought. Ill could they be content, born without and beyond the World. And their weak wings beat against their barriers – barriers of caste, of youth, of life; at last, in dangerous moments, against everything that opposed even a whim.

The ten years that follow youth, the years when first the realization comes that life is leading somewhere – these were the years that passed after I left my little school. When they were past, I came by chance once more to the walls of Fisk University, to the halls of the chapel of melody. As I lingered there in the joy and pain of meeting old school-friends, there swept over me a sudden longing to pass again beyond the blue hill, and to see the homes and the school of other days, and to learn how life had gone with my school-children; and I went.

Josie was dead, and the gray-haired mother said simply, "We've had a heap of trouble since you've been away." I had feared for Jim. With a cultured parentage and a

Notes

[87] *"the glory of the coming of the Lord"* from "The Battle Hymn of the Republic" (1861), by Julia Ward Howe (1819–1910).

social caste to uphold him, he might have made a venturesome merchant or a West Point cadet. But here he was, angry with life and reckless; and when Farmer Durham charged him with stealing wheat, the old man had to ride fast to escape the stones which the furious fool hurled after him. They told Jim to run away; but he would not run, and the constable came that afternoon. It grieved Josie, and great awkward John walked nine miles every day to see his little brother through the bars of Lebanon jail. At last the two came back together in the dark night. The mother cooked supper, and Josie emptied her purse, and the boys stole away. Josie grew thin and silent, yet worked the more. The hill became steep for the quiet old father, and with the boys away there was little to do in the valley. Josie helped them to sell the old farm, and they moved nearer town. Brother Dennis, the carpenter, built a new house with six rooms; Josie toiled a year in Nashville, and brought back ninety dollars to furnish the house and change it to a home.

When the spring came, and the birds twittered, and the stream ran proud and full, little sister Lizzie, bold and thoughtless, flushed with the passion of youth, bestowed herself on the tempter, and brought home a nameless child. Josie shivered and worked on, with the vision of schooldays all fled, with a face wan and tired – worked until, on a summer's day, someone married another; then Josie crept to her mother like a hurt child, and slept – and sleeps.

I paused to scent the breeze as I entered the valley. The Lawrences have gone – father and son forever – and the other son lazily digs in the earth to live. A new young widow rents out their cabin to fat Reuben. Reuben is a Baptist preacher now, but I fear as lazy as ever, though his cabin has three rooms; and little Ella has grown into a bouncing woman, and is ploughing corn on the hot hillside. There are babies a-plenty, and one half-witted girl. Across the valley is a house I did not know before, and there I found, rocking one baby and expecting another, one of my schoolgirls, a daughter of Uncle Bird Dowell. She looked somewhat worried with her new duties, but soon bristled into pride over her neat cabin and the tale of her thrifty husband, the horse and cow, and the farm they were planning to buy.

My log schoolhouse was gone. In its place stood Progress; and Progress, I understand, is necessarily ugly. The crazy foundation stones still marked the former site of my poor little cabin, and not far away, on six weary boulders, perched a jaunty board house, perhaps twenty by thirty feet, with three windows and a door that locked. Some of the window-glass was broken, and part of an old iron stove lay mournfully under the house. I peeped through the window half reverently, and found things that were more familiar. The blackboard had grown by about two feet, and the seats were still without backs. The county owns the lot now, I hear, and every year there is a session of school. As I sat by the spring and looked on the Old and the New I felt glad, very glad, and yet–

After two long drinks I started on. There was the great double log-house on the corner. I remembered the broken, blighted family that used to live there. The strong, hard face of the mother, with its wilderness of hair, rose before me. She had driven her husband away, and while I taught school a strange man lived there, big and jovial, and people talked. I felt sure that Ben and 'Tildy would come to naught from such a home. But this is an odd world; for Ben is a busy farmer in Smith County, "doing well, too," they say, and he had cared for little 'Tildy until last spring, when a lover married her. A hard life the lad had led, toiling for meat, and laughed at because he was homely and crooked. There was Sam Carlon, an impudent old skinflint, who had definite notions about "niggers," and hired Ben a summer and would not pay him. Then the hungry boy gathered his sacks together, and in broad daylight went into Carlon's corn; and when the hard-fisted farmer set upon him, the angry boy flew at him like a beast. Doc Burke saved a murder and a lynching that day.

The story reminded me again of the Burkes, and an impatience seized me to know who won in the battle, Doc or the seventy-five acres. For it is a hard thing to make a farm out of nothing, even in fifteen years. So I hurried on, thinking of the Burkes. They used to have a certain magnificent barbarism about them that I liked. They were never vulgar, never immoral, but rather rough and primitive, with an unconventionality that spent itself in loud guffaws, slaps on the back, and naps in the corner. I hurried by the cottage of the misborn Neill boys. It was empty, and they were grown into fat, lazy farm-hands. I saw the home of the Hickmans, but Albert, with his stooping shoulders, had passed from the world. Then I came to the Burkes' gate and peered through; the inclosure looked rough and untrimmed, and yet there were the same fences around the old farm save to the left, where lay twenty-five other acres. And lo! the cabin in the hollow had climbed the hill and swollen to a half-finished six-room cottage.

The Burkes held a hundred acres, but they were still in debt. Indeed, the gaunt father who toiled night and day would scarcely be happy out of debt, being so used to it. Some day he must stop, for his massive frame is showing decline. The mother wore shoes, but the lion-like physique of other days was broken. The children had grown up. Rob, the image of his father, was loud and rough with laughter. Birdie, my school baby of six, had grown to a picture of maiden beauty, tall and tawny. "Edgar is gone," said the mother, with head half bowed – "gone to work in Nashville; he and his father couldn't agree."

Little Doc, the boy born since the time of my school, took me on horseback[88] down the creek next morning toward Farmer Dowell's. The road and the stream were battling for mastery, and the stream had the better of it. We splashed and waded, and the merry boy, perched behind me, chattered and laughed. He showed me where Simon Thompson had bought a bit of ground and a home; but his daughter Lana, a plump, brown, slow girl, was not there. She had married a man and a farm twenty miles away. We wound on down the stream till we came to a gate that I did not recognize, but the boy insisted that it was "Uncle Bird's." The farm was fat with the growing crop. In that little valley was a strange stillness as I rode up; for death and marriage had stolen youth and left age and childhood there. We sat and talked that night after the chores were done. Uncle Bird was grayer, and his eyes did not see so well, but he was still jovial. We talked of the acres bought – one hundred and twenty-five – of the new guest-chamber added, of Martha's marrying. Then we talked of death: Fanny and Fred were gone; a shadow hung over the other daughter, and when it lifted she was to go to Nashville to school. At last we spoke of the neighbors, and as night fell, Uncle Bird told me how, on a night like that, 'Thenie came wandering back to her home over yonder, to escape the blows of her husband. And next morning she died in the home that her little bow-legged brother, working and saving, had bought for their widowed mother.

My journey was done, and behind me lay hill and dale, and Life and Death. How shall man measure Progress there where the dark-faced Josie lies? How many heartfuls of sorrow shall balance a bushel of wheat? How hard a thing is life to the lowly, and yet how human and real! And all this life and love and strife and failure – is it the twilight of nightfall or the flush of some faint-dawning day?

Thus sadly musing, I rode to Nashville in the Jim Crow car.[89]

Notes

[88] *Original reads*: took me horseback [ed.].

[89] *Jim Crow car* segregated car for African Americans.

Chapter 5

Of the Wings of Atalanta

O black boy of Atlanta!
But half was spoken;
The slave's chains and the master's
Alike are broken;
The one curse of the races
Held both in tether;
They are rising – all are rising –
The black and white together.
Whittier.[90]

South of the North, yet north of the South, lies the City of a Hundred Hills, peering out from the shadows of the past into the promise of the future. I have seen her in the morning, when the first flush of day had half-roused her; she lay gray and still on the crimson soil of Georgia; then the blue smoke began to curl from her chimneys, the tinkle of bell and scream of whistle broke the silence, the rattle and roar of busy life slowly gathered and swelled, until the seething whirl of the city seemed a strange thing in a sleepy land.

Once, they say, even Atlanta slept dull and drowsy at the foot-hills of the Alleghanies, until the iron baptism of war awakened her with its sullen waters, aroused and maddened her, and left her listening to the sea. And the sea cried to the hills and the hills answered the sea, till the city rose like a widow and cast away her weeds, and toiled for her daily bread; toiled steadily, toiled cunningly – perhaps with some bitterness, with a touch of *réclame*[91] – and yet with real earnestness, and real sweat.

It is a hard thing to live haunted by the ghost of an untrue dream; to see the wide vision of empire fade into real ashes and dirt; to feel the pang of the conquered, and yet know that with all the Bad that fell on one black day, something was vanquished that deserved to live, something killed that injustice had not dared to die; to know that with the Right that triumphed, triumphed something of Wrong, something sordid and mean, something less than the broadest and best. All this is bitter hard; and many a man and city and people have found in it excuse for sulking, and brooding, and listless waiting.

Such are not men of the sturdier make; they of Atlanta turned resolutely toward the future; and that future held aloft vistas of purple and gold:– Atlanta, Queen of the cotton kingdom; Atlanta, Gateway to the Land of the Sun; Atlanta, the new Lachesis, spinner of web and woof[92] for the world. So the city crowned her hundred hills with factories, and stored her shops with cunning handiwork, and stretched long iron ways to greet the busy Mercury[93] in his coming. And the Nation talked of her striving.

Notes

[90] John Greenleaf Whittier (1807–1892), American poet and abolitionist; the lines quoted are from "Howard at Atlanta" (1869).

[91] *réclame* (French) publicity.

[92] *Lachesis, spinner of the web and woof* in Greek mythology, one of the Three Fates, who determines the destiny of lives.

[93] *Mercury* the Roman god of commerce.

Perhaps Atlanta was not christened for the winged maiden of dull Bœotia;[94] you know the tale – how swarthy Atalanta, tall and wild, would marry only him who outraced her; and how the wily Hippomenes[95] laid three apples of gold in the way. She fled like a shadow, paused, startled over the first apple, but even as he stretched his hand, fled again; hovered over the second, then, slipping from his hot grasp, flew over river, vale, and hill; but as she lingered over the third, his arms fell round her, and looking on each other, the blazing passion of their love profaned the sanctuary of Love, and they were cursed. If Atlanta be not named for Atalanta, she ought to have been.

Atalanta is not the first or the last maiden whom greed of gold has led to defile the temple of Love; and not maids alone, but men in the race of life, sink from the high and generous ideals of youth to the gambler's code of the Bourse;[96] and in all our Nation's striving is not the Gospel of Work befouled by the Gospel of Pay? So common is this that one-half think it normal; so unquestioned, that we almost fear to question if the end of racing is not gold, if the aim of man is not rightly to be rich. And if this is the fault of America, how dire a danger lies before a new land and a new city, lest Atlanta, stooping for mere gold, shall find that gold accursed!

It was no maiden's idle whim that started this hard racing; a fearful wilderness lay about the feet of that city after the War – feudalism, poverty, the rise of the Third Estate,[97] serfdom, the re-birth of Law and Order, and above and between all, the Veil of Race. How heavy a journey for weary feet! what wings must Atalanta have to flit over all this hollow and hill, through sour wood and sullen water, and by the red waste of sun-baked clay! How fleet must Atalanta be if she will not be tempted by gold to profane the Sanctuary!

The Sanctuary of our fathers has, to be sure, few Gods – some sneer, "all too few." There is the thrifty Mercury of New England, Pluto of the North, and Ceres of the West; and there, too, is the half-forgotten Apollo of the South, under whose ægis the maiden ran – and as she ran she forgot him, even as there in Bœotia Venus was forgot.[98] She forgot the old ideal of the Southern gentleman – that new-world heir of the grace and courtliness of patrician, knight, and noble; forgot his honor with his foibles, his kindliness with his carelessness, and stooped to apples of gold – to men busier and sharper, thriftier and more unscrupulous. Golden apples are beautiful – I remember the lawless days of boyhood, when orchards in crimson and gold tempted me over fence and field – and, too, the merchant who has dethroned the planter is no despicable *parvenu*.[99] Work and wealth are the mighty levers to lift this old new land; thrift and toil and saving are the highways to new hopes and new possibilities; and yet the warning is needed lest the wily Hippomenes tempt Atalanta to thinking that golden apples are the goal of racing, and not mere incidents by the way.

Atlanta must not lead the South to dream of material prosperity as the touchstone of all success; already the fatal might of this idea is beginning to spread; it is replacing the finer type of Southerner with vulgar money-getters; it is burying the sweeter beauties of Southern life beneath pretence and ostentation. For every social ill the panacea of Wealth has been urged – wealth to overthrow the remains of the slave feudalism; wealth to raise the "cracker"[100] Third Estate; wealth to employ the black serfs, and the prospect of wealth to keep them working; wealth as the end and aim of politics, and

Notes

[94] *Bœotia* a region in central Greece.

[95] *Hippomenes* Greek mythology states that Hippomenes, the youthful descendant of Poseidon, god of the sea, fell in love with Atalanta.

[96] *Bourse* the stock market.

[97] *Third Estate* middle class.

[98] *Pluto ... Ceres ... Apollo ... Bœtia Venus* the Roman god of the underworld, the Roman goddess of farming, the Greek god of music and poetry, the Roman goddess of love, respectively.

[99] *parvenu* one who has only recently become wealthy.

[100] *cracker* low-class white person.

as the legal tender for law and order; and, finally, instead of Truth, Beauty, and Goodness, wealth as the ideal of the Public School.

Not only is this true in the world which Atlanta typifies, but it is threatening to be true of a world beneath and beyond that world – the Black World beyond the Veil. To-day it makes little difference to Atlanta, to the South, what the Negro thinks or dreams or wills. In the soul-life of the land he is to-day, and naturally will long remain, unthought of, half forgotten; and yet when he does come to think and will and do for himself – and let no man dream that day will never come – then the part he plays will not be one of sudden learning, but words and thoughts he has been taught to lisp in his race-childhood. To-day the ferment of his striving toward self-realization is to the strife of the white world like a wheel within a wheel: beyond the Veil are smaller but like problems of ideals, of leaders and the led, of serfdom, of poverty, of order and subordination, and, through all, the Veil of Race. Few know of these problems, few who know notice them; and yet there they are, awaiting student, artist, and seer – a field for somebody sometime to discover. Hither has the temptation of Hippomenes penetrated; already in this smaller world, which now indirectly and anon directly must influence the larger for good or ill, the habit is forming of interpreting the world in dollars. The old leaders of Negro opinion, in the little groups where there is a Negro social consciousness, are being replaced by new; neither the black preacher nor the black teacher leads as he did two decades ago. Into their places are pushing the farmers and gardeners, the well-paid porters and artisans, the businessmen – all those with property and money. And with all this change, so curiously parallel to that of the Other-world, goes too the same inevitable change in ideals. The South laments to-day the slow, steady disappearance of a certain type of Negro – the faithful, courteous slave of other days, with his incorruptible honesty and dignified humility. He is passing away just as surely as the old type of Southern gentleman is passing, and from not dissimilar causes – the sudden transformation of a fair far-off ideal of Freedom into the hard reality of bread-winning and the consequent deification of Bread.

In the Black World, the Preacher and Teacher embodied once the ideals of this people – the strife for another and a juster[101] world, the vague dream of righteousness, the mystery of knowing; but to-day the danger is that these ideals, with their simple beauty and weird inspiration, will suddenly sink to a question of cash and a lust for gold. Here stands this black young Atalanta, girding herself for the race that must be run; and if her eyes be still toward the hills and sky as in the days of old, then we may look for noble running; but what if some ruthless or wily or even thoughtless Hippomenes lay golden apples before her? What if the Negro people be wooed from a strife for righteousness, from a love of knowing, to regard dollars as the be-all and end-all of life? What if to the Mammonism[102] of America be added the rising Mammonism of the re-born South, and the Mammonism of this South be reinforced by the budding Mammonism of its half-awakened black millions? Whither, then, is the new-world quest of Goodness and Beauty and Truth gone glimmering? Must this, and that fair flower of Freedom which, despite the jeers of latter-day striplings, sprang[103] from our fathers' blood, must that too degenerate into a dusty quest of gold – into lawless lust with Hippomenes?

The hundred hills of Atlanta are not all crowned with factories. On one, toward the west, the setting sun throws three buildings in bold relief against the sky. The beauty of the group lies in its simple unity:– a broad lawn of green rising from the red street with mingled roses and peaches; north and south, two plain and stately halls; and in the midst, half hidden in ivy, a larger building, boldly graceful, sparingly decorated, and with one low

Notes

[101] *juster* more just.

[102] *Mammonism* the worship of riches.

[103] *Original reads*: sprung [ed.].

spire. It is a restful group – one never looks for more; it is all here, all intelligible. There I live, and there I hear from day to day the low hum of restful life. In winter's twilight, when the red sun glows, I can see the dark figures pass between the halls to the music of the night-bell. In the morning, when the sun is golden, the clang of the day-bell brings the hurry and laughter of three hundred young hearts from hall and street, and from the busy city below – children all dark and heavy-haired – to join their clear young voices in the music of the morning sacrifice. In a half-dozen class-rooms they gather then – here to follow the Love-song of Dido, here to listen to the tale of Troy divine;[104] there to wander among the stars, there to wander among men and nations – and elsewhere other well-worn ways of knowing this queer world. Nothing new, no time-saving devices – simply old time-glorified methods of delving for Truth, and searching out the hidden beauties of life, and learning the good of living. The riddle of existence is the college curriculum that was laid before the Pharaohs, that was taught in the groves by Plato,[105] that formed the *trivium* and *quadrivium*[106] and is to-day laid before the freedmen's sons by Atlanta University. And this course of study will not change; its methods will grow more deft and effectual, its content richer by toil of scholar and sight of seer; but the true college will ever have one goal – not to earn meat, but to know the end and aim of that life which meat nourishes.

The vision of life that rises before these dark eyes has in it nothing mean or selfish. Not at Oxford or at Leipsic, not at Yale or Columbia, [107] is there an air of higher resolve or more unfettered striving; the determination to realize for men, both black and white, the broadest possibilities of life, to seek the better and the best, to spread with their own hands the Gospel of Sacrifice – all this is the burden of their talk and dream. Here, amid a wide desert of caste and proscription, amid the heart-hurting slights and jars and vagaries of a deep race-dislike, lies this green oasis, where hot anger cools, and the bitterness of disappointment is sweetened by the springs and breezes of Parnassus;[108] and here men may lie and listen, and learn of a future fuller than the past, and hear the voice of Time:

> "Entbehren sollst du, sollst entbehren."[109]

They made their mistakes, those who planted Fisk and Howard and Atlanta before the smoke of battle had lifted; they made their mistakes, but those mistakes were not the things at which we lately laughed somewhat uproariously. They were right when they sought to found a new educational system upon the University: where, forsooth, shall we ground knowledge save on the broadest and deepest knowledge? The roots of the tree, rather than the leaves, are the sources of its life; and from the dawn of history, from Academus to Cambridge,[110] the culture of the University has been the broad foundation-stone on which is built the kindergarten's A B C.

But these builders did make a mistake in minimizing the gravity of the problem before them; in thinking it a matter of years and decades; in therefore building quickly and laying their foundation carelessly, and lowering the standard of knowing, until they had scattered haphazard through the South some dozen poorly equipped high

Notes

[104] *the Love-song of Dido… the tale of Troy divine* Virgil's *The Aeneid* and Homer's *The Iliad*, respectively; epic poems of antiquity.

[105] Plato (427–348 BC), Greek philosopher.

[106] *trivium and quadrivium* the seven liberal arts of the Renaissance (grammar, logic, and rhetoric; arithmetic, geometry, music, and astronomy).

[107] *Oxford or at Leipsic, not at Yale or Columbia* preeminent universities in England, Germany (Leipzig), Connecticut, and New York, respectively.

[108] *Parnassus* mountain in Greece, in legend the home of the Muses.

[109] *"Entbehren … entbehren"* (German) "Deny yourself, you must deny yourself." A line from Johann Wolfgang von Goethe's (1749–1832) tragic play *Faust* (1808).

[110] *from Academus to Cambridge* from Plato's Academy (in ancient Athens) to Harvard University (in Cambridge, Massachusetts).

schools and miscalled them universities. They forgot, too, just as their successors are forgetting, the rule of inequality:– that of the million black youth, some were fitted to know and some to dig; that some had the talent and capacity of university men, and some the talent and capacity of blacksmiths; and that true training meant neither that all should be college men nor all artisans, but that the one should be made a missionary of culture to an untaught people, and the other a free workman among serfs. And to seek to make the blacksmith a scholar is almost as silly as the more modern scheme of making the scholar a blacksmith; almost, but not quite.

The function of the university is not simply to teach bread-winning, or to furnish teachers for the public schools, or to be a centre of polite society; it is, above all, to be the organ of that fine adjustment between real life and the growing knowledge of life, an adjustment which forms the secret of civilization. Such an institution the South of to-day sorely needs. She has religion, earnest, bigoted:– religion that on both sides the Veil often omits the sixth, seventh, and eighth commandments,[111] but substitutes a dozen supplementary ones. She has, as Atlanta shows, growing thrift and love of toil; but she lacks that broad knowledge of what the world knows and knew of human living and doing, which she may apply to the thousand problems of real life to-day confronting her. The need of the South is knowledge and culture – not in dainty limited quantity, as before the war, but in broad busy abundance in the world of work; and until she has this, not all the Apples of Hesperides,[112] be they golden and bejewelled, can save her from the curse of the Bœotian lovers.

The Wings of Atalanta are the coming universities of the South. They alone can bear the maiden past the temptation of golden fruit. They will not guide her flying feet away from the cotton and gold; for – ah, thoughtful Hippomenes! – do not the apples lie in the very Way of Life? But they will guide her over and beyond them, and leave her kneeling in the Sanctuary of Truth and Freedom and broad Humanity, virgin and undefiled. Sadly did the Old South err in human education, despising the education of the masses, and niggardly in the support of colleges. Her ancient university foundations dwindled and withered under the foul breath of slavery; and even since the war they have fought a failing fight for life in the tainted air of social unrest and commercial selfishness, stunted by the death of criticism, and starving for lack of broadly cultured men. And if this is the white South's need and danger, how much heavier the danger and need of the freedmen's sons! how pressing here the need of broad ideals and true culture, the conservation of soul from sordid aims and petty passions! Let us build the Southern university – William and Mary, Trinity, Georgia, Texas, Tulane, Vanderbilt, and the others – fit to live; let us build, too, the Negro universities: Fisk, whose foundation was ever broad; Howard, at the heart of the Nation; Atlanta at Atlanta, whose ideal of scholarship has been held above the temptation of numbers. Why not here, and perhaps elsewhere, plant deeply and for all time centres of learning and living, colleges that yearly would send into the life of the South a few white men and a few black men of broad culture, catholic tolerance, and trained ability, joining their hands to other hands, and giving to this squabble of the Races a decent and dignified peace?

Patience, Humility, Manners, and Taste, common schools and kindergartens, industrial and technical schools, literature and tolerance – all these spring from knowledge and culture, the children of the university. So must men and nations build, not otherwise, not upside down.

Notes

[111] *The sixth, seventh and eighth commandments* from The Ten Commandments, those forbidding killing, adultery, and theft.

[112] *Hesperides* in Greek mythology, nymphs living in the gardens of the Arcadian Mountains or Mount Atlas.

Teach workers to work – a wise saying; wise when applied to German boys and American girls; wiser when said of Negro boys, for they have less knowledge of working and none to teach them. Teach thinkers to think – a needed knowledge in a day of loose and careless logic; and they whose lot is gravest must have the most careful[113] training to think aright. If these things are so, how foolish to ask what is the best education for one or seven or sixty million souls! shall we teach them trades, or train them in liberal arts? Neither and both: teach the workers to work and the thinkers to think; make carpenters of carpenters, and philosophers of philosophers, and fops of fools. Nor can we pause here. We are training not isolated men but a living group of men – nay, a group within a group. And the final product of our training must be neither a psychologist nor a brickmason, but a man. And to make men, we must have ideals, broad, pure, and inspiring ends of living – not sordid money-getting, not apples of gold. The worker must work for the glory of his handiwork, not simply for pay; the thinker must think for truth, not for fame. And all this is gained only by human strife and longing; by ceaseless training and education; by founding Right on righteousness and Truth on the unhampered search for Truth; by founding the common school on the university, and the industrial school on the common school; and weaving thus a system, not a distortion, and bringing a birth, not an abortion.

When night falls on the City of a Hundred Hills, a wind gathers itself from the seas and comes murmuring westward. And at its bidding, the smoke of the drowsy factories sweeps down upon the mighty city and covers it like a pall, while yonder at the University the stars twinkle above Stone Hall. And they say that yon gray mist is the tunic of Atalanta pausing over her golden apples. Fly, my maiden, fly, for yonder comes Hippomenes!

Chapter 6

Of the Training of Black Men

Why, if the Soul can fling the Dust aside,
And naked on the Air of Heaven ride,
Were't not a Shame – were't not a Shame for him
In this clay carcase crippled to abide?
Omar Khayyám (Fitzgerald).[114]

Notes

[113] *Original reads*: carefulest [ed.].

[114] Omar Khayyám (*c.*1048–1131), Persian poet and polymath, whose *Rubaiyat of Omar Khayyám* was translated into English in 1859 by Edward FitzGerald.

From the shimmering swirl of waters where many, many thoughts ago the slave-ship first saw the square tower of Jamestown,[115] have flowed down to our day three streams of thinking: one swollen from the larger world here and overseas, saying, the multiplying of human wants in culture-lands calls for the world-wide cooperation of men in satisfying them. Hence arises a new human unity, pulling the ends of earth nearer, and all men, black, yellow, and white. The larger humanity strives to feel in this contact of living Nations and sleeping hordes a thrill of new life in the world, crying, "If the contact of Life and Sleep be Death, shame on such Life." To be sure, behind this thought lurks the afterthought of force and dominion – the making of brown men to delve when the temptation of beads and red calico cloys.

The second thought streaming from the death-ship and the curving river is the thought of the older South – the sincere, and passionate belief that somewhere between men and cattle, God created a *tertium quid*,[116] and called it a Negro – a clownish, simple creature, at times even lovable within its limitations, but straitly foreordained to walk within the Veil. To be sure, behind the thought lurks the afterthought – some of them with favoring chance might become men, but in sheer self-defence we dare not let them, and we build about them walls so high, and hang between them and the light a veil so thick, that they shall not even think of breaking through.

And last of all there trickles down that third and darker thought – the thought of the things themselves, the confused, half-conscious mutter of men who are black and whitened, crying "Liberty, Freedom, Opportunity – vouchsafe to us, O boastful World, the chance of living men!" To be sure, behind the thought lurks the afterthought – suppose, after all, the World is right and we are less than men? Suppose this mad impulse within is all wrong, some mock mirage from the untrue?

So here we stand among thoughts of human unity, even through conquest and slavery; the inferiority of black men, even if forced by fraud; a shriek in the night for the freedom of men who themselves are not yet sure of their right to demand it. This is the tangle of thought and afterthought wherein we are called to solve the problem of training men for life.

Behind all its curiousness, so attractive alike to sage and *dilettante*,[117] lie its dim dangers, throwing across us shadows at once grotesque and awful. Plain it is to us that what the world seeks through desert and wild we have within our threshold – a stalwart laboring force, suited to the semitropics; if, deaf to the voice of the Zeitgeist,[118] we refuse to use and develop these men, we risk poverty and loss. If, on the other hand, seized by the brutal afterthought, we debauch the race thus caught in our talons, selfishly sucking their blood and brains in the future as in the past, what shall save us from national decadence? Only that saner selfishness, which Education teaches men, can find the rights of all in the whirl of work.

Again, we may decry the color-prejudice of the South, yet it remains a heavy fact. Such curious kinks of the human mind exist and must be reckoned with soberly. They cannot be laughed away, nor always successfully stormed at, nor easily abolished by act of legislature. And yet they must not be encouraged by being let alone. They must be recognized as facts, but unpleasant facts; things that stand in the way of civilization and religion and common decency. They can be met in but one way – by the breadth and broadening of human reason, by catholicity of taste and culture. And so, too, the

Notes

[115] *Jamestown* in Virginia, the first English settlement in the future United States.

[116] *tertium quid* (Latin) third thing.

[117] *dilettante* an amateur or dabbler.

[118] *Zeitgeist* (German) the spirit of the age.

native ambition and aspiration of men, even though they be black, backward, and ungraceful, must not lightly be dealt with. To stimulate wildly weak and untrained minds is to play with mighty fires; to flout their striving idly is to welcome a harvest of brutish crime and shameless lethargy in our very laps. The guiding of thought and the deft coordination of deed is at once the path of honor and humanity.

And so, in this great question of reconciling three vast and partially contradictory streams of thought, the one panacea of Education leaps to the lips of all: such human training as will best use the labor of all men without enslaving or brutalizing; such training as will give us poise to encourage the prejudices that bulwark society, and to stamp out those that in sheer barbarity deafen us to the wail of prisoned souls within the Veil, and the mounting fury of shackled men.

But when we have vaguely said that Education will set this tangle straight, what have we uttered but a truism? Training for life teaches living; but what training for the profitable living together of black men and white? A hundred and fifty years ago our task would have seemed easier. Then Dr. Johnson[119] blandly assured us that education was needful solely for the embellishments of life, and was useless for ordinary vermin. To-day we have climbed to heights where we would open at least the outer courts of knowledge to all, display its treasures to many, and select the few to whom its mystery of Truth is revealed, not wholly by birth or the accidents of the stock market, but at least in part according to deftness and aim, talent and character. This programme, however, we are sorely puzzled in carrying out through that part of the land where the blight of slavery fell hardest, and where we are dealing with two backward peoples. To make here in human education that ever necessary combination of the permanent and the contingent – of the ideal and the practical in workable equilibrium – has been there, as it ever must be in every age and place, a matter of infinite experiment and frequent mistakes.

In rough approximation we may point out four varying decades of work in Southern education since the Civil War. From the close of the war until 1876, was the period of uncertain groping and temporary relief. There were army schools, mission schools, and schools of the Freedman's Bureau in chaotic disarrangement seeking system and cooperation. Then followed ten years of constructive definite effort toward the building of complete school systems in the South. Normal schools and colleges were founded for the freedmen, and teachers trained there to man the public schools. There was the inevitable tendency of war to underestimate the prejudices of the master and the ignorance of the slave, and all seemed clear sailing out of the wreckage of the storm. Meantime, starting in this decade yet especially developing from 1885 to 1895, began the industrial revolution of the South. The land saw glimpses of a new destiny and the stirring of new ideals. The educational system striving to complete itself saw new obstacles and a field of work ever broader and deeper. The Negro colleges, hurriedly founded, were inadequately equipped, illogically distributed, and of varying efficiency and grade; the normal and high schools were doing little more than common-school work, and the common schools were training but a third of the children who ought to be in them, and training these too often poorly. At the same time the white South, by reason of its sudden conversion from the slavery ideal, by so much the more became set and strengthened in its racial prejudice, and crystallized it into harsh law and harsher custom; while the marvellous pushing forward of the poor white daily threatened to take even bread and butter from the mouths of the heavily handicapped

Notes

[119] *Dr. Johnson* Samuel Johnson (1709–1784), English writer, lexicographer, and critic.

sons of the freedmen. In the midst, then, of the larger problem of Negro education sprang up the more practical question of work, the inevitable economic quandary that faces a people in the transition from slavery to freedom, and especially those who make that change amid hate and prejudice, lawlessness and ruthless competition.

The industrial school springing to notice in this decade, but coming to full recognition in the decade beginning with 1895, was the proffered answer to this combined educational and economic crisis, and an answer of singular wisdom and timeliness. From the very first in nearly all the schools some attention had been given to training in handiwork, but now was this training first raised to a dignity that brought it in direct touch with the South's magnificent industrial development, and given an emphasis which reminded black folk that before the Temple of Knowledge swing the Gates of Toil.

Yet after all they are but gates, and when turning our eyes from the temporary and the contingent in the Negro problem to the broader question of the permanent uplifting and civilization of black men in America, we have a right to inquire, as this enthusiasm for material advancement mounts to its height, if after all the industrial school is the final and sufficient answer in the training of the Negro race; and to ask gently, but in all sincerity, the ever-recurring query of the ages, Is not life more than meat, and the body more than raiment?[120] And men ask this to-day all the more eagerly because of sinister signs in recent educational movements. The tendency is here, born of slavery and quickened to renewed life by the crazy imperialism of the day, to regard human beings as among the material resources of a land to be trained with an eye single to future dividends. Race-prejudices, which keep brown and black men in their "places," we are coming to regard as useful allies with such a theory, no matter how much they may dull the ambition and sicken the hearts of struggling human beings. And above all, we daily hear that an education that encourages aspiration, that sets the loftiest of ideals and seeks as an end culture and character rather than bread-winning, is the privilege of white men and the danger and delusion of black.

Especially has criticism been directed against the former educational efforts to aid the Negro. In the four periods I have mentioned, we find first, boundless, planless enthusiasm and sacrifice; then the preparation of teachers for a vast public-school system; then the launching and expansion of that school system amid increasing difficulties; and finally the training of workmen for the new and growing industries. This development has been sharply ridiculed as a logical anomaly and flat reversal of nature. Soothly[121] we have been told that first industrial and manual training should have taught the Negro to work, then simple schools should have taught him to read and write, and finally, after years, high and normal schools could have completed the system, as intelligence and wealth demanded.

That a system logically so complete was historically impossible, it needs but a little thought to prove. Progress in human affairs is more often a pull than a push, surging forward of the exceptional man, and the lifting of his duller brethren slowly and painfully to his vantage-ground. Thus it was no accident that gave birth to universities centuries before the common schools, that made fair Harvard the first flower of our wilderness. So in the South: the mass of the freedmen at the end of the war lacked the intelligence so necessary to modern workingmen. They must first have the common school to teach them to read, write, and cipher; and they must have higher schools to teach teachers for the common schools. The white teachers who flocked South went to establish such a common-school system. Few held the idea of founding colleges;

Notes

[120] *"Is not life more than meat ... raiment?"* Matthew 6:25.

[121] *Soothly* truly.

most of them at first would have laughed at the idea. But they faced, as all men since them have faced, that central paradox of the South – the social separation of the races. At that time it was the sudden volcanic rupture of nearly all relations between black and white, in work and government and family life. Since then a new adjustment of relations in economic and political affairs has grown up – an adjustment subtle and difficult to grasp, yet singularly ingenious, which leaves still that frightful chasm at the color-line across which men pass at their peril. Thus, then and now, there stand in the South two separate worlds; and separate not simply in the higher realms of social intercourse, but also in church and school, on railway and street-car, in hotels and theatres, in streets and city sections, in books and newspapers, in asylums and jails, in hospitals and graveyards. There is still enough of contact for large economic and group cooperation, but the separation is so thorough and deep that it absolutely precludes for the present between the races anything like that sympathetic and effective group-training and leadership of the one by the other, such as the American Negro and all backward peoples must have for effectual progress.

This the missionaries of '68 soon saw; and if effective industrial and trade schools were impracticable before the establishment of a common-school system, just as certainly no adequate common schools could be founded until there were teachers to teach them. Southern whites would not teach them; Northern whites in sufficient numbers could not be had. If the Negro was to learn, he must teach himself, and the most effective help that could be given him was the establishment of schools to train Negro teachers. This conclusion was slowly but surely reached by every student of the situation until simultaneously, in widely separated regions, without consultation or systematic plan, there arose a series of institutions designed to furnish teachers for the untaught. Above the sneers of critics at the obvious defects of this procedure must ever stand its one crushing rejoinder: in a single generation they put thirty thousand black teachers in the South; they wiped out the illiteracy of the majority of the black people of the land, and they made Tuskegee possible.

Such higher training-schools tended naturally to deepen broader development: at first they were common and grammar schools, then some became high schools. And finally, by 1900, some thirty-four had one year or more of studies of college grade. This development was reached with different degrees of speed in different institutions: Hampton is still a high school, while Fisk University started her college in 1871, and Spelman Seminary[122] about 1896. In all cases the aim was identical – to maintain the standards of the lower training by giving teachers and leaders the best practicable training; and above all, to furnish the black world with adequate standards of human culture and lofty ideals of life. It was not enough that the teachers of teachers should be trained in technical normal methods; they must also, so far as possible, be broad-minded, cultured men and women, to scatter civilization among a people whose ignorance was not simply of letters, but of life itself.

It can thus be seen that the work of education in the South began with higher institutions of training, which threw off as their foliage common schools, and later industrial schools, and at the same time strove to shoot their roots ever deeper toward college and university training. That this was an inevitable and necessary development, sooner or later, goes without saying; but there has been, and still is, a question in many minds if the natural growth was not forced, and if the higher training was not either overdone or

Notes

[122] *Spelman Seminary* Atlanta school for African American women, founded in 1881.

done with cheap and unsound methods. Among white Southerners this feeling is widespread and positive. A prominent Southern journal voiced this in a recent editorial.

> "The experiment that has been made to give the colored students classical training has not been satisfactory. Even though many were able to pursue the course, most of them did so in a parrot-like way, learning what was taught, but not seeming to appropriate the truth and import of their instruction, and graduating without sensible aim or valuable occupation for their future. The whole scheme has proved a waste of time, efforts, and the money of the state."

While most fair-minded men would recognize this as extreme and overdrawn, still without doubt many are asking, Are there a sufficient number of Negroes ready for college training to warrant the undertaking? Are not too many students prematurely forced into this work? Does it not have the effect of dissatisfying the young Negro with his environment? And do these graduates succeed in real life? Such natural questions cannot be evaded, nor on the other hand must a Nation naturally skeptical as to Negro ability assume an unfavorable answer without careful inquiry and patient openness to conviction. We must not forget that most Americans answer all queries regarding the Negro *a priori*,[123] and that the least that human courtesy can do is to listen to evidence.

The advocates of the higher education of the Negro would be the last to deny the incompleteness and glaring defects of the present system: too many institutions have attempted to do college work, the work in some cases has not been thoroughly done, and quantity rather than quality has sometimes been sought. But all this can be said of higher education throughout the land; it is the almost inevitable incident of educational growth, and leaves the deeper question of the legitimate demand for the higher training of Negroes untouched. And this latter question can be settled in but one way – by a first-hand study of the facts. If we leave out of view all institutions which have not actually graduated students from a course higher than that of a New England high school, even though they be called colleges; if then we take the thirty-four remaining institutions, we may clear up many misapprehensions by asking searchingly, What kind of institutions are they? what do they teach? and what sort of men do they graduate?

And first we may say that this type of college, including Atlanta, Fisk, and Howard, Wilberforce and Lincoln, Biddle, Shaw,[124] and the rest, is peculiar, almost unique. Through the shining trees that whisper before me as I write, I catch glimpses of a boulder of New England granite, covering a grave, which, graduates of Atlanta University have placed there, with this inscription:

"IN GRATEFUL MEMORY OF THEIR
FORMER TEACHER AND FRIEND
AND OF THE UNSELFISH LIFE HE
LIVED, AND THE NOBLE WORK HE
WROUGHT; THAT THEY, THEIR
CHILDREN, AND THEIR CHILDREN'S
CHILDREN MIGHT BE BLESSED."[125]

Notes

[123] *a priori* from presuppositions.

[124] *Atlanta, Fisk and Howard, Wilberforce and Lincoln, Biddle, Shaw* African American colleges in Georgia, Tennessee, Virginia, Ohio, Pennsylvania, and North Carolina.

[125] "IN GRATEFUL MEMORY … BLESSED." the memorial is to the founder of Atlanta University, Edmund Asa Ware (1837–1885).

This was the gift of New England to the freed Negro: not alms, but a friend; not cash, but character. It was not and is not money these seething millions want, but love and sympathy, the pulse of hearts beating with red blood – a gift which to-day only their own kindred and race can bring to the masses, but which once saintly souls brought to their favored children in the crusade of the sixties, that finest thing in American history, and one of the few things untainted by sordid greed and cheap vainglory. The teachers in these institutions came not to keep the Negroes in their place, but to raise them out of the defilement of the places where slavery had wallowed them. The colleges they founded were social settlements; homes where the best of the sons of the freedmen came in close and sympathetic touch with the best traditions of New England. They lived and ate together, studied and worked, hoped and harkened in the dawning light. In actual formal content their curriculum was doubtless old-fashioned, but in educational power it was supreme, for it was the contact of living souls.

From such schools about two thousand Negroes have gone forth with the bachelor's degree. The number in itself is enough to put at rest the argument that too large a proportion of Negroes are receiving higher training. If the ratio to population of all Negro students throughout the land, in both college and secondary training, be counted, Commissioner Harris assures us "it must be increased to five times its present average" to equal the average of the land.

Fifty years ago the ability of Negro students in any appreciable numbers to master a modern college course would have been difficult to prove. To-day it is proved by the fact that four hundred Negroes, many of whom have been reported as brilliant students, have received the bachelor's degree from Harvard, Yale, Oberlin, and seventy other leading colleges. Here we have, then, nearly twenty-five hundred Negro graduates, of whom the crucial query must be made, How far did their training fit them for life? It is of course extremely difficult to collect satisfactory data on such a point – difficult to reach the men, to get trustworthy testimony, and to gauge that testimony by any generally acceptable criterion of success. In 1900, the Conference at Atlanta University undertook to study these graduates, and published the results. First they sought to know what these graduates were doing, and succeeded in getting answers from nearly two-thirds of the living. The direct testimony was in almost all cases corroborated by the reports of the colleges where they graduated, so that in the main the reports were worthy of credence. Fifty-three per cent of these graduates were teachers – presidents of institutions, heads of normal schools, principals of city school-systems, and the like. Seventeen per cent were clergymen; another seventeen per cent were in the professions, chiefly as physicians. Over six per cent were merchants, farmers, and artisans, and four per cent were in the government civil-service. Granting even that a considerable proportion of the third unheard from are unsuccessful, this is a record of usefulness. Personally I know many hundreds of these graduates, and have corresponded with more than a thousand; through others I have followed carefully the life-work of scores; I have taught some of them and some of the pupils whom they have taught, lived in homes which they have builded, and looked at life through their eyes. Comparing them as a class with my fellow students in New England and in Europe, I cannot hesitate in saying that nowhere have I met men and women with a broader spirit of helpfulness, with deeper devotion to their life-work, or with more consecrated determination to succeed in the face of bitter difficulties than among Negro college-bred men. They have, to be sure, their proportion of ne'er-do-wells,[126]

Notes

[126] *Original reads*: ne'er-do-weels [ed.].

their pedants and lettered fools, but they have a surprisingly small proportion of them; they have not that culture of manner which we instinctively associate with university men, forgetting that in reality it is the heritage from cultured homes, and that no people a generation removed from slavery can escape a certain unpleasant rawness and *gaucherie*,[127] despite the best of training.

With all their larger vision and deeper sensibility, these men have usually been conservative, careful leaders. They have seldom been agitators, have withstood the temptation to head the mob, and have worked steadily and faithfully in a thousand communities in the South. As teachers, they have given the South a commendable system of city schools and large numbers of private normal-schools and academies. Colored college-bred men have worked side by side with white college graduates at Hampton; almost from the beginning the back-bone of Tuskegee's teaching force has been formed of graduates from Fisk and Atlanta. And to-day the institute is filled with college graduates, from the energetic wife of the principal down to the teacher of agriculture, including nearly half of the executive council and a majority of the heads of departments. In the professions, college men are slowly but surely leavening the Negro church, are healing and preventing the devastations of disease, and beginning to furnish legal protection for the liberty and property of the toiling masses. All this is needful work. Who would do it if Negroes did not? How could Negroes do it if they were not trained carefully for it? If white people need colleges to furnish teachers, ministers, lawyers, and doctors, do black people need nothing of the sort?

If it is true that there are an appreciable number of Negro youth in the land capable by character and talent to receive that higher training, the end of which is culture, and if the two and a half thousand who have had something of this training in the past have in the main proved themselves useful to their race and generation, the question then comes, What place in the future development of the South ought the Negro college and college-bred man to occupy? That the present social separation and acute race-sensitiveness must eventually yield to the influences of culture, as the South grows civilized, is clear. But such transformation calls for singular wisdom and patience. If, while the healing of this vast sore is progressing, the races are to live for many years side by side, united in economic effort, obeying a common government, sensitive to mutual thought and feeling, yet subtly and silently separate in many matters of deeper human intimacy – if this unusual and dangerous development is to progress amid peace and order, mutual respect and growing intelligence, it will call for social surgery at once the most delicate[128] and nicest in modern history. It will demand broad-minded, upright men, both white and black, and in its final accomplishment American civilization will triumph. So far as white men are concerned, this fact is to-day being recognized in the South, and a happy renaissance of university education seems imminent. But the very voices that cry hail to this good work are, strange to relate, largely silent or antagonistic to the higher education of the Negro.

Strange to relate! for this is certain, no secure civilization can be built in the South with the Negro as an ignorant, turbulent proletariat. Suppose we seek to remedy this by making them laborers and nothing more: they are not fools, they have tasted of the Tree of Life, and they will not cease to think, will not cease attempting to read the riddle of the world. By taking away their best equipped teachers and leaders, by slamming the door of opportunity in the faces of their bolder and brighter minds, will you make them satisfied with their lot? or will you not rather transfer their leading from the hands of

Notes

[127] *gaucherie* lack of grace or tact.

[128] *Original reads*: delicatest [ed.].

men taught to think to the hands of untrained demagogues? We ought not to forget that despite the pressure of poverty, and despite the active discouragement and even ridicule of friends, the demand for higher training steadily increases among Negro youth: there were, in the years from 1875 to 1880, 22 Negro graduates from Northern colleges; from 1885 to 1890 there were 43, and from 1895 to 1900, nearly 100 graduates. From Southern Negro colleges there were, in the same three periods, 143, 413, and over 500 graduates. Here, then, is the plain thirst for training; by refusing to give this Talented Tenth the key to knowledge, can any sane man imagine that they will lightly lay aside their yearning and contentedly become hewers of wood and drawers of water?

No. The dangerously clear logic of the Negro's position will more and more loudly assert itself in that day when increasing wealth and more intricate social organization preclude the South from being, as it so largely is, simply an armed camp for intimidating black folk. Such waste of energy cannot be spared if the South is to catch up with civilization. And as the black third of the land grows in thrift and skill, unless skilfully guided in its larger philosophy, it must more and more brood over the red past and the creeping, crooked present, until it grasps a gospel of revolt and revenge and throws its new-found energies athwart the current of advance. Even to-day the masses of the Negroes see all too clearly the anomalies of their position and the moral crookedness of yours. You may marshal strong indictments against them, but their counter-cries, lacking though they be in formal logic, have burning truths within them which you may not wholly ignore, O Southern Gentlemen! If you deplore their presence here, they ask, Who brought us? When you cry, Deliver us from the vision of intermarriage, they answer that legal marriage is infinitely better than systematic concubinage[129] and prostitution. And if in just fury you accuse their vagabonds of violating women, they also in fury quite as just may reply: The wrong which your gentlemen have done against helpless black women in defiance of your own laws is written on the foreheads of two millions of mulattoes, and written in ineffaceable blood. And finally, when you fasten crime upon this race as its peculiar trait, they answer that slavery was the arch-crime, and lynching and lawlessness its twin abortion; that color and race are not crimes, and yet they it is which in this land receives most unceasing condemnation, North, East, South, and West.

I will not say such arguments are wholly justified – I will not insist that there is no other side to the shield; but I do say that of the nine millions of Negroes in this nation, there is scarcely one out of the cradle to whom these arguments do not daily present themselves in the guise of terrible truth. I insist that the question of the future is how best to keep these millions from brooding over the wrongs of the past and the difficulties of the present, so that all their energies may be bent toward a cheerful striving and cooperation with their white neighbors toward a larger, juster, and fuller future. That one wise method of doing this lies in the closer knitting of the Negro to the great industrial possibilities of the South is a great truth. And this the common schools and the manual training and trade schools are working to accomplish. But these alone are not enough. The foundations of knowledge in this race, as in others, must be sunk deep in the college and university if we would build a solid, permanent structure. Internal problems of social advance must inevitably come – problems of work and wages, of families and homes, of morals and the true valuing of the things of life; and all these and other inevitable problems of civilization the Negro must meet and solve largely for himself, by reason of his isolation; and can there be any possible solution other than by study and thought and an appeal to the rich experience of the past?

Notes

129 *concubinage* cohabitation without marriage.

Is there not, with such a group and in such a crisis, infinitely more danger to be apprehended from half-trained minds and shallow thinking than from over-education and over-refinement? Surely we have wit enough to found a Negro college so manned and equipped as to steer successfully between the *dilettante* and the fool. We shall hardly induce black men to believe that if their stomachs be full, it matters little about their brains. They already dimly perceive that the paths of peace winding between honest toil and dignified manhood call for the guidance of skilled thinkers, the loving, reverent comradeship between the black lowly and the black men emancipated by training and culture.

The function of the Negro college, then, is clear: it must maintain the standards of popular education, it must seek the social regeneration of the Negro, and it must help in the solution of problems of race contact and cooperation. And finally, beyond all this, it must develop men. Above our modern socialism, and out of the worship of the mass, must persist and evolve that higher individualism which the centres of culture protect; there must come a loftier respect for the sovereign human soul that seeks to know itself and the world about it; that seeks a freedom for expansion and self-development; that will love and hate and labor, in its own way, untrammeled alike by old and new. Such souls aforetime have inspired and guided worlds, and if we be not wholly bewitched by our Rhine-gold,[130] they shall again. Herein the longing of black men must have respect: the rich and bitter depth of their experience, the unknown treasures of their inner life, the strange rendings of nature they have seen, may give the world new points of view and make their loving, living, and doing precious to all human hearts. And to themselves in these the days that try their souls, the chance to soar in the dim blue air above the smoke is to their finer spirits boon and guerdon for what they lose on earth by being black.

I sit with Shakespeare and he winces not. Across the color line I move arm in arm with Balzac and Dumas,[131] where smiling men and welcoming women glide in gilded halls. From out the caves of evening that swing between the strong-limbed earth and the tracery of the stars, I summon Aristotle and Aurelius[132] and what soul I will, and they come all graciously with no scorn nor condescension. So, wed with Truth, I dwell above the Veil. Is this the life you grudge us, O knightly America? Is this the life you long to change into the dull red hideousness of Georgia? Are you so afraid lest peering from this high Pisgah, between Philistine and Amalekite,[133] we sight the Promised Land?

Chapter 7

Of the Black Belt

I am black but comely, O ye daughters of Jerusalem,
As the tents of Kedar, as the curtains of Solomon.
Look not upon me, because I am black,

Notes

[130] *Rhine-gold* German composer Richard Wagner's (1813–1883) opera *The Rhine-Gold* (1853); its plot involves the pursuit and concealment of a great amount of gold.

[131] *Balzac and Dumas* Honoré de Balzac (1799–1850) and Alexandre Dumas (1802–1870), French novelists.

[132] *Aristotle and Aurelius* Aristotle (384–322 BC), Greek philosopher; Marcus Aurelius Antoninus (AD 121–180), stoic philosopher and Roman emperor.

[133] *This high Pisgah, between Philistine and Amalekite* Moses looked from Mount Pisgah onto the Promised Land; the Israelites had to battle the Philistines and Amalekites for control of it.

Because the sun hath looked upon me:
My mother's children were angry with me;
They made me the keeper of the vineyards;
But mine own vineyard have I not kept.
The Song of Solomon.[134]

Out of the North the train thundered, and we woke to see the crimson soil of Georgia stretching away bare and monotonous right and left. Here and there lay straggling, unlovely villages, and lean men loafed leisurely at the depots; then again came the stretch of pines and clay. Yet we did not nod, nor weary of the scene; for this is historic ground. Right across our track, three hundred and sixty years ago, wandered the cavalcade of Hernando de Soto,[135] looking for gold and the Great Sea; and he and his foot sore captives disappeared yonder in the grim forests to the west. Here sits Atlanta, the city of a hundred hills, with something Western, something Southern, and something quite its own, in its busy life. And a little past Atlanta, to the southwest, is the land of the Cherokees, and there, not far from where Sam Hose[136] was crucified, you may stand on a spot which is to-day the centre of the Negro problem – the centre of those nine million men who are America's dark heritage from slavery and the slave-trade.

Not only is Georgia thus the geographical focus of our Negro population, but in many other respects, both now and yesterday, the Negro problems have seemed to be centered in this State. No other State in the Union can count a million Negroes among its citizens – a population as large as the slave population of the whole Union in 1800; no other State fought so long and strenuously to gather this host of Africans. Oglethorpe[137] thought slavery against law and gospel; but the circumstances which gave Georgia its first inhabitants were not calculated to furnish citizens over-nice in their ideas about rum and slaves. Despite the prohibitions of the trustees, these Georgians, like some of their descendants, proceeded to take the law into their own hands; and so pliant were the judges, and so flagrant the smuggling, and so earnest were the prayers of

Notes

[134] Song of Solomon 1:5–6.

[135] Hernando de Soto (1496–1542), Spanish explorer who discovered the Mississippi river.

[136] *Sam Hose* a Georgia laborer accused in 1899 of killing his employer and raping the employer's wife. Hose confessed to the murder, and was tortured and killed in a lynching viewed by over 2,000 people.

[137] *Oglethorpe* James Edward Olgethorpe (1696–1785), founder of Georgia (in 1733).

Whitefield,[138] that by the middle of the eighteenth century all restrictions were swept away, and the slave-trade went merrily on for fifty years and more.

Down in Darien, where the Delegal riots[139] took place some summers ago, there used to come a strong protest against slavery from the Scotch Highlanders; and the Moravians of Ebenezea[140] did not like the system. But not till the Haytian Terror of Toussaint was the trade in men even checked; while the national statute of 1808[141] did not suffice to stop it. How the Africans poured in! – fifty thousand between 1790 and 1810, and then, from Virginia and from smugglers, two thousand a year for many years more. So the thirty thousand Negroes of Georgia in 1790 were doubled in a decade – were over a hundred thousand in 1810, had reached two hundred thousand in 1820, and half a million at the time of the war. Thus like a snake the black population writhed upward.

But we must hasten on our journey. This that we pass as we leave Atlanta is the ancient land of the Cherokees – that brave Indian nation which strove so long for its fatherland, until Fate and the United States Government drove them beyond the Mississippi. If you wish to ride with me you must come into the "Jim Crow Car." There will be no objection – already four other white men, and a little white girl with her nurse, are in there. Usually the races are mixed in there; but the white coach is all white. Of course this car is not so good as the other, but it is fairly clean and comfortable. The discomfort lies chiefly in the hearts of those four black men yonder – and in mine.

We rumble south in quite a business-like way. The bare red clay and pines of Northern Georgia begin to disappear, and in their place appears a rich rolling land, luxuriant, and here and there well tilled. This is the land of the Creek Indians; and a hard time the Georgians had to seize it. The towns grow more frequent and more interesting, and brand-new cotton mills rise on every side. Below Macon the world grows darker; for now we approach the Black Belt – that strange land of shadows, at which even slaves paled in the past, and whence come now only faint and half-intelligible murmurs to the world beyond. The "Jim Crow Car" grows larger and a shade better; three rough field-hands and two or three white loafers accompany us, and the newsboy still spreads his wares at one end. The sun is setting, but we can see the great cotton country as we enter it – the soil now dark and fertile, now thin and gray, with fruit-trees and dilapidated buildings – all the way to Albany.

At Albany, in the heart of the Black Belt, we stop. Two hundred miles south of Atlanta, two hundred miles west of the Atlantic, and one hundred miles north of the Great Gulf lies Dougherty County, with ten thousand Negroes and two thousand whites. The Flint River winds down from Andersonville, and, turning suddenly at Albany, the county-seat, hurries on to join the Chattahoochee and the sea. Andrew Jackson[142] knew the Flint well, and marched across it once to avenge the Indian Massacre at Fort Mims. That was in 1814, not long before the battle of New Orleans; and by the Creek treaty that followed this campaign, all Dougherty County, and much other rich land, was ceded to Georgia. Still, settlers fought shy of this land, for the Indians were all about, and they were unpleasant neighbors in those days.

Notes

[138] *prayers of Whitefield* George Whitefield (1714–1770), English evangelist, advocated for the re-legalization of slavery in Georgia.

[139] *Delegal riots* In August 1899, hundreds of African Americans thwarted a lynch mob that sought to extract a black prisoner from jail; many of them were sentenced to labor on a convict farm for insurrection.

[140] *Moravians of Ebenezea* a European Protestant sect that settled in Georgia.

[141] *national statute of 1808* an act of Congress prohibiting slave importation into the United States.

[142] Andrew Jackson (1767–1845), President of the United States (1829–1837).

The panic of 1837, which Jackson bequeathed to Van Buren,[143] turned the planters from the impoverished lands of Virginia, the Carolinas, and east Georgia, toward the West. The Indians were removed to Indian Territory, and settlers poured into these coveted lands to retrieve their broken fortunes. For a radius of a hundred miles about Albany, stretched a great fertile land, luxuriant with forests of pine, oak, ash, hickory, and poplar; hot with the sun and damp with the rich black swamp-land; and here the corner-stone of the Cotton Kingdom was laid.

Albany is to-day a wide-streeted, placid, Southern town, with a broad sweep of stores and saloons, and flanking rows of homes – whites usually to the north, and blacks to the south. Six days in the week the town looks decidedly too small for itself, and takes frequent and prolonged naps. But on Saturday suddenly the whole county disgorges itself upon the place, and a perfect flood of black peasantry pours through the streets, fills the stores, blocks the sidewalks, chokes the thoroughfares, and takes full possession of the town. They are black, sturdy, uncouth country folk, good-natured and simple, talkative to a degree, and yet far more silent and brooding than the crowds of the Rhine-Pfalz,[144] or Naples, or Cracow. They drink considerable quantities of whiskey, but do not get very drunk; they talk and laugh loudly at times, but seldom quarrel or fight. They walk up and down the streets, meet and gossip with friends, stare at the shop windows, buy coffee, cheap candy, and clothes, and at dusk drive home – happy? well no, not exactly happy, but much happier than as though they had not come.

Thus Albany is a real capital – a typical Southern county town, the centre of the life of ten thousand souls; their point of contact with the outer world, their centre of news and gossip, their market for buying and selling, borrowing and lending, their fountain of justice and law. Once upon a time we knew country life so well and city life so little, that we illustrated city life as that of a closely crowded country district. Now the world has well-nigh forgotten what the country is, and we must imagine a little city of black people scattered far and wide over three hundred lonesome square miles of land, without train or trolley, in the midst of cotton and corn, and wide patches of sand and gloomy soil.

It gets pretty hot in Southern Georgia in July – a sort of dull, determined heat that seems quite independent of the sun; so it took us some days to muster courage enough to leave the porch and venture out on the long country roads, that we might see this unknown world. Finally we started. It was about ten in the morning, bright with a faint breeze, and we jogged leisurely southward in the valley of the Flint. We passed the scattered box-like cabins of the brick-yard hands, and the long tenement-row facetiously called "The Ark," and were soon in the open country, and on the confines of the great plantations of other days. There is the "Joe Fields place"; a rough old fellow was he, and had killed many a "nigger" in his day. Twelve miles his plantation used to run – a regular barony. It is nearly all gone now; only straggling bits belong to the family, and the rest has passed to Jews and Negroes. Even the bits which are left are heavily mortgaged, and, like the rest of the land, tilled by tenants. Here is one of them now – a tall brown man, a hard worker and a hard drinker, illiterate, but versed in farm-lore, as his nodding crops declare. This distressingly new board house is his, and he has just moved out of yonder moss-grown cabin with its one square room.

From the curtains in Benton's house, down the road, a dark comely face is staring at the strangers; for passing carriages are not every-day occurrences here. Benton is an

Notes

[143] Martin Van Buren (1782–1862), succeeded Andrew Jackson as President (1837–1841).

[144] *Original reads*: Rhine-pfalz [ed.].

intelligent yellow man with a good-size family, and manages a plantation blasted by the war and now the broken staff of the widow. He might be well-to-do, they say; but he carouses too much in Albany. And the half-desolate spirit of neglect born of the very soil seems to have settled on these acres. In times past there were cotton-gins and machinery here but they have rotted away.

The whole land seems forlorn and forsaken. Here are the remnants of the vast plantations of the Sheldons, the Pellots, and the Rensons; but the souls of them are passed. The houses lie in half ruin, or have wholly disappeared; the fences have flown, and the families are wandering in the world. Strange vicissitudes have met these whilom[145] masters. Yonder stretch the wide acres of Bildad Reasor; he died in war-time, but the upstart overseer hastened to wed the widow. Then he went, and his neighbors too, and now only the black tenant remains; but the shadow-hand of the master's grand-nephew or cousin or creditor stretches out of the gray distance to collect the rack-rent[146] remorselessly, and so the land is uncared-for and poor. Only black tenants can stand such a system, and they only because they must. Ten miles we have ridden to-day and have seen no white face.

A resistless feeling of depression falls slowly upon us, despite the gaudy sunshine and the green cotton-fields. This, then, is the Cotton Kingdom – the shadow of a marvellous dream. And where is the King? Perhaps this is he – the sweating ploughman, tilling his eighty acres with two lean mules, and fighting a hard battle with debt. So we sit musing, until, as we turn a corner on the sandy road, there comes a fairer scene suddenly in view – a neat cottage snugly ensconced by the road, and near it a little store. A tall bronzed man rises from the porch as we hail him, and comes out to our carriage. He is six feet in height, with a sober face that smiles gravely. He walks too straight to be a tenant – yes, he owns two hundred and forty acres. "The land is run down since the boom-days of eighteen hundred and fifty," he explains, and cotton is low. Three black tenants live on his place, and in his little store he keeps a small stock of tobacco, snuff, soap, and soda, for the neighborhood. Here is his gin-house with new machinery just installed. Three hundred bales of cotton went through it last year. Two children he has sent away to school. Yes, he says sadly, he is getting on, but cotton is down to four cents; I know how Debt sits staring at him.

Wherever the King may be, the parks and palaces of the Cotton Kingdom have not wholly disappeared. We plunge even now into great groves of oak and towering pine, with an undergrowth of myrtle and shrubbery. This was the "home-house" of the Thompsons – slave-barons who drove their coach and four in the merry past. All is silence now, and ashes, and tangled weeds. The owner put his whole fortune into the rising cotton industry of the fifties, and with the falling prices of the eighties he packed up and stole away. Yonder is another grove, with unkempt lawn, great magnolias, and grass-grown paths. The Big House stands in half-ruin, its great front door staring blankly at the street, and the back part grotesquely restored for its black tenant. A shabby, well-built Negro he is, unlucky and irresolute. He digs hard to pay rent to the white girl who owns the remnant of the place. She married a policeman, and lives in Savannah.

Now and again we come to churches. Here is one now – Shepherd's, they call it – a great whitewashed barn of a thing, perched on stilts of stone, and looking for all the world as though it were just resting here a moment and might be expected to waddle off down the road at almost any time. And yet it is the centre of a hundred cabin

Notes

[145] *whilom* former.

[146] *rack-rent* exorbitant rent.

homes; and sometimes, of a Sunday, five hundred persons from far and near gather here and talk and eat and sing. There is a schoolhouse near – a very airy, empty shed; but even this is an improvement, for usually the school is held in the church. The churches vary from log-huts to those like Shepherd's, and the schools from nothing to this little house that sits demurely on the county line. It is a tiny plank-house, perhaps ten by twenty, and has within a double row of rough unplaned benches, resting mostly on legs, sometimes on boxes. Opposite the door is a square home-made desk. In one corner are the ruins of a stove, and in the other a dim blackboard. It is the most cheerful[147] schoolhouse I have seen in Dougherty, save in town. Back of the schoolhouse is a lodge-house two stories high and not quite finished. Societies meet there – societies "to care for the sick and bury the dead"; and these societies grow and flourish.

We had come to the boundaries of Dougherty, and were about to turn west along the county line, when all these sights were pointed out to us by a kindly old man, black, white-haired, and seventy. Forty-five years he had lived here, and now supports himself and his old wife by the help of the steer tethered yonder and the charity of his black neighbors. He shows us the farm of the Hills just across the county line in Baker – a widow and two strapping sons, who raised ten bales (one need not add "cotton" down here) last year. There are fences and pigs and cows, and the soft-voiced, velvet-skinned young Memnon, who sauntered half-bashfully over to greet the strangers, is proud of his home. We turn now to the west along the county line. Great dismantled trunks of pines tower above the green cotton-fields, cracking their naked gnarled fingers toward the border of living forest beyond. There is little beauty in this region, only a sort of crude abandon that suggests power – a naked grandeur, as it were. The houses are bare and straight; there are no hammocks or easy-chairs, and few flowers. So when, as here at Rawdon's, one sees a vine clinging to a little porch, and home-like windows peeping over the fences, one takes a long breath. I think I never before quite realized the place of the Fence in civilization. This is the Land of the Unfenced, where crouch on either hand scores of ugly one-room cabins, cheerless and dirty. Here lies the Negro problem in its naked dirt and penury. And here are no fences. But now and then the criss-cross rails or straight palings break into view, and then we know a touch of culture is near. Of course Harrison Gohagen – a quiet yellow man, young, smooth-faced, and diligent – of course he is lord of some hundred acres, and we expect to see a vision of well-kept rooms and fat beds and laughing children. For has he not fine fences? And those over yonder, why should they build fences on the rack-rented land? It will only increase their rent.

On we wind, through sand and pines and glimpses of old plantations, till there creeps into sight a cluster of buildings – wood and brick, mills and houses, and scattered cabins. It seemed quite a village. As it came nearer and nearer, however, the aspect changed: the buildings were rotten, the bricks were falling out, the mills were silent, and the store was closed. Only in the cabins appeared now and then a bit of lazy life. I could imagine the place under some weird spell, and was half-minded to search out the princess. An old ragged black man, honest, simple, and improvident, told us the tale. The Wizard of the North – the Capitalist – had rushed down in the seventies to woo this coy dark soil. He bought a square mile or more, and for a time the field-hands sang, the gins groaned, and the mills buzzed. Then came a change. The agent's son embezzled the funds and ran off with them. Then the agent himself disappeared. Finally the new agent stole even the books, and the company in wrath closed its business

Notes

[147] *Original reads*: cheerfulest [ed.].

and its houses, refused to sell, and let houses and furniture and machinery rust and rot. So the Waters-Loring plantation was stilled by the spell of dishonesty, and stands like some gaunt rebuke to a scarred land.

Somehow that plantation ended our day's journey; for I could not shake off the influence of that silent scene. Back toward town we glided, past the straight and thread-like pines, past a dark tree-dotted pond where the air was heavy with a dead sweet perfume. White slender-legged curlews flitted by us, and the garnet blooms of the cotton looked gay against the green and purple stalks. A peasant girl was hoeing in the field, white-turbaned and black-limbed. All this we saw, but the spell still lay upon us.

How curious a land is this – how full of untold story, of tragedy and laughter, and the rich legacy of human life; shadowed with a tragic past, and big with future promise! This is the Black Belt of Georgia. Dougherty County is the west end of the Black Belt, and men once called it the Egypt of the Confederacy. It is full of historic interest. First there is the Swamp, to the west, where the Chickasawhatchee flows sullenly southward. The shadow of an old plantation lies at its edge, forlorn and dark. Then comes the pool; pendent gray moss and brackish waters appear, and forests filled with wildfowl. In one place the wood is on fire, smouldering in dull red anger; but nobody minds. Then the swamp grows beautiful; a raised road, built by chained Negro convicts, dips down into it, and forms a way walled and almost covered in living green. Spreading trees spring from a prodigal luxuriance of undergrowth; great dark green shadows fade into the black background, until all is one mass of tangled semitropical foliage, marvellous in its weird savage splendour. Once we crossed a black silent stream, where the sad trees and writhing creepers, all glinting fiery yellow and green, seemed like some vast cathedral – some green Milan builded of wildwood. And as I crossed, I seemed to see again that fierce tragedy of seventy years ago. Osceola,[148] the Indian-Negro chieftain, had risen in the swamps of Florida, vowing vengeance. His war-cry reached the red Creeks of Dougherty, and their war-cry rang from the Chattahoochee to the sea. Men and women and children fled and fell before them as they swept into Dougherty. In yonder shadows a dark and hideously painted warrior glided stealthily on – another and another, until three hundred had crept into the treacherous swamp. Then the false slime closing about them called the white men from the east. Waist-deep, they fought beneath the tall trees, until the war-cry was hushed and the Indians glided back into the west. Small wonder the wood is red.

Then came the black slaves. Day after day the clank of chained feet marching from Virginia and Carolina to Georgia was heard in these rich swamp lands. Day after day the songs of the callous, the wail of the motherless, and the muttered curses of the wretched echoed from the Flint to the Chickasawhatchee, until by 1860 there had risen in West Dougherty perhaps the richest slave kingdom the modern world ever knew. A hundred and fifty barons commanded the labor of nearly six thousand Negroes, held sway over farms with ninety thousand acres of tilled land, valued even in times of cheap soil at three millions of dollars. Twenty thousand bales of ginned cotton went yearly to England, New and Old; and men that came there bankrupt made money and grew rich. In a single decade the cotton output increased four-fold and the value of lands was tripled. It was the heyday of the *nouveau riche*, and a life of careless extravagance reigned among the masters. Four and six bobtailed thoroughbreds rolled their coaches to town; open hospitality and gay entertainment were the rule. Parks and

Notes

[148] *Osceola* (1804–1838), Seminole war chief.

groves were laid out, rich with flower and vine, and in the midst stood the low wide-hailed "big house," with its porch and columns and great fireplaces.

And yet with all this there was something sordid, something forced – a certain feverish unrest and recklessness; for was not all this show and tinsel built upon a groan? "This land was a little Hell," said a ragged, brown, and grave-faced man to me. We were seated near a roadside blacksmith-shop, and behind was the bare ruin of some master's home. "I've seen niggers drop dead in the furrow, but they were kicked aside, and the plough never stopped. And down in the guardhouse, there's where the blood ran."

With such foundations a kingdom must in time sway and fall. The masters moved to Macon and Augusta, and left only the irresponsible overseers on the land. And the result is such ruin as this, the Lloyd "home-place": great waving oaks, a spread of lawn, myrtles and chestnuts, all ragged and wild; a solitary gate-post standing where once was a castle entrance; an old rusty anvil lying amid rotting bellows and wood in the ruins of a blacksmith shop; a wide rambling old mansion, brown and dingy, filled now with the grandchildren of the slaves who once waited on its tables; while the family of the master has dwindled to two lone women, who live in Macon and feed hungrily off the remnants of an earldom. So we ride on, past phantom gates and falling homes – past the once flourishing farms of the Smiths, the Gandys, and the Lagores – and find all dilapidated and half ruined, even there where a solitary white woman, a relic of other days, sits alone in state among miles of Negroes and rides to town in her ancient coach each day.

This was indeed the Egypt of the Confederacy – the rich granary whence potatoes and corn and cotton poured out to the famished and ragged Confederate troops as they battled for a cause lost long before 1861. Sheltered and secure, it became the place of refuge for families, wealth, and slaves. Yet even then the hard ruthless rape of the land began to tell. The red-clay sub-soil already had begun to peer above the loam. The harder the slaves were driven the more careless and fatal was their farming. Then came the revolution of war and Emancipation, the bewilderment of Reconstruction – and now, what is the Egypt of the Confederacy, and what meaning has it for the nation's weal or woe?

It is a land of rapid contrasts and of curiously mingled hope and pain. Here sits a pretty blue-eyed quadroon hiding her bare feet; she was married only last week, and yonder in the field is her dark young husband, hoeing to support her, at thirty cents a day without board. Across the way is Gatesby, brown and tall, lord of two thousand acres shrewdly won and held. There is a store conducted by his black son, a blacksmith shop, and a ginnery. Five miles below here is a town owned and controlled by one white New Englander. He owns almost a Rhode Island county, with thousands of acres and hundreds of black laborers. Their cabins look better than most, and the farm, with machinery and fertilizers, is much more business-like than any in the county, although the manager drives hard bargains in wages. When now we turn and look five miles above, there on the edge of town are five houses of prostitutes – two of blacks and three of whites; and in one of the houses of the whites a worthless black boy was harbored too openly two years ago; so he was hanged for rape. And here, too, is the high whitewashed fence of the "stockade," as the county prison is called; the white folks say it is ever full of black criminals – the black folks say that only colored boys are sent to jail, and they not because they are guilty, but because the State needs criminals to eke out its income by their forced labor.

The Jew is the heir of the slave-baron in Dougherty; and as we ride westward, by wide stretching cornfields and stubby orchards of peach and pear, we see on all sides within the circle of dark forest a Land of Canaan. Here and there are tales of projects for money-getting, born in the swift days of Reconstruction – "improvement companies, wine companies, mills and factories, nearly all failed, and the Jew fell heir. It is a beautiful land, this Dougherty, west of the Flint. The forests are wonderful, the solemn pines have disappeared, and this is the "Oakey Woods," with its wealth of hickories, beeches, oaks, and palmettos. But a pall of debt hangs over the beautiful land; the merchants are in debt to the wholesalers, the planters are in debt to the merchants, the tenants owe the planters, and laborers bow and bend beneath the burden of it all. Here and there a man has raised his head above these murky waters. We passed one fenced stock-farm, with grass and grazing cattle, that looked very homelike after endless corn and cotton. Here and there are black freeholders: there is the gaunt dull-black Jackson, with his hundred acres. "I says, 'Look up! If you don't look up you can't get up,'" remarks Jackson, philosophically. And he's gotten up. Dark Carter's neat barns would do credit to New England. His master helped him to get a start, but when the black man died last fall the master's sons immediately laid claim to the estate. "And them white folks will get it, too," said my yellow gossip.

I turn from these well-tended acres with a comfortable feeling that the Negro is rising. Even then, however, the fields, as we proceed, begin to redden and the trees disappear. Rows of old cabins appear filled with renters and laborers – cheerless, bare, and dirty, for the most part, although here and there the very age and decay makes the scene picturesque. A young black fellow greets us. He is twenty-two, and just married. Until last year he had good luck renting; then cotton fell, and the sheriff seized and sold all he had. So he moved here, where the rent is higher, the land poorer, and the owner inflexible; he rents a forty-dollar mule for twenty dollars a year. Poor lad! – a slave at twenty-two. This plantation, owned now by a Russian Jew, was a part of the famous Bolton estate. After the war it was for many years worked by gangs of Negro convicts – and black convicts then were even more plentiful than now; it was a way of making Negroes work, and the question of guilt was a minor one. Hard tales of cruelty and mistreatment of the chained freemen are told, but the county authorities were deaf until the free-labor market was nearly ruined by wholesale migration. Then they took the convicts from the plantations, but not until one of the fairest regions of the "Oakey Woods" had been ruined and ravished into a red waste, out of which only a Yankee or a Jew could squeeze more blood from debt-cursed tenants.

No wonder that Luke Black, slow, dull, and discouraged, shuffles to our carriage and talks hopelessly. Why should he strive? Every year finds him deeper in debt. How strange that Georgia, the world-heralded refuge of poor debtors, should bind her own to sloth and misfortune as ruthlessly as ever England did! The poor land groans with its birth-pains, and brings forth scarcely a hundred pounds of cotton to the acre, where fifty years ago it yielded eight times as much. Of this meagre yield the tenant pays from a quarter to a third in rent, and most of the rest in interest on food and supplies bought on credit. Twenty years yonder sunken-cheeked, old black man has labored under that system, and now, turned day-laborer, is supporting his wife and boarding himself on his wages of a dollar and a half a week, received only part of the year.

The Bolton convict farm formerly included the neighboring plantation. Here it was that the convicts were lodged in the great log prison still standing. A dismal place it still remains, with rows of ugly huts filled with surly ignorant tenants. "What rent do you pay here?" I inquired. "I don't know – what is it, Sam?" "All we make," answered Sam. It is a depressing place – bare, unshaded, with no charm of past association, only a memory of forced human toil – now, then, and before the war. They are not happy, these black men whom we meet throughout this region. There is little of the joyous abandon and playfulness which we are wont to associate with the plantation Negro. At best, the natural good-nature is edged with complaint or has changed into sullenness and gloom. And now and then it blazes forth in veiled but hot anger. I remember one big red-eyed black whom we met by the roadside. Forty-five years he had labored on this farm, beginning with nothing, and still having nothing. To be sure, he had given four children a common-school training, and perhaps if the new fence-law had not allowed unfenced crops in West Dougherty he might have raised a little stock and kept ahead. As it is, he is hopelessly in debt, disappointed, and embittered. He stopped us to inquire after the black boy in Albany, whom it was said a policeman had shot and killed for loud talking on the sidewalk. And then he said slowly: "Let a white man touch me, and he dies; I don't boast this – I don't say it around loud, or before the children – but I mean it. I've seen them whip my father and my old mother in them cotton-rows till the blood ran; by – " and we passed on.

Now Sears, whom we met next lolling under the chubby oak-trees, was of quite different fibre. Happy? – Well, yes; he laughed and flipped pebbles, and thought the world was as it was. He had worked here twelve years and has nothing but a mortgaged mule. Children? Yes, seven; but they hadn't been to school this year – couldn't afford books and clothes, and couldn't spare their work. There go part of them to the fields now – three big boys astride mules, and a strapping girl with bare brown legs. Careless ignorance and laziness here, fierce hate and vindictiveness there – these are the extremes of the Negro problem which we met that day, and we scarce knew which we preferred.

Here and there we meet distinct characters quite out of the ordinary. One came out of a piece of newly cleared ground, making a wide detour to avoid the snakes. He was an old, hollow-cheeked man, with a drawn and characterful brown face. He had a sort of self-contained quaintness and rough humor impossible to describe; a certain cynical earnestness that puzzled one. "The niggers were jealous of me over on the other place," he said, "and so me and the old woman begged this piece of woods, and I cleared it up myself. Made nothing for two years, but I reckon I've got a crop now." The cotton looked tall and rich, and we praised it. He curtsied low, and then bowed almost to the ground, with an imperturbable gravity that seemed almost suspicious. Then he continued, "My mule died last week" – a calamity in this land equal to a devastating fire in town – "but a white man loaned me another." Then he added, eyeing us, "Oh, I gets along with white folks." We turned the conversation. "Bears? deer?" he answered, "well, I should say there were," and he let fly a string of brave oaths, as he told hunting-tales of the swamp. We left him standing still in the middle of the road looking after us, and yet apparently not noticing us.

The Whistle place, which includes his bit of land, was bought soon after the war by an English syndicate, the "Dixie Cotton and Corn Company." A marvellous deal of style their factor put on, with his servants and coach-and-six; so much so that the concern soon landed in inextricable bankruptcy. Nobody lives in the old house now, but a man comes each winter out of the North and collects his high rents. I know not which are the more touching, such old empty houses, or the homes of the masters' sons. Sad and bitter tales lie hidden back of those white doors – tales of poverty, of struggle, of disappointment. A revolution such as that of '63 is a terrible thing; they that rose rich in the morning often slept in paupers' beds. Beggars and vulgar speculators rose to rule over them, and their children went astray. See yonder sad-colored house, with its cabins and fences and glad crops? It is not glad within; last month the prodigal son of the struggling father wrote home from the city for money. Money! Where was it to come from? And so the son rose in the night and killed his baby, and killed his wife, and shot himself dead. And the world passed on.

I remember wheeling around a bend in the road beside a graceful bit of forest and a singing brook. A long low house faced us, with porch and flying pillars, great oaken door, and a broad lawn shining in the evening sun. But the window-panes were gone, the pillars were worm-eaten; and the moss-grown roof was falling in. Half curiously I peered through the unhinged door, and saw where, on the wall across the hall, was written in once gay letters a faded "Welcome."

Quite a contrast to the southwestern part of Dougherty County is the northwest. Soberly timbered in oak and pine, it has none of that half-tropical luxuriance of the southwest. Then, too, there are fewer signs of a romantic past, and more of systematic modern land-grabbing and money-getting. White people are more in evidence here, and farmer and hired labor replace to some extent the absentee landlord and rack-rented tenant. The crops have neither the luxuriance of the richer land nor the signs of neglect so often seen, and there were fences and meadows here and there. Most of this land was poor, and beneath the notice of the slave-baron, before the war. Since then his nephews and the poor whites and the Jews have seized it. The returns of the farmer are too small to allow much for wages, and yet he will not sell off small farms. There is the Negro Sanford; he has worked fourteen years as overseer on the Ladson place, and "paid out enough for fertilizers to have bought a farm," but the owner will not sell off a few acres.

Two children – a boy and a girl – are hoeing sturdily in the fields on the farm where Corliss works. He is smooth-faced and brown, and is fencing up his pigs. He used to run a successful cotton-gin, but the Cotton Seed Oil Trust has forced the price of ginning so low that he says it hardly pays him. He points out a stately old house over the way as the home of "Pa Willis." We eagerly ride over, for "Pa Willis" was the tall and powerful black Moses who led the Negroes for a generation, and led them well. He was a Baptist preacher, and when he died two thousand black people followed him to the grave; and now they preach his funeral sermon each year. His widow lives here – a weazened, sharp-featured little woman, who curtsied quaintly as we greeted her. Further on lives Jack Delson, the most prosperous Negro farmer in the county. It is a joy to meet him – a great broad-shouldered, handsome black man, intelligent and jovial. Six hundred and fifty acres he owns, and has eleven black tenants. A neat and tidy home nestled in a flower-garden, and a little store stands beside it.

We pass the Munson place, where a plucky white widow is renting and struggling; and the eleven hundred acres of the Sennet plantation, with its Negro overseer. Then the character of the farms begins to change. Nearly all the lands belong to Russian Jews; the overseers are white, and the cabins are bare board-houses scattered here and there. The rents are high, and day-laborers and "contract" hands abound. It is a keen, hard struggle for living here, and few have time to talk. Tired with the long ride, we gladly drive into Gillonsville. It is a silent cluster of farm-houses standing on the cross-roads, with one of its stores closed and the other kept by a Negro preacher. They tell great tales of busy times at Gillonsville before all the railroads came to Albany; now it is chiefly a memory. Riding down the street, we stop at the preacher's and seat ourselves before the door. It was one of those scenes one cannot soon forget: a wide, low, little house, whose motherly roof reached over and sheltered a snug little porch. There we sat, after the long hot drive, drinking cool water – the talkative little storekeeper who is my daily companion; the silent old black woman patching pantaloons and saying never a word; the ragged picture of helpless misfortune who called in just to see the preacher; and finally the neat matronly preacher's wife, plump, yellow, and intelligent. "Own land?" said the wife; "well, only this house." Then she added quietly, "We did buy seven hundred acres up yonder, and paid for it; but they cheated us out of it. Sells was the owner." "Sells!" echoed the ragged misfortune, who was leaning against the balustrade and listening, "he's a regular cheat. I worked for him thirty-seven days this spring, and he paid me in cardboard checks which were to be cashed at the end of the month. But he never cashed them – kept putting me off. Then the sheriff came and took my mule and corn and furniture – " "Furniture?" I asked; "but furniture is exempt from seizure by law." "Well, he took it just the same," said the hard-faced man.

Chapter 8

Of the Quest of the Golden Fleece

> But the Brute, said in his breast, "Till the mills I grind have ceased, The riches shall be dust of dust, dry ashes be the feast!
>
> "On the strong and cunning few
> Cynic favors I will strew;
> I will stuff their maw with overplus until their spirit dies;
> From the patient and the low
> I will take the joys they know;
> They shall hunger after vanities and still an-hungered go.
> Madness shall be on the people, ghastly jealousies arise;
> Brother's blood shall cry on brother up the dead and empty skies."
>
> William Vaughn Moody.[149]

Have you ever seen a cotton-field white with the harvest – its golden fleece hovering above the black earth like a silvery cloud, edged with dark green, its bold white signals waving like the foam of billows from Carolina to Texas across that Black and human Sea? I have sometimes half suspected that here the winged ram Chrysomallus left that Fleece after which Jason and his Argonauts[150] went vaguely wandering into the shadowy East three thousand years ago; and certainly one might frame a pretty and not far-fetched analogy of witchery and dragon's teeth, and blood and armed men, between the ancient and the modern Quest of the Golden Fleece in the Black Sea.

And now the golden fleece is found; not only found, but, in its birthplace, woven. For the hum of the cotton-mills is the newest and most significant thing in the New

Notes

[149] William Vaughn Moody (1869–1910), American poet and dramatist. The lines come from "The Brute" (1901).

[150] *Jason and his Argonauts* in Greek mythology, Jason attempts to earn the throne by going on a quest for the Golden Fleece of Chrysomallus, a flying ram.

South today. All through the Carolinas and Georgia, away down to Mexico, rise these gaunt red buildings, bare and homely, and yet so busy and noisy withal that they scarce seem to belong to the slow and sleepy land. Perhaps they sprang from dragons' teeth. So the Cotton Kingdom still lives; the world still bows beneath her sceptre. Even the markets that once defied the *parvenu* have crept one by one across the seas, and then slowly and reluctantly, but surely, have started toward the Black Belt.

To be sure, there are those who wag their heads knowingly and tell us that the capital of the Cotton Kingdom has moved from the Black to the White Belt – that the Negro of to-day raises not more than half of the cotton crop. Such men forget that the cotton crop has doubled, and more than doubled, since the era of slavery, and that, even granting their contention, the Negro is still supreme in a Cotton Kingdom larger than that on which the Confederacy builded its hopes. So the Negro forms to-day one of the chief figures in a great world-industry; and this, for its own sake, and in the light of historic interest, makes the field-hands of the cotton country worth studying.

We seldom study the condition of the Negro to-day honestly and carefully. It is so much easier to assume that we know it all. Or perhaps, having already reached conclusions in our own minds, we are loth to have them disturbed by facts. And yet how little we really know of these millions – of their daily lives and longings, of their homely joys and sorrows, of their real shortcomings and the meaning of their crimes! All this we can only learn by intimate contact with the masses, and not by wholesale arguments covering millions separate in time and space, and differing widely in training and culture. To-day, then, my reader, let us turn our faces to the Black Belt of Georgia and seek simply to know the condition of the black farm-laborers of one county there.

Here in 1890 lived ten thousand Negroes and two thousand whites. The country is rich, yet the people are poor. The keynote of the Black Belt is debt; not commercial credit, but debt in the sense of continued inability on the part of the mass of the population to make income cover expense. This is the direct heritage of the South from the wasteful economies of the slave *régime*; but it was emphasized and brought to a crisis by the Emancipation of the slaves. In 1860, Dougherty County had six thousand slaves, worth at least two and a half millions of dollars; its farms were estimated at three millions – making five and a half millions of property, the value of which depended largely on the slave system, and on the speculative demand for land once marvellously rich but already partially devitalized by careless and exhaustive culture. The war then meant a financial crash; in place of the five and a half millions of 1860, there remained in 1870 only farms valued at less than two millions. With this came increased competition in cotton culture from the rich lands of Texas; a steady fall in the normal price of cotton followed, from about fourteen cents a pound in 1860 until it reached four cents in 1898. Such a financial revolution was it that involved the owners of the cotton-belt in debt. And if things went ill with the master, how fared it with the man?

The plantations of Dougherty County in slavery days were not as imposing and aristocratic as those of Virginia. The Big House was smaller and usually one-storied, and sat very near the slave cabins. Sometimes these cabins stretched off on either side like wings; sometimes only on one side, forming a double row, or edging the road that turned into the plantation from the main thoroughfare. The form and disposition of the laborers' cabins throughout the Black Belt is to-day the same as in slavery days. Some live in the selfsame cabins, others in cabins rebuilt on the sites of the old. All are sprinkled in little groups over the face of the land, centering about some dilapidated Big House where the head-tenant or agent lives. The general character and arrangement of these dwellings remains on the whole unaltered. There were in the county, outside the corporate town of Albany, about fifteen hundred Negro families in 1898.

Out of all these, only a single family occupied a house with seven rooms; only fourteen have five rooms or more. The mass live in one- and two-room homes.

The size and arrangements of a people's homes are no unfair index of their condition. If, then, we inquire more carefully into these Negro homes, we find much that is unsatisfactory. All over the face of the land is the one-room cabin – now standing in the shadow of the Big House, now staring at the dusty road, now rising dark and sombre amid the green of the cotton-fields. It is nearly always old and bare, built of rough boards, and neither plastered nor ceiled. Light and ventilation are supplied by the single door and by the square hole in the wall with its wooden shutter. There is no glass, porch, or ornamentation without. Within is a fireplace, black and smoky, and usually unsteady with age. A bed or two, a table, a wooden chest, and a few chairs compose the furniture; while a stray show-bill or a newspaper makes up the decorations for the walls. Now and then one may find such a cabin kept scrupulously neat, with merry steaming fireplace and hospitable door; but the majority are dirty and dilapidated, smelling of eating and sleeping, poorly ventilated, and anything but homes.

Above all, the cabins are crowded. We have come to associate crowding with homes in cities almost exclusively. This is primarily because we have so little accurate knowledge of country life. Here in Dougherty County one may find families of eight and ten occupying one or two rooms, and for every ten rooms of house accommodation for the Negroes there are twenty-five persons. The worst tenement abominations of New York do not have above twenty-two persons for every ten rooms. Of course, one small, close room in a city, without a yard, is in many respects worse than the larger single country room. In other respects it is better; it has glass windows, a decent chimney, and a trustworthy floor. The single great advantage of the Negro peasant is that he may spend most of his life outside his hovel, in the open fields.

There are four chief causes of these wretched homes: First, long custom born of slavery has assigned such homes to Negroes; white laborers would be offered better accommodations, and might, for that and similar reasons, give better work. Secondly; the Negroes, used to such accommodations, do not as a rule demand better; they do not know what better houses mean. Thirdly, the landlords as a class have not yet come to realize that it is a good business investment to raise the standard of living among labor by slow and judicious methods; that a Negro laborer who demands three rooms and fifty cents a day would give more efficient work and leave a larger profit than a discouraged toiler herding his family in one room and working for thirty cents. Lastly, among such conditions of life there are few incentives to make the laborer become a better farmer. If he is ambitious, he moves to town or tries other labor; as a tenant-farmer his outlook is almost hopeless, and following it as a makeshift, he takes the house that is given him without protest.

In such homes, then, these Negro peasants live. The families are both small and large; there are many single tenants – widows and bachelors, and remnants of broken groups. The system of labor and the size of the houses both tend to the breaking up of family groups: the grown children go away as contract hands or migrate to town, the sister goes into service; and so one finds many families with hosts of babies, and many newly married couples, but comparatively few families with half-grown and grown sons and daughters. The average size of Negro families has undoubtedly decreased since the war, primarily from economic stress. In Russia over a third of the bridegrooms and over half the brides are under twenty; the same was true of the antebellum Negroes. To-day, however, very few of the boys and less than a fifth of the Negro girls under twenty are married. The young men marry between the ages of twenty-five and thirty-five; the young women between twenty and thirty. Such postponement is due to the difficulty of earning sufficient to rear and support a family; and it undoubtedly leads, in the country districts, to sexual immorality. The form of this immorality, however, is very seldom that of prostitution, and less frequently that of illegitimacy than one would imagine. Rather, it takes the form of separation and desertion after a family group has been formed. The number of separated persons is thirty-five to the thousand – a very large number. It would of course be unfair to compare this number with divorce statistics, for many of these separated women are in reality widowed, were the truth known, and in other cases the separation is not permanent. Nevertheless, here lies the seat of greatest moral danger. There is little or no prostitution among these Negroes, and over three-fourths of the families, as found by house-to-house investigation, deserve to be classed as decent people with considerable regard for female chastity. To be sure, the ideas of the mass would not suit New England, and there are many loose habits and notions. Yet the rate of illegitimacy is undoubtedly lower than in Austria or Italy, and the women as a class are modest. The plague-spot in sexual relations is easy marriage, and easy separation. This is no sudden development, nor the fruit of Emancipation. It is the plain heritage from slavery. In those days Sam, with his master's consent, "took up" with Mary. No ceremony was necessary, and in the busy life of the great plantations of the Black Belt it was usually dispensed with. If now the master needed Sam's work in another plantation or in another part of the same plantation, or if he took a notion to sell the slave, Sam's married life with Mary was usually unceremoniously broken, and then it was clearly to the master's interest to have both of them take new mates. This widespread custom of two centuries has not been eradicated in thirty years. Today Sam's grandson "takes up" with a woman without license or ceremony; they live together decently and honestly, and are, to all intents and purposes, man and wife. Sometimes these unions are never broken, until death; but in too many cases family quarrels, a roving spirit, a rival suitor, or perhaps more frequently the hopeless battle to support a family, lead to separation, and a broken household is the result. The Negro church has done much to stop this practice, and now most marriage ceremonies are performed by the pastors. Nevertheless, the evil is still deep seated, and only a general raising of the standard of living will finally cure it.

Looking now at the county black population as a whole, it is fair to characterize it as poor and ignorant. Perhaps ten per cent compose the well-to-do and the best of the laborers, while at least nine per cent are thoroughly lewd and vicious. The rest, over eighty per cent, are poor and ignorant, fairly honest and well meaning, plodding, and to a degree shiftless, with some but not great sexual looseness. Such class lines are by no means fixed; they vary, one might almost say, with the price of cotton. The degree of ignorance cannot easily be expressed. We may say, for instance, that nearly two-thirds of them cannot read or write. This but partially expresses the fact. They are ignorant of the world about them, of modern economic organization, of the function of government, of individual worth and possibilities – of nearly all those things which slavery in self-defence had to keep them from learning. Much that the white boy imbibes from his earliest social atmosphere forms the puzzling problems of the black boy's mature years. America is not another word for Opportunity to *all* her sons.

It is easy for us to lose ourselves in details in endeavoring to grasp and comprehend the real condition of a mass of human beings. We often forget that each unit in the mass is a throbbing human soul. Ignorant it may be, and poverty stricken, black and curious in limb and ways and thought and yet it loves and hates, it toils and tires, it laughs and weeps its bitter tears, and looks in vague and awful longing at the grim horizon of its life – all this, even as you and I. These black thousands are not in reality lazy; they are improvident and careless; they insist on breaking the monotony of toil with a glimpse at the great town-world on Saturday; they have their loafers and their rascals; but the great mass of them work continuously and faithfully for a return, and under circumstances that would call forth equal voluntary effort from few if any other modern laboring class. Over eighty-eight per cent of them – men, women, and children – are farmers. Indeed, this is almost the only industry. Most of the children get their schooling after the "crops are laid by," and very few there are that stay in school after the spring work has begun. Child-labor is to be found here in some of its worst phases, as fostering ignorance and stunting physical development. With the grown men of the county there is little variety in work: thirteen hundred are farmers, and two hundred are laborers, teamsters, etc., including twenty-four artisans, ten merchants, twenty-one preachers, and four teachers. This narrowness of life reaches its maximum among the women: thirteen hundred and fifty of these are farm laborers, one hundred are servants and washerwomen, leaving sixty-five housewives, eight teachers, and six seamstresses.

Among this people there is no leisure class. We often forget that in the United States over half the youth and adults are not in the world earning incomes, but are making homes, learning of the world, or resting after the heat of the strife. But here ninety-six per cent are toiling; no one with leisure to turn the bare and cheerless cabin into a home, no old folks to sit beside the fire and hand down traditions of the past; little of careless happy childhood and dreaming youth. The dull monotony of daily toil is broken only by the gayety of the thoughtless and the Saturday trip to town. The toil, like all farm toil, is monotonous, and here there are little machinery and few tools to relieve its burdensome drudgery. But with all this, it is work in the pure open air, and this is something in a day when fresh air is scarce.

The land on the whole is still fertile, despite long abuse. For nine or ten months in succession the crops will come if asked: garden vegetables in April, grain in May, melons in June and July, hay in August, sweet potatoes in September, and cotton from then to Christmas. And yet on two thirds of the land there is but one crop, and that leaves the toilers in debt. Why is this?

Away down the Baysan road, where the broad flat fields are flanked by great oak forests, is a plantation; many thousands of acres it used to run, here and there, and beyond the great wood. Thirteen hundred human beings here obeyed the call of one – were his in body, and largely in soul. One of them lives there yet – a short, stocky man, his dull-brown face seamed and drawn, and his tightly curled hair gray-white. The crops? Just tolerable, he said; just tolerable. Getting on? No – he wasn't getting on at all. Smith of Albany "furnishes" him, and his rent is eight hundred pounds of cotton. Can't make anything at that. Why didn't he buy land? *Humph!* Takes money to buy land. And he turns away. Free! The most piteous thing amid all the black ruin of wartime, amid the broken fortunes of the masters, the blighted hopes of mothers and maidens, and the fall of an empire – the most piteous thing amid all this was the black freedman who threw down his hoe because the world called him free. What did such a mockery of freedom mean? Not a cent of money, not an inch of land, not a mouthful of victuals – not even ownership of the rags on his back. Free! On Saturday, once or twice a month, the old master, before the war, used to dole out bacon and meal to his Negroes. And after the first flush of freedom wore off, and his true helplessness dawned on the freedman, he came back and picked up his hoe, and old master still doled out his bacon and meal. The legal form of service was theoretically far different; in practice, task-work or "cropping" was substituted for daily toil in gangs; and the slave gradually became a metayer, or tenant on shares, in name, but a laborer with indeterminate wages in fact.

Still the price of cotton fell, and gradually the landlords deserted their plantations, and the reign of the merchant began. The merchant of the Black Belt is a curious institution – part banker, part landlord, part contractor, and part despot. His store, which used most frequently to stand at the crossroads and become the centre of a weekly village, has now moved to town; and thither the Negro tenant follows him. The merchant keeps everything – clothes and shoes, coffee and sugar, pork and meal, canned and dried goods, wagons and ploughs, seed and fertilizer – and what he has not in stock he can give you an order for at the store across the way. Here, then, comes the tenant, Sam Scott, after he has contracted with some absent landlord's agent for hiring forty acres of land; he fingers his hat nervously until the merchant finishes his morning chat with Colonel Sanders, and calls out, "Well, Sam, what do you want?" Sam wants him to "furnish" him – *i.e.*, to advance him food and clothing for the year, and perhaps seed and tools, until his crop is raised and sold. If Sam seems a favorable subject, he and the merchant go to a lawyer, and Sam executes a chattel mortgage on his mule and wagon in return for seed and a week's rations. As soon as the green cotton-leaves appear above the ground, another mortgage is given on the "crop." Every Saturday, or at longer intervals, Sam calls upon the merchant for his "rations"; a family of five usually gets about thirty pounds of fat side-pork and a couple of bushels of corn-meal a month. Besides this, clothing and shoes must be furnished; if Sam or his family is sick, there are orders on the druggist and doctor; if the mule wants shoeing, an order on the blacksmith, etc. If Sam is a hard worker and crops promise well, he is often encouraged to buy more – sugar, extra clothes, perhaps a buggy. But he is seldom encouraged to save. When cotton rose to ten cents last fall, the shrewd merchants of Dougherty County sold a thousand buggies in one season, mostly to black men.

The security offered for such transactions – a crop and chattel mortgage – may at first seem slight. And, indeed, the merchants tell many a true tale of shiftlessness and cheating; of cotton picked at night, mules disappearing, and tenants absconding. But on the whole the merchant of the Black Belt is the most prosperous man in the section. So skilfully and so closely has he drawn the bonds of the law about the tenant, that the black man has often simply to choose between pauperism and crime; he "waives" all homestead exemptions in his contract; he cannot touch his own mortgaged crop, which the laws put almost in the full control of the landowner and of the merchant. When the crop is growing the merchant watches it like a hawk; as soon as it is ready for market he takes possession of it, sells it, pays the land-owner his rent, subtracts his bill for supplies, and if, as sometimes happens, there is anything left, he hands it over to the black serf for his Christmas celebration.

The direct result of this system is an all-cotton scheme of agriculture and the continued bankruptcy of the tenant. The currency of the Black Belt is cotton. It is a crop always salable for ready money, not usually subject to great yearly fluctuations in price, and one which the Negroes know how to raise. The landlord therefore demands his rent in cotton, and the merchant will accept mortgages on no other crop. There is no use asking the black tenant, then, to diversify his crops – he cannot under this system. Moreover, the system is bound to bankrupt the tenant. I remember once meeting a little one-mule wagon on the River road. A young black fellow sat in it driving listlessly, his elbows on his knees. His dark-faced wife sat beside him, stolid, silent.

"Hello!" cried my driver – he has a most impudent way of addressing these people, though they seem used to it – "what have you got there?"

"Meat and meal," answered the man, stopping. The meat lay uncovered in the bottom of the wagon – a great thin side of fat pork covered with salt; the meal was in a white bushel bag.

"What did you pay for that meat?"

"Ten cents a pound." It could have been bought for six or seven cents cash.

"And the meal?"

"Two dollars." One dollar and ten cents is the cash price in town. Here was a man paying five dollars for goods which he could have bought for three dollars cash, and raised for one dollar or one dollar and a half.

Yet it is not wholly his fault. The Negro farmer started behind – started in debt. This was not his choosing, but the crime of this happy-go-lucky nation which goes blundering along with its Reconstruction tragedies, its Spanish war interludes and Philippine matinees, just as though God really were dead. Once in debt, it is no easy matter for a whole race to emerge.

In the year of low-priced cotton, 1898, out of three hundred tenant families one hundred and seventy-five ended their year's work in debt to the extent of fourteen thousand dollars; fifty cleared nothing, and the remaining seventy-five made a total profit of sixteen hundred dollars. The net indebtedness of the black tenant families of the whole county must have been at least sixty thousand dollars. In a more prosperous year the situation is far better; but on the average the majority of tenants end the year even, or in debt, which means that they work for board and clothes. Such an economic organization is radically wrong. Whose is the blame?

The underlying causes of this situation are complicated but discernible. And one of the chief, outside the carelessness of the nation in letting the slave start with nothing, is the widespread opinion among the merchants and employers of the Black Belt that only by the slavery of debt can the Negro be kept at work. Without doubt, some pressure was necessary at the beginning of the free-labor system to keep the listless and lazy at work; and even to-day the mass of the Negro laborers need stricter guardianship than most Northern laborers. Behind this honest and widespread opinion dishonesty and cheating of the ignorant laborers have a good chance to take refuge. And to all this must be added the obvious fact, that a slave ancestry and a system of unrequited toil has not improved the efficiency or temper of the mass of black laborers. Nor is this peculiar to Sambo; it has in history been just as true of John and Hans, of Jacques and Pat, of all ground-down peasantries. Such is the situation of the mass of the Negroes in the Black Belt to-day; and they are thinking about it. Crime, and a cheap and dangerous socialism, are the inevitable results of this pondering. I see now that ragged black man sitting on a log, aimlessly whittling a stick. He muttered to me with the murmur of many ages, when he said: "White man sit down whole year; Nigger work day and night and make crop; Nigger hardly gits bread and meat; white man sittin' down gits all. *It's wrong.*" And what do the better classes of Negroes do to improve their situation? One of two things: if any way possible, they buy land; if not, they migrate to town. Just as centuries ago it was no easy thing for the serf to escape into the freedom of town-life, even so today there are hindrances laid in the way of county laborers. In considerable parts of all the Gulf States, and especially in Mississippi, Louisiana, and Arkansas, the Negroes on the plantations in the back-country districts are still held at forced labor practically without wages. Especially is this true in districts where the farmers are composed of the more ignorant class of poor whites, and the Negroes are beyond the reach of schools and intercourse with their advancing fellows. If such a peon should run away, the sheriff, elected by white suffrage, can usually be depended on to catch the fugitive, return him, and ask no questions. If he escape to another county, a charge of petty thieving, easily true, can be depended upon to secure his return. Even if some unduly officious person insist upon a trial, neighborly comity will probably make his conviction sure, and then the labor due the county can easily be bought by the master. Such a system is impossible in the more civilized parts of the South, or near the large towns and cities; but in those vast stretches of land beyond the telegraph and the newspaper the spirit of the Thirteenth Amendment is sadly broken. This represents the lowest economic depths of the black American peasant; and in a study of the rise and condition of the Negro freeholder we must trace his economic progress from this modern serfdom.

Even in the better-ordered country districts of the South the free movement of agricultural laborers is hindered by the migration-agent laws. The "Associated Press" recently informed the world of the arrest of a young white man in Southern Georgia who represented the "Atlantic Naval Supplies Company," and who "was caught in the act of enticing hands from the turpentine farm of Mr. John Greer." The crime for which this young man was arrested is taxed five hundred dollars for each county in which the employment agent proposes to gather laborers for work outside the State. Thus the Negroes' ignorance of the labor-market outside his own vicinity is increased rather than diminished by the laws of nearly every Southern State.

Similar to such measures is the unwritten law of the back districts and small towns of the South, that the character of all Negroes unknown to the mass of the community must be vouched for by some white man. This is really a revival of the old Roman idea of the patron under whose protection the new-made freedman was put. In many instances this system has been of great good to the Negro, and very often under the protection and guidance of the former master's family, or other white friends, the freedman progressed in wealth and morality. But the same system has in other cases resulted in the refusal of whole communities to recognize the right of a Negro to change his habitation and to be master of his own fortunes. A black stranger in Baker County, Georgia, for instance, is liable to be stopped anywhere on the public highway and made to state his business to the satisfaction of any white interrogator. If he fails to give a suitable answer, or seems too independent or "sassy," he may be arrested or summarily driven away.

Thus it is that in the country districts of the South, by written or unwritten law, peonage, hindrances to the migration of labor, and a system of white patronage exists over large areas. Besides this, the chance for lawless oppression and illegal exactions is vastly greater in the country than in the city, and nearly all the more serious race disturbances of the last decade have arisen from disputes in the county between master and man – as, for instance, the Sam Hose affair. As a result of such a situation, there arose, first, the Black Belt; and, second, the Migration to Town. The Black Belt was not, as many assumed, a movement toward fields of labor under more genial climatic conditions; it was primarily a huddling for self-protection – a massing of the black population for mutual defence in order to secure the peace and tranquillity necessary to economic advance. This movement took place between Emancipation and 1880, and only partially accomplished the desired results. The rush to town since 1880 is the counter-movement of men disappointed in the economic opportunities of the Black Belt.

In Dougherty County, Georgia, one can see easily the results of this experiment in huddling for protection. Only ten per cent of the adult population was born in the county, and yet the blacks outnumber the whites four or five to one. There is undoubtedly a security to the blacks in their very numbers – a personal freedom from arbitrary treatment, which makes hundreds of laborers cling to Dougherty in spite of low wages and economic distress. But a change is coming, and slowly but surely even here the agricultural laborers are drifting to town and leaving the broad acres behind. Why is this? Why do not the Negroes become landowners, and build up the black landed peasantry, which has for a generation and more been the dream of philanthropist and statesman?

To the car-window sociologist, to the man who seeks to understand and know the South by devoting the few leisure hours of a holiday trip to unravelling the snarl of centuries – to such men very often the whole trouble with the black fieldhand may be summed up by Aunt Ophelia's word,[151] "Shiftless!" They have noted repeatedly scenes like one I saw last summer. We were riding along the highroad to town at the close of a long hot day. A couple of young black fellows passed us in a mule-team, with several bushels of loose corn in the ear. One was driving, listlessly bent forward, his elbows on his knees – a happy-go-lucky, careless picture of irresponsibility. The other was fast asleep in the bottom of the wagon. As we passed we noticed an ear of corn fall from the wagon. They never saw it – not they. A rod farther on we noted another ear on the ground; and between that creeping mule and town we counted twenty-six ears of corn. Shiftless? Yes, the personification of shiftlessness. And yet follow those boys: they are not lazy; to-morrow morning they'll be up with the sun; they work hard when they do work, and they work willingly. They have no sordid, selfish, money-getting ways, but rather a fine disdain for mere cash. They'll loaf before your face and work behind your back with good-natured honesty. They'll steal a watermelon, and hand you back your lost purse intact. Their great defect as laborers lies in their lack of incentive to work beyond the mere pleasure of physical exertion. They are careless because they have not found that it pays to be careful; they are improvident because the improvident ones of their acquaintance get on about as well as the provident. Above all, they cannot see why they should take unusual pains to make the white man's land better, or to fatten his mule, or save his corn. On the other hand, the white land-owner argues that any attempt to improve these laborers by increased responsibility, or higher wages, or better homes, or land of their own, would be sure to result in failure. He shows his Northern visitor the scarred and wretched land; the ruined mansions, the worn-out soil and mortgaged acres, and says, This is Negro freedom!

Now it happens that both master and man have just enough argument on their respective sides to make it difficult for them to understand each other. The Negro dimly personifies in the white man all his ills and misfortunes; if he is poor, it is because the white man seizes the fruit of his toil; if he is ignorant, it is because the white man gives him neither time nor facilities to learn; and, indeed, if any misfortune happens to him, it is because of some hidden machinations of "white folks." On the other hand, the masters and the masters' sons have never been able to see why the Negro, instead of settling down to be day-laborers for bread and clothes, are infected with a silly desire to rise in the world, and why they are sulky, dissatisfied, and careless, where their fathers were happy and dumb and faithful. "Why, you niggers have an easier time than I do," said a puzzled Albany merchant to his black customer. "Yes," he replied, "and so does yo' hogs."

Taking, then, the dissatisfied and shiftless field-hand as a starting-point, let us inquire how the black thousands of Dougherty have struggled from him up toward their ideal, and what that ideal is. All social struggle is evidenced by the rise, first of economic, then of social classes, among a homogeneous population. To-day the following economic classes are plainly differentiated among these Negroes.

A "submerged tenth" of croppers, with a few paupers; forty per cent who are metayers and thirty-nine per cent of semi-metayers and wage-laborers. There are left five per cent of money-renters and six per cent of freeholders – the "Upper Ten" of the land. The croppers are entirely without capital, even in the limited sense of food or money to keep them from seed-time to harvest. All they furnish is their labor; the land-owner

Notes

[151] *Aunt Ophelia's word* Ophelia St. Clare, a New England abolitionist in Harriet Beecher Stowe's *Uncle Tom's Cabin* (1852).

furnishes land, stock, tools, seed, and house; and at the end of the year the laborer gets from a third to a half of the crop. Out of his share, however, comes pay and interest for food and clothing advanced him during the year. Thus we have a laborer without capital and without wages, and an employer whose capital is largely his employees' wages. It is an unsatisfactory arrangement, both for hirer and hired, and is usually in vogue on poor land with hard-pressed owners.

Above the croppers come the great mass of the black population who work the land on their own responsibility, paying rent in cotton and supported by the crop-mortgage system. After the war this system was attractive to the freedmen on account of its larger freedom and its possibilities for making a surplus. But with the carrying out of the crop-lien system, the deterioration of the land, and the slavery of debt, the position of the metayers has sunk to a dead level of practically unrewarded toil. Formerly all tenants had some capital, and often considerable; but absentee landlordism, rising rack-rent, and falling cotton have stripped them well-nigh of all, and probably not over half of them to-day own their mules. The change from cropper to tenant was accomplished by fixing the rent. If, now, the rent fixed was reasonable, this was an incentive to the tenant to strive. On the other hand, if the rent was too high, or if the land deteriorated, the result was to discourage and check the efforts of the black peasantry. There is no doubt that the latter case is true; that in Dougherty County every economic advantage of the price of cotton in market and of the strivings of the tenant has been taken advantage of by the landlords and merchants, and swallowed up in rent and interest. If cotton rose in price, the rent rose even higher; if cotton fell, the rent remained or followed reluctantly. If a tenant worked hard and raised a large crop, his rent was raised the next year; if that year the crop failed, his corn was confiscated and his mule sold for debt. There were, of course, exceptions to this – cases of personal kindness and forbearance; but in the vast majority of cases the rule was to extract the uttermost farthing from the mass of the black farm laborers.

The average metayer pays from twenty to thirty per cent of his crop in rent. The result of such rack-rent can only be evil – abuse and neglect of the soil, deterioration in the character of the laborers, and a widespread sense of injustice. "Wherever the country is poor," cried Arthur Young,[152] "it is in the hands of metayers," and "their condition is more wretched than that of day-laborers." He was talking of Italy a century ago; but he might have been talking of Dougherty County to-day. And especially is that true to-day which he declares was true in France before the Revolution: "The metayers are considered as little better than menial servants, removable at pleasure, and obliged to conform in all things to the will of the landlords." On this low plane half the black population of Dougherty County – perhaps more than half the black millions of this land – are to-day struggling.

A degree above these we may place those laborers who receive money wages for their work. Some receive a house with perhaps a garden-spot; then supplies of food and clothing are advanced, and certain fixed wages are given at the end of the year, varying from thirty to sixty dollars, out of which the supplies must be paid for, with interest. About eighteen per cent of the population belong to this class of semi-metayers, while twenty-two per cent are laborers paid by the month or year, and are either "furnished" by their own savings or perhaps more usually by some merchant who takes his chances of payment. Such laborers receive from thirty-five to fifty cents a day

Notes

[152] Arthur Young (1741–1820), English author of *Travels in France* (1792).

during the working season. They are usually young unmarried persons, some being women; and when they marry they sink to the class of metayers, or, more seldom, become renters.

The renters for fixed money rentals are the first of the emerging classes, and form five per cent of the families. The sole advantage of this small class is their freedom to choose their crops, and the increased responsibility which comes through having money transactions. While some of the renters differ little in condition from the metayers, yet on the whole they are more intelligent and responsible persons, and are the ones who eventually become land-owners. Their better character and greater shrewdness enable them to gain, perhaps to demand, better terms in rents; rented farms, varying from forty to a hundred acres, bear an average rental of about fifty-four dollars a year. The men who conduct such farms do not long remain renters; either they sink to metayers, or with a successful series of harvests rise to be land-owners.

In 1870 the tax-books of Dougherty report no Negroes as landholders. If there were any such at that time – and there may have been a few – their land was probably held in the name of some white patron – a method not uncommon during slavery. In 1875 ownership of land had begun with seven hundred and fifty acres; ten years later this had increased to over sixty-five hundred acres, to nine thousand acres in 1890 and ten thousand in 1900. The total assessed property has in this same period risen from eighty thousand dollars in 1875 to two hundred and forty thousand dollars in 1900.

Two circumstances complicate this development and make it in some respects difficult to be sure of the real tendencies; they are the panic of 1893, the low price of cotton in 1898. Besides this, the system of assessing property in the country districts of Georgia is somewhat antiquated and of uncertain statistical value; there are no assessors, and each man makes a sworn return to a tax-receiver. Thus public opinion plays a large part, and the returns vary strangely from year to year. Certainly these figures show the small amount of accumulated capital among the Negroes, and the consequent large dependence of their property on temporary prosperity. They have little to tide over a few years of economic depression, and are at the mercy of the cotton-market far more than the whites. And thus the landowners, despite their marvellous efforts, are really a transient class, continually being depleted by those who fall back into the class of renters or metayers, and augmented by newcomers from the masses. Of the one hundred land-owners in 1898, half had bought their land since 1893, a fourth between 1890 and 1893, a fifth between 1884 and 1890, and the rest between 1870 and 1884. In all, one hundred and eighty-five Negroes have owned land in this county since 1875.

If all the black land-owners who had ever held land here had kept it or left it in the hands of black men, the Negroes would have owned nearer thirty thousand acres than the fifteen thousand they now hold. And yet these fifteen thousand acres are a creditable showing – a proof of no little weight of the worth and ability of the Negro people. If they had been given an economic start at Emancipation, if they had been in an enlightened and rich community which really desired their best good, then we might perhaps call such a result small or even insignificant. But for a few thousand poor ignorant field-hands, in the face of poverty, a falling market, and social stress, to save and capitalize two hundred thousand dollars in a generation has meant a tremendous effort. The rise of a nation, the pressing forward of a social class, means a bitter struggle, a hard and soul-sickening battle with the world such as few of the more favored classes know or appreciate.

Out of the hard economic conditions of this portion of the Black Belt, only six per cent of the population have succeeded in emerging into peasant proprietorship; and these are not all firmly fixed, but grow and shrink in number with the wavering of the cotton-market. Fully ninety-four per cent have struggled for land and failed, and half of them sit in hopeless serfdom. For these there is one other avenue of escape toward which they have turned in increasing numbers, namely, migration to town. A glance at the distribution of land among the black owners curiously reveals this fact. In 1898 the holdings were as follows: Under forty acres, forty-nine families; forty to two hundred and fifty acres, seventeen families; two hundred and fifty to one thousand acres, thirteen families; one thousand or more acres, two families. Now in 1890 there were forty-four holdings, but only nine of these were under forty acres. The great increase of holdings, then, has come in the buying of small homesteads near town, where their owners really share in the town life; this is a part of the rush to town. And for every land-owner who has thus hurried away from the narrow and hard conditions of country life, how many field-hands, how many tenants, how many ruined renters, have joined that long procession? Is it not strange compensation? The sin of the country districts is visited on the town, and the social sores of city life to-day may, here in Dougherty County, and perhaps in many places near and far, look for their final healing without the city walls.

Chapter 9

Of the Sons of Master and Man

Life treads on life, and heart on heart;
We press too close in church and mart
To keep a dream or grave apart.

Mrs. Browning.[153]

The world-old phenomenon of the contact of diverse races of men is to have new exemplification during the new century. Indeed, the characteristic of our age is the contact of European civilization with the world's undeveloped peoples. Whatever we may say of the results of such contact in the past, it certainly forms a chapter in human action not pleasant to look back upon. War, murder, slavery, extermination, and debauchery – this has again and again been the result of carrying civilization and the blessed gospel to the isles of the sea and the heathen without the law. Nor does it altogether satisfy the conscience of the modern world to be told complacently that all this has been right and proper, the fated triumph of strength over weakness, of righteousness over evil, of superiors over inferiors. It would certainly be soothing if one could

Notes

[153] Elizabeth Barrett Browning (1806–1861), English poet; the lines come from "A Vision of Poets" (1844).

readily believe all this; and yet there are too many ugly facts for everything to be thus easily explained away. We feel and know that there are many delicate differences in race psychology, numberless changes that our crude social measurements are not yet able to follow minutely, which explain much of history and social development. At the same time, too, we know that these considerations have never adequately explained or excused the triumph of brute force and cunning over weakness and innocence.

It is, then, the strife of all honorable men of the twentieth century to see that in the future competition of races the survival of the fittest shall mean the triumph of the good, the beautiful, and the true; that we may be able to preserve for future civilization all that is really fine and noble and strong, and not continue to put a premium on greed and impudence and cruelty. To bring this hope to fruition, we are compelled daily to turn more and more to a conscientious study of the phenomena of race-contact – to a study frank and fair, and not falsified and colored by our wishes or our fears. And we have in the South as fine a field for such a study as the world affords – a field, to be sure, which the average American scientist deems somewhat beneath his dignity, and which the average man who is not a scientist knows all about, but nevertheless a line of study which by reason of the enormous race complications with which God seems about to punish this nation must increasingly claim our sober attention, study, and thought, we must ask, what are the actual relations of whites and blacks in the South? and we must be answered, not by apology or fault-finding, but by a plain, unvarnished tale.

In the civilized life of to-day the contact of men and their relations to each other fall in a few main lines of action and communication: there is, first, the physical proximity of homes and dwelling-places, the way in which neighborhoods group themselves, and the contiguity of neighborhoods. Secondly, and in our age chiefest, there are the economic relations – the methods by which individuals cooperate for earning a living, for the mutual satisfaction of wants, for the production of wealth. Next, there are the political relations, the cooperation in social control, in group government, in laying and paying the burden of taxation. In the fourth place there are the less tangible but highly important forms of intellectual contact and commerce, the interchange of ideas through conversation and conference, through periodicals and libraries; and, above all, the gradual formation for each community of that curious *tertium quid*[154] which we call public opinion. Closely allied with this come the various forms of social contact in everyday life, in travel, in theatres, in house gatherings, in marrying and giving in marriage. Finally, there are the varying forms of religious enterprise, of moral teaching and benevolent endeavor. These are the principal ways in which men living in the same communities are brought into contact with each other. It is my present task, therefore, to indicate, from my point of view, how the black race in the South meet and mingle with the whites in these matters of everyday life.

First, as to physical dwelling. It is usually possible to draw in nearly every Southern community a physical color-line on the map, on the one side of which whites dwell and on the other Negroes. The winding and intricacy of the geographical color line varies, of course, in different communities. I know some towns where a straight line drawn through the middle of the main street separates nine-tenths of the whites from nine-tenths of the blacks. In other towns the older settlement of whites has been encircled by a broad band of blacks; in still other cases little settlements or nuclei of blacks have sprung up amid surrounding whites. Usually in cities each street has its distinctive

Notes

[154] *tertium quid* (Latin) third thing.

color, and only now and then do the colors meet in close proximity. Even in the country something of this segregation is manifest in the smaller areas, and of course in the larger phenomena of the Black Belt.

All this segregation by color is largely independent of that natural clustering by social grades common to all communities. A Negro slum may be in dangerous proximity to a white residence quarter, while it is quite common to find a white slum planted in the heart of a respectable Negro district. One thing, however, seldom occurs: the best of the whites and the best of the Negroes almost never live in anything like close proximity. It thus happens that in nearly every Southern town and city, both whites and blacks see commonly the worst of each other. This is a vast change from the situation in the past, when, through the close contact of master and house-servant in the patriarchal big house, one found the best of both races in close contact and sympathy, while at the same time the squalor and dull round of toil among the field-hands was removed from the sight and hearing of the family. One can easily see how a person who saw slavery thus from his father's parlors, and sees freedom on the streets of a great city, fails to grasp or comprehend the whole of the new picture. On the other hand, the settled belief of the mass of the Negroes that the Southern white people do not have the black man's best interests at heart has been intensified in later years by this continual daily contact of the better class of blacks with the worst representatives of the white race.

Coming now to the economic relations of the races, we are on ground made familiar by study, much discussion, and no little philanthropic effort. And yet with all this there are many essential elements in the cooperation of Negroes and whites for work and wealth that are too readily overlooked or not thoroughly understood. The average American can easily conceive of a rich land awaiting development and filled with black laborers. To him the Southern problem is simply that of making efficient workingmen out of this material, by giving them the requisite technical skill and the help of invested capital. The problem, however, is by no means as simple as this, from the obvious fact that these workingmen have been trained for centuries as slaves. They exhibit, therefore, all the advantages and defects of such training; they are willing and good-natured, but not self-reliant, provident, or careful. If now the economic development of the South is to be pushed to the verge of exploitation, as seems probable, then we have a mass of workingmen thrown into relentless competition with the workingmen of the world, but handicapped by a training the very opposite to that of the modern self-reliant democratic laborer. What the black laborer needs is careful personal guidance, group leadership of men with hearts in their bosoms, to train them to foresight, carefulness, and honesty. Nor does it require any fine-spun theories of racial differences to prove the necessity of such group training after the brains of the race have been knocked out by two hundred and fifty years of assiduous education in submission, carelessness, and stealing. After Emancipation, it was the plain duty of someone to assume this group leadership and training of the Negro laborer. I will not stop here to inquire whose duty it was – whether that of the white ex-master who had profited by unpaid toil, or the Northern philanthropist whose persistence brought on the crisis, or the National Government whose edict freed the bondmen; I will not stop to ask whose duty it was, but I insist it was the duty of someone to see that these workingmen were not left alone and unguided, without capital, without land, without skill, without economic organization, without even the bald protection of law, order, and decency – left in a great land, not to settle down to slow and careful internal development, but destined to be thrown almost immediately into relentless and sharp competition with the best of modern workingmen under an economic system where every participant is fighting for himself, and too often utterly regardless of the rights or welfare of his neighbor.

For we must never forget that the economic system of the South to-day which has succeeded the old *régime* is not the same system as that of the old industrial North, of England, or of France, with their trades-unions, their restrictive laws, their written and unwritten commercial customs, and their long experience. It is, rather, a copy of that England of the early nineteenth century, before the factory acts – the England that wrung pity from thinkers and fired the wrath of Carlyle.[155] The rod of empire that passed from the hands of Southern gentlemen in 1865, partly by force, partly by their own petulance, has never returned to them. Rather it has passed to those men who have come to take charge of the industrial exploitation of the New South – the sons of poor whites fired with a new thirst for wealth and power, thrifty and avaricious Yankees, shrewd and unscrupulous Jews. Into the hands of these men the Southern laborers, white and black, have fallen; and this to their sorrow. For the laborers as such there is in these new captains of industry neither love nor hate, neither sympathy nor romance; it is a cold question of dollars and dividends. Under such a system all labor is bound to suffer. Even the white laborers are not yet intelligent, thrifty, and well trained enough to maintain themselves against the powerful inroads of organized capital. The results among them, even, are long hours of toil, low wages, child labor, and lack of protection against usury and cheating. But among the black laborers all this is aggravated, first, by a race prejudice which varies from a doubt and distrust among the best element of whites to a frenzied hatred among the worst; and, secondly, it is aggravated, as I have said before, by the wretched economic heritage of the freedmen from slavery. With this training it is difficult for the freedman to learn to grasp the opportunities already opened to him; and the new opportunities are seldom given him, but go by favor to the whites.

Left by the best elements of the South with little protection or oversight, he has been made in law and custom the victim of the worst and most unscrupulous men in each community. The crop-lien system which is depopulating the fields of the South is not simply the result of shiftlessness on the part of Negroes, but is also the result of cunningly devised laws as to mortgages, liens, and misdemeanors, which can be made by conscienceless men to entrap and snare the unwary until escape is impossible, further toil a farce, and protest a crime. I have seen, in the Black Belt of Georgia, an ignorant, honest Negro buy and pay for a farm in installments three separate times, and then in the face of law and decency the enterprising Russian Jew who sold it to him pocketed money and deed and left the black man landless, to labor on his own land at thirty cents a day. I have seen a black farmer fall in debt to a white storekeeper, and that storekeeper go to his farm and strip it of every single marketable article – mules, ploughs, stored crops, tools, furniture, bedding, clocks, looking-glass – and all this without a warrant, without process of law, without a sheriff or officer, in the face of the law for homestead exemptions, and without rendering to a single responsible person any account or reckoning. And such proceedings can happen, and will happen, in any community where a class of ignorant toilers are placed by custom and race-prejudice beyond the pale of sympathy and race-brotherhood. So long as the best elements of a community do not feel in duty bound to protect and train and care for the weaker members of their group, they leave them to be preyed upon by these swindlers and rascals.

Notes

[155] *the factory acts … wrath of Carlyle* The Factory Acts of 1833 sought to curb rampant labor abuse by placing limits on the hours that women and children could work; Thomas Carlyle (1795–1881), Scottish essayist and satirist whose *Sartor Resartus* (1836) critiqued British commerce.

This unfortunate economic situation does not mean the hindrance of all advance in the black South, or the absence of a class of black landlords and mechanics who, in spite of disadvantages, are accumulating property and making good citizens. But it does mean that this class is not nearly so large as a fairer economic system might easily make it, that those who survive in the competition are handicapped so as to accomplish much less than they deserve to, and that, above all, the *personnel* of the successful class is left to chance and accident, and not to any intelligent culling or reasonable methods of selection. As a remedy for this, there is but one possible procedure. We must accept some of the race prejudice in the South as a fact – deplorable in its intensity, unfortunate in results, and dangerous for the future, but nevertheless a hard fact which only time can efface. We cannot hope, then, in this generation, or for several generations, that the mass of the whites can be brought to assume that close sympathetic and self-sacrificing leadership of the blacks which their present situation so eloquently demands. Such leadership, such social teaching and example, must come from the blacks themselves. For some time men doubted as to whether the Negro could develop such leaders; but to-day no one seriously disputes the capability of individual Negroes to assimilate the culture and common sense of modern civilization, and to pass it on, to some extent at least, to their fellows. If this is true, then here is the path out of the economic situation, and here is the imperative demand for trained Negro leaders of character and intelligence – men of skill, men of light and leading, college-bred men, black captains of industry, and missionaries of culture; men who thoroughly comprehend and know modern civilization, and can take hold of Negro communities and raise and train them by force of precept and example, deep sympathy, and the inspiration of common blood and ideals. But if such men are to be effective they must have some power – they must be backed by the best public opinion of these communities, and able to wield for their objects and aims such weapons as the experience of the world has taught are indispensable to human progress.

Of such weapons the greatest, perhaps, in the modern world is the power of the ballot; and this brings me to a consideration of the third form of contact between whites and blacks in the South – political activity.

In the attitude of the American mind toward Negro suffrage can be traced with unusual accuracy the prevalent conceptions of government. In the fifties we were near enough the echoes of the French Revolution to believe pretty thoroughly in universal suffrage. We argued, as we thought then rather logically, that no social class was so good, so true, and so disinterested as to be trusted wholly with the political destiny of its neighbors; that in every state the best arbiters of their own welfare are the persons directly affected; consequently that it is only by arming every hand with a ballot – with the right to have a voice in the policy of the state – that the greatest good to the greatest number could be attained. To be sure, there were objections to these arguments, but we thought we had answered them tersely and convincingly; if someone complained of the ignorance of voters, we answered, "Educate them." If another complained of their venality, we replied, "Disfranchise them or put them in jail." And, finally, to the men who feared demagogues and the natural perversity of some human beings we insisted that time and bitter experience would teach the most hardheaded. It was at this time that the question of Negro suffrage in the South was raised. Here was a defenceless people suddenly made free. How were they to be protected from those who did not believe in their freedom and were determined to thwart it? Not by force, said the North; not by government guardianship, said the South; then by the ballot, the sole and legitimate defence of a free people, said the Common Sense of the Nation. No one thought, at the time, that the ex-slaves could use the ballot intelligently or very effectively; but they did think that the possession of so great power by a great class in the nation would compel their fellows to educate this class to its intelligent use.

Meantime, new thoughts came to the nation: the inevitable period of moral retrogression and political trickery that ever follows in the wake of war overtook us. So flagrant became the political scandals that reputable men began to leave politics alone, and politics consequently became disreputable. Men began to pride themselves on having nothing to do with their own government, and to agree tacitly with those who regarded public office as a private perquisite. In this state of mind it became easy to wink at the suppression of the Negro vote in the South, and to advise self-respecting Negroes to leave politics entirely alone. The decent and reputable citizens of the North who neglected their own civic duties grew hilarious over the exaggerated importance with which the Negro regarded the franchise. Thus it easily happened that more and more the better class of Negroes followed the advice from abroad and the pressure from home, and took no further interest in politics, leaving to the careless and the venal of their race the exercise of their rights as voters. The black vote that still remained was not trained and educated, but further debauched by open and unblushing bribery, or force and fraud; until the Negro voter was thoroughly inoculated with the idea that politics was a method of private gain by disreputable means.

And finally, now, to-day, when we are awakening to the fact that the perpetuity of republican institutions on this continent depends on the purification of the ballot, the civic training of voters, and the raising of voting to the plane of a solemn duty which a patriotic citizen neglects to his peril and to the peril of his children's children – in this day, when we are striving for a renaissance of civic virtue, what are we going to say to the black voter of the South? Are we going to tell him still that politics is a disreputable and useless form of human activity? Are we going to induce the best class of Negroes to take less and less interest in government, and to give up their right to take such an interest, without a protest? I am not saying a word against all legitimate efforts to purge the ballot of ignorance, pauperism, and crime. But few have pretended that the present movement for disfranchisement in the South is for such a purpose; it has been plainly and frankly declared in nearly every case that the object of the disfranchising laws is the elimination of the black man from politics.

Now, is this a minor matter which has no influence on the main question of the industrial and intellectual development of the Negro? Can we establish a mass of black laborers and artisans and landholders in the South who, by law and public opinion, have absolutely no voice in shaping the laws under which they live and work? Can the modern organization of industry, assuming as it does free democratic government and the power and ability of the laboring classes to compel respect for their welfare – can this system be carried out in the South when half its laboring force is voiceless in the public councils and powerless in its own defence? To-day the black man of the South has almost nothing to say as to how much he shall be taxed, or how those taxes shall be expended; as to who shall execute the laws, and how they shall do it; as to who shall make the laws, and how they shall be made. It is pitiable that frantic efforts must be made at critical times to get law-makers in some States even to listen to the respectful presentation of the black man's side of a current controversy. Daily the Negro is coming more and more to look upon law and justice, not as protecting safeguards, but as sources of humiliation and oppression. The laws are made by men who have little interest in him; they are executed by men who have absolutely no motive for treating the black people with courtesy or consideration; and, finally, the accused law-breaker is tried, not by his peers, but too often by men who would rather punish ten innocent Negroes than let one guilty one escape.

I should be the last one to deny the patent weaknesses and shortcomings of the Negro people; I should be the last to withhold sympathy from the white South in its efforts to solve its intricate, social problems. I freely acknowledge that it is possible, and sometimes best, that a partially undeveloped people should be ruled by the best of their stronger and better neighbors for their own good, until such time as they can start and fight the world's battles alone. I have already pointed out how sorely in need of such economic and spiritual guidance the emancipated Negro was, and I am quite willing to admit that if the representatives of the best white Southern public opinion were the ruling and guiding powers in the South to-day the conditions indicated would be fairly well fulfilled. But the point I have insisted upon, and now emphasize again, is that the best opinion of the South to-day is not the ruling opinion. That to leave the Negro helpless and without a ballot to-day is to leave him, not to the guidance of the best, but rather to the exploitation and debauchment of the worst; that this is no truer of the South than of the North – of the North than of Europe: in any land, in any country under modern free competition, to lay any class of weak and despised people, be they white, black, or blue, at the political mercy of their stronger, richer, and more resourceful fellows, is a temptation which human nature seldom has withstood and seldom will withstand.

Moreover, the political status of the Negro in the South is closely connected with the question of Negro crime. There can be no doubt that crime among Negroes has sensibly increased in the last thirty years, and that there has appeared in the slums of great cities a distinct criminal class among the blacks. In explaining this unfortunate development, we must note two things: (1) that the inevitable result of Emancipation was to increase crime and criminals, and (2) that the police system of the South was primarily designed to control slaves. As to the first point, we must not forget that under a strict slave system there can scarcely be such a thing as crime. But when these variously constituted human particles are suddenly thrown broadcast on the sea of life, some swim, some sink, and some hang suspended, to be forced up or down by the chance currents of a busy hurrying world. So great an economic and social revolution as swept the South in '63 meant a weeding out among the Negroes of the incompetents and vicious, the beginning of a differentiation of social grades. Now a rising group of people are not lifted bodily from the ground like an inert solid mass, but rather stretch upward like a living plant with its roots still clinging in the mould. The appearance, therefore, of the Negro criminal was a phenomenon to be awaited; and while it causes anxiety, it should not occasion surprise.

Here again the hope for the future depended peculiarly on careful and delicate dealing with these criminals. Their offences at first were those of laziness, carelessness, and impulse, rather than of malignity or ungoverned viciousness. Such misdemeanors needed discriminating treatment, firm but reformatory, with no hint of injustice, and full proof of guilt. For such dealing with criminals, white or black, the South had no machinery, no adequate jails or reformatories; its police system was arranged to deal with blacks alone, and tacitly assumed that every white man was *ipso facto*[156] a member of that police. Thus grew up a double system of justice, which erred on the white side by undue leniency and the practical immunity of red-handed criminals, and erred on the black side by undue severity, injustice, and lack of discrimination. For, as I have said, the police system of the South was originally designed to keep track of all Negroes, not simply of criminals; and when the Negroes were freed and the whole

Notes

[156] *ipso facto* (Latin) by the fact itself.

South was convinced of the impossibility of free Negro labor, the first and almost universal device was to use the courts as a means of reenslaving the blacks. It was not then a question of crime, but rather one of color, that settled a man's conviction on almost any charge. Thus Negroes came to look upon courts as instruments of injustice and oppression, and upon those convicted in them as martyrs and victims.

When, now, the real Negro criminal appeared, and instead of petty stealing and vagrancy we began to have highway robbery, burglary, murder, and rape, there was a curious effect on both sides of the color-line:[157] the Negroes refused to believe the evidence of white witnesses or the fairness of white juries, so that the greatest deterrent to crime, the public opinion of one's own social caste, was lost, and the criminal was looked upon as crucified rather than hanged. On the other hand, the whites, used to being careless as to the guilt or innocence of accused Negroes, were swept in moments of passion beyond law, reason, and decency. Such a situation is bound to increase crime, and has increased it. To natural viciousness and vagrancy are being daily added motives of revolt and revenge which stir up all the latent savagery of both races and make peaceful attention to economic development often impossible.

But the chief problem in any community cursed with crime is not the punishment of the criminals, but the preventing of the young from being trained to crime. And here again the peculiar conditions of the South have prevented proper precautions. I have seen twelve-year-old boys working in chains on the public streets of Atlanta, directly in front of the schools, in company with old and hardened criminals; and this indiscriminate mingling of men and women and children makes the chain-gangs perfect schools of crime and debauchery. The struggle for reformatories, which has gone on in Virginia, Georgia, and other States, is the one encouraging sign of the awakening of some communities to the suicidal results of this policy.

It is the public schools, however, which can be made, outside the homes, the greatest means of training decent self-respecting citizens. We have been so hotly engaged recently in discussing trade-schools and the higher education that the pitiable plight of the public-school system in the South has almost dropped from view. Of every five dollars spent for public education in the State of Georgia, the white schools get four dollars and the Negro one dollar; and even then the white public-school system, save in the cities, is bad and cries for reform. If this is true of the whites, what of the blacks? I am becoming more and more convinced, as I look upon the system of common-school training in the South, that the national government must soon step in and aid popular education in some way. To-day it has been only by the most strenuous efforts on the part of the thinking men of the South that the Negro's share of the school fund has not been cut down to a pittance in some half-dozen States; and that movement not only is not dead, but in many communities is gaining strength. What in the name of reason does this nation expect of a people, poorly trained and hard pressed in severe economic competition, without political rights, and with ludicrously inadequate common-school facilities? What can it expect but crime and listlessness, offset here and there by the dogged struggles of the fortunate and more determined who are themselves buoyed by the hope that in due time the country will come to its senses?

I have thus far sought to make clear the physical, economic, and political relations of the Negroes and whites in the South, as I have conceived them, including, for the reasons set forth, crime and education. But after all that has been said on these more tangible matters of human contact, there still remains a part essential

Notes

[157] *Original reads*: sides the color-line [ed.].

to a proper description of the South which it is difficult to describe or fix in terms easily understood by strangers. It is, in fine, the atmosphere of the land, the thought and feeling, the thousand and one little actions which go to make up life. In any community or nation it is these little things which are most elusive to the grasp and yet most essential to any clear conception of the group life taken as a whole. What is thus true of all communities is peculiarly true of the South, where, outside of written history and outside of printed law, there has been going on for a generation as deep a storm and stress of human souls, as intense a ferment of feeling, as intricate a writhing of spirit, as ever a people experienced. Within and without the sombre veil of color vast social forces have been at work – efforts for human betterment, movements toward disintegration and despair, tragedies and comedies in social and economic life, and a swaying and lifting and sinking of human hearts which have made this land a land of mingled sorrow and joy, of change and excitement and unrest.

The centre of this spiritual turmoil has ever been the millions of black freedmen and their sons, whose destiny is so fatefully bound up with that of the nation. And yet the casual observer visiting the South sees at first little of this. He notes the growing frequency of dark faces as he rides along – but otherwise the days slip lazily on, the sun shines, and this little world seems as happy and contented as other worlds he has visited. Indeed, on the question of questions – the Negro problem – he hears so little that there almost seems to be a conspiracy of silence; the morning papers seldom mention it, and then usually in a far-fetched academic way, and indeed almost everyone seems to forget and ignore the darker half of the land, until the astonished visitor is inclined to ask if after all there *is* any problem here. But if he lingers long enough there comes the awakening: perhaps in a sudden whirl of passion which leaves him gasping at its bitter intensity; more likely in a gradually dawning sense of things he had not at first noticed. Slowly but surely his eyes begin to catch the shadows of the color-line: here he meets crowds of Negroes and whites; then he is suddenly aware that he cannot discover a single dark face; or again at the close of a day's wandering he may find himself in some strange assembly, where all faces are tinged brown or black, and where he has the vague, uncomfortable feeling of the stranger. He realizes at last that silently, resistlessly, the world about flows by him in two great streams: they ripple on in the same sunshine, they approach and mingle their waters in seeming carelessness – then they divide and flow wide apart. It is done quietly; no mistakes are made, or if one occurs, the swift arm of the law and of public opinion swings down for a moment, as when the other day a black man and a white woman were arrested for talking together on Whitehall Street in Atlanta.

Now if one notices carefully one will see that between these two worlds, despite much physical contact and daily intermingling, there is almost no community of intellectual life or point of transference where the thoughts and feelings of one race can come into direct contact and sympathy with the thoughts and feelings of the other. Before and directly after the war, when all the best of the Negroes were domestic servants in the best of the white families, there were bonds of intimacy, affection, and sometimes blood relationship, between the races. They lived in the same home, shared in the family life, often attended the same church, and talked and conversed with each other. But the increasing civilization of the Negro since then has naturally meant the development of higher classes: there are increasing numbers of ministers, teachers, physicians, merchants, mechanics, and independent farmers, who by nature and training are the aristocracy and leaders of the blacks. Between them, however, and the best element of the whites, there is little or no intellectual commerce. They go to separate churches, they live in separate sections, they are strictly separated in all public gatherings, they travel separately, and they are beginning to read different papers and books. To most libraries, lectures, concerts, and museums, Negroes are either not admitted at all, or on terms peculiarly galling to the pride of the very classes who might otherwise be attracted. The daily paper chronicles the doings of the black world from afar with no great regard for accuracy; and so on, throughout the category of means for intellectual communication – schools, conferences, efforts for social betterment, and the like – it is usually true that the very representatives of the two races, who for mutual benefit and the welfare of the land ought to be in complete understanding and sympathy, are so far strangers that one side thinks all whites are narrow and prejudiced, and the other thinks educated Negroes dangerous and insolent. Moreover, in a land where the tyranny of public opinion and the intolerance of criticism is for obvious historical reasons so strong as in the South, such a situation is extremely difficult to correct. The white man, as well as the Negro, is bound and barred by the color-line, and many a scheme of friendliness and philanthropy, of broad-minded sympathy and generous fellowship between the two has dropped still-born because some busybody has forced the color-question to the front and brought the tremendous force of unwritten law against the innovators.

It is hardly necessary for me to add very much in regard to the social contact between the races. Nothing has come to replace that finer sympathy and love between some masters and house servants which the radical and more uncompromising drawing of the color-line in recent years has caused almost completely to disappear. In a world where it means so much to take a man by the hand and sit beside him, to look frankly into his eyes and feel his heart beating with red blood; in a world where a social cigar or a cup of tea together means more than legislative halls and magazine articles and speeches – one can imagine the consequences of the almost utter absence of such social amenities between estranged races, whose separation extends even to parks and street-cars.

Here there can be none of that social going down to the people – the opening of heart and hand of the best to the worst, in generous acknowledgment of a common humanity and a common destiny. On the other hand, in matters of simple almsgiving, where there can be no question of social contact, and in the succor of the aged and sick, the South, as if stirred by a feeling of its unfortunate limitations, is generous to a fault. The black beggar is never turned away without a good deal more than a crust, and a call for help for the unfortunate meets quick response. I remember, one cold winter, in Atlanta, when I refrained from contributing to a public relief fund lest Negroes should be discriminated against, I afterward inquired of a friend: "Were any black people receiving aid?" "Why," said he, "they were *all* black."

And yet this does not touch the kernel of the problem. Human advancement is not a mere question of almsgiving, but rather of sympathy and cooperation among classes who would scorn charity. And here is a land where, in the higher walks of life, in all the higher striving for the good and noble and true, the color-line comes to separate natural friends and co-workers; while at the bottom of the social group, in the saloon, the gambling-hell, and the brothel, that same line wavers and disappears.

I have sought to paint an average picture of real relations between the sons of master and man in the South. I have not glossed over matters for policy's sake, for I fear we have already gone too far in that sort of thing. On the other hand, I have sincerely sought to let no unfair exaggerations creep in. I do not doubt that in some Southern communities conditions are better than those I have indicated; while I am no less certain that in other communities they are far worse.

Nor does the paradox and danger of this situation fail to interest and perplex the best conscience of the South. Deeply religious and intensely democratic as are the mass of the whites, they feel acutely the false position in which the Negro problems place them. Such an essentially honest-hearted and generous people cannot cite the caste-levelling precepts of Christianity, or believe in equality of opportunity for all men, without coming to feel more and more with each generation that the present drawing of the color-line is a flat contradiction to their beliefs and professions. But just as often as they come to this point, the present social condition of the Negro stands as a menace and a portent before even the most open-minded: if there were nothing to charge against the Negro but his blackness or other physical peculiarities, they argue, the problem would be comparatively simple; but what can we say to his ignorance, shiftlessness, poverty, and crime? can a self-respecting group hold anything but the least possible fellowship with such persons and survive? and shall we let a mawkish sentiment sweep away the culture of our fathers or the hope of our children? The argument so put is of great strength, but it is not a whit stronger than the argument of thinking Negroes: granted, they reply, that the condition of our masses is bad; there is certainly on the one hand adequate historical cause for this, and unmistakable evidence that no small number have, in spite of tremendous disadvantages, risen to the level of American civilization. And when, by proscription and prejudice, these same Negroes are classed with and treated like the lowest of their people, simply *because* they are Negroes, such a policy not only discourages thrift and intelligence among black men, but puts a direct premium on the very things you complain of – inefficiency and crime. Draw lines of crime, of incompetency, of vice, as tightly and uncompromisingly as you will, for these things must be proscribed; but a color-line not only does not accomplish this purpose, but thwarts it.

In the face of two such arguments, the future of the South depends on the ability of the representatives of these opposing views to see and appreciate and sympathize with each other's position – for the Negro to realize more deeply than he does at present the need of uplifting the masses of his people, for the white people to realize more vividly than they have yet done the deadening and disastrous effect of a color-prejudice that classes Phillis Wheatley and Sam Hose in the same despised class.

It is not enough for the Negroes to declare that color-prejudice is the sole cause of their social condition, nor for the white South to reply that their social condition is the main cause of prejudice. They both act as reciprocal cause and effect, and a change in neither alone will bring the desired effect. Both must change, or neither can improve to any great extent. The Negro cannot stand the present reactionary tendencies and unreasoning drawing of the color-line indefinitely without discouragement and retrogression. And the condition of the Negro is ever the excuse for further discrimination. Only by a union of intelligence and sympathy across the color-line in this critical period of the Republic shall justice and right triumph–

"That mind and soul according well,
May make one music as before,
But vaster."[158]

Notes

[158] *"That mind and soul ... vaster"* from the prologue to Alfred Lord Tennyson's "In Memoriam A.H.H." (1850).

Chapter 10

Of the Faith of the Fathers

Dim face of Beauty haunting all the world,
Fair face of Beauty all too fair to see,
Where the lost stars adown the heavens are hurled –
There, there alone for thee
May white peace be.

Beauty, sad face of Beauty, Mystery, Wonder,
What are these dreams to foolish babbling men
Who cry with little noises 'neath the thunder
Of Ages ground to sand,
To a little sand.

Fiona Macleod.[159]

It was out in the country, far from home, far from my foster home, on a dark Sunday night. The road wandered from our rambling log-house up the stony bed of a creek, past wheat and corn, until we could hear dimly across the fields a rhythmic cadence of song – soft, thrilling, powerful, that swelled and died sorrowfully in our ears. I was a country school-teacher then, fresh from the East, and had never seen a Southern Negro revival. To be sure, we in Berkshire were not perhaps as stiff and formal as they in Suffolk of olden time; yet we were very quiet and subdued, and I know not what would have happened those clear Sabbath mornings had someone punctuated the sermon with a wild scream, or interrupted the long prayer with a loud Amen! And so most striking to me, as I approached the village and the little plain church perched aloft, was the air of intense excitement that possessed that mass of black folk. A sort of suppressed terror hung in the air and seemed to seize us – a pythian madness,[160] a demoniac possession, that lent terrible reality to song and word. The black and massive form of the preacher swayed and quivered as the words crowded to his lips and flew at us in singular eloquence. The people moaned and fluttered, and then the gaunt-cheeked brown woman beside me suddenly leaped straight into the air and shrieked like a lost soul, while round about came wail and groan and outcry, and a scene of human passion such as I had never conceived before.

Those who have not thus witnessed the frenzy of a Negro revival in the untouched backwoods of the South can but dimly realize the religious feeling of the slave; as described, such scenes appear grotesque and funny, but as seen they are awful. Three things characterized this religion of the slave – the Preacher, the Music, and the Frenzy.

Notes

[159] Fiona Macleod, pseudonym of English poet and novelist William Sharp (1855–1905). The poem is called "Dim Face of Beauty" (1895).

[160] *Pythian madness* in ancient Greece, Pythia was the priestess of Delphi, who would give forth oracular sayings in a trance.

The Preacher is the most unique personality developed by the Negro on American soil. A leader, a politician, an orator, a "boss," an intriguer, an idealist – all these he is, and ever, too, the centre of a group of men, now twenty, now a thousand in number. The combination of a certain adroitness with deep-seated earnestness, of tact with consummate ability, gave him his preeminence, and helps him maintain it. The type, of course, varies according to time and place, from the West Indies in the sixteenth century to New England in the nineteenth, and from the Mississippi bottoms to cities like New Orleans or New York.

The Music of Negro religion is that plaintive, rhythmic melody, with its touching minor cadences, which, despite caricature and defilement, still remains the most original and beautiful expression of human life and longing yet born on American soil. Sprung from the African forests, where its counterpart can still be heard, it was adapted, changed, and intensified by the tragic soul-life of the slave, until, under the stress of law and whip, it became the one true expression of a people's sorrow, despair, and hope.

Finally the Frenzy or "Shouting," when the Spirit of the Lord passed by, and, seizing the devotee, made him mad with supernatural joy, was the last essential of Negro religion and the one more devoutly believed in than all the rest. It varied in expression from the silent rapt countenance or the low murmur and moan to the mad abandon of physical fervor – the stamping, shrieking, and shouting, the rushing to and fro and wild waving of arms, the weeping and laughing, the vision and the trance. All this is nothing new in the world, but old as religion, as Delphi and Endor.[161] And so firm a hold did it have on the Negro, that many generations firmly believed that without this visible manifestation of the God there could be no true communion with the Invisible.

These were the characteristics of Negro religious life as developed up to the time of Emancipation. Since under the peculiar circumstances of the black man's environment they were the one expression of his higher life, they are of deep interest to the student of his development, both socially and psychologically. Numerous are the attractive lines of inquiry that here group themselves. What did slavery mean to the African savage? What was his attitude toward the World and Life? What seemed to him good and evil – God and Devil? Whither went his longings and strivings, and wherefore were his heart-burnings and disappointments? Answers to such questions can come only from a study of Negro religion as a development, through its gradual changes from the heathenism of the Gold Coast to the institutional Negro church of Chicago.

Moreover, the religious growth of millions of men, even though they be slaves, cannot be without potent influence upon their contemporaries. The Methodists and Baptists of America owe much of their condition to the silent but potent influence of their millions of Negro converts. Especially is this noticeable in the South, where theology and religious philosophy are on this account a long way behind the North, and where the religion of the poor whites is a plain copy of Negro thought and methods. The mass of "gospel" hymns which has swept through American churches and well-nigh ruined our sense of song consists largely of debased imitations of Negro melodies, made by ears that caught the jingle but not the music, the body but not the soul, of the Jubilee songs.[162] It is thus clear that the study of Negro religion is not only a vital part of the history of the Negro in America, but no uninteresting part of American history.

Notes

[161] *Delphi and Endor* Delphi was the site of the ancient Greek shrine to Apollo; in 1 Samuel 28:7–14, King Saul finds in Endor a sorceress to summon up the prophet Samuel from the dead.

[162] *Jubilee songs* African American southern spirituals.

The Negro church of to-day is the social centre of Negro life in the United States, and the most characteristic expression of African character. Take a typical church in a small Virginian town: it is the "First Baptist" – a roomy brick edifice seating five hundred or more persons, tastefully finished in Georgia pine, with a carpet, a small organ, and stained-glass windows. Underneath is a large assembly room with benches. This building is the central club-house of a community of a thousand or more Negroes. Various organizations meet here – the church proper, the Sunday-school, two or three insurance societies, women's societies, secret societies, and mass meetings of various kinds. Entertainments, suppers, and lectures are held beside the five or six regular weekly religious services. Considerable sums of money are collected and expended here, employment is found for the idle, strangers are introduced, news is disseminated and charity distributed. At the same time this social, intellectual, and economic centre is a religious centre of great power. Depravity, Sin, Redemption, Heaven, Hell, and Damnation are preached twice a Sunday with much fervor, and revivals take place every year after the crops are laid by; and few indeed of the community have the hardihood to withstand conversion. Back of this more formal religion, the Church often stands as a real conserver of morals, a strengthener of family life, and the final authority on what is Good and Right.

Thus one can see in the Negro church to-day, reproduced in microcosm, all that great world from which the Negro is cut off by color-prejudice and social condition. In the great city churches the same tendency is noticeable and in many respects emphasized. A great church like the Bethel of Philadelphia has over eleven hundred members, an edifice seating fifteen hundred persons and valued at one hundred thousand dollars, an annual budget of five thousand dollars, and a government consisting of a pastor with several assisting local preachers, an executive and legislative board, financial boards and tax collectors; general church meetings for making laws; subdivided groups led by class leaders, a company of militia, and twenty-four auxiliary societies. The activity of a church like this is immense and far-reaching, and the bishops who preside over these organizations throughout the land are among the most powerful Negro rulers in the world.

Such churches are really governments of men, and consequently a little investigation reveals the curious fact that, in the South, at least, practically every American Negro is a church member. Some, to be sure, are not regularly enrolled, and a few do not habitually attend services; but, practically, a proscribed people must have a social centre, and that centre for this people is the Negro church. The census of 1890 showed nearly twenty-four thousand Negro churches in the country, with a total enrolled membership of over two and a half millions, or ten actual church members to every twenty-eight persons, and in some Southern States one in every two persons. Besides these there is the large number who, while not enrolled as members, attend and take part in many of the activities of the church. There is an organized Negro church for every sixty black families in the nation, and in some States for every forty families, owning, on an average, a thousand dollars' worth of property each, or nearly twenty-six million dollars in all.

Such, then, is the large development of the Negro church since Emancipation. The question now is, What have been the successive steps of this social history and what are the present tendencies? First, we must realize that no such institution as the Negro church could rear itself without definite historical foundations. These foundations we can find if we remember that the social history of the Negro did not start in America. He was brought from a definite social environment – the polygamous clan life under the headship of the chief and the potent influence of the priest. His religion was nature-worship, with profound belief in invisible surrounding influences, good and bad, and his worship was through incantation and sacrifice. The first rude change in this life was the slave ship and the West Indian sugar-fields. The plantation organization replaced the clan and tribe, and the white master replaced the chief with far greater and more despotic powers. Forced and long-continued toil became the rule of life, the old ties of blood relationship and kinship disappeared, and instead of the family appeared a new polygamy and polyandry,[163] which, in some cases, almost reached promiscuity. It was a terrific social revolution, and yet some traces were retained of the former group life, and the chief remaining institution was the Priest or Medicine-man. He early appeared on the plantation and found his function as the healer of the sick, the interpreter of the Unknown, the comforter of the sorrowing, the supernatural avenger of wrong, and the one who rudely but picturesquely expressed the longing, disappointment, and resentment of a stolen and oppressed people. Thus, as bard, physician, judge, and priest, within the narrow limits allowed by the slave system, rose the Negro preacher, and under him the first Afro-American institution, the Negro church. This church was not at first by any means Christian nor definitely organized; rather it was an adaptation and mingling of heathen rites among the members of each plantation, and roughly designated as Voodooism. Association with the masters, missionary effort and motives of expediency gave these rites an early veneer of Christianity, and after the lapse of many generations the Negro church became Christian.

Two characteristic things must be noticed in regard to this church. First, it became almost entirely Baptist and Methodist in faith; secondly, as a social institution it antedated by many decades the monogamic Negro home. From the very circumstances of its beginning, the church was confined to the plantation, and consisted primarily of a series of disconnected units; although, later on, some freedom of movement was allowed, still this geographical limitation was always important and was one cause of the spread of the decentralized and democratic Baptist faith among the slaves. At the same time, the visible rite of baptism appealed strongly to their mystic temperament. To-day the Baptist Church is still largest in membership among Negroes, and has a million and a half communicants. Next in popularity came the churches organized in connection with the white neighboring churches, chiefly Baptist and Methodist, with a few Episcopalian and others. The Methodists still form the second greatest denomination, with nearly a million members. The faith of these two leading denominations was more suited to the slave church from the prominence they gave to religious feeling and fervor. The Negro membership in other denominations has always been small and relatively unimportant, although the Episcopalians and Presbyterians are gaining among the more intelligent classes to-day, and the Catholic Church is making headway in certain sections. After Emancipation, and still earlier in the North, the Negro churches largely severed such affiliations as they had had with the white churches, either by choice or by compulsion. The Baptist churches became independent, but the Methodists were compelled early to unite for purposes of episcopal government. This gave rise to the great African Methodist Church, the greatest Negro organization in the world, to the Zion Church and the Colored Methodist, and to the black conferences and churches in this and other denominations.

Notes

[163] *polygamy and polyandry* having more than one wife or husband, respectively, at the same time.

The second fact noted, namely, that the Negro church antedates the Negro home, leads to an explanation of much that is paradoxical in this communistic institution and in the morals of its members. But especially it leads us to regard this institution as peculiarly the expression of the inner ethical life of a people in a sense seldom true elsewhere. Let us turn, then, from the outer physical development of the church to the more important inner ethical life of the people who compose it. The Negro has already been pointed out many times as a religious animal – a being of that deep emotional nature which turns instinctively toward the supernatural. Endowed with a rich tropical imagination and a keen, delicate appreciation of Nature, the transplanted African lived in a world animate with gods and devils, elves and witches; full of strange influences – of Good to be implored, of Evil to be propitiated. Slavery, then, was to him the dark triumph of Evil over him. All the hateful powers of the Under-world were striving against him, and a spirit of revolt and revenge filled his heart. He called up all the resources of heathenism to aid – exorcism and witchcraft, the mysterious Obi worship with its barbarous rites, spells, and blood-sacrifice even, now and then, of human victims. Weird midnight orgies and mystic conjurations were invoked, the witch-woman and the voodoo-priest became the centre of Negro group life, and that vein of vague superstition which characterizes the unlettered Negro even to-day was deepened and strengthened.

In spite, however, of such success as that of the fierce Maroons, the Danish blacks, and others, the spirit of revolt gradually died away under the untiring energy and superior strength of the slave masters. By the middle of the eighteenth century the black slave had sunk, with hushed murmurs, to his place at the bottom of a new economic system, and was unconsciously ripe for a new philosophy of life. Nothing suited his condition then better than the doctrines of passive submission embodied in the newly learned Christianity. Slave masters early realized this, and cheerfully aided religious propaganda within certain bounds. The long system of repression and degradation of the Negro tended to emphasize the elements in his character which made him a valuable chattel: courtesy became humility, moral strength degenerated into submission, and the exquisite native appreciation of the beautiful became an infinite capacity for dumb suffering. The Negro, losing the joy of this world, eagerly seized upon the offered conceptions of the next; the avenging Spirit of the Lord enjoining patience in this world, under sorrow and tribulation until the Great Day when He should lead His dark children home – this became his comforting dream. His preacher repeated the prophecy, and his bards sang–

> "Children, we all shall be free
> When the Lord shall appear!"[164]

This deep religious fatalism, painted so beautifully in "Uncle Tom,"[165] came soon to breed, as all fatalistic faiths will, the sensualist side by side with the martyr. Under the lax moral life of the plantation, where marriage was a farce, laziness a virtue, and property a theft, a religion of resignation and submission degenerated easily, in less strenuous minds, into a philosophy of indulgence and crime. Many of the worst characteristics of the Negro masses of to-day had their seed in this period of the slave's ethical growth. Here it was that the Home was ruined under the very shadow of the

Notes

[164] *"Children, we shall … appear!"* a Negro spiritual.

[165] *"Uncle Tom"* the devout and submissive slave in Harriet Beecher Stowe's *Uncle Tom's Cabin* (1852).

Church, white and black; here habits of shiftlessness took root, and sullen hopelessness replaced hopeful strife.

With the beginning of the abolition movement and the gradual growth of a class of free Negroes came a change. We often neglect the influence of the freedman before the war, because of the paucity of his numbers and the small weight he had in the history of the nation. But we must not forget that his chief influence was internal – was exerted on the black world; and that there he was the ethical and social leader. Huddled as he was in a few centres like Philadelphia, New York, and New Orleans, the masses of the freedmen sank into poverty and listlessness; but not all of them. The free Negro leader early arose and his chief characteristic was intense earnestness and deep feeling on the slavery question. Freedom became to him a real thing and not a dream. His religion became darker and more intense, and into his ethics crept a note of revenge, into his songs a day of reckoning close at hand. The "Coming of the Lord" swept this side of Death, and came to be a thing to be hoped for in this day. Through fugitive slaves and irrepressible discussion this desire for freedom seized the black millions still in bondage, and became their one ideal of life. The black bards caught new notes, and sometimes even dared to sing –

> "O Freedom, O Freedom, O Freedom over me!
> Before I'll be a slave
> I'll be buried in my grave,
> And go home to my Lord
> And be free."[166]

For fifty years Negro religion thus transformed itself and identified itself with the dream of Abolition, until that which was a radical fad in the white North and an anarchistic plot in the white South had become a religion to the black world. Thus, when Emancipation finally came, it seemed to the freedman a literal Coming of the Lord. His fervid imagination was stirred as never before, by the tramp of armies, the blood and dust of battle, and the wail and whirl of social upheaval. He stood dumb and motionless before the whirlwind: what had he to do with it? Was it not the Lord's doing, and marvellous in his eyes? Joyed and bewildered with what came, he stood awaiting new wonders till the inevitable Age of Reaction swept over the nation and brought the crisis of to-day.

It is difficult to explain clearly the present critical stage of Negro religion. First, we must remember that living as the blacks do in close contact with a great modem nation, and sharing, although imperfectly, the soul-life of that nation, they must necessarily be affected more or less directly by all the religious and ethical forces that are to-day moving the United States. These questions and movements are, however, overshadowed and dwarfed by the (to them) all-important question of their civil, political, and economic status. They must perpetually discuss the "Negro Problem" – must live, move, and have their being in it, and interpret all else in its light or darkness. With this come, too, peculiar problems of their inner life, of the status of women, the maintenance of Home, the training of children, the accumulation of wealth, and the prevention of crime. All this must mean a time of intense ethical ferment, of religious heart-searching and intellectual unrest. From the double life every American Negro must live, as a Negro and as an American, as swept on by the current of the nineteenth while yet struggling in the eddies of the fifteenth century – from this must arise a painful self-consciousness, an almost morbid sense of personality and a moral hesitancy

Notes

[166] *"O Freedom … be free"* a Negro spiritual.

which is fatal to self-confidence. The worlds within and without the Veil of Color are changing, and changing rapidly, but not at the same rate, not in the same way; and this must produce a peculiar wrenching of the soul, a peculiar sense of doubt and bewilderment. Such a double life, with double thoughts, double duties, and double social classes, must give rise to double words and double ideals, and tempt the mind to pretence or to revolt, to hypocrisy or to radicalism.

In some such doubtful words and phrases can one perhaps most clearly picture the peculiar ethical paradox that faces the Negro of to-day and is tingeing and changing his religious life. Feeling that his rights and his dearest ideals are being trampled upon, that the public conscience is ever more deaf to his righteous appeal, and that all the reactionary forces of prejudice, greed, and revenge are daily gaining new strength and fresh allies, the Negro faces no enviable dilemma. Conscious of his impotence, and pessimistic, he often becomes bitter and vindictive; and his religion, instead of a worship, is a complaint and a curse, a wail rather than a hope, a sneer rather than a faith. On the other hand, another type of mind, shrewder and keener and more tortuous too, sees in the very strength of the anti-Negro movement its patent weaknesses, and with Jesuitic casuistry[167] is deterred by no ethical considerations in the endeavor to turn this weakness to the black man's strength. Thus we have two great and hardly reconcilable streams of thought and ethical strivings; the danger of the one lies in anarchy, that of the other in hypocrisy. The one type of Negro stands almost ready to curse God and die, and the other is too often found a traitor to right and a coward before force; the one is wedded to ideals remote, whimsical, perhaps impossible of realization; the other forgets that life is more than meat and the body more than raiment. But, after all, is not this simply the writhing of the age translated into black – the triumph of the Lie which to-day, with its false culture, faces the hideousness of the anarchist assassin?

To-day the two groups of Negroes, the one in the North, the other in the South, represent these divergent ethical tendencies, the first tending toward radicalism, the other toward hypocritical compromise. It is no idle regret with which the white South mourns the loss of the old-time Negro – the frank, honest, simple old servant who stood for the earlier religious age of submission and humility. With all his laziness and lack of many elements of true manhood, he was at least open-hearted, faithful, and sincere. To-day he is gone, but who is to blame for his going? Is it not those very persons who mourn for him? Is it not the tendency, born of Reconstruction and Reaction, to found a society on lawlessness and deception, to tamper with the moral fibre of a naturally honest and straightforward people until the whites threaten to become ungovernable tyrants and the blacks criminals and hypocrites? Deception is the natural defence of the weak against the strong, and the South used it for many years against its conquerors; to-day it must be prepared to see its black proletariat turn that same two-edged weapon against itself. And how natural this is! The death of Denmark Vesey and Nat Turner proved long since to the Negro the present hopelessness of physical defence. Political defence is becoming less and less available, and economic defence is still only partially effective. But there is a patent defence at hand – the defence of deception and flattery, of cajoling and lying. It is the same defence which the Jews of the Middle Age used and which left its stamp on their character for centuries. Today the young Negro of the South who would succeed cannot be frank and outspoken, honest and self-assertive, but rather he is daily tempted to be silent and wary, politic and sly; he must flatter and be pleasant, endure petty insults with a smile, shut his eyes to wrong; in too many cases he sees positive personal advantage in

Notes

[167] *Jesuitic casuistry* clever but misleading reasoning.

deception and lying. His real thoughts, his real aspirations, must be guarded in whispers; he must not criticize, he must not complain. Patience, humility, and adroitness must, in these growing black youth, replace impulse, manliness, and courage. With this sacrifice there is an economic opening, and perhaps peace and some prosperity. Without this there is riot, migration, or crime. Nor is this situation peculiar to the Southern United States – is it not rather the only method by which undeveloped races have gained the right to share modern culture? The price of culture is a Lie.

On the other hand, in the North the tendency is to emphasize the radicalism of the Negro. Driven from his birthright in the South by a situation at which every fibre of his more outspoken and assertive nature revolts, he finds himself in a land where he can scarcely earn a decent living amid the harsh competition and the color discrimination. At the same time, through schools and periodicals, discussions and lectures, he is intellectually quickened and awakened. The soul, long pent up and dwarfed, suddenly expands in new-found freedom. What wonder that every tendency is to excess – radical complaint, radical remedies, bitter denunciation or angry silence. Some sink, some rise. The criminal and the sensualist leave the church for the gambling-hell and the brothel, and fill the slums of Chicago and Baltimore; the better classes segregate themselves from the group-life of both white and black, and form an aristocracy, cultured but pessimistic, whose bitter criticism stings while it points out no way of escape. They despise the submission and subserviency of the Southern Negroes, but offer no other means by which a poor and oppressed minority can exist side by side with its masters. Feeling deeply and keenly the tendencies and opportunities of the age in which they live, their souls are bitter at the fate which drops the Veil between; and the very fact that this bitterness is natural and justifiable only serves to intensify it and make it more maddening.

Between the two extreme types of ethical attitude which I have thus sought to make clear wavers the mass of the millions of Negroes, North and South; and their religious life and activity partake of this social conflict within their ranks. Their churches are differentiating – now into groups of cold, fashionable devotees, in no way distinguishable from similar white groups save in color of skin; now into large social and business institutions catering to the desire for information and amusement of their members, warily avoiding unpleasant questions both within and without the black world, and preaching in effect if not in word: *Dum vivimus, vivamus*.[168]

But back of this still broods silently the deep religious feeling of the real Negro heart, the stirring, unguided might of powerful human souls who have lost the guiding star of the past and are seeking in the great night a new religious ideal. Someday the Awakening will come, when the pent-up vigor of ten million souls shall sweep irresistibly toward the Goal, out of the Valley of the Shadow of Death, where all that makes life worth living – Liberty, Justice, and Right – is marked "For White People Only."

Chapter 11

Of the Passing of the First-Born

O sister, sister, thy first-begotten,
The hands that cling and the feet that follow,
The voice of the child's blood crying yet,

Notes

[168] *Dum vivimus, vivamus* (Latin) While we live, let us live.

Who hath remembered me? who hath forgotten?
Thou hast forgotten, O summer swallow,
But the world shall end when I forget.
Swinburne.[169]

"Unto you a child is born," sang the bit of yellow paper that fluttered into my room one brown October morning. Then the fear of fatherhood mingled wildly with the joy of creation; I wondered how it looked and how it felt – what were its eyes, and how its hair curled and crumpled itself. And I thought in awe of her – she who had slept with Death to tear a man-child from underneath her heart, while I was unconsciously wandering. I fled to my wife and child, repeating the while to myself half wonderingly, "Wife and child? Wife and child?" – fled fast and faster than boat and steamcar, and yet must ever impatiently await them; away from the hard-voiced city, away from the flickering sea into my own Berkshire Hills that sit all sadly guarding the gates of Massachusetts.

Up the stairs I ran to the wan mother and whimpering babe, to the sanctuary on whose altar a life at my bidding had offered itself to win a life, and won. What is this tiny formless thing, this new-born wail from an unknown world – all head and voice? I handle it curiously, and watch perplexed its winking, breathing, and sneezing. I did not love it then; it seemed a ludicrous thing to love; but her I loved, my girl-mother, she whom now I saw unfolding like the glory of the morning – the transfigured woman.

Through her I came to love the wee thing, as it grew and waxed strong; as its little soul unfolded itself in twitter and cry and half-formed word, and as its eyes caught the gleam and flash of life. How beautiful he was, with his olive-tinted flesh and dark gold ringlets, his eyes of mingled blue and brown, his perfect little limbs, and the soft voluptuous roll which the blood of Africa had moulded into his features! I held him in my arms, after we had sped far away to our Southern home – held him, and glanced at the hot red soil of Georgia and the breathless city of a hundred hills, and felt a vague unrest. Why was his hair tinted with gold? An evil omen was golden hair in my life. Why had not the brown of his eyes crushed out and killed the blue? – for brown were his father's eyes, and his father's father's. And thus in the Land of the Color-line I saw, as it fell across my baby, the shadow of the Veil.

Within the Veil was he born, said I; and there within shall he live – a Negro and a Negro's son. Holding in that little head – ah, bitterly! – the unbowed pride of a hunted race, clinging with that tiny dimpled hand – ah, wearily! – to a hope not hopeless but unhopeful, and seeing with those bright wondering eyes that peer into my soul a land whose freedom is to us a mockery and whose liberty a lie. I saw the shadow of the Veil as it passed over my baby, I saw the cold city towering above the

Notes

[169] Charles Algernon Swinburne (1837–1909), English poet. The lines quoted are from his 1866 poem "Itylus."

blood-red land. I held my face beside his little cheek, showed him the star-children and the twinkling lights as they began to flash, and stilled with an even-song the unvoiced terror of my life.

So sturdy and masterful he grew, so filled with bubbling life so tremulous with the unspoken wisdom of a life but eighteen months distant from the All-life – we were not far from worshipping this revelation of the divine, my wife and I. Her own life builded and moulded itself upon the child; he tinged her every dream and idealized her every effort. No hands but hers must touch and garnish those little limbs; no dress or frill must touch them that had not wearied her fingers; no voice but hers could coax him off to Dreamland, and she and he together spoke some soft and unknown tongue and in it held communion. I too mused above his little white bed; saw the strength of my own arm stretched onward through the ages through the newer strength of his; saw the dream of my black fathers stagger a step onward in the wild phantasm of the world; heard in his baby voice the voice of the Prophet that was to rise within the Veil.

And so we dreamed and loved and planned by fall and winter, and the full flush of the long Southern spring, till the hot winds rolled from the fetid Gulf, till the roses shivered and the still stern sun quivered its awful light over the hills of Atlanta. And then one night the little feet pattered wearily to the wee white bed, and the tiny hands trembled; and a warm flushed face tossed on the pillow, and we knew baby was sick. Ten days he lay there – a swift week and three endless days, wasting, wasting away. Cheerily the mother nursed him the first days, and laughed into the little eyes that smiled again. Tenderly then she hovered round him, till the smile fled away and Fear crouched beside the little bed.

Then the day ended not, and night was a dreamless terror, and joy and sleep slipped away. I hear now that Voice at midnight calling me from dull and dreamless trance – crying, "The Shadow of Death! The Shadow of Death!" Out into the starlight I crept, to rouse the gray physician – the Shadow of Death, the Shadow of Death. The hours trembled on; the night listened; the ghastly dawn glided like a tired thing across the lamplight. Then we two alone looked upon the child as he turned toward us with great eyes, and stretched his string-like hands – the Shadow of Death! And we spoke no word, and turned away.

He died at eventide, when the sun lay like a brooding sorrow above the western hills, veiling its face; when the winds spoke not, and the trees, the great green trees he loved, stood motionless. I saw his breath beat quicker and quicker, pause, and then his little soul leapt like a star that travels in the night and left a world of darkness in its train. The day changed not; the same tall trees peeped in at the windows, the same green grass glinted in the setting sun. Only in the chamber of death writhed the world's most piteous thing – a childless mother.

I shirk not. I long for work. I pant for a life full of striving. I am no coward, to shrink before the rugged rush of the storm, nor even quail before the awful shadow of the Veil. But hearken, O Death! Is not this my life hard enough – is not that dull land that stretches its sneering web about me cold enough – is not all the world beyond these four little walls pitiless enough, but that thou must needs enter here – thou, O Death? About my head the thundering storm beat like a heartless voice, and the crazy forest pulsed with the curses of the weak; but what cared I, within my home beside my wife and baby boy? Wast thou so jealous of one little coign of happiness that thou must needs enter there – thou, Death?

A perfect life was his, all joy and love, with tears to make it brighter – sweet as a summer's day beside the Housatonic. The world loved him; the women kissed his curls, the men looked gravely into his wonderful eyes, and the children hovered and fluttered about him. I can see him now, changing like the sky from sparkling laughter to darkening frowns, and then to wondering thoughtfulness as he watched the world. He knew no color-line, poor dear – and the Veil, though it shadowed him, had not yet darkened half his sun. He loved the white matron, he loved his black nurse; and in his little world walked souls alone, uncolored and unclothed. I – yea, all men – are larger and purer by the infinite breadth of that one little life. She who in simple clearness of vision sees beyond the stars said when he had flown, "He will be happy There; he ever loved beautiful things." And I, far more ignorant, and blind by the web of mine own weaving, sit alone winding words and muttering, "If still he be, and he be There, and there be a There, let him be happy, O Fate!"

Blithe was the morning of his burial, with bird and song and sweet-smelling flowers. The trees whispered to the grass, but the children sat with hushed faces. And yet it seemed a ghostly unreal day – the wraith of Life. We seemed to rumble down an unknown street behind a little white bundle of posies, with the shadow of a song in our ears. The busy city dinned about us; they did not say much, those pale-faced hurrying men and women; they did not say much – they only glanced and said, "Niggers!"

We could not lay him in the ground there in Georgia, for the earth there is strangely red; so we bore him away to the northward, with his flowers and his little folded hands. In vain, in vain! – for where, O God! beneath thy broad blue sky shall my dark baby rest in peace – where Reverence dwells, and Goodness, and a Freedom that is free?

All that day and all that night there sat an awful gladness in my heart – nay, blame me not if I see the world thus darkly through the Veil – and my soul whispers ever to me, saying, "Not dead, not dead, but escaped; not bond, but free." No bitter meanness now shall sicken his baby heart till it die a living death, no taunt shall madden his happy boyhood. Fool that I was to think or wish that this little soul should grow choked and deformed within the Veil! I might have known that yonder deep unworldly look that ever and anon floated past his eyes was peering far beyond this narrow Now. In the poise of his little curl-crowned head did there not sit all that wild pride of being which his father had hardly crushed in his own heart? For what, forsooth, shall a Negro want with pride amid the studied humiliations of fifty million fellows? Well sped, my boy, before the world had dubbed your ambition insolence, had held your ideals unattainable, and taught you to cringe and bow. Better far this nameless void that stops my life than a sea of sorrow for you.

Idle words; he might have borne his burden more bravely than we – aye, and found it lighter too, someday; for surely, surely this is not the end. Surely there shall yet dawn some mighty morning to lift the Veil and set the prisoned free. Not for me – I shall die in my bonds – but for fresh young souls who have not known the night and waken to the morning; a morning when men ask of the workman, not "Is he white?" but "Can he work?" When men ask artists, not "Are they black?" but "Do they know?" Some morning this may be, long, long years to come. But now there wails, on that dark shore within the Veil, the same deep voice, *Thou shalt forego!* And all have I foregone at that command, and with small complaint – all save that fair young form that lies so coldly wed with death in the nest I had builded.

If one must have gone, why not I? Why may I not rest me from this restlessness and sleep from this wide waking? Was not the world's alembic, Time, in his young hands, and is not my time waning? Are there so many workers in the vineyard that the fair promise of this little body could lightly be tossed away? The wretched of my race that line the alleys of the nation sit fatherless and unmothered; but Love sat beside his cradle, and in his ear Wisdom waited to speak. Perhaps now he knows the All-love, and needs not to be wise. Sleep, then, child – sleep till I sleep and waken to a baby voice and the ceaseless patter of little feet – above the Veil.

Chapter 12

Of Alexander Crummell[170]

Then from the Dawn it seemed there came, but faint
As from beyond the limit of the world,
Like the last echo born of a great cry,
Sounds, as if some fair city were one voice
Around a king returning from his wars.

Tennyson.[171]

This is the history of a human heart – the tale of a black boy who many long years ago began to struggle with life that he might know the world and know himself. Three temptations he met on those dark dunes that lay gray and dismal before the wonder-eyes of the child: the temptation of Hate, that stood out against the red dawn; the temptation of Despair, that darkened noonday; and the temptation of Doubt, that ever steals along with twilight. Above all, you must hear of the vales he crossed – the Valley of Humiliation and the Valley of the Shadow of Death.

I saw Alexander Crummell first at a Wilberforce commencement season, amid its bustle and crush. Tall, frail, and black he stood, with simple dignity and an unmistakable air of good breeding. I talked with him apart, where the storming of the lusty young orators could not harm us. I spoke to him politely, then curiously, then eagerly, as I began to feel the fineness of his character – his calm courtesy, the sweetness of his strength, and his fair blending of the hope and truth of life. Instinctively I bowed before this man, as one bows before the prophets of the world. Some seer he seemed, that came not from the crimson Past or the gray To-come, but from the pulsing Now – that mocking world which seemed to me at once so light and dark, so splendid and sordid. Four-score years had he wandered in this same world of mine, within the Veil.

He was born with the Missouri Compromise[172] and lay a-dying amid the echoes of Manila and El Caney:[173] stirring times for living, times dark to look back upon, darker to look forward to. The black-faced lad that paused over his mud and marbles seventy years ago saw puzzling vistas as he looked down the world. The slave-ship still groaned across the Atlantic, faint cries burdened the Southern breeze, and the great black father whispered mad tales of cruelty into those young ears. From the low doorway the

Notes

[170] Alexander Crummell (1819–1898), an African American Episcopal priest and African nationalist and missionary.

[171] Alfred Lord Tennyson (1809–1892), British poet; the lines come from "The Passing of Arthur" in *Idylls of the King* (1869).

[172] *Missouri Compromise* legislation passed by Congress in 1820 to allow Missouri to enter the Union as a slave state.

[173] *Manila and El Caney* locations in the Philippines and Cuba of important US victories in the Spanish–American War in 1898.

mother silently watched her boy at play, and at nightfall sought him eagerly lest the shadows bear him away to the land of slaves.

So his young mind worked and winced and shaped curiously a vision of Life; and in the midst of that vision ever stood one dark figure alone – ever with the hard, thick countenance of that bitter father, and a form that fell in vast and shapeless folds. Thus the temptation of Hate grew and shadowed the growing child – gliding stealthily into his laughter, fading into his play, and seizing his dreams by day and night with rough, rude turbulence. So the black boy asked of sky and sun and flower the never-answered Why? and loved, as he grew, neither the world nor the world's rough ways.

Strange temptation for a child, you may think; and yet in this wide land to-day a thousand thousand dark children brood before this same temptation, and feel its cold and shuddering arms. For them, perhaps, someone will someday lift the Veil – will come tenderly and cheerily into those sad little lives and brush the brooding hate away, just as Beriah Green strode in upon the life of Alexander Crummell. And before the bluff, kind-hearted man the shadow seemed less dark. Beriah Green had a school in Oneida County, New York, with a score of mischievous boys. "I'm going to bring a black boy here to educate," said Beriah Green, as only a crank and an abolitionist would have dared to say. "Oho!" laughed the boys. "Ye-es," said his wife; and Alexander came. Once before, the black boy had sought a school, had travelled, cold and hungry, four hundred miles up into free New Hampshire, to Canaan. But the godly farmers hitched ninety yoke of oxen to the abolition schoolhouse and dragged it into the middle of the swamp. The black boy trudged away.

The nineteenth was the first century of human sympathy – the age when half wonderingly we began to descry in others that transfigured spark of divinity which we call Myself; when clodhoppers and peasants, and tramps and thieves, and millionaires and – sometimes – Negroes, became throbbing souls whose warm pulsing life touched us so nearly that we half gasped with surprise, crying, "Thou too! Hast Thou seen Sorrow and the dull waters of Hopelessness? Hast Thou known Life?" And then all helplessly we peered into those Other-worlds, and wailed, "O World of Worlds, how shall man make you one?"

So in that little Oneida school there came to those schoolboys a revelation of thought and longing beneath one black skin, of which they had not dreamed before. And to the lonely boy came a new dawn of sympathy and inspiration. The shadowy, formless thing – the temptation of Hate, that hovered between him and the world – grew fainter and less sinister. It did not wholly fade away, but diffused itself and lingered thick at the edges. Through it the child now first saw the blue and gold of life – the sun-swept road that ran 'twixt heaven and earth until in one far-off wan wavering line they met and kissed. A vision of life came to the growing boy – mystic, wonderful. He raised his head, stretched himself, breathed deep of the fresh new air. Yonder, behind the forests, he heard strange sounds; then glinting through the trees he saw, far, far away, the bronzed hosts of a nation calling – calling faintly, calling loudly. He heard the hateful clank of their chains, he felt them cringe and grovel, and there rose within him a protest and a prophecy. And he girded himself to walk down the world.

A voice and vision called him to be a priest – a seer to lead the uncalled out of the house of bondage. He saw the headless host turn toward him like the whirling of mad waters – he stretched forth his hands eagerly, and then, even as he stretched them, suddenly there swept across the vision the temptation of Despair.

They were not wicked men – the problem of life is not the problem of the wicked – they were calm, good men, Bishops of the Apostolic Church of God, and strove toward righteousness. They said slowly, "It is all very natural – it is even commendable; but the General Theological Seminary of the Episcopal Church cannot admit a Negro."

And when that thin, half-grotesque figure still haunted their doors, they put their hands kindly, half sorrowfully, on his shoulders, and said, "Now – of course, we – we know how *you* feel about it; but you see it is impossible – that is – well – it is premature. Sometime, we trust – sincerely trust – all such distinctions will fade away; but now the world is as it is."

This was the temptation of Despair; and the young man fought it doggedly. Like some grave shadow he flitted by those halls, pleading, arguing, half angrily demanding admittance, until there came the final *No*; until men hustled the disturber away, marked him as foolish, unreasonable, and injudicious, a vain rebel against God's law. And then from that Vision Splendid all the glory faded slowly away, and left an earth gray and stern rolling on beneath a dark despair. Even the kind hands that stretched themselves toward him from out the depths of that dull morning seemed but parts of the purple shadows. He saw them coldly, and asked, "Why should I strive by special grace when the way of the world is closed to me?" All gently yet, the hands urged him on – the hands of young John Jay,[174] that daring father's daring son; the hands of the good folk of Boston, that free city. And yet, with a way to the priesthood of the Church open at last before him, the cloud lingered there; and even when in old St. Paul's the venerable Bishop raised his white arms above the Negro deacon – even then the burden had not lifted from that heart, for there had passed a glory from the earth.

And yet the fire through which Alexander Crummell went did not burn in vain. Slowly and more soberly he took up again his plan of life. More critically he studied the situation. Deep down below the slavery and servitude of the Negro people he saw their fatal weaknesses, which long years of mistreatment had emphasized. The dearth of strong moral character, of unbending righteousness, he felt, was their great shortcoming, and here he would begin. He would gather the best of his people into some little Episcopal chapel and there lead, teach, and inspire them, till the leaven spread, till the children grew, till the world hearkened, till – till – and then across his dream gleamed some faint after-glow of that first fair vision of youth – only an after-glow, for there had passed a glory from the earth.

One day – it was in 1842, and the springtide was struggling merrily with the May winds of New England – he stood at last in his own chapel in Providence, a priest of the Church. The days sped by, and the dark young clergyman labored; he wrote his sermons carefully; he intoned his prayers with a soft, earnest voice; he haunted the streets and accosted the wayfarers; he visited the sick, and knelt beside the dying. He worked and toiled, week by week, day by day, month by month. And yet month by month the congregation dwindled, week by week the hollow walls echoed more sharply, day by day the calls came fewer and fewer, and day by day the third temptation sat clearer and still more clearly within the Veil; a temptation, as it were, bland and smiling, with just a shade of mockery in its smooth tones. First it came casually, in the cadence of a voice: "Oh, colored folks? Yes." Or perhaps more definitely: "What do you *expect*?" In voice and gesture lay the doubt – the temptation of Doubt. How he hated it, and stormed at it furiously! "Of course they are capable," he cried; "of course they can learn and strive and achieve – " and "Of course," added the temptation softly, "they do nothing of the sort." Of all the three temptations, this one struck the deepest. Hate? He had outgrown so childish a thing. Despair? He had steeled his right arm against it, and fought it with the vigor of determination. But to doubt the worth of his life-work – to doubt the destiny and capability of the race his soul loved because it was his; to find listless squalor

Notes

[174] John Jay (1817–1894), politician and abolitionist.

instead of eager endeavor; to hear his own lips whispering, "They do not care; they cannot know; they are dumb driven cattle – why cast your pearls before swine?" – this, this seemed more than man could bear; and he closed the door, and sank upon the steps of the chancel, and cast his robe upon the floor and writhed.

The evening sunbeams had set the dust to dancing in the gloomy chapel when he arose. He folded his vestments, put away the hymn-books, and closed the great Bible. He stepped out into the twilight, looked back upon the narrow little pulpit with a weary smile, and locked the door. Then he walked briskly to the Bishop, and told the Bishop what the Bishop already knew. "I have failed," he said simply. And gaining courage by the confession, he added: "What I need is a larger constituency. There are comparatively few Negroes here, and perhaps they are not of the best. I must go where the field is wider, and try again." So the Bishop sent him to Philadelphia, with a letter to Bishop Onderdonk.

Bishop Onderdonk lived at the head of six white steps – corpulent, red-faced, and the author of several thrilling tracts on Apostolic Succession. It was after dinner, and the Bishop had settled himself for a pleasant season of contemplation, when the bell must needs ring, and there must burst in upon the Bishop a letter and a thin, ungainly Negro. Bishop Onderdonk read the letter hastily and frowned. Fortunately, his mind was already clear on this point; and he cleared his brow and looked at Crummell. Then he said, slowly and impressively: "I will receive you into this diocese on one condition: no Negro priest can sit in my church convention, and no Negro church must ask for representation there."

I sometimes fancy I can see that tableau: the frail black figure, nervously twitching his hat before the massive abdomen of Bishop Onderdonk; his threadbare coat thrown against the dark woodwork of the book-cases, where Fox's "Lives of the Martyrs"[175] nestled happily beside "The Whole Duty of Man."[176] I seem to see the wide eyes of the Negro wander past the Bishop's broadcloth to where the swinging glass doors of the cabinet glow in the sunlight. A little blue fly is trying to cross the yawning keyhole. He marches briskly up to it, peers into the chasm in a surprised sort of way, and rubs his feelers reflectively; then he essays its depths, and, finding it bottomless, draws back again. The dark-faced priest finds himself wondering if the fly too has faced its Valley of Humiliation, and if it will plunge into it when lo! it spreads its tiny wings and buzzes merrily across, leaving the watcher wingless and alone.

Then the full weight of his burden fell upon him. The rich walls wheeled away, and before him lay the cold rough moor winding on through life, cut in twain by one thick granite ridge – here, the Valley of Humiliation; yonder, the Valley of the Shadow of Death. And I know not which be darker – no, not I. But this I know: in yonder Vale of the Humble stand today a million swarthy men, who willingly would

"… bear the whips and scorns of time,
The oppressor's wrong, the proud man's contumely,
The pangs of despised love, the law's delay,
The insolence of office, and the spurns
That patient merit of the unworthy takes,"[177]

Notes

[175] *Fox's "Lives of the Martyrs" The Book of Martyrs* by English clergyman John Foxe (1516–1578).

[176] *"The Whole Duty of Man"* an anonymous Christian devotional book published in 1658.

[177] *"… bear the whips … unworthy takes"* Shakespeare, *Hamlet* 3.1.69–73.

all this and more would they bear did they but know that this were sacrifice and not a meaner thing. So surged the thought within that lone black breast. The Bishop cleared his throat suggestively; then, recollecting that there was really nothing to say, considerately said nothing, only sat tapping his foot impatiently. But Alexander Crummell said, slowly and heavily: "I will never enter your diocese on such terms." And saying this, he turned and passed into the Valley of the Shadow of Death. You might have noted only the physical dying, the shattered frame and hacking cough; but in that soul lay deeper death than that. He found a chapel in New York – the church of his father; he labored for it in poverty and starvation, scorned by his fellow priests. Half in despair, he wandered across the sea, a beggar with outstretched hands. Englishmen clasped them – Wilberforce and Stanley,[178] Thirwell and Ingles,[179] and even Froude and Macaulay;[180] Sir Benjamin Brodie[181] bade him rest awhile at Queen's College in Cambridge, and there he lingered, struggling for health of body and mind, until he took his degree in '53. Restless still and unsatisfied, he turned toward Africa, and for long years, amid the spawn of the slave-smugglers, sought a new heaven and a new earth.

So the man groped for light; all this was not Life – it was the world-wandering of a soul in search of itself, the striving of one who vainly sought his place in the world, ever haunted by the shadow of a death that is more than death – the passing of a soul that has missed its duty. Twenty years he wandered – twenty years and more; and yet the hard rasping question kept gnawing within him, "What, in God's name, am I on earth for?" In the narrow New York parish his soul seemed cramped and smothered. In the fine old air of the English University he heard the millions wailing over the sea. In the wild fever-cursed swamps of West Africa he stood helpless and alone.

You will not wonder at his weird pilgrimage – you who in the swift whirl of living, amid its cold paradox and marvellous vision, have fronted life and asked its riddle face to face. And if you find that riddle hard to read, remember that yonder black boy finds it just a little harder; if it is difficult for you to find and face your duty, it is a shade more difficult for him; if your heart sickens in the blood and dust of battle, remember that to him the dust is thicker and the battle fiercer. No wonder the wanderers fall! No wonder we point to thief and murderer, and haunting prostitute, and the never-ending throng of unhearsed dead! The Valley of the Shadow of Death gives few of its pilgrims back to the world.

But Alexander Crummell it gave back. Out of the temptation of Hate, and burned by the fire of Despair, triumphant over Doubt, and steeled by Sacrifice against Humiliation, he turned at last home across the waters, humble and strong, gentle and determined. He bent to all the gibes and prejudices, to all hatred and discrimination, with that rare courtesy which is the armor of pure souls. He fought among his own, the low, the grasping, and the wicked, with that unbending righteousness which is the sword of the just. He never faltered, he seldom complained; he simply worked, inspiring the young, rebuking the old, helping the weak, guiding the strong.

So he grew, and brought within his wide influence all that was best of those who walk within the Veil. They who live without knew not nor dreamed of that full power within, that mighty inspiration which the dull gauze of caste decreed that most men should not know. And now that he is gone, I sweep the Veil away and cry, Lo! the soul to whose dear memory I bring this little tribute. I can see his face still, dark and heavy-lined beneath his

Notes

[178] *Wilberforce and Stanley* William Wilberforce (1759–1833), English politician and abolitionist; Arthur Penrhyn Stanley (1815–1881), English churchman and historian.

[179] *Thirwell and Ingles* Connop Thirwall (1797–1875), English bishop and historian; John Eardley Inglis (1814–1862), British military officer.

[180] *Froude and Macaulay* James Anthony Froude (1818–1894) and Thomas Babington Macaulay (1800–1859), British historians.

[181] Sir Benjamin Brodie (1783–1862), English surgeon.

snowy hair; lighting and shading, now with inspiration for the future, now in innocent pain at some human wickedness, now with sorrow at some hard memory from the past. The more I met Alexander Crummell, the more I felt how much that world was losing which knew so little of him. In another age he might have sat among the elders of the land in purple-bordered toga;[182] in another country mothers might have sung him to the cradles.

He did his work – he did it nobly and well; and yet I sorrow that here he worked alone, with so little human sympathy. His name to-day, in this broad land, means little, and comes to fifty million ears laden with no incense of memory or emulation. And herein lies the tragedy of the age: not that men are poor – all men know something of poverty; not that men are wicked – who is good? not that men are ignorant – what is Truth? Nay, but that men know so little of men.

He sat one morning gazing toward the sea. He smiled and said, "The gate is rusty on the hinges." That night at star-rise a wind came moaning out of the west to blow the gate ajar, and then the soul I loved fled like a flame across the Seas, and in its seat sat Death.

I wonder where he is to-day? I wonder if in that dim world beyond, as he came gliding in, there rose on some wan throne a King – a dark and pierced Jew, who knows the writhings of the earthly damned, saying, as he laid those heart-wrung talents down, "Well done!" while round about the morning stars sat singing.

Chapter 13

Of the Coming of John

What bring they 'neath the midnight,
  Beside the River-sea?
They bring the human heart wherein
  No nightly calm can be;
That droppeth never with the wind,
  Nor drieth with the dew;
O calm it, God; thy calm is broad
  To cover spirits too.
    The river floweth on.
      Mrs. Browning.[183]

Notes

[182] *purple-bordered toga* the garb of Roman nobility.

[183] The epigraph comes from Elizabeth Barrett Browning's "A Romance of the Ganges" (1838).

Carlisle Street runs westward from the centre of Johnstown, across a great black bridge, down a hill and up again, by little shops and meat-markets, past single-storied homes, until suddenly it stops against a wide green lawn. It is a broad, restful place, with two large buildings outlined against the west. When at evening the winds come swelling from the east, and the great pall of the city's smoke hangs wearily above the valley, then the red west glows like a dreamland down Carlisle Street, and, at the tolling of the supper-bell, throws the passing forms of students in dark silhouette against the sky. Tall and black, they move slowly by, and seem in the sinister light to flit before the city like dim warning ghosts. Perhaps they are; for this is Wells Institute, and these black students have few dealings with the white city below.

And if you will notice, night after night, there is one dark form that ever hurries last and late toward the twinkling lights of Swain Hall – for Jones is never on time. A long, straggling fellow he is, brown and hard-haired, who seems to be growing straight out of his clothes, and walks with a half-apologetic roll. He used perpetually to set the quiet dining-room into waves of merriment, as he stole to his place after the bell had tapped for prayers; he seemed so perfectly awkward. And yet one glance at his face made one forgive him much – that broad, good-natured smile in which lay no bit of art or artifice, but seemed just bubbling good-nature and genuine satisfaction with the world.

He came to us from Altamaha, away down there beneath the gnarled oaks of Southeastern Georgia, where the sea croons to the sands and the sands listen till they sink half drowned beneath the waters, rising only here and there in long, low islands. The white folk of Altamaha voted John a good boy – fine plough-hand, good in the rice-fields, handy everywhere, and always good-natured and respectful. But they shook their heads when his mother wanted to send him off to school. "It'll spoil him – ruin him," they said; and they talked as though they knew. But full half the black folk followed him proudly to the station, and carried his queer little trunk and many bundles. And there they shook and shook hands, and the girls kissed him shyly and the boys clapped him on the back. So the train came, and he pinched his little sister lovingly, and put his great arms about his mother's neck, and then was away with a puff and a roar into the great yellow world that flamed and flared about the doubtful pilgrim. Up the coast they hurried, past the squares and palmettos of Savannah, through the cotton-fields and through the weary night, to Millville, and came with the morning to the noise and bustle of Johnstown.

And they that stood behind, that morning in Altamaha, and watched the train as it noisily bore playmate and brother and son away to the world, had thereafter one ever-recurring word – "When John comes." Then what parties were to be, and what speakings in the churches; what new furniture in the front room – perhaps even a new front room; and there would be a new schoolhouse, with John as teacher; and then perhaps a big wedding; all this and more – when John comes. But the white people shook their heads.

At first he was coming at Christmas-time – but the vacation proved too short; and then, the next summer – but times were hard and schooling costly, and so, instead, he worked in Johnstown. And so it drifted to the next summer, and the next – till playmates scattered, and mother grew gray, and sister went up to the Judge's kitchen to work. And still the legend lingered – "When John comes."

Up at the Judge's they rather liked this refrain; for they too had a John – a fair-haired, smooth-faced boy, who had played many a long summer's day to its close with his darker namesake. "Yes, sir! John is at Princeton, sir," said the broad-shouldered gray-haired Judge every morning as he marched down to the post-office. "Showing the Yankees what a Southern gentleman can do," he added; and strode home again with his letters and papers. Up at the great pillared house they lingered long over the Princeton letter – the Judge and his frail wife, his sister and growing daughters. "It'll make a man of him," said the Judge, "college is the place." And then he asked the shy little waitress, "Well, Jennie, how's your John?" and added reflectively, "Too bad, too bad your mother sent him off – it will spoil him." And the waitress wondered.

Thus in the far-away Southern village the world lay waiting, half consciously, the coming of two young men, and dreamed in an inarticulate way of new things that would be done and new thoughts that all would think. And yet it was singular that few thought of two Johns – for the black folk thought of one John, and he was black; and the white folk thought of another John, and he was white. And neither world thought the other world's thought, save with a vague unrest.

Up in Johnstown, at the Institute, we were long puzzled at the case of John Jones. For a long time the clay seemed unfit for any sort of moulding. He was loud and boisterous, always laughing and singing, and never able to work consecutively at anything. He did not know how to study; he had no idea of thoroughness; and with his tardiness, carelessness, and appalling good-humor, we were sore perplexed. One night we sat in faculty-meeting, worried and serious; for Jones was in trouble again. This last escapade was too much, and so we solemnly voted "that Jones, on account of repeated disorder and inattention to work, be suspended for the rest of the term."

It seemed to us that the first time life ever struck Jones as a really serious thing was when the Dean told him he must leave school. He stared at the gray-haired man blankly, with great eyes. "Why – why," he faltered, "but – I haven't graduated!" Then the Dean slowly and clearly explained, reminding him of the tardiness and the carelessness, of the poor lessons and neglected work, of the noise and disorder, until the fellow hung his head in confusion. Then he said quickly, "But you won't tell mammy and sister – you won't write mammy, now will you? For if you won't I'll go out into the city and work, and come back next term and show you something." So the Dean promised faithfully, and John shouldered his little trunk, giving neither word nor look to the giggling boys, and walked down Carlisle Street to the great city, with sober eyes and a set and serious face.

Perhaps we imagined it, but someway it seemed to us that the serious look that crept over his boyish face that afternoon never left it again. When he came back to us he went to work with all his rugged strength. It was a hard struggle, for things did not come easily to him – few crowding memories of early life and teaching came to help him on his new way; but all the world toward which he strove was of his own building, and he builded slow and hard. As the light dawned lingeringly on his new creations, he sat rapt and silent before the vision, or wandered alone over the green campus peering through and beyond the world of men into a world of thought. And the thoughts at times puzzled him sorely; he could not see just why the circle was not square, and carried it out fifty-six decimal places one midnight – would have gone further, indeed, had not the matron rapped for lights out. He caught terrible colds lying on his back in the meadows of nights, trying to think out the solar system; he had grave doubts as to the ethics of the Fall of Rome, and strongly suspected the Germans of being thieves and rascals, despite his text-books; he pondered long over every new Greek word, and wondered why this meant that and why it couldn't mean something else, and how it must have felt to think all things in Greek. So he thought and puzzled along for himself – pausing perplexed where others skipped merrily, and walking steadily through the difficulties where the rest stopped and surrendered.

Thus he grew in body and soul, and with him his clothes seemed to grow and arrange themselves; coat sleeves got longer, cuffs appeared, and collars got less soiled. Now and then his boots shone, and a new dignity crept into his walk. And we who saw daily a new thoughtfulness growing in his eyes began to expect something of this plodding boy. Thus he passed out of the preparatory school into college, and we who watched him felt four more years of change, which almost transformed the tall, grave man who bowed to us commencement morning. He had left his queer thought-world and come back to a world of motion and of men. He looked now for the first time sharply about him, and wondered he had seen so little before. He grew slowly to feel almost for the first time the Veil that lay between him and the white world; he first noticed now the oppression that had not seemed oppression before, differences that erstwhile seemed natural, restraints and slights that in his boyhood days had gone unnoticed or been greeted with a laugh. He felt angry now when men did not call him "Mister," he clenched his hands at the "Jim Crow" cars, and chafed at the color-line that hemmed in him and his. A tinge of sarcasm crept into his speech, and a vague bitterness into his life; and he sat long hours wondering and planning a way around these crooked things. Daily he found himself shrinking from the choked and narrow life of his native town. And yet he always planned to go back to Altamaha – always planned to work there. Still, more and more as the day approached he hesitated with a nameless dread; and even the day after graduation he seized with eagerness the offer of the Dean to send him North with the quartette during the summer vacation, to sing for the Institute. A breath of air before the plunge, he said to himself in half apology.

It was a bright September afternoon, and the streets of New York were brilliant with moving men. They reminded John of the sea, as he sat in the square and watched them, so changelessly changing, so bright and dark, so grave and gay. He scanned their rich and faultless clothes, the way they carried their hands, the shape of their hats; he peered into the hurrying carriages. Then, leaning back with a sigh, he said, "This is the World." The notion suddenly seized him to see where the world was going; since many of the richer and brighter seemed hurrying all one way. So when a tall, light-haired young man and a little talkative lady came by, he rose half hesitatingly and followed them. Up the street they went, past stores and gay shops, across a broad square, until with a hundred others they entered the high portal of a great building.

He was pushed toward the ticket-office with the others, and felt in his pocket for the new five-dollar bill he had hoarded. There seemed really no time for hesitation, so he drew it bravely out, passed it to the busy clerk, and received simply a ticket but no change. When at last he realized that he had paid five dollars to enter he knew not what, he stood stock-still amazed. "Be careful," said a low voice behind him; "you must not lynch the colored gentleman simply because he's in your way," and a girl looked up roguishly into the eyes of her fair-haired escort. A shade of annoyance passed over the escort's face. "You *will* not understand us at the South," he said half impatiently, as if continuing an argument. "With all your professions, one never sees in the North so cordial and intimate relations between white and black as are everyday occurrences with us. Why, I remember my closest play-fellow in boyhood was a little Negro named after me, and surely no two – *well!*" The man stopped short and flushed to the roots of his hair, for there directly beside his reserved orchestra chairs sat the Negro he had stumbled over in the hallway. He hesitated and grew pale with anger, called the usher and gave him his card, with a few peremptory words, and slowly sat down. The lady deftly changed the subject.

All this John did not see, for he sat in a half-maze minding the scene about him; the delicate beauty of the hall, the faint perfume, the moving myriad of men, the rich clothing and low hum of talking seemed all a part of a world so different from his, so strangely more beautiful than anything he had known, that he sat in dreamland, and started when, after a hush, rose high and clear the music of Lohengrin's swan.[184] The

Notes

[184] *Lohengrin's swan* a swan guides the hero of Wagner's *Lohengrin* (1850).

infinite beauty of the wail lingered and swept through every muscle of his frame, and put it all a-tune. He closed his eyes and grasped the elbows of the chair, touching unwittingly the lady's arm. And the lady drew away. A deep longing swelled in all his heart to rise with that clear music out of the dirt and dust of that low life that held him prisoned and befouled. If he could only live up in the free air where birds sang and setting suns had no touch of blood! Who had called him to be the slave and butt of all? And if he had called, what right had he to call when a world like this lay open before men?

Then the movement changed, and fuller, mightier harmony swelled away. He looked thoughtfully across the hall, and wondered why the beautiful gray-haired woman looked so listless, and what the little man could be whispering about.

He would not like to be listless and idle, he thought, for he felt with the music the movement of power within him. If he but had some master-work, some life-service, hard – aye, bitter hard, but without the cringing and sickening servility, without the cruel hurt that hardened his heart and soul. When at last a soft sorrow crept across the violins, there came to him the vision of a far-off home – the great eyes of his sister, and the dark drawn face of his mother. And his heart sank below the waters, even as the sea-sand sinks by the shores of Altamaha, only to be lifted aloft again with that last ethereal wail of the swan that quivered and faded away into the sky.

It left John sitting so silent and rapt that he did not for some time notice the usher tapping him lightly on the shoulder and saying politely, "Will you step this way, please, sir?" A little surprised, he arose quickly at the last tap, and, turning to leave his seat, looked full into the face of the fair-haired young man. For the first time the young man recognized his dark boyhood playmate, and John knew that it was the Judge's son. The white John started, lifted his hand, and then froze into his chair; the black John smiled lightly, then grimly, and followed the usher down the aisle. The manager was sorry, very, very sorry – but he explained that some mistake had been made in selling the gentleman a seat already disposed of; he would refund the money, of course – and indeed felt the matter keenly, and so forth, and – before he had finished John was gone, walking hurriedly across the square and down the broad streets, and as he passed the park he buttoned his coat and said, "John Jones, you're a natural-born fool." Then he went to his lodgings and wrote a letter, and tore it up; he wrote another, and threw it in the fire. Then he seized a scrap of paper and wrote: "Dear Mother and Sister – I am coming – John."

"Perhaps," said John, as he settled himself on the train, "perhaps I am to blame myself in struggling against my manifest destiny simply because it looks hard and unpleasant. Here is my duty to Altamaha plain before me; perhaps they'll let me help settle the Negro problems there –perhaps they won't. 'I will go in to the King, which is not according to the law; and if I perish, I perish.' "[185] And then he mused and dreamed, and planned a life-work; and the train flew south.

Down in Altamaha, after seven long years, all the world knew John was coming. The homes were scrubbed and scoured – above all, one; the gardens and yards had an unwonted trimness, and Jennie bought a new gingham. With some finesse and negotiation, all the dark Methodists and Presbyterians were induced to join in a monster welcome at the Baptist Church; and as the day drew near, warm discussions arose on every corner as to the exact extent and nature of John's accomplishments. It was noontide on a gray and cloudy day when he came. The black town flocked to the depot, with a little of the white at the edges – a happy throng, with "Good-mawnings" and

Notes

[185] *'if I perish, I perish'* Esther 4:16.

"Howdys" and laughing and joking and jostling. Mother sat yonder in the window watching; but sister Jennie stood on the platform, nervously fingering her dress – tall and lithe, with soft brown skin and loving eyes peering from out a tangled wilderness of hair. John rose gloomily as the train stopped, for he was thinking of the "Jim Crow" car; he stepped to the platform, and paused: a little dingy station, a black crowd gaudy and dirty, a half-mile of dilapidated shanties along a straggling ditch of mud. An overwhelming sense of the sordidness and narrowness of it all seized him; he looked in vain for his mother, kissed coldly the tall, strange girl who called him brother, spoke a short, dry word here and there; then, lingering neither for hand-shaking nor gossip, started silently up the street, raising his hat merely to the last eager old aunty, to her open-mouthed astonishment. The people were distinctly bewildered. This silent, cold man – was this John? Where was his smile and hearty hand-grasp? "'Peared kind o' down in the mouf," said the Methodist preacher thoughtfully. "Seemed monstus stuck up," complained a Baptist sister. But the white postmaster from the edge of the crowd expressed the opinion of his folks plainly. "That damn Nigger," said he, as he shouldered the mail and arranged his tobacco, "has gone North and got plum full o' fool notions; but they won't work in Altamaha." And the crowd melted away.

The meeting of welcome at the Baptist Church was a failure. Rain spoiled the barbecue, and thunder turned the milk in the ice-cream. When the speaking came at night, the house was crowded to overflowing. The three preachers had especially prepared themselves, but somehow John's manner seemed to throw a blanket over everything – he seemed so cold and preoccupied, and had so strange an air of restraint that the Methodist brother could not warm up to his theme and elicited not a single "Amen"; the Presbyterian prayer was but feebly responded to, and even the Baptist preacher, though he wakened faint enthusiasm, got so mixed up in his favorite sentence that he had to close it by stopping fully fifteen minutes sooner than he meant. The people moved uneasily in their seats as John rose to reply. He spoke slowly and methodically. The age, he said, demanded new ideas; we were far different from those men of the seventeenth and eighteenth centuries – with broader ideas of human brotherhood and destiny. Then he spoke of the rise of charity and popular education, and particularly of the spread of wealth and work. The question was, then, he added reflectively, looking at the low discolored ceiling, what part the Negroes of this land would take in the striving of the new century. He sketched in vague outline the new Industrial School that might rise among these pines, he spoke in detail of the charitable and philanthropic work that might be organized, of money that might be saved for banks and business. Finally he urged unity, and deprecated especially religious and denominational bickering. "To-day," he said, with a smile, "the world cares little whether a man be Baptist or Methodist, or indeed a churchman at all, so long as he is good and true. What difference does it make whether a man be baptized in river or wash-bowl, or not at all? Let's leave all that littleness, and look higher." Then, thinking of nothing else, he slowly sat down. A painful hush seized that crowded mass. Little had they understood of what he said, for he spoke an unknown tongue, save the last word about baptism; that they knew, and they sat very still while the clock ticked. Then at last a low suppressed snarl came from the Amen corner, and an old bent man arose, walked over the seats, and climbed straight up into the pulpit. He was wrinkled and black, with scant gray and tufted hair; his voice and hands shook as with palsy; but on his face lay the intense rapt look of the religious fanatic. He seized the Bible with his rough, huge hands; twice he raised it inarticulate, and then fairly burst into the words, with rude and awful eloquence. He quivered, swayed, and bent; then rose aloft in perfect majesty, till the people moaned and wept, wailed and shouted, and a wild shrieking arose from the corners where all the pent-up feeling of the hour gathered itself and rushed into the air. John never knew clearly what the old man said; he only felt himself held up to scorn and scathing denunciation for trampling on the true Religion, and he realized with amazement that all unknowingly he had put rough, rude hands on something this little world held sacred. He arose silently, and passed out into the night. Down toward the sea he went, in the fitful starlight, half conscious of the girl who followed timidly after him. When at last he stood upon the bluff, he turned to his little sister and looked upon her sorrowfully, remembering with sudden pain how little thought he had given her. He put his arm about her and let her passion of tears spend itself on his shoulder.

Long they stood together, peering over the gray unresting water.

"John," she said, "does it make everyone – unhappy when they study and learn lots of things?"

He paused and smiled. "I am afraid it does," he said.

"And, John, are you glad you studied?"

"Yes," came the answer, slowly but positively.

She watched the flickering lights upon the sea, and said thoughtfully, "I wish I was unhappy – and – and," putting both arms about his neck, "I think I am, a little, John."

It was several days later that John walked up to the Judge's house to ask for the privilege of teaching the Negro school. The Judge himself met him at the front door, stared a little hard at him, and said brusquely, "Go 'round to the kitchen door, John, and wait." Sitting on the kitchen steps, John stared at the corn, thoroughly perplexed. What on earth had come over him? Every step he made offended someone. He had come to save his people, and before he left the depot he had hurt them. He sought to teach them at the church, and had outraged their deepest feelings. He had schooled himself to be respectful to the Judge, and then blundered into his front door. And all the time he had meant right – and yet, and yet, somehow he found it so hard and strange to fit his old surroundings again, to find his place in the world about him. He could not remember that he used to have any difficulty in the past, when life was glad and gay. The world seemed smooth and easy then. Perhaps – but his sister came to the kitchen door just then and said the Judge awaited him.

The Judge sat in the dining-room amid his morning's mail, and he did not ask John to sit down. He plunged squarely into the business. "You've come for the school, I suppose. Well, John, I want to speak to you plainly. You know I'm a friend to your people. I've helped you and your family, and would have done more if you hadn't got the notion of going off. Now I like the colored people, and sympathize with all their reasonable aspirations; but you and I both know, John, that in this country the Negro must remain subordinate, and can never expect to be the equal of white men. In their place, your people can be honest and respectful; and God knows, I'll do what I can to help them. But when they want to reverse nature, and rule white men, and marry white women, and sit in my parlor, then, by God! we'll hold them under if we have to lynch every Nigger in the land. Now, John, the question is, are you, with your education and Northern notions, going to accept the situation and teach the darkies to be faithful servants and laborers as your fathers were – I knew your father, John, he belonged to my brother, and he was a good Nigger. Well – well, are you going to be like him, or are you going to try to put fool ideas of rising and equality into these folks' heads, and make them discontented and unhappy?"

"I am going to accept this situation, Judge Henderson," answered John, with a brevity that did not escape the keen old man. He hesitated a moment, and then said shortly, "Very well – we'll try you awhile. Good-morning."

It was a full month after the opening of the Negro school that the other John came home, tall, gay, and headstrong. The mother wept, the sisters sang. The whole white town was glad. A proud man was the Judge, and it was a goodly sight to see the two swinging down Main Street together. And yet all did not go smoothly between them, for the younger man could not and did not veil his contempt for the little town, and plainly had his heart set on New York. Now the one cherished ambition of the Judge was to see his son mayor of Altamaha, representative to the legislature, and – who could say? – governor of Georgia. So the argument often waxed hot between them. "Good heavens, father," the younger man would say after dinner, as he lighted a cigar and stood by the fireplace, "you surely don't expect a young fellow like me to settle down permanently in this – this God-forgotten town with nothing but mud and Negroes?" "*I* did," the Judge would answer laconically; and on this particular day it seemed from the gathering scowl that he was about to add something more emphatic, but neighbors had already begun to drop in to admire his son, and the conversation drifted.

"Heah that John is livenin' things up at the darky school," volunteered the postmaster, after a pause.

"What now?" asked the Judge, sharply.

"Oh, nothin' in particulah – just his almighty air and uppish ways. B'lieve I did heah somethin' about his givin' talks on the French Revolution, equality, and such like. He's what I call a dangerous Nigger."

"Have you heard him say anything out of the way?"

"Why, no – but Sally, our girl, told my wife a lot of rot. Then, too, I don't need to heah: a Nigger what won't say 'sir' to a white man, or – "

"Who is this John?" interrupted the son.

"Why, it's little black John, Peggy's son – your old play-fellow."

The young man's face flushed angrily, and then he laughed.

"Oh," said he, "it's the darky that tried to force himself into a seat beside the lady I was escorting – "

But Judge Henderson waited to hear no more. He had been nettled all day, and now at this he rose with a half-smothered oath, took his hat and cane, and walked straight to the schoolhouse.

For John, it had been a long, hard pull to get things started in the rickety old shanty that sheltered his school. The Negroes were rent into factions for and against him, the parents were careless, the children irregular and dirty, and books, pencils, and slates largely missing. Nevertheless, he struggled hopefully on, and seemed to see at last some glimmering of dawn. The attendance was larger and the children were a shade cleaner this week. Even the booby class in reading showed a little comforting progress. So John settled himself with renewed patience this afternoon.

"Now, Mandy," he said cheerfully, "that's better; but you mustn't chop your words up so: 'If – the – man – goes." Why, your little brother even wouldn't tell a story that way, now would he?"

"Naw, suh, he cain't talk."

"All right; now let's try again: 'If the man – '"

"John!"

The whole school started in surprise, and the teacher half arose, as the red, angry face of the Judge appeared in the open doorway.

"John, this school is closed. You children can go home and get to work. The white people of Altamaha are not spending their money on black folks to have their heads crammed with impudence and lies. Clear out! I'll lock the door myself."

Up at the great pillared house the tall young son wandered aimlessly about after his father's abrupt departure. In the house there was little to interest him; the books were old and stale, the local newspaper flat, and the women had retired with headaches and sewing. He tried a nap, but it was too warm. So he sauntered out into the fields, complaining disconsolately, "Good Lord! how long will this imprisonment last!" He was not a bad fellow – just a little spoiled and self-indulgent, and as headstrong as his proud father. He seemed a young man pleasant to look upon, as he sat on the great black stump at the edge of the pines idly swinging his legs and smoking. "Why, there isn't even a girl worth getting up a respectable flirtation with," he growled. Just then his eye caught a tall, willowy figure hurrying toward him on the narrow path. He looked with interest at first, and then burst into a laugh as he said, "Well, I declare, if it isn't Jennie, the little brown kitchen-maid! Why, I never noticed before what a trim little body she is. Hello, Jennie! Why, you haven't kissed me since I came home," he said gaily. The young girl stared at him in surprise and confusion – faltered something inarticulate, and attempted to pass. But a wilful mood had seized the young idler, and he caught at her arm. Frightened, she slipped by; and half mischievously he turned and ran after her through the tall pines.

Yonder, toward the sea, at the end of the path, came John slowly, with his head down. He had turned wearily homeward from the schoolhouse; then, thinking to shield his mother from the blow, started to meet his sister as she came from work and break the news of his dismissal to her. "I'll go away," he said slowly; "I'll go away and find work, and send for them. I cannot live here longer." And then the fierce, buried anger surged up into his throat. He waved his arms and hurried wildly up the path.

The great brown sea lay silent. The air scarce breathed. The dying day bathed the twisted oaks and mighty pines in black and gold. There came from the wind no warning, not a whisper from the cloudless sky. There was only a black man hurrying on with an ache in his heart, seeing neither sun nor sea, but starting as from a dream at the frightened cry that woke the pines, to see his dark sister struggling in the arms of a tall and fair-haired man.

He said not a word, but, seizing a fallen limb, struck him with all the pent-up hatred of his great black arm; and the body lay white and still beneath the pines, all bathed in sunshine and in blood. John looked at it dreamily, then walked back to the house briskly, and said in a soft voice, "Mammy, I'm going away – I'm going to be free."

She gazed at him dimly and faltered, "No'th, honey, is yo' gwine No'th agin?"

He looked out where the North Star glistened pale above the waters, and said, "Yes, mammy, I'm going – North."

Then, without another word, he went out into the narrow lane, up by the straight pines, to the same winding path, and seated himself on the great black stump, looking at the blood where the body had lain. Yonder in the gray past he had played with that dead boy, romping together under the solemn trees. The night deepened; he thought of the boys at Johnstown. He wondered how Brown had turned out, and Carey? And Jones – Jones? Why, *he* was Jones, and he wondered what they would all say when they knew, when they knew, in that great long dining-room with its hundreds of merry eyes. Then as the sheen of the starlight stole over him, he thought of the gilded ceiling of that vast concert hall, and heard stealing toward him the faint sweet music of the swan. Hark! was it music, or the hurry and shouting of men? Yes, surely! Clear and high the faint sweet melody rose and fluttered like a living thing, so that the very earth trembled as with the tramp of horses and murmur of angry men.

He leaned back and smiled toward the sea, whence rose the strange melody, away from the dark shadows where lay the noise of horses galloping, galloping on. With an effort he roused himself, bent forward, and looked steadily down the pathway, softly humming the "Song of the Bride" –

"Freudig geführt, ziehet dahin."[186]

Notes

[186] *"Freudig geführt, ziehet dahin."* (German) "Joyfully led, enter within." A slight modification of the opening line of the "Wedding March" in *Lohengrin*.

Amid the trees in the dim morning twilight he watched their shadows dancing and heard their horses thundering toward him, until at last they came sweeping like a storm, and he saw in front that haggard white-haired man, whose eyes flashed red with fury. Oh, how he pitied him – pitied him – and wondered if he had the coiling twisted rope. Then, as the storm burst round him, he rose slowly to his feet and turned his closed eyes toward the Sea.

And the world whistled in his ears.

Chapter 14

The Sorrow Songs

I walk through the churchyard
  To lay this body down;
I know moon-rise, I know star-rise;
I walk in the moonlight, I walk in the starlight;
I'll lie in the grave and stretch out my arms,
I'll go to judgment in the evening of the day,
And my soul and thy soul shall meet that day,
  When I lay this body down.

Negro Song.[187]

They that walked in darkness sang songs in the olden days – Sorrow Songs – for they were weary at heart. And so before each thought that I have written in this book I have set a phrase, a haunting echo of these weird old songs in which the soul of the black slave spoke to men. Ever since I was a child these songs have stirred me strangely. They came out of the South unknown to me, one by one, and yet at once I knew them as of me and of mine. Then in after years when I came to Nashville I saw the great temple builded of these songs towering over the pale city. To me Jubilee Hall[188] seemed ever made of the songs themselves, and its bricks were red with the blood and dust of toil. Out of them rose for me morning, noon, and night, bursts of wonderful melody, full of the voices of my brothers and sisters, full of the voices of the past.

Little of beauty has America given the world save the rude grandeur God himself stamped on her bosom; the human spirit in this new world has expressed itself in vigor and ingenuity rather than in beauty. And so by fateful chance the Negro folk-song – the

Notes

[187] The epigraph comes from "Lay This Body Down," a Negro spiritual.

[188] *Jubilee Hall* at the center of Fisk University, a building constructed with funds earned by the Fisk Jubilee Singers.

rhythmic cry of the slave – stands to-day not simply as the sole American music, but as the most beautiful expression of human experience born this side the seas. It has been neglected, it has been, and is, half despised, and above all it has been persistently mistaken and misunderstood; but notwithstanding, it still remains as the singular spiritual heritage of the nation and the greatest gift of the Negro people.

Away back in the thirties the melody of these slave songs stirred the nation, but the songs were soon half forgotten. Some, like "Near the lake where drooped the willow," passed into current airs and their source was forgotten; others were caricatured on the "minstrel" stage and their memory died away. Then in war-time came the singular Port Royal experiment after the capture of Hilton Head, and perhaps for the first time the North met the Southern slave face to face and heart to heart with no third witness. The Sea Islands of the Carolinas, where they met, were filled with a black folk of primitive type, touched and moulded less by the world about them than any others outside the Black Belt. Their appearance was uncouth, their language funny, but their hearts were human and their singing stirred men with a mighty power. Thomas Wentworth Higginson[189] hastened to tell of these songs, and Miss McKim[190] and others urged upon the world their rare beauty. But the world listened only half credulously until the Fisk Jubilee Singers[191] sang the slave songs so deeply into the world's heart that it can never wholly forget them again.

There was once a blacksmith's son born at Cadiz, New York, who in the changes of time taught school in Ohio and helped defend Cincinnati from Kirby Smith.[192] Then he fought at Chancellorsville and Gettysburg and finally served in the Freedman's Bureau at Nashville. Here he formed a Sunday-school class of black children in 1866, and sang with them and taught them to sing. And then they taught him to sing, and when once the glory of the Jubilee songs passed into the soul of George L. White,[193] he knew his life-work was to let those Negroes sing to the world as they had sung to him. So in 1871 the pilgrimage of the Fisk Jubilee Singers began. North to Cincinnati they rode – four half-clothed black boys and five girl-women – led by a man with a cause and a purpose. They stopped at Wilberforce, the oldest of Negro schools, where a black bishop blessed them. Then they went, fighting cold and starvation, shut out of hotels, and cheerfully sneered at, ever northward; and ever the magic of their song kept thrilling hearts, until a burst of applause in the Congregational Council at Oberlin revealed them to the world. They came to New York and Henry Ward Beecher[194] dared to welcome them, even though the metropolitan dailies sneered at his "Nigger Minstrels." So their songs conquered till they sang across the land and across the sea, before Queen and Kaiser, in Scotland and Ireland, Holland and Switzerland. Seven years they sang, and brought back a hundred and fifty thousand dollars to found Fisk University.

Since their day they have been imitated – sometimes well, by the singers of Hampton and Atlanta, sometimes ill, by straggling quartettes. Caricature has sought again to spoil the quaint beauty of the music, and has filled the air with many debased melodies which

Notes

189 Thomas Wentworth Higginson (1823–1911), Civil War commander of the first black regiment, who wrote widely on spirituals and folk songs in *Army Life in a Southern Regiment* (1870).

190 *Miss McKim* Lucy McKim Garrison (1842–1877), musician and collector of black folk songs.

191 *Fisk Jubilee Singers* a traveling chorus established at Fisk University in 1867.

192 *Kirby Smith* Edmund Kirby Smith (1824–1893), Confederate general who besieged Cincinnati in 1862.

193 George L. White (1838–1895), founder and director of the Fisk Jubilee Singers.

194 Henry Ward Beecher (1813–1887), Congregationalist clergyman and prominent abolitionist.

vulgar ears scarce know from the real. But the true Negro folk-song still lives in the hearts of those who have heard them truly sung and in the hearts of the Negro people.

What are these songs, and what do they mean? I know little of music and can say nothing in technical phrase, but I know something of men, and knowing them, I know that these songs are the articulate message of the slave to the world. They tell us in these eager days that life was joyous to the black slave, careless and happy. I can easily believe this of some, of many. But not all the past South, though it rose from the dead, can gainsay the heart-touching witness of these songs. They are the music of an unhappy people, of the children of disappointment; they tell of death and suffering and unvoiced longing toward a truer world, of misty wanderings and hidden ways.

The songs are indeed the siftings of centuries; the music is far more ancient than the words, and in it we can trace here and there signs of development. My grandfather's grandmother was seized by an evil Dutch trader two centuries ago; and coming to the valleys of the Hudson and Housatonic, black, little, and lithe, she shivered and shrank in the harsh north winds, looked longingly at the hills, and often crooned a heathen melody to the child between her knees, thus:

The child sang it to his children and they to their children's children, and so two hundred years it has travelled down to us and we sing it to our children, knowing as little as our fathers what its words may mean, but knowing well the meaning of its music.

This was primitive African music; it may be seen in larger form in the strange chant which heralds "The Coming of John":

> "You may bury me in the East,
> You may bury me in the West,
> But I'll hear the trumpet sound in that morning,"

– the voice of exile.

Ten master songs, more or less, one may pluck from this forest of melody – songs of undoubted Negro origin and wide popular currency, and songs peculiarly characteristic of the slave. One of these I have just mentioned. Another, whose strains begin this book, is "Nobody knows the trouble I've seen." When, struck with a sudden poverty, the United States refused to fulfil its promises of land to the freedmen, a brigadier-general went down to the Sea Islands to carry the news. An old woman on the outskirts of the throng began singing this song; all the mass joined with her, swaying. And the soldier wept.

The third song is the cradle-song of death which all men know – "Swing low, sweet chariot" – whose bars begin the life story of "Alexander Crummell." Then there is the song of many waters, "Roll, Jordan, roll," a mighty chorus with minor cadences. There were many songs of the fugitive like that which opens "The Wings of Atalanta," and the more familiar "Been a-listening." The seventh is the song of the End and the Beginning – "My Lord, what a mourning! when the stars begin to fall"; a strain of this is placed before "The Dawn of Freedom." The song of groping – "My way's cloudy" – begins "The Meaning of Progress"; the ninth is the song of this chapter – "Wrestlin' Jacob, the day is a-breaking" – a pæan of hopeful strife. The last master song is the song of songs – "Steal away" – sprung from "The Faith of the Fathers."

There are many others of the Negro folk-songs as striking and characteristic as these, as, for instance, the three strains in the third, eighth, and ninth chapters; and others I am sure could easily make a selection on more scientific principles. There are, too, songs that seem to me a step removed from the more primitive types: there is the maze-like medley, "Bright sparkles," one phrase of which heads "The Black Belt"; the Easter carol, "Dust, dust and ashes"; the dirge, "My mother's took her flight and gone home"; and that burst of melody hovering over "The Passing of the First-Born" – "I hope my mother will be there in that beautiful world on high."

These represent a third step in the development of the slave song, of which "You may bury me in the East" is the first, and songs like "March on" (chapter six) and "Steal away" are the second. The first is African music, the second Afro-American, while the third is a blending of Negro music with the music heard in the foster land. The result is still distinctively Negro and the method of blending original, but the elements are both Negro and Caucasian. One might go further and find a fourth step in this development, where the songs of white America have been distinctively influenced by the slave songs or have incorporated whole phrases of Negro melody, as "Swanee River" and "Old Black Joe."[195] Side by side, too, with the growth has gone the debasements and imitations – the Negro "minstrel" songs, many of the "gospel" hymns, and some of the contemporary "coon" songs – a mass of music in which the novice may easily lose himself and never find the real Negro melodies.

In these songs, I have said, the slave spoke to the world. Such a message is naturally veiled and half articulate. Words and music have lost each other and new and cant phrases of a dimly understood theology have displaced the older sentiment. Once in a while we catch a strange word of an unknown tongue, as the "Mighty Myo," which figures as a river of death; more often slight words or mere doggerel are joined to music of singular sweetness. Purely secular songs are few in number, partly because many of them were turned into hymns by a change of words, partly because the frolics were seldom heard by the stranger, and the music less often caught. Of nearly all the songs, however, the music is distinctly sorrowful. The ten master songs I have mentioned tell in word and music of trouble and exile, of strife and hiding; they grope toward some unseen power and sigh for rest in the End.

The words that are left to us are not without interest, and, cleared of evident dross, they conceal much of real poetry and meaning beneath conventional theology and unmeaning rhapsody. Like all primitive folk, the slave stood near to Nature's heart. Life was a "rough and rolling sea" like the brown Atlantic of the Sea Islands; the "Wilderness" was the home of God, and the "lonesome valley" led to the way of life. "Winter'll soon be over," was the picture of life and death to a tropical imagination. The sudden

Notes

195 *"Swanee River" and "Old Black Joe"* popular minstrel songs by Stephen Foster (1826–1864).

wild thunderstorms of the South awed and impressed the Negroes – at times the rumbling seemed to them "mournful," at times imperious:

"My Lord calls me,
He calls me by the thunder,
The trumpet sounds it in my soul."

The monotonous toil and exposure is painted in many words. One sees the ploughmen in the hot, moist furrow, singing:

"Dere's no rain to wet you,
Dere's no sun to burn you,
Oh, push along, believer,
I want to go home."

The bowed and bent old man cries, with thrice-repeated wail:

"O Lord, keep me from sinking down,"

and he rebukes the devil of doubt who can whisper:

"Jesus is dead and God's gone away."

Yet the soul-hunger is there, the restlessness of the savage, the wail of the wanderer, and the plaint is put in one little phrase:

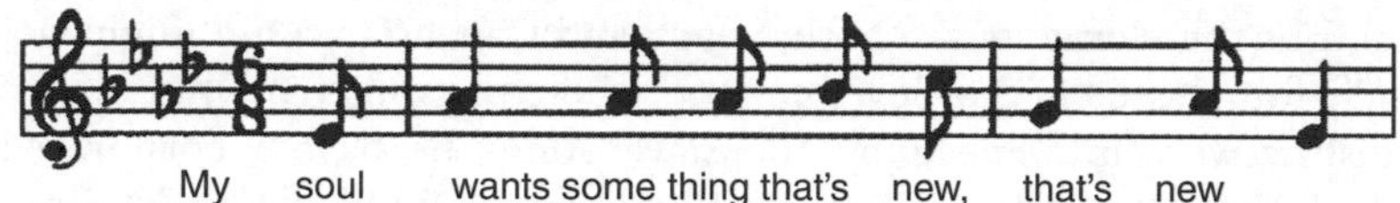
My soul wants some thing that's new, that's new

Over the inner thoughts of the slaves and their relations one with another the shadow of fear ever hung, so that we get but glimpses here and there, and also with them, eloquent omissions and silences. Mother and child are sung, but seldom father; fugitive and weary wanderer call for pity and affection, but there is little of wooing and wedding; the rocks and the mountains are well known, but home is unknown. Strange blending of love and helplessness sings through the refrain:

"Yonder's my ole mudder,
Been waggin' at de hill so long;
'Bout time she cross over,
Git home bime-by."

Elsewhere comes the cry of the "motherless" and the "Farewell, farewell, my only child."

Love-songs are scarce and fall into two categories – the frivolous and light, and the sad. Of deep successful love there is ominous silence, and in one of the oldest of these songs there is a depth of history and meaning:

Poor Ro - sy, Poor gal; Poor Ro - sy,
Poor gal; Ro - sy break my poor heart.
Heav'n shall - a - be my home.

A black woman said of the song, "It can't be sung without a full heart and a troubled sperrit." The same voice sings here that sings in the German folk-song:

"Jetz Geh i' an's brunele, trink' aber net."[196]

Of death the Negro showed little fear, but talked of it familiarly and even fondly as simply a crossing of the waters, perhaps – who knows? – back to his ancient forests again. Later days transfigured his fatalism, and amid the dust and dirt the toiler sang:

"Dust, dust and ashes, fly over my grave,
But the Lord shall bear my spirit home."

The things evidently borrowed from the surrounding world undergo characteristic change when they enter the mouth of the slave. Especially is this true of Bible phrases. "Weep, O captive daughter of Zion," is quaintly turned into "Zion, weep-a-low," and the wheels of Ezekiel are turned every way in the mystic dreaming of the slave, till he says:

"There's a little wheel a-turnin' in-a-my heart."

As in olden time, the words of these hymns were improvised by some leading minstrel of the religious band. The circumstances of the gathering, however, the rhythm of the songs, and the limitations of allowable thought, confined the poetry for the most part to single or double lines, and they seldom were expanded to quatrains or longer tales, although there are some few examples of sustained efforts, chiefly paraphrases of the Bible. Three short series of verses have always attracted me – the one that heads this chapter, of one line of which Thomas Wentworth Higginson has fittingly said, "Never, it seems to me, since man first lived and suffered was his infinite longing for peace uttered more plaintively." The second and third are descriptions of the Last Judgment – the one a late improvisation, with some traces of outside influence:

"Oh, the stars in the elements are falling,
And the moon drips away into blood,
And the ransomed of the Lord are returning unto God,
Blessed be the name of the Lord."

And the other earlier and homelier picture from the low coast lands:

"Michael, haul the boat ashore,
Then you'll hear the horn they blow,
Then you'll hear the trumpet sound,
Trumpet sound the world around,
Trumpet sound for rich and poor,
Trumpet sound the Jubilee,

Notes

[196] *"Jetz Geh i' an's brunele, trink' aber net."* (German) "Now I'm going to the well, but I'm not going to drink."

Trumpet sound for you and me."

Through all the sorrow of the Sorrow Songs there breathes a hope – a faith in the ultimate justice of things. The minor cadences of despair change often to triumph and calm confidence. Sometimes it is faith in life, sometimes a faith in death, sometimes assurance of boundless justice in some fair world beyond. But whichever it is, the meaning is always clear: that sometime, somewhere, men will judge men by their souls and not by their skins. Is such a hope justified? Do the Sorrow Songs sing true?

The silently growing assumption of this age is that the probation of races is past, and that the backward races of today are of proven inefficiency and not worth the saving. Such an assumption is the arrogance of peoples irreverent toward Time and ignorant of the deeds of men. A thousand years ago such an assumption, easily possible, would have made it difficult for the Teuton to prove his right to life. Two thousand years ago such dogmatism, readily welcome, would have scouted the idea of blond races ever leading civilization. So woefully[197] unorganized is sociological knowledge that the meaning of progress, the meaning of "swift" and "slow" in human doing, and the limits of human perfectibility,[198] are veiled, unanswered sphinxes on the shores of science. Why should Æschylus[199] have sung two thousand years before Shakespeare was born? Why has civilization flourished in Europe, and flickered, flamed, and died in Africa? So long as the world stands meekly dumb before such questions, shall this nation proclaim its ignorance and unhallowed prejudices by denying freedom of opportunity to those who brought the Sorrow Songs to the Seats of the Mighty?

Your country? How came it yours? Before the Pilgrims landed we were here. Here we have brought our three gifts and mingled them with yours: a gift of story and song – soft, stirring melody in an ill-harmonized and unmelodious land; the gift of sweat and brawn to beat back the wilderness, conquer the soil, and lay the foundations of this vast economic empire two hundred years earlier than your weak hands could have done it; the third, a gift of the Spirit. Around us the history of the land has centred for thrice a hundred years; out of the nation's heart we have called all that was best to throttle and subdue all that was worst; fire and blood, prayer and sacrifice, have billowed over this people, and they have found peace only in the altars of the God of Right. Nor has our gift of the Spirit been merely passive. Actively we have woven ourselves with the very warp and woof of this nation – we fought their battles, shared their sorrow, mingled our blood with theirs, and generation after generation have pleaded with a headstrong, careless people to despise not Justice, Mercy, and Truth, lest the nation be smitten with a curse. Our song, our toil, our cheer, and warning have been given to this nation in blood-brotherhood. Are not these gifts worth the giving? Is not this work and striving? Would America have been America without her Negro people?

Even so is the hope that sang in the songs of my fathers well sung. If somewhere in this whirl and chaos of things there dwells Eternal Good, pitiful yet masterful, then anon in His good time America shall rend the Veil and the prisoned shall go free. Free, free as the sunshine trickling down the morning into these high windows of mine, free as yonder fresh young voices welling up to me from the caverns of brick and mortar below – swelling with song, instinct with life, tremulous treble and darkening bass. My children, my little children, are singing to the sunshine, and thus they sing:

Notes

[197] *Original reads*: wofully [ed.].

[198] *Original reads*: perfectability, [ed.].

[199] Æschylus (525–456 BC), Greek dramatist.

Let us cheer the wea - ry tray - el - ler,
Cheer the wea - ry tray el - ler, let us
Cheer the wea - ry tray - el - ler A
- Long the heav - en - ly way,

And the traveller girds himself, and sets his face toward the Morning, and goes his way.

The After-thought

Hear my cry, O God the Reader, vouchsafe that this my book fall not still-born into the world-wilderness. Let there spring, Gentle One, from out its leaves vigor of thought and thoughtful deed to reap the harvest wonderful. (Let the ears of a guilty people tingle with truth, and seventy millions sigh for the righteousness which exalteth nations, in this drear day when human brotherhood is mockery and a snare.) Thus in Thy good time may infinite reason turn the tangle straight, and these crooked marks on a fragile leaf be not indeed

THE END

1903

James Weldon Johnson (1871–1938)

Few were as influential as James Weldon Johnson was over the generation of writers coming of age in the New Negro Renaissance. In addition to the novel he published first anonymously in 1912 and then under his own name in 1927, *The Autobiography of an Ex-Colored Man*, Johnson authored multiple books of poetry, a pioneering work of cultural history, an autobiography, and a book on race relations. He also edited the first major anthology of African American poetry and two anthologies of African American sacred music. Not only a man of letters, he was also a successful songwriter, a lawyer, and a diplomat. A "renaissance man" rivaled perhaps only by W.E.B. Du Bois and Alain Locke, he also served as United States consul to Venezuela and Nicaragua, and for a decade was the field secretary of the National Association for the Advancement of Colored People (NAACP). Of the novels published by African American writers between the Civil War and the New Negro Renaissance, none would have a greater impact upon the subsequent shape of African American fiction than Johnson's *The Autobiography of an Ex-Colored Man*.

James Williams Johnson was born in Jacksonville, Florida, in 1871, the second of three children in a middle-class household. His parents, James and Helen Louise (Dillet) Johnson, had emigrated from the Bahamas in 1866. His father served as a head waiter in a luxury hotel, while his mother was the first African American female public school teacher in Florida. Young James graduated at age 16 from Jacksonville's largest all-black grammar school, the Stanton School, and enrolled in 1887 at Atlanta University. There he excelled, both as an outstanding scholar-athlete (he delivered the commencement oration in 1894) and as a member of the Atlanta University Quartet that toured New England during the long vacations. After college, Johnson returned to Jacksonville to become principal of his former grammar school, serving from 1894 until 1901. During this time he founded and edited a newspaper, *The Daily American* (1895–1896), and, in 1898, became the first African American lawyer admitted to the bar in Duval County, Florida. Johnson formed a legal partnership with Judson Douglas Wetmore, an old friend from Atlanta University who had passed for white at the School of Law at the University of Michigan, and twice married a white woman. Most scholars agree that the protagonist of *The Autobiography* was inspired by Wetmore's experiences across the color line.

Between 1902 and 1906, Johnson, his brother John Rosamond, and their friend Bob Cole joined together to form a highly successful songwriting partnership. Their song "Lift Every Voice and Sing," initially composed for a Stanton School celebration of Abraham Lincoln's birthday, became known as the "Negro National Anthem" when the NAACP adopted it. "Under the Bamboo Tree," which Marie Cahill used in her musical *Sally in Our Alley* in 1902, sold approximately 400,000 copies in just one year. Johnson left his position at Stanton and moved to New York. During this time, Johnson studied literature at Columbia University for three years with Brander Matthews, a pioneering advocate of American realism. His career as a student and Broadway songwriter ended in 1906, when he sailed to Venezuela to assume a position as US consul at Puerto Cabello. Johnson had become actively involved with the

The Wiley Blackwell Anthology of African American Literature: Volume 1, 1746–1920, First Edition.
Edited by Gene Andrew Jarrett.

Republican Party in 1904, serving as treasurer of the Colored Republican Club, and writing the two campaign songs for Theodore Roosevelt's 1904 presidential campaign ("You're All Right, Teddy" and "The Old Flag Never Touched the Ground"). With these credentials (and, more importantly, with a weighty recommendation from Booker T. Washington that he receive consular appointment), Johnson served in Venezuela between 1906 and 1909, and in Nicaragua between 1909 and 1912, when he took leave to join his wife, Grace Nail, in New York.

During his stay in Nicaragua, Johnson wrote *The Autobiography of an Ex-Colored Man*, which he published anonymously in 1912 with the small Boston house of Sherman, French. The book purported to be an actual autobiography, written by an African American man who was racially passing as white. Although several reviewers speculated about its status as fiction, the strategy was remarkably successful – perhaps particularly because autobiography had been the dominant mode of writing in the African American literary tradition, from the slave narratives of Frederick Douglass and Harriet Jacobs to Washington's *Up from Slavery* (1901). Only in 1927, at the height of the New Negro Renaissance, was the novel republished under Johnson's name by Alfred A. Knopf with an introduction by Carl Van Vechten. Van Vechten hailed it "a composite autobiography of the Negro race in the United States in modern times."

The years between 1912 and 1914 were momentous for Johnson. His father died in 1912, the year of the publication of *The Autobiography*. His poem "Fifty Years," commemorating the fiftieth anniversary of the Emancipation Proclamation, was published on the January 1, 1913, editorial page of *The New York Times*, eliciting widespread praise from such public figures as Theodore Roosevelt, Charles Chesnutt, Washington, and Du Bois. Later that year he changed his middle name to Weldon, which he thought to be more "literary" than Williams. In 1914, he became editor of *The New York Age*, the major African American newspaper in the United States. Through his editorials and his column, "Views and Reviews," Johnson became an influential voice both within the African American community and as an interpreter of race relations to the broader nation. In December 1916, at Du Bois's urging, he became a field organizer for the NAACP. Up to this point, Johnson had deftly occupied a middle ground between Du Bois's ideological stance of political activism, and the social "accommodation" epitomized by Washington. After Washington's death in 1915, Johnson became an activist more in the mold of Du Bois: his NAACP fieldwork led to the creation of hundreds of new branches. Johnson also organized in 1917 the historic "silent protest march" against lynching in New York City. In 1920 he published four essays, based upon an on-site investigation, protesting the colonialism and violence endemic to the US occupation of Haiti. Two months after this four-part exposé appeared in *The Nation*, Johnson became the secretary of the NAACP. For the next decade, he would remain one of the most dynamic and effective secretaries in the history of the organization.

Johnson's lively political career occurred in tandem with enormous artistic output. One of the most prolific figures of the New Negro Renaissance, he published several books of poetry, including *Fifty Years and Other Poems* (1917), *God's Trombones: Seven Sermons in Verse* (1927), and *Saint Peter Relates an Incident* (1934). He also edited *The Book of American Negro Poetry* (1922; 1931 revised edition), *The Book of American Negro Spirituals* (1925), and *The Second Book of Negro Spirituals* (1926). He published a major work of cultural history, *Black Manhattan* (1930), and a number of seminal essays on Harlem, African American authorship, and lynching. He released an autobiography, *Along This Way*, in 1933, and returned to race issues the following year in *Negro Americans, What Now?* Despite the depth of his political involvement, Johnson was able to allow his political convictions to inform his theory and practice of art without succumbing to the temptation of becoming "propagandistic" or overtly didactic. He rarely forced rhetoric to do the difficult and subtle work of art.

In 1930 Johnson resigned his position at the NAACP to become the Adam K. Spence Professor of Creative Literature and Writing at Fisk University – a chair essentially created for him. There, he delivered lectures on "Life, Art, and Letters." Between 1934 and 1937, Johnson lectured annually during the fall term at New York University on African American literature and culture, perhaps the first African American professor to do so at an elite research university. Only an untimely death could halt his productivity: Johnson was killed, tragically, in an automobile accident in 1938. He was buried as he had requested, wearing a lounging robe and formal trousers.

Further reading

Andrade, Heather Russell. "Revising Critical Judgments of *The Autobiography of an Ex-Coloured Man*." *African American Review* 40.2 (2006): 257–270.

Blandón, Ruth. "'¿Qué Dice?': Latin America and the Transnational in James Weldon Johnson's *Autobiography of an Ex-Coloured Man* and *Along This Way*." *Representing Segregation: Toward an Aesthetics of Living Jim Crow, and Other Forms of Racial Division*. Eds. Brian Norman and Piper Kendrix Williams. Albany: State University of New York Press, 2010. 201–219.

Goldsby, Jacqueline. *A Spectacular Secret: Lynching in American Life and Literature*. Chicago: University of Chicago Press, 2006. Ch. 4.

Lamothe, Daphne. *Inventing the New Negro: Narrative, Culture, and Ethnography*. Philadelphia: University of Pennsylvania Press, 2008. Ch. 4.

Nowlin, Michael. "James Weldon Johnson's *Black Manhattan* and the Kingdom of American Culture." *African American Review* 39.3 (2005): 315–325.

Page, Amanda M. "The Ever-Expanding South: James Weldon Johnson and the Rhetoric of the Global Color Line." *Southern Quarterly: A Journal of the Arts in the South* 46.3 (2009): 26–46.

Roberts, Brian Russell. "Passing into Diplomacy: U.S. Consul James Weldon Johnson and *The Autobiography of an Ex-Colored Man*." *MFS: Modern Fiction Studies* 56.2 (2010): 290–316.

Ross, Marlon B. "Racial Uplift and the Literature of the New Negro." *A Companion to African American Literature*. Ed. Gene Andrew Jarrett. Malden, MA: Wiley-Blackwell, 2010. 151–168.

Russell, Heather. *Legba's Crossing: Narratology in the African Atlantic*. Athens: University of Georgia Press, 2009. Ch. 1.

Stecopoulos, Harilaos. *Reconstructing the World: Southern Fictions and U.S. Imperialisms, 1898–1976*. Ithaca: Cornell University Press, 2008. Ch. 2.

Sugimori, Masami. "Narrative Order, Racial Hierarchy, and 'White' Discourse in James Weldon Johnson's *The Autobiography of an Ex-Colored Man* and *Along this Way*." *MELUS: The Journal of the Society for the Study of the Multi-Ethnic Literature of the United States* 36.3 (2011): 37–62.

Taketani, Etsuko. "The Cartography of the Black Pacific: James Weldon Johnson's *Along This Way*." *American Quarterly* 59.1 (2007): 79–106.

Wandler, Steven. "'A Negro's Chance': Ontological Luck in *The Autobiography of an Ex-Colored Man*." *African American Review* 42.3–4 (2008): 579–594.

Washington, Salim. "Of Black Bards, Known and Unknown: Music as Racial Metaphor in James Weldon Johnson's *The Autobiography of an Ex-Colored Man*." *Callaloo* 25.1 (2002): 233–256.

Wilson, Sarah. *Melting-Pot Modernism*. Ithaca: Cornell University Press, 2010. Ch. 3.

The Autobiography of an Ex-Colored Man

Chapter 1

I know that in writing the following pages I am divulging the great secret of my life, the secret which for some years I have guarded far more carefully than any of my earthly possessions; and it is a curious study to me to analyze the motives which prompt me to do it. I feel that I am led by the same impulse which forces the unfound-out criminal to take somebody into his confidence, although he knows that the act is liable, even almost certain, to lead to his undoing. I know that I am playing with fire, and I feel the thrill which accompanies that most fascinating pastime; and, back of it all, I think I find a sort of savage and diabolical desire to gather up all the little tragedies of my life, and turn them into a practical joke on society.

And, too, I suffer a vague feeling of unsatisfaction, of regret, of almost remorse from which I am seeking relief, and of which I shall speak in the last paragraph of this account.

I was born in a little town of Georgia a few years after the close of the Civil War. I shall not mention the name of the town, because there are people still living there who could be connected with this narrative. I have only a faint recollection of the place of my birth. At times I can close my eyes, and call up in a dream-like way things that seem to have happened ages ago in some other world. I can see in this half vision a little house – I am quite sure it was not a large one; I can remember that flowers grew in the front yard, and that around each bed of flowers was a hedge of vari-colored glass bottles stuck in the ground neck down. I remember that once, while playing around in the sand, I became curious to know whether or not the bottles grew as the flowers did, and I proceeded to dig them up to find out; the investigation brought me a terrific spanking which indelibly fixed the incident in my mind. I can remember, too, that behind the house was a shed under which stood two or three wooden wash-tubs. These tubs were the earliest aversion of my life, for regularly on certain evenings I was plunged into one of them, and scrubbed until my skin ached. I can remember to this day the pain caused by the strong, rank soap getting into my eyes.

Back from the house a vegetable garden ran, perhaps, seventy-five or one hundred feet; but to my childish fancy it was an endless territory. I can still recall the thrill of joy, excitement and wonder it gave me to go on an exploring expedition through it, to find the blackberries, both ripe and green, that grew along the edge of the fence.

I remember with what pleasure I used to arrive at, and stand before, a little enclosure in which stood a patient cow chewing her cud, how I would occasionally offer her through the bars a piece of my bread and molasses, and how I would jerk back my hand in half fright if she made any motion to accept my offer.

I have a dim recollection of several people who moved in and about this little house, but I have a distinct mental image of only two; one, my mother, and the other, a tall man with a small, dark mustache. I remember that his shoes or boots were always shiny, and that he wore a gold chain and a great gold watch with which he was always willing to let me play. My admiration was almost equally divided between the watch and chain and the shoes. He used to come to the house evenings, perhaps two or three times a week; and it became my appointed duty whenever he came to bring him a pair of slippers, and to put the shiny shoes in a particular corner; he often gave me in return for this service a bright coin which my mother taught me to promptly drop in a little tin bank. I remember distinctly the last time this tall man came to the little house in Georgia; that evening before I went to bed he took me up in his arms, and squeezed me very tightly; my mother stood behind his chair wiping tears from her eyes. I remember how I sat upon his knee, and watched him laboriously drill a hole through a ten-dollar gold piece, and then tie the coin around my neck with a string. I have worn that gold piece around my neck the greater part of my life, and still possess it, but more than once I have wished that some other way had been found of attaching it to me besides putting a hole through it.

On the day after the coin was put around my neck my mother and I started on what seemed to me an endless journey. I knelt on the seat and watched through the train window the corn and cotton fields pass swiftly by until I fell asleep. When I fully awoke we were being driven through the streets of a large city – Savannah. I sat up and blinked at the bright lights. At Savannah we boarded a steamer which finally landed us in New York. From New York we went to a town in Connecticut, which became the home of my boyhood.

My mother and I lived together in a little cottage which seemed to me to be fitted up almost luxuriously; there were horse-hair covered chairs in the parlor, and a little square piano; there was a stairway with red carpet on it leading to a half second story; there were pictures on the walls, and a few books in a glass-doored case. My mother dressed me very neatly, and I developed that pride which well-dressed boys generally have. She was careful about my associates, and I myself was quite particular. As I look back now I can see that I was a perfect little aristocrat. My mother rarely went to anyone's house, but she did sewing, and there were a great many ladies coming to our cottage. If I were around they would generally call me, and ask me my name and age and tell my mother what a pretty boy I was. Some of them would pat me on the head and kiss me.

My mother was kept very busy with her sewing; sometimes she would have another woman helping her, I think she must have derived a fair income from her work. I know, too, that at least once each month she received a letter; I used to watch for the postman, get the letter, and run to her with it; whether she was busy or not she would take it and instantly thrust it into her bosom. I never saw her read one of them. I knew later that these letters contained money and, what was to her, more than money. As busy as she generally was she, however, found time to teach me my letters and figures and how to spell a number of easy words. Always on Sunday evenings she opened the little square piano, and picked out hymns. I can recall now that whenever she played hymns from the book her tempos were always decidedly largo.[1] Sometimes on other evenings when she was not sewing she would play simple accompaniments to some old southern songs which she sang. In these songs she was freer, because she played them by ear. Those evenings on which she opened the little piano were the happiest hours of my childhood. Whenever she started toward the instrument I used to follow her with all the interest and irrepressible joy that a pampered pet dog shows when a package is opened in which he knows there is a sweet bit for him. I used to stand by her side, and often interrupt and annoy her by chiming in with strange harmonies which I found either on the high keys of the treble or low keys of the bass. I remember that I had a particular fondness for the black keys. Always on such evenings, when the music was over, my mother would sit with me in her arms often for a very long time. She would hold me close, softly crooning some old melody without words, all the while gently stroking her face against my head; many and many a night I thus fell asleep. I can see her now, her great dark eyes looking into the fire, to where? No one knew but she. The memory of that picture has more than once kept me from straying too far from the place of purity and safety in which her arms held me.

At a very early age I began to thump on the piano alone, and it was not long before I was able to pick out a few tunes. When I was seven years old I could play by ear all of the hymns and songs that my mother knew. I had also learned the names of the notes in both clefs, but I preferred not to be hampered by notes. About this time several ladies for whom my mother sewed heard me play, and they persuaded her that I should at once be put under a teacher; so arrangements were made for me to study the piano with a lady who was a fairly good musician; at the same time arrangements were made

Notes

[1] *largo* (Italian) slow and dignified.

for me to study my books with this lady's daughter. My music teacher had no small difficulty at first in pinning me down to the notes. If she played my lesson over for me I invariably attempted to reproduce the required sounds without the slightest recourse to the written characters. Her daughter, my other teacher, also had her worries. She found that, in reading, whenever I came to words that were difficult or unfamiliar I was prone to bring my imagination to the rescue and read from the picture. She has laughingly told me, since then, that I would sometimes substitute whole sentences and even paragraphs from what meaning I thought the illustrations conveyed. She said she sometimes was not only amused at the fresh treatment I would give an author's subject, but that when I gave some new and sudden turn to the plot of the story she often grew interested and even excited in listening to hear what kind of a denouement I would bring about. But I am sure this was not due to dullness, for I made rapid progress in both my music and my books.

And so, for a couple of years my life was divided between my music and my school books. Music took up the greater part of my time. I had no playmates, but amused myself with games – some of them my own invention – which could be played alone. I knew a few boys whom I had met at the church which I attended with my mother, but I had formed no close friendships with any of them. Then, when I was nine years old, my mother decided to enter me in the public school, so all at once I found myself thrown among a crowd of boys of all sizes and kinds; some of them seemed to me like savages. I shall never forget the bewilderment, the pain, the heart-sickness of that first day at school. I seemed to be the only stranger in the place; every other boy seemed to know every other boy. I was fortunate enough, however, to be assigned to a teacher who knew me; my mother made her dresses. She was one of the ladies who used to pat me on the head and kiss me. She had the tact to address a few words directly to me; this gave me a certain sort of standing in the class, and put me somewhat at ease.

Within a few days I had made one staunch friend, and was on fairly good terms with most of the boys. I was shy of the girls, and remained so; even now, a word or look from a pretty woman sets me all a-tremble. This friend I bound to me with hooks of steel in a very simple way. He was a big awkward boy with a face full of freckles and a head full of very red hair. He was perhaps fourteen years of age; that is, four or five years older than any other boy in the class. This seniority was due to the fact that he had spent twice the required amount of time in several of the preceding classes. I had not been at school many hours before I felt that "Red Head" – as I involuntarily called him – and I were to be friends. I do not doubt that this feeling was strengthened by the fact that I had been quick enough to see that a big, strong boy was a friend to be desired at a public school; and, perhaps, in spite of his dullness, "Red Head" had been able to discern that I could be of service to him. At any rate there was a simultaneous mutual attraction.

The teacher had strung the class promiscuously round the walls of the room for a sort of trial heat for places of rank; when the line was straightened out I found that by skillful maneuvering I had placed myself third, and had piloted "Red Head" to the place next to me. The teacher began by giving us to spell the words corresponding to our order in the line. "Spell first." "Spell second." "Spell third." I rattled off, "t-h-i-r-d, third," in a way which said, "Why don't you give us something hard?" As the words went down the line I could see how lucky I had been to get a good place together with an easy word. As young as I was I felt impressed with the unfairness of the whole proceeding when I saw the tailenders going down before "twelfth" and "twentieth," and I felt sorry for those who had to spell such words in order to hold a low position. "Spell fourth." "Red Head," with his hands clutched tightly behind his back, began bravely, "f-o-r-t-h." Like a flash a score of hands went up, and the teacher began saying,

"No snapping of fingers, no snapping of fingers." This was the first word missed, and it seemed to me that some of the scholars were about to lose their senses; some were dancing up and down on one foot with a hand above their heads, the fingers working furiously, and joy beaming all over their faces; others stood still, their hands raised not so high, their fingers working less rapidly, and their faces expressing not quite so much happiness; there were still others who did not move nor raise their hands, but stood with great wrinkles on their foreheads, looking very thoughtful.

The whole thing was new to me, and I did not raise my hand, but slyly whispered the letter "u" to "Red Head" several times. "Second chance," said the teacher. The hands went down and the class became quiet. "Red Head," his face now red, after looking beseechingly at the ceiling, then pitiably at the floor, began very haltingly, "f-u-." Immediately an impulse to raise hands went through the class, but the teacher checked it, and poor "Red Head," though he knew that each letter he added only took him farther out of the way, went doggedly on and finished, "r-t-h." The hand raising was now repeated with more hubbub and excitement than at first. Those who before had not moved a finger were now waving their hands above their heads. "Red Head" felt that he was lost. He looked very big and foolish, and some of the scholars began to snicker. His helpless condition went straight to my heart, and gripped my sympathies. I felt that if he failed it would in some way be my failure. I raised my hand, and under cover of the excitement and the teacher's attempts to regain order, I hurriedly shot up into his ear twice, quite distinctly, "f-o-u-r-t-h," "f-o-u-r-t-h." The teacher tapped on her desk and said, "Third and last chance." The hands came down, the silence became oppressive. "Red Head" began, "f" – Since that day I have waited anxiously for many a turn of the wheel of fortune, but never under greater tension than I watched for the order in which those letters would fall from "Red's" lips – "o-u-r-t-h." A sigh of relief and disappointment went up from the class. Afterwards, through all our school days, "Red Head" shared my wit and quickness and I benefited by his strength and dogged faithfulness.

There were some black and brown boys and girls in the school, and several of them were in my class. One of the boys strongly attracted my attention from the first day I saw him. His face was as black as night, but shone as though it was polished; he had sparkling eyes, and when he opened his mouth he displayed glistening white teeth. It struck me at once as appropriate to call him "Shiny face," or "Shiny eyes," or "Shiny teeth," and I spoke of him often by one of these names to the other boys. These terms were finally merged into "Shiny," and to that name he answered good naturedly during the balance of his public school days.

"Shiny" was considered without question to be the best speller, the best reader, the best penman, in a word, the best scholar, in the class. He was very quick to catch anything; but, nevertheless, studied hard; thus he possessed two powers very rarely combined in one boy. I saw him year after year, on up into the high school, win the majority of the prizes for punctuality, deportment, essay writing and declamation. Yet it did not take me long to discover that, in spite of his standing as a scholar, he was in some way looked down upon.

The other black boys and girls were still more looked down upon. Some of the boys often spoke of them as "niggers." Sometimes on the way home from school a crowd would walk behind them repeating:

"Nigger, nigger, never die,
Black face and shiny eye."

On one such afternoon one of the black boys turned suddenly on his tormentors, and hurled a slate; it struck one of the white boys in the mouth, cutting a slight gash in his lip. At sight of the blood the boy who had thrown the slate ran, and his companions quickly followed. We ran after them pelting them with stones until they separated in several directions. I was very much wrought up over the affair, and went home and told my mother how one of the "niggers" had struck a boy with a slate. I shall never forget how she turned on me. "Don't you ever use that word again," she said, "and don't you ever bother the colored children at school. You ought to be ashamed of yourself." I did hang my head in shame, but not because she had convinced me that I had done wrong, but because I was hurt by the first sharp word she had ever given me.

My school days ran along very pleasantly. I stood well in my studies, not always so well with regard to my behavior. I was never guilty of any serious misconduct, but my love of fun sometimes got me into trouble. I remember, however, that my sense of humor was so sly that most of the trouble usually fell on the head of the other fellow. My ability to play on the piano at school exercises was looked upon as little short of marvelous in a boy of my age. I was not chummy with many of my mates, but, on the whole, was about as popular as it is good for a boy to be.

One day near the end of my second term at school the principal came into our room, and after talking to the teacher, for some reason said, "I wish all of the white scholars to stand for a moment." I rose with the others. The teacher looked at me, and calling my name said, "You sit down for the present, and rise with the others." I did not quite understand her, and questioned, "Ma'm?" She repeated with a softer tone in her voice, "You sit down now, and rise with the others." I sat down dazed. I saw and heard nothing. When the others were asked to rise I did not know it. When school was dismissed I went out in a kind of stupor. A few of the white boys jeered me, saying, "Oh, you're a nigger too." I heard some black children say, "We knew he was colored." "Shiny" said to them, "Come along, don't tease him," and thereby won my undying gratitude.

I hurried on as fast as I could, and had gone some distance before I perceived that "Red Head" was walking by my side. After a while he said to me, "Le' me carry your books." I gave him my strap without being able to answer. When we got to my gate he said as he handed me my books, "Say, you know my big red agate? I can't shoot with it any more. I'm going to bring it to school for you to-morrow." I took my books and ran into the house. As I passed through the hallway I saw that my mother was busy with one of her customers; I rushed up into my own little room, shut the door, and went quickly to where my looking-glass hung on the wall. For an instant I was afraid to look, but when I did I looked long and earnestly. I had often heard people say to my mother, "What a pretty boy you have." I was accustomed to hear remarks about my beauty; but, now, for the first time, I became conscious of it, and recognized it. I noticed the ivory whiteness of my skin, the beauty of my mouth, the size and liquid darkness of my eyes, and how the long black lashes that fringed and shaded them produced an effect that was strangely fascinating even to me. I noticed the softness and glossiness of my dark hair that fell in waves over my temples, making my forehead appear whiter than it really was. How long I stood there gazing at my image I do not know. When I came out and reached the head of the stairs, I heard the lady who had been with my mother going out. I ran downstairs, and rushed to where my mother was sitting with a piece of work in her hands. I buried my head in her lap and blurted out, "Mother, mother, tell me, am I a nigger?" I could not see her face, but I knew the piece of work dropped to the floor, and I felt her hands on my head. I looked up into her face and repeated, "Tell me, mother, am I a nigger?" There were tears in her eyes, and I could see that she was suffering for me. And then it was that I looked at her critically for the first time. I had thought of her in a childish way only as the most beautiful woman in the world; now I looked at her searching for defects. I could see that her skin was almost brown, that her hair was not so soft as mine, and that she did differ in some way from the other ladies who came to the house; yet, even so, I could see that she was very beautiful, more beautiful than any of them. She must have felt that I was examining her, for she hid her face in my hair, and said with difficulty, "No, my darling, you are not a nigger." She went on, "You are as good as anybody; if anyone calls you a nigger don't notice them." But the more she talked the less was I reassured, and I stopped her by asking, "Well, mother, am I white? Are you white?" She answered tremblingly, "No, I am not white, but you – your father is one of the greatest men in the country – the best blood of the South is in you – " This suddenly opened up in my heart a fresh chasm of misgiving and fear, and I almost fiercely demanded, "Who is my father? Where is he?" She stroked my hair and said, "I'll tell you about him some day." I sobbed, "I want to know now." She answered, "No, not now."

Perhaps it had to be done, but I have never forgiven the woman who did it so cruelly. It may be that she never knew that she gave me a sword-thrust that day in school which was years in healing.

Chapter 2

Since I have grown older I have often gone back and tried to analyze the change that came into my life after that fateful day in school. There did come a radical change, and, young as I was, I felt fully conscious of it, though I did not fully comprehend it. Like my first spanking, it is one of the few incidents in my life that I can remember clearly. In the life of everyone there is a limited number of unhappy experiences which are not written upon the memory, but stamped there with a die; and in long years after they can be called up in detail, and every emotion that was stirred by them can be lived through anew; these are the tragedies of life. We may grow to include some of them among the trivial incidents of childhood – a broken toy, a promise made to us which was not kept, a harsh, heart-piercing word – but these, too, as well as the bitter experiences and disappointments of mature years, are the tragedies of life.

And so I have often lived through that hour, that day, that week in which was wrought the miracle of my transition from one world into another; for I did indeed pass into another world. From that time I looked out through other eyes, my thoughts were colored, my words dictated, my actions limited by one dominating, all-pervading idea which constantly increased in force and weight until I finally realized in it a great, tangible fact.

And this is the dwarfing, warping, distorting influence which operates upon each colored man in the United States. He is forced to take his outlook on all things, not from the viewpoint of a citizen, or a man, nor even a human being, but from the viewpoint of a *colored* man. It is wonderful to me that the race has progressed so broadly as it has, since most of its thought and all of its activity must run through the narrow neck of one funnel.

And it is this, too, which makes the colored people of this country, in reality, a mystery to the whites. It is a difficult thing for a white man to learn what a colored man really thinks; because, generally, with the latter an additional and different light must be brought to bear on what he thinks; and his thoughts are often influenced by considerations so delicate and subtle that it would be impossible for him to confess or explain them to one of the opposite race. This gives to every colored man, in proportion to his intellectuality, a sort of dual personality; there is one phase of him which is disclosed only in the freemasonry of his own race. I have often watched with interest and sometimes with amazement even ignorant colored men under cover of broad grins and minstrel antics maintain this dualism in the presence of white men.

I believe it to be a fact that the colored people of this country know and understand the white people better than the white people know and understand them.

I now think that this change which came into my life was at first more subjective than objective. I do not think my friends at school changed so much toward me as I did toward them. I grew reserved, I might say suspicious. I grew constantly more and more afraid of laying myself open to some injury to my feelings or my pride. I frequently saw or fancied some slight where, I am sure, none was intended. On the other hand, my friends and teachers were, if anything different, more considerate of me; but I can remember that it was against this very attitude in particular that my sensitiveness revolted. "Red" was the only one who did not so wound me; up to this day I recall with a swelling heart his clumsy efforts to make me understand that nothing could change his love for me.

I am sure that at this time the majority of my white schoolmates did not understand or appreciate any differences between me and themselves; but there were a few who had evidently received instructions at home on the matter, and more than once they displayed their knowledge in word and action. As the years passed I noticed that the most innocent and ignorant among the others grew in wisdom.

I, myself, would not have so clearly understood this difference had it not been for the presence of the other colored children at school; I had learned what their status was, and now I learned that theirs was mine. I had had no particular like or dislike for these black and brown boys and girls; in fact, with the exception of "Shiny," they had occupied very little of my thought, but I do know that when the blow fell I had a very strong aversion to being classed with them. So I became something of a solitary. "Red" and I remained inseparable, and there was between "Shiny" and me a sort of sympathetic bond, but my intercourse with the others was never entirely free from a feeling of constraint. But I must add that this feeling was confined almost entirely to my intercourse with boys and girls of about my own age; I did not experience it with my seniors. And when I grew to manhood I found myself freer with elderly white people than with those near my own age.

I was now about eleven years old, but these emotions and impressions which I have just described could not have been stronger or more distinct at an older age. There were two immediate results of my forced loneliness; I began to find company in books, and greater pleasure in music. I made the former discovery through a big, gilt-bound, illustrated copy of the Bible, which used to lie in splendid neglect on the center table in our little parlor. On top of the Bible lay a photograph album. I had often looked at the pictures in the album, and one day after taking the larger book down, and opening it on the floor, I was overjoyed to find that it contained what seemed to be an inexhaustible supply of pictures. I looked at these pictures many times; in fact, so often that I knew the story of each one without having to read the subject, and then, somehow, I picked up the thread of history on which is strung the trials and tribulations of the Hebrew children; this I followed with feverish interest and excitement. For a long time King David,[2] with Samson[3] a close second, stood at the head of my list of heroes; he was not displaced until I came to know Robert the Bruce.[4] I read a good portion of the Old Testament, all that part treating of wars and rumors of wars, and then started

Notes

[2] King David (*c.*1040–972 BC), biblical hero and second king of Israel.

[3] *Samson* an ancient Israelite leader with superhuman strength (Judges 13–16).

[4] Robert the Bruce (1274–1329), king of Scotland.

in on the New. I became interested in the life of Christ, but became impatient and disappointed when I found that, notwithstanding the great power he possessed, he did not make use of it when, in my judgment, he most needed to do so. And so my first general impression of the Bible was what my later impression has been of a number of modern books, that the authors put their best work in the first part, and grew either exhausted or careless toward the end.

After reading the Bible, or those parts which held my attention, I began to explore the glass-doored book-case which I have already mentioned. I found there "Pilgrim's Progress,"[5] "Peter Parley's History of the United States,"[6] Grimm's "Household Stories,"[7] "Tales of a Grandfather,"[8] a bound volume of an old English publication, I think it was called "The Mirror,"[9] a little volume called "Familiar Science,"[10] and somebody's "Natural Theology," which latter, of course, I could not read, but which, nevertheless, I tackled, with the result of gaining a permanent dislike for all kinds of theology. There were several other books of no particular name or merit, such as agents sell to people who know nothing of buying books. How my mother came by this little library which, considering all things, was so well suited to me, I never sought to know. But she was far from being an ignorant woman, and had herself, very likely, read the majority of these books, though I do not remember ever having seen her with a book in her hand, with the exception of the Episcopal Prayer-book. At any rate she encouraged in me the habit of reading, and when I had about exhausted those books in the little library which interested me, she began to buy books for me. She also regularly gave me money to buy a weekly paper which was then very popular for boys.

At this time I went in for music with an earnestness worthy of maturer years; a change of teachers was largely responsible for this. I began now to take lessons of the organist of the church which I attended with my mother; he was a good teacher and quite a thorough musician. He was so skillful in his instruction, and filled me with such enthusiasm that my progress – these are his words – was marvelous. I remember that when I was barely twelve years old I appeared on a program with a number of adults at an entertainment given for some charitable purpose, and carried off the honors. I did more; I brought upon myself through the local newspapers the handicapping title of "Infant prodigy."

I can believe that I did astonish my audience, for I never played the piano like a child, that is, in the "one-two-three" style with accelerated motion. Neither did I depend upon mere brilliancy of technic, a trick by which children often surprise their listeners, but I always tried to interpret a piece of music; I always played with feeling. Very early I acquired that knack of using the pedals which makes the piano a sympathetic, singing instrument; quite a different thing from the source of hard or blurred sounds it so generally is. I think this was due not entirely to natural artistic temperament, but largely to the fact that I did not begin to learn the piano by counting out exercises, but by trying to reproduce the quaint songs which my mother used to sing, with all their pathetic turns and cadences.

Notes

[5] *"Pilgrim's Progress"* (1678) popular Christian allegorical narrative by English writer Paul Bunyan (1628–1688).

[6] *"Peter Parley's History of the United States"* American publisher Samuel Griswold Goodrich (1793–1860) published various texts for the young under the Peter Parley name, including *Peter Parley's Book of the United States, Geographical, Political and Historical* (1837).

[7] *"Grimm's Household Stories"* an 1812 collection of German folk tales published by Wilhelm and Jacob Grimm.

[8] *"Tales of a Grandfather"* (1827–1831), a series of books on Scottish history by Sir Walter Scott (1771–1832).

[9] *"The Mirror"* Nathaniel Parker Willis, magazine writer and editor of the *Evening Mirror*, published texts in the Mirror Library series in the 1840s.

[10] *"Familiar Science"* R.E. Peterson's *Familiar Science, or the Scientific Explanation of Common Things* (1851).

Even at a tender age, in playing, I helped to express what I felt by some of the mannerisms which I afterwards observed in great performers; I had not copied them. I have often heard people speak of the mannerisms of musicians as affectations adopted for mere effect; in some cases this may be so; but a true artist can no more play upon the piano or violin without putting his whole body in accord with the emotions he is striving to express than a swallow can fly without being graceful. Often when playing I could not keep the tears which formed in my eyes from rolling down my cheeks. Sometimes at the end or even in the midst of a composition, as big a boy as I was, I would jump from the piano, and throw myself sobbing into my mother's arms. She, by her caresses and often her tears, only encouraged these fits of sentimental hysteria. Of course, to counteract this tendency to temperamental excesses I should have been out playing ball or in swimming with other boys of my age; but my mother didn't know that. There was only once when she was really firm with me, making me do what she considered was best; I did not want to return to school after the unpleasant episode which I have related, and she was inflexible.

I began my third term, and the days ran along as I have already indicated. I had been promoted twice, and had managed each time to pull "Red" along with me. I think the teachers came to consider me the only hope of his ever getting through school, and I believe they secretly conspired with me to bring about the desired end. At any rate, I know it became easier in each succeeding examination for me not only to assist "Red," but absolutely to do his work. It is strange how in some things honest people can be dishonest without the slightest compunction. I knew boys at school who were too honorable to tell a fib even when one would have been just the right thing, but could not resist the temptation to assist or receive assistance in an examination. I have long considered it the highest proof of honesty in a man to hand his street-car fare to the conductor who had overlooked it.

One afternoon after school, during my third term, I rushed home in a great hurry to get my dinner, and go to my music teacher's. I was never reluctant about going there, but on this particular afternoon I was impetuous. The reason of this was, I had been asked to play the accompaniment for a young lady who was to play a violin solo at a concert given by the young people of the church and on this afternoon we were to have our first rehearsal. At that time playing accompaniments was the only thing in music I did not enjoy; later this feeling grew into positive dislike. I have never been a really good accompanist because my ideas of interpretation were always too strongly individual. I constantly forced my accelerandos[11] and rubatos[12] upon the soloist, often throwing the duet entirely out of gear.

Perhaps the reader has already guessed why I was so willing and anxious to play the accompaniment to this violin solo; if not – the violinist was a girl of seventeen or eighteen whom I had first heard play a short time before on a Sunday afternoon at a special service of some kind, and who had moved me to a degree which now I can hardly think of as possible. At present I do not think it was due to her wonderful playing, though I judge she must have been a very fair performer, but there was just the proper setting to produce the effect upon a boy such as I was; the half dim church, the air of devotion on the part of the listeners, the heaving tremor of the organ under the clear wail of the violin, and she, her eyes almost closing, the escaping strands of her dark hair wildly framing her pale face, and her slender body swaying to the tones

Notes

[11] *accelerandos* (Italian) gradual increases of tempo.

[12] *rubatos* (Italian) rhythmic manipulations and nuances expressed by a slight speeding up and then slowing down.

she called forth, all combined to fire my imagination and my heart with a passion though boyish, yet strong and, somehow, lasting. I have tried to describe the scene; if I have succeeded it is only half success, for words can only partially express what I would wish to convey. Always in recalling that Sunday afternoon I am subconscious of a faint but distinct fragrance which, like some old memory-awakening perfume, rises and suffuses my whole imagination, inducing a state of reverie so airy as to just evade the powers of expression.

She was my first love, and I loved her as only a boy loves. I dreamed of her, I built air castles for her, she was the incarnation of each beautiful heroine I knew; when I played the piano it was to her, not even did music furnish an adequate outlet for my passion; I bought a new note-book, and, to sing her praises, made my first and last attempts at poetry. I remember one day at school, after having given in our note-books to have some exercises corrected, the teacher called me to her desk and said, "I couldn't correct your exercises because I found nothing in your book but a rhapsody on somebody's brown eyes." I had passed in the wrong note-book. I don't think I have felt greater embarrassment in my whole life than I did at that moment. I was not only ashamed that my teacher should see this nakedness of my heart, but that she should find out that I had any knowledge of such affairs. It did not then occur to me to be ashamed of the kind of poetry I had written.

Of course, the reader must know that all of this adoration was in secret; next to my great love for this young lady was the dread that in some way she would find it out. I did not know what some men never find out, that the woman who cannot discern when she is loved has never lived. It makes me laugh to think how successful I was in concealing it all; within a short time after our duet all of the friends of my dear one were referring to me as her "little sweetheart," or her "little beau," and she laughingly encouraged it. This did not entirely satisfy me; I wanted to be taken seriously. I had definitely made up my mind that I should never love another woman, and that if she deceived me I should do something desperate – the great difficulty was to think of something sufficiently desperate – and the heartless jade,[13] how she led me on!

So I hurried home that afternoon, humming snatches of the violin part of the duet, my heart beating with pleasurable excitement over the fact that I was going to be near her, to have her attention placed directly upon me; that I was going to be of service to her, and in a way in which I could show myself to advantage – this last consideration has much to do with cheerful service. The anticipation produced in me a sensation somewhat between bliss and fear. I rushed through the gate, took the three steps to the house at one bound, threw open the door, and was about to hang my cap on its accustomed peg of the hall rack when I noticed that that particular peg was occupied by a black derby hat. I stopped suddenly, and gazed at this hat as though I had never seen an object of its description. I was still looking at it in open-eyed wonder when my mother, coming out of the parlor into the hallway, called me, and said there was someone inside who wanted to see me. Feeling that I was being made a party to some kind of mystery I went in with her, and there I saw a man standing leaning with one elbow on the mantel, his back partly turned toward the door. As I entered he turned, and I saw a tall, handsome, well-dressed gentleman of perhaps thirty-five; he advanced a step toward me with a smile on his face. I stopped and looked at him with the same feelings with which I had looked at the derby hat, except that they were greatly magnified.

Notes

[13] *jade* a disreputable woman.

I looked at him from head to foot, but he was an absolute blank to me until my eyes rested on his slender, elegant, polished shoes; then it seemed that indistinct and partly obliterated films of memory began at first slowly then rapidly to unroll, forming a vague panorama of my childhood days in Georgia.

My mother broke the spell by calling me by name, and saying, "This is your father."

"Father, Father," that was the word which had been to me a source of doubt and perplexity ever since the interview with my mother on the subject. How often I had wondered about my father, who he was, what he was like, whether alive or dead, and above all, why she would not tell me about him. More than once I had been on the point of recalling to her the promise she had made me, but I instinctively felt that she was happier for not telling me and that I was happier for not being told; yet I had not the slightest idea what the real truth was. And here he stood before me, just the kind of looking father I had wishfully pictured him to be; but I made no advance toward him; I stood there feeling embarrassed and foolish, not knowing what to say or do. I am not sure but that he felt pretty much the same. My mother stood at my side with one hand on my shoulder almost pushing me forward, but I did not move. I can well remember the look of disappointment, even pain, on her face; and I can now understand that she could expect nothing else but that at the name "father" I should throw myself into his arms. But I could not rise to this dramatic or, better, melodramatic climax. Somehow I could not arouse any considerable feeling of need for a father. He broke the awkward tableau by saying, "Well, boy, aren't you glad to see me?" He evidently meant the words kindly enough, but I don't know what he could have said that would have had a worse effect; however, my good breeding came to my rescue, and I answered, "Yes, sir," and went to him and offered him my hand. He took my hand into one of his, and, with the other, stroked my head saying that I had grown into a fine youngster. He asked me how old I was; which, of course, he must have done merely to say something more, or perhaps he did so as a test of my intelligence. I replied, "Twelve, sir." He then made the trite observation about the flight of time, and we lapsed into another awkward pause.

My mother was all in smiles; I believe that was one of the happiest moments of her life. Either to put me more at ease or to show me off, she asked me to play something for my father. There is only one thing in the world that can make music, at all times and under all circumstances, up to its general standard, that is a hand-organ, or one of its variations. I went to the piano and played something in a listless, halfhearted way. I simply was not in the mood. I was wondering, while playing, when my mother would dismiss me and let me go; but my father was so enthusiastic in his praise that he touched my vanity – which was great – and more than that; he displayed that sincere appreciation which always arouses an artist to his best effort, and, too, in an unexplainable manner, makes him feel like shedding tears. I showed my gratitude by playing for him a Chopin waltz with all the feeling that was in me. When I had finished my mother's eyes were glistening with tears; my father stepped across the room, seized me in his arms, and squeezed me to his breast. I am certain that for that moment he was proud to be my father. He sat and held me standing between his knees while he talked to my mother. I, in the meantime, examined him with more curiosity, perhaps, than politeness. I interrupted the conversation by asking, "Mother, is he going to stay with us now?" I found it impossible to frame the word "father"; it was too new to me; so I asked the question through my mother. Without waiting for her to speak, my father answered, "I've got to go back to New York this afternoon, but I'm coming to see you again." I turned abruptly and went over to my mother, and almost in a whisper reminded her that I had an appointment which I should not miss; to my pleasant surprise she said that she would give me something to eat at once so that I might go. She went out of the room, and I began to gather from off the piano the music I needed. When I had finished, my father, who had been watching me, asked, "Are you going?" I replied, "Yes, sir, I've got to go to practice for a concert." He spoke some words of advice to me about being a good boy and taking care of my mother when I grew up, and added that he was going to send me something nice from New York. My mother called, and I said good-by to him, and went out. I saw him only once after that.

I quickly swallowed down what my mother had put on the table for me, seized my cap and music, and hurried off to my teacher's house. On the way I could think of nothing but this new father, where he came from, where he had been, why he was here, and why he would not stay. In my mind I ran over the whole list of fathers I had become acquainted with in my reading, but I could not classify him. The thought did not cross my mind that he was different from me, and even if it had the mystery would not thereby have been explained; for notwithstanding my changed relations with most of my schoolmates, I had only a faint knowledge of prejudice and no idea at all how it ramified and affected the entire social organism. I felt, however, that there was something about the whole affair which had to be hid.

When I arrived I found that she of the brown eyes had been rehearsing with my teacher, and was on the point of leaving. My teacher with some expressions of surprise asked why I was late, and I stammered out the first deliberate lie of which I have any recollection. I told him that when I reached home from school I found my mother quite sick, and that I had stayed with her a while before coming. Then unnecessarily and gratuitously, to give my words force of conviction, I suppose, I added, "I don't think she'll be with us very long." In speaking these words I must have been comical; for I noticed that my teacher, instead of showing signs of anxiety or sorrow, half hid a smile. But how little did I know that in that lie I was speaking a prophecy.

She of the brown eyes unpacked her violin, and we went through the duet several times. I was soon lost to all other thoughts in the delights of music and love. I say delights of love without reservation; for at no time of life is love so pure, so delicious, so poetic, so romantic, as it is in boyhood. A great deal has been said about the heart of a girl when she stands "where the brook and river meet," but what she feels is negative; more interesting is the heart of a boy when just at the budding dawn of manhood he stands looking wide-eyed into the long vistas opening before him; when he first becomes conscious of the awakening and quickening of strange desires and unknown powers; when what he sees and feels is still shadowy and mystical enough to be intangible, and, so, more beautiful; when his imagination is unsullied, and his faith new and whole – then it is that love wears a halo – the man who has not loved before he was fourteen has missed a fore-taste of Elysium.[14]

When I reached home it was quite dark, and I found my mother without a light, sitting rocking in a chair as she so often used to do in my childhood days, looking into the fire and singing softly to herself. I nestled close to her, and with her arms around me she haltingly told me who my father was – a great man, a fine gentleman – he loved me and loved her very much; he was going to make a great man of me. All she said was so limited by reserve and so colored by her feelings that it was but half truth; and so, I did not yet fully understand.

Notes

[14] *Elysium* in Greek mythology, the afterlife abode of heroes.

Chapter 3

Perhaps I ought not pass on this narrative without mentioning that the duet was a great success; so great that we were obliged to respond with two encores. It seemed to me that life could hold no greater joy than it contained when I took her hand and we stepped down to the front of the stage bowing to our enthusiastic audience. When we reached the little dressing-room, where the other performers were applauding as wildly as the audience, she impulsively threw both her arms around me, and kissed me, while I struggled to get away.

One day a couple of weeks after my father had been to see us, a wagon drove up to our cottage loaded with a big box. I was about to tell the man on the wagon that they had made a mistake, when my mother, acting darkly wise, told them to bring their load in; she had them to unpack the box, and quickly there was evolved from the boards, paper and other packing material, a beautiful, brand new, upright piano. Then she informed me that it was a present to me from my father. I at once sat down and ran my fingers over the keys; the full, mellow tone of the instrument was ravishing. I thought, almost remorsefully, of how I had left my father; but, even so, there momentarily crossed my mind a feeling of disappointment that the piano was not a grand. The new instrument greatly increased the pleasure of my hours of study and practice at home.

Shortly after this I was made a member of the boys' choir, it being found that I possessed a clear, strong soprano voice. I enjoyed the singing very much. About a year later I began the study of the pipe organ and the theory of music; and before I finished the grammar school I had written out several simple preludes for organ which won the admiration of my teacher, and which he did me the honor to play at services.

The older I grew the more thought I gave to the question of my and my mother's position, and what was our exact relation to the world in general. My idea of the whole matter was rather hazy. My study of United States history had been confined to those periods which were designated in my book as "Discovery," "Colonial," "Revolutionary," and "Constitutional." I now began to study about the Civil War, but the story was told in such a condensed and skipping style that I gained from it very little real information. It is a marvel how children ever learn any history out of books of that sort. And, too, I began now to read the newspapers; I often saw articles which aroused my curiosity, but did not enlighten me. But, one day, I drew from the circulating library a book that cleared the whole mystery, a book that I read with the same feverish intensity with which I had read the old Bible stories, a book that gave me my first perspective of the life I was entering; that book was "Uncle Tom's Cabin."[15]

This work of Harriet Beecher Stowe has been the object of much unfavorable criticism. It has been assailed, not only as fiction of the most imaginative sort, but as being a direct misrepresentation. Several successful attempts have lately been made to displace the book from northern school libraries. Its critics would brush it aside with the remark that there never was a Negro as good as Uncle Tom, nor a slave-holder as bad as Lagree. For my part, I was never an admirer of Uncle Tom, nor of his type of goodness; but I believe that there were lots of old Negroes as foolishly good as he; the proof of which is that they knowingly stayed and worked the plantations that furnished sinews for the army which was fighting to keep them enslaved. But, in these later years,

Notes

[15] *Uncle Tom's Cabin* (1852), popular abolitionist novel by Harriet Beecher Stowe (1811–1896).

several cases have come to my personal knowledge in which old Negroes have died and left what was a considerable fortune to the descendants of their former masters. I do not think it takes any great stretch of the imagination to believe there was a fairly large class of slave-holders typified in Lagree. And we must also remember that the author depicted a number of worthless if not vicious Negroes, and a slave-holder who was as much of a Christian and a gentleman as it was possible for one in his position to be; that she pictured the happy, singing, shuffling darkey as well as the mother waiting for her child sold "down river."

I do not think it is claiming too much to say that "Uncle Tom's Cabin" was a fair and truthful panorama of slavery; however that may be, it opened my eyes as to who and what I was and what my country considered me; in fact, it gave me my bearing. But there was no shock; I took the whole revelation in a kind of stoical way. One of the greatest benefits I derived from reading the book was that I could afterwards talk frankly with my mother on all the questions which had been vaguely troubling my mind. As a result, she was entirely freed from reserve, and often herself brought up the subject, talking of things directly touching her life and mine and of things which had come down to her through the "old folks." What she told me interested and even fascinated me; and, what may seem strange, kindled in me a strong desire to see the South. She spoke to me quite frankly about herself, my father and myself; she, the sewing girl of my father's mother; he, an impetuous young man home from college; I, the child of this unsanctioned love. She told me even the principal reason for our coming North. My father was about to be married to a young lady of another great Southern family. She did not neglect to add that another reason for our being in Connecticut was that he intended to give me an education, and make a man of me. In none of her talks did she ever utter one word of complaint against my father. She always endeavored to impress upon me how good he had been and still was, and that he was all to us that custom and the law would allow. She loved him; more, she worshiped him, and she died firmly believing that he loved her more than any other woman in the world. Perhaps she was right. Who knows?

All of these newly awakened ideas and thoughts took the form of a definite aspiration on the day I graduated from the grammar school. And what a day that was! The girls in white dresses[16] with fresh ribbons in their hair; the boys in new suits and creaky shoes; the great crowd of parents and friends, the flowers, the prizes and congratulations, made the day seem to me one of the greatest importance. I was on the programme, and played a piano solo which was received by the audience with that amount of applause which I had come to look upon as being only the just due to my talent.

But the real enthusiasm was aroused by "Shiny." He was the principal speaker of the day, and well did he measure up to the honor. He made a striking picture, that thin little black boy standing on the platform, dressed in clothes that did not fit him any too well, his eyes burning with excitement, his shrill, musical voice vibrating in tones of appealing defiance, and his black face alight with such great intelligence and earnestness as to be positively handsome. What were his thoughts when he stepped forward and looked into that crowd of faces, all white with the exception of a score or so that were lost to view. I do not know, but I fancy he felt his loneliness. I think there must have rushed over him a feeling akin to that of a gladiator tossed into the arena and bade to fight for his life. I think that solitary little black figure standing there felt that for the particular time and place he bore the weight and responsibility of his race;

Notes

[16] *Original reads*: dresess [ed.].

that for him to fail meant general defeat; but he won, and nobly. His oration was Wendell Phillips' "Toussant L'Ouverture,"[17] a speech which may now be classed as rhetorical, even, perhaps, bombastic; but as the words fell from "Shiny's" lips their effect was magical. How so young an orator could stir so great enthusiasm was to be wondered at. When in the famous peroration,[18] his voice trembling with suppressed emotion rose higher and higher and then rested on the name Toussant L'Ouverture, it was like touching an electric button which loosed the pent-up feelings of his listeners. They actually rose to him.

I have since known of colored men who have been chosen as class orators in our leading universities, of others who have played on the 'Varsity foot-ball and base-ball teams, of colored speakers who have addressed great white audiences. In each of these instances I believe the men were stirred by the same emotions which actuated "Shiny" on the day of his graduation; and, too, in each case where the efforts have reached any high standard of excellence they have been followed by the same phenomenon of enthusiasm. I think the explanation of the latter lies in what is a basic, though often dormant, principle of the Anglo-Saxon heart, love of fair play. "Shiny," it is true, was what is so common in his race, a natural orator; but I doubt that any white boy of equal talent could have wrought the same effect. The sight of that boy gallantly waging with puny, black arms, so unequal a battle, touched the deep springs in the hearts of his audience, and they were swept by a wave of sympathy and admiration.

But the effect upon me of "Shiny's" speech was double; I not only shared the enthusiasm of his audience, but he imparted to me some of his own enthusiasm. I felt leap within me pride that I was colored; and I began to form wild dreams of bringing glory and honor to the Negro race. For days I could talk of nothing else with my mother except my ambitions to be a great man, a great colored man, to reflect credit on the race, and gain fame for myself. It was not until years after that I formulated a definite and feasible plan for realizing my dreams.

I entered the high school with my class, and still continued my study of the piano, the pipe organ and the theory of music. I had to drop out of the boys' choir on account of a changing voice; this I regretted very much. As I grew older my love for reading grew stronger. I read with studious interest everything I could find relating to colored men who had gained prominence. My heroes had been King David, then Robert the Bruce; now Frederick Douglass[19] was enshrined in the place of honor. When I learned that Alexander Dumas[20] was a colored man, I re-read "Monte Cristo" and "The Three Guardsmen" with magnified pleasure. I lived between my music and books, on the whole a rather unwholesome life for a boy to lead. I dwelt in a world of imagination, of dreams and air castles – the kind of atmosphere that sometimes nourishes a genius, more often men unfitted for the practical struggles of life. I never played a game of ball, never went fishing or learned to swim; in fact, the only outdoor exercise in which I took any interest was skating. Nevertheless, though slender, I grew well-formed and in perfect health. After I entered the high school I began to notice the change in my mother's health, which I suppose had been going on for some years. She began to complain a little and to cough a great deal; she tried several remedies, and finally went to see a

Notes

[17] *Wendell Phillips' "Toussant L'Ouverture"* Toussaint L'Ouverture (*c.*1743–1803) led the successful Haitian revolution, establishing the independent black state of Haiti; Phillips (1811–1884) was an American abolitionist and orator.

[18] *peroration* conclusion of a speech.

[19] Frederick Douglass (1818–1895), African American writer, orator, and civil rights leader.

[20] Alexandre Dumas (1802–1870), French writer whose novels include *The Count of Monte Cristo* (1845–1846) and *The Three Musketeers* (1844).

doctor; but though she was failing in health she kept her spirits up. She still did a great deal of sewing, and in the busy seasons hired two women to help her. The purpose she had formed of having me go through college without financial worries kept her at work when she was not fit for it. I was so fortunate as to be able to organize a class of eight or ten beginners on the piano, and so start a separate little fund of my own. As the time for my graduation from the high school grew nearer, the plans for my college career became the chief subject of our talks. I sent for catalogues of all the prominent schools in the East, and eagerly gathered all the information I could concerning them from different sources. My mother told me that my father wanted me to go to Harvard or Yale; she herself had a half desire for me to go to Atlanta University, and even had me write for a catalogue of that school. There were two reasons, however, that inclined her to my father's choice: the first, that at Harvard or Yale I should be near her; the second, that my father had promised to pay a part of my college education.

Both "Shiny" and "Red" came to my house quite often of evenings, and we used to talk over our plans and prospects for the future. Sometimes I would play for them, and they seemed to enjoy the music very much. My mother often prepared sundry southern dishes for them, which I am not sure but that they enjoyed more. "Shiny" had an uncle in Amherst, Mass., and he expected to live with him and work his way through Amherst College. "Red" declared that he had enough of school and that after he got his high school diploma he would get a position in a bank. It was his ambition to become a banker, and he felt sure of getting the opportunity through certain members of his family.

My mother barely had strength to attend the closing exercises of the high school when I graduated; and after that day she was seldom out of bed. She could no longer direct her work, and under the expense of medicines, doctors, and someone to look after her, our college fund began to diminish rapidly. Many of her customers and some of the neighbors were very kind, and frequently brought her nourishment of one kind or another. My mother realized what I did not, that she was mortally ill, and she had me write a long letter to my father. For some time past she had heard from him only at irregular intervals; we never received an answer. In those last days I often sat at her bedside and read to her until she fell asleep. Sometimes I would leave the parlor door open and play on the piano, just loud enough for the music to reach her. This she always enjoyed.

One night, near the end of July, after I had been watching beside her for some hours, I went into the parlor, and throwing myself into the big armchair dozed off into a fitful sleep. I was suddenly aroused by one of the neighbors, who had come in to sit with her that night. She said, "Come to your mother at once." I hurried upstairs, and at the bedroom door met the woman who was acting as nurse. I noted with a dissolving heart the strange look of awe on her face. From my first glance at my mother, I discerned the light of death upon her countenance. I fell upon my knees beside the bed, and burying my face in the sheets sobbed convulsively. She died with the fingers of her left hand entwined in my hair.

I will not rake over this, one of the two sacred sorrows of my life; nor could I describe the feeling of unutterable loneliness that fell upon me. After the funeral I went to the house of my music teacher; he had kindly offered me the hospitality of his home for so long as I might need it. A few days later I moved my trunk, piano, my music and most of my books to his home; the rest of my books I divided between "Shiny" and "Red." Some of the household effects I gave to "Shiny's" mother and to two or three of the neighbors who had been kind to us during my mother's illness; the others I sold. After settling up my little estate I found that besides a good supply of clothes, a piano, some books and other trinkets, I had about two hundred dollars in cash.

The question of what I was to do now confronted me. My teacher suggested a concert tour; but both of us realized that I was too old to be exploited as an infant prodigy and too young and inexperienced to go before the public as a finished artist. He, however, insisted that the people of the town would generously patronize a benefit concert, so took up the matter, and made arrangements for such an entertainment. A more than sufficient number of people with musical and elocutionary talent volunteered their services to make a programme. Among these was my brown-eyed violinist. But our relations were not the same as they were when we had played our first duet together. A year or so after that time she had dealt me a crushing blow by getting married. I was partially avenged, however, by the fact that, though she was growing more beautiful, she was losing her ability to play the violin.

I was down on the programme for one number. My selection might have appeared at that particular time as a bit of affectation, but I considered it deeply appropriate; I played Beethoven's "Sonata Pathétique."[21] When I sat down at the piano, and glanced into the faces of the several hundreds of people who were there solely on account of love or sympathy for me, emotions swelled in my heart which enabled me to play the "Pathétique" as I could never again play it. When the last tone died away the few who began to applaud were hushed by the silence of the others; and for once I played without receiving an encore.

The benefit yielded me a little more than two hundred dollars, thus raising my cash capital to about four hundred dollars. I still held to my determination of going to college; so it was now a question of trying to squeeze through a year at Harvard or going to Atlanta where the money I had would pay my actual expenses for at least two years. The peculiar fascination which the South held over my imagination and my limited capital decided me in favor of Atlanta University; so about the last of September I bade farewell to the friends and scenes of my boyhood, and boarded a train for the South.

Chapter 4

The farther I got below Washington the more disappointed I became in the appearance of the country. I peered through the car windows, looking in vain for the luxuriant semi-tropical scenery which I had pictured in my mind. I did not find the grass so green, nor the woods so beautiful, nor the flowers so plentiful, as they were in Connecticut. Instead, the red earth partly covered by tough, scrawny grass, the muddy straggling roads, the cottages of unpainted pine boards, and the clay-daubed huts imparted a "burnt up" impression. Occasionally we ran through a little white and green village that was like an oasis in a desert.

When I reached Atlanta my steadily increasing disappointment was not lessened. I found it a big, dull, red town. This dull red color of that part of the South I was then seeing had much, I think, to do with the extreme depression of my spirits – no public squares, no fountains, dingy street-cars and, with the exception of three or four principal thoroughfares, unpaved streets. It was raining when I arrived and some of these unpaved streets were absolutely impassable. Wheels sank to the hubs in red mire, and I actually stood for an hour and watched four or five men work to save a mule, which

Notes

[21] *Beethoven's "Sonata Pathétique"* Ludwig Van Beethoven (1770–1827), German composer, published Piano Sonata No. 8 in C Minor, Op. 13 in 1799.

had stepped into a deep sink, from drowning, or, rather, suffocating in the mud. The Atlanta of to-day is a new city.

On the train I had talked with one of the Pullman car porters, a bright young fellow who was himself a student, and told him that I was going to Atlanta to attend school. I had also asked him to tell me where I might stop for a day or two until the University opened. He said I might go with him to the place where he stopped during his "layovers" in Atlanta. I gladly accepted his offer, and went with him along one of those muddy streets until we came to a rather rickety-looking frame house, which we entered. The proprietor of the house was a big, fat, greasy-looking brown-skinned man. When I asked him if he could give me accommodation he wanted to know how long I would stay. I told him perhaps two days, not more than three. In reply he said, "Oh, dat's all right den," at the same time leading the way up a pair of creaky stairs. I followed him and the porter to a room, the door of which the proprietor opened while continuing, it seemed, his remark, "Oh, dat's all right den," by adding, "You kin sleep in dat cot in de corner der. Fifty cents please." The porter interrupted by saying, "You needn't collect from him now, he's got a trunk." This seemed to satisfy the man, and he went down leaving me and my porter friend in the room. I glanced around the apartment and saw that it contained a double bed and two cots, two wash-stands, three chairs, and a time-worn bureau with a looking-glass that would have made Adonis[22] appear hideous. I looked at the cot in which I was to sleep and suspected, not without good reasons, that I should not be the first to use the sheets and pillow-case since they had last come from the wash. When I thought of the clean, tidy, comfortable surroundings in which I had been reared, a wave of homesickness swept over me that made me feel faint. Had it not been for the presence of my companion, and that I knew this much of his history – that he was not yet quite twenty, just three years older than myself, and that he had been fighting his own way in the world, earning his own living and providing for his own education since he was fourteen – I should not have been able to stop the tears that were welling up in my eyes.

I asked him why it was that the proprietor of the house seemed unwilling to accommodate me for more than a couple of days. He informed me that the man ran a lodging house especially for Pullman porters, and as their stays in town were not longer than one or two nights it would interfere with his arrangements to have anyone stay longer. He went on to say, "You see this room is fixed up to accommodate four men at a time. Well, by keeping a sort of table of trips, in and out, of the men, and working them like checkers, he can accommodate fifteen or sixteen in each week, and generally avoid having an empty bed. You happen to catch a bed that would have been empty for a couple of nights." I asked him where he was going to sleep. He answered, "I sleep in that other cot to-night; to-morrow night I go out." He went on to tell me that the man who kept the house did not serve meals, and that if I was hungry we would go out and get something to eat.

We went into the street, and in passing the railroad station I hired a wagon to take my trunk to my lodging place. We passed along until, finally, we turned into a street that stretched away, up and down hill, for a mile or two; and here I caught my first sight of colored people in large numbers. I had seen little squads around the railroad stations on my way south; but here I saw a street crowded with them. They filled the shops and thronged the sidewalks and lined the curb. I asked my companion if all the

Notes

[22] *Adonis* in Greek mythology, a beautiful youth loved by the goddess Aphrodite.

colored people in Atlanta lived in this street. He said they did not, and assured me that the ones I saw were of the lower class. I felt relieved, in spite of the size of the lower class. The unkempt appearance, the shambling, slouching gait and loud talk and laughter of these people aroused in me a feeling of almost repulsion. Only one thing about them awoke a feeling of interest; that was their dialect. I had read some Negro dialect and had heard snatches of it on my journey down from Washington; but here I heard it in all of its fullness and freedom. I was particularly struck by the way in which it was punctuated by such exclamatory phrases as "Lawd a mussy!" "G'wan man!" "Bless ma soul!" "Look heah chile!" These people talked and laughed without restraint. In fact, they talked straight from their lungs, and laughed from the pits of their stomachs. And this hearty laughter was often justified by the droll humor of some remark. I paused long enough to hear one man say to another, "W'at's de mattah wid you an' yo' fr'en' Sam?" and the other came back like a flash, "Ma fr'en? He ma fr'en? Man! I'd go to his funeral jes de same as I'd go to a minstrel show." I have since learned that this ability to laugh heartily is, in part, the salvation of the American Negro; it does much to keep him from going the way of the Indian.

The business places of the street along which we were passing consisted chiefly of low bars, cheap dry-goods and notion stores, barber shops, and fish and bread restaurants. We, at length, turned down a pair of stairs that led to a basement, and I found myself in an eating-house somewhat better than those I had seen in passing; but that did not mean much for its excellence. The place was smoky, the tables were covered with oilcloth, the floor covered with sawdust, and from the kitchen came a rancid odor of fish fried over several times, which almost nauseated me. I asked my companion if this were the place where we were to eat. He informed me that it was the best place in town where a colored man could get a meal. I then wanted to know why somebody didn't open a place where respectable colored people who had money could be accommodated. He answered, "It wouldn't pay; all the respectable colored people eat at home, and the few who travel generally have friends in the towns to which they go, who entertain them." He added, "Of course, you could go in any place in the city; they wouldn't know you from white."

I sat down with the porter at one of the tables, but was not hungry enough to eat with any relish what was put before me. The food was not badly cooked; but the iron knives and forks needed to be scrubbed, the plates and dishes and glasses needed to be washed and well dried. I minced over what I took on my plate while my companion ate. When we finished we paid the waiter twenty cents each and went out. We walked around until the lights of the city were lit. Then the porter said that he must get to bed and have some rest, as he had not had six hours' sleep since he left Jersey City. I went back to our lodging-house with him.

When I awoke in the morning there were, besides my new found friend, two other men in the room, asleep in the double bed. I got up and dressed myself very quietly, so as not to awake anyone. I then drew from under the pillow my precious roll of greenbacks, took out a ten dollar bill, and very softly unlocking my trunk, put the remainder, about three hundred dollars, in the inside pocket of a coat near the bottom; glad of the opportunity to put it unobserved in a place of safety. When I had carefully locked my trunk, I tiptoed toward the door with the intention of going out to look for a decent restaurant where I might get something fit to eat. As I was easing the door open, my porter friend said with a yawn, "Hello! You're going out?" I answered him, "Yes." "Oh!" he yawned again, "I guess I've had enough sleep; wait a minute, I'll go with you." For the instant his friendship bored and embarrassed me. I had visions of another meal in the greasy restaurant of the day before. He must have divined my thoughts; for he went on to say, "I know a woman across town who takes a few boarders; I think we can go over there and get a good breakfast." With a feeling of mingled fears and doubts regarding what the breakfast might be, I waited until he had dressed himself.

When I saw the neat appearance of the cottage we entered my fears vanished, and when I saw the woman who kept it my doubts followed the same course. Scrupulously clean, in a spotless white apron and colored head handkerchief, her round face beaming with motherly kindness, she was picturesquely beautiful. She impressed me as one broad expanse of happiness and good nature. In a few minutes she was addressing me as "chile" and "honey." She made me feel as though I should like to lay my head on her capacious bosom and go to sleep.

And the breakfast, simple as it was, I could not have had at any restaurant in Atlanta at any price. There was fried chicken, as it is fried only in the South, hominy boiled to the consistency where it could be eaten with a fork, and biscuits so light and flaky that a fellow with any appetite at all would have no difficulty in disposing of eight or ten. When I had finished I felt that I had experienced the realization of, at least, one of my dreams of Southern life.

During the meal we found out from our hostess, who had two boys in school, that Atlanta University opened on that very day. I had somehow mixed my dates. My friend the porter suggested that I go out to the University at once and offered to walk over and show me the way. We had to walk because, although the University was not more than twenty minutes distance from the center of the city, there were no street-cars running in that direction. My first sight of the school grounds made me feel that I was not far from home; here the red hills had been terraced and covered with green grass; clean gravel walks, well shaded, led[23] up to the buildings; indeed, it was a bit of New England transplanted. At the gate my companion said he would bid me good-by, because it was likely that he would not see me again before his car went out. He told me that he would make two more trips to Atlanta, and that he would come out and see me; that after his second trip he would leave the Pullman service for the winter and return to school in Nashville. We shook hands, I thanked him for all his kindness, and we said good-by.

I walked up to a group of students and made some inquiries. They directed me to the president's office in the main building. The president gave me a cordial welcome; it was more than cordial; he talked to me, not as the official head of a college, but as though he were adopting me into what was his large family, to personally look after my general welfare as well as my education. He seemed especially pleased with the fact that I had come to them all the way from the North. He told me that I could have come to the school as soon as I had reached the city, and that I had better move my trunk out at once. I gladly promised him that I would do so. He then called a boy and directed him to take me to the matron, and to show me around afterwards. I found the matron even more motherly than the president was fatherly. She had me to register, which was in effect to sign a pledge to abstain from the use of intoxicating beverages, tobacco, and profane language, while I was a student in the school. This act caused me no sacrifice; as, up to that time, I was free from either habit. The boy who was with me then showed me about the grounds. I was especially interested in the industrial building.

The sounding of a bell, he told me, was the signal for the students to gather in the general assembly hall, and he asked me if I would go. Of course I would. There were

Notes

[23] *Original reads*: lead [ed.].

between three and four hundred students and perhaps all of the teachers gathered in the room. I noticed that several of the latter were colored. The president gave a talk addressed principally to newcomers; but I scarcely heard what he said, I was so much occupied in looking at those around me. They were of all types and colors, the more intelligent types predominating. The colors ranged from jet black to pure white, with light hair and eyes. Among the girls especially there were many so fair that it was difficult to believe that they had Negro blood in them. And, too, I could not help but notice that many of the girls, particularly those of the delicate brown shades, with black eyes and wavy dark hair, were decidedly pretty. Among the boys, many of the blackest were fine specimens of young manhood, tall, straight, and muscular, with magnificent heads; these were the kind of boys who developed into the patriarchal "uncles" of the old slave régime.

When I left the University it was with the determination to get my trunk, and move out to the school before night. I walked back across the city with a light step and a light heart. I felt perfectly satisfied with life for the first time since my mother's death. In passing the railroad station I hired a wagon and rode with the driver as far as my stopping place. I settled with my landlord and went upstairs to put away several articles I had left out. As soon as I opened my trunk a dart of suspicion shot through my heart; the arrangement of things did not look familiar. I began to dig down excitedly to the bottom till I reached the coat in which I had concealed my treasure. My money was gone! Every single bill of it. I knew it was useless to do so, but I searched through every other coat, every pair of trousers, every vest, and even into each pair of socks. When I had finished my fruitless search I sat down dazed and heartsick. I called the landlord up, and informed him of my loss; he comforted me by saying that I ought to have better sense than to keep money in a trunk, and that he was not responsible for his lodgers' personal effects. His cooling words brought me enough to my senses to cause me to look and see if anything else was missing. Several small articles were gone, among them a black and gray necktie of odd design upon which my heart was set; almost as much as the loss of my money, I felt the loss of my tie.

After thinking for a while[24] as best I could, I wisely decided to go at once back to the University and lay my troubles before the president. I rushed breathlessly back to the school. As I neared the grounds the thought came across me, would not my story sound fishy? Would it not place me in the position of an impostor or beggar? What right had I to worry these busy people with the results of my carelessness? If the money could not be recovered, and I doubted that it could, what good would it do to tell them about it. The shame and embarrassment which the whole situation gave me caused me to stop at the gate. I paused, undecided, for a moment; then turned and slowly retraced my steps, and so changed the whole course of my life.

If the reader has never been in a strange city without money or friends, it is useless to try to describe what my feelings were; he could not understand. If he has been, it is equally useless, for he understands more than words could convey. When I reached my lodgings I found in the room one of the porters who had slept there the night before. When he heard what misfortune had befallen me he offered many words of sympathy and advice. He asked me how much money I had left, I told him that I had ten or twelve dollars in my pocket. He said, "That won't last you very long here, and you will hardly be able to find anything to do in Atlanta. I'll tell you what you do, go down to Jacksonville and you won't have any trouble to get a job in one of the big hotels there,

Notes

[24] *Original reads*: awhile [ed.].

or in St. Augustine." I thanked him, but intimated my doubts of being able to get to Jacksonville on the money I had. He reassured me by saying, "Oh, that's all right. You express your trunk on through, and I'll take you down in my closet." I thanked him again, not knowing then, what it was to travel in a Pullman porter's closet. He put me under a deeper debt of gratitude by lending me fifteen dollars, which he said I could pay back after I had secured work. His generosity brought tears to my eyes, and I concluded that, after all, there were some kind hearts in the world.

I now forgot my troubles in the hurry and excitement of getting my trunk off in time to catch the train, which went out at seven o'clock. I even forgot that I hadn't eaten anything since morning. We got a wagon – the porter went with me – and took my trunk to the express office. My new friend then told me to come to the station at about a quarter of seven, and walk straight to the car where I should see him standing, and not to lose my nerve. I found my rôle not so difficult to play as I thought it would be, because the train did not leave from the central station, but from a smaller one, where there were no gates and guards to pass. I followed directions, and the porter took me on his car, and locked me in his closet. In a few minutes the train pulled out for Jacksonville.

I may live to be a hundred years old, but I shall never forget the agonies I suffered that night. I spent twelve hours doubled up in the porter's basket for soiled linen, not being able to straighten up on account of the shelves for clean linen just over my head. The air was hot and suffocating and the smell of damp towels and used linen was sickening. At each lurch of the car over the none too smooth track, I was bumped and bruised against the narrow walls of my narrow compartment. I became acutely conscious of the fact that I had not eaten for hours. Then nausea took possession of me, and at one time I had grave doubts about reaching my destination alive. If I had the trip to make again, I should prefer to walk.

Chapter 5

The next morning I got out of the car at Jacksonville with a stiff and aching body. I determined to ask no more porters, not even my benefactor, about stopping places; so I found myself on the street not knowing where to go. I walked along listlessly until I met a colored man who had the appearance of a preacher. I asked him if he could direct me to a respectable boarding-house for colored people. He said that if I walked along with him in the direction he was going he would show me such a place. I turned and walked at his side. He proved to be a minister, and asked me a great many direct questions about myself. I answered as many as I saw fit to answer; the others I evaded or ignored. At length we stopped in front of a frame house, and my guide informed me that it was the place. A woman was standing in the doorway, and he called to her saying that he had brought her a new boarder. I thanked him for his trouble, and after he had urged upon me to attend his church while I was in the city, he went on his way.

I went in and found the house neat and not uncomfortable. The parlor was furnished with cane-bottomed chairs, each of which was adorned with a white crocheted tidy. The mantel over the fireplace had a white crocheted cover; a marble-topped center table held a lamp, a photograph album and several trinkets, each of which was set upon a white crocheted mat. There was a cottage organ in a corner of the room, and I noted that the lamp-racks upon it were covered with white crocheted mats. There was a matting on the floor, but a white crocheted carpet would not have been out of keeping. I made arrangements with the landlady for my board and lodging; the amount was, I think, three dollars and a half a week. She was a rather fine looking, stout, brown-skinned woman of about forty years of age. Her husband was a light colored Cuban, a man about one half her size, and one whose age could not be guessed from his appearance. He was small in size, but a handsome black mustache and typical Spanish eyes redeemed him from insignificance.

I was in time for breakfast, and at the table I had the opportunity to see my fellow-boarders. There were eight or ten of them. Two, as I afterwards learned, were colored Americans. All of them were cigar makers and worked in one of the large factories – cigar making is the one trade in which the color-line is not drawn. The conversation was carried on entirely in Spanish, and my ignorance of the language subjected me more to alarm than embarrassment. I had never heard such uproarious conversation; everybody talked at once, loud exclamations, rolling *"carambas,"*[25] menacing gesticulations with knives, forks, and spoons. I looked every moment for the clash of blows. One man was emphasizing his remarks by flourishing a cup in his hand, seemingly forgetful of the fact that it was nearly full of hot coffee. He ended by emptying it over what was, relatively, the only quiet man at the table excepting myself, bringing from him a volley of language which made the others appear dumb by comparison. I soon learned that in all of this clatter of voices and table utensils they were discussing purely ordinary affairs and arguing about mere trifles, and that not the least ill-feeling was aroused. It was not long before I enjoyed the spirited chatter and badinage[26] at the table as much as I did my meals – and the meals were not bad.

I spent the afternoon in looking around the town. The streets were sandy, but were well shaded by fine oak trees, and far preferable to the clay roads of Atlanta. One or two public squares with green grass and trees gave the city a touch of freshness. That night after supper I spoke to my landlady and her husband about my intentions. They told me that the big winter hotels would not open within two months. It can easily be imagined what effect this news had on me. I spoke to them frankly about my financial condition and related the main fact of my misfortune in Atlanta. I modestly mentioned my ability to teach music and asked if there was any likelihood of my being able to get some scholars. My landlady suggested that I speak to the preacher who had shown me her house; she felt sure that through his influence I should be able to get up a class in piano. She added, however, that the colored people were poor, and that the general price for music lessons was only twenty-five cents. I noticed that the thought of my teaching white pupils did not even remotely enter her mind. None of this information made my prospects look much brighter.

The husband, who up to this time had allowed the woman to do most of the talking, gave me the first bit of tangible hope; he said that he could get me a job as a "stripper" in the factory where he worked, and that if I succeeded in getting some music pupils I could teach a couple of them every night, and so make a living until something better turned up. He went on to say that it would not be a bad thing for me to stay at the factory and learn my trade as a cigar maker, and impressed on me that, for a young man knocking about the country, a trade was a handy thing to have. I determined to accept his offer and thanked him heartily. In fact, I became enthusiastic, not only because I saw a way out of my financial troubles, but also because I was eager and curious over the new experience I was about to enter. I wanted to know all about the cigar making business. This narrowed the conversation down to the husband and myself, so the wife went in and left us talking.

Notes

[25] *"carambas"* (Spanish) interjections denoting surprise or pain.

[26] *badinage* (French) witty banter.

He was what is called a *regaliá*[27] workman, and earned from thirty-five to forty dollars a week. He generally worked a sixty dollar job; that is, he made cigars for which he was paid at the rate of sixty dollars per thousand. It was impossible for him to make a thousand in a week because he had to work very carefully and slowly. Each cigar was made entirely by hand. Each piece of filler and each wrapper had to be selected with care. He was able to make a bundle of one hundred cigars in a day, not one of which could be told from the others by any difference in size or shape, or even by any appreciable difference in weight. This was the acme of artistic skill in cigar making. Workmen of this class were rare, never more than three or four of them in one factory, and it was never necessary for them to remain out of work. There were men who made two, three, and four hundred cigars of the cheaper grades in a day; they had to be very fast in order to make a decent week's wages.[28] Cigar making was a rather independent trade; the men went to work when they pleased and knocked off when they felt like doing so. As a class the workmen were careless and improvident; some very rapid makers would not work more than three or four days out of the week, and there were others who never showed up at the factory on Mondays. "Strippers" were the boys who pulled the long stems from the tobacco leaves. After they had served at that work for a certain time they were given tables as apprentices.

All of this was interesting to me; and we drifted along in conversation until my companion struck the subject nearest his heart, the independence of Cuba. He was an exile from the island, and a prominent member of the Jacksonville *Junta*.[29] Every week sums of money were collected from *juntas* all over the country. This money went to buy arms and ammunition for the insurgents. As the man sat there nervously smoking his long, "green" cigar, and telling me of the Gomezes,[30] both the white one and the black one, of Maceo and Bandera,[31] he grew positively eloquent. He also showed that he was a man of considerable education and reading. He spoke English excellently, and frequently surprised me by using words one would hardly expect from a foreigner. The first one of this class of words he employed almost shocked me, and I never forgot it, 'twas "ramify." We sat on the piazza until after ten o'clock. When we arose to go in to bed it was with the understanding that I should start in the factory on the next day.

I began work the next morning seated at a barrel with another boy, who showed me how to strip the stems from the leaves, to smooth out each half leaf, and to put the "rights" together in one pile, and the "lefts" together in another pile on the edge of the barrel. My fingers, strong and sensitive from their long training, were well adapted to this kind of work; and within two weeks I was accounted the fastest "stripper" in the factory. At first the heavy odor of the tobacco almost sickened me; but when I became accustomed to it I liked the smell. I was now earning four dollars a week, and was soon able to pick up a couple more by teaching a few scholars at night, whom I had secured through the good offices of the preacher I had met on my first morning in Jacksonville.

At the end of about three months, through my skill as a "stripper" and the influence of my landlord, I was advanced to a table, and began to learn my trade; in fact, more than my trade; for I learned not only to make cigars, but also to smoke, to swear, and to speak Spanish. I discovered that I had a talent for languages as well as for music. The rapidity and ease with which I acquired Spanish astonished my associates. In a short

Notes

[27] *regaliá* fine cigar.

[28] *Original reads*: make decent week's wages [ed.].

[29] *Junta* Cuban exiles seeking to bring about the end of Spanish colonial rule in Cuba.

[30] *Gomezes* José Miguel Gómez y Gómez (1858–1921) and Máximo Gómez y Báez (1836–1905), Cuban revolutionaries.

[31] *Maceo and Banderas* Antonio Maceo y Grajales (1845–1896) and José Quintino "Quintín" Bandera Betancourt (1834–1906), officers of the Cuban revolutionary armies.

time I was able not only to understand most of what was said at the table during meals, but to join in the conversation. I bought a method for learning the Spanish language, and with the aid of my landlord as a teacher, by constant practice with my fellow workmen, and by regularly reading the Cuban newspapers, and finally some books of standard Spanish literature which were at the house, I was able in less than a year to speak like a native. In fact, it was my pride that I spoke better Spanish than many of the Cuban workmen at the factory.

After I had been in the factory a little over a year, I was repaid for all the effort I had put forth to learn Spanish by being selected as "reader." The "reader" is quite an institution in all cigar factories which employ Spanish-speaking workmen. He sits in the center of the large room in which the cigar makers work and reads to them for a certain number of hours each day all the important news from the papers and whatever else he may consider would be interesting. He often selects an exciting novel, and reads it in daily installments. He must, of course, have a good voice, but he must also have a reputation among the men for intelligence, for being well posted and having in his head a stock of varied information. He is generally the final authority on all arguments which arise; and, in a cigar factory, these arguments are many and frequent, ranging from discussions on the respective and relative merits of rival baseball clubs to the duration of the sun's light and energy – cigar-making is a trade in which talk does not interfere with work. My position as "reader" not only released me from the rather monotonous work of rolling cigars, and gave me something more in accord with my tastes, but also added considerably to my income. I was now earning about twenty-five dollars a week, and was able to give up my peripatetic[32] method of giving music lessons. I hired a piano and taught only those who could arrange to take their lessons where I lived. I finally gave up teaching entirely; as what I made scarcely paid for my time and trouble. I kept the piano, however, in order to keep up my own studies, and occasionally I played at some church concert or other charitable entertainment.

Through my music teaching and my not absolutely irregular attendance at church I became acquainted with the best class of colored people in Jacksonville. This was really my entrance into the race. It was my initiation into what I have termed the freemasonry of the race. I had formulated a theory of what it was to be colored, now I was getting the practice. The novelty of my position caused me to observe and consider things which, I think, entirely escaped the young men I associated with; or, at least, were so commonplace to them as not to attract their attention. And of many of the impressions which came to me then I have realized the full import only within the past few years, since I have had a broader knowledge of men and history, and a fuller comprehension of the tremendous struggle which is going on between the races in the South.

It is a struggle; for though the black man fights passively he nevertheless fights; and his passive resistance is more effective at present than active resistance could possibly be. He bears the fury of the storm as does the willow tree.

It is a struggle; for though the white man of the South may be too proud to admit it, he is, nevertheless, using in the contest his best energies; he is devoting to it the greater part of his thought and much of his endeavor. The South to-day stands panting and almost breathless from its exertions.

And how the scene of the struggle has shifted! The battle was first waged over the right of the Negro to be classed as a human being with a soul; later, as to whether he

Notes

[32] *peripatetic* traveling from place to place.

had sufficient intellect to master even the rudiments of learning; and to-day it is being fought out over his social recognition.

I said somewhere in the early part of this narrative that because the colored man looked at everything through the prism of his relationship to society as a *colored* man, and because most of his mental efforts ran through the narrow channel bounded by his rights and his wrongs, it was to be wondered at that he has progressed so broadly as he has. The same thing may be said of the white man of the South; most of his mental efforts run through one narrow channel; his life as a man and a citizen, many of his financial activities and all of his political activities are impassably limited by the ever present "Negro question." I am sure it would be safe to wager that no group of Southern white men could get together and talk for sixty minutes without bringing up the "race question." If a Northern white man happened to be in the group the time could be safely cut to thirty minutes. In this respect I consider the condition of the whites more to be deplored than that of the blacks. Here, a truly great people, a people that produced a majority of the great historic Americans from Washington to Lincoln now forced to use up its energies in a conflict as lamentable as it is violent.

I shall give the observations I made in Jacksonville as seen through the light of after years; and they apply generally to every Southern community. The colored people may be said to be roughly divided into three classes, not so much in respect to themselves as in respect to their relations with the whites. There are those constituting what might be called the desperate class – the men who work in the lumber and turpentine camps, the ex-convicts, the bar-room loafers are all in this class. These men conform to the requirements of civilization much as a trained lion with low muttered growls goes through his stunts under the crack of the trainer's whip. They cherish a sullen hatred for all white men, and they value life as cheap. I have heard more than one of them say, "I'll go to hell for the first white man that bothers me." Many who have expressed that sentiment have kept their word; and it is that fact which gives such prominence to this class; for in numbers it is but a small proportion of the colored people, but it often dominates public opinion concerning the whole race. Happily, this class represents the black people of the South far below their normal physical and moral condition, but in its increase lies the possibility of grave dangers. I am sure there is no more urgent work before the white South, not only for its present happiness, but its future safety, than the decreasing of this class of blacks. And it is not at all a hopeless class; for these men are but the creatures of conditions, as much so as the slum and criminal elements of all the great cities of the world are creatures of conditions. Decreasing their number by shooting and burning them off will not be successful; for these men are truly desperate, and thoughts of death, however terrible, have little effect in deterring them from acts the result of hatred or degeneracy. This class of blacks hate everything covered by a white skin, and in return they are loathed by the whites. The whites regard them just about as a man would a vicious mule, a thing to be worked, driven and beaten, and killed for kicking.

The second class, as regards the relation between blacks and whites, comprises the servants, the washer-women, the waiters, the cooks, the coachmen, and all who are connected with the whites by domestic service. These may be generally characterized as simple, kindhearted and faithful; not over fine in their moral deductions, but intensely religious, and relatively – such matters can be judged only relatively – about as honest and wholesome in their lives as any other grade of society. Any white person is "good" who treats them kindly, and they love them for that kindness. In return, the white people with whom they have to do regard them with indulgent affection. They come into close daily contact with the whites, and may be called the connecting link between whites and blacks; in fact, it is through them that the whites know the rest of their colored neighbors. Between this class of the blacks and the whites there is little or no friction.

The third class is composed of the independent workmen and tradesmen, and of the well-to-do and educated colored people; and, strange to say, for a directly opposite reason they are as far removed from the whites as the members of the first class I mentioned. These people live in a little world of their own; in fact, I concluded that if a colored man wanted to separate himself from his white neighbors he had but to acquire some money, education and culture, and to live in accordance. For example, the proudest and fairest lady in the South could with propriety – and it is what she would most likely do – go to the cabin of Aunt Mary, her cook, if Aunt Mary were sick, and minister to her comfort with her own hands; but if Mary's daughter, Eliza, a girl who used to run around my lady's kitchen, but who has received an education and married a prosperous young colored man, were at death's door, my lady would no more think of crossing the threshold of Eliza's cottage than she would of going into a bar-room for a drink.

I was walking down the street one day with a young man who was born in Jacksonville, but had been away to prepare himself for a professional life. We passed a young white man, and my companion said to me, "You see that young man? We grew up together, we have played, hunted, and fished together, we have even eaten and slept together, and now since I have come back home he barely speaks to me." The fact that the whites of the South despise and ill-treat the desperate class of blacks is not only explainable according to the ancient laws of human nature, but it is not nearly so serious or important as the fact that as the progressive colored people advance they constantly widen the gulf between themselves and their white neighbors. I think that the white people somehow feel that colored people who have education and money, who wear good clothes and live in comfortable houses, are "putting on airs," that they do these things for the sole purpose of "spiting the white folks," or are, at best, going through a sort of monkey-like imitation. Of course, such feelings can only cause irritation or breed disgust. It seems that the whites have not yet been able to realize and understand that these people, in striving to better their physical and social surroundings in accordance with their financial and intellectual progress, are simply obeying an impulse which is common to human nature the world over. I am in grave doubt as to whether the greater part of the friction in the South is caused by the whites having a natural antipathy to Negroes as a race, or an acquired antipathy to Negroes in certain relations to themselves. However that may be, there is to my mind no more pathetic side of this many-sided question than the isolated position into which are forced the very colored people who most need and who could best appreciate sympathetic cooperation; and their position grows tragic when the effort is made to couple them, whether or no, with the Negroes of the first class I mentioned.

This latter class of colored people are well disposed towards the whites, and always willing to meet them more than halfway. They, however, feel keenly any injustice or gross discrimination, and generally show their resentment. The effort is sometimes made to convey the impression that the better class of colored people fight against riding in "jim crow" cars because they want to ride with white people or object to being with humbler members of their own race. The truth is they object to the humiliation of being forced to ride in a *particular* car, aside from the fact that that car is distinctly inferior, and that they are required to pay full first-class fare. To say that the whites are forced to ride in the superior car is less than a joke. And, too, odd as it may sound, refined colored people get no more pleasure out of riding with offensive Negroes than anybody else would get.

I can realize more fully than I could years ago that the position of the advanced element of the colored race is often very trying. They are the ones among the blacks who carry the entire weight of the race question; it worries the others very little, and I believe the only thing which at times sustains them is that they know that they are in the right. On the other hand, this class of colored people get a good deal of pleasure out of life; their existence is far from being one long groan about their condition. Out of a chaos of ignorance and poverty they have evolved a social life of which they need not be ashamed. In cities where the professional and well-to-do class is large, they have formed society – society as discriminating as the actual conditions will allow it to be; I should say, perhaps, society possessing discriminating tendencies which become rules as fast as actual conditions allow. This statement will, I know, sound preposterous, even ridiculous, to some persons; but as this class of colored people is the least known of the race it is not surprising. These social circles are connected throughout the country, and a person in good standing in one city is readily accepted in another. One who is on the outside will often find it a difficult matter to get in. I know of one case personally in which money to the extent of thirty or forty thousand dollars and a fine house, not backed up by a good reputation, after several years of repeated effort, failed to gain entry for the possessor. These people have their dances and dinners and card parties, their musicals and their literary societies. The women attend social affairs dressed in good taste, and the men in evening dress-suits which they own; and the reader will make a mistake to confound these entertainments with the "Bellman's Balls" and "Whitewashers' Picnics" and "Lime Kiln Clubs" with which the humorous press of the country illustrates "Cullud Sassiety."

Jacksonville, when I was there, was a small town, and the number of educated and well-to-do colored people was few; so this society phase of life did not equal what I have since seen in Boston, Washington, Richmond, and Nashville; and it is upon what I have more recently seen in these cities that I have made the observations just above. However, there were many comfortable and pleasant homes in Jacksonville to which I was often invited. I belonged to the literary society – at which we generally discussed the race question – and attended all of the church festivals and other charitable entertainments. In this way I passed three years which were not at all the least enjoyable of my life. In fact, my joy took such an exuberant turn that I fell in love with a young school teacher and began to have dreams of matrimonial bliss; but another turn in the course of my life brought these dreams to an end.

I do not wish to mislead my readers into thinking that I led a life in Jacksonville which would make copy as the hero of a Sunday School library book. I was a hale fellow well met with all of the workmen at the factory, most of whom knew little and cared less about social distinctions. From their example I learned to be careless about money; and for that reason I constantly postponed and finally abandoned returning to Atlanta University. It seemed impossible for me to save as much as two hundred dollars. Several of the men at the factory were my intimate friends, and I frequently joined them in their pleasures. During the summer months we went almost every Monday on an excursion to a seaside resort called Pablo Beach. These excursions were always crowded. There was a dancing pavilion, a great deal of drinking and generally a fight or two to add to the excitement. I also contracted the cigar-maker's habit of riding around in a hack[33] on Sunday afternoons. I sometimes went with my cigar-maker friends to public balls that were given at a large hall on one of the main streets. I learned to take a drink occasionally and paid for quite a number that my friends took; but strong liquors never appealed to my appetite. I drank them only when the

Notes

[33] *hack* vehicle for hire.

company I was in required it, and suffered for it afterwards. On the whole, though I was a bit wild, I can't remember that I ever did anything disgraceful, or, as the usual standard for young men goes, anything to forfeit my claim to respectability.

At one of the first public balls I attended I saw the Pullman car porter who had so kindly assisted me in getting to Jacksonville. I went immediately to one of my factory friends and borrowed fifteen dollars with which to repay the loan my benefactor had made me. After I had given him the money, and was thanking him, I noticed that he wore what was, at least, an exact duplicate of my lamented black and gray tie. It was somewhat worn, but distinct enough for me to trace the same odd design which had first attracted my eye. This was enough to arouse my strongest suspicions, but whether it was sufficient for the law to take cognizance of I did not consider. My astonishment and the ironical humor of the situation drove everything else out of my mind.

These balls were attended by a great variety of people. They were generally given by the waiters of some one of the big hotels, and were often patronized by a number of hotel guests who came to "see the sights." The crowd was always noisy, but good-natured; there was much quadrille dancing,[34] and a strong-lunged man called figures in a voice which did not confine itself to the limits of the hall. It is not worth the while for me to describe in detail how these people acted; they conducted themselves in about the same manner as I have seen other people at similar balls conduct themselves. When one has seen something of the world and human nature he must conclude, after all, that between people in like stations of life there is very little difference the world over.

However, it was at one of these balls that I first saw the cake-walk.[35] There was a contest for a gold watch, to be awarded to the hotel head-waiter receiving the greatest number of votes. There was some dancing while the votes were being counted. Then the floor was cleared for the cake-walk. A half-dozen guests from some of the hotels took seats on the stage to act as judges, and twelve or fourteen couples began to walk for a "sure enough" highly decorated cake, which was in plain evidence. The spectators crowded about the space reserved for the contestants and watched them with interest and excitement. The couples did not walk around in a circle, but in a square, with the men on the inside. The fine points to be considered were the bearing of the men, the precision with which they turned the corners, the grace of the women, and the ease with which they swung around the pivots. The men walked with stately and soldierly step, and the women with considerable grace. The judges arrived at their decision by a process of elimination. The music and the walk continued for some minutes; then both were stopped while the judges conferred; when the walk began again several couples were left out. In this way the contest was finally narrowed down to three or four couples. Then the excitement became intense; there was much partisan cheering as one couple or another would execute a turn in extra elegant style. When the cake was finally awarded the spectators were about evenly divided between those who cheered the winners and those who muttered about the unfairness of the judges. This was the cake-walk in its original form, and it is what the colored performers on the theatrical stage developed into the prancing movements now known all over the world, and which some Parisian critics pronounced the acme of poetic motion.

There are a great many colored people who are ashamed of the cake-walk, but I think they ought to be proud of it. It is my opinion that the colored people of this

Notes

[34] *quadrille dancing* a square dance performed by four couples.

[35] *cake-walk* a late nineteenth-century popular African American dance style and competition.

country have done four things which refute the oft advanced theory that they are an absolutely inferior race, which demonstrate that they have originality and artistic conception; and, what is more, the power of creating that which can influence and appeal universally. The first two of these are the Uncle Remus stories, collected by Joel Chandler Harris,[36] and the Jubilee songs,[37] to which the Fisk singers[38] made the public and the skilled musicians of both America and Europe listen. The other two are ragtime[39] music and the cake-walk. No one who has traveled can question the world-conquering influence of ragtime; and I do not think it would be an exaggeration to say that in Europe the United States is popularly known better by ragtime than by anything else it has produced in a generation. In Paris they call it American music. The newspapers have already told how the practice of intricate cake-walk steps has taken up the time of European royalty and nobility. These are lower forms of art, but they give evidence of a power that will someday be applied to the higher forms. In this measure, at least, and aside from the number of prominent individuals the colored people of the United States have produced, the race has been a world influence; and all of the Indians between Alaska and Patagonia[40] haven't done as much.

Just when I was beginning to look upon Jacksonville as my permanent home, and was beginning to plan about marrying the young school teacher, raising a family, and working in a cigar factory the rest of my life, for some reason, which I do not now remember, the factory at which I worked was indefinitely shut down. Some of the men got work in other factories in town, some decided to go to Key West and Tampa, others made up their minds to go to New York for work. All at once a desire like a fever seized me to see the North again, and I cast my lot with those bound for New York.

Chapter 6

We steamed up into New York harbor late one afternoon in spring. The last efforts of the sun were being put forth in turning the waters of the bay to glistening gold; the green islands on either side, in spite of their warlike mountings, looked calm and peaceful; the buildings of the town shone out in a reflected light which gave the city an air of enchantment; and, truly, it is an enchanted spot. New York City is the most fatally fascinating thing in America. She sits like a great witch at the gate of the country, showing her alluring white face, and hiding her crooked hands and feet under the folds of her wide garments – constantly enticing thousands from far within, and tempting those who come from across the seas to go no farther. And all these become the victims of her caprice. Some she at once crushes beneath her cruel feet; others she condemns to a fate like that of galley slaves; a few she favors and fondles, riding them high on the bubbles of fortune; then with a sudden breath she blows the bubbles out and laughs mockingly as she watches them fall.

Twice I had passed through it; but this was really my first visit to New York; and as I walked about that evening I began to feel the dread power of the city; the crowds, the lights, the excitement, the gayety and all its subtler stimulating influences began to take effect upon me. My blood ran quicker, and I felt that I was just beginning to live.

Notes

[36] *Uncle Remus stories, collected by Joel Chandler Harris* Joel Chandler Harris (1848–1908), an American journalist and folklorist best known for his adaptation of African American folktales in *Uncle Remus: His Songs and His Sayings* (1881).

[37] *Jubilee songs* African American religious folk songs.

[38] *Fisk singers* an a cappella ensemble formed in 1871 to raise money for Fisk University.

[39] *ragtime* a syncopated style of piano music developed by African American players in the 1890s.

[40] *Patagonia* a region of southern Argentina.

To some natures this stimulant of life in a great city becomes a thing as binding and necessary as opium is to one addicted to the habit. It becomes their breath of life; they cannot exist outside of it; rather than be deprived of it they are content to suffer hunger, want, pain and misery; they would not exchange even a ragged and wretched condition among the great crowd for any degree of comfort away from it.

As soon as we landed, four of us went directly to a lodging-house in 27th Street, just west of Sixth Avenue. The house was run by a short, stout mulatto man, who was exceedingly talkative and inquisitive. In fifteen minutes he not only knew the history of the past life of each one of us, but had a clearer idea of what we intended to do in the future than we ourselves. He sought this information so much with an air of being very particular as to whom he admitted into his house that we tremblingly answered every question that he asked. When we had become located we went out and got supper; then walked around until about ten o'clock. At that hour we met a couple of young fellows who lived in New York and were known to one of the members of our party. It was suggested we go to a certain place which was known by the proprietor's name. We turned into one of the cross streets and mounted the stoop of a house in about the middle of a block between Sixth and Seventh Avenues. One of the young men whom we had met rang a bell, and a man on the inside cracked the door a couple of inches; then opened it and let us in. We found ourselves in the hallway of what had once been a residence. The front parlor had been converted into a bar, and a half dozen or so of well-dressed men were in the room. We went in, and after a general introduction had several rounds of beer. In the back parlor a crowd was sitting and standing around the walls of the room watching an exciting and noisy game of pool. I walked back and joined this crowd to watch the game, and principally to get away from the drinking party. The game was really interesting, the players being quite expert, and the excitement was heightened by the bets which were being made on the result. At times the antics and remarks of both players and spectators were amusing. When, at a critical point, a player missed a shot he was deluged by those financially interested in his making it with a flood of epithets synonymous to "chump"; while from the others he would be jeered by such remarks as "Nigger, dat cue ain't no hoe-handle." I noticed that among this class of colored men the word "nigger" was freely used in about the same sense as the word "fellow," and sometimes as a term of almost endearment; but I soon learned that its use was positively and absolutely prohibited to white men.

I stood watching this pool game until I was called by my friends, who were still in the bar-room, to go upstairs. On the second floor there were two large rooms. From the hall I looked into the one on the front. There was a large, round table in the center, at which five or six men were seated playing poker. The air and conduct here were greatly in contrast to what I had just seen in the pool-room; these men were evidently the aristocrats of the place; they were well, perhaps a bit flashily, dressed and spoke in low modulated voices, frequently using the word "gentlemen"; in fact, they seemed to be practicing a sort of Chesterfieldian politeness[41] towards each other. I was watching these men with a great deal of interest and some degree of admiration, when I was again called by the members of our party, and I followed them on to the back room. There was a doorkeeper at this room, and we were admitted only after inspection. When we got inside I saw a crowd of men of all ages and kinds grouped about an old

Notes

[41] *Chesterfieldian politeness* the fourth Earl of Chesterfield (1694–1773) was a writer on etiquette and manners.

billiard table, regarding some of whom, in supposing them to be white, I made no mistake. At first I did not know what these men were doing; they were using terms that were strange to me. I could hear only a confusion of voices exclaiming, "Shoot the two!" "Shoot the four!" "Fate me!" "Fate me!" "I've got you fated!" "Twenty-five cents he don't turn!" This was the ancient and terribly fascinating game of dice, popularly known as "craps." I, myself, had played pool in Jacksonville; it is a favorite game among cigar-makers, and I had seen others play cards; but here was something new. I edged my way in to the table and stood between one of my new-found New York friends and a tall, slender, black fellow, who was making side bets while the dice were at the other end of the table. My companion explained to me the principles of the game; and they are so simple that they hardly need to be explained twice. The dice came around the table until they reached the man on the other side of the tall, black fellow. He lost, and the latter said, "Gimme the bones."[42] He threw a dollar on the table and said, "Shoot the dollar." His style of play was so strenuous that he had to be allowed plenty of room. He shook the dice high above his head, and each time he threw them on the table he emitted a grunt such as men give when they are putting forth physical exertion with a rhythmic regularity. He frequently whirled completely around on his heels, throwing the dice the entire length of the table, and talking to them as though they were trained animals. He appealed to them in short singsong phrases. "Come dice," he would say. "Little Phoebe," "Little Joe," "'Way down yonder in the cornfield." Whether these mystic incantations were efficacious or not I could not say, but, at any rate, his luck was great, and he had what gamblers term "nerve." "Shoot the dollar!" "Shoot the two!" "Shoot the four!" "Shoot the eight!" came from his lips as quickly as the dice turned to his advantage. My companion asked me if I had ever played. I told him no. He said that I ought to try my luck; that everybody won at first. The tall man at my side was waving his arms in the air exclaiming "Shoot the sixteen!" "Shoot the sixteen!" "Fate me!" Whether it was my companion's suggestion or some latent daredevil strain in my blood which suddenly sprang into activity I do not know; but with a thrill of excitement which went through my whole body I threw a twenty dollar bill on the table and said in a trembling voice, "I fate you,"

I could feel that I had gained the attention and respect of everybody in the room, every eye was fixed on me, and the widespread question, "Who is he?" went around. This was gratifying to a certain sense of vanity of which I have never been able to rid myself, and I felt that it was worth the money even if I lost. The tall man with a whirl on his heels and a double grunt threw the dice; four was the number which turned up. This is considered as a hard "point" to make. He redoubled his contortions and his grunts and his pleadings to the dice; but on his third or fourth throw the fateful seven turned up, and I had won. My companion and all my friends shouted to me to follow up my luck. The fever was on me. I seized the dice. My hands were so hot that the bits of bone felt like pieces of ice. I shouted as loudly as I could, "Shoot it all!" but the blood was tingling so about my ears that I could not hear my own voice. I was soon "fated." I threw the dice – seven – I had won. "Shoot it all!" I cried again. There was a pause; the stake was more than one man cared to or could cover. I was finally "fated" by several men taking "a part" of it. I then threw the dice again. Seven. I had won. "Shoot it all!" I shouted excitedly. After a short delay I was "fated." Again I rolled the dice. Eleven. Again I had won. My friends now surrounded me and, much against my inclination, forced me to take down all of the money except five dollars. I tried my luck

Notes

[42] *"the bones"* (slang) dice.

once more, and threw some small "Point" which I failed to make, and the dice passed on to the next man.

In less than three minutes I had won more than two hundred dollars, a sum which afterwards cost me dearly. I was the hero of the moment, and was soon surrounded by a group of men who expressed admiration for my "nerve" and predicted for me a brilliant future as a gambler. Although at the time I had no thought of becoming a gambler I felt proud of my success. I felt a bit ashamed, too, that I had allowed my friends to persuade me to take down my money so soon. Another set of men also got around me, and begged me for twenty-five or fifty cents to put them back into the game. I gave each of them something. I saw that several of them had on linen dusters,[43] and as I looked about I noticed that there were perhaps a dozen men in the room similarly clad. I asked the fellow who had been my prompter at the dice table why they dressed in such a manner. He told me that men who had lost all the money and jewelry they possessed, frequently, in an effort to recoup their losses, would gamble away all their outer clothing and even their shoes; and that the proprietor kept on hand a supply of linen dusters for all who were so unfortunate. My informant went on to say that sometimes a fellow would become almost completely dressed and then, by a turn of the dice, would be thrown back into a state of semi-nakedness. Some of them were virtually prisoners and unable to get into the streets for days at a time. They ate at the lunch counter, where their credit was good so long as they were fair gamblers and did not attempt to jump their debts, and they slept around in chairs. They importuned friends and winners to put them back in the game, and kept at it until fortune again smiled on them. I laughed heartily at this, not thinking the day was coming which would find me in the same ludicrous predicament.

On passing downstairs I was told that the third and top floor of the house was occupied by the proprietor. When we passed through the bar I treated everybody in the room – and that was no small number, for eight or ten had followed us down. Then our party went out. It was now about half-past twelve, but my nerves were at such a tension that I could not endure the mere thought of going to bed. I asked if there was no other place to which we could go; our guides said yes, and suggested that we go to the "Club." We went to Sixth Avenue, walked two blocks, and turned to the west into another street. We stopped in front of a house with three stories and a basement. In the basement was a Chinese Chop-suey restaurant. There was a red lantern at the iron gate to the areaway, inside of which the Chinaman's name was printed. We went up the steps of the stoop, rang the bell, and were admitted without any delay. From the outside the house bore a rather gloomy aspect, the windows being absolutely dark, but within it was a veritable house of mirth. When we had passed through a small vestibule and reached the hallway we heard mingled sounds of music and laughter, the clink of glasses and the pop of bottles. We went into the main room, and I was little prepared for what I saw. The brilliancy of the place, the display of diamond rings, scarf-pins, ear-rings and breast-pins, the big rolls of money that were brought into evidence when drinks were paid for, and the air of gayety that pervaded, all completely dazzled and dazed me. I felt positively giddy, and it was several minutes before I was able to make any clear and definite observations.

We at length secured places at a table in a corner of the room, and as soon as we could attract the attention of one of the busy waiters ordered a round of drinks. When I had somewhat collected my senses I realized that in a large back room into which the

Notes

[43] *linen dusters* loose full-length coats.

main room opened, there was a young fellow singing a song, accompanied on the piano by a short, thick-set, dark man. Between each verse he did some dance steps, which brought forth great applause and a shower of small coins at his feet. After the singer had responded to a rousing encore, the stout man at the piano began to run his fingers up and down the keyboard. This he did in a manner which indicated that he was master of a good deal of technic. Then he began to play; and such playing! I stopped talking to listen. It was music of a kind I had never heard before. It was music that demanded physical response, patting of the feet, drumming of the fingers, or nodding of the head in time with the beat. The barbaric harmonies, the audacious resolutions often consisting of an abrupt jump from one key to another, the intricate rhythms in which the accents fell in the most unexpected places, but in which the beat was never lost, produced a most curious effect. And, too, the player – the dexterity of his left hand in making rapid octave runs and jumps was little short of marvelous; and, with his right hand, he frequently swept half the keyboard with clean cut chromatics[44] which he fitted in so nicely as never to fail to arouse in his listeners a sort of pleasant surprise at the accomplishment of the feat.

This was ragtime music, then a novelty in New York, and just growing to be a rage which has not yet subsided. It was originated in the questionable resorts about Memphis and St. Louis by Negro piano players, who knew no more of the theory of music than they did of the theory of the universe, but were guided by natural musical instinct and talent. It made its way to Chicago, where it was popular some time before it reached New York. These players often improvised crude and, at times, vulgar words to fit the melodies. This was the beginning of the ragtime song. Several of these improvisations were taken down by white men, the words slightly altered, and published under the names of the arrangers. They sprang into immediate popularity and earned small fortunes, of which the Negro originators got only a few dollars. But I have learned that since that time a number of colored men, of not only musical talent, but training, are writing out their own melodies and words and reaping the reward of their work. I have learned also that they have a large number of white imitators and adulterators.

American musicians, instead of investigating ragtime, attempt to ignore it or dismiss it with a contemptuous word. But that has always been the course of scholasticism[45] in every branch of art. Whatever new thing the *people* like is pooh-poohed; whatever is *popular* is spoken of as not worth the while. The fact is, nothing great or enduring, especially in music, has ever sprung full-fledged and unprecedented from the brain of any master; the best that he gives to the world he gathers from the hearts of the people, and runs it through the alembic[46] of his genius. In spite of the bans which musicians and music teachers have placed upon it, the people still demand and enjoy ragtime. One thing cannot be denied; it is music which possesses at least one strong element of greatness; it appeals universally; not only the American, but the English, the French, and even the German people, find delight in it. In fact, there is not a corner of the civilized world in which it is not known, and this proves its originality; for if it were an imitation, the people of Europe, anyhow, would not have found it a novelty. Anyone who doubts that there is a peculiar heel-tickling, smile-provoking, joy-awakening charm in ragtime needs only to hear a skillful performer play the genuine article to be convinced. I believe that it has its place as well as the music which draws from us sighs and tears.

Notes

[44] *chromatics* musical semitones produced by the black and white keys on a piano.

[45] *scholasticism* adherence to tradition.

[46] *alembic* a distilling apparatus.

I became so interested in both the music and the player that I left the table where I was sitting, and made my way through the hall into the back room, where I could see as well as hear. I talked to the piano player between the musical numbers, and found out that he was just a natural musician, never having taken a lesson in his life. Not only could he play almost anything he heard, but could accompany singers in songs he had never heard. He had by ear alone, composed some pieces, several of which he played over for me; each of them was properly proportioned and balanced. I began to wonder what this man with such a lavish natural endowment would have done had he been trained. Perhaps he wouldn't have done anything at all; he might have become, at best, a mediocre imitator of the great masters in what they have already done to a finish, or one of the modern innovators who strive after originality by seeing how cleverly they can dodge about through the rules of harmony, and at the same time avoid melody. It is certain that he would not have been so delightful as he was in ragtime.

I sat by watching and listening to this man until I was dragged away by my friends. The place was now almost deserted; only a few stragglers hung on, and they were all the worse for drink. My friends were well up in this class. We passed into the street; the lamps were pale against the sky; day was just breaking. We went home and got into bed. I fell into a fitful sort of sleep with ragtime music ringing continually in my ears.

Chapter 7

I shall take advantage of this pause in my narrative to more closely describe the "Club" spoken of in the latter part of the preceding chapter – to describe it, as I afterwards came to know it, as an habitue.[47] I shall do this, not only because of the direct influence it had on my life, but also because it was at that time the most famous place of its kind in New York, and was well known to both white and colored people of certain classes.

I have already stated that in the basement of the house there was a Chinese restaurant. The Chinaman who kept it did an exceptionally good business; for chop-suey was a favorite dish among the frequenters of the place. It is a food that, somehow, has the power of absorbing alcoholic liquors that have been taken into the stomach. I have heard men claim that they could sober up on chop-suey. Perhaps that accounted, in some degree, for its popularity. On the main floor there were two large rooms, a parlor about thirty feet in length and a large square back room into which the parlor opened. The floor of the parlor was carpeted; small tables and chairs were arranged about the room; the windows were draped with lace curtains, and the walls were literally covered with photographs or lithographs of every colored man in America who had ever "done anything." There were pictures of Frederick Douglass and of Peter Jackson,[48] of all the lesser lights of the prizefighting ring, of all the famous jockeys and the stage celebrities, down to the newest song and dance team. The most of these photographs were autographed and, in a sense, made a really valuable collection. In the back room there was a piano; and tables were placed around the wall. The floor was bare and the center was left vacant for singers, dancers and others who entertained the patrons. In a closet in this room which jutted out into the hall the proprietor kept his buffet. There was no open bar, because the place had no liquor license. In this back room the tables were sometimes pushed aside, and the floor given over to general dancing. The front room on the next floor was a sort of private party room; a back room on the same

Notes

[47] *habitue* (French) frequent visitor or resident.

[48] Peter Jackson (1861–1901), African American boxing champion.

floor contained no furniture, and was devoted to the use of new and ambitious[49] performers. In this room song and dance teams practiced their steps, acrobatic teams practiced their tumbles, and many other kinds of "acts" rehearsed their "turns." The other rooms of the house were used as sleeping apartments.

No gambling was allowed, and the conduct of the place was surprisingly orderly. It was, in short, a center of colored Bohemians and sports.[50] Here the great prize fighters were wont to come, the famous jockeys, the noted minstrels, whose names and faces were familiar on every bill-board in the country; and these drew a multitude of those who love to dwell in the shadow of greatness. There were then no organizations giving performances of such order as are now given by several colored companies; that was because no manager could imagine that audiences would pay to see Negro performers in any other rôle than that of Mississippi River roustabouts; but there was lots of talent and ambition. I often heard the younger and brighter men discussing the time when they would compel the public to recognize that they could do something more than grin and cut pigeon wings.[51]

Sometimes one or two of the visiting stage professionals, after being sufficiently urged, would go into the back room, and take the places of the regular amateur entertainers, but they were very sparing with these favors, and the patrons regarded them as special treats. There was one man, a minstrel, who, whenever he responded to a request to "do something," never essayed anything below a reading from Shakespeare. How well he read I do not know, but he greatly impressed me; and I can, at least, say that he had a voice which strangely stirred those who heard it. Here was a man who made people laugh at the size of his mouth, while he carried in his heart a burning ambition to be a tragedian; and so after all he did play a part in a tragedy.

These notables of the ring, the turf and the stage, drew to the place crowds of admirers, both white and colored. Whenever one of them came in there were awe-inspired whispers from those who knew him by sight, in which they enlightened those around them as to his identity, and hinted darkly at their great intimacy with the noted one. Those who were on terms of approach immediately showed their privilege over others less fortunate by gathering around their divinity. I was, at first, among those who dwelt in darkness. Most of these celebrities I had never heard of. This made me an object of pity among many of my new associates. I, however, soon learned to fake a knowledge for the benefit of those who were greener than I; and, finally, I became personally acquainted with the majority of the famous personages who came to the "Club."

A great deal of money was spent here; so many of the patrons were men who earned large sums. I remember one night a dapper little brown-skinned fellow was pointed out to me, and I was told that he was the most popular jockey of the day, and that he earned $12,000 a year. This latter statement I couldn't doubt, for with my own eyes I saw him spending at about that rate. For his friends and those who were introduced to him be bought nothing but wine – in the sporting circle, "wine" means champagne – and paid for it at five dollars a quart. He sent a quart to every table in the place with his compliments; and on the table at which he and his party were seated there were more than a dozen bottles. It was the custom at the "Club" for the waiter not to remove the bottles when champagne was being drunk until the party had finished.

Notes

[49] *Original reads*: ambitions [ed.].

[50] *Bohemians and sports* non-conformists and revelers. *Original reads*: bohemians [ed.].

[51] *pigeon wings* a jumping dance step.

There were reasons for this; it advertised the brand of wine, it advertised that the party was drinking wine, and advertised how much they had bought. This jockey had won a great race that day, and he was rewarding his admirers for the homage they paid him, all of which he accepted with a fine air of condescension.

Besides the people I have just been describing there was at the place almost every night one or two parties of white people, men and women, who were out sight-seeing, or slumming. They generally came in cabs; some of them would stay only for a few minutes, while others sometimes stayed until morning. There was also another set of white people who came frequently; it was made up of variety performers and others who delineated darky characters; they came to get their imitations[52] first hand from the Negro entertainers they saw there.

There was still another set of white patrons, composed of women; these were not occasional visitors, but five or six of them were regular habitues. When I first saw them I was not sure that they were white. In the first place, among the many colored women who came to the "Club" there were several just as fair; and, secondly, I always saw these women in company with colored men. They were all good-looking and well dressed, and seemed to be women of some education. One of these in particular attracted my attention; she was an exceedingly beautiful woman of perhaps thirty-five; she had glistening copper-colored hair, very white skin and eyes very much like Du Maurier's[53] conception of Trilby's "twin gray stars." When I came to know her I found that she was a woman of considerable culture; she had traveled in Europe, spoke French, and played the piano well. She was always dressed elegantly, but in absolute good taste. She always came to the "Club" in a cab, and was soon joined by a well set up, very black young fellow. He was always faultlessly dressed; one of the most exclusive tailors in New York made his clothes, and he wore a number of diamonds in about as good taste as they could be worn by a man. I learned that she paid for his clothes and his diamonds. I learned, too, that he was not the only one of his kind. More that I learned would be better suited to a book on social phenomena than to a narrative of my life.

This woman was known at the "Club" as the rich widow. She went by a very aristocratic sounding name, which corresponded to her appearance. I shall never forget how hard it was for me to get over my feelings of surprise, perhaps more than surprise, at seeing her with her black companion; somehow I never exactly enjoyed the sight. I have devoted so much time to this pair, the "widow" and her companion, because it was through them that another decided turn was brought about in my life.

Chapter 8

On the day following our night at the "Club" we slept until late in the afternoon; so late that beginning of search for work was entirely out of the question. This did not cause me much worry, for I had more than three hundred dollars, and New York had impressed me as a place where there was lots of money and not much difficulty in getting it. It is needless to inform my readers that I did not long hold this opinion. We got out of the house about dark, went round to a restaurant on Sixth Avenue and ate something, then walked around for a couple of hours. I finally suggested that we visit

Notes

[52] *Original reads*: imitatations [ed.].

[53] George Du Maurier (1834–1896), British author whose novel *Trilby* (1894) was a best-seller.

the same places we had been in the night before. Following my suggestion we started first to the gambling house. The man on the door let us in without any question; I accredited this to my success of the night before. We went straight to the "crap" room, and I at once made my way to a table, where I was rather flattered by the murmur of recognition which went around. I played in up and down luck for three or four hours; then, worn with nervous excitement, quit, having lost about fifty dollars. But I was so strongly possessed with the thought that I would make up my losses the next time I played that I left the place with a light heart.

When we got into the street our party was divided against itself; two were for going home at once and getting to bed. They gave as a reason that we were to get up early and look for jobs. I think the real reason was that they had each lost several dollars in the game. I lived to learn that in the world of sport all men win alike but lose differently; and so gamblers are rated, not by the way in which they win, but by the way in which they lose. Some men lose with a careless smile, recognizing that losing is a part of the game; others curse their luck and rail at fortune; and others, still, lose sadly; after each such experience they are swept by a wave of reform; they resolve to stop gambling and be good. When in this frame of mind it would take very little persuasion to lead them into a prayer-meeting. Those in the first class are looked upon with admiration; those in the second class are merely commonplace; while those in the third are regarded with contempt. I believe these distinctions hold good in all the ventures of life. After some minutes one of my friends and I succeeded in convincing the other two that a while at the "Club" would put us all in better spirits; and they consented to go on our promise not to stay longer than an hour. We found the place crowded, and the same sort of thing going on which we had seen the night before. I took a seat at once by the side of the piano player, and was soon lost to everything else except the novel charm of the music. I watched the performer with the idea of catching the trick; and, during one of his intermissions, I took his place at the piano and made an attempt to imitate him, but even my quick ear and ready fingers were unequal to the task on first trial.

We did not stay at the "Club" very long, but went home to bed in order to be up early the next day. We had no difficulty in finding work, and my third morning in New York found me at a table rolling cigars. I worked steadily for some weeks, at the same time spending my earnings between the "crap" game and the "Club." Making cigars became more and more irksome to me; perhaps my more congenial work as a "reader" had unfitted me for work at the table. And, too, the late hours I was keeping made such a sedentary occupation almost beyond the powers of will and endurance. I often found it hard to keep my eyes open and sometimes had to get up and move around to keep from falling asleep. I began to miss whole days from the factory, days on which I was compelled to stay at home and sleep.

My luck at the gambling table was varied; sometimes I was fifty to a hundred dollars ahead, and at other times I had to borrow money from my fellow workmen to settle my room rent and pay for my meals. Each night after leaving the dice game I went to the "Club" to hear the music and watch the gayety. If I had won, this was in accord with my mood; if I had lost, it made me forget. I at last realized that making cigars for a living and gambling for a living could not both be carried on at the same time, and I resolved to give up the cigar-making. This resolution led me into a life which held me bound more than a year. During that period my regular time for going to bed was somewhere between four and six o'clock in the mornings. I got up late in the afternoons, walked about a little, then went to the gambling house or the "Club.' My New York was limited to ten blocks; the boundaries were Sixth Avenue from Twenty-third to Thirty-third Streets, with the cross streets one block to the west. Central Park was a distant forest, and the lower part of the city a foreign land. I look back upon the life I then led with a shudder when I think what would have been had I not escaped it. But had I not escaped it, I would have been no more unfortunate than are many young colored men who come to New York. During that dark period I became acquainted with a score of bright, intelligent young fellows who had come up to the great city with high hopes and ambitions, and who had fallen under the spell of this underlife, a spell they could not throw off. There was one popularly known as "the doctor"; he had had two years in the Harvard Medical School; but here he was, living this gas-light life, his will and moral sense so enervated and deadened that it was impossible for him to break away. I do not doubt that the same thing is going on now, but I have rather sympathy than censure for these victims, for I know how easy it is to slip into a slough from which it takes a Herculean[54] effort to leap.

I regret that I cannot contrast my views of life among colored people of New York; but the truth is, during my entire stay in this city I did not become acquainted with a single respectable family. I knew that there were several colored men worth a hundred or so thousand dollars each, and some families who proudly dated their free ancestry back a half-dozen generations. I also learned that in Brooklyn there lived quite a large colony in comfortable homes, most of which they owned; but at no point did my life come in contact with theirs.

In my gambling experiences I passed through all the states and conditions that a gambler is heir to. Some days found me able to peel ten and twenty dollar bills from a roll, and others found me clad in a linen duster and carpet slippers. I finally caught up another method of earning money, and so did not have to depend entirely upon the caprices of fortune at the gaming table. Through continually listening to the music at the "Club," and through my own previous training, my natural talent and perseverance, I developed into a remarkable player of ragtime; indeed, I had the name at that time of being the best ragtime player in New York. I brought all my knowledge of classic music to bear and, in so doing, achieved some novelties which pleased and even astonished my listeners. It was I who first made ragtime transcriptions of familiar classic selections. I used to play Mendelssohn's[55] "Wedding March" in a manner that never failed to arouse enthusiasm among the patrons of the "Club." Very few nights passed during which I was not asked to play it. It was no secret that the great increase in slumming visitors was due to my playing. By mastering ragtime I gained several things; first of all, I gained the title of professor. I was known as the "professor" as long as I remained in that world. Then, too, I gained the means of earning a rather fair livelihood. This work took up much of my time and kept me almost entirely away from the gambling table. Through it I also gained a friend who was the means by which I escaped from this lower world. And, finally, I secured a wedge which has opened to me more doors and made me a welcome guest than my playing of Beethoven and Chopin[56] could ever have done.

The greater part of the money I now began to earn came through the friend to whom I alluded in the foregoing paragraph. Among the other white "slummers" there came into the "Club" one night a clean-cut, slender, but athletic looking man, who would have been taken for a youth had it not been for the tinge of gray about his temples. He was clean shaven, had regular features, and all of his movements bore the indefinable but unmistakable stamp of culture. He spoke to no one, but sat languidly

Notes

[54] *Original reads*: herculean [ed.].

[55] Felix Mendelssohn (1809–1847), German composer.

[56] Frédéric Chopin (1810–1849), Polish composer and pianist.

puffing cigarettes and sipping a glass of beer. He was the center of a great deal of attention, all of the old timers were wondering who he was. When I had finished playing he called a waiter and by him sent me a five dollar bill. For about a month after that he was at the "Club" one or two nights each week, and each time after I had played he gave me five dollars. One night he sent for me to come to his table; he asked me several questions about myself; then told me that he had an engagement which he wanted me to fill. He gave me a card containing his address and asked me to be there on a certain night.

I was on hand promptly, and found that he was giving a dinner in his own apartments to a party of ladies and gentlemen, and that I was expected to furnish the musical entertainment. When the grave, dignified man at the door let me in, the place struck me as being almost dark, my eyes had been so accustomed to the garish light of the "Club." He took my coat and hat, bade me take a seat, and went to tell his master that I had come. When my eyes were adjusted to the soft light I saw that I was in the midst of elegance and luxury in such a degree as I had never seen; but not the elegance which makes one ill at ease. As I sank into a great chair, the subdued tone, the delicately sensuous harmony of my surroundings, drew from me a deep sigh of relief and comfort. How long the man was gone I do not know; but I was startled by a voice saying, "Come this way, if you please, sir," and I saw him standing by my chair. I had been asleep; and I awoke very much confused and a little ashamed, because I did not know how many times he may have called me. I followed him through into the dining-room, where the butler was putting the finishing touches to a table which already looked like a big jewel. The doorman turned me over to the butler, and I passed with the butler on back to where several waiters were busy polishing and assorting table utensils. Without being asked whether I was hungry or not, I was placed at a table and given something to eat. Before I had finished eating I heard the laughter and talk of the guests who were arriving. Soon afterwards I was called in to begin my work.

I passed in to where the company was gathered, and went directly to the piano. According to a suggestion from the host I began with classic music. During the first number there was absolute quiet and appreciative attention, and when I had finished I was given a round of generous applause. After that the talk and the laughter began to grow until the music was only an accompaniment to the chatter. This, however, did not disconcert me as it once would have done, for I had become accustomed to playing in the midst of uproarious noise. As the guests began to pay less attention to me I was enabled to pay more to them. There were about a dozen of them. The men ranged in appearance from a girlish looking youth to a big grizzled man whom everybody addressed as "Judge." None of the women appeared to be under thirty, but each of them struck me as being handsome. I was not long in finding out that they were all decidedly blasé. Several of the women smoked cigarettes, and with a careless grace which showed they were used to the habit. Occasionally a "damn it!" escaped from the lips of some one of them, but in such a charming way as to rob it of all vulgarity. The most notable thing which I observed was that the reserve of the host increased in direct proportion with the hilarity of his guests. I thought that there was something going wrong which displeased him. I afterwards learned that it was his habitual manner on such occasions. He seemed to take cynical delight in watching and studying others indulging in excess. His guests were evidently accustomed to his rather non-participating attitude, for it did not seem in any degree to dampen their spirits.

When dinner was served the piano was moved and the door left open, so that the company might hear the music while eating. At a word from the host I struck up one of my liveliest ragtime pieces. The effect was perhaps surprising, even to the host; the ragtime music came very near spoiling the party so far as eating the dinner was concerned. As soon as I began the conversation stopped suddenly. It was a pleasure to me to watch the expression of astonishment and delight that grew on the faces of everybody. These were people – and they represented a large class – who were ever expecting to find happiness in novelty, each day restlessly exploring and exhausting every resource of this great city that might possibly furnish a new sensation or awaken a fresh emotion, and who were always grateful to anyone who aided them in their quest. Several of the women left the table and gathered about the piano. They watched my fingers, asked what kind of music it was that I was playing, where I had learned it and a host of other questions. It was only by being repeatedly called back to the table that they were induced to finish their dinner. When the guests arose I struck up my ragtime transcription of Mendelssohn's "Wedding March," playing it with terrific chromatic octave runs in the base. This raised everybody's spirits to the highest point of gayety, and the whole company involuntarily and unconsciously did an impromptu cake-walk. From that time on until the time of leaving they kept me so busy that my arms ached. I obtained a little respite when the girlish looking youth and one or two of the ladies sang several songs, but after each of these it was, "back to ragtime."

In leaving, the guests were enthusiastic in telling the host that he had furnished them the most unique entertainment they had "ever" enjoyed. When they had gone, my millionaire friend – for he was reported to be a millionaire – said to me with a smile, "Well, I have given them something they've never had before." After I had put on my coat and was ready to leave he made me take a glass of wine; he then gave me a cigar and twenty dollars in bills. He told me that he would give me lots of work, his only stipulation being that I should not play any engagements such as I had just filled for him, except by his instructions. I readily accepted the proposition, for I was sure that I could not be the loser by such a contract.

I afterwards played for him at many dinners and parties of one kind or another. Occasionally he "loaned" me to some of his friends. And, too, I often played for him alone at his apartments. At such times he was quite a puzzle to me until I became accustomed to his manners. He would sometimes sit for three or four hours hearing me play, his eyes almost closed, making scarcely a motion except to light a fresh cigarette, and never commenting one way or another on the music. At first, I used sometimes to think that he had fallen asleep and would pause in playing. The stopping of the music always aroused him enough to tell me to play this or that; and I soon learned that my task was not to be considered finished until he got up from his chair and said, "That will do." The man's powers of endurance in listening often exceeded mine in performing – yet I am not sure that he was always listening. At times I became so oppressed with fatigue and sleepiness that it took almost superhuman effort to keep my fingers going; in fact, I believe I sometimes did so while dozing. During such moments, this man sitting there so mysteriously silent, almost hid in a cloud of heavy-scented smoke, filled me with a sort of unearthly terror. He seemed to be some grim, mute, but relentless tyrant, possessing over me a supernatural power which he used to drive me on mercilessly to exhaustion. But these feelings came very rarely; besides, he paid me so liberally I could forget much. There at length grew between us a familiar and warm relationship; and I am sure he had a decided personal liking for me. On my part, I looked upon him at that time as about all a man could wish to be.

The "Club" still remained my headquarters, and when I was not playing for my good patron I was generally to be found there. However, I no longer depended on playing at the "Club" to earn my living; I rather took rank with the visiting celebrities and, occasionally, after being sufficiently urged, would favor my old and new admirers with a number or two. I say, without any egotistic pride, that among my admirers were several of the best-looking women who frequented the place, and who made no secret of the fact that they admired me as much as they did my playing. Among these was the "widow"; indeed, her attentions became so marked that one of my friends warned me to beware of her black companion, who was generally known as a "bad man." He said there was much more reason to be careful because the pair had lately quarreled, and had not been together at the "Club" for some nights. This warning greatly impressed me and I resolved to stop the affair before it should go any further; but the woman was so beautiful that my native gallantry and delicacy would not allow me to repulse her; my finer feelings entirely overcame my judgment. The warning also opened my eyes sufficiently to see that though my artistic temperament and skill made me interesting and attractive to the woman, she was, after all, using me only to excite the jealousy of her companion and revenge herself upon him. It was this surly black despot who held sway over her deepest emotions.

One night, shortly afterwards, I went into the "Club" and saw the "widow" sitting at a table in company with another woman. She at once beckoned for me to come to her. I went, knowing that I was committing worse than folly. She ordered a quart of champagne and insisted that I sit down and drink with her. I took a chair on the opposite side of the table and began to sip a glass of the wine. Suddenly I noticed by an expression on the "widow's" face that something had occurred. I instinctively glanced around and saw that her companion had just entered. His ugly look completely frightened me. My back was turned to him, but by watching the "widow's" eyes I judged that he was pacing back and forth across the room. My feelings were far from being comfortable; I expected every moment to feel a blow on my head. She, too, was very nervous; she was trying hard to appear unconcerned, but could not succeed in hiding her real feelings. I decided that it was best to get out of such a predicament even at the expense of appearing cowardly, and I made a motion to rise. Just as I partly turned in my chair, I saw the black fellow approaching; he walked directly to our table and leaned over. The "Widow" evidently feared he was going to strike her, and she threw back her head. Instead of striking her he whipped out a revolver and fired; the first shot went straight into her throat. There were other shots fired, but how many I do not know; for the first knowledge I had of my surroundings and actions was that I was rushing through the chop-suey restaurant into the street. Just which streets I followed when I got outside I do not know, but I think I must have gone towards Eighth Avenue, then down towards Twenty-third Street and across towards Fifth Avenue. I traveled not by sight, but instinctively. I felt like one fleeing in a horrible nightmare.

How long and far I walked I cannot tell; but on Fifth Avenue, under a light, I passed a cab containing a solitary occupant, who called to me, and I recognized the voice and face of my millionaire friend. He stopped the cab and asked, "What on earth are you doing strolling in this part of the town?" For answer I got into the cab and related to him all that had happened. He reassured me by saying that no charge of any kind could be brought against me; then added, "But, of course, you don't want to be mixed up in such an affair." He directed the driver to turn around and go into the park, and then went on to say, "I decided last night that I'd go to Europe to-morrow. I think I'll take you along instead of Walter." Walter was his valet. It was settled that I should go to his apartments for the rest of the night and sail with him in the morning.

We drove around through the park, exchanging only an occasional word. The cool air somewhat calmed my nerves and I lay back and closed my eyes; but still I could see that beautiful white throat with the ugly wound. The jet of blood pulsing from it had placed an indelible red stain on my memory.

Chapter 9

I did not feel at ease until the ship was well out of New York harbor; and, notwithstanding the repeated reassurances of my millionaire friend and my own knowledge of the facts in the case, I somehow could not rid myself of the sentiment that I was, in a great degree, responsible for the widow's tragic end. We had brought most of the morning papers aboard with us, but my great fear of seeing my name in connection with the killing would not permit me to read the accounts, although, in one of the papers, I did look at the picture of the victim, which did not in the least resemble her. This morbid state of mind, together with seasickness, kept me miserable for three or four days. At the end of that time my spirits began to revive, and I took an interest in the ship, my fellow passengers, and the voyage in general. On the second or third day out we passed several spouting whales; but I could not arouse myself to make the effort to go to the other side of the ship to see them. A little later we ran in close proximity to a large iceberg. I was curious enough to get up and look at it, and I was fully repaid for my pains. The sun was shining full upon it, and it glistened like a mammoth diamond, cut with a million facets. As we passed it constantly changed its shape; at each different angle of vision it assumed new and astonishing forms of beauty. I watched it through a pair of glasses, seeking to verify my early conception of an iceberg – in the geographies of my grammar-school days the pictures of icebergs always included a stranded polar bear, standing desolately upon one of the snowy crags. I looked for the bear, but if he was there he refused to put himself on exhibition.

It was not, however, until the morning that we entered the harbor of Havre[57] that I was able to shake off my gloom. Then the strange sights, the chatter in an unfamiliar tongue and the excitement of landing and passing the customs officials caused me to forget completely the events of a few days before. Indeed, I grew so light-hearted that when I caught my first sight of the train which was to take us to Paris, I enjoyed a hearty laugh. The toy-looking engine, the stuffy little compartment cars with tiny, old-fashioned wheels, struck me as being extremely funny. But before we reached Paris my respect for our train rose considerably. I found that the "tiny" engine made remarkably fast time, and that the old-fashioned wheels ran very smoothly. I even began to appreciate the "stuffy" cars for their privacy. As I watched the passing scenery from the car window it seemed too beautiful to be real. The bright-colored houses against the green background impressed me as the work of some idealistic painter. Before we arrived in Paris there was awakened in my heart a love for France which continued to grow stronger, a love which today makes that country for me the one above all others to be desired.

We rolled into the station Saint Lazare about four o'clock in the afternoon, and drove immediately to the Hotel Continental. My benefactor, humoring my curiosity and enthusiasm, which seemed to please him very much, suggested that we take a short walk before dinner. We stepped out of the hotel and turned to the right into the Rue de Rivoli. When the vista of the Place de la Concorde and the Champs Elysées[58] suddenly burst on me I could hardly credit my own eyes. I shall attempt no such supererogatory[59] task as a description of Paris. I wish only to give briefly the impressions which that wonderful city made upon me. It impressed me as the perfect and perfectly beautiful city; and even after I had been there for some time, and seen not only its

Notes

[57] *Havre* a French seaport.

[58] *Champs Elysées* a luxurious avenue in Paris.

[59] *supererogatory* superfluous. *Original reads*: superogatory [ed.].

avenues and palaces, but its most squalid alleys and hovels, this impression was not weakened. Paris became for me a charmed spot, and whenever I have returned there I have fallen under the spell, a spell which compels admiration for all of its manners and customs and justification of even its follies and sins.

We walked a short distance up the Champs Elysées and sat for a while in chairs along the sidewalk, watching the passing crowds on foot and in carriages. It was with reluctance that I went back to the hotel for dinner. After dinner we went to one of the summer theaters, and after the performance my friend took me to a large café on one of the grand boulevards. Here it was that I had my first glimpse of the French life of popular literature, so different from real French life. There were several hundred people, men and women, in the place drinking, smoking, talking, and listening to the music. My millionaire friend and I took seats at a table where we sat smoking and watching the crowd. It was not long before we were joined by two or three good-looking, well-dressed young women. My friend talked to them in French and bought drinks for the whole party. I tried to recall my high school French, but the effort availed me little. I could stammer out a few phrases, but, very naturally, could not understand a word that was said to me. We stayed at the café a couple of hours, then went back to the hotel. The next day we spent several hours in the shops and at the tailors. I had no clothes except what I had been able to gather together at my benefactor's apartments the night before we sailed. He bought me the same kind of clothes which he himself wore, and that was the best; and he treated me in every way as he dressed me, as an equal, not as a servant. In fact, I don't think anyone could have guessed that such a relation existed. My duties were light and few, and he was a man full of life and vigor, who rather enjoyed doing things for himself. He kept me supplied with money far beyond what ordinary wages would have amounted to. For the first two weeks we were together almost constantly, seeing the sights, sights old to him, but from which he seemed to get new pleasure in showing them to me. During the day we took in the places of interest, and at night the theaters and cafés. This sort of life appealed to me as ideal, and I asked him one day how long he intended to stay in Paris. He answered, "Oh, until I get tired of it." I could not understand how that could ever happen. As it was, including several short trips to the Mediterranean, to Spain, to Brussels, and to Ostend,[60] we did remain there fourteen or fifteen months. We stayed at the Hotel Continental about two months of this time. Then my millionaire took apartments, hired a piano, and lived almost the same life he lived in New York. He entertained a great deal, some of the parties being a good deal more blasé than the New York ones. I played for the guests at all of them with an effect which to relate would be but a tiresome repetition to the reader. I played not only for the guests, but continued, as I used to do in New York, to play often for the host when he was alone. This man of the world, who grew weary of everything, and was always searching for something new, appeared never to grow tired of my music; he seemed to take it as a drug. He fell into a habit which caused me no little annoyance; sometimes he would come in during the early hours of the morning, and finding me in bed asleep, would wake me up and ask me to play something. This, so far as I can remember, was my only hardship during my whole stay with him in Europe.

After the first few weeks spent in sight-seeing, I had a great deal of time left to myself; my friend was often I did not know where. When not with him I spent the day nosing about all the curious nooks and corners of Paris; of this I never grew tired.

Notes

[60] *Brussels ... Ostend* Belgian cities.

At night I usually went to some theater, but always ended up at the big café on the Grand Boulevards. I wish the reader to know that it was not alone the gayety which drew me there; aside from that I had a laudable purpose. I had purchased an English-French conversational dictionary, and I went there every night to take a language lesson. I used to get three or four of the young women who frequented the place at a table and buy beer and cigarettes for them. In return I received my lesson. I got more than my money's worth; for they actually compelled me to speak the language. This, together with reading the papers every day, enabled me within a few months to express myself fairly well, and, before I left Paris, to have more than an ordinary command of French. Of course, every person who goes to Paris could not dare to learn French in this manner, but I can think of no easier or quicker way of doing it. The acquiring of another foreign language awoke me to the fact that with a little effort I could secure an added accomplishment as fine and as valuable as music; so I determined to make myself as much of a linguist as possible. I bought a Spanish newspaper every day in order to freshen my memory on that language, and, for French, devised what was, so far as I knew, an original system of study. I compiled a list which I termed "Three hundred necessary words." These I thoroughly committed to memory, also the conjugation of the verbs which were included in the list. I studied these words over and over, much like children of a couple of generations ago studied the alphabet. I also practiced a set of phrases like the following: "How?" "What did you say?" "What does the word —— mean?" "I understand all you say except ——." "Please repeat." "What do you call ——?" "How do you say ——?" These I called my working sentences. In an astonishingly short time I reached the point where the language taught itself – where I learned to speak merely by speaking. This point is the place which students taught foreign languages in our schools and colleges find great difficulty in reaching. I think the main trouble is that they learn too much of a language at a time. A French child with a vocabulary of two hundred words can express more spoken ideas than a student of French can with a knowledge of two thousand. A small vocabulary, the smaller the better, which embraces the common, everyday-used ideas, thoroughly mastered, is the key to a language. When that much is acquired the vocabulary can be increased simply by talking. And it is easy. Who cannot commit three hundred words to memory? Later I tried my method, if I may so term it, with German, and found that it worked in the same way.

I spent a good many evenings at the Grand Opera. The music there made me strangely reminiscent of my life in Connecticut; it was an atmosphere in which I caught a fresh breath of my boyhood days and early youth. Generally, in the morning, after I had attended a performance, I would sit at the piano and for a couple of hours play the music which I used to play in my mother's little parlor.

One night I went to hear "Faust."[61] I got into my seat just as the lights went down for the first act. At the end of the act I noticed that my neighbor on the left was a young girl. I cannot describe her either as to feature, color of her hair, or of her eyes; she was so young, so fair, so ethereal, that I felt to stare at her would be a violation; yet I was distinctly conscious of her beauty. During the intermission she spoke English in a low voice to a gentleman and a lady who sat in the seats to her left, addressing them as father and mother. I held my programme as though studying it, but listened to catch every sound of her voice. Her observations on the performance and the audience were

Notes

[61] *Faust* 1859 opera by French composer Charles Gounod (1818–1893).

so fresh and naïve as to be almost amusing. I gathered that she was just out of school, and that this was her first trip to Paris. I occasionally stole a glance at her, and each time I did so my heart leaped into my throat. Once I glanced beyond to the gentleman who sat next to her. My glance immediately turned into a stare. Yes, there he was, unmistakably, my father! looking hardly a day older than when I had seen him some ten years before. What a strange coincidence! What should I say to him? What would he say to me? Before I had recovered from my first surprise there came another shock in the realization that the beautiful, tender girl at my side was my sister. Then all the springs of affection in my heart, stopped since my mother's death, burst out in fresh and terrible torrents, and I could have fallen at her feet and worshiped her. They were singing the second act, but I did not hear the music. Slowly the desolate loneliness of my position became clear to me. I knew that I could not speak, but I would have given a part of my life to touch her hand with mine and call her sister. I sat through the opera until I could stand it no longer. I felt that I was suffocating. Valentine's[62] love seemed like mockery, and I felt an almost uncontrollable impulse to rise up and scream to the audience, "Here, here in your very midst, is a tragedy, a real tragedy!" This impulse grew so strong that I became afraid of myself, and in the darkness of one of the scenes I stumbled out of the theater. I walked aimlessly about for an hour or so, my feelings divided between a desire to weep and a desire to curse. I finally took a cab and went from café to café, and for one of the very few times in my life drank myself into a stupor.

It was unwelcome news for me when my benefactor – I could not think of him as employer – informed me that he was at last tired of Paris. This news gave me, I think, a passing doubt as to his sanity. I had enjoyed life in Paris, and, taking all things into consideration, enjoyed it wholesomely. One thing which greatly contributed to my enjoyment was the fact that I was an American. Americans are immensely popular in Paris; and this is not due solely to the fact that they spend lots of money there; for they spend just as much or more in London, and in the latter city they are merely tolerated because they do spend. The Londoner seems to think that Americans are people whose only claim to be classed as civilized is that they have money, and the regrettable thing about that is that the money is not English. But the French are more logical and freer from prejudices than the British; so the difference of attitude is easily explained. Only once in Paris did I have cause to blush for my American citizenship. I had become quite friendly with a young man from Luxembourg whom I had met at the big café. He was a stolid, slow-witted fellow, but, as we say, with a heart of gold. He and I grew attached to each other and were together frequently. He was a great admirer of the United States and never grew tired of talking to me about the country and asking for information. It was his intention to try his fortune there some day. One night he asked me in a tone of voice which indicated that he expected an authoritative denial of an ugly rumor, "Did they really burn a man alive in the United States?" I never knew what I stammered out to him as an answer. I should have felt relieved if I could even have said to him, "Well, only one."

When we arrived in London my sadness at leaving Paris was turned into despair. After my long stay in the French capital, huge, ponderous, massive London seemed to me as ugly a thing as man could contrive to make. I thought of Paris as a beauty spot on the face of the earth, and of London as a big freckle. But soon London's massiveness, I might say its very ugliness, began to impress me. I began to experience that

Notes

[62] *Valentine* brother of *Faust*'s heroine, Marguerite.

sense of grandeur which one feels when he looks at a great mountain or a mighty river. Beside London Paris becomes a toy, a pretty plaything. And I must own that before I left the world's metropolis I discovered much there that was beautiful. The beauty in and about London is entirely different from that in and about Paris; and I could not but admit that the beauty of the French city seemed hand-made, artificial, as though set up for the photographer's camera, everything nicely adjusted so as not to spoil the picture; while that of the English city was rugged, natural and fresh.

How these two cities typify the two peoples who built them! Even the sounds[63] of their names express a certain racial difference. Paris is the concrete expression of the gayety, regard for symmetry, love of art and, I might well add, of the morality of the French people. London stands for the conservatism, the solidarity, the utilitarianism and, I might well add, the hypocrisy of the Anglo-Saxon. It may sound odd to speak of the morality of the French, if not of the hypocrisy of the English; but this seeming paradox impressed me as a deep truth. I saw many things in Paris which were immoral according to English standards, but the absence of hypocrisy, the absence of the spirit to do the thing if it might only be done in secret, robbed these very immoralities of the damning influence of the same evils in London. I have walked along the terrace cafés of Paris and seen hundreds of men and women sipping their wine and beer, without observing a sign of drunkenness. As they drank, they chatted and laughed and watched the passing crowds; the drinking seemed to be a secondary thing. This I have witnessed, not only in the cafés along the Grand Boulevards, but in the out-of-way places patronized by the working classes. In London I have seen in the "Pubs" men and women crowded in stuffy little compartments, drinking seemingly only for the pleasure of swallowing as much as they could hold. I have seen there women from eighteen to eighty, some in tatters, and some clutching babes in their arms, drinking the heavy English ales and whiskies served to them by women. In the whole scene, not one ray of brightness, not one flash of gayety, only maudlin joviality or grim despair. And I have thought, if some men and women will drink – and it is certain that some will – is it not better that they do so under the open sky, in the fresh air, than huddled together in some close, smoky room? There is a sort of frankness about the evils of Paris which robs them of much of the seductiveness of things forbidden, and with that frankness goes a certain cleanliness of thought belonging to things not hidden. London will do whatever Paris does, provided exterior morals are not shocked. As a result, Paris has the appearance only of being the more immoral city. The difference may be summed up in this: Paris practices its sins as lightly as it does its religion, while London practices both very seriously.

I should not neglect to mention what impressed me most forcibly during my stay in London. It was not St. Paul's nor the British Museum nor Westminster Abbey. It was nothing more or less than the simple phrase "Thank you," or sometimes more elaborated, "Thank you very kindly, sir." I was continually surprised by the varied uses to which it was put; and, strange to say, its use as an expression of politeness seemed more limited than any other. One night I was in a cheap music hall and accidentally bumped into a waiter who was carrying a tray-load of beer, almost bringing him to several shillings' worth of grief. To my amazement he righted himself and said, "Thank ye, sir," and left me wondering whether he meant that he thanked me for not completely spilling his beer, or that he would thank me for keeping out of his way.

Notes

[63] *Original reads*: sound [ed.].

I also found cause to wonder upon what ground the English accuse Americans of corrupting the language by introducing slang words. I think I heard more and more different kinds of slang during my few weeks' stay in London than in my whole "tenderloin"[64] life in New York. But I suppose the English feel that the language is theirs, and that they may do with it as they please without at the same time allowing that privilege to others.

My "millionaire" was not so long in growing tired of London, as of Paris. After a stay of six or eight weeks we went across into Holland. Amsterdam was a great surprise to me. I had always thought of Venice as the city of canals; but it had never entered my mind that I should find similar conditions in a Dutch town. I don't suppose the comparison goes far beyond the fact that there are canals in both cities – I have never seen Venice – but Amsterdam struck me as being extremely picturesque. From Holland we went to Germany, where we spent five or six months, most of the time in Berlin. I found Berlin more to my taste than London, and occasionally I had to admit that in some things it was superior to Paris.

In Berlin I especially enjoyed the orchestral concerts, and I attended a large number of them. I formed the acquaintance of a good many musicians, several of whom spoke of my playing in high terms. It was in Berlin that my inspiration was renewed. One night my "millionaire" entertained a party of men composed of artists, musicians, writers and, for aught I know, a count or two. They drank and smoked a great deal, talked art and music, and discussed, it seemed to me, everything that ever entered man's mind. I could only follow the general drift of what they were saying. When they discussed music it was more interesting to me; for then some fellow would run excitedly to the piano and give a demonstration of his opinions, and another would follow quickly doing the same. In this way, I learned that, regardless of what his specialty might be, every man in the party was a musician. I was at the same time impressed with the falsity of the general idea that Frenchmen are excitable and emotional, and that Germans are calm and phlegmatic.[65] Frenchmen are merely gay and never overwhelmed by their emotions. When they talk loud and fast it is merely talk, while Germans get worked up and red in the face when sustaining an opinion; and in heated discussions are likely to allow their emotions to sweep them off their feet.

My "millionaire" planned, in the midst of the discussion on music, to have me play the "new American music" and astonish everybody present. The result was that I was more astonished than anyone else. I went to the piano and played the most intricate ragtime piece I knew. Before there was time for anybody to express an opinion on what I had done, a big bespectacled, bushy-headed man rushed over, and, shoving me out of the chair, exclaimed, "Get up! Get up!" He seated himself at the piano, and taking the theme of my ragtime, played it through first in straight chords; then varied and developed it through every known musical form. I sat amazed. I had been turning classic music into ragtime, a comparatively easy task; and this man had taken ragtime and made it classic. The thought came across me like a flash. It can be done, why can't I do it? From that moment my mind was made up. I clearly saw the way of carrying out the ambition I had formed when a boy.

I now lost interest in our trip. I thought, here I am a man, no longer a boy, and what am I doing but wasting my time and abusing my talent. What use am I making of my gifts? What future have I before me following my present course? These thoughts

Notes

[64] *"tenderloin"* a midtown-Manhattan district renowned for vice and corruption.

[65] *phlegmatic* unemotional.

made me feel remorseful, and put me in a fever to get to work, to begin to do something. Of course I know now that I was not wasting time; that there was nothing I could have done at that age which would have benefited me more than going to Europe as I did. The desire to begin work grew stronger each day. I could think of nothing else. I made up my mind to go back into the very heart of the South, to live among the people, and drink in my inspiration first-hand. I gloated over the immense amount of material I had to work with, not only modern ragtime, but also the old slave songs – material which no one had yet touched.

The more decided and anxious I became to return to the United States, the more I dreaded the ordeal of breaking with my "millionaire." Between this peculiar man and me there had grown a very strong bond of affection, backed up by a debt which each owed to the other. He had taken me from a terrible life in New York and by giving me the opportunity of traveling and of coming in contact with the people with whom he associated, had made me a polished man of the world. On the other hand, I was his chief means of disposing of the thing which seemed to sum up all in life that he dreaded – Time. As I remember him now, I can see that time was what he was always endeavoring to escape, to bridge over, to blot out; and it is not strange that some years later he did escape it forever, by leaping into eternity.

For some weeks I waited for just the right moment in which to tell my patron of my decision. Those weeks were a trying time to me. I felt that I was playing the part of a traitor to my best friend. At length, one day, he said to me, "Well, get ready for a long trip; we are going to Egypt, and then to Japan." The temptation was for an instant almost overwhelming, but I summoned determination enough to say, "I don't think I want to go." "What!" he exclaimed, "you want to go back to your dear Paris? You still think that the only spot on earth? Wait until you see Cairo and Tokio[66], you may change your mind." "No," I stammered, "it is not because I want to go back to Paris. I want to go back to the United States." He wished to know my reason, and I told him, as best I could, my dreams, my ambition, and my decision. While I was talking he watched me with a curious, almost cynical, smile growing on his lips. When I had finished he put his hand on my shoulder. This was the first physical expression of tender regard he had ever shown me – and looking at me in a big-brotherly way, said, "My boy, you are by blood, by appearance, by education and by tastes, a white man. Now why do you want to throw your life away amidst the poverty and ignorance, in the hopeless struggle of the black people of the United States? Then look at the terrible handicap you are placing on yourself by going home and working as a Negro composer; you can never be able to get the hearing for your work which it might deserve. I doubt that even a white musician of recognized ability could succeed there by working on the theory that American music should be based on Negro themes. Music is a universal art; anybody's music belongs to everybody; you can't limit it to race or country. Now, if you want to become a composer, why not stay right here in Europe? I will put you under the best teachers on the continent. Then if you want to write music on Negro themes, why, go ahead and do it."

We talked for some time on music and the race question. On the latter subject I had never before heard him express any opinion. Between him and me no suggestion of racial differences had ever come up. I found that he was a man entirely free from prejudice, but he recognized that prejudice was a big stubborn entity which had to be taken into account. He went on to say, "This idea you have of making a Negro out of yourself

Notes

[66] *Tokio* Tokyo.

is nothing more than a sentiment; and you do not realize the fearful import of what you intend to do. What kind of a Negro would you make now, especially in the South? If you had remained there, or perhaps even in your club in New York, you might have succeeded very well; but now you would be miserable. I can imagine no more dissatisfied human being than an educated, cultured and refined colored man in the United States. I have given more study to the race question in the United States than you may suppose, and I sympathize with the Negroes there; but what's the use? I can't right their wrongs, and neither can you; they must do that themselves. They are unfortunate in having wrongs to right, and you would be foolish to unnecessarily take their wrongs on your shoulders. Perhaps someday, through study and observation, you will come to see that evil is a force and, like the physical and chemical forces, we cannot annihilate it; we may only change its form. We light upon one evil and hit it with all the might of our civilization, but only succeed in scattering it into a dozen of other forms. We hit slavery through a great civil war. Did we destroy it? No, we only changed it into hatred between sections of the country: in the South, into political corruption and chicanery, the degradation of the blacks through peonage,[67] unjust laws, unfair and cruel treatment; and the degradation of the whites by their resorting to these practices; the paralyzation of the public conscience, and the ever overhanging dread of what the future may bring. Modern civilization hit ignorance of the masses through the means of popular education. What has it done but turn ignorance into anarchy, socialism, strikes, hatred between poor and rich, and universal discontent. In like manner, modern philanthropy hit at suffering and disease through asylums and hospitals; it prolongs the sufferers' lives, it is true; but is, at the same time, sending down strains of insanity and weakness into future generations. My philosophy of life is this: make yourself as happy as possible, and try to make those happy whose lives come into touch with yours; but to attempt to right the wrongs and ease the sufferings of the world in general, is a waste of effort. You had just as well try to bale the Atlantic by pouring the water into the Pacific."

This tremendous flow of serious talk from a man I was accustomed to see either gay or taciturn so surprised and overwhelmed me that I could not frame a reply. He left me thinking over what he had said. Whatever was the soundness of his logic or the moral tone of his philosophy, his argument greatly impressed me. I could see, in spite of the absolute selfishness upon which it was based, that there was reason and common sense in it. I began to analyze my own motives, and found that they, too, were very largely mixed with selfishness. Was it more a desire to help those I considered my people or more a desire to distinguish myself, which was leading me back to the United States? That is a question I have never definitely answered.

For several weeks longer I was in a troubled state of mind. Added to the fact that I was loath to leave my good friend, was the weight of the question he had aroused in my mind, whether I was not making a fatal mistake. I suffered more than one sleepless night during that time. Finally, I settled the question on purely selfish grounds, in accordance with my "millionaire's" philosophy. I argued that music offered me a better future than anything else I had any knowledge of, and, in opposition to my friend's opinion, that I should have greater chances of attracting attention as a colored composer than as a white one. But I must own that I also felt stirred by an unselfish desire to voice all the joys and sorrows, the hopes and ambitions, of the American Negro, in classic musical form.

Notes

[67] *peonage* debt slavery.

When my mind was fully made up I told my friend. He asked me when I intended to start. I replied that I would do so at once. He then asked me how much money I had. I told him that I had saved several hundred dollars out of sums he had given me. He gave me a check for $500, told me to write to him care of his Paris bankers if I ever needed his help, wished me good luck, and bade me good-by. All this he did almost coldly; and I often wondered whether he was in a hurry to get rid of what he considered a fool, or whether he was striving to hide deeper feelings of sorrow.

And so I separated from the man who was, all in all, the best friend I ever had, except my mother, the man who exerted the greatest influence ever brought into my life, except that exerted by my mother. My affection for him was so strong, my recollections of him are so distinct; he was such a peculiar and striking character, that I could easily fill several chapters with reminiscences of him; but for fear of tiring the reader I shall go on with my narration.

I decided to go to Liverpool[68] and take ship for Boston. I still had an uneasy feeling about returning to New York; and in a few days I found myself aboard ship headed for home.

Chapter 10

Among the first of my fellow passengers of whom I took any particular notice, was a tall, broad-shouldered, almost gigantic, colored man. His dark-brown face was clean shaven; he was well dressed and bore a decidedly distinguished air. In fact, if he was not handsome, he at least compelled admiration for his fine physical proportions. He attracted general attention as he strode the deck in a sort of majestic loneliness. I became curious to know who he was and determined to strike up an acquaintance with him at the first opportune moment. The chance came a day or two later. He was sitting in the smoking-room, with a cigar in his mouth which had gone out, reading a novel. I sat down beside him and, offering him a fresh cigar, said, "You don't mind my telling you something unpleasant, do you?" He looked at me with a smile, accepted the proffered cigar, and replied in a voice which comported perfectly with his size and appearance, "I think my curiosity overcomes any objections I might have." "Well," I said, "have you noticed that the man who sat at your right in the saloon during the first meal has not sat there since?"

He frowned slightly without answering my question. "Well," I continued, "he asked the steward to remove him; and not only that, he attempted to persuade a number of the passengers to protest against your presence in the dining-saloon." The big man at my side took a long draw from his cigar, threw his head back and slowly blew a great cloud of smoke toward the ceiling. Then turning to me he said, "Do you know, I don't object to anyone having prejudices so long as those prejudices don't interfere with my personal liberty. Now, the man you are speaking of had a perfect right to change his seat if I in any way interfered with his appetite or his digestion. I would have no reason to complain if he removed to the farthest corner of the saloon, or even if he got off the ship; but when his prejudice attempts to move *me* one foot, one inch, out of the place where I am comfortably located, then I object." On the word "object" he brought his great fist down on the table in front of us with such a crash that everyone in the room turned to look. We both covered up the slight embarrassment with a laugh, and strolled out on the deck.

Notes

[68] *Liverpool* seaport in northern England.

We walked the deck for an hour or more, discussing different phases of the Negro question. I, in referring to the race, used the personal pronoun "we"; my companion made no comment about it, nor evinced any surprise, except to slightly raise his eyebrows the first time he caught the significance of the word. He was the broadest-minded colored man I have ever talked with on the Negro question. He even went so far as to sympathize with and offer excuses for some white Southern points of view. I asked him what were his main reasons for being so hopeful. He replied, "In spite of all that is written, said and done, this great, big, incontrovertible fact stands out – the Negro is progressing, and that disproves all the arguments in the world that he is incapable of progress. I was born in slavery, and at emancipation was set adrift a ragged, penniless bit of humanity. I have seen the Negro in every grade, and I know what I am talking about. Our detractors point to the increase of crime as evidence against us; certainly we have progressed in crime as in other things; what less could be expected? And yet, in this respect, we are far from the point which has been reached by the more highly civilized white race. As we continue to progress, crime among us will gradually lose much of its brutal, vulgar, I might say healthy, aspect, and become more delicate, refined and subtile. Then it will be less shocking and noticeable, although more dangerous to society." Then dropping his tone of irony, he continued with some show of eloquence, "But, above all, when I am discouraged and disheartened, I have this to fall back on: if there is a principle of right in the world, which finally prevails, and I believe that there is; if there is a merciful but justice-loving God in heaven, and I believe that there is, we shall win; for we have right on our side; while those who oppose us can defend themselves by nothing in the moral law, nor even by anything in the enlightened thought of the present age."

For several days, together with other topics, we discussed the race problem, not only of the United States, but the race problem as it affected native Africans and Jews. Finally, before we reached Boston, our conversation had grown familiar and personal. I had told him something of my past and much about my intentions for the future. I learned that he was a physician, a graduate of Howard University, Washington, and had done post-graduate work in Philadelphia; and this was his second trip abroad to attend professional courses. He had practiced for some years in the city of Washington, and though he did not say so, I gathered that his practice was a lucrative one. Before we left the ship he had made me promise that I would stop two or three days in Washington before going on South.

We put up at a hotel in Boston for a couple of days, and visited several of my new friend's acquaintances; they were all people of education and culture and, apparently, of means. I could not but help being struck by the great difference between them and the same class of colored people in the South. In speech and thought they were genuine Yankees. The difference was especially noticeable in their speech. There was none of that heavy-tongued enunciation which characterizes even the best educated colored people of the South. It is remarkable, after all, what an adaptable creature the Negro is. I have seen the black West India gentleman in London, and he is in speech and manners a perfect Englishman. I have seen natives of Haiti and Martinique[69] in Paris, and they are more Frenchy than a Frenchman. I have no doubt that the Negro would make a good Chinaman, with exception of the pigtail.

My stay in Washington, instead of being two or three days, was two or three weeks. This was my first visit to the National Capital, and I was, of course, interested in seeing

Notes

[69] *Haiti and Martinique* French Caribbean colonies.

the public buildings and something of the working of the government; but most of my time I spent with the doctor among his friends and acquaintances. The social phase of life among colored people, which I spoke of in an earlier chapter, is more developed in Washington than in any other city in the country. This is on account of the large number of individuals earning good salaries and having a reasonable amount of leisure time to be drawn from. There are dozens of physicians and lawyers, scores of school teachers and hundreds of clerks in the departments. As to the colored department clerks, I think it fair to say that in educational equipment they average above the white clerks of the same grade; for, whereas a colored college graduate will seek such a job, the white university man goes into one of the many higher vocations which are open to him.

In a previous chapter I spoke of social life among colored people; so there is no need to take it up again here. But there is one thing I did not mention: among Negroes themselves there is the peculiar inconsistency of a color question. Its existence is rarely admitted and hardly ever mentioned; it may not be too strong a statement to say that the greater portion of the race is unconscious of its influence; yet this influence, though silent, is constant. It is evidenced most plainly in marriage selection; thus the black men generally marry women fairer than themselves; while, on the other hand, the dark women of stronger mental endowment are very often married to light-complexioned men; the effect is a tendency toward lighter complexions, especially among the more active elements in the race. Some might claim that this is a tacit admission of colored people among themselves of their own inferiority judged by the color line. I do not think so. What I have termed an inconsistency is, after all, most natural; it is, in fact, a tendency in accordance with what might be called an economic necessity. So far as racial differences go, the United States puts a greater premium on color, or better, lack of color, than upon anything else in the world. To paraphrase, "Have a white skin, and all things else may be added unto you."[70] I have seen advertisements in newspapers for waiters, bell boys or elevator men, which read, "Light colored man wanted," It is this tremendous pressure which the sentiment of the country exerts that is operating on the race. There is involved not only the question of higher opportunity, but often the question of earning a livelihood; and so I say it is not strange, but a natural tendency. Nor is it any more a sacrifice of self-respect that a black man should give to his children every advantage he can which complexion of the skin carries, than that the new or vulgar rich should purchase for their children the advantages which ancestry, aristocracy, and social position carry. I once heard a colored man sum it up in these words, "It's no disgrace to be black, but it's often very inconvenient."

Washington shows the Negro not only at his best, but also at his worst. As I drove around with the doctor, he commented rather harshly on those of the latter class which we saw. He remarked: "You see those lazy, loafing, good-for-nothing darkies, they're not worth digging graves for; yet they are the ones who create impressions of the race for the casual observer. It's because they are always in evidence on the street corners, while the rest of us are hard at work, and you know a dozen loafing darkies make a bigger crowd and a worse impression in this country than fifty white men of the same class. But they ought not to represent the race. We are the race, and the race ought to be judged by us, not by them. Every race and every nation is judged by the best it has been able to produce, not by the worst."

Notes

[70] *"Have a white skin ... you"* Luke 12:31; "Seek ye the kingdom of God; and all these things will be added unto you."

The recollection of my stay in Washington is a pleasure to me now. In company with the doctor I visited Howard University, the public schools, the excellent colored hospital, with which he was in some way connected, if I remember correctly, and many comfortable and even elegant homes. It was with some reluctance that I continued my journey south. The doctor was very kind in giving me letters to people in Richmond and Nashville when I told him that I intended to stop in both of these cities. In Richmond a man who was then editing a very creditable colored newspaper, gave me a great deal of his time, and made my stay there of three or four days very pleasant. In Nashville I spent a whole day at Fisk University, the home of the "Jubilee Singers," and was more than repaid for my time. Among my letters of introduction was one to a very prosperous physician. He drove me about the city and introduced me to a number of people. From Nashville I went to Atlanta, where I stayed long enough to gratify an old desire to see Atlanta University again. I then continued my journey to Macon.

During the trip from Nashville to Atlanta I went into the smoking compartment of the car to smoke a cigar. I was traveling in a Pullman, not because of an abundance of funds, but because through my experience with my "millionaire," a certain amount of comfort and luxury had become a necessity to me whenever it was obtainable. When I entered the car I found only a couple of men there; but in a half hour there were half a dozen or more. From the general conversation I learned that a fat Jewish-looking man was a cigar manufacturer, and was experimenting in growing Havana tobacco in Florida; that a slender bespectacled young man was from Ohio and a professor in some State institution in Alabama; that a white-mustached, well-dressed man was an old Union soldier who had fought through the Civil War; and that a tall, raw-boned, red-faced man, who seemed bent on leaving nobody in ignorance of the fact that he was from Texas, was a cotton planter.

In the North men may ride together for hours in a "smoker" and unless they are acquainted with each other never exchange a word; in the South, men thrown together in such manner are friends in fifteen minutes. There is always present a warm-hearted cordiality which will melt down the most frigid reserve. It may be because Southerners are very much like Frenchmen in that they must talk; and not only must they talk, but they must express their opinions.

The talk in the car was for a while miscellaneous – on the weather, crops, business prospects – the old Union soldier had invested capital in Atlanta, and he predicted that that city would soon be one of the greatest in the country – finally the conversation drifted to politics; then, as a natural sequence, turned upon the Negro question.

In the discussion of the race question, the diplomacy of the Jew was something to be admired; he had the faculty of agreeing with everybody without losing his allegiance to any side. He knew that to sanction Negro oppression would be to sanction Jewish oppression, and would expose him to a shot along that line from the old soldier, who stood firmly on the ground of equal rights and opportunity to all men; yet long traditions and business instincts told him, when in Rome to act as a Roman. Altogether his position was a delicate one, and I gave him credit for the skill he displayed in maintaining it. The young professor was apologetic. He had had the same views as the G.A.R.[71] man; but a year in the South had opened his eyes, and he had to confess that the problem could hardly be handled any better than it was being handled by the Southern whites. To which the G.A.R. man responded somewhat rudely that he had spent ten times as many years in the South as his young friend, and that he could easily

Notes

[71] *G.A.R.* Grand Army of the Republic.

understand how holding a position in a State institution in Alabama would bring about a change of views. The professor turned very red and had very little more to say. The Texan was fierce, eloquent and profane in his argument and, in a lower sense, there was a direct logic in what he said, which was convincing; it was only by taking higher ground, by dealing in what Southerners call "theories," that he could be combatted. Occasionally some one of the several other men in the "smoker" would throw in a remark to reinforce what he said, but he really didn't need any help; he was sufficient in himself.

In the course of a short time the controversy narrowed itself down to an argument between the old soldier and the Texan. The latter maintained hotly that the Civil War was a criminal mistake on the part of the North, and that the humiliation which the South suffered during Reconstruction could never be forgotten. The Union man retorted just as hotly that the South was responsible for the war, and that the spirit of unforgetfulness on its part was the greatest cause of present friction; that it seemed to be the one great aim of the South to convince the North that the latter made a mistake in fighting to preserve the Union and liberate the slaves. "Can you imagine," he went on to say, "what would have been the condition of things eventually if there had been no war, and the South had been allowed to follow its course? Instead of one great, prosperous country with nothing before it but the conquests of peace, a score of petty republics, as in Central and South America, wasting their energies in war with each other or in revolutions."

"Well," replied the Texan, "anything – no country at all is better than having niggers over you. But anyhow, the war was fought and the niggers were freed; for it's no use beating around the bush, the niggers, and not the Union, was the cause of it; and now do you believe that all the niggers on earth are worth the good white blood that was spilt? You freed the nigger and you gave him the ballot, but you couldn't make a citizen out of him. He don't know what he's voting for, and we buy 'em like so many hogs. You're giving 'em education, but that only makes slick rascals out of 'em."

"Don't fancy for a moment," said the Northern man, "that you have any monopoly in buying ignorant votes. The same thing is done on a larger scale in New York and Boston, and in Chicago and San Francisco; and they are not black votes either. As to education making the Negro worse, you had just as well tell me that religion does the same thing. And, by the way, how many educated colored men do you know personally?"

The Texan admitted that he knew only one, and added that he was in the penitentiary. "But," he said, "do you mean to claim, ballot or no ballot, education or no education, that niggers are the equals of white men?"

"That's not the question," answered the other, "but if the Negro is so distinctly inferior, it is a strange thing to me that it takes such tremendous effort on the part of the white man to make him realize it, and to keep him in the same place into which inferior men naturally fall. However, let us grant for sake of argument that the Negro is inferior in every respect to the white man; that fact only increases our moral responsibility in regard to our actions toward him. Inequalities of numbers, wealth and power, even of intelligence and morals, should make no difference in the essential rights of men."

"If he's inferior and weaker, and is shoved to the wall, that's his own lookout," said the Texan. "That's the law of nature; and he's bound to go to the wall; for no race in the world has ever been able to stand competition with the Anglo-Saxon. The Anglo-Saxon race has always been and always will be the masters of the world, and the niggers in the South ain't going to change all the records of history."

"My friend," said the old soldier slowly, "if you have studied history, will you tell me, as confidentially between white men, what the Anglo-Saxon has ever done?"

The Texan was too much astonished by the question to venture any reply.

His opponent continued, "Can you name a single one of the great fundamental and original intellectual achievements which have raised man in the scale of civilization that may be credited to the Anglo-Saxon? The art of letters, of poetry, of music, of sculpture, of painting, of the drama, of architecture; the science of mathematics, of astronomy, of philosophy, of logic, of physics, of chemistry, the use of the metals and the principles of mechanics, were all invented or discovered by darker and what we now call inferior races and nations. We have carried many of these to their highest point of perfection, but the foundation was laid by others. Do you know the only original contribution to civilization we can claim is what we have done in steam and electricity and in making implements of war more deadly; and there we worked largely on principles which we did not discover. Why, we didn't even originate the religion we use. We are a great race, the greatest in the world to-day, but we ought to remember that we are standing on a pile of past races, and enjoy our position with a little less show of arrogance. We are simply having our turn at the game, and we were a long time getting to it. After all, racial supremacy is merely a matter of dates in history. The man here who belongs to what is, all in all, the greatest race the world ever produced, is almost ashamed to own it. If the Anglo-Saxon is the source of everything good and great in the human race from the beginning, why wasn't the German forest the birthplace of civilization?"

The Texan was somewhat disconcerted, for the argument had passed a little beyond his limits, but he swung it back to where he was sure of his ground by saying, "All that may be true, but it hasn't got much to do with us and the niggers here in the South. We've got 'em here, and we've got 'em to live with, and it's a question of white man or nigger, no middle ground. You want us to treat niggers as equals. Do you want to see 'em sitting around in our parlors? Do you want to see a mulatto South? To bring it right home to you, would you let your daughter marry a nigger?"

"No, I wouldn't consent to my daughter's marrying a nigger, but that doesn't prevent my treating a black man fairly. And I don't see what fair treatment has to do with niggers sitting around in your parlors; they can't come there unless they're invited. Out of all the white men I know, only a hundred or so have the privilege of sitting around in my parlor. As to the mulatto South, if you Southerners have one boast that is stronger than another, it is your women; you put them on a pinnacle of purity and virtue and bow down in a chivalric worship before them; yet you talk and act as though, should you treat the Negro fairly and take the anti-intermarriage laws off your statute books, these same women would rush into the arms of black lovers and husbands. It's a wonder to me that they don't rise up and resent the insult."

"Colonel," said the Texan, as he reached into his handbag and brought out a large flask of whiskey, "you might argue from now until hell freezes over, and you might convince me that you're right, but you'll never convince me that I'm wrong. All you say sounds very good, but it's got nothing to do with facts. You can say what men ought to be, but they ain't that; so there you are. Down here in the South we're up against facts, and we're meeting 'em like facts. We don't believe the nigger is or ever will be the equal of the white man, and we ain't going to treat him as an equal; I'll be damned if we will. Have a drink." Everybody, except the professor, partook of the generous Texan's flask, and the argument closed in a general laugh and good feeling.

I went back into the main part of the car with the conversation on my mind. Here I had before me the bald, raw, naked aspects of the race question in the South; and, in consideration of the step I was just taking, it was far from encouraging. The sentiments of the Texan – and he expressed the sentiments of the South – fell upon me like a chill. I was sick at heart. Yet, I must confess that underneath it all I felt a certain sort of admiration for the man who could not be swayed from what he held as his principles. Contrasted with him, the young Ohio professor was indeed a pitiable character. And all along, in spite of myself, I have been compelled to accord the same kind of admiration to the Southern white man for the manner in which he defends not only his virtues but his vices. He knows, that judged by a high standard, he is narrow and prejudiced, that he is guilty of unfairness, oppression and cruelty, but this he defends as stoutly as he would his better qualities. This same spirit obtains in a great degree among the blacks; they, too, defend their faults and failings. This spirit carries them so far at times as to make them sympathizers with members of their race who are perpetrators of crime. And, yet, among themselves they are their own most merciless critics. I have never heard the race so terribly arraigned as I have by colored speakers to strictly colored audiences. It is the spirit of the South to defend everything belonging to it. The North is too cosmopolitan and tolerant for such a spirit. If you should say to an Easterner that Paris is a gayer city than New York he would be likely to agree with you, or at least to let you have your way; but to suggest to a South Carolinian that Boston is a nicer city to live in than Charleston would be to stir his greatest depths of argument and eloquence.

But, to-day, as I think over that smoking-car argument, I can see it in a different light. The Texan's position does not render things so hopeless, for it indicates that the main difficulty of the race question does not lie so much in the actual condition of the blacks as it does in the mental attitude of the whites; and a mental attitude, especially one not based on truth, can be changed more easily than actual conditions. That is to say, the burden of the question is not that the whites are struggling to save ten million despondent and moribund people from sinking into a hopeless slough of ignorance, poverty and barbarity in their very midst, but that they are unwilling to open certain doors of opportunity and to accord certain treatment to ten million aspiring, education-and-property-acquiring people. In a word, the difficulty of the problem is not so much due to the facts presented, as to the hypothesis assumed for its solution. In this it is similar to the problem of the Solar System. By a complex, confusing and almost contradictory mathematical process, by the use of zigzags instead of straight lines, the earth can be proven to be the center of things celestial; but by an operation so simple that it can be comprehended by a schoolboy, its position can be verified among the other worlds which revolve about the sun, and its movements harmonized with the laws of the universe. So, when the white race assumes as a hypothesis that it is the main object of creation, and that all things else are merely subsidiary to its wellbeing, sophism, subterfuge, perversion of conscience, arrogance, injustice, oppression, cruelty, sacrifice of human blood, all are required to maintain the position, and its dealings with other races become indeed a problem, a problem which, if based on a hypothesis of common humanity, could be solved by the simple rules of justice.

When I reached Macon I decided to leave my trunk and all my surplus belongings, to pack my bag, and strike out into the interior. This I did; and by train, by mule and ox-cart, I traveled through many counties. This was my first real experience among rural colored people, and all that I saw was interesting to me; but there was a great deal which does not require description at my hands; for log cabins and plantations and dialect-speaking darkies are perhaps better known in American literature than any other single picture of our national life. Indeed, they form an ideal and exclusive literary concept of the American Negro to such an extent that it is almost impossible to get the reading public to recognize him in any other setting; but I shall endeavor to avoid giving the reader any already overworked and hackneyed descriptions. This generally accepted literary ideal of the American Negro constitutes what is really an obstacle in the way of the thoughtful and progressive element of the race. His character has been established as a happy-go-lucky, laughing, shuffling, banjo-picking being, and the reading public has not yet been prevailed upon to take him seriously. His efforts to elevate himself socially are looked upon as a sort of absurd caricature of "white civilization." A novel dealing with colored people who lived in respectable homes and amidst a fair degree of culture and who naturally acted "just like white folks" would be taken in a comic opera sense. In this respect the Negro is much in the position of a great comedian who gives up the lighter rôles to play tragedy. No matter how well he may portray the deeper passions, the public is loath to give him up in his old character; they even conspire to make him a failure in serious work, in order to force him back into comedy. In the same respect, the public is not too much to be blamed, for great comedians are far more scarce than mediocre tragedians; every amateur actor is a tragedian. However, this very fact constitutes the opportunity of the future Negro novelist and poet to give the country something new and unknown, in depicting the life, the ambitions, the struggles and the passions of those of their race who are striving to break the narrow limits of traditions. A beginning has already been made in that remarkable book by Dr. Du Bois, "The Souls of Black Folk."[72]

Much, too, that I saw while on this trip, in spite of my enthusiasm, was disheartening. Often I thought of what my "millionaire" had said to me, and wished myself back in Europe. The houses in which I had to stay were generally uncomfortable, sometimes worse. I often had to sleep in a division or compartment with several other people. Once or twice I was not so fortunate as to find divisions; everybody slept on pallets on the floor. Frequently I was able to lie down and contemplate the stars which were in their zenith. The food was at times so distasteful and poorly cooked that I could not eat it. I remember that once I lived for a week or more on buttermilk, on account of not being able to stomach the fat bacon, the rank turnip tops and the heavy damp mixture of meal, salt and water, which was called corn bread. It was only my ambition to do the work which I had planned that kept me steadfast to my purpose. Occasionally I would meet with some signs of progress and uplift in even one of these backwood settlements – houses built of boards, with windows, and divided into rooms, decent food and a fair standard of living. This condition was due to the fact that there was in the community some exceptionally capable Negro farmer whose thrift served as an example. As I went about among these dull, simple people, the great majority of them hard working; in their relations with the whites, submissive, faithful, and often affectionate, negatively content with their lot, and contrasted them with those of the race who had been quickened by the forces of thought, I could not but appreciate the logic of the position held by those Southern leaders who have been bold enough to proclaim against the education of the Negro. They are consistent in their public speech with Southern sentiment and desires. Those public men of the South who have not been daring or heedless enough to defy the ideals of twentieth century civilization and of modern humanitarianism and philanthropy, find themselves in the embarrassing situation of preaching one thing and praying for another. They are in the position of the fashionable woman who is compelled by the laws of polite society to say to her dearest enemy, "How happy I am to see you."

And yet in this respect how perplexing is Southern character; for in opposition to the above, it may be said that the claim of the Southern whites that they love the Negro better than the Northern whites do, is in a manner true. Northern white people

Notes

[72] *The Souls of Black Folk* 1903 seminal essay collection by W.E.B. Du Bois.

love the Negro in a sort of abstract way, as a race; through a sense of justice, charity and philanthropy, they will liberally assist in his elevation. A number of them have heroically spent their lives in this effort (and just here I wish to say that when the colored people reach the monument building stage, they should not forget the men and women who went South after the war and founded schools for them). Yet, generally speaking, they have no particular liking for individuals of the race. Southern white people despise the Negro as a race, and will do nothing to aid in his elevation as such; but for certain individuals they have a strong affection, and are helpful to them in many ways. With these individual members of the race they live on terms of the greatest intimacy; they intrust to them their children, their family treasures and their family secrets; in trouble they often go to them for comfort and counsel: in sickness they often rely upon their care. This affectionate relation between the Southern whites and those blacks who come into close touch with them has not been overdrawn even in fiction.

This perplexity of Southern character extends even to the mixture of the races. That is spoken of as though it were dreaded worse than smallpox, leprosy or the plague. Yet, when I was in Jacksonville I knew several prominent families there with large colored branches, which went by the same name and were known and acknowledged as blood relatives. And what is more, there seemed to exist between these black brothers and sisters and uncles and aunts a decided friendly feeling.

I said above that Southern whites would do nothing for the Negro as a race. I know the South claims that it has spent millions for the education of the blacks, and that it has of its own free will shouldered this awful burden. It seems to be forgetful of the fact that these millions have been taken from the public tax funds for education, and that the law of political economy which recognizes the land owner as the one who really pays the taxes is not tenable. It would be just as reasonable for the relatively few landowners of Manhattan to complain that they had to stand the financial burden of the education of the thousands and thousands of children whose parents pay rent for tenements and flats. Let the millions of producing and consuming Negroes be taken out of the South, and it would be quickly seen how much less of public funds there would be to appropriate for education or any other purpose.

In thus traveling about through the country, I was sometimes amused on arriving at some little railroad-station town to be taken for and treated as a white man, and six hours later, when it was learned that I was stopping at the house of the colored preacher or school teacher, to note the attitude of the whole town change. At times this led even to embarrassment. Yet it cannot be so embarrassing for a colored man to be taken for white as for a white man to be taken for colored; and I have heard of several cases of the latter kind.

All this while I was gathering material for work, jotting down in my note-book themes and melodies, and trying to catch the spirit of the Negro in his relatively primitive state. I began to feel the necessity of hurrying so that I might get back to some city like Nashville to begin my compositions, and at the same time earn at least a living by teaching and performing before my funds gave out. At the last settlement in which I stopped I found a mine of material. This was due to the fact that "big meeting" was in progress. "Big meeting" is an institution something like camp-meeting; the difference being that it is held in a permanent church, and not in a temporary structure. All the churches of some one denomination – of course, either Methodist or Baptist – in a county or, perhaps, in several adjoining counties, are closed, and the congregations unite at some centrally located church for a series of meetings lasting a week. It is really a social as well as a religious function. The people come in great numbers, making the trip, according to their financial status, in buggies drawn by sleek, fleet-footed mules, in ox-teams, or on foot. It was amusing to see some of the latter class trudging down the hot and dusty road with their shoes, which were brand new, strung across their shoulders. When they got near the church they sat on the side of the road and, with many grimaces, tenderly packed their feet into those instruments of torture. This furnished, indeed, a trying test of their religion. The famous preachers come from near and far, and take turns in warning sinners of the day of wrath. Food, in the form of those two Southern luxuries, fried chicken and roast pork, is plentiful, and no one need go hungry. On the opening Sunday the women are immaculate in starched stiff white dresses adorned with ribbons either red or blue. Even a great many of the men wear streamers of vari-colored ribbons in the button-holes of their coats. A few of them carefully cultivate a forelock of hair by wrapping it in twine, and on such festive occasions decorate it with a narrow ribbon streamer. Big meetings afford a fine opportunity to the younger people to meet each other dressed in their Sunday clothes, and much rustic courting, which is as enjoyable as any other kind, is indulged in.

This big meeting which I was lucky enough to catch was particularly well attended; the extra large attendance was due principally to two attractions, a man by name of John Brown, who was renowned as the most powerful preacher for miles around; and a wonderful leader of singing, who was known as "Singing Johnson." These two men were a study and a revelation to me. They caused me to reflect upon how great an influence their types have been in the development of the Negro in America. Both these types are now looked upon generally with condescension or contempt by the progressive element among the colored people; but it should never be forgotten that it was they who led the race from paganism, and kept it steadfast to Christianity through all the long, dark years of slavery.

John Brown was a jet black man of medium size, with a strikingly intelligent head and face, and a voice like an organ peal. He preached each night after several lesser lights successively held the pulpit during an hour or so. As far as subject matter is concerned, all of the sermons were alike; each began with the fall of man, ran through various trials and tribulations of the Hebrew children, on to the redemption by Christ, and ended with a fervid picture of the judgment day and the fate of the damned. But John Brown possessed magnetism and an imagination so free and daring that he was able to carry through what the other preachers would not attempt. He knew all the arts and tricks of oratory, the modulation of the voice to almost a whisper, the pause for effect, the rise through light, rapid-fire sentences to the terrific, thundering outburst of an electrifying climax. In addition, he had the intuition of a born theatrical manager. Night after night this man held me fascinated. He convinced me that, after all, eloquence consists more in the manner of saying than in what is said. It is largely a matter of tone pictures.

The most striking example of John Brown's magnetism and imagination was his "heavenly march"; I shall never forget how it impressed me when I heard it. He opened his sermon in the usual way; then proclaiming to his listeners that he was going to take them on the heavenly march, he seized the Bible under his arm and began to pace up and down the pulpit platform. The congregation immediately began with their feet a tramp, tramp, tramp, in time with the preacher's march in the pulpit, all the while singing in an undertone a hymn about marching to Zion. Suddenly he cried, "Halt!" Every foot stopped with the precision of a company of well drilled soldiers, and the singing ceased. The morning star had been reached. Here the preacher described the beauties of that celestial body. Then the march, the tramp, tramp, tramp, and the singing was again taken up. Another "Halt!" They had reached the evening star. And so on, past the sun and the moon – the intensity of religious emotion all the time increasing – along the Milky Way,[73] on up to the gates of heaven. Here the halt was longer, and the preacher described at length the gates and walls of the New Jerusalem. Then he took his hearers through the pearly gates, along the golden streets, pointing out the glories of the City, pausing occasionally to greet some patriarchal members of the church, well known to most of his listeners in life, who had had "the tears wiped from their eyes, were clad in robes of spotless white, with crowns of gold upon their heads and harps within their hands," and ended his march before the great white throne. To the reader this may sound ridiculous, but listened to under the circumstances, it was highly and effectively dramatic. I was a more or less sophisticated and non-religious man of the world, but the torrent of the preacher's words, moving with the rhythm and glowing with the eloquence of primitive poetry, swept me along, and I, too, felt like joining in the shouts of "Amen! Hallelujah!"

John Brown's powers in describing the delights of heaven were no greater than those in depicting the horrors of hell. I saw great, strapping fellows, trembling and weeping like children at the "mourners' bench." His warnings to sinners were truly terrible. I shall never forget one expression that he used, which for originality and aptness could not be excelled. In my opinion, it is more graphic and, for us, far more expressive than St. Paul's "It is hard to kick against the pricks."[74] He struck the attitude of a pugilist and thundered out, "Young man, yo' arm's too short to box wid God!"

As interesting as was John Brown to me, the other man, "Singing Johnson," was more so. He was a small, dark-brown, one-eyed man, with a clear, strong, high-pitched voice, a leader of singing, a maker of songs, a man who could improvise at the moment lines to fit the occasion. Not so striking a figure as John Brown, but, at "big meetings,' equally important. It is indispensable to the success of the singing, when the congregation is a large one made up of people from different communities, to have someone with a strong voice who knows just what hymn to sing and when to sing it, who can pitch it in the right key, and who has all the leading lines committed to memory. Sometimes it devolves upon the leader to "sing down" a long-winded, or uninteresting speaker. Committing to memory the leading lines of all the Negro spiritual songs is no easy task, for they run up into the hundreds. But the accomplished leader must know them all, because the congregation sings only the refrains and repeats; every ear in the church is fixed upon him, and if he becomes mixed in his lines or forgets them, the responsibility falls directly on his shoulders.

For example, most of these hymns are constructed to be sung in the following manner:

Leader – "Swing low, sweet chariot."
Congregation – "Coming for to carry me home."
Leader – "Swing low, sweet chariot."
Congregation – "Coming for to carry me home."
Leader – "I look over yonder, what do I see?"
Congregation – "Coming for to carry me home."
Leader – "Two little angels coming after me."
Congregation – "Coming for to carry me home."
– etc., etc., etc.

Notes

[73] *Original reads*: milky way [ed.].

[74] *"kick against the pricks"* Acts 9:5.

The solitary and plaintive voice of the leader is answered by a sound like the roll of the sea, producing a most curious effect.

In only a few of these songs do the leader and the congregation start off together. Such a song is the well-known "Steal away to Jesus."

The leader and the congregation begin:

"Steal away, steal away,
Steal away to Jesus;
Steal away, steal away home,
I ain't got long to stay here."

Then the leader alone:

"My Lord he calls me,
He calls me by the thunder,
The trumpet sounds within-a my soul."

Then all together:

"I ain't got long to stay here."

The leader and the congregation again take up the opening refrain; then the leader sings three more leading lines alone, and so on almost ad infinitum. It will be seen that even here most of the work falls upon the leader, for the congregation sings the same lines over and over, while his memory and ingenuity are taxed to keep the songs going.

Generally, the parts taken up by the congregation are sung in a three-part harmony, the women singing the soprano and a transposed tenor, the men with high voices singing the melody, and those with low voices, a thundering bass. In a few of these songs, however, the leading part is sung in unison by the whole congregation, down to the last line, which is harmonized. The effect of this is intensely thrilling. Such a hymn is "Go down Moses." It stirs the heart like a trumpet call.

"Singing Johnson" was an ideal leader; and his services were in great demand. He spent his time going about the country from one church to another. He received his support in much the same way as the preachers – part of a collection, food and lodging. All of his leisure time he devoted to originating new words and melodies and new lines for old songs. He always sang with his eyes – or to be more exact – his eye closed, indicating the tempo by swinging his head to and fro. He was a great judge of the proper hymn to sing at a particular moment; and I noticed several times, when the preacher reached a certain climax, or expressed a certain sentiment, that Johnson broke in with a line or two of some appropriate hymn. The speaker understood, and would pause until the singing ceased.

As I listened to the singing of these songs, the wonder of their production grew upon me more and more. How did the men who originated them manage to do it? The sentiments are easily accounted for; they are mostly taken from the Bible; but the melodies, where did they come from? Some of them so weirdly sweet, and others so wonderfully strong. Take, for instance, "Go down Moses." I doubt that there is a stronger theme in the whole musical literature of the world. And so many of these songs contain more than mere melody; there is sounded in them that elusive undertone, the note in music which is not heard with the ears. I sat often with the tears rolling down my cheeks and my heart melted within me. Any musical person who has never heard a Negro congregation under the spell of religious fervor sing these old songs, has missed one of the most thrilling emotions which the human heart may experience. Anyone who can listen to Negroes sing, "Nobody knows de trouble I see, Nobody knows but Jesus," without shedding tears, must indeed have a heart of stone.

As yet, the Negroes themselves do not fully appreciate these old slave songs. The educated classes are rather ashamed of them, and prefer to sing hymns from books. This feeling is natural; they are still too close to the conditions under which the songs were produced; but the day will come when this slave music will be the most treasured heritage of the American Negro.

At the close of the "big meeting" I left the settlement where it was being held, full of enthusiasm. I was in that frame of mind which, in the artistic temperament, amounts to inspiration. I was now ready and anxious to get to some place where I might settle down to work, and give expression the ideas which were teeming in my head; but I strayed into another deviation from my path of life as I had it marked out, which led me into an entirely different road. Instead of going to the nearest and most convenient railroad station, I accepted the invitation of a young man who had been present the closing Sunday at the meeting, to drive with him some miles farther to the town in which he taught school, and there take the train. My conversation with this young man as we drove along through the country was extremely interesting. He had been a student in one of the Negro colleges – strange coincidence, in the very college, as I learned through him, in which "Shiny" was now a professor. I was, of course, curious to hear about my boyhood friend; and had it not been vacation time, and that I was not sure that I would find him, I should have gone out of my way to pay him a visit; but I determined to write to him as soon as the school opened. My companion talked to me about his work among the people, of his hopes and his discouragements. He was tremendously in earnest; I might say, too much so. In fact, it may be said that the majority of intelligent colored people are, in some degree, too much in earnest over the race question. They assume and carry so much that their progress is at times impeded, and they are unable to see things in their proper proportions. In many instances, a slight exercise of the sense of humor would save much anxiety of soul. Anyone who marks the general tone of editorials in colored newspapers is apt to be impressed with this idea. If the mass of Negroes took their present and future as seriously as do the most of their leaders, the race would be in no mental condition to sustain the terrible pressure which it undergoes; it would sink of its own weight. Yet, it must be acknowledged that in the making of a race over-seriousness is a far lesser failing than its reverse, and even the faults resulting from it lean toward the right.

We drove into the town just before dark. As we passed a large, unpainted church, my companion pointed it out as the place where he held his school. I promised that I would go there with him the next morning and stay a while. The town was of that kind which hardly requires or deserves description; a straggling line of brick and wooden stores on one side of the railroad track and some cottages of various sizes on the other side constituted about the whole of it. The young school teacher boarded at the best house in the place owned by a colored man. It was painted, had glass windows, contained "store bought" furniture, an organ, and lamps with chimneys. The owner held a job of some kind on the railroad. After supper it was not long before everybody was sleepy. I occupied the room with the school teacher. In a few minutes after we got into the room he was in bed and asleep; but I took advantage of the unusual luxury of a lamp which gave light, and sat looking over my notes and jotting down some ideas which were still fresh in my mind. Suddenly I became conscious of that sense of alarm which is always aroused by the sound of hurrying footsteps on the silence of the night. I stopped work, and looked at my watch. It was after eleven. I listened, straining every nerve to hear above the tumult of my quickening pulse. I caught the murmur of voices, then the gallop of a horse, then of another and another. Now thoroughly alarmed, I woke my companion, and together we both listened. After a moment he put out the light, softly opened the window-blind, and we cautiously peeped out. We saw men moving in one direction, and from the mutterings we vaguely caught the rumor that some terrible crime had been committed, murder! rape! I put on my coat and hat. My friend did all in his power to dissuade me from venturing out; but it was impossible for me to remain in the house under such tense excitement. My nerves would not have stood it. Perhaps what bravery I exercised in going out was due to the fact that I felt sure my identity as a colored man had not yet become known in the town.

I went out, and, following the drift, reached the railroad station. There was gathered there a crowd of men, all white, and others were steadily arriving, seemingly from all the surrounding country. How did the news spread so quickly? I watched these men moving under the yellow glare of the kerosene lamps about the station, stern, comparatively silent, all of them armed, some of them in boots and spurs; fierce, determined men. I had come to know the type well, blond, tall and lean, with ragged mustache and beard, and glittering gray eyes. At the first suggestion of daylight they began to disperse in groups, going in several directions. There was no extra noise or excitement, no loud talking, only swift, sharp words of command given by those who seemed to be accepted as leaders by mutual understanding. In fact, the impression made upon me was that everything was being done in quite an orderly manner. In spite of so many leaving, the crowd around the station continued to grow; at sunrise there were a great many women and children. By this time I also noticed some colored people; a few seemed to be going about customary tasks, several were standing on the outskirts of the crowd; but the gathering of Negroes usually seen in such towns was missing.

Before noon they brought him in. Two horsemen rode abreast; between them, half dragged, the poor wretch made his way through the dust. His hands were tied behind him, and ropes around his body were fastened to the saddle horns of his double guard. The men who at midnight had been stern and silent were now emitting that terror-instilling sound known as the "rebel yell." A space was quickly cleared in the crowd, and a rope placed about his neck; when from somewhere came the suggestion, "Burn him!" It ran like an electric current. Have you ever witnessed the transformation of human beings into savage beasts? Nothing can be more terrible. A railroad tie was sunk into the ground, the rope was removed and a chain brought and securely coiled around the victim and the stake. There he stood, a man only in form and stature, every sign of degeneracy stamped upon his countenance. His eyes were dull and vacant, indicating not a single ray of thought. Evidently the realization of his fearful fate had robbed him of whatever reasoning power he had ever possessed. He was too stunned and stupefied even to tremble. Fuel was brought from everywhere, oil, the torch; the flames crouched for an instant as though to gather strength, then leaped up as high as their victim's head. He squirmed, he writhed, strained at his chains, then gave out cries and groans that I shall always hear. The cries and groans were choked off by the fire and smoke; but his eyes bulging from their sockets, rolled from side to side, appealing in vain for help. Some of the crowd yelled and cheered, others seemed appalled at what they had done, and there were those who turned away sickened at the sight. I was fixed to the spot where I stood, powerless to take my eyes from what I did not want to see.

It was over before I realized that time had elapsed. Before I could make myself believe that what I saw was really happening, I was looking at a scorched post, a smoldering fire, blackened bones, charred fragments sifting down through coils of chain, and the smell of burnt flesh – human flesh – was in my nostrils.

I walked a short distance away, and sat down in order to clear my dazed mind. A great wave of humiliation and shame swept over me. Shame that I belonged to a race that could be so dealt with; and shame for my country, that it, the great example of democracy to the world, should be the only civilized, if not the only state on earth, where a human being would be burned alive. My heart turned bitter within me. I could understand why Negroes are led to sympathize with even their worst criminals, and to protect them when possible. By all the impulses of normal human nature they can and should do nothing less.

Whenever I hear protests from the South that it should be left alone to deal with the Negro question, my thoughts go back to that scene of brutality and savagery. I do not see how a people that can find in its conscience any excuse whatever for slowly burning to death a human being, or to tolerate such an act, can be entrusted with the salvation of a race. Of course, there are in the South men of liberal thought who do not approve of lynching;[75] but I wonder how long they will endure the limits which are placed upon free speech. They still cower and tremble before "Southern opinion." Even so late as the recent Atlanta riot,[76] those men who were brave enough to speak a word in behalf of justice and humanity felt called upon, by way of apology, to preface what they said with a glowing rhetorical tribute to the Anglo-Saxon's superiority, and to refer to the "great and impassable gulf" between the races "fixed by the Creator at the foundation of the world." The question of the relative qualities of the two races is still an open one. The reference to the "great gulf" loses force in face of the fact that there are in this country perhaps three or four million people with the blood of both races in their veins; but I fail to see the pertinency of either statement, subsequent to the beating and murdering of scores of innocent people in the streets of a civilized and Christian city.

The Southern whites are in many respects a great people. Looked at from a certain point of view, they are picturesque. If one will put himself in a romantic frame of mind, he can admire their notions of chivalry and bravery and justice. In this same frame of mind an intelligent man can go to the theater and applaud the impossible hero, who with his single sword slays everybody in the play except the equally impossible heroine. So can an ordinary peace-loving citizen sit by a comfortable fire and read with enjoyment of the bloody deeds of pirates and the fierce brutality of Vikings. This is the way in which we gratify the old, underlying animal instincts and passions; but we should shudder with horror at the mere idea of such practices being realities in this day of enlightened and humanitarianized thought. The Southern whites are not yet living quite in the present age; many of their general ideas hark back to a former century, some of them to the Dark Ages. In the light of other days, they are sometimes magnificent. To-day they are often ludicrous and cruel.

How long I sat with bitter thoughts running through my mind, I do not know; perhaps an hour or more. When I decided to get up and go back to the house I found that I could hardly stand on my feet. I was as weak as a man who had lost blood. However, I dragged myself along, with the central idea of a general plan well fixed in my mind. I did not find my school teacher friend at home, so did not see him again. I swallowed a few mouthfuls of food, packed my bag, and caught the afternoon train.

When I reached Macon, I stopped only long enough to get the main part of my luggage, and to buy a ticket for New York. All along the journey I was occupied in debating

Notes

[75] *Original reads*: approve lynching [ed.].

[76] *Atlanta riot* the Atlanta Race Riot of September 1906 resulted in the death of dozens of African Americans.

with myself the step which I had decided to take. I argued that to forsake one's race to better one's condition was no less worthy an action than to forsake one's country for the same purpose. I finally made up my mind that I would neither disclaim the black race nor claim the white race; but that I would change my name, raise a mustache, and let the world take me for what it would; that it was not necessary for me to go about with a label of inferiority pasted across my forehead. All the while, I understood that it was not discouragement, or fear, or search for a larger field of action and opportunity, that was driving me out of the Negro race. I knew that it was shame, unbearable shame. Shame at being identified with a people that could with impunity be treated worse than animals. For certainly the law would restrain and punish the malicious burning alive of animals.

So once again, I found myself gazing at the towers of New York, and wondering what future that city held in store for me.

Chapter 11

I have now reached that part of my narrative where I must be brief, and touch only lightly on important facts; therefore, the reader must make up his mind to pardon skips and jumps and meager details.

When I reached New York I was completely lost. I could not have felt more a stranger had I been suddenly dropped into Constantinople.[77] I knew not where to turn or how to strike out. I was so oppressed by a feeling of loneliness that the temptation to visit my old home in Connecticut was well-nigh irresistible. I reasoned, however, that unless I found my old music teacher, I should be, after so many years of absence, as much of a stranger there as in New York; and, furthermore, that in view of the step which I had decided to take, such a visit would be injudicious. I remembered, too, that I had some property there in the shape of a piano and a few books, but decided that it would not be worth what it might cost me to take possession.

By reason of the fact that my living expenses in the South had been very small, I still had nearly four hundred dollars of my capital left. In contemplation of this, my natural and acquired Bohemian tastes asserted themselves, and I decided to have a couple of weeks' good time before worrying seriously about the future. I went to Coney Island[78] and the other resorts, took in the pre-season shows along Broadway, and ate at first class restaurants; but I shunned the old Sixth Avenue district as though it were pest infected. My few days of pleasure made appalling inroads upon what cash I had, and caused me to see that it required a good deal of money to live in New York as I wished to live, and that I should have to find, very soon, some more or less profitable employment. I was sure that unknown, without friends or prestige, it would be useless to try to establish myself as a teacher of music; so I gave that means of earning a livelihood scarcely any consideration. And even had I considered it possible to secure pupils, as I then felt, I should have hesitated about taking up a work in which the chances for any considerable financial success are necessarily so small. I had made up my mind that since I was not going to be a Negro, I would avail myself of every possible opportunity to make a white man's success; and that, if it can be summed up in any one word, means "money."

Notes

[77] *Constantinople* present-day Istanbul, Turkey.

[78] *Coney Island* a beach and amusement park in Brooklyn, NY.

I watched the "want" columns in the newspapers and answered a number of advertisements; but in each case found the positions were such as I could not fill or did not want. I also spent several dollars for "ads" which brought me no replies. In this way I came to know the hopes and disappointments of a large and pitiable class of humanity in this great city, the people who look for work through the newspapers. After some days of this sort of experience, I concluded that the main difficulty with me was that I was not prepared for what I wanted to do. I then decided upon a course which, for an artist, showed an uncommon amount of practical sense and judgment. I made up my mind to enter a business college. I took a small room, ate at lunch counters, in order to economize, and pursued my studies with the zeal that I have always been able to put into any work upon which I set my heart. Yet, in spite of all my economy, when I had been at the school for several months, my funds gave out completely. I reached the point where I could not afford sufficient food for each day. In this plight, I was glad to get, through one of the teachers, a job as an ordinary clerk in a downtown wholesale house. I did my work faithfully, and received a raise of salary before I expected it. I even managed to save a little money out of my modest earnings. In fact, I began then to contract the money fever, which later took strong possession of me. I kept my eyes open, watching for a chance to better my condition. It finally came in the form of a position with a house which was at the time establishing a South American department. My knowledge of Spanish was, of course, the principal cause of my good luck; and it did more for me; it placed me where the other clerks were practically put out of competition with me. I was not slow in taking advantage of the opportunity to make myself indispensable to the firm.

What an interesting and absorbing game is money making! After each deposit at my savings-bank, I used to sit and figure out, all over again, my principal and interest, and make calculations on what the increase would be in such and such time. Out of this I derived a great deal of pleasure. I denied myself as much as possible in order to swell my savings. Even so much as I enjoyed smoking, I limited myself to an occasional cigar, and that was generally of a variety which in my old days at the "Club" was known as a "Henry Mud." Drinking I cut out altogether, but that was no great sacrifice.

The day on which I was able to figure up $1,000.00 marked an epoch in my life. And this was not because I had never before had money. In my gambling days and while I was with my "millionaire" I handled sums running high up into the hundreds; but they had come to me like fairy god-mother's gifts, and at a time when my conception of money was that it was made only to spend. Here, on the other hand, was a thousand dollars which I had earned by days of honest and patient work, a thousand dollars which I had carefully watched grow from the first dollar; and I experienced, in owning them, a pride and satisfaction which to me was an entirely new sensation. As my capital went over the thousand dollar mark, I was puzzled to know what to do with it, how to put it to the most advantageous use. I turned down first one scheme and then another, as though they had been devised for the sole purpose of gobbling up my money. I finally listened to a friend who advised me to put all I had in New York real estate; and under his guidance I took equity in a piece of property on which stood a rickety old tenement-house. I did not regret following this friend's advice, for in something like six months I disposed of my equity for more than double my investment. From that time on I devoted myself to the study of New York real estate, and watched for opportunities to make similar investments. In spite of two or three speculations which did not turn out well, I have been remarkably successful. To-day I am the owner and part-owner of several flat-houses. I have changed my place of employment four times since returning to New York, and each change has been a decided advancement.

Concerning the position which I now hold, I shall say nothing except that it pays extremely well.

As my outlook on the world grew brighter, I began to mingle in the social circles of the men with whom I came in contact; and gradually, by a process of elimination, I reached a grade of society of no small degree of culture. My appearance was always good and my ability to play on the piano, especially ragtime, which was then at the height of its vogue, made me a welcome guest. The anomaly of my social position often appealed strongly to my sense of humor. I frequently smiled inwardly at some remark not altogether complimentary to people of color; and more than once I felt like declaiming, "I am a colored man. Do I not disprove the theory that one drop of Negro blood renders a man unfit?" Many a night when I returned to my room after an enjoyable evening, I laughed heartily over what struck me as the capital joke I was playing.

Then I met her, and what I had regarded as a joke was gradually changed into the most serious question of my life. I first saw her at a musical which was given one evening at a house to which I was frequently invited. I did not notice her among the other guests before she came forward and sang two sad little songs. When she began I was out in the hallway where many of the men were gathered; but with the first few notes I crowded with others into the doorway to see who the singer was. When I saw the girl, the surprise which I had felt at the first sound of her voice was heightened; she was almost tall and quite slender, with lustrous yellow hair and eyes so blue as to appear almost black. She was as white as a lily, and she was dressed in white. Indeed, she seemed to me the most dazzlingly white thing I had ever seen. But it was not her delicate beauty which attracted me most; it was her voice, a voice which made one wonder how tones of such passionate color could come from so fragile a body.

I determined that when the programme was over I would seek an introduction to her; but at the moment, instead of being the easy man of the world, I became again the bashful boy of fourteen, and my courage failed me. I contented myself with hovering as near her as politeness would permit; near enough to hear her voice, which in conversation was low, yet thrilling, like the deeper middle tones of a flute. I watched the men gather around her talking and laughing in an easy manner, and wondered how it was possible for them to do it. But destiny, my special destiny, was at work. I was standing near, talking with affected gayety to several young ladies, who, however, must have remarked my preoccupation; for my second sense of hearing was alert to what was being said by the group of which the girl in white was the center, when I heard her say, "I think his playing of Chopin is exquisite." And one of my friends in the group replied, "You haven't met him? Allow me – " then turning to me, "Old man, when you have a moment I wish you to meet Miss ——." I don't know what she said to me or what I said to her. I can remember that I tried to be clever, and experienced a growing conviction that I was making myself appear more and more idiotic. I am certain, too, that, in spite of my Italian-like complexion, I was as red as a beet.

Instead of taking the car I walked home. I needed the air and exercise as a sort of sedative. I am not sure whether my troubled condition of mind was due to the fact that I had been struck by love or to the feeling that I had made a bad impression upon her.

As the weeks went by, and when I had met her several more times, I came to know that I was seriously in love; and then began for me days of worry, for I had more than the usual doubts and fears of a young man in love to contend with.

Up to this time I had assumed and played my rôle as a white man with a certain degree of nonchalance, a carelessness as to the outcome, which made the whole thing more amusing to me than serious; but now I ceased to regard "being a white man" as a sort of practical joke. My acting had called for mere external effects. Now I began to doubt my ability to play the part. I watched her to see if she was scrutinizing me, to see if she was looking for anything in me which made me differ from the other men she knew. In place of an old inward feeling of superiority over many of my friends, I began to doubt myself. I began even to wonder if I really was like the men I associated with; if there was not, after all, an indefinable something which marked a difference.

But, in spite of my doubts and timidity, my affair progressed; and I finally felt sufficiently encouraged to decide to ask her to marry me. Then began the hardest struggle of my life, whether to ask her to marry me under false colors or to tell her the whole truth. My sense of what was exigent made me feel there was no necessity of saying anything; but my inborn sense of honor rebelled at even indirect deception in this case. But however much I moralized on the question, I found it more and more difficult to reach the point of confession. The dread that I might lose her took possession of me each time I sought to speak, and rendered it impossible for me to do so. That moral courage requires more than physical courage is no mere poetic fancy. I am sure I would have found it easier to take the place of a gladiator, no matter how fierce the Numidian[79] lion, than to tell that slender girl that I had Negro blood in my veins. The fact which I had at times wished to cry out, I now wished to hide forever.

During this time we were drawn together a great deal by the mutual bond of music. She loved to hear me play Chopin, and was herself far from being a poor performer of his compositions. I think I carried her every new song that was published which I thought suitable to her voice, and played the accompaniment for her. Over these songs we were like two innocent children with new toys. She had never been anything but innocent; but my innocence was a transformation wrought by my love for her, love which melted away my cynicism and whitened my sullied soul and gave me back the wholesome dreams of my boyhood. There is nothing better in all the world that a man can do for his moral welfare than to love a good woman.

My artistic temperament also underwent an awakening. I spent many hours at my piano, playing over old and new composers. I also wrote several little pieces in a more or less Chopinesque style, which I dedicated to her. And so the weeks and months went by. Often words of love trembled on my lips, but I dared not utter them, because I knew they would have to be followed by other words which I had not the courage to frame. There might have been some other woman in my set with whom I could have fallen in love and asked to marry me without a word of explanation; but the more I knew this girl, the less could I find it in my heart to deceive her. And yet, in spite of this specter that was constantly looming up before me, I could never have believed that life held such happiness as was contained in those dream days of love.

One Saturday afternoon, in early June, I was coming up Fifth Avenue, and at the corner of Twenty-third Street I met her. She had been shopping. We stopped to chat for a moment, and I suggested that we spend half an hour at the Eden Musée.[80] We were standing leaning on the rail in front of a group of figures, more interested in what we had to say to each other than in the group, when my attention became fixed upon a man who stood at my side studying his catalogue. It took me only an instant to recognize in him my old friend "Shiny." My first impulse was to change my position at once. As quick as a flash I considered all the risks I might run in speaking to him, and most especially the delicate question of introducing him to her. I must confess that in my embarrassment and confusion I felt small and mean. But before I could decide what

Notes

[79] *Numidian* of the ancient African kingdom of Numidia (present-day Algeria).

[80] *Eden Musée* a Manhattan wax museum.

to do he looked around at me and, after an instant, said, "Pardon me; but isn't this ——?" The nobler part in me responded to the sound of his voice, and I took his hand in a hearty clasp. Whatever fears I had felt were quickly banished, for he seemed, at a glance, to divine my situation, and let drop no word that would have aroused suspicion as to the truth. With a slight misgiving I presented him to her, and was again relieved of fear. She received the introduction in her usual gracious manner, and without the least hesitancy or embarrassment joined in the conversation. An amusing part about the introduction was that I was upon the point of introducing him as "Shiny," and stammered a second or two before I could recall his name. We chatted for some fifteen minutes. He was spending his vacation North, with the intention of doing four or six weeks' work in one of the summer schools; he was also going to take a bride back with him in the fall. He asked me about myself, but in so diplomatic a way that I found no difficulty in answering him. The polish of his language and the unpedantic manner in which he revealed his culture greatly impressed her; and after we had left the Musée she showed it by questioning me about him. I was surprised at the amount of interest a refined black man could arouse. Even after changes in the conversation she reverted several times to the subject of "Shiny." Whether it was more than mere curiosity I could not tell; but I was convinced that she herself knew very little about prejudice.

Just why it should have done so I do not know; but somehow the "Shiny" incident gave me encouragement and confidence to cast the die of my fate; but I reasoned that since I wanted to marry her only, and since it concerned her alone, I would divulge my secret to no one else, not even her parents.

One evening, a few days afterwards, at her home, we were going over some new songs and compositions, when she asked me, as she often did, to play the "13th Nocturne."[81] When I began she drew a chair near to my right, and sat leaning with her elbow on the end of the piano, her chin resting on her hand, and her eyes reflecting the emotions which the music awoke in her. An impulse which I could not control rushed over me, a wave of exaltation, the music under my fingers sank almost to a whisper, and calling her for the first time by her Christian name, but without daring to look at her, I said, "I love you, I love you, I love you." My fingers were trembling, so that I ceased playing. I felt her hand creep to mine, and when I looked at her, her eyes were glistening with tears. I understood, and could scarcely resist the longing to take her in my arms; but I remembered, remembered that which has been the sacrificial altar of so much happiness – Duty; and bending over her hand in mine, I said, "Yes, I love you; but there is something more, too, that I must tell you." Then I told her, in what words I do not know, the truth. I felt her hand grow cold, and when I looked up she was gazing at me with a wild, fixed stare as though I was some object she had never seen. Under the strange light in her eyes I felt that I was growing black and thick-featured and crimp-haired. She appeared not to have comprehended what I had said. Her lips trembled and she attempted to say something to me; but the words stuck in her throat. Then dropping her head on the piano she began to weep with great sobs that shook her frail body. I tried to console her, and blurted out incoherent words of love; but this seemed only to increase her distress, and when I left her she was still weeping.

When I got into the street I felt very much as I did the night after meeting my father and sister at the opera in Paris, even a similar desperate inclination to get drunk; but my self-control was stronger. This was the only time in my life that I ever felt absolute regret at being colored, that I cursed the drops of African blood in my veins, and

Notes

[81] *13th Nocturne* a Chopin piano piece.

wished that I were really white. When I reached my rooms I sat and smoked several cigars while I tried to think out the significance of what had occurred. I reviewed the whole history of our acquaintance, recalled each smile she had given me, each word she had said to me that nourished my hope. I went over the scene we had just gone through, trying to draw from it what was in my favor and what was against me. I was rewarded by feeling confident that she loved me, but I could not estimate what was the effect upon her of my confession. At last, nervous and unhappy, I wrote her a letter, which I dropped into the mail-box before going to bed, in which I said:

"I understand, understand even better than you, and so I suffer even more than you. But why should either of us suffer for what neither of us is to blame? If there is any blame, it belongs to me, and I can only make the old, yet strongest plea that can be offered; I love you; and I know that my love, my great love, infinitely overbalances that blame, and blots it out. What is it that stands in the way of our happiness? It is not what you feel or what I feel; it is not what you are or what I am. It is what others feel and are. But, oh! is that a fair price? In all the endeavors and struggles of life, in all our strivings and longings there is only one thing worth seeking, only one thing worth winning, and that is love. It is not always found; but when it is, there is nothing in all the world for which it can be profitably exchanged."

The second morning after, I received a note from her which stated briefly that she was going up in New Hampshire to spend the summer with relatives there. She made no reference to what had passed between us; nor did she say exactly when she would leave the city. The note contained no single word that gave me any clue to her feelings. I could only gather hope from the fact that she had written at all. On the same evening, with a degree of trepidation which rendered me almost frightened, I went to her house.

I met her mother, who told me that she had left for the country that very afternoon. Her mother treated me in her usual pleasant manner, which fact greatly reassured me; and I left the house with a vague sense of hope stirring in my breast, which sprang from the conviction that she had not yet divulged my secret. But that hope did not remain with me long. I waited one, two, three weeks, nervously examining my mail every day, looking for some word from her. All of the letters received by me seemed so insignificant, so worthless, because there was none from her. The slight buoyancy of spirit which I had felt gradually dissolved into gloomy heartsickness. I became preoccupied, I lost appetite, lost sleep, and lost ambition. Several of my friends intimated to me that perhaps I was working too hard.

She stayed away the whole summer. I did not go to the house, but saw her father at various times, and he was as friendly as ever. Even after I knew that she was back in town I did not go to see her. I determined to wait for some word or sign. I had finally taken refuge and comfort in my pride, pride which, I suppose, I came by naturally enough.

The first time I saw her after her return was one night at the theater. She and her mother sat in company with a young man whom I knew slightly, not many seats away from me. Never did she appear more beautiful and yet, it may have been my fancy, she seemed a trifle paler and there was a suggestion of haggardness in her countenance. But that only heightened her beauty; the very delicacy of her charm melted down the strength of my pride. My situation made me feel weak and powerless, like a man trying with his bare hands to break the iron bars of his prison cell. When the performance was over I hurried out and placed myself where, unobserved, I could see her as she passed out. The haughtiness of spirit in which I had sought relief was all gone, and I was willing and ready to undergo any humiliation.

Shortly afterward we met at a progressive card party, and during the evening we were thrown together at one of the tables as partners. This was really our first meeting since the eventful night at her house. Strangely enough, in spite of our mutual nervousness, we won every trick of the game, and one of our opponents jokingly quoted the old saw, "Lucky at cards, unlucky in love." Our eyes met, and I am sure that in the momentary glance my whole soul went out to her in one great plea. She lowered her eyes and uttered a nervous little laugh. During the rest of the game I fully merited the unexpressed and expressed abuse of my various partners; for my eyes followed her wherever she was, and I played whatever card my fingers happened to touch.

Later in the evening she went to the piano and began to play very softly, as to herself, the opening bars of the 13th Nocturne. I felt that the psychic moment of my life had come, a moment which if lost could never be called back; and, in as careless a manner as I could assume, I sauntered over to the piano and stood almost bending over her. She continued playing; but, in a voice that was almost a whisper, she called me by my Christian name and said, "I love you, I love you, I love you." I took her place at the piano and played the Nocturne in a manner that silenced the chatter of the company both in and out of the room; involuntarily closing it with the major triad.

We were married the following spring, and went to Europe for several months. It was a double joy for me to be in France again under such conditions.

First there came to us a little girl, with hair and eyes dark like mine, but who is growing to have ways like her mother. Two years later there came a boy, who has my temperament, but is fair like his mother, a little golden-headed god, a face and head that would have delighted the heart of an old Italian master. And this boy, with his mother's eyes and features, occupies an inner sanctuary of my heart; for it was for him that she gave all; and that is the second sacred sorrow of my life.

The few years of our married life were supremely happy, and, perhaps she was even happier than I; for after our marriage, in spite of all the wealth of her love which she lavished upon me, there came a new dread to haunt me, a dread which I cannot explain and which was unfounded, but one that never left me. I was in constant fear that she would discover in me some shortcoming which she would unconsciously attribute to my blood rather than to a failing of human nature. But no cloud ever came to mar our life together; her loss to me is irreparable. My children need a mother's care, but I shall never marry again. It is to my children that I have devoted my life. I no longer have the same fear for myself of my secret being found out; for since my wife's death I have gradually dropped out of social life; but there is nothing I would not suffer to keep the "brand" from being placed upon them.

It is difficult for me to analyze my feelings concerning my present position in the world. Sometimes it seems to me that I have never really been a Negro, that I have been only a privileged spectator of their inner life; at other times I feel that I have been a coward, a deserter, and I am possessed by a strange longing for my mother's people.

Several years ago I attended a great meeting in the interest of Hampton Institute[82] at Carnegie Hall. The Hampton students sang the old songs and awoke memories that left me sad. Among the speakers were R.C. Ogden,[83] Ex-Ambassador Choate,[84] and Mark Twain;[85] but the greatest interest of the audience was centered in Booker

Notes

[82] *Hampton Institute* an African American vocational school in Hampton, Virginia.

[83] *R.C. Ogden* Robert Curtis Ogden (1836–1913), business leader and education reformer.

[84] *Ex-Ambassador Choate* Joseph Hodges Choate (1832–1917), diplomat.

[85] *Mark Twain* the nom de plume of Samuel Langhorne Clemens (1835–1910), American author and humorist.

T. Washington;[86] and not because he so much surpassed the others in eloquence, but because of what he represented with so much earnestness and faith. And it is this that all of that small but gallant band of colored men who are publicly fighting the cause of their race have behind them. Even those who oppose them know that these men have the eternal principles of right on their side, and they will be victors even though they should go down in defeat. Beside them I feel small and selfish. I am an ordinarily successful white man who has made a little money. They are men who are making history and a race. I, too, might have taken part in a work so glorious.

My love for my children makes me glad that I am what I am, and keeps me from desiring to be otherwise; and yet, when I sometimes open a little box in which I still keep my fast yellowing manuscripts, the only tangible remnants of a vanished dream, a dead ambition, a sacrificed talent, I cannot repress the thought, that, after all, I have chosen the lesser part, that I have sold my birthright for a mess of pottage.[87]

1912, 1927

Notes

[86] Booker T. Washington (1856–1915), African American educator, author, and political leader.

[87] *a mess of pottage* In Genesis 25:26, Esau sells his birthright to his younger brother Jacob for a bowl of stew.

Glossary

Abolitionism: A prospective movement or doctrine, overlapping with antislavery, that indicts the immorality of the slave trade and slavery while proposing arguments that slaves deserve equal rights upon emancipation.

African American literature: Literature written by authors who both identify themselves and are publicly identified as African Americans.

African American Press: Newspapers and periodicals, sometimes with transnational circulations, in which African-descended people played significant roles as publishers, editors, contributors, and/or readers.

African American Studies: An interdisciplinary field of scholarly or intellectual study, instituted at United States colleges and universities beginning in the 1970s, concentrating on the historical, current, or future experiences of African Americans.

Antebellum: The period of nineteenth-century American history before the Civil War.

Antislavery: An ethos, overlapping with abolitionism by the 1830s, opposing the trade and enslavement of Africans and their descendants.

Assimilation: The process by which one group adopts the customs and attitudes of a newfound society.

Authenticity: The empirical or symbolic quality by which a literary text or author is deemed to possess an incontrovertible origin.

Black: Used interchangeably across history with "Negro," "Afro-American," and "African American," a term that entered mainstream usage especially during the rise of the Black Power, Black Aesthetic, and Black Studies Movements in the 1960s and 1970s to describe authentic African American identity.

The Wiley Blackwell Anthology of African American Literature: Volume 1, 1746–1920, First Edition.
Edited by Gene Andrew Jarrett.

Black Aesthetic: Established during the Black Arts Movement, a joint principle of racial politics and art rooted in both an authentic African American heritage and in opposition to myths of Eurocentric heritage.

Black Arts Movement: A connected series of events and activities in the 1960s and 1970s in which African American art and artists largely promoted the Black Aesthetic.

Black Atlantic: A trope referring to the voluntary or involuntary migration of Africans and their African American descendants across the Atlantic Ocean.

Black Church: A historic institution of African American denominational worship, education, community organization, racial uplift, and racial politics.

Black nationalism: A philosophy of group identity and political self-determination based in racial rather than traditionally "national" categories, seeking to unify people of African descent in a collective effort for social, political, and economic rights. Black nationalism has taken the form of "Back-to-Africa" movements and separatism, but also of emphasizing racial pride in a distinct black culture.

Blackness: **See Black**

Black Power Movement: A series of connected events and activities in the 1960s and 1970s in which African Americans promoted a doctrine of self-determination historically overlapping with, but fundamentally in contrast to, the Civil Rights Movement struggles of the 1950s.

Black Press: **See African American Press**

Black Studies: **See African American Studies**

Blues: The musical composition and performance style rooted in southern African American oral tradition, collective consciousness, and traditional African performance style. Characterized by a pentatonic scale, call-and-response pattern, and three-line stanzas with statement, restatement, and conclusion, it describes a worldliness born of loss and experience.

British abolitionism: A movement in late eighteenth-century Britain that sought an end to both enslavement and the Atlantic Slave Trade, originating in the James Somersett case of 1772 and concluding with the Slavery Abolition Act of 1833. British abolitionists included William Wilberforce, Olaudah Equiano, and Thomas Clarkson, and their tactics inspired American abolitionists in the 1830s.

Chicago Renaissance: A period of African American cultural activity in Chicago, Illinois, between the mid-1930s and early 1950s, marked by literary realism, jazz and gospel music, as well as sociological investigation. Comparable to the New Negro Renaissance in its literary and cultural dynamics, the Chicago Renaissance was characterized particularly by racial and social realism.

Civil Rights Act: An act passed by Congress establishing or protecting equal rights under the law in voting, public accommodation, employment, and housing. Various Civil Rights Acts have been passed since 1866, when Congress first extended citizenship to African Americans; the 1964 Civil Rights Act prohibiting major forms of discrimination was a primary achievement of the Civil Rights Movement.

Civil Rights Movement: An organized social, cultural, and political movement following World War II that partnered legal challenges to segregation, discrimination, and disfranchisement with grass-roots, non-violent direct action against unequal laws and practices, institutional and local. The Civil Rights Movement of the 1950s and early 1960s was unique in its national and international impact, its major campaigns of civil resistance (led by Dr Martin Luther King, Jr), and its tenuous relationship with political liberalism.

Civil War: A war in the United States between the northern Union and the southern Confederacy between 1861 and 1865, fought over economic and legal issues pertaining to slavery. The triumph of the Union over the Confederate secessionists signaled the end of centuries of slavery on North American soil, and initiated the process of Reconstruction.

Cold War: A sustained period of political, economic, and military tension between the Western Bloc (the United States and European NATO allies) and the Eastern Bloc (the Soviet Union and its satellite states) between 1945 and 1991. Cast as the worldwide struggle between communism and democracy, the Cold War proceeded as a series of proxy wars and crises behind which lay the threat of mutually assured nuclear destruction. In the United States, it led to state surveillance of those with leftist sympathies, including Richard Wright, Chester Himes, and singer Paul Robeson.

Colonization: The movement of African Americans to resettle outside of the United States, primarily in Western Africa or the Caribbean, spurred on by the seeming intractability of American racism.

Color line (African Americans): A metaphor signifying a measurement of individual identity and social status according to skin pigmentation, whereby inter- and intra-racial relationships are structured by the derogation of dark skin and African ancestry. In addition to legitimating white/black hierarchies and discrimination, the color line sometimes operated within African American communities as colorism, which internalized white supremacy to privilege those of lighter skin color.

Conjure tales: Traditional African American stories, myths, and fables originating in southern slave culture characterized by magical or supernatural powers used to subvert relationships of power.

Conversion narrative: A testimony of personal spiritual conviction marked by religious rebirth and individual salvation.

Cultural nationalism: A national identity based on shared language, belief, religion, and history rather than ancestry.

Dialect: A linguistic distinction, or vernacular, based on a special assortment of grammar, syntax, and vocabulary marking a specific region, class, or culture for the speaker.

Diaspora (African Diaspora): From the Greek word meaning "dispersion," it refers to groups of people (involuntarily) scattered far from their ancestral homeland, and was first applied to the Jews exiled after the dissolution of their nation. African Diaspora describes the scattering of people of African descent across the globe, and draws attention to the potential shared historical and cultural experience of these peoples.

Discrimination: The prejudicial treatment of an individual or group based on their membership in a certain category.

Domestic realism: A sentimental literary genre characterized by the heroine's struggle to balance social demands with personal desires, meant to evoke sympathy from a predominantly female audience during the nineteenth century.

Double consciousness: The notion that African American identity is marked by internal tensions and divisions. The term was coined by W.E.B. Du Bois, who found a "two-ness" within the African American consciousness in terms of conflicts between personal self and racially stereotyped self, "American" identity and "African" identity, and the "American" and "not-American" ways of life enforced by racial segregation.

Dred Scott: An African American slave whose suit for his freedom in 1850 led to a seminal Supreme Court ruling in 1857 that African Americans were not citizens, and that slavery could exist wherever slaves were brought by their owners. Chief Justice Roger B. Taney stated in his majority ruling that African Americans "have no rights that a white man is bound to respect." The Dred Scott decision overturned the 1820 Missouri Compromise and incited anti- and proslavery passions.

Emancipation: The action of setting free or delivering freedom for a group of people previously held in bondage, granted finally to American slaves with the Thirteenth Amendment in 1865.

Emancipation Proclamation: A federal document signed by President Abraham Lincoln on January 1, 1863, declaring that all slaves in rebelling areas of the Confederacy were free and precipitating the end of chattel slavery in North America. The Proclamation rhetorically positioned the war as a battle over slavery, and also allowed freed African Americans to enlist in segregated units in the Union Army.

Emigration: The movement by African Americans seeking greater cultural, economic, and political autonomy by leaving the United States for another nation.

Ethiopianism: The nineteenth-century idea that located African historical identity and promise of redemption in the ancient civilization of Ethiopia. Ethiopia was invoked rhetorically to connote Africans around the world, and posited as a "cradle of civilization" against racist theories of African inferiority.

Ethnicity: Group identification based on culture – as distinguished by family life, religion, literature, ritual, food, and material culture – that creates a "people."

Exoticism: In literature, the objectification of a cultural "other" for consumption by the dominant culture.

Federal Art Project: The first federal patronage of the visual arts in the United States, founded in 1935 as part of President Franklin D. Roosevelt's Works Progress Administration, which employed artists from the public relief rolls and established community art centers and galleries.

Folklore: The legends, stories, and traditions belonging to a defined community.

Harlem Renaissance: **See New Negro Renaissance**

Hip hop: A subculture that emerged from rap music, graffiti art, and urban unrest in the South Bronx, New York City, during the 1970s amongst African American and Latino youth. Originally characterized by opposition to mainstream culture and social criticism, hip hop underwent a period of commercialization during the 1980s and 1990s and is now a dominant form of pop music around the world.

Hoodoo: A form of folk magic that developed among enslaved peoples in the southeastern United States, marked by its incorporation of African and Native American traditions syncretized with Old Testament Christianity. **See Conjure tales**

Intelligentsia: A class of people distinguished by their accomplishments in intellectual or academic culture, or by their involvement in an artistic or intellectual movement, such as the New Negro Renaissance.

Jazz: A musical tradition, created in late nineteenth-century New Orleans, that combines several musical types: blues, ragtime, brass band, and dance music. Rooted in musical improvisation, jazz rhythm, and hybridity, it has informed African American literary works from the poetry of Langston Hughes to the prose of Toni Morrison.

Jim Crow: A system of laws, ideas, and social norms created after the Civil War to maintain white control over African Americans despite the abolition of slavery. Originally a blackface minstrel show character, Jim Crow came to mean the racial segregation, institutionalized discrimination, and violent oppression of African Americans, legally bookended by the Supreme Court rulings in *Plessy v. Ferguson* in 1896 upholding the separate-but-equal policy and *Brown v. Board of Education* in 1954 outlawing it.

Ku Klux Klan: A white secret society founded after the Civil War to restore white supremacy and prevent African American enfranchisement in the former Confederacy by means of terror, political outrage, and murder.

Literacy: The ability to reason, understand, and express rational thought through the written word. Because of Enlightenment assumptions that human reason was essential for the economic, political, and social health of communities and individuals, many African American writers used literacy to challenge their exclusion from racialized definitions of humanity.

Lynching: Acts of public and extra-legal violent punishment, typically carried out by mobs in retaliation for perceived social, political, and racial transgressions. Lynching, in the form of hanging, shooting, or burning at the stake, was used by white civilian mobs to quash African American social mobility, economic success, or political action.

Middle Passage: From the sixteenth to the nineteenth century, the liminal and traumatic journey of about 12 million western and west-central Africans, who were abducted, enslaved, and traded during their transportation from their native continent, across the Atlantic Ocean, and to the New World Americas.

Migration: The movement, displacement, mobility, and dispersal of people of African descent that has characterized their long history in the Americas, including the Middle Passage through the twentieth-century movement from the rural South to the urban North and West in the United States.

Militancy: **See Black nationalism**

Minstrelsy: An American form of stage entertainment that emerged in the antebellum era, performed by white Americans in blackface makeup and dress, that lampooned African Americans as dim-witted comic buffoons, lazy man-children, or desexualized, overbearing "mammies." Minstrelsy also refers to the practice of performing a stereotypical blackness for comic relief or monetary gain.

Miscegenation: The genetic mingling of races through interracial sex and procreation, and the various socio-psychological consequences of this mixture in a country committed to a binary conception of race.

Modernism: A literary and cultural impulse marked by a deliberate break with tradition, fueled in part by the technological and sociological upheavals that accompanied the turn of the twentieth century.

Mulatto: A person with one white and one black parent, or more generally a racially mixed person; the genealogical hybridity undermines racial essentialism by calling that person's fixed racial identity into question.

Nationalism: **See Black nationalism**

Naturalism: A literary movement of the late nineteenth and early twentieth centuries that conceived of human character as largely determined by social conditions, environment, and hereditary forces; closely related to realism in its commitment to quotidian and unflinching detail.

Negritude: A movement among African-descended artists and intellectuals in France in the 1930s and 1940s that valorized a common cultural identity of "blackness" and African heritage against the prejudices and history of European colonialism.

Neo-slave narrative: A literary work published after slavery that reconstructs the tropes of the antebellum slave narrative to reanimate the experience and examine the consequences of slavery.

New Negro: A term that gained widespread use after the Civil War's end with the rise of the New South during Reconstruction, and continued through the middle of the twentieth century, New Negroes were largely middle-class, educated, civically responsible, and politically enfranchised African Americans who embodied racial pride and social advancement, in contrast to the putatively lowly "Old Negro" beholden to slavery and ostracism.

New Negro Renaissance: Also called "Harlem Renaissance," a period of immense cultural activity in the 1920s that reconceived and promoted African American arts and letters. Although the era arose partly out of the Great Migration of African Americans from the rural South to the urban North and spanned areas across the United States and as far away as Europe, the epicenter of the movement was in Harlem, New York City.

Old Negro: Figures of social and cultural degradation and inferiority, invoked rhetorically in contradistinction to the culturally proud, politically conscious, racially aware generation that left the South and embraced cultural modernism.

One-drop rule: The classification of individuals as "black" or "negro" if they possessed any trace of African ancestry, no matter how minuscule. The one-drop rule was the logical extension of racial essentialism.

Oral tradition: A set of orally transmitted expressions of beliefs, ideas, stories, and sentiments particular to a certain people's worldview.

Pan-Africanism: The idea that all people of African descent, whether on the African continent or across the diaspora, share a political, cultural, and economic destiny linked to their common history of forced migration, enslavement, colonialism, second-class citizenship, and economic exploitation.

Passing: The act of one's crossing the metaphorical "color line," and representing oneself as, or being accepted as, a member of a group opposite from one's racial origin. While historically motivated by social incentives or threats, passing as a literary trope serves to highlight the constructed nature of race and identity.

Postbellum: The period of nineteenth-century US history after the Civil War.

Post-race/Postracial: Pertaining to the notion that, as the Civil Rights Movement recedes from historical view in the early twenty-first century, people have begun to move beyond race as a basis for social preference, discrimination, and prejudice.

Prejudice: Antagonism toward a group or class of people and its members based on irrational or stereotypical belief rather than experience or reality. **See Stereotyping**

Protest Literature: Writing meant to challenge or condemn not only social, political, cultural, or economic inequities but also the causes or institutions that create them.

Racial essentialism: The belief that human beings are divided into races with essential, inheritable differences.

Racial uplift: The ideology that believes a race can be improved in aesthetic, intellectual, cultural, economic, and political ways, in contrast to historical allegations of that race's inferiority.

Racism: Accepting the premise of racial essentialism, the belief that some races are innately inferior to others and should be treated accordingly. **See Racial essentialism**

Radical Reconstruction: **See Reconstruction Era**

Realism: A literary movement in the United States arising first in the latter half of the nineteenth century that sought to depict reality faithfully and in quotidian detail, in opposition to the fanciful tendencies of romanticism.

Reconstruction Era: The post-Civil War era until 1877, when the Confederate states that had seceded were reorganized and transformed within the federal government, with a special emphasis on the citizenship and enfranchisement of African American former slaves. Unfulfilled political and economic promises overshadow the legal advancement of African American civil rights, leading into an era, in the late nineteenth century, of racial violence and segregation.

Segregation: The separation of African American and European American citizens by law, policy, or social practice in housing, education, and public or private accommodation. While outlawed with the 1964 Civil Rights Act, de facto segregation in public spaces continued after the legal gains of the Civil Rights Movement.

Slave narrative: A nineteenth-century literary form in which formerly enslaved African Americans recounted their journey from enslavement to freedom. The most popular African American literary form of the antebellum era, these narratives employed common motifs, including descriptions of the brutality of enslavement, personal realization of one's humanity and self-determination, and a dramatic escape to freedom.

Slave trade: The commercial exchange of Africans and their descendants across Europe, Africa, and the Americas between the sixteenth and the nineteenth centuries that resulted in the transportation of over 12 million across the Atlantic world. Between 10 and 20% of Africans died aboard slave ships prior to landing in the Americas. **See Middle Passage**

Slavery: A system of involuntary labor forced upon millions of Africans and their descendants in the Americas from the early days of colonization until 1865, when the United States formally abolished slavery under the Thirteenth Amendment to the Constitution.

Stereotyping: In printing, a process of fixing stereotype plates for reprinting, which serves more broadly as a metaphor of the act of associating ideas and characteristics with individuals, groups, circumstances, or actions that may not accurately reflect of reality. Whereas prejudice is an emotional response to one's belief about a certain type of person, a stereotype is the expectation or belief itself on which prejudice may be predicated.

Uncle Tom: The title character in Harriet Beecher Stowe's best-selling novel *Uncle Tom's Cabin* (1852), as an epithet it now connotes excessive and willful African American subservience to figures of white authority.

Underground Railroad: The covert network in which abolitionists, antislavery sympathizers, and even former slaves assisted runaway slaves in their flight from their owners in the South to free territories in the North and Canada.

White supremacy: A belief and practice of racism promoting the superiority of Anglo-Saxon whites over non-whites.

Works Progress Administration (WPA): The largest agency formed under President Franklin D. Roosevelt's New Deal, the Works Progress Administration (renamed the Works Project Administration in 1939) employed millions of unemployed people on public works projects, including the construction of bridges and roads, and the establishment of arts, drama, and literacy projects across the country. The WPA created eight million jobs in its operation between 1935 and 1943, and helped launch the careers of a number of African American writers and scholars.

Timeline: 1746 to 1920

1740s–1760s	
American Politics, History, Culture	
1740s–1780s	The Great Awakening in North America spreads ideas of egalitarianism through religious revivals that prepare many colonists for the republican ideals of the American Revolution.
1750	The British mainland American colonies have a population of 1.5 million, of which 300,000 (or nearly 20%) are enslaved people of African descent. Of these British North American slaves, 145,000 live in Virginia and Maryland, primarily working in the tobacco fields.
1754–1763	French and Indian War. At the same time that the American colonies move toward greater economic and political autonomy that will eventually lead to the rise in republicanism, people of African descent face increasing restrictions on their rights. In 1740, Georgia and Carolina attempt to invade Florida in retaliation for the Spanish territory's policy of emancipation for escaped slaves. In 1760, New Jersey prohibits slave enlistment without the permission of slave masters.
African American Literary History	
1746	Lucy Terry writes "Bars Fight" about a Native American attack on Deerfield, Massachusetts. The poem is published in 1850.
1760	Briton Hammon's *The Narrative of the Uncommon Sufferings and Surprizing Deliverance of Briton Hammon, a Negro Man* published.
1768	Samson Occom's *A Short Narrative of My Life* published.
1770s–1780s	
American Politics, History, Culture	
March 5, 1770	Escaped slave Crispus Attucks, of Native American and African descent, is killed in the Boston Massacre.

The Wiley Blackwell Anthology of African American Literature: Volume 1, 1746–1920, First Edition.
Edited by Gene Andrew Jarrett.

1773	Slaves in Massachusetts, including future founder of African American Freemasonry, Prince Hall, unsuccessfully petition Massachusetts for their freedom. On December 16, the Boston Tea Party occurs, during which angry colonists dump 342 casks of tea into the Boston Harbor after Governor Thomas Hutchinson declares that the British ship *Dartmouth* must remain until taxes are paid.
1775	Peter Salem, an African American patriot, fights at the battle of Lexington and Concord.
July, 1775	George Washington announces a ban on the enlistment of free blacks and slaves in the colonial army. In a speech before the Virginia Legislature on March 23, slave owner Patrick Henry encourages colonists to bear arms to protect themselves, using the famous words "give me liberty or give me death."
November 7, 1775	Lord Dunmore issues his proclamation promising freedom to slaves who flee their masters to join the royal forces. In South Carolina alone, nearly 30% of the enslaved population (25,000 men, women, and children) flee, migrate, or die in an attempt to take advantage of the chaos caused by the war.
July 4, 1776	The Second Continental Congress adopts the Declaration of Independence, written by Virginia slaveholder (and future president) Thomas Jefferson.
1776	The Society of Friends in Philadelphia, also known as the Quakers, prohibits members from holding slaves.
1776	Thomas Paine's *Common Sense* published.
1777	Prince Hall, founder of the first African Masonic Lodge in the United States, leads a petition to the Massachusetts state legislature protesting against slavery in the Commonwealth.
1780	Pennsylvania begins gradual emancipation, with a law that says all children of African descent born as slaves shall be freed at age 28.
1780–1783	A series of court decisions, initiated by enslaved woman Elizabeth "Mum Bet" Freeman and Framingham slave Quok Walker, lead Massachusetts to interpret slavery as illegal in the state.
October 19, 1781	General Cornwallis signs surrender papers after American and French forces successfully seize York Town on September 28. This concludes the last major battle of the Revolutionary War.
1784	Rhode Island and Connecticut pass gradual emancipation laws.
1785	New York State outlaws slavery.
1785	Thomas Jefferson's *Notes on the State of Virginia* published.
September 17, 1787	The Constitution of the United States is approved by the Federal Convention in Philadelphia and it is sent to the states for ratification. Although the Constitution never mentions the word "slavery," it provides for the continuation of the Atlantic slave trade for 20 years, allows the federal government to use force to put down slave insurrections, creates a federal fugitive slave law, and counts the slave population as "3/5ths" of the total population to calculate southern states' representation in Congress.
October 1787–May 1788	The Federalist Papers, written by James Madison, Alexander Hamilton, and John Jay, appear in New York newspapers under the pseudonym, Publius.

January 21, 1789	William Hill Brown's *The Power of Sympathy: or, The Triumph of Nature Founded in Truth* published. It is the first published American novel.
African American Literary History	
1772	The first autobiographical slave narrative, by James Albert Ukawsaw Gronniosaw, is published.
1773	Phillis Wheatley, enslaved to the loyalist Wheatley family in Boston, becomes the first published African American poet when a London publishing company releases *Poems on Various Subjects.*
1778	Jupiter Hammon's *An Address to Miss Phillis Wheatly* published.
1785	John Marrant's *A Narrative of the Lord's Wonderful Dealings with John Marrant, a Black* published.
1789	Olaudah Equiano's *Interesting Narrative of the Life of Olaudah Equiano, or Gustavus Vassa, the African* is published in England. It appears in America in 1791.
1790s–1800s	
American Politics, History, Culture	
1790	The first United States Census lists the US population at 3,929,214. The African American population is 757, 208, or 19% of the total population; 59,000 African Americans are free, 27,000 of whom live in the North.
1794	Richard Allen, a former slave in Delaware, establishes the African Methodist Episcopal Church in Philadelphia.
1794	Susanna Rowson's *Charlotte Temple* appears in the United States. Originally published in London in 1791 as *Charlotte: A Tale of Truth,* it was the best-selling novel of the nineteenth century prior to Harriet Beecher Stowe's *Uncle Tom's Cabin* (1852)
1800	Gabriel's Conspiracy is uncovered in Virginia. Inspired by the revolt in St Domingue, which led to the founding of the Haitian Republic in 1804, Gabriel and 25 of his followers are executed.
1803	The Louisiana Purchase doubles the size of the United States. New Orleans, founded by the French Mississippi Company in 1718, will become a center of southern African American culture.
1809	Washington Irving's *A History of New York from the Beginning of the World to the End of the Dutch Dynasty, by Diedrich Knickerbocker* published.
African American Literary History	
1798	*Narrative of the Life of Venture Smith* is published by a white schoolteacher in Connecticut. A native of Guinea, West Africa, Smith (1729–1805) was enslaved at the age of eight and spent much of his adult life in New York and Connecticut. After purchasing his own freedom in the 1760s, by 1775 he earned enough money to free his entire family.
1810s–1820s	
American Politics, History, Culture	
1810	The 1810 US Census lists the population at 7,239,881. African Americans are 1,377,808, or 19% of the population; 186,446, or 13.5% of this population, are free.

1817	The American Colonization Society is founded by Reverend Robert Finley to help free African Americans emigrate to Africa. Although some prominent African Americans, including whaling entrepreneur Paul Cuffe and sail-maker James Forten, had supported colonization since the 1780s, many African Americans rejected the idea.
1820	The 1820 US Census lists the American population at 9,638,543. African Americans number 1,771,656, or 18% of the population; 233,634, or 13.2% of all African Americans, are free.
1822	Demark Vesey's conspiracy is uncovered in Charleston, South Carolina.
March 16, 1827	John Brown Russwurm, a graduate of Bowdoin College, and Samuel Cornish publish the first African American newspaper in the United States, *Freedom's Journal*.
African American Literary History	
1826	James Fenimore Cooper's *The Last of the Mohicans* published.
1829	David Walker's *An Appeal to the Colored Citizens of the World* published.
1829	George Moses Horton's *The Hope of Liberty* published.
1830s	
American Politics, History, Culture	
1830	The 1830 US Census lists the population at 12,860,702. African Americans number 2,328,642, or 18% of the population; 319,599, or 13.7% of all African Americans, are free.
1830	Congress passes the Indian Removal Act, which allows President Andrew Jackson to relocate eastern Indians west of the Mississippi River.
September 1830	Philadelphia hosts the first meeting of the American Society of Free Persons of Colour, which eventually became the National Negro Convention. The organization of over 100 beneficial societies founded by free African Americans sought access to education, employment, and economic relief for communities from Philadelphia to Cleveland.
January 1, 1831	William Lloyd Garrison publishes the first issue of *The Liberator* in Boston, the most influential abolitionist newspaper of the era.
August 1831	Nat Turner leads a slave rebellion in Virginia in which over 55 whites are killed.
1835	Catharine Maria Sedgwick's "A Reminiscence of Federalism" published in *Tales and Sketches*.
1836	Ralph Waldo Emerson's essay "Nature" is published anonymously.
1836	Transcendentalists meet informally in Boston and Concord.
1838–1839	"Trail of Tears" forces thousands of Cherokees from their homeland in the Southeast to Indian Territory.
African American Literary History	
1831	Omar ibn Said's *Autobiography of Omar ibn Said, Slave in North Carolina* published.
1831	Maria Stewart's *Religion and the Pure Principles of Morality, the Sure Foundation on Which We Build* published.

1833	Richard Allen's *The Life, Experience, and Gospel Labors of the Rt. Rev. Richard Allen* published.
1837	Victor Séjour Marcou et Ferrand's "The Mulatto" is published in France. It is the earliest known work of fiction by an African American.
1840s	
American Politics, History, Culture	
1840	The 1840 US Census lists the population at 17,063, 353. African Americans number 2,873,648, or 17% of the population; 386,293, or 13.4% of all African Americans, are free.
1843	Henry Highland Garnet gives "An Address to the Slaves of the united States" at the National Negro Convention in Buffalo, New York.
1844	Samuel Morse invents the telegraph.
1845	Edgar Allan Poe's *The Raven* published.
1847	Henry Wadsworth Longfellow's *Evangeline* published.
1848	The Seneca Falls Convention inaugurates the campaign for women's rights.
1849	In *Roberts v. Massachusetts,* the state Supreme Court rules that separation of students based on race in Boston's public schools is constitutional provided that the facilities for both races are equal. Although Boston's public schools are legally desegregated in 1855, the legal concept in the Roberts case will form a precedent for the "separate-but-equal" ruling in the 1896 Federal Supreme Court's *Plessy v. Ferguson* case.
African American Literary History	
1845	Frederick Douglass's *Narrative of the Life of Frederick Douglass, an American Slave. Written by Himself.* published.
1849	William Wells Brown's *Narrative of William Wells Brown, an American Slave. Written by Himself.* published.
1850s	
American Politics, History, Culture	
1850	The 1850 US Census lists the population at 23,191,876. African Americans number 3,638,808, or 16% of the population; 434,495, or 11.9% of all African Americans, are free.
1850	The Fugitive Slave Law, part of the Compromise of 1850, allows federal judges to oversee African Americans accused of being fugitive slaves in the North, which jeopardizes the lives of every African American living outside of the enslaved South. As a result, many African American communities are radicalized as they defend themselves from kidnapping by white slave catchers.
1850	Nathaniel Hawthorne's *The Scarlett Letter* published.
1851	Herman Melville's *Moby Dick* published.
1851	Sojourner Truth gives speech "Ain't I A Woman?" at the Women's Rights Conference in Akron, Ohio.
1852	Harriet Beecher Stowe's *Uncle Tom's Cabin* published. The novel was serialized, beginning in 1851, in the antislavery *The National Era.*

1854	Henry David Thoreau's *Walden; or, Life in the Woods* published.
1855	Henry Wadsworth Longfellow's "The Song of Hiawatha" published.
1855	Walt Whitman's *Leaves of Grass* (1st edition) published.
1857	*The Atlantic Monthly* is founded.
1857	*Harper's Weekly* (1857–1916) is founded.
1857	The Supreme Court rules in *Dred Scott v. Sandford* that people of African descent are not citizens, and that they have "no rights that a white man is bound to respect."
African American Literary History	
1852	Martin Robison Delany's *The Condition, Elevation, Emigration, and Destiny of the Colored People of the United States* published.
1852	Frederick Douglass's essay "What to the Slave Is the Fourth of July?" published.
1853	Solomon Northup's *Twelve Years a Slave* published.
1853	William Wells Brown's *Clotel; or, The President's Daughter* published. It is the first published novel by an African American.
1853	J.M. Whitfield's *America and Other Poems* published.
1854	Frances Ellen Watkins Harper's *Poems on Miscellaneous Subjects* published.
1855	Frederick Douglass's *My Bondage and My Freedom* published.
1857	Frank J. Webb's *The Garies and Their Friends* is published in England.
1858	William Wells Brown's *The Escape; or, a Leap for Freedom: A Drama in Five Acts* published.
1859	Frances Ellen Watkins Harper's "The Two Offers" is the first short story published by an African American woman when it appears in the weekly *Christian Recorder*.
1859	Harriet E. Adams Wilson's *Our Nig; or, Sketches from the Life of a Free Black* published.
1859	Martin Robinson Delany's *Blake; or The Huts of America* published.
1860s	
US Politics, History, Culture	
1860	The 1860 US Census lists the population at 31,191,876. African Americans number 4,441,830, or 14.2% of the population; 488,070, or 11% of all African Americans, are free.
April 12, 1861	Confederate forces attack Fort Sumter in South Carolina, signaling the start of the Civil War. Over 200,000 African Americans fight for the Union Army.
January 1, 1863	Lincoln signs the Emancipation Proclamation, freeing slaves in the rebelling areas of the South. Although the Proclamation signals the death of over 250 years of slavery on North American soil, it is not until the Thirteenth Amendment is ratified, in December 1865, that slavery is abolished in the United States.

December 18, 1865	Congress passes the Thirteenth Amendment to the Constitution, outlawing slavery in the United States. Congress also establishes the Bureau of Freedman and Abandoned Lands to assist freed people in the economic transition from slavery to freedom.
1865	Union General William T. Sherman issues his "Field Order 15," which provides acres of abandoned land to freed people in South Carolina, Georgia, and Florida.
1865	The Freedman's Savings and Trust Company, also known as the Freedman's Bank, is established in New York City. By 1866, it moves to Washington, DC.
November 6, 1865	Mark Twain's "The Celebrated Jumping Frog of Calaveras County" is published in the *New York Saturday Press.*
1866	Legislatures in the former Confederacy pass "Black Codes" that curtail African American freedom. That same year, the white terrorist organization, the Ku Klux Klan, is established in Pulaski, Tennessee.
1867	Five African American colleges are founded, primarily through northern philanthropists and former abolitionists. They include Howard University, Morgan State College, Talladega College, St Augustine's College, and Johnson C. Smith College.
July 28, 1868	The Fourteenth Amendment is ratified, establishing due process and equal protection under the law. Because the amendment places civil rights under the federal rather than the state government, it overturns the 1857 Dred Scott decision, which denied African Americans citizenship even if they had previously been granted citizenship by the state.
African American Literary History	
1861	Harriet Ann Jacobs's *Incidents in the Life of a Slave Girl. Written by Herself.* published.
1861	Frances Ellen Watkins Harper's "The Two Offers" is the first short story published by an African American woman.
1865	Julia C. Collins's *The Curse of Caste* is serialized in the *Christian Recorder.*
1868	Elizabeth Keckley's *Behind the Scenes; or, Thirty Years a Slave, and Four Years in the White House* published.
1870s–1880s	
US Politics, History, Culture	
1870	The 1870 Census lists the population at 38,558,371. African Americans number 4,880,009, or 12.7% of the total population.
March 30, 1870	The Fifteenth Amendment is ratified, granting the right to vote to all male citizens regardless of "race, color, or previous condition of servitude."
1874	Collapse of the Freedman's Bank.
February 6, 1877	The Compromise of 1877 between the Democratic and Republican Parties leads to the Presidency of Rutherford B. Hayes in exchange for withdrawal of federal troops from the South. In addition to signaling the beginning of federal investment in southern industry, the compromise effectively ends federal protection for African Americans in the former Confederacy and leads to the long nadir in African American political, cultural, and economic history.

1878	Thomas Edison forms the Edison Electric Light Company in New York City.
1879	Thousands of African Americans, resisting racial violence, segregation, and economic exploitation, flee Texas, Louisiana, and Tennessee for the West in what businessmen like Benjamin "Pap" Singleton call the Exoduster movement.
1880	The 1880 Census lists the American population at 49,371,340. African Americans number 6,580,793, or 13.1% of the total population.
1880	Henry Ossian Flipper is the first African American to graduate from West Point.
1880	George Washington Cable's *The Grandissimes: A Story of Creole Life* published.
1880	Joel Chandler Harris's *Uncle Remus: His Songs and His Sayings* published.
July 4, 1881	Booker T. Washington, protégé of Hampton Institute founder and Civil War veteran Samuel Chapman Armstrong, establishes the Tuskegee Institute.
1881	Tennessee becomes the first state to pass segregation legislation when the legislature approves a measure segregating railroad passengers by race.
1882	George Washington Williams' *History of the Negro Race in America from 1619 to 1880*. It is the first comprehensive and objective general history of African Americans published in the United States.
1883	Mark Twain's *Life on the Mississippi* published.
October 15, 1883	In the famous Civil Rights Cases before the Federal Supreme Court, the 1875 Civil Rights Act is ruled unconstitutional. Another federal law guaranteeing civil rights will not be passed until 1957.
1884	Helen Hunt Jackson's *Ramona* published.
1885	Mark Twain's *The Adventures of Huckleberry Finn* published.
1885	William Dean Howells's *The Rise of Silas Lapham* published.
October 28, 1886	The Statue of Liberty is dedicated in New York Harbor.
1888	Edward Bellamy's *Looking Backward* published.
African American Literary History	
1870	Frank J. Webb's *Two Wolves and a Lamb* and *Marvin Hayle* published.
1879	Pauline Elizabeth Hopkins's *Peculiar Sam, or the Underground Railroad: A Musical Drama in Four Acts* published.
1881	Frederick Douglass's *Life and Times of Frederick Douglass* published.
1890s	
US History, Politics, Culture	
1890	The 1890 Census lists the population at 62,979,766. African Americans number 7,488,788, or 11.9% of the total population.
December 29, 1890	The Wounded Knee Massacre at which 200 Sioux are killed by Federal soldiers in South Dakota.
1891	First International Copyright Law.

1893	Stephen Crane's *Maggie: A Girl of the Streets* published.
June 1895	William Edward Burghardt Du Bois becomes the first African American to receive a PhD from Harvard University.
September 18, 1895	Booker T. Washington, principal of the Tuskegee Normal Institute, delivers his Atlanta Exposition Speech before the Cotton States International Exposition in Atlanta.
May 18, 1896	In *Plessy v. Ferguson*, the United States Supreme Court upholds the doctrine of "separate but equal", which will legalize segregationist policy across the country until the 1950s.
March 5, 1897	African American intellectuals, led by Reverend Alexander Crummell, found the American Negro Academy in Washington, DC, to challenge racial inequality, segregation, and racial violence through intellectual engagement and study.
February 15, 1898	The sinking of the Battleship *Maine* in Havana Harbor, Cuba leads to 260 deaths. Secretary of the Navy Theodore Roosevelt sends the Pacific Fleet to the Philippines 10 days later, and by April the US is at war with Spain.
1898	Henry James's *The Turn of the Screw* published.
1899	Kate Chopin's *The Awakening* published.
1899	Charlotte Perkins Gilman's *The Yellow Wallpaper* published.
1899–1902	The Philippine Insurrection ends with US occupation of the Philippines. Many writers (including Mark Twain and William Dean Howells) oppose American imperialism.
African American Literary History	
1891	Frances Ellen Watkins Harper's *Sketches of Southern Life* published.
1892	Frances Ellen Watkins Harper's *Iola Leroy, or Shadows Uplifted* published.
1892	Anna Julia Cooper's *A Voice from the South* published.
1893	Paul Laurence Dunbar's *Oak and Ivy* published.
1895	Alice Moore Dunbar Nelson's *Violets and Other Tales* published.
1895	Ida B. Wells-Barnett's *A Red Record* published.
1896	Paul Laurence Dunbar's *Lyrics of Lowly Life* published.
1899	Charles Waddell Chesnutt's *The Conjure Woman* and *The Wife of His Youth and Other Stories of the Color Line* and his essay "What is a White Man?" published.
1899	Alice Dunbar-Nelson's *The Goodness of St. Rocque and Other Stories* published.
1900s–1910s	
US History, Politics, Culture	
1900	The 1900 Census lists the population at 76,212,168. African Americans number 8,833,994, or 11.6% of the total population.
1900	Theodore Dreiser's *Sister Carrie* published.
1901	Frank Norris's *The Octopus* published.

September 14, 1901	President William McKinley dies of wounds sustained after Leon Czogloz shot him at the Pan-American Exposition in Buffalo, New York. Vice-President Theodore Roosevelt is sworn in as president.
October 16, 1901	President Roosevelt invites Booker T. Washington to dinner at the White House.
1902	Henry James's *The Wings of the Dove* published.
1902	Upton Sinclair's *The Jungle* published.
July 11–13, 1905	The Niagara Movement, led by W.E.B. Du Bois, William Monroe Trotter, and J. Max Barber, is founded to challenge the conservative accommodationism of Booker T. Washington, and to fight for racial equality.
1905	Edith Wharton's *The House of Mirth* published.
1906	Death of Paul Laurence Dunbar.
October, 1908	Henry Ford introduces the Model T.
February 12, 1909	The National Association for the Advancement of Colored People (NAACP) is founded to enforce the Fourteenth and Fifteenth Amendments to the Constitution through legal action. Although the organization is initially led by white Progressives (including Boston attorney Moorfield Storey and William Lloyd Garrison's grandson, Oswald Garrison Villard), African Americans like Ida B. Wells and William Monroe Trotter are present at the initial meeting. W.E.B. Du Bois is the only African American to head a committee in the new organization.
1910	The 1910 Census lists the American population at 92,228,496. African Americans number 9,827,763, or 10.7% of the total population.
April, 1910	The National Urban League is founded in New York City to assist southern migrants to the North.
1910	The NAACP's official newspaper, *The Crisis*, begins publication, with W.E.B. Du Bois as editor.
1911	Founding of *The Masses*.
1912	Founding of *Poetry Magazine*.
1913	Robert Frost's *A Boy's Will* published.
1914	Carl Sandburg's *Chicago* published.
1915	D.W. Griffith's film *The Birth of A Nation* is released.
April 2, 1917	After running for re-election under his pledge to keep America out of war, President Woodrow Wilson asks Congress to declare war on Germany. The US enters the war on April 16. During the conflict, approximately 300,000 African Americans will serve in the US military.
November 5, 1917	The Supreme Court rules in *Buchanan v. Warley* that a Louisville, Kentucky law compelling racial segregation in residential zoning is unconstitutional.
1917	Pulitzer Prizes are established.
1918	O. Henry Awards are established.
1919	Sherwood Anderson's *Winesburg, Ohio* published.
February 19–21, 1918	The First Pan-African Congress, led by W.E.B. Du Bois, met in Paris, with delegates from the West Indies, Africa, and America.

July 13–October 1, 1918	Over 25 race riots, leaving 100 dead and 1,000 wounded, erupt across the country. The violence in cities from Washington, DC, to Chicago leads James Weldon Johnson to coin the term "Red Summer" to describe the racial turmoil in cities across the country.
African American Literary History	
1900	Charles Waddell Chesnutt's *The House Behind the Cedars* published.
1900	Pauline Elizabeth Hopkins's *Contending Forces* published.
1901	Charles Waddell Chesnutt's *The Marrow of Tradition* published.
1901	Booker T. Washington's *Up from Slavery* published.
1903	W.E.B. Du Bois's *The Souls of Black Folk* published.
1904	William Stanley Braithwaite's *Lyrics of Life and Love* published.
1905	Sutton E. Griggs's *The Hindered Hand; or, The Reign of the Repressionist* published.
1908	William Stanley Braithwaite's *The House of Falling Leaves with Other Poems* published.
1912	James Weldon Johnson's *The Autobiography of an Ex-Colored Man* published.
1912	Claude McKay's *Songs of Jamaica* and *Constab Ballads* published.
1913	Fenton Johnson's *A Little Dreaming* published.
1916	Performed in Washington, DC, Angela Weld Grimke's *Rachel* is the first play written, produced, and performed by African Americans in the twentieth century.
1920	W.E.B. Du Bois's *Darkwater: Voices from Within the Veil* published.

Name Index

Full index entries for titles of works reproduced in this anthology can be found in the subject index. In the following name index, only the starting page number indicates the link between an author and the title of his/her work(s).

The Wiley Blackwell Anthology of African American Literature: Volume 1, 1746–1920, First Edition.
Edited by Gene Andrew Jarrett.

Subject Index

The Wiley Blackwell Anthology of African American Literature: Volume 1, 1746–1920, First Edition.
Edited by Gene Andrew Jarrett.

Wiley Blackwell Anthologies

Editorial Advisers

Wiley Blackwell Anthologies are a series of extensive and comprehensive volumes designed to address the numerous issues raised by recent debates regarding the literary canon, value, text, context, gender, genre, and period. While providing the reader with key canonical writings in their entirety, the series is also ambitious in its coverage of hitherto marginalized texts, and flexible in the overall variety of its approaches to periods and movements. Each volume has been thoroughly researched to meet the current needs of teachers and students.

Old and Middle English *c.*890–*c.*1450: An Anthology. Third Edition
edited by Elaine Treharne

Medieval Drama: An Anthology
edited by Greg Walker

Chaucer to Spenser: An Anthology of English Writing 1375–1575
edited by Derek Pearsall

Renaissance Literature: An Anthology of Poetry and Prose. Second Edition
edited by John C. Hunter

Renaissance Drama: An Anthology of Plays and Entertainments. Second Edition
edited by Arthur F. Kinney

Restoration Drama: An Anthology
edited by David Womersley

British Literature 1640–1789: An Anthology. Third Edition
edited by Robert DeMaria, Jr

Romanticism: An Anthology. Fourth Edition
edited by Duncan Wu

Irish Literature 1750–1900: An Anthology
edited by Julia Wright

Children's Literature: An Anthology 1801–1902
edited by Peter Hunt

Victorian Women Poets: An Anthology
edited by Angela Leighton and Margaret Reynolds

Modernism: An Anthology
edited by Lawrence Rainey

The Literatures of Colonial America: An Anthology
edited by Susan Castillo and Ivy T. Schweitzer

African American Literature: Volume 1, 1746–1920
edited by Gene Andrew Jarrett

African American Literature: Volume 2, 1920 to the Present
edited by Gene Andrew Jarrett

American Gothic: An Anthology from Salem Witchcraft to H. P. Lovecraft. Second Edition.
edited by Charles L. Crow

Nineteenth-Century American Women Writers: An Anthology
edited by Karen L. Kilcup

Nineteenth-Century American Women Poets: An Anthology
edited by Paula Bernat Bennett

Native American Women's Writing: An Anthology of Works *c.*1800–1924
edited by Karen L. Kilcup

The Wiley Blackwell Anthology of African American Literature: Volume 1, 1746–1920, First Edition.
Edited by Gene Andrew Jarrett.